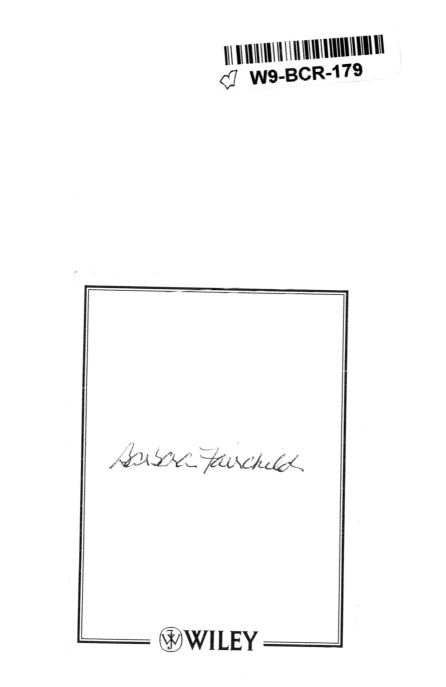

The Bon Appétit Cookbook

BON APPÉTIT BON APPÉTIT BON
APPÉTIT BON APPÉTIT BON APP
ON APPÉTIT BON APPÉTIT BON A
BON APPÉTIT BON APPÉTIT BON
APPÉTIT BON APPÉTIT BON APP
ON APPÉTIT BON APPÉTIT BON A
BON APPÉTIT BON APPÉTIT BON
APPÉTIT BON APPÉTIT BON APP
ON APPÉTIT BON APPÉTIT BON A
BON APPÉTIT BON APPÉTIT BON
APPÉTIT BON APPÉTIT BON APP
ON APPÉTIT BON APPÉTIT BON A
BON APPÉTIT BON APPÉTIT BON

The Bon Appétit Cookbook

BARBARA FAIRCHILD

Photographs by Pornchai Mittongtare
Illustrations by Narda Lebo
Design by Vertigo Design, NYC

This book is printed on acid-free paper. ∞

Published by John Wiley & Sons, Inc., Hoboken, New Jersey
Published simultaneously in Canada

LIBRARY OF CONGRESS CATALOGING-IN-PUBLICATION DATA:

Fairchild, Barbara, 1951-
The Bon appétit cookbook / Barbara Fairchild.
p. cm.
Includes index.
ISBN-13: 978-0-7645-9686-5 (cloth)
ISBN-10: 0-7645-9686-1 (cloth)
ISBN-13: 978-0-470-09710-6 (special edition)
ISBN-10: 0-470-09710-8 (special edition)
1. Cookery. I. Bon appétit. II. Title.
TX714.F3356 2006
641.5—dc22

2005005181

PRINTED IN THE UNITED STATES OF AMERICA

10 9 8 7 6 5 4 3 2 1

Contents

Recipes

Shellfish 402

13 Potatoes 415

15 Breads, jams, and condiments 469

Jams and condiments 496

16 Cakes 501

Acknowledgments

The creation of this book has been both an adventure and an education for me. And while some adventures can be solitary, this one had behind it a most impressive team, many of whom did double duty working on THE BON APPÉTIT COOKBOOK while also handling their "day jobs" at the magazine. BON APPÉTIT Managing Editor Laurie Glenn Buckle spearheaded the original proposal, and also coordinated the first list of recipes. She was passionate about this book, and that passion really helped get the ball rolling. The fact that we have more than 1,200 outstanding recipes in this book is a tribute to the extraordinary work of the BON APPÉTIT food department, which for the past 23 years has been directed by Food Editor Kristine Kidd. Kristine and her team have a gift—truly—for creating, testing, analyzing, tweaking, enhancing, and perfecting recipes so that every single one that runs in the magazine is a winner. Needless to say, narrowing them down to 1,200+ was a feat in itself—more on that in a second. But before we could even put pen to paper, so to speak, or even consider going further into the project, Editorial Operations Director Marcy MacDonald took charge of clearing all of the rights, working with attorneys, and making sure that every detail was in place. Marcy is the queen of the BON APPÉTIT COOKBOOK business universe, and we could not have moved forward on this book without her fastidious preliminary efforts.

Senior Food Editor Sarah Tenaglia then took on the enormous challenge of selecting and balancing the recipes, deciding which would need retesting, which would not make the cut, and where new material would be needed. Sarah was the perfect person for this job; she seems to have about 20 years of recipe content stored in her head. A typical conversation with Sarah went something like this:

ME: I think we need another green bean recipe.

SARAH: Great idea—we ran a terrific one in February of 1983, let me go get it.

Hers was a huge task, and I think that as a result Sarah is now definitely the historian among us.

With Sarah, Senior Associate Food Editors Selma Brown Morrow and Lena Cedarham Birnbaum helped edit all of the recipes so they were brought into current BON APPÉTIT style, and Contributing Editor Jeanne Thiel Kelley did any retesting necessary—given the BON APPÉTIT track record, this was minimal—as well as writing some of the recipe headnotes.

We were fortunate to have veteran food writer Christopher Styler lead the way with the chapter introductions, and we assembled a wonderful group of BON APPÉTIT veterans past and present to write recipe headnotes: Contributing Editor Tricia Callas O'Donnell, Norman Kolpas (himself a noted cookbook author), Rochelle Palermo Torres, Monica Parcell, and our current Assistant Managing Editor, Katie O'Kennedy. It is their words—written with a depth of precision and care that is so very impressive—that will help guide you along the way, ensuring success after success.

After all of that writing, it fell to Executive Editor Victoria von Biel to take on the initial editing of the chapter work, as well as our first marketing materials and promotional pieces. Victoria is a quick, savvy, and facile writer and editor, and she was the ideal person to have on board here.

Bon Appétit photo editor Liz Mathews helped bring vision to the gorgeous photographs in this book. She was involved in deciding which recipes to photograph, as well as directing the exquisite work of photographer Pornchai Mittongtare and the food and prop stylists—making sure the photos were beautiful, of course, but also that they accurately reflected the recipes so that the readers could expect similar results in their own kitchens. In other words, in true Bon Appétit fashion, the food in these pictures tastes as good as it looks.

Illustrator Narda Lebo—who created the drawings of cooking techniques, ingredients, and equipment that you'll find throughout the book—managed to pull off an artistic trifecta: Her illustrations are simple, technically precise, and also lovely to look at. And designer Alison Lew and her talented team at Vertigo Design in New York achieved something truly extraordinary: They took thousands of manuscript pages (the stack was about two feet high) full of diverse elements (text, recipes, subrecipes, headnotes, illustrations) and created a book that is elegant, airy, beautiful, and most important—easy to use. I'm both impressed and grateful, as I am to Wiley art director Jeff Faust, who created our fantastic eye-catching cover.

Throughout this process, someone had to oversee and coordinate the entire book, working with our publisher, John Wiley & Sons. What we needed was a smart liaison, a good diplomat, and a great schedule-watcher, all rolled into one. How lucky for us that former Bon Appétit Managing Editor Susan Champlin was available. Having someone familiar with the magazine, who also happens to be a terrific editor herself, made my job—and the completion of this book—that much easier. Susan had my utmost trust and confidence, and now she has my utmost thanks.

Those mentioned here were the people whom I worked with most directly on this adventure, but there were scores of others who helped make this book come to fruition: designers, copy editors, researchers, technical, production, and business people; you will find them listed elsewhere (pages 751–753). To them all I add my sincere appreciation for the obvious pride they took in their work, as well as the pride they feel for Bon Appétit. I appreciated their dedication, and I never took it for granted.

During this "excellent adventure" also came my own excellent (and rapid) education into book publishing. It was provided by two people in particular: Pam Chirls and David Black. They helped me immeasurably, giving me a crash course in the inner workings of books while I kept my other hand steady on the magazine. It was Pam—our smart, calm, talented, and highly skilled editor at John Wiley & Sons—

who said, "Bon Appétit feels like a community to me, more than any other magazine I have had contact with, because many of the contributors and many of the staff members have been a part of it for so long." That sense of community that we create with our loyal readership is of prime importance, and obviously, Pam understood this. Her commitment to this project was an inspiration to us all, and she logged many, many hours seeing it through.

David Black is more than the book agent that any writer could dream about: He is a terrific sounding board—both brainiac professor and sometime confessor—a tough but fair businessman, and now, a friend. I hope this book is not our last project together.

Yes, the creation of The Bon Appétit Cookbook has most definitely been an adventure and an education. For me professionally and personally, it has also been a long-time dream fulfilled. At 50 years and counting, Bon Appétit magazine and the influence it has had on modern American food, cooking, entertaining, wines and spirits, and travel and restaurants deserves its due. How fitting that this magnificent book should come out in the magazine's 50th anniversary year.

And it's been a busy 50 years: Bon Appétit launched in 1956 as a bimonthly publication, and was later owned by and published by the Pillsbury company. In 1975, Los Angeles businessman Bud Knapp bought the Bon Appétit name, and helped launch the magazine into its modern incarnation. (Knapp already owned *Architectural Digest*, and its editor-in-chief Paige Rense—who is still its editor-in-chief—devised the Bon Appétit prototype.) I joined Bon Appétit as an Editorial Assistant in 1978. In 1993, Si Newhouse bought both magazines for Condé Nast, and it was Si, James Truman, and Steve Florio who, in 2000, made it possible for me to lead Bon Appétit. Today it remains the largest food and entertaining magazine in the world.

Finally, on a strictly personal note, I would like to thank my executive assistant, Dennis O'Brien: He is super-organized, remains his personable self under pressure, and is a multi-tasker extraordinaire. And I would like to acknowledge and thank those I consider my mentors, J. Walter Flynn, Paige Rense, Bill Garry, and Zack Hanle. Somehow, they always knew.

Barbara Fairchild

BARBARA FAIRCHILD
Editor-in-Chief
Los Angeles, California

Introduction

I love to cook. That may seem like an obvious thing for the editor of a food magazine to say, but I think it bears mentioning, and here's why: Cooking is one of the most thoroughly enjoyable, satisfying, hands-on creative experiences that I know of—*and* you've got something great to eat at the end of it. Now, here's the best part: *Anybody can do it.* We may not all be able to sculpt or compose a piece of music or write a novel, but we can chop and slice and stir and blend, winding up with a delicious dish that brings real pleasure to the people around us.

For 50 years, BON APPÉTIT has celebrated that experience, with recipes that make cooking a pleasure and a triumph for every home cook, regardless of experience level. Now we've collected more than 1,200 of our very best recipes in this definitive book, so that cooks everywhere can enjoy the same gratifying success, whether braising lamb shanks or baking brownies.

This book is also the story of cooking at BON APPÉTIT—really, the story of food and cooking in this country—over the years.

When I started at the magazine in 1978, food magazines were geared toward the home cook who was expected to make *everything.* There was no good bread available in the supermarkets, no pâté; there were no farmers' markets down the block every Saturday morning. If you were a cook, you made it all—from, well, soup to nuts. And in the late '70s, that meant *French:* Everything was French-inspired, French-looking, French-tasting.

Since then, Americans have become much more knowledgeable, sophisticated, and adventurous about food. We're dining out more, traveling more, tasting new things. Throughout all the changes, BON APPÉTIT has provided the road map to the shifting landscape of food. We've been helping to define and develop this new American way of cooking and eating—which means incorporating regional and international influences and flavors, adapting the techniques of the world's great chefs, and expanding our culinary vocabulary in ways that are comfortable and accessible to the home cook.

BON APPÉTIT has even been at the forefront of what I call the supermarket revolution: As the magazine encouraged Americans to tackle more adventuresome recipes, people went on the hunt for new ingredients. If they couldn't find them, they asked their supermarket manager to stock them—and you can believe that the shelves of local markets are now filled with all kinds of herbs, spices, and ingredients I never would have found in 1978.

Today, if I could use three words to describe BON APPÉTIT, they would be *approachable, relevant,* and *fun. Approachable* because we make all of our content, including the recipes, as lively and as straightforward as possible. *Relevant* because we keep in touch with all parts of popular culture and how they feed into—pun intended—the worlds of food, cooking, and entertaining. And *fun* because we welcome people into our magazine and invite them to participate, whether they're cooks or travelers or restaurant-goers or wine aficionados.

But at the magazine we know that at the heart of it all are...the *recipes.* Readers love our recipes—and so do their family, friends, neighbors, and anyone else who gets to sample a bite. You can always tell a Bon Appétit recipe: It's a sophisticated twist on a beloved classic, and it's easy to make.

Our readers love food, they love to cook, they enjoy getting into the kitchen and trying new dishes. Yet they are also busy—they don't have all day to put dinner on the table. That's why our recipes feature ingredients you can find in any well-stocked supermarket. You can decide at 4:00 in the afternoon to make something to serve at 7:00—without worrying about having to give the recipe a trial run. I travel a great deal on behalf of the magazine, and I talk with our readers all the time. The one comment I hear over and over again is, "When I make a dish from Bon Appétit, I know it's going to be delicious, first time out."

I think that's why our readers are so loyal. I can't tell you how many times I've gone into people's homes and discovered decades' worth of Bon Appétit issues lined up on their kitchen shelves. People have success after success with Bon Appétit—the recipes become standards in our readers' repertoires, familiar favorites to turn to time and again.

After five decades of producing these great recipes, we knew it was time to compile our greatest hits into one comprehensive package—one that would put the cumulative expertise of Bon Appétit at the fingertips of every home cook.

To come up with the definitive list of the all-time-favorite Bon Appétit recipes, we went to several sources—first among them, the readers. Which recipes generated the most phone calls? Put those in. We also polled every member of our staff, engaged in endless discussions (not to say arguments), and even checked in with our own family members and friends to see which dishes made the greatest impression. It wasn't easy—but it was a huge amount of fun. I think you'll love the list we came up with (and I know you'll let me know).

We feel that this book is our way of saying "Thank you" to the readers who have made Bon Appétit a part of their lives for decades—and "Welcome" to those cooks and readers discovering the magic of Bon Appétit recipes for the very first time. We look forward to having you join us for years to come.

BARBARA FAIRCHILD

1 Notes from the test kitchen

Tips, techniques, and advice from the experts at *Bon Appétit*

A carpenter wouldn't begin work without a hammer and saw, nor a painter without a canvas, brushes, and paint. To do more than boil water—or even to boil water, for that matter—you'll need some basic equipment and tools at hand. Recipe preparation also goes a lot more quickly when the home cook has a variety of ingredients at the ready in the pantry, fridge, and freezer.

Starting with equipment, we have compiled a list of the items we use on a regular basis in the Bon Appétit test kitchen. There are many more items out there, of course, and tempting new gadgets appear in cookware stores all the time; stocking your own kitchen is both an ongoing process and a matter of personal preference. But these are the items we reach for most often, and they will be the most useful for preparing the recipes in this book.

Likewise, the ingredients we suggest stocking up on are those that are used regularly in this book. (You don't need to purchase every item in every category, and naturally you'll choose the foods that suit your tastes.) Keeping an assortment of high-quality dry ingredients and refrigerated and frozen foods on hand allows for more spontaneous and creative cooking—whether or not you're following a recipe.

We've also provided an overview of cooking terms—from the basics (boil, sauté, steam) to the more sophisticated (braise, brine, poach)—that should be part of every home cook's vocabulary.

Finally, we share some of our test kitchen "secrets," with how-tos that demystify and simplify more than three dozen techniques—such as peeling a tomato, deveining shrimp, melting chocolate, rolling out a pie crust, and uncorking a bottle of Champagne—for both novice cooks and seasoned experts.

The well-stocked kitchen

Major equipment

Blender: Of course you can make milk shakes, smoothies, Margaritas, and other icy blended drinks with it, but a blender—which can chop, blend, or puree foods—is also great for making soups. An **immersion blender**—a tall and narrow handheld blender with a blade at one end—can be used to puree soups and sauces directly in their pots. Many immersion blenders come with whisk attachments for whipping cream and egg whites.

Electric mixers: A heavy-duty **standing mixer** has a stainless steel bowl and adjustable attachments (such as a whisk, paddle, and dough hook). Its powerful motor is ideal for making bread or cookie dough. Another benefit: Because the mixer is freestanding, you can add ingredients while the motor is running. A portable or **handheld mixer** has a smaller motor and is better for lighter tasks, such as whipping cream. It's also well suited to beating mixtures over simmering water, as when making zabaglione. It's best to have both kinds of mixers.
TIP: *Though an immersion blender and a handheld mixer can do some of the same things—whipping cream and egg whites, for instance—they're not interchangeable. The handheld mixer is more powerful, and can beat heavier ingredients.*

Food processor: With its many attachments (metal blade, plastic dough blade, shredding disks, slicing disks, grating disks), a processor is invaluable for chopping ingredients, pureeing mixtures, and making dough. Attach the grating disk to grate vegetables or large amounts of cheese quickly.

Ice cream maker: Electric ice cream makers with self-contained refrigeration are ideal because they're so easy to use, requiring only the switch of a button to start the chilling and churning process. However, they are very expensive. The more basic and less expensive machines require advance planning, as the canister needs to chill overnight in the freezer before the custard is added and churned—but they're fine if you're making ice cream just a few times a year.

Small equipment

Colander: This bowl-shaped metal or plastic device perforated with small holes is used for rinsing fruits and vegetables or for draining boiled vegetables and pastas.

Juicer: Manual and electric juicers feature ridged cones that extract juice, primarily from citrus fruits.

Mixing bowls: Stainless steel is the best choice for mixing bowls for several reasons: They're inexpensive, lightweight, and stackable (they are sold in graduated sizes), and stainless steel does not react with food.
TIP: *Having a variety of sizes on hand simplifies the preparation of a multicourse meal.*

Salad spinner: A plastic spinner allows you to dry greens quickly. Most spinners have an inner basket that is pulled or turned to remove the water from the greens as they are spun.

Steamer basket: A collapsible metal steamer basket, with feet that keep the basket above the water, can be used in pots and pans to create a steamer.
TIP: *If using a collapsible basket, add about ½ inch of water and replace the water as it evaporates during cooking.*

Strainer (also called a sieve): This is used for separating solids from liquids—for instance, when straining particles from custards and sauces. Use a coarse sieve for straining custards and berry purees, and for general straining purposes. A small, fine-mesh sieve allows you to remove even smaller particles from sauces; it's also best for sifting dry ingredients together.

Pots and pans

Double boiler: A set of two pans, one sitting atop the other. The lower pan is filled with water that is brought to a simmer, while ingredients placed in the upper pan heat gently. This is a great way to melt chocolate or make delicate sauces such as hollandaise sauce.
TIP: *If you don't have a double boiler, place a metal mixing bowl atop a saucepan of simmering water—but do not allow the bottom of the bowl to touch the water. You want indirect heat, not direct.*

Dutch oven (also called a **heavy casserole**): This large pot has a tightly fitting lid and is used for slow cooking on the stove or in the oven; it's made of enameled cast iron, regular cast iron, or metal, and is round or oval in shape.

Roasting pan: This heavy-duty metal pan should be large enough to hold a turkey or beef roast. Large handles are important for lifting the heavy pan from the oven.
TIP: *Use an uncoated metal roasting pan, not nonstick, for the best browning.*

Saucepans: Large saucepans hold 3 to 4 quarts; medium, 2 to 3 quarts; small, 4 to 6 cups. Select top-quality heavy-duty pans to prevent scorching—preferably a "sandwich" construction featuring an aluminum core sandwiched between a stainless steel interior and an anodized aluminum, stainless steel, or copper exterior. The bottom and sides should be of uniform thickness.

Skillets (also called **frying pans**): Sloped shallow sides allow moisture to escape more easily, resulting in foods that brown better. Large skillets measure 12 to 14 inches in diameter across the top; medium skillets, about 10 inches; and small skillets, 7 to 8 inches. Keep several sizes of nonstick skillets on hand—they're easy to clean, and allow you to cook with much less oil or butter.
TIP: *Never heat an empty nonstick skillet over high heat, and never use metal utensils with a nonstick pan or skillet. If the nonstick coating gets scratched or damaged, discard the pan.*

Stockpot: A tall, deep, large-capacity pot (10 to 12 quarts is a useful size) with a tightly fitting lid is used for making stocks or soups, or for boiling or braising large cuts of meat. This is also a good choice for cooking large amounts of pasta. Stockpots can be useful for brining large pieces of meat, such as roasts or turkey.

Bakeware

Baking dishes: Select an assortment of tempered glass, metal, or heavy-duty glazed porcelain, stoneware, or earthenware in a variety of shapes and sizes. BON APPÉTIT recipes routinely call for the following sizes: 8x8x2, 11x7x2, 13x9x2, and 15x10x2 inches.

Baking sheets: Choose heavy-duty metal sheets with raised edges in a variety of sizes. Thin sheets have a tendency to buckle or turn in the oven.
TIP: *Rimless baking sheets are useful for transferring large baked items (such as crostatas) to cooling racks.*

Cake pans: The most commonly used pan sizes are 8- or 9-inch round pans with 1½- or 2-inch-high sides. Having three of each size is useful for making layer cakes. Look for good-quality metal pans—but not the dark-colored variety, which tend to absorb heat more quickly and can cause overbrowning.

Loaf pans: Standard loaf pans are approximately 9x5x3 inches and are made of tempered glass or metal. Bread bakers will want more than one.

Muffin (or **cupcake**) **pans:** These come in a variety of sizes: standard, jumbo (for oversize muffins), and miniature (for bite-size treats or hors d'oeuvres).

Pie dishes: These are made of metal and glass, and the most standard size is 9 inches in diameter. Many recipes call for a deep-dish pie dish, so be sure to have one on hand.

Soufflé dishes and **custard cups:** Made of porcelain or tempered glass, these are also great for making individual pot pies. We use the 6-ounce and 1-cup sizes most often.

TIP: *These individual dishes are perfect for holding small quantities of chopped vegetables and herbs when you prepare a meal. Tiny ones (2-tablespoon capacity or so) are extremely handy for dressings and dipping sauces and make for a pretty presentation.*

Springform pans: These round pans, with a spring-clip side that locks onto a bottom and releases, allow for easy unmolding of cakes, cheesecakes, and frozen desserts. Recipes most frequently call for 9- or 10-inch-diameter pans.

Tart and tartlet pans: The best and most useful are made of metal with removable bottoms for easy release after baking. You'll find them in round, square, and rectangular shapes.
TIP: *Wash and dry them well after each use and store between sheets of paper towels to absorb moisture and prevent rusting.*

General tools

Corkscrews: There are many kinds, but our favorites are the waiter's knife and the lever-style corkscrew. The waiter's knife—which folds easily and is the most portable—has a handle that attaches to the rim of the bottle, while a screw is turned and pushed into the cork. The lever-style opener, though pricey, is the choice of pros: It is durable and opens bottles easily. Simply clamp it around the neck of the bottle, and then pull the long lever up and down; the cork is removed with virtually no effort.

Ice cream scoops: Sturdy metal scoops are ideal for serving ice cream as they won't bend.
TIP: *Smaller scoops can be used to scoop cookie dough onto baking sheets.*

Kitchen scales: Now available at reasonable prices, digital or mechanical kitchen scales ensure accuracy in measuring all kinds of ingredients, such as chocolate, butter, vegetables, and nuts.

Ladle: Choose a ladle with a heat-resistant handle; the ladle should be large enough to scoop up good-size portions of soups or stews.

Measuring cups: There are two kinds of measuring cups, those for measuring dry ingredients and those for measuring liquids. Dry measures, made of plastic or metal, are bundled as a set, in graduated sizes. The best liquid measures are made of tempered glass and are sold in 1-, 2-, 4-, and 8-cup sizes. You'll need both dry and liquid measures.

Measuring spoons: These come in sets that generally range from ⅛ teaspoon to 1 tablespoon. Stainless steel is preferable to plastic because it does not absorb flavors.

Pepper mill: The BON APPÉTIT test kitchen uses freshly ground pepper. Use a standard pepper mill (or the disposable kind now available at most supermarkets) to grind whole peppercorns into various degrees of coarseness or fineness.
TIP: *When grinding large amounts, use a spice grinder or a clean coffee mill.*

Potato masher: The best are made of stainless steel with a wire grid.

Pot holders and **oven mitts:** Choose thickly padded, moisture-resistant pads or gloves. Extra-long mitts are designed for reaching into the oven or working over a hot grill.

Ruler: Have a ruler handy to measure accurately the diameter of any dough or crust, or the size of a pan.

Spatulas: Either solid or slotted, **basic spatulas** made of metal or heat-resistant plastic are ideal for turning foods during cooking. Long, thin **metal** (or **icing**) **spatulas** are used for icing cakes and other desserts; many find that **offset spatulas** (which are Z-shaped when viewed from the side) offer greater maneuverability. Keep a variety of sizes of **rubber spatulas** on hand to suit different tasks. Use a large flexible rubber spatula to scrape out mixtures from bowls. When scraping hot mixtures from saucepans or skillets, use heat-resistant spatulas made of silicone.

Spoons: Wooden spoons and spatulas are best for stirring thick mixtures, such as polenta or mashed potatoes—because they "clean" the bottom of a pot with every turn, preventing burning and sticking.

Keep an assortment of sizes of **metal spoons,** both solid and slotted, for a variety of purposes. Use slotted spoons for removing solid foods from liquids, such as boiling water or hot oil.

Thermometers: A **candy thermometer** (or **deep-fry thermometer**) gauges the temperature of boiled syrups, sauces, candy mixtures, and oil for deep-frying foods. A clip-on thermometer allows you to monitor the temperature of a mixture while stirring constantly. **Instant read thermometers** are designed to measure the internal temperature of foods or liquids. When the metal stem is inserted into the food, it produces an instant reading. Unlike standard meat thermometers, which gauge the temperature gradually while the meat is baking, instant-read thermometers can't be put in the oven; the plastic dial will melt.
TIP: *To make sure that your thermometer is accurate, attach it to the inside of a medium saucepan and fill the pan with cold water. Bring the water to a boil and boil for three minutes. The thermometer should register 212°F; if it doesn't, take the difference into account when reading ingredient temperatures.*

Timers: Digital timers with magnets adhere to metal. Clip-on timers attach to your apron or clothing so you can do other tasks while food is cooking.

Tongs: This hinged, V-shaped metal device is used to turn meats or vegetables in a skillet, on the grill, under the broiler, or over a gas flame. It's also useful for tossing and serving salads.

Whisk: For most recipes, use a standard whisk—about 2 to 3 inches wide at the large end.

Knives and other slicing tools

Bread knife: A long (8 inches or more) serrated knife used for cutting through crusty bread or delicate items, like tomatoes, using a sawing motion.

Carving knife: A long, sturdy-but-flexible blade that slices easily through beef roasts, ham, and turkey.

Chef's knife: All-purpose knife (usually with an 8-inch blade) for chopping, slicing, and dicing large items or large quantities of ingredients.

Paring knife: A 3- to 4-inch tapered blade, used for peeling fruits and vegetables or cutting slits in meats for stuffing.

Scissors and poultry shears: Scissors are for general cutting, sturdy poultry shears for cutting up chicken and game hens.

Box grater: A four-sided stainless steel grater. Each side is designed for a different purpose—such as shredding, grating, or slicing.

Microplane graters: Razor-sharp stainless steel graters ideal for grating all kinds of citrus rinds, as well as cheeses (especially Parmesan), nutmeg, ginger, and more.

V-slicer: A manually operated slicer with adjustable blades. Hard vegetables such as carrots, potatoes, or beets are run across the blade to obtain even slices, baton shapes, or julienne strips.
TIP: *Some chefs and home cooks use a mandoline, a pricey and complex piece of machinery that can make plain, crinkle-, or waffle-cut slices and julienne strips in a range of thicknesses from paper-thin to chunky. In the* BON APPÉTIT *test kitchen, we prefer the simpler and less expensive V-slicer, which is much easier to use. It is fine for the recipes in this book.*

Carving fork: A sturdy two-pronged fork used to steady roasts during carving.

Cutting boards: Choose large wood cutting boards for efficient cutting without damaging knives or kitchen counters. Flexible plastic cutting boards can be bent after chopping, so that ingredients can be easily transferred to bowls or skillets.
TIP: *Always use separate cutting boards for raw meat and for other foods to avoid cross-contamination; wash boards thoroughly after each use.*

Baking tools

Cardboard cake rounds: Putting a fragile cake layer or a tart on a cardboard round allows for easy transfer from one surface to another.

Cookie and **biscuit cutters:** The best cutters are made of metal, which result in a clean cut. Keep an assortment of shapes and sizes on hand, and be sure to include several sizes of biscuit cutters.

Cooling racks: Placing cakes, pies, and other baked goods on racks allows air to circulate underneath for quick, even cooling.

Parchment and **waxed paper:** Use waxed paper to line cake pans (it helps remove the cake layer from the pan); parchment paper, which is heatproof, can be used to line baking sheets.

Pastry bag and **tips:** Used for more than just decorating cakes, pies, and other desserts, a pastry bag with a variety of tips is terrific for piping out cookie batter, meringue, and dough into various shapes. Purchase both plain and star tips in large, medium, and small sizes.

Pastry brushes: Use these for jobs like brushing down pan sides when making sugar syrups, for applying egg washes to loaves of bread, and for brushing butter over layers of pastry.

Pie weights: These small metal or ceramic pellets are used to keep the sides of pie and tart crusts from shrinking during "blind baking" (see "How-Tos" for more on blind baking).
TIP: *If you don't have pie weights, dried beans can be used as a substitute.*

Rolling pin: French-style pins without handles offer better control. Choose a heavy one for more efficiency.

Silpats: These nonstick silicone baking mats (used on top of metal baking sheets) are great for baking cookies. The cookies slide right off.

Wooden skewers: Slender skewers are best for testing cakes and other baked goods.

Fruit and vegetable tools

Garlic press: A press is used to "mince" garlic cloves by squeezing them through perforated holes with a plunger—without getting garlic all over a knife, your counter, or your fingers.
TIP: *Choose a heavy-duty metal press that comes with a self-cleaning tool; too lightweight a press will only mash the garlic, not mince it.*

Melon baller: Used primarily to scoop out decorative balls of melon, it can also be used to core fruits such as pears.

Vegetable peeler: A swivel-bladed peeler is more maneuverable than other types, following the contours of vegetables and fruits so that just the skins are removed.
TIP: *A vegetable peeler can also be used to create long, thin ribbons of cucumbers, carrots, and zucchini, as well as chocolate curls.*

Zester: The five-pronged zester will remove the colored peel from citrus in long thin strips, leaving the bitter white pith behind.

Meat and poultry tools

Bulb baster (also known as a **turkey baster**): With a plastic, glass, or metal tube and a squeezable end, this is used to baste turkeys and other meats. Glass or metal is preferable; the plastic ones can become warped by the heat of the basting liquid.

Kitchen string: Use food-safe string to tie roasts and chickens.

Meat mallet: A mallet is used primarily for pounding boneless meat and poultry into thinner pieces. Mallets often have two sides, one with a ridged surface that breaks down the meat, thus tenderizing it, and a smooth side for flattening.
TIP: *Mallets can also be used to crush candies or spices in resealable plastic bags.*

Metal skewers: For grilling and serving kebabs, metal skewers are preferable to wooden ones because they can take more weight and won't burn on the barbecue.

The well-stocked pantry, refrigerator, and freezer

TIP: *When preparing your shopping list, divide the items according to how they are stored—in the pantry, fridge, or freezer. After marketing, tape the lists to the inside of the cupboard, and to the side of the fridge and the freezer. As you use each item, cross it off the list, so that you always know what you have in the house.*

Stocking the pantry

Asian ingredients: black bean sauce, chili-garlic sauce, hoisin sauce, mirin, Asian sesame oil, oyster sauce, panko (Japanese breadcrumbs), plum sauce, rice vinegar, sake, soy sauce, Thai red curry paste, wasabi (horseradish powder).

Bottled and jarred items: artichoke hearts (marinated), clam juice, pesto, roasted red peppers, sun-dried tomatoes, tapenade.

Bottled sauces and dressings: barbecue sauce, ketchup, mayonnaise, prepared horseradish, soy sauce, teriyaki sauce, Worcestershire sauce.

Canned items: anchovies, beans (black beans, garbanzo beans [chickpeas], kidney beans, white beans), broth (beef broth, low-salt chicken broth, vegetable broth), coconut milk (unsweetened), tomatoes (diced), tomato paste, tuna.

Chocolate: bittersweet chocolate, chocolate chips, unsweetened chocolate, unsweetened cocoa powder.

Dried beans, grains, and pasta: barley, beans (various types), bulgur, couscous, grits, lentils, pasta (various types), rice (arborio rice, brown rice, jasmine rice, wild rice).
TIP: *When cooking rice, make extra. Later in the week, turn the leftover rice into a fried rice dish by adding chicken and vegetables and flavoring it with ginger and teriyaki, hoisin, or soy sauce (which will rehydrate it).*

Dried fruit: apricots, cherries, cranberries, currants, dates, figs, raisins.

Dried herbs and spices: dill, *herbes de Provence*, oregano, rosemary, tarragon, thyme; allspice, caraway seed, cardamom pods, chili powder, Chinese five-spice powder, cinnamon, cloves, coriander (whole), cumin, curry powder, dried crushed red pepper, fennel seeds, ginger, nutmeg, saffron, vanilla beans.
TIP: *These are some of our favorites, but choose your own based on the way you like to cook.*

Dried wild mushrooms: morels, porcini, shiitakes.

Dry ingredients: baking powder, baking soda, cornmeal, cornstarch, dry yeast, flour (all purpose flour, cake flour, whole wheat flour), unflavored gelatin.

Extracts: almond, peppermint, vanilla.

Hot sauce and chiles: canned chipotle chiles in *adobo* sauce, canned diced green chiles, hot pepper sauce, salsa verde.

Kitchen products: aluminum foil, plastic wrap, resealable plastic bags.

Mustard: Dijon mustard, honey mustard, whole grain mustard, yellow mustard.

Oil and vinegar: Asian toasted sesame oil, nut oils (such as walnut or pistachio), olive oil, vegetable oil; balsamic vinegar, red and white wine vinegars, rice vinegar, Sherry wine vinegar; cooking spray.
TIP: *Never aim cooking spray toward an open flame, and use caution with it when grilling or cooking on a gas burner. A flame can travel up the stream of spray and cause burns or an explosion—so you should spray only a* cold *pan or grill,* then *light the burner or barbecue.*

Pickled foods: capers, cornichons, olives, peperoncini, pickles.

Salt and pepper: sea salt, kosher salt; black peppercorns, green peppercorns, white peppercorns; cayenne pepper.

Sweeteners: corn syrup (light and dark), honey, jams and preserves (assorted), maple syrup, molasses (light and dark), pomegranate molasses, sugar (golden and dark brown sugar, granulated sugar, powdered sugar, raw sugar).

Wine and spirits: brandy or Cognac, cassis syrup, Grand Marnier or other orange liqueur, Marsala, Madeira, Port (ruby and tawny), red wine, rum, dry Sherry, white wine, whiskey.

Stocking the refrigerator

Dairy: butter, cheese (blue cheese, cheddar, feta, goat cheese, Monterey Jack, mozzarella, Parmesan); buttermilk, crème fraîche, milk, whipping cream, sour cream, yogurt.

Fruit: apples, lemons, limes, oranges, other seasonal fresh fruits.

Sauces: marinara, pesto, salsas (fresh, such as mango or fire-roasted salsas).

Smoked foods: bacon, Black Forest ham, prosciutto, smoked salmon, smoked sausages.

Vegetables: Belgian endive, cabbage, romaine lettuce, baby spinach leaves; bell peppers (green and red), carrots, cherry tomatoes, cucumbers, herbs (fresh, such as basil, dill, Italian parsley, marjoram, thyme), garlic, ginger root, onions, potatoes.
TIP: *When boiling or steaming potatoes, boil extra and keep some in large pieces. They can be sautéed in olive oil or butter with diced prosciutto and herbs for a quick side dish later in the week.*

Miscellaneous: eggs, pita bread rounds, tortillas (corn and flour).

Stocking the freezer

TIP: *Make sure to wrap items well (that is, in a resealable plastic bag) when storing them in the freezer, and write the date on the outside of the bag. Storage times listed below are conservative; some items may last longer, but these are the times we feel will ensure a good-quality product when you take it out of the freezer. Obviously, the shelf life decreases when items such as ice cream or sorbet or frozen fruits or vegetables are opened and then re-frozen.*

Bread: French-bread baguettes, ciabatta, or other breads. Wrapped in aluminum foil and stored in resealable plastic bags, they should last up to a month in the freezer.

Desserts: chocolate chips, ice cream and sorbet, pound cake. Unopened bags of chocolate chips can last three to six months; ice cream, one month; pound cake, three months in a sealed container.

Dough: phyllo pastry, pie dough, puff pastry sheets; these can last up to three months.

Frozen fruits: blueberries, boysenberries, cranberries, mango, peaches, pineapple, raspberries, strawberries; all can last up to three months.
TIP: *Make a delicious and easy sauce or syrup substitute by sautéeing some frozen berries or other fruits with a little butter and sugar.*

Frozen juice concentrates: apple, cranberry, lemonade, limeade, orange, passion fruit.

Frozen meats, poultry, and shellfish: pork potstickers, pork tenderloin, rack of lamb, steaks; chicken breasts, chicken thighs; peeled and deveined cooked shrimp. All can last up to three months.
TIP: *Remember to add another layer of wrapping to the supermarket packaging—preferably a resealable plastic freezer bag.*

Frozen vegetables: artichoke hearts, corn (petite white), edamame (shelled), green beans (French-cut), peas, spinach; can last up to three months.

Nuts and seeds: almonds, cashews, hazelnuts, macadamia nuts, peanuts, pecans, pine nuts, walnuts; pepitas (pumpkin seeds). Stored airtight, these can last up to six months.

Cooking terminology

Bake: To cook foods in the oven using dry heat.
TIP: *Use an oven thermometer to make sure that your oven's temperature setting is accurate.*

Baste: To drizzle, brush, or spoon liquid—such as melted butter, drippings, or broth—over poultry or meat as it cooks. This adds great flavor and can help the meat brown evenly. A bulb baster (or turkey baster) is useful for gathering up the accumulated pan juices and pouring them over the meat.

Blanch: To immerse foods (most commonly vegetables or fruit) in boiling water for a short period of time, usually less than a minute. This cooks them only slightly. The vegetables or fruits are then transferred to ice water to cool them quickly and preserve their color.

Boil: To heat water until air bubbles break through the surface (at sea level, this occurs at 212°F). If the water continues to bubble even when it is stirred, this is known as a "full" or "rolling" boil. Boiling is best for dried pasta and hardy vegetables like artichokes, potatoes, and corn on the cob.

Braise: To cook food slowly in a small amount of simmering liquid. This long cooking process makes tough cuts of meat (such as brisket, shanks, or pot roasts) quite tender. The meat is often browned first in fat to give it color, and it is then cooked, covered, either on the stovetop or in the oven. Adding onions, carrots, and herbs to the braising liquid enhances flavor.

Brine: To soak raw meat, poultry, or shellfish in a brine—a mixture of water, salt, and often seasonings. The water, salt, and seasonings are brought to a simmer and stirred to dissolve the salt; then the brine is cooled and chilled before the food is added. *(To do this quickly, start with less water and cool it by adding ice cubes.)* Brining time can range from 30 minutes (for shellfish) to several days for meat and poultry. After soaking in brine, the foods are drained and cooked. This technique produces tender, juicy results as the salt from the brine penetrates the meat and draws in moisture.
TIP: *To brine a large item, such as a turkey or a roast, without taking up valuable refrigerator space, place the item in a food-safe plastic bag, add the brine, and seal the bag; then place the bag in a large cooler. Cover the bag with ice and replenish the ice as necessary to maintain a temperature of 40°F or below.*

Broil: To cook meat, fish, or other foods in the oven under an open flame. The intense heat browns the outside quickly, while keeping the inside moist. Thicker pieces of meat or fish should be cooked farther away from the heat source, to avoid burning the outside before the inside has had a chance to cook.

Chop: To cut ingredients into bite-size pieces. *Coarsely chopped* indicates ingredient pieces about ⅓ inch in size. *Finely chopped* indicates pieces between ⅛ inch and ¼ inch in size. *Minced* indicates pieces that are 1/16 inch to ⅛ inch in size.

Deep-fry: To cook foods—such as doughnuts, french fries, and tempura—in a large amount of hot fat for a short period of time. This technique produces a golden-brown exterior and tender interior.
TIP: *Choose an oil or fat with a high smoke point, such as peanut oil or grapeseed oil.*

Grill: To cook foods on a metal grill (or barbecue) over hot coals, a gas flame, or other heat source. Grilling is a great way to cook meats, fish, poultry, and vegetables, as it imparts a nice smoky flavor, and requires no fat.
TIP: *To prevent foods from sticking to the grill, spray the cold grill with nonstick spray, then light the coals or turn on the gas.*

Pan-fry: Similar to sautéing but using more oil or fat, pan-frying involves cooking foods in a moderate amount of fat over medium heat. (Unlike deep-frying, the foods are not completely immersed in the fat.) Pan-frying is an effective cooking method for thicker pieces of meat such as pork chops.

Poach: To cook foods gently in hot liquid kept just below a simmer. This technique is ideal for delicate foods, such as fish and eggs, that can easily become overcooked. The gentle heat keeps these foods from falling apart.

Roast: To cook foods using dry heat in an uncovered pan in the oven. Tender cuts of meat and poultry are well suited to this cooking method.

Sauté: A dry-heat cooking method in which foods are cooked in a small amount of fat; usually done quickly over high heat.

Sear: To brown foods quickly over very high heat. This technique gives foods a deeper, more complex flavor and visual appeal. Seared foods such as tuna are often served rare. Other foods, such as short ribs, shanks, and chicken, are seared first before a secondary cooking, such as braising.
TIP: *Before searing, pat foods dry. When working with a large volume of food, sear it in batches; overcrowding foods will create steam and prevent proper browning.*

Simmer: "To bring to a simmer" means to bring water or another liquid to near-boiling, at which point small bubbles rise to the surface—without letting the water get so hot that large air bubbles break through the surface (boiling).

Steam: A moist-heat cooking method in which foods are cooked on a rack or in a steamer basket in a covered pan over simmering or boiling water. Steaming provides a moist, gentle heat that is especially good for fish and vegetables.

Stew: To cook meat, poultry, fish, and/or vegetables slowly in liquid (which may include broth, water, and/or wine) in a covered pot, so that the ingredients become tender, the liquid thickens, and the flavors meld. Hearty stews are generally served as a main course.

Stir-fry: A dry-heat cooking method in which small pieces of food are cooked in a large pan (usually a wok, sometimes with a small amount of oil) over very high heat while stirring constantly.

How-to . . .

Trim an artichoke and remove the choke

Starting at the base, pull off the tough outer leaves. Using a heavy large knife, cut off the stem at the base of the artichoke. Cut off the top 1½ inches of the artichoke. Using scissors, trim off the sharp, pointed tip of each leaf. Rub all cut sides of artichoke with a halved lemon to prevent discoloration. To remove the choke from whole artichokes, pull back the inner leaves from the top of the artichoke and scoop out the fuzzy choke with a spoon; squeeze lemon juice over the cavity. The cavity is now ready to be stuffed, if desired.

Pit an avocado

Using a large knife, cut the unpeeled avocado lengthwise in half, cutting around the pit in the center. Using both hands, gently grasp both sides of the avocado and turn the halves in opposite directions to separate them. Using the same knife, tap it into the pit so that it sticks, and then twist the knife to loosen and remove the pit. Slide the pit against the inside rim of the sink to release it from the knife.

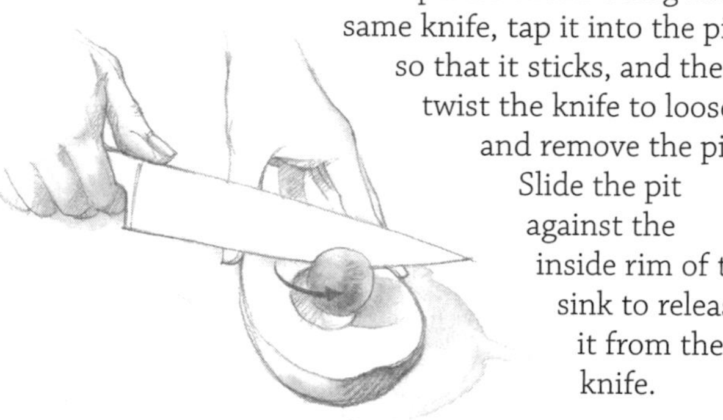

Roast, peel, and seed bell peppers

Roasting peppers is a technique that makes peeling them easy, and also imparts a smoky flavor to the peppers. Char the peppers over a gas flame or in the broiler until completely blackened on all sides, turning frequently with tongs. Enclose the peppers in a paper bag; let stand for ten minutes—this will steam and loosen their skins. Check to see if they are cool enough to touch. Using your fingertips, peel off the blackened skins, rinsing your fingertips under running water to wash away blackened pepper skin (do not rinse the pepper itself, as this will wash away flavorful juices). Using a small sharp knife, cut off the stem; remove the membrane and seeds.

Cut corn off the cob

Husk and remove the silk from the corn, then cut off the stem. Stand the ear up on its flat end on a work surface. Using a heavy large knife and beginning at the tip of the ear, cut all the way down one side between the base of the kernels and the cob, releasing the kernels onto the work surface. Repeat on the remaining sides.

Pit an olive or a cherry

Place the olive or cherry on a work surface and cover with the flat side of a heavy large knife. Using the fist of your opposite hand, tap firmly on the wide flat side of the knife to split the olive or cherry open, then remove the pit.

Seed a cucumber

Using a large knife, cut the cucumber lengthwise in half. Run a spoon along the middle of each half, scraping out the seeds.

TIP: *If using English hothouse cucumbers, it will not be necessary to peel the skin or remove their seeds, as the skin is tender and the few seeds are very small.*

Seed a tomato

Cut tomatoes crosswise in half. Squeeze each tomato half gently, using your index finger to push out seeds and pulp.

Peel garlic

Place garlic cloves on a work surface and cover with the flat side of a heavy large knife. Using the fist of your opposite hand, tap firmly on the flat side of the blade to loosen the skins from the garlic. Peel off the skin.

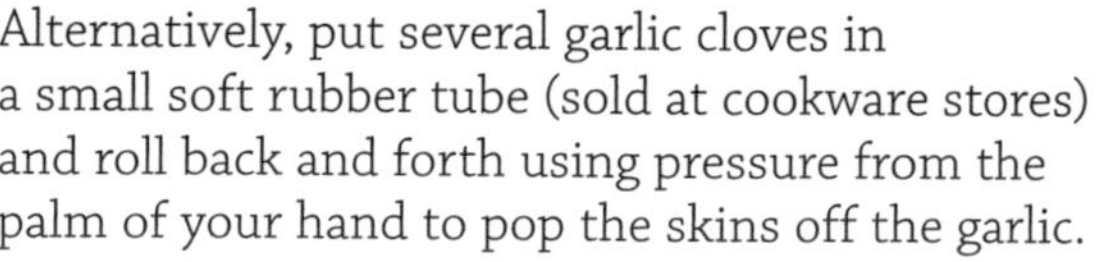

Alternatively, put several garlic cloves in a small soft rubber tube (sold at cookware stores) and roll back and forth using pressure from the palm of your hand to pop the skins off the garlic.

Remove peel from citrus fruits

Depending on how the peel is to be used, it can be removed in several ways. When a recipe calls for grated citrus peel, use a *Microplane,* a long, slender, and very sharp handheld grater that is ideal for this task. Run the sharp edges along the peel only (not the bitter white pith beneath) to produce finely grated peel. When the recipe calls for citrus peel to be removed in long, thin strips, run a *vegetable peeler* across the colored peel to create strips. To create long, thin, curly strips of peel (usually used to decorate desserts), run the holes of a *zester* across the skin of the citrus.

Cut winter squash

Winter squash (such as butternut, kabocha, and acorn) have hard flesh that can be difficult to cut. Using a large sharp knife, cut the squash lengthwise in half, using a mallet if necessary to tap on the top edge of the knife and force it through the squash.

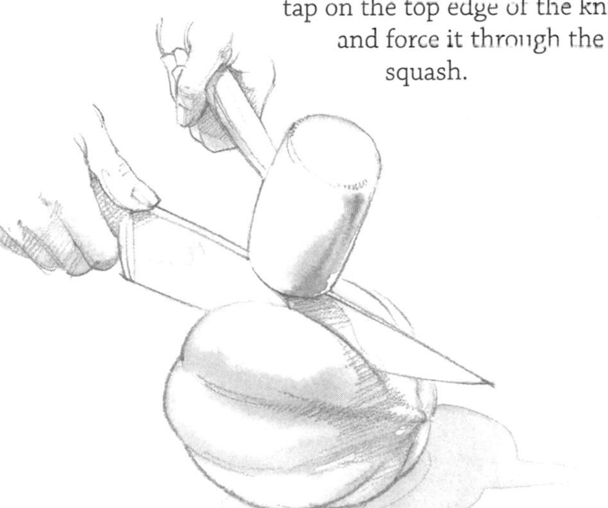

Peel peaches and tomatoes

Blanching helps remove skins quickly and easily from fresh peaches and tomatoes. Using a small sharp knife, cut a very shallow X opposite the stem end. Gently lower the fruit into boiling water and cook until the skin begins to wrinkle—about 15 to 60 seconds, depending on the ripeness and quantity of the fruit. Using a slotted spoon or strainer, transfer the peaches or tomatoes to a bowl of ice water to cool quickly. Drain. When cool, peel off the skins using a small sharp knife.

Peel a pineapple

Using a heavy large knife, cut off the leafy top from the pineapple. Cut off the base of the pineapple and stand it up on its wide base end. Starting at the top of the pineapple, cut off the skin in a curving motion to conform to the shape and cutting just below the surface of the skin to expose the brown eyes. Turn the pineapple on its side; make shallow diagonal cuts along both sides of each row of eyes and remove.

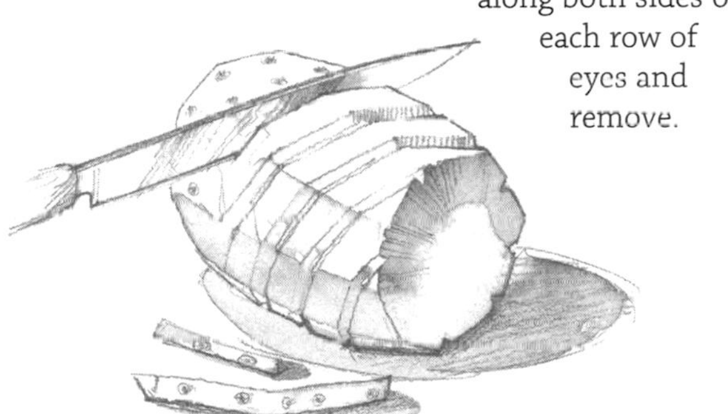

Store fresh herbs

There are several ways to store fresh herbs. The most common is to wrap each bunch of herbs in damp paper towels and then place in a resealable plastic bag; store in the refrigerator up to four days. Herbs with tender stems, such as basil, parsley, mint, and cilantro, can be kept in water. Trim half an inch off the stem of each bunch and place in a cup of water. Cover with a plastic bag and refrigerate up to one week.

Make breadcrumbs

When our recipes call for *fresh breadcrumbs,* we mean soft, moist crumbs made from fresh bread. Tear bread (with crusts, unless the recipe specifies "crustless") into pieces and grind in batches in a processor fitted with a metal blade to a fine or coarse texture. To make *dry breadcrumbs,* cut fresh bread into cubes and spread them on a rimmed baking sheet. Bake at 300°F until dry but not colored, about 15 minutes. Cool, then grind in processor to crumbs.
TIP: *If using packaged breadcrumbs, we recommend panko (Japanese breadcrumbs), which are unseasoned.*

Quick-soak dried beans

This method is terrific when you don't have time to let beans soak overnight. Put the beans in a large pot and add enough cold water to cover by three inches. Do not cover. Bring the water to a simmer over medium-high heat. Continue simmering for two minutes. Remove from the heat. Cover and let stand for two hours. Drain.

Loosen the skin on chicken or turkey

Many recipes require that poultry skin be loosened in order to create a space in which to place herb sprigs, or to spread a flavored butter or marinade. To do this, find an area on the side of the breast where the skin can be lifted easily to create a space. Slide two to three fingertips between the chicken breast skin and meat and move from side to side to loosen (the skin stretches easily, but be careful to move slowly to prevent tears).

Peel and devein shrimp

Carefully pull off the shrimp legs. Beginning at the wide end, peel off the entire shell. If the recipe calls for the tails to be left intact, firmly grasp the tail before beginning to remove the shell (this will ensure that the tail stays attached). Holding the shrimp between the thumb and index finger, use a small sharp knife to make a shallow slit along the center back of the shrimp to expose the vein. Place the shrimp under running water and pull out the vein.

Remove cooked lobster meat from the tail

Lobster cooking instructions often suggest cutting straight down the middle of the lobster; we use a different technique that enables you to remove the tail in one piece. Place the lobster tail on a work surface, shell side down. Using kitchen scissors and starting at the wide end, cut all the way down one side to the end of the tail. Repeat on the opposite side. Pull back the membrane to free the tail meat. Pull out the tail meat in one piece. The tail can now be sliced into medallions.

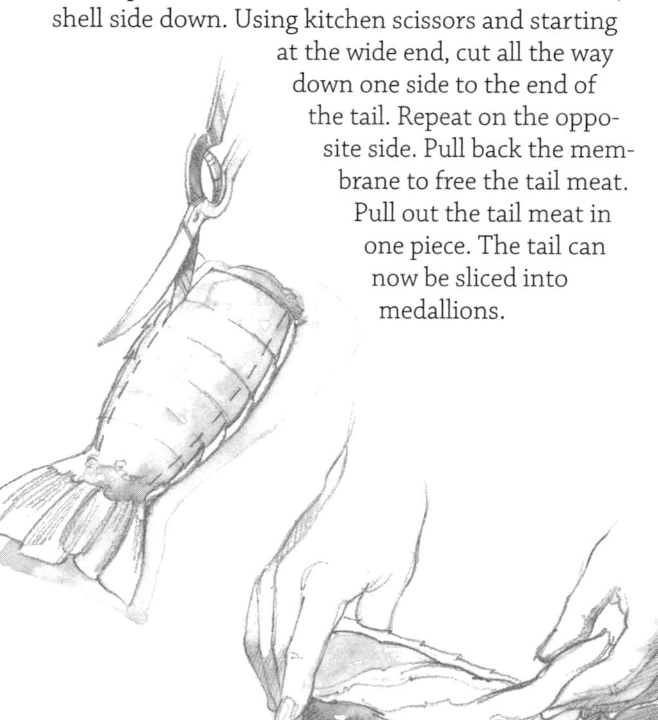

Split king crab shells

Removing the meat from king crab legs can be challenging. To make it easier and still present the crab attractively, use kitchen scissors to cut along one long side of each crab leg from end to end. Repeat, making a second cut parallel to the first cut, about half an inch away. Remove the cut section of the shell to expose the meat. The crabmeat can then be removed with a fork in whole long pieces. If serving crab legs on their own, present them in their split shells, allowing guests to remove the meat themselves.

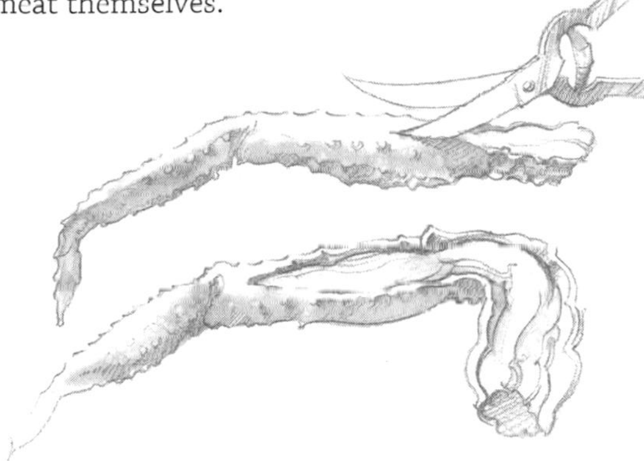

Toast nuts

Spread the nuts in a single layer on a rimmed baking sheet and roast them in a 350°F oven until they are golden and fragrant. The cooking time varies depending on the nut (times are approximate; check the nuts periodically):

Almonds (sliced): 7 to 10 minutes
Almonds (whole): 10 minutes
Chestnuts: 25 minutes
Hazelnuts:* 12 to 15 minutes
Macadamia nuts: 12 to 15 minutes
Pecans: 10 to 15 minutes
Pine nuts: 5 minutes
Walnuts: 10 to 15 minutes

**To skin hazelnuts after toasting, let them cool a bit, and then pour the nuts onto a clean kitchen towel spread out on a work surface. Gather the towel around the nuts and rub together until most of the skins have come off (don't worry about getting off every bit).*

Make a cookie crumb crust

Crumble the cookies into a food processor fitted with a metal blade; process until fine crumbs form. Or place the cookies in a heavy resealable plastic bag and use a rolling pin to crush the cookies into small pieces by rolling back and forth. Mix the crumbs with melted butter, and they are ready to be pressed into a pan.

TIP: *To do this quickly and easily, cover your hand with a plastic bag and press the crumbs firmly onto the pan. The plastic will keep the crumbs from sticking to your hand and enable you to compact the crust nicely.*

Roll out pie dough

Flatten the dough into a disk and chill for about one hour before rolling (the time will vary depending on the recipe). Using a rolling pin, flatten the dough disk slightly by tapping on it several times from one side to the other, and then give the dough a quarter turn and tap on it in the opposite direction. When rolling out the dough, start in the center of the disk and roll out away from you, almost to the opposite edge. Bring the rolling pin back to the center of the round, and roll it toward you almost to the edge. Turn the dough a quarter turn, and repeat rolling and turning until the dough is rolled to the proper diameter or thickness.

Transfer pie dough to a pie dish

There are several ways to transfer pie dough to a pie dish or pie plate. One is to roll the dough between sheets of waxed paper or parchment paper into a round. Peel off the top sheet of paper. Turn the dough over into the pie dish and carefully peel off the bottom paper. Another way is to roll the dough out on a lightly floured surface into a round. Roll the dough loosely up onto the rolling pin. Center the pin above one end of the pie dish and unroll, draping the dough loosely over the pie dish. Or you can roll the dough out on a lightly floured surface into a round, and fold the dough in half, then into quarters. Position one corner of the folded dough in the center of the dish, then unfold. Using scissors, trim the edge of the dough, leaving the desired overhang specified in the recipe. Fold the overhang under itself to form a high-standing rim.

Crimp a pie crust edge

Gently press the thumb of one hand into the crust edge while pressing the opposite thumb and index finger into it, creating a V-shaped indent. Repeat all around the edge of the crust.

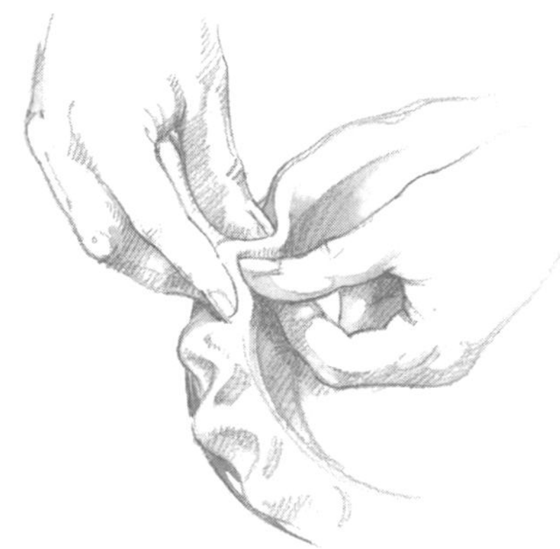

Blind-bake

Blind baking is partially or completely baking a pie or tart shell before filling it. Line a pie dish or tart pan with the dough, and chill the dough about 30 minutes to firm up. Cover the dough with a sheet of parchment paper or aluminum foil large enough to stand about one or two inches above the sides of the pan. Add enough pie weights or dried beans to fill the crust. If partially baking the crust, follow the recipe, removing the paper and weights after the crust sides are set but still pale. To prebake the crust completely, continue baking the pie (without paper and weights) until golden or dark brown, using a fork to pierce any bubbles that may form. In many Bon Appétit recipes, you'll find that we've eliminated the need for blind baking by chilling the dough first and by extending the dough slightly above the edge of the pie plate, which allows for some sinking during the baking. However, if there's a blind-baking instruction in the recipe, don't ignore it—it's there for a reason.

Remove a baked cake from a pan

Follow the recipe cooling instructions (typical cooling time for a cake layer is ten to fifteen minutes before unmolding). Push a small sharp knife between the side of the pan and the cake and cut all the way around the sides to loosen. Place a cardboard cake round over the cake. Using oven mitts, hold the cardboard round to the cake and turn upside down, shaking the pan gently, if necessary, to release the cake. Some recipes require the cake to cool completely in the pan on a rack before it is removed from the pan.

TIP: *If using a metal cake pan and the cake won't release, try placing the pan briefly over a gas flame or electric burner and moving it from side to side to warm slightly. (Do* not *use this technique with a glass pan.) Turn the cake upside down to unmold.*

Cut a cake into two layers

Mark the cake halfway down the side with toothpicks inserted into the side of the cake and spaced about three inches apart. Following the toothpicks as markers, use a long serrated knife to cut the cooled cake horizontally in half, using a sawing motion and turning the cake as necessary, while keeping the opposite hand atop the cake to steady it. Slide a tart pan bottom between the layers to remove the top layer.

Apply a crumb coat

A crumb coat is a very thin layer of frosting applied to a cake to secure any crumbs and keep them from showing through on the finished cake, while provid-

ing a smooth surface for the final frosting layer. Using an icing spatula, gently apply a small amount of frosting to the top and sides of the cake.
TIP: *If necessary, chill the cake briefly to allow the crumb coat to set, and then finish frosting.*

Frost a layer cake

If you have a decorating turntable it will make frosting the cake easier, as the cake can be turned while you work. If frosting a cake directly on a platter, keep the platter clean by sliding wide strips of waxed paper ¼ to ½ inch under the cake on all sides to cover the platter (angle the strips if working with a round cake layer). Spread the frosting (the amount will vary depending on the recipe) atop the first cake layer, and then top with the second cake layer, cut side down. Apply the crumb coat, if desired, and then cover the sides and top with the remaining frosting. Apply the frosting on the sides first, spreading up to the top edge of the cake. Drop a mound of frosting on top of the cake and use an icing spatula to spread it out to the edge of the cake. Carefully remove the waxed paper strips.

Glaze a cake

Some cakes are given a finished coating in a thin, rich chocolate glaze. Place the cake on a cardboard round that is slightly smaller than the diameter of the cake. Set the cake on a rack over a rimmed baking sheet. Pour the glaze over the center of the cake, allowing it to drip over the sides. Use an icing spatula to coax it over and smooth the sides as necessary (the less the glaze is worked, the shinier it will remain). Allow the glaze to set, and then transfer the cake to a platter.

Fill a pastry bag

Using a pastry bag to pipe batter, cookie dough, and frosting requires some practice. Drop the desired pastry tip into the pastry bag. Cup one hand about halfway down the bag and fold the overhanging portion of the bag over the cupped hand. Using a rubber spatula, fill the pastry bag about halfway. Fold the overhang back up and shake the bag to lodge the mixture firmly in the bottom half of the bag. Use your fingertips to squeeze the bag from the top, sliding them down to compact the frosting and remove any air pockets. Twist the bag at the filled point and grasp with one hand to secure tightly. Place the fingertips of your other hand under the tip end to steady and guide the bag as the mixture is piped.

Work with phyllo

Phyllo is a paper-thin dough; you must work with it quickly or it will dry out. The best phyllo is purchased fresh at Greek and Middle Eastern markets. If using frozen phyllo, thaw it overnight in its box in the refrigerator, and then let it stand a few hours at room temperature before using it. Remove the phyllo from the package and unfold it. Cover the stack of phyllo with plastic wrap and a damp towel. Pull out one sheet at a time and arrange it on a work surface or baking sheet. Use a pastry brush to apply melted butter or oil (depending on the recipe) to the pastry, covering completely. Repeat with the remaining phyllo, stacking sheets (or not) depending on the recipe. Be aware that phyllo sheets have a tendency to tear as they dry out, so treat them gently; in some cases a little tearing won't matter (as when stacking sheets to make baklava).

Knead dough by hand

When a recipe calls for kneading bread dough by hand, gather the dough into a ball and place it on a lightly floured work surface. Push the heel of your hand firmly into the center of the dough. At the same time, use your other hand to push the outside edge of the dough back toward the center in a folding motion. Repeat the process, kneading the dough as instructed (for example, "until smooth and elastic") and lightly dusting with flour as necessary to prevent sticking.

Caramelize sugar

This is one of the trickiest techniques to master, as getting the caramel syrup to the precise color requires practice. If it is not cooked far enough, the caramel flavor will be weak; if taken too far, a burned flavor may result. Be sure to use a heavy saucepan so that the sugar caramelizes evenly, but avoid pans with a dark interior as this will make it difficult to assess the actual color of the caramel. If adding cream or another liquid to the caramelized sugar, use a large enough saucepan to accommodate the increase in volume that will occur when the liquid is added (it will bubble up vigorously).
TIP: *Use great caution when working with caramelized sugar, as it can cause severe burns.*

Stir the designated amounts of sugar and water in a heavy enameled cast-iron or stainless steel saucepan (the size will vary depending on the recipe) over low heat until sugar dissolves; do not let the syrup come to a simmer until the sugar has dissolved. Brush down the sides of the pan (where sugar crystals have a tendency to form) with a pastry brush dipped in water, repeating as necessary. To test that the sugar has dissolved, rub a small amount of the syrup between your fingertips. If no granules are present, proceed with the recipe. Increase the heat and boil without stirring (stirring will encourage the formation of unwanted sugar crystals) until the syrup turns a deep amber color, swirling the pan occasionally and using a pastry brush dipped in water to brush down any sugar crystals that may accumulate on the sides of the pan. How long it takes to reach the proper caramel color will vary greatly depending on the volume of the mixture and the amount of water that was used. Once the desired color is reached, proceed quickly with the recipe's next steps or the syrup may burn.

Melt chocolate

Melting chocolate can be done in different ways. Begin by chopping the chocolate using a heavy large knife.

Stove-top method: Place the chopped chocolate in the top of a double boiler set over one or two inches of barely simmering water. Stir the chocolate until melted and smooth. Do not allow the water to boil as steam could billow out and settle on the chocolate, causing it to seize (stiffen). For the same reason, chocolate should never be covered during melting or cooling.
TIP: *If your melted bittersweet or semisweet chocolate does seize, don't throw it out—it can be turned into a delicious sauce. Simply stir in enough cream by tablespoonfuls to make it liquid and drizzle over ice cream, or use as a fondue and serve with strawberry, banana, and pineapple slices.*

Microwave method: Place the chopped chocolate in a microwave-safe bowl and heat on a low or medium setting for short periods of time until it begins to soften (the chocolate will look glossy, but will retain its shape). Microwaves vary tremendously in their power, so check frequently (about every 30 seconds) to avoid scorching. Remove the chocolate before it has fully melted and stir until smooth.

Make chocolate curls

The key to making nice chocolate curls is to have the chocolate at the proper temperature. If making curls from a solid two-inch chunk of chocolate, place it on a paper plate and microwave it on low for five-second intervals until it is barely warm. To create the curls, run a vegetable peeler along one edge of a chocolate bar or block of chocolate. If the chocolate breaks into short pieces, it may be too hard. Continue to warm it in the microwave for five-second intervals on low before continuing. To make long chocolate ruffles, hold the handle of a heavy large chef's knife in one hand and the top edge of the tip of the knife with the fingers of the other hand. Drag or pull the knife across the chocolate to create decorative chocolate shavings.

Soften ice cream

To soften ice cream or sorbet for use in ice cream cakes or pies, microwave a one-pint container for 10-second intervals on low power (or the defrost setting) until the ice cream is just soft enough to spread.

Uncork a bottle of Champagne safely

To open Champagne or sparkling wine: Stand the bottle upright on a counter top. Peel off the foil cover, and then place a folded kitchen towel or cloth napkin over the cork. Twist off and remove the wire cage. With one hand, hold the bottle steady and point it away from you at a slight angle. Grasp the cork firmly with the other hand. Gently twist the bottle to loosen the cork, gradually releasing the pressure while still maintaining a gentle hold on the cork. Resist the temptation to pop the cork out of the bottle as it can release abruptly, leaving you little control over where it may travel.

Tips for getting the most out of this book

Recipe preparation

- Read the entire recipe before you begin.
- Make sure you have all the equipment you'll need to prepare the recipe.
- Assemble and prepare all ingredients ahead of time (traditionally, this is known as *mise en place.*)

Ingredients

- When an ingredient quantity is described as *divided* (as in "3 tablespoons butter, divided"), portions of the total quantity will be used at different stages of recipe preparation. (However, if the ingredient is simply used in batches during a single stage, we don't use the word *divided.*)
- For best results, use the exact ingredients called for in the recipe. Egg substitutes do not perform like real eggs in baked goods. Nondairy liquids are chemically different from natural milk products. Stick margarine can often stand in for butter, but soft-spread margarine products cannot.
- Use any brand-name ingredients called for in the recipes. For cheesecakes and frostings, we have found that the best results come from Philadelphia brand cream cheese. When making a recipe with white or milk chocolate, we use high-quality chocolate, such as Lindt or Perugina.
- When an ingredient is not readily available at all supermarkets, the recipe headnote will tell you where to obtain it. For example, "Niçoise olives, small brine-cured black olives, are available at Italian markets, specialty foods stores, and some supermarkets." Specialty foods stores are either upscale stores (such as Whole Foods Markets, Central Market, and others) that carry a wider range of gourmet products than the average supermarket, or dedicated product stores—such as cheese shops, meat and

sausage shops, fish markets, or candy stores. See "Finding Ingredients Online" for mail-order sources of specialized ingredients.

Measuring

- Measurements indicate a full container that has been leveled off. For example, to measure one teaspoon of ground cinnamon, dip a teaspoon into the jar and use a straight edge to level it off.
- Unless otherwise specified, one cup of all purpose flour is measured using the "scoop and level" technique: Dip a one-cup measure into a sack of flour and scoop out the flour. Then level off the top by sweeping a straight edge over the cup.
- Do not sift flour before measuring unless specified in the recipe.
- If an ingredient is described as (for example), "1 cup pecans, chopped," that means the pecans should be measured whole and *then* chopped. If the ingredient is intended to be chopped and then measured, it will be described as "1 cup chopped pecans."
- For accurate measuring, use the correct type of measuring cup. (See "The Well-Stocked Kitchen" for information on dry and liquid measuring cups.) When measuring a liquid, place the cup on a flat surface, let the liquid settle, and then read it at eye level.

Cooking

- Unless otherwise specified, most baking is done with the oven rack at the center position.
- Preheat an oven for at least 20 minutes, preferably using an oven thermometer for accuracy.
- To account for variations in ovens everywhere, recipe instructions will give an approximate time *and* a visual clue. For example, if a recipe calls for a cake to bake "until tester comes out clean, about 1 hour," begin checking at least 5 minutes *before* the hour is up, and take the cake out of the oven when the tester comes out clean—whether it's less than an hour or more than an hour.

Finding ingredients online

Bakeware and dessert ingredients
Sweet Celebrations: sweetc.com

Baking flours and grains
The Baker's Catalogue: bakerscatalogue.com

Cookware
Chef's Resource: chefsresource.com

Fresh produce
Frieda's: friedas.com
Melissa's: melissas.com

Gourmet products
Adriana's Caravan: adrianascaravan.com
Earthy Delights: earthy.com

Grocery
Chef Shop: chefshop.com

International ingredients and products
Kalustyan's: kalustyans.com

Italian ingredients and products
AG Ferrari: agferrari.com

Mexican ingredients and products
MexGrocer: mexgrocer.com

Spanish ingredients and products
La Tienda: tienda.com
The Spanish Table: thespanishtable.com

Breakfast and brunch 2

A chicken-or-egg question: Do morning people make breakfast because they're already up, or is it breakfast that gets them out of bed in the first place?

Certainly the vision of Gingerbread Waffles, Skillet-Poached Eggs with Prosciutto and Arugula, or Maple-Pecan Sticky Buns would have most people throwing aside the covers in anticipation. But even coffee and granola are worth waking up for if the coffee is good and the granola is homemade. Regardless of whether it's "the most important meal of the day," breakfast should be both an enticement to and a reward for a day well started.

We'll admit it: We're partial to those weekend brunches that give both hosts and guests a chance to relax over coffee, good conversation, fresh fruit, and a variety of dishes, savory and sweet. In fact, the laid-back brunch is the secret weapon of casual entertainers. And it seems easier these days to round up a group of friends late on a weekend morning than on a weekend evening.

The recipes in this chapter offer a wealth of flavors while being easy to prepare (think of scrambled eggs, omelets, stratas and frittatas, with ingredients like andouille sausage, smoked salmon, asparagus, and goat cheese). They're gorgeous to look at—who could resist those buttermilk pancakes with jewel-colored blueberry compote? Many have do-ahead suggestions that simplify the preparation and timing so that you can enjoy your own party.

But all of this focus on brunch is not to suggest that a satisfying weekday breakfast is outside the realm of possibility. Yes, our modern lives are busy and we're all moving fast. Fortunately, there are plenty of quick and easy dishes here, too, along with recipes that can be assembled the night before and enjoyed in the morning before everyone heads out the door.

Skillet-poached eggs with prosciutto and arugula

STEAMING EGGS in custard cups is a no-muss, no-fuss way to "poach" eggs. Green-onion oil brushed over the custard cups flavors the eggs while they cook, then becomes a topping once the eggs are turned out. This stylish breakfast and brunch dish is also perfectly suitable for lunch or even a light supper.

4 SERVINGS

1 cup finely chopped green onion tops
½ cup extra-virgin olive oil
¼ cup minced fresh Italian parsley
½ teaspoon coarse kosher salt

4 ½-inch-thick slices country-style sourdough bread, each about 4x6 inches
3 ounces arugula leaves (about 4 cups)
8 thin slices prosciutto (about 4 ounces)

8 large eggs

Fresh Italian parsley sprigs

COMBINE chopped green onion tops, olive oil, minced parsley, and coarse salt in small bowl; whisk to blend. *(Can be prepared 3 hours ahead. Let stand at room temperature.)*

LIGHTLY toast sourdough bread slices. Spread each with 1 tablespoon green onion oil. Arrange ¼ of arugula on each toast slice. Top each with 2 slices prosciutto. Transfer 1 prepared toast slice to each of 4 plates.

DIVIDE remaining green onion oil equally among four 10-ounce custard cups or ramekins. Using pastry brush, spread green onion oil over inside of each cup to coat (most will fall back to bottom of cup). Break open 2 eggs into each prepared cup. Place cups in large skillet. Pour enough water into skillet to reach halfway up sides of cups.

SET skillet over medium-high heat and bring water to simmer. Reduce heat to medium-low. Cover skillet and gently cook eggs until whites are just firm to touch and yolks are set to desired consistency, about 6 minutes.

USING spatula and oven mitt or hand towel as aids, lift cups with eggs from water. Cut around eggs to loosen. Turn 2 eggs out onto each prepared toast slice. Garnish with parsley sprigs.

Smoked salmon benedict

HERE IS A DELICIOUS UPDATE of the classic eggs Benedict. Brioche slices replace the English muffin, smoked salmon takes the place of Canadian bacon, and the traditional blanket of thick, rich hollandaise sauce gives way to a light cream sauce flavored with wine and dill. If you prefer, the eggs can be fried instead of poached.

6 SERVINGS

3 tablespoons minced shallots
2 teaspoons dry mustard
1½ cups dry white wine
¾ cup whipping cream

3 tablespoons white wine vinegar
12 large eggs

6 ¾-inch-thick slices brioche loaf or egg bread, lightly toasted, each slice halved diagonally
8 ounces thinly sliced smoked salmon (not lox)
3 large egg yolks
3 tablespoons chopped fresh dill
Fresh dill sprigs (optional)

COMBINE shallots and mustard in medium saucepan. Gradually whisk in wine. Boil over high heat until mixture is reduced to ½ cup, whisking often, about 10 minutes. Whisk in cream. Season with salt and pepper. *(Sauce can be made 1 day ahead. Cover; chill.)*

FILL large bowl with cold water. Bring large skillet of water to boil; add vinegar. Reduce heat to medium-low. Working in batches, crack eggs open and add to simmering water. Cook until whites are set, about 3 minutes. Using slotted spoon, transfer 1 egg at a time to cold water. Reserve skillet with vinegar water. *(Eggs can be prepared 1 hour ahead. Let stand at room temperature.)*

PLACE 2 toast triangles on each of 6 plates. Top with salmon. Bring vinegar water in skillet to simmer. Transfer cream sauce to top of double boiler set over saucepan of simmering water. Whisk 3 raw egg yolks into cream sauce. Whisk constantly until sauce thickens and instant-read thermometer inserted into sauce registers 160°F, about 4 minutes. Remove from heat. Add chopped dill and whisk 1 minute. Using slotted spoon, gently transfer poached eggs, 1 at a time, from bowl of cold water to skillet of simmering vinegar water. Cook eggs until warm, about 30 seconds. Using slotted spoon, transfer 1 poached egg to each toast triangle. Spoon sauce over. Garnish with dill sprigs, if desired.

Broiled portobellos topped with creamy scrambled eggs

IN THIS INVENTIVE BREAKFAST, a broiled mushroom serves as an edible dish or "low-carb caddy" for scrambled eggs. To achieve the creamiest scrambled eggs, stir the eggs gently while cooking slowly over medium-low heat; a heat-resistant rubber spatula is the perfect tool for the job.

6 SERVINGS

6 4- to 5-inch-diameter portobello mushrooms
Olive oil
3 garlic cloves, minced

12 large eggs
4 tablespoons grated Parmesan cheese, divided
1½ teaspoons chopped fresh rosemary
¾ teaspoon salt
½ teaspoon ground black pepper
6 tablespoons (¾ stick) butter, divided

PREHEAT broiler. Line large baking sheet with foil. Remove and discard mushroom stems. Scoop out and discard tough inside centers where mushroom stems were attached. Brush both sides of mushrooms generously with olive oil. Place mushrooms, dark gill side up, on prepared baking sheet. Sprinkle mushrooms with minced garlic, then sprinkle generously with salt and pepper. Broil mushrooms about 5 inches from heat source until beginning to soften, about 5 minutes. Turn mushrooms over; broil until tender when pierced with knife, about 7 minutes longer. *(Can be made 2 hours ahead. Let stand at room temperature. Before continuing, rewarm in 350°F oven until heated through, about 10 minutes.)*

WHISK eggs, 2 tablespoons Parmesan cheese, rosemary, salt, and pepper in large bowl to blend. Melt 5 tablespoons butter in large nonstick skillet over medium-low heat. Add egg mixture and cook until eggs are softly set, stirring frequently, about 4 minutes. Dot with remaining 1 tablespoon butter.

ARRANGE hot portobello mushrooms, gill side up, on plates. Top with eggs, dividing equally. Sprinkle with remaining 2 tablespoons Parmesan cheese, dividing equally, and serve.

Scrambled eggs with smoked salmon and chives

THOUGH SIMPLE TO PREPARE, scrambled eggs can be as elegant as the additions you dress them up with. Here, smoked salmon and chives do the trick, but you can use your imagination (as well as what's available in your refrigerator) to create a quick and satisfying start to the day.

4 SERVINGS

8 large eggs
4 tablespoons chopped fresh chives, divided
3 tablespoons milk
5 tablespoons butter
1 large onion, chopped
6 ounces thinly sliced smoked salmon, cut into strips

WHISK eggs, 2 tablespoons chives, and milk in bowl to blend. Melt butter in large nonstick skillet over medium heat. Add onion and sauté until golden, about 15 minutes. Add egg mixture and cook until eggs are softly set, stirring frequently, about 3 minutes. Mix in salmon. Season to taste with salt and pepper. Transfer eggs to platter; sprinkle with remaining 2 tablespoons chives.

Scrambled eggs with tomato, goat cheese, and mint

FRESH MINT gives this egg dish an exotic Middle Eastern or Mediterranean flair. Crumbled feta cheese would make a robust substitution for the milder goat cheese. For a complete meal, accompany the eggs with sliced cucumbers, fresh olive bread, and honey-drizzled fresh or dried figs, and pour sweetened black tea.

4 SERVINGS

10 large eggs
1 large tomato, seeded, chopped
¼ cup coarsely crumbled soft fresh goat cheese
¼ cup chopped green onions
¼ cup chopped fresh mint
1 teaspoon salt
½ teaspoon ground black pepper
3 tablespoons butter, divided
2 shallots, chopped

Fresh mint sprigs (optional)

WHISK eggs in large bowl to blend. Add tomato, goat cheese, green onions, chopped mint, salt, and pepper; whisk just to blend. Melt 1 tablespoon butter in 12-inch nonstick skillet over medium heat. Add shallots; sauté 3 minutes. Add remaining 2 tablespoons butter to skillet and let melt. Add egg mixture; cook 2 minutes without stirring. Using spatula, gently stir and turn over portions of the egg mixture until softly set, about 4 minutes.

DIVIDE scrambled eggs among 4 plates. Garnish with mint sprigs, if desired, and serve.

Southwestern breakfast scramble

WHEN SERVED with refried beans or black beans, this breakfast scramble is a wonderful brunch or lunch dish. Feel free to substitute your favorite red salsa for the green tomatillo salsa.

6 SERVINGS

1 cup purchased tomatillo salsa
½ cup chopped fresh cilantro, divided
2 tablespoons (¼ stick) butter
2 5-inch-diameter corn tortillas, cut into ½-inch strips
8 ounces pork chorizo sausage, casings removed
½ cup chopped red onion
12 large eggs, beaten to blend
1 cup grated white cheddar cheese (about 4 ounces)

Sour cream
1 avocado, halved, pitted, peeled, sliced

MIX salsa and ¼ cup cilantro in bowl. Set salsa mixture aside. Melt butter in large nonstick skillet over medium-high heat. Add tortillas; sauté until brown, about 3 minutes. Using slotted spoon, transfer tortillas to plate. Add chorizo to skillet and sauté until cooked through, breaking up with back of spoon, about 12 minutes. Add onion; sauté 1 minute. Return tortillas to skillet. Add eggs and remaining ¼ cup cilantro; cook until eggs are softly set, stirring frequently, about 3 minutes. Mix in cheese.

TRANSFER egg mixture to platter. Season to taste with salt and pepper. Top with sour cream and avocado. Serve, passing salsa mixture.

Wild mushroom, shallot, and Gruyère omelets

IN FRANCE, mushroom omelets made with cèpes (porcini mushrooms) are served at dinner along with a tossed green salad, a baguette, and a glass of wine. For this omelet, the mushroom filling can be cooked and refrigerated up to a day ahead for a super-quick breakfast. If wild mushrooms are unavailable, button mushrooms are a good substitute.

2 SERVINGS; CAN BE DOUBLED OR TRIPLED

4 tablespoons (½ stick) butter, divided
4 ounces fresh wild mushrooms (such as stemmed shiitake, oyster, or porcini), sliced
2 large shallots, minced
1 tablespoon minced fresh parsley

6 large eggs
4 teaspoons cold water, divided
⅔ cup grated Gruyère cheese (about 2 ounces), divided
Additional minced fresh parsley

MELT 1 tablespoon butter in heavy small skillet over medium heat. Add mushrooms and shallots; sauté until mushrooms are tender, about 2 minutes. Remove from heat and mix in 1 tablespoon parsley. Season to taste with salt and pepper.

WHISK 3 eggs and 2 teaspoons cold water in small bowl to blend. Heat small nonstick skillet over medium-high heat. Add 1½ tablespoons butter and heat until foam begins to subside. Add egg mixture and stir with back of fork until eggs begin to set. Cook until mixture is set, lifting edges occasionally with spatula to let uncooked egg run under cooked portion. Spoon half of cheese, then half of mushroom mixture down center of omelet. Fold sides of omelet over filling to enclose. Transfer omelet to plate. Cover with foil to keep warm. Make second omelet with remaining eggs, cold water, 1½ tablespoons butter, mushrooms, and cheese. Garnish with additional parsley.

Bell pepper, tomato, and cheese omelets

THIS RECIPE YIELDS two individual omelets, but you can also make one big omelet in a large skillet if you prefer. Using a nonstick skillet makes omelet fixing easy, and preparing the filling the night before cuts down on cooking time in the morning. You can also add half a cup of diced ham, if you like.

2 SERVINGS; CAN BE DOUBLED

2 tablespoons olive oil, divided
1 small onion, chopped
1 small green bell pepper, chopped
2 tomatoes, seeded, chopped
1 teaspoon dried oregano
Large pinch of cayenne pepper

4 large eggs
1 tablespoon water
½ cup grated Fontina or Monterey Jack cheese (about 2 ounces), divided
4 tablespoons grated Parmesan cheese, divided

HEAT 1½ tablespoons oil in medium nonstick skillet over medium heat. Add onion and bell pepper; sauté until almost soft, about 5 minutes. Add tomatoes, oregano, and cayenne; simmer until vegetables are very soft and filling is thick, about 3 minutes. Season to taste with salt and pepper. Transfer filling to small bowl; do not clean skillet.

WHISK eggs and 1 tablespoon water in small bowl to blend. Mix in ¼ cup Fontina cheese. Heat same skillet over medium-high heat. Add half of egg mixture and stir with back of fork until eggs begin to set. Cook until mixture is set, lifting edges occasionally with spatula to let uncooked egg run under cooked portion, about 2 minutes. Spoon half of vegetable filling, half of remaining Fontina, and 2 tablespoons Parmesan down center of omelet. Fold sides of omelet over filling to enclose. Transfer omelet to plate. Cover with foil to keep warm. Add remaining ½ tablespoon oil to skillet. Make second omelet with remaining egg mixture, filling, and cheeses.

Potato omelet with olives

THIS IS A VERSION of the classic Spanish dish called *tortilla* (not the thin cornmeal or flour round, but a creation similar to an omelet). In Spain the potatoes are mixed with the eggs, cooked until set, and served at room temperature as a tapa or appetizer. Here, the potatoes are combined with other Spanish favorites—nutty Manchego sheep's milk cheese and zesty green olives—to make a wonderful vegetarian omelet filling. Look for Manchego at specialty foods stores and some supermarkets.

2 SERVINGS

- **1 8-ounce russet potato**
- **2 tablespoons olive oil, divided**
- **½ small onion, chopped**
- **¼ small green bell pepper, diced**
- **¼ cup sliced pimiento-stuffed green Spanish olives**
- **1 tablespoon minced fresh oregano or 1 teaspoon dried**
- **¾ cup grated Manchego or white cheddar cheese (about 2½ ounces)**
- **6 large eggs**

COOK potato in boiling salted water until just tender when pierced with sharp knife, about 25 minutes. Drain potato. Cool, peel, and dice.

HEAT 1 tablespoon olive oil in heavy medium saucepan over medium-high heat. Add onion and bell pepper; sauté until vegetables are soft, about 10 minutes. Mix in potato, olives, and oregano; cook until mixture is heated through, stirring occasionally, about 5 minutes. Remove from heat. Gently mix in cheese. Season to taste with salt and pepper and cover to keep warm.

HEAT remaining 1 tablespoon olive oil in 10-inch nonstick skillet over medium-high heat. Whisk eggs in large bowl to blend. Add eggs to skillet and stir with back of fork until eggs begin to set. Cook until mixture is set, lifting edges occasionally with spatula to let uncooked egg run under cooked portion, about 3 minutes. Spoon filling over half of eggs. Using spatula, fold plain side of eggs over filling. Transfer to platter. Cut omelet in half and serve.

Asparagus omelet

THIS OMELET is cooked like a pancake, with the "filling" mixed in. It's a wonderful use for leftover asparagus. Served with fresh strawberries and lemon muffins or scones, it makes a perfect springtime breakfast.

2 SERVINGS

- **10 ounces asparagus, trimmed, cut into ⅓-inch pieces**
- **6 large eggs**
- **⅓ cup freshly grated Parmesan cheese (about 1 ounce)**
- **½ teaspoon salt**
- **¼ teaspoon ground black pepper**
- **4 bacon slices, cut into ½-inch pieces**
- **4 green onions (white parts only), thinly sliced**

STEAM asparagus until crisp-tender, about 5 minutes. Drain.

WHISK eggs, Parmesan, salt, and pepper in large bowl to blend. Sauté bacon pieces in large ovenproof nonstick skillet over medium-high heat until golden brown, about 3 minutes. Add green onions and sauté until onions are translucent, about 3 minutes. Add cooked asparagus; sauté until heated through. Reduce heat to medium. Spread asparagus mixture in single layer in same skillet. Pour egg mixture over asparagus, bacon, and green onions. Cook until eggs are set, tilting skillet and lifting edges occasionally with spatula to let uncooked egg run under cooked portion, about 4 minutes. Tilt skillet and slide omelet out onto platter, then fold omelet in half. Cut omelet in half and serve.

Andouille sausage and potato omelet

HERE ARE your eggs, home fries, and sausage together in one delicious open-face omelet. Andouille is spicy smoked pork sausage from Louisiana; kielbasa, linguiça, or any other smoked (fully cooked) sausage can be used instead. If you love cheese in your omelets, a packed half-cup of grated cheese can be sprinkled over the filling before baking.

2 SERVINGS

1 tablespoon olive oil
1 cup ½-inch cubes peeled small red-skinned potatoes
½ cup ⅛-inch cubes andouille sausage (about 2 ounces)
¼ cup chopped red bell pepper
¼ cup chopped onion
2 tablespoons minced green onion
¼ teaspoon ground cumin

6 large eggs
½ teaspoon salt
¼ teaspoon ground black pepper
1 tablespoon butter

PREHEAT oven to 375°F. Heat oil in large nonstick skillet over medium heat. Add potatoes and sauté until brown, about 7 minutes. Add sausage, bell pepper, and onion; sauté until vegetables are soft, about 6 minutes. Stir in green onion and cumin. Season sausage mixture to taste with salt and pepper. Remove from heat; keep warm.

WHISK eggs, salt, and pepper in large bowl to blend. Melt butter in heavy large ovenproof skillet over medium heat. Add egg mixture and cook until eggs are almost set in center, tilting skillet and lifting edges occasionally with spatula to let uncooked portion run under cooked portion, about 3 minutes. Distribute sausage mixture over eggs. Transfer skillet to oven; bake until eggs are completely set, about 3 minutes. Run spatula under outer edges of omelet to loosen and slide onto platter. Cut in half and serve.

Sausage and cheese strata with sun-dried tomatoes

A *STRATA* is best described as a savory bread pudding. It's well suited to morning parties as it can be assembled the night before. This adaptable dish makes excellent use of leftover bread. Add a layer of salsa and replace the mozzarella with shredded hot pepper Monterey Jack cheese for a Southwestern flair; or replace the sausage and sun-dried tomatoes with some caramelized onions and Gruyère cheese for a French touch.

8 SERVINGS

½ cup sun-dried tomatoes (not oil-packed), chopped

12 ounces hot Italian sausages, casings removed

8 large eggs
3½ cups whole milk
2 teaspoons minced fresh thyme or ¾ teaspoon dried
1½ teaspoons salt
¼ teaspoon ground black pepper
11 slices white sandwich bread (about 1 pound), crusts trimmed, bread cut into 1-inch pieces
½ cup chopped onion
½ cup freshly grated Parmesan cheese (about 1½ ounces)

1 cup (packed) grated mozzarella cheese (about 4 ounces)
¼ cup crumbled soft fresh goat cheese
Chopped fresh parsley

PLACE sun-dried tomatoes in medium bowl. Pour enough boiling water over to cover. Let stand until softened, about 15 minutes. Drain.

SAUTÉ sausage in heavy medium skillet over medium heat until cooked through, breaking up with back of spoon, about 5 minutes. Using slotted spoon, transfer sausage to paper towels to drain well.

BUTTER 13x9x2-inch glass baking dish. Whisk eggs, milk, thyme, salt, and pepper in large bowl to blend.

Add sun-dried tomatoes, sausage, bread, onion, and Parmesan cheese; stir to blend. Transfer to prepared dish. Cover and refrigerate at least 4 hours and up to 1 day.

PREHEAT oven to 375°F. Bake strata uncovered until puffed and golden brown, about 45 minutes. Sprinkle with mozzarella and goat cheeses and bake until mozzarella melts, about 5 minutes. Transfer pan to rack and cool 5 minutes. Sprinkle with parsley.

Prosciutto and goat cheese strata

BEGIN PREPARING this soufflé-like strata the day before you plan to serve it. As a brunch dish, it would go nicely with slices of honeydew melon and cantaloupe and some chocolate-dipped biscotti. For lunch or dinner, serve with a salad of arugula, radicchio, and artichoke hearts tossed with a garlicky vinaigrette.

6 SERVINGS

18 slices firm white bread (such as English muffin bread), crusts removed
6 ounces prosciutto, thinly sliced
8 ounces soft fresh goat cheese, crumbled
4 ounces provolone cheese, grated (about 1½ cups)
¼ cup chopped green onions

6 tablespoons thinly sliced fresh basil
5 large eggs
2 cups whole milk
1 tablespoon Dijon mustard
½ teaspoon salt
3 tablespoons butter, melted

LINE bottom of 13x9x2-inch glass baking dish completely with 1 layer of bread, cutting some slices to fit. Arrange half of prosciutto evenly over bread. Sprinkle half of goat cheese and half of provolone over. Sprinkle with half of green onions and half of basil. Top with second layer of bread. Layer remaining prosciutto, goat cheese, provolone, green onions, and basil atop bread. Cut remaining bread into ¼-inch cubes. Sprinkle over top.

WHISK eggs, milk, mustard, and salt in bowl. Season with pepper. Pour egg mixture over strata; press down on bread with spatula. Drizzle melted butter over strata. Cover and refrigerate overnight.

PREHEAT oven to 350°F. Uncover strata and let stand at room temperature 30 minutes. Bake until center is set, about 1 hour. Remove from oven. Preheat broiler. Cook strata in broiler until top is golden, about 30 seconds. Cut into large squares and serve.

Frittata with pancetta and mint

A *FRITTATA* is an Italian omelet in which the vegetable, meat, and cheese components are mixed with the beaten eggs and then cooked and broiled in a skillet until set. It is served in wedges. *Pancetta* is salt-cured Italian bacon (it differs from American bacon in that it is not smoked), available at Italian markets and in the deli case at many supermarkets.

6 SERVINGS

1½ tablespoons olive oil
6 ounces pancetta or bacon, cut into ¼-inch pieces (about 1½ cups)
1½ cups chopped red onion

12 large eggs
¼ cup cold water
¾ teaspoon salt
⅛ teaspoon ground black pepper
½ cup plus 2 tablespoons chopped fresh mint

HEAT olive oil in large nonstick ovenproof skillet over medium heat. Add pancetta and onion; sauté until onion is soft, about 10 minutes.

PREHEAT broiler. Whisk eggs, ¼ cup cold water, salt, and pepper in medium bowl to blend. Pour eggs into skillet with onion and pancetta. Stir 1 minute. Add ½ cup chopped mint; stir 30 seconds. Reduce heat to low and cook without stirring until almost set, about 10 minutes.

TRANSFER skillet to broiler and cook frittata just until firm, about 1 minute. Using spatula as aid, transfer frittata to serving platter. Sprinkle with remaining 2 tablespoons chopped mint. Cut frittata into wedges and serve.

Fresh corn, brie, and jalapeño frittata

PLACE THE BRIE in the freezer briefly to facilitate trimming and dicing. You can double the recipe; just use a 12-inch skillet. Enjoy with hearty multi-grain toast for breakfast, lunch, or dinner.

2 SERVINGS; CAN BE DOUBLED

3 tablespoons butter, divided
½ cup minced onion
¾ cup fresh corn kernels (cut from 1 large ear of corn) or frozen, thawed
2 jalapeño chiles, seeded, finely chopped

5 large eggs
6 ounces Brie cheese, rind trimmed, finely diced
¼ teaspoon salt
⅛ teaspoon ground black pepper

6 fresh basil leaves, shredded

MELT 1 tablespoon butter in heavy small skillet over medium-low heat. Add onion and stir 3 minutes. Add corn and jalapeños; cook until corn is tender, stirring occasionally, about 5 minutes. Cool slightly.

PREHEAT broiler. Beat eggs lightly in medium bowl to blend. Stir in corn mixture, cheese, salt, and pepper. Melt remaining 2 tablespoons butter in heavy 9-inch-diameter ovenproof skillet over medium heat. Add egg mixture. Pierce holes in egg mixture and lift up edges with spatula, tipping pan to allow uncooked egg to run under until edge forms, about 1 minute; do not stir. Cover skillet and continue cooking until eggs are almost set, about 5 minutes.

TRANSFER skillet to broiler and cook frittata until eggs are set and top is golden brown, watching carefully, about 1 minute. Garnish with basil.

Vegetable frittata with herbs and goat cheese

THIS HEARTY FRITTATA is perfect for a picnic breakfast or brunch as it can be made ahead and kept at room temperature up to two hours. A nonstick skillet and a heatproof flexible silicone spatula are must-haves. If the goat cheese is well chilled, it will crumble easily.

6 SERVINGS

1 tablespoon plus 2 teaspoons olive oil
2 medium-size red-skinned potatoes (about 9 ounces total), cut crosswise into ⅛-inch-thick rounds
1 medium onion, halved, thinly sliced
1 red bell pepper, cut into ⅓-inch-wide strips
1 yellow bell pepper, cut into ⅓-inch-wide strips
1 tablespoon chopped fresh marjoram or 1 teaspoon dried
2 teaspoons minced fresh rosemary or ¾ teaspoon dried
1¼ teaspoons salt, divided
¼ teaspoon dried rubbed sage

9 large eggs
1 tablespoon chopped fresh dill or 1 teaspoon dried dillweed
½ teaspoon ground black pepper
4 ounces chilled soft fresh goat cheese, crumbled (about 1 cup), divided

Fresh herb sprigs and chopped fresh herbs such as rosemary, dill, and marjoram (optional)

HEAT 1 tablespoon oil in 12-inch-diameter nonstick ovenproof skillet over medium-low heat. Add potatoes, onion, red and yellow bell peppers, marjoram, rosemary, ½ teaspoon salt, and sage. Cook 5 minutes, stirring occasionally. Cover and cook until potatoes are tender, stirring occasionally, about 15 minutes. Cool vegetable mixture in skillet 5 minutes. *(Can be prepared 2 hours ahead. Let stand at room temperature.)*

PREHEAT oven to 350°F. Whisk eggs, dill, remaining ¾ teaspoon salt, and pepper in large bowl to blend. Mix in 3 ounces goat cheese. Transfer several potato slices and bell pepper strips to small dish and reserve. Stir remaining vegetable mixture into egg mixture.

WIPE same 12-inch skillet clean. Add remaining 2 teaspoons oil; heat over medium-high heat, tilting skillet to coat bottom with oil. Pour egg-vegetable mixture into skillet, stirring vegetables to distribute. Arrange reserved vegetables on top in attractive pattern; sprinkle with remaining 1 ounce goat cheese. Cook until sides of frittata begin to set, about 2 minutes. Transfer skillet to oven; bake until frittata is set in center, about 15 minutes.

RUN spatula around edge of frittata to loosen from skillet. Slide out onto platter. Serve hot, or cover loosely with foil and let stand at room temperature up to 2 hours.

GARNISH frittata with herb sprigs and chopped herbs, if desired. Cut frittata into wedges and serve.

Salmon hash with horseradish-dill cream

HASH GETS ITS NAME from the French *hacher*, meaning "to chop." Though once considered an economy meal, usually made with corned or boiled beef and cooked potatoes, a good hash is delicious comfort food. This elegant version could make excellent use of leftover cooked salmon and potatoes.

2 SERVINGS

1 12-ounce salmon fillet (about 1 inch thick)
12 ounces small white-skinned potatoes

6 tablespoons chilled whipping cream, divided
4 tablespoons prepared white horseradish, divided
3 tablespoons chopped fresh dill, divided
½ teaspoon white wine vinegar

½ cup chopped green onions

2 tablespoons (¼ stick) butter

PREHEAT oven to 350°F. Place salmon on baking sheet; sprinkle with salt and pepper. Bake just until cooked through, about 18 minutes. Transfer to plate. Cover; chill until cold. Flake salmon into ½-inch pieces. Cook potatoes in pot of boiling salted water until just tender, about 10 minutes. Drain potatoes well; cool, peel, and dice.

WHISK 5 tablespoons cream, 2 tablespoons horseradish, and 2 tablespoons dill in small bowl until very thick. Whisk in vinegar. Season horseradish cream to taste with salt and pepper. Chill.

MASH ¾ cup diced potatoes with remaining 1 tablespoon whipping cream, 2 tablespoons horseradish, and 1 tablespoon dill in medium bowl until almost smooth. Lightly mix in salmon, green onions, and remaining potatoes. Season with salt and pepper.

MELT butter in heavy medium nonstick skillet over high heat. Add hash; press to compact. Reduce heat to medium and cook until bottom is brown and crusty, about 10 minutes. Using large spatula, turn over hash in sections. Press lightly and cook until bottom is brown, about 5 minutes. Turn out hash onto 2 plates. Serve with horseradish cream.

Blue and red flannel hash

THIS GREAT-TASTING HASH gets its red from red bell pepper and beets, and its blue from blue cheese. Maytag blue cheese is creamy, American-made blue cheese; a medium-sharp blue cheese such as a Danish blue or Gorgonzola can also be used in its place.

4 SERVINGS

- **8 ounces turkey hot Italian sausages, casings removed**
- **1 cup chopped red onion**
- **3 tablespoons butter, divided**
- **3/4 teaspoon dried thyme**
- **1 10-ounce russet potato, peeled, cut into 1/2-inch cubes**
- **1 cup chopped red bell pepper**
- **1 15-ounce can sliced pickled beets, drained, cut into 1/2-inch pieces**
- **4 tablespoons chopped fresh parsley, divided**
- **3/4 cup crumbled Maytag blue cheese**

- **4 large eggs**

HEAT large nonstick skillet over medium-high heat. Add sausage and sauté until cooked through, breaking up with back of spoon, about 10 minutes. Using slotted spoon, transfer sausage to bowl. Add onion, 1 tablespoon butter, and thyme to same skillet; sauté 3 minutes. Add potato and bell pepper; season with salt and pepper. Reduce heat to low, cover, and cook until potato is tender, stirring occasionally, about 10 minutes. Increase heat to medium-high. Stir sausage, beets, and half of parsley into potato. Cook without stirring until hash begins to brown on bottom, about 5 minutes. Using spatula, turn hash over in sections and cook without stirring until brown on bottom, about 5 minutes. Sprinkle cheese over. Remove from heat; cover and let stand 5 minutes.

MELT remaining 2 tablespoons butter in medium skillet over medium-high heat. Add eggs and fry to desired doneness.

DIVIDE hash among plates; top with eggs. Sprinkle with remaining parsley.

Baked eggs with artichokes and Parmesan

THESE EGGS are super-fast to make—and get even faster if you assemble them the night before so they're ready to bake in the morning. For a festive brunch, serve with toasted sliced ciabatta, grilled Italian sweet sausages, and Bellinis, the peach and Champagne cocktail from Venice.

2 SERVINGS

- **1 tablespoon unsalted butter, room temperature**
- **2 teaspoons chopped fresh chives**
- **1 teaspoon chopped fresh parsley**
- **1 teaspoon chopped fresh oregano**
- **8 frozen artichoke heart quarters, thawed**
- **2 large eggs**
- **2 tablespoons (packed) freshly grated Parmesan cheese**

RUB butter over bottom and sides of two 6-ounce soufflé dishes or custard cups, dividing equally. Sprinkle with herbs, dividing equally. Place 4 artichoke pieces in each dish. Crack 1 egg into each dish, being careful not to break yolk. Sprinkle eggs with salt, pepper, and cheese. *(Can be prepared 1 day ahead. Cover; chill.)*

PREHEAT oven to 400°F. Bake until eggs are softly set and cheese is golden, about 9 minutes. Serve immediately.

Gruyère and Parmesan cheese soufflé

THE KEY HERE is to have your guests assembled *before* the soufflé has finished baking: That way they can enjoy the fluffy texture, delicate flavor, lovely aroma—and its fully risen glory. Because soufflés are sensitive to temperature changes, don't open the oven to check on it until just a few minutes before it should be done. The following recipe can be used to make one large soufflé or six smaller individual soufflés.

4 TO 6 SERVINGS

- **Freshly grated Parmesan cheese**
- **1/4 cup (1/2 stick) butter**
- **5 tablespoons all purpose flour**
- **Pinch of cayenne pepper**
- **Pinch of ground nutmeg**
- **1 1/4 cups whole milk**
- **1/4 cup dry white wine**
- **6 large egg yolks**
- **1 teaspoon salt**
- **1/4 teaspoon ground black pepper**
- **1 1/4 cups plus 2 tablespoons (packed) coarsely grated Gruyère cheese (about 6 ounces)**
- **1/4 cup finely grated Parmesan cheese**

- **8 large egg whites**

POSITION rack in center of oven and preheat to 400°F. Generously butter one 10-cup soufflé dish or six 10-ounce soufflé dishes; sprinkle with Parmesan cheese to coat. (If using individual dishes, place all 6 on rimmed baking sheet.) Melt butter in heavy large saucepan over medium heat. Add flour, cayenne, and nutmeg. Cook, whisking constantly, until mixture begins to bubble but does not brown, about 1 minute. Gradually whisk in milk, then wine. Cook until smooth, thick, and beginning to boil, whisking constantly, about 2 minutes. Remove from heat. Mix yolks, salt, and pepper in small bowl. Add yolk mixture all at once to sauce and whisk quickly to blend. Fold in 1¼ cups Gruyère cheese and ¼ cup Parmesan cheese (cheeses do not need to melt).

USING electric mixer, beat egg whites in large bowl until stiff but not dry. Fold ¼ of whites into lukewarm soufflé base to lighten. Fold in remaining whites. Transfer soufflé mixture to prepared dish or dishes. Sprinkle with remaining 2 tablespoons Gruyère cheese.

PLACE soufflé in oven; reduce heat to 375°F. Bake soufflé until puffed, golden, and gently set in center, about 40 minutes for large soufflé or 25 minutes for small soufflés. Using oven mitts, transfer to platter and serve immediately.

Breakfast polenta with sausage, onion, and peppers

A ZIPPY ITALIAN VERSION of old fashioned cornmeal mush—make it a day ahead to allow enough time for chilling. If you prefer a less spicy but equally delicious breakfast treat, you can substitute Italian sweet sausages for the hot sausages, or use a combination. Turkey or chicken Italian sausages can be used as well.

6 SERVINGS

- **3 hot Italian sausages (about 8 ounces), casings removed**
- **3/4 cup chopped onion**
- **3/4 cup chopped green bell pepper**
- **1 teaspoon dried oregano**

- **3 1/2 cups water**
- **1 cup yellow cornmeal**
- **1/2 cup grated Parmesan cheese (about 1 1/2 ounces)**

- **4 tablespoons (1/2 stick) butter**

BUTTER 11x7x2-inch glass baking dish. Sauté sausage in skillet over medium heat until cooked through, breaking up sausage with back of fork, about 8 minutes. Add onion, bell pepper, and oregano. Sauté until vegetables are tender, about 8 minutes.

BRING 3½ cups water to boil in medium saucepan. Gradually whisk in cornmeal. Reduce heat to medium-low; whisk until cornmeal is tender and very thick, about 7 minutes. Stir in cheese and sausage mixture. Season to taste with salt and pepper. Pour into prepared dish. Cover and chill at least 1 hour and up to 1 day.

CUT polenta into 2-inch squares. Melt 2 tablespoons butter in large nonstick skillet over medium-high heat. Sauté half of squares until brown, about 5 minutes per side. Transfer to platter; tent with foil. Repeat with remaining butter and squares. Serve hot.

Tortillas in black bean sauce

THIS OAXACAN BREAKFAST and snack dish—known as *enfrijoladas*—begins like so many in Mexico: with an assemblage of fried tortillas. In Oaxaca, the lightly fried tortillas, still warm and pliable, are coated with a smoky puree of black beans before thick crema mexicana, chopped cilantro, and onion are added. While it is traditional to fold the tortillas into quarters or into thirds like an omelet, you can also fold them over once.

Wait to season the beans with salt until they are just soft; this will ensure the creamiest texture. Epazote and queso fresco are available at Latin markets and at some supermarkets.

6 SERVINGS

- **1 pound dried black beans, rinsed**
- **1 cup chopped white onion, divided**
- **4 large fresh epazote sprigs or marjoram sprigs**
- **2 tablespoons lard or corn oil**
- **2 large garlic cloves, halved**
- **1¼ teaspoons aniseed, ground or finely crushed in plastic bag or in mortar with pestle**
- **½ cup corn oil (for frying)**
- **18 5- to 6-inch-diameter white corn tortillas**
- **1½ cups crumbled queso fresco or feta cheese (about 6 ounces)**
- **½ cup chopped fresh cilantro**
- **6 tablespoons crema mexicana or sour cream**
- **3 pickled jalapeño chiles, halved lengthwise**

PLACE beans in heavy large pot. Add enough cold water to cover by 2 inches. Add ½ cup onion, epazote, lard, garlic, and aniseed; bring to boil over high heat. Reduce heat to low, cover, and simmer until beans are just tender, adding more boiling water by cupfuls if less than 1 inch of water covers beans and stirring occasionally, about 1 hour (beans should have soupy consistency). Season beans generously with salt; continue to simmer until very tender, about 15 minutes longer. *(Can be made 2 days ahead. Cool slightly, cover, and chill. Rewarm before continuing.)*

DRAIN beans, reserving bean cooking liquid. Place 3 cups beans (about half) and 1½ cups bean cooking liquid in blender. Puree until smooth. Transfer bean sauce to large saucepan. Repeat with remaining beans and bean cooking liquid, supplementing with water if necessary. Season sauce to taste with salt and pepper. Bring sauce to simmer; reduce heat and keep warm over low heat.

HEAT oil in heavy medium skillet over medium heat. Add 1 tortilla and heat 20 seconds. Using tongs, turn tortilla over and cook until beginning to bubble and soften, about 20 seconds longer. Dip tortilla into warm bean sauce to coat. Place tortilla on plate; fold into quarters. Repeat with remaining tortillas and sauce, arranging 3 folded tortillas in center of each of 6 plates. Spoon additional bean sauce over. Top with cheese, remaining ½ cup onion, cilantro, and crema, dividing equally, then pickled jalapeño chile halves.

Mushroom crepes with poblano chile sauce

THE CREPES AND SAUCE can be prepared ahead of time, making this south-of-the-border dish excellent for entertaining. Wild mushrooms stand in for *cuitlacoche* (corn fungus), which is a delicacy in Mexico. *Poblanos* (dark green, shiny heart-shaped chiles) can be found in Latin markets and some supermarkets, as can the herb epazote. Manchego is a Spanish sheep's milk cheese available at specialty foods stores and some supermarkets. The recipe makes a few more crepes than you need in case any go awry—and if they all come out perfectly, just drizzle some maple syrup over the extras.

6 SERVINGS

Crepes

- **2 cups whole milk**
- **3 large eggs**
- **2 tablespoons (¼ stick) unsalted butter, melted, cooled**
- **1 teaspoon fine sea salt**
- **2 cups sifted all purpose flour**

Additional melted butter

Sauce

- **6 large fresh poblano chiles**

- **2 tablespoons (¼ stick) unsalted butter**
- **¼ cup chopped white onion**
- **1 small garlic clove, minced**
- **3 tablespoons all purpose flour**
- **2 cups warm whole milk**
- **½ cup whipping cream**

Mushroom filling

- **⅓ cup corn oil**
- **2 cups chopped white onions**
- **1 pound fresh shiitake mushrooms, stemmed, caps thinly sliced**
- **2 tablespoons minced fresh epazote or fresh cilantro**
- **4 teaspoons finely chopped garlic**
- **1 cup coarsely grated Manchego or white cheddar cheese (about 4 ounces)**

- **3 tablespoons corn oil**
- **½ cup fresh corn kernels**
- **Fresh cilantro sprigs**

FOR CREPES: Blend milk, eggs, 2 tablespoons melted butter, and salt in blender 5 seconds. Add flour, ½ cup at a time, blending batter until smooth after each addition. Let rest 1 to 2 hours. Reblend batter 5 seconds before using.

HEAT nonstick skillet with 7- to 8-inch-diameter bottom over medium-high heat; brush with melted butter. Pour 3 tablespoons batter into skillet; swirl skillet to coat bottom evenly. Cook until bottom of crepe is golden, about 30 seconds. Loosen edges gently with spatula and turn crepe over. Cook until bottom is brown in spots, about 30 seconds. Turn crepe out onto paper towel. Repeat, making about 16 crepes and stacking between paper towels. *(Can be made 2 days ahead. Wrap and chill.)*

FOR SAUCE: Char chiles directly over gas flame or in broiler until blackened on all sides. Enclose in paper bag 10 minutes. Peel, seed, and thinly slice chiles.

MELT butter in medium saucepan over medium heat. Add onion; sauté until soft, about 2 minutes. Add garlic; stir 30 seconds. Stir in flour (mixture may be firm). Sauté 1 minute longer. Whisk in warm milk and bring to boil, whisking constantly. Reduce heat to medium-low; simmer until sauce thickens, whisking occasionally, about 5 minutes. Pour sauce into blender. Add cream and half of roasted chiles (reserve remaining chiles for garnish). Blend sauce until smooth. Season with salt and pepper. *(Can be made 1 day ahead. Cover and chill. Whisk over medium heat until just warm before continuing.)*

FOR MUSHROOM FILLING: Heat oil in large skillet over medium-high heat. Add onions and sauté until translucent, about 3 minutes. Add mushrooms, epazote, and garlic. Sauté until mushrooms are brown and mushroom liquid has evaporated, about 10 minutes. Season with salt and pepper.

BRUSH small baking sheet with oil. Arrange 1 crepe, brown spots up, on work surface. Place 2 packed tablespoons filling in center. Fold crepe in half. Fold in half again, forming triangle. Place filled crepe on prepared sheet. Repeat with 11 more crepes and all of filling. *(Can be made 1 day ahead. Cover with foil and chill.)*

PREHEAT oven to 350°F. Pour ¼ cup warm sauce into center of each of 6 ovenproof plates. Top each with 2 filled crepes. Pour ¼ cup sauce over. Sprinkle with cheese. Bake until cheese melts, about 12 minutes.

MEANWHILE, heat 3 tablespoons oil in heavy medium skillet over medium-high heat. Add reserved poblano chiles and corn kernels; sauté until heated through, about 2 minutes. Sprinkle with salt.

GARNISH crepes with sautéed chiles and corn, then cilantro sprigs, and serve.

Giant Sunday pancakes

SIX-INCH-DIAMETER PANCAKES will delight both young and old. Be sure to use a heavy nonstick skillet for even cooking. This perfect pancake can be varied, if desired, by sprinkling a quarter-cup blueberries, raisins, or even chocolate chips over each pancake before turning it to finish cooking.

MAKES 6

- **3 large eggs**
- **½ cup sugar**
- **6 tablespoons (¾ stick) butter, melted**
- **1½ cups all purpose flour**
- **1 cup milk**
- **1 tablespoon baking powder**
- **¼ teaspoon salt**

Butter
Pure maple syrup, warmed

PREHEAT oven to 250°F. Whisk eggs, sugar, and melted butter in medium bowl to blend. Add flour alternately with milk in 3 additions, whisking to blend after each addition. Whisk in baking powder and salt.

MELT enough butter in heavy medium nonstick skillet over medium heat just to coat bottom. Ladle scant ¾ cup batter into skillet, rotating skillet to spread batter to about 6-inch-diameter round. Cook pancake until bubbles form and break on surface and bottom is brown, about 2 minutes. Turn over pancake and cook until bottom is brown and pancake is cooked through, about 2 minutes. Transfer to large baking sheet. Place in oven to keep warm. Repeat with remaining batter to form 5 more pancakes, adding more butter to skillet as necessary. Serve with syrup.

Banana cream pancakes

HERE BANANAS ARE ENJOYED two ways: cooked into the griddle cake and pureed and mixed with rich whipped cream. If you're short on time and long on bananas, the pancakes are great on their own with maple syrup and additional sliced bananas.

4 SERVINGS

- **3 cups buttermilk**
- **2 large eggs, separated**
- **2½ cups all purpose flour**
- **2 tablespoons sugar**
- **1½ teaspoons baking powder**
- **1 teaspoon baking soda**
- **1 teaspoon salt**

- **6 tablespoons (¾ stick) butter**
- **4 ripe medium bananas, thinly sliced**

Banana Cream (see recipe)
Pure maple syrup (optional)

WHISK buttermilk and egg yolks in large bowl to blend. Whisk flour, sugar, baking powder, baking soda, and salt in medium bowl to blend. Gradually whisk flour mixture into buttermilk mixture. Beat egg whites in medium bowl until stiff but not dry. Gently fold whites into batter.

PREHEAT oven to 250°F. Melt 2 tablespoons butter in large nonstick skillet over medium heat. Working in batches, drop batter by ½ cupfuls into skillet. Place 8 banana slices on each pancake, spacing evenly. Cook until pancakes are light golden, about 3 minutes per side. Transfer pancakes to baking sheet; keep warm in oven. Repeat with remaining butter, batter, and banana slices.

TOP pancakes with dollops of Banana Cream. Serve pancakes warm with maple syrup, if desired.

Banana cream

THIS DO-AHEAD CREAM is also delicious spooned into goblets with layers of fresh tropical fruits.

MAKES ABOUT 5 CUPS

- **4 ripe bananas (about 1¼ pounds), peeled, sliced**
- **1 cup apple juice**
- **⅔ cup powdered sugar**
- **¼ cup fresh lemon juice**

- **1½ cups chilled whipping cream**

COMBINE first 4 ingredients in medium saucepan over medium heat. Cook until bananas are very soft, about 3 minutes. Using slotted spoon, transfer bananas to processor. Add ⅓ cup liquid from pan to bananas (discard remaining liquid). Puree until smooth. Transfer to large bowl. Chill until cold.

BEAT cream in medium bowl until stiff peaks form. Fold whipped cream into chilled banana puree. *(Can be made 2 days ahead. Cover with plastic wrap; chill.)*

Whole grain–buttermilk pancakes

THESE HEARTY HOTCAKES are excellent served fresh off the griddle with butter and maple syrup, but they also make a delicious base for yogurt, fresh fruit, chopped nuts, and a drizzle of honey—the perfect pre-hike weekend breakfast.

MAKES ABOUT 20

- **1 cup whole wheat flour**
- **⅓ cup quick-cooking oats**
- **⅓ cup yellow cornmeal**
- **⅓ cup all purpose flour**
- **2 teaspoons baking powder**
- **¼ teaspoon baking soda**
- **¼ teaspoon salt**
- **2 cups buttermilk**
- **2 large eggs**
- **4 tablespoons (about) butter, melted, divided**
- **2 tablespoons mild-flavored (light) molasses**
- **Pure maple syrup**

MIX first 7 ingredients in medium bowl to blend. Whisk buttermilk, eggs, 2 tablespoons melted butter, and molasses in large bowl to blend. Add dry ingredients; mix just until blended. Heat griddle or heavy large skillet over medium heat. Brush with some of remaining butter. Working in batches, drop scant ¼ cup batter onto griddle for each pancake. Cook until brown, about 3 minutes per side, brushing griddle with more butter as needed between batches. Serve with syrup.

Buttermilk pancakes with blueberry compote

SOUR CREAM AND BUTTERMILK give these pancakes a delicate texture and rich, tangy flavor. The easy-to-make blueberry compote is a wonderful accompaniment; the pancakes are also great served with butter and jam or maple syrup.

MAKES ABOUT 18

2½ cups all purpose flour
¼ cup sugar
2 teaspoons baking powder
2 teaspoons baking soda
1 teaspoon salt
2 cups buttermilk
2 cups sour cream
2 large eggs
4 teaspoons vanilla extract

3 tablespoons (about) unsalted butter

Additional unsalted butter
Blueberry Compote (see recipe)

WHISK first 5 ingredients in large bowl to blend. Whisk buttermilk, sour cream, eggs, and vanilla in another large bowl. Add to dry ingredients. Stir until batter is just blended but still lumpy (do not overmix).

MELT ½ tablespoon butter in heavy large skillet over medium heat. Pour batter by ⅓ cupfuls into skillet, spacing pancakes 2 inches apart. Cook until bubbles break on surface, about 3 minutes. Turn pancakes over. Cook until bottoms are golden, 3 minutes. Transfer to plates. Repeat with remaining batter, adding more butter to skillet as needed.

SERVE pancakes immediately, topped with additional butter and compote.

Blueberry compote

THIS WOULD ALSO BE a good topping for plain yogurt or oatmeal.

MAKES ABOUT 1½ CUPS

2½ cups frozen blueberries, unthawed, divided
⅓ cup sugar
⅓ cup water

COMBINE 1½ cups blueberries, ⅓ cup sugar, and ⅓ cup water in heavy small saucepan. Simmer over medium heat until berries burst, stirring often, about 10 minutes. Add remaining 1 cup berries. Cook until compote coats spoon, stirring often, about 8 minutes. *(Can be made 3 days ahead. Cover and chill; rewarm before using.)* Serve warm.

Baked apple pancakes

THIS RECIPE MAKES two brown-sugar-glazed cakes that melt in your mouth. You will need two small ovenproof skillets. Paired with vanilla ice cream, these pancakes can be served as a comforting dessert.

2 SERVINGS

1 Granny Smith apple, cored, peeled, cut into ¼-inch-thick slices
2 teaspoons fresh lemon juice
4 large eggs
¾ cup whole milk
¾ cup all purpose flour
1 tablespoon plus ¼ cup sugar
¼ teaspoon salt
¼ cup (packed) dark brown sugar
1¼ teaspoons ground cinnamon

4 tablespoons (½ stick) unsalted butter

PREHEAT oven to 450°F. Toss apple slices with lemon juice in medium bowl. Whisk eggs and milk in large bowl to blend. Add flour, 1 tablespoon sugar, and salt; whisk until batter is almost smooth (small lumps of flour will remain). Mix brown sugar, cinnamon, and remaining ¼ cup sugar in small bowl.

MELT 1 tablespoon butter in each of two 6-inch ovenproof nonstick skillets over medium heat. Pour half of batter into each skillet. Arrange half of apple slices evenly over batter in each skillet.

TRANSFER skillets to oven and bake until pancakes are set around edges but still wet in center, about 8 minutes. Remove from oven; sprinkle half of brown sugar mixture over each pancake. Dot each with 1 tablespoon butter. Using spatula, carefully turn pancakes over. Return to oven. Bake until pancakes rise, sugar mixture melts to sauce consistency, and top is golden, about 6 minutes. Invert onto plates and serve warm.

Blintz casserole

A SPECIALTY OF JEWISH COOKING, traditional cheese blintzes are thin pancakes filled with a sweet or savory cheese filling, then fried in butter until golden brown and crisp. Here, the cheese filling is sandwiched between layers of a light, buttery cake-like batter. Be sure to make the filling ahead, and work quickly when assembling the casserole. Serve it as soon as it comes out of the oven with sour cream and your favorite jam.

12 SERVINGS

Cheese filling

- **24 ounces (1½ pounds) ricotta cheese**
- **2 8-ounce packages cream cheese, room temperature**
- **2 large eggs**
- **¼ cup sugar**
- **3½ tablespoons fresh lemon juice**
- **1 teaspoon grated lemon peel**
- **1 teaspoon grated orange peel**
- **⅛ teaspoon salt**

Batter

- **1 cup all purpose flour, sifted**
- **1 tablespoon baking powder**
- **⅛ teaspoon salt**
- **1 cup (2 sticks) unsalted butter, melted**
- **½ cup sugar**
- **3 large eggs**
- **¼ cup milk**
- **1 teaspoon vanilla extract or ½ teaspoon almond extract**

- **⅓ cup blanched slivered almonds, toasted**
- **Sour cream**
- **Strawberry jam**

FOR CHEESE FILLING: Using electric mixer, beat all ingredients in large bowl until blended. *(Can be prepared 1 day ahead. Cover and refrigerate.)*

FOR BATTER: Preheat oven to 300°F. Butter 13x9x2-inch baking dish. Combine flour, baking powder, and salt in large bowl. Mix in butter, sugar, eggs, milk, and vanilla extract.

POUR half of batter into prepared dish. Spoon cheese filling over, gently spreading without mixing into batter. Pour remaining batter over. Bake casserole until set, about 1½ hours. Sprinkle with almonds. Cut into squares. Serve warm, passing sour cream and jam separately.

Baked French toast with cardamom and marmalade

THIS FESTIVELY FLAVORED FRENCH TOAST serves a crowd, bakes in the oven (rather than being cooked a few pieces at a time on a griddle), and can be assembled the night before–which makes it the perfect centerpiece for a holiday breakfast or a brunch party. Serve with bacon or sausage and fruit compote. Any leftover citrus syrup would be nice poured over peeled, sliced oranges.

10 SERVINGS

French toast

- **1 1/4 cups orange marmalade**
- **10 4x4x1-inch slices egg bread**
- **1 1/4 cups whole milk**
- **3/4 cup whipping cream**
- **1/2 cup sugar**
- **3 large egg yolks**
- **3 large eggs**
- **1 1/4 teaspoons ground cardamom**
- **1 teaspoon grated orange peel**
- **1 teaspoon grated lemon peel**

Citrus syrup

- **1 1/4 cups light corn syrup**
- **3 tablespoons fresh lemon juice**
- **2 tablespoons grated orange peel**
- **4 teaspoons sugar**
- **1 tablespoon grated lemon peel**

Powdered sugar

FOR FRENCH TOAST: Butter 15x10x2-inch glass baking dish. Spread marmalade evenly over 1 side of each bread slice. Cut slices diagonally in half, forming triangles. Arrange triangles crosswise in dish, marmalade side up and overlapping slightly. Whisk milk and next 7 ingredients in large bowl. Pour custard over bread. Let bread stand 1 hour, basting occasionally, or cover and refrigerate overnight.

FOR CITRUS SYRUP: Mix corn syrup, lemon juice, orange peel, sugar, and lemon peel in small bowl, stirring until sugar dissolves. Let stand at least 1 hour. *(Can be made 1 day ahead. Cover and refrigerate.)*

PREHEAT oven to 350°F. Bake French toast, uncovered, until puffed and golden brown, about 50 minutes. Sprinkle with powdered sugar; serve with citrus syrup.

Banana-berry French toast

A LIGHT, FUN, AND ELEGANT French toast "sandwich" stuffed with banana and strawberry slices—the perfect breakfast in bed for a special someone. The recipe also doubles easily: Just prepare the egg mixture in a 13x9x2-inch baking dish and cook the French toast on a large griddle or in two batches.

2 SERVINGS; CAN BE DOUBLED

- **1/3 cup half and half**
- **2 large eggs**
- **1/2 teaspoon vanilla extract**
- **1/4 teaspoon ground cinnamon**
- **8 slices egg bread (each about 1/2 inch thick)**
- **4 large strawberries, hulled, sliced**
- **1/2 medium banana, peeled, sliced**

- **1 tablespoon butter**

Additional strawberries
Pure maple syrup

WHISK half and half, eggs, vanilla, and cinnamon in 8-inch square baking dish to blend. Using 3-inch round cookie cutter, cut 1 round from each bread slice. Divide 4 sliced strawberries and banana slices equally over 4 bread rounds. Top each with another bread round, creating 4 sandwiches. Press on bread to compact. Place sandwiches in egg mixture; let stand 2 minutes. Turn sandwiches over; let stand additional 2 minutes.

MELT butter in large nonstick skillet over medium heat. Add sandwiches to skillet and cook until golden brown, about 2 minutes per side.

TRANSFER sandwiches to plates. Garnish with additional strawberries and serve with maple syrup.

Pomegranate, Beet, and Blood Orange Salad (page 133)
Grilled Asian-Style Scallop and Asparagus Salad (page 149)

Buttermilk Pancakes with Blueberry Compote (page 38)

Skillet-Poached Eggs with Prosciutto and Arugula (page 23)

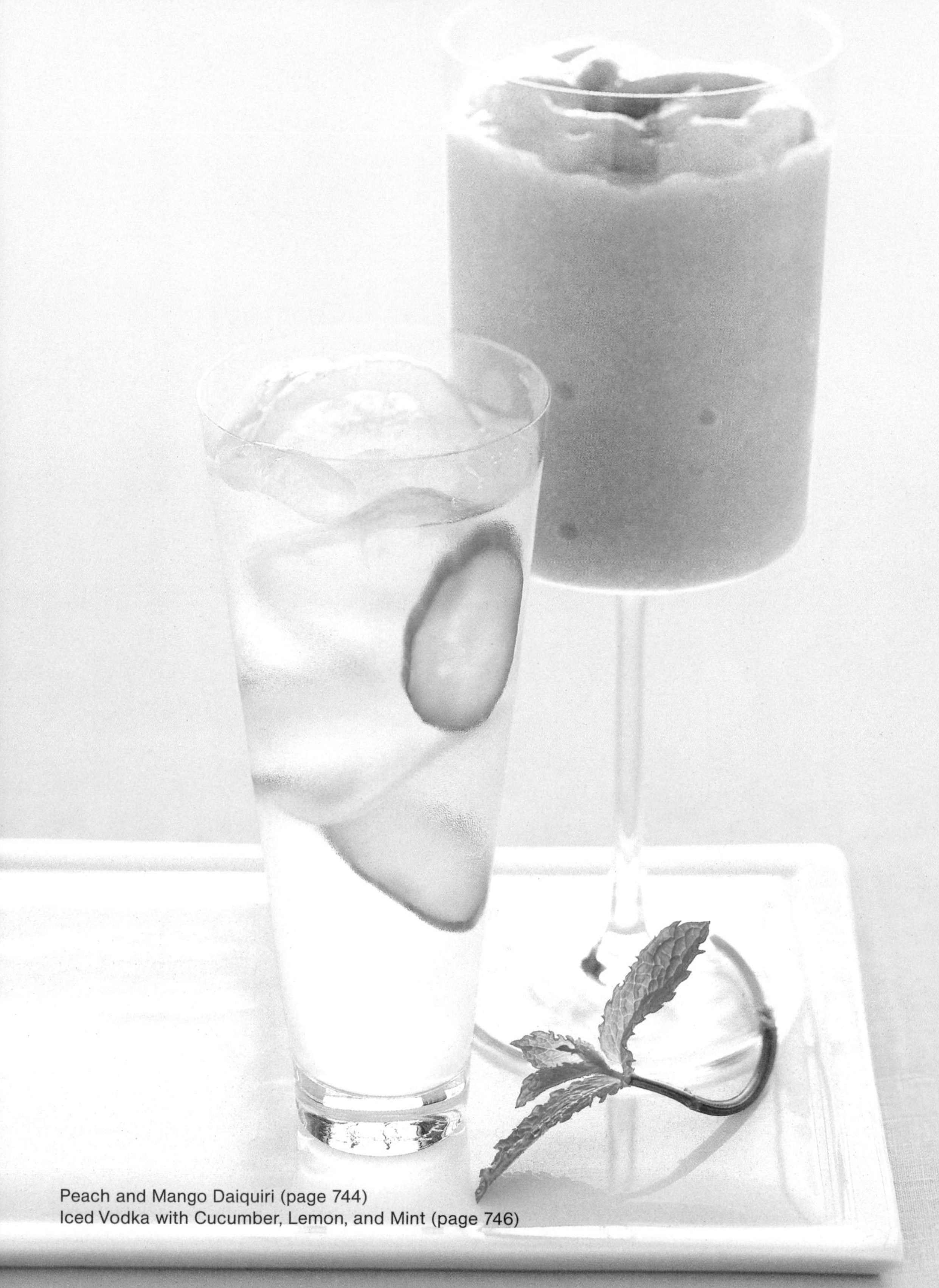

Peach and Mango Daiquiri (page 744)
Iced Vodka with Cucumber, Lemon, and Mint (page 746)

Shrimp Rice-Paper Rolls with Vietnamese Dipping Sauce (page 63)
Tamarind-Glazed Lamb Skewers with Dried Apricot Relish (page 71)

Crab-and-Corn Chowder with Bacon and Chanterelle Mushrooms (page 91)

Chicken Tagine with Vegetable Couscous (page 119)

Grilled Prosciutto and Fontina Sandwiches (page 173)
Tuna Salad on Olive Bread with Arugula (page 165)

Double cinnamon French toast

FOR A VARIATION, try a cinnamon-raisin bread and sprinkle with chopped toasted pecans. For a "skinny" version—just as tasty though not quite as rich—use milk in place of the whipping cream or half and half. The cinnamon-infused maple syrup keeps well in the refrigerator and is wonderful poured over hot oatmeal.

2 TO 4 SERVINGS

- **1 cup pure maple syrup**
- **3 tablespoons unsalted butter, divided**
- **2 teaspoons ground cinnamon, divided**
- **3 large eggs**
- **1 cup whipping cream or half and half**
- **2 teaspoons vanilla extract**
- **4 ¾- to 1-inch-thick slices cinnamon bread or egg bread**

BRING syrup, 1 tablespoon butter, and 1 teaspoon cinnamon to boil in heavy medium saucepan. Boil 2 minutes. Whisk eggs, cream, vanilla, 3 tablespoons maple syrup mixture, and remaining 1 teaspoon cinnamon in medium bowl. Place bread slices in large baking dish. Pour egg mixture over; turn to coat. Pierce bread in several places with fork. Let stand 5 minutes.

MELT 1 tablespoon butter in heavy large skillet over medium-high heat. Add bread and cook until brown, about 3 minutes. Add 1 tablespoon butter to skillet. Turn bread over and cook until brown, about 3 minutes longer.

TRANSFER to plates. Serve with remaining syrup.

Gingerbread waffles

THE AROMA that these tender, exceptionally flavorful waffles sends through the home will get even the sleepiest heads out of bed and into the kitchen. Since waffles tend to cool rather quickly, serve them on heated plates. A spoonful of whipped cream and a drizzle of maple syrup or a dollop of applesauce make these an excellent breakfast or any-time treat.

MAKES ABOUT 12 WAFFLES

- **⅓ cup (firmly packed) golden brown sugar**
- **1 large egg**
- **¾ cup buttermilk**
- **¼ cup mild-flavored (light) molasses**
- **3 tablespoons butter, melted**
- **1 cup all purpose flour**
- **1½ teaspoons baking powder**
- **1 teaspoon ground ginger**
- **1 teaspoon ground cinnamon**
- **½ teaspoon ground allspice**
- **½ teaspoon baking soda**
- **¼ teaspoon dry mustard**
- **¼ teaspoon salt**
- **⅓ cup chopped raisins**
- **2 tablespoons minced crystallized ginger**

Additional melted butter
Whipped cream
Pure maple syrup or applesauce

WHISK sugar and egg in medium bowl to blend well, about 2 minutes. Mix in buttermilk, molasses, and butter. Combine flour, baking powder, spices, baking soda, mustard, and salt in small bowl. Add to liquid ingredients and whisk to blend. Stir in raisins and crystallized ginger.

PREHEAT waffle maker according to manufacturer's instructions. Brush waffle maker with melted butter. Spoon some batter onto waffle maker (amount of batter will vary depending on size of waffle maker). Cover and cook waffle until golden and cooked through (cooking time will vary depending on waffle maker). Repeat with remaining batter. Serve waffles immediately with whipped cream and maple syrup.

Macadamia nut waffles with papaya and strawberries

ANY COMBINATION OF TROPICAL FRUITS, such as bananas or mangoes, would also be delicious with these light and crisp Belgian-style waffles. Although the waffles won't be as tall, you can cook the batter in a standard waffle maker. Unsweetened coconut milk is available at Indian, Southeast Asian, and Latin markets and at many supermarkets.

4 SERVINGS

1½ cups cake flour
2 tablespoons golden brown sugar
2½ teaspoons baking powder
¼ teaspoon salt
1¼ cups canned unsweetened coconut milk, room temperature
3 eggs, separated, room temperature
5 tablespoons unsalted butter, melted
1 teaspoon vanilla extract

⅓ cup ground toasted macadamia nuts

1 papaya, peeled, seeded, sliced
1 pint strawberries, hulled, quartered
Pure maple syrup

SIFT flour, sugar, baking powder, and salt into large bowl. Make well in center. Mix coconut milk, yolks, butter, and vanilla in another bowl; pour into well. Whisk into dry ingredients until just blended.

PREHEAT Belgian waffle maker (medium heat). Beat egg whites in another bowl to medium peaks. Gently fold whites and nuts into batter (several lumps may remain). Ladle 1 cup batter onto center of waffle maker and cook until waffle is golden brown. Transfer to warmed plate. Repeat with remaining batter.

GARNISH waffles with papaya and strawberries. Serve, passing syrup separately.

Toffee bar coffee cake

THIS CRUMB CAKE–STYLE coffee cake is a snap to prepare; the topping and batter are both made from the same butter, sugar, and flour mixture. Enjoy with coffee at your next brunch party, or wrap up squares to put in the kids' lunch boxes.

MAKES 16 SQUARES

2 cups all purpose flour
1 cup (packed) dark brown sugar
½ cup sugar
½ cup (1 stick) unsalted butter, room temperature
½ teaspoon salt
4 1.4-ounce chocolate-covered English toffee bars (such as Heath Bars), chopped (about 1 cup)
1 cup chopped pecans
1 teaspoon baking soda
1 cup buttermilk
1 large egg
1 teaspoon vanilla extract

PREHEAT oven to 350°F. Butter 13x9x2-inch glass baking dish. Using electric mixer on low speed, beat flour, both sugars, butter, and salt in large bowl until mixture resembles coarse meal. Transfer ½ cup butter-sugar mixture to medium bowl and mix in toffee and pecans. Set toffee topping aside. Stir baking soda into remaining butter-sugar mixture in large bowl. Add buttermilk, egg, and vanilla, beating until just combined. Transfer batter to prepared dish. Sprinkle toffee topping evenly over batter.

BAKE coffee cake until topping is golden brown and toothpick inserted into center of cake comes out clean, about 35 minutes. Cool completely in dish. Cut into 16 squares. *(Coffee cake can be prepared 1 day ahead. Store in airtight container at room temperature.)*

Sour cream–streusel coffee cake

A CLASSIC BUNDT-STYLE CAKE with two layers of dark, sweetly spiced streusel, this is elegant enough for brunch or afternoon tea. It would even make a nice host or hostess gift. If you're running short on time, simply sprinkle the cake with powdered sugar and skip the icing.

8 TO 10 SERVINGS

1¼ cups coarsely chopped walnuts
1¼ cups (packed) golden brown sugar
6 tablespoons dried currants
4½ teaspoons ground cinnamon
4½ teaspoons unsweetened cocoa powder
3 cups cake flour
1½ teaspoons baking soda
1½ teaspoons baking powder
¾ teaspoon salt
¾ cup (1½ sticks) unsalted butter, room temperature
1½ cups sugar
3 large eggs
1 tablespoon vanilla extract
1 16-ounce container sour cream

1 cup powdered sugar
1 tablespoon milk

PREHEAT oven to 350°F. Butter 12-cup Bundt pan. Mix first 5 ingredients in small bowl. Set nut mixture aside. Sift flour, baking soda, baking powder, and salt into medium bowl. Using electric mixer, beat butter and 1½ cups sugar in large bowl to blend. Beat in eggs 1 at a time. Mix in vanilla. Mix dry ingredients and sour cream alternately into butter mixture in 3 additions. Beat batter on high 1 minute.

POUR ⅓ of batter into prepared pan. Sprinkle with half of nut mixture. Spoon ⅓ of batter over. Sprinkle with remaining nut mixture. Spoon remaining batter over. Bake cake until tester inserted near center comes out clean, about 1 hour. Cool cake in pan on rack 10 minutes. Cut around pan sides to loosen cake. Turn cake out onto rack and cool 1 hour. Transfer to platter.

WHISK powdered sugar and milk in small bowl until smooth. Drizzle over coffee cake. Serve slightly warm or at room temperature. *(Can be prepared 1 day ahead. Cool completely. Wrap in foil and let stand at room temperature.)*

Ginger scones

FANS OF CRYSTALLIZED GINGER will love these tender, buttery scones. The subtle citrus and bold ginger flavors go particularly well with a freshly brewed pot of Earl Grey tea. The scones can be baked ahead and reheated, making them great for entertaining.

MAKES 12

2¼ cups all purpose flour
⅓ cup sugar
1 tablespoon baking powder
¼ teaspoon grated lemon peel
11 tablespoons chilled unsalted butter, cut into small pieces
¾ cup plus 2 tablespoons whipping cream
⅔ cup diced crystallized ginger

PREHEAT oven to 400°F. Lightly butter baking sheet. Blend flour, sugar, baking powder, and lemon peel in processor. Add butter; using on/off turns, cut in until mixture resembles coarse meal. Transfer mixture to large bowl. Make well in center; add ¾ cup cream. Using fork, stir until just moist. Mix in ginger.

TRANSFER dough to floured surface and knead gently until smooth, about 8 turns. Divide dough in half; pat each portion into ¾-inch-thick round. Cut each round into 6 wedges and transfer to prepared baking sheet, spacing 1 inch apart. Brush tops with remaining 2 tablespoons cream.

BAKE scones until light brown, about 18 minutes. *(Can be made 1 day ahead. Cool completely. Store in airtight container at room temperature. Rewarm in 350°F oven before serving.)*

Heart-shaped chocolate chip–orange scones

THESE SCONES can be cut out the night before, refrigerated unbaked on a baking sheet, and then popped into the oven in the morning. They will be ready in ready in just 15 minutes. The sugar topping gives these hearts a delightful sweet crust. If you like nuts, try adding 3/4 cup chopped toasted hazelnuts along with the chocolate chips.

MAKES ABOUT 12

- **2 cups unbleached all purpose flour**
- **1/3 cup plus 3 tablespoons sugar**
- **1 teaspoon baking powder**
- **3/4 teaspoon salt**
- **1/2 teaspoon baking soda**
- **1/2 cup (1 stick) chilled unsalted butter, diced**
- **3 teaspoons grated orange peel, divided**
- **1 cup miniature semisweet chocolate chips**
- **2/3 cup chilled buttermilk**
- **1 large egg yolk**
- **1 teaspoon vanilla extract**

Additional buttermilk (for glaze)

BUTTER and flour baking sheet. Whisk flour, 1/3 cup sugar, baking powder, salt, and baking soda in large bowl. Add butter and 2 teaspoons orange peel; rub in with fingertips until mixture resembles coarse meal. Mix in chocolate chips. Whisk 2/3 cup buttermilk, egg yolk, and vanilla extract in small bowl to blend. Add buttermilk mixture to dry ingredients; stir with fork until dough comes together in moist clumps. Gather dough into ball. Press out dough on lightly floured surface to 3/4-inch thickness. Using 2-inch heart-shaped cookie cutter, cut out scones. Gather scraps, press out dough, and cut out additional scones. Transfer to baking sheet, spacing 1 inch apart. *(Can be prepared 1 day ahead. Cover; chill.)*

PREHEAT oven to 400°F. Mix remaining 3 tablespoons sugar with remaining 1 teaspoon orange peel in small bowl. Brush scones lightly with buttermilk; sprinkle with orange-sugar. Bake until scones are crusty on top and tester inserted into centers comes out clean, about 15 minutes (or up to 20 minutes if refrigerated). Serve warm or at room temperature.

Treacle scones

IN SCOTLAND, where they originated, scones are a favorite for breakfast, but even more so at teatime. One popular variety is made with treacle, a thick semiliquid syrup that is a by-product of refining cane sugar. Treacle is not commonly found in the United States, but molasses makes a good substitute. Offer these scones with butter and marmalade.

MAKES 8

- **2 cups all purpose flour**
- **1/4 cup (firmly packed) dark brown sugar**
- **2 1/2 teaspoons baking powder**
- **1/2 teaspoon baking soda**
- **1/4 teaspoon ground cinnamon**
- **1/4 teaspoon ground nutmeg**
- **1/4 teaspoon salt**
- **1/2 cup dried currants**
- **1/4 cup (1/2 stick) unsalted butter**
- **2 tablespoons mild-flavored (light) molasses (do not use blackstrap)**
- **3/4 cup buttermilk**

Melted butter
Sugar

PREHEAT oven to 425°F. Sift flour, brown sugar, baking powder, baking soda, cinnamon, nutmeg, and salt into large bowl. Add currants. Melt 1/4 cup butter with molasses in heavy small saucepan over low heat. Combine molasses mixture with buttermilk and add to dry ingredients. Mix until just blended.

GENTLY knead dough on generously floured surface until smooth, about 20 turns. Divide dough in half.

Pat out each dough piece to 5-inch-diameter round. Cut each round into 4 wedges. Transfer wedges to ungreased baking sheet, spacing 2 inches apart. Brush with melted butter and sprinkle with sugar. Bake until scones are just firm to touch, about 20 minutes. Serve hot.

Glazed maple-walnut scones

THESE OVERSIZED SCONES have a light muffin-like texture. The golden glaze adds a sweet, firm coating. Pack them along with a thermos of hot coffee for any early-morning outing.

MAKES 6

- **2 cups all purpose flour**
- **¾ cup (packed) golden brown sugar, divided**
- **1 teaspoon baking powder**
- **½ teaspoon baking soda**
- **½ teaspoon salt**
- **10 tablespoons (1¼ sticks) chilled unsalted butter, cut into ½-inch cubes, divided**
- **¾ cup walnuts, toasted, broken into pieces**
- **⅔ cup buttermilk**
- **2 large egg yolks**
- **1 teaspoon maple extract**

- **2 tablespoons whipping cream**
- **⅔ cup powdered sugar**
- **½ teaspoon mild-flavored (light) molasses**

POSITION rack in center of oven and preheat to 400°F. Combine flour, ¼ cup brown sugar, baking powder, baking soda, and salt in large bowl; whisk to blend. Add 6 tablespoons butter; using fingertips, rub in until butter is reduced to pea-size pieces. Mix in walnuts. Whisk buttermilk, egg yolks, and maple extract in medium bowl. Add to flour mixture. Toss with fork until dough comes together in moist clumps. Gather dough into ball. Press out dough on lightly floured surface to 8-inch round; cut into 6 wedges.

ARRANGE wedges 1 inch apart on ungreased baking sheet. Bake until tester inserted into centers comes out clean, about 16 minutes; transfer to rack.

WHISK remaining ½ cup brown sugar, 4 tablespoons butter, and cream in heavy small saucepan over low heat until sugar dissolves. Remove pan from heat. Whisk in powdered sugar and molasses. Spread glaze over warm scones. Let stand until glaze sets, at least 30 minutes.

Tart cherry and almond muffins

ALMOND PASTE adds wonderful flavor and keeps the muffins moist for days. Look for it in the baking-products section of your local market or specialty foods store.

MAKES 10

- **6 tablespoons orange juice**
- **¾ cup dried tart cherries (about 4 ounces)**

- **1 cup plus 2 tablespoons all purpose flour**
- **½ cup sugar**
- **1½ teaspoons baking powder**
- **¼ teaspoon salt**
- **1 7-ounce package almond paste, crumbled**
- **6 tablespoons (¾ stick) unsalted butter, melted, hot**
- **3 large eggs**
- **1½ teaspoons grated orange peel**

POSITION rack in center of oven and preheat to 375°F. Butter ten ⅓-cup metal muffin cups. Bring juice to simmer in small saucepan. Remove from heat. Add cherries; let stand until softened, about 10 minutes.

MIX flour, sugar, baking powder, and salt in medium bowl. Using electric mixer, beat almond paste and melted butter in large bowl to blend well (mixture will still have some small pieces of almond paste). Add eggs 1 at a time, beating well after each addition. Mix in cherry mixture and orange peel. Add flour mixture and mix just until blended.

DIVIDE batter among prepared muffin cups. Bake until tester inserted into center of muffins comes out clean but slightly moist to touch, about 20 minutes. *(Muffins can be made 2 days ahead. Cool. Wrap in foil and store at room temperature. Rewarm in foil in 350°F oven 5 minutes.)* Serve warm.

Spiced pumpkin muffins

THE ADDITION OF whole wheat flour gives these muffins a full, earthy flavor that complements the pumpkin. *Pepitas* are shelled green pumpkin seeds; if they're unavailable at the supermarket, you'll find them at a natural foods store. Omit the spray and line the muffins cups with decorative muffin papers if desired.

MAKES 15

- **Nonstick vegetable oil spray**
- **1 cup all purpose flour**
- **1/2 cup whole wheat flour**
- **1/3 cup sugar**
- **1/4 cup (packed) golden brown sugar**
- **2 1/2 teaspoons baking powder**
- **1 teaspoon ground cinnamon**
- **1/4 teaspoon ground cloves**
- **1/2 teaspoon salt**
- **1/3 cup pepitas (shelled pumpkin seeds), lightly toasted, divided**
- **1/3 cup coarsely chopped walnuts, lightly toasted, divided**
- **1 1/4 cups canned pure pumpkin**
- **1 cup whole milk**
- **2 large eggs**
- **6 tablespoons (3/4 stick) unsalted butter, melted**
- **2 teaspoons grated peeled fresh ginger**

PREHEAT oven to 375°F. Spray 15 standard muffin cups (1/3-cup capacity) with nonstick spray. Whisk both flours, both sugars, baking powder, spices, and salt in large bowl to blend. Mix in half of pumpkin seeds and half of walnuts. Whisk pumpkin, milk, eggs, butter, and ginger in medium bowl to blend. Add to dry ingredients and stir just until incorporated (do not overmix).

SPOON 1/4 cup batter into each muffin cup. Sprinkle remaining pumpkin seeds and walnuts over. Bake until muffins are golden and tester inserted into center comes out clean, about 25 minutes. Turn muffins out onto rack and cool. *(Can be made 1 day ahead. Store muffins airtight at room temperature.)*

Maple-pecan sticky buns

HIGH-RISING YEAST DOUGH is rolled with a filling of pecans, raisins, and cinnamon, then the buns are baked in an irresistible "sticky" maple-syrup glaze. They can be completely assembled a day before baking, or baked and then frozen up to two weeks, making this home-baked, old-fashioned treat as convenient as a stop at the bakery.

MAKES 12

Dough

- **1/4 cup warm water (105°F to 115°F)**
- **1 envelope dry yeast**

- **1/3 cup old-fashioned oats**
- **1/3 cup sugar**
- **3 tablespoons unsalted butter, cut into pieces**
- **2 teaspoons grated lemon peel**
- **1 1/2 teaspoons salt**
- **1 1/4 cups whole milk (do not use low-fat or nonfat)**

- **1 large egg**
- **1 large egg yolk**
- **2 teaspoons vanilla extract**
- **4 1/2 cups (about) unbleached all purpose flour**

Syrup

- **1 cup pure maple syrup**
- **9 tablespoons (1 stick plus 1 tablespoon) unsalted butter**

- 1 cup (packed) golden brown sugar
- 1/2 cup coarsely chopped pecans

Filling

- 3/4 cup pecans
- 1/2 cup (packed) golden brown sugar
- 1/2 cup raisins
- 2 teaspoons ground cinnamon

- 3 tablespoons unsalted butter, melted

FOR DOUGH: Place ¼ cup warm water in small bowl. Sprinkle yeast over and stir to blend. Let stand until yeast dissolves, about 8 minutes.

COMBINE oats, sugar, butter, lemon peel, and salt in large bowl. Heat milk in small saucepan until bubbles form around edge of pan. Pour hot milk over oat mixture and stir until butter melts and sugar dissolves. Cool mixture to 105°F to 115°F, about 10 minutes.

ADD egg, egg yolk, vanilla, and dissolved yeast to oat mixture; stir to blend. Mix in 3 cups flour. Using firm rubber spatula or large wooden spoon, beat batter 100 strokes. Cover bowl with plastic wrap; let batter rest 10 minutes.

USING spatula, mix enough flour into batter, ¼ cupful at a time, to form soft dough. Turn dough out onto floured surface. Knead gently until smooth and slightly sticky dough forms, adding more flour if very sticky, about 8 minutes.

LIGHTLY oil large bowl. Place dough in bowl; turn to coat with oil. Cover bowl with plastic wrap, then with towel. Let dough rise in warm draft-free area until doubled in volume, about 1½ hours.

MEANWHILE, PREPARE SYRUP: Butter two 13x9x2-inch glass baking dishes. Combine maple syrup and butter in heavy medium skillet. Stir over medium heat until butter melts. Remove from heat. Mix in brown sugar. Pour half of syrup into each prepared dish; tilt to coat bottom of dishes evenly. Sprinkle each with half of nuts; cool.

FOR FILLING: Combine pecans, brown sugar, raisins, and cinnamon in processor. Using on/off turns, blend until pecans are finely chopped.

CAREFULLY turn risen dough out onto floured surface (do not punch down dough). Roll dough gently to flatten slightly. Using hands, pull and stretch dough to 12x18-inch rectangle. Brush dough with all of melted butter. Sprinkle filling evenly over dough, leaving ½-inch plain border on 1 long side. Starting at long side opposite plain border, roll up dough jelly-roll style, forming log. Pinch seam to seal. Using heavy large knife, score log in 12 places, spacing evenly. Cut log at scores. Arrange 6 pieces, cut side up and evenly spaced, in each prepared baking dish. Lightly press down on buns with palm of hand. Cover pans tightly with plastic wrap. *(Can be prepared 1 day ahead. Refrigerate overnight.)* Let buns rise in warm draft-free area until light and puffy, about 50 minutes if buns are at room temperature or 1 hour 15 minutes if refrigerated.

POSITION rack in center of oven and preheat to 375°F. Bake buns uncovered until tops are golden brown and syrup is bubbling thickly, rotating dishes halfway through baking, about 25 minutes.

REMOVE dishes from oven. Immediately place large baking sheet over 1 baking dish. Using oven mitts as aid, grasp dish and baking sheet together and turn over, releasing buns and topping onto sheet. Turn second dish of buns out onto another baking sheet. Cool buns 5 minutes. *(Buns can be made ahead. Cool completely. Wrap tightly with foil on baking sheet and freeze up to 2 weeks. Bake frozen buns, covered, at 375°F until heated through, about 15 minutes.)* Serve buns hot.

Raisin-nut breakfast rings

MAKING THESE TASTY BREAKFAST RINGS couldn't be any easier: The dough requires no kneading, and the filling can be made ahead. Just be sure to prepare the dough the day before, as it needs to be refrigerated overnight. In the morning just bake, glaze, and enjoy.

MAKES 2

Dough

- **1/4 cup warm water (105°F to 115°F)**
- **1 envelope dry yeast**

- **2 1/4 cups all purpose flour**
- **2 tablespoons sugar**
- **1 teaspoon salt**
- **1/2 cup (1 stick) chilled unsalted butter, cut into 1/2-inch cubes**
- **1 large egg**
- **1/4 cup evaporated milk**
- **1/4 cup chopped raisins**

Filling

- **1/2 cup (packed) golden brown sugar**
- **1/2 cup chopped pecans**
- **1/4 cup (1/2 stick) chilled unsalted butter, cut into 1/2-inch cubes**

Glaze

- **2 tablespoons (1/4 stick) unsalted butter**
- **1 cup powdered sugar**
- **1/2 teaspoon vanilla extract**
- **2 tablespoons (about) whole milk**

FOR DOUGH: Place ¼ cup warm water in small bowl; sprinkle yeast over. Let stand until yeast softens, about 8 minutes.

SIFT flour, sugar, and salt into large bowl. Add butter; rub in with fingertips until mixture resembles coarse meal. Add egg, evaporated milk, raisins, and yeast mixture; stir well (dough will be sticky). Cover; chill overnight.

FOR FILLING: Using fingertips, rub sugar, pecans, and butter in medium bowl until mixture comes together in small clumps. *(Filling can be prepared 1 day ahead. Cover and refrigerate.)*

LINE heavy large baking sheet with foil. Divide dough in half. Roll out each half between sheets of floured parchment paper to 16x12-inch rectangle; peel off paper and sprinkle each with half of filling. Starting at 12-inch sides, roll up rectangles into logs and seal ends. Place logs on prepared baking sheet. Using sharp knife and starting at sealed end, divide each log into 1-inch sections, cutting to within ½ inch of opposite side. Shape each cut log into ring; turn cut sections onto sides. Cover rings with kitchen towels and let rise in warm draft-free area until light and puffy, about 45 minutes.

PREHEAT oven to 350°F. Bake rings until golden brown, about 18 minutes. Cool 30 minutes on baking sheet.

FOR GLAZE: Melt butter in heavy small skillet over medium-low heat. Cook until butter browns, about 2 minutes. Remove from heat. Add powdered sugar, vanilla, and 1 tablespoon milk. Stir until smooth, adding more milk by teaspoonfuls until glaze has spreadable consistency. Drizzle glaze over rings. Serve warm or at room temperature, preferably within 8 hours. *(Can be made 1 day ahead. Cool completely. Wrap in foil; store at room temperature.)*

Kirsch and dried cherry kugelhupf

A *KUGELHUPF* is a rich and delicate yeast cake baked in a tall decorative ring. Enjoyed in Austria, Poland, and Germany's Black Forest region, it is most popular in Alsace, where a festival is held in its honor. Traditionally made for breakfast on Sundays, when the village baker had the day off, it is wonderful on any morning (or at any time of day). The tall fluted kugelhupf pan can be ordered from a specialty cookware store, but a 12-cup Bundt pan also works.

10 TO 12 SERVINGS

Cake

- **1 cup dried tart cherries**
- **½ cup golden raisins**
- **4 tablespoons kirsch (clear cherry brandy)**
- **¼ cup warm water (105°F to 115°F)**
- **Pinch of sugar**
- **2 envelopes dry yeast**
- **8 tablespoons (1 stick) unsalted butter, room temperature, divided**
- **¾ cup sugar**
- **4 large egg yolks**
- **1 tablespoon grated lemon peel**
- **2 teaspoons vanilla extract**
- **1 teaspoon almond extract**
- **1 teaspoon salt**
- **¾ cup lukewarm milk**
- **3½ cups all purpose flour, divided**
- **1 cup almonds, toasted, finely chopped**

Glaze

- **1 cup powdered sugar**
- **2 tablespoons kirsch**
- **2 teaspoons milk**

FOR CAKE: Combine first 3 ingredients in medium bowl. Let stand 15 minutes. Combine ¼ cup warm water and pinch of sugar in bowl. Sprinkle yeast over; stir to dissolve. Let stand 10 minutes.

MEANWHILE, in bowl of large mixer fitted with dough hook, beat 6 tablespoons butter, ¾ cup sugar, egg yolks, lemon peel, vanilla extract, almond extract, and salt to blend well. Add yeast mixture, milk, and 1 cup flour; beat until smooth. Beat in dried fruits and their soaking liquid. Gradually add remaining 2½ cups flour and beat until very soft dough forms, about 6 minutes. Let stand 15 minutes.

BUTTER 12-cup kugelhupf or Bundt pan with remaining 2 tablespoons butter. Add almonds; tilt pan to coat bottom and sides. Spoon dough into pan. Cover with plastic wrap and towel. Let dough rise in warm place until within 1 inch of top of pan, about 2½ hours.

PREHEAT oven to 350°F. Bake kugelhupf until tester inserted near center comes out clean, about 35 minutes. Let stand 10 minutes. Turn out onto rack; cool completely.

FOR GLAZE: Combine sugar and kirsch in bowl. Add milk; stir. Spoon glaze over cooled kugelhupf. *(Can be prepared 8 hours ahead; let stand uncovered at room temperature.)*

Chunky date, coconut, and almond granola

GRANOLA IS WONDERFUL served as cereal in a bowl with milk, spooned over plain yogurt and fresh fruit, sprinkled over vanilla ice cream, or even eaten by the handful as a quick snack. When preparing the granola, be sure to stir frequently during the last 15 minutes of baking to avoid burning.

MAKES ABOUT 6 CUPS

- **2 cups old-fashioned oats**
- **¾ cup whole almonds, halved**

- **½ cup sweetened flaked coconut**
- **½ cup raw cashews**
- **⅓ cup (firmly packed) golden or dark brown sugar**
- **1½ teaspoons ground allspice**
- **1 teaspoon ground cinnamon**
- **¼ cup (½ stick) unsalted butter**
- **2 tablespoons honey**
- **1 cup (packed) pitted dates, each cut crosswise into thirds**

PREHEAT oven to 300°F. Mix first 7 ingredients in large bowl. Melt butter with honey in heavy small saucepan over low heat. Pour over granola mixture and toss well. Spread out mixture on baking sheet. Bake 20 minutes, stirring occasionally. Add dates; mix to separate any clumps. Continue to bake until granola is golden brown, stirring frequently, about 15 minutes longer. Cool. *(Can be made 1 week ahead. Store airtight at room temperature.)*

Dried-cranberry granola

MAKING YOUR OWN GRANOLA is easy and economical, and the results are far better than anything you can get from a box. Feel free to experiment with different combinations of dried fruits and nuts—such as walnuts instead of pecans, or cherries in place of cranberries. Large-shred coconut and pepitas are available at natural foods stores.

MAKES ABOUT 7½ CUPS

- **2½ cups old-fashioned oats**
- **1 cup unsweetened large-shred coconut (about ½-inch wide)**
- **1 cup coarsely chopped pecans**
- **½ cup pepitas (shelled pumpkin seeds)**
- **1 teaspoon ground cinnamon**
- **1 cup (packed) dark brown sugar**
- **¼ cup water**
- **3 tablespoons vegetable oil**
- **⅔ cup dried cranberries**

POSITION rack in top third of oven and preheat to 325°F. Grease heavy large baking sheet. Combine first 5 ingredients in large bowl. Bring sugar, ¼ cup water, and oil to boil in heavy medium saucepan, stirring occasionally. Add sugar mixture to oat mixture and stir with fork to combine well. Spread evenly on prepared baking sheet. Bake 15 minutes; stir mixture with spatula. Bake 10 minutes longer, then stir in cranberries. Bake until golden brown, stirring frequently, about 10 minutes longer. Stir mixture; cool completely. *(Can be made 1 week ahead. Store airtight at room temperature.)*

Creole-style oven hash browns

THIS FOOLPROOF OVEN METHOD for making the popular breakfast potato dish frees up the stove top for frying eggs. Creole or Cajun seasoning is available in the spice section of most supermarkets. You can vary the flavor by using different herb and spice blends; try extra chili powder, *herbes de Provence*, or even just salt and pepper.

4 SERVINGS

- **6 large red-skinned potatoes (about 2½ pounds), peeled, cut into ½-inch pieces**
- **1 teaspoon paprika**
- **1 teaspoon chili powder**
- **1 teaspoon Creole or Cajun seasoning**
- **¼ cup olive oil**

PREHEAT oven to 400°F. Cook potatoes in medium pot of boiling salted water until almost tender, about 5 minutes. Drain well. Spread potatoes on heavy large baking sheet. Sprinkle with paprika, chili powder, and Creole seasoning. Season to taste with salt. Drizzle oil over potatoes and stir to coat.

BAKE potatoes until crisp, turning with metal spatula every 10 minutes, about 40 minutes.

Andouille grits

GRITS—A HOT CEREAL made from ground white hominy or maize—are a breakfast staple across the South. This "souped-up" version features andouille, a spicy, smoked pork link sausage from Louisiana. Find it at specialty foods stores and some supermarkets.

4 SERVINGS

- **4 tablespoons (1/2 stick) butter, divided**
- **8 ounces andouille sausage or hot links, cut into small cubes**
- **3 3/4 cups (or more) low-salt chicken broth**
- **1 cup instant grits**

MELT 1 tablespoon butter in heavy large saucepan over medium-high heat. Add sausage and sauté until brown, about 3 minutes. Add 3¾ cups broth and bring to boil. Gradually whisk in grits. Reduce heat to medium and simmer until mixture is thick, stirring occasionally, about 8 minutes. Mix in more broth by ¼ cupfuls to thin, if desired. Stir in remaining 3 tablespoons butter. Season grits to taste with salt and pepper and serve.

Caramelized bacon

COOKED IN THE OVEN, this bacon is dark, super-crunchy, and slightly sweet. Because it can be made ahead, it's great for large morning gatherings, where it complements any number of breakfast dishes. Leftovers (if there are any) can be added to sandwiches or crumbled into salad later in the day.

8 SERVINGS

- **1 1/2 cups (packed) golden brown sugar**
- **1 pound bacon (do not use thick-sliced)**

PREHEAT oven to 350°F. Place sugar in shallow dish. Add strips of bacon to dish and turn to coat completely with sugar. Transfer bacon to large broiler pan or rack set over rimmed baking sheet.

BAKE bacon until dark golden brown, turning once, about 8 minutes per side. Using tongs, transfer to rack and cool. *(Can be prepared 2 hours ahead. Store in airtight container at room temperature.)* Serve at room temperature.

Paprika pork patties

FOR SPICY PORK SAUSAGE that will transport you to Budapest, use both sweet and hot Hungarian paprika, which can be found at specialty foods stores. Great at breakfast time, these patties also can be assembled into amazing sandwiches with toasted rye bread, grilled onions, roasted red peppers, and sauerkraut.

6 SERVINGS

- **6 large garlic cloves**
- **4 ounces bacon, diced**
- **6 tablespoons ice water**
- **4 teaspoons sweet Hungarian paprika**
- **1 teaspoon hot Hungarian paprika**
- **3/4 teaspoon coarse salt**
- **1/2 teaspoon ground black pepper**
- **1/2 teaspoon ground allspice**
- **1 pound ground pork**
- **1/2 cup chopped drained sauerkraut**

WITH processor running, drop garlic through feed tube and mince. Add next 7 ingredients and process until thick paste forms. Add pork and combine, using on/off turns. Add sauerkraut and process until just mixed in. With moistened hands, shape mixture into six ¾-inch-thick patties; arrange on plate.

HEAT large nonstick skillet over medium heat. Add sausage patties and fry until brown and just cooked through, about 6 minutes per side. Drain on paper towels. Transfer to platter and serve.

Fresh country pork sausage with pepper and sage

ASK YOUR BUTCHER to set aside some pork fat for you, then mix up this country-style "bulk" sausage three days ahead to allow the flavors to develop. Skillet-fried into crispy patties, the sausage can be served with eggs and hot grits for a Southern-style breakfast.

MAKES ABOUT 28 PATTIES

- **2 pounds boneless pork shoulder, cut into 1-inch cubes, chilled**
- **1 pound fresh pork fat, cut into 1-inch pieces, chilled**
- **3 tablespoons cold water**
- **1 tablespoon dried rubbed sage**
- **1 tablespoon salt**
- **1½ teaspoons dried crushed red pepper**
- **1 teaspoon ground black pepper**

COMBINE ⅓ of pork shoulder and ⅓ of pork fat in processor. Using on/off turns, process mixture until finely ground. Transfer to large bowl. Repeat with remaining pork shoulder and pork fat in 2 more batches. Sprinkle 3 tablespoons cold water, sage, salt, and red and black pepper over pork. Using moistened hands, mix sausage just until blended. Wrap sausage in plastic and chill. *(Sausage can be prepared up to 3 days ahead. Keep refrigerated.)*

FORM sausage into 3-inch-diameter patties. Heat heavy large skillet over medium heat. Fry patties in batches until brown and cooked through, about 5 minutes per side. Drain on paper towels. Transfer to platter and serve.

Fruit salad with honey-lime dressing

THIS LIGHT AND DELICIOUS SALAD is best if perfectly ripe fruit is used. When choosing melons, pick those that are heavy for their size; cantaloupes should have a nice (not too strong) fragrance, and should give slightly when pressed at the stem end. Pineapples should also give slightly when squeezed gently; look for those with bright green leaves.

8 SERVINGS

- **½ cup plain yogurt**
- **¼ cup fresh lime juice**
- **¼ cup honey**
- **1 teaspoon grated lime peel**
- **2 cups diced peeled cantaloupe**
- **2 cups diced peeled honeydew melon**
- **2 cups seedless red or green grapes**
- **2 cups diced peeled, cored pineapple**
- **1½ cups diced peeled, seeded papaya**
- **1 cup halved hulled fresh strawberries**

WHISK yogurt and next 3 ingredients in small bowl to blend; set dressing aside. Combine all fruit in large bowl. Cover dressing and fruit separately and chill until ready to serve, up to 6 hours. Mix dressing into fruit. Let stand 15 minutes to blend flavors.

Appetizers 3

Great things start small. Great parties and great meals, for instance, start with sensational appetizers or first courses small enough to tantalize while leaving room for what's to come. An entire food revolution can even start with a few tiny bites. Appetizers provide excellent entrée–so to speak–to a wide variety of ethnic cuisines, as we sample flavors from every corner of the globe and then adopt them as our own.

Now for a few definitions. The terms *hors d'oeuvres* and *appetizers* tend to be used interchangeably to mean bite-size or finger foods served hot or cold. A *first course* is a plated dish served at the beginning of a meal. To make things easy, we've divided this chapter into "Cold Appetizers," "Hot Appetizers," and "First Courses."

When picking a first course, consider the components of the menu. Flavor balances and compatible ingredients are important considerations, but so is timing. Choose a starter that needs last-minute attention, such as goat-cheese soufflés, only when you have a ready-to-go main course. More demanding entrées call for a done-in-advance first course, like Shrimp Marinated with Capers and Olive Oil.

Besides supplying the opening act at dinner or keeping a cocktail company, these dishes, grouped creatively, can *be* dinner. The "small-plate" supper is perfectly familiar to Spanish, Turkish, and Greek cooks, who entertain guests with a parade of savory bites to keep everyone happy and keep the conversation flowing. To do a small-plate meal, it helps to pick a theme–perhaps room-temperature Mediterranean dishes–then pair a drink to go with it (maybe a cool rosé?). Or host a salsa tasting, complete with warm chips in a rainbow of colors and freshly shaken Sweet-and-Sour Margaritas (see the Drinks chapter). The key is to provide a variety of dishes that can be cut, spooned, or picked up in small portions.

However you use these recipes, guests will respond with enthusiasm and alacrity. After all, they don't call them *appetizers* for nothing.

Cold appetizers

Caesar dip with crudités

USE THE INNER LEAVES, also known as the heart, of a head of romaine lettuce as dippers. They're smaller, as well as crisper and more succulent, than the outer leaves. Reserve the outer leaves for sandwiches, or chop and toss them in a mixed greens salad.

8 TO 10 SERVINGS

1 cup mayonnaise
½ cup sour cream
½ cup freshly grated Parmesan cheese (about 1½ ounces)
1 tablespoon fresh lemon juice
1 garlic clove, pressed
1 anchovy fillet, mashed

Small romaine lettuce leaves
Assorted fresh vegetables

MIX first 6 ingredients in small bowl. Season dip with salt and pepper.

SERVE with lettuce and vegetables.

Crudités with herbed dipping sauce

THIS DIPPING SAUCE is a cinch to put together and can be made two days ahead. In fact, allow at least a few hours for the flavors to marry. Accompany this colorful green sauce with red bell pepper spears, cherry tomatoes, and radishes for a festive touch. Cooked shrimp and crab claws make ideal companions, too. If there's any leftover sauce, mix it with cooked chicken or tuna for a delicious salad sandwich.

MAKES ABOUT 2¼ CUPS

2 cups mayonnaise
⅓ cup chopped fresh parsley or basil
½ cup chopped green onions
⅓ cup chopped spinach leaves
¼ cup sour cream
¼ cup fresh lemon juice
Dash of Worcestershire sauce
Assorted fresh vegetables

PROCESS first 7 ingredients in blender until smooth, stopping occasionally to scrape down sides. Transfer dip to bowl. Season to taste with salt and pepper. Cover and refrigerate at least 2 hours to allow flavors to develop. *(Can be made 2 days ahead. Keep refrigerated.)* Serve dip with vegetables.

Fig and walnut tapenade with goat cheese

CALIMYRNA FIGS ARE GROWN IN CALIFORNIA—hence the *cali* in the name. The dried variety is widely available, but the recipe would also be good with black Mission figs. Likewise, toasted pine nuts make a good substitute for the walnuts. Don't skip the step of toasting the nuts, though, as this brings out their rich flavor. This is a great party appetizer; serve any leftover tapenade with chicken, pork, or lamb.

20 SERVINGS

1 cup chopped stemmed dried Calimyrna figs
⅓ cup water
⅓ cup chopped pitted Kalamata olives
2 tablespoons extra-virgin olive oil
1 tablespoon balsamic vinegar
1 tablespoon drained capers, chopped
1½ teaspoons chopped fresh thyme

2 5.5-ounce logs soft fresh goat cheese, each cut crosswise into ½-inch-thick rounds
½ cup chopped toasted walnuts
¼ cup toasted walnut halves
Fresh thyme sprigs (optional)
Assorted breads and/or crackers

COMBINE chopped figs and ⅓ cup water in heavy medium saucepan. Cook over medium-high heat until liquid evaporates and figs are soft, about 7 minutes. Transfer to medium bowl. Mix in olives, oil, vinegar, capers, and chopped thyme. Season tapenade to taste with salt and pepper. *(Can be made 3 days ahead. Cover and refrigerate. Bring to room temperature before serving.)*

ARRANGE overlapping cheese rounds in circle in center of medium platter. Stir chopped walnuts into tapenade; spoon into center of cheese circle. Garnish with walnut halves, and thyme sprigs, if desired. Serve with breads and/or crackers.

Guacamole with lime and roasted chiles

THE ROASTED CHILE MIXTURE adds a boost of flavor to the creamy guacamole; you'll find poblanos (fresh green chiles) at Latin markets and some supermarkets. The onion and fresh lime juice help keep the guacamole from turning brown; also press a sheet of plastic wrap directly onto the surface of the guacamole until ready to serve. Serve with corn tortilla chips, cooked shrimp, and jicama sticks.

6 SERVINGS

3 poblano chiles (about 12 ounces)
1 large jalapeño chile
8 tablespoons fresh lime juice, divided
1 large plum tomato, seeded, chopped
2 small green onions, finely chopped
1 teaspoon grated lime peel
2 large ripe avocados, halved, pitted, peeled
⅔ cup finely chopped onion
½ cup (packed) coarsely chopped fresh cilantro
¼ teaspoon ground cumin

CHAR all chiles directly over gas flame or in broiler until blackened on all sides. Enclose in paper bag at least 10 minutes and up to 1 hour. Peel, seed, and finely chop chiles. Mix chiles, 1 tablespoon lime juice, tomato, green onions, and lime peel in small bowl. Season chile mixture with salt.

PUREE avocados and next 3 ingredients with remaining 7 tablespoons lime juice in processor until almost smooth. Season with salt. *(Can be made 1 day ahead. Cover chile mixture and refrigerate. Press plastic wrap onto surface of guacamole and refrigerate.)*

SPOON guacamole into wide, shallow bowl. Spoon chile mixture into center.

Layered bean, guacamole, and salsa dip

THE CLASSIC CROWD-PLEASER gets a modern kick with tomatillo salsa and jalapeños. The use of purchased refried beans, guacamole, and salsa makes this a breeze to assemble; if you can't find refried beans with bacon, regular refried beans will work as well. To continue the Mexican theme, layer the ingredients in an attractive terracotta dish (rather than the glass bowl suggested here) and offer a refreshing sangria or Margarita alongside.

8 SERVINGS

1½ 16-ounce cans refried beans with bacon
1¾ teaspoons chili powder
2 cups purchased guacamole
⅓ cup purchased tomatillo salsa
1 teaspoon minced garlic
2 cups grated cheddar cheese (about 8 ounces)

- **2 14.5-ounce cans diced tomatoes with jalapeños, well drained**
- **¾ cup chopped green onions**
- **1½ cups sour cream**
- **⅔ cup chopped fresh cilantro**
- **1 3.8-ounce can sliced black olives, drained**
- **Corn tortilla chips**

MIX beans and chili powder in medium bowl to blend. Mix guacamole, tomatillo salsa, and garlic in another medium bowl. Spread half of bean mixture in bottom of 2- to 2½-quart glass bowl. Sprinkle with 1 cup cheese. Spread guacamole mixture over. Spoon half of drained tomatoes over. Sprinkle with green onions. Spread remaining bean mixture over. Stir sour cream to loosen. Spread over bean mixture, covering completely. Arrange cilantro, remaining cheese, olives, and remaining drained tomatoes in concentric circles atop sour cream. Cover; refrigerate at least 2 hours. *(Dip can be assembled 1 day ahead; keep refrigerated.)* Serve dip with chips.

Low-fat avocado and yogurt dip with jalapeño and cilantro

ENJOY THIS DIP to your heart's content: Avocados contain monounsaturated fat, which is said to reduce cholesterol. They are also a source of dietary fiber and vitamin C. Draining the liquid from the yogurt makes this dip extra-creamy. Serve it with skinny dippers such as green, red, or yellow bell pepper wedges, cherry tomatoes, and Belgian endive leaves.

MAKES ABOUT 1½ CUPS

- **1 16-ounce container plain nonfat yogurt (scant 2 cups)**
- **1 teaspoon ground cumin**
- **1 large avocado, halved, pitted, peeled, coarsely chopped**
- **4 tablespoons chopped fresh cilantro, divided**
- **2 teaspoons minced jalapeño chile**
- **1 small garlic clove, minced**

SET strainer over medium bowl; line with double layer of cheesecloth. Place yogurt in cloth-lined strainer. Cover with plastic wrap; chill overnight.

DISCARD liquid drained from yogurt. Transfer yogurt to processor. Stir cumin in small dry skillet over medium-low heat until fragrant, about 1 minute. Add cumin to processor, then avocado, 3 tablespoons cilantro, jalapeño, and garlic. Process until smooth. Season with salt and pepper. Transfer dip to small bowl. *(Can be prepared 6 hours ahead. Press plastic wrap onto surface of dip and chill.)* Sprinkle with remaining 1 tablespoon cilantro.

Smoky chipotle hummus with garlic bagel chips

THIS TRADITIONAL BEAN DIP marries well with a variety of flavors. Here, we've added smoky chipotle chiles; canned in a spicy tomato sauce called *adobo,* chipotles are available at Latin markets, specialty foods stores, and some supermarkets. You'll find tahini in Middle Eastern markets, natural foods stores, and some supermarkets. This hummus can also serve as a spread for pita sandwiches with grilled chicken.

20 SERVINGS

- **2 15- to 16-ounce cans garbanzo beans (chickpeas), drained**
- **½ cup water**
- **¼ cup plus 2 tablespoons tahini (sesame seed paste)**
- **3 tablespoons plus 2 teaspoons fresh lemon juice**
- **2 tablespoons olive oil**
- **2½ teaspoons minced canned chipotle chiles**
- **1 large garlic clove, minced**
- **1½ teaspoons ground cumin**
- **1 4-ounce jar sliced pimientos, drained**
- **⅓ cup chopped fresh cilantro**
- **2 6-ounce packages roasted-garlic bagel chips**

RESERVE 3 tablespoons garbanzo beans for garnish. Blend remaining garbanzo beans and next 7 ingredients in processor until smooth. Add pimientos; using on/off turns, process until pimientos are coarsely chopped. Transfer hummus to medium bowl. Stir in cilantro. Season hummus to taste with salt and pepper. Sprinkle with reserved garbanzo beans. *(Can be made 1 day ahead. Cover and chill. Bring to room temperature before serving.)* Accompany with bagel chips.

Caramelized onion and sour cream spread

SOUR-CREAM-AND-ONION DIP has been a party favorite for nearly 50 years. Here, the dip gets a zesty Mediterranean makeover and crostini replace potato chips. If you can't find olive bread, use ciabatta or a French-bread baguette. *Herbes de Provence* is a dried herb mixture available at specialty foods stores and some supermarkets. A combination of dried thyme, basil, savory, and fennel seeds can be substituted.

6 TO 8 SERVINGS

- **3 tablespoons plus 1/3 cup olive oil**
- **1 large red onion, thinly sliced**
- **1 large red bell pepper, thinly sliced**
- **1/2 fennel bulb, cored, thinly sliced**
- **2 teaspoons herbes de Provence**
- **1 teaspoon sugar**
- **8 garlic cloves, finely chopped**

- **1/3 cup sour cream**
- **1 tablespoon drained capers**

- **18 4x1 1/2x1/4-inch slices olive bread**

HEAT 3 tablespoons oil in heavy large skillet over medium heat. Add onion and next 4 ingredients. Cover; cook until vegetables release their juices, stirring occasionally, about 12 minutes. Uncover; sauté until juices evaporate, about 10 minutes. Add garlic; cook until vegetables are very tender and just beginning to brown, about 12 minutes longer. Cool completely.

PUREE vegetable mixture and sour cream in processor until almost smooth. Season spread generously with salt and pepper. Transfer to bowl. Sprinkle with capers.

PREHEAT broiler. Arrange bread slices on baking sheet. Brush both sides of bread slices with remaining ⅓ cup oil. Broil until golden, about 2 minutes per side. Cool. Serve with spread.

Provençal vegetable and goat cheese terrine

TAKE THIS COLORFUL APPETIZER ALONG to your next potluck. It can be made up to two days ahead, transported in the pan, and unmolded onto a platter when you arrive. Drizzle a little extra-virgin olive oil over and around the terrine and garnish with Niçoise olives.

6 SERVINGS

- **2 red bell peppers**

- **1 large eggplant, cut lengthwise into 3/8-inch-thick slices**
- **Olive oil**
- **2 large zucchini, cut lengthwise into 1/4-inch-thick slices**

- **1 11-ounce log soft fresh goat cheese, room temperature**
- **3 tablespoons olive oil**
- **2 tablespoons chopped fresh thyme**

- **1 cup fresh arugula, chopped (about 3/4 ounce)**
- **1/2 cup chopped pitted Niçoise or Kalamata olives**

- **Additional fresh arugula leaves**
- **French bread**

CHAR peppers over gas flame or in broiler until blackened on all sides. Place in bag and let stand 10 minutes. Peel and seed peppers. Cut into ½-inch pieces.

PREHEAT broiler. Brush both sides of eggplant slices with oil. Season with salt and pepper. Broil until cooked through and golden, about 3 minutes per side. Drain on paper towels. Brush both sides of zucchini slices with oil. Season with salt and pepper. Broil until cooked through, about 3 minutes per side. Drain on paper towels.

PUREE cheese in processor until smooth. With machine running, add 3 tablespoons oil through feed tube. Add bell peppers; using on/off turns, process until peppers are coarsely chopped and cheese mixture begins to color. Add thyme. Season with salt and pepper.

LINE 9x5-inch glass loaf pan with plastic wrap, leaving 4-inch overhang. Place single layer of zucchini in bottom of pan, covering completely and trimming to fit. Spread ⅓ of cheese mixture over. Top with ⅓ of chopped arugula and ⅓ of olives. Cover with single layer of eggplant, trimming to fit. Spread ⅓ of cheese mixture over; top with ⅓ of chopped arugula and ⅓ of olives. Repeat with remaining zucchini, cheese, chopped arugula, and olives. Finish with layer of eggplant. Fold plastic wrap over to cover; press down gently on eggplant. Cover; chill until firm, at least 6 hours. *(Can be made 2 days ahead. Keep chilled. Let stand at room temperature 30 minutes before serving.)*

LINE platter with arugula leaves. Open plastic wrap on top of terrine. Unmold terrine onto platter, lift off pan, and peel off plastic. Serve with bread.

Country mushroom and nut pâté

THIS PÂTÉ HAS a nice old-fashioned appeal, made contemporary with the addition of chopped mushrooms for flavor and texture. Using shiitake mushrooms would add even more intense flavor.

8 SERVINGS

- **3 tablespoons butter**
- **1½ pounds mushrooms, sliced**
- **1 small onion, finely chopped**
- **1 garlic clove, minced**

- **¾ cup slivered almonds, toasted**
- **¼ cup hazelnuts, toasted**
- **2 tablespoons peanut oil**
- **4 ounces cream cheese, room temperature**
- **1 teaspoon salt**
- **¼ teaspoon cayenne pepper**
- **¼ teaspoon dried thyme**
- **3 tablespoons chopped fresh parsley**

Assorted crackers or French-bread baguette slices

LINE 1-quart bowl or loaf pan with plastic wrap, extending over sides. Melt butter in heavy large skillet over medium-high heat. Add mushrooms, onion, and garlic; sauté until liquid has evaporated and mushrooms are golden brown, about 20 minutes. Cool slightly.

COARSELY chop almonds and hazelnuts in processor; remove 2 tablespoonfuls and set aside. Continue chopping nuts, slowly adding oil until mixture is well blended. Set aside 1 cup mushroom mixture. Add remaining mushroom mixture, cream cheese, salt, cayenne, and thyme to nut mixture and blend thoroughly. Transfer to medium bowl; mix in parsley and reserved 1 cup mushroom mixture and nuts. Transfer mixture to prepared bowl; smooth top. Cover and chill at least 4 hours or overnight.

TURN pâté out onto platter. Peel off plastic wrap. Surround with crackers or baguette slices.

Smoked fish pâté with pita chips

FOR AN ELEGANT PRESENTATION, serve this pâté unmolded at a cocktail party. Line a bowl with plastic wrap, allowing the plastic to hang over the edges. Spoon the pâté into the lined bowl and cover. Refrigerate until the pâté is cold, then uncover and invert it onto an attractive platter. Remove the bowl and peel off the plastic wrap. Garnish the pâté with more green onions and fresh herbs.

6 SERVINGS

4 pita bread rounds, each cut into 8 wedges
3 tablespoons olive oil
Garlic salt

1 pound smoked fish (such as bluefish, trout, or chub), skinned, boned, chopped
½ cup chopped green onions
¼ cup fresh lemon juice
¼ cup cream cheese, room temperature

PREHEAT oven to 350°F. Place pita wedges on baking sheet. Brush with olive oil. Season with garlic salt. Bake pita wedges until crisp, about 7 minutes.

MIX fish, green onions, lemon juice, and cream cheese in medium bowl to blend. Spoon pâté into bowl. *(Pita chips and pâté can be prepared 1 day ahead. Store chips in airtight container at room temperature. Cover and refrigerate pâté.)*

PLACE pâté on platter. Surround with pita chips.

Caviar pie

USE GOOD-QUALITY GOLDEN WHITEFISH CAVIAR and pale orange salmon caviar for this easy, colorful, and festive appetizer, and reserve your premium beluga caviar to serve with toast points.

16 SERVINGS

Nonstick vegetable oil spray
1 small onion, finely chopped
½ teaspoon sugar
10 hard-boiled eggs, peeled
¼ cup low-fat mayonnaise
2 tablespoons sweet pickle relish

1 8-ounce package Neufchâtel cheese (reduced-fat cream cheese), room temperature
1 tablespoon milk

8 ounces caviar (preferably 2 or more colors)
Lemon slices
Chopped parsley
Assorted crackers

SPRAY 9-inch-diameter tart pan with removable bottom or 9-inch-diameter springform pan with nonstick spray. Combine onion and sugar in medium bowl. Place 10 egg whites and 6 yolks in processor (reserve remaining yolks for another use). Chop coarsely. Add mayonnaise and relish; using on/off turns, process just until combined (do not overmix). Add to bowl with onion and blend well. Spread over bottom of prepared pan. Refrigerate 15 minutes.

COMBINE Neufchâtel cheese and milk in clean processor. Blend well. Drop cheese mixture by teaspoonfuls over chilled egg layer and spread gently to cover. Refrigerate until firm, about 1 hour. *(Can be prepared 1 day ahead. Cover and keep refrigerated.)*

SPOON caviar decoratively atop cheese layer. Garnish with lemon slices and parsley. Press bottom of tart pan up or remove sides of springform pan, releasing pie. Place pie on platter; surround with crackers.

Sesame-eggplant salsa with Parmesan pita crisps

SOY SAUCE, GINGER, RICE VINEGAR, and sesame oil accent this Asian-inspired salsa. Chili-garlic sauce and the dark, fragrant sesame oil are available at Asian markets and in the Asian foods section of many supermarkets.

MAKES ABOUT 4 CUPS

- **2 1- to 1¼-pound eggplants**
- **1 tablespoon vegetable oil**
- **¾ cup (packed) plus 1 tablespoon minced green onions**
- **2½ tablespoons minced peeled fresh ginger**
- **4 garlic cloves, minced**
- **1 teaspoon chili-garlic sauce**
- **3 tablespoons (packed) golden brown sugar**
- **2 tablespoons soy sauce**
- **1 tablespoon rice vinegar**
- **2 teaspoons fresh lemon juice**
- **2 large plum tomatoes, seeded, chopped**
- **¾ cup (packed) plus 1 tablespoon finely chopped fresh cilantro**
- **1½ teaspoons Asian sesame oil**

Parmesan Pita Crisps (see recipe)

PREHEAT oven to 425°F. Pierce eggplants all over with fork. Place on baking sheet. Roast in oven until eggplants are very soft and deflated, turning once, about 1 hour. Cool slightly.

CUT eggplants in half; scrape flesh into strainer set over large bowl (do not allow bottom of strainer to touch bowl). Let eggplant drain 30 minutes. Transfer eggplant to processor. Using on/off turns, process until almost smooth.

HEAT vegetable oil in heavy large skillet over medium-high heat. Add ¾ cup green onions, ginger, garlic, and chili-garlic sauce; sauté just until onions soften, about 45 seconds. Stir in brown sugar, soy sauce, vinegar, and lemon juice. Bring to simmer, stirring constantly. Mix in eggplant puree and cook until heated through, about 2 minutes. Remove from heat. Stir in tomatoes, ¾ cup cilantro, and sesame oil. Cool to room temperature. Season with salt and pepper. Transfer to medium bowl. *(Can be prepared 1 day ahead. Cover and refrigerate. Bring to room temperature before serving.)*

GARNISH eggplant salsa with remaining 1 tablespoon each green onions and cilantro. Serve with pita crisps.

Parmesan pita crisps

THESE CRISPS ARE GREAT by themselves and would also be excellent with hummus.

MAKES 6 DOZEN

- **6 pita bread rounds**
- **6 tablespoons olive oil**
- **1¼ cups freshly grated Parmesan cheese**

PREHEAT oven to 325°F. Cut each pita bread horizontally in half, forming 2 pita disks. Brush cut sides with olive oil. Sprinkle with Parmesan cheese, then pepper. Cut each disk into 6 wedges. Arrange pita wedges in single layer on large baking sheets.

BAKE until pita wedges are golden and just crisp, about 12 minutes. *(Can be prepared 3 days ahead. Cool completely. Store airtight at room temperature. Rewarm in 325°F oven about 5 minutes.)*

Peach and cucumber salsa

CHIPOTLE CHILES are simply dried smoked jalapeño chiles. While they are available in their dried form, they are more commonly found—at Latin markets, specialty foods stores, and some supermarkets—canned in a thick and spicy sauce called *adobo,* which makes them easy to chop and add to soups and salsas such as this one. To remove the skin from the peaches, submerge them in a pot of boiling water for 20 seconds, then transfer them to a bowl of ice water to cool. The skin will peel away easily from the flesh.

MAKES ABOUT 3 CUPS

2 cups diced peeled pitted peaches (about 1½ pounds)
1 cup diced unpeeled English hothouse cucumber
¾ cup diced red bell pepper
⅓ cup chopped fresh cilantro
2 tablespoons fresh lime juice
2 tablespoons apricot preserves
1 teaspoon chopped canned chipotle chiles
Tortilla chips

MIX first 7 ingredients in medium bowl. Season salsa to taste with salt and pepper. *(Can be prepared 2 hours ahead. Cover and refrigerate.)* Serve salsa with tortilla chips.

Spicy black bean salsa

IF YOU MAKE THIS SALSA more than two hours ahead, stir in the avocado just before serving. Use thick corn tortilla chips to scoop up the chunky salsa. While the recipe can easily be cut in half, any remaining salsa is good spooned into a warm corn tortilla for a light snack, or served alongside grilled steaks or chicken. Chipotle chiles canned in *adobo* (a spicy tomato sauce) are available at Latin markets, specialty foods stores, and some supermarkets.

MAKES ABOUT 8 CUPS

¼ cup fresh lime juice
¼ cup chopped fresh cilantro
2 tablespoons olive oil
4 teaspoons minced canned chipotle chiles
1 tablespoon red wine vinegar
1 teaspoon ground cumin
2 15- to 16-ounce cans black beans, rinsed, drained
1½ cups fresh corn kernels, blanched, or frozen corn kernels, thawed
1½ cups chopped red onion
1½ cups chopped tomatoes (about 3 medium)
1 cup chopped green bell pepper
1 large ripe avocado, halved, pitted, peeled, diced
Tortilla chips

WHISK first 6 ingredients in large bowl to blend. Stir in beans, corn, onion, tomatoes, and bell pepper. Mix in avocado; season to taste with salt and pepper. *(Can be prepared 2 hours ahead. Cover and refrigerate.)* Transfer salsa to serving bowl. Serve with tortilla chips.

Mango-curry shrimp salad in wonton cups

THESE ONE-BITERS pack a powerful punch thanks to the Thai green curry paste, which is made with green chiles, garlic, onion, and spices; you can find it at Asian markets and in the Asian foods section of some supermarkets. If you don't have a miniature muffin tin to prepare the wonton cups, serve the shrimp salad atop fried wonton squares or diagonal slices of English hothouse cucumber. The shrimp salad can also be spooned into small butter lettuce leaves and served as a first-course salad.

MAKES 48

12 wonton wrappers (from one 12-ounce package), each cut into 4 squares
Vegetable oil

- ½ cup mayonnaise
- 2 tablespoons chopped fresh cilantro
- 5 teaspoons fresh lime juice
- 2 teaspoons mango chutney
- ¾ teaspoon Thai green curry paste
- 12 ounces peeled cooked medium shrimp, coarsely chopped

Fresh cilantro leaves

PREHEAT oven to 325°F. Place wonton squares on work surface; brush lightly with oil. Press each into miniature muffin cup, oiled side down. Bake until wonton cups are golden brown, about 10 minutes. Cool completely in tins. *(Can be made 3 days ahead. Remove cups from tins and store airtight at room temperature.)*

WHISK mayonnaise, chopped cilantro, lime juice, chutney, and curry paste in medium bowl to blend. Stir in shrimp. Season salad to taste with salt and pepper. *(Salad can be prepared up to 1 day ahead. Cover and refrigerate.)*

PLACE wonton cups on serving platter. Spoon 1 teaspoon shrimp salad into each cup. Garnish with cilantro leaves.

Shrimp rice-paper rolls with Vietnamese dipping sauce

NUOC CHAM, the dipping sauce in this recipe, is indispensable in Vietnamese cuisine. This sweet, salty, and spicy dipping sauce features the fish sauce known in Vietnam as *nuoc nam* or in Thailand as *nam pla* (and which is available, along with the *maifun* and rice-paper sheets, at Asian markets and in the Asian foods section of some supermarkets). Use a mandoline or V-slicer to cut the vegetables into matchstick-size strips. Arrange the softened rice-paper sheets in a single layer to keep them from sticking together.

MAKES 36 PIECES

Dipping sauce

- ½ cup fresh lime juice
- ¼ cup sugar
- 3 tablespoons fermented fish sauce (nam pla or nuoc nam)
- 1 tablespoon unseasoned rice vinegar
- 1 tablespoon chopped fresh cilantro
- 2 garlic cloves, minced
- 1 teaspoon minced jalapeño chile with seeds

Rice-paper rolls

- 1½ tablespoons olive oil
- 6 ounces fresh shiitake mushrooms, stemmed, caps thinly sliced
- 4 ounces dried thin Chinese rice sticks (maifun)
- 12 8- to- 9-inch round rice-paper sheets
- 1 cup fresh mint leaves
- 1 cup fresh cilantro leaves
- 1 cup small fresh basil leaves
- 1 cup finely shredded iceberg lettuce or green cabbage
- 1 cup mung bean sprouts or daikon (Japanese white radish) sprouts
- 1 cup matchstick-size strips seeded English hothouse cucumber
- 1 cup matchstick-size strips peeled carrot or jicama
- 8 ounces cooked peeled deveined medium shrimp, cut lengthwise in half

FOR DIPPING SAUCE: Whisk all ingredients in medium bowl until sugar dissolves. Let stand at least 30 minutes. *(Can be made 1 day ahead. Cover; chill.)*

FOR RICE-PAPER ROLLS: Heat oil in medium skillet over medium-high heat. Add mushrooms and sauté until soft, about 5 minutes. Cool.

PLACE rice sticks in large bowl; add enough hot water to cover. Let stand until softened, about 30 minutes. Drain. Cut into 6-inch lengths; set aside. Fill same bowl with warm water. Add 1 rice-paper sheet and turn until beginning to soften, about 30 seconds (sheet will still be stiff in a few spots). Remove from water; drain on kitchen towel. Repeat with 5 more rice-paper sheets, arranging in single layer.

DIVIDE half of mint, cilantro, and basil equally among softened rice-paper sheets, arranging in line across bottom third of each sheet and leaving 1-inch plain border at each end. Top with half of rice sticks, shaping into compact log. Top with half of lettuce, sprouts, cucumber, carrot, shrimp, and mushrooms. Fold bottom of each rice sheet over filling, then fold in ends and roll into tight cylinder. Place rolls, seam side down, on platter. Repeat soaking with remaining rice-paper sheets, then top with remaining filling to form 6 more rolls. *(Can be made 6 hours ahead. Cover with damp paper towel and plastic wrap; chill.)* Cut each roll diagonally into thirds. Arrange on platter and serve with sauce.

Mussels on the half shell with pesto

LIVE, FRESH MUSSELS will close tightly when they are jostled, then open once they are cooked. If the mussels do not close when live, or open when cooked, they should be discarded. The "beard" is the fuzzy appendage protruding between the shells. If the mussels are not debearded when you purchase them, remove the beards just before cooking. Use black mussels or green-lipped mussels from New Zealand, and line a platter with rock salt to keep the mussels in place when serving.

MAKES ABOUT 40

- **1 cup dry white wine**
- **1 cup water**
- **1/4 cup chopped shallots**
- **2 tablespoons white wine vinegar**
- **4 garlic cloves, crushed with side of knife**
- **40 fresh mussels, scrubbed, debearded**

- **4 cups fresh basil leaves**
- **4 garlic cloves, chopped**
- **3 tablespoons olive oil**
- **6 tablespoons freshly grated Parmesan cheese**
- **2 tablespoons low-fat mayonnaise**

BRING first 5 ingredients to boil in large pot. Carefully add mussels to pot. Cover; cook until mussels open, about 4 minutes. Using slotted spoon, transfer mussels to large bowl, discarding any that do not open. Cool mussels. Strain cooking liquid, reserving 1 cup.

REMOVE mussels from shells, reserving half of each shell. Transfer mussels to medium bowl; refrigerate.

FINELY chop basil and garlic in processor. With machine running, gradually add reserved 1 cup cooking liquid and oil; process until well blended. Blend in cheese and mayonnaise. Transfer pesto to large bowl. Season with salt and pepper. Add mussels and toss to coat. Chill at least 1 hour. *(Can be prepared 1 day ahead. Refrigerate reserved shells.)*

SPOON mussels and pesto into reserved shells. Arrange on platter.

Prosciutto rolls with arugula and figs

PROSCIUTTO DI PARMA is Italy's finest ham and is available at the deli counter of most specialty markets and some supermarkets. Usually it's sliced paper-thin, but for this recipe be sure the slices are not too thin or they will tear when you spread the cheese on them. Ask that the prosciutto slices be separated by deli paper so that the slices do not stick together.

MAKES 24

- **1/4 cup extra-virgin olive oil**
- **2 tablespoons fresh lemon juice**
- **4 teaspoons grated lemon peel**
- **12 thin (not paper-thin) slices prosciutto**
- **6 ounces soft fresh goat cheese, room temperature**
- **16 dried black Mission figs, quartered**
- **4 large bunches (about) arugula, stems trimmed**

WHISK oil, lemon juice, and lemon peel in medium bowl to blend. Lay prosciutto on work surface, spacing slices 2 inches apart. Spread cheese evenly over prosciutto. Arrange figs over cheese, dividing and spacing evenly. Drizzle lemon mixture over. Sprinkle with pepper. Arrange 6 arugula leaves atop each prosciutto slice, alternating stems and tops and allowing tops to extend 1 inch over long sides of prosciutto.

STARTING at 1 short end of each prosciutto slice, roll up tightly jelly-roll style. Cut rolls crosswise in half. Transfer to platter. *(Can be made 2 hours ahead. Cover with damp paper towels, then plastic wrap; chill.)*

Brochettes of melon, prosciutto, and fresh mozzarella

SELECT A CANTALOUPE that is fragrant and heavy for its size and that yields when pressed gently with your thumb at the stem end. The small balls of water-packed mozzarella may be labeled as *bocconcini,* and are found at Italian markets, cheese shops, and some supermarkets.

MAKES 6

- **½ cup olive oil**
- **⅓ cup (packed) fresh basil leaves**
- **1 medium shallot, quartered**
- **1 small (about 2-pound) cantaloupe, halved crosswise, seeded, cut into 6 wedges, peeled**
- **6 small fresh water-packed mozzarella balls or one 8-ounce ball, drained**
- **6 thin slices prosciutto, halved lengthwise, gathered into ruffle**
- **6 8-inch wooden skewers**

Basil sprigs for garnish

USING on/off turns, puree olive oil, ⅓ cup basil, and shallot in processor until basil and shallot are finely chopped. Cut each cantaloupe wedge crosswise in half. If using large mozzarella ball, trim and cut into 6 cubes. Alternate 1 melon piece, 1 piece ruffled prosciutto, 1 mozzarella ball or cube, 1 more prosciutto piece, and 1 more melon piece on each skewer. *(Can be prepared 2 hours ahead; cover and refrigerate. Bring to room temperature 15 minutes before serving.)*

ARRANGE skewers on platter. Drizzle with basil oil and sprinkle with cracked black pepper. Garnish with basil sprigs.

Chicken, wild rice, and pecan salad in romaine spears

WILD RICE is not actually a type of rice, but rather a long-grain marsh grass native to the northern Great Lakes area. Using a purchased roast chicken from the deli counter makes this a snap to prepare. Stir the toasted pecans into the salad just before serving so that they remain crunchy. Radicchio leaves or Belgian endive spears could also stand in for the romaine.

12 SERVINGS

- **6 cups low-salt chicken broth**
- **8 ounces wild rice**

- **1 2½-pound roasted chicken, skinned, boned, meat cut into ⅓-inch pieces**
- **1 red bell pepper, chopped**
- **4 cups chopped arugula (about 3 ounces)**
- **¼ cup chopped green onions**
- **3 tablespoons soy sauce**
- **3 tablespoons rice vinegar**
- **3 tablespoons Asian sesame oil**

- **2 cups pecans, toasted, chopped**
- **3 hearts of romaine lettuce (any large outer leaves removed)**

BRING broth to boil in medium saucepan. Add rice and return to boil. Reduce heat to low, cover, and cook until just tender, about 50 minutes. Drain well.

TRANSFER rice to large bowl. Mix in chicken, bell pepper, arugula, and green onions. Mix soy sauce, vinegar, and oil in small bowl. Pour over salad and mix to coat. Season with salt and pepper. *(Can be made 4 hours ahead. Cover and chill.)*

MIX nuts into salad. Arrange hearts of romaine on platter. Spoon salad into romaine leaves and serve.

Chive tartines with smoked salmon

TARTINES ARE SLICES OF buttered bread topped with cheese, honey, jams, or other spreads. Goat cheese, chive oil, and smoked salmon turn this simple French snack into a sophisticated appetizer.

MAKES 20

1 cup 1-inch pieces fresh chives
3/4 cup extra-virgin olive oil

6 tablespoons crumbled soft fresh goat cheese
2 tablespoons minced shallot
20 3/4-inch-thick diagonal slices French-bread baguette

6 ounces thinly sliced smoked salmon
Additional chopped fresh chives

PUREE 1 cup chives and oil in blender 2 minutes. Pour through fine sieve set over medium bowl. Let drain 1 hour (do not press on solids). Discard solids.

PREHEAT oven to 400°F. Mix goat cheese and shallot in small bowl; season to taste with pepper. Place bread slices on large baking sheet. Brush both sides of bread lightly with chive oil. Spread each slice with 1½ teaspoons cheese mixture.

BAKE bread until bread and cheese mixture are light golden, about 5 minutes. Transfer to platter. Drape 1 salmon slice over each, trimming to fit if necessary. Sprinkle with additional chopped chives.

Tomato and basil bruschetta

PERFECTLY RIPENED TOMATOES will give this classic bruschetta the best flavor. After purchasing tomatoes, let them continue to ripen at room temperature for a few days. A combination of red and yellow tomatoes offers an appealing color contrast.

MAKES 24

12 6x2x1/2-inch slices country bread, cut crosswise in half
6 tablespoons olive oil, divided
3 garlic cloves, peeled, cut in half lengthwise

2 pounds tomatoes, seeded, cut into 1/3-inch cubes
1/4 cup chopped fresh basil

PREHEAT oven to 375°F. Arrange bread slices on large rimmed baking sheet. Brush bread with 3 tablespoons oil. Bake until bread is toasted and golden brown, about 10 minutes. Rub toasts with cut sides of garlic.

MIX tomatoes, basil, and remaining 3 tablespoons oil in large bowl. Season topping to taste with salt and pepper. Spoon 2 tablespoons tomato topping on each toast. Arrange bruschetta on platter and serve.

Pine nut dolmades with yogurt-feta dip

FOR A BUFFET of Greek mezedes (appetizers), serve the dolmades and the dip with a platter of crudités, pita chips, hummus, assorted olives, and a traditional fish roe spread called *taramasalata*, which can be found at a Greek market or restaurant.

MAKES ABOUT 40

1 14.5-ounce can diced tomatoes
1 cup uncooked long-grain white rice
1 cup thinly sliced green onions

½ cup (packed) finely chopped fresh mint (about 3 bunches)
½ cup (packed) finely chopped fresh dill (about 4 bunches)
½ cup pine nuts, toasted
⅓ cup extra-virgin olive oil
2 large garlic cloves, minced

52 (about) grape leaves from jar (about two 2-pound jars)

¼ cup fresh lemon juice

Yogurt-Feta Dip (see recipe)

PLACE tomatoes with juice in large bowl. Add next 7 ingredients and mix to blend. Season with salt and pepper.

RINSE grape leaves under cold water. Drain. Cover bottom of heavy large pot with grape leaves (using about 6). Place 1 grape leaf on work surface, vein side up; cut off stem. Place about 1 tablespoon rice mixture in center of leaf toward stem end. Fold sides over filling. Starting at stem end of leaf, roll up tightly as for egg roll. Place in leaf-lined pot, seam side down. Repeat with more leaves and rice mixture, layering dolmades when bottom of pot is filled.

POUR lemon juice over dolmades. Cover with grape leaves (using about 6). Add enough water to pot almost to cover dolmades. Place heatproof plate atop dolmades to weigh down. Cover pot and bring to boil. Reduce heat to low; simmer until rice is tender and almost all liquid is absorbed, about 35 minutes.

REMOVE from heat; uncover. Allow dolmades to cool in pot. Drain any liquid remaining in pot. *(Can be prepared 2 days ahead. Cover and chill.)* Arrange dolmades on platter. Serve with dip.

Yogurt-feta dip

MAKE THE DIP at least two hours and up to two days ahead so that it has plenty of time to chill before being served. If desired, mix in chopped fresh dill or oregano.

MAKES ABOUT 1½ CUPS

1 cup plain whole-milk yogurt (do not use low-fat or nonfat)
4 ounces feta cheese, crumbled
1 large green onion, cut into 1-inch pieces
¼ teaspoon grated lemon peel

Place all ingredients in processor and puree until almost smooth. Season with pepper. Chill until cold, about 2 hours. *(Can be made 2 days ahead. Keep chilled.)*

Herb-marinated feta and olives

MAKE THIS EASY APPETIZER at least one day and up to one week before serving to allow the herbs and spices to flavor the oil, cheese, and olives. You can substitute lemon peel for the orange peel, and replace the cilantro with fresh oregano or parsley, if desired.

6 SERVINGS

1 tablespoon whole cumin seeds
2 teaspoons whole coriander seeds
1 teaspoon dried crushed red pepper
2 garlic cloves, minced
2 teaspoons grated orange peel
1½ cups extra-virgin olive oil
10 ounces assorted brine-cured green and black olives
3 tablespoons minced fresh basil
2 tablespoons minced fresh cilantro
8 ounces feta cheese, cut into ½-inch squares

1 French-bread baguette, sliced

COMBINE cumin, coriander, and crushed red pepper in heavy small skillet over medium-high heat. Shake skillet gently until spices are fragrant, about 1 minute. Transfer to bowl. Add garlic, orange peel, and oil; stir to combine. Mix in olives, basil, and cilantro. Gently stir in feta. Cover and refrigerate at least 1 day. *(Can be made 1 week ahead. Keep refrigerated.)* Bring olive and cheese mixture to room temperature before serving.

TRANSFER mixture to bowl and place on platter. Surround with baguette slices.

Deviled eggs with tarragon and capers

WHEN MAKING ANY TYPE OF deviled egg, you don't need to use the freshest eggs, as they are usually the hardest to peel. But stirring the eggs gently as they cook helps ensure that the yolks set in the center of the egg, which will provide usable receptacles for stuffing.

6 SERVINGS

- **6 hard-boiled eggs, peeled, halved lengthwise**
- **3 tablespoons sour cream**
- **2 tablespoons mayonnaise**
- **2 teaspoons fresh lemon juice**
- **¼ teaspoon dry mustard**
- **2 tablespoons minced green onion**
- **4 teaspoons drained capers**
- **1 teaspoon minced fresh tarragon**

SPOON yolks from egg halves into small bowl; mash yolks to smooth paste. Add sour cream, mayonnaise, lemon juice, and mustard; blend well. Mix in green onion, capers, and tarragon. Season with salt and pepper. Spoon yolk mixture back into whites, mounding in center. *(Can be made 8 hours ahead. Cover; refrigerate.)*

Crab and wild mushroom cheesecake

IF YOU CAN'T FIND smoked Gouda cheese, use regular Gouda or smoked mozzarella instead. Just as with its sweet counterparts, this cheesecake is done when the center moves slightly when the pan is gently shaken. As the cheesecake chills, it will become firm but retain its creamy texture.

16 TO 20 SERVINGS

Crust

- **1¾ cups fresh breadcrumbs made from French bread**
- **1 cup freshly grated Parmesan cheese (about 3 ounces)**
- **6 tablespoons (¾ stick) butter, melted**

Filling

- **1 tablespoon olive oil**
- **1 cup chopped onion**
- **1 cup chopped red bell pepper**
- **4 cups coarsely chopped assorted fresh wild mushrooms (such as crimini, oyster, and stemmed shiitake)**

- **3 8-ounce packages cream cheese, room temperature**
- **4 ounces cream cheese, room temperature**
- **2 teaspoons salt**
- **1 teaspoon ground black pepper**
- **4 large eggs**
- **½ cup whipping cream**
- **10 ounces crabmeat (about 2 cups), drained well, picked over**
- **1 cup grated smoked Gouda cheese (about 4 ounces)**
- **½ cup chopped fresh parsley**

- **1 French-bread baguette, sliced, toasted**

FOR CRUST: Preheat oven to 350°F. Mix all crust ingredients in medium bowl until well blended. Press mixture over bottom (not sides) of 9-inch-diameter springform pan with 2¾-inch-high sides.

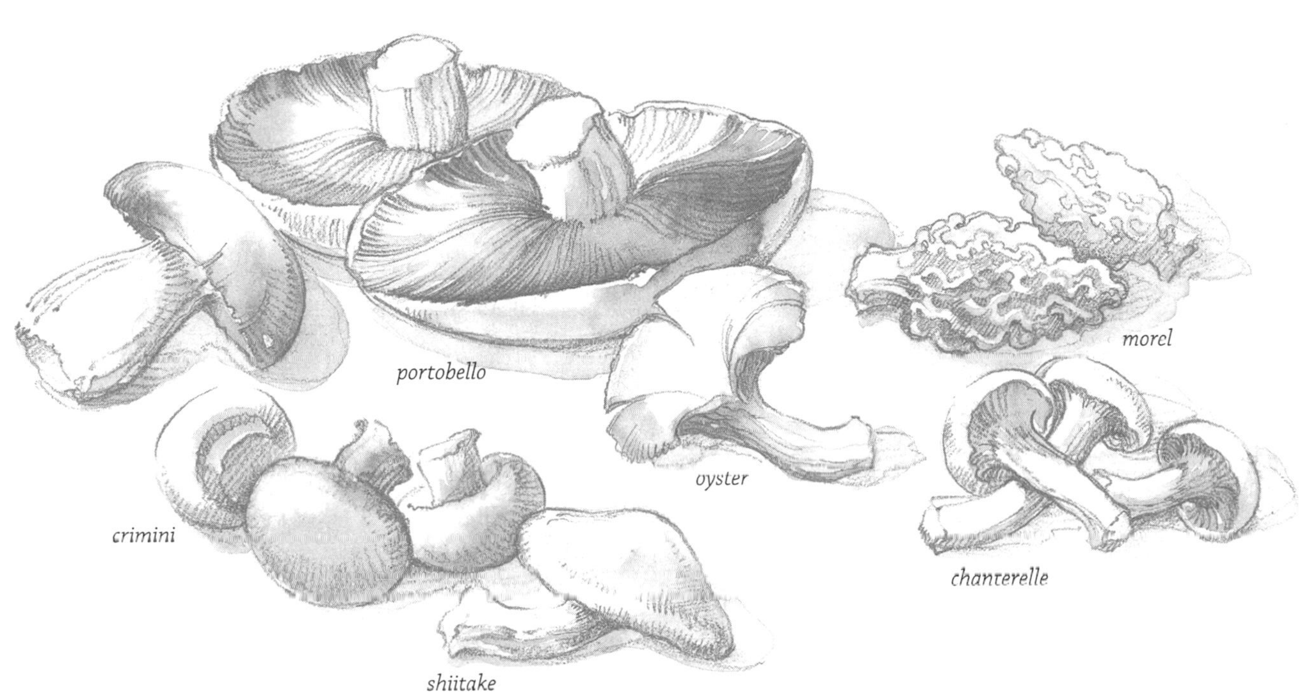

Bake crust until golden brown, about 15 minutes. Cool crust while preparing filling. Maintain oven temperature.

FOR FILLING: Heat oil in heavy large skillet over medium-high heat. Add onion and bell pepper; sauté 2 minutes. Add mushrooms and sauté until liquid evaporates and mushrooms begin to brown, about 10 minutes. Cool.

USING electric mixer, beat cream cheese, salt, and pepper in large bowl until mixture is fluffy. Beat in eggs 1 at a time, then whipping cream. Mix in vegetable mixture, crabmeat, smoked Gouda, and parsley.

POUR filling over crust. Place cheesecake on baking sheet. Bake until cake puffs and browns on top but center moves slightly when pan is shaken, about 1 hour 30 minutes. Transfer pan to rack and cool completely. *(Cheesecake can be prepared 1 day ahead. Cover and refrigerate.)*

RUN small sharp knife around pan sides to loosen cheesecake. Release pan sides. Transfer cheesecake to platter. Serve cold or at room temperature with baguette slices.

Spiced pecans

THESE NUTS ARE GREAT to nibble on with Champagne, and delicious in a salad. Chinese five-spice powder—a blend of ground anise, cinnamon, star anise, cloves, and ginger—is available in the spice section of most supermarkets. Substitute one or more of these individual spices for the five-spice powder, adjusting the quantities to your taste, or try with other spices, such as paprika, cayenne pepper, or chili powder.

MAKES 4 CUPS

- **¼ cup (½ stick) butter**
- **½ cup (packed) golden brown sugar**
- **¼ cup water**
- **1 teaspoon salt**
- **2 teaspoons Chinese five-spice powder**
- **½ teaspoon ground cumin**
- **½ teaspoon ground black pepper**
- **4 cups pecan halves**

PREHEAT oven to 350°F. Butter 2 large baking sheets. Melt ¼ cup butter in large skillet over medium heat. Add brown sugar, ¼ cup water, salt, and spices; stir until sugar dissolves. Add nuts to sugar mixture and cook until syrup thickly coats nuts, stirring frequently, about 5 minutes.

TRANSFER nuts to prepared baking sheets, spreading in single layer. Bake until golden, about 10 minutes. Cool. *(Can be prepared 3 days ahead. Store airtight at room temperature.)*

Glazed red pepper–fennel almonds

AS WITH MOST spiced or candied nuts, these can be made up to a week ahead if stored airtight at room temperature. Lining the baking sheet with foil makes cleanup a snap, and spraying the foil helps release the sticky nuts. As the nuts cool, the sticky glaze will harden, so separate the nuts as soon as you remove them from the oven.

MAKES 1 CUP

- **Nonstick vegetable oil spray**
- **3 tablespoons sugar**
- **2 teaspoons fennel seeds**
- **1 teaspoon dried crushed red pepper**
- **1 teaspoon salt**
- **1 cup whole almonds**
- **1 tablespoon water**

PREHEAT oven to 325°F. Line heavy baking sheet with foil; coat with nonstick spray. Combine sugar, fennel seeds, crushed red pepper, and salt in medium bowl. Mix in almonds and 1 tablespoon water. Spread mixture on prepared baking sheet in single layer. Bake until sugar melts and almonds are deep golden brown and glazed, stirring often, about 22 minutes. Separate almonds with fork; cool completely on sheet. *(Can be prepared 1 week ahead. Store in plastic bag.)* Transfer almonds to bowl and serve.

Hot appetizers

Pepperoni and Asiago pinwheels

PURCHASED FROZEN PUFF PASTRY makes these light and flaky hors d'oeuvres simple to prepare, and the Asiago cheese makes them absolutely addictive. Asiago is available at Italian markets, specialty foods stores, and some supermarkets; if you can't find it, use Parmesan instead.

MAKES ABOUT 60

- **½ cup grated Asiago cheese**
- **¾ teaspoon dried thyme**
- **¾ teaspoon dried oregano**
- **¼ teaspoon ground black pepper**
- **1 sheet frozen puff pastry (half of 17.3-ounce package), thawed**
- **2 tablespoons honey-Dijon mustard, divided**
- **2 ounces packaged sliced pepperoni (about twenty-four 1½-inch-diameter slices)**
- **1 large egg, beaten to blend**
- **Nonstick vegetable oil spray**

MIX first 4 ingredients in medium bowl. Cut puff pastry crosswise in half to form 2 rectangles. Spread 1 tablespoon mustard over 1 puff pastry rectangle, leaving 1-inch plain border at 1 long edge. Place half of pepperoni in single layer atop mustard. Top pepperoni with half of cheese mixture. Brush plain border with egg. Starting at side opposite plain border, roll up pastry, sealing at egg-coated edge. Transfer pastry roll, seam side down, to medium baking sheet. Repeat with remaining pastry rectangle, mustard, pepperoni, cheese mixture, and egg. Chill rolls until firm, about 30 minutes, or wrap in plastic and chill up to 1 day.

PREHEAT oven to 400°F. Line 2 baking sheets with foil. Lightly coat with nonstick spray. Cut each pastry roll into about thirty ¼-inch-thick rounds. Transfer pinwheels to prepared sheets. Bake until golden, about 15 minutes. Transfer to platter and serve.

Tamarind-glazed lamb skewers with dried apricot relish

TAMARIND PASTE HAS a sweet-and-sour flavor that it lends to this glaze. It is available at Indian markets and some Asian markets. Be sure to brush the glaze over the lamb skewers during the last minute of grilling; otherwise the sugar in the glaze will burn. Substitute chicken or beef for the lamb, if desired. Partner with basmati rice and purchased *naan* (Indian flatbread) for a delicious entrée. Serve with California Zinfandel, an Alsatian Pinot Gris, or a pale ale.

10 SERVINGS

Glaze

- **½ cup seedless unsweetened tamarind paste**
- **½ cup fresh orange juice**
- **⅓ cup mild-flavored (light) molasses**
- **1 teaspoon dried crushed red pepper**
- **3 tablespoons fresh lime juice**

Apricot relish

- **2 cups chopped dried apricots**
- **6 tablespoons fresh lemon juice**
- **⅓ cup chopped fresh cilantro**
- **2 tablespoons minced seeded red jalapeño chiles**
- **2 tablespoons (packed) golden brown sugar**
- **2 tablespoons cracked coriander seeds**

Skewers

- **2 pounds boneless leg of lamb, cut into ½-inch pieces; or 4 pounds lamb shoulder chops, fat trimmed, meat cut into ½-inch pieces**
- **1 large red onion, cut into ½-inch cubes**
- **20 12-inch metal skewers**

FOR GLAZE: Bring first 4 ingredients to boil in small saucepan over high heat. Reduce heat and simmer until reduced to 1 cup, stirring occasionally, about 8 minutes. Remove from heat. Stir in lime juice.

FOR APRICOT RELISH: Mix apricots and next 5 ingredients in medium bowl to blend. Season relish to taste with salt and pepper. *(Glaze and relish can be made 1 day ahead; cover separately and chill. Bring relish to room temperature. Stir glaze over medium heat until heated through.)*

FOR SKEWERS: Thread lamb and onion pieces onto skewers, using about 6 onion and 6 lamb pieces per skewer. *(Skewers can be prepared 1 day ahead. Cover and chill.)*

PREPARE barbecue (medium-high heat). Sprinkle skewers with salt and pepper. Grill lamb to desired doneness, turning once and basting with glaze during last minute of grilling, about 2 minutes total for medium-rare. Transfer skewers to platter. Serve with relish.

Peppered tuna skewers with wasabi mayonnaise

WASABI POWDER AND PICKLED GINGER are available at Japanese markets and specialty foods stores and in the Asian foods section of some supermarkets. Use fresh wasabi powder, as it can become bitter over time. The wasabi mayonnaise can also be used in sandwiches, such as cucumber or smoked salmon tea sandwiches.

MAKES 28

- **2 tablespoons wasabi powder (horseradish powder)**
- **1½ tablespoons water**
- **½ cup mayonnaise**

- **1 pound fresh tuna steaks, cut into ¾-inch cubes**
- **2½ tablespoons soy sauce**

- **28 large slices pickled ginger**
- **28 8-inch wooden skewers**

- **1 bunch watercress**
- **1 teaspoon freshly ground black pepper**
- **1 tablespoon vegetable oil**

MIX wasabi powder and 1½ tablespoons water in small bowl to blend. Whisk in mayonnaise. Cover wasabi mayonnaise and refrigerate at least 30 minutes. *(Can be made 1 day ahead. Keep refrigerated.)*

COMBINE tuna and soy sauce in medium bowl; toss to coat. Marinate tuna 30 minutes at room temperature, stirring occasionally.

MEANWHILE, thread 1 ginger slice onto each skewer 2 inches from tip.

LINE platter with watercress. Place bowl of wasabi mayonnaise on platter. Drain tuna; pat dry. Return to medium bowl. Sprinkle with pepper; toss to coat. Heat oil in large skillet over medium-high heat. Add tuna and sear until browned on all sides but still pink inside, about 2 minutes total. Thread 1 tuna cube onto each prepared skewer next to ginger. Arrange skewers on platter and serve.

Indian-spiced chicken kebabs with cilantro-mint chutney

TIKKA CURRY PASTE is available at Asian markets, but any mild Indian curry paste can be substituted. Pair this exotic appetizer with a white wine that has ripe fruit and crisp acidity to balance the spices. Good choices include Alsace Pinot Gris, New Zealand Sauvignon Blanc, or an extra-dry sparkling wine. The cilantro-mint chutney is a popular Indian condiment that is also delicious with other curry dishes.

MAKES ABOUT 24

Cilantro-mint chutney

- **½ cup (packed) fresh mint leaves**
- **½ cup (packed) fresh cilantro**
- **1 tablespoon fresh lemon juice**
- **2½ teaspoons minced fresh ginger**
- **1 jalapeño chile, seeded, minced**
- **2 tablespoons (or more) plain yogurt**

Chicken
- 1/2 cup plain yogurt
- 3 tablespoons tikka paste or mild curry paste (such as Patak's)
- 1 tablespoon olive oil
- 2 garlic cloves, minced
- 2 teaspoons minced fresh ginger
- 1/4 teaspoon cayenne pepper
- 1 1/2 pounds skinless boneless chicken breasts, cut into 2-inch cubes

- 24 (about) 6-inch bamboo skewers, soaked in water 30 minutes
- Butter lettuce leaves
- 1/2 small English hothouse cucumber, halved lengthwise, thinly sliced crosswise
- 2 limes, cut into wedges

FOR CHUTNEY: Blend first 5 ingredients and 2 tablespoons yogurt in blender or processor. Blend in more yogurt if necessary to make smooth paste. *(Chutney can be made 1 day ahead. Cover and refrigerate.)*

FOR CHICKEN: Whisk first 6 ingredients in large bowl to blend. Add chicken and toss to coat. Cover and refrigerate at least 2 hours and up to 12 hours.

PREHEAT broiler. Thread 1 chicken piece onto each skewer. Cover exposed part of skewers with foil. Broil chicken until cooked through, turning occasionally, about 8 minutes. Arrange lettuce and cucumber on platter. Top with chicken. Squeeze lime over. Serve chicken with chutney.

Cajun grilled shrimp

SERVE THE SHRIMP as an appetizer along with some grilled crusty bread for sopping up the flavorful dressing. Creole or Cajun seasoning can be found in the spice section of most supermarkets.

8 TO 10 SERVINGS

- 2 pounds uncooked shrimp, peeled, deveined
- 3/4 cup olive oil
- 3/4 cup red wine vinegar
- 1/4 cup Creole or Cajun seasoning
- 6 large garlic cloves, finely chopped

- 6 metal skewers

PLACE shrimp in large resealable plastic bag. Whisk oil, vinegar, seasoning, and garlic in medium bowl to blend. Transfer half of dressing to bag with shrimp; reserve remaining dressing. Seal bag. Marinate shrimp at room temperature 1 hour or refrigerate up to 2 hours, turning bag occasionally.

PREPARE barbecue (medium-high heat). Thread shrimp closely together onto skewers; discard marinade in bag. Grill until shrimp are just opaque in center, about 4 minutes per side. Push shrimp off skewers onto platter. Drizzle shrimp with some of reserved dressing. Serve, passing remaining dressing separately.

Pork satay with peanut dipping sauce

SOAKING THE BAMBOO SKEWERS in water helps prevent charring; you can also use metal skewers. If desired, the pork satay can be grilled rather than broiled. To turn these delicious appetizers into a light dinner, serve them with steamed rice and a salad of chopped cucumber, sliced red onion, and cilantro leaves, with a sweet-and-sour dressing made of vinegar, sugar, water, and chiles.

6 SERVINGS

- 1 tablespoon plus 1/3 cup minced fresh lemongrass (from bottom 6 inches of stalk)
- 3 tablespoons fresh lime juice, divided
- 2 tablespoons dark brown sugar, divided
- 1 tablespoon soy sauce

- 2 garlic cloves, minced
- 3/4 pound pork tenderloin, trimmed, cut into 3x1/2x1/4-inch slices

- 1 cup (or more) low-salt chicken broth
- 1/2 cup creamy peanut butter (do not use old-fashioned style or freshly ground)
- 1/2 cup chopped onion
- 1 tablespoon coriander seeds
- 1/2 jalapeño chile, minced

- 12 8-inch bamboo skewers, soaked in water 30 minutes
- Minced green onion tops

MIX 1 tablespoon lemongrass, 1 tablespoon lime juice, 1 tablespoon brown sugar, soy sauce, and garlic in large bowl. Add pork; toss to coat with marinade. Let stand 30 minutes to 1 hour.

MEANWHILE, mix remaining 1/3 cup lemongrass, 2 tablespoons lime juice, 1 tablespoon sugar, 1 cup broth, peanut butter, onion, coriander, and jalapeño in heavy medium saucepan. Bring to boil, whisking frequently. Transfer mixture to blender and puree. Strain into heavy small saucepan, pressing on solids with back of spoon; discard solids. Simmer until reduced to thick sauce consistency, stirring frequently, about 6 minutes. *(Dipping sauce can be prepared 1 day ahead. Cover and refrigerate. Reheat before using, thinning with more chicken broth if necessary.)*

PREHEAT broiler. Thread 3 pork strips on each skewer. Broil until cooked through, about 3 minutes per side. Pour dipping sauce into bowl; set in center of platter. Sprinkle with green onion. Surround with pork skewers and serve.

Phyllo-wrapped Brie with apricot and rosemary chutney

ORDER AN UNCUT WHEEL of Brie from the cheese shop or specialty foods store, and allow frozen phyllo dough to defrost overnight in the refrigerator. Check the expiration date on the box of phyllo, as it tends to stick together when it's not absolutely fresh. Have all of your ingredients and equipment ready before unwrapping the phyllo dough: It dries out quickly and can become difficult to handle shortly after it is opened.

16 SERVINGS

Chutney

- 12 ounces dried apricots, chopped
- 1 large red onion, chopped
- 1 cup water
- 2/3 cup cider vinegar
- 2/3 cup (packed) golden brown sugar
- 3 ounces dried tart cherries (3/4 cup)
- 1 1/2 tablespoons chopped fresh rosemary
- 3 large garlic cloves, finely chopped
- 2 teaspoons grated lemon peel
- 1/2 teaspoon salt
- 1/8 teaspoon cayenne pepper
- 1/2 cup blanched slivered almonds, toasted

Phyllo-wrapped cheese

- 1 cup (2 sticks) unsalted butter, melted
- 1 pound sheets fresh phyllo pastry or frozen, thawed
- 4 1/2 tablespoons chopped fresh rosemary
- 1 8-inch-diameter, 32- to 36-ounce wheel of Brie

- Fresh herb sprigs (such as rosemary, sage and chives)
- Additional dried apricots and dried cherries
- Fresh French-bread baguettes, thinly sliced
- Thinly sliced apples

FOR CHUTNEY: Combine all chutney ingredients except almonds in heavy large saucepan. Bring to boil over medium-high heat, stirring until sugar dissolves. Reduce heat to medium-low; simmer until almost all liquid has evaporated and chutney is thick, stirring occasionally, about 25 minutes. Mix in almonds. Transfer chutney to bowl. Chill until cold, about 3 hours. *(Can be made 1 week ahead. Cover; keep chilled.)*

FOR CHEESE: Brush heavy large baking sheet with butter; set aside. Unroll pastry. Cover with plastic wrap and damp kitchen towel. Transfer 2 stacked phyllo sheets to work surface, arranging 1 short side parallel to edge of work surface. Arrange 2 more stacked phyllo sheets on work surface, overlapping long side of first sheets by about 5 to 7 inches and forming rectangle about 18x17 inches. Brush pastry with butter; sprinkle 1½ tablespoons rosemary over. Place 2 more stacked sheets atop first set of 2 sheets, then 2 more stacked sheets atop second set of 2 sheets. Brush with butter and sprinkle with 1½ tablespoons rosemary. Repeat layering 1 more time with phyllo, butter, and 1½ tablespoons rosemary. (You will use a total of 12 sheets.)

USING sharp knife or scissors, trim phyllo corners, forming approximately 17-inch oval. Place Brie in center of phyllo. Spread 1⅓ cups chutney evenly over cheese. Slide hand under 1 rounded corner of phyllo. Lift phyllo and fold over top of cheese. Brush folded pastry with butter. Continue to lift phyllo in sections and fold snugly over top of cheese, brushing with butter and pressing each section to adhere, until cheese is wrapped (the top center 2 to 3 inches of cheese will not be covered). Use hands and metal spatula to transfer wrapped cheese to prepared baking sheet.

PLACE 1 phyllo sheet on work surface. Brush with butter. Starting at 1 long side, fold 1 inch of pastry over. Continue folding pastry loosely over itself, forming 1-inch-wide strip of pastry. Stand strip on edge and roll up into loose coil. Gather bottom edge of coil together, pinching to force top slightly open, forming a rose. Place rose atop uncovered center of cheese. Brush with butter. Repeat with 2 more sheets of phyllo, forming 2 more roses. Place atop cheese, covering opening completely. Chill 3 hours. *(Can be made 1 day ahead. Cover with plastic wrap; keep chilled.)*

POSITION rack in center of oven and preheat to 400°F. Bake cheese until pastry is deep golden brown, covering roses loosely with foil if browning too quickly, about 25 minutes. (If cheese leaks from pastry during baking, press piece of foil over tear in pastry; continue baking.) Cool cheese on sheet 45 minutes.

USING metal spatula, transfer warm cheese to large platter. Arrange herbs, dried fruit, baguette slices, and apple slices around cheese. Cut cheese into wedges.

Baked Brie with caramelized onions

SERVE AN ASSORTMENT of crudités and slices of French-bread baguettes alongside this rich fondue-like appetizer.

8 TO 10 SERVINGS

- **2 tablespoons (¼ stick) butter**
- **8 cups sliced onions (about 4 large)**
- **1 tablespoon minced fresh thyme**
- **4 garlic cloves, chopped**
- **½ cup dry white wine, divided**
- **1 teaspoon sugar**

- **1 8-inch-diameter, 32- to 36-ounce French Brie, packed in wooden box (do not discard box)**
- **2 French-bread baguettes, sliced**

MELT butter in heavy very large skillet over medium-high heat. Add onions; sauté until just tender, about 6 minutes. Add thyme; reduce heat to medium and cook until onions are golden, stirring often, about 25 minutes. Add garlic and sauté 2 minutes. Add ¼ cup wine; stir until almost all liquid evaporates, about 2 minutes. Sprinkle sugar over onions and sauté until soft and brown, about 10 minutes. Add remaining ¼ cup wine; stir just until liquid evaporates, about 2 minutes. Season to taste with salt and pepper. Cool. *(Can be prepared 2 days ahead. Cover and refrigerate.)*

PREHEAT oven to 350°F. Unwrap Brie, reserving bottom of wooden box. Cut away only top rind of cheese, leaving rind on sides and bottom intact. Return Brie to box, rind side down. Place box on baking sheet. Top Brie evenly with onion mixture. Bake until cheese just melts, about 30 minutes. Transfer Brie in box to platter. Surround with baguette slices.

Rosemary cheese straws

THESE FLAKY TWISTS are almost too good to be true: They require only four easy-to-find ingredients, they can be made two days ahead, and they are absolutely delicious. Serve them on their own as an appetizer, or team them with a salad or soup.

MAKES ABOUT 44

1 cup (packed) chilled grated Parmesan cheese (about 3 ounces)
¾ cup (packed) chilled grated white cheddar cheese (about 3 ounces)
1 tablespoon plus 1 teaspoon dried rosemary

1 sheet frozen puff pastry (half of 17.3-ounce package), thawed

POSITION rack in center of oven and preheat to 425°F. Line 3 heavy large baking sheets with parchment. Grind both cheeses and rosemary in processor until coarse powder forms. Transfer cheese mixture to small bowl.

PLACE pastry on lightly floured surface. Roll out pastry to 11x18-inch rectangle. Arrange 1 long side of pastry parallel to edge of work surface. Cover right half of pastry with ⅓ of cheese mixture. Fold left half of pastry over, covering cheese completely; press lightly all over to seal. Repeat rolling out to 11x18-inch rectangle, sprinkling with ⅓ of cheese, folding, and pressing 2 more times (for a total of 3 times; let pastry rest a few minutes if difficult to roll.) Roll out dough to 11x18-inch rectangle. Cut in half crosswise, forming two 11x9-inch pieces. Cut each dough piece crosswise into about 22 strips, each½ inch wide by 9 inches long. Twist each strip a few times and place on prepared sheets, pressing ends onto parchment and spacing evenly.

BAKE 1 sheet of cheese straws at a time until golden, about 8 minutes. Cool 5 minutes. Serve warm or at room temperature. *(Can be made 2 days ahead. Store airtight at room temperature. Rewarm in 350°F oven 5 minutes, if desired.)*

Walnut, arugula, and Gorgonzola crostini

A SIMPLE MIXTURE of tangy blue cheese, toasted walnuts, and peppery arugula turns baguette slices into irresistible *crostini*. Toasted pine nuts make a good substitute for the walnuts, and any creamy blue cheese can replace the Gorgonzola.

6 SERVINGS

Butter, room temperature
18 ¼-inch-thick diagonal French-bread baguette slices

6 tablespoons chopped toasted walnuts
3 ounces Gorgonzola cheese, crumbled
3 tablespoons finely chopped arugula
Arugula leaves

PREHEAT oven to 400°F. Spread butter over 1 side of each baguette slice. Arrange baguette slices on baking sheet, butter side up. Bake baguette slices until golden, about 12 minutes. Cool.

REDUCE oven temperature to 350°F. Mix walnuts, Gorgonzola, and arugula in medium bowl. Spoon nut-cheese mixture evenly atop baguette toasts, pressing to adhere. Season toasts with pepper. Bake toasts just until cheese melts, about 6 minutes. Cool crostini slightly. Arrange crostini on platter. Garnish platter with arugula leaves and serve.

Shiitake scrambled eggs and caviar on toasts

UNLIKE MOST MUSHROOMS, shiitakes have stems that become very tough and inedible when cooked, so be sure to trim them from the caps. If shiitake mushrooms are unavailable, use crimini or button mushrooms instead. Take care when cooking the eggs: They should be just softly set and still slightly creamy when served.

14 SERVINGS

6 tablespoons (3/4 stick) butter, divided
10 ounces shiitake mushrooms, stemmed, thinly sliced
1 teaspoon grated lemon peel

10 large eggs
1/4 cup minced fresh chives
1/2 teaspoon salt
1/2 teaspoon ground black pepper

28 1/3-inch-thick diagonal slices French-bread baguette, toasted
Sour cream
Caviar

MELT 3 tablespoons butter in heavy large skillet over medium heat. Add mushrooms and sauté until tender and beginning to brown, about 6 minutes. Mix in lemon peel. Set aside.

WHISK eggs, chives, salt, and pepper in large bowl to blend. Melt remaining 3 tablespoons butter in large nonstick skillet over medium heat. Add egg mixture and cook until eggs are softly set, stirring often, about 2 minutes. Mix in mushrooms.

SPOON egg mixture onto toasts. Top with sour cream and caviar. Transfer to platter and serve.

Stuffed mushrooms with bacon and olives

CHOOSE WHITE MUSHROOMS that are firm and evenly colored with tightly closed caps, and avoid rinsing them with water, since this may cause them to become waterlogged. Instead, wipe any dirt away with a clean moist cloth. Use a melon baller to scoop out the mushroom stems and form neat bowls for stuffing.

MAKES 18

18 large mushrooms (each about 2 inches in diameter)
4 bacon slices
3 garlic cloves, chopped
1 teaspoon chopped fresh rosemary or 1/2 teaspoon dried
1/4 cup chopped pitted Kalamata olives
2 ounces cream cheese, room temperature

Olive oil

REMOVE stems from mushrooms. Coarsely chop stems and set aside. Cook bacon in heavy large skillet over medium heat until crisp. Using tongs, transfer bacon to paper towels to drain. Pour off all but 1 tablespoon drippings from skillet. Add chopped mushroom stems, garlic, and rosemary; sauté over medium heat until tender, about 10 minutes. Crumble bacon and add to skillet. Add olives and stir to combine. Mix cream cheese in medium bowl until smooth. Add mushroom mixture and stir to blend. Season to taste with salt and pepper.

LIGHTLY brush rounded side of mushroom caps with oil. Place rounded side down on large baking sheet. Spoon filling into caps, mounding in center. *(Can be prepared 1 day ahead. Cover stuffed mushrooms with plastic wrap and chill.)*

PREHEAT oven to 375°F. Bake stuffed mushrooms until heated through, about 20 minutes. Transfer mushrooms to platter and serve.

Parsnip chips

CUTTING THE PARSNIPS into very thin slices is crucial in order to get a crunchy, delicate chip. Using a mandoline, or a less expensive V-slicer, makes it easy; look for these tools in the housewares section of department stores or at specialty cookware stores.

6 SERVINGS

1½ pounds large parsnips, peeled
8 cups (64 ounces) peanut oil
Salt

CUT parsnips lengthwise into ¹⁄₁₆-inch-thick slices, using V-slicer or very sharp knife. *(Can be prepared 4 hours ahead. Place in large bowl and cover with cold water. Drain thoroughly and pat dry before continuing.)*

HEAT oil in deep-fryer or large saucepan to 325°F. Add parsnips in batches (do not crowd) and fry until limp, about 30 seconds. Using slotted spoon, transfer to paper towels.

HEAT oil to 375°F. Add partially cooked parsnips in batches (do not crowd) and fry until golden brown and crisp, about 2 minutes. Drain on paper towels. Sprinkle lightly with salt and serve.

Gruyère, white wine, and mustard fondue

IF YOU DON'T HAVE a fondue pot, simply put the fondue in a decorative microwavable bowl, and serve it warm. When the fondue gets too cold, just rewarm it in the microwave. In addition to the steamed red-skinned baby potatoes, bread cubes, and grilled sausages, steamed broccoli and cauliflower make great dippers for this appetizer. Serve it also as an easy main course for casual weeknight entertaining.

6 TO 8 SERVINGS

5 cups (lightly packed) grated Gruyère cheese (about 13 ounces)
2½ tablespoons all purpose flour
1¾ cups dry white wine
2 garlic cloves, pressed
1 tablespoon Dijon mustard
Steamed red-skinned baby potatoes, bread cubes, and/or grilled sausages

COMBINE Gruyère cheese and flour in large bowl, tossing to coat cheese with flour. Simmer wine and garlic in heavy medium saucepan or fondue pot 1 minute. Reduce heat to medium-low. Add Gruyère cheese mixture to saucepan 1 handful at a time, stirring constantly until cheese melts before adding another handful. Whisk in mustard. Boil until smooth and thick, stirring constantly, about 2 minutes. Place pot over canned heat burner to keep warm. Serve with potatoes, bread, and/or sausages.

Tomato-dill fritters

KNOWN IN SANTORINI, GREECE, as *pseftokeftedes*—"false fritters"—because they don't contain meat as *keftedes* do, this mezede has become one of the island's signature dishes. Serve the fritters on their own or with a simple dip of yogurt mixed with fresh dill.

MAKES 24

1½ pounds plum tomatoes, halved, seeded, chopped (about 4 cups)
1 cup chopped red onion
2 tablespoons extra-virgin olive oil
2 tablespoons chopped fresh dill, divided
1 teaspoon dried oregano
1 cup all purpose flour
1¼ teaspoons salt
½ teaspoon coarsely ground black pepper

8 tablespoons (about) olive oil, divided

MIX tomatoes, onion, 2 tablespoons extra-virgin olive oil, 1 tablespoon dill, and oregano in large bowl. Let stand 30 minutes. Mix in flour, salt, and pepper. Let stand until mixture becomes moist, about 1 hour.

PREHEAT oven to 300°F. Heat 6 tablespoons oil in large skillet over medium-high heat. Drop 1 heaping tablespoon batter into oil. Repeat, forming 8 fritters total. Using slotted spatula, flatten each to 2-inch-diameter round. Cook fritters until brown, about 3 minutes per side. Transfer to paper towels to drain. Transfer to baking sheet and place in oven to keep warm. Repeat with remaining batter in 2 more batches, adding more oil to skillet as necessary. Arrange fritters on platter. Sprinkle with remaining 1 tablespoon dill.

First courses

Asparagus with hazelnuts and tarragon vinaigrette

ASPARAGUS IS COMBINED with other typically French ingredients in this lovely dish. During the spring use either green asparagus or the delicately flavored white asparagus, which are available at some farmer's markets and specialty markets. Hazelnut and walnut oils tend to spoil easily, so store them in the refrigerator to extend their shelf life.

4 SERVINGS

1 pound fresh asparagus, trimmed

¼ cup minced shallots
3 tablespoons tarragon-white wine vinegar
4 teaspoons chopped fresh tarragon or 1¼ teaspoons dried
1 teaspoon Dijon mustard
7 tablespoons hazelnut oil, walnut oil, or olive oil

4 cups baby lettuces or inner leaves of curly endive
¼ cup hazelnuts, toasted, skinned, coarsely chopped

POUR water into large pot to depth of 1 inch and bring to boil. Place asparagus on steamer rack set over water in pot. Cover pot and steam until asparagus is crisp-tender, about 4 minutes. Transfer asparagus to bowl of ice water and cool. Drain. Place asparagus on paper towels. *(Can be prepared 6 hours ahead. Cover and refrigerate.)*

COMBINE shallots, vinegar, tarragon, and mustard in bowl. Gradually whisk in oil. Season to taste with salt and pepper.

DIVIDE baby lettuces among 4 plates. Arrange asparagus atop lettuces. Drizzle with vinaigrette. Sprinkle with hazelnuts.

Shellfish with spicy island sauce

JALAPEÑO CHILES CARRY most of the heat in their seeds and veins. If you'd like this sauce to be extra-spicy, use the seeds. The sauce can be made two days ahead and kept covered in the refrigerator.

4 SERVINGS

- **1 cup canned crushed tomatoes with added puree**
- **½ cup chopped onion**
- **⅓ cup chopped pimiento-stuffed green olives**
- **2 jalapeño chiles, seeded but not deveined, minced**
- **1½ teaspoons cider vinegar**

- **12 snow crab claws or cooked jumbo shrimp, peeled, deveined**

COMBINE first 5 ingredients in medium bowl. Cover and refrigerate. *(Can be prepared 2 days ahead. Keep refrigerated.)*

SERVE shellfish with sauce.

Clams with saffron and tomatoes

HARVESTING SAFFRON is very labor-intensive, which is one reason it's among the most expensive spices in the world. Fortunately, a little saffron goes a long way. Look for it in the spice section of most supermarkets.

4 SERVINGS

- **½ cup white wine vinegar**
- **½ teaspoon crushed saffron threads**
- **1 cup extra-virgin olive oil**

- **4 pounds littleneck clams, scrubbed**
- **1½ cups cherry tomatoes (about one 12-ounce basket), halved**
- **2 large shallots, thinly sliced**
- **4 garlic cloves, finely chopped, divided**
- **2 tablespoons fresh lemon juice**

- **4 6x4-inch sourdough bread slices, cut into thirds**
- **½ cup chopped fresh Italian parsley**
- **Lemon wedges**

PLACE vinegar and saffron in heavy large nonreactive pot over low heat. Cook 1 minute to blend flavors. Remove from heat; let cool. Whisk in olive oil. Season vinaigrette to taste with salt and pepper.

PREHEAT broiler. Add clams, tomatoes, shallots, and 3 chopped garlic cloves to vinaigrette in pot. Cover and cook over high heat until clams open, about 8 minutes (discard any clams that do not open). Remove pot from heat. Using tongs, arrange clams in large serving bowl. Add lemon juice to saffron-tomato broth in pot.

MEANWHILE, brush sourdough bread slices lightly with olive oil. Rub bread with remaining chopped garlic. Broil bread until golden, about 2 minutes.

SPRINKLE clams with chopped parsley. Pour saffron-tomato broth over clams. Garnish with sourdough toasts and lemon wedges and serve.

Vegetable sushi rolls with sesame-miso sauce

YOU CAN INCORPORATE YOUR FAVORITE or seasonal produce into this vegetarian sushi. You'll find miso and somen noodles at Asian markets, specialty foods stores, and some supermarkets.

4 SERVINGS

Sauce

- **¼ cup rice vinegar**
- **¼ cup low-salt chicken broth**
- **2 tablespoons yellow or white miso**
- **2 tablespoons sugar**

Rolls

- **8 large Napa cabbage leaves or beet leaves, stemmed**

- **5 ounces (about 2½ bundles) somen noodles**
- **2 cups cold water**

- **16 matchstick-size strips red bell pepper**
- **16 matchstick-size strips English hothouse cucumber**

16 **matchstick-size strips green onion**
16 **enoki mushrooms or matchstick-size strips carrot**

2 **teaspoons sesame seeds**

FOR SAUCE: Whisk all sauce ingredients in small bowl to blend. Cover and refrigerate. *(Can be prepared 2 days ahead. Keep chilled.)*

FOR ROLLS: Fill large skillet ⅔ full with water. Bring to boil. Add half of cabbage leaves and simmer until leaves are just pliable, about 1 minute. Using slotted spoon, transfer cabbage to colander to drain. Repeat with remaining cabbage. Dry leaves thoroughly.

RETURN water in skillet to boil. Add noodles and bring to boil. Stir in 1 cup cold water and return to boil. Stir in remaining 1 cup cold water and return to boil. Drain noodles. Rinse under cold water to cool. Drain well.

PLACE clean damp towel on work surface. Arrange 1 cabbage leaf atop towel. Place ¼ cup noodles across width of leaf, 1 inch in from stem. Top noodles with 2 strips each red bell pepper, cucumber, and green onion and 2 enoki mushrooms. Fold stem end in over filling, then continue to roll up tightly jelly roll style, using towel as aid. Repeat filling and rolling with remaining cabbage, noodles, and vegetables. Cover and chill 1 to 4 hours.

SLICE rolls into 1-inch rounds. Arrange rounds cut side up on 4 plates. Sprinkle sesame seeds over sauce. Serve, passing sauce separately.

Shrimp marinated with capers and olive oil

BEGIN PREPARING THIS dish at least three hours and up to one day before serving, to allow the flavors to infuse the shrimp. Serve with crusty bread to soak up the marinade.

6 SERVINGS

1 **cup extra-virgin olive oil**
¾ **cup white wine vinegar**
¼ **cup capers with brine**
¼ **cup sugar**
2 **teaspoons salt**
1 **teaspoon chopped fresh parsley**
1 **teaspoon dry mustard**
3 **bay leaves**
1 **garlic clove, pressed**
2 **pounds cooked peeled deveined medium shrimp**
1 **onion, thinly sliced**
Niçoise olives
Lemon slices

MIX first 9 ingredients in large bowl. Add shrimp and onion and toss to coat. Cover and refrigerate at least 3 hours or overnight. Divide shrimp and marinade among 6 plates. Garnish with olives and lemon.

Twice-baked goat cheese soufflés

THESE FIRST-COURSE SOUFFLÉS are perfect for entertaining because most of the preparation can be done two hours ahead. Serve them unmolded or keep them in their soufflé dishes—in which case the cream can be spooned into the soufflés when served.

MAKES 8

1¾ **cups whole milk**
¾ **cup coarsely chopped onion**
2 **whole cloves**
⅛ **teaspoon ground nutmeg**

6 **tablespoons (¾ stick) butter**
9 **tablespoons all purpose flour**
¼ **teaspoon dry mustard**
2 **cups crumbled soft fresh goat cheese (about 9 ounces), divided**
6 **large egg yolks**
1¼ **teaspoons salt, divided**
¾ **teaspoon ground black pepper**

8 **large egg whites**

1 **cup whipping cream**

COMBINE milk, onion, cloves, and nutmeg in heavy medium saucepan over medium heat. Bring to boil. Remove from heat, cover, and let stand 30 minutes. Strain; discard solids.

PREHEAT oven to 350°F. Butter eight 10-ounce soufflé dishes. Melt 6 tablespoons butter in heavy large saucepan over medium heat. Add flour and dry mustard; whisk 2 minutes. Gradually whisk in strained milk. Boil until mixture is very thick and smooth, whisking constantly, about 2 minutes. Transfer soufflé base to large bowl. Gradually add 1½ cups cheese, whisking until melted and smooth. Add yolks, 1 teaspoon salt, and pepper; whisk until smooth. Cool to lukewarm.

BEAT egg whites and remaining ¼ teaspoon salt in another large bowl until stiff but not dry. Gently fold beaten whites into cheese mixture in 3 additions.

DIVIDE batter equally among prepared soufflé dishes. Arrange dishes in heavy 17x12-inch roasting pan. Pour enough hot water into pan to come halfway up sides of dishes. Bake until soufflés are puffed and just firm to touch on top, about 20 minutes. Transfer pan to rack and cool soufflés completely in water. *(Can be prepared 2 hours ahead. Let stand at room temperature.)*

PREHEAT oven to 425°F. Butter heavy large baking sheet. Using small knife, cut around sides of soufflés to loosen. Invert each soufflé onto spatula and slide onto prepared sheet, spacing evenly. Sprinkle with remaining½ cup cheese. Bake until soufflés are puffed, about 10 minutes.

MEANWHILE, bring cream to boil in heavy small saucepan. Remove from heat and season with salt and pepper.

USING spatula, transfer soufflés to plates. Spoon seasoned cream around soufflés and serve hot.

Crab and corn puddings

DUNGENESS CRAB from the Pacific coast lends rich taste and a nice texture to these comforting savory corn puddings; you can also use blue crab from the Gulf of Mexico or Atlantic coast. Purchase fresh crabmeat or buy cooked crab legs and extract the meat yourself by cutting the shells down the length of the legs with scissors (or breaking them with your hands) and picking out the prized meat. Poblanos are fresh green chiles available at Latin markets and some supermarkets. Serve these puddings as a first course for dinner, or team them with a mixed baby green salad accented with avocado, shaved fennel, and segmented grapefruit for a luxurious luncheon entrée.

8 SERVINGS

2 tablespoons (¼ stick) butter
½ cup minced shallots
¼ cup minced seeded fresh poblano chile

12 ounces frozen corn kernels (about 3 cups), thawed
1¾ cups half and half
6 large eggs
3 tablespoons all purpose flour
1½ teaspoons salt
1 teaspoon sugar
¼ teaspoon ground nutmeg
¼ teaspoon ground white pepper
1½ cups (packed) fresh crabmeat (about 8 ounces)

4 tablespoons freshly grated Parmesan cheese

PREHEAT oven to 350°F. Lightly butter eight 6-ounce custard cups or soufflé dishes. Melt 2 tablespoons butter in heavy small skillet over medium heat. Add shallots and chile; sauté until chile is tender, about 3 minutes.

PUREE corn in processor. Add half and half and next 6 ingredients. Using on/off turns, process until mixture is smooth. Transfer to large bowl. Add crabmeat and chile mixture; stir to blend. *(Custard can be prepared 8 hours ahead. Cover; chill.)*

DIVIDE custard among prepared cups. Sprinkle ½ tablespoon cheese over each. Place cups in large roasting pan. Pour enough hot water into pan to come halfway up sides of cups. Bake until custards are set in center and knife inserted into center comes out clean, about 50 minutes.

Bacon, green onion, and Port-Salut quiche

PORT-SALUT IS a mild-flavored cheese from the northern part of France. It has a smooth and semisoft texture that melts into a silky consistency. If you can't find Port-Salut, substitute Muenster or Monterey Jack cheese.

6 TO 8 SERVINGS

- **6 thick bacon slices, cut into ⅓-inch-wide pieces**
- **1 frozen 9-inch deep-dish pie crust, baked according to package instructions**
- **1 bunch green onions, sliced**
- **3 large eggs**
- **1½ cups half and half**
- **½ teaspoon salt**
- **Pinch of freshly grated nutmeg**
- **8 ounces Port-Salut or Muenster cheese, trimmed and grated**

PREHEAT oven to 375°F. Cook bacon in heavy medium skillet over medium-low heat until crisp. Using slotted spoon, transfer to paper towels. Sprinkle bacon over baked crust. Pour off all but 1 tablespoon fat from skillet. Add green onions. Cook over medium heat until tender, stirring frequently, about 2 minutes. Transfer to medium bowl. Add eggs, half and half, salt, and nutmeg; whisk to blend. Sprinkle cheese over crust. Pour in egg mixture. Sprinkle top liberally with pepper. Place quiche on baking sheet. Cook until top is beginning to puff and knife inserted into center comes out clean, covering edges with foil if browning too quickly, about 40 minutes. Cool slightly. Cut into wedges and serve.

Asparagus-Parmesan tart

BOILING THE ASPARAGUS actually removes the excess water from the stalks that might otherwise leak out while the tart bakes. This easy first course would also be nice for a weekend brunch.

6 SERVINGS

- **1 All Ready Pie Crust (half of 15-ounce package), room temperature**
- **1 teaspoon all purpose flour**
- **14 ounces asparagus, each spear trimmed to 3 inches long**
- **⅔ cup half and half**
- **2 large eggs**
- **½ cup freshly grated Parmesan cheese (about 4 ounces)**
- **1 tablespoon chopped fresh tarragon or 1 teaspoon dried**
- **½ teaspoon salt**

PREHEAT oven to 450°F. Open crust on work surface. Press out any cracks. Rub with 1 teaspoon flour. Arrange dough, flour side down, in 9-inch-diameter tart pan with removable bottom. Press dough into pan. Fold excess dough border over to form double-thick sides. Pierce dough all over with fork. Bake until golden, about 15 minutes. Cool on rack. Reduce oven temperature to 375°F.

COOK asparagus in pot of boiling salted water until just crisp-tender, about 2 minutes. Drain well. Place on paper towels. Whisk half and half, eggs, cheese, tarragon, and salt in bowl. Season with pepper. Arrange asparagus like spokes of wheel in crust, tips toward edge and ends meeting in center. Pour custard over. Bake tart until top puffs and browns, about 35 minutes. Cool slightly. Cut into wedges and serve.

Wild mushroom tart

DRIED PORCINI MUSHROOMS lend a rich, earthy flavor to this tart. They are available at Italian markets and specialty foods stores, and in the produce section of many supermarkets; you can also substitute other dried mushrooms, such as shiitakes. Use a mixture of chopped fresh herbs such as thyme, rosemary, and Italian parsley.

6 SERVINGS

Crust

- **1¼ cups all purpose flour**
- **½ teaspoon salt**
- **½ cup (1 stick) chilled unsalted butter, cut into pieces**
- **2 tablespoons (or more) ice water**

Filling

- **1 cup water**
- **1 ounce dried porcini mushrooms**

- **¼ cup (½ stick) unsalted butter**
- **10 ounces crimini or button mushrooms, sliced**
- **¼ cup minced shallots**
- **2 tablespoons Cognac or brandy**
- **2 tablespoons chopped fresh herbs, divided**

- **⅔ cup grated Gruyère cheese, divided**
- **¾ cup whipping cream**
- **2 large egg yolks**
- **1 large egg**

FOR CRUST: Blend flour and salt in processor. Using on/off turns, cut in butter until mixture resembles coarse meal. Add 2 tablespoons ice water and process until moist clumps form, adding more ice water by teaspoonfuls if dough is dry. Gather dough into ball; flatten into disk. Wrap in plastic and chill 45 minutes.

ROLL out dough on floured surface to 12-inch round. Transfer to 9-inch-diameter tart pan with removable bottom. Trim edges, leaving ½-inch overhang. Fold overhang in to form double-thick sides. Press tart edges to raise dough ⅛ inch above pan. Chill 30 minutes.

FOR FILLING: Bring 1 cup water to boil in saucepan. Add porcini; remove from heat and let stand 30 minutes. Spoon porcini from liquid; reserve liquid. Coarsely chop porcini.

MELT butter in heavy large skillet over high heat. Add porcini and crimini mushrooms. Season with salt; sauté until deep golden, about 10 minutes. Add shallots; sauté 2 minutes. Add Cognac and reserved porcini liquid, leaving any grit behind in saucepan. Boil until almost all liquid is absorbed, about 3 minutes. Mix in 1 tablespoon herbs. Cool.

PREHEAT oven to 375°F. Line crust with foil. Fill with dried beans or pie weights. Bake 15 minutes. Remove foil and beans; bake until golden, about 15 minutes longer. Maintain oven temperature.

SPRINKLE ⅓ cup cheese in crust. Cover with mushroom mixture. Whisk cream, egg yolks, egg, and remaining 1 tablespoon herbs in bowl. Pour custard over mushrooms. Top with remaining cheese. Bake until filling is set and top is golden, about 30 minutes. Cool on rack 15 minutes.

Seafood cakes with cilantro butter sauce

FOR BEST RESULTS, look for scallops that are pale beige or creamy pink in color. Scallops that are milky white have either been soaked in water, which increases their weight and dilutes their flavor, or treated with a preservative. You can also use bay scallops, though they tend to be more expensive because they are less plentiful than sea scallops. Japanese breadcrumbs, called *panko*, give a crunchy coating to the seafood cakes; they are available at Asian markets and specialty foods stores, and in the Asian foods section of most supermarkets. Use very coarse dried white breadcrumbs as a substitute.

6 SERVINGS

Seafood cakes

- **6 ounces sea scallops**
- **2 cups panko (Japanese breadcrumbs), divided**
- **1 large egg**
- **2 tablespoons whipping cream**
- **1 tablespoon chopped shallot**
- **2 garlic cloves, minced**
- **¾ teaspoon salt**
- **½ teaspoon ground black pepper**
- **5 ounces cooked peeled deveined shrimp, coarsely chopped**
- **⅓ cup chopped fresh cilantro**
- **2 tablespoons chopped fresh chives**
- **2 tablespoons chopped fresh parsley**

Cilantro sauce

- **2 cups dry white wine**
- **½ cup white wine vinegar**
- **2 shallots, minced**
- **½ cup whipping cream**

- **4 tablespoons vegetable oil**

- **½ cup (1 stick) chilled unsalted butter, cut into 8 pieces**
- **1 cup coarsely chopped fresh cilantro**

FOR SEAFOOD CAKES: Blend scallops, ½ cup panko, egg, cream, shallot, garlic, salt, and pepper in processor until smooth. Add shrimp and herbs; using on/off turns, process until shrimp is finely chopped (do not puree). Transfer to bowl. Cover and chill until cold, about 2 hours (mixture will be soft).

PLACE remaining 1½ cups panko in bowl. Drop ⅓ cup seafood mixture into panko; turn to coat. Press gently between hands into 3-inch-diameter cake. Transfer cake to baking sheet. Repeat with remaining seafood mixture and panko to form 6 cakes total. *(Can be prepared 1 day ahead. Cover and chill.)*

FOR CILANTRO SAUCE: Boil wine, vinegar, and shallots in heavy medium nonreactive saucepan until liquid is reduced to ¼ cup, about 18 minutes. Add cream and boil until sauce coats spoon, about 3 minutes longer. *(Cilantro sauce can be prepared 1 day ahead. Cover and chill.)*

PREHEAT oven to 350°F. Heat 2 tablespoons oil in large nonstick skillet over medium heat. Add 3 seafood cakes and cook until golden, about 4 minutes per side. Transfer to baking sheet. Repeat with remaining 2 tablespoons oil and 3 cakes. Bake until cooked through, about 5 minutes.

MEANWHILE, bring sauce to simmer. Remove from heat. Add butter 1 piece at a time; whisk just until melted. Immediately transfer to blender. Add cilantro; blend until cilantro is minced, about 10 seconds. Season with salt and pepper.

SPOON sauce onto 6 plates. Top each with 1 seafood cake and serve.

Potato galette with smoked salmon and dill crème fraîche

A *GALETTE* IS A ROUND, somewhat flat cake that can be made with an endless array of ingredients, and may be sweet or savory. This one, made with grated potatoes, resembles a large ring of golden hash browns. Topped with smoked salmon and a decadent crème fraîche sauce, it makes an easy, sophisticated first course. Serve it with poached eggs and toasted brioche bread for a special-occasion brunch. Crème fraîche is available at some supermarkets, but sour cream works as well.

4 SERVINGS

- **¼ cup crème fraîche or sour cream**
- **3 tablespoons minced shallots**
- **2 tablespoons minced fresh dill**
- **1½ tablespoons fresh lemon juice, divided**

- **2½ cups grated peeled russet potatoes (about 19 ounces)**
- **¼ cup (½ stick) butter, melted, divided**

- **3 ounces thinly sliced smoked salmon**
- **1½ teaspoons olive oil**
- **1½ ounces salmon caviar**
- **1 tablespoon chopped fresh chives**

MIX first 3 ingredients and 1 tablespoon lemon juice in bowl. Season mixture with salt and pepper. Cover and refrigerate until ready to use.

PREHEAT oven to 425°F. Toss potatoes with half of melted butter in bowl. Season with salt and pepper. Heat large ovenproof nonstick skillet over high heat. Add remaining melted butter; swirl to coat pan. Add potatoes. Using metal spatula, press and flatten potatoes into pancake. Cook 2 minutes. Reduce heat to medium-high and cook until bottom is golden, about 4 minutes. Slide galette onto plate. Place skillet upside-down atop plate; grasp plate and skillet with oven mitts and invert galette into skillet. Remove plate. Cook until bottom is golden, about 4 minutes. Transfer skillet to oven; cook until galette is crisp, about 10 minutes longer.

PLACE galette on platter. Spread with crème fraîche mixture. Top with salmon. Drizzle with oil and remaining ½ tablespoon lemon juice. Season with pepper. Garnish with caviar and chives. Cut into quarters and serve.

Classic saganaki with olives and lemon

SAGANAKI IS PAN-FRIED RECTANGLES of cheese such as *kasseri* or *kefalotyri*, which can be found at Greek markets and many supermarkets. If you can't find these cheeses, use another firm sheep's milk cheese such as pecorino Romano. These simple mezedes, or appetizers, are standard fare at Greek cafés, along with another Greek classic—ouzo, a clear, sweet, anise-flavored liqueur. Accompany the cheese with tomato wedges, olives, and pita bread.

4 TO 6 SERVINGS

- **1 8-ounce package kasseri cheese or pecorino Romano, cut into ½-inch-thick rectangular slices**
- **All purpose flour**
- **3 tablespoons (about) olive oil**
- **½ lemon**
- **1 tablespoon chopped fresh oregano**
- **Tomato wedges**
- **Pita bread triangles**
- **Kalamata olives**

RINSE cheese slices under cold water (do not pat dry). Coat with flour. Heat oil in heavy large skillet over medium-high heat until almost smoking. Add cheese and cook until beginning to brown, about 1 minute per side. Transfer to plates.

SQUEEZE lemon over cheese; sprinkle with oregano and pepper. Serve with tomatoes, pita, and olives.

Queso fundido with sausage and chipotle chiles

LITERALLY "MELTED CHEESE," *queso fundido* is particularly popular in and around Guadalajara, where it is traditionally served with roasted baby goat. The chipotle chiles (available canned in a spicy tomato sauce called *adobo* at Latin markets, specialty foods stores, and some supermarkets) give it a twist, but may be replaced with diced roasted green chiles, if desired. Warming and comforting, this makes a crowd-pleasing appetizer, and a perfect lunch or light supper when accompanied by a simple salad. Offer salsa alongside, and serve with cold beer or a Homemade Sweet-and-Sour Margarita (page 746).

6 SERVINGS

- **8 ounces Italian hot sausages, casings removed**
- **1¾ cups chopped onions**
- **1 cup chopped fresh cilantro, divided**
- **2 teaspoons chopped canned chipotle chiles, divided**
- **10 ounces Monterey Jack cheese, grated (2½ cups packed)**
- **12 6-inch-diameter flour or corn tortillas**

PREHEAT oven to 350°F. Sauté sausages and onion in large skillet over medium-high heat until brown, breaking up clumps of sausage with back of spoon, about 10 minutes. Mix in ½ cup cilantro and 1 teaspoon chipotle chiles. Transfer mixture to 9-inch-diameter baking dish. Mix cheese with remaining ½ cup cilantro and 1 teaspoon chipotle chiles in medium bowl.

SPRINKLE cheese mixture over sausage mixture. Bake casserole 10 minutes.

WRAP tortillas in aluminum foil. Place tortillas in oven to heat through. Continue to bake casserole until cheese bubbles, about 10 minutes longer. Serve casserole with warm tortillas.

Grilled marinated vegetables with fresh mozzarella

THE HERB OILS used to marinate the vegetables in this grilled antipasto double as dressings. Serve the antipasto as a first course, or offer it as a side dish with grilled steaks or lamb. Place any leftover vegetables and cheese between slices of ciabatta bread to make a delicious grilled vegetable sandwich.

8 SERVINGS

18 tablespoons extra-virgin olive oil
¼ cup chopped fresh mint
¼ cup chopped fresh basil
6 large garlic cloves, chopped
½ teaspoon dried crushed red pepper

6 medium zucchini (about 1 pound total), trimmed, each cut lengthwise into 4 strips
4 medium Japanese eggplants (about 1 pound total), trimmed, each cut lengthwise into 4 strips
4 medium red bell peppers (about 1¾ pounds total), stemmed, seeded, each cut lengthwise into 6 strips

2 8-ounce balls fresh water-packed mozzarella cheese, thinly sliced

SPOON 6 tablespoons oil into each of 3 small bowls. Add chopped mint to first bowl. Add basil and half of garlic to second bowl, and add dried crushed red pepper and remaining garlic to third bowl. Season each oil with salt and pepper.

COMBINE zucchini and 2 tablespoons mint marinade in medium bowl; toss to coat. Combine eggplants and 2 tablespoons basil marinade in another bowl; toss to coat. Combine bell peppers and 2 tablespoons crushed pepper marinade in third bowl; toss to coat. *(Can be prepared 2 hours ahead. Let stand at room temperature, tossing occasionally.)*

PREPARE barbecue (medium-high heat). Grill vegetables until just charred and tender, turning occasionally, about 5 minutes. Arrange vegetables on platter; sprinkle with salt and pepper. Drizzle each with remaining 4 tablespoons of its marinade. *(Can be prepared 2 hours ahead. Let stand at room temperature.)* Add cheese to platter and serve.

Spicy chicken, eggplant, and red onion quesadillas

A CILANTRO-JALAPEÑO MARINADE gives a spicy kick to the chicken in these quesadillas, but also makes a delicious marinade for other meats, especially flank steak. Broil or grill the chicken or steak and use it for other Mexican specialties such as tacos, nachos, or tostadas.

4 SERVINGS

¼ cup water
2 tablespoons chopped fresh cilantro
1 jalapeño chile, sliced
1 tablespoon fresh lime juice
1 tablespoon olive oil
8 ounces chicken tenders

4 ¼-inch-thick slices red onion
4 ¼-inch-thick crosswise slices eggplant
Vegetable oil

8 6-inch-diameter flour tortillas
½ cup grated Monterey Jack cheese
½ cup grated sharp cheddar cheese

Sour cream

COMBINE ¼ cup water, cilantro, jalapeño, lime juice, and olive oil in blender. Blend until smooth. Season to taste with salt and pepper. Place chicken in shallow baking dish. Pour marinade over, coating completely. Cover and refrigerate 4 hours.

PREHEAT broiler. Remove chicken from marinade; discard marinade. Broil chicken until cooked through, about 3 minutes per side. Set chicken aside. Lightly brush both sides of onion and eggplant slices with vegetable oil. Sprinkle both sides with salt and pepper. Broil vegetables until tender and golden, about 2 minutes per side.

LIGHTLY brush 4 tortillas with vegetable oil. Place tortillas, oil side down, on baking sheet. Combine grated Monterey Jack and cheddar cheeses in small bowl. Sprinkle ¼ cup cheese mixture over each tortilla. Place chicken atop cheese, dividing equally. Place 1 onion slice and 1 eggplant slice atop each. Top each eggplant slice with 1 tortilla. Lightly brush tops of tortillas with oil. *(Can be prepared 6 hours ahead. Cover and refrigerate.)*

PREHEAT oven to 450°F. Bake quesadillas until tortillas are slightly crisp and cheese melts, about 10 minutes. Cut quesadillas into quarters. Serve with sour cream.

Artichokes with Romano, cracked pepper, and olive oil

SELECT ARTICHOKES that are heavy and round, with tightly closed leaves. Do not use a pot made of a reactive metal (such as aluminum, copper, or cast iron) to cook artichokes, as these metals will discolor the artichokes and impart a metallic flavor. Instead, use either a stainless steel or enamel-coated pot.

4 SERVINGS

2 lemons, halved
4 artichokes (about 10 ounces each)

¾ cup extra-virgin olive oil
¾ cup grated pecorino Romano cheese
1½ teaspoons cracked black pepper
¾ teaspoon salt

SQUEEZE juice from lemon halves into large bowl of cold water; add squeezed lemons. Cut off stem and top ¾ inch of 1 artichoke and discard. Using scissors, trim sharp tips from leaves. Place artichoke in lemon water until ready to cook. Repeat with remaining artichokes.

DRAIN artichokes and cook in large pot of boiling salted water until base of each is tender when pierced with knife and leaves pull away easily, about 25 minutes. Drain artichokes well. *(Can be prepared 8 hours ahead. Cover and refrigerate. Steam artichokes 10 minutes to rewarm before continuing.)*

MIX oil, cheese, pepper, and salt in small bowl to blend. Gently press artichoke leaves outward from center to open artichokes slightly. Pull out small purple-tipped leaves, then scoop out fibrous choke. Place 1 artichoke on each of 4 plates. Sprinkle artichoke cavities with salt and pepper. Drizzle 1 tablespoon cheese dressing over each artichoke. Divide remaining cheese dressing equally among 4 small ramekins and serve with artichokes.

4 Soups, stews, and chilies

You eat them with a spoon. That's about all the great big world of soups has in common. After that, all bets are off: Whether the soup of choice is hot, cold, smooth, chunky, spicy, mild, clear, or creamed depends on some combination of personal preference, family favorites, geography, and the calendar.

Cold soups are ideal for warm-weather parties, and not just for formal affairs. Sneak one in when nobody's expecting it—say, at the next backyard barbecue. Poured from a pitcher into chilled mugs, cold soups are simplicity to serve and sip. And the fact that they need time to chill means that they *must* be made ahead, another reason to turn to cold soups for entertaining.

Hot soups run the gamut from smooth and sophisticated to chunky and down-home. When serving one as a first course, pair a lighter, more elegant soup, such as one with roasted red peppers and eggplant, with a hearty or richly flavored entrée. Follow a sturdier selection, such as Cheese Tortellini Soup with Cannellini, Kielbasa, and Kale, with a simple second course, like broiled salmon or sautéed chicken. Thicker, more satisfying soups, stews, and chilies—usually containing meats, beans, or potatoes—can also be the main course, followed by a simple green salad and light dessert. Crusty bread, still warm from the oven, should accompany any of the three.

So where is the line between soup and stew? Couldn't a hearty Beef-Barley Soup with Wild Mushrooms and Parsnips easily double as a main course? Here's one way to think about it: Stews tend to contain ingredients that need extended cooking to make them tender—oxtails, for instance, or largish cuts of chicken and pork. Here's another way to approach the issue: Make whichever of these dishes appeals, and don't worry about the semantics.

Hot soups

Classic New England clam chowder

THIS RICH AND CREAMY CHOWDER—with just the right proportion of potatoes to clams—is excellent as either a starter or a main course. Purists are welcome to shuck and chop fresh clams, but this version, with easier-to-use canned clams, is equally delicious (and puts the soup on the table faster). Save even more time by preparing the soup a day before you plan to serve it; simply refrigerate, then return it to a simmer. Oyster crackers are a traditional accompaniment.

8 FIRST-COURSE OR 4 MAIN-COURSE SERVINGS

- **3 cups bottled clam juice**
- **1 pound russet potatoes, peeled, cut into ½-inch cubes**

- **2 tablespoons (¼ stick) butter**
- **3 bacon slices, finely chopped**
- **2 cups chopped onions**
- **1¼ cups chopped celery with leaves**
- **2 garlic cloves, chopped**
- **1 bay leaf**
- **¼ cup all purpose flour**
- **6 6.5-ounce cans chopped clams, drained, juice reserved**
- **1¼ cups half and half**
- **1 teaspoon hot pepper sauce**

BRING bottled clam juice and potatoes to boil in heavy large saucepan over high heat. Reduce heat to medium-low, cover, and simmer until potatoes are tender, about 10 minutes. Remove from heat.

MELT butter in heavy large pot over medium heat. Add bacon and cook until bacon begins to brown, about 8 minutes. Add onions, celery, garlic, and bay leaf; sauté until vegetables soften, about 6 minutes. Add flour; stir 2 minutes (do not allow flour to brown). Gradually whisk in reserved juice from canned clams. Add potato mixture, clams, half and half, and hot pepper sauce. Simmer chowder 5 minutes to blend flavors, stirring frequently. Discard bay leaf. Season to taste with salt and pepper. *(Can be prepared 1 day ahead. Cool slightly. Refrigerate uncovered until cold, then cover and keep refrigerated. Bring to simmer before serving.)*

Crab-and-corn chowder with bacon and chanterelle mushrooms

WITH A POUND OF FRESH CRABMEAT and fresh chanterelle mushrooms, this is a luxurious and elegant special-occasion soup. For the best results, use Dungeness crab from the Pacific Coast or blue crab from the Gulf of Mexico or the Atlantic Coast. If chanterelles are unavailable, oyster mushrooms or stemmed shiitakes are good substitutes.

8 FIRST-COURSE SERVINGS

- **6 ears fresh yellow corn**
- **4 cups low-salt chicken broth**
- **3 cups whipping cream**

- **2 tablespoons olive oil**
- **7 bacon slices, cut crosswise into ¼-inch-wide strips**
- **1½ cups finely chopped onions**
- **1½ cups finely chopped leeks (white and pale green parts only; about 2 medium)**
- **¾ cup finely chopped celery**
- **1 teaspoon fennel seeds**
- **1¾ pounds white-skinned potatoes, peeled, cut into ½-inch cubes**

- **2 tablespoons (¼ stick) butter**
- **6 ounces fresh chanterelle mushrooms, thickly sliced**
- **2 tablespoons dry Sherry**
- **1 teaspoon fresh thyme leaves**

- **1 pound fresh crabmeat, picked over**
- **2 tablespoons chopped fresh parsley**

CUT kernels off corn cobs. Set kernels aside. Combine cobs, broth, and cream in heavy large saucepan. Simmer 5 minutes. Remove from heat.

HEAT oil in heavy large pot over medium-high heat. Add bacon and sauté until crisp, about 8 minutes. Transfer bacon to paper towels to drain. Pour off all but 3 tablespoons bacon drippings; add onion, leeks, celery, and fennel seeds to pot. Sauté until vegetables are crisp-tender, about 4 minutes. Stir in potatoes. Discard cobs from cream mixture; strain cream mixture into potato mixture. Simmer until potatoes are almost tender, stirring occasionally, about 10 minutes. Stir in corn kernels. Simmer chowder until potatoes are tender, about 5 minutes longer. *(Can be prepared 1 day ahead. Cover and chill bacon. Cool soup slightly. Refrigerate uncovered until cold, then cover and keep refrigerated. Bring to simmer before continuing.)*

MELT butter in heavy large skillet over medium heat. Add mushrooms and sauté until tender, about 5 minutes. Stir in Sherry and thyme. Add mushroom mixture to chowder. Season to taste with salt and pepper.

SAUTÉ crabmeat in same large skillet over medium-low heat just until heated through, about 3 minutes. Divide crabmeat, reserved bacon, and parsley among bowls. Ladle chowder over and serve.

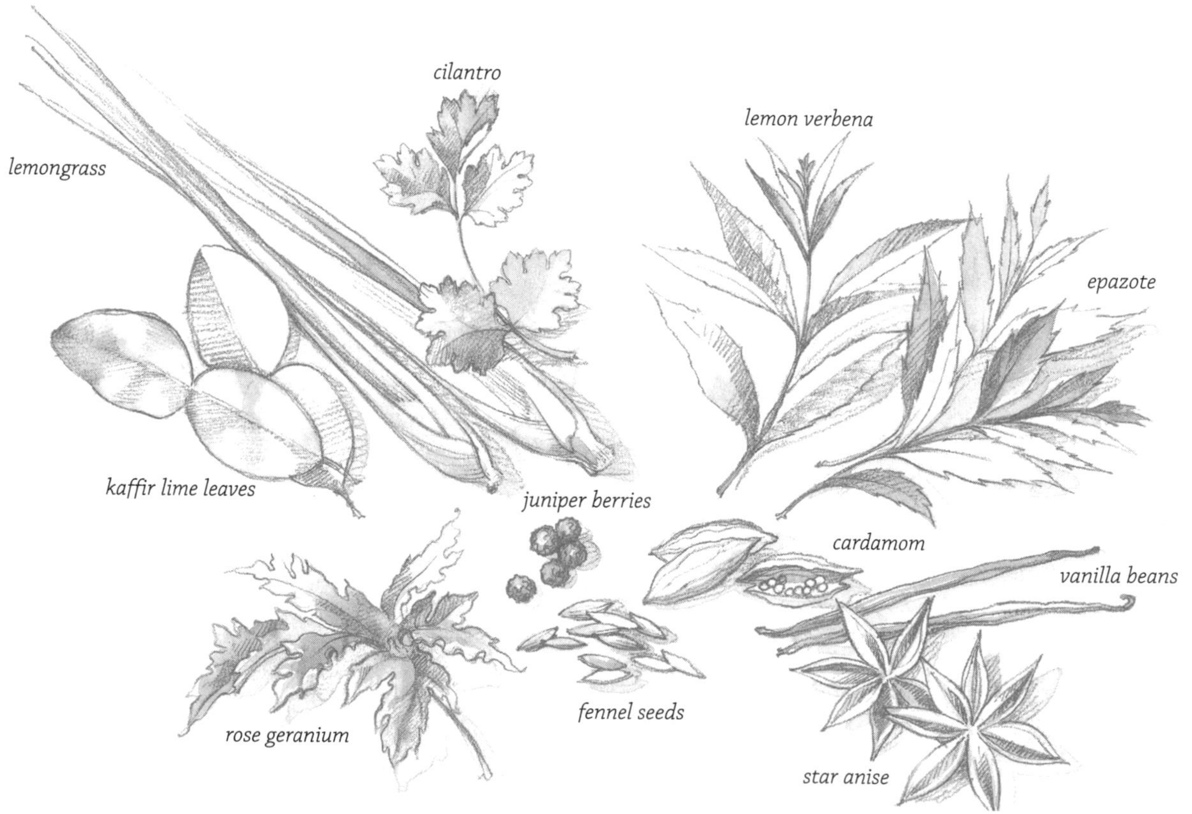

Thai curried seafood soup

A WONDERFULLY EXOTIC TWIST on a classic seafood soup—the combined aromas and flavors of coconut milk, clam juice, curry powder, and saffron will transport you to another land. Using the clams and mussels in their shells accentuates the freshness of the soup, and adding the rice to the broth makes this a substantial meal all by itself. Simply serve with bread or biscuits (and salad if desired). The unsweetened coconut milk can be found at Indian, Southeast Asian, or Latin markets and many supermarkets.

4 MAIN-COURSE SERVINGS

- **2 tablespoons vegetable oil**
- **1 cup chopped leek (white and pale green parts only; about 1 large)**
- **4 teaspoons minced peeled fresh ginger**
- **1 tablespoon curry powder**
- **1½ teaspoons minced red jalapeño chile with seeds, divided**
- **2½ cups canned unsweetened coconut milk**
- **2½ cups bottled clam juice**
- **⅓ cup long-grain white rice**
- **Generous pinch of saffron threads (optional)**
- **1½ tablespoons fresh lime juice**
- **½ teaspoon grated lime peel**
- **12 small clams, scrubbed**
- **8 mussels, scrubbed, debearded**
- **16 uncooked medium shrimp, peeled, deveined**
- **⅓ pound bay scallops**
- **Chopped fresh chives**

HEAT oil in heavy large pot over medium heat. Add leek, ginger, curry, and 1 teaspoon jalapeño; sauté 5 minutes. Stir in coconut milk, clam juice, rice, and saffron, if desired; bring to boil. Reduce heat, cover, and simmer until rice is tender, about 15 minutes. Mix in lime juice and peel. Add clams and mussels; cover and cook 4 minutes. Add shrimp and scallops; cover and cook until clams and mussels open, about 3 minutes longer (discard any clams or mussels that do not open).

LADLE soup into bowls. Garnish with remaining ½ teaspoon jalapeño and chives.

Cheese tortellini soup with cannellini, kielbasa, and kale

MAKING SOUP FROM SCRATCH is fast and easy with the use of prepared broth, canned beans, and purchased tortellini. (For a nice change of pace, use pumpkin tortellini instead.) You can also make the soup a day ahead and have it ready to go. Asiago cheese is available at most well-stocked supermarkets or at Italian markets, but Parmesan works equally well.

6 MAIN-COURSE SERVINGS

- **2 tablespoons olive oil**
- **12 ounces fully cooked smoked kielbasa sausage, thinly sliced**
- **1 onion, chopped**
- **1 cup chopped fresh fennel bulb**
- **4 garlic cloves, minced**
- **1½ tablespoons chopped fresh thyme**
- **½ teaspoon dried crushed red pepper**
- **10 cups low-salt chicken broth**
- **4 cups chopped kale (about ½ bunch)**
- **1 15-ounce can cannellini (white kidney beans), rinsed, drained**

- **1 9-ounce package cheese tortellini**
- **1 cup grated Asiago cheese or Parmesan cheese**

HEAT oil in heavy large pot over medium high heat. Add next 6 ingredients and sauté until vegetables are soft and kielbasa is brown, about 12 minutes. Add broth and bring to boil. Stir in kale and cannellini. Reduce heat to low and simmer until kale is wilted, about 4 minutes. *(Can be prepared 1 day ahead. Cool slightly. Refrigerate uncovered until cold, then cover and keep refrigerated. Bring to simmer before continuing.)*

ADD tortellini to soup. Simmer until pasta is tender but still firm to bite, about 5 minutes.

LADLE soup into bowls. Serve, passing grated cheese separately.

Smoky shrimp, hominy, and tortilla soup

IF YOU'RE LOOKING FOR a flavorful soup full of the tastes of the West, this is one you won't forget. The tortilla strips need to dry overnight, so begin making the soup one day (or up to three days) ahead. Chipotle chiles canned in a spicy tomato sauce called *adobo*, are available at Latin markets, specialty foods stores, and some supermarkets.

10 FIRST-COURSE SERVINGS

4 5- to 6-inch-diameter corn tortillas, halved, cut crosswise into thin strips

2 tablespoons olive oil
1 cup finely chopped onion
1 cup finely chopped peeled carrot
½ cup finely chopped celery
6 garlic cloves, minced
½ teaspoon dried oregano
7 cups low-salt chicken broth
2 15-ounce cans golden hominy, drained
⅓ cup canned crushed tomatoes with added puree
2 teaspoons chopped canned chipotle chiles

1 pound uncooked small shrimp, peeled, deveined
½ cup chopped fresh cilantro
Lime wedges

SPREAD tortilla strips in single layer on paper towels. Let tortilla strips stand at room temperature overnight to dry.

HEAT oil in heavy large pot over medium heat. Add onion, carrot, celery, garlic, and oregano. Sauté until vegetables are crisp-tender, about 10 minutes. Add broth, hominy, crushed tomatoes, and chipotle chiles; bring to simmer. Reduce heat, cover, and simmer 30 minutes. Season to taste with salt and pepper. *(Can be prepared 3 days ahead. Cool slightly. Refrigerate uncovered until cold, then cover and keep refrigerated. Bring to simmer before continuing.)*

ADD shrimp to soup and simmer until shrimp are opaque in center, stirring occasionally, about 3 minutes. Stir in cilantro. Divide soup among 10 bowls. Top with tortilla strips. Serve, passing lime wedges separately.

Cabbage and blue cheese soup

THE FLAVORS OF FALL—cabbage and caraway—highlight this rich first-course soup. (*Rich* is the operative word: Serve this in small cups.) Surprisingly easy to make, this soup gets even simpler if you purchase pre-shredded cabbage from the supermarket, and if you prepare it one day ahead. Just refrigerate, then bring to a simmer, and stir in the cheese, cream, and Sherry.

8 FIRST-COURSE SERVINGS

¼ cup (½ stick) unsalted butter
2 large onions, chopped
2 bay leaves
7 cups thinly sliced green cabbage (about 12 ounces)
1 tablespoon caraway seeds
5 cups low-salt chicken broth

2 cups crumbled blue cheese (about 8 ounces)
1 cup whipping cream
1 tablespoon dry Sherry

MELT butter in heavy large pot over medium heat. Add onions and bay leaves; sauté until onions are translucent, about 15 minutes. Add cabbage and caraway seeds; sauté until cabbage wilts, about 5 minutes. Add broth and bring to boil. Reduce heat and simmer 15 minutes to blend flavors. *(Can be prepared 1 day ahead. Cool slightly. Refrigerate uncovered until cold, then cover and keep refrigerated. Bring to simmer before continuing.)*

ADD cheese to soup and stir over medium heat until melted. Add cream and stir until heated through; do not boil. Season to taste with pepper. Mix in Sherry. Discard bay leaves. Ladle soup into cups and serve.

Creamy cilantro and almond soup

THIS FAST AND EASY SOUP offers intense Mexican flavor, and is ready in less than an hour. Toasting the almonds and simmering the soup enrich their flavors. When buying cilantro and parsley, look for bunches with bright green, unwilted leaves.

6 FIRST-COURSE SERVINGS

6½ cups (or more) low-salt chicken broth, divided
4 cups (packed) fresh cilantro, divided
2 cups (packed) fresh Italian parsley
6 ounces cream cheese, cubed
½ cup slivered almonds, toasted
1 fresh marjoram sprig

COMBINE 2 cups broth, 2 cups cilantro, parsley, cream cheese, and almonds in blender; blend until smooth. Heat 4½ cups broth in large saucepan. Whisk in herb-cheese mixture and marjoram. Simmer 25 minutes to blend flavors. Transfer 1 cup soup and remaining 2 cups cilantro to blender; puree until smooth. Add puree to soup in pan. Season to taste with salt and pepper. Bring soup to simmer, thinning with more broth if desired.

Corn and wild rice soup with smoked sausage

AN EXCELLENT STARTER for a Midwestern-style Sunday supper—or just a warmer-upper any night of the week—this soup features three classic heartland ingredients: corn, smoked sausage, and wild rice. The combination gives this appealing soup its sweet-spicy flavor and interesting texture. To keep things easy for the busy cook, the soup can be made up to two days ahead.

12 FIRST-COURSE OR 6 MAIN-COURSE SERVINGS

12½ cups (or more) low-salt chicken broth, divided
1¼ cups wild rice (about 7½ ounces)

6¼ cups frozen corn kernels (about 2½ pounds), thawed, divided
2 tablespoons vegetable oil
10 ounces fully cooked smoked sausage (such as kielbasa), cut into ½-inch cubes
3 carrots, peeled, diced
2 medium onions, chopped

1½ cups half and half

Chopped fresh chives or parsley

BRING 5 cups broth to simmer in heavy medium saucepan over medium heat. Add wild rice and simmer uncovered until all liquid evaporates and rice is almost tender, stirring occasionally, about 40 minutes.

MEANWHILE, blend 3¾ cups corn and 1½ cups broth in processor until thick, almost smooth puree forms. Heat oil in heavy large pot over medium-high heat. Add sausage and sauté until beginning to brown, about 5 minutes. Add carrots and onions; sauté 3 minutes. Add 6 cups broth and bring soup to simmer. Reduce heat to low and simmer 15 minutes.

ADD cooked wild rice, corn puree, and remaining 2½ cups corn kernels to soup. Cook until rice is very tender and flavors blend, about 15 minutes longer. Mix in half and half. Thin soup with more broth, if desired. Season soup to taste with salt and pepper. *(Can be prepared 2 days ahead. Cool slightly. Refrigerate uncovered until cold, then cover and keep refrigerated. Bring to simmer over medium-low heat before serving.)*

LADLE soup into bowls. Garnish with chives or parsley and serve.

Chicken-orecchiette soup with cilantro and lemon

FEATURING BOTH GREEK AND ASIAN herbs and spices, this aromatic soup is a delightfully exotic take on chicken noodle. Lemongrass can be found at Asian markets and in the produce section of some supermarkets. Orecchiette pasta (whose name and shape suggest "little ears") should be easy to find, but any other small pasta shells will work as well.

6 FIRST-COURSE SERVINGS

- **1 tablespoon olive oil**
- **2 skinless boneless chicken breast halves (about 12 ounces total)**

- **3 cups coarsely chopped onions**
- **3 plum tomatoes, sliced**
- **2 stalks lemongrass, thinly sliced (about ½ cup)**
- **2 tablespoons coriander seeds**
- **2 teaspoons cumin seeds**
- **2 teaspoons fennel seeds**
- **8 cups low-salt chicken broth**
- **½ cup chopped fresh cilantro, divided**

- **8 ounces orecchiette (little ear-shaped pasta), freshly cooked**
- **3 plum tomatoes, seeded, chopped**
- **½ cup fresh lemon juice**
- **Lemon slices (optional)**

HEAT oil in heavy large pot over medium-high heat. Sprinkle chicken with salt and pepper; add to pot and sauté until cooked through, about 4 minutes per side. Transfer chicken to plate. Cool.

ADD onions and next 5 ingredients to pot; sauté over medium heat until fragrant, about 4 minutes. Add broth and ¼ cup chopped cilantro. Simmer 20 minutes to blend flavors.

STRAIN broth into heavy large saucepan; discard solids in strainer. Slice cooked chicken crosswise into thin strips; add to broth. *(Can be prepared 1 day ahead. Refrigerate uncovered until cold, then cover and keep refrigerated. Bring to simmer before continuing.)*

ADD cooked pasta, chopped tomatoes, lemon juice, and remaining ¼ cup cilantro to soup; simmer just until heated through. Season to taste with salt and pepper. Ladle soup into bowls; garnish with lemon slices, if desired.

Beef-barley soup with wild mushrooms and parsnips

THIS RECIPE YIELDS ENOUGH for leftovers the next day. It makes a warming autumn supper with bread and a crisp salad. Dried porcini mushrooms are available at Italian markets and specialty foods stores, and in the produce section of many supermarkets. The soup can be made up to two days ahead.

8 MAIN-COURSE SERVINGS

- **3 tablespoons olive oil**
- **1½ pounds assorted fresh wild mushrooms (such as crimini and oyster), sliced**
- **¾ pound onions, chopped**
- **2 celery stalks, chopped**
- **4 garlic cloves, chopped**
- **3½ pounds center-cut beef shank slices (about ¾- to 1-inch thick)**
- **8 cups beef broth**
- **7 cups water**
- **1¼ pounds red bell peppers, chopped**
- **1 pound parsnips, peeled, cut into ½-inch pieces**
- **½ pound carrots, peeled, cut into ½-inch pieces**
- **1¾ cups pearl barley (about 9 ounces)**
- **1½ cups canned crushed tomatoes with added puree**
- **2 ¾-ounce packages dried porcini mushrooms, brushed clean of any grit, coarsely chopped**
- **2 tablespoons dried marjoram**
- **1 tablespoon dried thyme**

HEAT oil in heavy large pot over medium-high heat. Add fresh wild mushrooms and onions. Sauté until mushrooms brown, about 18 minutes. Add celery and garlic; stir 1 minute. Add beef shank slices and all remaining ingredients. Bring to boil. Reduce heat to medium-low, cover, and simmer until meat is tender, about 1½ hours. Remove from heat.

USING tongs, remove meat from pot. Cool slightly. Remove meat from bones; discard bones and any tough connective tissue. Cut meat into bite-size pieces and return to soup. Season soup to taste with salt and pepper. *(Can be prepared 2 days ahead. Cool slightly. Refrigerate uncovered until cold, then cover and keep refrigerated. Bring to simmer before serving.)*

Brandied onion soup with croque-monsieur croutons

THE RESTAURANT FAVORITE known as French onion soup gets a truly authentic Gallic twist here: In France, the popular *croque-monsieur* is a grilled ham-and-cheese sandwich. In this recipe, the ham and cheese top small slices of baguette, which are then broiled and added to the richly flavored onion soup.

6 FIRST-COURSE SERVINGS

- **3 tablespoons butter**
- **2½ pounds onions, thinly sliced**
- **7¼ cups beef broth**
- **¾ cup dry white wine**
- **2 teaspoons Dijon mustard**
- **1 to 2 tablespoons brandy**

- **18 ⅓-inch-thick slices French-bread baguette**
- **2 cups grated Swiss cheese (about 8 ounces)**
- **1 cup coarsely chopped ham (about 7 ounces)**

MELT butter in heavy large pot over medium-high heat. Add onions and sauté until deep brown, about 30 minutes. Add broth, wine, and mustard; bring to boil. Reduce heat to medium and simmer until flavors blend, about 15 minutes. Add brandy to taste and simmer 5 minutes. Season soup to taste with salt and pepper.

MEANWHILE, preheat broiler. Arrange bread slices on baking sheet. Broil until beginning to color, about 1 minute. Mound cheese and ham on bread; sprinkle with pepper. Broil until cheese melts, turning baking sheet for even cooking, about 2 minutes.

LADLE soup into deep bowls. Top each with 3 croutons and serve.

Caramelized onion and roasted shallot cream soup

THE ULTIMATE ONION SOUP—caramelizing the onions and roasting the shallots first imparts abundant flavor. Consider saving this soup for company: Its richness (finished with a little Sherry) makes a dramatic impression at a dinner party. The soup would also be nice garnished with croutons.

8 FIRST-COURSE SERVINGS

- **16 large shallots, peeled**
- **1 tablespoon olive oil**

- **¾ cup (1½ sticks) unsalted butter**
- **3½ pounds onions, thinly sliced**
- **2 tablespoons (packed) golden brown sugar**

- **¾ cup cream Sherry, divided**
- **1 tablespoon dried thyme**
- **1 tablespoon dried rubbed sage**
- **2 cups low-salt chicken broth**
- **1 cup beef broth**
- **3 cups whipping cream**

- **3 tablespoons minced fresh thyme (optional)**
- **2 tablespoons chopped fresh parsley**
- **½ teaspoon hot pepper sauce**
- **8 fresh sage leaves (optional)**

PREHEAT oven to 375°F. Toss shallots with oil in bowl. Arrange shallots on large rimmed baking sheet, spacing evenly. Bake until golden brown, turning occasionally, about 30 minutes.

MELT butter in heavy large pot over medium-high heat. Add onions and sugar; cook until onions are deep golden brown, stirring frequently to prevent sticking, about 50 minutes.

ADD whole shallots, ½ cup Sherry, and dried herbs to onions. Cook until almost all liquid evaporates, stirring occasionally, about 5 minutes. Add both broths and simmer 25 minutes. Add cream and simmer until soup thickens, about 10 minutes. *(Can be prepared 1 day ahead. Cool slightly. Refrigerate uncovered until cold, then cover and keep refrigerated. Bring to simmer before continuing.)*

ADD fresh thyme, if desired, parsley, hot pepper sauce, and remaining ¼ cup Sherry to soup. Season to taste with salt and pepper. Ladle soup into bowls. Garnish with sage leaves, if desired, and serve.

Smoky split pea and root vegetable soup

THIS SOUP IS A MEAL unto itself—just round it out with some savory scones or biscuits and maybe a salad. Smoked turkey wings or drumsticks, or the meaty bone of a ham, can replace the ham hocks.

8 MAIN-COURSE SERVINGS

- **6 tablespoons (¾ stick) butter**
- **3 medium carrots, peeled, chopped**
- **2 large parsnips, peeled, chopped**
- **1½ cups chopped leeks (white and pale green parts only; about 2 medium)**
- **1 large onion, chopped**
- **2½ teaspoons dried thyme**
- **2 teaspoons dried marjoram**
- **3 bay leaves**
- **11 cups low-salt chicken broth**
- **3 cups dried split peas**
- **1¼ pounds smoked ham hocks**
- **½ cup chopped fresh Italian parsley**

MELT butter in heavy large pot over low heat. Add carrots, parsnips, leeks, onion, thyme, marjoram, and bay leaves. Cover and cook until vegetables are tender, stirring occasionally, about 20 minutes. Add broth, peas, and ham hocks. Bring to simmer; cover partially and cook until peas are tender and soup thickens slightly, stirring occasionally, about 45 minutes. Remove ham hocks and cut meat into small pieces. Discard bone and fat. Return meat to soup. Season to taste with salt and pepper. *(Can be prepared 2 days ahead. Cool slightly. Refrigerate uncovered until cold, then cover and keep refrigerated. Bring soup to simmer, thinning with water if needed, before continuing.)*

DISCARD bay leaves. Mix parsley into soup. Ladle into bowls and serve.

Cumin-spiced black bean soup

IF YOU KEEP a few staples on hand in your pantry—cans of black beans, low-salt chicken broth, diced tomatoes—this soup is quick enough to make from scratch even on a weeknight. Offer sour cream and chopped cilantro in separate bowls on the table, so diners can add toppings at their discretion.

6 FIRST-COURSE SERVINGS

- **2 tablespoons olive oil**
- **1¼ cups chopped onions**
- **4 garlic cloves, chopped**
- **1 tablespoon chopped fresh thyme, or 1½ teaspoons dried**
- **3 15-ounce cans black beans, drained, 1 cup liquid reserved**
- **3½ cups (or more) low-salt chicken broth**
- **1 28-ounce can diced tomatoes in juice**
- **2 teaspoons ground cumin**
- **1½ teaspoons hot pepper sauce**

HEAT oil in heavy large pot over medium heat. Add onion, garlic, and thyme; sauté until onion is golden, about 8 minutes. Add beans, reserved 1 cup bean liquid, 3½ cups broth, tomatoes with juice, cumin, and hot pepper sauce. Bring soup to boil. Reduce heat to medium-low and simmer until flavors blend and soup thickens slightly, stirring occasionally, about 20 minutes. Cool slightly.

WORKING in 2 batches, puree 2½ cups soup in blender until smooth. Mix puree back into soup pot. Bring to simmer. Season to taste with salt and pepper. *(Can be made 1 day ahead. Cool slightly. Refrigerate uncovered until cold, then cover and keep refrigerated. Bring soup to simmer, thinning with more broth if needed, before serving.)*

LADLE soup into bowls and serve.

Lentil soup with minted yogurt

COOL AND REFRESHING YOGURT enhanced with fresh mint, cilantro, and basil tops this hearty curry-flavored soup. Fresh peppermint, with its bright green leaves and purple stems, is more pungent than spearmint, but either will work here. For ease of preparation, the yogurt mixture and the soup can each be made ahead, but refrigerate them separately.

10 FIRST-COURSE SERVINGS

- **1½ tablespoons olive oil**
- **2 medium onions, chopped**
- **2 large carrots, peeled, chopped**
- **3 garlic cloves, minced**
- **4 teaspoons curry powder**
- **1 16-ounce package dried lentils**
- **9 cups (or more) low-salt chicken broth or vegetable broth**

- **1½ cups plain yogurt**
- **¼ cup chopped fresh mint**
- **¼ cup chopped fresh cilantro**
- **¼ cup chopped fresh basil**

HEAT oil in heavy large pot over medium heat. Add onions, carrots, and garlic; sauté until vegetables begin to soften, about 10 minutes. Add curry, then lentils, and stir 2 minutes. Add 9 cups broth and bring to boil. Reduce heat, cover, and simmer until lentils are tender, adding more broth if soup is too thick and stirring occasionally, about 1 hour 15 minutes. Season soup to taste with salt and pepper.

WHISK yogurt, mint, cilantro, and basil in small bowl to blend. Season herbed yogurt to taste with salt and pepper. *(Soup and herbed yogurt can be prepared 1 day ahead. Cool soup slightly. Refrigerate uncovered until cold, then cover and keep refrigerated. Cover herbed yogurt and chill. Bring soup to simmer, thinning with more broth if needed, before serving.)*

LADLE soup into bowls. Spoon generous dollops of herbed yogurt atop soup and serve.

Butternut squash soup with cider cream

SQUASH SOUPS ARE always a fall treat, and this one gets extra interest and pleasant sweetness from apples and apple cider. It would make an excellent starter for Thanksgiving dinner. The soup and cider cream can both be prepared one day ahead and stored separately in the refrigerator.

10 FIRST-COURSE SERVINGS

- **5 tablespoons butter**
- **2½ pounds butternut squash, halved, peeled, seeded, cut into ½-inch pieces (about 6 cups)**
- **2 cups chopped leeks (white and pale green parts only; about 2 large)**
- **½ cup chopped peeled carrot**
- **½ cup chopped celery**
- **2 small Granny Smith apples, peeled, cored, chopped**
- **1½ teaspoons dried thyme**
- **½ teaspoon dried sage leaves**

5 cups low-salt chicken broth
1½ cups apple cider, divided
⅔ cup sour cream
½ cup whipping cream
Chopped fresh chives

MELT butter in heavy large pot over medium-high heat. Add squash, leeks, carrot, and celery; sauté until slightly softened, about 15 minutes. Mix in apples, thyme, and sage. Add broth and 1 cup cider; bring to boil. Reduce heat to medium-low, cover, and simmer until apples are tender, stirring occasionally, about 30 minutes. Cool slightly.

WORKING in batches, puree soup in blender until smooth. Return soup to pot.

SEASON to taste with salt and pepper.

BOIL remaining ½ cup cider in heavy small saucepan until reduced to ¼ cup, about 5 minutes. Cool. Place sour cream in small bowl. Whisk in reduced cider. *(Soup and cider cream can be prepared 1 day ahead. Cool soup slightly. Refrigerate uncovered until cold, then cover and keep refrigerated. Cover cider cream and chill. Bring soup to simmer before continuing.)*

MIX whipping cream into soup. Ladle soup into bowls. Drizzle with cider cream. Top with chives.

Kabocha squash and chestnut soup with chipotle crème fraîche

THIS LUSCIOUS SOUP uses kabocha squash, a beautiful jade-green winter squash with deep orange flesh. If crème fraîche is hard to come by, substitute sour cream. Chipotle chiles canned in a spicy tomato sauce called *adobo*, are available at Latin markets, specialty foods stores, and many supermarkets.

10 TO 12 FIRST-COURSE SERVINGS

Chipotle crème fraîche

1 cup ruby Port
½ cup dry red wine
1 teaspoon chopped canned chipotle chiles
2 tablespoons tomato paste
1 cup crème fraîche or sour cream

Soup

Vegetable oil
2 2½-pound kabocha squash, halved horizontally, seeded
8 cups low-salt chicken broth
1½ 7.4-ounce jars whole roasted chestnuts
2 tablespoons pure maple syrup

FOR CHIPOTLE CRÈME FRAÎCHE: Combine Port, red wine, chiles, and tomato paste in heavy small saucepan. Simmer over medium heat until reduced to thick paste, stirring often, about 12 minutes. Transfer to small bowl; cool. Fold in crème fraîche. Cover and chill at least 1 hour and up to 1 week.

FOR SOUP: Preheat oven to 350°F. Brush baking sheet with oil. Place squash halves, cut side down, on prepared sheet. Bake squash until very tender, about 1 hour.

SCOOP squash from skins. Measure 6 cups squash and transfer to large pot (reserve any remaining squash for another use). Add broth and chestnuts to pot. Bring to boil over high heat. Reduce heat to medium-low. Simmer soup uncovered until chestnuts are very tender, about 30 minutes. Mix maple syrup into soup. Cool slightly. Working in batches, puree soup in blender until very smooth; return to same pot. Season to taste with salt and pepper. *(Soup can be prepared 1 day ahead. Cool slightly. Refrigerate uncovered until cold, then cover and keep refrigerated. Bring to simmer before serving.)*

LADLE soup into bowls. Top each serving with chipotle crème fraîche.

Spiced pumpkin soup

A MEDLEY OF EXOTIC SPICES plus coconut milk and banana add complexity and rich flavor to this smooth fall soup. Look for the canned unsweetened coconut milk at Indian, Southeast Asian, or Latin markets; many supermarkets carry it as well.

8 FIRST-COURSE SERVINGS

- **1½ tablespoons butter**
- **¾ cup chopped peeled carrot**
- **¾ cup chopped celery**
- **¾ cup chopped ripe banana**
- **½ onion, chopped**
- **1 garlic clove, minced**
- **1 bay leaf**
- **1 whole clove**
- **5 cups low-salt chicken broth**
- **2 cups canned pure pumpkin**
- **¾ cup canned unsweetened coconut milk**
- **¼ cup sweetened condensed milk**
- **1 teaspoon ground nutmeg**
- **½ teaspoon ground cinnamon**
- **½ teaspoon ground coriander**
- **½ teaspoon dried sage leaves**
- **¼ teaspoon ground allspice**
- **¼ teaspoon curry powder**
- **¼ cup chopped fresh cilantro**

MELT butter in heavy large pot over medium-high heat. Add carrot and next 6 ingredients; sauté until vegetables are soft, about 10 minutes. Add broth and all remaining ingredients except cilantro. Simmer soup over medium heat 15 minutes to blend flavors. Discard bay leaf. Cool slightly. Working in batches, puree soup in blender until smooth. Return soup to pot. Season to taste with salt and pepper. *(Can be prepared 1 day ahead. Cool slightly. Refrigerate uncovered until cold, then cover and keep refrigerated. Bring to simmer before serving.)* Divide soup among 8 bowls. Sprinkle with cilantro and serve.

Curried parsnip soup

CURRY POWDER nicely complements the slight sweetness of the parsnips in this elegant—and extremely easy to make—soup. Whipping cream adds a little richness. As a first course, the soup would be lovely followed by simple roast chicken and rice pilaf.

6 FIRST-COURSE SERVINGS

- **3 tablespoons butter**
- **1 pound parsnips, peeled, sliced**
- **1 cup chopped onion**
- **1 garlic clove, chopped**
- **1 tablespoon all purpose flour**
- **2 teaspoons curry powder**
- **4 cups beef broth**

- **½ cup whipping cream**

Chopped fresh chives or green onions

MELT butter in heavy large saucepan over low heat. Add parsnips, onion, and garlic. Cover and cook until vegetables begin to soften but not color, stirring occasionally, about 10 minutes. Mix in flour and curry powder; stir 2 minutes. Gradually mix in beef broth. Increase heat to medium, cover, and simmer until parsnips are tender, about 15 minutes. Cool slightly.

WORKING in batches, puree soup in blender until smooth. Return soup to same saucepan. Stir in cream; bring to simmer. Season to taste with salt and pepper. *(Can be prepared 1 day ahead. Cool slightly. Refrigerate uncovered until cold, then cover and keep refrigerated. Bring soup to simmer before serving.)*

LADLE soup into bowls. Garnish with chives or green onions and serve.

Cream of mushroom soup

THE SURPRISING SECRET of this rich-tasting soup is that it contains only half a cup of whipping cream. The "creaminess" actually comes from rice, which is cooked in broth and then pureed. Using two pounds of mushrooms lends an intense mushroom flavor. Feel free to substitute any of your favorite wild mushrooms.

8 FIRST-COURSE SERVINGS

- **2 tablespoons (1/4 stick) butter**
- **3 cups chopped leeks (white and pale green parts only; about 3 large)**
- **2 pounds mushrooms, sliced**
- **2 garlic cloves, minced**
- **1/4 cup long-grain white rice**
- **3 1/4 cups (or more) low-salt chicken broth**
- **3 1/4 cups beef broth**
- **1/2 cup whipping cream**
- **1/4 cup chopped fresh chives**

MELT butter in heavy large pot over medium heat. Add leeks and sauté until tender, about 5 minutes. Increase heat to medium-high. Add mushrooms and sauté until mushrooms are soft and dry, about 10 minutes. Add garlic; sauté 1 minute. Stir in rice. Add 3¼ cups chicken broth and beef broth to pot. Bring to boil. Reduce heat to low, cover, and simmer until rice is very tender, about 30 minutes. Cool slightly.

WORKING in batches, puree soup in blender until smooth. Return soup to pot. Stir in cream. Thin with more chicken broth, if desired. *(Can be prepared 1 day ahead. Cool slightly. Refrigerate uncovered until cold, then cover and keep refrigerated. Bring to simmer before serving.)*

LADLE soup into 8 bowls. Sprinkle with chives and serve.

Leek, potato, and tarragon soup

LEEKS ARE NOT BEAUTIFUL VEGETABLES, but they have a sweet mellow flavor, less assertive than onions, that works well in a variety of preparations. Plus they're available all year, making this a good "any-time" soup. Just be sure to wash the leeks with care: Remove the tough green leaves, then halve the leeks lengthwise and rinse thoroughly in the sink or a bowl of water to remove all dirt.

6 FIRST-COURSE SERVINGS

- **3 tablespoons butter**
- **2 cups chopped leeks (white and pale green parts only; about 2 large)**
- **1 small onion, chopped**
- **4 garlic cloves, sliced**
- **2 tablespoons water**
- **1/2 pound red-skinned potatoes, unpeeled, cut into 1/2-inch pieces**
- **4 cups low-salt chicken broth or vegetable broth**
- **2 teaspoons chopped fresh tarragon**
- **1/2 cup whipping cream**
- **1/2 cup plain yogurt**

MELT butter in heavy large pot over medium heat. Add leeks, onion, garlic, and 2 tablespoons water. Cook until leeks are golden, about 10 minutes. Add potatoes and broth; bring to boil. Reduce heat to low and simmer until potatoes are tender, about 10 minutes. Mix in tarragon. *(Can be prepared 1 day ahead. Cool slightly. Refrigerate uncovered until cold, then cover and keep refrigerated. Bring to simmer before continuing.)*

STIR cream and yogurt into soup. Season soup to taste with salt and pepper.

Roasted red pepper and eggplant soup

EGGPLANT ADDS A NUTTY FLAVOR to this delicious soup, which gets its texture not from cream (there's none in the recipe) but from pureeing. Some Parmesan cheese shavings make a savory garnish. This would be a great starter for a hearty Italian dinner.

8 FIRST-COURSE SERVINGS

2 eggplants (about 2½ pounds total), halved lengthwise

4 red bell peppers

¼ cup olive oil
2 medium onions, chopped
2 cups chopped leeks (white and pale green parts only; about 2 large)
6 garlic cloves, minced
8½ cups low-salt chicken broth
3 tablespoons tomato paste
¼ cup chopped fresh basil
2 tablespoons chopped fresh thyme

3 tablespoons unsalted butter
1½ tablespoons fresh lemon juice

Parmesan cheese shavings

PREHEAT oven to 450°F. Line rimmed baking sheet with parchment paper. Pierce eggplants all over with fork. Place cut side down on prepared baking sheet. Roast until tender, about 45 minutes. Cool slightly. Remove peel and discard. Cut eggplants into large pieces. Set aside.

CHAR bell peppers over gas flame or in broiler until blackened on all sides. Enclose in paper bag 10 minutes. Peel, seed, and coarsely chop peppers.

HEAT oil in large pot over medium-high heat. Add onions and leeks; sauté until tender, about 5 minutes. Add garlic and stir 1 minute. Stir in eggplant, peppers, broth, and tomato paste. Bring to boil. Reduce heat to medium and simmer uncovered until vegetables are very tender and flavors blend, about 45 minutes. Stir in basil and thyme. Cool slightly.

WORKING in batches, puree soup in blender until smooth. Return soup to pot. Season to taste with salt and pepper. Add butter and lemon juice; stir over low heat until soup is heated through, about 5 minutes. *(Can be prepared 1 day ahead. Cool slightly. Refrigerate uncovered until cold, then cover and keep refrigerated. Bring to simmer before continuing.)*

TRANSFER soup to large bowl; garnish with Parmesan shavings.

Garbanzo bean soup with saffron

THIS SOUP IS both delicious and good for you (garbanzo beans contain fiber, iron, and vegetable protein). It's also nicely filling, so all you need is a salad and some bread. Then treat yourself to dessert; you've earned it.

6 FIRST-COURSE OR 4 MAIN-COURSE SERVINGS

1 tablespoon olive oil
1 medium onion, chopped
2 garlic cloves, minced
½ teaspoon saffron threads
5 cups vegetable broth
1 28-ounce can diced tomatoes in juice
5 cups ½-inch pieces peeled butternut squash
1 12- to 14-ounce russet potato, peeled, cut into ½-inch pieces
1 cinnamon stick
2 teaspoons ground cumin
1 15- to 16-ounce can garbanzo beans (chickpeas), drained

½ cup chopped fresh cilantro

HEAT oil in heavy large pot over medium heat. Add onion and garlic; sauté until tender, about 6 minutes. Add saffron and stir 1 minute. Add broth and next 5 ingredients; bring to boil. Reduce heat, cover, and simmer until vegetables are very tender, about 30 minutes. Stir in garbanzo beans. Simmer 10 minutes. Season to taste with salt and pepper.

LADLE soup into bowls. Sprinkle with chopped cilantro and serve.

Escarole and orzo soup with turkey-Parmesan meatballs

A COMPLETE MEAL in a bowl, this healthful and flavorful soup can be made using several of the staples you probably have on hand: low-salt chicken broth, breadcrumbs, ground turkey, Parmesan cheese. If desired, grate a little extra Parmesan for passing; a sprinkling over the soup will echo the flavor in the meatballs.

4 MAIN-COURSE SERVINGS

- **1 large egg**
- **2 tablespoons water**
- **1/4 cup plain dried breadcrumbs**
- **12 ounces lean ground turkey**
- **1/4 cup freshly grated Parmesan cheese**
- **2 tablespoons chopped fresh Italian parsley**
- **2 garlic cloves, minced**
- **3/4 teaspoon salt**
- **1/4 teaspoon ground black pepper**

- **8 cups (or more) low-salt chicken broth**
- **1 cup chopped peeled carrots**
- **3/4 cup orzo (rice-shaped pasta)**
- **4 cups coarsely chopped escarole (about 1/2 medium head)**

WHISK egg and 2 tablespoons water in medium bowl to blend. Mix in breadcrumbs; let stand 5 minutes. Add turkey, Parmesan cheese, parsley, garlic, salt, and pepper; stir gently to blend. Using wet hands, shape turkey mixture into 1¼-inch-diameter meatballs. Place meatballs on baking sheet; cover and chill 30 minutes.

BRING 8 cups chicken broth to boil in large pot. Add carrots and orzo; reduce heat to medium and simmer uncovered 8 minutes. Add turkey meatballs and simmer 10 minutes. Stir in chopped escarole and simmer until turkey meatballs, orzo, and escarole are tender, about 5 minutes longer. Season soup to taste with salt and pepper. *(Can be prepared 2 hours ahead. Let stand uncovered at room temperature. Bring to simmer over medium heat, thinning with more broth if desired, before serving.)*

LADLE soup into bowls and serve.

Spicy Vietnamese beef and noodle soup

THIS IS A ROBUST stew like soup inspired by Vietnamese *pho*. The broth needs to be refrigerated overnight, so start preparing this recipe one day before serving. Lemongrass, whole star anise, fish sauce, and udon can be found at Asian markets and some supermarkets.

6 MAIN-COURSE SERVINGS

- **5 tablespoons peanut oil**
- **3 1/4 pounds meaty oxtails, patted dry**
- **2 large onions, chopped**
- **1 large carrot, peeled, chopped**
- **3 stalks lemongrass, chopped**
- **2/3 cup chopped peeled fresh ginger**
- **8 garlic cloves, chopped**
- **7 whole star anise (star-shaped spice)**
- **1 tablespoon whole black peppercorns**
- **12 cups water**
- **7 cups beef broth**
- **3 tablespoons fish sauce (such as nam pla or nuoc nam)**

- **1 12-ounce package fresh udon (Japanese wheat noodles) or fresh linguine**
- **1 tablespoon Asian sesame oil**

- **3 cups fresh mung bean sprouts**
- **6 radishes, thinly sliced**

4 green onions, thinly sliced
4 serrano chiles, thinly sliced
6 tablespoons chopped fresh basil
6 tablespoons chopped fresh mint
6 tablespoons chopped fresh cilantro
Lime wedges
Additional fish sauce (nam pla or nuoc nam)

HEAT peanut oil in heavy large pot over medium-high heat. Sprinkle oxtails with salt and pepper. Add oxtails to pot and brown on all sides, about 20 minutes. Transfer oxtails to large bowl. Add onions and next 6 ingredients to same pot. Sauté until vegetables are tender, about 8 minutes. Return oxtails to pot. Add 12 cups water, beef broth, and 3 tablespoons fish sauce. Cover and simmer gently until oxtails are very tender, about 3 hours.

USING tongs, transfer oxtails to large bowl. Strain broth into another large pot; discard solids. Remove meat from oxtails; discard bones. Add meat to broth. Cool slightly. Refrigerate uncovered until cold, then cover and refrigerate overnight. Spoon solid fat off top of soup.

COOK noodles in large pot of boiling salted water until tender. Drain; rinse under cold water. Return to same pot. Toss noodles with sesame oil.

BRING soup to boil. Divide noodles, sprouts, and next 6 ingredients among 6 bowls. Ladle soup into bowls. Serve with lime wedges and additional fish sauce.

Cold soups

Chilled Indian-spiced tomato soup with crabmeat

HERE'S WHERE a few specialized kitchen products come in handy: A spice mill makes it easy to grind the toasted whole spices and peppercorns—thereby getting the freshest, most intense flavor from them. They can also be ground in a mortar with a pestle. A food mill is useful for pureeing the soup; you can also press the soup through a strainer, or puree it in a blender and then strain it.

8 FIRST-COURSE SERVINGS

Spice mix

1 tablespoon cumin seeds
1 tablespoon coriander seeds
1 tablespoon fennel seeds
1 teaspoon yellow mustard seeds
1 teaspoon whole black peppercorns

Soup

6 tablespoons extra-virgin olive oil
2 cups chopped celery
1½ cups chopped onions
1 cup chopped carrots
¼ cup chopped peeled fresh ginger (from about 3-inch-long piece)
6 garlic cloves, chopped
1 pound red bell peppers, chopped
1¾ cups chopped fresh fennel bulb
3 pounds plum tomatoes, diced (about 8 cups)
5¼ cups vegetable broth

2 teaspoons (about) hot pepper sauce

1 pound fresh crabmeat, picked over
Thinly sliced radishes
Chopped fresh chives

FOR SPICE MIX: Toast all ingredients in heavy medium skillet over medium heat until spices darken slightly in color and start to pop, stirring occasionally, about 7 minutes. Cool in skillet. Transfer to spice mill and grind finely.

FOR SOUP: Heat oil in heavy large pot over medium-high heat. Add celery, onions, and carrots. Sauté until vegetables soften slightly, about 8 minutes. Add ginger and garlic; sauté 3 minutes. Add bell peppers and fennel. Stir 2 minutes to coat. Add tomatoes; cook until tomatoes soften and break down, stirring often, about 8 minutes. Add broth and bring soup to boil. Reduce heat to medium; simmer until all vegetables are tender, about 25 minutes. Add ground spice mix; return soup to boil. Remove from heat; cover and let steep 20 minutes.

PLACE coarse sieve over large bowl. Working with 2 cups at a time, strain soup into bowl, pressing liquid and most of solids through sieve. Discard remaining solids. Season soup to taste with hot pepper sauce, salt, and pepper. Cool slightly. Refrigerate soup uncovered until cold, at least 3 hours. *(Can be prepared 1 day ahead; cover and keep refrigerated.)*

LADLE soup into 8 shallow bowls. Divide crabmeat among bowls. Garnish with radish slices and chives.

Tomato-chipotle soup with fresh peach salsa

THE SWEETNESS of the fresh peach salsa contrasts nicely with the smoky chipotle chiles. (Chipotles, canned in a spicy tomato sauce called *adobo,* are available at Latin markets, specialty foods stores, and some supermarkets.)

4 FIRST-COURSE SERVINGS

- **2½ pounds plum tomatoes, seeded, chopped (about 6 cups), divided**
- **1 cup (about) tomato juice**
- **4 tablespoons chopped onion, divided**
- **3 tablespoons chopped fresh cilantro, divided**
- **2 teaspoons (or more) chopped canned chipotle chiles**
- **1 garlic clove, minced**

- **1 ripe peach, peeled, pitted, diced**
- **1 teaspoon minced jalapeño chile**

RESERVE 1 cup chopped tomatoes for peach salsa. Place remaining tomatoes in processor and puree until smooth. Transfer puree to 2-quart glass measuring cup. Add enough tomato juice to puree to equal 5 cups tomato mixture. Place 2 cups tomato mixture in blender. Add 2 tablespoons onion, 2 tablespoons cilantro, 2 teaspoons chipotle chiles, and garlic to blender. Puree until very smooth. Stir puree back into tomato mixture in measuring cup. Season to taste with salt and pepper. Add more chopped chipotles, if desired. Cover; refrigerate until well chilled, about 1 hour. *(Can be prepared 1 day ahead. Keep soup refrigerated. Cover reserved chopped tomatoes and chill.)*

MIX reserved chopped tomatoes, peach, jalapeño, and remaining 2 tablespoons onion and 1 tablespoon cilantro in small bowl. Ladle tomato soup into bowls. Sprinkle with peach salsa; serve.

Great gazpacho

ONE OF THE NICE THINGS about this version of gazpacho is that it can be made as spicy or as mild as you and your guests desire—the hot sauce is added to taste at the end. For toppings, provide some diced avocado and extra chopped cilantro.

8 TO 10 FIRST-COURSE SERVINGS

- **4 cups tomato juice**
- **2 cups purchased fresh mild salsa**
- **2 red bell peppers, chopped**
- **1 cucumber, peeled, seeded, chopped**
- **1 cup onion- and garlic-seasoned croutons**

½ **cup low-salt chicken broth**
⅓ **cup chopped fresh cilantro**
4 **large garlic cloves**
2 **tablespoons balsamic vinegar**
1 **tablespoon olive oil**
1 **teaspoon ground cumin**
Hot pepper sauce

WORKING in batches, blend all ingredients except hot sauce in processor to coarse puree. Transfer gazpacho to large bowl. Season to taste with hot sauce, salt, and pepper. Refrigerate until well chilled, about 2 hours. *(Can be prepared 1 day ahead; cover and keep refrigerated.)*

LADLE soup into bowls and serve.

Chilled tomatillo and cucumber soup

TOMATILLOS, LIKE THEIR COUSINS the tomatoes, are fruits—small, green, and pleasantly tart. Pick the ones with snug-fitting, dry husks. You can find tomatillos and poblanos at Latin markets and some supermarkets.

6 FIRST-COURSE SERVINGS

2 **poblano chiles**

1 **tablespoon olive oil**
1 **cup chopped onion**
2 **garlic cloves, minced**
½ **pound tomatillos, husked, rinsed, cut into ½-inch pieces**
1 **English hothouse cucumber, peeled, chopped (about 2 cups)**
4 **cups low-salt chicken broth**
2 **tablespoons minced seeded jalapeño chiles**
2 **tablespoons fresh lime juice**
2 **tablespoons chopped fresh cilantro**

½ **cup whipping cream**

2 **green onions, chopped**

CHAR poblano chiles over gas flame or in broiler until blackened on all sides. Enclose in paper bag 10 minutes. Peel and seed chiles, then cut into 1-inch pieces.

HEAT oil in heavy large saucepan over medium heat. Add 1 cup chopped onion and garlic; sauté 5 minutes. Add tomatillos and cucumber; sauté 5 minutes. Add broth and poblano chiles; bring to boil. Reduce heat to medium-low and simmer until tomatillos are tender, about 10 minutes. Stir in jalapeños, lime juice, and cilantro. Cool completely.

WORKING in batches, puree soup in blender. Transfer to large bowl; stir in cream. Season to taste with salt and pepper. Cover and refrigerate soup until cold, at least 3 hours or overnight.

DIVIDE soup among 6 bowls. Sprinkle with green onions and serve.

Cucumber soup with smoked salmon and dill

CUCUMBER JOINS the classic combination of salmon and dill in this cool summer soup. This would make an excellent beginning to a light supper featuring the fresh vegetables of the summer season.

6 FIRST-COURSE SERVINGS

1½ **tablespoons butter**
1 **cup chopped onion**
4 **cucumbers, peeled, halved, seeded, cut crosswise into ½-inch-thick slices (about 5 cups)**
1 **8-ounce russet potato, peeled, cut into ½-inch dice**
3½ **cups low-salt chicken broth**
3 **large fresh dill sprigs**
1 **teaspoon (or more) salt**

1 **cup crème fraîche or sour cream, divided**
6 **tablespoons minced fresh dill, divided**

3 **ounces smoked salmon, cut into ½-inch pieces**

MELT butter in heavy large pot over medium heat. Add onion and sauté until slightly softened, about 3 minutes. Add cucumbers and potato; stir 1 minute. Add broth, dill sprigs, and 1 teaspoon salt. Increase heat and bring to simmer. Reduce heat to low, cover, and simmer until cucumbers and potato are tender, stirring occasionally, about 25 minutes. Cool slightly.

WORKING in batches, puree soup in processor until smooth. Return to pot. Whisk in ½ cup crème fraîche and 4 tablespoons minced dill. Refrigerate uncovered until cold, about 4 hours. *(Can be prepared 1 day ahead. Cover and keep refrigerated.)*

TASTE soup, adding more salt if desired. Ladle soup into 6 bowls. Place dollop of remaining crème fraîche in center of each bowl; sprinkle with smoked salmon and remaining 2 tablespoons minced dill.

Chilled red pepper soup with basil and croutons

A LOVELY WARM-WEATHER SOUP, this makes a great starter for a menu featuring grilled chicken and fresh fruit for dessert. The recipe can easily be doubled to serve eight, and it can be prepared a day before serving (no need to rewarm!).

4 FIRST-COURSE SERVINGS; CAN BE DOUBLED

4 large red bell peppers (about 2¼ pounds total)

4 tablespoons olive oil, divided
1 onion, cut into ¾-inch pieces
3 cups (or more) low-salt chicken broth
⅛ teaspoon dried crushed red pepper

1½ cups ½-inch French bread cubes
Thinly sliced fresh basil

CHAR peppers over gas flame or in broiler until blackened on all sides. Enclose in paper bag 10 minutes. Peel and seed peppers. Cut into ½-inch pieces.

HEAT 2 tablespoons oil in heavy large saucepan over medium-high heat. Add onion and sauté until brown on edges, about 6 minutes. Add bell peppers and 3 cups broth. Simmer until vegetables are tender, about 5 minutes. Using slotted spoon, transfer peppers and onion to processor; puree. With machine running, add broth from saucepan and process until smooth. Mix in crushed red pepper. Season to taste with salt and pepper. Refrigerate uncovered until cold. *(Can be made 1 day ahead; cover and keep refrigerated.)*

HEAT remaining 2 tablespoons oil in medium skillet over medium heat. Add bread; stir until golden brown, about 5 minutes. Whisk cold soup to blend; thin with more broth if desired. Ladle soup into bowls. Top with bread and basil.

Velvety chilled corn soup

THIS ELEGANT FIRST COURSE is ideal for entertaining, because everything can be prepared a day ahead—just chop the toppings and refrigerate them until ready to use. To select the freshest corn, look for ears that are cool to the touch, with tender, slightly damp green husks and golden brown, slightly sticky tassels. Squeeze the ear to feel for full, firm kernels. Then store the corn in the refrigerator and use as soon as possible.

6 FIRST-COURSE SERVINGS

6 ears fresh corn, husked
6 cups (about) low-salt chicken broth, divided
3 shallots, chopped
1 onion, chopped

6 tablespoons crème fraîche or sour cream
¼ cup minced English hothouse cucumber
2 tablespoons chopped fresh chives

USING cleaver or heavy large knife, cut each ear of corn crosswise in half. Place corn in heavy large pot. Add 5 cups broth, shallots, and onion; bring to boil. Reduce heat, cover, and simmer until corn is very tender, about 25 minutes. Using tongs, transfer corn to large bowl to cool; reserve broth.

CUT corn kernels off cobs. Return 4 cups corn kernels to broth (reserve any remaining corn for another use). Working in batches, puree soup in blender until very smooth. Strain soup through fine sieve set over large bowl, pressing on solids with back of spoon; discard solids. Mix in enough additional chicken broth to thin soup to consistency of heavy cream. Season to taste with salt and pepper. Refrigerate uncovered until cold, about 4 hours. *(Can be prepared 1 day ahead. Cover and keep refrigerated.)*

LADLE soup into 6 bowls. Top each with dollop of crème fraîche. Sprinkle with cucumber and chives and serve.

Chilled carrot and cauliflower soup

A PERFECT PARTY SOUP. Prepare a day ahead, then garnish at the last minute with a dollop of sour cream and a spoonful of the lively mixture of onions, mint, and lemon.

8 FIRST-COURSE SERVINGS

2 tablespoons (1/4 stick) butter
1 tablespoon olive oil
2 medium white onions, chopped (about 3 1/2 cups)
2 pounds carrots, peeled, cut into 1-inch pieces (about 5 cups)
4 1/2 cups cauliflower florets (from 1 large head)
7 1/2 cups (or more) low-salt chicken broth
1/2 teaspoon cayenne pepper

3/4 cup buttermilk

6 tablespoons chopped red onion
6 tablespoons chopped green onions
2 tablespoons chopped fresh mint
2 tablespoons fresh lemon juice
1/2 cup sour cream

MELT butter with oil in heavy large pot over medium heat. Add white onions; sauté until golden, about 10 minutes. Add carrots and cauliflower; sauté 5 minutes. Add 7½ cups broth; bring to boil. Reduce heat, cover, and simmer until vegetables are very tender, about 45 minutes. Stir in cayenne. Cool slightly.

WORKING in batches, puree soup in blender until smooth. Transfer to large bowl. Stir in buttermilk. Thin with more broth, if desired. Season to taste with salt and pepper. Refrigerate uncovered until cold, at least 6 hours. *(Can be prepared 1 day ahead. Cover and keep refrigerated.)*

MIX red onion, green onions, mint, and lemon juice in small bowl. Season to taste with salt and pepper. Ladle soup into 8 bowls. Top each with dollop of sour cream and 1 tablespoon onion mixture.

Southwestern avocado soup

CHILI POWDER and chopped jalapeño chile add a touch of heat to this smooth appetizer. Sprinkle it with chopped red onion for some crunch and color. Then round out a Mexican-themed menu with tostadas and cinnamon-accented brownies.

4 FIRST-COURSE SERVINGS

2 ripe medium avocados, halved, pitted
3/4 cup buttermilk
1/2 cup plain yogurt
2 tablespoons fresh lime juice
1 1/2 tablespoons chopped seeded jalapeño chile
1/2 teaspoon chili powder
1/2 cup (or more) low-salt chicken broth

Chopped red onion

SCRAPE avocados from skin into processor. Add buttermilk and yogurt; puree until smooth. Mix in lime juice, jalapeño, and chili powder. With machine running, blend in ½ cup broth. Season to taste with salt and pepper. Cover and refrigerate soup until cold, at least 4 hours. *(Can be made 1 day ahead. Keep chilled.)*

THIN soup with more broth, if desired. Spoon into bowls. Sprinkle with onion.

Chilled beet soup with dill and sour cream

A REFRESHING FIRST COURSE, this eye-catching soup would make an excellent beginning to a dinner of pasta with fresh spring vegetables, followed by strawberry shortcake for dessert. The soup can be prepared up to two days ahead of time, then garnished just before serving.

4 FIRST-COURSE SERVINGS

- **4 cups (or more) low-salt chicken broth**
- **1 pound beets, peeled, chopped**
- **1 cup chopped onion**
- **¾ cup peeled chopped carrot**
- **2 garlic cloves, minced**
- **1 teaspoon sugar**
- **2 tablespoons chopped fresh dill or 2 teaspoons dried dillweed**
- **2 tablespoons chopped fresh chives or green onions**
- **Sour cream**

COMBINE 4 cups broth, beets, onion, carrot, and garlic in medium saucepan. Bring to boil. Reduce heat to medium-low, cover, and simmer until vegetables are very tender, about 35 minutes. Cool slightly.

WORKING in batches, puree soup in blender until smooth. Transfer to bowl. Thin with more broth if soup is too thick. Mix in sugar. Season to taste with salt and pepper. Refrigerate uncovered until cold, at least 4 hours. *(Can be prepared 2 days ahead. Cover and keep refrigerated.)*

LADLE soup into bowls. Sprinkle with dill and chives. Top with sour cream.

Chilled zucchini-cumin soup

YOU WOULD NEVER KNOW that this flavorful soup is also healthful and extremely low in fat (no need to tell your guests that it's good for them). Ground spices can be stored up to three years—but it's a good idea to check the expiration date anyway.

4 FIRST-COURSE SERVINGS

- **1 tablespoon olive oil**
- **1 large onion, chopped**
- **1½ teaspoons ground cumin**
- **1½ pounds zucchini, trimmed, cut into ¾-inch pieces**
- **3½ cups low-salt chicken broth**
- **⅓ cup chopped fresh basil**
- **4 tablespoons plain nonfat yogurt**
- **Sliced fresh basil**

HEAT oil in heavy medium saucepan over medium heat. Add onion and sauté until tender, about 5 minutes. Add cumin; stir until aromatic, about 30 seconds. Mix in zucchini. Add broth; bring soup to boil. Reduce heat and simmer until zucchini is very tender, about 30 minutes. Cool slightly.

MIX ⅓ cup chopped basil into soup. Working in batches, puree soup in blender until smooth. Transfer to bowl. Season to taste with salt and pepper. Refrigerate uncovered until cold, at least 4 hours. *(Can be prepared 1 day ahead. Cover and keep refrigerated.)*

LADLE soup into bowls. Top each with 1 tablespoon yogurt and sliced basil.

Fresh fennel vichyssoise

CLASSIC VICHYSSOISE is a creamy chilled potato and leek soup. Here, it gets a sophisticated spin with the delicate licorice flavors of fennel and Pernod. When preparing the fennel bulb, remove the feathery tops (they can be used as a garnish if you wish).

8 FIRST-COURSE SERVINGS

- **2 tablespoons (¼ stick) butter**
- **2 tablespoons olive oil**
- **5 cups thinly sliced fennel bulbs (about 3 small)**
- **2 onions, sliced**
- **1 pound white-skinned potatoes, unpeeled, cut into ½-inch pieces**
- **4 cups low-salt chicken broth**
- **2 tablespoons Pernod or other anise-flavored liqueur**
- **2 cups half and half**

MELT butter with olive oil in heavy large pot over medium heat. Add fennel and onions. Cover and cook until fennel is tender, stirring occasionally, about 15 minutes. Add potatoes and broth; increase heat and bring to boil. Reduce heat, cover, and simmer until potatoes are very tender, about 30 minutes. Remove from heat. Mix in Pernod. Cool slightly.

WORKING in batches, puree soup in blender. Transfer soup to large bowl. Mix in half and half. Season soup to taste with salt and pepper. Refrigerate soup uncovered until cold, at least 4 hours. *(Can be prepared 1 day ahead. Cover and keep refrigerated.)*

Chilled watercress-potato soup

THE PEPPERY TASTE of fresh watercress gives this soup a nice, cool snap. When buying watercress in bunches, make sure the leaves are healthy and green; avoid bunches with yellowing leaves. You can make watercress last longer by keeping the bunch in a bowl of water in the refrigerator—leaves down, stems up.

6 TO 8 FIRST-COURSE SERVINGS

- **3 cups (packed) watercress, thick stems trimmed**
- **2 tablespoons (¼ stick) butter**
- **1¼ pounds russet potatoes, peeled, sliced into ¼-inch-thick rounds**
- **3 cups sliced leeks (white and pale green parts only; about 3 large)**
- **6 cups (or more) low-salt chicken broth**
- **½ cup whipping cream**
- **3 tablespoons minced fresh chives**

COOK watercress in pot of boiling salted water 30 seconds. Drain; set aside.

MELT butter in heavy large pot over medium heat. Add potatoes and leeks; sauté 4 minutes. Stir in 6 cups broth. Bring to boil. Reduce heat, cover partially, and simmer until vegetables are tender, about 20 minutes. Add watercress and simmer uncovered 5 minutes. Cool slightly.

WORKING in batches, puree soup in blender until smooth. Return soup to pot. Mix in cream. Season to taste with salt and pepper. Refrigerate soup uncovered until cold, at least 4 hours. *(Can be prepared 1 day ahead. Cover and keep refrigerated.)*

THIN soup with more broth, if desired. Ladle soup into bowls. Sprinkle with chives.

Stews

Beef bourguignon

"BEEF BURGUNDY" is the most famous dish of the Burgundy region of France, southeast of Paris. The locals use the lean beef from the Charolais steer; while you probably won't find that in your local supermarket, try to trim as much fat off the chuck roast as possible. Then again, the French would tell you it's all about the wine, anyway: It doesn't have to be the best, but it definitely shouldn't be the worst.

8 SERVINGS

- **8 ounces bacon, coarsely chopped**
- **3 pounds well-trimmed boneless beef chuck, cut into 1½-inch cubes**
- **⅓ cup all purpose flour**
- **1¼ pounds boiling onions, peeled**
- **¾ pound large carrots, peeled, cut into 1-inch pieces**
- **12 garlic cloves, peeled**

- **3 cups beef broth, divided**
- **½ cup Cognac or brandy**
- **2 750-ml bottles red Burgundy wine**
- **1¼ pounds mushrooms**
- **⅓ cup chopped fresh thyme or 2 tablespoons dried**
- **1 tablespoon dark brown sugar**
- **1 tablespoon tomato paste**

PREHEAT oven to 325°F. Sauté bacon in heavy large ovenproof pot over high heat until brown and crisp, about 8 minutes. Using slotted spoon, transfer bacon to paper towels to drain. Sprinkle beef generously with salt and pepper; coat with ⅓ cup flour. Working in 3 batches, brown beef in same pot over high heat, about 5 minutes per batch. Transfer beef to large bowl. Add onions and carrots to same pot; sauté until light brown, about 6 minutes. Add whole garlic cloves and sauté 1 minute. Transfer vegetables to bowl with beef.

ADD 1 cup broth and Cognac to pot; boil until reduced to glaze, scraping up any browned bits, about 8 minutes. Return beef and vegetables and their juice to pot. Add wine, mushrooms, thyme, sugar, tomato paste, remaining 2 cups broth, and bacon. Bring to boil, stirring occasionally. Cover pot and place in oven. Cook until beef is tender, about 1 hour 20 minutes.

LADLE liquid from stew into large saucepan. Spoon off fat. Boil liquid until reduced to 2¾ cups, about 40 minutes. Season to taste with salt and pepper. Pour liquid back over beef and vegetables. *(Can be prepared 1 day ahead. Cool stew slightly. Refrigerate uncovered until cold, then cover and keep refrigerated. Rewarm over low heat before serving.)*

Oxtail stew with tomatoes and bacon

BRAISING BRINGS OUT THE BEST in oxtails, the star of this long-simmered stew. It is garnished with bright green sugar snap peas for a contemporary touch. Serve it over mashed potatoes and parsnips to catch the sauce.

6 SERVINGS

- **4½ pounds oxtails**
- **Paprika**
- **All purpose flour**
- **6 bacon slices, chopped**

- **2 large onions, chopped**
- **2 garlic cloves, minced**
- **¼ cup tomato paste**
- **4 teaspoons plus 2 tablespoons chopped fresh rosemary or 1 teaspoon plus 2 teaspoons dried**
- **2 cups dry red wine**

- **1 28-ounce can Italian-style tomatoes in juice, drained**
- **1¾ cups beef broth**
- **¾ pound sugar snap peas, trimmed**

SPRINKLE oxtails with paprika, salt and pepper. Coat with flour. Cook bacon in heavy large pot over medium heat until fat is rendered, about 5 minutes. Using slotted spoon, transfer bacon to paper towels to drain. Increase heat to high. Working in batches, add oxtails to pot and cook until brown on all sides, about 10 minutes. Transfer oxtails to bowl.

ADD onions and garlic to pot; reduce heat to medium and cook until tender, stirring occasionally, about 8 minutes. Mix in tomato paste and 4 teaspoons rosemary. Add wine and bring to boil, scraping up any browned bits. Boil until liquid is reduced by half, about 6 minutes. Add tomatoes, breaking up with back of spoon. Add broth. Return oxtails with any accumulated juice and bacon to pot. Bring to boil. Reduce heat, cover, and simmer until meat is tender, about 2½ hours. Uncover and simmer until liquid is slightly thickened, about 30 minutes longer. *(Can be prepared 1 day ahead. Cool slightly. Refrigerate uncovered until cold, then cover and keep refrigerated. Before continuing, rewarm over medium heat, stirring occasionally.)*

ADD sugar snap peas to stew. Simmer uncovered until peas are just crisp-tender, about 3 minutes. Sprinkle stew with remaining 2 tablespoons rosemary.

Mahogany beef stew with red wine and hoisin sauce

HOISIN—THE SWEET-SPICY CHINESE SAUCE made from soybeans, garlic, chiles, and spices—adds complexity to this rich stew. You'll find hoisin sauce at Asian markets and in the Asian foods section of many supermarkets. Save yourself time and tears by chopping the onions in the processor in two batches.

6 SERVINGS

- **4 tablespoons olive oil, divided**
- **3½ pounds boneless beef chuck roast, trimmed, cut into 2½-inch pieces**
- **3½ cups chopped onions**
- **2 cups Cabernet Sauvignon, divided**
- **1 14.5-ounce can diced tomatoes with Italian herbs**
- **½ cup hoisin sauce**
- **2 bay leaves**
- **1 pound slender carrots, peeled, cut diagonally into 1-inch lengths**
- **1 tablespoon cornstarch mixed with 1 tablespoon water**
- **2 tablespoons chopped fresh parsley**

HEAT 2 tablespoons oil in heavy large pot over high heat. Sprinkle meat with salt and pepper. Add meat to pot; sauté until brown on all sides, about 10 minutes. Push meat to sides of pot. Reduce heat to medium; add remaining 2 tablespoons oil to pot. Add onions and sauté until golden brown, about 15 minutes. Mix meat into onions. Add 1 cup wine, tomatoes with juice, hoisin sauce, and bay leaves; bring to boil. Reduce heat to low, cover, and simmer 45 minutes, stirring occasionally. Add carrots and remaining 1 cup wine. Cover and simmer 30 minutes, stirring occasionally. Uncover and increase heat to high; boil until sauce thickens slightly, stirring occasionally, about 15 minutes longer. Reduce heat to medium, add cornstarch mixture and simmer until sauce thickens, stirring occasionally, about 8 minutes. Discard bay leaves. Season stew to taste with salt and pepper. *(Can be prepared 1 day ahead. Cool slightly. Refrigerate uncovered until cold, then cover and keep refrigerated. Before continuing, rewarm over medium heat, stirring occasionally.)*

TRANSFER stew to large bowl. Sprinkle with parsley.

Spicy lamb stew with apricots and cardamom

CARDAMOM, A RICHLY AROMATIC SPICE from the ginger family, is used widely in Indian, Middle Eastern, and Scandinavian cooking. Here it's combined with cinnamon, ginger, cloves, and cayenne pepper to give the stew a North African flavor, and it enhances the accompanying rice. You can use purchased ground cardamom or buy whole pods, crush them and remove the green outer husks, then grind the seeds. The seeds from eight pods will equal approximately ½ teaspoon when ground.

4 SERVINGS

½ teaspoon ground cardamom
½ teaspoon ground cinnamon
½ teaspoon cayenne pepper
¼ teaspoon ground cloves
3½ pounds lamb shoulder round-bone chops, trimmed, boned, cut into 1-inch pieces
2 tablespoons vegetable oil
5 cups chopped onions
2 teaspoons minced peeled fresh ginger
1 cup water

⅔ cup dried apricots, quartered
1 teaspoon white wine vinegar
1 teaspoon sugar
Saffron-Cardamom Rice (see recipe)

MIX first 4 ingredients in large bowl. Add lamb and toss to coat. Heat oil in heavy large pot over medium-high heat. Add onions and sauté until tender and golden, about 10 minutes. Add lamb and sprinkle with salt. Sauté until brown, about 5 minutes. Add ginger and stir 1 minute. Add 1 cup water and bring to boil. Reduce heat, cover, and simmer until lamb is tender, stirring occasionally, about 1 hour. *(Can be prepared 1 day ahead. Cool slightly. Refrigerate uncovered until cold, then cover and keep refrigerated. Before continuing, rewarm over medium heat, stirring occasionally.)*

ADD apricots to pot and simmer uncovered until liquid is slightly thickened and reduced, about 10 minutes. Stir in vinegar and sugar. Season to taste with salt. Divide Saffron-Cardamom Rice among 4 bowls; top with stew.

Saffron-cardamom rice

THIS COLORFUL, AROMATIC RICE would also be delicious with broiled chicken, fish, or vegetables.

4 SERVINGS

3 teaspoons butter, divided
¼ cup pine nuts

½ cup chopped red onion
1 cup basmati rice
1½ cups water
2 tablespoons golden raisins
1 teaspoon sugar
¾ teaspoon salt
¼ teaspoon crumbled saffron threads
¼ teaspoon ground cardamom

MELT 1 teaspoon butter in small skillet over medium heat. Add pine nuts; sauté until golden, about 5 minutes. Cool.

MELT remaining 2 teaspoons butter in heavy medium saucepan over medium heat. Add onion and sauté until slightly softened, about 5 minutes. Add rice and stir 2 minutes. Add 1½ cups water, raisins, sugar, salt, saffron, and cardamom. Bring to boil. Reduce heat, cover, and simmer until rice is tender, about 15 minutes. Remove from heat; let stand covered 10 minutes. Stir in pine nuts.

Swedish lamb stew with dill sauce

DILL HAS BEEN USED as everything from a digestive aid to a love potion ingredient, but it has also been known to add bright flavor to a vast variety of dishes, as in this succulent lamb stew. Thanks to the long cooking time, the lamb becomes meltingly tender. Serve with noodles.

4 SERVINGS

2½ pounds boneless leg of lamb, cut into 1-inch cubes
4 cups water
1 large onion, chopped
1 large carrot, peeled, chopped
1 large bunch fresh dill
8 whole white peppercorns
2 teaspoons salt

2 tablespoons (¼ stick) butter
2 tablespoons all purpose flour
1 tablespoon white wine vinegar
2 teaspoons sugar
¼ cup chopped fresh dill
2 tablespoons whipping cream

PLACE lamb, 4 cups water, onion, carrot, bunch of dill, peppercorns, and salt in heavy large pot. Bring to boil over medium-high heat, skimming off foam. Reduce heat to medium-low, cover, and simmer until meat is tender, stirring occasionally, about 1½ hours. Strain broth into medium saucepan. Boil broth until reduced to 2⅓ cups, about 8 minutes.

MEANWHILE, remove lamb from vegetable mixture; discard vegetable mixture.

MELT butter in heavy medium saucepan over medium heat. Add flour and whisk 1 minute. Whisk in 2⅓ cups reduced broth. Cook until sauce thickens and boils, whisking occasionally, about 6 minutes. Whisk in vinegar, sugar, and chopped dill. Simmer 3 minutes to blend flavors. Stir in cream and lamb; simmer until heated through, about 2 minutes.

Season to taste with salt and pepper. Transfer to serving bowl. *(Can be prepared 1 day ahead. Cool slightly. Refrigerate uncovered until cold, then cover and keep refrigerated. Before serving, rewarm over medium heat, stirring often.)*

Hearty veal stew with red wine and sweet peppers

CAPERS LEND TANGY CONTRAST to the sweet bell peppers in this recipe. Serve the stew over egg noodles. If you're looking for an appropriate starter, small appetizer pizzas would be an excellent complement, rounding out the Italian theme.

6 SERVINGS

2 pounds 1-inch pieces trimmed veal stew meat
¼ cup all purpose flour
2 tablespoons extra-virgin olive oil
3 garlic cloves, peeled, flattened
2 tablespoons (¼ stick) butter
¾ cup dry red wine
2 cups canned Italian-style tomatoes in juice
1 tablespoon dried sage leaves

2 red bell peppers, cut into 2x½-inch strips
2 tablespoons drained capers

TOSS veal with flour in medium bowl; shake off excess. Sprinkle veal with salt and pepper. Heat oil in heavy large pot over medium-high heat. Add garlic; sauté 1 minute. Discard garlic. Add butter to same pot and let melt. Working in batches, add veal to pot and sauté until brown, about 6 minutes per batch. Using slotted spoon, transfer veal to bowl. Add wine, tomatoes with juice, and sage to pot, breaking up tomatoes with back of spoon and scraping up any browned bits. Return veal and any accumulated juices to pot; bring to boil. Reduce heat to medium-low, cover, and simmer 30 minutes.

ADD bell peppers to stew; cover and simmer until veal and peppers are very tender, stirring frequently, about 50 minutes. Stir in capers. Season to taste with salt and pepper. *(Can be prepared 1 day ahead. Cool slightly. Refrigerate uncovered until cold, then cover and keep refrigerated. Before serving, rewarm over medium heat, stirring often.)*

Winter squash and chicken stew with Indian spices

CURRY POWDER, CUMIN, AND CINNAMON give this dish a hint of the exotic. Either butternut or acorn squash works equally well in this recipe; you could also try it with other winter squash, such as delicata (an oval-shaped squash with a green-striped orange skin) or kabocha (a round, green squash with golden, rich-tasting flesh).

6 SERVINGS

- **2 teaspoons olive oil, divided**
- **6 chicken thighs with bones, skin removed**

- **1⅓ cups chopped onions**
- **3 garlic cloves, minced**
- **1½ teaspoons curry powder**
- **1½ teaspoons ground cumin**
- **1 teaspoon ground cinnamon**
- **4 cups 1-inch pieces peeled butternut or acorn squash**
- **2 cups 1-inch pieces peeled russet potatoes**
- **1 cup low-salt chicken broth**
- **1 14.5-ounce can diced tomatoes in juice**
- **2 tablespoons chopped fresh cilantro**

HEAT 1 teaspoon oil in heavy large pot over medium-high heat. Sprinkle chicken with salt and pepper. Add to pot; sauté until brown on all sides, about 8 minutes. Transfer to plate.

HEAT remaining 1 teaspoon oil in same pot over medium-high heat. Add onion and garlic; sauté until golden, about 5 minutes. Add curry powder, cumin, and cinnamon; stir 1 minute. Return chicken and any accumulated juices to pot. Add squash, potatoes, broth, and tomatoes with juice. Cover and simmer 15 minutes. Uncover and simmer until chicken and potatoes are cooked through and liquid is slightly reduced, about 8 minutes. Season to taste with salt and pepper. *(Can be prepared 1 day ahead. Cool slightly. Refrigerate uncovered until cold, then cover and keep refrigerated. Before serving, rewarm over medium heat, stirring often.)*

SPRINKLE with cilantro and serve.

Classic coq au vin

MARINATING THE CHICKEN in the wine mixture adds flavor. Starting two days ahead and rewarming the dish improves that flavor. To divide the chicken into eight pieces, cut through the meat and bone on each side of the backbone, then discard the backbone. Open the chicken flat, and cut in half through the breast. Cut off each leg, then each thigh. Cut off the wings with top quarter of each breast still attached.

4 TO 6 SERVINGS

- **1 750-ml bottle French Burgundy or California Pinot Noir**
- **1 large onion, sliced**
- **2 celery stalks, sliced**
- **1 large carrot, peeled, sliced**
- **1 garlic clove, peeled, flattened**
- **1 teaspoon whole black peppercorns**
- **3 tablespoons olive oil, divided**
- **1 6-pound roasting chicken, backbone removed, cut into 8 pieces (2 drumsticks, 2 thighs, 2 wings with top quarter of adjoining breast, 2 breasts)**

- **6 ounces thick-cut bacon slices, cut crosswise into strips**
- **3 tablespoons all purpose flour**

- **2 large shallots, chopped**
- **2 garlic cloves, chopped**
- **4 large fresh thyme sprigs**
- **4 large fresh parsley sprigs**
- **2 small bay leaves**
- **2 cups low-salt chicken broth**

- **4 tablespoons (½ stick) butter, divided**
- **1 pound assorted fresh wild mushrooms (such as crimini and stemmed shiitake)**
- **20 1-inch-diameter pearl onions or boiling onions, peeled**

Chopped fresh parsley

COMBINE first 6 ingredients in large pot. Bring to boil over high heat. Reduce heat to medium and simmer 5 minutes. Cool completely; mix in 2 tablespoons oil. Place chicken pieces in large glass bowl. Pour wine mixture over chicken; stir to coat. Cover and refrigerate at least 1 day and up to 2 days, turning chicken occasionally.

USING tongs, transfer chicken pieces from marinade to paper towels to drain; pat dry. Strain marinade; reserve vegetables and liquid separately.

HEAT remaining 1 tablespoon oil in heavy large pot (wide enough to hold chicken in single layer) over medium-high heat. Add bacon and sauté until crisp and brown. Using slotted spoon, transfer bacon to small bowl. Add chicken, skin side down, to drippings in pot. Sauté until brown, about 8 minutes per side. Transfer chicken to large bowl. Add vegetables reserved from marinade to pot. Sauté until brown, about 10 minutes. Mix in flour; stir 2 minutes. Gradually whisk in reserved marinade liquid. Bring to boil, whisking frequently. Cook until sauce thickens, whisking occasionally, about 2 minutes. Mix in shallots, chopped garlic, herb sprigs, and bay leaves, then broth. Return chicken to pot, arranging skin side up in single layer; bring to simmer. Reduce heat to medium-low, cover pot, and simmer chicken 30 minutes. Using tongs, turn chicken over. Cover and simmer until tender, about 15 minutes longer.

MEANWHILE, melt 3 tablespoons butter in heavy large skillet over medium heat. Add mushrooms; sauté until tender, about 8 minutes. Transfer mushrooms to plate. Melt remaining 1 tablespoon butter in same skillet. Add pearl onions and sauté until beginning to brown, about 8 minutes. Transfer onions to plate alongside mushrooms; reserve skillet.

USING tongs, transfer chicken to plate. Strain sauce from pot into reserved skillet, pressing on solids in strainer to extract all sauce; discard solids. Bring sauce to simmer, scraping up any browned bits. Return sauce to pot. Add onions to pot and bring to simmer over medium heat. Cover and cook until onions are almost tender, about 8 minutes. Add mushrooms and bacon. Simmer uncovered until onions are very tender and sauce is slightly reduced, about 12 minutes. Tilt pot and spoon off excess fat from top of sauce. Season sauce to taste with salt and pepper. Return chicken to sauce. *(Can be prepared 1 day ahead. Cool slightly. Refrigerate uncovered until cold, then cover and keep refrigerated. Before continuing, rewarm over low heat.)*

ARRANGE chicken on large rimmed platter. Spoon sauce and vegetables over. Sprinkle with parsley.

Chicken mole with chipotles

MOLE, A CLASSIC Mexican chile sauce, gets streamlined here. Chipotle chiles (available canned in *adobo* sauce at Latin markets and some supermarkets) add heat, while unsweetened chocolate provides subtle richness. Serve the stew in shallow bowls with steamed rice. Add an arugula, orange, and red onion salad and a basket of warm corn tortillas.

4 SERVINGS

- **6 skinless boneless chicken thighs, each cut crosswise into 3 pieces**
- **2 tablespoons ground cumin**

- **1 tablespoon olive oil**
- **1 large onion, thinly sliced**
- **2 14.5-ounce cans chili-style chunky tomatoes in juice**
- **1 cup low-salt chicken broth**
- **2 tablespoons minced canned chipotle chiles plus 1 tablespoon adobo sauce**
- **1 ounce unsweetened chocolate, chopped**

COAT chicken on all sides with cumin. Sprinkle with salt and pepper. Heat oil in heavy large pot over medium-high heat. Add chicken; sauté until browned on all sides, about 5 minutes. Add onion and sauté until beginning to brown, about 3 minutes. Add tomatoes with juice, broth, chipotle chiles, adobo sauce, and chocolate; bring to simmer. Reduce heat to medium-low and simmer until chicken is cooked through and sauce thickens slightly, about 20 minutes. Season with salt and pepper.

Chicken and andouille sausage ragù

ANDOUILLE SAUSAGE lends rich, smoky flavor to this hearty winter stew. And the flavors will only improve if the stew rests in the refrigerator overnight.

6 SERVINGS

- **9 chicken thighs with skin and bones (about 4 pounds), well trimmed**
- **2 tablespoons olive oil**
- **1 pound chicken andouille sausage or other fully cooked, spicy smoked sausage, cut into ½-inch-thick rounds**
- **3 medium carrots, peeled, diced**
- **2 large onions, chopped**
- **½ cup chopped fresh marjoram (from about 2 large bunches), divided**
- **6 garlic cloves, minced**
- **1 teaspoon grated lemon peel**
- **¼ teaspoon dried crushed red pepper**
- **1 cup dry white wine**
- **2 14.5-ounce cans diced tomatoes in juice**
- **2 cups low-salt chicken broth**

Campanelle Pasta with Parsley Butter (see recipe)

PLACE chicken thighs, skin side down, on work surface. Using sharp knife, cut each thigh lengthwise along each side of bone, forming 2 pieces of meat (some meat may remain on bones); reserve bones.

HEAT oil in heavy large pot over medium-high heat. Sprinkle chicken and bones with salt and pepper. Working in batches, sauté in pot until brown, about 6 minutes per batch. Transfer to bowl. Add sausage to pot and sauté until brown, about 5 minutes. Using slotted spoon, transfer to bowl with chicken. Add carrots and onions to pot and sauté until onions are tender and golden, about 10 minutes. Stir in ¼ cup marjoram, garlic, lemon peel, and crushed red pepper; sauté 2 minutes. Add wine and boil until reduced by half, about 3 minutes. Stir in tomatoes with juice and broth; bring to boil. Add chicken, bones, sausage, and any accumulated juice from bowl. Reduce heat, cover, and simmer until chicken is cooked through, about 35 minutes.

USING slotted spoon, transfer chicken and sausage to bowl; discard bones. Boil liquid in pot until reduced to 3 cups, about 20 minutes. Stir in remaining ¼ cup marjoram. Season to taste with salt and pepper. Return chicken and sausage to pot. *(Can be prepared 1 day ahead. Cool slightly. Refrigerate uncovered until cold, then cover and keep refrigerated. Before continuing, rewarm over medium heat, stirring occasionally.)*

SPOON ragù over pasta.

Campanelle pasta with parsley butter

THE PARSLEY BUTTER can be made three days ahead, making this pasta quick and easy to prepare. Its simple flavors make it an excellent complement to a variety of complex stews.

6 SERVINGS

Parsley butter

- **1 cup (packed) coarsely chopped fresh Italian parsley**
- **2 teaspoons (packed) grated lemon peel**
- **1 garlic clove, peeled**
- **½ cup (1 stick) unsalted butter, room temperature**

Pasta

- **1 pound campanelle (trumpet-shaped pasta), fiori, or fusilli pasta**

FOR PARSLEY BUTTER: Finely chop parsley, lemon peel, and garlic in processor. Add butter and process until well blended. Season parsley butter to taste with salt and pepper. *(Can be prepared 3 days ahead. Cover and refrigerate. Bring to room temperature before using.)*

FOR PASTA: Cook pasta in large pot of boiling salted water until tender but still firm to bite. Drain. Transfer pasta to large serving bowl. Add half of parsley butter (about ⅓ cup) to pasta (reserve remainder for another use); toss to coat. Season to taste with salt and pepper.

Chicken tagine with vegetable couscous

A *TAGINE* IS A highly seasoned Moroccan stew traditionally simmered in a shallow clay pot with a tall, conical lid, also called a tagine. There are hundreds of variations on the theme; this one features authentic Moroccan flavors while being quite easy to prepare. Make it even simpler by asking the butcher to quarter the chickens for you.

6 SERVINGS

- **3 tablespoons olive oil**
- **2 3-pound chickens, quartered**
- **2 onions, chopped**
- **4 teaspoons paprika**
- **2 teaspoons ground ginger**
- **½ teaspoon turmeric**
- **¼ teaspoon cayenne pepper**
- **2 cups low-salt chicken broth**
- **3 lemons, each cut lengthwise into 6 wedges**
- **1 cup Kalamata olives**
- **1 cup imported green olives (such as Sicilian or Greek)**

Vegetable Couscous (see recipe)
Chopped fresh cilantro

HEAT oil in heavy large pot over high heat. Sprinkle chicken pieces with salt and pepper. Working in batches, add chicken to pot and brown, about 5 minutes per side. Transfer chicken to platter. Pour off all but thin film of fat from pot. Add onions. Reduce heat to medium and sauté until tender, about 8 minutes. Add all spices and stir until fragrant, about 30 seconds. Return chicken pieces to pot, in single layer if possible. Add chicken broth, lemons, and all olives. Bring to boil. Reduce heat to medium-low, cover, and simmer until chicken is cooked through, basting and turning occasionally, about 30 minutes. Season tagine to taste with salt and pepper. *(Can be prepared 1 day ahead. Refrigerate uncovered until cold, then cover and keep refrigerated. Reheat gently before continuing.)*

MOUND Vegetable Couscous on platter. Surround with chicken and lemons. Spoon olives and some sauce over to moisten. Sprinkle with cilantro. Serve, passing remaining sauce separately.

Vegetable couscous

TAGINES ARE OFTEN PAIRED with couscous—the Moroccan national dish made from semolina wheat flour. Couscous can be prepared with many different ingredients; this version, with onion, red bell pepper, carrots, zucchini, and raisins, would also be a good accompaniment to other chicken, beef, or lamb dishes.

6 SERVINGS

- **2 tablespoons olive oil**
- **1 large onion, coarsely chopped**
- **1 large red bell pepper, coarsely chopped**
- **4 carrots, peeled, cut into ½-inch-thick rounds**
- **2 zucchini, quartered lengthwise, cut into 1-inch pieces**
- **2¼ cups low-salt chicken broth**
- **1 cup golden raisins**
- **¾ teaspoon ground cinnamon**
- **¼ teaspoon turmeric**
- **1½ cups couscous**

HEAT oil in heavy large saucepan over medium heat. Add onion and sauté 5 minutes. Add bell pepper and carrots; sauté 5 minutes. Add zucchini and cook 5 minutes, stirring occasionally. Add broth, raisins, cinnamon, and turmeric. Bring to boil. Mix in couscous. Cover, remove from heat and let stand 10 minutes. Season to taste with salt and pepper. Fluff couscous with fork.

Chicken vindaloo

INTRODUCED TO INDIA by Portuguese settlers, this spicy stew can also be made with pork, beef, or lamb. Serve it over basmati rice. Yellow mustard seeds are commonly sold at supermarkets, but specialty foods stores, Asian markets, and Indian markets would have them, too.

4 SERVINGS

- **⅓ cup white wine vinegar**
- **6 garlic cloves, peeled**
- **3 tablespoons chopped peeled fresh ginger**
- **1½ tablespoons curry powder**
- **2 teaspoons ground cumin**
- **¾ teaspoon ground cardamom**
- **¼ teaspoon ground cloves**
- **¼ teaspoon (generous) dried crushed red pepper**
- **2 tablespoons yellow mustard seeds, divided**
- **2 pounds skinless boneless chicken thighs (about 10), cut into 1- to 1½-inch pieces**
- **4 tablespoons olive oil, divided**

- **2½ cups chopped onions**
- **1 14.5-ounce can diced tomatoes in juice**
- **1 cinnamon stick**
- **½ cup chopped fresh cilantro**

PLACE vinegar and next 7 ingredients in blender. Add 1 tablespoon mustard seeds and blend until smooth paste forms. Transfer paste to large bowl. Add chicken and 2 tablespoons oil; toss to coat.

HEAT remaining 2 tablespoons oil in heavy large pot over medium-high heat. Add onions and sauté until golden, about 5 minutes. Add chicken mixture and stir 3 minutes to combine flavors. Add tomatoes with juice and cinnamon stick; bring to boil. Reduce heat, cover, and simmer until chicken is tender, stirring occasionally, about 30 minutes. Mix in remaining 1 tablespoon mustard seeds. Simmer uncovered until sauce is slightly thickened, about 8 minutes. Remove cinnamon stick. Season to taste with salt and pepper. Stir in cilantro and serve.

Pork and hominy stew

THE FLAVORS OF MEXICO come through in this comforting winter stew. Poblanos are fresh green chiles available at Latin markets and some supermarkets. Serve the stew with warm corn bread or spooned over steamed rice.

4 SERVINGS

1 tablespoon plus 2 teaspoons chili powder
1 teaspoon salt
½ teaspoon ground black pepper
2½ pounds boneless country-style pork spareribs, cut into 2-inch pieces
3 bacon slices, chopped

1 large onion, thinly sliced
1 cup diced smoked ham
1 medium carrot, peeled, chopped
6 garlic cloves, chopped
2 poblano chiles, seeded, cut into 2x¼-inch strips
2 cups drained canned hominy (from two 15-ounce cans)
1 cup canned diced tomatoes in juice
1 cup beer
1 cup low-salt chicken broth
1 teaspoon dried marjoram

¼ cup chopped fresh cilantro

MIX 1 tablespoon chili powder, salt, and pepper in bowl. Rub spice mixture all over pork. Sauté bacon in heavy large pot over medium heat until crisp, about 5 minutes. Transfer bacon to paper towels to drain. Working in batches, add pork to drippings in pot and sauté until brown on all sides, about 10 minutes per batch. Using slotted spoon, transfer pork to bowl.

REDUCE heat to medium. Add onion, ham, carrot, and garlic to pot; cover and cook 5 minutes, stirring occasionally and scraping up any browned bits. Add chiles; stir 1 minute. Stir in hominy, tomatoes with juice, beer, broth, marjoram, pork and any accumulated juices, and remaining 2 teaspoons chili powder; bring to boil. Reduce heat, cover, and simmer until pork is very tender, about 1 hour. *(Can be prepared 1 day ahead. Cover and chill bacon. Cool stew slightly. Refrigerate uncovered until cold, then cover and keep refrigerated.)*

SIMMER stew uncovered until liquid is slightly reduced and thickened, about 10 minutes. Season to taste with salt and pepper. Transfer to bowl. Sprinkle with reserved bacon and cilantro.

Lobster and shrimp cioppino

WE RECOMMEND USING a sturdy food mill (available at cookware stores) to help produce a thick stew base from simmered vegetables and fish. Alternatively, use a large heavy-duty mesh sieve to strain the seafood broth. Then push through enough fish and vegetables to make 13 cups of stew base. Serve cioppino with sourdough toasts.

8 SERVINGS

Stew base

2 1⅓- to 1½-pound live lobsters

2 pounds uncooked large shrimp with shells

1¼ cups olive oil
2 medium onions, chopped
1 cup chopped celery
1 cup chopped fresh fennel bulb
12 garlic cloves, peeled, flattened
¼ cup tomato paste
1 28-ounce can plus 2 cups diced tomatoes in juice
1 bunch fresh basil
4 large fresh thyme sprigs
4 large fresh parsley sprigs
2 large fresh oregano sprigs
2 bay leaves
1 teaspoon dried crushed red pepper
4 cups bottled clam juice
2 cups dry white wine
2 pounds red snapper, cod, or orange roughy fillets

Stew

- **16 large sea scallops**
- **1 pound large lump crabmeat (optional)**
- **½ cup all purpose flour**
- **6 tablespoons olive oil, divided**
- **3 tablespoons unsalted butter, divided**
- **6 tablespoons chopped fresh parsley, divided**
- **2 garlic cloves, minced, divided**
- **1 large shallot, minced, divided**
- **½ cup dry white wine**

FOR STEW BASE: Bring large pot of water to boil. Add 1 lobster headfirst. Cover pot; cook lobster 5 minutes. Transfer lobster to large bowl of ice. Cook remaining lobster; cool. Working over rimmed baking sheet, twist tail and large claws off lobsters. Using lobster cracker or nutcracker, crack claws; remove meat in 1 piece. Remove tail meat from shell; slice each tail crosswise into 6 medallions. Place lobster meat in small bowl; cover and chill. Place lobster shells and juice in heavy-duty resealable plastic bag; using mallet, smash shells into smaller pieces and reserve.

PEEL and devein shrimp, leaving tails intact; reserve shells. Place shrimp in medium bowl; cover and chill.

HEAT 1¼ cups oil in large pot (at least 8-quart capacity) over medium-high heat. Add onions, celery, fennel, and flattened garlic; sauté 5 minutes. Mix in tomato paste; sauté 5 minutes. Add tomatoes with juice, herbs, and crushed red pepper; cook 5 minutes. Add clam juice, 2 cups wine, snapper, lobster shells and juice, and shrimp shells; bring to boil. Reduce heat and simmer uncovered 1 hour.

WORKING in batches, strain stew base through large sieve into second large pot, reserving solids. Set food mill over second pot. Working with 2 cups at a time, press reserved stew-base solids through food mill to extract remaining broth and some fish and vegetables, making 13 cups stew base. Discard remaining solids.

BOIL stew base until reduced to 10 cups, stirring occasionally, about 15 minutes. *(Can be prepared 1 day ahead. Refrigerate stew base uncovered until cold, then cover and keep refrigerated. Keep lobster and shrimp chilled.)*

TO FINISH STEW: Bring stew base to simmer; keep warm. Combine scallops, crabmeat if desired, shrimp, and lobster meat in large bowl. Add flour; toss gently to coat. Place seafood in sieve; shake off excess flour. Heat 3 tablespoons oil in heavy large skillet over medium-high heat. Add half of seafood and sauté 1 minute. Add half of butter, then 2 tablespoons parsley, half of minced garlic, and half of shallot. Sauté until scallops and shrimp are just opaque in center and all seafood is beginning to brown, about 4 minutes. Transfer to large bowl. Repeat with remaining oil, butter, seafood, 2 tablespoons parsley, garlic, and shallot; transfer to same bowl. Add ½ cup wine to skillet and boil until reduced to glaze, scraping up any browned bits, about 3 minutes. Mix glaze into seafood.

LADLE stew base into shallow bowls. Arrange seafood in center. Sprinkle with remaining 2 tablespoons parsley.

Thai fish curry

THE MILD SPICE PASTE can also be used as a base for chicken and shrimp curries. And it can be prepared three days ahead to save time. Canned unsweetened coconut milk can be found at Indian, Southeast Asian, or Latin markets and many supermarkets. Lemongrass is available at Asian markets and at some supermarkets.

2 SERVINGS

- **⅓ cup finely chopped onion**
- **2 tablespoons minced fresh cilantro stems**
- **2 tablespoons minced fresh lemongrass (from bottom 6 inches of stalk)**
- **1 tablespoon turmeric**

- **1 tablespoon minced peeled fresh ginger**
- **1 tablespoon ground cumin**
- **3 garlic cloves, halved**
- **3/4 teaspoon dried crushed red pepper**

- **1 tablespoon vegetable oil**
- **12 ounces 1 1/2-inch-thick sea bass or halibut fillets, cut into 3-inch pieces**
- **1 cup canned unsweetened coconut milk**
- **2/3 cup bottled clam juice**
- **Minced fresh cilantro**
- **Freshly cooked rice**

BLEND first 8 ingredients in processor to dry paste, stopping frequently to scrape down sides of work bowl. *(Paste can be prepared 3 days ahead. Cover and chill.)*

HEAT oil in medium nonstick skillet over medium-high heat. Add 2 rounded tablespoons spice paste; stir 1 minute. Add fish and cook 1 minute per side. Add coconut milk and clam juice; simmer until fish is just opaque in center, about 3 minutes per side. Using slotted spoon, transfer fish to plate. Boil liquid until reduced to thick sauce, about 8 minutes. Season with salt. Return fish and any accumulated juices to sauce and heat through. Sprinkle with cilantro. Serve over rice.

Manhattan-style seafood stew

THIS STEW can be prepared up to the point of adding the seafood, then refrigerated and returned to a simmer before continuing with the clams, scallops, and shrimp.

4 SERVINGS

- **5 bacon slices, chopped**
- **1 1/2 large onions, chopped**
- **5 large shallots or green onions, chopped**
- **3 28-ounce cans Italian-style tomatoes in juice, drained, chopped in processor**
- **3 cups bottled clam juice**
- **3/4 cup dry white wine**
- **3 bay leaves**
- **1/4 teaspoon (generous) dried crushed red pepper**

- **1 pound white-skinned potatoes, peeled, quartered lengthwise, thinly sliced**

- **24 clams (about 3 1/2 pounds), well scrubbed**
- **8 ounces sea scallops, halved crosswise**
- **8 ounces uncooked medium shrimp, peeled, deveined (tails left intact)**
- **30 fresh basil leaves, thinly sliced, divided**

- **1 tablespoon matchstick-size strips lemon peel**

COOK bacon in heavy large pot over medium heat until fat renders, about 5 minutes. Add onions and shallots; sauté until tender, about 8 minutes. Add chopped tomatoes, clam juice, wine, bay leaves, and crushed red pepper to pot. Simmer 20 minutes, stirring occasionally.

ADD potatoes to stew and simmer until tender, about 20 minutes. *(Can be prepared 1 day ahead. Cool slightly. Refrigerate uncovered until cold, then cover and keep refrigerated. Bring to simmer before continuing.)*

ADD clams to stew. Cover and simmer until clams begin to open, about 5 minutes. Add scallops and shrimp; cover and simmer until clams open and scallops and shrimp are just opaque in center, about 3 minutes (discard any clams that do not open). Discard bay leaves. Mix in half of basil. Season to taste with salt and pepper.

TRANSFER stew to large serving bowl. Sprinkle with remaining basil and lemon peel.

Seafood stew with fennel and thyme

FROM THE COASTAL REGION of Normandy, France, this stew features fresh mussels and scallops in a sauce richly flavored with fennel and crème fraîche. Crème fraîche is sold at many supermarkets, but if it's unavailable, heat one cup whipping cream to lukewarm (85°F). Remove it from the heat and mix in two tablespoons buttermilk. Cover and let stand in a warm, draft-free area until slightly thickened, 24 to 48 hours, depending on room temperature. Refrigerate it until ready to use.

6 SERVINGS

1½ pounds mussels, scrubbed, debearded
2½ cups chopped onions, divided
1 cup dry white wine
12 parsley sprigs, divided, plus ½ cup chopped parsley

2 tablespoons (¼ stick) butter
2 cups finely chopped leeks (white and pale green parts only)
2 cups diced trimmed fennel bulb
4 8-ounce bottles clam juice
4 large fresh thyme sprigs
2 bay leaves
1¾ pounds thick halibut fillets, cut into 1½-inch pieces
10 ounces sea scallops

1 cup crème fraîche
2 large egg yolks

COMBINE mussels, 1¼ cups onions, wine, and 8 parsley sprigs in large pot; bring to boil. Cover and cook until mussels open, shaking pot often, about 5 minutes. Using slotted spoon, transfer mussels to large bowl to cool (discard any mussels that do not open). Strain cooking liquid into large measuring cup; discard vegetables in strainer. Add enough water to cooking liquid to measure 2 cups total. Remove mussels from shells if desired.

MELT butter in same large pot over medium heat. Add remaining 1¼ cups onions, leeks, and fennel; sauté until leeks are soft, stirring frequently, about 7 minutes. Add reserved mussel cooking liquid, 4 parsley sprigs, clam juice, thyme sprigs, and bay leaves. Simmer uncovered until vegetables are tender and liquid has reduced by ⅓, about 25 minutes. Add halibut and scallops to broth and simmer until just opaque in center, about 4 minutes. Using slotted spoon, transfer halibut and scallops to bowl. Discard parsley sprigs, thyme sprigs, and bay leaves.

WHISK crème fraîche and egg yolks in medium bowl to blend. Whisk in ½ cup hot cooking liquid from pot. Gradually stir yolk mixture into stew. Cook over medium heat until liquid thickens slightly, stirring constantly, about 5 minutes (do not allow mixture to boil). Return halibut, scallops, and mussels to pan. Cook until halibut is heated through, stirring often, about 5 minutes. Stir in ½ cup chopped parsley. Season with salt and pepper. Serve in warmed shallow bowls.

Salt cod, potato, and olive stew

THIS HEARTY ITALIAN-STYLE STEW delivers great flavor in a short amount of time. Salt cod, known as *baccalà* in Italian, can be found loose at Italian and Latin markets, and packed in a wooden box or plastic bag in the seafood department of the supermarket.

4 SERVINGS

1 1-pound package boned salted codfish, cut into ½-inch pieces

3 tablespoons olive oil
2 large celery stalks, chopped
1 small onion, chopped
3 russet potatoes (about 1¾ pounds), peeled, cut into ½-inch pieces
16 Sicilian or Greek green olives, pitted
2 Turkish bay leaves
¼ teaspoon dried crushed red pepper
2½ cups water
1¼ cups whipping cream

PLACE fish in large pot; fill pot with cold water. Bring just to simmer; cook 3 minutes. Drain fish and rinse well. Repeat 1 more time.

HEAT oil in same pot over medium heat. Add celery and onion; sauté 5 minutes. Add potatoes, olives, bay leaves, and crushed red pepper; stir 1 minute. Add 2½ cups water and bring to boil. Cover and boil 5 minutes. Add fish and cream. Reduce heat to medium-low, cover, and simmer until fish and potatoes are tender, about 15 minutes longer. Discard bay leaves; season stew to taste with pepper.

Ragout of halibut and cabbage

THIS RECIPE IS QUICK and easy enough to serve on a weeknight after work—hence the two servings. But it can easily be doubled if you want to invite a couple of friends over. Begin by offering crisp breadsticks with roasted red peppers, black olives, and marinated artichoke hearts on a bed of arugula.

2 SERVINGS; CAN BE DOUBLED

- **4 bacon slices, coarsely chopped**
- **1 large onion, sliced**
- **2 cups bottled clam juice**
- **1 12-ounce russet potato, peeled, cut into ¾-inch pieces**
- **3 cups (packed) thinly sliced green cabbage**
- **1 8- to 10-ounce halibut fillet, cut into 1-inch pieces**
- **½ cup half and half**

SAUTÉ bacon in heavy large saucepan over medium-high heat until brown and crisp, about 3 minutes. Using slotted spoon, transfer bacon to paper towel to drain. Add onion to drippings in pan and sauté until beginning to color, about 4 minutes. Add clam juice and potato; bring to boil. Reduce heat to medium, cover, and simmer until potato is almost tender, about 8 minutes. Add cabbage and fish; simmer uncovered until potato is tender, fish is just opaque in center, and cabbage is wilted, about 5 minutes. Add half and half and bacon; simmer 1 minute to blend flavors. Season to taste with salt and pepper. Ladle ragout into bowls.

White bean, butternut squash, kale, and olive stew

VEGETABLE STEWS have made their way into many culinary repertoires. Aside from their obvious healthful qualities, they're easy to whip up at the last minute with whatever you may have on hand. The combination of vegetables here produces a robust stew, but feel free to experiment with favorites of your own.

6 SERVINGS

- **¼ cup olive oil**
- **3 large onions, chopped**
- **6 garlic cloves, minced**
- **1 3¼- to 3½-pound butternut squash, halved, peeled, seeded, cut into 1½-inch cubes**
- **3 red bell peppers, seeded, cut into 1½-inch pieces**
- **1½ cups vegetable broth**
- **1½ large bunches kale, thick stems trimmed, leaves cut crosswise into 2-inch strips**
- **1 tablespoon dried rubbed sage**
- **5 15-ounce cans cannellini (white kidney beans), rinsed, drained**
- **1 cup Kalamata olives, pitted, halved**

Freshly grated pecorino Romano cheese

HEAT oil in heavy large pot over medium-high heat. Add onions and garlic; sauté until tender, about 10 minutes. Add squash; sauté 10 minutes. Add bell peppers and stir to coat with onion mixture. Add broth. Cover and simmer until squash is just tender, about 10 minutes. Mix kale and sage into stew. Cover and cook until kale wilts, stirring occasionally, about 8 minutes. Add beans and olives; stir until heated through. Season to taste with salt and pepper.

TRANSFER stew to large shallow bowl. Sprinkle generously with cheese.

Garbanzo bean, lentil, and vegetable stew

THERE'S VERY LITTLE FAT—and no cholesterol—in this full-flavored meatless stew, which is based on a Tunisian specialty called *tbikha*. Serve it with steamed rice.

4 SERVINGS

2 tablespoons olive oil
2 cups chopped onions
3 garlic cloves, chopped
3 tablespoons tomato paste
2 teaspoons ground coriander
1 teaspoon caraway seeds
½ teaspoon cayenne pepper
2 ¼ cups canned vegetable broth
2 ¼ cups water
1 cup dried lentils
1 15- to 16-ounce can garbanzo beans (chickpeas), rinsed, drained
1 ½ carrots, peeled, cut into ¼-inch-thick rounds
1 cup frozen lima beans
½ cup chopped fresh parsley

1 10-ounce bag fresh spinach leaves
Lemon wedges

HEAT oil in heavy large pot over medium-low heat. Add onions and garlic; sauté until soft and golden, about 10 minutes. Add tomato paste, coriander, caraway, and cayenne; stir 1 minute. Stir in broth, 2¼ cups water, and lentils. Increase heat to high; bring to boil. Reduce heat, cover, and simmer until lentils are almost tender, stirring occasionally, about 15 minutes. Add garbanzo beans, carrots, lima beans, and parsley. Cover and simmer until carrots are very tender, about 20 minutes. *(Can be prepared 1 day ahead. Cool slightly. Cover and refrigerate. Bring to simmer before continuing.)*

STIR spinach into stew. Cover and cook just until spinach wilts, about 3 minutes. Season to taste with salt and pepper. Ladle stew into bowls; serve with lemon wedges.

Chilies

Two-bean chili in bread bowls

THE BREAD BOWLS make for a clever presentation for this party chili. There are two ways to make the bowls: Purchase twenty 8-ounce round bread loaves, cut off the tops, and scoop out the centers so that each person has a separate "bowl"; or buy ten 1-pound loaves, cut in half horizontally, scoop out the centers, and use each half as a bowl. You can add sweet or hot Italian sausages here (or a combination), according to your preference.

20 SERVINGS

2¼ pounds dried Great Northern beans
2¼ pounds dried pinto beans

½ cup olive oil
7 large onions, chopped (about 14 cups)
½ cup chili powder
5 tablespoons tomato paste
9 garlic cloves, minced
3 tablespoons ground cumin
1½ tablespoons dried oregano
1½ tablespoons dried basil
¾ teaspoon cayenne pepper
14 cups (or more) chicken broth or vegetable broth
3 15-ounce cans corn kernels (undrained)
5 6-ounce jars roasted red bell peppers, drained
3 8-ounce cans tomato sauce

20 8-ounce round sourdough bread loaves or ten 1-pound round sourdough bread loaves

1 cup (2 sticks) butter, melted

3 pounds Italian sausages

2½ cups chopped fresh cilantro
4 cups grated cheddar cheese (about 16 ounces)
2½ cups chopped red onions
2 cups sour cream

PLACE all beans in large pot with enough cold water to cover by at least 3 inches. Let stand overnight.

DRAIN beans. Divide beans between 2 large pots. Add enough cold water to each pot to cover beans by 3 inches. Simmer until beans are almost tender, stirring occasionally, about 1 hour. Drain. Transfer beans to large bowl. Wipe pots dry.

HEAT ¼ cup oil in each pot over medium-high heat. Add half of onions to each pot and sauté until tender, about 15 minutes. Add half of chili powder, tomato paste, garlic, cumin, oregano, basil, and cayenne to each pot; stir 1 minute. Divide beans, 14 cups broth, corn with liquid, bell peppers, and tomato sauce between pots. Bring to boil. Reduce heat to medium and simmer until beans are tender and chili thickens, stirring occasionally, about 1½ hours. Season to taste with salt and pepper. *(Can be prepared 1 day ahead. Cool slightly. Refrigerate uncovered until cold, then cover and keep refrigerated. Bring to simmer before serving, thinning with more broth if necessary.)*

IF USING twenty 8-ounce bread loaves, cut off tops. Using small knife, cut out center, leaving 1-inch shell. If using ten 1-pound loaves, cut each horizontally in half. Cut off thin slice from top half of each loaf. Turn top of loaf trimmed side down. Cut out center of top and bottom halves, leaving 1-inch shell. Reserve trimmings for another use. *(Bread bowls can be prepared 1 day ahead. Cover; let stand at room temperature.)*

PREHEAT oven to 400°F. Brush insides of bread bowls with melted butter. Place bread bowls on oven racks. Bake until crusty and brown, about 15 minutes. Transfer bread bowls to plates.

MEANWHILE, working in batches, cook sausages in heavy large skillet over medium-high heat until cooked through, turning occasionally, about 15 minutes. Cut into rounds. Transfer to bowl.

MIX cilantro into chili. Ladle chili into bread bowls. Serve, passing sausages, cheese, red onions, and sour cream separately.

Pork chili with tomatoes

THIS FULL-BODIED GREEN CHILI gets a fantastic kick from the poblano chiles; poblanos are available at Latin markets and some supermarkets. For a milder chili, replace some of the poblanos with green bell peppers. Serve the chili with warm corn tortillas, and pass bowls of chopped fresh cilantro, chopped green onions, and sour cream for garnishes. This recipe can easily be halved for a smaller crowd.

12 SERVINGS; CAN BE HALVED

3 pounds poblano chiles (about 12 large)

7½ pounds boneless country-style pork spareribs, trimmed, cut into 1-inch pieces
6 tablespoons all purpose flour
6 tablespoons (about) vegetable oil

6 cups coarsely chopped onions
12 garlic cloves, chopped
2 tablespoons dried oregano
2 tablespoons ground cumin
10 cups low-salt chicken broth
1 28-ounce can diced tomatoes in juice

CHAR chiles over gas flame or in broiler until blackened on all sides. Enclose in paper bag; let stand 10 minutes. Peel and seed chilies. Cut into 1-inch pieces.

PLACE pork in large bowl. Sprinkle with salt and pepper. Add flour and toss to coat. Heat 4 tablespoons oil in heavy large wide pot over high heat. Working in batches and adding more oil as needed, cook pork until brown on all sides, about 6 minutes per batch. Using slotted spoon, transfer pork to large bowl.

REDUCE heat to medium. Add onions to same pot and sauté until tender, about 10 minutes. Add garlic, oregano, and cumin; stir 2 minutes. Return pork and any accumulated juice to pot; add broth, chiles, and tomatoes with juice. Bring to boil. Reduce heat and simmer uncovered until chili thickens and meat is very tender, stirring occasionally, about 2 hours. Season to taste with salt and pepper. *(Can be prepared 1 day ahead. Cool slightly. Refrigerate uncovered until cold, then cover and keep refrigerated. Before serving, rewarm over medium heat, stirring occasionally.)*

Spicy lamb and chorizo chili

CILANTRO, SOUR CREAM, grated cheddar or Monterey Jack cheese, chopped red or green onion, and salsa would be great toppings for this hearty one-dish supper. Toss a quick salad, throw in a purchased dessert, and you're done. Look for chorizo in the refrigerated meat or deli case, and for dried ancho chiles at Latin markets, specialty foods stores, and some supermarkets.

6 TO 8 SERVINGS

2¼ cups low-salt chicken broth
3 ounces dried ancho chiles (about 5 large), stemmed, seeded, torn into pieces
1 teaspoon cayenne pepper

2 1-pound beef or pork chorizo sausages, casings removed

2 cups coarsely chopped red onions
12 garlic cloves, chopped
1 tablespoon dried oregano
1 tablespoon ground cumin
3¼ pounds lamb shoulder round-bone chops, trimmed, boned, cut into ¾-inch cubes
2 15-ounce cans golden hominy, rinsed, drained

COMBINE first 3 ingredients in heavy medium saucepan. Cover and simmer over medium heat until chiles soften, about 12 minutes. Puree chile mixture in batches in blender.

SAUTÉ chorizo in heavy large pot over medium-high heat until drippings come to simmer, breaking up meat with back of spoon. Transfer to fine strainer set over bowl. Let chorizo drain 10 minutes.

RETURN ¼ cup chorizo drippings to same pot and heat over medium-high heat (discard remaining drippings). Add onions, garlic, oregano, and cumin. Sauté until onions begin to soften, about 5 minutes. Sprinkle lamb with salt and pepper; add to pot. Sauté until lamb is no longer pink on outside, about 10 minutes. Add chile puree and drained chorizo. Bring chili to boil, stirring occasionally. Reduce heat to medium-low, cover, and simmer 1 hour. Add hominy. Simmer uncovered until lamb is tender and liquid thickens, stirring occasionally, about 15 minutes. Season chili to taste with salt and pepper. *(Can be prepared 3 days ahead. Cool slightly. Refrigerate uncovered until cold, then cover and keep refrigerated. Before serving, rewarm over medium heat, stirring occasionally.)*

Turkey chili with white beans

BY CALLING FOR TURKEY rather than beef or pork and using only one tablespoon of oil, this chili manages to be both satisfying and healthful; it's extremely low in saturated fat. If you have leftover chili (doubtful), serve it over turkey or chicken franks the next day—they may just be the best-tasting and best-for-you chili dogs you'll ever eat.

8 SERVINGS

1 tablespoon vegetable oil
2 medium onions, chopped
1½ teaspoons dried oregano
1½ teaspoons ground cumin
1½ pounds lean ground turkey
¼ cup chili powder
2 bay leaves
1 tablespoon unsweetened cocoa powder
1½ teaspoons salt
¼ teaspoon ground cinnamon
1 28-ounce can whole tomatoes in juice
3 cups beef broth
1 8-ounce can tomato sauce

3 15-ounce cans small white beans, rinsed, drained

Chopped red onion
Chopped fresh cilantro
Plain low-fat yogurt or light sour cream

HEAT oil in heavy large pot over medium heat. Add onions; sauté until light brown and tender, about 10 minutes. Add oregano and cumin; stir 1 minute. Increase heat to medium-high. Add turkey; stir until no longer pink, breaking up with back of spoon. Stir in chili powder, bay leaves, cocoa powder, salt, and cinnamon. Add tomatoes with juice, breaking up with back of spoon. Mix in broth and tomato sauce. Bring to boil. Reduce heat; simmer 45 minutes, stirring occasionally.

ADD beans to chili and simmer until flavors blend, about 10 minutes. Discard bay leaves. *(Can be prepared 1 day ahead. Cool slightly. Refrigerate uncovered until cold, then cover and keep refrigerated. Before continuing, bring to simmer over medium-low heat.)*

LADLE chili into bowls. Pass red onion, cilantro, and yogurt separately.

Black bean and espresso chili

THIS UNIQUE CHILI is excellent served over polenta (see "Rice, Grains, and Beans" chapter for recipes) and seasoned with any—or all—of the suggested toppings. If you're wondering about the shaved bittersweet chocolate: It adds Mexican *mole* flavor.

8 SERVINGS

- **½ cup olive oil**
- **5 large onions, chopped**
- **¼ cup instant espresso powder**
- **¼ cup chili powder**
- **¼ cup ground cumin**
- **¼ cup dried oregano leaves**
- **2 28-ounce cans crushed tomatoes with added puree**
- **⅓ cup honey**
- **6 garlic cloves, minced**
- **7 15-ounce cans black beans, rinsed, drained**
- **2 cups water**
- **2 teaspoons salt**
- **¼ teaspoon ground chipotle chile powder or chili powder**
- **Large pinch of ground cinnamon**
- **Assorted toppings (such as sour cream, chopped fresh cilantro, chopped green onions, shredded cheese, sliced jalapeño chiles, and shaved bittersweet chocolate)**

HEAT oil in heavy large pot over medium-high heat. Add onions and sauté until tender, about 8 minutes. Mix in espresso powder, ¼ cup chili powder, cumin, and oregano. Cook 1 minute. Mix in tomatoes, honey, and garlic. Bring to simmer. Reduce heat to medium-low, cover, and simmer 30 minutes. Add beans, 2 cups water, 2 teaspoons salt, chipotle chile powder, and cinnamon. Bring to boil over high heat. Reduce heat to medium and simmer uncovered until mixture thickens slightly, stirring often, about 30 minutes. Season to taste with more salt. *(Can be prepared 1 day ahead. Cool slightly. Refrigerate uncovered until cold, then cover and keep refrigerated. Bring to simmer over medium heat before serving.)*

PLACE chili toppings in individual condiment bowls. Ladle chili into large bowl and serve toppings alongside.

Salads 5

Once salads were simple combinations of leafy greens and vegetables, dressed with salt and little else. (In fact, the word *salad* itself comes from the Latin *salata,* meaning "salted things.") Now that definition has expanded to include all manner of additions—meats, seafood, beans, other vegetables—and dressings, but we haven't lost our love for the basics. There is something remarkably satisfying about a salad of tender greens, picked from the garden or a farmers' market stand and dressed with the best olive oil you can get your hands on and a dash of good vinegar, a little salt, and fresh pepper. Shredded carrots, thinly sliced cukes, and perfectly ripe tomatoes never hurt, either.

Making a great salad is not dependent on hard-and-fast rules; it's about the art of pairing ingredients. Simply said, a salad should balance flavor, color, and texture. Think of the French bistro classic: bitter, pale green and yellow *frisée* tossed with chunks of smoky-sweet bacon and nutty-fruity olive oil dressing. Even Mom's potato salad likely contains a little celery for crunch and pimientos for sweetness and color.

Like soups, salads can start the meal or *be* the meal. Add—for instance—shrimp, legumes (such as garbanzos), or chunks of potato, and there's a meal in a bowl. But unlike a soup, where the goal is to simmer and stir until all flavors are blended, the key to a great salad lies in clever juxtaposition of ingredients so that each remains distinctive—crisp with juicy, tart with sweet, delicate with assertive. (Think of yourself as half matchmaker, half cook.) Each bite should be a mini meal.

Use the recipes in this chapter as a springboard for creating your own new classics. The freewheeling ease with which a salad can be put together makes it a prime candidate for that meal you eat when there's "nothing in the house."

Pomegranate, beet, and blood orange salad

YOU CAN USE WHICHEVER color of beets you prefer in this vibrant salad. Pomegranate molasses, a rich and tangy syrup, may be at your local supermarket; if not, look for it at a Middle Eastern market or specialty foods store. Blood oranges can be found at supermarkets in the winter season , but super-sweet oranges are a suitable stand-in year round. Seeding pomegranates can be tricky; wear an apron and kitchen gloves to avoid staining clothes and fingers. Cut around the circumference of the fruit, making sure the knife is inserted only half an inch deep. Use the palms of your hands to break the membranes into pieces, then use your fingers to separate the seeds from the membranes. Discard the membranes and strain the seeds.

4 FIRST-COURSE SERVINGS

4 medium beets, tops trimmed
3 tablespoons vegetable oil, divided
¼ cup water

¼ cup blood orange juice (from about 1 blood orange) or regular orange juice
1 tablespoon pomegranate molasses
1 tablespoon white wine vinegar

1 medium red onion, thinly sliced
3 blood oranges or small navel oranges, peeled, cut into ¼-inch-thick slices
1 cup pomegranate seeds (from one 11-ounce pomegranate)

PREHEAT oven to 400°F. Place beets in 13x9x2-inch metal pan. Toss with 1 tablespoon oil; sprinkle with salt and pepper. Add ¼ cup water. Cover pan with foil; roast until beets are tender, about 50 minutes. Cool. Peel beets and cut into ⅓-inch-thick wedges.

WHISK orange juice, pomegranate molasses, vinegar, and remaining 2 tablespoons oil in large bowl to blend. Season vinaigrette to taste with salt and pepper.

PLACE onion in small bowl; cover with cold water. Soak onion 1 minute, then drain and pat dry. Add beets, onion, orange slices, and pomegranate seeds to vinaigrette in bowl; toss to blend. Season salad to taste with salt and pepper.

Jicama, spinach, and pineapple salad with cilantro vinaigrette

THE SWEETNESS of the pineapple and jicama is a sensational foil to the distinctively aromatic cilantro, which is found chopped in the dressing and in whole-leaf form in the salad itself. Cumin rounds out the Mexican flavors in this inventive salad.

4 SERVINGS

⅓ cup vegetable oil
3 tablespoons white wine vinegar
1 tablespoon minced shallot
¼ cup chopped fresh cilantro
¼ teaspoon ground cumin
1 6-ounce package baby spinach leaves
1 small jicama, peeled, cut into 3-inch-long matchstick-size strips
1 cup cubed peeled fresh pineapple
½ cup fresh cilantro leaves

WHISK first 5 ingredients in small bowl to blend. Season vinaigrette to taste with salt and pepper. Combine all remaining ingredients in large bowl. Toss salad with enough vinaigrette to coat. Divide salad among 4 plates.

Spinach, pear, and pancetta salad

SWEET ASIAN PEARS and the salt-cured Italian bacon called pancetta play off each other deliciously in this first-course salad. Asian pears are shaped like apples, with a flavor very much like the typical pear, but they are known most for their crunchy texture and nectar-like juice. If you can't find them at your favorite market, use Bosc pears instead. You can find pancetta at Italian markets and in the refrigerated deli case of many supermarkets, but classic American bacon is a reliable, if less peppery, substitute.

10 SERVINGS

- **1 cup diced pancetta or bacon (about 5 ounces)**
- **¼ cup minced shallots**
- **3 tablespoons Sherry wine vinegar**
- **2 teaspoons Dijon mustard**
- **2 teaspoons minced fresh thyme**
- **½ cup extra-virgin olive oil**

- **1½ 10-ounce packages spinach leaves**
- **2 Asian pears or Bosc pears, halved, cored, thinly sliced**
- **1 medium red onion, thinly sliced**
- **1 head of radicchio, separated into leaves**

SAUTÉ pancetta in medium nonstick skillet over medium heat until crisp, about 6 minutes. Using slotted spoon, transfer to paper towels to drain. Pour drippings from skillet into medium bowl. Add shallots, vinegar, mustard, and thyme to bowl; whisk to blend. Add oil; whisk to blend. Season dressing to taste with salt and pepper. *(Can be made 1 day ahead. Cover pancetta and dressing separately and chill. Bring to room temperature before continuing.)*

COMBINE spinach, pears, red onion, and pancetta in large bowl. Toss with enough dressing to coat. Surround salad with radicchio leaves.

Radicchio, grapefruit, and spinach salad

SLIGHTLY BITTER AND SOFTLY CRUNCHY, radicchio has long been a popular addition to Italian salad bowls, but has only been grown stateside since the 1980s. Radicchio's deep red color makes it a beautiful component of this refreshing salad, a dramatic counterpoint to the bright green spinach and tangy white grapefruit. Crushing the fennel seeds in a plastic bag helps contain the seeds.

6 SERVINGS

- **5 tablespoons red wine vinegar**
- **1 teaspoon fennel seeds, crushed**
- **½ cup olive oil**
- **2 white grapefruits**

- **1 10-ounce head of radicchio, torn into bite-size pieces**
- **1½ 6-ounce packages baby spinach leaves**
- **½ cup Kalamata olives, pitted**

COMBINE vinegar and fennel seeds in medium bowl. Gradually whisk in oil. Season dressing to taste with salt and pepper. Cut all peel and white pith from grapefruits. Working over bowl, cut grapefruits between membranes to release segments. Stir segments into dressing. Let stand at least 15 minutes and up to 1 hour.

TOSS radicchio, spinach, and olives in large bowl. Add grapefruit segments and dressing; toss to coat.

Arugula, fennel, and orange salad

SIMPLE TO PREPARE, this salad showcases a complex flavor combination that's pleasing to the eye and the palate. It makes a nice first course for a Provençal menu, as fennel and orange often come together in the popular seafood soups and stews of the region.

6 SERVINGS

¼ cup minced shallots
3 tablespoons extra-virgin olive oil
1½ tablespoons fresh lemon juice

2 large oranges

7 cups arugula
1 large fennel bulb, trimmed, quartered lengthwise, cored, thinly sliced
1 small red onion, thinly sliced

WHISK shallots, olive oil, and lemon juice in medium bowl to blend. Season dressing to taste with salt and pepper.

CUT all peel and white pith from oranges. Working over bowl and using small, sharp knife, cut between membranes to release segments.

COMBINE arugula, fennel, and onion in large bowl. Toss with enough dressing to coat. Add orange segments; toss to combine.

Frisée salad with prosciutto, roasted figs, and walnuts

THE CLASSIC ITALIAN first-course combination of figs and prosciutto is teamed with blue cheese and walnuts for a salad that's ideal for a special occasion. It's best to buy the prosciutto from a good Italian deli, but if that's not an option, you should be able to find the prepackaged variety in the refrigerated deli section of your market, alongside other cured meats.

12 SERVINGS

36 whole fresh figs, stems trimmed
2 tablespoons plus ½ cup extra-virgin olive oil

¼ cup red wine vinegar
½ cup crumbled blue cheese (about 2 ounces)

6 cups torn frisée lettuce leaves
4 cups mixed baby greens
4 cups trimmed watercress sprigs
8 ounces thinly sliced prosciutto, cut crosswise into thin strips
1½ cups walnuts, toasted, coarsely chopped

PREHEAT oven to 350°F. Toss figs with 2 tablespoons oil in large bowl to coat. Arrange figs on rimmed baking sheet. Roast until figs are tender and shiny, about 12 minutes. Cool. Cut figs lengthwise in half.

WHISK remaining ½ cup oil and vinegar in small bowl to blend. Add cheese and whisk to blend. Season dressing to taste with salt and pepper. *(Figs and dressing can be prepared 1 day ahead. Cover separately and refrigerate. Bring to room temperature and rewhisk dressing before using.)*

COMBINE frisée, baby greens, watercress sprigs, prosciutto, and walnuts in large bowl. Add dressing; toss to coat. Gently mix in figs. Transfer salad to serving bowl.

Salad of fall greens with persimmons and hazelnuts

FRESH TANGERINE JUICE is boiled with grated tangerine peel and then whisked together with balsamic vinegar, hazelnut oil, and cinnamon for an outstanding and innovative dressing. It makes a stellar counterpoint to the honey-like persimmon and crunchy toasted hazelnuts. Persimmons have a narrow window of availability—late fall and winter—so substitute sliced and seeded papayas or mangoes the rest of the year.

10 TO 12 SERVINGS

¾ cup fresh tangerine juice
1 tablespoon finely grated tangerine peel
¾ cup vegetable oil
2 tablespoons hazelnut oil or walnut oil
2 tablespoons balsamic vinegar
¼ teaspoon ground cinnamon

- **1 head of escarole (about 11 ounces), torn into 2-inch pieces**
- **6 cups watercress, thick stems trimmed (from about 2 bunches)**
- **1 5-ounce bag mixed baby greens**
- **2 ripe Fuyu persimmons, peeled, halved, thinly sliced, divided**
- **½ cup hazelnuts, toasted, skinned**

BOIL tangerine juice and tangerine peel in heavy small saucepan over medium-high heat until reduced to ¼ cup, about 5 minutes. Transfer to medium bowl. Whisk in next 4 ingredients. Season dressing to taste with salt and pepper. *(Can be made 1 day ahead. Cover; chill. Bring to room temperature and rewhisk before using.)*

PLACE all greens and half of persimmon slices in large bowl. Add dressing and toss to coat. Divide salad among plates. Top each with remaining persimmon slices and hazelnuts.

Tijuana tangerine and mixed green salad

THE LATIN ACCENT in this dish can be found in the dressing's cumin, chili powder, and cayenne pepper, as well as the salad's avocado, jicama, and tangerine. The combination makes a good partner for chili or grilled meats and fish. Put the aniseed in a plastic bag to crush them—it simplifies the crushing and the clean-up.

6 SERVINGS

Dressing

- **7 tablespoons corn oil**
- **¼ cup red wine vinegar**
- **3 tablespoons (scant) honey**
- **1¼ teaspoons ground cumin**
- **1¼ teaspoons chili powder**
- **½ teaspoon (generous) aniseed, crushed**
- **Pinch of cayenne pepper**

Salad

- **1 small head of romaine lettuce**
- **1 head of curly endive, outer leaves discarded**
- **1 small head of red leaf lettuce**
- **4 seedless tangerines, peeled**
- **1 small red onion, thinly sliced**
- **1 avocado, halved, pitted, peeled, cut into ½-inch cubes**
- **1 cup coarsely grated peeled jicama (about 6 ounces)**
- **2 green onions, minced**

FOR DRESSING: Whisk oil, vinegar, honey, and spices in medium bowl to blend. Season dressing to taste with salt and pepper. *(Can be prepared 2 days ahead. Cover tightly and let stand at room temperature.)*

FOR SALAD: Tear all greens into bite-size pieces and place in large bowl. Separate tangerines into segments. Add tangerine segments, red onion, avocado, and jicama to greens. Toss gently to combine. Whisk green onions into dressing. Pour over salad and toss to coat.

Hearts of romaine salad with apple, red onion, and cider vinaigrette

RICH WITH FALL AND WINTER ingredients, this salad just begs to be part of cold-weather menus. The cider vinaigrette is enhanced with apple juice concentrate and red onion, as well as nutmeg and ginger—classic holiday spices that make the dressing surprisingly aromatic. For an elegant presentation, the salad can be arranged on individual plates instead of one large platter. When cutting the romaine hearts, be sure to leave a small part of the base attached to each piece to hold the leaves together.

10 SERVINGS

- **1¼ cups vegetable oil**
- **⅓ cup apple cider vinegar**
- **3 tablespoons frozen apple juice concentrate, thawed**
- **2 tablespoons minced red onion**

1¾ teaspoons salt
½ teaspoon ground nutmeg
½ teaspoon ground ginger
¼ teaspoon ground black pepper

1 cup thinly sliced red onion

2 Gala apples, peeled, halved, cored, cut into ¼-inch dice
5 hearts of romaine lettuce, halved lengthwise
¾ cup pecans, toasted, coarsely chopped

WHISK first 8 ingredients in small bowl to blend. *(Dressing can be made 1 day ahead. Cover and refrigerate. Bring to room temperature and rewhisk before using.)*

PLACE sliced onion in medium bowl. Cover with cold water; let stand 30 minutes. Drain well; pat dry.

PLACE ⅓ cup dressing in another medium bowl. Add apples; toss to coat. Cut each romaine half lengthwise into 3 wedges. Fan wedges on large platter. Top with red onion slices. Drizzle salad with dressing, then sprinkle with apples and pecans.

Corn, tomato, and basil salad

THIS COLORFUL AND SIMPLE SALAD is the essence of summer, when corn and tomatoes are at their finest. When buying corn, look for green and moist husks, golden brown, slightly sticky tassels, and a plump feel. Under the husk, the kernels should be fat with no spaces between the rows, and when you pierce a kernel, the juice that runs out should be milky.

6 SERVINGS

- **6 large ears white corn, husked**
- **5 tablespoons olive oil, divided**
- **3 garlic cloves, finely chopped**
- **½ cup (packed) thinly sliced fresh basil, divided**
- **5 plum tomatoes, seeded, chopped**
- **3 tablespoons balsamic vinegar**

Using large knife, cut corn kernels from cobs. Heat 2 tablespoons oil in heavy large skillet over medium-high heat. Add garlic; sauté 1 minute. Add corn; sauté until just cooked through, about 5 minutes. Remove skillet from heat. Add ¼ cup basil. Transfer corn mixture to large bowl. Cool slightly, stirring occasionally. Stir in tomatoes, vinegar, and remaining 3 tablespoons oil and ¼ cup basil. Season salad to taste with salt and pepper. Cover; chill at least 3 hours and up to 8 hours.

Brussels sprout and apple salad with blue cheese and walnuts

CLASSIC COMBINATIONS—celery and blue cheese, walnuts and blue cheese, apples and walnuts—team up with brussels sprouts in a terrific salad that will win over even those who shy away from the cabbage-like vegetable. If brussels sprouts are lightly cooked and then paired with strongly flavored foods, such as the blue cheese in this salad, their intense taste is nicely balanced. When buying brussels sprouts, look for them still on the stalk, which indicates freshness and better flavor. If you can't find them on the stalk, look at their stem ends—if they are dried out or brown, they were cut from the stalk long ago.

12 SERVINGS

- **2 pounds small brussels sprouts, quartered through stem end**
- **2 tablespoons Sherry wine vinegar**
- **1½ tablespoons mayonnaise**
- **½ cup olive oil**
- **4 large red-skinned apples, quartered, cored, cut into ½-inch cubes**
- **¾ cup chopped celery leaves**
- **1⅔ cups crumbled blue cheese (about 7 ounces)**
- **1½ cups walnuts, toasted, coarsely chopped**
- **Radicchio leaves**

STEAM brussels sprouts until just tender, about 12 minutes. Transfer to large bowl; cool.

MIX vinegar and mayonnaise in small bowl. Gradually whisk in oil. Season dressing to taste with salt and pepper. *(Brussels sprouts and dressing can be made 1 day ahead. Cover separately and chill.)*

ADD apples and celery leaves to brussels sprouts. Add dressing; toss to combine. Mix in blue cheese and walnuts. Season salad to taste with salt and pepper. Line serving bowl with radicchio leaves. Spoon in salad.

Tomato, cucumber, and red onion salad with mint

LIGHT AND REFRESHING, this salad is an ideal accompaniment for smoky and succulent barbecue dishes. The English hothouse cucumbers called for in this recipe are longer and thinner than the standard American supermarket cucumber, which has a dark, thick, waxed skin. The hothouse cucumber also has fewer seeds.

6 SERVINGS

2 **large English hothouse cucumbers**
1/3 **cup red wine vinegar**
1 **tablespoon sugar**
1 **teaspoon salt**

3 **large tomatoes, seeded, coarsely chopped**
2/3 **cup coarsely chopped red onion**
1/2 **cup chopped fresh mint**
3 **tablespoons olive oil**

CUT cucumbers in half lengthwise; scrape out seeds. Cut halves on diagonal into ½-inch-thick pieces. Place in large bowl. Add vinegar, sugar, and salt. Let stand at room temperature 1 hour, tossing occasionally.

ADD tomatoes, onion, mint, and oil to cucumbers and toss to blend. Season salad to taste with salt and pepper.

Pipérade salad with olives

A SPIN ON THE CLASSIC Basque dish of red and green bell peppers sautéed in olive oil, this colorful salad takes advantage of Sherry wine vinegar, another popular Spanish ingredient. The vinegar teams with brine-cured black olives for a sweet-tangy-salty accent. At the market, avoid peppers that have soft or dark spots and wrinkled skin.

8 SERVINGS

1/3 **cup extra-virgin olive oil**
2 **garlic cloves, thinly sliced**
1 **large red onion, halved, sliced**
2 **large red bell peppers, cut into 1/2-inch-wide strips**
1 **large yellow bell pepper, cut into 1/2-inch-wide strips**
1 **large green bell pepper, cut into 1/2-inch-wide strips**
2 **tablespoons Sherry wine vinegar**
1/2 **cup coarsely chopped pitted Kalamata olives**

HEAT olive oil in heavy large skillet over medium-high heat. Add garlic and stir 30 seconds. Add onion slices and sauté until beginning to soften, about 5 minutes. Add all bell peppers and sauté until crisp-tender, about 7 minutes. Stir in vinegar, then olives. Season salad generously to taste with salt and pepper. Cool completely. *(Salad can be made 1 day ahead. Cover and refrigerate. Bring to room temperature before serving.)*

Antipasto salad with basil dressing

LITERALLY TRANSLATED AS "before the meal," *antipasto* refers to the platters of hot or cold appetizers that precede many Italian meals. This salad features a variety of the foods found on a typical antipasto platter: prosciutto, mozzarella cheese, olives, and roasted red bell peppers. When buying your peppers, try to select ones with flat sides so that they will be easier to roast and peel. Water-packed fresh mozzarella is available at Italian markets, specialty foods stores, and some supermarkets.

6 SERVINGS

2 **large red bell peppers**

1 **cup (packed) fresh basil leaves**
1 **garlic clove**
1/2 **teaspoon salt**
3/4 **cup extra-virgin olive oil**

8 **ounces thinly sliced prosciutto**
2 **8-ounce balls water-packed fresh mozzarella cheese, drained, thinly sliced into rounds**
4 **large tomatoes, thinly sliced**
6 **hard-boiled eggs, peeled, sliced into 1/4-inch-thick rounds**
1/4 **cup Kalamata olives, pitted, coarsely chopped**

CHAR bell peppers directly over gas flame or in broiler until blackened on all sides. Enclose in paper bag; let stand 10 minutes. Peel, seed, and slice peppers thinly.

COMBINE basil, garlic, and salt in processor and blend to coarse puree. With machine running, gradually blend in oil. Transfer basil dressing to small bowl; season to taste with salt and pepper. *(Peppers and dressing can be made 1 day ahead. Cover separately and chill.)*

ARRANGE prosciutto around edge of platter. Arrange cheese slices within circle of prosciutto and tomatoes within circle of cheese. Tuck in egg slices; top with pepper strips. Sprinkle salad with olives; drizzle with some basil dressing. Serve, passing remaining dressing separately.

Curried couscous with roasted vegetables, peach chutney, and cilantro yogurt

A SIGNATURE ELEMENT of the North African culinary repertoire, couscous takes on Indian flavors—including curry, yogurt, cilantro, and lime—in this salad, which is substantial enough to be a main course.

6 TO 8 SERVINGS

Cilantro yogurt

- **3 cups (loosely packed) fresh cilantro leaves (from 3 large bunches)**
- **1 tablespoon fresh lime juice**
- **3/4 teaspoon salt**
- **1/2 cup plain whole-milk yogurt**
- **1/2 cup sour cream**

Roasted vegetables

- **Nonstick vegetable oil spray**
- **2 1-pound eggplants, unpeeled, cut into 1-inch cubes**
- **6 tablespoons corn oil, divided**
- **1 1/4 pounds medium zucchini, halved lengthwise, cut crosswise into 1-inch-thick pieces**

- **3 large red bell peppers**

Couscous

- **2 tablespoons corn oil, divided**
- **1 medium onion, chopped**
- **1 tablespoon curry powder**
- **3 cups water**

- **2 cups plain couscous**
- **1/2 cup coarsely chopped roasted, salted cashews**
- **1/4 cup dried currants**

- **Peach Chutney (see recipe)**

FOR CILANTRO YOGURT: Combine cilantro, lime juice, and salt in processor; blend to coarse puree. Transfer to medium bowl; mix in yogurt and sour cream. Season to taste with pepper. *(Cilantro yogurt can be prepared 1 day ahead. Cover and chill.)*

FOR ROASTED VEGETABLES: Preheat oven to 400°F. Spray 2 large rimmed baking sheets with nonstick spray. Mound eggplant cubes on 1 prepared sheet; drizzle with 4 tablespoons oil. Sprinkle with salt and pepper; toss to coat. Spread out evenly. Mound zucchini on second prepared sheet; drizzle with remaining 2 tablespoons oil. Sprinkle with salt and pepper; toss to coat. Spread out evenly. Roast eggplant and zucchini until golden and tender, turning occasionally with spatula, about 25 minutes for zucchini and 50 minutes for eggplant. Transfer vegetables to bowl and cool.

MEANWHILE, char peppers directly over gas flame or in broiler until blackened on all sides. Enclose in paper bag; let stand 10 minutes. Peel and seed peppers. Cut 2 peppers into 1-inch pieces. Thinly slice remaining pepper and reserve for garnish.

FOR COUSCOUS: Heat 1 tablespoon oil in heavy large saucepan over medium-high heat. Add onion; sauté until soft, about 5 minutes. Mix in curry powder; stir 1 minute. Add 3 cups water; bring to simmer. Cover, reduce heat to medium-low, and simmer 10 minutes.

HEAT remaining 1 tablespoon oil in heavy large pot over medium-high heat. Add couscous and stir constantly until color darkens slightly and couscous is toasted, about 3 minutes. Mix in hot curry water. Turn off heat, cover pot, and let stand until couscous is tender and liquid is absorbed, about 10 minutes. Fluff couscous with fork to separate grains. Mix in cashews and currants and cool completely. Mix in eggplant, zucchini, and bell pepper pieces. Season salad to taste with salt and pepper.

MOUND salad on large platter; garnish with reserved bell pepper slices. Serve with cilantro yogurt and peach chutney.

Peach chutney

MIX DICED COOKED CHICKEN and some mayo into the chutney for a stylish chicken salad. Or mix the chutney and some toasted almonds into cooked white rice for a Middle Eastern–style pilaf.

MAKES ABOUT 4 CUPS

- **4 green onions, chopped**
- **¼ cup dried currants**
- **1 tablespoon Sherry wine vinegar**
- **2 teaspoons grated peeled fresh ginger**
- **1¾ pounds peaches (about 4 medium), peeled, halved, pitted**

COMBINE green onions, currants, vinegar, and ginger in medium bowl. Cut peaches into ⅓-inch cubes. Add to onion mixture and toss to coat. Season chutney to taste with salt and pepper. Cover; chill at least 1 hour and up to 6 hours, tossing occasionally.

Tomato and bread salad with basil and red onion

IN TUSCANY, leftover bread is put to many uses, including this sensational salad, a classic dish of the region. Called *panzanella*—a play on the word *pantanella,* which means "little swamp"—the salad calls for the bread to be softened in water, then squeezed dry and tossed with the salad, where it soaks up the delicious vinaigrette. It is important that the bread be a few days old and coarse in texture; keep the crusts on when cutting it into pieces.

6 FIRST-COURSE SERVINGS

- **⅓ cup red wine vinegar**
- **½ cup extra-virgin olive oil**

- **8 ounces stale Italian bread, cut into 2-inch pieces**
- **8 cups (about) cold water**
- **2 pounds plum tomatoes, coarsely chopped (about 5 cups)**
- **1 small red onion, thinly sliced**
- **1 cup (loosely packed) fresh basil leaves, torn into bite-size pieces**

POUR vinegar into small bowl. Gradually whisk in oil. Season vinaigrette to taste with salt and pepper.

PLACE bread in large bowl. Pour in enough cold water (about 8 cups) to cover bread. Soak 5 minutes. Drain well; squeeze bread to remove as much water as possible. Wipe bowl dry. Coarsely crumble bread into same bowl. Add tomatoes, onion, and basil. Toss with enough vinaigrette to coat. Season salad generously to taste with salt and pepper. *(Salad can be made 8 hours ahead. Cover and refrigerate. Let stand 1 hour at room temperature before serving.)*

Fennel, watercress, radicchio, and Parmesan salad

CRUNCHY LIKE CELERY and flavored like licorice, fennel is a distinctive and delicious vegetable that works beautifully in salads. At the market, avoid fennel bulbs that are brown or cracked or have moist areas. For ease of crushing and clean-up, crush the fennel seeds in a plastic bag.

4 SERVINGS

- **¼ cup olive oil**
- **3 tablespoons balsamic vinegar**
- **2 tablespoons grated Parmesan cheese**
- **½ teaspoon fennel seeds, crushed**
- **1 large fresh fennel bulb, trimmed, thinly sliced**
- **1 large bunch watercress, thick stems trimmed**
- **1 small head of radicchio, thinly sliced**

- **1 4-ounce piece Parmesan cheese**

WHISK oil, vinegar, 2 tablespoons grated cheese, and fennel seeds in small bowl to blend. Season dressing to taste with salt and pepper. Toss sliced fennel, watercress, and radicchio in large bowl. *(Can be prepared 8 hours ahead. Cover dressing and salad mixture separately. Refrigerate salad mixture.)*

USING vegetable peeler, shave cheese piece into strips. Rewhisk dressing to blend. Toss fennel, watercress, and radicchio with enough dressing to coat lightly. Add cheese strips and toss to blend. Serve, passing remaining dressing separately.

Caesar salad with sourdough croutons

TO KEEP ROMAINE LETTUCE as fresh as possible, rinse it in cold water, then dry it. Wrap the leaves in a few dry paper towels, place in a plastic bag, squeeze out as much air as possible, and seal the bag tightly. The lettuce should keep about one week in the refrigerator.

6 SERVINGS

- **½ cup fresh lemon juice**
- **2 tablespoons Worcestershire sauce**
- **4 garlic cloves, coarsely chopped**
- **½ teaspoon hot pepper sauce**
- **1 cup olive oil**

- **2 large heads of romaine lettuce, torn into bite-size pieces**
- **1 red onion, thinly sliced**
- **Sourdough Croutons (see recipe)**
- **1 cup freshly grated Parmesan cheese (about 3 ounces)**

BLEND first 4 ingredients in processor or blender. With machine running, gradually add oil in thin steady stream and blend well. Season dressing to taste with salt and pepper. (Can be prepared 1 day ahead. Cover and chill. Bring to room temperature and rewhisk before using.)

COMBINE lettuce, onion, and croutons in large bowl. Toss with enough dressing to coat. Sprinkle salad with cheese.

Sourdough croutons

FRESH HOMEMADE CROUTONS, so simple to prepare, can transform a salad—there'll be no reason to use a stale-tasting store-bought variety after you've tried these. Keep the crusts on when making the croutons.

MAKES ABOUT 6 CUPS

6 **cups 3/4-inch cubes sourdough bread (about 6 ounces)**
1/2 **teaspoon garlic powder**
1/4 **cup olive oil**
6 **tablespoons freshly grated Parmesan cheese (about 1 1/2 ounces)**

PREHEAT oven to 350°F. Place bread cubes in large bowl. Sprinkle with garlic powder. Drizzle oil over and toss to coat evenly. Add Parmesan cheese and toss to coat. Spread out cubes on heavy large baking sheet; sprinkle with salt and pepper. Bake until golden brown, using metal spatula to turn bread cubes occasionally, about 15 minutes. Cool croutons completely. *(Can be prepared 1 day ahead. Store in airtight container at room temperature.)*

Prosciutto-wrapped shrimp with garbanzo bean and artichoke salad

THIS FIRST-COURSE SALAD features freshly cooked shrimp wrapped in prosciutto, then arranged atop a simple salad of roasted red bell peppers, garbanzo beans, and artichoke hearts, accented with a garlicky dressing.

10 FIRST-COURSE SERVINGS

2 **small red bell peppers**
3 **15- to 16-ounce cans garbanzo beans (chickpeas), rinsed, drained**
10 **canned whole artichoke hearts, drained, patted dry, quartered**

20 **uncooked large shrimp, peeled, deveined (tails left intact)**
5 **paper-thin slices prosciutto, each slice cut lengthwise into 4 strips**

10 **radicchio leaves**
Balsamic Dressing (see recipe)
Pickled hot or sweet cherry peppers, drained
Kalamata olives

CHAR bell peppers directly over gas flame or in broiler until blackened on all sides. Enclose in paper bag; let stand 10 minutes. Peel and seed peppers, then cut into matchstick-size strips. Transfer to large bowl. Add garbanzo beans and artichoke hearts.

BRING large saucepan of salted water to boil. Remove from heat and add shrimp. Let stand until shrimp are just opaque in center, stirring occasionally, about 5 minutes. Drain. Pat shrimp dry with paper towels. Transfer shrimp to medium bowl and chill until cold. Wrap each shrimp with 1 prosciutto strip; return to same bowl. *(Can be prepared 8 hours ahead. Cover garbanzo bean mixture and prosciutto-wrapped shrimp separately and refrigerate.)*

PLACE radicchio leaves on plates. Toss garbanzo bean mixture with enough balsamic dressing to coat. Season to taste with salt and pepper. Spoon salad into radicchio leaves, dividing equally. Top with prosciutto-wrapped shrimp. Drizzle some dressing over shrimp. Garnish salads with pickled peppers and olives.

Balsamic dressing

THIS SIMPLE, TANGY balsamic vinaigrette can become a staple in your salad repertoire. It makes an excellent partner for any tossed green salad.

MAKES ABOUT 3/4 CUP

3 **tablespoons balsamic vinegar**
2 **tablespoons fresh lemon juice**
1 **tablespoon Dijon mustard**
2 **garlic cloves, minced**
1/2 **cup olive oil**

WHISK first 4 ingredients in medium bowl to blend. Gradually whisk in oil. Season dressing to taste with salt and pepper. *(Can be prepared 8 hours ahead. Cover and chill. Bring to room temperature and rewhisk before using.)*

Marinated shrimp, scallop, and caper salad with Sherry vinaigrette

THE RED PEPPER–INFUSED DRESSING also acts as a marinade for the seafood. Sherry wine vinegar, widely used in Spain and made from the fortified wine produced in Jerez, has become very popular in the United States and is now made here. It can be an excellent substitute for fine red wine vinegar.

4 SERVINGS

1 tablespoon plus ½ cup olive oil
12 ounces uncooked large shrimp, peeled, deveined
12 ounces bay scallops

3½ tablespoons Sherry wine vinegar
2 garlic cloves, minced
½ teaspoon dried crushed red pepper
½ medium red onion, sliced
⅓ cup drained capers

8 cups mixed baby greens
3 medium tomatoes, sliced
1 large avocado, peeled, pitted, sliced

HEAT 1 tablespoon oil in heavy large skillet over high heat. Add shrimp to skillet; sauté 2 minutes. Add scallops and sprinkle with salt and pepper. Sauté until shrimp and scallops are just opaque in center, about 2 minutes. Transfer to medium bowl; cool. Drain off any accumulated juice.

WHISK vinegar, garlic, and crushed red pepper in small bowl to blend. Whisk in remaining ½ cup oil. Add to shrimp mixture. Mix in onion and capers. Season to taste with salt and pepper. Chill at least 1 hour or up to 3 hours, tossing occasionally.

PLACE greens in large bowl. Drizzle with some vinaigrette from shrimp mixture, tossing to coat. Using slotted spoon, arrange shrimp mixture atop greens. Place tomato and avocado slices around edge of salad, overlapping slightly. Drizzle with any remaining vinaigrette.

Smoked trout, watercress, and apple salad with creamy horseradish dressing

SWEET APPLE (any kind of red apple will do), smoked trout, and peppery watercress team up in a sophisticated salad that would make a terrific first course for any special-occasion meal. If you can't find smoked trout or whitefish chubs at your local supermarket, check your favorite delicatessen or specialty foods store. If using chubs, you'll need to skin and bone them.

6 SERVINGS

1 cup whipping cream
⅓ cup prepared white horseradish
4 tablespoons olive oil, divided
2 tablespoons plus 2 teaspoons apple cider vinegar
2 teaspoons finely chopped fresh dill
⅛ teaspoon cayenne pepper

6 cups trimmed watercress sprigs (from about 2 bunches)
½ cup very thinly sliced red onion
2 red apples, halved, cored, thinly sliced
9 ounces smoked trout or smoked whitefish chubs, coarsely flaked (about 1½ cups)
Fresh dill sprigs (optional)

WHISK cream, horseradish, 2 tablespoons oil, 2 tablespoons vinegar, chopped dill, and cayenne in small bowl to blend. Season dressing with salt and pepper.

PLACE watercress in large bowl. Add ⅓ cup dressing, remaining 2 tablespoons oil, and 2 teaspoons vinegar; toss to coat. Mound watercress in center of each of 6 plates. Top with sliced onion. Fan apple slices atop salad. Top with trout. Spoon dressing over. Garnish salads with dill sprigs, if desired.

Salad of mixed greens with salmon rillettes

RILLETTES IS THE TERM for a French pâté that is usually made with pork or rabbit combined with fat and seasonings. It is presented in little pots or ramekins as an appetizer spread. This adaptation is prepared with smoked salmon, and uses Dijon mustard and olive oil for lighter texture and flavor. It is then spread on baguette slices and goes on top of a simple salad of mixed lettuces.

4 FIRST-COURSE SERVINGS

3 tablespoons Dijon mustard
1/3 cup olive oil
1/4 cup finely chopped fresh chives
3 ounces smoked salmon, finely chopped

4 1/2-inch-thick slices French bread baguette, toasted
6 cups mixed baby greens

PLACE mustard in small bowl. Gradually add oil, whisking until well blended and thick. Whisk in chives. Season dressing to taste with salt and pepper. Place salmon in small bowl. Stir 2 tablespoons dressing into salmon. *(Can be prepared 6 hours ahead. Cover dressing and salmon separately. Refrigerate salmon.)*

SPREAD salmon rillettes on toasted baguette slices, mounding slightly. Toss greens with remaining dressing. Divide salad among plates. Top with salmon toasts.

Fiesta chicken salad with lime-cilantro vinaigrette

QUESO AÑEJO IS A dry, white aged cheese available at Latin markets. Shelled pumpkin seeds, or *pepitas*, can be found there too, as well as at natural foods stores.

6 SERVINGS

Vinaigrette

1/2 cup chopped shallots
1/4 cup fresh lime juice
1/4 cup chopped fresh cilantro
3 garlic cloves, minced
1/2 cup vegetable oil

Salad

3 cups thinly sliced red leaf lettuce
3 cups thinly sliced Napa cabbage
1 cup diced cooked chicken breast
2 plum tomatoes, seeded, chopped
1/2 red bell pepper, thinly sliced
1/2 yellow bell pepper, thinly sliced
1/2 avocado, halved, pitted, peeled, diced
1/3 cup crumbled tortilla chips
1/4 cup cooked fresh corn kernels or frozen, thawed
1/4 cup pumpkin seeds (pepitas), toasted
1/4 cup thinly sliced onion
1/2 cup crumbled queso añejo or feta cheese (about 2 ounces)

FOR VINAIGRETTE: Combine first 4 ingredients in medium bowl. Gradually whisk in oil. Season vinaigrette to taste with salt and pepper. *(Can be made 1 day ahead. Cover and chill. Bring to room temperature and rewhisk before using.)*

FOR SALAD: Combine all ingredients except cheese in large bowl. Toss with enough vinaigrette to coat. Sprinkle with cheese.

Roasted chicken, bell pepper, and onion salad

THE CHICKEN, BELL PEPPERS, and onions are roasted after being tossed with a delicious sauce of balsamic vinegar, olive oil, and fresh rosemary. The roasting reduces the coating to a glaze that echoes the balsamic dressing the salad gets tossed with before serving.

8 SERVINGS

Chicken and vegetables

- **2/3 cup olive oil**
- **2/3 cup balsamic vinegar**
- **1/4 cup chopped fresh rosemary or 2 tablespoons dried**
- **5 garlic cloves, minced**
- **1/2 teaspoon dried crushed red pepper**
- **4 pounds chicken breast halves with skin and bones**
- **3 large red bell peppers, cut into 1/2-inch-wide strips**
- **2 large yellow bell peppers, cut into 1/2-inch-wide strips**
- **3 large red onions, cut into 1/2-inch-thick rounds**

Dressing

- **2 teaspoons Dijon mustard**
- **2 teaspoons balsamic vinegar or red wine vinegar**
- **1/4 cup olive oil**
- **4 teaspoons finely grated orange peel**
- **1 teaspoon chopped fresh rosemary**

Ornamental kale leaves
Fresh rosemary sprigs

FOR CHICKEN AND VEGETABLES: Preheat oven to 425°F. Whisk first 5 ingredients in medium bowl to blend. Place chicken breasts in large roasting pan. Brush chicken on both sides with oil mixture. Sprinkle both sides with salt and pepper. Arrange chicken skin side up in pan. Divide vegetables between 2 large rimmed baking sheets. Drizzle remaining oil mixture over vegetables; toss to coat. Sprinkle vegetables with salt and pepper. Bake chicken until just cooked through, about 35 minutes. Bake vegetables until edges are brown, stirring occasionally, about 40 minutes. Cool slightly.

MEANWHILE PREPARE DRESSING: Combine mustard and vinegar in large bowl. Whisk in oil. Add orange peel and rosemary. Season with salt and pepper.

REMOVE skin and bones from chicken. Cut chicken into ½-inch-wide strips. Add chicken to dressing and toss to coat. Mix in roasted vegetables. Season salad to taste with salt and pepper. *(Salad can be prepared 1 day ahead. Cover and refrigerate.)*

LINE platter with kale. Spoon salad over. Garnish with rosemary sprigs.

Grilled chicken salad with mustard-rosemary dressing

BEFORE GRILLING, the chicken is rubbed with a mixture of Dijon mustard, fresh rosemary, and garlic. The meaty shiitake mushroom is available almost year-round in many supermarkets; select plump mushrooms with edges that curl under, and be sure to cut off the woody stem.

2 SERVINGS

- **5 teaspoons Dijon mustard, divided**
- **4 teaspoons minced fresh rosemary, divided**
- **3 garlic cloves, pressed**
- **2 boneless chicken breast halves with skin**
- **1 tablespoon plus 1/2 cup olive oil**

- **3 tablespoons fresh lemon juice**
- **2 teaspoons coarse-grained Dijon mustard**
- **2 teaspoons minced shallot**

- **6 shiitake mushrooms, stemmed**
- **4 cups mixed baby greens (such as frisée, arugula, radicchio, and oakleaf lettuce)**
- **8 asparagus spears, trimmed, blanched**
- **1 tomato, peeled, seeded, chopped**

MIX 1 teaspoon Dijon mustard, 2 teaspoons rosemary, and garlic in small bowl. Run fingertips between chicken skin and meat to loosen. Rub mustard mixture under and over skin. Place chicken on plate. Drizzle 1 tablespoon oil over chicken. Cover and refrigerate at least 2 hours and up to 1 day.

WHISK remaining 4 teaspoons Dijon mustard, 2 teaspoons rosemary, lemon juice, coarse-grained mustard, and shallot in small bowl to blend. Whisk in remaining ½ cup oil. Season dressing to taste with salt and pepper.

PREPARE barbecue (medium-high heat). Sprinkle chicken with salt and pepper. Grill until cooked through, turning occasionally, about 15 minutes. Transfer to cutting board; tent with foil to keep warm. Toss mushrooms and 1 tablespoon dressing in medium bowl to coat. Grill mushrooms until soft, turning once, about 3 minutes. Toss greens in large bowl with enough dressing to coat. Divide greens between 2 plates. Cut chicken crosswise on diagonal into thin slices and fan atop greens. Spoon more dressing over chicken. Garnish salads with mushrooms, asparagus, and tomato.

Grilled steak salad with green beans and blue cheese

THE THIN, DELICATE French green beans called haricots verts are perfect for this salad, but if you can't find them, look for the skinniest American green beans you can find–they are the most tender. Also look for beans that are crisp, and put aside ones that have brown spots.

6 SERVINGS

1 pound slender green beans, trimmed

6 cups baby arugula (about 6 ounces)
4 cups cherry tomatoes, halved
1¼ cups pitted Kalamata olives, halved
½ cup plus 1 tablespoon olive oil
3 tablespoons balsamic vinegar

3 8- to 9-ounce strip loin steaks

1 cup crumbled blue cheese (about 4 ounces)

COOK green beans in pot of boiling salted water until crisp-tender, about 4 minutes. Drain. Transfer to bowl of ice water and cool. Drain.

PREPARE barbecue (medium-high heat). Combine beans, arugula, tomatoes, and olives in large bowl. Whisk ½ cup oil and vinegar in small bowl to blend. Season dressing to taste with salt and pepper.

BRUSH steaks with remaining 1 tablespoon oil; sprinkle with salt and pepper. Grill to desired doneness, about 4 minutes per side for medium-rare. Transfer steaks to work surface; let stand 5 minutes. Cut steaks crosswise into thin strips.

TOSS salad with enough dressing to coat. Divide salad among 6 plates. Top with steak strips. Sprinkle cheese over.

Southwestern grilled beef salad with corn salsa and chipotle dressing

CHIPOTLE CHILES are smoked jalapeños, available packed in complexly spiced *adobo* sauce; they are sold at Latin markets and specialty foods stores, and in the Latin American section of the supermarket. An extra layer of spice can be found in the rub for the steak. (The rub is also excellent on chicken, pork, shrimp, or firm fish like swordfish or halibut.) All that spicy flavor is cooled down nicely by greens, avocado, and mangoes. When preparing the mangoes, peel them first and set on their largest end. Separate the fruit from the pit with a sharp knife by cutting straight down along the outside of the pit.

6 SERVINGS

Dressing

¼ cup fresh lime juice
¼ cup chopped fresh cilantro
1 tablespoon chopped canned chipotle chiles
2 large garlic cloves, pressed
1 cup olive oil

Salsa

2 ears fresh corn, husked
4 plum tomatoes, seeded, chopped
1 cup chopped peeled jicama
½ cup chopped red onion
¼ cup chopped fresh cilantro

Steak

1½ tablespoons fresh lime juice
1 tablespoon ground cumin
1 tablespoon chili powder
3 large garlic cloves, pressed
2 pounds 1-inch-thick beef tenderloin steaks

Assembly

- **1 avocado, halved, pitted, peeled, diced**
- **10 cups mixed baby greens**
- **2 small mangoes, peeled, pitted, thinly sliced**

FOR DRESSING: Whisk first 4 ingredients in medium bowl to blend. Gradually whisk in oil. Season dressing to taste with salt and pepper. *(Can be made 1 day ahead. Cover and refrigerate.)*

FOR SALSA: Cook corn in large pot of boiling salted water 2 minutes. Drain. Cool. Cut corn kernels from cob. Transfer corn kernels to large bowl. Add tomatoes, jicama, onion, and cilantro; mix. *(Salsa can be prepared 6 hours ahead. Cover and chill.)*

FOR STEAK: Whisk first 4 ingredients in small bowl to blend. Sprinkle steaks with salt and pepper. Spread spice paste over both sides of steaks. Cover and refrigerate at least 2 hours and up to 6 hours.

TO ASSEMBLE: Prepare barbecue (medium-high heat). Grill steaks to desired doneness, about 5 minutes per side for medium-rare. Transfer steaks to cutting board and let stand 5 minutes.

MEANWHILE, mix avocado and 2 tablespoons dressing into salsa. Season to taste with salt and pepper. Place greens in large bowl and toss with enough dressing to coat. Divide greens equally among 6 plates. Fan some mango slices on 1 side of each salad. Top each salad with ½ cup salsa.

THINLY slice steaks crosswise. Arrange atop greens. Serve, passing remaining dressing separately.

Grilled shrimp, corn, and black bean tostada salad

THIS SPIN on the classic tostada features many of the traditional elements—lettuce, chopped tomatoes, and onions—but showcases black beans instead of refried beans, as well as grilled shrimp and corn.

4 SERVINGS

Dressing

- **5 tablespoons fresh lime juice**
- **¾ cup olive oil**
- **6 tablespoons chopped fresh cilantro**
- **1½ tablespoons minced seeded jalapeño chile (preferably red)**
- **1 tablespoon ground cumin**

Salad

- **3 cups chopped seeded tomatoes**
- **1 15-ounce can black beans, rinsed, drained**
- **1 cup chopped green onions**
- **¾ cup chopped fresh cilantro**
- **¾ cup chopped red onion**

- **6 cups shredded iceberg lettuce (about 1 small head)**
- **2 ears fresh corn, husked**
- **24 uncooked large shrimp (about 1½ pounds), peeled, deveined (tails left intact)**

- **24 large tortilla chips**
- **Additional chopped fresh cilantro (optional)**

FOR DRESSING: Place lime juice in medium bowl. Gradually whisk in olive oil. Mix in cilantro, jalapeño, and cumin. Season dressing to taste with salt and pepper.

FOR SALAD: Combine tomatoes, beans, green onions, ¾ cup chopped cilantro, and red onion in large bowl. *(Dressing and salad can be prepared 6 hours ahead. Cover dressing and let stand at room temperature. Cover salad and refrigerate.)*

PREPARE barbecue (medium-high heat). Mix lettuce into salad. Pour ¼ cup dressing into small bowl; reserve remainder for salad. Brush corn with dressing from small bowl. Grill corn until beginning to brown, turning often, about 5 minutes. Transfer corn to work surface. Brush shrimp with dressing from small bowl. Grill until just opaque in center, turning occasionally, about 5 minutes.

CUT kernels from corn and add to salad. Toss salad with enough reserved dressing to coat. Top salad with shrimp. Garnish with tortilla chips; sprinkle with additional cilantro, if desired.

Grilled Asian-style scallop and asparagus salad

THIS LIGHT SALAD features a wonderful medley of flavors, including soy sauce, shallot, ginger, and sesame oil. Sesame oil is dark and richly flavored, and a little goes a long way. The scallops don't need to be cooked long; be sure to remove them from the grill when they still feel a bit soft to the touch. And before grilling, if there is a chewy side hinge connecting the mollusk to its shell, peel it away with your fingers.

4 SERVINGS

Dressing

- **3 tablespoons balsamic vinegar**
- **1½ tablespoons soy sauce**
- **1 large shallot, minced**
- **1 large garlic clove, minced**
- **1½ teaspoons grated peeled fresh ginger**
- **¾ teaspoon Asian sesame oil**
- **6 tablespoons vegetable oil**

Salad

- **24 sea scallops, connective muscle removed**
- **4 tablespoons vegetable oil, divided**
- **1 teaspoon Asian sesame oil**

- **1 pound thin asparagus, trimmed**
- **10 cups mixed baby greens**
- **⅓ cup fresh cilantro leaves**

FOR DRESSING: Combine first 6 ingredients in small bowl. Gradually whisk in vegetable oil. Season dressing to taste with salt and pepper. *(Can be prepared 3 days ahead; cover and refrigerate. Bring to room temperature and rewhisk before using.)*

FOR SALAD: Combine scallops, 2 tablespoons vegetable oil, and sesame oil in medium bowl; toss to coat. Refrigerate 20 minutes.

PREPARE barbecue (medium-high heat). Brush asparagus with remaining 2 tablespoons vegetable oil. Sprinkle with salt and pepper. Grill asparagus and scallops until asparagus is brown and crisp-tender and scallops are just opaque in center, turning occasionally, about 4 minutes. Transfer asparagus and scallops to plate. Drizzle with 3 tablespoons dressing.

MEANWHILE, combine greens and cilantro in large bowl. Toss with enough remaining dressing to coat. Divide salad among plates. Arrange asparagus and scallops decoratively atop salads.

Grilled vegetable salad with greens, tomatoes, herbs, olives, and cheese

RED ONION, BEETS, ZUCCHINI, eggplants, and red bell peppers are grilled and then arranged atop greens, and complemented with tomatoes, herbs, and olives. You can add and subtract any vegetables you like—the beauty of this salad lies in its versatility.

6 SERVINGS

- **¾ cup olive oil**
- **¼ cup balsamic vinegar**
- **12 baby beets, stems trimmed to 1 inch, peeled, halved lengthwise**
- **3 small zucchini, each cut lengthwise into 4 slices**
- **3 Japanese eggplants, each cut lengthwise into 4 slices**
- **2 large red bell peppers, cut into 1-inch-wide strips**
- **1 large red onion, cut into ¾-inch-thick rounds**
- **6 slices crusty country-style French bread**
- **Additional olive oil**

- **10 cups mixed baby greens**
- **4 large tomatoes, sliced**
- **3 tablespoons chopped fresh basil**
- **2 tablespoons chopped fresh chives**
- **1 tablespoon chopped fresh marjoram**
- **¾ cup soft fresh goat cheese, crumbled (about 3 ounces)**

½ cup freshly grated pecorino Romano cheese (about 1½ ounces)
¾ cup Kalamata olives

PREPARE barbecue (medium-high heat). Whisk ¾ cup oil and vinegar in medium bowl to blend. Season vinaigrette to taste with salt and pepper. Place beets, zucchini, eggplants, red bell peppers, and onion on 2 large rimmed baking sheets. Brush both sides of vegetables with some of vinaigrette; sprinkle with salt and pepper. Grill vegetables until just cooked through, about 10 minutes per side for beets, 6 minutes per side for onion, and 4 minutes per side for zucchini, eggplants, and peppers. Return to same baking sheets. *(Vegetables can be grilled 1 hour ahead. Let stand at room temperature.)* Brush bread with additional olive oil; sprinkle with salt and pepper. Grill bread until beginning to brown, about 2 minutes per side. Transfer to basket.

ARRANGE greens on large platter. Overlap tomatoes atop greens in center of platter. Sprinkle tomatoes with salt and pepper. Arrange grilled vegetables atop greens around tomatoes. Drizzle remaining vinaigrette over tomatoes and grilled vegetables. Sprinkle tomatoes and vegetables with herbs. Sprinkle tomatoes with goat cheese. Sprinkle Romano cheese over all. Garnish with olives. Serve with grilled bread.

Warm goat cheese salad with pears and walnuts

MIXED GREENS ARE TOSSED with sliced Belgian endive—an elegant addition that complements the pears and sautéed walnuts nicely. The warm goat cheese rounds crown the salad with a special-occasion touch, but they don't take long to prepare.

4 SERVINGS

1¼ cups fresh breadcrumbs made from crustless country-style French bread
2 tablespoons minced fresh thyme
1 11-ounce log soft fresh goat cheese, cut into 8 rounds
1 egg, beaten to blend

2 tablespoons plus ¾ teaspoon white wine vinegar
1 tablespoon Dijon mustard
½ cup plus 3 tablespoons walnut oil
8 cups mixed baby greens
2 heads of Belgian endive, cut crosswise into ½-inch pieces
2 large ripe pears, peeled, cored, cut into ¼-inch-thick slices

⅓ cup chopped walnuts

MIX breadcrumbs and thyme in glass pie dish. Sprinkle cheese rounds with salt and pepper. Dip rounds into beaten egg, then into breadcrumbs, coating completely. Transfer to plate. Cover and refrigerate until ready to use. *(Can be prepared 4 hours ahead.)*

WHISK vinegar and mustard in small bowl to blend. Gradually whisk in ½ cup oil. Season dressing to taste with salt and pepper. Combine mixed greens, endive, and pears in large bowl.

HEAT remaining 3 tablespoons oil in heavy large nonstick skillet over medium-high heat. Add walnuts and sauté until lightly toasted, about 2 minutes. Using slotted spoon, transfer walnuts to plate. Reduce heat to medium. Add cheese rounds to skillet and cook until crisp, brown, and warmed through, about 2 minutes per side.

TOSS salad with enough dressing to coat. Divide among 4 plates. Using metal spatula, place 2 cheese rounds in center of each salad. Sprinkle with walnuts.

Goat cheese salad with pancetta, dried cherry, and Port dressing

THIS SALAD IS DRESSED with a sensational cooked dressing that begins with the sautéing of pancetta (an Italian salt-cured bacon available at Italian markets and in the refrigerated deli case of many supermarkets). Olive oil, red wine vinegar, and sugar come next, then dried cherries macerated in tawny Port. If dried cherries are difficult to find, dried cranberries are a good alternative.

4 SERVINGS

1¼ cups dried tart cherries
½ cup tawny Port

5 ounces pancetta or bacon, chopped
2 shallots, minced
1 garlic clove, minced
⅓ cup olive oil
¼ cup red wine vinegar
2 teaspoons sugar

1 5.5-ounce log soft fresh goat cheese, cut into ½-inch-thick rounds

1 5-ounce bag mixed baby greens
½ cup pine nuts, toasted

COMBINE cherries and Port in heavy small saucepan. Bring to simmer over medium heat. Remove from heat; let stand until cherries soften, about 15 minutes.

SAUTÉ pancetta in heavy large skillet over medium-low heat until crisp, about 8 minutes. Add shallots and garlic; sauté 2 minutes. Add oil, then vinegar and sugar; stir until sugar dissolves. Stir in cherry mixture. Season dressing to taste with salt and pepper. *(Can be made 2 hours ahead. Set aside in skillet at room temperature.)*

PREHEAT oven to 350°F. Place goat cheese rounds on rimmed nonstick baking sheet. Bake until just warm, about 10 minutes.

MEANWHILE, combine greens and pine nuts in large bowl. Rewarm dressing in skillet and pour over salad; toss to blend. Top with warm goat cheese.

Curly endive and bacon salad with mustard-anchovy dressing

HERE'S A VERSION of the quintessential Parisian bistro salad. Dijon mustard, lemon juice, and anchovy paste give the dressing robust flavor, as do homemade garlicky croutons and smoky bacon. Curly endive has a softly bitter taste that is bracing in salads.

8 SERVINGS

2 tablespoons Dijon mustard
2 tablespoons fresh lemon juice
1 tablespoon anchovy paste
¾ teaspoon ground black pepper
⅔ cup plus ¼ cup olive oil

12 ounces ¼-inch-thick bacon slices, cut into ½-inch pieces
2 garlic cloves, lightly crushed
4 cups ¾-inch cubes crustless country-style French bread
1 head of curly endive, torn into bite-size pieces

WHISK first 4 ingredients in small bowl. Gradually whisk in ⅔ cup oil. Season dressing to taste with salt. *(Can be prepared 1 day ahead. Cover and refrigerate. Bring to room temperature and rewhisk before using.)*

COOK bacon in heavy large skillet over medium heat until crisp and brown. Using slotted spoon, transfer bacon to paper towels to drain. Pour off all but 2 tablespoons fat from skillet. Add remaining ¼ cup oil and garlic to same skillet; sauté over medium heat until garlic is golden, about 5 minutes. Using slotted spoon, remove garlic from skillet and discard. Add bread to skillet and toss to coat with garlic oil. Cook until crisp and golden, about 10 minutes. Transfer croutons to large bowl. Add endive and bacon. Toss with enough dressing to coat. Divide salad among plates.

Pasta salad with mozzarella, sun-dried tomatoes, and olives

THIS EASY SALAD has a wonderful medley of assertive flavors, contrasting with the water-packed fresh mozzarella, which is made from whole milk and features a softer texture and a more delicate flavor than regular mozzarella. If you can't find fresh mozzarella at your local supermarket, check the nearest Italian delicatessen or specialty foods store, or substitute regular mozzarella. You can use any kind of tomatoes and olives you like.

8 SERVINGS

½ cup drained oil-packed sun-dried tomatoes
6 tablespoons olive oil
¼ cup red wine vinegar
1 tablespoon drained capers
1 garlic clove, minced

1 pound fusilli pasta
12 ounces tomatoes, coarsely chopped
8 ounces water-packed fresh mozzarella cheese, drained, cut into ½-inch cubes
1 cup (packed) fresh basil leaves, thinly sliced
1 cup freshly grated Parmesan cheese (about 3 ounces)
½ cup minced pitted oil-cured black olives

BLEND first 5 ingredients in processor until dried tomatoes are coarsely chopped. Season dressing to taste with salt and pepper.

COOK pasta in large pot of boiling salted water until tender but still firm to bite, stirring occasionally. Drain. Transfer to large bowl. Add dressing to hot pasta; toss to coat. Cool, stirring occasionally. Add fresh tomatoes, mozzarella, basil, Parmesan, and olives; toss to blend. Season to taste with salt and pepper. *(Salad can be made 6 hours ahead. Cover; chill. Bring to room temperature before serving.)*

Orzo with everything

EVERYTHING MEANS a lot of delicious ingredients, such as sun-dried tomatoes, balsamic vinegar, Kalamata olives, radicchio, pine nuts, basil, and Parmesan cheese. Pine nuts have a high fat content, so they turn rancid quickly at room temperature. After buying them, store them in an airtight container in the refrigerator up to three months or in the freezer up to nine months.

6 SERVINGS

1½ cups orzo (rice-shaped pasta; about 10 ounces)
⅓ cup (packed) chopped drained oil-packed sun-dried tomatoes
5 tablespoons extra-virgin olive oil
¼ cup balsamic vinegar
¼ cup (packed) chopped pitted Kalamata olives

1 cup finely chopped radicchio (from 1 small head)
½ cup pine nuts, toasted
½ cup chopped fresh basil
½ cup freshly grated Parmesan cheese (about 1½ ounces)
2 large garlic cloves, minced

COOK orzo in pot of boiling salted water until tender but still firm to bite, stirring occasionally. Drain well. Transfer to large bowl. Add sun-dried tomatoes, oil, vinegar, and olives; toss to blend. Let stand until cool. *(Can be prepared 6 hours ahead. Cover and refrigerate. Bring to room temperature before continuing.)*

MIX radicchio, pine nuts, basil, Parmesan, and garlic into orzo mixture. Season salad to taste with salt and pepper.

Greek orzo and shrimp salad

THE INGREDIENTS of the classic Greek village salad—tomato, cucumber, onion, and feta cheese—are rounded out with shrimp and fresh dill in this light pasta salad. It serves a crowd—or a small village.

20 SERVINGS

- 1½ 1-pound packages orzo (rice-shaped pasta)
- 1½ bunches green onions (about 8 green onions), chopped
- 3 cups crumbled feta cheese (about 12 ounces)
- ¾ cup chopped fresh dill
- 7 tablespoons fresh lemon juice
- 6 tablespoons olive oil
- 3 pounds uncooked medium shrimp, peeled, deveined

- 1½ English hothouse cucumbers, quartered lengthwise, cut crosswise into ¼-inch-thick pieces
- 2 12-ounce baskets cherry tomatoes, halved, divided
- ½ English hothouse cucumber, sliced into thin rounds
- Fresh dill sprigs

COOK orzo in large pot of boiling salted water until tender but still firm to bite, stirring occasionally. Drain. Rinse with cold water to cool; drain well. Transfer to large bowl. Add green onions, feta cheese, chopped dill, lemon juice, and oil; mix well. Cook shrimp in large pot of boiling salted water until just opaque in center, about 2 minutes. Drain. Rinse with cold water to cool; drain well. Mix into salad. Season to taste with salt and pepper. *(Salad can be prepared 8 hours ahead. Cover and refrigerate.)*

MIX cucumber pieces and ¾ of cherry tomatoes into salad. Transfer salad to serving bowl. Arrange cucumber rounds and remaining cherry tomato halves around edge of bowl. Garnish salad with dill sprigs.

White beans with ham, cilantro, and mint

THIS MAKE-AHEAD SALAD is refreshing and satisfying at the same time. The starchy beans and rich ham give the dish real substance, and the Sherry wine vinegar, fresh mint, and cilantro provide the zest. Dried beans can be stored in an airtight container for up to a year.

8 SERVINGS

- 1 pound dried white beans (such as Great Northern), rinsed, picked over

- ¾ cup diced ham (about 6 ounces)
- ½ cup chopped fresh mint
- ½ cup chopped fresh cilantro
- ½ cup (about) olive oil
- ¼ cup (about) Sherry wine vinegar

PLACE beans in large pot. Add enough cold water to cover beans by at least 3 inches. Let stand overnight.

DRAIN beans. Return to same pot and add enough fresh cold water to cover by 3 inches. Simmer over medium heat until just tender, stirring occasionally, about 1 hour. Drain beans. Transfer to large bowl, sprinkle generously with salt and pepper, and cool slightly.

ADD ham, mint, cilantro, ½ cup oil, and ¼ cup vinegar; toss gently. Season salad to taste with salt and pepper. Cool completely. *(Salad can be prepared 1 day ahead. Cover and refrigerate. Bring to room temperature before serving, adding more oil and vinegar to moisten, if desired.)*

Lentil and celery root salad

FRANCE'S DRIED GREEN LENTILS are renowned throughout that country for their color (which changes to brown after cooking), and for their rich texture. They can be found at specialty foods stores and some supermarkets, but if green lentils are unavailable, standard brown lentils can be used. On the outside, the knobby, brown celery root is rather ugly. But on the inside it has a distinctively delicious flavor—a cross between parsley and strong celery—and can be eaten raw or cooked. The roots range in size from as small as an apple to as large as a small cantaloupe; the best ones are smooth and firm with a minimum of knobs.

4 SERVINGS

- **1 1- to 1¼-pound celery root (celeriac)**
- **1 cup French green lentils**
- **6 tablespoons olive oil**
- **3 tablespoons white wine vinegar**
- **2 garlic cloves, minced**
- **1 teaspoon minced fresh rosemary**
- **Large pinch of ground nutmeg**
- **½ cup crumbled blue cheese (about 2 ounces)**

COOK celery root in pot of boiling salted water until tender, about 45 minutes. Drain, cool, and peel. Cut enough of root into ¼-inch cubes to yield 1½ cups.

COOK lentils in medium saucepan of boiling salted water until tender but still firm to bite, about 20 minutes. Drain; cool.

WHISK oil, vinegar, garlic, rosemary, and nutmeg in small bowl to blend. Season dressing to taste with salt and pepper; add cheese.

MIX celery root, lentils, and dressing in medium bowl to blend. *(Salad can be made 4 hours ahead. Cover and refrigerate. Bring to room temperature before serving.)*

Chickpea salad with parsley, lemon, and sun-dried tomatoes

THIS NORTH AFRICAN–INFLUENCED SALAD is drenched in aromatic ingredients: cumin-flavored olive oil combines with lemon juice, sun-dried tomatoes, garlic, and crushed red pepper to coat mildly nutty chickpeas. It's super-easy to make and especially convenient for buffet-style entertaining, since it is served at room temperature.

6 SERVINGS

- **¼ cup olive oil**
- **1 tablespoon cumin seeds**
- **2 15- to 16-ounce cans garbanzo beans (chickpeas), rinsed, drained**
- **1 cucumber, peeled, seeded, chopped (about 1⅓ cups)**
- **½ cup chopped fresh parsley**
- **⅓ cup drained oil-packed sun-dried tomatoes, thinly sliced**
- **¼ cup fresh lemon juice**
- **1 garlic clove, minced**
- **¼ teaspoon dried crushed red pepper**

COMBINE oil and cumin seeds in heavy small saucepan. Cook over medium heat 5 minutes to blend flavors, stirring occasionally. Cool completely.

COMBINE remaining ingredients in large bowl. Add cumin oil and toss to blend. Season salad to taste with salt and pepper. *(Can be made 1 day ahead. Cover and refrigerate. Bring to room temperature before serving.)*

Couscous salad with cinnamon vinaigrette

RAISINS ARE A TYPICAL ADDITION to couscous dishes, but tangy dried cranberries are used here instead for more depth of flavor. They make a wonderful accent to the cinnamon-cumin dressing. This innovative salad would be a terrific side dish to grilled lamb or chicken.

4 SERVINGS

- **⅓ cup canola oil**
- **2 teaspoons ground cinnamon**
- **1 teaspoon ground cumin**
- **2⅓ cups low-salt chicken broth**
- **1 10-ounce box plain couscous**
- **¾ cup dried cranberries or dried currants**
- **3 tablespoons minced shallot**
- **2 tablespoons white wine vinegar**
- **5 green onions, chopped**
- **1 15- to 16-ounce can garbanzo beans (chickpeas), rinsed, drained**
- **5 tablespoons chopped fresh mint**

BRING first 3 ingredients to boil in heavy small saucepan, stirring constantly. Pour into small bowl; cool.

BRING broth to boil in heavy medium saucepan. Mix in couscous and cranberries. Cover; remove from heat. Let stand until broth is absorbed and couscous is tender, about 10 minutes. Transfer couscous to large bowl; fluff with fork to separate grains. Cool. Whisk shallot and vinegar into oil mixture. Season vinaigrette to taste with salt and pepper. Pour over couscous. Mix in green onions, garbanzos, and mint. Serve at room temperature or chill up to 3 hours and serve cold.

State fair potato salad

HERE IS A SENSATIONAL SPIN on the old-fashioned, all-American potato salad. Dijon mustard gives the dressing some bite, and drizzling sweet pickle juice over the warm red potatoes adds tangy flavor so they stand up deliciously to the creamy mayonnaise dressing.

6 TO 8 SERVINGS

- **3½ pounds red-skinned potatoes, peeled, cut into ¾-inch cubes**
- **¼ cup juice from jar of sweet pickles**

- **¾ cup mayonnaise**
- **⅓ cup buttermilk**
- **4 teaspoons Dijon mustard**
- **1 teaspoon sugar**
- **½ teaspoon ground black pepper**
- **3 hard-boiled eggs, peeled, chopped**
- **½ cup chopped red onion**
- **½ cup chopped celery**
- **½ cup chopped sweet pickles**

COOK potatoes in large pot of boiling salted water until just tender, about 10 minutes. Drain; transfer to large bowl. Drizzle pickle juice over potatoes and sprinkle with salt and pepper. Toss gently to blend. Cool to room temperature.

WHISK mayonnaise, buttermilk, mustard, sugar, and pepper in medium bowl to blend. Season dressing to taste with salt and pepper. Pour over potatoes. Add eggs, onion, celery, and pickles; toss gently to blend. *(Salad can be made 8 hours ahead. Cover and chill. Bring to room temperature before serving.)*

Roasted-potato salad with haricots verts, Roquefort, and walnuts

THIS IS AN EXCELLENT picnic salad—just pack the prepared potatoes and beans separately, then arrange them on a platter before serving. If you can't find haricots verts, the slender French string beans, you can use thin green beans instead.

4 SERVINGS

Dressing

- **¼ cup Dijon mustard**
- **3 tablespoons white wine vinegar**
- **¾ cup olive oil**
- **⅔ cup chopped shallots**
- **2 tablespoons chopped fresh rosemary**
- **2 teaspoons chopped fresh sage**

Salad

- **2 pounds baby red-skinned potatoes, quartered**
- **⅔ cup crumbled Roquefort cheese (about 3 ounces), divided**

- **8 ounces haricots verts or small slender green beans, trimmed**
- **⅓ cup walnuts, toasted, chopped**

FOR DRESSING: Mix mustard and vinegar in medium bowl. Gradually whisk in oil, then shallots and herbs. Season dressing to taste with salt and pepper. *(Dressing can be made 1 day ahead. Cover and chill. Bring to room temperature and rewhisk before using.)*

FOR SALAD: Preheat oven to 450°F. Mix potatoes and 3 tablespoons dressing in 13x9x2-inch glass baking dish. Roast 20 minutes. Reduce oven temperature to 375°F and continue roasting until potatoes are tender, stirring occasionally, about 50 minutes longer.

Transfer to large bowl and cool slightly. Mix in 3 tablespoons dressing and ⅓ cup Roquefort cheese. Season to taste with salt and pepper.

COOK haricots verts in medium pot of boiling salted water until crisp-tender, about 3 minutes. Drain. Rinse under cold water to cool; drain well. Transfer to medium bowl. Mix in 3 tablespoons cheese, 2 tablespoons dressing, and walnuts. Season with salt and pepper. *(Beans and potatoes can be left at room temperature 1 hour. Keep remaining cheese refrigerated until ready to serve.)*

ARRANGE beans on platter. Mound potatoes in center of platter atop beans. Sprinkle with remaining Roquefort cheese.

Potato-cauliflower salad with marinated red onions

BECAUSE THEY MARINATE for quite a while, the onions are mellow and tangy rather than harsh in this "red, white, and blue" salad.

6 SERVINGS

- **9 tablespoons olive oil**
- **5 tablespoons prepared white horseradish**
- **3 tablespoons white wine vinegar**
- **1 8-ounce red onion, peeled, halved, thinly sliced**

- **3 cups small cauliflower florets (about 10 ounces)**
- **2 pounds small red-skinned potatoes (about 20), unpeeled**

- **½ cup crumbled blue cheese (about 2 ounces)**

WHISK oil, horseradish, and vinegar in medium bowl to blend. Mix in onion slices. Season generously with salt and pepper. Let stand 2 hours at room temperature or cover and refrigerate up to 1 day, tossing occasionally.

STEAM cauliflower until just tender, about 4 minutes. Cool 5 minutes, then add to red onion mixture. Steam potatoes until just tender, about 20 minutes. Cool 15 minutes.

SLICE potatoes thickly. Place in large bowl. Add onion mixture to potatoes. Add blue cheese; toss gently to blend. Season salad to taste with salt and pepper. *(Can be prepared 2 hours ahead. Let stand at room temperature.)*

Santa Fe potato salad

WONDERFULLY UNEXPECTED ingredients and flavors—hominy and cilantro, jicama and jalapenos—give this potato salad Southwestern style and spice. It would make an excellent side dish for grilled chili-rubbed steaks at a summer cookout.

6 SERVINGS

- **½ cup olive oil**
- **6 tablespoons fresh lime juice**
- **3 garlic cloves, peeled**
- **2 tablespoons chopped jalapeño chiles with seeds**
- **3½ teaspoons ground cumin**
- **1 teaspoon dried oregano**
- **1 15- to 16-ounce can golden hominy, drained**
- **¾ cup chopped fresh cilantro, divided**
- **⅔ cup diced peeled jicama**
- **½ cup chopped white onion**

- **2 pounds medium-large Yukon Gold potatoes, unpeeled**

PUREE first 6 ingredients in blender until almost smooth. Season dressing generously to taste with salt and pepper. Pour dressing into medium bowl. Mix in hominy, ½ cup cilantro, jicama, and onion. Let stand 30 minutes.

STEAM potatoes until tender, about 30 minutes. Cool 15 minutes; peel. Cut lengthwise in half, then crosswise into ½-inch-thick slices. Place in large bowl. Add hominy mixture and toss to blend. Season salad to taste with salt and pepper. Sprinkle with remaining ¼ cup cilantro. *(Salad can be prepared up to 2 hours ahead. Let stand at room temperature.)*

Warm red potatoes with olives, feta, and mint

THE HUMBLE RED-SKINNED POTATO gets a Mediterranean accent with the addition of Kalamata olives, feta cheese, and mint. This delicious salad is served warm, and would be particularly good paired with barbecued lamb.

6 SERVINGS

- **1 ¾ pounds small red-skinned potatoes, quartered**
- **6 tablespoons chopped fresh mint, divided**
- **2 cups crumbled feta cheese (about 8 ounces), divided**
- **¾ cup chopped pitted Kalamata olives, divided**
- **¼ cup extra-virgin olive oil**

COOK potatoes and 3 tablespoons mint in large pot of boiling salted water until potatoes are tender, about 12 minutes. Drain potatoes; transfer to large bowl.

RESERVE 2 tablespoons each of mint, cheese, and olives. Add remainder of each to warm potatoes. Mix in oil. Season salad to taste with salt and pepper. Garnish with reserved 1 tablespoon mint, cheese, and olives. Serve warm.

Potato salad with sugar snap peas and mustard seed dressing

THIS SPRINGTIME SALAD features a piquant dressing flavored with whole yellow mustard seeds, the kind most often used in American mustard and pickling spice. Mustard seeds can be kept up to a year if stored in a dry place in an airtight container.

4 SERVINGS

- **⅓ cup olive oil**
- **5 tablespoons whole-grain Dijon mustard**
- **3 tablespoons yellow mustard seeds**
- **3 tablespoons (packed) chopped fresh dill**
- **2 tablespoons white wine vinegar**
- **1½ pounds medium red-skinned potatoes, each cut into 6 wedges, each wedge cut crosswise in half**
- **8 ounces sugar snap peas, trimmed**
- **½ cup chopped red onion**

WHISK first 5 ingredients in small bowl to blend. Season dressing to taste with salt and pepper.

STEAM potatoes just until tender, about 10 minutes. Transfer to large bowl; add 3 tablespoons dressing and toss to coat. Steam sugar snap peas until just crisp-tender, about 2 minutes. Cool. Add to bowl with potatoes. Add red onion. Pour remaining dressing over salad; toss to coat. Season salad to taste with salt and pepper.

Potato-parsnip salad with aquavit dressing

LIKE RUSSIAN VODKA, Scandinavian aquavit is a strong clear liquor made from potatoes or grain; it is often used in cooking. It has a subtle flavor of caraway, which is heightened by the caraway seeds in this potato salad. Aquavit is available at some liquor stores and specialty foods stores.

4 TO 6 SERVINGS

- **¾ cup mayonnaise**
- **7 tablespoons aquavit (caraway spirit), divided**
- **3 tablespoons white wine vinegar**
- **½ medium red onion, thinly sliced**
- **1½ teaspoons caraway seeds**
- **1½ pounds baby red-skinned potatoes (about 18), halved**
- **1 pound medium parsnips, peeled, cut into ¼-inch-thick rounds**

WHISK mayonnaise, 3 tablespoons aquavit, and vinegar in medium bowl to blend. Season dressing to taste with salt and pepper. Transfer ¼ cup dressing to small bowl and reserve. Add onion and caraway seeds to remaining dressing in medium bowl. Mix well and let stand 30 minutes.

STEAM potatoes until tender, about 15 minutes. Transfer to large bowl. Gently mix in 2 tablespoons aquavit. Steam parsnips until just tender, about 5 minutes. Place parsnips atop potatoes in bowl. Sprinkle with remaining 2 tablespoons aquavit. Let cool 15 minutes. Pour onion-dressing mixture over and stir gently. Moisten with reserved dressing by tablespoonfuls, if desired. Season salad to taste with salt and pepper. Serve slightly warm or at room temperature.

Thai cabbage slaw

NOT YOUR GRANDMOTHER'S COLESLAW—this tangy Asian variant replaces mayonnaise with rice vinegar, soy sauce, and cilantro.

MAKES ABOUT 4 CUPS

- **4 cups finely shredded green cabbage**
- **2/3 cup matchstick-size strips peeled cucumber**
- **1/2 cup (loosely packed) fresh cilantro leaves**
- **1/2 cup (loosely packed) fresh mint leaves**
- **2 tablespoons unseasoned rice vinegar**
- **1 tablespoon soy sauce**

TOSS cabbage, cucumber, cilantro, and mint in large bowl to combine. Add vinegar and soy sauce to cabbage mixture and toss to coat. Season slaw to taste with salt and pepper.

Kohlrabi coleslaw with paprika dressing

PAPRIKA IS A STAPLE of Hungarian cooking, and Hungarian paprika is more pungent than the American version. You can find it at specialty foods stores, but if it's unavailable, regular paprika will work, too (the flavor will just be less intense). The use of paprika, horseradish, and kohlrabi—a relative of the turnip, with a similar taste—make this a wonderfully exotic, slightly spicy slaw.

4 SERVINGS

- **3 tablespoons white wine vinegar**
- **1 tablespoon Hungarian sweet paprika**
- **1/2 cup olive oil**
- **2 teaspoons prepared white horseradish**
- **1/2 teaspoon sugar**

- **2 large kohlrabi, trimmed (leafy tops reserved), peeled, cut into large pieces**
- **1 large carrot, peeled, cut into 2-inch lengths**

COMBINE vinegar and paprika in small bowl. Whisk in oil. Mix in horseradish and sugar. Season dressing to taste with salt and pepper.

USING medium shredding disk, shred kohlrabi, then carrot, in processor. Transfer vegetables to medium bowl. Thinly slice enough reserved kohlrabi leaves to make 1 cup; add to bowl. Toss with dressing. Let coleslaw stand at least 30 minutes and up to 1 hour before serving.

6 Sandwiches and burgers

The sandwich has become a thing of beauty. Once humble, now chic, decked out in great bread and a dazzling variety of ingredients, sandwiches appear everywhere from trendy restaurants to our dinner tables. We can still dress them down, but even today's simplest creation has a certain style.

Some sandwich combinations seem obvious. It could not have required too much imagination on the part of some long-ago chef to pile thin slices of cured ham on a slab of crusty bread. And egg salad had to have been invented to fill the void between two slices of white bread. But what mad culinary genius (maybe alchemist is closer to the mark) figured out that combining roast beef, marinated red onions, and blue cheese would yield a result so much greater than the sum of its parts? That quality of transcending their ingredients is what makes sandwiches irresistible.

When they can be anything from wafer-thin tea sandwiches to Dagwood's gravity-defying creations, it's hard to get a lock on just what sandwiches are. Yes, there's bread involved and, of course, a filling of some sort. But after that, the field is wide open. Think of the bread as a blank canvas. Scandinavian Open-Face Bay Shrimp Sandwiches are edible works of art. So are long, thin baguettes filled with smoked chicken salad, made with Granny Smith apples, atop a bed of sweet-and-sour cabbage.

Some sandwiches are best eaten right after they're made. Hamburgers and hot dogs fresh off the grill are a good example. (That may explain why you never found either in your lunch box.) Still other sandwiches might be best left to rest for a bit in order to give the juices—say, those from grilled portobellos or sliced flank steak—a chance to seep in a bit, soften the bread, and pull the flavors together.

Whoever assembled the first sandwich (and we could be here all day discussing *that*) couldn't have foreseen where the enterprise was headed. Today there is a bread, filling, and dressing for every whim and occasion. Herewith, the best.

Sandwiches

Smoked turkey pinwheel sandwiches with mango chutney

CRUNCHY, REFRESHING, and easy to eat, these exotic pinwheels are a great partner for cocktails. The Armenian flatbread called lavash is spread with a cream cheese–chutney mixture, layered with smoked turkey, cucumber, and arugula, then rolled up and cut into one-inch slices for eye-catching, colorful hors d'oeuvres. Look for lavash at well-stocked supermarkets or any Middle Eastern market. It comes in large oval sheets.

MAKES ABOUT 16

- **1 8-ounce package cream cheese, room temperature**
- **¼ cup chopped fresh cilantro**
- **¼ cup chopped green onion**
- **¼ cup mango chutney**
- **2 teaspoons curry powder**
- **1 jalapeño chile, seeded, minced**

- **2 lavash bread wraps (from one 16-ounce package)**
- **1½ cups thinly sliced English hothouse cucumber**
- **12 5½x3½x⅛-inch slices smoked turkey (about 10 ounces)**
- **1 cup arugula**

MIX first 6 ingredients in medium bowl. Season to taste with salt and pepper.

UNFOLD 1 lavash bread on work surface. Trim 14x11-inch rectangle from center of bread. Place rectangle on damp kitchen towel. Spread half of cream cheese mixture over bread, covering completely. Starting at 1 short side, arrange half of cucumber slices over half of cream cheese layer. Top with 6 slices of smoked turkey, covering cucumber and part of cream cheese layer. Sprinkle entire sandwich with half of arugula. Starting at short end with cucumbers, roll bread up tightly jelly-roll style. Repeat with remaining bread, cream cheese mixture, cucumber, smoked turkey, and arugula. *(Can be prepared 1 day ahead. Cover tightly with plastic and refrigerate.)* Cut rolls diagonally into 1-inch-thick slices. Arrange on platter.

Cucumber, radish, and watercress sandwiches with truffled goat cheese

WHO KNEW that tea sandwiches could get even more sophisticated? Radish and watercress add a peppery bite to the usual cool cucumber, and truffle oil gives these little bites an addictive, earthy flavor; look for truffle oil at Italian markets, specialty foods stores, and some supermarkets. (If you can't find this delicacy, the sandwiches will still be fantastic without it.) To keep the watercress fresh, store it leaf-end down in a bowl of water in the fridge; drain well on paper towels before using.

MAKES 24

- **9 ounces soft fresh goat cheese, room temperature**
- **½ cup chopped watercress**
- **1 teaspoon white truffle oil**
- **12 very thin slices white bread**
- **1 bunch radishes, very thinly sliced, divided**
- **½ English hothouse cucumber, peeled, thinly sliced**

BLEND first 3 ingredients in processor until just combined. Season to taste with salt and pepper. Place bread slices on work surface. Spread each with goat cheese mixture, dividing equally. Set aside 24 radish slices for garnish. Top 6 bread slices with cucumber slices, then remaining radish slices.

Sprinkle with pepper. Top with remaining bread slices, cheese side down. *(Can be made 2 hours ahead. Wrap individually in paper towels; chill.)*

TRIM sandwich crusts. Cut each sandwich into 4 squares. Transfer to platter. Top each with 1 radish slice and serve.

Tofu, avocado, and tahini pita sandwiches

THESE SANDWICHES are so rich and creamy that it seems they couldn't possibly be good for you, but in fact they are: Avocado is high in vitamin E and "good" fat, and tofu is a cholesterol-free source of protein. And since tofu soaks up the surrounding flavors—in this case a delectable yogurt-tahini dressing—a sandwich is an ideal spot for it. Be sure to drain the tofu very well; otherwise the sandwiches will get soggy. You'll find tahini, a nutty-tasting paste made from sesame seeds, at Middle Eastern markets, natural foods stores, and well-stocked supermarkets.

MAKES 4

1 cup plain nonfat yogurt
2 tablespoons tahini (sesame seed paste)
2 teaspoons fresh lemon juice
1 garlic clove, minced
Dash of hot pepper sauce

4 whole wheat pita bread rounds
8 ounces tofu (firm or medium-firm), drained, cut into ⅛-inch-thick slices
4 ¼-inch-thick slices ripe tomato
4 thin slices red onion
4 large lettuce leaves
1 cup alfalfa sprouts or sunflower sprouts
1 large avocado, halved, pitted, peeled, cut into thin wedges

MIX first 5 ingredients in small bowl to blend. Season to taste with salt and pepper. Set sauce aside.

CUT off top ¼ of each pita bread. Open pita pockets and insert ¼ of tofu, 1 tomato slice, 1 onion slice, 1 lettuce leaf, ¼ cup alfalfa sprouts, and 3 avocado slices into each. Spoon 2 tablespoons sauce into each sandwich and serve.

Peanut butter, banana, and date sandwiches

THESE TAKE THE PRIZE for best upscale (and good for your kids) after-school snack. Virtually any kind of honey will work in this recipe: Clover honey is the mild, in-every-grocery-store variety; orange blossom is a little sweeter and fruitier. Or try spun honey, a crystallized version that's more butter-like. The kids may also want to give hazelnut or almond butter a try.

MAKES 4

2 whole wheat pita bread rounds
8 tablespoons peanut butter
6 pitted dates, chopped
8 teaspoons honey
2 ripe bananas, peeled, sliced

Lightly toast pita breads; cut each in half crosswise. Open pita pockets. Spread 2 tablespoons peanut butter inside each pita pocket on 1 side. Sprinkle chopped dates over peanut butter, dividing equally. Drizzle 2 teaspoons honey over each. Divide banana slices among pita pockets; close sandwiches, pressing slightly to adhere.

Smoked salmon–wasabi tea sandwiches

HERE'S A TEA SANDWICH that even guys will like: The wasabi and salmon combination is reminiscent of sushi. Peppery-hot wasabi comes from the root of a Japanese plant that is similar to horseradish. This recipe calls for the dried powder, which is mixed with water to make a paste. The powder can be found on the spice aisle or in the Asian foods section of the supermarket or at Asian foods stores. You can assemble these sandwiches two hours ahead; wrap them in paper towels (to keep them from getting soggy) and hold them in the fridge.

MAKES 24

- **1 tablespoon wasabi powder**
- **2 teaspoons water**
- **1 8-ounce package cream cheese, room temperature**

- **12 very thin slices whole wheat bread**
- **8 ounces thinly sliced smoked salmon**
- **2 teaspoons grated lemon peel**
- **3 tablespoons chopped fresh cilantro**

MIX wasabi powder and 2 teaspoons water in medium bowl to form paste. Add cream cheese; using electric mixer, beat until well combined.

PLACE all bread slices on work surface. Spread each with wasabi cream cheese, dividing equally. Top 6 bread slices with smoked salmon, dividing equally. Sprinkle lemon peel, then cilantro over salmon. Top with remaining bread slices, cheese side down. *(Can be made 2 hours ahead. Wrap sandwiches individually in paper towels and refrigerate.)*

TRIM crusts. Cut each sandwich into 4 triangles. Transfer to platter, points up.

Roast beef sandwiches with marinated red onions and blue cheese

BLUE CHEESE, ROAST BEEF, and red onions—one of the most classic and satisfying combinations. The onions are marinated in sugar and red wine vinegar to sweeten and soften them. To slice the onions thinly and safely, cut off half an inch or so from one rounded side, creating a flat surface to steady the onion on the cutting board. Any blue cheese will do here, and feel free to experiment with different breads: Gorgonzola on ciabatta and Stilton on sourdough are excellent combinations.

MAKES 4

- **2 cups thinly sliced red onions**
- **2 tablespoons red wine vinegar**
- **1 teaspoon sugar**

- **4 large soft whole grain rolls, halved horizontally, toasted**
- **Olive oil (optional)**
- **½ cup crumbled blue cheese**
- **12 slices tomato**
- **8 ounces thinly sliced roast beef**
- **2 cups (packed) trimmed small watercress sprigs**

MIX first 3 ingredients in medium bowl; sprinkle with salt and pepper. Let stand until onions are soft, tossing occasionally, at least 1 hour and up to 4 hours.

PLACE bottom halves of rolls on work surface; brush with olive oil, if desired. Sprinkle with cheese. Top each with 3 tomato slices, then ¼ of roast beef. Top each with ½ cup watercress, then ¼ of pickled onions. Cover with tops of rolls. Cut each sandwich in half.

Smoked chicken salad with sweet-and-sour cabbage on baguettes

HERE'S A CHICKEN SALAD with a European accent, one that's reminiscent of the cuisines of Germany, Scandinavia, and Austria. Try it on rye bread to keep the theme going, and have dill pickles and German-style potato salad on the side. Of course, if you use bacon fat rather than butter, it couldn't hurt to throw the bacon on the sandwich as well.

MAKES 6

Sweet-and-sour cabbage

- **1 medium head of red cabbage, quartered, cored, thinly sliced**
- **1 onion, thinly sliced**
- **½ cup sugar**
- **⅓ cup red wine vinegar**
- **2 tablespoons (¼ stick) butter or rendered bacon fat**

Chicken salad

- **4 cups ½-inch dice smoked chicken or turkey**
- **3 Granny Smith apples, peeled, cored, cut into ¼-inch dice**
- **6 green onions, thinly sliced**
- **1 cup mayonnaise**
- **½ cup sour cream**
- **4 celery stalks, chopped**
- **2 tablespoons red wine vinegar**

- **2 large French-bread baguettes**
- **2 tablespoons coarse-grained mustard**
- **6 romaine lettuce leaves**

FOR SWEET-AND-SOUR CABBAGE: Combine all ingredients in heavy large nonreactive pot over medium heat. Cover and cook until cabbage is tender, stirring frequently, about 25 minutes. Transfer cabbage to medium bowl and cool. Cover and refrigerate until well chilled, about 3 hours. *(Can be prepared 1 day ahead. Keep refrigerated.)*

FOR CHICKEN SALAD: Mix first 7 ingredients in large bowl. Season to taste with salt and pepper. Cover and refrigerate until well chilled, about 3 hours. *(Can be prepared 4 hours ahead; keep refrigerated.)*

CUT each baguette crosswise into thirds, then halve each piece horizontally. Pull out half of center part of each piece of bread (reserve for another use). Spread mustard over each piece of bread, dividing equally. Cover bottom 6 pieces of bread with ¼ cup cabbage mixture. Top with chicken salad, then lettuce leaves. Top with remaining bread.

Lemon-tarragon chicken salad sandwiches

LEMON AND TARRAGON complement each other beautifully, and they take this chicken salad to an elegant level. If you're short on time, purchase roast chicken at the market or buy a very thick slice of smoked turkey breast at the deli counter. Helpful hint: Grate the lemon peel before juicing the lemon (hollow rinds are difficult to grate).

MAKES 6

- **1¼ pounds skinless boneless chicken breast halves (about 3)**

- **¾ cup finely chopped celery**
- **½ cup plus 3 tablespoons mayonnaise**
- **¼ cup finely chopped red onion**
- **2 tablespoons chopped fresh tarragon**
- **2 tablespoons fresh lemon juice**
- **1 teaspoon grated lemon peel**

- **12 slices rye bread with seeds**
- **2 cups thinly sliced romaine lettuce**

BRING large saucepan of salted water to boil. Add chicken breasts; reduce heat to medium-low, cover, and simmer until chicken is just cooked through, about 12 minutes. Using tongs, transfer chicken to plate; cool. Discard broth.

MIX celery, ½ cup mayonnaise, onion, tarragon, lemon juice, and lemon peel in large bowl to blend. Cut chicken into ½-inch cubes; stir into mayonnaise mixture. Season with salt and pepper. *(Can be made 4 hours ahead. Cover and refrigerate.)*

Arrange 6 bread slices on work surface. Spread with remaining 3 tablespoons mayonnaise. Divide salad among bread slices. Top each with lettuce and second bread slice. Cut sandwiches in half.

Tuna, pickle, and chopped-vegetable pita sandwiches

FINALLY—A GOOD LOW-FAT version of tuna salad. Nonfat yogurt stands in for some of the mayonnaise, and the chopped veggies add crunch and flavor. Tuna and pickle is a match made in heaven, and here the combo is enhanced with onion, apple, and cider vinegar (substitute dill pickles if you prefer them to the sweet variety).

MAKES 4 SERVINGS

- **1 6-ounce can albacore tuna packed in water, drained**
- **½ cup chopped drained sweet pickles**
- **3 tablespoons plain nonfat yogurt**
- **3 tablespoons light mayonnaise**

- **1 red bell pepper, chopped**
- **½ cup chopped sweet onion (such as Vidalia)**
- **½ cup chopped peeled, cored Granny Smith apple**
- **2 teaspoons apple cider vinegar**

- **2 cups thinly sliced red leaf lettuce**
- **4 pita bread rounds, halved crosswise, pockets opened**

MIX first 4 ingredients in small bowl to blend. Season tuna mixture to taste with salt and pepper.

MIX bell pepper, onion, and apple in medium bowl. Add half of vegetable mixture to tuna mixture and stir to blend. Add vinegar to remaining vegetable mixture; toss to combine. Season vegetable mixture to taste with salt and pepper.

PLACE ¼ cup lettuce inside each pita half. Spoon ⅛ of tuna mixture, then ⅛ of vegetable mixture into each pita half. Place 2 pita halves on each of 4 plates and serve.

Tuna salad on olive bread with arugula

THE BEST TUNA SALAD EVER. If you can't find olive bread, chop up some Kalamata olives and add them to the tuna mixture. And don't feel confined to canned tuna: This is a great way to use up leftover grilled tuna steak. Simply flake the fish as you would canned albacore. For an alternative presentation, serve this pretty salad atop a bed of arugula. You can prepare the tuna salad a day ahead; just give it a stir before making the sandwiches.

MAKES 6

- **2 6-ounce cans albacore tuna packed in water, drained**
- **½ cup chopped green onions**
- **¼ cup diced seeded English hothouse cucumber**
- **¼ cup minced fresh dill**
- **¼ cup drained capers**
- **2 tablespoons Dijon mustard**
- **2 tablespoons minced fresh tarragon**
- **¾ cup mayonnaise, divided**
- **12 ⅓-inch-thick slices olive bread**
- **1 cup arugula**

MIX first 7 ingredients and ¼ cup mayonnaise in medium bowl to blend. Season to taste with salt and pepper. Divide tuna salad among 6 bread slices; top with arugula leaves. Spread remaining mayonnaise on remaining 6 bread slices; place atop arugula, mayonnaise side down. Cut sandwiches in half; wrap each tightly in plastic wrap. *(Can be made 1 day ahead. Refrigerate.)*

Best-ever egg salad sandwiches

BACON AND PIMIENTO-STUFFED OLIVES earn these sandwiches their "best-ever" title. Be sure to use white bread: A more flavorful choice would interfere with the delicate egg salad. A foolproof method for hard-boiling is to bring the eggs to room temperature before boiling. Place them in a single layer in the bottom of a pot. Run cold water into the pot until it reaches about an inch over the eggs. Bring the water to a simmer over high heat, then turn off the heat, cover, and let the eggs sit in the very hot water for about 10 to 12 minutes.

MAKES 6

12 bacon slices

8 large hard-boiled eggs, peeled, coarsely chopped
⅓ cup finely chopped celery
¼ cup chopped pimiento-stuffed green olives
½ cup mayonnaise, divided
1 tablespoon Dijon mustard

12 slices white sandwich bread, toasted
12 red leaf lettuce leaves

COOK bacon in heavy large skillet over medium heat until brown and crisp, about 8 minutes. Using slotted spoon, transfer bacon to paper towels to drain. Cut bacon slices crosswise in half.

COMBINE chopped eggs, celery, and olives in bowl. Mix in ¼ cup mayonnaise and mustard. Season to taste with salt and pepper.

PLACE toast slices on work surface; spread lightly with remaining mayonnaise. Divide egg salad among 6 toast slices. Place 4 bacon pieces, then 2 lettuce leaves atop egg salad on each. Cover with remaining toast slices, mayonnaise side down. Cut sandwiches diagonally in half.

Greek salad submarine sandwiches

SALAD-IN-A-SANDWICH is a brilliant notion—and if egg salad, tuna salad, and chicken salad can do it, why not Greek salad? Most markets sell pitted Kalamata olives in jars or cans, but if you can't find them pitted, simply crush the olives with the side of a chef's knife and pop out the pits. For a party, double or triple this recipe—these are easy to assemble and they'll go like hotcakes.

MAKES 6

½ cup olive oil
6 tablespoons fresh lemon juice
¼ cup chopped fresh basil
2 tablespoons chopped fresh mint
2 tablespoons chopped fresh oregano or 2 teaspoons dried

1 1-pound loaf French bread (approximately 12x4 inches), halved horizontally
8 ounces feta cheese, crumbled (about 2 cups)
12 Kalamata olives, pitted, halved
3 large plum tomatoes, thinly sliced
1 green bell pepper, thinly sliced
½ red onion, thinly sliced
½ cucumber, peeled, thinly sliced
3 peperoncini from jar, drained, coarsely chopped

WHISK first 5 ingredients in small bowl to blend. Season dressing to taste with salt and pepper.

SPOON ¾ cup dressing evenly over cut side of bottom half of bread. Sprinkle cheese over bread. Top with even layers of olives, tomatoes, bell pepper, onion, cucumber, and peperoncini. Pull or cut away enough bread from top half to leave ½-inch-thick shell. Spoon remaining dressing over peperoncini. Place top of bread over filling. Press to compact. Cut crosswise into 6 sandwiches.

Italian deli sandwiches with marjoram-caper dressing

THE GREAT THING about these sandwiches is that no matter what combination of meats and cheese you choose—from the mortadella, salami, and provolone suggested in the recipe to *bresaola*, prosciutto, and mozzarella—they're guaranteed to taste fabulous. Marjoram adds a zesty kick to the dressing, and the sweet Vidalia onion (named after its birthplace in Georgia) provides a mellow counterpoint. If you can't find the Vidalia variety, try another sweet onion such as the Hawaiian Maui, or Walla Walla from Washington State.

MAKES 4

- **½ cup olive oil**
- **¼ cup chopped fresh Italian parsley**
- **¼ cup drained capers**
- **4 tablespoons chopped fresh marjoram, divided**
- **2 tablespoons red wine vinegar**

- **1 22-inch-long sourdough baguette, halved horizontally**
- **12 ounces assorted sliced deli meats and cheeses (such as mortadella, salami, and provolone)**
- **1 cup thinly sliced sweet onion (such as Vidalia)**

BLEND oil, parsley, capers, 3 tablespoons marjoram, and vinegar in food processor until herbs are finely chopped. Season with salt and pepper. Transfer dressing to small bowl. Let stand 30 minutes.

MIX remaining 1 tablespoon marjoram into dressing. Spoon dressing over cut sides of bread, dividing equally. Arrange meats, cheeses, and onion on bottom half of bread. Cover with top half of bread. Cut diagonally into 4 sandwiches. *(Sandwiches can be made 4 hours ahead. Wrap tightly in aluminum foil and refrigerate.)*

Chorizo, pepper, and onion sandwiches

THESE SANDWICHES highlight the flavors of Spain. Be sure to use Spanish chorizo, not Mexican, in this recipe; the Spanish kind is a fully cooked link sausage that can be easily sliced and grilled. Check Spanish markets, specialty foods stores, or the meat counter at the supermarket; if you can't find it, substitute another smoked sausage, such as andouille or kielbasa.

MAKES 2; CAN BE DOUBLED

- **1 tablespoon olive oil**
- **8 ounces Spanish chorizo sausage, halved lengthwise**
- **1 medium onion, thinly sliced**
- **½ green bell pepper, thinly sliced**
- **½ red bell pepper, thinly sliced**
- **½ cup dry red wine**
- **2 large sandwich rolls, halved horizontally**

HEAT oil in heavy large skillet over medium heat. Add chorizo to skillet and cook until beginning to brown, turning occasionally, about 5 minutes. Transfer chorizo to plate. Cut crosswise into 2- to 3-inch pieces. Pour off all but 2 tablespoons drippings from skillet. Add onion and bell pepper slices to skillet. Sauté until vegetables begin to soften, about 5 minutes. Return chorizo to skillet. Add wine and simmer to blend flavors, stirring frequently, about 3 minutes. Season sausage mixture to taste with salt and pepper. Place bottoms of rolls on 2 plates. Spoon sausage mixture over. Cover with tops of rolls and serve.

Meatball hero sandwiches

THIS TYPE OF SANDWICH goes by many different names—hoagie, po' boy, submarine, grinder. It was dubbed hero by some, reportedly because eating a whole one was such a feat. No matter what you call these creations, you'll have no problem finishing them. Use ground beef with 15 percent fat (a little fat will keep the meatballs moist). Cornflakes are a fun substitute for the usual breadcrumbs; they add body and extra flavor.

MAKES 6

- **Nonstick vegetable oil spray**
- **1½ pounds lean ground beef (15% fat)**
- **½ cup freshly grated Parmesan cheese (about 1½ ounces)**
- **2 large eggs**
- **¼ cup chopped fresh parsley (preferably Italian)**
- **¼ cup crushed cornflakes**
- **3 garlic cloves, minced**
- **2½ teaspoons dried oregano**
- **½ teaspoon ground white pepper**
- **½ teaspoon salt**

- **3 cups purchased marinara sauce**

- **6 long Italian or French rolls, halved horizontally, toasted**

PREHEAT oven to 350°F. Spray heavy large baking sheet with nonstick vegetable oil spray. Combine ground beef, Parmesan cheese, eggs, parsley, cornflakes, garlic, oregano, pepper and salt in large bowl; blend thoroughly. Using moistened hands, shape meat mixture into 30 to 36 1½-inch balls and place on prepared sheet, spacing evenly. Bake meatballs until just firm to touch and cooked through, about 20 minutes.

BRING marinara sauce to simmer in heavy large saucepan. Add meatballs to sauce and simmer until sauce thickens slightly, about 15 minutes. *(Can be prepared 1 day ahead. Cool slightly. Refrigerate uncovered until cold, then cover and refrigerate. Rewarm over low heat before continuing.)*

GENTLY press center of bottoms of rolls to compact slightly. Place 1 roll bottom on each of 6 plates. Spoon 5 or 6 meatballs into depression in each roll. Spoon over enough sauce to coat meatballs. Cover with tops of rolls.

BLT & G(uacamole)

FORGET MAYO: The classic bacon, lettuce, and tomato sandwich gets an unexpected boost here from luscious, spicy guacamole. Choose your avocados carefully: Look for fruit that gives easily when squeezed lightly (don't paw the poor things too much, though, or you'll bruise the flesh). Now would be the right time to try applewood-smoked bacon—the thicker cut and sweet flavor complement this sandwich very nicely.

MAKES 4

- **2 large ripe avocados, halved, pitted, peeled**
- **2 tablespoons minced fresh cilantro**
- **2 pickled jalapeño chiles, stemmed, minced**
- **2 teaspoons fresh lime juice**

- **12 thick-cut bacon slices**
- **8 slices whole grain bread**
- **8 thin slices tomato**
- **4 romaine lettuce leaves**

PREHEAT broiler. Mash avocados in medium bowl. Stir in cilantro, jalapeños and lime juice. Season to taste with salt and pepper.

COOK bacon in large skillet over medium-high heat until crisp, turning occasionally, about 7 minutes. Transfer bacon to paper towels to drain. Meanwhile, lightly toast bread slices on 1 side under broiler. Spread guacamole over untoasted side of each slice while still warm. Place 3 bacon slices on each of 4 bread slices. Top with tomatoes, then lettuce. Place remaining 4 bread slices atop lettuce.

Jamaican Jerk Burgers with Orange-Chipotle Mayonnaise (page 182)

Fettuccine Bolognese (page 203)

Smoked-Salmon Pizza with Red Onion and Dill (page 222)

Risotto Primavera (page 230)

Corn, Cheese, and Chile Tamales with Tomatillo-Avocado Salsa (page 251)

Herb- and Garlic-Crusted Beef Tenderloin with
Red and Yellow Bell Pepper Relish (page 281)

Cider-Brined Pork Chops with
Creamed Leeks and Apples (page 292)

Braised Lamb Shanks with
Winter Squash and Red Chard (page 309)

Canadian bacon, mustard greens, and fried egg on potato bread

LIKE BRUNCH IN A SANDWICH, these are nice at any time of day (turn this recipe into an elegant supper with a frisée salad and a good Pinot Noir). We break the yolks when frying the eggs (which makes it easier to use them in a sandwich), but you can fry them however you prefer. Look for oversize English muffins as a substitute for the potato bread, if you like. Mayo, mustard, and horseradish make a delicious, versatile spread. Whip up some extra and try it on roast beef, turkey, or tomato sandwiches.

MAKES 6

6 tablespoons mayonnaise
1½ tablespoons coarse-grained mustard
1½ tablespoons prepared horseradish
2 tablespoons (¼ stick) butter, divided
1 bunch mustard greens, stemmed, very thinly sliced
18 Canadian bacon slices

6 large eggs
12 slices potato bread, toasted
2 tomatoes, thinly sliced

PREHEAT broiler. Mix first 3 ingredients in small bowl. Melt 1 tablespoon butter in heavy medium skillet over medium-high heat. Add mustard greens and stir until wilted, about 2 minutes. Cover; remove from heat. Place Canadian bacon on large baking sheet. Broil until heated through, about 1 minute per side. Tent with aluminum foil to keep warm.

MELT remaining 1 tablespoon butter in large nonstick skillet over medium heat. Add eggs and break yolks using fork. Cook until yolks are just set, about 1 minute per side. Spread toast with mustard mayonnaise. Cover 6 pieces of toast with mustard greens, bacon, and tomato. Top each with fried egg and piece of toast.

Salade Niçoise sandwiches

SURPRISINGLY, THESE SANDWICHES actually get better the longer they sit—the flavors meld and intensify. *Olivada* is a black olive paste that's available at Italian markets, specialty foods stores, and well-stocked supermarkets. If you can't find it, puree pitted, brine-cured black olives in the processor.

MAKES 6

3 6-ounce cans albacore tuna packed in water, well drained
3 tablespoons drained capers
¼ cup mayonnaise
1½ tablespoons fresh lemon juice
2 1-pound loaves soft French or Italian bread (approximately 12x4 inches)
6 tablespoons (about) olivada
3 bunches arugula or 1 bunch watercress, thick stems trimmed
2 tomatoes, sliced
1 red onion, thinly sliced

MIX first 4 ingredients in medium bowl to blend. Season to taste with pepper. Cut each bread loaf crosswise into 3 pieces, then halve each piece horizontally. Pull out centers of bread pieces, leaving ½-inch-thick crusts. Spread olivada on inside of each bread piece. Cover olivada with generous layer of arugula. Spread ½ cup tuna mixture over each bottom piece of bread. Top with tomato and onion, then with top pieces of bread. Wrap each sandwich tightly in aluminum foil and refrigerate at least 1 hour. *(Sandwiches can be prepared 6 hours ahead; keep refrigerated.)*

Grilled salmon club sandwiches

THIS IS ONE CLUB you'll definitely want to join. The longer the salmon marinates, the more the flavors will penetrate the fish. To keep the salmon from sticking to the grill, spray the grates generously with nonstick spray before placing the fish on them. The lemon-basil mayonnaise would also make a good dressing for egg salad or chicken salad.

MAKES 4

6 tablespoons mayonnaise
5 tablespoons minced fresh basil, divided
1 teaspoon grated lemon peel

3 tablespoons olive oil
1 tablespoon fresh lemon juice
4 5- to 6-ounce skinless salmon fillets (each about ¾-inch thick)

8 bacon slices
1 small red onion, sliced

8 ½-inch-thick slices sourdough bread (each about 5x3 inches)
8 slices tomato
8 lettuce leaves

MIX mayonnaise, 2 tablespoons basil, and lemon peel in small bowl to blend. *(Lemon-basil mayonnaise can be made 1 day ahead. Cover and refrigerate.)*

MIX remaining 3 tablespoons basil, olive oil, and lemon juice in large glass baking dish. Add salmon to oil mixture; turn to coat. Cover; refrigerate at least 1 hour and up to 4 hours.

COOK bacon in heavy large skillet over medium-high heat until crisp. Using tongs, transfer bacon to paper towels to drain. Pour off all but 1 tablespoon drippings from skillet. Add onion to drippings in skillet. Sauté until onion is tender and beginning to brown, about 5 minutes. Season to taste with salt and pepper.

PREPARE barbecue (medium-high heat). Grill fish until just opaque in center, about 3 minutes per side. Grill bread just until golden, about 2 minutes per side. Spread mayonnaise mixture over 1 side of bread slices. Top each of 4 bread slices with 2 bacon slices, 2 tomato slices, ¼ of onion, 1 salmon fillet, and 2 lettuce leaves. Cover with remaining bread slices, mayonnaise side down.

Scandinavian open-face bay shrimp sandwiches

THESE COOL AND REFRESHING SANDWICHES piled high with cucumber, shrimp, and dill are an integral part of any Swedish smorgasbord. The shrimp salad would make a sophisticated appetizer atop cocktail-size bread or blini, too. Bay shrimp are the little guys that usually come about 100 to the pound. They're always sold cooked, so there's no peeling or deveining to be done.

MAKES 4

½ cup mayonnaise
½ cup chopped fresh dill
4 teaspoons Dijon mustard
2 teaspoons fresh lemon juice

4 slices egg or pumpernickel bread, toasted
1 pound cooked bay shrimp, drained, patted dry
4 butter lettuce leaves
½ English hothouse cucumber, thinly sliced
4 thin slices lemon
4 fresh dill sprigs

MIX first 4 ingredients in medium bowl. Season to taste with salt and pepper. *(Dill mayonnaise can be made 1 day ahead. Cover and refrigerate.)*

SPREAD 1 tablespoon dill mayonnaise over each bread slice. Mix shrimp into remaining mayonnaise. Place 1 lettuce leaf on each bread slice, pressing to adhere. Arrange 6 cucumber slices atop lettuce on each slice. Arrange shrimp mixture atop cucumber slices. Garnish each sandwich with lemon slice and dill sprig.

Add fillets; sauté until cooked through and brown, about 5 minutes per side.

PLACE fillets on bread bottoms. Top with tomato, lettuce, and bread tops.

Fried catfish sandwiches with curried mayonnaise

FLAVORFUL CATFISH is coated in cornmeal and sautéed until the crust is crunchy, then made into a sandwich with spicy curried mayonnaise. Make sure the oil in the skillet is nice and hot before adding the fish. That way, the crust will brown and crisp properly.

MAKES 4

- **½ cup mayonnaise**
- **1 tablespoon curry powder**
- **1 tablespoon fresh lemon juice**
- **1 18-inch-long French-bread baguette**

- **½ cup yellow cornmeal**
- **½ cup all purpose flour**
- **½ cup whole milk**
- **4 catfish fillets (each about 5 ounces)**
- **3 tablespoons olive oil**

- **1 large tomato, thinly sliced**
- **4 butter lettuce leaves**

STIR first 3 ingredients in small bowl to blend; season to taste with salt and pepper. Cut bread crosswise into 4 pieces, then halve each piece horizontally. Spread halves generously with curried mayonnaise.

WHISK cornmeal and flour in shallow bowl to blend. Pour milk into another shallow bowl. Dip each fillet into milk, then into cornmeal mixture, turning to coat. Sprinkle with salt and pepper. Heat oil in heavy large nonstick skillet over medium-high heat.

New England crab rolls

LOBSTER SALAD SANDWICHES (on buttered, toasted hot dog buns) can be found all along the Northeastern coast in the summer months. This is a more economical version that you can make at home. Be sure to get real crabmeat at the fish counter, and before making the salad, pick over the crab to remove any cartilage or shell. Hot dog buns are authentic, but if you prefer, pile the salad onto a crusty baguette or kaiser roll.

MAKES 4

- **6 tablespoons mayonnaise**
- **1 tablespoon fresh lemon juice**
- **1 teaspoon grated lemon peel**
- **⅛ teaspoon cayenne pepper**
- **¾ pound fresh crabmeat, picked over**
- **3 tablespoons finely chopped green onions**

- **2 tablespoons (¼ stick) butter, room temperature**
- **4 hot dog buns, split open**
- **4 butter lettuce leaves**

WHISK first 4 ingredients in medium bowl to combine. Mix in crabmeat and green onions. Season crab salad to taste with salt and pepper.

SPREAD butter on insides of buns. Preheat large skillet over medium heat. Place buns, buttered side down, in heated skillet and toast until golden, about 5 minutes. Place 1 toasted bun on each of 4 plates. Place 1 lettuce leaf inside each bun. Divide crab salad among buns and serve.

Grilled cheddar, tomato, and bacon sandwiches

THE CLASSIC GRILLED CHEESE is ratcheted up a notch here. Spreading mayonnaise on the outside of the sandwiches before grilling adds a little tang, a good toasty crunch, and an attractive golden color. Use this recipe as a jumping-off point to a world of grilled cheese sandwiches: Try cheddar and apple, Fontina and tomato, or mozzarella and sausage. While almost anything goes inside, we recommend using sourdough or crusty white bread on the outside.

MAKES 4

- **8 thick-cut bacon slices**
- **8 slices country-style sourdough bread (cut on deep diagonal into 5x3x½-inch slices)**
- **2 cups (packed) grated extra-sharp cheddar cheese (about 8 ounces)**
- **8 slices tomato, seeded, slices drained on paper towels**
- **4 tablespoons mayonnaise**

COOK bacon in heavy large skillet over medium heat until brown and crisp, turning occasionally, about 6 minutes. Transfer bacon to paper towels to drain. Wash and dry skillet.

PLACE 4 bread slices on work surface. Press ¼ cup grated cheese onto each slice. Top each with 2 tomato slices. Sprinkle with pepper. Place 2 bacon slices atop each, breaking into pieces if necessary to fit. Press ¼ cup grated cheese over bacon on each. Top sandwiches with remaining bread slices, then spread ½ tablespoon mayonnaise over top of each sandwich.

HEAT 2 heavy large skillets over medium heat. Add 2 sandwiches, mayonnaise side down, to each skillet. Place plate atop sandwiches to weigh down. Cook sandwiches until bottom is golden brown, about 2 minutes. Spread top of each sandwich with ½ tablespoon mayonnaise. Turn sandwiches over. Top with plate and cook until golden brown on bottom, about 2 minutes. Transfer sandwiches to work surface. Cut sandwiches crosswise in half.

Toasted blue cheese and caramelized onion sandwiches

ELEGANT PARTY NIBBLES, these are lovely with Champagne, a dry Martini, or a nice Zinfandel. Cambozola is a very mild blue cheese (it's like a cross between Camembert and Gorgonzola), and *Gorgonzola dolce* is the sweeter, less pungent version of the famous Italian blue. Don't be afraid to caramelize the onions thoroughly. The darker the better: the more intense the flavor will be, and the sweeter the onions will become. Caramelizing the onions ahead makes these a breeze to assemble just before guests arrive. If you don't like raisins, try dried figs or apricots.

MAKES 24 WEDGES

- **2 tablespoons olive oil**
- **2 large white onions, thinly sliced**
- **2 tablespoons (packed) golden brown sugar**
- **2 tablespoons unseasoned rice vinegar**
- **2 tablespoons chopped golden raisins**
- **8 5½x3x½-inch slices rustic country bread, such as walnut, pecan, or walnut-raisin**
- **2 6-ounce wedges soft blue cheese (such as Cambozola, rind trimmed, or Gorgonzola dolce), sliced**
- **4 tablespoons (½ stick) butter, room temperature, divided**

HEAT oil in heavy large skillet over medium heat. Add onions and sauté until just beginning to color, stirring often, about 20 minutes. Sprinkle sugar over and sauté until onions are deep golden brown and very soft, stirring occasionally, about 25 minutes longer. Remove from heat. Mix in vinegar and raisins. Season caramelized onions to taste with salt and pepper. Cool. *(Can be prepared 3 days ahead. Transfer to bowl. Cover and refrigerate.)*

ARRANGE 4 bread slices on work surface. Top with cheese, dividing equally. Top each with ¼ of caramelized onions. Top with remaining bread slices to form 4 sandwiches. Spread 2 tablespoons butter over tops of sandwiches. Heat heavy large skillet over medium heat. Add sandwiches, buttered side down. Spread remaining 2 tablespoons butter over tops of bread. Cover partially and cook until bottoms are brown, about 3 minutes. Turn sandwiches over. Cook until second sides are brown and cheese is melted, about 3 minutes. Transfer to cutting board. Cut each sandwich into 6 wedges.

Grilled prosciutto and Fontina sandwiches

THE HAM-AND-CHEESE gets fancy. The star, of course, is prosciutto. This famed Italian ham from Emilia-Romagna is salt-cured, air-dried, and aged for ten months to two years in a highly regulated, much-revered tradition. Buy it presliced in packages or ask the butcher to slice it paper-thin (otherwise it can be chewy and even a little bit gamy). You can make these into appetizer sandwiches by dividing the ingredients among baguette slices.

MAKES 2; CAN BE DOUBLED OR TRIPLED

- **4 ounces Fontina or Havarti cheese**
- **4 large slices sourdough bread**
- **¾ teaspoon chopped fresh thyme**
- **6 thin slices prosciutto**
- **Olive oil**

USING cheese plane or swivel-bladed vegetable peeler, thinly slice cheese. Divide half of cheese between 2 bread slices, covering completely. Sprinkle each with half of thyme, cover with half of prosciutto, and then remaining cheese. Top each sandwich with second bread slice.

HEAT heavy large skillet over medium heat. Brush 1 side of each sandwich with oil and sprinkle generously with pepper. Arrange sandwiches oiled side down in skillet. Brush top side with oil and sprinkle with pepper. Cook until bottom is golden brown, pressing down occasionally with spatula, about 3 minutes. Turn and cook until cheese has melted and bottom is golden brown, about 3 minutes longer. Transfer sandwiches to work surface. Cut each sandwich in half and serve immediately.

Prosciutto, mozzarella, tomato, and basil panini

PANINI—ITALIAN-STYLE SANDWICHES usually served grilled—are all the rage at restaurants and cafés. Here's one you can make at home. It's like a *caprese* salad in sandwich form, with the added bonus of prosciutto. Ciabatta is Italian "slipper" bread, named for the flat, slipper-like shape of the loaf. Use focaccia if you can't find ciabatta. These sandwiches take on a smoky nuance from the grilling, but you can use an indoor grill instead (or unpack that sandwich press you got for your birthday).

MAKES 4

- **½ cup olive oil**
- **3 tablespoons balsamic vinegar**
- **1 garlic clove, minced**
- **8 ounces thinly sliced prosciutto**
- **10 ounces thinly sliced whole-milk mozzarella cheese**
- **12 slices tomato**
- **12 large fresh basil leaves**
- **1 16-ounce ciabatta bread (13x6½x1½ inches), halved horizontally**

PREPARE barbecue (medium heat). Whisk olive oil, vinegar, and garlic in small bowl to blend; season dressing to taste with salt and pepper. Layer prosciutto, mozzarella, tomato, and basil over bottom of bread. Drizzle lightly with dressing, then sprinkle with salt and pepper. Press top of bread over. Cut bread into 4 sandwiches.

GRILL sandwiches until bread is golden brown and cheese has melted, pressing occasionally to compact with large spatula, about 5 minutes per side.

Texas-style steak sandwiches with tomato-olive relish

DON'T MESS WITH THIS SANDWICH—it's full of Texas-size flavors. The chili powder–brown sugar rub makes for a bold, tasty steak, and the tomato-olive relish packs a punch (try it on a tuna steak, too). The key components can be made ahead, so it's great for entertaining. Onion rings and beer are the proper accompaniments.

MAKES 4

- **1 teaspoon chili powder**
- **½ teaspoon dark brown sugar**
- **1 1½-pound top sirloin steak (about 1 inch thick), trimmed**

- **1 cup coarsely chopped seeded tomatoes**
- **½ cup pitted Kalamata olives**
- **5 tablespoons, divided, plus 2 teaspoons olive oil**
- **2 teaspoons red wine vinegar**
- **2 tablespoons minced red onion**

- **8 1-inch-thick slices French bread**

- **2 bunches watercress, thick stems trimmed**

MIX chili powder and brown sugar in small bowl to blend. Rub mixture over steak. Sprinkle with salt and pepper.

COMBINE tomatoes, olives, 2 tablespoons oil, and vinegar in processor. Using on/off turns, blend just until olives are coarsely chopped. Transfer to bowl. Stir in onion. Season relish to taste with salt and pepper. *(Steak and relish can be prepared 6 hours ahead. Cover separately and refrigerate.)*

HEAT 2 teaspoons oil in heavy large skillet over medium-high heat. Add steak and cook to desired doneness, about 3 minutes per side for medium-rare. Transfer steak to plate. Let stand 5 minutes. Wipe out skillet.

BRUSH 1 side of each bread slice with remaining 3 tablespoons oil. Heat same skillet over medium heat. Add bread, oiled side down, to skillet and cook until golden, about 2 minutes. Turn bread slices over and cook dry side until browned, about 2 minutes.

CUT steak across grain into ¼-inch-thick slices. Spread relish generously over oiled side of 4 toasts. Top with watercress, then steak slices. Top with a bit more relish, then remaining toasts.

Grilled skirt steak sandwiches on rye with horseradish mayonnaise

SKIRT STEAK CAN BE a tricky cut to work with, but when you marinate the steak overnight, the meat will be foolproof—tender and flavorful. When it comes time to slice the meat, cut it across the grain (perpendicular to the striations). That makes it much more tender than if you slice it with the grain. Use the mayonnaise with abandon on turkey, chicken, or roast beef sandwiches.

MAKES 4

- **4 6-ounce skirt steaks**
- **9 garlic cloves**
- **1¾ cups olive oil**
- **2 tablespoons soy sauce**
- **2 tablespoons distilled white vinegar**

- **1 tablespoon Worcestershire sauce**
- **1 tablespoon hot pepper sauce**
- **2¼ teaspoons dry mustard**

- **1 cup mayonnaise**
- **¼ cup prepared horseradish**
- **¼ cup Dijon or coarse-grained mustard**

- **Unsalted butter, room temperature**
- **8 large ½-inch-thick slices rye bread**
- **4 romaine lettuce leaves**
- **2 tomatoes, thinly sliced**

ARRANGE steaks in shallow glass dish just large enough to accommodate in single layer. Chop garlic in blender. Add next 6 ingredients; blend well. Pour over steaks. Cover and refrigerate overnight.

MIX mayonnaise, horseradish, and Dijon mustard in small bowl. Cover and refrigerate until ready to use. *(Horseradish mayonnaise can be prepared 1 day ahead; keep refrigerated.)*

PREPARE barbecue (high heat). Remove steaks from marinade and arrange on grill rack. Cook about 4 minutes per side for medium-rare. Lightly butter bread and grill until toasted on each side. Spread 1½ tablespoons horseradish mayonnaise over each piece of toast. Cover 4 pieces of toast with lettuce and tomato. Cut steak diagonally across grain into ⅓-inch-thick slices. Arrange steak over tomato. Top with remaining toasts, mayonnaise side down.

Tandoori chicken sandwiches

A *TANDOOR* IS A CLAY OVEN used often in Indian cooking, and chicken responds especially well to the oven's intense heat. Here a barbecue achieves the tandoor effect; the chicken is first marinated, then grilled and placed atop toasted bread slathered with a zesty cilantro-and-mint mayonnaise. Try this sandwich on naan, the soft, doughy Indian flatbread.

MAKES 6

- **6 skinless boneless chicken breast halves**
- **2 tablespoons fresh lemon juice**
- **1 cup plain yogurt**
- **2 tablespoons chopped fresh ginger**
- **2 garlic cloves, chopped**
- **½ teaspoon ground cumin**
- **½ teaspoon ground coriander**
- **¼ teaspoon cayenne pepper**
- **¼ teaspoon turmeric**

- **12 slices sourdough bread**
- **Indian-Spiced Mayonnaise (see recipe)**

ARRANGE chicken in single layer in large glass baking dish. Sprinkle with lemon juice and salt. Mix yogurt, ginger, garlic, cumin, coriander, cayenne, and turmeric in medium bowl. Pour yogurt marinade over chicken breasts and turn to coat. Cover and refrigerate chicken at least 3 and up to 8 hours.

PREPARE barbecue (medium-high heat) or preheat broiler. Remove chicken breasts from marinade (do not wipe clean). Grill or broil chicken until just cooked through, about 5 minutes per side. Cool slightly. *(Chicken can be prepared up to 2 hours ahead. Cover and let stand at room temperature.)*

LIGHTLY toast or grill bread. Spread 1 side of each piece of bread generously with Indian-Spiced Mayonnaise. Slice chicken breasts diagonally. Place slices from 1 breast atop each of 6 bread slices. Top with remaining bread slices, mayonnaise side down. Cut chicken sandwiches in half. Serve sandwiches warm or at room temperature.

Indian-spiced mayonnaise

IN ADDITION TO USING this condiment on the Tandoori Chicken Sandwiches, try it on lamb sandwiches, on roasted fish, or as a dip with crudités.

MAKES ABOUT 1 CUP

- **1 cup (packed) fresh mint leaves**
- **1 cup (packed) fresh cilantro leaves**
- **3 tablespoons chopped onion**
- **1 jalapeño chile, seeded, minced**
- **2 teaspoons apple cider vinegar**
- **½ cup mayonnaise**

COMBINE mint leaves, cilantro leaves, chopped onion, and jalapeño chile in processor; blend until very finely chopped. Mix in vinegar. Add mayonnaise and process just until combined. Season mayonnaise to taste with salt and pepper. *(Mayonnaise can be prepared 3 days ahead. Transfer to small bowl. Cover tightly and refrigerate.)*

Pork barbecue sandwiches with coleslaw

VINEGARY BARBECUE SAUCES—popular in many parts of the South—do their job best on succulent pulled pork, slowly smoked and infused with hickory-wood flavor. No worries if you don't have a smoker. A regular old grill can be converted; just follow the instructions here. What you will need, though, is a charcoal chimney. It's a metal cylinder that helps heat the coals quickly and keep them burning (you'll find chimneys at cookware stores and even some hardware stores).You'll also need a candy/deep-fry thermometer (with a metal stem and a dial face). A helping of coleslaw goes on top of the pork; use purchased slaw if you need to save a step.

MAKES 12

Barbecue sauce

- **¼ cup (½ stick) unsalted butter**
- **6 tablespoons minced onion**
- **1⅓ cups apple cider vinegar**
- **1⅓ cups ketchup**
- **1 cup (packed) dark brown sugar**
- **1 teaspoon Worcestershire sauce**
- **¼ teaspoon cayenne pepper**

Dry seasoning rub

- **3 tablespoons coarsely ground black pepper**
- **3 tablespoons dark brown sugar**
- **3 tablespoons paprika**
- **2 tablespoons salt**
- **1 teaspoon cayenne pepper**

Coleslaw

- **1 cup mayonnaise**
- **6 tablespoons apple cider vinegar**
- **3 tablespoons sugar**
- **12 cups (lightly packed) shredded green cabbage (about 2 small heads)**

Barbecue mop

- **1 cup apple cider vinegar**
- **½ cup water**
- **1 tablespoon Worcestershire sauce**
- **1 tablespoon coarsely ground black pepper**
- **1 tablespoon salt**
- **2 teaspoons vegetable oil**
- **½ teaspoon cayenne pepper**

Pork

- **2 untrimmed boneless pork shoulder halves (Boston butt; about 6 pounds total)**
- **1 20-pound bag charcoal briquettes**
- **4 cups hickory-wood chips, soaked in cold water 30 minutes, drained**
- **12 soft sesame-seed hamburger buns, warmed, split**

FOR BARBECUE SAUCE: Melt butter in heavy large saucepan over medium heat. Add onion and sauté 3 minutes. Add remaining ingredients and bring to boil, stirring frequently. Reduce heat and simmer until sauce is reduced to 2⅔ cups, stirring occasionally, about 30 minutes. Season to taste with salt and pepper. *(Barbecue sauce can be prepared 1 week ahead. Cover and refrigerate.)*

FOR SEASONING RUB: Mix all ingredients in small bowl. *(Seasoning rub can be made 1 week ahead. Store in airtight container at room temperature.)*

FOR COLESLAW: Mix mayonnaise, vinegar, sugar, and 6 tablespoons barbecue sauce in large bowl. Mix in cabbage. Season with salt and pepper. Chill at least 1 hour. *(Coleslaw can be made 1 day ahead. Keep refrigerated.)*

FOR BARBECUE MOP: Mix all ingredients in bowl. Set barbecue mop aside until ready to use.

FOR PORK: Place pork, fat side up, on work surface. Cut each pork piece lengthwise in half, forming 4 long strips total. Place pork on baking sheet. Sprinkle seasoning rub all over pork; rub into pork, covering completely. Cover and chill at least 2 hours and up to 6 hours.

PLACE handful of torn newspaper in bottom of charcoal chimney. Top with 25 charcoal briquettes. Remove top rack from grill. Place chimney on lower grill rack. Light newspaper and let charcoal burn until ash is gray, about 30 minutes.

OPEN 1 bottom grill vent. Turn out hot charcoal onto ½ of bottom rack. Using metal spatula, spread charcoal to cover approximately ⅓ of rack. Scatter 1 cup drained wood chips over coals (avoid using too many wet chips, which may douse the fire). Fill foil loaf pan halfway with water and place it opposite coals on bottom rack.

PLACE top rack on grill. Arrange pork, fat side up, on top rack above loaf pan. Cover grill with lid, positioning top vent directly over pork. Place stem of candy/deep-fry thermometer through top vent, with gauge on outside and tip near pork (thermometer should not touch meat or grill rack); leave in place during cooking. Check temperature after 5 minutes. Use top and bottom vents to maintain temperature range between 225°F and 250°F, opening vents wider to increase heat and closing to decrease heat. Leave any other vents closed. Check temperature every 20 minutes.

AFTER 30 minutes, use technique described above to light additional 15 charcoal briquettes in same charcoal chimney set atop bricks, cement or other nonflammable surface.

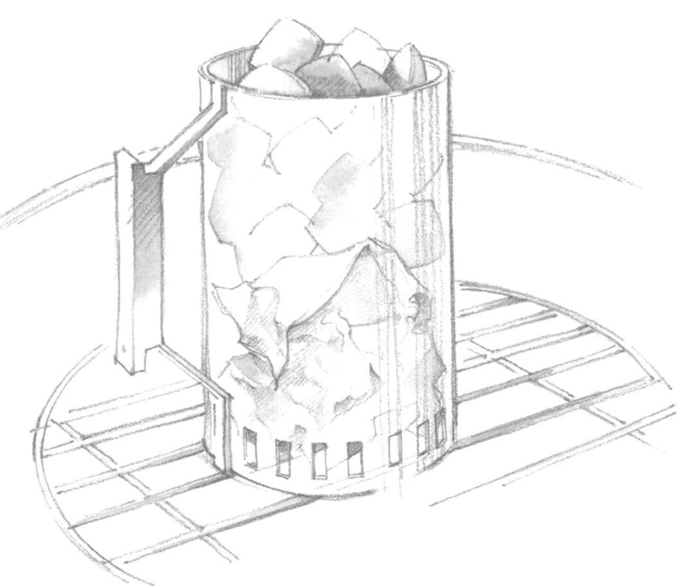

WHEN cooking temperature drops below 225°F, use oven mitts to lift off top rack with pork and place on heatproof surface. Using tongs, add hot ash-tinged briquettes to bottom rack. Sprinkle about 1 cup drained wood chips over charcoal. Reposition top rack with pork above loaf pan. Brush pork lightly with some of barbecue mop. Cover with lid.

ABOUT once an hour, light more charcoal in chimney and replenish charcoal and wood chips as necessary to maintain temperature between 225°F and 250°F, brushing pork lightly with barbecue mop each time grill is opened. Open grill only when necessary and cover as quickly as possible to minimize loss of heat and smoke. Cook pork until meat thermometer inserted into center of meat registers between 165°F and 170°F, turning occasionally, about 3 hours total.

TRANSFER pork to baking sheet. Let stand 10 minutes. When cool enough to handle, shred pork into bite-size pieces, discarding any fat. Mix any accumulated juices into pork. Spoon pork onto bottom halves of buns. Drizzle with barbecue sauce. Top with coleslaw and bun tops.

Grilled lamb sandwiches with grilled green onions

FOR THIS RECIPE you'll need butterflied leg of lamb (ask your butcher to bone and butterfly it for you). These are great for a warm-weather party: Set the components up as a backyard buffet; guests can pick up a sliced baguette, slather it with Aioli, Red Bell Pepper Sauce (see recipes), or tapenade (a thick paste of olives, anchovies, capers, and seasonings), then help themselves to sliced lamb and grilled green onions. Be sure to make enough for seconds. Tapenade is available at Italian markets, specialty foods stores, and some supermarkets.

MAKES 10

- **1 4½-pound butterflied boned leg of lamb, trimmed of excess fat**
- **6 garlic cloves, thinly sliced**
- **2 tablespoons minced fresh thyme**
- **1 tablespoon dried savory**
- **1 tablespoon minced fresh rosemary**

- **5 bunches green onions, trimmed**
- **¼ cup plus 3 tablespoons extra-virgin olive oil**
- **2 22-inch-long French-bread baguettes**
- **Aioli (see recipe)**
- **Red Bell Pepper Sauce (see recipe)**
- **1½ cups purchased tapenade**

USING sharp knife, cut ½-inch slits all over lamb. Insert garlic slices into slits. Sprinkle lamb with salt and pepper, then herbs, pressing herbs to adhere. *(Can be prepared 1 day ahead. Cover and refrigerate.)*

PREPARE barbecue (medium-high heat). Place green onions in large roasting pan. Drizzle ¼ cup oil over onions; toss to coat. Sprinkle with salt and pepper. Cut each baguette crosswise into 5 pieces, then cut each piece horizontally in half. Brush cut sides of bread with remaining 3 tablespoons oil.

GRILL lamb until meat thermometer inserted into thickest part registers 135°F for medium-rare, turning occasionally, about 30 minutes. Transfer to cutting board and tent with foil. Let stand 10 minutes.

WORKING in batches, arrange green onions in single layer on grill. Grill until beginning to brown, about 4 minutes per side. Transfer to cutting board. Grill baguettes, cut side down, until golden brown, about 2 minutes. Place bread in basket. Chop onions; place in bowl. Cut lamb diagonally into thin slices; arrange on platter. Serve with Aioli, Red Bell Pepper Sauce, and tapenade, allowing guests to assemble their own sandwiches.

Aioli

THIS CLASSIC PROVENÇAL CONDIMENT also dresses up steamed vegetables, steamed or roasted fish, or virtually any kind of sandwich.

MAKES ABOUT 2⅓ CUPS

- **6 garlic cloves**
- **⅓ cup extra-virgin olive oil**
- **2 cups mayonnaise**

FINELY chop garlic in processor; gradually blend in oil. Add mayonnaise and blend until smooth. Season to taste with salt and pepper. Transfer to bowl. *(Can be made 1 day ahead. Cover and refrigerate.)*

Red bell pepper sauce

EASY AS CAN BE: Jarred red bell peppers are pureed in the processor with aioli.

MAKES ABOUT 2 CUPS

- **1 15-ounce jar roasted red bell peppers, drained well, patted dry**
- **1 cup Aioli (see recipe)**

BLEND roasted peppers and 1 cup aioli in processor until mixture is smooth. Season to taste with salt and pepper. Transfer sauce to small bowl. *(Can be made 1 day ahead. Cover and refrigerate.)*

Grilled lamb and arugula sandwiches with spicy tomato jam

CUMIN, CILANTRO, AND GARLIC bring out the best in this lamb sandwich. Begin marinating the meat at least two hours ahead. And after it's grilled, be sure to let it sit for at least ten minutes. All the juices that rise to the surface during cooking will settle back into the meat, making for succulent sandwiches. Ciabatta is a rustic, chewy, oval-shaped Italian flatbread available at many bakeries and supermarkets; focaccia can be substituted.

MAKES 8

- **¼ cup olive oil**
- **½ bunch cilantro, stems trimmed**
- **8 garlic cloves**
- **2 tablespoons fresh lemon juice**
- **1 tablespoon ground cumin**
- **1 6-pound leg of lamb, boned, butterflied, trimmed**
- **Spicy Tomato Jam (see recipe)**
- **8 5x4-inch rectangles ciabatta (cut from 2 ciabatta loaves), halved horizontally**
- **5 cups arugula**

PUREE first 5 ingredients in blender. Place lamb in large glass baking dish. Pour marinade over; turn to coat. Cover and refrigerate at least 2 hours or overnight.

PREPARE barbecue (medium-high heat). Sprinkle lamb with salt and pepper. Grill lamb to desired doneness, turning occasionally, about 30 minutes for medium-rare.

TRANSFER lamb to cutting board and tent with aluminum foil; let stand 10 minutes. Cut lamb diagonally into thin slices. Spread Spicy Tomato Jam over cut sides of bread. Arrange lamb and arugula over bottom halves of bread. Cover with bread tops, jam side down.

Spicy tomato jam

THE TOMATO IS A FRUIT, after all, so why not turn it into a jam? This one is a little bit spicy, a little bit tart, and a little bit sweet. In addition to using it on the grilled lamb and arugula sandwiches, try it on chicken, pork, or fish.

MAKES ABOUT 3 CUPS

¼ cup olive oil
3 cups chopped onions
6 garlic cloves, minced
2 tablespoons minced jalapeño chiles with seeds
3½ pounds tomatoes, seeded, chopped
6 tablespoons red wine vinegar
1½ tablespoons sugar
½ cup chopped fresh cilantro

HEAT oil in heavy large pot over medium heat. Add onions and sauté until softened, about 8 minutes. Add garlic and jalapeños; sauté 4 minutes. Add tomatoes, vinegar, and sugar. Cook until almost dry, stirring frequently, about 40 minutes. Mix in cilantro. Season to taste with salt and pepper. Cool. *(Can be prepared 2 days ahead. Transfer to bowl. Cover and refrigerate.)*

Burgers

Grilled hamburgers with sour cream and herbs

THE ADDITION OF SOUR CREAM to these hamburger patties is inspired–it makes them so moist and tender. Don't buy ground beef that's too lean; you'll want about 15 percent fat so the burgers don't dry out. Also, refrain from pressing down the patties with a spatula while they grill (you know you want to): That squeezes out all the precious juices.

MAKES 8

2⅔ pounds lean ground beef (15% fat)
¼ cup sour cream
1 tablespoon minced fresh thyme or 1 teaspoon dried, crumbled
1 tablespoon minced fresh parsley
1 teaspoon minced fresh rosemary or ¼ teaspoon dried, crumbled
¾ teaspoon ground black pepper

8 hamburger buns, split

Grilled Red Onions (see recipe)
Three-Pepper Ketchup (see recipe)

COMBINE first 6 ingredients thoroughly in medium bowl. Shape beef mixture into eight 1-inch-thick patties. Cover and refrigerate at least 1 hour and up to 8 hours.

PREPARE barbecue (medium-high heat). Place burgers on grill. Cover grill and cook burgers 4 minutes. Turn burgers. Cover grill and cook burgers to desired doneness, about 4 minutes longer for medium-rare. Grill buns, inner sides down, during last 2 minutes, if desired.

ARRANGE burgers on bottom halves of buns. Cover burgers with bun tops and serve with Grilled Red Onions and Three Pepper Ketchup.

Grilled red onions

THE SIMPLE MARINADE mellows the onions, and a quick turn on the grill sweetens them. They're delicious on the Grilled Hamburgers with Sour Cream and Herbs, but also try them on grilled cheese sandwiches.

8 SERVINGS

- **4 medium-size red onions**
- **2 tablespoons Worcestershire sauce**
- **2 tablespoons balsamic vinegar**
- **2 tablespoons soy sauce**
- **2 tablespoons olive oil**
- **¾ teaspoon ground black pepper**

CUT ¼-inch slice off top and bottom of each onion and discard. Cut onions crosswise into ½-inch-thick rounds. Arrange onion rounds in single layer in shallow dish. Whisk Worcestershire sauce, vinegar, soy sauce, and oil in small bowl to blend. Pour over onions and let stand at room temperature at least 1 hour and up to 4 hours, basting occasionally.

PREPARE barbecue (medium-high heat). Using large spatula, arrange onions on grill. Cover grill and cook onions until brown, basting occasionally, about 4 minutes per side. Transfer onions to platter. Season to taste with pepper.

Three-pepper ketchup

RED BELL PEPPER, green chile peppers, and ground black pepper come together in this spicy condiment. It'll keep two weeks in the fridge, so there's plenty of time to use up any leftovers.

MAKES ABOUT 2¾ CUPS

- **2 tablespoons olive oil**
- **½ cup minced onion**
- **½ cup sliced green onions**
- **½ cup minced red bell pepper**
- **3 canned pickled jalapeño chiles, stemmed, seeded, minced**
- **2 garlic cloves, minced**
- **¼ teaspoon dried thyme**
- **1½ cups bottled ketchup**
- **¾ cup canned crushed tomatoes in puree**
- **½ teaspoon freshly ground black pepper**

HEAT oil in heavy medium saucepan over low heat. Add all onions, bell pepper, chiles, garlic, and thyme. Cover and cook until vegetables are tender, stirring occasionally, about 10 minutes. Mix in ketchup, tomatoes, and black pepper. Cover partially and simmer until thickened, stirring occasionally, about 5 minutes. Season to taste with salt. Transfer to bowl. Cover and refrigerate. *(Can be prepared 2 weeks ahead. Keep refrigerated.)*

Grilled burgers with blue cheese mayonnaise and barbecued red onions

THAT TIME-HONORED COMBINATION—beef, red onions, blue cheese—on a burger. If you're not a mayonnaise fan, sprinkle a little crumbled blue cheese atop the burgers just before they come off the grill. French fries or onion rings, beer for the grown-ups, and lemonade for the kids are all you need with these.

MAKES 8

- **8 thick slices red onions**
- **1⅓ cups bottled hickory-flavored barbecue sauce**
- **3 pounds ground round, formed into eight 4- to 5-inch-diameter patties**
- **8 4- to 5-inch-diameter hamburger buns, split**
- **Blue Cheese Mayonnaise (see recipe)**

PREPARE barbecue (medium heat). Brush onions generously with barbecue sauce. Grill until onions are tender, brown, and glazed, basting with barbecue sauce and turning occasionally, about 15 minutes.

SPRINKLE patties with salt and pepper. Grill patties until cooked through, about 5 minutes per side. Grill hamburger buns, inner sides down, until lightly toasted, about 2 minutes. Place patties on bottom halves of buns. Top each with 1 onion slice, Blue Cheese Mayonnaise, and then bun tops.

Blue cheese mayonnaise

ALSO TRY THIS on roast beef or turkey sandwiches, or as a dip for crudités.

MAKES ABOUT 1½ CUPS

8 ounces blue cheese, crumbled
⅔ cup mayonnaise
2 teaspoons red wine vinegar
1 teaspoon hot pepper sauce

MIX all ingredients in bowl to blend. *(Can be made 1 day ahead. Cover and refrigerate.)*

Jamaican jerk burgers with orange-chipotle mayonnaise

THESE BURGERS PRACTICALLY BURST with Caribbean flavors. Jerk seasoning is a Jamaican invention; it varies from place to place on the island, but the common denominators are thyme, chiles, allspice, and garlic. Chipotle chiles are smoked jalapeños packed in a spicy tomato sauce called *adobo*. They're usually in the aisle with the canned and jarred salsas. If your market doesn't carry them, check a Latin market. Here the chipotles mix with orange juice and mayonnaise for a sweet-hot burger topper. If you like, grill the onion slices.

MAKES 6

Orange-chipotle mayonnaise
1 cup mayonnaise
3 tablespoons orange juice
1 tablespoon minced canned chipotle chiles

Jerk sauce
1 bunch green onions, coarsely chopped (about 1½ cups)
1 tablespoon chopped fresh thyme
1 small habanero chile or 2 medium jalapeño chiles, seeded, chopped
1 garlic clove
½ cup (packed) golden brown sugar
½ cup vegetable oil
½ cup soy sauce
1 teaspoon ground allspice

2 pounds ground beef (15% fat)

6 sesame-seed hamburger buns, split, toasted
6 romaine lettuce leaves
3 tomatoes, sliced
1 onion, thinly sliced

FOR ORANGE-CHIPOTLE MAYONNAISE: Mix all ingredients in small bowl. Season to taste with salt and pepper. *(Mayonnaise can be prepared 1 day ahead. Cover and refrigerate.)*

FOR JERK SAUCE: Finely chop first 4 ingredients in processor. Add sugar and next 3 ingredients; process until almost smooth. Season sauce to taste with salt and pepper.

PREPARE barbecue (medium-high heat). Set aside ¾ cup jerk sauce.

SHAPE ground beef into six ½- to ¾-inch-thick patties; place in 13x9x2-inch glass baking dish. Pour ½ cup jerk sauce over patties and turn to coat; let stand 20 minutes.

SPRINKLE patties with salt and pepper. Grill to desired doneness, brushing occasionally with remaining jerk sauce from baking dish, about 4 minutes per side for medium.

SPREAD mayonnaise over inner surfaces of buns. Place lettuce on bottom halves of buns. Top with tomato, burgers, onion, and bun tops. Serve, passing reserved ¾ cup jerk sauce separately.

Beef and andouille burgers with Asiago cheese

PUNCHED UP WITH spicy andouille sausage and sharp Asiago cheese, and spread with a mayonnaise mixed with Dijon mustard and sun-dried tomatoes—these are like no cheeseburgers you've ever had. You'll find andouille, a smoked pork-and-beef sausage, at most supermarkets and butcher shops. Asiago will be available at some supermarkets and any good cheese store.

MAKES 6

- **4 oil-packed sun-dried tomatoes, drained**
- **½ cup mayonnaise**
- **1 tablespoon whole grain Dijon mustard**

- **8 ounces andouille sausages or hot links, cut into 1-inch pieces**
- **2½ pounds ground beef (15% fat)**
- **2 large shallots, minced**
- **2 teaspoons salt**
- **2 teaspoons ground black pepper**
- **1 teaspoon fennel seeds, crushed**

- **6 large sesame-seed hamburger buns, split**
- **6 ⅓-inch-thick slices red onion**
- **Olive oil**
- **1 cup coarsely grated Asiago cheese**

- **1 7- to 7.5-ounce jar roasted red peppers, drained**

FINELY chop sun-dried tomatoes in processor. Blend in mayonnaise and mustard. Transfer mayonnaise mixture to small bowl. *(Can be made 1 day ahead. Cover and refrigerate.)*

FINELY chop andouille sausages in clean processor. Transfer to large bowl. Add beef, shallots, salt, pepper, and crushed fennel seeds. Stir mixture with fork just until blended. Form mixture into six 1-inch-thick patties.

PREPARE barbecue (medium-high heat). Grill hamburger buns until golden, about 2 minutes. Transfer to platter. Brush onion slices with oil. Sprinkle with salt and pepper. Grill until golden, about 7 minutes per side. Grill hamburgers to desired doneness, about 5 minutes per side for medium-rare. Sprinkle cheese over top of burgers.

SPREAD inner sides of hamburger buns with mayonnaise mixture. Top bottom halves of buns with hamburgers, then red peppers. Top with onion slices. Cover with top halves of buns and serve.

Maple-barbecued pork burgers

TRUTH BE TOLD, these are really sausage burgers—and they're unbelievably easy to make. Bottled barbecue sauce, maple syrup, and apple cider vinegar mix with fresh sausage and fresh bell pepper. Purchased coleslaw makes for a one-step topping. Easy sides: corn on the cob, potato chips, and dill pickles.

MAKES 2; CAN BE DOUBLED

- **8 ounces pork sausage (preferably hot breakfast sausage)**
- **½ cup diced green bell pepper**

- **⅔ cup bottled barbecue sauce**
- **1½ tablespoons pure maple syrup**
- **1½ tablespoons apple cider vinegar**

- **2 onion rolls, split**
- **½ cup purchased coleslaw**

GENTLY mix sausage and green bell pepper in medium bowl. Form into two ½-inch-thick patties. *(Can be prepared 8 hours ahead. Cover and refrigerate.)*

PREPARE barbecue (medium-high heat). Whisk barbecue sauce, maple syrup, and vinegar in medium bowl to blend. Reserve ⅓ cup sauce for basting patties.

GRILL rolls until lightly toasted. Transfer to 2 plates. Grill patties 5 minutes. Turn patties over. Brush with sauce. Grill until cooked through, brushing occasionally with sauce, about 5 minutes longer. Place burgers on bottom halves of rolls. Top each burger with ¼ cup coleslaw and top half of roll. Serve, passing remaining sauce separately.

Spiced lamb burgers in pita

WHOLE WHEAT PITA BREAD makes it easy to pile on (or in) the garnishes: Try chopped tomato, sliced cucumber, shredded lettuce, and a creamy spoonful of yogurt. Even better, whip up a little *raita*—yogurt mixed with some finely chopped cucumber and crushed garlic. This recipe can be doubled and tripled—and beyond—to serve a crowd. Put out Indian beers on ice to drink alongside.

MAKES 2; CAN BE DOUBLED

- **12 ounces lean ground lamb**
- **½ cup finely chopped onion**
- **1 garlic clove, minced**
- **3 tablespoons chopped fresh mint or 1 teaspoon dried**
- **1 teaspoon ground cumin**
- **½ teaspoon ground coriander**
- **2 whole wheat pita bread rounds, top third cut off**

PREPARE barbecue (medium-high heat). Mix first 6 ingredients in medium bowl. Sprinkle with salt and pepper. Shape lamb into two ¾-inch-thick patties. Grill burgers to desired doneness, about 5 minutes per side for medium-rare. Open pita breads; place 1 burger in each.

Grilled open-face crab burgers

THESE OPEN-FACE SANDWICHES are like a crab cake on a bun. Serve them with fries for a New England version of fish and chips, or just accompany them with a simple green salad. If you use fresh crabmeat, be sure to remove any cartilage or shell before forming the patties. Old Bay seasoning, a zesty mixture of celery salt, red and black pepper, cloves, bay leaves, ginger, and paprika (among other things), is a must on the East Coast when it comes to shellfish. You'll find it in the supermarket spice aisle.

MAKES 2 SERVINGS; CAN BE DOUBLED

- **6 ounces fresh crabmeat, picked over**
- **1½ cups fresh breadcrumbs made from crustless French bread, divided**
- **½ cup chopped green onions**
- **4½ tablespoons mayonnaise, divided**
- **1 teaspoon Old Bay or other seafood seasoning**
- **1 egg yolk**
- **1½ tablespoons Dijon mustard**

Vegetable oil

- **4 large slices French bread**

MIX crabmeat, 1 cup breadcrumbs, green onions, 2 tablespoons mayonnaise, and Old Bay seasoning in medium bowl. Season with salt and pepper. Mix in egg yolk. Form mixture into four 2½-inch-diameter patties. Place remaining ½ cup breadcrumbs in shallow bowl. Dip patties into crumbs, turning to coat completely. Mix remaining 2½ tablespoons mayonnaise with mustard in small bowl to blend; set dressing aside.

PREPARE barbecue (medium-high heat) or preheat broiler. Brush barbecue rack with oil. Grill burgers until golden brown, about 4 minutes per side. Grill bread slices until lightly toasted, about 1 minute per side. Spread toasts with mustard dressing. Top each with burger.

Salmon burgers with hoisin and ginger

HOISIN IS A WONDERFUL, complex sauce of soybeans, garlic, chiles, sesame paste, and other flavors. Look for it in the Asian section of well-stocked supermarkets or at Asian markets. Kept in the fridge, it will last indefinitely. (It's usually packaged in glass jars, but you may find it in a can—if so, transfer any leftovers to a jar before refrigerating.) You'll find Asian sesame oil in the same places; it's worth seeking out because it has a toasted flavor that regular sesame oil doesn't. Sweet potato fries or chips and an Asian-style coleslaw are appropriate companions to this burger.

MAKES 4

- **1 pound skinless boneless salmon fillet, cut into 1-inch pieces**
- **¼ cup fresh cilantro leaves**
- **2 tablespoons hoisin sauce**
- **2 tablespoons mayonnaise**
- **¼ cup chopped green onions**
- **2 teaspoons minced peeled fresh ginger**
- **1 garlic clove, minced**
- **¾ teaspoon salt**
- **½ teaspoon ground black pepper**

- **2½ teaspoons Asian sesame oil**
- **4 large sesame-seed hamburger buns, split**
- **Additional hoisin sauce**
- **Additional mayonnaise**
- **8 butter lettuce leaves**

PLACE first 4 ingredients in processor. Using on/off turns, blend until coarsely ground. Transfer mixture to medium bowl. Mix in next 5 ingredients. Form into four ½-inch-thick patties. Cover; refrigerate at least 1 hour and up to 4 hours.

HEAT oil in large nonstick skillet over medium heat. Sauté patties until fish is cooked through, about 3 minutes per side. Meanwhile, toast hamburger buns. Spread bottom halves of buns with additional hoisin sauce. Spread top halves with additional mayonnaise. Transfer burgers to bottom halves of buns; top with lettuce leaves and top halves of buns.

Seared tuna burgers with ginger-garlic mayonnaise

ESSENTIALLY, THESE BURGERS ARE tuna steak sandwiches—whole pieces of tuna are grilled, then placed atop toasted sesame-seed buns. The recipe calls for cooking the tuna until it's opaque in the center, but if you or your guests prefer the fish pink or ruby-red in the middle, just reduce the cooking time.

MAKES 2; CAN BE DOUBLED

- **2 ¾-inch-thick tuna steaks (each about 5 to 6 ounces)**
- **2 teaspoons olive oil**

- **1 tablespoon minced peeled fresh ginger**
- **1 garlic clove, minced**
- **4 tablespoons mayonnaise**
- **1 tablespoon fresh lemon juice**

- **2 large sesame-seed sandwich rolls, split, toasted**
- **1 bunch arugula, stems trimmed**

SPRINKLE tuna with salt and pepper. Heat oil in heavy medium skillet over medium-high heat. Add tuna to skillet and cook until browned outside and just opaque in center, about 3 minutes per side. Transfer tuna to plate.

ADD ginger and garlic to same skillet; stir 30 seconds. Scrape into small bowl. Mix in mayonnaise and lemon juice. Season with salt and pepper.

SPREAD bottoms of rolls with mayonnaise mixture. Top with tuna, arugula, and tops of rolls.

Turkey burgers with chipotle tartar sauce

CHIPOTLE CHILES—jalapeños that have been smoked, dried, and then packed in a spicy tomato sauce called *adobo*—give these burgers their kick. You'll find them at Latin markets and near the canned salsas at some supermarkets. A tablespoon is usually about one chile, minced. Refrigerate the leftover chipotles and use them to make spicy mayo for other sandwiches; mix some of the sauce into sour cream for tacos or enchiladas; or chop a chile and throw it in the next time you make scrambled eggs. Serve the turkey burgers with a butter lettuce and avocado salad tossed in a citrus vinaigrette.

MAKES 4

- **3/4 cup mayonnaise**
- **2 tablespoons extra-virgin olive oil**
- **2 tablespoons minced red onion**
- **2 tablespoons chopped fresh dill**
- **1 tablespoon minced canned chipotle chiles**
- **1 tablespoon drained capers**

- **1 pound ground turkey**
- **4 whole wheat hamburger buns, split**
- **4 slices red onion**
- **8 slices plum tomato**
- **2 bunches arugula**

WHISK first 6 ingredients in small bowl. Season to taste with salt and pepper. *(Tartar sauce can be made 2 days ahead. Cover and refrigerate.)*

PREPARE barbecue (medium heat). Form ground turkey into four ½-inch-thick patties. Sprinkle with salt and pepper. Grill burgers until cooked through, about 5 minutes per side. Grill buns until just toasted. Spread 1 tablespoon tartar sauce on bottom half of each bun. Top each with 1 burger, then 1 tablespoon sauce. Top each with 1 onion slice, 2 tomato slices, then ½ bunch arugula. Cover with bun tops. Serve, passing remaining tartar sauce separately.

7 Pastas and pizzas

There may be debate over who first arrived on this continent, but there's no argument about who eventually conquered the country. The Italians—their pizzas and pastas, to be specific—have won the battle for American appetites.

Things have changed much since the waves of Italian immigrants, mostly from the south of Italy, started arriving here in the late nineteenth century. Once upon a time, pasta meant spaghetti with a slow-cooked red sauce. Menus still feature spaghetti in tomato sauce, but now it's between the rigatoni with prosciutto and the pappardelle in a rich quail ragù. The depth and diversity of our pasta dishes have been enhanced in two ways: first by a wave of chefs who arrived in America from all regions of Italy, bringing their treasured recipes with them, and second by eager American chefs who have traveled across Italy to hone their skills. Both have introduced us to pairings of pasta and sauce that go well beyond linguini and clams.

Pizza, too, used to be a pretty straightforward proposition: a tomato sauce and cheese pie with a chewy, thickish crust, topped with sausage, onion, anchovy, or pepperoni (still the most popular topping in the States). Then came the 1970s, California Cuisine, and the burst of creativity that followed. Today, for every traditional pizzeria there is a restaurant or café serving its own super-crispy, thin-crusted spin on the classic, finished with everything from roast duck to a salad of baby arugula tossed in an olive oil dressing.

The recipes in this chapter reflect the variety of pizzas found across the country. They also call for crusts made with yeast dough—hand-kneaded at home or store-bought—and the excellent baked crusts sold at most supermarkets. You'll even find here a few cousins of the pizza, like southern France's pissaladière, topped with richly caramelized onions and anchovies, and the calzone, the well-known pizza "turnover."

Pasta and pizza have achieved star status in this country. But they are still, no matter their trimmings, comfort foods that go directly to the soul.

Pastas

Upscale macaroni and cheese

EVERYONE'S FAVORITE CHILDHOOD DISH gets a sophisticated twist with blue cheese and the addition of red bell peppers and celery. But never fear: The kid in you—and all the kids in your life—will love it. You can use any type of blue cheese, but for more thorough melting and blending, choose one with a consistency that is more creamy than crumbly. Penne pasta, which gets its descriptive name from the Italian word for old-fashioned quill pens, may be replaced with elbow macaroni or other tube shapes.

12 SERVINGS

2 tablespoons (1/4 stick) butter
3 large red bell peppers (about 1 1/2 pounds), cut into 1/2-inch pieces
5 celery stalks, chopped

1 1/2 cups whipping cream
1 1/2 cups half and half
1 pound blue cheese, crumbled (about 4 cups)
1 teaspoon celery seeds
Cayenne pepper
3 large egg yolks
1/2 cup chopped celery leaves

1 pound penne pasta
3/4 cup freshly grated Parmesan cheese (about 2 1/2 ounces)

MELT butter in heavy large skillet over medium-high heat. Add bell peppers and celery; sauté until just beginning to soften, about 7 minutes. Remove from heat. Sprinkle vegetables with salt and pepper.

COMBINE cream, half and half, and blue cheese in heavy large saucepan. Stir over low heat until cheese melts. Remove from heat. Add celery seeds. Season sauce to taste with cayenne pepper, salt, and ground black pepper. Beat egg yolks in medium bowl to blend. Gradually whisk in half of cheese sauce. Return mixture to sauce in pan and whisk to blend. Add celery leaves.

BUTTER 13¾x10½x2¾-inch (4-quart-capacity) oval baking dish. Cook pasta in large pot of boiling salted water until tender but still firm to bite, stirring occasionally. Drain; return to same pot. Add sauce and vegetables; stir to blend. Transfer to prepared baking dish. *(Pasta can be prepared 1 day ahead. Cover and chill. Let stand at room temperature 1 hour before continuing.)*

PREHEAT oven to 400°F. Sprinkle Parmesan over surface of pasta. Bake uncovered until pasta is heated through, sauce is bubbling, and top is beginning to brown, about 25 minutes.

Macaroni and cheese with prosciutto

TANGY CHEESES AND PROSCIUTTO, the salt-cured, air-dried ham of Northern Italy, give pleasingly bold flavor to this hearty concoction. As you should for all baked pasta dishes, take care to boil the pasta only until it is tender but still slightly chewy—what the Italians call *al dente*, or "to the tooth." The pasta will continue to soften as it absorbs sauce during baking.

6 SERVINGS

8 ounces small elbow macaroni (about 2 cups)

1 1/2 cups (packed) coarsely grated Gruyère cheese (about 6 ounces), divided
1 cup whipping cream
1 cup whole milk

- **3 ounces thinly sliced prosciutto, coarsely chopped**
- **3 tablespoons freshly grated Parmesan cheese (scant 1 ounce)**
- **⅛ teaspoon ground nutmeg**

POSITION rack in bottom third of oven and preheat to 400°F. Butter 11x7-inch glass baking dish. Cook macaroni in large pot of boiling salted water until tender but still firm to bite, stirring occasionally. Drain well.

WHISK ½ cup Gruyère, cream, milk, prosciutto, Parmesan, and nutmeg in large bowl to blend. Add pasta and toss to coat. Season to taste with salt and pepper. Transfer to prepared baking dish. Sprinkle remaining 1 cup Gruyère over. Bake until cheese on top melts and pasta is heated through, about 20 minutes. Serve warm.

Spaghetti with butter, Parmesan, and pepper

ULTRA-RICH AND ready in a flash, this pasta dish just might be the ultimate comfort food. As in any recipe composed of only a few simple elements, the quality of the ingredients is paramount. Look for good-quality Parmesan cheese, such as Parmigiano-Reggiano imported from Italy, and buy it in block form if possible. That way, you will be able not only to grate it just before use for maximum flavor, but also to cut thin shavings from the block to garnish each serving, using a cheese plane or a swivel-bladed vegetable peeler.

4 TO 6 SERVINGS

- **1 pound spaghetti**
- **2 cups freshly grated Parmesan cheese (about 6 ounces)**
- **½ cup (1 stick) butter, diced, room temperature**
- **Freshly ground black pepper**
- **Fresh Parmesan cheese shavings (optional)**

COOK pasta in large pot of boiling salted water until tender but still firm to bite, stirring occasionally. Drain, reserving 1 cup pasta cooking liquid. Return pasta to same pot. Add ¼ cup reserved cooking liquid, grated cheese, and butter. Toss over medium heat until cheese melts and sauce coats pasta, adding more reserved cooking liquid by ¼ cupfuls if pasta is dry, about 3 minutes. Season to taste with salt and freshly ground black pepper. Transfer pasta to serving bowl. Garnish with Parmesan shavings, if desired, and serve.

Wild mushroom and orzo "risotto"

ORZO—RICE-SHAPED PASTA—is easier to find than arborio rice (the traditional ingredient in risotto) and makes a delicious risotto-style side dish. It also requires less frequent stirring as it cooks, leaving you more time and attention to prepare a quick main course to go with it, such as grilled shrimp or chicken. Packets of dried porcini mushrooms are available at Italian markets and specialty foods stores, and in the produce section of many supermarkets. For a vegetarian version, substitute vegetable broth.

6 SERVINGS

- **⅞ to 1 ounce dried porcini mushrooms**
- **1½ cups hot water**

- **3 tablespoons olive oil**
- **1 medium onion, chopped**
- **2 cups orzo (rice-shaped pasta; about 13 ounces)**

- **4 cups low-salt chicken broth**

- **½ cup freshly grated Parmesan cheese (about 1½ ounces)**
- **Minced fresh parsley**

PLACE mushrooms in small bowl. Add 1½ cups hot water and let stand until mushrooms soften, about 40 minutes. Drain mushrooms well, reserving soaking liquid. Chop mushrooms.

HEAT oil in heavy medium saucepan over medium heat. Add onion and sauté until tender, about 8 minutes. Add orzo and stir until coated with onion mixture. Stir in chopped mushrooms.

MEANWHILE, combine broth and reserved mushroom soaking liquid in another medium saucepan, leaving any mushroom sediment behind. Bring broth mixture to simmer; reduce heat to low and keep hot.

ADD 1 cup broth mixture to orzo. Simmer over medium-low heat until orzo absorbs broth mixture, stirring occasionally. Continue adding broth mixture 1 cup at a time, simmering until each addition is absorbed before adding next, stirring occasionally, until orzo is just tender and risotto is creamy, about 30 minutes. Stir in Parmesan. Season to taste with salt and pepper. Transfer to bowl; garnish with parsley.

Goat cheese–arugula ravioli with tomato-pancetta butter

NO ONE EXCEPT YOU will know how easy this elegant recipe is to make. The secret is using purchased wonton wrappers, found at Asian markets and in the refrigerated case of many supermarkets, so that you don't have to fuss with a pasta machine. Lightly brushing egg white over the wrappers provides a moisture barrier that keeps the filling from softening the wrappers and helps to seal the filling securely inside. Pancetta—Italian bacon cured in salt—is available at Italian markets and in the refrigerated deli case of many supermarkets.

4 TO 6 SERVINGS

Ravioli

- **2 tablespoons olive oil**
- **3 large shallots, minced**
- **8 ounces baby arugula (about 8 cups)**
- **6 ounces soft fresh goat cheese, crumbled (about 1½ cups)**
- **½ cup freshly grated Parmesan cheese (about 1½ ounces)**
- **Nonstick vegetable oil spray**
- **42 (about) wonton wrappers (from one 12-ounce package)**
- **2 large egg whites, whisked until foamy**

Tomato-pancetta butter

- **6 ounces thinly sliced pancetta or bacon, coarsely chopped**
- **¼ cup (½ stick) butter**
- **6 large plum tomatoes, quartered, seeds and membranes discarded, tomatoes diced**
- **1 teaspoon chopped fresh thyme**

Serving

- **5 tablespoons butter, melted**
- **12 fresh basil leaves**
- **Fresh thyme sprigs**

FOR RAVIOLI: Heat oil in heavy large skillet over medium heat. Add shallots; sauté 10 minutes. Add arugula; toss until wilted but still bright green, about 3 minutes. Transfer arugula mixture to large bowl to cool. Mix in goat cheese and Parmesan cheese. Season filling to taste with salt and pepper.

LINE 2 large rimmed baking sheets with heavy-duty aluminum foil; spray foil with nonstick spray. Place 4 wonton wrappers on work surface; cover remaining wrappers with plastic wrap to prevent drying. Lightly brush entire surface of each wrapper with egg white. Spoon 1 generous teaspoon filling into center of each wrapper. Fold wrappers diagonally in half, forming triangles. Press edges firmly to seal. Arrange ravioli in single layer on prepared baking sheets. Repeat with remaining wrappers and filling. *(Ravioli can be made ahead. Cover with plastic wrap and chill up to 1 day; or cover with plastic wrap, then heavy-duty foil, and freeze up to 1 week. If frozen, do not thaw before cooking.)*

FOR TOMATO BUTTER: Sauté chopped pancetta in large skillet over medium-high heat until crisp and brown. Using slotted spoon, transfer pancetta to paper towels to drain. Pour off all but 1 tablespoon drippings from skillet. Add butter to drippings in skillet; melt over medium-high heat. Add tomatoes and thyme; sauté until tomatoes are tender, about 5 minutes. Season to taste with salt and pepper. *(Butter and pancetta can be prepared 2 hours ahead. Let stand separately at room temperature.)*

TO SERVE: Place melted butter in large bowl. Cook half of ravioli in large pot of boiling salted water until just tender, about 4 minutes for fresh or 5 minutes for frozen. Using large strainer, transfer ravioli to colander and drain, then place in bowl with butter and toss to coat. Cover to keep warm. Cook remaining ravioli in same pot of boiling water. Drain and add to bowl of buttered ravioli. Toss gently to coat. Divide ravioli among shallow bowls. Rewarm tomato butter over medium heat. Add reserved pancetta and basil leaves; sauté 1 minute. Spoon sauce over ravioli; garnish with thyme sprigs.

Ravioli with herbed walnut sauce

PURCHASED CHEESE RAVIOLI get dressed up for dinner in a ten-minute sauce that combines wine, walnuts, garlic, and chopped fresh rosemary and parsley. The simple step of sautéing the walnuts until they turn golden dramatically enriches their flavor. For an attractive garnish, use a cheese plane or a swivel-bladed vegetable peeler to cut thin shavings from the side of a block of imported Parmesan cheese.

4 SERVINGS

1 pound purchased cheese ravioli

1/4 cup (1/2 stick) butter
3/4 cup coarsely chopped walnuts
3 garlic cloves, minced
1 cup dry white wine
1/4 cup chopped fresh parsley
1 tablespoon chopped fresh rosemary

COOK pasta in large pot of boiling salted water until tender but still firm to bite, or according to directions on package, stirring occasionally. Drain.

MELT butter in heavy large skillet over medium-high heat. Add walnuts; sauté until golden, about 2 minutes. Add garlic; sauté 30 seconds. Add wine. Simmer until sauce is slightly reduced, about 2 minutes. Add parsley and rosemary. Simmer 1 minute. Add pasta and toss to coat with sauce. Season to taste with salt and pepper. Transfer to bowl.

Spicy penne with tomatoes, olives, and two cheeses

A ROBUST ANTIDOTE to a chilly evening, this delicious and simple baked pasta dish is all the easier because you can make its sauce up to two days in advance. The final cooking of the pasta, assembly, and baking is left until less than an hour before dinner. Havarti, a widely available Danish cow's milk cheese also produced in America, has a mild yet pungent flavor and a semisoft texture that melts beautifully.

4 SERVINGS

6 tablespoons olive oil, divided
1 1/2 cups chopped onion
1 garlic clove, minced
3 28-ounce cans Italian plum tomatoes in juice, drained
2 teaspoons dried basil
1 1/2 teaspoons dried crushed red pepper
2 cups low-salt chicken broth

1 pound penne pasta or rigatoni
2 1/2 cups (packed) coarsely grated Havarti cheese (about 10 ounces)
1/3 cup sliced pitted Kalamata olives
1/3 cup freshly grated Parmesan cheese (about 1 ounce)
1/4 cup finely chopped fresh basil

HEAT 3 tablespoons oil in heavy large pot over medium-high heat. Add onion and garlic; sauté until onion is translucent, about 5 minutes. Mix in tomatoes, dried basil, and crushed red pepper. Bring to boil, breaking up tomatoes with back of fork. Add broth; return to boil. Reduce heat to medium; simmer until mixture thickens to chunky sauce consistency and is reduced to 6 cups, stirring occasionally, about 1 hour 10 minutes. Season to taste with salt and pepper. *(Sauce can be made 2 days ahead. Refrigerate uncovered until cold, then cover and keep refrigerated. Rewarm over low heat before using.)*

PREHEAT oven to 375°F. Cook pasta in large pot of boiling salted water until tender but still firm to bite, stirring occasionally. Drain; return to same pot. Toss with remaining 3 tablespoons oil. Pour sauce over and toss to blend. Mix in Havarti cheese. Transfer pasta to 13x9x2-inch glass baking dish. Sprinkle with olives, then Parmesan. Bake until pasta is heated through, about 30 minutes. Sprinkle with fresh basil.

Capellini with fresh tomato, caper, and basil sauce

THIS CLASSIC PASTA SAUCE gains tangy flavor from capers and Sherry wine vinegar. Angel hair pasta, slightly thinner than capellini, can be substituted. Use the ripest tomatoes you can find. To peel tomatoes, bring a pot of water to a boil and fill a mixing bowl with ice and water. With a sharp knife, core each tomato and score an X in its opposite end. Immerse the tomatoes in boiling water until their skins start to wrinkle, about 30 seconds; using a slotted spoon, transfer them to the ice water to cool. With the help of the knife, peel off the skin starting at the X. Or don't peel them, for a more rustic result.

6 SERVINGS

- **2 pounds plum tomatoes, peeled, seeded, coarsely chopped**
- **1 cup coarsely chopped fresh basil**

- **3 tablespoons Sherry wine vinegar**
- **1 3- to 4-ounce jar capers, drained**
- **1 pound capellini or angel hair**
- **3/4 to 1 cup olive oil (preferably extra-virgin)**

COMBINE chopped tomatoes and basil in medium bowl. Marinate at room temperature 2 hours, tossing occasionally.

STIR vinegar and capers into tomato mixture. Season to taste with salt and pepper. Cook pasta in large pot of boiling salted water until tender but still firm to bite, stirring occasionally. Drain; return to same pot. Add enough oil to coat. Stir in tomato mixture. Season to taste with salt and pepper. Transfer to large shallow bowl.

Rigatoni with tomatoes and vodka

MUCH OF THE VODKA'S alcohol content will evaporate during simmering, but it loses none of its refreshing edge of flavor, which spikes the creamy tomato-based sauce. Chopped prosciutto or ham adds its own salty-sweet, meaty taste, but you can leave it out for a vegetarian version of the recipe.

4 SERVINGS

- **8 ounces rigatoni or other tubular pasta**

- **2 tablespoons (1/4 stick) butter**
- **1 small onion, chopped**
- **2 garlic cloves, minced**
- **1 tablespoon dried Italian seasoning**
- **1 15- to 16-ounce can diced tomatoes in juice**
- **3 ounces sliced prosciutto or ham, chopped**
- **1/2 cup vodka**
- **3/4 cup whipping cream**
- **1 cup freshly grated Parmesan cheese (about 3 ounces), divided**

COOK pasta in large pot of boiling salted water until tender but still firm to bite, stirring occasionally. Drain well.

MEANWHILE, melt butter in heavy large skillet over medium-high heat. Add onion, garlic, and Italian seasoning; sauté until onion is translucent, about 4 minutes. Add tomatoes with juice and prosciutto; simmer 10 minutes, stirring occasionally. Add vodka and simmer 5 minutes. Add cream and ½ cup Parmesan; simmer until sauce thickens slightly, stirring occasionally, about 4 minutes. Add pasta and toss until sauce coats pasta. Season to taste with salt and pepper. Transfer to bowl. Serve, passing remaining ½ cup Parmesan separately.

Gemelli with artichokes, sugar snap peas, and Parmesan

HERE'S A DELICIOUS SPRINGTIME PASTA, with the edible pea pods and a generous sprinkling of freshly grated Parmesan cheese providing a nice contrast to the artichoke hearts. Gemelli, which means "twins" in Italian, is a pasta featuring two short strands twisted together.

4 SERVINGS

- **8 ounces gemelli or penne pasta**
- **2 tablespoons olive oil**
- **1 8-ounce package frozen artichoke hearts, thawed**
- **2 garlic cloves, minced**
- **½ pound sugar snap peas, trimmed**
- **½ cup whipping cream**
- **1 tablespoon minced fresh tarragon**
- **½ cup freshly grated Parmesan cheese (about 1½ ounces)**

COOK pasta in large pot of boiling salted water until tender but still firm to bite, stirring occasionally. Drain well.

HEAT oil in heavy large skillet over medium-high heat. Add artichokes and garlic; sauté until artichokes begin to brown, about 5 minutes. Add sugar snap peas; sauté 1 minute. Add cream and tarragon; bring to simmer. Mix in pasta, then cheese. Toss until heated through, about 2 minutes. Season to taste with salt and pepper. Transfer to bowl.

Farfalle with asparagus, roasted shallots, and blue cheese

WHEN TOSSED with the warm pasta, the blue cheese melts into a silky sauce. Roasting the shallots caramelizes their natural sugars, giving them a rich, sweet flavor that complements the tangy cheese and the fresh asparagus. A garnish of breadcrumbs browned in olive oil adds intriguing crunch to every bite.

6 SERVINGS

- **1½ pounds shallots (about 24), peeled, halved through root end**
- **4 tablespoons olive oil, divided**
- **1 cup fresh breadcrumbs made from crustless French bread**
- **1½ pounds farfalle (bow-tie pasta)**
- **2 pounds thin asparagus, trimmed, cut diagonally into 1½-inch pieces**
- **1 pound creamy blue cheese (such as Saga blue or Gorgonzola), cut into ½-inch cubes**

PREHEAT oven to 375°F. Toss shallots with 2 tablespoons oil on rimmed baking sheet; spread in single layer. Sprinkle with salt and pepper. Roast until tender and golden brown, stirring occasionally, about 35 minutes.

STIR remaining 2 tablespoons oil and breadcrumbs in small skillet over medium heat until crumbs brown, about 4 minutes. *(Shallots and crumbs can be prepared 8 hours ahead. Cover separately; let stand at room temperature.)*

COOK pasta in large pot of boiling salted water 8 minutes. Add asparagus; cook until asparagus is crisp-tender and pasta is tender but still firm to bite, stirring occasionally, about 4 minutes. Drain pasta and asparagus. Transfer to large bowl. Immediately add blue cheese and shallots. Toss until cheese melts and pasta is well coated. Season to taste with salt and pepper. Transfer pasta to bowls. Sprinkle with breadcrumbs.

Orecchiette with broccoli rabe

IN THE SOUTHEASTERN ITALIAN REGION of Apulia, women still make pasta at home, and their favorite shape is orecchiette ("little ears"). The sauces for this whimsical pasta are straightforward and usually contain vegetables, along with Apulia's famed olive oil. The broccoli rabe featured in this version is a leafy green stalk with scattered clusters of tiny broccoli-like florets. Sometimes called rapini, broccoli rabe is available at specialty foods stores and some supermarkets.

6 SERVINGS

- **¼ cup olive oil**
- **4 garlic cloves, minced**

- **12 ounces orecchiette or medium shell pasta**
- **1 pound broccoli rabe, trimmed, chopped**
- **⅔ cup freshly grated pecorino Romano cheese (about 2 ounces)**
- **⅓ cup freshly grated Parmesan cheese (about 1 ounce)**

HEAT oil in heavy small saucepan over medium heat. Add garlic and sauté until beginning to color, about 1 minute. Remove from heat.

COOK pasta in large pot of boiling salted water until just beginning to soften, stirring occasionally. Add broccoli rabe to same pot and cook until pasta is tender but still firm to bite, about 3 minutes. Drain pasta and broccoli rabe, reserving ½ cup pasta cooking liquid. Transfer pasta mixture to large bowl. Pour garlic oil over. Sprinkle with cheeses and toss to coat, adding reserved cooking liquid by tablespoonfuls to moisten if desired. Season to taste with salt and pepper and serve.

Fettuccine with pesto, green beans, and potatoes

THIS VERSION OF PESTO SAUCE includes walnuts, a variation on the classic recipe. To thin the thick pesto into a creamy sauce, reserve some of the cooking liquid when draining the pasta, then add the liquid little by little back into the pasta after you've combined it with the vegetables and sauce to reach the desired consistency.

4 TO 6 SERVINGS

- **3 cups (packed) fresh basil leaves (about 6 ounces)**
- **¾ cup olive oil, divided**
- **⅓ cup pine nuts**
- **3 tablespoons chopped walnuts**
- **2 garlic cloves**
- **1 cup freshly grated Parmesan cheese (about 3 ounces)**

- **8 ounces green beans, trimmed, halved crosswise**
- **8 ounces white-skinned potatoes, peeled, cut into ½-inch cubes**
- **12 ounces fettuccine**

BLEND basil, ¼ cup oil, pine nuts, walnuts, and garlic in processor until finely chopped. Add Parmesan cheese. With machine running, gradually add remaining ½ cup oil, blending until coarse paste forms. Season pesto to taste with salt and pepper. Set pesto aside.

COOK green beans in large pot of boiling salted water until crisp-tender, about 4 minutes. Using strainer, remove beans from pot and transfer to large bowl. Return cooking liquid to boil. Add potatoes and boil until tender, about 7 minutes. Using same strainer, transfer potatoes to bowl with beans. Return cooking liquid to boil. Add fettuccine to same pot. Boil until pasta is tender but still firm to bite, stirring occasionally. Drain pasta, reserving 1 cup cooking liquid. Return green beans, potatoes, and cooked pasta to same pot. Add pesto and toss to coat, gradually adding enough reserved cooking liquid to thin pesto and coat pasta with moist sauce. Season to taste with salt and pepper. Transfer to bowl and serve.

Fettuccine with greens, raisins, and pine nuts

THE GREENS CALLED FOR in this satisfying vegetarian pasta are Swiss chard, but you could substitute kale with equally good results. To prepare the greens for cooking, lay a leaf flat on a cutting board; with a sharp knife, cut the darker leafy portions away from the center stem. Using thinly sliced pieces of chard stem adds extra color and crunch, and the browned butter adds richness.

4 SERVINGS

¼ cup golden raisins

1 bunch green Swiss chard
6 tablespoons (¾ stick) unsalted butter
4 garlic cloves, minced
1 bunch spinach, trimmed
1½ teaspoons fresh lemon juice

12 ounces fettuccine
1⅓ cups freshly grated Parmesan cheese (about 4 ounces)
⅓ cup toasted pine nuts
1 tablespoon minced fresh chives
2 teaspoons minced fresh thyme
2 teaspoons minced fresh marjoram
Additional grated Parmesan cheese

PLACE raisins in small bowl. Add enough hot water to cover. Let stand until raisins are plump, about 10 minutes. Drain.

CUT stems from center of chard leaves. Thinly slice enough stems to measure ½ cup. Discard remaining stems. Slice chard leaves into ½-inch-wide strips. Melt butter in heavy large skillet over medium heat. Cook butter until golden brown, stirring constantly, about 7 minutes. Add garlic and sliced chard leaves; sauté until chard is tender and wilted, stirring frequently, about 3 minutes. Add spinach and stir until wilted, about 2 minutes. Stir in lemon juice and raisins.

MEANWHILE, bring large pot of salted water to boil. Add fettuccine and ½ cup chard stems and cook until pasta is tender but still firm to bite. Drain pasta and chard stems. Transfer to large bowl. Add spinach mixture, 1⅓ cups grated Parmesan cheese, pine nuts, and herbs. Toss thoroughly. Season pasta to taste with salt and pepper. Serve, passing additional Parmesan cheese separately.

Fettuccine with wild mushroom sauce

RIBBONS OF PASTA are tossed with an assortment of fresh mushrooms that cooks still refer to as "wild," even though most of them are cultivated commercially today and widely available at farmers' markets and well-stocked food stores. Dried porcini mushrooms—available at Italian markets and specialty foods stores, and in the produce section of many supermarkets—add their own intensely meaty flavor; you can also use fresh porcini when they are available in late spring or early autumn. Wide pappardelle noodles can be substituted for fettuccine.

4 SERVINGS

2 cups hot water
1 ounce dried porcini mushrooms

2 tablespoons olive oil
1 pound assorted fresh wild mushrooms (such as oyster, crimini, and stemmed shiitake), sliced
4 large garlic cloves, chopped

- **3 tablespoons butter**
- **1 tablespoon chopped fresh thyme**
- **¾ cup low-salt chicken broth**
- **8 tablespoons freshly grated Parmesan cheese, divided**

- **12 ounces fettuccine**

COMBINE 2 cups hot water and dried porcini in medium bowl. Let stand until porcini soften, about 40 minutes. Drain, reserving soaking liquid. Chop porcini coarsely.

HEAT oil in heavy large skillet over medium-high heat. Add fresh mushrooms and garlic; sauté until mushrooms brown, about 6 minutes. Add porcini and sauté until fragrant, about 4 minutes. Add butter and thyme; stir 1 minute. Add broth and 1¼ cups reserved mushroom soaking liquid, leaving any mushroom sediment behind. Boil until sauce thickens slightly, about 5 minutes. Mix in 4 tablespoons cheese. *(Sauce can be prepared 1 hour ahead. Let stand at room temperature.)*

COOK pasta in large pot of boiling salted water until tender but still firm to bite, stirring occasionally. Drain pasta; return to same pot. Bring sauce to simmer over medium-high heat. Add sauce to pasta; toss to coat. Season to taste with salt and pepper. Transfer pasta to bowl. Top with remaining 4 tablespoons cheese.

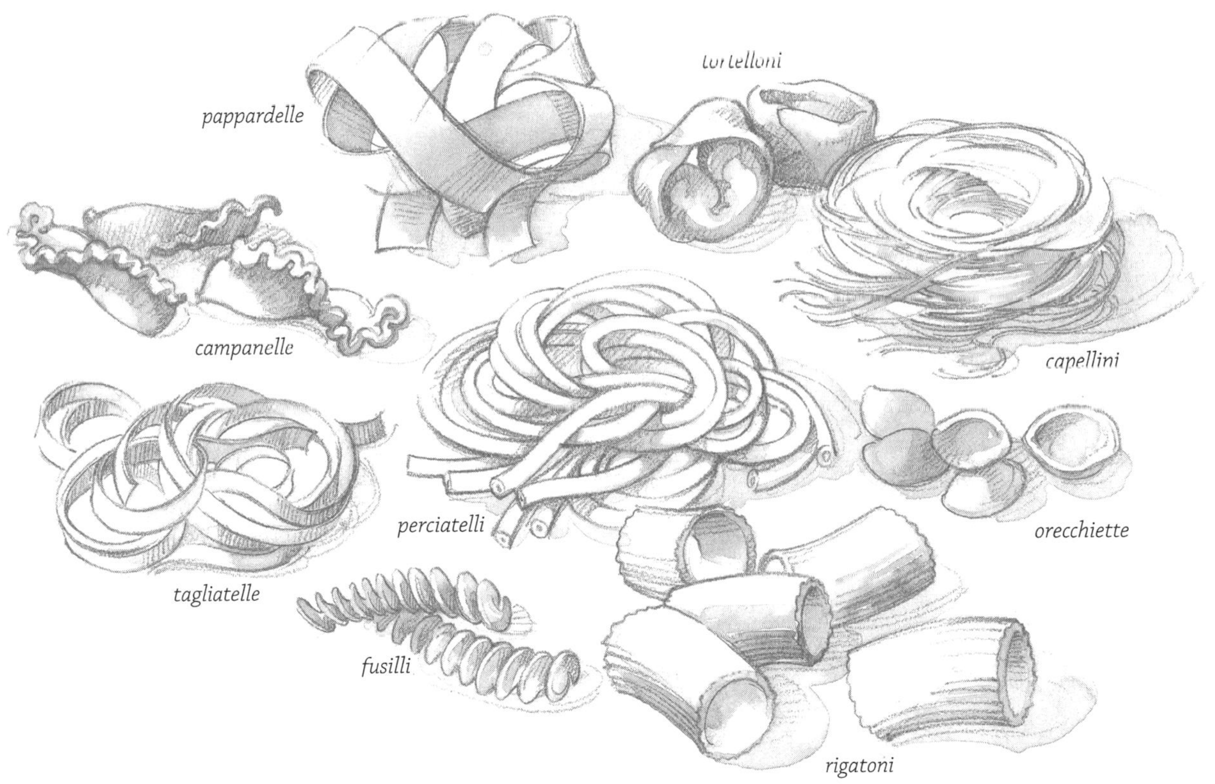

Linguine with peas and mint

BRIGHT-TASTING FRESH MINT LEAVES are a classic seasoning for springtime peas, and they go especially well with the sweet, crunchy, edible pea pods that star in this recipe along with the more familiar fresh or frozen shucked variety. If you would prefer a vegetarian version, substitute good-quality canned vegetable broth for the chicken broth.

2 SERVINGS

4 ounces sugar snap peas, trimmed

2 tablespoons (1/4 stick) butter
1 large shallot, minced
1/2 cup fresh or frozen peas
1/3 cup low-salt chicken broth
4 ounces plum tomatoes, peeled, seeded, thinly sliced
1/3 cup whipping cream
3 tablespoons chopped fresh mint

8 ounces linguine

1 1/2 tablespoons minced fresh parsley

COOK sugar snap peas in medium pot of boiling salted water until crisp-tender, about 4 minutes. Drain. Transfer to bowl of ice water and cool. Drain well. Thinly slice sugar snap peas lengthwise.

MELT butter in heavy medium skillet over medium-low heat. Add shallot and sauté until tender, about 3 minutes. Add ½ cup peas and broth; simmer until peas are tender, about 3 minutes. Add sugar snap peas, tomatoes, cream, and mint. Simmer until sauce thickens slightly, about 2 minutes. Season to taste with salt and pepper.

MEANWHILE, cook linguine in large pot of boiling salted water until tender but still firm to bite.

LADLE ¼ cup pasta cooking liquid into small bowl and reserve. Drain linguine; return to same pot. Add sauce and parsley to pasta; toss over low heat, thinning sauce with ¼ cup reserved cooking liquid if too thick. Transfer to bowl and serve.

Tortelloni with mushroom-sage sauce

PURCHASED FRESH STUFFED PASTA, found in the refrigerated section of many supermarkets, makes it fast and easy to serve a stylish, satisfying dinner. Fresh shiitake mushrooms, which have a meaty flavor and texture, are available in the produce departments of supermarkets. Be sure to cut off and discard the woody stems. If you can't find this variety, substitute portobello mushrooms or large white button mushrooms.

4 TO 6 SERVINGS

2 packages (about 9 ounces each) mushroom and cheese tortelloni

1/4 cup (1/2 stick) butter
1/2 cup chopped shallots
12 ounces fresh shiitake mushrooms, stemmed, caps thickly sliced
1 1/4 cups dry vermouth or dry white wine
3/4 cup whipping cream
1 1/2 tablespoons chopped fresh sage

COOK pasta in pot of boiling salted water according to package directions; drain.

MELT butter in heavy large skillet over medium-high heat. Add shallots and sauté 1 minute. Add mushrooms and sauté until brown, about 7 minutes. Add vermouth and cream. Boil until sauce thickens and coats spoon, about 5 minutes. Stir in sage. Season sauce to taste with salt and pepper. Add pasta; toss until heated through and coated with sauce. Transfer to bowl and serve.

Asian noodles with ginger-cilantro sauce

BURSTING WITH SPICY FLAVORS and aromas, this cold noodle side dish typifies the kind of lively, casual street food sold from market stalls all over Southeast Asia. Add chicken or pork to turn it into a satisfying main course. Chopped roasted peanuts are a nice garnish. You'll find all the ingredients at Asian markets or well-stocked supermarkets. Use any of a wide variety of fresh Asian noodles made simply from wheat flour and water, or substitute purchased fresh Italian pasta strands.

4 SERVINGS

- **1 12-ounce package fresh Asian-style water noodles or fresh linguine**
- **3 tablespoons Asian sesame oil, divided**
- **2½ tablespoons chopped peeled fresh ginger**
- **1 small jalapeño chile, seeded**
- **1 cup (packed) fresh cilantro leaves**
- **1 tablespoon soy sauce**
- **1 tablespoon unseasoned rice vinegar**
- **1 tablespoon creamy peanut butter**
- **3 tablespoons (or more) low-salt chicken broth**

COOK noodles in large pot of boiling salted water until tender but still firm to bite, stirring occasionally. Drain noodles. Rinse with cold water; drain well. Transfer to large bowl. Toss with 1 tablespoon sesame oil.

WITH processor running, drop ginger and chile through feed tube and mince. Add cilantro, soy sauce, vinegar, peanut butter, 3 tablespoons broth, and remaining 2 tablespoons sesame oil. Process until sauce is almost smooth, adding more broth by tablespoonfuls to thin, if desired. Season sauce to taste with salt and pepper. Add sauce to noodles and toss to coat.

Spaghetti with fresh clams, parsley, and lemon

LEMONS ARE THE SYMBOL and the signature flavor of Italy's romantic isle of Capri, the source of this simple, fresh-tasting, absolutely authentic pasta recipe. Freshly squeezed lemon juice is an integral part of its success. So is selecting the smallest fresh clams possible. Be sure not to overcook the shellfish: Remove them from the heat the moment most of them have opened, thus ensuring that they will be as tender as they are sweet. Discard any unopened clams before serving.

4 SERVINGS

- **½ cup extra-virgin olive oil**
- **8 garlic cloves, thinly sliced**
- **3 pounds fresh small clams (such as Manila or littleneck clams), scrubbed**
- **¼ cup plus 2 tablespoons chopped fresh Italian parsley**
- **½ cup dry white wine**
- **¼ cup fresh lemon juice**
- **1 pound spaghetti**

HEAT oil in heavy large pot over medium-high heat. Add garlic and sauté until light brown, about 1 minute. Add clams and ¼ cup parsley; stir 2 minutes. Add wine; simmer 2 minutes. Add lemon juice. Cover and simmer until clams open, about 6 minutes (discard any clams that do not open).

MEANWHILE, cook pasta in another large pot of boiling salted water until tender but still firm to bite, stirring occasionally. Drain. Add pasta to clam mixture and toss to coat. Season to taste with salt and pepper. Transfer to large bowl. Sprinkle with remaining 2 tablespoons parsley.

Pasta with grilled shrimp and basil vinaigrette

GRILLED ZUCCHINI adds extra flavor and texture to this light and pretty main course. When the weather isn't right for outdoor grilling, you can cook the shrimp under the broiler. You can even use one of the popular countertop double-sided grills, cutting the cooking time approximately in half for both the zucchini and the shrimp. Gnocchi-shaped pasta, found at Italian markets and some supermarkets, are in shapes reminiscent of shells, not to be confused with the plump bite-size Italian dumplings of the same name.

4 SERVINGS

5 tablespoons fresh lemon juice, divided
2 tablespoons Dijon mustard
⅓ cup plus 2 tablespoons olive oil
¾ cup chopped fresh basil (about 1 ounce)
1½ pounds uncooked medium shrimp, peeled, deveined

1 pound gnocchi-shaped pasta or orecchiette (little ear-shaped pasta)

4 zucchini, halved lengthwise
Additional olive oil

Freshly grated Parmesan cheese (optional)

PREPARE barbecue (medium-high heat) or preheat broiler. Combine 4 tablespoons lemon juice and Dijon mustard in small bowl. Gradually whisk in ⅓ cup olive oil. Mix in basil. Season vinaigrette to taste with salt and pepper. Place shrimp in medium bowl. Drizzle with remaining 1 tablespoon lemon juice and 2 tablespoons olive oil. Toss to coat. Sprinkle shrimp with salt and pepper.

COOK pasta in large pot of boiling salted water until tender but still firm to bite, stirring occasionally.

MEANWHILE, brush zucchini on both sides with additional oil. Sprinkle with salt and pepper. Grill or broil until charred, about 2 minutes per side. Transfer to plate. Add shrimp to grill or broiler and cook until just opaque in center, about 2 minutes per side. Transfer shrimp to large bowl. Cut zucchini crosswise into 1-inch pieces and add to shrimp.

DRAIN pasta well. Add pasta to bowl with shrimp and zucchini. Add basil vinaigrette and toss to coat. Season to taste with salt and pepper. Serve pasta warm or let stand up to 1 hour and serve at room temperature, passing grated Parmesan if desired.

Greek-style linguine with shrimp and feta

GARLIC, OREGANO, lemon juice, artichoke hearts, tomatoes, and the crumbly sheep's milk cheese called feta give a lively Greek personality to this simple recipe. Serve extra lemon wedges on the side for guests who want to add even zestier flavor to their servings.

4 SERVINGS

¼ cup olive oil
4 garlic cloves, minced
1 pound uncooked medium shrimp, peeled, deveined
1 8-ounce package frozen artichoke hearts, thawed, halved lengthwise
1½ cups crumbled feta cheese (about 6 ounces)
½ cup chopped seeded tomatoes
3 tablespoons fresh lemon juice
3 tablespoons chopped fresh parsley
2 tablespoons finely chopped fresh oregano

12 ounces linguine or angel hair pasta

HEAT oil in heavy large skillet over medium-high heat. Add garlic and sauté 30 seconds. Add shrimp and sauté 2 minutes. Add artichokes, feta, tomatoes, lemon juice, parsley, and oregano; sauté until shrimp are just opaque in center, about 2 minutes longer. Season sauce to taste with salt and pepper.

MEANWHILE, cook pasta in large pot of boiling salted water until tender but still firm to bite, stirring occasionally. Drain. Transfer pasta to large bowl.

ADD shrimp mixture to pasta and toss to coat. Season to taste with salt and pepper.

Tagliatelle with smoked salmon cream sauce

WIDELY AVAILABLE BOTTLED CLAM JUICE contributes a fresh taste of the sea to the cream sauce for this dish. Buy the best-quality smoked salmon you can find, as a little bit goes a long way. If you can, sample a small piece before deciding: It should taste clean and rich with a nice edge of smoke, and not too oily, fishy, or salty. Also, avoid salmon that appears dried or discolored. Season the finished dish to taste carefully, since you probably won't need too much additional salt.

4 FIRST-COURSE SERVINGS

12 ounces tagliatelle or linguine

1 cup bottled clam juice
1 cup whipping cream
¼ cup chopped fresh dill
1 teaspoon fresh lemon juice
4 ounces thinly sliced smoked salmon, cut into thin strips

Lemon wedges

COOK pasta in large pot of boiling salted water until tender but still firm to bite, stirring occasionally. Drain well.

BRING clam juice and cream to boil in heavy large skillet over high heat. Reduce heat and simmer until sauce thickens enough to coat spoon, whisking occasionally, about 10 minutes. Whisk in dill and lemon juice. Add pasta to sauce in skillet and toss to coat. Remove skillet from heat. Add salmon and toss to combine. Season pasta to taste with salt and pepper.

DIVIDE pasta among 4 plates. Serve with lemon.

Pasta with scallops and lemon-mustard butter sauce

THE LIGHT YET SATISFYING CHARACTER of this pasta-and-shellfish pairing results from first poaching sweet little bay scallops in white wine with lemon peel, and then boiling down the cooking liquid to a flavorful concentrate into which some mustard and butter are whisked, forming a smooth sauce. Be sure to whisk in the butter just one piece at a time, which will give the sauce a velvety consistency. The recipe also works well with small to medium fresh shrimp.

2 SERVINGS; CAN BE DOUBLED

1 cup dry white wine
½ teaspoon finely grated lemon peel
8 ounces bay scallops
2 teaspoons Dijon mustard
¼ cup (½ stick) chilled butter, cut into 4 pieces

5 ounces capellini or angel hair
1 tablespoon butter, room temperature
1 tablespoon chopped fresh chives

BRING wine and lemon peel to simmer in heavy medium skillet over medium heat. Add scallops and simmer until almost opaque in center, about 1 minute. Using slotted spoon, transfer scallops to medium bowl. Increase heat and boil until wine mixture is reduced to ¼ cup, about 6 minutes. Reduce heat to low. Whisk in mustard, then chilled butter, 1 piece at a time. Add scallops and any accumulated juices to sauce; heat through (do not boil). Season sauce to taste with salt and pepper.

MEANWHILE, cook pasta in large pot of boiling salted water until tender but still firm to bite, stirring occasionally. Drain; return to same pot. Toss with 1 tablespoon room-temperature butter. Divide pasta between plates. Spoon scallops and sauce over. Sprinkle with chives.

Pasta with smoked whitefish, tomatoes, and garlic

SMALL INDIVIDUAL SMOKED WHITEFISH, often referred to as chubs, are available at delicatessens, fish markets, and some supermarkets. The golden skin peels off readily by hand, and the bones separate easily from the firm flesh; use your fingertips to feel for and remove small bones as you separate the fish into flakes.

4 SERVINGS

- **6 tablespoons olive oil**
- **3/4 cup finely chopped shallots (about 3 large)**
- **6 garlic cloves, finely chopped**
- **1 1/2 pounds cherry tomatoes, halved**
- **1/2 cup plus 2 tablespoons finely chopped fresh parsley**
- **3/4 teaspoon dried crushed red pepper**
- **18 ounces smoked whitefish (chubs), skinned, boned, coarsely flaked**

- **1 9-ounce package fresh linguine**

HEAT oil in heavy large skillet over medium heat. Add shallots and garlic; sauté until shallots begin to soften, about 2 minutes. Reduce heat to medium-low. Add tomatoes, ½ cup parsley, and crushed red pepper; stir until tomatoes are just tender, about 8 minutes. Add whitefish and cook until heated through, about 3 minutes.

MEANWHILE, cook pasta in large pot of boiling salted water until tender but still firm to bite, stirring occasionally. Drain; return to same pot.

TOSS fish mixture with pasta. Season pasta to taste with salt and pepper. Transfer pasta to bowl. Sprinkle with remaining 2 tablespoons parsley.

Fettuccine with chicken, red onion, and peppers

TWO KINDS OF CHILE PEPPER give a pleasant kick to this recipe: Poblanos are mild to medium-hot fresh dark green chiles. Chipotles, the smoke-dried form of hot jalapeños, are often sold canned in a spicy tomato sauce called *adobo*. Both are available at Latin markets and some supermarkets. After handling any hot chiles, which contain capsaicin that can cause a burning sensation, avoid touching your eyes or other sensitive areas and wash your hands well with warm soapy water (or wear rubber gloves).

4 TO 6 SERVINGS

- **3 skinless boneless chicken breast halves, cut crosswise into strips**
- **1 tablespoon plus 1/2 cup chopped fresh cilantro**
- **4 tablespoons olive oil, divided**

- **2 large red bell peppers, seeded, thinly sliced**
- **1 large red onion, thinly sliced**
- **1 large poblano chile, seeded, thinly sliced**
- **6 garlic cloves, minced**
- **2 cups whipping cream**
- **1 tablespoon minced canned chipotle chiles**

- **1 pound fettuccine**

- **1 1/2 cups (packed) coarsely grated Monterey Jack cheese (about 6 ounces), divided**

TOSS chicken, 1 tablespoon cilantro, and 1 tablespoon oil in medium bowl to combine. Sprinkle with salt and pepper. Cover; chill 1 hour.

HEAT remaining 3 tablespoons oil in heavy large skillet over medium heat. Add bell peppers, onion, poblano chile, and garlic; sauté until just tender, about 10 minutes. Transfer vegetables to large bowl. Add chicken to same skillet; increase heat to high and sauté until cooked through and beginning to brown, about 4 minutes. Transfer chicken to bowl with vegetables. Add cream and chipotle chiles to skillet; boil until sauce is reduced enough to coat spoon thickly, about 4 minutes.

MEANWHILE, cook pasta in large pot of boiling salted water until tender but still firm to bite, stirring occasionally. Drain; return to same pot.

ADD chicken mixture, cream mixture, and remaining ½ cup cilantro to pasta in pot. Toss over medium-high heat until sauce coats pasta, about 3 minutes. Stir in 1 cup cheese and toss to blend. Season pasta to taste with salt and pepper. Transfer to large bowl. Sprinkle with remaining ½ cup cheese.

Fettuccine Bolognese

YOU CAN USE either dried fettuccine or purchased fresh fettuccine, sold packaged in the refrigerated cases of most supermarkets, for this recipe. A combination of ground veal and pork and chopped bacon results in a more complex, robust flavor than the usual meat sauce. The salt-cured Italian bacon called pancetta is available at Italian markets and in the refrigerated deli case of many supermarkets.

4 TO 6 SERVINGS

¼ cup extra-virgin olive oil
2 medium onions, chopped
2 cups chopped celery
6 garlic cloves, chopped
1 pound ground veal
1 pound ground pork
4 ounces pancetta or bacon, finely chopped
2 14.5-ounce cans whole tomatoes in juice
1¾ cups chicken stock or one 14-ounce can (or more) low-salt chicken broth
½ cup whole milk
5 teaspoons chopped fresh thyme

12 ounces fettuccine
1 cup freshly grated Parmesan cheese (about 3 ounces), divided

HEAT oil in heavy large pot over medium heat. Add onions, celery, and garlic; sauté until vegetables are tender and beginning to brown, about 10 minutes. Increase heat to high; add veal, pork, and pancetta. Sauté until meat browns, breaking up meat with back of fork, about 10 minutes. Add tomatoes with juice, 1¾ cups stock, milk, and thyme. Reduce heat to medium-low and simmer uncovered 1 hour 15 minutes, breaking up tomatoes with back of fork, adding more stock by ¼ cupfuls if ragù is too thick, and stirring occasionally. Season ragù to taste with salt and pepper.

COOK pasta in another large pot of boiling salted water until tender but still firm to bite, stirring occasionally. Drain. Add fettuccine to pot with ragù and toss to blend. Season pasta to taste with salt and pepper. Transfer to large bowl. Sprinkle with ½ cup Parmesan. Serve, passing remaining ½ cup Parmesan separately.

Fettuccine with prosciutto, peas, and lemon-chive sauce

THE BRIGHT GREEN SWEET PEAS and rose-hued slivers of salty, rich-tasting Italian cured ham harmonize to make a pasta dish that is delicately beautiful in both appearance and flavor. A small amount of the cooking liquid reserved from draining the pasta helps to thin the rich sauce so it coats the fettuccine more readily.

2 SERVINGS; CAN BE DOUBLED

6 ounces fettuccine
1 cup frozen petite peas (about 4½ ounces)

- 1/2 cup whipping cream
- 1/2 cup chopped fresh chives
- 3 tablespoons fresh lemon juice
- 1 1/2 teaspoons finely grated lemon peel
- 2 ounces thinly sliced prosciutto, cut crosswise into slivers

COOK pasta in large pot of boiling salted water until tender but still firm to bite, stirring occasionally. Add peas; cook 30 seconds. Drain, reserving ½ cup pasta cooking liquid. Return pasta and peas to same pot. Add cream, chives, lemon juice, and lemon peel to pasta. Toss over medium heat until sauce coats pasta, adding reserved cooking liquid by tablespoonfuls if pasta is dry, about 1 minute. Mix in prosciutto; season to taste with salt and pepper. Transfer pasta to bowl.

Spaghetti with Sicilian meatballs

WHEN ITALIAN RESTAURANTS began to spread across the United States in the 1920s, Americans couldn't understand the appeal of spaghetti and tomato sauce served in the Neapolitan style: Where was the meat? In response, chefs started topping their pasta with meatballs prepared in the style of their homeland, mixing the meat with breadcrumbs, herbs, garlic, and Parmesan cheese. This recipe reflects today's interest in the cooking of Italy's farther-flung regions, adding embellishments popular in Sicily: pine nuts and currants. Baking the meatballs in the oven before combining them with the sauce gives them a flavorful browned surface.

4 TO 6 SERVINGS

Sauce

- 2 tablespoons olive oil
- 1 1/2 cups chopped onion
- 2 garlic cloves, minced
- 2 28-ounce cans diced tomatoes in juice
- 4 tablespoons chopped fresh basil, divided

Meatballs

- 2/3 cup fresh breadcrumbs made from crustless French bread
- 3 tablespoons whole milk
- 1/3 cup freshly grated Parmesan cheese (about 1 ounce)
- 1/4 cup finely chopped onion
- 3 tablespoons chopped fresh basil
- 1 large egg
- 1 garlic clove, minced
- 1/2 teaspoon salt
- 1/4 teaspoon ground black pepper
- 1 pound sweet Italian sausages, casings removed
- 2 tablespoons pine nuts, toasted
- 2 tablespoons dried currants

- 1 pound spaghetti

FOR SAUCE: Heat oil in heavy large pot over medium-low heat. Add onion and sauté until golden, about 10 minutes. Add garlic and stir 1 minute. Add tomatoes with juice and 2 tablespoons basil; bring to boil. Reduce heat and simmer until sauce thickens, stirring occasionally, about 1 hour. Mix in remaining 2 tablespoons basil. Season sauce to taste with salt and pepper. Set aside.

FOR MEATBALLS: Preheat oven to 350°F. Lightly oil large rimmed baking sheet. Mix breadcrumbs and milk in medium bowl; let stand 5 minutes. Mix in Parmesan, onion, basil, egg, garlic, salt, and pepper. Add sausage, pine nuts, and currants; blend well. Using wet hands, form mixture into 1¼-inch meatballs. Place on prepared baking sheet. Bake until meatballs are light brown and cooked through, about 30 minutes. Add meatballs to sauce.

COOK pasta in large pot of boiling salted water until tender but still firm to bite, stirring occasionally. Drain. Mound pasta in large dish. Bring sauce and meatballs to simmer. Spoon over pasta.

Perciatelli with meatballs and tomato-porcini sauce

IF YOU'RE A FAN of spaghetti and meatballs, then you'll love this upmarket rendition featuring perciatelli—long, thin, hollow tubes of pasta. The noodles are topped with a tomato sauce enriched with meaty-tasting dried porcini mushrooms, available at Italian markets, specialty foods stores, and many supermarkets; the meatballs include ground veal, Italian sausage, and more porcini. Soaking in hot water reconstitutes the dried mushrooms; don't discard the water, which itself adds flavor to the tomato sauce.

6 SERVINGS

Mushrooms

- **2 ounces dried porcini mushrooms**
- **2 cups hot water**

Sauce

- **3 tablespoons olive oil**
- **1½ large onions, chopped**
- **3 garlic cloves, chopped**
- **1 tablespoon chopped fresh rosemary**
- **¼ teaspoon dried crushed red pepper**
- **1½ 28-ounce cans crushed tomatoes with added puree (about 4½ cups)**

Meatballs

- **4 slices English muffin toasting bread or white sandwich bread with crusts, torn into pieces**
- **2 cups whole milk**
- **12 ounces ground veal**
- **12 ounces Italian sweet sausages, casings removed**
- **¾ cup freshly grated pecorino Romano cheese (about 2½ ounces)**
- **3 large eggs**
- **1 tablespoon chopped fresh rosemary**
- **1 teaspoon salt**
- **1 teaspoon freshly ground black pepper**

Olive oil (for frying)

- **1¼ pounds perciatelli or spaghetti**
- **Additional freshly grated pecorino Romano cheese**

FOR MUSHROOMS: Place mushrooms in small bowl. Pour 2 cups hot water over; soak until mushrooms soften, about 40 minutes. Drain mushrooms well, reserving soaking liquid. Chop mushrooms.

FOR SAUCE: Heat oil in heavy large pot over medium-high heat. Add onions and garlic; sauté until tender, about 8 minutes. Add rosemary and crushed red pepper; stir 30 seconds. Add crushed tomatoes and 1 cup chopped mushrooms. Pour in reserved mushroom soaking liquid, leaving any mushroom sediment behind in bowl. Bring sauce to boil. Reduce heat and simmer 20 minutes, stirring occasionally.

MEANWHILE, PREPARE MEATBALLS: Place bread in medium bowl; pour milk over. Let stand until bread is very soft, about 15 minutes. Squeeze milk from bread; place bread in large bowl and discard milk. Add veal, sausage, ¾ cup cheese, eggs, rosemary, salt, pepper, and remaining mushrooms to bread. Using hands, combine veal mixture thoroughly.

ADD oil to heavy large skillet to depth of ¼ inch; heat over medium-high heat. Working in batches, form veal mixture into 1½-inch meatballs; add to skillet. Cook until browned, turning occasionally, about 4 minutes. Using slotted spoon, transfer meatballs to paper towels to drain.

ADD meatballs to tomato sauce. Simmer until sauce thickens and meatballs are cooked through, stirring occasionally, about 10 minutes. Season to taste with salt and pepper. *(Meatballs in sauce can be prepared 1 day ahead. Refrigerate uncovered until cold, then cover and keep refrigerated. Bring to simmer, stirring frequently, before using.)*

COOK pasta in large pot of boiling salted water until tender but still firm to bite, stirring occasionally. Drain. Transfer to platter. Spoon sauce and meatballs over pasta. Serve, passing additional grated cheese separately.

Pasta with sausage, bell peppers, and basil

GREAT FOR a casual dinner party, this recipe captures the appealing flavor combination of one of the all-time favorite street-festival sandwiches in New York's Little Italy: sweet pork sausage, caramelized onions, and colorful strips of sautéed red bell pepper. Feel free to substitute Italian-style fresh turkey or chicken sausage, found at upscale butcher shops, Italian delicatessens, and the meat departments of many supermarkets.

12 SERVINGS

- **¼ cup extra-virgin olive oil**
- **3 pounds sweet Italian sausages, casings removed**
- **5 cups sliced onions (about 1¼ pounds)**
- **2 red bell peppers, cut into strips**
- **1½ cups dry white wine**

- **2 pounds short pasta (such as fusilli)**
- **1½ cups freshly grated Parmesan cheese (about 4½ ounces)**
- **2 cups thinly sliced fresh basil, divided**
- **Additional freshly grated Parmesan cheese**

DIVIDE oil between 2 heavy large skillets and heat over medium heat. Divide sausage between skillets; cook until brown, breaking up with back of fork, about 12 minutes. Using slotted spoon, transfer sausage to large bowl. Add onions to skillets, dividing equally. Sauté until golden, about 10 minutes. Add bell peppers to onions, dividing equally. Sauté until tender, about 6 minutes. Pour ¾ cup wine into each skillet; boil 5 minutes to allow wine to evaporate slightly. Add vegetables to bowl with sausage.

COOK pasta in large pot of boiling salted water until tender but still firm to bite, stirring occasionally. Drain pasta; return to same pot. Add sausage and vegetables; toss to combine. Mix in 1½ cups cheese. Add 1½ cups basil; toss to combine. Season pasta to taste with salt and pepper. Mound in bowl. Sprinkle with remaining ½ cup basil. Serve, passing additional cheese separately.

Pasta fazool casserole

PASTA FAZOOL IS SLANG FOR the classic Italian *pasta e fagioli* (pasta and beans). The hearty main course becomes even more satisfying in a baked version that includes Italian sausage and beef along with kidney beans and pasta. If you like, try substituting canned Italian white beans, cannellini, for the kidney beans. The widely available pasta tubes known as mostaccioli ("moustaches") may be replaced with rigatoni—or even large macaroni or quill-shaped penne.

8 SERVINGS

- **1 pound hot or sweet Italian sausages, casings removed**
- **1 pound ground beef**
- **1 large onion, chopped**
- **4 garlic cloves, chopped**
- **1 teaspoon dried oregano**
- **½ teaspoon dried thyme**
- **1 28-ounce can Italian plum tomatoes, drained, chopped**
- **2 tablespoons tomato paste**
- **¼ teaspoon cayenne pepper**
- **1 15- to 16-ounce can kidney beans, rinsed, drained**

- **1 pound mostaccioli or rigatoni**
- **½ cup freshly grated Parmesan cheese (about 1½ ounces)**
- **¼ cup chopped fresh Italian parsley**
- **⅓ cup (packed) coarsely grated Fontina cheese or provolone cheese (about 1½ ounces)**

PREHEAT oven to 400°F. Sauté first 6 ingredients in heavy large pot over medium-high heat until sausage and beef are brown, breaking up meats with back of fork, about 5 minutes. Add tomatoes, tomato paste, and cayenne; simmer 5 minutes. Add kidney beans and heat through. Season sauce to taste with salt and pepper.

COOK pasta in another large pot of salted boiling water until tender but still firm to bite, stirring occasionally. Drain and return to same pot. Add meat sauce, Parmesan cheese, and parsley; toss to combine. Transfer to 13x9x2-inch glass baking dish. Sprinkle with Fontina cheese. Bake until casserole is heated through and cheese on top has melted, about 30 minutes.

Saffron pasta with pork and tomato sauce

ON THE ITALIAN ISLAND of Sardinia, cooks prepare a type of bite-size, thumbprint-shaped pasta called malloreddus, which gets a vibrant yellow color and heady fragrance from saffron included in the dough. For convenience, this version of a traditional Sardinian recipe uses widely available dried pasta of a similar shape, giving it color and flavor by adding saffron to the cooking water.

6 TO 8 FIRST-COURSE SERVINGS

- **2 tablespoons olive oil**
- **3 ounces pancetta or bacon, finely chopped**
- **1 medium onion, finely chopped**
- **¼ cup chopped fresh Italian parsley**
- **1 pound ground pork**
- **1 28-ounce can crushed tomatoes with added puree**
- **2 bay leaves**
- **2 teaspoons chopped fresh sage**

- **12 ounces gnocchi-shaped pasta or orecchiette (little ear-shaped pasta)**
- **1½ teaspoons whole saffron threads, crumbled**
- **1 cup freshly grated pecorino Sardo or pecorino Romano cheese (about 3 ounces), divided**

HEAT oil in heavy large skillet over medium heat. Add pancetta and sauté until fat is rendered, about 3 minutes. Add onion and parsley; sauté until onion is soft, about 5 minutes. Add ground pork and sauté until brown, breaking up with back of fork, about 8 minutes. Stir in crushed tomatoes, bay leaves, and sage. Reduce heat to medium-low and simmer until sauce thickens and flavors blend, stirring occasionally, about 25 minutes. Season sauce to taste with salt and pepper. *(Can be made 2 days ahead. Chill uncovered 1 hour, then cover and keep chilled. Rewarm over low heat before using.)*

COOK pasta with saffron in large pot of boiling salted water until pasta is tender but still firm to bite, stirring occasionally. Drain; return to same pot. Add sauce and ½ cup cheese; toss to blend. Season pasta to taste with salt and pepper. Transfer to bowl. Sprinkle with remaining ½ cup cheese and serve.

Pasta with caramelized onions, cabbage, and smoked ham

A CLASSIC COMBINATION of German ingredients is tossed with corkscrew-shaped pasta in a simple, robust recipe for a quick weeknight dinner. Be patient when sautéing the onions, because browning them well will give the finished dish a rich, mellow flavor that perfectly complements the cabbage and ham. Whole caraway seeds, a traditional German seasoning, add their own pungent bite.

4 TO 6 SERVINGS

- **4 bacon slices**
- **Vegetable oil**
- **2 pounds onions, thinly sliced**
- **½ teaspoon caraway seeds or fennel seeds**
- **4 cups thinly sliced green cabbage (about ¼ small head)**
- **1½ cups diced smoked ham (such as Black Forest; about 8 ounces)**

12 ounces fusilli or rotini pasta

- **⅓ cup freshly grated Parmesan cheese (about 1 ounce)**
- **½ cup (about) beef broth**

COOK bacon in heavy large skillet over medium-high heat until brown and crisp. Transfer bacon to paper towels to drain. Crumble bacon. Measure drippings from skillet; add enough vegetable oil to measure

¼ cup and return mixture to skillet. Add onions and caraway seeds; sauté until onions are dark brown, about 25 minutes. Add cabbage and ham; sauté until cabbage wilts, about 8 minutes.

MEANWHILE, cook pasta in large pot of boiling salted water until tender but still firm to bite, stirring occasionally. Drain; return to same pot.

ADD bacon, onion mixture, and cheese to pasta. Toss over medium heat until warmed through, adding broth by ¼ cupfuls to moisten if pasta is dry, about 4 minutes. Season pasta to taste with salt and pepper. Transfer to bowl.

Spaghetti carbonara

"CHARCOAL MAKER'S" SPAGHETTI, a humble yet luxurious-tasting dish that may have originated in the Lazio region of central Italy, is popular today throughout that country, and across America as well. For a more authentic flavor, instead of American smoked bacon use slices of pancetta, the Italian salt-cured, rolled bacon, available at Italian markets and in the refrigerated deli case of many supermarkets.

6 FIRST-COURSE SERVINGS

- **9 bacon slices, chopped**
- **1 tablespoon butter**
- **½ cup whipping cream**
- **½ cup freshly grated Parmesan cheese (about 1½ ounces)**
- **4 large egg yolks**

- **12 ounces spaghetti**
- **Additional freshly grated Parmesan cheese**

COMBINE bacon and butter in heavy large skillet. Sauté over medium heat until bacon is brown and crisp. Using slotted spoon, transfer bacon to paper towels to drain. Whisk cream, ½ cup grated cheese, and egg yolks in medium bowl to blend; whisk in 2 tablespoons drippings from skillet. Set cream mixture aside; discard remaining drippings.

COOK pasta in large pot of boiling salted water until tender but still firm to bite, stirring occasionally. Drain pasta; return to same pot. Add cream mixture to pasta. Toss over medium-low heat until sauce cooks through and coats pasta thickly, about 4 minutes (do not boil). Mix in bacon. Season to taste with salt and pepper. Divide pasta among 6 plates and serve, passing additional cheese separately.

Potato gnocchi with beef ragù

THE TRADITIONAL MANNER for shaping these traditional Italian dumplings is to press each short piece of dough against the tines of a fork, creating grooves to catch the sauce. Home cooks may find it simpler to roll the dough along the wires of a whisk, as outlined here. Also, if you can't get ground chuck, essential to the sauce's rich flavor and hearty consistency, buy a boneless chuck roast and ask the butcher to grind it for you. Pancetta—Italian bacon cured in salt—is available at Italian markets and in the refrigerated deli case of many supermarkets.

6 SERVINGS

Ragù

- **½ cup olive oil**
- **1¾ cups chopped onions**
- **3 ounces pancetta or bacon, finely chopped**
- **2 ounces prosciutto, finely chopped**
- **9 garlic cloves, chopped**
- **2 pounds ground chuck**
- **4 cups beef broth, divided**
- **1 ounce dried porcini mushrooms, broken into small pieces**
- **1 tablespoon dried sage leaves**
- **1 6-ounce can tomato paste**
- **1 28-ounce can diced tomatoes in juice**
- **3 cups (about) water**

Gnocchi

- **4 small russet potatoes (22 to 24 ounces total), peeled, cut into ½-inch cubes**
- **1 large egg**
- **2 tablespoons whipping cream**
- **1¼ teaspoons salt**
- **⅛ teaspoon ground nutmeg**
- **1½ cups (about) all purpose flour**

Serving

- **½ cup (1 stick) butter**
- **Wedge of Parmesan cheese**
- **Fresh sage sprigs (optional)**

FOR RAGÙ: Heat oil in heavy large pot over medium heat. Add onions, pancetta, prosciutto, and garlic; sauté until mixture begins to brown, about 10 minutes. Add chuck and cook until no longer pink, breaking up with back of fork, about 5 minutes. Add 1 cup broth, dried mushrooms, and sage. Simmer until almost all liquid is absorbed, about 4 minutes. Add remaining 3 cups stock, 1 cup at a time, simmering until almost all liquid is absorbed before adding more and stirring occasionally. Mix in tomato paste, then tomatoes with juice. Simmer until meat is very tender, stirring occasionally and thinning with about 1 cup water every 30 minutes, about 1½ hours (sauce should be medium-thick consistency). Season sauce to taste with salt and pepper. *(Sauce can be prepared 4 days ahead. Refrigerate uncovered until cold; cover and keep refrigerated.)*

FOR GNOCCHI: Steam potatoes until tender, about 12 minutes. Working in batches, press warm potatoes through ricer into large bowl (or place warm potatoes in large bowl and mash finely with potato masher). Cool to lukewarm, about 10 minutes. Add egg, cream, salt, and nutmeg to potatoes; blend well. Add 1½ cups flour and mix until soft and slightly sticky dough forms, adding more flour by tablespoonfuls if dough is too moist.

TURN dough out onto lightly floured work surface. Divide dough into 6 equal portions. Gently roll 1 dough portion between hands and work surface to ¾-inch-thick rope, about 20 inches long. Cut rope into ¾-inch-long pieces. Roll each piece over wires of slender whisk or tines of dinner fork to make grooves. Arrange gnocchi in single layer on floured baking sheet. Repeat rolling, cutting, and shaping with remaining 5 dough portions.

COOK ⅓ of gnocchi in large pot of boiling generously salted water until gnocchi rise to surface and are cooked through and tender, about 5 minutes (check at 4 minutes). Using large strainer or slotted spoon, transfer gnocchi to large baking dish; arrange gnocchi in single layer. Cook remaining gnocchi in 2 batches. *(Gnocchi can be prepared ahead. Let stand 1 hour at room temperature, or cover and refrigerate up to 2 days.)*

TO SERVE: Melt butter in very large skillet (about 14 inches in diameter) over medium heat. Add gnocchi and cook until heated through, tossing often, about 8 minutes.

MEANWHILE, rewarm ragù over medium-low heat, stirring occasionally. Season with salt and pepper.

LADLE ragù into large shallow bowls. Spoon gnocchi over. Using cheese plane or swivel-bladed vegetable peeler, shave Parmesan cheese over gnocchi. Garnish with fresh sage, if desired.

Spinach and ricotta gnocchi

GNOCCHI ARE AMONG the oldest foods in Italy, and this variety is a specialty of the Casentino, an area east of Florence where greens grow wild on the hillsides. Fortunately, the greens for this version, baby spinach, are easily gathered in the ready-to-use packages found at supermarkets everywhere. In different parts of Tuscany, these gnocchi are also known as *malfatti* (badly made), *ravioli nudi* (naked ravioli), or *topini verdi* (little green mice).

8 FIRST-COURSE SERVINGS

4 6-ounce packages baby spinach leaves
2 cups whole-milk ricotta cheese (about 16 ounces)
1 cup freshly grated Parmesan cheese (about 3 ounces), divided
½ cup (about) all purpose flour
2 large egg yolks
½ teaspoon salt
½ teaspoon ground black pepper
Generous pinch of ground nutmeg

¼ cup (½ stick) butter, melted

COOK spinach in large pot of boiling salted water just until wilted, stirring occasionally, about 2 minutes. Drain. Squeeze out as much liquid as possible. Chop spinach. Mix spinach, ricotta, ½ cup Parmesan, ½ cup flour, egg yolks, salt, pepper, and nutmeg in large bowl until slightly sticky dough forms.

DUST large rimmed baking sheet with flour. Using floured hands, roll ¼ cup dough between hands and work surface to 5-inch-long rope. Cut rope into 1-inch pieces. Roll each piece between palms to form oval. Transfer gnocchi to prepared baking sheet. Repeat rolling, cutting, and shaping with remaining dough.

WORKING in batches, cook gnocchi in large pot of boiling salted water until gnocchi rise to surface and are cooked through and tender, about 5 minutes (check at 4 minutes). Using large strainer or slotted spoon, remove gnocchi from water; drain. Place in ovenproof serving dish.

POUR butter over gnocchi; toss to coat. Season to taste with salt and pepper. *(Gnocchi can be made 1 day ahead. Cover; chill. Before serving, reheat in 400°F oven about 10 minutes.)* Sprinkle with remaining ½ cup Parmesan.

Lamb and zucchini fusilli tossed with basil butter

LAMB MIGHT NOT BE the first ingredient choice that comes to mind when you think of meat sauce. As this recipe reveals, however, ground lamb can form the basis for a very satisfying pasta dish, especially when joined by slender shreds of zucchini, Parmesan cheese, and a mixture of butter and fresh basil.

6 SERVINGS

¼ cup (½ stick) butter
½ cup chopped fresh basil

2 tablespoons olive oil
1 onion, chopped
3 large shallots, chopped
8 ounces ground lamb
1 pound zucchini, trimmed, coarsely grated (about 3½ cups)
¼ cup dry white wine or 2 tablespoons fresh lemon juice

1 pound fusilli or other corkscrew pasta
¾ cup freshly grated Parmesan cheese (about 2½ ounces)

MELT butter in small saucepan over medium heat. Stir in basil. Set basil butter aside.

HEAT oil in heavy large skillet over medium heat. Add onion and shallots; sauté until soft, about 5 minutes. Add lamb and sauté until cooked through, breaking up with back of fork, about 8 minutes. Increase heat to medium-high; add zucchini and sauté until wilted, about 7 minutes. Add wine; reduce heat and simmer until liquid is reduced by half, about 5 minutes.

COOK pasta in large pot of boiling salted water until tender but still firm to bite, stirring occasionally. Drain; return to same pot. Add zucchini-lamb mixture and basil butter to pasta; toss to coat. Season to taste with salt and pepper. Transfer pasta to large bowl. Sprinkle with Parmesan.

Pesto lasagna

RESTAURANTS THROUGHOUT ITALY offer specialties featuring the popular sauce of fresh basil, Parmesan, garlic, pine nuts, and olive oil. In this recipe, the pesto sauce adds its highly aromatic flavor and bright color to an elegantly simple vegetarian version of the classic layered and baked pasta dish.

8 SERVINGS

Pesto

- **2 cups (packed) fresh basil leaves**
- **1 cup freshly grated Parmesan cheese (about 3 ounces)**
- **½ cup olive oil**
- **¼ cup pine nuts**
- **4 garlic cloves, halved**
- **⅓ cup vegetable broth**

Béchamel sauce

- **½ cup (1 stick) butter**
- **⅓ cup minced shallots**
- **½ cup all purpose flour**
- **4 cups whole milk**
- **1 Turkish bay leaf**
- **¼ teaspoon ground nutmeg**

- **16 lasagna noodles**
- **1⅓ cups freshly grated Parmesan cheese (about 4 ounces)**

FOR PESTO: Blend basil and next 4 ingredients in processor until coarse puree forms. Season pesto to taste with salt and pepper. Transfer 1 cup pesto to medium bowl; mix in vegetable broth (reserve remaining pesto for another use).

FOR BÉCHAMEL SAUCE: Melt butter in heavy large saucepan over medium heat. Add shallots and sauté 2 minutes. Add flour and whisk until smooth. Reduce heat to low; whisk 1 minute. Gradually whisk in milk. Bring sauce to boil, whisking constantly. Add bay leaf. Reduce heat and simmer until slightly thickened, stirring often, about 5 minutes. Mix in nutmeg. Season to taste with salt and pepper. Cool sauce slightly. Discard bay leaf before using.

BUTTER 13x9x2-inch baking dish. Cook noodles in pot of boiling water until tender but still firm to bite. Drain. Rinse under cold water; drain again. Spread ½ cup béchamel sauce over bottom of prepared dish. Overlap 4 noodles atop sauce to cover. Spread 1 cup béchamel sauce over. Spoon ⅓ of pesto-broth mixture over. Sprinkle with ⅓ cup Parmesan. Repeat layering twice, using 4 noodles, 1 cup béchamel, ⅓ of pesto-broth mixture, and ⅓ cup cheese for each layer. Cover with remaining 4 noodles. Spread remaining béchamel over. Sprinkle with remaining ⅓ cup Parmesan. Cover lasagna loosely with foil. *(Can be prepared 1 day ahead. Refrigerate.)*

PREHEAT oven to 375°F. Bake lasagna covered 30 minutes (if refrigerated, bake 45 minutes). Uncover and bake until heated through and bubbling, about 20 minutes longer. Let stand 15 minutes. Cut into squares and serve.

Fontina, mushroom, and pancetta lasagna

A SIMPLE SALAD AND BREAD are all you need to transform this creative baked pasta into a perfect party meal. Be sure to drain any excess liquid from the ricotta and spinach before making the filling, so the finished lasagna will be firm enough to cut into neat squares. Pancetta—Italian bacon cured in salt—is available at Italian markets and in the refrigerated deli case of many supermarkets.

8 SERVINGS

Filling

- **2 15-ounce containers ricotta cheese**
- **1 10-ounce package frozen chopped spinach, cooked according to package directions, drained, squeezed dry**
- **½ cup freshly grated Parmesan cheese (about 1½ ounces)**
- **2 large eggs**

Mushrooms

- **1 tablespoon olive oil**
- **2 ounces pancetta or bacon, chopped**
- **2 teaspoons minced fresh rosemary**
- **12 ounces mushrooms, sliced**

Assembly and baking

- **12 (about) lasagna noodles**

- **Tomato, Porcini, and Pancetta Sauce (see recipe)**
- **4 cups (packed) coarsely grated Fontina cheese (about 1 pound), divided**
- **¾ cup freshly grated Parmesan cheese (about 2½ ounces), divided**
- **1 tomato, seeded, chopped**
- **2 teaspoons minced fresh rosemary**

FOR FILLING: Combine first 3 ingredients in large bowl. Season to taste with salt and pepper. Add eggs and mix well. *(Filling can be prepared 1 day ahead. Cover and chill.)*

FOR MUSHROOMS: Heat oil in heavy large skillet over medium heat. Add pancetta and rosemary; sauté until fat renders, about 3 minutes. Add mushrooms, sprinkle with salt and pepper, and cook until juices evaporate, stirring frequently, about 12 minutes.

FOR ASSEMBLY AND BAKING: Cook noodles in large pot of boiling salted water until tender but still firm to bite, stirring occasionally. Drain. Rinse under cold water to cool; drain again. Arrange noodles in single layer on sheet of aluminum foil.

OIL 13x9x2-inch glass baking dish. Spread 1 cup Tomato, Porcini, and Pancetta Sauce over bottom of dish. Arrange 3 to 4 noodles over, trimming to fit and covering completely. Spread half of ricotta filling over. Spoon 1 cup sauce over. Sprinkle with 1 cup Fontina and ¼ cup Parmesan. Cover with 3 to 4 noodles, trimming to fit. Spread remaining ricotta filling over noodles. Spoon 1 cup sauce over. Sprinkle with 1 cup Fontina and ¼ cup Parmesan. Reserve ½ cup sautéed mushrooms for garnish. Spread remaining mushrooms over cheese. Cover with remaining noodles. Spread remaining sauce over noodles. Sprinkle remaining Fontina and ¼ cup Parmesan over. Cover with aluminum foil. *(Lasagna can be prepared 1 day ahead. Refrigerate lasagna and reserved ½ cup mushrooms separately. Before continuing, let lasagna and mushrooms stand at room temperature 2 hours.)*

PREHEAT oven to 350°F. Bake covered lasagna 30 minutes. Uncover and continue baking until heated through and bubbling, about 20 minutes longer. Sprinkle reserved ½ cup mushrooms, tomato, and 2 teaspoons rosemary over. Let stand 10 minutes. Cut into squares.

Tomato, porcini, and pancetta sauce

THIS SAUCE ENRICHES the Fontina, Mushroom, and Pancetta Lasagna, and would also be delicious served over penne or rigatoni. Or bake chicken in the sauce for an easy company entrée. Pancetta, which is Italian unsmoked bacon cured in salt, and dried porcini mushrooms are available at Italian markets, specialty foods stores, and some supermarkets.

MAKES ABOUT 4 CUPS

- **1 1-ounce package dried porcini mushrooms**
- **1 cup hot water**

- **1 tablespoon olive oil**
- **2 ounces pancetta or bacon, chopped**
- **1 medium onion, chopped**
- **2 teaspoons minced fresh rosemary or 1 teaspoon dried**
- **⅛ teaspoon dried crushed red pepper**
- **1 28-ounce can crushed tomatoes with added puree**

RINSE mushrooms briefly under cold water if sandy. Place in small bowl. Pour 1 cup hot water over and let soak until soft, about 30 minutes. Drain mushrooms; reserve soaking liquid. Cut hard stems from mushrooms.

HEAT oil in heavy medium saucepan over medium heat. Add pancetta and sauté 2 minutes. Add onion and rosemary; sauté until onion is translucent, stirring occasionally, about 8 minutes. Add crushed red pepper and sauté 20 seconds. Add tomatoes and porcini. Carefully pour in reserved mushroom soaking liquid, leaving any sediment in bowl. Simmer until sauce is thick, stirring occasionally, about 35 minutes. Season to taste with salt and pepper. *(Can be prepared 2 days ahead. Refrigerate until cold, then cover and keep refrigerated.)*

Sausage, cheese, and basil lasagna

NO-BOIL LASAGNA NOODLES, found at most supermarkets, and a flavorful three-cheese filling in place of the usual béchamel sauce result in a lasagna that takes only about 45 minutes to put together, and needs only about an hour in the oven after that. The biggest surprise, however, is that the results are twice as good as many lasagnas that take twice as long to prepare.

6 TO 8 SERVINGS

Sauce

2 tablespoons olive oil
1 pound hot Italian sausages, casings removed
1 cup chopped onion
3 large garlic cloves, chopped
2 teaspoons dried oregano
1/4 teaspoon dried crushed red pepper
1 28-ounce can crushed tomatoes with added puree
1 14.5-ounce can diced tomatoes with green pepper and onion

Filling

1 1/2 cups (packed) fresh basil leaves
1 15-ounce container plus 1 cup part-skim ricotta cheese
1 1/2 cups (packed) coarsely grated mozzarella cheese (about 6 ounces)
3/4 cup freshly grated Parmesan cheese (about 2 1/2 ounces)
1 large egg
1/2 teaspoon salt
1/4 teaspoon ground black pepper

Assembly and baking

12 no-boil lasagna noodles (from one 8- to 9-ounce package)
3 cups (packed) coarsely grated mozzarella cheese (about 12 ounces)
1 cup freshly grated Parmesan cheese (about 3 ounces)
Nonstick olive oil spray

FOR SAUCE: Heat oil in heavy large pot over medium-high heat. Add sausage, onion, garlic, oregano, and crushed red pepper; sauté until sausage is cooked through, breaking up sausage with back of fork, about 10 minutes. Add crushed tomatoes and diced tomatoes with juice. Bring sauce to boil. Reduce heat to medium and simmer 5 minutes to blend flavors. Season with salt and pepper. *(Sauce can be made 1 day ahead. Chill until cold, then cover, and keep chilled.)*

FOR FILLING: Using on/off turns, chop basil leaves finely in processor. Add ricotta, mozzarella, Parmesan, egg, salt, and pepper. Using on/off turns, process until filling is just blended and texture is still chunky.

FOR ASSEMBLY AND BAKING: Preheat oven to 375°F. Spread 1¼ cups sauce in 13x9x2-inch glass baking dish. Arrange 3 noodles, side by side, atop sauce. Drop 1½ cups filling by tablespoonfuls over noodles, then spread evenly to cover. Sprinkle with ¾ cup mozzarella cheese and ¼ cup Parmesan cheese. Repeat layering of sauce, noodles, filling, and cheeses 2 more times. Top with remaining 3 noodles. Spoon remaining sauce atop noodles. Sprinkle with remaining cheeses. Spray large piece of aluminum foil with nonstick olive oil spray. Cover lasagna with foil, sprayed side down.

BAKE lasagna 40 minutes. Carefully uncover. Increase oven temperature to 400°F. Bake until noodles are tender, sauce is bubbling thickly, and edges of lasagna are golden and puffed, about 20 minutes longer. Transfer to work surface; let stand 15 minutes.

Pizzas

Pizza bianca with goat cheese and greens

THE TERM *WHITE PIZZA* generally refers to any version of the dish that does not include the familiar tomato-based sauce. Some white pizzas use no sauce at all, but most replace the pizza sauce with a brushing of flavored olive oil. Allow about five and a half hours total for the pizza dough to rise twice. The small quantity of yeast and a long, slow rise give the crust its great flavor and texture. Kale could be used in place of the Swiss chard.

4 SERVINGS

Seasoned oil

- **2 tablespoons extra-virgin olive oil**
- **1 garlic clove, minced**
- **¼ teaspoon dried crushed red pepper**

Crust

- **¾ cup warm water (105°F to 115°F)**
- **1½ teaspoons dry yeast (from 1 envelope)**
- **1 tablespoon extra-virgin olive oil**
- **1 teaspoon salt**
- **1¾ cups (about) unbleached all purpose flour, divided**

Topping

- **1 bunch Swiss chard (about 10 ounces), white ribs cut away**
- **2 tablespoons extra-virgin olive oil**
- **1 garlic clove, minced**
- **Yellow cornmeal**
- **8 ounces whole-milk mozzarella cheese, coarsely grated (about 2 cups packed)**
- **4 ounces soft fresh goat cheese, crumbled (about 1 cup)**

FOR SEASONED OIL: Mix oil, garlic, and crushed red pepper in small bowl. Cover and refrigerate until needed, up to 1 day.

FOR CRUST: Pour ¾ cup warm water into large bowl. Sprinkle yeast over and stir to blend. Let stand until yeast dissolves, about 10 minutes. Add oil and salt, then 1½ cups flour. Stir until well blended (dough will be sticky). Turn dough out onto generously floured surface and knead until smooth and elastic, adding just enough additional flour by tablespoonfuls to keep dough from sticking, about 5 minutes (dough will be soft). Shape dough into ball; place in large oiled bowl and turn to coat. Cover bowl with plastic wrap, then kitchen towel. Let dough rise at cool room temperature until almost doubled in volume, about 2 hours. Punch dough down; shape into ball. Return to bowl; cover with plastic wrap, then towel, and let rise again until doubled in volume, about 3 hours.

FOR TOPPING: Cook chard in large pot of boiling salted water until just tender, about 2 minutes. Drain. Rinse under cold water; drain again. Squeeze dry, then chop coarsely. Heat 2 tablespoons oil in small skillet over medium heat. Add garlic and stir 30 seconds. Add chard and stir 1 minute. Remove from heat. Season topping to taste with salt.

PREHEAT oven to 500°F. Punch down dough. Shape into ball; place on floured work surface. Cover with kitchen towel; let rest 30 minutes.

SPRINKLE rimless baking sheet with cornmeal. Roll out dough on floured surface to 13-inch round. Transfer to prepared baking sheet. Sprinkle mozzarella over dough, leaving 1-inch plain border. Scatter chard topping over mozzarella. Top with goat cheese. Brush plain border with some of seasoned oil. Measure 2 teaspoons seasoned oil and reserve; drizzle remaining seasoned oil over pizza.

BAKE pizza until crust is brown, about 15 minutes. Remove from oven; brush edge with reserved seasoned oil and serve.

Grilled rosemary-crust pizzas with sausage, bell peppers, onions, and cheese

PIZZAS COOKED ON top of an outdoor grill develop a crisp texture and a wonderfully smoky flavor. The dough won't fall through into the fire, because it begins to firm up the moment it comes into contact with the intense heat. Individual-serving pizzas are easier to manage; and since the sausages and colorful summer vegetables in this recipe are also grilled, there's almost nothing to clean up. (Prepare the toppings while the dough is rising.)

MAKES FOUR 8-INCH PIZZAS

Dough

- **1 cup warm water (105°F to 115°F)**
- **1 tablespoon sugar**
- **1 envelope dry yeast**
- **3 tablespoons olive oil**
- **3 cups (or more) all purpose flour**
- **1½ teaspoons salt**
- **1 tablespoon chopped fresh rosemary**

Toppings

- **¾ cup olive oil**
- **9 garlic cloves, minced**
- **6 tablespoons balsamic vinegar**
- **2 tablespoons chopped fresh rosemary**

- **1 pound hot Italian sausages**
- **2 yellow or red bell peppers, quartered lengthwise**
- **1 large red onion, peeled, cut through root end into ½-inch-thick wedges**

Assembly and grilling

- **2 cups (packed) coarsely grated mozzarella cheese (about 8 ounces)**
- **½ cup freshly grated Parmesan cheese (about 1½ ounces)**
- **2 cups crumbled chilled soft fresh goat cheese (about 8 ounces)**
- **4 plum tomatoes, halved, seeded, chopped**
- **¾ cup chopped green onions**

FOR DOUGH: Combine 1 cup warm water and sugar in processor. Sprinkle yeast over; let stand until yeast dissolves and mixture is foamy, about 10 minutes. Add oil, then 3 cups flour and salt. Process until dough comes together, about 1 minute. Turn dough out onto floured work surface. Sprinkle with rosemary. Knead until dough is smooth and elastic, adding more flour by tablespoonfuls if dough is sticky, about 5 minutes. Lightly oil large bowl. Add dough and turn to coat. Cover bowl with plastic wrap, then clean kitchen towel. Let stand in warm draft-free area until dough doubles in volume, about 1 hour.

PUNCH down dough. Knead dough in bowl until smooth, about 2 minutes. Cover loosely with towel and set aside.

FOR TOPPINGS: Whisk oil, garlic, vinegar, and rosemary in medium bowl to blend. Let vinaigrette stand 15 minutes at room temperature or refrigerate up to 2 hours.

PREPARE barbecue (medium heat). Arrange sausages, peppers, and red onion on baking sheet. Brush with some of vinaigrette. Sprinkle with salt and pepper. Grill sausages until cooked through and peppers and red onion until slightly charred and crisp-tender, turning and basting occasionally with vinaigrette, about 12 minutes for sausages and 8 minutes for peppers and red onion.

TRANSFER sausages and vegetables to cutting board. Cut sausages into ½-inch cubes and peppers into thin strips.

FOR ASSEMBLY AND GRILLING: Add coals to barbecue, if necessary. Divide dough into 4 equal pieces. Working on floured surface, stretch out each piece to 9-inch round.

PLACE 2 dough rounds on barbecue rack. Grill over medium heat until top of dough puffs and underside is crisp, about 3 minutes. Using tongs, turn rounds over. Grill 1 minute. Transfer to baking sheet, well-grilled side up. Repeat with remaining 2 dough rounds. Sprinkle each with ¼ of mozzarella and Parmesan. Top each with ¼ of sausage, peppers, and red onion, then with ¼ of goat cheese, tomatoes, and green onions. Drizzle each with 1½ tablespoons vinaigrette.

USING large metal spatula, return 2 pizzas to barbecue rack. Close grill or cover pizzas loosely with aluminum foil. Grill until cheeses melt and dough is cooked through and browned on bottom, using tongs to rotate pizzas for even cooking, about 5 minutes. Transfer to plates. Repeat grilling for remaining 2 pizzas.

Mozzarella and prosciutto pizza with balsamic onions

MANY PIZZA RECIPES call for baking on a ceramic pizza stone or baking tiles, which simulate the radiant dry heat of a traditional pizza oven. As this recipe demonstrates, a heavy baking sheet preheated in the oven can be used to approximate a pizza stone. And if you don't have a pizza peel (the wooden paddle that slides a pizza into and out of the oven), you can easily use a large rimless baking sheet instead.

4 SERVINGS

Dough

1½ cups unbleached all purpose flour
1½ teaspoons coarse kosher salt
½ cup warm water (105°F to 115°F)
1 teaspoon dry yeast (from 1 envelope)
1½ tablespoons olive oil
1 tablespoon honey

Toppings

2 tablespoons plus ½ cup olive oil
1 12-ounce red onion, thinly sliced
2 tablespoons balsamic vinegar
2 teaspoons Worcestershire sauce
4 garlic cloves, chopped
1 large red bell pepper

Assembly and baking

All purpose flour
1 cup (packed) coarsely grated whole-milk mozzarella cheese (about 4 ounces)
3 tablespoons coarsely grated Parmesan cheese (about 1 ounce)
4 thin slices prosciutto, sliced crosswise into thin strips
2 teaspoons chopped fresh thyme
Balsamic vinegar

FOR DOUGH: Mix flour and salt in large bowl. Pour ½ cup warm water into small bowl. Sprinkle yeast over water and stir to blend. Let stand until yeast dissolves, about 10 minutes. Pour yeast mixture into bowl with flour. Add oil and honey. Using flexible spatula, stir until coarse dough forms. Knead dough in bowl until smooth and elastic, about 6 minutes. Cover bowl with plastic wrap, then clean kitchen towel. Let dough stand 30 minutes. Refrigerate dough in bowl, still covered, at least 2 hours (dough will rise very little). *(Dough can be prepared 2 days ahead; keep refrigerated.)*

FOR TOPPINGS: Heat 2 tablespoons oil in heavy medium skillet over medium-high heat. Add onion and sauté until golden, about 12 minutes. Add vinegar and Worcestershire sauce. Reduce heat to medium-low; simmer until liquid evaporates and onion is very tender, about 4 minutes. Season onion to taste with salt and pepper.

HEAT remaining ½ cup oil in heavy small skillet over medium-low heat. Add garlic and sauté just until garlic begins to brown, about 4 minutes. Using slotted spoon, transfer garlic to custard cup. Pour garlic oil into separate small bowl.

CHAR bell pepper over gas flame or in broiler until blackened on all sides. Enclose in paper bag; let stand 10 minutes. Peel, seed, and slice thinly.

(Onion, garlic, garlic oil, and roasted pepper can be prepared 1 day ahead. Cover separately; chill.)

FOR ASSEMBLY AND BAKING: Place chilled dough on work surface. Cover with plastic wrap; let stand at room temperature until malleable, about 1 hour.

POSITION rack in bottom third of oven. Place heavy large rimless baking sheet on rack (invert sheet if rimmed). Preheat oven to 500°F at least 30 minutes. Roll out dough on lightly floured surface to 12-inch round, allowing dough to rest a few minutes any time it springs back. Sprinkle flour on pizza paddle or another rimless baking sheet. Slide paddle under dough. Brush 1 tablespoon reserved garlic oil over dough, leaving ½-inch plain border. Sprinkle dough with mozzarella, then reserved garlic and balsamic onion. Top with roasted pepper strips in spoke pattern. Sprinkle with Parmesan. Slide knife under dough to loosen from paddle, if sticking.

POSITION paddle at far edge of hot baking sheet in oven. Tilt paddle slightly and pull back slowly, allowing pizza to slide onto hot sheet. Bake 6 minutes. Rotate pizza half a turn. Bake until crust is deep brown, about 6 minutes longer. Arrange prosciutto atop pizza. Bake until prosciutto softens, about 30 seconds. Using paddle, transfer pizza to cutting board. Sprinkle with thyme. Cut into 8 wedges. Serve, passing more balsamic vinegar and remaining garlic oil separately.

Asian-style barbecued pork pizza

A PURCHASED FULLY BAKED pizza crust, bottled barbecue and hoisin sauces, and preshredded mozzarella cheese make short work of preparing this delicious and contemporary pizza. It also works well as an appetizer if it's cut into bite-size pieces or narrow wedges after baking. Look for hoisin sauce at Asian markets or in the Asian foods section of the supermarket.

6 APPETIZER OR 4 MAIN-COURSE SERVINGS

3 tablespoons olive oil, divided
8 ounces pork tenderloin, cut into ½-inch cubes
2 teaspoons minced peeled fresh ginger
1 garlic clove, minced

1 cup chopped onion
1½ cups ½-inch pieces bok choy (about 2 large leaves)
2 cups (packed) coarsely shredded mozzarella cheese (about 8 ounces)
⅓ cup plus 3 tablespoons chopped fresh cilantro

1 10-ounce purchased fully baked thin pizza crust
3 tablespoons purchased barbecue sauce
3 tablespoons hoisin sauce

PREHEAT oven to 450°F. Heat 2 tablespoons oil in heavy medium skillet over medium-high heat. Sprinkle pork with salt and pepper. Add pork, ginger, and garlic to skillet. Sauté until pork is cooked through, about 5 minutes. Transfer pork mixture to large bowl.

ADD remaining 1 tablespoon oil and onion to same skillet; sauté over medium-high heat 3 minutes. Add bok choy; sauté until vegetables are crisp-tender, about 1 minute. Transfer vegetable mixture to bowl with pork and cool. Mix in cheese and ⅓ cup cilantro. Season topping to taste with salt and pepper.

PLACE pizza crust on heavy large baking sheet. Blend barbecue sauce and hoisin sauce in small bowl; spread 4 tablespoons over crust. Spread topping over. Drizzle with remaining 2 tablespoons sauce. Bake pizza until crust is crisp, topping is heated through, and cheese is melted, about 15 minutes. Transfer to cutting board. Sprinkle with remaining 3 tablespoons cilantro. Cut into wedges or bite-size pieces and serve.

Mexican chicken pizza with salsa verde

THE FLAVORS of cumin and cilantro, along with the piquant green tomatillo sauce known as *salsa verde*—and the use of a purchased fully baked pizza crust and a rotisserie chicken—make this a quick weeknight trip to Mexico. *Queso fresco* (also known as *queso blanco*) is available at Latin markets and some supermarkets, but a mild feta works well, too.

6 APPETIZER OR 4 MAIN-COURSE SERVINGS

3 tablespoons olive oil, divided
2 garlic cloves, minced
½ teaspoon ground cumin
¾ cup bottled or canned salsa verde
½ cup chopped fresh cilantro, divided
2 cups shredded purchased rotisserie chicken
1 cup chopped onion
1 zucchini, cut into thin rounds
1½ cups (packed) coarsely grated Monterey Jack cheese (about 6 ounces)
2 tablespoons chopped fresh oregano

1 10-ounce purchased fully baked thin pizza crust
½ cup crumbled queso fresco or feta cheese (about 2 ounces)

PREHEAT oven to 450°F. Heat 1 tablespoon oil in heavy large nonstick skillet over medium heat. Add garlic and cumin; sauté 30 seconds. Scrape contents of skillet into large bowl. Add salsa, ¼ cup cilantro, then chicken to bowl; toss to combine. Heat remaining 2 tablespoons oil in same skillet over medium-high heat. Add onion and sauté until golden, about 4 minutes. Add zucchini and sauté until crisp-tender, about 3 minutes. Add zucchini mixture to chicken mixture and stir to combine. Cool 15 minutes. Mix in Monterey Jack cheese and oregano.

PLACE pizza crust on heavy large baking sheet. Spread chicken topping over. Sprinkle with queso fresco. Bake pizza until crust is crisp, topping is heated through, and cheeses are melted, about 15 minutes. Transfer pizza to cutting board. Sprinkle with remaining ¼ cup cilantro. Cut into wedges and serve.

Gouda and red salad pizza

A PREBAKED PIZZA CRUST provides the ideal base for an out-of-the-ordinary but easy topping composed of fresh, raw vegetables marinated in a light vinaigrette dressing. A layer of melted cheese helps seal the purchased baked crust from some of the salad's juices during baking.

4 SERVINGS

1 medium head of radicchio, thinly sliced
½ red onion, thinly sliced
½ large red bell pepper, thinly sliced
2 large plum tomatoes, seeded, thinly sliced
1 large red jalapeño chile, seeded, minced
2½ tablespoons balsamic vinegar
2 tablespoons olive oil
¾ teaspoon salt
½ teaspoon ground black pepper
¼ teaspoon sugar

2½ cups (packed) coarsely shredded Gouda cheese (about 10 ounces), divided
1 14-ounce purchased fully baked pizza crust

TOSS first 10 ingredients in large bowl to combine. Marinate until juices begin to accumulate in bowl, tossing occasionally, at least 45 minutes and up to 2 hours.

MEANWHILE, position rack in center of oven. Place heavy large rimless baking sheet on rack (invert if rimmed). Preheat oven to 500°F for 30 minutes.

DRAIN vegetables well. Mix in 1 cup Gouda. Spread 1 cup Gouda over crust. Cover with vegetable mixture, spreading evenly. Top with remaining ½ cup Gouda. Transfer pizza to heated baking sheet in oven. Bake until cheese is melted and edges of crust are crisp, about 12 minutes. Transfer pizza to platter. Let stand 5 minutes before serving.

Eggplant and tomato pizza

PREPARED PIZZA DOUGH from the supermarket refrigerator case makes this delicious pizza a snap. For extra ease, the dough is pressed into a metal baking pan, and the pizza is cut into neat squares when it comes out of the oven. When preparing the topping, cut the cubes of eggplant to a uniform size and not too big, so they will all be completely cooked through and full of flavor.

2 SERVINGS; CAN BE DOUBLED

- **2 tablespoons olive oil**
- **2 cups ½-inch cubes unpeeled Japanese eggplant (about 8 ounces)**
- **1 medium onion, thinly sliced**

- **1 10-ounce tube refrigerated pizza dough**
- **8 ounces plum tomatoes (about 3 medium), thinly sliced into rounds**
- **3 tablespoons freshly grated Parmesan cheese (scant 1 ounce)**
- **¾ teaspoon dried marjoram**

PREHEAT oven to 450°F. Lightly oil 9x9x2-inch metal baking pan. Heat 2 tablespoons oil in heavy medium skillet over medium-high heat. Add eggplant and onion; sauté until vegetables soften and brown lightly, about 10 minutes. Sprinkle with salt and pepper.

UNROLL pizza dough. Fit into prepared pan, pressing upward at edges of pan to create 1-inch high dough border. Spread eggplant mixture evenly over bottom of crust. Arrange tomatoes over. Sprinkle with cheese and marjoram.

BAKE until topping is heated through and edges of pizza are brown and crisp, about 15 minutes. Cut into squares in pan.

Artichoke pizza with goat cheese and sausage

THE INVENTIVE MEDLEY OF FLAVORS atop this pizza includes brine-cured black Greek-style Kalamata olives. For an even bolder flavor, substitute bottled marinated artichoke hearts, well drained, for the canned. A good meatless version can be made simply by omitting the Italian sausages. Use either a thick or a thin purchased crust.

MAKES 1 LARGE PIZZA

- **½ pound sweet Italian sausages, casings removed**

- **1 13.75- to 14-ounce can artichoke hearts, drained**
- **⅓ cup drained roasted red peppers from jar**
- **20 Kalamata olives, pitted, divided**
- **2 tablespoons chopped fresh basil**
- **1 cup (packed) coarsely grated mozzarella cheese (about 4 ounces)**
- **⅓ cup freshly grated Parmesan cheese (about 1 ounce)**

- **1 14-ounce purchased fully baked pizza crust**
- **1 tablespoon Garlic Oil (see recipe)**
- **½ cup crumbled soft fresh goat cheese (about 2 ounces)**

SAUTÉ sausage in heavy medium skillet over medium heat until cooked through, breaking up sausage with back of fork, about 10 minutes. Using slotted spoon, transfer sausage to paper towels to drain.

COMBINE artichoke hearts, peppers, 12 olives, and basil in processor. Using on/off turns, process until finely chopped. Transfer mixture to large bowl. Stir in sausage, mozzarella, and Parmesan. *(Topping can be prepared 1 day ahead. Cover and refrigerate.)*

PREHEAT oven to 450°F. Place crust on heavy large baking sheet. Brush with Garlic Oil. Spread artichoke topping over crust. Dot with goat cheese. Top with remaining 8 olives. Sprinkle with ground pepper. Bake pizza until crust is golden, topping is heated through, and mozzarella is bubbling, about 15 minutes. Transfer to cutting board; cool 5 minutes. Cut into wedges.

Garlic oil

HERE'S AN EASY, FLAVORFUL OIL that can be used for other homemade pizzas. Or to make bruschetta, just brush the oil on crusty Italian bread slices, place them under the broiler until they're lightly toasted, and top with chopped tomatoes and basil. Be sure to prepare the oil the day before using and to store it in the refrigerator.

MAKES ½ CUP

- **½ cup olive oil**
- **6 garlic cloves, pressed**

COMBINE olive oil and garlic in small bowl. Cover and refrigerate overnight. *(Can be prepared 2 days ahead. Keep refrigerated.)* Let stand at room temperature 30 minutes before using.

Rustic green pepper and olive skillet pizza

CONVENIENT INGREDIENTS from the supermarket compose an absolutely easy weeknight main course. To vary the recipe, top the pizza with vegetables from the market's salad bar, such as broccoli florets or halved cherry tomatoes. Frying the dough in olive oil gives this pizza a crisp outer crust. You can use chopped fresh oregano in place of the marjoram.

2 SERVINGS

- **2 tablespoons extra-virgin olive oil**
- **1 10-ounce tube refrigerated pizza dough, rolled out to 12-inch square**
- **1 garlic clove, minced**
- **1 8-ounce package shredded pizza blend cheese**
- **1 small green or red bell pepper, thinly sliced**
- **1 small red onion, thinly sliced**
- **⅓ cup sliced pitted black olives**
- **1 tablespoon chopped fresh marjoram**

PREHEAT oven to 400°F. Heat oil in medium (10-inch-diameter) ovenproof nonstick skillet over medium-high heat, tilting skillet to coat. Ease dough into skillet (dough will extend partway up sides). Cook until golden on bottom, about 4 minutes. Using tongs, turn dough over in skillet. Top dough with remaining ingredients. Transfer skillet to oven. Bake pizza until cheese is melted and toppings are hot, about 10 minutes. Cut into quarters in skillet.

Pizza with sautéed endive, bacon, and Fontina

WHEN BUYING BELGIAN ENDIVE, remember that the paler the vegetable is, the less bitter it tastes. So look for tender, creamy-white leaves tipped in yellow. Store the endive wrapped in paper towels inside a plastic bag in the refrigerator once you get it home, to help safeguard its mild flavor, and use the heads within a day.

MAKES 1 LARGE PIZZA

- **1 teaspoon olive oil**
- **2 bacon slices, cut into ¼-inch pieces**
- **6 medium heads of Belgian endive, cut crosswise into ½-inch-thick slices (about 6 cups)**
- **3 tablespoons freshly grated Parmesan cheese (scant 1 ounce)**
- **1 teaspoon fresh lemon juice**

- **1 14-ounce purchased fully baked pizza crust**
- **1½ cups (packed) coarsely grated Fontina cheese (about 6 ounces)**

HEAT oil in heavy large skillet over medium-high heat. Add bacon and sauté until crisp, about 3 minutes. Add endive and sauté until endive is golden, about 5 minutes. Reduce heat to medium and cook until endive is tender, about 5 minutes. Transfer mixture to medium bowl. Stir in Parmesan and lemon juice. Season topping to taste with salt and pepper. *(Topping can be prepared 4 hours ahead. Cover and chill.)*

PREHEAT oven to 500°F. Place crust on heavy large baking sheet. Spoon topping over crust, leaving 1-inch plain border. Sprinkle Fontina over topping. Bake pizza until cheese is melted and crust is crisp, about 10 minutes. Transfer to cutting board. Cut pizza into wedges.

Pizza squares with Stilton and caramelized onion

THE METHOD FOR CARAMELIZING ONIONS in this recipe—which involves cooking them with sugar, Sherry, and vinegar, and repeatedly adding and evaporating white wine—produces a deep brown color and sweet, mellow flavor. Combining them with blue-veined Stilton cheese on a purchased baked pizza crust yields a lively hors d'oeuvre to serve with cocktails.

10 APPETIZER SERVINGS

- **3 tablespoons olive oil, divided**
- **1 garlic clove, pressed**
- **1 tablespoon butter**
- **1 very large onion, thinly sliced (about 2 cups)**
- **2¼ cups dry white wine, divided**
- **½ cup Sherry wine vinegar**
- **2 tablespoons sugar**
- **1 tablespoon dry Sherry**

- **1 14-ounce purchased fully baked pizza crust**
- **3 ounces Stilton cheese or other blue cheese, crumbled (about ¾ cup)**
- **2 teaspoons chopped fresh rosemary**

COMBINE 2 tablespoons oil and garlic in bowl. Set garlic oil aside. Melt butter with remaining 1 tablespoon oil in heavy large skillet over medium-high heat. Add onion, ¾ cup wine, vinegar, sugar, and Sherry. Boil until almost all liquid evaporates, stirring often, about 10 minutes. Add 1 cup wine, ½ cup at a time, boiling until liquid almost evaporates after each addition. Add remaining ½ cup wine; cook until onions are brown and liquid is thick and syrupy, stirring often, about 5 minutes. Season with salt and pepper. *(Garlic oil and caramelized onion can be made 3 days ahead. Cover separately and chill.)*

PREHEAT oven to 350°F. Brush crust with garlic oil. Cut into squares or diamonds, approximately 2 inches each. Arrange squares on large baking sheet. Divide caramelized onion equally among squares. Top with Stilton and sprinkle with rosemary. Bake until cheese begins to melt and crust is crispy, about 12 minutes. Arrange on platter and serve warm.

Wild mushroom and Fontina pizza

THE SHIITAKE AND OYSTER MUSHROOMS called for in this casual party appetizer are widely cultivated commercially and are sold at many farmers' markets and supermarkets. Other wild mushrooms, such as chanterelles or morels, can also be used. You may want to double this recipe if your friends particularly like pizza.

12 APPETIZER SERVINGS

- **2 tablespoons olive oil**
- **3 large shallots, thinly sliced**
- **8 ounces assorted fresh wild mushrooms (such as oyster and stemmed shiitake), sliced**
- **3 plum tomatoes, seeded, chopped**
- **2 tablespoons chopped fresh thyme**
- **2 tablespoons balsamic vinegar**

- **1 14-ounce purchased fully baked pizza crust**
- **2½ cups (packed) coarsely grated Fontina cheese (about 10 ounces), divided**
- **½ cup freshly grated Parmesan cheese (about 1½ ounces)**
- **Fresh thyme sprigs**

HEAT olive oil in heavy large skillet over medium-high heat. Add shallots and sauté until tender, about 4 minutes. Add mushrooms and sauté until just tender, about 5 minutes. Add tomatoes, chopped thyme, and vinegar; stir to combine. Remove skillet from heat. Season to taste with salt and pepper. *(Vegetable mixture can be prepared 1 day ahead. Cover and refrigerate.)*

PREHEAT oven to 500°F. Place crust on pizza stone or heavy large baking sheet. Top with ¾ of Fontina cheese. Drain vegetable mixture if very wet, and arrange atop cheese. Top with Parmesan and remaining Fontina. Bake until crust is crisp and cheeses are melted, about 12 minutes. Transfer to cutting board; cool 5 minutes. Cut pizza into wedges. Garnish with thyme sprigs.

Smoked-salmon pizza with red onion and dill

THIS IS AN EASY TWIST on the classic companion for a glass of chilled Champagne: buckwheat pancakes called blini topped with sour cream and smoked salmon. Here a purchased pizza crust replaces the traditional blini as the base for the salmon; the sour cream is replaced by cream cheese enhanced with the piquant flavors of red onion, horseradish, fresh dill, and lemon peel. Be sure to let the crust cool a bit after you crisp it in the oven, so its heat won't melt the cream cheese topping or partially cook the salmon.

6 APPETIZER SERVINGS

1 10-ounce purchased fully baked thin pizza crust

4 ounces cream cheese, room temperature
¼ cup minced red onion
1 tablespoon chopped fresh dill
2 teaspoons finely grated lemon peel
1 teaspoon prepared white horseradish

6 ounces thinly sliced smoked salmon

PREHEAT oven to 450°F. Place pizza crust on heavy large baking sheet. Bake until crisp at edges, about 13 minutes. Transfer crust to rack; cool to lukewarm.

STIR cream cheese with next 4 ingredients to combine. Season to taste with salt and pepper.

SPREAD cheese topping over crust, leaving 1-inch plain border. Top with salmon. Cut pizza into wedges; transfer to platter.

Pizza with feta, tomatoes, and shrimp

ROBUST INGREDIENTS that often accompany shrimp in Greek cooking—tomatoes, feta cheese, black olives, and oregano—top this Mediterranean-inspired pie. Adding the tender precooked shrimp to the pizza about two thirds of the way through its baking time ensures that they heat through perfectly without drying out.

MAKES 1 LARGE PIZZA

1 14-ounce purchased fully baked pizza crust
8 ounces mozzarella cheese, coarsely grated (about 2 cups packed)
1 pound plum tomatoes, thinly sliced
8 ounces feta cheese, crumbled (about 2 cups)
16 Kalamata olives, pitted
½ cup chopped green onions, divided
2 tablespoons chopped fresh oregano

8 ounces cooked peeled deveined large shrimp

PREHEAT oven to 450°F. Place pizza crust on heavy large baking sheet. Sprinkle mozzarella over. Arrange tomatoes atop cheese. Sprinkle feta over tomatoes. Sprinkle olives, ⅓ cup green onions, and oregano over pizza.

BAKE pizza 10 minutes. Remove pizza from oven and arrange shrimp atop pizza. Continue baking until crust is golden and mozzarella is melted, about 4 minutes longer. Cool pizza on sheet 5 minutes. Sprinkle remaining green onions over pizza. Cut into wedges and serve.

Pissaladière

PISSALADIÈRE, A CLASSIC DISH of Provence, is pizza's French cousin. The thin pizza-like crust, traditionally baked in a large rectangular pan and cut into squares for serving, is piled high with caramelized onions, then topped with anchovy fillets, olives, and fresh herbs.

12 APPETIZER SERVINGS

Onion topping

- **¼ cup (½ stick) butter**
- **6 pounds onions, thinly sliced**
- **6 fresh thyme sprigs**
- **4 fresh rosemary sprigs**
- **2 bay leaves**
- **6 tablespoons extra-virgin olive oil**

Crust

- **1 cup warm water (105°F to 115°F)**
- **1 tablespoon dry yeast (from 2 envelopes)**
- **1 teaspoon sugar**
- **2¾ cups (or more) all purpose flour**
- **1 teaspoon salt**
- **3 tablespoons extra-virgin olive oil, divided**

- **Yellow cornmeal**
- **20 drained anchovy fillets**
- **20 oil-cured black olives, pitted**
- **1 tablespoon chopped fresh thyme**

FOR ONION TOPPING: Preheat oven to 350°F. Place butter on heavy large rimmed baking sheet; place in oven until butter melts, about 5 minutes. Spread half of onions on baking sheet; top with 3 thyme sprigs, 2 rosemary sprigs, and 1 bay leaf. Sprinkle with salt and pepper. Drizzle with 3 tablespoons oil. Top with remaining onions, 3 thyme sprigs, 2 rosemary sprigs, and 1 bay leaf. Sprinkle with salt and pepper. Drizzle with remaining 3 tablespoons oil (onion topping will be about 2½ inches thick but will settle during baking). Bake until onions are very tender and golden, stirring and turning every 30 minutes, about 2 hours total. Cool. Discard herb sprigs and bay leaves. *(Onion topping can be made 1 day ahead. Cover and chill. Bring to room temperature before using.)*

FOR CRUST: Pour 1 cup warm water into small bowl; sprinkle yeast and sugar over. Stir to blend. Let stand until yeast dissolves and mixture is foamy, about 10 minutes.

BLEND 2¾ cups flour and salt in processor. Add yeast mixture and 2 tablespoons oil. Using on/off turns, process until dough comes together in moist clumps, adding more flour by tablespoonfuls if dough is sticky. Process until ball forms, about 1 minute. Turn dough out onto floured work surface and knead until smooth and elastic, about 5 minutes. Coat large bowl with remaining 1 tablespoon oil. Add dough to bowl; turn to coat with oil. Cover with plastic wrap, then clean kitchen towel. Let rise in warm draft-free area until doubled in volume, about 1½ hours. Punch down dough; cover and let rise until puffed and almost doubled in volume, about 1 hour.

SPRINKLE heavy 17x11x1-inch baking sheet with cornmeal. Roll out dough on lightly floured surface to 18x12-inch rectangle. Transfer to prepared baking sheet; press edges of dough up along sides and corners of sheet. Cover with dry kitchen towel; let rise until slightly puffed, about 1 hour.

PREHEAT oven to 475°F. Spread onion topping over dough. Arrange anchovies and olives atop. Bake pissaladière until crust is golden, about 15 minutes. Sprinkle with chopped thyme. Cut into squares. Serve warm or at room temperature. *(Can be made 4 hours ahead; let stand at room temperature.)*

Alsatian onion and bacon tart

ALTHOUGH THE PIZZA is distinctively Italian, other cultures also relish flatbreads with savory toppings, such as this classic from northeastern France. Crème fraîche is sold at some supermarkets. If unavailable, heat 1 cup whipping cream to lukewarm (85°F). Remove it from the heat and mix in 2 tablespoons buttermilk. Cover and let stand in a warm, draft-free area until slightly thickened and tangy, 24 to 48 hours, depending on room temperature. Refrigerate until ready to use, up to one week.

6 SERVINGS

2¼ cups (or more) all purpose flour, divided
1 cup warm water (105°F to 115°F)
1 teaspoon dry yeast (from 1 envelope)
½ teaspoon fine sea salt

¾ cup crème fraîche
⅓ cup large-curd cottage cheese
⅓ cup sour cream
2 small white onions, very thinly sliced (about 1½ cups)
12 ounces ¼-inch-thick bacon slices, cut crosswise into ½-inch-wide strips

COMBINE 1 cup flour, 1 cup warm water, and yeast in large bowl; stir to blend well. Cover bowl with plastic wrap and let stand until mixture is foamy, about 30 minutes. Stir in salt, then 1¼ cups flour. Mix until soft, slightly sticky dough forms, adding more flour by tablespoonfuls if dough is very sticky. Cover bowl with plastic wrap. Let dough rise in warm draft-free area until doubled in volume, about 1½ hours.

PREHEAT oven to 500°F. Lightly flour 2 heavy large baking sheets. Lightly flour hands; punch down dough and divide in half. Roll out each half on lightly floured surface to thin 16x10-inch rectangle. Transfer each rectangle to 1 prepared baking sheet. If dough shrinks, let rest several minutes, then roll or stretch back to size. Puree crème fraîche, cottage cheese, and sour cream in processor until smooth. Season to taste with salt and pepper. Spread cream mixture over crusts, leaving 1-inch plain border. Sprinkle onions and raw bacon over cream mixture, dividing equally. Bake tarts until edges of crusts are crisp and brown, about 14 minutes. Sprinkle generously with freshly ground black pepper. Cut into pieces and serve.

Calzones with four cheeses, eggplant, and basil

AS THIS RECIPE DEMONSTRATES, a pizza turnover can hold a generous quantity of filling. These capacious calzones call for an especially diligent method of sealing to keep the filling from leaking. First, the edges of the dough are brushed with water; then the lower edge is folded over the upper edge, before they are crimped together. The baking stones or tiles called for in the recipe, which simulate the dry, radiant heat of a brick pizza oven, may be found at cookware stores and many department stores.

MAKES 4

Eggplant mixture

7 tablespoons olive oil
4 garlic cloves, minced
1 12-ounce eggplant, unpeeled, cut into 1-inch cubes
1 tablespoon balsamic vinegar
¼ cup pine nuts (about 1 ounce)

Dough

1 cup warm water (105°F to 115°F), divided
1 envelope dry yeast
3 tablespoons olive oil
¾ teaspoon salt
3 cups (or more) bread flour

Assembly and baking

1½ cups (packed) coarsely grated Fontina cheese (about 6 ounces)
1½ cups (packed) coarsely grated mozzarella cheese (about 6 ounces)
1 3.5- to 4-ounce log soft fresh goat cheese, crumbled (about 1 cup)
¼ cup freshly grated Parmesan cheese (about ¾ ounce)

1 red bell pepper, cut into strips
½ cup thinly sliced fresh basil leaves

Fresh basil sprigs

FOR EGGPLANT: Combine oil and garlic in small bowl. Let stand 30 minutes. Place eggplant in colander. Sprinkle with salt and let stand 30 minutes.

TOSS eggplant in colander to drain further; pat dry. Heat half of garlic oil in heavy large skillet over medium heat. Add eggplant and sauté until tender, about 8 minutes. Increase heat to high. Add vinegar and cook until almost all liquid evaporates, about 1 minute. Season eggplant to taste with pepper. Transfer to large bowl.

HEAT 1 teaspoon garlic oil in heavy small skillet over medium heat. Add pine nuts and sauté until golden, about 2 minutes. Add nuts to eggplant. *(Garlic oil and eggplant mixture can be prepared 1 day ahead. Cover separately and refrigerate. Bring to room temperature before continuing.)*

FOR DOUGH: Place ¼ cup warm water in bowl of heavy-duty mixer; sprinkle yeast over and stir to combine. Let stand until yeast dissolves, about 10 minutes. Add remaining ¾ cup warm water, oil, salt, and 3 cups flour; stir to combine. Attach dough hook to mixer and beat until dough pulls away from sides of bowl, about 2 minutes. Turn dough out onto lightly floured surface and knead until smooth and elastic, adding more flour by tablespoonfuls if dough is sticky, about 10 minutes.

LIGHTLY oil large bowl. Add dough, turning to coat. Cover with plastic wrap, then clean kitchen towel. Let rise in warm draft-free area until doubled in volume, about 1 hour. While dough rises, begin preparation for assembly and baking.

FOR ASSEMBLY AND BAKING: Position rack in bottom third of oven. Place baking stone, baking tiles, or heavy large rimless baking sheet on rack. Preheat oven to 450°F for 30 minutes. Mix cheeses together in bowl.

PUNCH down dough. Divide into 4 pieces. Roll out 1 dough piece on lightly floured surface to 8-inch round. Brush dough with some of garlic oil, leaving 1-inch plain border. Spread ¼ of cheese mixture over half of dough, leaving 1-inch plain border. Cover cheese with ¼ of eggplant mixture, ¼ of bell pepper, and ¼ of sliced basil. Brush border of dough with water. Fold plain dough half over filling, allowing bottom edge of dough to show. Fold bottom edge over top edge and crimp to seal. Repeat with remaining dough pieces, garlic oil, cheese mixture, eggplant mixture, bell pepper, and sliced basil, forming total of 4 calzones. Cover calzones with kitchen towels and let stand 15 minutes.

USING large metal spatula, transfer calzones to preheated baking stone or baking sheet in oven. Bake until golden brown and crisp, about 12 minutes. Transfer calzones to platter. Garnish with basil sprigs and serve.

Calzones with cheese, sausage, and roasted red pepper

FOLD A PIZZA IN HALF to enclose its filling and you have the savory turnover known in Italian as a calzone. Baked in a hot oven, calzones puff up impressively while turning golden brown. To keep them from opening during baking, close the seam by pinching the edges of the dough together tightly.

MAKES 4

- **1½ cups warm water (105°F to 115°F)**
- **1 envelope dry yeast**
- **4 tablespoons olive oil, divided**
- **1½ teaspoons salt**
- **4 cups (about) all purpose flour**

- **1 large red bell pepper**

- **1¼ pounds red onions, sliced**
- **4 sweet or hot Italian sausages, casings removed**
- **3 cups (packed) coarsely grated mozzarella cheese (about 12 ounces)**
- **1½ cups ricotta cheese (about 12 ounces)**
- **4 teaspoons dried oregano**

POUR 1½ cups warm water into large bowl. Sprinkle yeast over; stir to blend. Let stand until yeast dissolves, about 10 minutes. Mix in 2 tablespoons oil and salt. Add 3¾ cups flour, about ½ cup at a time, stirring until blended after each addition. Turn dough out onto floured surface. Knead until smooth and elastic, sprinkling with more flour by tablespoonfuls if sticky, about 10 minutes.

PLACE dough in large oiled bowl; turn to coat. Cover bowl with plastic wrap, then kitchen towel. Let dough rise in warm draft-free area until doubled in volume, about 1 hour 15 minutes.

MEANWHILE, char bell pepper over gas flame or in broiler until blackened on all sides. Enclose in paper bag and let stand 10 minutes. Peel, seed, and slice.

HEAT remaining 2 tablespoons oil in heavy large skillet over medium-high heat. Add red onions; sauté until brown, about 25 minutes. Set aside. Cook sausage in heavy medium skillet over medium heat until cooked through, breaking into ½-inch pieces with back of fork, about 15 minutes. Set aside. Mix both cheeses and oregano in medium bowl; sprinkle with salt and pepper.

POSITION 1 rack in top third and 1 rack in bottom third of oven and preheat to 400°F. Dust 2 heavy large baking sheets with flour. Punch down dough. Knead on lightly floured surface until smooth, about 1 minute. Divide into 4 equal portions; shape each into ball. Roll out dough balls on lightly floured surface to 9-inch rounds. Spread ⅓ cup cheese mixture over half of each round, leaving ¾-inch plain border. Cover cheese on each with ¼ of onions, ⅓ cup cheese mixture, ¼ of sausage, ⅓ cup cheese mixture, then ¼ of bell pepper. Fold plain dough halves over filling, forming half circles. Pinch edges of dough firmly together to seal.

USING large spatula, transfer 2 calzones to each prepared baking sheet. Pierce tops in several places with small knife for steam to escape. Bake calzones 15 minutes. Reverse positions of baking sheets and bake until calzones are golden brown, about 15 minutes longer.

8 Rice, grains, and beans

There is an everyday sort of magic in rice, grains, and beans. With some gentle simmering, a few minutes of stirring, or an overnight soaking, these humble ingredients can yield astonishing results.

Take risotto, for instance. While it has acquired something of a diva reputation—touchy, difficult to handle, requiring a lot of coaxing and pleading—risotto is simply misunderstood. If you start with the right kind of rice—a short-grain or medium-grain variety like arborio or Vialone—and take it through a few simple steps (outlined in this chapter), you are guaranteed a bravura performance: a potful of creamy, firm rice with unforgettable flavor. And once you get the knack of when to add certain types of ingredients, the variations are endless.

Corn is another good example. It not only adds sweetness and texture to everything from corn bread to an airy soufflé, it also yields sandy, coarse-ground cornmeal. With a little patience and some stirring, cornmeal is transformed into comforting grits or polenta, which—like mashed potatoes—can be enriched with any number of additions, from butter and grated Parmesan cheese to sausage, pancetta, and Asiago. Served hot and creamy, polenta is a delicious "sponge" for the juices from all kinds of roasted meats, such as chicken and herbed pork. Or if left to firm up, it is easily sliced and grilled or quickly browned in a pan slicked with hot olive oil.

And then there's the basic bean. If you're starting with dried beans, a soak and a simmer can turn the toughest customer into a silky-smooth wonder, ready for seasoning, adding to soups, or whipping into a velvety puree, as in the White Bean Puree with Rosemary in this chapter. Even better when time is an issue are canned beans, available in a rainbow of varieties. Keep the pantry stocked with them and—through an everyday kind of magic—you'll have a head start on a variety of quick fixes and vegetarian meals.

Rice

Roasted garlic and wild mushroom risotto

DRIED PORCINI MUSHROOMS add depth of flavor to this risotto. Try substituting the porcini soaking liquid for some of the chicken broth to yield an even more pronounced mushroom flavor. Look for dried porcini mushrooms at Italian markets and specialty foods stores, and in the produce section of supermarkets.

6 FIRST-COURSE OR SIDE-DISH SERVINGS

- **2 large heads of garlic (about 40 cloves), cloves separated, unpeeled**
- **4 tablespoons olive oil, divided**
- **¾ ounce dried porcini mushrooms**
- **12 ounces assorted fresh wild mushrooms (such as crimini and stemmed shiitake), sliced**
- **1 cup chopped shallots (about 6 large)**
- **2 tablespoons chopped fresh thyme**
- **1½ cups arborio rice or medium-grain white rice**
- **½ cup dry white wine**
- **3½ to 4 cups low-salt chicken broth**
- **2 cups thinly sliced fresh spinach leaves**
- **⅓ cup freshly grated Parmesan cheese (about 1 ounce)**

PREHEAT oven to 400°F. Combine garlic and 2 tablespoons oil in small baking dish. Cover with aluminum foil and bake until garlic is golden and tender when pierced with small sharp knife, about 50 minutes. Cool slightly; peel garlic. Chop enough garlic to measure ¼ cup packed (refrigerate any remaining garlic for another use).

PLACE porcini in small bowl. Pour enough hot water over to cover. Let stand until porcini are soft, about 30 minutes. Drain. Squeeze porcini dry and chop coarsely.

HEAT 1 tablespoon oil in large nonstick skillet over medium-high heat. Add fresh mushrooms and sauté until mushrooms are golden and juices have evaporated, about 7 minutes. Add porcini and stir 1 minute. Season with salt and pepper. Set aside.

HEAT remaining 1 tablespoon oil in heavy medium saucepan over medium-high heat. Add shallots and thyme; sauté until shallots are tender, about 4 minutes. Add rice and stir to coat with shallot mixture. Add wine and cook until almost evaporated. Mix in chopped garlic and 3½ cups broth; bring to boil. Reduce heat to medium and cook until rice is tender and mixture is creamy, stirring occasionally and adding more broth if risotto is dry, about 20 minutes. Add mushroom mixture and spinach. Stir until spinach wilts. Stir in Parmesan cheese. Season to taste with salt and pepper.

Truffled lobster risotto

LOBSTER AND TRUFFLE OIL give this risotto a luxurious twist. Be sure to purchase uncooked lobster tails in their shells, as the shells enrich the broth for the risotto. And chopping the baked lobster shells in the blender with the broth helps extract every morsel of lobster flavor. You'll find both white and black truffle oils in small bottles at Italian markets, specialty foods stores, and some supermarkets. Try them in mashed potatoes or drizzled over steamed asparagus. A little oil goes a long way, so use it sparingly.

4 FIRST-COURSE SERVINGS

- **2 8-ounce uncooked lobster tails**
- **3½ cups low-salt chicken broth, divided**
- **3 tablespoons white or black truffle oil, divided**
- **¾ cup chopped peeled carrots**

1/4 cup chopped shallots
1 cup arborio rice or medium-grain white rice
1/4 cup brandy
1/3 cup whipping cream
1/3 cup chopped fresh chives

PREHEAT oven to 425°F. Cook lobster tails in large pot of simmering salted water until cooked through, about 10 minutes. Transfer lobster to bowl of cold water to cool. Drain. Remove meat from shells; reserve shells. Cut meat into ½-inch pieces. Refrigerate lobster pieces.

BREAK shells into large pieces. Place shells on rimmed baking sheet; bake 15 minutes. Blend shells with 1 cup chicken broth in blender until finely chopped. Strain through fine sieve. Reserve lobster broth; discard shells.

BRING remaining 2½ cups chicken broth to simmer in medium saucepan. Reduce heat to low, cover, and keep hot. Heat 1 tablespoon truffle oil in heavy large saucepan over medium heat. Add carrots and shallots; sauté 2 minutes. Add rice and stir 2 minutes. Add brandy; reduce heat to medium-low and simmer until brandy is absorbed, stirring constantly, about 2 minutes. Add lobster broth and ¾ of hot chicken broth. Simmer until rice is just tender and mixture is creamy, adding remaining broth by ¼ cupfuls as broth is absorbed and stirring often, about 20 minutes. Add lobster and cream; stir until heated through. Remove from heat. Stir in remaining 2 tablespoons truffle oil and chives. Season to taste with salt and pepper and serve.

Risotto primavera

ARBORIO RICE, a starchy short-grain white rice, is now readily available at most supermarkets. Otherwise, you're sure to find it at Italian markets and specialty foods stores. If you don't have arborio, a medium-grain white rice makes a good substitute. Do not rinse the rice before using it, as this will remove the necessary starches that help create its creamy consistency; and use hot broth in order to maintain the temperature of the risotto as it cooks. This recipe uses a shortcut technique—almost all the hot broth is added at once—rather than the traditional method of adding it gradually.

6 SERVINGS

Artichokes

1 lemon, halved, divided
3 artichokes

Risotto

7¼ cups (about) low-salt chicken broth

3 tablespoons olive oil
1 large onion, chopped
2 cups arborio rice or medium-grain white rice
4 ounces sliced prosciutto, chopped, divided
1 pound slender asparagus, trimmed, cut into 1-inch pieces
1 cup frozen peas, thawed
1 bunch green onions, chopped

½ cup thinly sliced fresh basil, divided
2 cups freshly grated Parmesan cheese (about 6 ounces)
Additional freshly grated Parmesan cheese

FOR ARTICHOKES: Fill large bowl halfway with cold water. Squeeze in juice from 1 lemon half. Cut off stem from 1 artichoke and rub exposed area with cut side of second lemon half. Starting from base of artichoke, bend each leaf back and snap off where it breaks naturally. Continue until light green leaves are exposed. Cut off top 2 inches of leaves above heart. Using small sharp knife, cut off all dark green areas. Cut artichoke into quarters. Rub all cut surfaces with lemon half. Cut out choke and purple inner leaves from each quarter. Cut each quarter lengthwise into ¼-inch-thick slices and place in lemon water. Repeat with remaining artichokes. *(Can be prepared 3 hours ahead. Let stand in water.)*

FOR RISOTTO: Pour broth into saucepan; bring to simmer. Reduce heat to low, cover, and keep hot.

HEAT oil in heavy large saucepan over medium-high heat. Add onion and cook until tender, stirring frequently, about 5 minutes. Drain artichokes and add to saucepan. Cook until almost tender, stirring occasionally, about 14 minutes. Add rice and half of prosciutto; stir 2 minutes. Add ¾ of hot broth to saucepan and reduce heat to simmer. Cook 10 minutes, stirring frequently. Add asparagus and continue cooking until rice is tender but still slightly firm to bite and mixture is creamy, stirring frequently and adding remaining broth by ¼ cupfuls as liquid is absorbed, about 15 minutes. Add peas and green onions; stir until heated through, about 2 minutes.

SET aside 2 tablespoons basil and 1 tablespoon prosciutto for garnish. Stir remaining basil and prosciutto and 2 cups Parmesan cheese into risotto. Season to taste with salt and pepper. Garnish with reserved basil and prosciutto. Serve immediately, passing additional Parmesan cheese separately.

Lamb risotto with bacon, herbs, and tomatoes

RISOTTO IS THE PERFECT BACKDROP for a variety of meats, seasonal vegetables, and fresh herbs. Here, adding lamb, fresh tomatoes, dill, mint, and feta cheese creates a risotto with Mediterranean accents. If you can't find a small piece of boneless leg of lamb, use two pounds of lamb chops, and cut enough meat off the bones in small cubes to measure 1½ cups packed.

6 FIRST-COURSE OR 4 MAIN-COURSE SERVINGS

- **2 tablespoons olive oil**
- **12 ounces boneless leg of lamb, chopped into small cubes**
- **2 cups chopped onions**
- **3 bacon slices, chopped**
- **4 garlic cloves, chopped**
- **¼ teaspoon ground nutmeg**
- **1½ cups arborio rice or medium-grain white rice**
- **5½ cups (about) low-salt chicken broth**
- **2 large plum tomatoes, seeded, chopped**
- **¼ cup chopped fresh dill**
- **2 tablespoons chopped fresh mint**
- **Grated Parmesan cheese or crumbled feta cheese**

HEAT oil in heavy large skillet over medium-high heat. Add lamb; sprinkle with salt and pepper. Sauté until brown, about 4 minutes. Add onions, bacon, garlic, and nutmeg; sauté until mixture is deep brown, about 12 minutes. Mix in rice and stir 1 minute. Add ½ cup broth; simmer until absorbed, stirring often, about 2 minutes. Continue to add broth ½ cup at a time until rice is just tender and risotto is creamy, stirring often and allowing almost all broth to be absorbed before adding more, about 25 minutes longer. Mix in tomatoes, dill, and mint. Season to taste with salt and pepper. Spoon risotto into large shallow bowls; top with cheese and serve.

Crispy garlic risotto cakes

ALMOST ANY LEFTOVER RISOTTO can be formed into patties and pan-fried, as in these delicious skillet cakes. The cakes can also be prepared hours ahead, then fried just before serving. Don't be put off by the amount of garlic used in this recipe: Roasted garlic is milder than fresh garlic, and it lends a nutty and somewhat sweet flavor.

6 SERVINGS

- **14 whole garlic cloves, unpeeled**
- **2 teaspoons olive oil**

- **4 cups water**

- 4 tablespoons (1/2 stick) butter, divided
- 1/4 cup finely chopped onion
- 1 cup arborio rice or medium-grain white rice
- 1/2 cup dry white wine

- 1/4 cup freshly grated Parmesan cheese (scant 1 ounce)
- 2 tablespoons chopped fresh parsley

All purpose flour

PREHEAT oven to 375°F. Toss garlic cloves with oil in small baking dish. Cover with aluminum foil and bake until garlic is tender, about 30 minutes. Uncover and bake until garlic is very tender, about 10 minutes longer. Cool garlic; peel. Puree half of garlic in processor. Thinly slice remaining garlic. Set garlic puree and slices aside.

BRING 4 cups water to simmer in medium saucepan. Reduce heat to low, cover, and keep hot.

MELT 2 tablespoons butter in heavy large saucepan over medium-high heat. Add onion and sauté until tender, about 3 minutes. Add rice and stir until golden, about 3 minutes. Add wine and stir until absorbed, about 2 minutes. Add 1 cup hot water. Reduce heat to simmer and stir until liquid is absorbed. Continue adding hot water 1 cup at a time, simmering until liquid is absorbed before each addition and stirring frequently, until rice is just tender and mixture is very thick, about 25 minutes. Transfer risotto to large bowl. Cool 30 minutes.

MIX cheese, parsley, garlic puree, and garlic slices into risotto. Season to taste with salt and pepper. Cover and refrigerate until cold, about 2 hours.

SHAPE risotto into six 3-inch-diameter, ¾-inch-thick patties, using about ⅓ cup risotto for each. Place risotto cakes on baking sheet. Cover and refrigerate 1 hour. *(Can be prepared 8 hours ahead. Keep refrigerated.)*

PLACE flour in shallow dish. Lightly coat each risotto cake with flour. Melt 1 tablespoon butter in large nonstick skillet over medium heat. Add 3 risotto cakes and cook until golden brown and heated through, about 3 minutes per side. Transfer risotto cakes to plate lined with paper towels to drain. Repeat with remaining 1 tablespoon butter and 3 risotto cakes. Transfer risotto cakes to platter and serve.

Jasmine rice timbales with black and white sesame seeds

JASMINE RICE is a fragrant long-grain rice from Thailand with an aroma and flavor comparable to basmati rice from India. Both the jasmine rice and the black sesame seeds can be found at Asian markets, specialty foods stores, and some supermarkets. Although the black sesame seeds add a dramatic touch to this simple side dish, it's fine to use all toasted white sesame seeds. Brushing the dishes with sesame oil not only allows the rice timbales to release easily from the dishes, but also imparts another dimension of flavor.

6 SERVINGS

- 2 1/2 cups water
- 1 1/2 cups jasmine rice or long-grain white rice
- 2 tablespoons (1/4 stick) butter, divided
- 3 teaspoons Asian sesame oil, divided
- 1/4 teaspoon salt

- 1/4 cup finely chopped chives
- 2 tablespoons white sesame seeds, toasted
- 1 tablespoon black sesame seeds

COMBINE 2½ cups water, rice, 1 tablespoon butter, 1 teaspoon sesame oil, and salt in large saucepan. Bring to boil. Reduce heat to low, cover, and simmer until rice is tender, stirring once, about 15 minutes.

ADD remaining 1 tablespoon butter, chives, and all sesame seeds to rice. Fluff with fork. Cover and let stand 5 minutes. Fluff rice again. Season to taste with salt and pepper.

BRUSH six ¾-cup soufflé dishes or custard cups with remaining 2 teaspoons sesame oil. Divide rice among dishes. Pack rice tightly into dishes. Turn timbales out onto plates and serve.

Spinach and ginger fried rice

GINGER, GARLIC, SESAME OIL, and oyster sauce turn cold, steamed long-grain rice into a simple but delicious fried rice that's perfect with grilled shrimp or salmon. As a rule of thumb, one cup of uncooked rice yields about three cups of cooked rice. When chilled, cooked long-grain rice becomes firm, so it's the best choice when making fried rice. By contrast, short-grain and medium-grain rice stay tender when cold and are therefore better to use when making chilled rice puddings or custards. Oyster sauce is available at Asian markets and at some supermarkets.

4 SERVINGS

- **1 tablespoon vegetable oil**
- **1 9- to 10-ounce bag fresh spinach leaves**

- **1 tablespoon Asian sesame oil**
- **1 tablespoon chopped peeled fresh ginger**
- **3 garlic cloves, chopped**
- **3 cups unsalted cooked basmati or long-grain rice, chilled (about 1 cup uncooked rice)**
- **2 tablespoons oyster sauce**

HEAT vegetable oil in large nonstick skillet over medium-high heat. Add half of spinach and toss until wilted but still bright green, about 2 minutes. Transfer spinach to sieve; set over bowl and drain well. Repeat with remaining spinach.

HEAT sesame oil in same skillet over medium-high heat. Add ginger and garlic; sauté until fragrant, about 30 seconds. Add rice and toss to coat. Add drained spinach and oyster sauce. Toss until combined and heated through, about 5 minutes. Transfer to bowl and serve.

Fried rice with peppers, green onions, and shiitake mushrooms

THIS FRIED RICE is filled with fresh vegetables and fortified with eggs, making it a quick and satisfying main course for two. For heartier appetites, serve it as a side dish alongside pork tenderloin. Use a mixture of red and yellow peppers to add color, which you can enhance with some chopped fresh cilantro if you desire.

2 SERVINGS; CAN BE DOUBLED

- **1½ cups water**
- **½ teaspoon salt**
- **¾ cup long-grain white rice**

- **2½ tablespoons vegetable oil, divided**
- **2 large eggs, beaten to blend**

- **8 ounces fresh shiitake mushrooms, stems removed, caps sliced**
- **1 large red or yellow bell pepper, thinly sliced**
- **2 teaspoons minced peeled fresh ginger**
- **2 green onions, chopped**
- **1 tablespoon (or more) soy sauce**

BRING 1½ cups water and ½ teaspoon salt to boil in medium saucepan over high heat. Stir in rice. Reduce heat to low, cover, and cook until rice is tender and water is absorbed, about 18 minutes.

MEANWHILE, heat 1 tablespoon oil in medium nonstick skillet over medium heat. Add eggs. Cook without stirring until eggs are set and bottom is golden brown, lifting edge of eggs occasionally to let uncooked portion run underneath, about 3 minutes. Turn out egg pancake onto work surface. Cut egg pancake in half, then cut crosswise into thin strips.

HEAT remaining 1½ tablespoons oil in same skillet over medium-high heat. Add mushrooms and sauté 4 minutes. Add bell pepper and ginger; sauté 3 minutes. Add rice, egg strips, green onions, and 1 tablespoon soy sauce; toss to combine. Season to taste with salt and pepper. Serve, passing more soy sauce if desired.

Spicy Mexican rice with cilantro

WHEN MAKING MEXICAN RICE and most rice dishes, it is important that the mixture be allowed to cook covered and undisturbed until the rice is tender. Removing the lid before the rice is done releases valuable steam and lengthens the amount of cooking time needed. Most important, never stir the rice while it cooks, as doing so will make the rice sticky. To make the rice ahead of time, remove it from the heat and fluff it with a fork, which allows the steam to escape and keeps the grains separated. Lay a clean kitchen towel over the rice, then cover it with the lid. The towel absorbs the condensation that forms on the lid, which could overcook the rice and make it sticky.

6 SERVINGS

- **2 tablespoons olive oil**
- **1 large red bell pepper, chopped**
- **1 cup chopped green onions**
- **2 garlic cloves, chopped**
- **1 cup long-grain white rice**
- **1½ cups low-salt chicken broth**
- **1 10-ounce can diced tomatoes with green chiles**
- **1 teaspoon dried oregano**
- **½ teaspoon Creole seasoning**
- **1 small bay leaf**
- **¼ cup chopped fresh cilantro**

HEAT oil in heavy large saucepan over medium-high heat. Add bell pepper, green onions, and garlic; sauté 5 minutes. Add rice and stir to coat. Mix in broth, tomatoes, oregano, Creole seasoning, and bay leaf. Bring to boil. Reduce heat to medium-low, cover, and simmer until rice is tender and liquid is absorbed, about 15 minutes. Mix in cilantro. Remove from heat; cover and let stand 10 minutes. Discard bay leaf. Season to taste with salt and pepper and serve.

Spiced wild and brown rice pilaf with butternut squash and dried cranberries

THIS HEALTHFUL PILAF uses only two tablespoons of olive oil and is made with long-grain brown rice, which includes the nutritious high-fiber bran that has been removed from white rice. Brown rice pairs well with wild rice (which is not actually a rice, but rather the seeds of a marsh grass), as both impart a nutty flavor and chewy texture and take about the same extended amount of time to cook. The pilaf can be prepared two hours ahead.

8 SERVINGS

- **2 tablespoons olive oil**
- **1 cup chopped onion**
- **½ cup chopped peeled carrot**
- **1 tablespoon minced peeled fresh ginger**
- **1 tablespoon curry powder**
- **1 teaspoon ground cumin**
- **1 garlic clove, minced**
- **3 cups ½-inch cubes peeled seeded butternut squash**
- **1 cup wild rice**
- **1 cup long-grain brown rice**
- **1 Fuji apple, peeled, cored, diced**
- **1 cinnamon stick**
- **3¾ cups low-salt chicken broth**
- **1 teaspoon salt**
- **1 cup dried cranberries**

HEAT oil in heavy large saucepan over medium heat. Add onion and carrot; sauté 5 minutes. Add ginger, curry powder, cumin, and garlic; stir 1 minute. Stir in squash and next 4 ingredients. Add broth and 1 teaspoon salt. Bring to boil. Reduce heat to medium-low, cover, and simmer until broth is absorbed and rice is tender, about 45 minutes. Remove from heat. Stir in cranberries. Cover and let stand until cranberries soften, about 10 minutes. Season to taste with salt and pepper. Transfer to bowl. *(Can be prepared 2 hours ahead. Let stand uncovered at room temperature. Before serving, cover with plastic wrap and rewarm in microwave.)*

Lemon-pistachio pilaf

A PILAF, *pilau, pilafi,* or *pilav* is a classic dish in regions extending from Greece to India, and therefore has many different names. Pilaf differs from other rice dishes in that the rice is sautéed in butter or oil before the broth is added. It can contain various herbs, spices, nuts, and seasonings. This one, using pistachio nuts and lemon zest, makes a perfect accompaniment to spiced grilled chicken or lamb kebabs. Be sure to use only the yellow part of the lemon peel, as the white pith is bitter. For a nuttior taste, toast the pistachios or sauté the rice in the oil a few minutes longer until it is golden brown before adding the broth.

8 SERVINGS

- **4 teaspoons extra-virgin olive oil**
- **2 large shallots, minced**
- **1½ cups long-grain white rice**
- **8 tablespoons chopped unsalted pistachios, divided**
- **1 14-ounce can (or more) low-salt chicken broth**
- **½ cup fresh lemon juice**
- **½ teaspoon salt**
- **2½ tablespoons 1x⅛-inch strips lemon peel (yellow part only), divided**

HEAT oil in heavy large saucepan over medium heat. Add shallots and sauté 3 minutes. Add rice and 2 tablespoons pistachios; stir 2 minutes. Stir in 1 can broth, lemon juice, and ½ teaspoon salt; bring to boil. Reduce heat to low, cover, and cook until liquid is absorbed and rice is tender, about 20 minutes. Mix in 4 tablespoons pistachios and 2 tablespoons lemon peel. Season to taste with salt and pepper. *(Can be prepared 2 hours ahead. Spread rice out on baking sheet; cool. Before continuing, drizzle with additional broth and rewarm tightly covered with aluminum foil in 400°F oven until heated through, about 10 minutes.)* Transfer rice to bowl. Sprinkle with remaining 2 tablespoons pistachios and ½ tablespoon lemon peel.

Curried rice with cauliflower, bell pepper, and green onions

USE AROMATIC BASMATI RICE HERE: The aged long-grain rice, grown in the Himalayan foothills, imparts a fragrance and flavor that enhances this Indian-style pilaf. Turn it into a satisfying meal by adding some cooked garbanzo beans with the peas and serving it with a dollop of yogurt mixed with diced cucumbers.

4 TO 6 SERVINGS

- **¼ cup (½ stick) butter**
- **1 tablespoon finely chopped peeled fresh ginger**
- **1¼ teaspoons curry powder**
- **½ teaspoon grated lemon peel**
- **2 cups small cauliflower florets**
- **½ cup diced red bell pepper**
- **⅓ cup chopped green onions**
- **1½ cups long-grain white rice or basmati rice**
- **2 cups water**
- **¾ teaspoon salt**
- **1 cup frozen peas, thawed**

MELT butter in heavy large saucepan over medium heat. Add ginger, curry powder, and lemon peel; stir 30 seconds. Mix in cauliflower, bell pepper, and green onions, then rice. Add 2 cups water and salt; bring to boil, stirring occasionally. Reduce heat to medium low, cover, and simmer until water is absorbed and rice is tender, about 18 minutes. Remove from heat. Mix in peas; season to taste with pepper. Cover and let stand 5 minutes.

Wild rice and jasmine rice pilaf with apricots and cashews

BECAUSE WILD RICE TAKES LONGER to cook than jasmine rice, they are cooked separately in this recipe. When combined, they give the dish a wonderful chewy texture and delicate aroma. Cool the rice before combining it with the hot vegetable mixture to keep it from overcooking. Various dried fruits and nuts may be used in place of the apricots and cashews. Try golden raisins or currants along with toasted pecans.

6 SERVINGS

- **1 cup wild rice (about 6 ounces)**
- **1 14-ounce can low-salt chicken broth**
- **1 cup jasmine rice (about 6½ ounces)**

- **¼ cup (½ stick) butter**
- **1 cup chopped green onions**
- **½ cup diced dried apricots**
- **½ cup coarsely chopped roasted salted cashews**
- **2 teaspoons grated lemon peel**

COOK wild rice in large saucepan of boiling salted water until just tender, about 45 minutes. Drain well. Bring broth to boil in medium saucepan over high heat. Mix in jasmine rice. Reduce heat to medium-low, cover, and cook until rice is tender and broth is absorbed, about 18 minutes. Let all rice cool at least 1 hour and up to 2 hours.

MELT butter in heavy large skillet over medium-high heat. Add green onions, apricots, cashews, and lemon peel. Stir until onions are soft, about 1 minute. Add all rice; toss to blend and heat through, about 3 minutes. Season with salt and pepper.

Toasted-garlic rice with fresh herbs and lime

THE SNOWY WHITE RICE contrasts well with the golden bits of garlic. In this recipe, the rice is first rinsed under cold water until the water runs clear, which removes any excess starch surrounding the rice and results in a fluffier finished dish. Use a heavy saucepan with a tightly fitting lid to keep the steam from escaping and to ensure that the rice cooks properly. If you ever find that your rice is still firm but the liquid has been absorbed, pour a quarter-cup of hot broth or water into the rice mixture without stirring, then cover and continue cooking until the rice is tender, repeating if necessary.

6 SERVINGS

- **1½ cups long-grain white rice**
- **3 cups low-salt chicken broth**
- **2 tablespoons fresh lime juice**

- **2 tablespoons vegetable oil**
- **12 garlic cloves, minced**
- **¾ teaspoon salt**
- **¼ cup chopped fresh cilantro**
- **¼ cup chopped fresh Italian parsley**
- **2 tablespoons chopped fresh mint**
- **1 tablespoon chopped fresh marjoram**
- **1½ teaspoons grated lime peel**

PLACE rice in strainer. Rinse under cold water until water runs clear. Drain well. Bring broth and lime juice to simmer in medium saucepan.

HEAT oil in heavy large saucepan over medium heat. Add garlic; sauté until golden and sticky, about 1 minute. Add rice and stir 2 minutes. Add hot broth mixture and ¾ teaspoon salt; bring to boil. Reduce heat to low; cover and cook until rice is tender, about 25 minutes. Turn off heat; let stand, covered, 10 minutes. Add herbs and lime peel to rice; fluff with fork. Season with additional salt, if desired.

Grains

Barley with caramelized onions and bow-tie pasta

SIX EASY-TO-FIND INGREDIENTS create a satisfying pasta dish that's loaded with flavor. Sauté the onions until they are a deep brown and well caramelized, and cook the mushrooms and barley until they brown as well, as it is the browning that lends flavor to this simple recipe. Kasha—roasted buckwheat groats—may be used instead of pearl barley, if desired.

6 TO 8 SERVINGS

- **2 tablespoons olive oil**
- **2 large onions, chopped**
- **1 cup pearl barley**
- **8 ounces mushrooms, sliced**
- **2 cups vegetable broth**

- **1 cup small bow-tie pasta**

HEAT oil in heavy large saucepan over medium-high heat. Add onions and sauté until deep brown, about 15 minutes. Add barley and stir 30 seconds. Add mushrooms; sauté until barley browns and mushrooms begin to soften, about 5 minutes. Add broth; bring mixture to boil. Cover pan, reduce heat to medium-low, and simmer until barley is tender and broth is absorbed, about 25 minutes.

MEANWHILE, cook pasta in medium saucepan of boiling salted water until tender but still firm to bite, stirring occasionally. Drain.

MIX pasta into barley. Season to taste with salt and pepper and serve.

Lemon couscous with peas and carrots

COUSCOUS IS ACTUALLY small granular bits of semolina dough; it's a staple in the North African diet. Here it is combined with peas and carrots for a colorful side dish that can be made within 15 minutes. To make the preparation even easier, mince the carrots in a food processor using on/off turns. Mix in fresh herbs such as chopped parsley or mint for wonderful twists of flavor. Serve this couscous with broiled or grilled salmon for a quick and delicious weeknight dinner.

6 SERVINGS

- **1½ cups low-salt chicken broth**
- **¼ cup water**
- **2 carrots (about 8 ounces), peeled, finely chopped**
- **1 cup frozen green peas**
- **1¼ cups couscous**
- **3 tablespoons fresh lemon juice**
- **1½ tablespoons grated lemon peel**
- **1½ tablespoons butter**

BRING broth and ¼ cup water to boil in medium saucepan over medium-high heat. Add carrots; cook 2 minutes. Add peas; cook 1 minute. Add couscous; stir 30 seconds. Add lemon juice, lemon peel, and butter; stir until butter melts. Remove from heat, cover, and let stand 5 minutes.

FLUFF couscous with fork. Season to taste with salt and pepper. Transfer to bowl and serve.

Couscous with garbanzo beans, prunes, and almonds

UNLIKE OTHER PASTAS AND GRAINS, couscous is not boiled in its cooking liquid. Rather, it is added to the hot cooking liquid and allowed to stand, covered and off the heat. After just 10 to 15 minutes, the couscous absorbs the liquid and is tender. Serve this couscous at room temperature as a side dish or salad.

6 SERVINGS

- **¼ cup olive oil**
- **4 cups chopped onions**
- **1 15- to 16-ounce can garbanzo beans (chickpeas), drained**
- **1 cup chopped pitted prunes (about 6 ounces)**
- **3 cups low-salt chicken broth**
- **½ teaspoon ground cinnamon**
- **2 cups couscous**

- **⅓ cup chopped fresh mint**
- **½ cup slivered almonds, toasted, divided**

HEAT oil in heavy large pot over medium-high heat. Add onions and sauté until very tender and beginning to brown, about 25 minutes. Add garbanzo beans and prunes; stir 1 minute. Add broth and cinnamon; bring to boil. Mix in couscous. Cover pot and remove from heat. Let stand 10 minutes.

FLUFF couscous with fork. Mix in mint and half of almonds. Season to taste with salt and pepper. Mound couscous in bowl. Sprinkle with remaining almonds and serve.

Golden couscous with olives and fresh herbs

TURMERIC GIVES THIS COUSCOUS its golden hue. For a variation, pearl couscous—a large type of couscous also known as Israeli or Middle Eastern couscous—can substitute for regular couscous. This larger type is about the size of pearl barley, and is available at Middle Eastern markets. To substitute, omit the broth from the recipe; boil the pearl couscous separately in salted water and drain it well before adding it to the remaining ingredients.

8 SERVINGS

- **½ cup (1 stick) butter**
- **6 cups chopped onions**
- **¾ teaspoon ground ginger**
- **½ teaspoon turmeric**
- **2¼ cups low-salt chicken broth**
- **1 cup pitted halved Kalamata olives**
- **½ cup chopped fresh basil**
- **⅓ cup chopped fresh mint**
- **¼ cup fresh lemon juice**
- **2 cups couscous**

MELT butter in heavy large pot over medium-low heat. Add onions and stir to coat. Cover pot and cook onions until very tender but not brown, stirring occasionally, about 35 minutes. Mix in ginger and turmeric. Add broth, olives, basil, mint, and lemon juice; bring to simmer. Mix in couscous. Cover pot, turn off heat, and let stand until all liquid is absorbed and couscous is tender, about 10 minutes.

FLUFF couscous with fork. Season to taste with salt and pepper. Mound couscous in bowl and serve.

Tabbouleh with avocado and feta cheese

THE VEGETARIAN MOVEMENT of the early 1970s spurred a growing interest in Middle Eastern cuisine and brought tabbouleh to the American table. Still popular today, the refreshing parsley and bulgur wheat salad is given a nice twist with the addition of avocado and feta cheese. Bulgur is available at natural foods stores and some supermarkets. Serve the salad with crisp flatbread or spoon it into small romaine lettuce leaves.

4 TO 6 SERVINGS

1½ cups hot water
½ cup bulgur

12 ounces plum tomatoes, seeded, chopped
1 cup chopped fresh Italian parsley
4 green onions, chopped
½ cucumber, peeled, seeded, finely chopped
4 radishes, chopped
½ cup crumbled feta cheese (about 2 ounces)
¼ cup chopped fresh mint
1 tablespoon grated lemon peel

6 tablespoons olive oil
3 tablespoons fresh lemon juice

2 avocados, halved, pitted, peeled, sliced

COMBINE 1½ cups hot water and bulgur in large bowl. Cover tightly and let stand until bulgur is tender, about 45 minutes.

DRAIN bulgur. Place in clean, dry kitchen towel and squeeze out any excess liquid. Return bulgur to dry bowl. Add tomatoes, parsley, onions, cucumber, radishes, cheese, mint, and lemon peel to bulgur. Stir to combine.

WHISK oil and lemon juice in medium bowl to blend. Season dressing to taste with salt and pepper. Add all but 2 tablespoons dressing to bulgur mixture; toss to combine. Season tabbouleh to taste with salt and pepper.

ADD avocado slices to remaining dressing; toss gently to coat. Mound tabbouleh on platter. Garnish with avocado slices and serve.

Overnight tabbouleh

THIS TABBOULEH IS ASSEMBLED and refrigerated overnight to allow the bulgur time to soften and the flavors in the salad to blend. Don't worry about cutting the vegetables perfectly, since the food processor does all the fine chopping for you. Bulgur, sometimes referred to as cracked wheat, is a nutritious grain that can be found at natural foods stores, Middle Eastern markets, and some supermarkets.

6 SERVINGS

2½ cups bulgur
⅓ cup chopped green onions
3½ cups (packed) fresh parsley leaves (from about 3 large bunches)
2 large carrots, peeled, cut into 1-inch pieces (about 2 cups)
1 large red bell pepper, cut into 1-inch pieces (about 1 cup)
2 cups tomato juice
1½ cups water
½ cup extra-virgin olive oil
½ cup fresh lemon juice
1 teaspoon salt
½ teaspoon ground black pepper
3 tablespoons chopped fresh thyme

PLACE bulgur and onions in large bowl. Finely chop parsley in processor; add to bulgur. Finely chop carrots in processor; add to bulgur. Finely chop bell pepper in processor; add to bulgur. Add tomato juice and next 5 ingredients; toss to combine. Cover and chill overnight. Mix thyme into tabbouleh. Season to taste with additional salt and pepper.

Bulgur pilaf with dates, dried apricots, and toasted walnuts

BULGUR IS WHEAT KERNELS that have had the bran removed, and which are then steamed, dried, and cut into coarse, medium, or fine grinds. (Bulgur is available at natural foods stores and some supermarkets.) Coarse- and medium-ground bulgur hold up well to simmering and work best in this pilaf. Use the finer grind of bulgur for recipes in which the bulgur is not cooked, such as in tabbouleh. Serve this healthful pilaf with roasted pork loin or grilled leg of lamb.

8 SERVINGS

- **2 tablespoons olive oil**
- **1 cup chopped onion**
- **2 garlic cloves, minced**
- **2 cups coarse or medium bulgur**
- **½ cup chopped pitted dates**
- **½ cup chopped dried apricots**
- **1 cinnamon stick, broken in half**
- **2 teaspoons curry powder**
- **2 14-ounce cans low-salt chicken broth**

- **½ cup chopped green onions**
- **½ cup coarsely chopped walnuts, toasted**

HEAT oil in heavy large saucepan over medium heat. Add onion and sauté until golden, about 5 minutes. Add garlic and stir 1 minute. Add bulgur and sauté 5 minutes. Stir in dates, apricots, cinnamon stick, and curry powder. Add broth; bring to boil. Reduce heat to medium-low, cover, and simmer until broth is absorbed and bulgur is tender, about 15 minutes.

STIR in green onions. Season to taste with salt and pepper. Transfer pilaf to bowl. Sprinkle with walnuts and serve.

Polenta with sausage and Asiago

SINCE THIS DISH IS LOADED with pancetta, sausage, and salami, it's no wonder that its Italian name, *smacafam,* translates to "hunger killer" in the dialect of the Trentino part of the northern region of Trentino-Alto Adige, where polenta has been a staple longer than pasta. Asiago cheese and pancetta, an Italian salt-cured bacon, can be found at Italian markets and in the refrigerated deli case of many supermarkets; or you can substitute Parmesan cheese and thick-cut bacon if desired. Or use more Italian sweet sausage to fill in for the pancetta.

8 SERVINGS

- **8 ounces Asiago cheese**

- **3 tablespoons butter, divided**
- **1 3-ounce piece pancetta, cut into ½-inch cubes**
- **1 2-ounce piece hard Italian salami, cut into ½-inch cubes**
- **8 ounces sweet Italian sausages, casings removed, crumbled**

- **7 cups water**
- **1½ cups yellow cornmeal**

PREHEAT oven to 400°F. Butter 13x9x2-inch glass baking dish. Grate enough Asiago cheese to measure ¼ cup. Cut remaining cheese into ½-inch cubes.

MELT 1 tablespoon butter in heavy large skillet over medium-high heat. Add pancetta and stir until golden, about 3 minutes. Add salami and stir 1 minute. Transfer pancetta mixture and pan drippings to bowl. Add sausage to same skillet; sauté until cooked through, breaking up with back of fork, about 8 minutes. Using slotted spoon, transfer sausage to paper towels to drain.

BRING 7 cups water to boil in heavy large saucepan. Gradually whisk in cornmeal. Reduce heat to low; cook until polenta thickens and starts to pull away from sides of pan, stirring frequently, about 20 minutes. Stir in pancetta mixture, diced Asiago cheese, and remaining 2 tablespoons butter. Transfer polenta to prepared baking dish. Arrange sausage over polenta; sprinkle with grated Asiago cheese. Bake until polenta is set and cheese is melted, about 25 minutes.

Creamy baked polenta with herbs and green onions

BAKING THE POLENTA in the oven eliminates the labor of stirring it as it cooks. Serve this in place of mashed potatoes or as a bed for oven-roasted vegetables or sautéed greens. Polenta has numerous uses and pairs especially well with roasted, stewed, or braised meats. Any leftover polenta can be chilled, then sliced and grilled, or cut into small squares and fried to make croutons for salads. In addition, the chilled sliced polenta can be layered with cheese and marinara sauce and baked like lasagna.

6 SERVINGS

6 cups water
1½ cups polenta (coarse cornmeal) or yellow cornmeal
2 teaspoons salt
¼ teaspoon ground black pepper

2 tablespoons (¼ stick) butter
4 green onions, thinly sliced
3 tablespoons minced fresh Italian parsley
1½ teaspoons minced fresh thyme
¼ cup whipping cream

¾ cup grated dry Jack cheese or freshly grated Parmesan cheese
1 teaspoon grated lemon peel

PREHEAT oven to 350°F. Pour 6 cups water into 13x9x2-inch glass baking dish. Whisk polenta, 2 teaspoons salt, and ¼ teaspoon pepper into water. Bake uncovered 40 minutes.

MEANWHILE, melt butter in small skillet over medium heat. Add green onions and sauté 2 minutes. Stir in parsley and thyme, then cream. Season to taste with salt and pepper. Remove from heat.

STIR polenta to blend. Stir green onion mixture, cheese, and lemon peel into polenta. Continue to bake uncovered until polenta is creamy and liquid is completely absorbed, about 10 minutes longer. Let stand 5 minutes.

Soft polenta with leeks

THERE ARE TWO MAIN TYPES of cornmeal used for making polenta: a stone-ground cornmeal and a steel-ground cornmeal, which is the most widely available variety. However, the stone-ground type is coarser and retains some of the corn's hull and germ, which makes it more nutritious and creates a heartier polenta. It's available at Italian markets, natural foods stores, and some supermarkets; if you're not able to find coarse stone-ground polenta, substitute an equal quantity of regular yellow cornmeal, and cook the leek-cornmeal mixture for about 15 minutes rather than 35 minutes.

4 SERVINGS

3 tablespoons butter, divided
3 cups thinly sliced leeks (white and pale green parts only; about 3 large)
2¼ cups (or more) water
2 cups low-salt chicken broth
1 bay leaf
1 cup polenta (coarse cornmeal)

⅓ cup freshly grated Parmesan cheese

MELT 2 tablespoons butter in heavy large saucepan over medium heat. Add leeks; stir to coat. Cover and cook until leeks soften, stirring occasionally, about 10 minutes. Add 2¼ cups water, broth, and bay leaf. Bring to boil. Gradually whisk in polenta. Reduce heat to medium-low and cook until mixture is thick and creamy, stirring often and thinning with more water if necessary, about 35 minutes.

REMOVE pan from heat. Discard bay leaf. Stir in remaining 1 tablespoon butter and Parmesan cheese. Season polenta to taste with salt and pepper. Transfer to bowl and serve.

Baked grits with Parmesan and black pepper

COARSELY GROUND GRAINS such as corn, oats, or rice are referred to as grits, but hominy grits are most common. In this recipe, quick-cooking hominy grits, which cook within ten minutes, take on a light, soufflé-like texture, turning this Southern staple into a spectacular side dish (which would be great for a party). Beat the egg whites with an electric mixer just until they hold their shape when the beaters are lifted, then immediately—but gently—fold the beaten egg whites into the grits in three additions using a large flat rubber spatula. These steps will help maintain the volume of the egg whites and create a desirable airy texture.

16 SERVINGS

- **3 cups whole milk**
- **3 cups water**
- **2 teaspoons salt**
- **1½ cups quick-cooking grits**
- **6 tablespoons (¾ stick) butter**
- **6 large eggs, separated**
- **1½ cups finely chopped shallots (about 7 large)**
- **1¼ cups freshly grated Parmesan cheese, divided**
- **¾ teaspoon ground black pepper**

PREHEAT oven to 350°F. Butter two 6-cup soufflé dishes. Bring milk, 3 cups water, and salt to simmer in heavy large saucepan. Gradually whisk in grits. Cook until thickened, stirring constantly, about 10 minutes. Remove from heat. Add butter; stir until melted. Cool slightly. Whisk egg yolks to blend in small bowl. Add to grits. Whisk in shallots, 1 cup Parmesan, and pepper. Beat egg whites in large bowl until stiff but not dry. Fold whites into grits in 3 additions. Divide mixture between soufflé dishes.

BAKE grits 30 minutes. Sprinkle with remaining ¼ cup Parmesan, dividing equally. Continue baking until grits are puffed, brown, and set in center, about 30 minutes longer.

Herbed quinoa with pine nuts

A PROMINENT STAPLE in the South American diet dating back to the ancient Incas, quinoa (pronounced *keen-wa*) is quickly gaining popularity within the United States. These tiny grains are similar in size to couscous and are immensely healthful, as they contain more protein than any other grain; they are considered to be a complete source of protein since they include all eight essential amino acids. Quinoa is available at natural foods stores and some supermarkets. For a toasted flavor, stir the rinsed quinoa in a heavy large dry skillet until it is golden and begins to pop, then proceed as directed in the recipe. This easy and delicious quinoa salad can be made up to six hours ahead. Keep it covered and refrigerated, and serve it cold or at room temperature.

12 SERVINGS

- **4 cups quinoa (about 18 ounces)**
- **4½ cups water**
- **¾ teaspoon salt**
- **3 tablespoons extra-virgin olive oil**
- **1½ tablespoons fresh lemon juice**
- **1½ cups pine nuts, lightly toasted**
- **¾ cup finely chopped red onion**
- **1½ cups chopped fresh basil**

PLACE quinoa in large fine mesh strainer. Rinse under cold running water until water is clear. Transfer quinoa to large saucepan; add 4½ cups water and ¾ teaspoon salt. Bring to boil. Reduce heat to medium-low, cover, and simmer until water is absorbed and quinoa is tender, about 20 minutes. Transfer quinoa to large bowl; fluff with fork. Stir in oil and lemon juice. Cool to room temperature. Mix in pine nuts and red onion. Season to taste with salt and pepper. *(Can be prepared 6 hours ahead. Cover and refrigerate.)* Mix in basil.

Beans

Hot and smoky baked beans

CHIPOTLE CHILES, which are actually dried, smoked jalapeños, lend both the heat and the smoky flavor to these sweet and spicy baked beans. Canned in a spicy tomato sauce called *adobo*, chipotle chiles can be found at Latin markets and most supermarkets. Be sure to use some of the bacon drippings, as they will also give the dish a smoky flavor. Serve these beans hot or at room temperature.

8 TO 10 SERVINGS

- **6 bacon slices**
- **1½ cups chopped onion**
- **1¼ cups purchased barbecue sauce**
- **¾ cup dark beer**
- **¼ cup mild-flavored (light) molasses**
- **3 tablespoons Dijon mustard**
- **3 tablespoons (packed) dark brown sugar**
- **2 tablespoons Worcestershire sauce**
- **1 tablespoon soy sauce**
- **4 to 6 teaspoons minced canned chipotle chiles**
- **6 15- to 16-ounce cans Great Northern beans, drained**
- **Chopped fresh parsley**

PREHEAT oven to 350°F. Cook bacon in large skillet over medium heat until crisp. Transfer to paper towels to drain. Transfer 2½ tablespoons bacon drippings from skillet to large bowl. Finely chop bacon; add to bowl. Add onion and next 7 ingredients to bowl and whisk to blend. Whisk in 4 to 6 teaspoons chipotle chiles, depending on spiciness desired. Stir in beans.

TRANSFER bean mixture to 13x9x2-inch glass baking dish. Bake uncovered until liquid is bubbling and slightly thickened, about 1 hour. Cool 10 minutes.

SPRINKLE with parsley and serve.

Ranch-style poquito beans

POQUITO BEANS are small, pinkish-brown beans indigenous to California's Santa Ynez Valley. If you're not able to find them, use dried pink beans, which are readily available at most supermarkets. While cooking the beans, maintain the heat at a simmer rather than a boil, as boiling breaks the beans apart and loosens the skins. Also, avoid salting the beans until after they have been cooked, as the salt will toughen the beans and prolong the cooking time. Chipotle chiles canned in a spicy tomato sauce called *adobo* are available at Latin markets, specialty foods stores, and most supermarkets.

8 TO 10 SERVINGS

1 pound dried poquito beans or pink beans

1 pound smoked bacon, chopped
1 large red onion, chopped
1 tablespoon ground cumin
2 cups orange juice
1 tablespoon minced canned chipotle chiles

1 large red onion, thinly sliced

PLACE beans in large bowl. Pour enough cold water over to cover beans by 1½ inches; let stand overnight. Do not drain.

COOK bacon in large pot over medium heat until crisp, about 12 minutes. Using slotted spoon, transfer bacon to paper towels to drain. Transfer 3 tablespoons bacon drippings to small bowl. Heat remaining drippings in pot over medium-high heat. Add chopped onion and cumin; sauté 5 minutes. Stir in juice and chiles; boil 5 minutes. Add beans and soaking liquid; bring to boil. Reduce heat to medium, cover partially, and simmer 2 hours. Uncover and simmer until beans are tender and liquid has thickened, about 30 minutes longer. Stir in bacon. Season to taste with salt and pepper.

COMBINE reserved bacon drippings and sliced onion in large skillet. Sauté over medium heat until onion is soft and brown, about 25 minutes. Season to taste with salt and pepper.

TRANSFER beans to large bowl. Top with caramelized onion and serve.

White bean puree with rosemary

CANNELLINI, ALSO KNOWN AS large white Italian kidney beans, create a creamy puree that pairs perfectly with sautéed scallops and shrimp, as well as with roasted lamb or chicken. Since beans are high in protein and iron, this rich-tasting side dish makes a nutritious alternative to mashed potatoes.

MAKES 4 TO 6 SERVINGS

1 tablespoon olive oil
¼ cup chopped bacon
½ carrot, peeled, finely chopped
½ cup chopped onion
1 tablespoon chopped fresh rosemary
3 15-ounce cans cannellini (white kidney beans), rinsed, drained
1 cup low-salt chicken broth

HEAT oil in heavy large saucepan over medium-high heat. Add bacon; sauté until brown, about 3 minutes. Reduce heat to low. Add carrot, onion, and rosemary; sauté until vegetables are tender, about 5 minutes. Increase heat to high. Add cannellini and broth; bring to boil. Reduce heat to low; cook until almost all liquid has evaporated, stirring often, about 20 minutes. Transfer mixture to processor and puree until almost smooth. Season to taste with salt and pepper.

Baja's best pinto beans

THESE MASHED BEANS have a luxurious creamy texture and a slightly sweet flavor from the brown sugar (though you can omit the sugar, if you prefer). Bean dishes, like this recipe, make a great do-ahead side dish. But in order to prevent spoilage, it's important to cool the beans slightly, then refrigerate them *uncovered* until they are cold. Once the beans are cold, cover them. To reheat these beans, simply stir them in a nonstick saucepan over medium heat until hot.

6 SERVINGS

2 tablespoons vegetable oil
1 cup chopped white onion
4 garlic cloves, chopped
1 large jalapeño chile with seeds, cut lengthwise in half
1 tablespoon dried oregano
1 teaspoon ground cumin

9½ **cups water**
1 **pound dried pinto beans, rinsed**

2 **tablespoons (packed) dark brown sugar**
1 **teaspoon salt**

HEAT oil in heavy large pot over medium-high heat. Add onion and sauté until translucent, about 3 minutes. Add garlic, chile, oregano, and cumin; sauté 1 minute. Add 9½ cups water and beans. Bring to boil. Reduce heat to medium-low, cover, and simmer 1 hour.

DISCARD chile. Add sugar and 1 teaspoon salt to bean mixture. Simmer uncovered over medium heat until beans are tender and almost all liquid has evaporated, stirring occasionally, about 1 hour longer. Remove from heat. Using potato masher, coarsely mash most of beans. Season with additional salt, if desired. *(Can be prepared 1 day ahead. Cool slightly. Refrigerate uncovered until cold, then cover and keep refrigerated. Rewarm in nonstick saucepan over medium heat, stirring frequently.)*

Cannellini in tomato-sage sauce

BECAUSE THE BEANS should be soaked overnight, start making this dish a day or two before you plan to serve it. But if you don't have time to soak the beans overnight, use the quick-soak method: Cover them by an inch or two with water and bring to a boil. Remove the pot from the heat, cover, and let the beans soak for one to two hours in the hot water. Drain the soaking liquid and proceed with the recipe as directed.

8 SERVINGS

Beans

3 **cups (about 21 ounces) dried cannellini (white kidney beans)**

3 **quarts cold water**
5 **tablespoons olive oil**
4 **whole garlic cloves, peeled**
1 **large bunch fresh sage leaves**
16 **whole black peppercorns**
1 **tablespoon salt**

Sauce

¼ **cup extra-virgin olive oil**
12 **large fresh sage leaves**
8 **whole garlic cloves, peeled**
2 **pounds plum tomatoes, seeded, coarsely chopped**

FOR BEANS: Place beans in large bowl; cover generously with water. Let stand at room temperature overnight.

DRAIN beans; transfer to heavy large pot. Add 3 quarts water, oil, garlic, sage bunch, and peppercorns. Bring to boil over medium-high heat. Reduce heat to medium-low and simmer uncovered until beans are tender, about 1 hour 5 minutes. Remove from heat and mix in 1 tablespoon salt. Cool beans 1 hour. *(Can be prepared 1 day ahead. Refrigerate uncovered in water.)*

FOR SAUCE: Heat oil in heavy large skillet over medium heat. Add sage and garlic; sauté 2 minutes. Add tomatoes and sauté until tomatoes soften and begin to release juices, about 8 minutes.

DRAIN beans, reserving cooking liquid. Discard sage bunch. Mix beans into tomato sauce. Simmer over medium-low heat until sauce thickens slightly and flavors blend, adding reserved cooking liquid by half-cupfuls if mixture is dry, about 30 minutes (beans should have slightly soupy consistency). Season to taste with salt and pepper. Serve beans warm or at room temperature.

Cuban-style black beans

SIMMERED WITH ONIONS, green bell peppers, and garlic, these black beans take on the flavors of Cuban cuisine. Using canned black beans makes the recipe quick and easy to prepare. You can serve the beans as a dinnertime side dish with fluffy white rice—as the Cubans do—or alongside ham and eggs for a satisfying breakfast.

6 SERVINGS

- **¼ cup olive oil**
- **1 large onion, chopped**
- **1 large green bell pepper, cut into ½-inch pieces**
- **6 large garlic cloves, chopped**
- **1 tablespoon dried oregano**
- **3 15- to 16-ounce cans black beans, rinsed, drained**
- **¾ cup vegetable broth or water**
- **1½ tablespoons apple cider vinegar**
- **1 teaspoon sugar (optional)**

HEAT oil in heavy large saucepan over medium heat. Add onion, bell pepper, garlic, and oregano; sauté until vegetables begin to soften, about 5 minutes. Add 1 cup beans to pan. Using back of fork, mash beans coarsely. Add remaining beans, broth, and vinegar; simmer until mixture thickens and flavors blend, stirring occasionally, about 15 minutes. Mix in sugar, if desired. Season with salt and pepper.

Lentils with Port-glazed shallots

LENTILS ARE NOT ACTUALLY BEANS, but rather small flat legume seeds. Like beans and other legumes, lentils are high in soluble fiber, which is helpful for reducing cholesterol. But unlike beans, lentils do not need to be soaked before using, making them a good choice for a quick side dish like this one. The lentils sold at most U.S. markets are yellowish brown in color; you can also use green lentils in this dish, or try red lentils, which lend a vibrant color and may be found at Indian markets, natural foods stores, and some supermarkets. Cook the lentils until they are just tender but not falling apart. Since times may vary, check the lentils frequently to be sure they are cooked to the correct doneness.

4 SERVINGS

- **1½ cups ruby Port**
- **8 ounces small shallots, peeled**
- **3 cups water**
- **1½ cups dried lentils (about 12 ounces), rinsed, drained**
- **1 large shallot, peeled, finely chopped**
- **1 tablespoon olive oil**

COMBINE Port and small shallots in heavy medium saucepan. Simmer over medium heat until shallots are tender and glazed, stirring occasionally, about 35 minutes. Set Port mixture aside. *(Can be prepared 8 hours ahead. Keep at room temperature.)*

COMBINE 3 cups water, lentils, and shallot in heavy large saucepan; bring to boil. Reduce heat to medium-low, cover saucepan, and simmer until lentils are just tender, about 30 minutes.

REWARM Port mixture over medium-low heat. Stir oil and Port mixture into lentils. Season with salt and pepper. Transfer lentils to bowl and serve.

9 Meatless main courses

Today's meatless main courses are more notable for what's in them than for what's not.

Our repertoire expands continuously as we experiment with new ingredients and new cuisines, and as we explore familiar cuisines (such as Italian) more thoroughly. Since much of the world is less meat-focused and more enamored of vegetables than we are, there is a lot to learn. Each culture has its own alluring take on preparing vegetarian main courses—and Asian cultures have turned them into an art form.

If you're new to the land of meatless entrées, you'll do well to learn what vegetarians have known for ages: Having a variety of colors and textures makes a dish enticing and can go a long way toward weaning even the most carnivorous off meat-centric meals. Lasagna, to many Americans, is a rich and meaty affair. But in Italy, lasagna is just as often replete with vegetables, as in the Artichoke and Mushroom Lasagna offered here. In this chapter you'll even find a kind of "lasagna" made with firm golden-yellow polenta layered with sautéed escarole and three cheeses.

You can also travel south of the border for dynamic vegetarian main-course options. Consider *Chilaquiles,* crispy tortillas bathed in a spicy roasted tomato-chipotle sauce, *crema mexicana,* and *queso fresco* (fresh white cheese). There's a whole world—literally—of artful grain, noodle, bean, and vegetable-based main courses.

Looking at the table of contents at the front of this book, you'll find plenty of other meatless options. The chapters on Soups and Stews and on Salads, for example, are full of great vegetarian choices. This chapter showcases the dishes that feel the most substantial—meatier, if you will.

While health concerns may have started the ball rolling on meatless dining, the trend is now inspiring new heights of culinary creativity. It's time to join the revolution.

Baked polenta with escarole and three cheeses

GOLDEN POLENTA, or coarse cornmeal, is a comforting mainstay of Northern Italian cooking, whether simmered to a creamy consistency and served alongside roasted meats, or molded and cut into squares, then grilled or baked between layers of sauce and cheese. Slightly bitter escarole, a bright green leafy endive, responds brilliantly to cooking; its flavors mellow, and it has enough heft to stand up to its braise in the sauce. This entire dish can be assembled and chilled in the refrigerator the day before baking and serving. Neufchâtel is a lighter style of cream cheese; it's available at most supermarkets.

8 SERVINGS

3¾ cups water
1½ cups yellow cornmeal
1 teaspoon salt

3 tablespoons olive oil
1 medium head of escarole, chopped
1 cup chopped onion
1 28-ounce can crushed tomatoes with added puree
½ cup chopped fresh basil
2 tablespoons tomato paste
4 garlic cloves, minced

6 ounces Neufchâtel cheese, room temperature
1 large egg
1 cup freshly grated Parmesan cheese (about 3 ounces)

2 cups freshly grated Monterey Jack cheese (about 8 ounces)

BUTTER 9x5x2½-inch loaf pan. Bring 3¾ cups water, cornmeal, and salt to boil in heavy large saucepan, whisking constantly. Reduce heat to medium-low; cook until mixture is very thick, whisking frequently, about 5 minutes. Transfer to prepared pan; smooth top. Cover and refrigerate until firm, at least 3 hours or overnight.

HEAT oil in large pot over medium heat. Add escarole; sauté until wilted, about 3 minutes. Add onion; sauté until tender, about 8 minutes. Mix in crushed tomatoes, basil, tomato paste, and garlic. Simmer 10 minutes to blend flavors. Season sauce to taste with salt and pepper.

USING electric mixer, beat Neufchâtel cheese in large bowl until fluffy. Beat in egg, then Parmesan cheese.

PREHEAT oven to 400°F. Oil 8x8x2-inch glass baking dish. Turn polenta out onto work surface. Using serrated knife, cut into 20 slices. Spoon ⅓ of sauce over bottom of prepared dish. Arrange 10 polenta slices atop sauce, overlapping slightly. Spoon ⅓ sauce over. Drop cheese mixture by small spoonfuls over sauce. Arrange remaining 10 polenta slices atop cheese. Spoon remaining sauce over. Sprinkle Jack cheese over. *(Can be prepared 1 day ahead; cool 2 hours, then cover and refrigerate.)* Place dish on baking sheet. Bake casserole until cheese melts and sauce is bubbling around edges, about 35 minutes (or up to 45 minutes if chilled). Cool 10 minutes and serve.

Artichoke and mushroom lasagna

A WHITE SAUCE made with Parmesan cheese gives this springtime lasagna a particularly luxurious creaminess and refinement. Freshly grated nutmeg has a sweet pungency that the jarred stuff just can't match (nutmeg quickly loses its essential oils once grated); buy whole nutmeg kernels if you can (in the spice section of the supermarket) and use them to season the sauce to taste, starting with a few swipes across a spice grater or the smallest holes of a box grater. A wonderful dish for entertaining, this can be assembled and chilled one day before it's baked and served. Round out the meal with a salad of mixed field greens and radicchio, along with crusty bread.

8 SERVINGS

Filling

- **2 tablespoons (1/4 stick) butter**
- **1 pound mushrooms, sliced**
- **3 garlic cloves, minced**
- **2 8-ounce packages frozen artichoke hearts, thawed, coarsely chopped**
- **1 cup dry vermouth**

Sauce

- **4 1/2 tablespoons butter**
- **4 1/2 tablespoons all purpose flour**
- **4 1/2 cups whole milk**
- **2 1/2 cups freshly grated Parmesan cheese (about 7 1/2 ounces), divided**
- **Ground nutmeg**

- **1 8- to 9-ounce package oven-ready (no-boil) lasagna noodles**
- **1 pound whole-milk mozzarella cheese, thinly sliced**

FOR FILLING: Melt butter in large skillet over medium-high heat. Add mushrooms and garlic; sauté until mushrooms release juices and begin to brown, about 7 minutes. Add artichokes and vermouth. Cook until liquid is absorbed, stirring occasionally, about 10 minutes. Season with salt and pepper.

FOR SAUCE: Melt butter in heavy medium saucepan over medium-high heat. Add flour and stir 1 minute. Gradually whisk in milk. Reduce heat to medium and simmer until sauce thickens and lightly coats spoon, stirring occasionally, about 20 minutes. Stir in 1½ cups Parmesan. Season sauce to taste with salt, pepper, and ground nutmeg.

SPREAD ⅔ cup sauce over bottom of 13x9x2-inch glass baking dish. Top with enough noodles to cover bottom of dish in single layer. Spread ¼ of artichoke filling over. Spoon ⅔ cup sauce over. Top sauce with ¼ of mozzarella. Sprinkle with 3 tablespoons Parmesan. Top with enough noodles to cover in single layer. Repeat layering 3 more times, finishing with noodle layer, then remaining sauce. Sprinkle with remaining Parmesan. *(Lasagna can be prepared 1 day ahead. Cover with aluminum foil and refrigerate.)*

PREHEAT oven to 350°F. Bake lasagna covered with foil 1 hour (or 1 hour 15 minutes if chilled). Remove foil. Increase temperature to 450°F. Bake lasagna until golden on top, about 10 minutes longer. Cool 20 minutes and serve.

Spring vegetable paella

THIS IS A BEAUTIFUL centerpiece dish, the classic saffron-scented Spanish rice studded with colorful spring vegetables instead of the traditional meat and/or seafood. Once the vegetables are prepped, everything comes together very quickly. Some markets sell fennel bulbs with the fronds still attached; farmers' markets always do. To trim fennel, lay the bulb on its side and trim off the stalks and fronds. Next, cut off the root end, halve the bulb lengthwise, and slice into wedges. Use any type of paprika—sweet or spicy—that you prefer; for an infusion of deep, smoky flavor, use *Pimentón de la Vera,* a Spanish smoked paprika available at specialty foods stores.

6 SERVINGS

- **2 large fennel bulbs (about 1 1/2 pounds total), trimmed, each cut into 8 wedges; 2 tablespoons chopped fronds reserved**
- **12 ounces baby carrots (from about 4 bunches), trimmed, peeled**
- **8 ounces turnips, peeled, cut into 3/4-inch pieces (about 1 1/2 cups)**
- **8 ounces 1 1/2-inch red-skinned potatoes, halved**
- **1/4 cup plus 3 tablespoons olive oil**

- **1/4 cup plus 1 tablespoon chopped fresh parsley**
- **4 garlic cloves, chopped**
- **1 tablespoon paprika**
- **1 teaspoon saffron threads, crushed**
- **1 teaspoon salt**

1 onion, chopped
4 plum tomatoes, chopped
2¼ cups arborio rice or medium-grain white rice
1 14-ounce can vegetable broth
2 cups water
¾ cup dry white wine
1 pound asparagus, trimmed, cut into 1-inch pieces
1 cup drained canned garbanzo beans (chickpeas)

PREHEAT oven to 450°F. Toss fennel wedges, carrots, turnips, potatoes, and ¼ cup oil in large bowl. Sprinkle generously with salt and pepper. Transfer to large rimmed baking sheet. Roast until vegetables are tender and brown around edges, about 1 hour.

FINELY mince ¼ cup parsley and garlic together. Transfer to small bowl. Stir in paprika, saffron, and 1 teaspoon salt.

HEAT remaining 3 tablespoons oil in large deep skillet over medium-high heat. Add onion and sauté until soft, about 8 minutes. Add tomatoes; sauté 2 minutes. Add rice and parsley mixture; stir 2 minutes. Stir in broth, 2 cups water, and wine; bring to boil. Reduce heat to low, cover, and simmer 15 minutes. Stir in asparagus, garbanzo beans, and roasted vegetables. Increase heat to medium-low, cover, and simmer until liquid is absorbed, stirring often, about 20 minutes. Season paella to taste with salt and pepper. Transfer to large platter. Sprinkle with fennel fronds and remaining 1 tablespoon parsley and serve.

Corn, cheese, and chile tamales with tomatillo-avocado salsa

TAMALES ARE A TRADITIONAL fiesta dish in Mexico, and they add a celebratory air to any dinner. In Mexican homes, there is often a pre-party, occasioned by the tamale making itself, and the process does lend itself to taking advantage of several cooks in the kitchen. But tamales can also be made completely ahead of time and simply reheated once the party has started. Traditional sides are *frijoles refritos* (refried beans) or whole beans. Use Hass avocados if available; they add an unequaled nutty, buttery creaminess to the salsa. Avocados are ripe when they yield to gentle pressure. Poblano chiles (fresh green chiles), tomatillos (green tomato-like fruits with thin husks), dried corn husks, and Masa Harina (corn tortilla mix) are found at many supermarkets and Latin markets.

MAKES 18

Tomatillo-avocado salsa

12 tomatillos, husked, rinsed well
1 small onion, quartered
6 garlic cloves
2 serrano chiles, stemmed
2 ripe avocados, halved, pitted, peeled, sliced
½ cup chopped fresh cilantro
2 tablespoons fresh lime juice

Tamales

1 6-ounce package dried corn husks
1 pound large fresh poblano chiles
2 cups Masa Harina (corn tortilla mix)
6 tablespoons (¾ stick) unsalted butter, room temperature
3 tablespoons sugar
2¼ teaspoons salt, divided
½ cup canned vegetable broth
5 cups frozen white corn kernels (about 25 ounces), thawed, divided

- **3 cups (packed) coarsely grated sharp cheddar cheese, divided**
- **1 teaspoon baking powder**
- **⅛ teaspoon ground black pepper**

FOR SALSA: Cook first 4 ingredients in heavy large skillet over high heat until charred in spots but still firm, turning occasionally, about 5 minutes. Transfer to processor; using on/off turns, chop coarsely. Add all remaining ingredients. Blend to coarse puree. Season to taste with salt and pepper. *(Salsa can be made 1 day ahead. Cover; chill.)*

FOR TAMALES: Selecting the largest and cleanest husks, place half of husks in large bowl; fill bowl with warm water. Weigh husks down with plate; soak husks until soft, separating occasionally, about 2 hours. Form 36 ties by tearing several husks into ½-inch-wide strips.

CHAR chiles directly over gas flame or in broiler until blackened on all sides. Place in medium bowl; cover tightly with plastic wrap. Let stand 10 minutes. Peel, seed, and chop chiles.

TO make dough, blend Masa Harina, butter, sugar, and 1 teaspoon salt in processor until coarse meal forms. Add broth and blend in (mixture will be crumbly). Transfer masa mixture to large bowl. Blend 2½ cups corn, 1 cup cheese, baking powder, pepper, and remaining 1¼ teaspoons salt in processor until coarse puree forms. Stir puree, then remaining 2½ cups corn into masa.

FOR each tamale, open 1 large softened husk. Place ⅓ cup tamale dough in center of husk. Make depression in center of dough; fill with 1 tablespoon chiles, then 1 tablespoon cheese. Using moistened fingertips, press dough over filling to cover; shape filled dough into 3-inch-long log parallel to 1 long edge of husk. Fold 1 long side of husk over filling and roll up to enclose. Tie ends of filled husks tightly with husk strips.

ADD enough water to large pot containing steamer insert to reach bottom of insert. Layer tamales in steamer insert. Bring water to boil; cover pot. Steam until tamales are firm, removing insert and adding boiling water to pot to maintain water level as needed, about 1 hour. *(Can be made 1 day ahead. Cool 2 hours, then cover and refrigerate. Before serving, re-steam 45 minutes to heat through.)* Serve tamales in husks with salsa.

Chilaquiles in chipotle sauce

CHILAQUILES ARE ONE OF THOSE culinary inventions born of necessity, and they are among a handful of Mexican breakfast and snack dishes that begin with a cluster of fried tortillas. Early versions used day-old tortillas that were dried in the sun before being broken into pieces and coated with a piquant tomato-chile sauce, then topped with *crema mexicana* (a kind of Mexican crème fraîche), fresh cilantro, and chopped raw onion. These days, the tortillas are freshly fried before being covered with the sauce. Generally served for breakfast or brunch, chilaquiles are delicious at any time of day and make a great light supper when paired with a green salad. Be sure to eat these immediately; the sauce should soften the chips just slightly until the texture is al dente. Crema mexicana, *queso fresco* (a fresh white crumbly cheese), and chipotle chiles (smoked jalapeños canned in a spicy *adobo* sauce) are available at Latin markets and some supermarkets. Epazote is the distinctive herb that traditionally flavors black beans; it is available at Latin markets and specialty produce stores.

6 SERVINGS

- **Canola oil (for frying)**
- **18 5- to 6-inch-diameter white corn tortillas, each cut into 8 triangles**
- **Chipotle Sauce (see recipe)**
- **3 large fresh epazote sprigs, stemmed, or 3 fresh oregano sprigs**

½ **cup chopped fresh cilantro**
1 **cup crema mexicana or sour cream**
1 **cup crumbled queso fresco**
½ **cup chopped white onion**

POUR enough oil into heavy large deep skillet to reach depth of 1 inch. Attach deep-fry thermometer; heat oil over medium-high heat to 350°F. Add 12 tortilla triangles at a time to oil. Fry until golden, turning occasionally, about 1 minute. Using slotted spoon, transfer chips to paper towels; cool.

BRING Chipotle Sauce to boil in another heavy large deep skillet over medium-high heat. Add epazote; simmer 2 minutes. Season to taste with salt; stir in fried chips. Immediately divide among 6 plates. Top with cilantro, then crema, queso fresco, and onion.

Chipotle sauce

YOU COULD ALSO serve this sauce over grilled chicken or fish.

MAKES ABOUT 7 CUPS

1 **small white onion, quartered**
5 **garlic cloves, unpeeled**

4 **pounds tomatoes (about 15 medium)**
2 **tablespoons chopped canned chipotle chiles**

2 **tablespoons canola oil**
1 **teaspoon fine sea salt**

LINE heavy large skillet with aluminum foil; heat over medium heat. Place onion and garlic in skillet; cook until onion softens and blackens in spots, turning often with tongs, about 15 minutes. Transfer onion and garlic to medium bowl. Peel garlic.

PLACE same foil-lined skillet over medium-high heat. Working in 2 batches, cook tomatoes in skillet until tomatoes are tender and skins blister and blacken, turning occasionally, about 20 minutes. Transfer to large bowl; cool and peel. Working in batches, puree tomatoes, onion, garlic, and chiles in blender until smooth.

HEAT oil in heavy large deep skillet over medium-high heat. Carefully add tomato puree to skillet (mixture will bubble vigorously). Stir in sea salt. Reduce heat; simmer gently until sauce thickens slightly, stirring often, about 15 minutes. *(Can be prepared 1 day ahead. Cool slightly, then cover and refrigerate.)*

Huevos rancheros verdes

THE SAUCE THAT MAKES huevos rancheros *huevos rancheros*—the Mexican and Southwestern breakfast dish of fried eggs atop lightly fried tortillas—is usually a tangy, ranch-style red sauce (hence the name) or salsa. In this version, a green sauce of citrusy tomatillos is drizzled over the golden yolks. Tomatillos resemble small green tomatoes underneath their parchment-like husks; they are available at Latin markets and in the exotic produce section of some supermarkets. Serrano chiles (fresh green chiles) are available in the produce section of many supermarkets and at Latin markets. To make it easier to get every serving on the table at the same time, heat two large skillets and cook four eggs in each. And huevos rancheros aren't complete without refried beans.

4 SERVINGS

8 **ounces tomatillos, husked, rinsed**
1½ **cups (packed) fresh cilantro leaves, divided**
¾ **cup diced peeled avocado**
½ **cup chopped onion**
2 **tablespoons fresh lime juice**
4 **teaspoons minced seeded serrano chiles**
2 **garlic cloves**
1 **teaspoon ground cumin**

- **3 tablespoons (or more) butter, divided**
- **4 corn tortillas**
- **8 large eggs**
- **1½ cups (packed) grated Monterey Jack cheese (about 6 ounces)**

COOK tomatillos in large saucepan of simmering water until soft, about 20 minutes. Drain. Transfer tomatillos to blender; add 1 cup cilantro, avocado, onion, lime juice, chiles, garlic and cumin; puree. Season sauce to taste with salt and pepper.

MELT 1 tablespoon butter in large nonstick skillet over medium-high heat. Add 2 tortillas; cook about 1 minute per side. Transfer to baking sheet. Repeat with remaining tortillas, adding more butter to skillet as necessary. Melt 1 tablespoon butter in same skillet over medium heat. Crack 4 eggs into skillet; cover and cook eggs to desired doneness. Sprinkle fried eggs with salt and pepper. Using spatula, place 2 eggs on each of 2 fried tortillas. Repeat with remaining eggs and 1 tablespoon butter. Top eggs on each tortilla with ¼ of sauce and ¼ of cheese. Using spatula, return 2 huevos rancheros to same skillet. Cover and cook over medium heat until cheese melts, about 3 minutes. Transfer to 2 plates. Repeat with remaining huevos rancheros. Sprinkle with remaining ½ cup cilantro and serve.

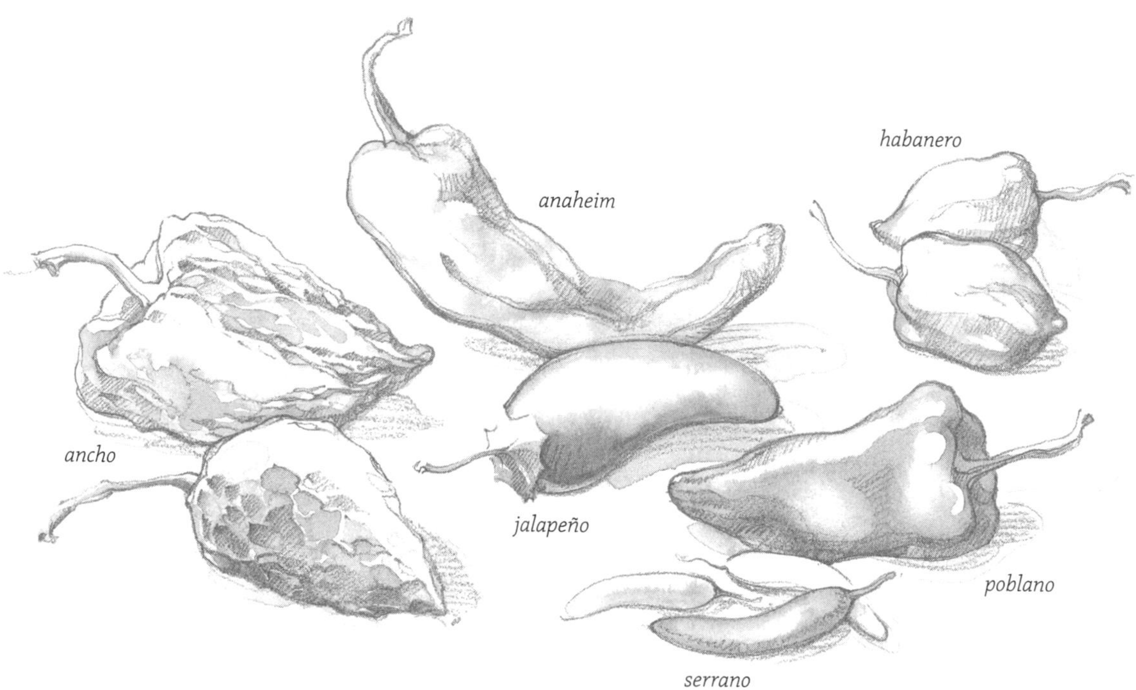

Deep-fried lemongrass tofu with red bell pepper

CUBES OF DEEP-FRIED TOFU are combined with mushrooms and red pepper strips in this aromatic Thai-inspired stir-fry. Pair it with Thailand's fragrant jasmine rice for a delicious meal. To prepare the lemongrass for cooking, trim off the spiky top leaves and woody core at the bottom, then peel off any tough outer layers. Thinly slice the remaining tender leaves crosswise and mince. Asian groceries will probably have the freshest selection of lemongrass, but many supermarkets now carry it in the produce section. The fish sauce known in Vietnam as *nuoc nam* and in Thailand as *nam pla* is available at Asian markets and in the Asian foods section of many supermarkets.

2 MAIN-COURSE OR 4 SIDE-DISH SERVINGS

Vegetable oil (for frying)
12 to 14 ounces firm tofu, drained, patted dry, cut into ¾-inch cubes

3 tablespoons vegetable oil
2 tablespoons minced fresh lemongrass
2 garlic cloves, minced
1 teaspoon (heaping) chopped seeded jalapeño chile
1 onion, thinly sliced
½ red bell pepper, cut into ¾-inch pieces
4 ounces shiitake mushrooms, stemmed, thickly sliced
2 teaspoons fish sauce (nam pla or nuoc nam)
1 tablespoon sugar
1½ tablespoons chopped fresh cilantro

ADD enough vegetable oil to heavy medium saucepan to reach depth of 2 inches. Heat vegetable oil over medium-high heat to 350°F. Deep-fry tofu squares in 2 batches until golden, about 2 minutes. Using slotted spoon, transfer tofu to paper towels to drain. Sprinkle with salt and pepper.

HEAT 3 tablespoons vegetable oil in heavy large skillet over medium heat. Add lemongrass, garlic, and jalapeño; sauté until fragrant, about 1 minute. Add onion, red bell pepper, and shiitake mushrooms; sauté until vegetables are crisp-tender, about 3 minutes. Add fish sauce and sugar; sauté 1 minute. Add fried tofu squares and sauté until heated through, about 1 minute. Transfer to bowl. Sprinkle with cilantro and serve.

Stir-fried tofu and shiitake mushrooms in spicy black bean sauce

BEEFY SHIITAKE MUSHROOMS stand in for the standard ground pork in this version of *ma po* tofu. Serve with steamed rice. Fermented black beans, chili-garlic sauce, and Szechuan peppercorns (sometimes called wild pepper) are available at Asian markets and in the Asian foods section of many supermarkets.

6 SERVINGS

18 dried shiitake mushrooms
3 cups boiling water

1 tablespoon cornstarch
1 cup canned vegetable broth
2 tablespoons soy sauce
1 tablespoon rice vinegar
1½ teaspoons sugar
¼ teaspoon coarse sea salt

3 tablespoons peanut oil
1 small leek (white and pale green parts only), cut into matchstick-size strips
2 tablespoons Asian fermented black beans, minced
2 tablespoons minced peeled fresh ginger
3 garlic cloves, minced
2 teaspoons chili-garlic sauce
¼ teaspoon finely crushed Szechuan peppercorns or coarsely cracked black pepper
2 12- to 14-ounce containers soft tofu, drained, patted dry, cut into ½-inch cubes

Fresh cilantro sprigs (for garnish)

PLACE mushrooms in large bowl. Pour 3 cups boiling water over; let soak until mushrooms soften, at least 25 minutes and up to 4 hours. Drain. Cut off stems and discard; finely chop caps.

DISSOLVE cornstarch in 2 tablespoons vegetable broth in 2-cup measuring cup. Stir in remaining broth, soy sauce, vinegar, sugar, and sea salt.

HEAT oil in heavy large wok or nonstick skillet over high heat until very hot. Add mushrooms and stir-fry until browned, about 3 minutes. Add leek and stir-fry until beginning to brown, about 1 minute. Add black beans, ginger, garlic, chili-garlic sauce, and peppercorns; stir-fry 30 seconds. Stir cornstarch mixture to blend, then stir into vegetable mixture. Add tofu; toss gently to coat with sauce. Reduce heat to low, cover, and simmer until sauce thickens slightly, about 4 minutes.

SPOON tofu mixture into serving bowl. Garnish with cilantro and serve.

Coconut curried tofu with green jasmine rice

THIS STIR-FRY CROSSES BORDERS, combining South Asian and Southeast Asian flavors and ingredients. Warm, pungent spices such as curry and cumin are softened by velvety coconut milk in the mixture, which is served on a bed of "green" rice—cooked jasmine rice enhanced with an aromatic puree of cilantro, more coconut milk, garlic, and ginger. The final touch is a garnish of chopped peanuts sprinkled on top. Unsweetened shredded coconut is sold at specialty foods stores and natural foods stores. Canned unsweetened coconut milk is available at Indian, Southeast Asian, and Latin markets as well as many supermarkets.

4 SERVINGS

¼ cup unsweetened shredded coconut

1¾ cups water
1 teaspoon salt
1 cup jasmine or basmati rice

1 cup (packed) coarsely chopped fresh cilantro
¾ cup canned light unsweetened coconut milk, divided
4 teaspoons minced peeled fresh ginger, divided
1 tablespoon fresh lime juice
2 garlic cloves, minced, divided

2 tablespoons vegetable oil
1⅓ 12- to 14-ounce packages extra-firm tofu, drained, patted dry, cut into ½-inch cubes
½ cup thinly sliced green onions
2 teaspoons curry powder
1 teaspoon ground cumin
⅛ teaspoon dried crushed red pepper
1 cup small cherry tomatoes

2 tablespoons chopped peanuts

STIR shredded coconut in small nonstick skillet over medium heat until light golden, about 5 minutes. Transfer to bowl.

BRING 1¾ cups water and salt to boil in heavy medium saucepan. Stir in rice; return to boil. Reduce heat to low, cover, and simmer until water is absorbed and rice is tender, about 18 minutes.

MEANWHILE, puree cilantro, ½ cup coconut milk, 1 teaspoon ginger, lime juice, and half of garlic in blender. Mix puree and coconut into rice. Set aside.

HEAT oil in large nonstick skillet over high heat. Add tofu; stir-fry until golden, about 6 minutes. Add green onions, curry, cumin, crushed red pepper, remaining 3 teaspoons ginger, and remaining half of garlic. Stir-fry 1 minute. Stir in tomatoes and remaining ¼ cup coconut milk. Season to taste with salt and pepper.

DIVIDE rice among 4 plates. Top with tofu mixture. Sprinkle with peanuts and serve.

Peanut noodles with gingered vegetables and tofu

IF YOU LIKE your noodles spicier, just add more chili-garlic sauce (available at Asian markets and in the Asian foods section of many supermarkets) to the peanut sauce. Any peanut butter will work well, but freshly ground peanut butter would provide a really nutty flavor. Dried *futonaga udon* noodles (Japanese wheat noodles) are available at Asian markets and in the Asian foods section of some supermarkets. If you can't find them, use linguine instead. A crisp cucumber salad dressed with rice vinegar makes a nice side dish.

6 SERVINGS

Peanut sauce

½ cup peanut butter
2 tablespoons soy sauce
4 garlic cloves, minced
⅔ cup hot water
¼ cup chopped fresh cilantro
2 tablespoons golden brown sugar
1 tablespoon rice vinegar
1 tablespoon chili-garlic sauce

Noodles and vegetables

3 tablespoons peanut oil, divided
3 tablespoons minced peeled fresh ginger, divided
3 garlic cloves, minced, divided
8 ounces broccoli, tops cut into florets, stems peeled, cut into matchstick-size strips
1 large carrot, peeled, cut into matchstick-size strips
8 green onions, white parts cut into matchstick-size strips, green parts chopped
1 zucchini, cut lengthwise in half, then crosswise into ⅓-inch-thick slices
8 ounces sugar snap peas, trimmed
1 red bell pepper, cut into matchstick-size strips
2 tablespoons dry Sherry
12 ounces extra-firm or firm tofu, drained, patted dry, cut into ½-inch cubes
12 ounces dried futonaga udon noodles (Asian-style spaghetti)
1 cup lightly salted roasted peanuts

FOR PEANUT SAUCE: Mix peanut butter, soy sauce, and garlic in medium bowl. Whisk in ⅔ cup hot water. Add remaining ingredients and whisk to blend. Season to taste with salt and pepper. Let peanut sauce stand at room temperature 1 hour. *(Can be made 1 day ahead. Cover and refrigerate. Bring to room temperature before using.)*

FOR NOODLES AND VEGETABLES: Heat 2 tablespoons oil in large nonstick skillet over medium-high heat. Add 2 tablespoons ginger and 2 minced garlic cloves; stir 30 seconds. Add broccoli and carrot; sauté 5 minutes. Add white parts of green onions, zucchini, sugar snap peas, bell pepper, and Sherry; sauté until vegetables are crisp-tender, about 3 minutes longer. Remove from heat.

MEANWHILE, heat remaining 1 tablespoon oil in medium nonstick skillet over medium-high heat. Add remaining 1 tablespoon ginger and 1 minced garlic clove; sauté 30 seconds. Add tofu and sauté until golden, about 5 minutes. Season to taste with salt and pepper.

MEANWHILE, cook noodles in large pot of boiling salted water until tender but still firm to bite, stirring occasionally. Drain.

RETURN noodles to pot. Add vegetables, tofu, and peanut sauce; toss to coat. Transfer to platter. Sprinkle with peanuts and chopped green parts of green onions and serve.

Wild-mushroom bread pudding

THIS RICH AND SAVORY bread pudding puffs dramatically like a soufflé and is topped with a golden-brown Parmesan crust. It is a lovely brunch or supper dish, served with an herb salad dressed with a lemon or Sherry vinaigrette. Combine butter lettuces with radicchio and a mixture of herbs, such as Italian parsley leaves, tarragon, chopped chives, and basil.

4 SERVINGS

- **3 tablespoons olive oil**
- **6 ounces fresh shiitake mushrooms, stemmed, caps thickly sliced**
- **6 ounces oyster mushrooms, thickly sliced**
- **6 ounces crimini mushrooms, thickly sliced**
- **2 portobello mushrooms, stems and gills removed, caps thickly sliced**
- **2 garlic cloves, chopped**
- **1 tablespoon chopped fresh basil**
- **1 tablespoon chopped fresh parsley**
- **1 teaspoon dried rubbed sage**
- **1 teaspoon dried thyme**

- **5 large eggs**
- **2 cups whipping cream**
- **1 cup whole milk**
- **¼ cup plus 2 tablespoons freshly grated Parmesan cheese**
- **¾ teaspoon salt**
- **½ teaspoon ground pepper**
- **6 cups 1-inch cubes crustless day-old French bread (about 6 ounces)**

PREHEAT oven to 350°F. Lightly butter 8x8x2-inch glass baking dish. Heat oil in heavy large pot over medium-high heat. Add all mushrooms, garlic, basil, parsley, sage, and thyme; sauté until mushrooms are tender and brown, about 15 minutes. Remove pot from heat. Season mixture to taste with salt and pepper.

WHISK eggs, cream, milk, ¼ cup Parmesan, salt, and pepper in large bowl to blend. Add bread cubes and toss to coat. Let stand 15 minutes. Stir in mushroom mixture. Transfer to prepared dish. Sprinkle remaining 2 tablespoons cheese over. Bake until pudding is brown, puffed, and set in center, about 1 hour. Serve warm.

Sweet potatoes topped with vegetarian black bean chili

IN CARIBBEAN COOKING, sweet potatoes are often combined with chiles and spices and used in savory dishes—in soups or stews, or even sliced and french-fried. Here, each serving is a whole baked potato topped with a spicy chili. Tangy yogurt and chopped cilantro can dress it up, if you like. It's a surprisingly satisfying one-dish meal loaded with big flavors and great textures. Either tan-skinned sweet potatoes or yams (red-skinned sweet potatoes) would be delicious here.

4 SERVINGS

- **4 large sweet potatoes**

- **1 tablespoon olive oil**
- **2 cups diced red bell pepper**
- **1½ cups chopped onion**
- **3 garlic cloves, minced**
- **1 tablespoon chili powder**
- **2 teaspoons ground cumin**
- **1 14.5- to 15-ounce can diced tomatoes in juice**
- **1 15- to 16-ounce can black beans, rinsed thoroughly, drained**
- **2 cups diced yellow crookneck squash**
- **1 tablespoon minced seeded jalapeño chile**

- **4 lime wedges**
- **Plain nonfat yogurt (optional)**
- **Chopped fresh cilantro (optional)**

PREHEAT oven to 400°F. Place sweet potatoes in baking dish. Pierce potatoes with fork and bake until tender, about 1 hour 15 minutes.

MEANWHILE, heat oil in large nonstick skillet over medium-low heat. Add bell pepper and onion; sauté until golden, about 10 minutes. Add garlic and stir 2 minutes. Stir in chili powder and cumin, then tomatoes with juice and beans; bring mixture to simmer. Reduce heat to low, cover, and cook 20 minutes. Mix squash and jalapeños into chili; cover and cook until squash is crisp-tender, about 6 minutes.

ARRANGE 1 sweet potato on each of 4 plates. Split potatoes open; mash flesh slightly. Spoon some chili into center of each. Squeeze lime juice over. Top with yogurt and chopped cilantro, if desired. Pass remaining chili separately.

Oven-roasted winter vegetables with rigatoni

THIS MAIN-COURSE PASTA makes a delicious and substantial weeknight dinner. Roasting is one of the easiest and most healthful ways to amplify the flavors in winter vegetables (it caramelizes their sugars). Using wild mushrooms will add extra smoky, earthy flavor: crimini (a young portobello with a coffee-colored cap) and shiitake (which has a large dark brown cap) are good choices and available at most supermarkets. Before using, be sure to remove the woody stems of the shiitakes where they meet the cap. You can add a salad if you like, but this is a perfectly filling meal on its own.

6 SERVINGS

- **1 small eggplant (about 12 ounces), cut into ¾-inch pieces**
- **2 small red-skinned potatoes, unpeeled, cut into ¾-inch pieces**
- **2 medium carrots, thinly sliced diagonally**
- **1½ medium red onions, cut into 1-inch pieces**
- **1 cup quartered mushrooms**
- **8 garlic cloves, minced**
- **½ teaspoon dried thyme**
- **½ teaspoon dried rosemary**
- **¼ cup extra-virgin olive oil**
- **2 cups broccoli florets**

- **1 pound rigatoni, shell, or fusilli pasta**
- **Freshly grated Parmesan cheese**

PREHEAT oven to 400°F. Combine first 8 ingredients in large roasting pan. Add olive oil and toss to coat well. Sprinkle generously with salt and pepper. Roast until vegetables are tender and beginning to brown, stirring occasionally, about 45 minutes. Add broccoli to pan and roast until broccoli is crisp-tender, about 10 minutes.

MEANWHILE, cook pasta in large pot of boiling salted water until tender but still firm to bite, stirring occasionally. Add ½ cup pasta cooking liquid to vegetables in roasting pan. Drain pasta and add to roasting pan. Toss pasta with vegetables to combine. Transfer mixture to serving dish; sprinkle pasta with Parmesan cheese and serve.

Falafel with cilantro yogurt in pita bread

THE MIDDLE EASTERN pita sandwich featuring deep-fried rounds of spiced ground chickpeas and a yogurt dressing becomes a fast weeknight supper in this easy-to-prepare recipe. The sandwiches make for an intriguing—and healthier—variation on burgers. Add other toppings if you like, such as chopped pickle, grated cheddar, or crumbled feta cheese, or additional chopped fresh cilantro.

4 SERVINGS

- **1 cup plain yogurt**
- **1 cup chopped fresh cilantro, divided**
- **1 cup chopped onion, divided**
- **5 garlic cloves, chopped, divided**
- **1 tablespoon fresh lemon juice**
- **½ teaspoon cayenne pepper, divided**

- **2 15- to 16-ounce cans garbanzo beans (chickpeas), drained**

3 tablespoons plus 1/2 cup all purpose flour
2 teaspoons ground cumin
1 large egg

Olive oil
4 warm pita bread rounds, top third cut off
Sliced tomatoes
Crisp lettuce leaves

WHISK yogurt, ½ cup cilantro, ¼ cup onion, 1 garlic clove, lemon juice, and ¼ teaspoon cayenne in medium bowl to blend; season with salt and pepper. Refrigerate until ready to serve.

BLEND garbanzo beans, 3 tablespoons flour, cumin, remaining ½ cup cilantro, 4 garlic cloves, and ¼ teaspoon cayenne in processor until almost smooth. Add egg and remaining ¾ cup onion; using on/off turns, blend until onion is finely chopped. Transfer mixture to bowl; sprinkle with salt and pepper. Shape mixture into four ½-inch-thick patties. Turn patties in remaining ½ cup flour to coat on both sides.

POUR enough oil into heavy large skillet to coat bottom; heat over medium-high heat. Add patties and cook until crisp and golden, about 8 minutes per side. Open pita breads; slide 1 patty, sliced tomato, and lettuce into each. Spoon in some yogurt mixture.

Toasted-almond tofu burgers

THESE SUCCULENT BURGERS are inspired by the fresh and creative sandwiches and other fare you find at cafés in California and Hawaii—wherever Asian cuisines meet surfers and health-food enthusiasts. Toast the sesame seeds on a rimmed baking sheet in a 350°F oven, stirring occasionally, just until golden, three to four minutes. If grilling the burgers, spray the grill rack with nonstick spray, then prepare the barbecue (medium heat). An Asian-style cabbage slaw would be great on the side.

4 SERVINGS

1 12- to 14-ounce package firm tofu, drained, patted dry, cut into 1-inch-thick slices

2 teaspoons vegetable oil, divided
1/2 cup grated carrot
1/2 cup thinly sliced green onions
2 teaspoons minced peeled fresh ginger
1 garlic clove, minced
1/2 cup almonds, toasted, finely chopped
1 large egg white, beaten to blend
4 teaspoons soy sauce
1 1/2 teaspoons Asian sesame oil, divided
1 teaspoon sesame seeds, toasted

4 sesame seed buns, split, toasted
4 tomato slices
1 cup alfalfa sprouts

WRAP tofu in doubled dish towel. Place on work surface. Weigh down with board topped with food cans or weights and let stand for 1 hour. Squeeze towel-wrapped tofu to extract as much liquid as possible from tofu. Transfer tofu to medium bowl. Using fork, mash into small pieces.

HEAT 1 teaspoon vegetable oil in medium nonstick skillet over medium heat. Add carrot, green onions, ginger, and garlic; sauté until slightly softened, about 3 minutes. Cool. Stir carrot mixture, almonds, egg white, soy sauce, 1 teaspoon sesame oil, and sesame seeds into tofu. Season with salt and pepper. Shape mixture into four ½-inch-thick patties. *(Can be prepared 4 hours ahead. Cover and chill.)*

HEAT remaining 1 teaspoon vegetable oil and ½ teaspoon sesame oil in large nonstick skillet over medium heat. Add patties to skillet and cook until golden brown and heated through, about 3 minutes per side. Place 1 burger on each bun bottom. Top each with 1 tomato slice, ¼ of sprouts, and bun top.

Rosemary portobello burgers

ROBUST, SUN-DRENCHED ITALIAN FLAVORS are featured in these stylish burgers. Grilling meaty portobello mushrooms enhances their earthy taste. If you'd like to make your own balsamic vinaigrette, simply whisk one part balsamic vinegar into three parts extra-virgin olive oil. Feel free to use whole milk mozzarella, Fontina, Italian Stracchino, or any other melting cheese you prefer on the burgers. Make it a meal with an orzo salad tossed with slivered basil and Kalamata olives, and a few grilled red bell pepper quarters per person.

2 SERVINGS; CAN BE DOUBLED

⅓ cup purchased balsamic vinaigrette
1 tablespoon chopped fresh rosemary
2 round crusty rolls, split

2 large portobello mushrooms (about 5 inches in diameter), stemmed
4 slices deli-style mozzarella cheese
1 tomato, thinly sliced
1 cup (loosely packed) arugula leaves

PREPARE barbecue (medium-high heat). Whisk vinaigrette and rosemary in small bowl. Brush cut sides of rolls with vinaigrette. Place rolls on grill, cut side down. Grill until lightly toasted, about 1 minute. Transfer to 2 plates.

BRUSH mushrooms on both sides with vinaigrette. Sprinkle generously with salt and pepper. Place mushrooms on grill, dark gill side down. Close grill or cover mushrooms with small metal roasting pan; cook until mushrooms begin to soften, brushing with vinaigrette once more, about 5 minutes. Turn mushrooms over. Cover; grill until tender when pierced with knife, about 7 minutes longer. Place 2 cheese slices on each mushroom. Cover; grill until cheese melts, about 1 minute.

PLACE 1 mushroom on bottom half of each roll. Top each with tomato, arugula, and top half of roll.

Spiced basmati rice with lentils and caramelized onions

THE RICE IS SCENTED with cardamom, a spice native to India that has a pungent aroma and a sweet and spicy flavor. It can be found at Indian markets and in the spice section of many supermarkets. Use whatever color of lentils are easiest to find; any will work fine in this dish. Pick up a container of raita, the refreshing foil to spicy Indian curries, to serve on the side–or make your own by combining yogurt with chopped seeded cucumber and chopped cilantro. Add a little fragrant spice to it if you like: Toss some ground cumin in a dry skillet over medium heat for 30 seconds before adding to the yogurt.

4 SERVINGS

1 tablespoon butter
4 cups sliced onions

½ cup dried lentils

2½ cups water
3 whole cardamom pods
2 whole allspice
1 bay leaf
1 teaspoon salt
1 cup basmati rice or long-grain white rice

MELT butter in 10-inch-diameter ovenproof nonstick skillet over medium-low heat. Add onions and stir 1 minute. Cover and cook until onions are tender, stirring occasionally, about 15 minutes. Uncover and sauté until onions are deep golden, about 5 minutes longer. Season to taste with salt and pepper. Remove from heat. Spread onions in even layer in same skillet; set aside.

MEANWHILE, cook lentils in saucepan of boiling water until almost tender but still firm to bite, about 20 minutes. Drain.

COMBINE 2½ cups water, cardamom, allspice, bay leaf, and salt in heavy medium saucepan; bring to boil. Add rice and lentils; bring to boil. Reduce heat to low, cover, and simmer until water is absorbed and rice is tender, about 15 minutes. Discard cardamom, allspice, and bay leaf.

SPOON rice mixture atop onions in skillet, pressing with back of spoon to compact rice; smooth top. *(Can be prepared 2 hours ahead. Cool, then cover and let stand at room temperature.)*

PREHEAT oven to 400°F. Cover skillet tightly with double layer of aluminum foil. Bake rice mixture until heated through, about 35 minutes. Remove foil; let stand 5 minutes. Place plate over skillet; invert skillet, releasing rice and onions onto plate and scraping any onions remaining in skillet onto rice. Spoon rice and onions onto plates and serve.

Yellow rice salad with roasted peppers and spicy black beans

THIS DISH COMBINES two Cuban classics—black beans and yellow rice—in a beautiful composed salad. The beans are mounded in the center of a platter and the bright yellow rice salad, which gets its color from turmeric, is arranged around them. Using canned black beans (try organic brands for best flavor) makes it very easy to put together. Chipotle chiles canned in a spicy tomato sauce called *adobo* are available at Latin markets, specialty foods stores, and some supermarkets. To complete the meal, add corn or flour tortillas, warmed briefly over a gas flame to enhance their flavor, and a simple green salad.

4 MAIN-COURSE SERVINGS

4 teaspoons ground cumin, divided
¼ cup fresh lime juice
2½ tablespoons vegetable oil

½ teaspoon turmeric
2 cups water
1 cup basmati rice
1 teaspoon salt
½ cup thinly sliced green onions

1 15- to 16-ounce can black beans, rinsed, drained
½ cup chopped roasted red peppers from jar
½ cup chopped green bell pepper
⅓ cup chopped fresh cilantro
1½ teaspoons minced canned chipotle chiles

STIR 3 teaspoons cumin in small dry skillet over medium heat just until fragrant, about 1 minute. Remove from heat. Whisk lime juice and oil into cumin in skillet. Set dressing aside.

STIR turmeric and remaining 1 teaspoon cumin in heavy medium saucepan over medium heat until fragrant, about 1 minute. Add 2 cups water, rice, and 1 teaspoon salt; bring to boil. Reduce heat to low, cover, and simmer until water is absorbed, about 15 minutes. Cool rice. Mix green onions and half of dressing into rice. Season to taste with salt and pepper.

COMBINE black beans, all peppers, cilantro, chipotle chiles, and remaining dressing in medium bowl. Toss to coat. Season to taste with salt and pepper.

MOUND bean mixture in center of platter. Surround with rice salad and serve.

Summer vegetable stir-fry with couscous

IF YOU MAKE THIS DISH during the summer months when eggplant is at its freshest, take the opportunity to experiment with a selection of varieties available at your local farmers' market: Choose Thai or slender Japanese eggplants, which sauté beautifully, or mix in a few of the round, pale green or white fruits. In general, Asian eggplants are the sweetest and may not require salting (which helps leech out bitterness) when cooked in season. Likewise peeling: The skins are beautiful and delicious, so leave them on if you prefer.

4 SERVINGS

2 cups diced peeled eggplant
1½ teaspoons salt, divided

1½ cups water
1 cup couscous

2½ tablespoons canola oil, divided
2½ tablespoons red wine vinegar
1 cup diced peeled carrots
1 cup diced zucchini
1 cup diced yellow crookneck squash
1 cup small broccoli florets
1 cup diced red bell pepper
½ cup diced red onion
2 garlic cloves, minced
4 tablespoons chopped fresh basil
2 tablespoons chopped fresh mint
2 tablespoons pine nuts, toasted

TOSS eggplant and 1 teaspoon salt in medium bowl; let stand 30 minutes. Rinse and drain eggplant. Pat eggplant dry.

BRING 1½ cups water and remaining ½ teaspoon salt to boil in large saucepan. Stir in couscous. Remove from heat, cover, and let stand 10 minutes. Uncover; fluff with fork.

WHISK 1½ tablespoons oil with vinegar in small bowl. Heat remaining 1 tablespoon oil in wok or large nonstick skillet over medium-high heat. Add eggplant and carrots; stir-fry 3 minutes. Add zucchini and next 5 ingredients; stir-fry until vegetables are crisp-tender, about 2 minutes. Add couscous and vinegar mixture; stir-fry 1 minute. Stir in basil and mint. Season to taste with salt and pepper. Sprinkle with pine nuts.

Grilled-vegetable tostadas with two salsas

WHEN SUMMER PRODUCE is at its peak it should be the main attraction, not just a garnish, and that's the idea behind these meatless tostadas. The vegetables are grilled, then piled on crispy tortillas and topped with homemade red and green salsas. Tomatillos, which resemble small green tomatoes underneath their thin husks, are available at Latin markets and in the exotic produce section of some supermarkets. Dried ancho chiles are sold at Latin markets and some supermarkets.

4 SERVINGS

Tomatillo salsa
2 tablespoons olive oil
1 medium onion, chopped
2 garlic cloves, minced
1 pound fresh tomatillos, husked, rinsed, quartered
⅔ cup vegetable broth

⅓ cup chopped fresh cilantro
½ teaspoon chili powder
Hot pepper sauce

Tomato-chile salsa
2 large dried ancho chiles

1½ pounds tomatoes

2 green onions, finely chopped
3 tablespoons chopped fresh cilantro
1 garlic clove, minced
¾ teaspoon sugar
½ teaspoon ground cumin

Tortillas
3 tablespoons vegetable oil
4 8-inch-diameter flour tortillas

Grilled vegetables
¾ cup olive oil
6 garlic cloves, minced
1½ teaspoons chili powder
1¼ teaspoons salt

- **3 large zucchini, cut on deep diagonal into ¼-inch-thick slices**
- **2 large red bell peppers, seeded, cut into 1-inch-wide strips**
- **1 large eggplant, halved lengthwise, cut crosswise into ¼-inch-thick slices**
- **12 large oyster mushrooms**
- **1 large onion, cut into thin rounds**

FOR TOMATILLO SALSA: Heat oil in large saucepan over medium-high heat. Add onion and garlic; sauté 5 minutes. Add tomatillos; sauté 3 minutes. Add broth. Reduce heat, cover, and simmer until tomatillos are soft, about 8 minutes.

BLEND tomatillo mixture and cilantro in food processor until almost smooth. Transfer to bowl. Mix in chili powder. Season to taste with hot pepper sauce and salt. Cover and chill up to 2 days.

FOR TOMATO-CHILE SALSA: Place chiles in bowl. Cover with hot water and soak until soft, about 20 minutes. Drain. Cut open; scrape out seeds. Cut off stems and coarsely chop chiles.

COOK tomatoes in boiling water 20 seconds. Drain and peel tomatoes. Cut in half; squeeze out seeds. Chop tomatoes.

COMBINE chiles and ¾ cup tomatoes in processor; puree until smooth. Transfer to bowl. Mix in remaining tomatoes, green onions, cilantro, garlic, sugar, and cumin. Season to taste with salt. *(Can be prepared 1 day ahead. Cover and refrigerate.)*

FOR TORTILLAS: Line baking sheet with paper towels. Heat oil in large skillet over medium-high heat. Add 1 tortilla; fry until crisp and golden, about 30 seconds per side. Transfer tortilla to paper-towel-lined sheet to drain. Repeat frying and draining with remaining tortillas.

FOR GRILLED VEGETABLES: Preheat oven to 350°F. Prepare barbecue (medium-high heat). Mix olive oil, garlic, chili powder, and salt in large bowl. Pour ¼ cup oil mixture into small bowl and reserve. Add zucchini, bell peppers, and eggplant to oil mixture in large bowl; toss to coat. Grill zucchini, bell peppers, and eggplant in batches until light brown, about 3 minutes per side. Place on baking sheet and tent with aluminum foil to keep warm. Brush mushrooms and onion rounds with reserved ¼ cup oil mixture. Grill until light brown, about 3 minutes per side. Place on baking sheet with other vegetables.

MEANWHILE, transfer tortillas to clean baking sheet and rewarm in oven until hot, about 5 minutes.

PLACE 1 tortilla on each of 4 plates. Top with vegetables and serve with salsas.

Bulgur with garbanzo beans, feta, and plum tomatoes

A CREATIVE RIFF on tabbouleh (the Middle Eastern salad of bulgur, parsley, mint, tomatoes, and lemon juice), this recipe adds a punch of protein with feta cheese and garbanzo beans to make a fresh, light one-dish meal. Bulgur, also called cracked wheat, is sold at natural foods stores and supermarkets. You could easily turn this salad into a vegetarian feast by adding purchased hummus with crudités, *tzatziki* (Greek yogurt-cucumber salad), a bowl of Kalamata olives, and warm pita bread.

4 SERVINGS

- **2 cups water**
- **1 cup bulgur**
- **1 teaspoon salt**
- **1 15- to 16-ounce can garbanzo beans (chickpeas), rinsed, drained**
- **1 cup diced plum tomatoes**
- **½ cup crumbled feta cheese**
- **½ cup chopped green onions**
- **⅓ cup chopped fresh mint**
- **⅓ cup chopped fresh Italian parsley**
- **3 tablespoons fresh lemon juice**
- **1½ tablespoons olive oil**
- **2 teaspoons grated lemon peel**

BRING 2 cups water to boil in medium saucepan. Remove from heat; add bulgur and salt and stir. Cover and let stand until bulgur is just tender, about 20 minutes. Drain well, pressing to extract excess water. Transfer bulgur to large bowl and cool. Mix in all remaining ingredients. Season to taste with salt and pepper.

Cannellini and fennel salad with roasted peppers, mushrooms, and zucchini

THIS STUNNING COMPOSED SALAD with its Mediterranean accents makes a delightful centerpiece dish for summer entertaining. Fresh thyme, mint, and orange peel add a vibrant note to the roasted vegetables. To trim fennel, lay the bulb on its side and cut off the stalks and fronds. Next, cut off the root end and halve the bulb lengthwise. Place the bulb, cut side down, on a work surface and slice thinly, then chop the slices.

4 SERVINGS

Nonstick vegetable oil spray
2 large red bell peppers, quartered
2 large portobello mushrooms, stemmed, caps quartered
4 small zucchini, halved lengthwise
1 tablespoon chopped fresh thyme
1 tablespoon chopped fresh mint
2 teaspoons grated orange peel

1/4 cup extra-virgin olive oil
1/4 cup red wine vinegar
1/2 teaspoon fennel seeds, crushed
2 15-ounce cans cannellini (white kidney beans), drained
2 cups chopped fresh fennel
1/2 cup chopped red onion

6 cups mixed baby greens
4 plum tomatoes, cut into wedges

PREHEAT oven to 400°F. Spray heavy large rimmed baking sheet with nonstick spray. Arrange bell peppers, mushrooms, and zucchini on prepared sheet; sprinkle with salt and pepper. Roast until peppers and zucchini are brown in spots, turning twice, about 35 minutes. Sprinkle with thyme, mint, and orange peel.

WHISK oil, vinegar, and fennel seeds to blend in small bowl. Season dressing to taste with salt and pepper. Mix beans, fennel, onion, and all but 1 tablespoon dressing in medium bowl. Season salad to taste with salt and pepper. Spoon salad into center of large platter

TOSS greens with remaining 1 tablespoon dressing in large bowl; arrange greens around bean salad. Place roasted peppers, mushrooms, and zucchini atop greens. Garnish with tomato wedges and serve.

Spicy orecchiette with white beans, tomatoes, and broccoli

ORECCHIETTE IS ITALIAN FOR "little ears," a lighthearted description of this pasta's shape. It is a specialty of the Apulia region of Italy, where it is traditionally paired with broccoli rabe and a pinch of crushed red pepper. This recipe calls for the more commonly found broccoli crowns, but feel free to substitute broccoli rabe.

4 SERVINGS

3 tablespoons olive oil
1 cup chopped onion
3 garlic cloves, minced
1/2 teaspoon dried crushed red pepper
1 28-ounce can diced tomatoes in juice
1/4 cup water
1 15-ounce can cannellini (white kidney beans), drained
1/2 cup chopped fresh basil

8 ounces orecchiette (little ear-shaped pasta; about 2 cups) or medium pasta shells
1 pound broccoli crowns, separated into small florets (about 5 cups)

Freshly shaved Parmesan cheese

HEAT oil in large nonstick skillet over medium-high heat. Add onion and sauté until tender, about 5 minutes. Add garlic and crushed red pepper; stir 1 minute. Stir in tomatoes with juice and ¼ cup water. Bring to boil. Reduce heat to medium and simmer until sauce thickens, stirring occasionally, about 10 minutes. Stir in beans and basil. Season sauce to taste with salt and pepper.

MEANWHILE, cook orecchiette in large pot of boiling salted water until almost tender, about 15 minutes. Add broccoli florets; cook until pasta is tender but still firm to bite and broccoli florets are crisp-tender, about 2 minutes longer. Ladle out ½ cup pasta cooking liquid and reserve. Drain orecchiette and broccoli florets; return to pot. Add tomato sauce and reserved pasta cooking liquid; toss to combine. Season to taste with salt and pepper.

TRANSFER pasta to bowl. Sprinkle with cheese and serve.

Caribbean black beans and rice with red onion–jalapeño relish

THIS RECIPE FOR BLACK BEANS begins with the traditional *sofrito,* a flavor base of sautéed aromatics such as garlic and onion essential to many dishes of Spanish origin, then it takes a shortcut by adding canned beans. A quick red onion–jalapeño relish adds a textural contrast and fresh, bright flavor. Offer buttered, grilled Cuban (or French) bread with the beans and rice.

4 SERVINGS

¼ cup olive oil
1 large onion, chopped
2 garlic cloves, chopped
1½ teaspoons chili powder
2 15- to 16-ounce cans black beans, well drained
3 cups water, divided
1 bay leaf
1 tablespoon red wine vinegar
½ teaspoon hot pepper sauce
Pinch of sugar

1 cup long-grain white rice
½ teaspoon turmeric

¾ cup chopped red onion
2 jalapeño chiles, seeded, minced

HEAT oil in heavy large saucepan over medium heat. Add onion and sauté until beginning to soften, about 5 minutes. Add garlic and chili powder; sauté 1 minute, stirring constantly. Add beans, 1 cup water, and bay leaf. Simmer until reduced to thick soup consistency, about 20 minutes. Discard bay leaf. Add vinegar, pepper sauce, and sugar. Season beans to taste with salt and pepper.

MEANWHILE, bring remaining 2 cups water to boil in heavy medium saucepan. Add rice, turmeric, and pinch of salt; stir. Reduce heat to low, cover, and cook until liquid is absorbed and rice is tender, about 20 minutes.

MIX chopped red onion and chiles in small bowl. Mound rice in center of platter. Spoon beans around rice. Serve, passing red onion relish separately.

Meats 10

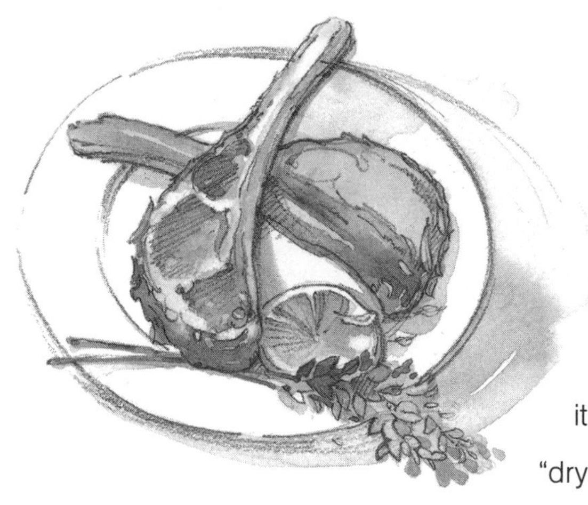

Beef, pork, lamb, veal; steaks, chops, ribs, roasts; grilling, braising, roasting, brining…the world of meats is a world of extraordinary variety. It's no wonder that this is one of the most extensive chapters in this book.

For each cut of meat, there is a preparation that shows it off to its best advantage. For instance, roasting and grilling—"dry-heat" methods in culinary jargon—use high heat to add flavor and a crispy, crusty exterior to tender cuts like tenderloins, chops, and steaks. Both methods work best if the meat is seasoned or marinated before cooking. Cuts such as pork spare ribs and short ribs of beef can be braised to tenderize them before they're seared to mahogany on a hot grill. This precooking adds a tremendous amount of flavor, too.

Braising, stewing, and pot-roasting—the "wet heat" trio—yield delicious results with tougher cuts of meat. These cooking methods offer perhaps the greatest room for improvisation. The flavor of the liquids and seasonings you use with these cuts of meat will penetrate the entire portion. And the savory cooking liquid that bubbles on the stove or in the oven doubles as a sauce. Taste the Braised Lamb Shanks with Winter Squash and Red Chard or one of the other braises in this chapter, and you'll be an instant convert.

Then there are the marinades and brines that both tenderize and add deep flavor before you even start to cook. The Cider-Brined Pork Chops with Creamed Leeks and Apples is a delectable example—and a great dinner-party entrée.

A world of extraordinary variety comes down to one delicious meal at a time.

Beef

Rib-eye steaks with béarnaise butter

MADE WITH A REDUCTION of wine, tarragon, shallots, and sometimes vinegar, then finished with butter, the classic French béarnaise sauce is excellent with steaks—it mingles with the meat's pan juices to create extravagant flavor. Round out the meal with creamy mashed potatoes, frisée salad, and a rich Bordeaux.

2 SERVINGS

- **¼ cup dry white wine**
- **1 tablespoon minced shallot**
- **¼ teaspoon dried tarragon**

- **5 tablespoons butter, room temperature**
- **1 tablespoon minced fresh tarragon**

- **Olive oil**
- **2 12-ounce rib-eye steaks (each 1 to 1¼ inches thick)**

BOIL wine, shallot, and dried tarragon in heavy small saucepan until liquid reduces to glaze, about 2 minutes. Cool completely.

WHISK butter and fresh tarragon into shallot mixture. Season to taste with salt and pepper. Shape butter mixture into log; wrap in plastic and chill until firm. *(Can be made 3 days ahead. Keep chilled.)* Cut cold butter crosswise into ⅓-inch-thick slices. Bring to room temperature before using.

BRUSH large nonstick skillet with oil; heat over medium-high heat. Sprinkle steaks with salt and pepper; add to skillet. Cook to desired doneness, about 5 minutes per side for medium-rare. Transfer steaks to plates. Overlap butter slices atop steaks and serve.

Spencer steaks with red wine–shiitake sauce

A CLASSIC AMERICAN ENTRÉE—steak with sautéed mushrooms—gets updated in a delicious way: Shiitake mushrooms are sautéed with shallots, red wine, thyme, and soy sauce. Even better, this go-with sauce can be prepared ahead of time. Spencer steaks (also called boneless rib-eye steaks, or entrecotes by the French) are flavorful, juicy cuts from the rib section.

4 SERVINGS

- **10 tablespoons (1¼ sticks) butter, divided**
- **12 ounces fresh shiitake mushrooms, stemmed, caps sliced**
- **⅓ cup minced shallots**
- **1½ cups dry red wine, divided**
- **3¼ cups low-salt or unsalted beef broth, divided**
- **4 fresh thyme sprigs**
- **2 tablespoons minced fresh thyme**
- **2 teaspoons light soy sauce**

- **4 6- to 8-ounce Spencer steaks (boneless rib-eye steaks; each about 1 inch thick)**
- **1 tablespoon vegetable oil**

- **Chopped fresh thyme**

MELT 4 tablespoons butter in heavy large skillet over medium-high heat. Add mushrooms and shallots; sauté until tender, about 4 minutes. Add ¾ cup wine and boil until reduced to glaze, about 4 minutes. Add remaining ¾ cup wine and boil until reduced to glaze, about 4 minutes longer. Add 3 cups broth and thyme sprigs; boil until sauce is syrupy and coats spoon, about 20 minutes. Add minced thyme and soy sauce. *(Mushroom sauce can be made 2 hours ahead. Cover and let stand at room temperature.)*

SPRINKLE steaks generously with ground black pepper. Melt 2 tablespoons butter with oil in another heavy large skillet over high heat. Add steaks and brown, about 2 minutes per side. Reduce heat to medium and cook steaks to desired doneness, about 3 minutes longer per side for medium-rare. Transfer to heated plates and cover loosely with aluminum foil to keep warm.

POUR off drippings from skillet with steaks. Add remaining ¼ cup broth and bring to boil, scraping up any browned bits. Boil until syrupy, about 1 minute. Add mushroom sauce to same skillet. Bring to simmer. Whisk in remaining 4 tablespoons butter. Season sauce to taste with salt and pepper and discard thyme sprigs. Spoon sauce over steaks. Sprinkle with chopped thyme.

Cowboy steaks with tomato-lime salsa and red chili onion rings

THE FLAVORS OF THE SOUTHWEST come through in a salsa prepared with tomatoes, onion, lime juice, cilantro, and jalapeños, and in sensational onion rings seasoned with chili powder and cumin. This recipe calls for large T-bone or porterhouse steaks, big enough for a cowboy; have your butcher cut them for you. If you prefer smaller portions, buy standard-size steaks and grill them for a shorter time. The steaks are also terrific pan-fried in a small amount of olive oil.

2 SERVINGS

1 small red onion, diced
3 cups water
1 pound tomatoes, cut into ¼-inch cubes
3 tablespoons fresh lime juice
3 tablespoons finely chopped fresh cilantro
1 tablespoon finely chopped seeded jalapeño chiles
1 tablespoon olive oil

2 1½-inch-thick T-bone or porterhouse steaks, room temperature
Red Chili Onion Rings (see recipe)

SOAK red onion in 3 cups water in large bowl 1 hour. Drain onion thoroughly; transfer to medium bowl. Add tomatoes, lime juice, cilantro, chiles, and oil; combine well. Season salsa to taste with salt and pepper. *(Salsa can be prepared 6 hours ahead. Cover and chill.)*

PREPARE barbecue (medium-high heat). Sprinkle steaks with salt and pepper. Grill steaks to desired doneness, about 7 minutes per side for medium-rare. Transfer to plates. Drain salsa and spoon onto plates. Serve steaks immediately with onion rings.

Red chili onion rings

THESE ONION RINGS would also be great with burgers—or all by themselves.

2 SERVINGS

2 white onions, cut into ⅛-inch-thick rounds
1½ cups whole milk
1½ cups sifted all purpose flour
¼ cup chili powder
1 tablespoon plus 1 teaspoon cornstarch
1½ teaspoons salt
1½ teaspoons ground cumin
1 teaspoon (generous) sugar
1 teaspoon (generous) Hungarian hot paprika
Vegetable oil (for deep-frying)

SOAK onions in milk in large bowl 1 hour, separating into rings. Drain thoroughly. Mix all remaining ingredients except oil in another large bowl. Dredge onions in flour mixture; shake off excess. Pour enough oil into heavy large saucepan to reach depth of 2 inches. Attach deep-fry thermometer and heat oil to 360°F. Working in batches, add onions and cook until golden brown, about 45 seconds. Using slotted spoon, transfer onions to paper towels to drain. Mound onions in bowl; serve immediately.

Porterhouse steak with arugula and Parmesan cheese

IN FLORENCE, ITALY, where this recipe originated, the steaks are traditionally cooked over a grate in the fireplace. Fortunately, you can prepare them instead on an outdoor grill with equally appealing results. Use a swivel-bladed vegetable peeler to cut thin strips from a wedge of Parmesan to make the cheese shavings. To give the meal an authentic Italian flair, team the steaks with a Chianti Classico.

8 SERVINGS

3 2- to 2½-inch-thick porterhouse steaks (each about 3 pounds)
Olive oil

5 ounces arugula (about 5 cups packed)
1 cup Parmesan cheese shavings

PREPARE barbecue (medium-high heat). Rub steaks with oil and sprinkle lightly with salt and pepper. Grill until steaks are brown and crusty and thermometer inserted into thickest part registers 120°F to 125°F for rare, turning every 5 minutes, about 25 minutes total. Using tongs, transfer steaks to cutting board; let rest 10 minutes.

COARSELY chop enough arugula to measure 2 cups and set aside. Arrange remaining arugula on platter and sprinkle with oil, salt, and pepper. Cut meat away from bones. Slice meat thinly. Overlap slices atop arugula. Sprinkle reserved chopped arugula and cheese shavings over steak and serve.

Steaks de Burgo

THIS REGIONAL AMERICAN SPECIALTY hails from central Iowa, where the steaks are topped with butter, Italian herbs, and garlic. The recipe's name and origin are a mystery, but there's no mystery to its appeal: The steaks are simple to prepare and filled with flavor.

4 SERVINGS

½ cup (1 stick) unsalted butter
6 garlic cloves, thinly sliced

4 6- to 8-ounce beef tenderloin steaks (each about 1 inch thick)

¼ cup chopped fresh oregano
¼ cup chopped fresh basil

MELT butter in heavy small saucepan over medium heat. Remove from heat; add garlic. Season to taste with salt and pepper. Let garlic butter stand 2 hours at room temperature.

PREPARE barbecue (medium-high heat). Place saucepan of garlic butter at edge of grill to rewarm. Sprinkle steaks with salt and pepper. Grill steaks to desired doneness, about 4 minutes per side for medium-rare.

TRANSFER steaks to plates. Spoon warmed garlic butter over. Sprinkle with herbs and serve.

Garlic and rosemary steak with potato–green onion cakes

AFTER THE STEAK HAS MARINATED overnight in olive oil, soy sauce, balsamic vinegar, garlic, and rosemary, the marinade is boiled to become a sauce. With two flavorful side dishes–a sauté of bell peppers and onions, and cumin-seasoned potato–green onion cakes–this is a terrific special-occasion meal.

6 SERVINGS

Steak

- **½ cup olive oil**
- **½ cup soy sauce**
- **¼ cup balsamic vinegar**
- **8 garlic cloves, minced**
- **4 teaspoons dried rosemary**
- **1 2-inch-thick boneless top sirloin steak (about 3½ pounds)**

Peppers and onions

- **⅓ cup olive oil**
- **2 large onions, cut into 1-inch pieces**
- **2 red bell peppers, cut into 1-inch pieces**
- **1 green bell pepper, cut into 1-inch pieces**
- **¾ teaspoon dried marjoram**
- **⅛ teaspoon dried crushed red pepper**

Potato–Green Onion Cakes (see recipe)

FOR STEAK: Whisk first 5 ingredients in 13x9x2-inch glass baking dish to blend. Add steak and turn to coat. Sprinkle generously with pepper. Cover and refrigerate steak overnight, turning occasionally.

FOR PEPPERS AND ONIONS: Heat oil in heavy large skillet over medium-high heat. Add onions and sauté 4 minutes. Add all bell peppers and sauté until beginning to soften, about 8 minutes. Add marjoram and crushed red pepper; stir 2 minutes. Season to taste with salt and pepper. Remove from heat.

BRING steak to room temperature. Preheat broiler 5 minutes. Remove steak from marinade and pat dry. Transfer marinade to heavy small saucepan. Broil steak to desired degree of doneness, about 10 minutes per side for rare (meat thermometer inserted into thickest part registers 125°F). Transfer steak to platter. Let stand 10 minutes.

MEANWHILE, reheat bell peppers and onions in skillet. Bring marinade to boil and boil 1 minute.

THINLY slice steak across grain. Arrange slices on large platter. Surround with potato cakes, peppers, and onions. Serve, passing marinade separately.

Potato–green onion cakes

THESE SIMPLE POTATO PANCAKES can accompany a variety of meat and chicken dishes. And they can be assembled up to six hours ahead, simplifying dinner preparation considerably.

MAKES ABOUT 14

- **3 pounds large white-skinned potatoes**

- **12 green onions, chopped**
- **2 large eggs**
- **2 teaspoons ground cumin**

- **3 tablespoons (about) olive oil**

COOK potatoes in large pot of boiling salted water until just tender, about 20 minutes. Drain. Cover and refrigerate until well chilled. *(Potatoes can be prepared 1 day ahead. Keep refrigerated.)*

PEEL potatoes. Using hand grater, coarsely grate cold potatoes into large bowl. Gently mix in green onions. Season to taste with salt and pepper. Beat eggs and cumin in small bowl to blend; gently stir into potato mixture. Form potato mixture into 2½-inch-diameter cakes (each about 1 inch thick). Place cakes on baking sheet. Cover and refrigerate until ready to cook. *(Cakes can be prepared 6 hours ahead.)*

HEAT 2 tablespoons oil in heavy large skillet over medium-high heat. Working in batches, add potato cakes and fry until golden brown, about 8 minutes per side, adding more oil as necessary.

Marinated flank steak with horseradish sauce

FLANK STEAK IS A LEAN, flat, boneless steak that comes from the underside of the steer. It has great flavor and responds well to marinades, but should be cooked quickly. It is best rare or medium-rare and sliced thinly across the grain to ensure tenderness. This rendition, perfect for summer barbecues, is a snap to prepare. The sour cream-horseradish sauce gives it a kick.

6 SERVINGS

Steak

- **½ cup soy sauce**
- **½ cup dry white wine**
- **½ onion, chopped**
- **3 tablespoons chopped fresh rosemary**
- **2 tablespoons olive oil**
- **2 garlic cloves, chopped**
- **1 2-pound flank steak, trimmed**

Sauce

- **½ cup sour cream**
- **2 green onions, chopped**
- **1 tablespoon plus 1 teaspoon prepared white horseradish**

Romaine lettuce leaves

FOR STEAK: Whisk first 6 ingredients in 13x9x2-inch glass baking dish to blend. Add steak and turn to coat. Cover and refrigerate overnight, turning occasionally.

FOR SAUCE: Mix sour cream, green onions, and horseradish in small bowl. Season to taste with coarsely ground black pepper. *(Sauce can be prepared 1 day ahead. Cover and refrigerate.)*

PREPARE barbecue (high heat). Drain steak. Pour marinade into small saucepan and boil 1 minute. Sprinkle steak generously with pepper. Grill to desired doneness, basting occasionally with marinade, about 6 minutes per side for medium-rare. Transfer steak to plate and let stand at least 15 minutes. Cut steak across grain and on slight diagonal into thin slices. Line platter with romaine leaves. Top with steak. Serve warm or at room temperature with horseradish sauce.

Herbed flank steak with cherry tomato and olive relish

HERE'S AN EXCELLENT summertime dinner: Fresh herbs—thyme, rosemary, and tarragon—accent the steak, which should marinate one hour to one day before being grilled. The steak slices (cut across the grain to make them especially tender) are then topped with colorful cherry tomatoes, brine-cured black and green olives, and fresh basil. Serve with a pale ale for a perfect backyard barbecue.

6 SERVINGS

Steak

- **2 tablespoons chopped fresh thyme**
- **2 tablespoons chopped fresh rosemary**
- **1 tablespoon chopped fresh tarragon**
- **2 garlic cloves, minced**
- **2 teaspoons salt**
- **1½ teaspoons ground black pepper**
- **2 1½-pound flank steaks**
- **1 tablespoon olive oil**

Tomato and olive relish

- **2 cups halved cherry tomatoes (about 10 ounces)**
- **1 cup chopped fresh Italian parsley**
- **¼ cup coarsely chopped pitted Kalamata olives**
- **¼ cup coarsely chopped pitted imported green olives**
- **¼ cup chopped fresh basil**
- **¼ cup extra-virgin olive oil**
- **2 tablespoons Sherry wine vinegar**

FOR STEAK: Mix first 6 ingredients in small bowl. Place steaks in single layer in 15x10x2-inch glass baking dish. Brush steaks with oil. Rub with herb mixture. Cover with plastic wrap and refrigerate at least 1 hour and up to 1 day.

FOR TOMATO AND OLIVE RELISH: Mix all ingredients in large bowl; season to taste with salt and pepper. *(Relish can be made 2 hours ahead. Let stand at room temperature.)*

PREPARE barbecue (medium-high heat). Grill steaks with herb mixture still clinging until cooked to desired doneness, about 4 minutes per side for medium-rare. Transfer steaks to cutting board. Let stand 5 minutes.

CUT steaks across grain and on slight diagonal into ½-inch-thick slices. Arrange steak slices on large platter. Spoon tomato and olive relish with juices over steaks and serve.

Spicy steak and corn soft tacos

THESE QUICK TACOS are easy enough for a weeknight supper. And with their combination of sautéed steak, onion, bell pepper, corn, cheddar cheese, and fresh tomatoes, they can be a whole meal unto themselves.

2 SERVINGS; CAN BE DOUBLED

- **2 tablespoons olive oil**
- **1 medium red onion, sliced**
- **1 red bell pepper, sliced**
- **½ pound top sirloin, flank, or skirt steak, cut into ¼-inch-thick, long narrow strips**
- **¾ cup frozen corn kernels, cooked according to package directions, drained**
- **1 jalapeño chile, stemmed, minced with seeds**
- **½ teaspoon ground cumin**
- **½ teaspoon chili powder**
- **1½ tablespoons minced fresh cilantro**

Corn or flour tortillas
Grated cheddar cheese
Chopped fresh tomatoes
Sour cream

HEAT oil in heavy large skillet over medium heat. Add onion and bell pepper; sauté until soft, about 10 minutes. Transfer to plate. Add steak to same skillet and sauté until no longer pink, about 1 minute. Return onion and pepper to skillet. Add corn, jalapeño, cumin, and chili powder; stir until heated through. Season to taste with salt and pepper. Remove from heat and mix in cilantro. Transfer steak mixture to bowl. Cover loosely with aluminum foil to keep warm.

COOK tortillas directly over gas flame or electric burner until just beginning to char in spots, about 30 seconds per side. Transfer to napkin-lined basket. Serve hot tortillas, steak mixture, cheese, tomatoes, and sour cream separately, so tacos can be assembled at table.

Grilled skirt steaks with cilantro chimichurri sauce

IN ARGENTINA, the mixture of olive oil, vinegar, and herbs known as *chimichurri* is practically required as an accompaniment to grilled meats. The fresh and assertive flavors in this version—cilantro, garlic, and jalapeños—are an ideal foil to the steak. Complete the meal with black beans and rice.

6 SERVINGS

- **½ cup (packed) fresh cilantro leaves, divided**
- **6 garlic cloves**
- **2 jalapeño chiles, stemmed, halved**
- **4 large bay leaves, center stem removed, leaves crumbled**
- **1 tablespoon dried oregano**
- **1 teaspoon salt**
- **1 cup (packed) fresh Italian parsley leaves**
- **½ cup distilled white vinegar**
- **½ cup olive oil**

- **6 5- to 6-ounce skirt steaks**

Tomato wedges (optional)
Watercress sprigs (optional)

COMBINE ¼ cup cilantro, garlic, jalapeños, bay leaves, oregano, and salt in processor. Blend until mixture is finely chopped, scraping down sides of bowl occasionally. Add parsley, vinegar, oil, and remaining ¼ cup cilantro. Blend until herbs are coarsely chopped. Season chimichurri sauce to taste with pepper. *(Sauce can be made 8 hours ahead. Cover and chill.)*

PREPARE barbecue (medium-high heat) or preheat broiler. Sprinkle steaks with salt and pepper. Cook to desired doneness, about 3 minutes per side for medium-rare. Transfer to plates. Spoon some sauce over. Garnish with tomatoes and watercress, if desired. Serve, passing remaining sauce separately.

Southwestern-style Salisbury steaks

SALISBURY STEAK was introduced around the beginning of the twentieth century, but there is nothing old-fashioned about this recipe. Zesty pickled red onions replace the familiar mushroom gravy, and the "steaks" themselves (actually ground chuck patties) feature such contemporary accents as Monterey Jack cheese, cilantro, green chiles, green onions, and tequila.

4 SERVINGS

- **1½ pounds ground beef chuck or ground beef sirloin**
- **½ cup (packed) coarsely shredded Monterey Jack cheese (about 2 ounces)**
- **¼ cup chopped fresh cilantro**
- **1 4-ounce can diced mild green chiles**
- **2 tablespoons minced green onions**
- **1 tablespoon tequila**
- **2 teaspoons chili powder**
- **1 teaspoon salt**

- **1 avocado, halved, pitted, peeled, sliced**
- **Lime-Pickled Red Onions (see recipe)**
- **Purchased salsas**

USING hands, gently mix first 8 ingredients in large bowl just until combined. Form beef mixture into four ¾-inch-thick oval patties. Arrange on plate. *(Patties can be made 1 day ahead. Cover and chill.)*

PREPARE barbecue (medium-high heat). Grill patties until cooked to desired doneness, about 6 minutes per side for medium.

TRANSFER steaks to plates. Top with avocado slices and pickled red onions. Serve, passing salsas.

Lime-pickled red onions

ALLOW TIME for the onions to marinate; they need to stand for at least one hour before serving.

MAKES ABOUT 2 CUPS

- **1 large red onion, thinly sliced**
- **¼ cup fresh lime juice**
- **2 tablespoons chopped fresh cilantro**
- **2 teaspoons olive oil**
- **½ teaspoon dried oregano**
- **½ teaspoon salt**

MIX all ingredients in medium bowl. Cover and let stand at room temperature at least 1 hour and up to 3 hours, stirring occasionally. *(Onions can be made 2 days ahead. Cover and refrigerate.)*

Beef brisket braised with root vegetables

THIS IMPRESSIVE ENTRÉE can be prepared up to two days ahead, making it ideal for a holiday or special-occasion meal. The brisket cooks for three and a half hours, creating a rich sauce that also gives the vegetables—potatoes, rutabagas, carrots, and parsnips—deep, full flavor.

8 SERVINGS

3 tablespoons vegetable oil
3 medium onions, chopped
4 garlic cloves, minced
2 tablespoons tomato paste
1 tablespoon paprika
½ teaspoon ground ginger
3½ cups beef broth
1½ cups dry red wine
3 small bay leaves
2 teaspoons dried thyme
1 4- to 4½-pound boneless flat-cut beef brisket
Additional paprika

2 pounds red-skinned potatoes, cut into 1½-inch pieces
2 pounds rutabagas, peeled, cut into 1½-inch pieces
4 large carrots, peeled, cut into 1½-inch pieces
4 large parsnips, peeled, cut into 1½-inch pieces

Minced fresh parsley

PREHEAT oven to 325°F. Heat oil in heavy large saucepan over medium heat. Add onions and garlic; sauté until beginning to brown, about 20 minutes. Add tomato paste, 1 tablespoon paprika, and ginger; stir 20 seconds. Add beef broth, wine, bay leaves, and thyme; boil 10 minutes to blend flavors. Transfer broth mixture to large roasting pan. Sprinkle brisket all over with salt, pepper, and additional paprika, and rub in. Arrange brisket fat side up in broth mixture in roasting pan. Cover and bake 1 hour.

ARRANGE potatoes, rutabagas, carrots, and parsnips around brisket. Cover and bake until brisket is tender, about 2½ hours longer.

TRANSFER brisket to cutting board and cool 30 minutes. Transfer vegetables to bowl; cover. Tilt pan and spoon fat off top of cooking liquid. Pour cooking liquid into blender or processor and puree. Transfer to heavy medium saucepan and boil over high heat until reduced to 3½ cups sauce, stirring occasionally, about 10 minutes. Season sauce to taste with salt and pepper. Thinly slice brisket across grain. Arrange slices, overlapping, in large ovenproof dish. Arrange vegetables around brisket. Spoon sauce over. *(Brisket can be prepared 2 days ahead. Cover with aluminum foil and refrigerate. Reheat covered in 350°F oven about 40 minutes.)* Sprinkle with parsley.

Brisket with dried apricots, prunes, and aromatic spices

AN INVENTIVE PUREE of dried fruits and spices flavors the brisket before it is cooked and rounds out the sauce in which the meat braises. The brisket is refrigerated overnight because it's easier to slice when it's cold and firm; so begin preparing this at least one day ahead.

8 SERVINGS

⅔ cup quartered dried apricots (about 4 ounces), divided
9 garlic cloves, divided
3½ teaspoons ground cumin, divided
1 teaspoon salt
¼ teaspoon ground cinnamon
¼ teaspoon ground black pepper
1 4½- to 5-pound flat-cut beef brisket

3 tablespoons olive oil
4 cups chopped onions
2 medium carrots, peeled, coarsely chopped
1 tablespoon minced peeled fresh ginger
1 teaspoon ground coriander
⅛ teaspoon cayenne pepper
1 cup dry red wine
3 cups low-salt beef broth

⅔ cup pitted prunes (about 4 ounces), quartered

Chopped fresh cilantro

COMBINE ⅓ cup apricots, 3 garlic cloves, 1 teaspoon cumin, salt, cinnamon, and ¼ teaspoon pepper in processor. Using on/off turns, chop to coarse paste. Using small sharp knife, make ½-inch-deep slits all over brisket. Measure 1 tablespoon apricot mixture and reserve. Press remaining apricot mixture into slits in brisket.

POSITION rack in bottom third of oven and preheat to 300°F. Heat oil in heavy large ovenproof pot over medium-high heat. Sprinkle brisket all over with salt and pepper. Add brisket to pot and sauté until brown, about 5 minutes per side. Transfer to plate, fat side up; spread with reserved 1 tablespoon apricot mixture. Add onions to same pot and sauté over medium-high heat 5 minutes. Add carrots, ginger, coriander, cayenne, and remaining 6 garlic cloves and 2½ teaspoons cumin; sauté 3 minutes. Add wine and boil until reduced almost to glaze, scraping up any browned bits, about 5 minutes. Return brisket to pot. Add broth and bring to simmer, spooning some of vegetable mixture over brisket.

COVER pot and place in oven. Roast brisket 2½ hours, basting every 30 minutes with pan juices. Add prunes and remaining ⅓ cup apricots. Cover and roast until brisket is tender, about 30 minutes longer. Cool brisket uncovered 1 hour. Place in refrigerator and chill uncovered until cold, then cover and keep chilled overnight.

SPOON off any solid fat from top of gravy; discard fat. Using tongs, lift brisket slightly and scrape attached gravy off into pot. Place brisket on work surface. Slice brisket thinly across grain. Bring gravy in pot to boil over medium-high heat. Boil until slightly thickened, if desired. Season gravy to taste with salt and pepper. Arrange sliced brisket in large ovenproof dish. Spoon gravy over. Cover with aluminum foil. *(Can be made 2 days ahead; refrigerate.)*

PREHEAT oven to 350°F. Rewarm covered brisket about 30 minutes (or 40 minutes if chilled). Sprinkle with cilantro and serve.

Barbecued Texas beef brisket

TEXANS LIKE THEIR BARBECUE SPICY, in the tradition of the Southwest, which is chile pepper country. For this recipe, you'll need to order a USDA "choice" grade, packer-trimmed whole brisket: That's a brisket with none of the fat cut off. Before being cooked, the meat is seasoned with a dry rub; during cooking, it is brushed regularly with a beer-based mop. You'll need to use a smoker for the brisket (a converted barbecue won't maintain the very low heat required), and to get the most authentic Texas flavor, seek out the natural lump charcoal specified in the recipe; it is available at barbecue stores, some natural foods stores, and some supermarkets.

12 SERVINGS

Dry rub

- **½ cup paprika**
- **3 tablespoons ground black pepper**
- **3 tablespoons coarse kosher salt**
- **3 tablespoons sugar**
- **2 tablespoons chili powder**

- **1 7½- to 8-pound untrimmed whole beef brisket**

Mop

- **1 12-ounce can or bottle of beer**
- **½ cup apple cider vinegar**
- **½ cup water**
- **¼ cup vegetable oil**
- **2 tablespoons Worcestershire sauce**
- **2 tablespoons minced jalapeño chiles with seeds**

- **5 pounds (about) 100% natural lump charcoal**
- **4 cups (about) oak or hickory-wood smoke chips, soaked in cold water at least 30 minutes**

- **1 cup purchased barbecue sauce (such as Bull's-Eye)**
- **1 tablespoon chili powder**

FOR DRY RUB: Mix first 5 ingredients in small bowl to combine. Transfer 1 tablespoon dry rub to another small bowl and reserve for mop.

SPREAD remaining dry rub all over brisket. Place brisket on rimmed baking sheet. Cover with plastic wrap and chill overnight.

FOR MOP: Mix first 6 ingredients plus 1 tablespoon reserved dry rub in heavy medium nonreactive saucepan. Stir over low heat 5 minutes. Pour ½ cup mop into small bowl; cover, chill, and reserve for sauce. Cover and chill remaining mop in saucepan.

FOLLOWING manufacturer's instructions and using some of natural lump charcoal, start fire in smoker. When charcoal is ash-gray, drain ½ cup wood chips and scatter over charcoal. Bring smoker to 200°F to 225°F, regulating temperature by opening vents wider to increase temperature and closing slightly to reduce temperature.

PLACE brisket, fat side up, on rack in smoker. Cover and cook until tender and meat thermometer inserted into center registers 185°F, about 10 hours (turn brisket over for last 30 minutes). Every 1½ to 2 hours, add enough charcoal to maintain single layer and to maintain 200°F to 225°F temperature, and add ½ cup drained wood chips. Brush brisket with chilled mop in saucepan each time smoker is opened. Transfer brisket to platter; let stand 15 minutes. *(Can be made 1 day ahead. Cool 1 hour. Wrap in aluminum foil and chill. Before continuing, rewarm brisket, still wrapped, in 350°F oven about 45 minutes.)*

COMBINE barbecue sauce and chili powder in heavy small saucepan. Add any accumulated juices from brisket and bring to boil, thinning sauce with some of reserved ½ cup mop if desired.

THINLY slice brisket across grain. Arrange on platter. Serve, passing sauce separately.

Rib roast with fresh thyme-mustard jus

HERE IS A CLASSIC special-occasion main course: The rib roast may be the finest and most impressive cut of meat. And the boneless rib roast, trimmed of the cap meat and excess fat, features only the tender rib-eye meat. As in this recipe, the roast needs little adornment to let the incredible flavor and texture come through.

6 SERVINGS

½ cup honey-Dijon mustard
3 teaspoons chopped fresh thyme, divided
1 3½- to 4-pound boneless prime rib beef roast, excess fat trimmed

½ cup water
¼ cup dry white wine

MIX mustard and 2 teaspoons thyme in small bowl. Place beef in heavy large roasting pan. Coat beef with mustard mixture. Cover and let stand 1½ hours at room temperature or refrigerate overnight.

PREHEAT oven to 375°F. Scrape marinade off beef; reserve marinade. Roast beef 1 hour. Brush reserved marinade over beef. Roast until thermometer inserted into center of meat registers 120°F for rare, about 10 minutes longer. Transfer beef to cutting board. Tent loosely with aluminum foil to keep warm and let stand 15 minutes.

POUR pan juices into 1-cup glass measuring cup. Spoon off fat from top of pan juices. Return juices to same roasting pan. Place pan atop 2 burners on medium-high heat. Add ½ cup water and wine. Boil until juices are reduced to ½ cup, scraping up any browned bits. Stir in remaining 1 teaspoon thyme. Season pan juices to taste with salt and pepper. Cut beef crosswise into ½-inch-thick slices. Arrange on platter. Sprinkle with salt and pepper. Serve beef with reduced pan juices.

Grilled tri-tip roast with tequila marinade and cherry tomato relish

THE TRI-TIP comes from the bottom of the sirloin and features less marbling than the top sirloin steak. It has excellent meaty flavor, which stands up well to this assertive marinade. Let it marinate at least two hours before grilling.

8 SERVINGS

- **½ cup fresh lime juice**
- **⅓ cup chopped fresh cilantro**
- **½ cup olive oil**
- **⅓ cup soy sauce**
- **¼ cup tequila**
- **7 garlic cloves, finely chopped**
- **2 teaspoons grated lime peel**
- **2 teaspoons ground cumin**
- **2 teaspoons dried oregano**
- **1 teaspoon ground black pepper**
- **2 2-pound beef loin tri-tip roasts, trimmed**

Cherry Tomato Relish (see recipe)

WHISK first 10 ingredients in medium bowl to blend for marinade. Using small sharp knife, pierce meat all over. Place meat in large resealable plastic bag; add marinade. Seal bag. Refrigerate at least 2 hours or overnight, turning bag occasionally.

PREPARE barbecue (medium-high heat). Remove meat from marinade; discard marinade. Grill meat to desired doneness, about 10 minutes per side for medium-rare. Transfer to cutting board. Tent loosely with aluminum foil; let stand 10 minutes. Cut meat thinly across grain on slight diagonal. Arrange meat on platter; serve with tomato relish.

Cherry tomato relish

THIS SPRIGHTLY RELISH can accessorize a variety of grilled meats, chicken, or fish.

MAKES ABOUT 4 CUPS

- **¼ cup balsamic vinegar**
- **4 teaspoons chopped fresh oregano**
- **¾ cup olive oil**
- **⅔ cup drained canned diced mild green chiles (about 6 ounces)**
- **4 green onions, finely chopped**
- **4 cups halved cherry tomatoes (about 20 ounces)**

WHISK vinegar and oregano in medium bowl to blend. Gradually whisk in oil. Mix in chiles and green onions. *(Relish base can be made 6 hours ahead. Cover and chill.)* Add tomatoes to relish base and toss to combine. Season to taste with salt and pepper.

Roast prime rib with Madeira sauce and horseradish-chive sauce

A SIMPLY SEASONED and prepared prime rib is paired with two contrasting yet complementary sauces: One features Madeira, a medium-sweet fortified wine from Portugal; the other stars horseradish, a classic beef accompaniment, combined with crème fraîche, chives, and lemon juice. You'll want a hearty red wine, such as Cabernet Sauvignon, to go with this dish.

8 SERVINGS

- **1 9- to 9½-pound prime rib beef roast, excess fat trimmed**
- **1 tablespoon olive oil**
- **6 medium onions, peeled, quartered**

- **2½ cups beef broth**
- **1¾ cups Madeira**

1¼ cups dry red wine
4 large fresh thyme sprigs
4 large fresh parsley sprigs
3 large fresh rosemary sprigs
1 bay leaf

2 tablespoons (¼ stick) butter, room temperature
2 tablespoons all purpose flour
Horseradish-Chive Sauce (see recipe)

POSITION rack in center of oven and preheat to 450°F. Place beef, fat side up, on heavy large rimmed baking sheet. Rub with oil; sprinkle generously with salt and pepper. Roast beef 20 minutes. Reduce oven temperature to 350°F. Place onions on sheet around beef. Continue to roast until thermometer inserted into center of meat registers 125°F for rare, stirring onions occasionally, about 2 hours 5 minutes.

MEANWHILE, combine broth, Madeira, wine, thyme, parsley, rosemary, and bay leaf in heavy large saucepan. Boil until mixture is reduced to 2 cups, about 25 minutes. Remove Madeira sauce from heat. Discard herbs.

TRANSFER beef to platter. Using slotted spoon, transfer onions to same platter; tent loosely with aluminum foil to keep warm. Let stand 30 minutes.

POUR off fat from baking sheet. Scrape juices and any browned bits from baking sheet into sauce; bring to boil. Mix butter and flour in small bowl to combine. Whisk into sauce. Simmer until sauce is smooth and slightly thickened, whisking occasionally, about 2 minutes. Season sauce to taste with salt and pepper. Carve beef and serve with Madeira and Horseradish-Chive sauces.

Horseradish-chive sauce

HORSERADISH FANS WILL love this simple sauce, which you can use with your favorite meat or fish dishes.

MAKES ABOUT 2 CUPS

1½ cups crème fraîche or sour cream (about 12 ounces)
½ cup prepared white horseradish
6 tablespoons chopped fresh chives
4 teaspoons fresh lemon juice

WHISK all ingredients to blend in small bowl. Season sauce to taste with salt and pepper. *(Can be made 2 days ahead. Cover and chill.)*

Roast prime rib au poivre

AU POIVRE MEANS the dish is prepared with pepper, and there's plenty of it in this very special roast. If possible, buy the prime rib from a butcher who carries dry-aged beef: It's more tender, flavorful, and juicy than the unaged variety. Crushing the peppercorns in a plastic bag helps contain the pepper and simplifies clean-up.

8 SERVINGS

1 9-pound prime rib beef roast (about 4 ribs), excess fat trimmed
2 tablespoons Dijon mustard
4 teaspoons minced garlic
2 tablespoons plus 1 teaspoon mixed whole peppercorns, coarsely crushed

⅓ cup minced shallots
3½ cups beef broth
⅓ cup Cognac or brandy

POSITION oven rack in center of oven and preheat to 450°F. Place beef, fat side up, in shallow roasting pan. Sprinkle beef all over with salt. Mix mustard and garlic in small bowl. Spread mustard mixture over top of beef. Sprinkle 2 tablespoons crushed peppercorns over mustard mixture.

ROAST beef 15 minutes. Reduce oven temperature to 325°F. Roast until meat thermometer inserted into center of meat registers 125°F for rare, tenting loosely with aluminum foil if crust browns too quickly, about 2 hours 45 minutes. Transfer beef to platter. Tent loosely with foil to keep warm. Let stand 30 minutes.

POUR pan juices into 2-cup glass measuring cup (reserve roasting pan). Spoon off fat from top of pan juices, returning 1 tablespoon fat to roasting pan. Reserve pan juices.

PLACE roasting pan over 2 burners on medium-high heat. Add shallots and sauté until soft, scraping up any browned bits from bottom of pan, about 2 minutes. Remove pan from heat. Add beef broth, then Cognac or brandy (mixture may ignite). Return pan to heat and boil until mixture is reduced to 2 cups, stirring occasionally, about 15 minutes. Add reserved pan juices and remaining 1 teaspoon crushed peppercorns; whisk to blend. Transfer pan juices to sauceboat.

CARVE roast and serve with pan juices.

Roast tenderloin of beef with mushroom-port sauce

THE FILET, or tenderloin, is known for its tenderness (hence the name) and its mild flavor. The intensity of the sauce in this recipe—a Port and red wine reduction paired with sautéed wild mushrooms and onions—provides an excellent counterpoint to the meat.

10 SERVINGS

- **2 750-ml bottles dry red wine (such as Cabernet Sauvignon)**
- **1 750-ml bottle tawny Port**
- **4 cups beef broth**

- **6 tablespoons (¾ stick) butter, divided**
- **1½ pounds onions, chopped**
- **2 tablespoons chopped fresh thyme or 2 teaspoons dried**
- **2 pounds assorted fresh wild mushrooms (such as crimini and stemmed shiitake), thickly sliced**
- **2 tablespoons all purpose flour**
- **2 2- to 2¼-pound well-trimmed beef tenderloin roasts (from center or thick end)**
- **2 tablespoons olive oil**

BOIL wine, Port, and broth in heavy large pot until reduced to 6 cups, about 40 minutes.

MEANWHILE, melt 4 tablespoons butter in heavy large skillet over medium-high heat. Add onions and sauté until soft, about 15 minutes. Mix in thyme and sauté until onions are deep brown, about 10 minutes longer. Transfer onions to bowl. Melt remaining 2 tablespoons butter in same skillet. Add mushrooms and sauté until tender, about 15 minutes. Return onions to skillet. Add flour and stir 3 minutes. Stir mushroom mixture into wine mixture in pot. Simmer sauce over medium heat until thickened and reduced to 6 cups, stirring occasionally, about 1 hour. Season sauce to taste with salt and pepper. *(Can be prepared 1 day ahead. Refrigerate until cold, then cover and keep refrigerated.)*

PREHEAT oven to 400°F. Rub tenderloins with oil. Sprinkle with salt and pepper. Place in roasting pan. Roast until thermometer inserted into thickest part of meat registers 125°F for rare, about 40 minutes. Remove from oven and let stand 15 minutes.

REWARM sauce over low heat; mix in any juices from roasting pan. Cut tenderloins crosswise into ½-inch-thick slices. Overlap beef slices on platter. Spoon some sauce over. Serve, passing remaining sauce.

Herb- and garlic-crusted beef tenderloin with red and yellow bell pepper relish

A MIXTURE OF garlic, thyme, rosemary, and Dijon mustard coats the beef before it goes in the oven, creating a delicious crust for the roast.

10 SERVINGS

- **8 tablespoons olive oil, divided**
- **2 2¼- to 2¾-pound trimmed beef tenderloin roasts (from center or thick end)**

- **6 garlic cloves, minced**
- **2½ tablespoons minced fresh thyme, divided**
- **2½ tablespoons minced fresh rosemary, divided**
- **6 tablespoons Dijon mustard**

Red and Yellow Bell Pepper Relish (see recipe)

PREHEAT oven to 375°F. Rub 1 tablespoon oil over each beef roast. Sprinkle with salt and pepper. Heat 2 large nonstick skillets over high heat. Add 1 roast to each; brown beef on all sides, about 10 minutes.

PLACE beef roasts in large roasting pan. Mix remaining 6 tablespoons oil, garlic, 2 tablespoons thyme, and 2 tablespoons rosemary in small bowl. Coat top and sides of beef pieces with mustard, then herb mixture. Roast until meat thermometer inserted into center of meat registers 125°F for rare, about 45 minutes. Transfer to platter. Let stand 15 minutes.

CUT beef crosswise into ½-inch-thick slices. Sprinkle with remaining ½ tablespoon each thyme and rosemary; serve with bell pepper relish.

Red and yellow bell pepper relish

THIS RELISH would be outstanding with most roasted meats, and also as a topper for crostini. Begin preparing it one day ahead.

MAKES ABOUT 2 CUPS

- **2 tablespoons (¼ stick) butter**
- **2 tablespoons olive oil**
- **1 large onion, thinly sliced**
- **1 red bell pepper, coarsely chopped**
- **1 yellow bell pepper, coarsely chopped**
- **⅓ cup coarsely chopped pitted Kalamata olives**
- **1 tablespoon Dijon mustard**
- **1 garlic clove, chopped**

MELT butter with oil in heavy large skillet over medium-high heat. Add onion and sauté until golden, about 5 minutes. Add all peppers and sauté until just tender, about 3 minutes. Add olives, mustard, and garlic; stir 1 minute. Remove from heat. Season to taste with salt and pepper. Transfer relish to bowl. Cool, then cover and refrigerate overnight. *(Relish can be made 2 days ahead. Keep refrigerated.)* Bring to room temperature before serving.

Beef tenderloin with Italian green herb salsa

YOU'VE GOT the best of both worlds here: vibrant flavors (thyme, capers, parsley, shallots) and a dish that's simple to prepare. But while it's not complicated, it still requires some time—after the tenderloin has been rolled in the spice mixture, it needs to chill for three hours.

6 SERVINGS

- **3 tablespoons chopped fresh thyme, divided**
- **2 tablespoons coarse kosher salt**
- **1 tablespoon ground black pepper**
- **1 2½-pound trimmed beef tenderloin roast**

- **¾ cup extra-virgin olive oil**
- **2 tablespoons drained capers**
- **2 tablespoons chopped fresh Italian parsley**
- **2 tablespoons chopped shallot**

- **1 tablespoon vegetable oil**

SPRINKLE 2 tablespoons thyme, coarse salt, and pepper on baking sheet. Roll tenderloin in spice mixture to coat. Cover and chill 3 hours.

MIX olive oil, capers, parsley, shallot, and remaining 1 tablespoon thyme in small bowl to combine. Season salsa to taste with salt and pepper. Let stand 1 hour.

PREHEAT oven to 400°F. Heat vegetable oil in heavy large skillet over high heat. Add tenderloin; cook until brown on all sides, about 10 minutes. Transfer to rimmed baking sheet. Roast until thermometer inserted into center of meat registers 125°F for rare, about 12 minutes. Remove from oven and let stand 15 minutes. Slice tenderloin and serve with salsa.

Roast New York strip loin with garlic-herb crust

ALSO CALLED top loin of beef, the New York strip loin is a succulent, elegant roast. At the market, have your butcher trim some of the fat, leaving about a quarter of an inch, for the best flavor. If you'd like to have enough for left-overs, use a seven-pound roast and multiply the seasonings by one and a half.

10 SERVINGS

- **4 garlic cloves**
- **8 fresh sage leaves**
- **4 teaspoons fresh thyme leaves**
- **4 teaspoons olive oil**
- **4 teaspoons salt**
- **1½ teaspoons ground black pepper**

- **1 4- to 5-pound boneless New York strip loin (beef top loin) roast, fat trimmed to ¼ inch**

WITH machine running, drop garlic into processor through feed tube and chop finely. Scrape down sides of bowl. Add sage, thyme, oil, salt, and pepper; process until paste forms.

PAT meat dry with paper towels. Place meat, fat side up, on rack in roasting pan. Rub meat all over with herb paste. Cover and chill at least 3 hours and up to 1 day.

PREHEAT oven to 450°F. Uncover meat and roast 15 minutes. Reduce oven temperature to 350°F. Roast until instant-read thermometer inserted into thickest part of meat registers 130°F for medium-rare, about 35 minutes (or 140°F for medium, about 40 minutes). Remove from oven; let stand 20 minutes. Cut meat crosswise into ⅓-inch-thick slices. Arrange slices on platter and serve.

Stir-fried lemongrass beef with Asian greens

FREEZING THE TOP SIRLOIN for 30 minutes makes it firm and easier to slice thinly before marinating. The marinade itself is made up of a number of classic Asian ingredients, including lemongrass and the fermented fish sauce known in Thailand as *nam pla;* fish sauce can be found at Asian markets and in the Asian foods section of some supermarkets. The mustard greens and bok choy are treated like a salad, tossed with red onions and opal basil, which has purple leaves and a milder flavor than sweet basil; it is available at Asian markets and some supermarkets.

6 SERVINGS

- **1½ pounds beef top sirloin steak, fat trimmed, cut lengthwise in half**
- **3 tablespoons minced fresh lemongrass (from about 4 large stalks)**
- **4 tablespoons Thai fish sauce (nam pla), divided**
- **1½ tablespoons soy sauce**
- **1½ teaspoons sugar, divided**
- **3 garlic cloves, minced**

- **4 tablespoons peanut oil, divided**
- **3 tablespoons fresh lime juice**
- **1 large shallot, minced**
- **1 tablespoon minced seeded serrano chile**

- **1 bunch mustard greens, torn into 1-inch pieces**
- **1 head of bok choy, torn into 1-inch pieces**
- **2 cups thinly sliced red onions**
- **1 cup (packed) fresh opal basil leaves or regular basil leaves**

FREEZE beef 30 minutes. Using large knife, thinly slice beef crosswise. Mix meat, lemongrass, 3 tablespoons fish sauce, soy sauce, ¾ teaspoon sugar, and garlic in large bowl. Sprinkle generously with black pepper. Let stand at room temperature 30 minutes or cover and chill up to 3 hours, tossing occasionally.

WHISK 3 tablespoons oil, lime juice, shallot, chile, and remaining 1 tablespoon fish sauce and ¾ teaspoon sugar in small bowl to blend. Season dressing to taste with salt and pepper. Let stand at room temperature 30 minutes.

PLACE mustard greens, bok choy, onions, and basil in large bowl. Add ¾ of dressing; toss to coat. Season salad to taste with salt and pepper.

HEAT remaining 1 tablespoon oil in heavy large skillet over high heat. Working in 2 batches, stir-fry beef until cooked to desired doneness, about 35 seconds per batch for rare. Add to salad. Add remaining dressing, toss to combine, and serve.

Beef short ribs in chipotle and green chile sauce

SLOW BRAISING makes this "offcut" of beef moist and tender. Buy ribs with a thick, solid portion of meat on the bone. The robust flavor of the short ribs stands up well to the chipotle and Anaheim chiles in the sauce. You'll find Anaheim chiles and chipotles, the latter canned in a spicy tomato sauce called *adobo*, at Latin markets, specialty foods stores, and some supermarkets.

4 SERVINGS

1 teaspoon salt
1 teaspoon ground black pepper
1 teaspoon ground cumin
1 teaspoon chili powder
½ teaspoon ground coriander
8 3-inch-long meaty beef short ribs
2 tablespoons olive oil
1½ cups chopped onion
6 garlic cloves, minced
1 14-ounce can low-salt chicken broth
1 cup drained canned diced tomatoes
¼ cup fresh lime juice
1½ tablespoons chopped canned chipotle chiles

3 large fresh Anaheim (California) chiles, stemmed, seeded, cut into ¼-inch-thick rings
Chopped fresh cilantro
Lime wedges

MIX salt and next 4 ingredients in bowl; sprinkle all over short ribs. Place ribs on plate; cover and refrigerate 1 hour. *(Can be prepared 1 day ahead. Keep refrigerated.)*

PREHEAT oven to 350°F. Heat oil in large ovenproof pot over medium-high heat. Add half of ribs and brown on all sides, about 9 minutes; transfer to plate. Repeat with remaining ribs. Reduce heat to medium. Add onion and garlic to same pot; cover and cook until onion is soft, stirring occasionally, about 5 minutes. Add broth and bring to boil, scraping up any browned bits. Add tomatoes, lime juice, and chipotle chiles. Return ribs to pot, meaty side down, in single layer. Bring to boil; cover and cook in oven until ribs are just tender, about 1½ hours.

REMOVE pot from oven. Tilt pot and spoon off fat. Place pot over medium heat and simmer uncovered until sauce coats spoon and ribs are very tender, about 25 minutes. Season sauce with salt and pepper. *(Can be prepared 1 day ahead. Cool 30 minutes, refrigerate uncovered until cold, and then cover and keep refrigerated.)*

BRING ribs to simmer over medium heat; add chile rings. Simmer until chiles soften, about 10 minutes. Transfer ribs and sauce to large bowl. Sprinkle with cilantro; garnish with lime wedges and serve.

Morel-crusted beef short ribs with polenta

DRIED MOREL MUSHROOMS lend their earthy, smoky flavor to both the sauce and the breadcrumb crust for the short ribs. The ribs can be braised one day ahead then topped with the morel-breadcrumb mixture shortly before you serve them.

4 SERVINGS

1 ounce dried morel mushrooms
1½ cups boiling water

2 teaspoons chopped fresh thyme, divided
1 teaspoon chopped fresh rosemary
1 teaspoon salt
1 teaspoon ground black pepper
3½ to 4 pounds meaty beef short ribs (each 3 to 4 inches long), fat and membranes trimmed
2 tablespoons olive oil

1 large onion, chopped
1 medium carrot, peeled, chopped
1½ ounces prosciutto, finely chopped
3 garlic cloves, minced
1 cup dry white wine
2 cups low-salt chicken broth
1 bay leaf

2 tablespoons (¼ stick) butter, room temperature
2 cups fresh breadcrumbs made from crustless French bread
¼ cup (about) Dijon mustard

Polenta (see recipe)

PLACE morels in small bowl. Pour 1½ cups boiling water over; let soak until mushrooms soften, at least 40 minutes and up to 4 hours. Drain mushrooms, reserving soaking liquid. Rinse mushrooms under cold water to remove any dirt, if necessary.

PREHEAT oven to 350°F. Mix 1 teaspoon thyme, rosemary, salt, and pepper in small bowl. Rub herb mixture all over short ribs. Heat oil in heavy large ovenproof pot over medium-high heat. Working in batches, add ribs to pot and cook until brown on all sides, about 10 minutes per batch. Transfer ribs to large bowl.

POUR off all but 2 tablespoons fat from pot. Reduce heat to medium. Add onion, carrot, prosciutto, and garlic to pot; sauté until vegetables begin to soften, about 5 minutes. Add wine and bring to boil, scraping up any browned bits from bottom of pot. Add broth, bay leaf, morel mushrooms, reserved morel soaking liquid (leaving any sediment behind), and remaining 1 teaspoon thyme to pot. Return ribs to pot, arranging meat side down in single layer. Bring to boil; cover pot tightly and transfer to oven. Bake until ribs are very tender, about 1 hour 45 minutes. Remove from oven. *(Ribs can be braised 1 day ahead. Uncover and cool slightly. Refrigerate uncovered until cold, then cover and keep chilled. Rewarm enough to loosen ribs from sauce before continuing.)*

PREHEAT oven to 450°F. Using tongs, transfer ribs to large roasting pan, bone side down; reserve pot. Remove 5 large morels from pot and chop finely. Place in medium bowl. Add butter and mix with fork to blend. Mix in breadcrumbs. Season mixture to taste with salt and pepper. Spread mustard over top of each rib. Spread breadcrumb mixture over mustard on each rib, pressing to adhere. Bake ribs until topping is crisp and golden, about 10 minutes.

MEANWHILE, spoon off any fat from top of sauce in pot and discard. Boil sauce until slightly thickened and reduced to generous 2 cups, about 10 minutes. Season sauce to taste with salt and pepper.

SPOON polenta into bowls. Top with short ribs. Spoon sauce over and serve.

Polenta

POLENTA, OR COARSE CORNMEAL, is sold at Italian markets, natural foods stores, and some supermarkets. If it's unavailable, substitute an equal amount of regular yellow cornmeal and cook it about half as long.

4 SERVINGS

6 cups water, divided
1½ cups polenta (coarse cornmeal)
1 teaspoon salt

WHISK 1½ cups water, polenta, and salt in heavy large saucepan to combine. Stir over medium heat until mixture comes to simmer. Gradually whisk in remaining 4½ cups water. Bring to boil, whisking polenta often. Reduce heat to low, cover, and cook until polenta is thick, soft, and creamy, whisking often, about 30 minutes.

Provençal-style short ribs with crème fraîche mashed potatoes

HUMBLE SHORT RIBS get dressed up for a dinner party. Ask your butcher for meaty short ribs that are three to four inches long; they make a handsome presentation. *Herbes de Provence* is a dried herb mixture featuring lavender, the essence of the region. It is available at specialty foods stores and in the spice section of some markets; you may substitute a mix of dried thyme, basil, savory, and fennel seeds. Niçoise olives are small brine-cured black olives, available at Italian markets, specialty foods stores, and some supermarkets; Kalamata olives can be used instead.

6 SERVINGS

2 tablespoons (or more) olive oil
6 pounds meaty beef short ribs (each 3 to 4 inches long), fat and membranes trimmed
1 large onion, finely chopped
1 medium carrot, peeled, finely chopped
1 celery stalk, finely chopped
12 whole garlic cloves, peeled
2 tablespoons all purpose flour
1 tablespoon dried herbes de Provence
2½ cups beef broth, divided
2 cups dry red wine (such as Zinfandel)
1 14.5-ounce can diced tomatoes in juice
1 bay leaf
½ cup (about) water

24 baby carrots, peeled
½ cup Niçoise olives, pitted
3 tablespoons chopped fresh parsley
Crème Fraîche Mashed Potatoes (see recipe)

PREHEAT oven to 325°F. Heat 2 tablespoons oil in heavy large ovenproof pot over medium-high heat. Sprinkle ribs with salt and pepper. Working in batches, add ribs to pot and brown well, turning often, about 8 minutes per batch. Using tongs, transfer ribs to large bowl.

POUR off all but 2 tablespoons drippings from pot or add oil if necessary to measure 2 tablespoons. Add onion, chopped carrot, and celery; cook over medium-low heat until vegetables are soft, stirring frequently, about 10 minutes. Add garlic, flour, and herbes de Provence; stir 1 minute. Add 2 cups broth and wine; bring to boil over high heat, scraping up any browned bits. Add tomatoes with juice and bay leaf. Return ribs and any accumulated juices to pot, arranging meat side down in single layer. If necessary, add enough water to pot to barely cover ribs. Return to boil.

COVER pot tightly and transfer to oven. Bake until ribs are very tender, stirring occasionally, about 2 hours. *(Ribs can be prepared 1 day ahead. Cool slightly; refrigerate uncovered until cold, then cover and keep refrigerated. Bring to simmer before continuing.)*

PREHEAT oven to 350°F. Add remaining ½ cup broth, baby carrots, and olives to pot; press carrots gently to submerge. Cover pot, return to oven, and continue cooking until carrots are tender, about 15 minutes. Transfer short ribs and carrots to platter; tent loosely with aluminum foil to keep warm. Discard bay leaf. If desired, tilt pot and spoon off fat from top of sauce, then boil sauce to thicken slightly. Season sauce to taste with salt and pepper. Pour sauce over short ribs and carrots. Sprinkle with parsley. Serve with mashed potatoes.

Crème fraîche mashed potatoes

THESE RICH AND MILD mashed potatoes contrast perfectly with the robust short rib sauce. Indeed, they'd be excellent paired with most beef or lamb stews.

6 SERVINGS

- **3½ pounds russet potatoes, peeled, quartered**
- **⅔ cup crème fraîche or sour cream (about 5½ ounces)**
- **¼ cup (½ stick) butter**

COOK potatoes in large pot of boiling salted water until just tender, about 25 minutes. Drain. Return potatoes to same pot. Add crème fraîche and butter; mash until smooth. Season to taste with salt and pepper. *(Potatoes can be made 2 hours ahead. Let stand at room temperature. Rewarm over low heat, stirring frequently.)*

Beef short rib tagine with honey-glazed buttternut squash

DRIED FRUITS AND HONEY are teamed with meat dishes of all kinds in Moroccan cooking, and in this rich stew, or tagine, the dates, dried pears, and honey impart complex flavor and sweetness. The ribs can be prepared two days ahead, and then simply reheated before serving.

8 SERVINGS

Short ribs

- **5 tablespoons olive oil, divided**
- **1 pound onions, chopped**
- **16 3- to 4-inch-long meaty beef short ribs, fat and membranes trimmed**
- **3 tablespoons all purpose flour**
- **4 cups low-salt chicken broth, divided**
- **1½ cups dry red wine**
- **1 cup prune juice**
- **1 tablespoon tomato paste**
- **½ teaspoon ground cumin**
- **½ teaspoon ground allspice**
- **½ teaspoon ground ginger**
- **½ teaspoon ground cinnamon**
- **2 ounces pitted dates, diced (about ⅓ cup)**
- **2 ounces dried pears, diced (about ⅓ cup)**
- **1 tablespoon honey**

Squash

- **¼ cup olive oil**
- **2 medium butternut squash, peeled, seeded, cut into ¾-inch cubes (about 6 cups)**
- **¼ cup honey**
- **Fresh parsley sprigs**

FOR SHORT RIBS: Preheat oven to 325°F. Heat 3 tablespoons oil in heavy large ovenproof pot over medium-high heat. Add onions and sauté until brown, about 20 minutes. Using slotted spoon, transfer onions to large bowl. Sprinkle short ribs with salt and pepper. Add 1 tablespoon oil to same pot. Add 8 short ribs and brown on all sides, about 10 minutes. Transfer ribs to bowl with onions. Add remaining 1 tablespoon oil to pot. Add remaining 8 ribs and brown on all sides, about 10 minutes. Transfer ribs to same bowl.

WHISK flour into drippings in pot. Whisk in 2 cups broth. Bring to boil, scraping up browned bits. Mix in remaining 2 cups broth, wine, prune juice, tomato paste, and spices. Return ribs to pot, arranging close together on sides in single layer if possible. Add dates and pears, then onions and accumulated juices.

BRING to boil. Cover pot and transfer to oven; bake until ribs are tender, about 1 hour 45 minutes.

USING tongs, transfer ribs to large bowl. Strain cooking liquid into medium bowl, pressing on solids in strainer to release as much liquid as possible. Tilt bowl and spoon off fat from surface. Return liquid to pot. Add 1 tablespoon honey; boil until sauce is reduced to 3 cups and thick enough to coat spoon, about 12 minutes. Season to taste with salt and pepper. Return ribs to pot, spooning sauce over to coat. *(Short ribs can be made 2 days ahead. Refrigerate uncovered until cold; then cover and keep chilled.)*

FOR SQUASH: Heat oil in heavy large nonstick skillet over medium heat. Add squash; cover and cook until squash is just tender and beginning to brown, stirring occasionally, about 12 minutes. Add ¼ cup honey; toss until squash is glazed. Season to taste with salt and pepper.

REWARM ribs over medium-low heat, stirring occasionally. Mound ribs on platter. Top with squash; garnish with parsley and serve.

Beer-braised beef short ribs with spicy molasses mop

A MOP IS A thin basting sauce, in this case a slightly sweet and spicy blend of molasses and hot pepper sauce. After the braising process, which produces lusciously tender meat, the ribs are given a ten-minute finish on the grill, creating a crispy exterior while the mop glazes them a rich dark brown.

6 SERVINGS

- **5 pounds meaty beef short ribs (each 3 to 4 inches long), fat and membranes trimmed**
- **3½ cups beef broth**
- **1 12-ounce bottle dark beer**
- **1 medium onion, sliced**
- **2 teaspoons salt, divided**
- **½ teaspoon dried thyme**
- **¼ cup mild-flavored (light) molasses**
- **2 tablespoons balsamic vinegar**
- **2½ teaspoons hot pepper sauce**

PREHEAT oven to 350°F. Combine first 4 ingredients in heavy large pot; add 1 teaspoon salt and thyme. Bring to boil over medium heat. Cover pot and transfer to oven; bake until ribs are very tender, turning occasionally, about 2 hours 50 minutes. Uncover and cool 1 hour. Refrigerate uncovered until cold. *(Ribs can be prepared 2 days ahead. Cover and keep refrigerated.)*

SPOON off fat from surface of braising liquid. Rewarm ribs enough to loosen from liquid. Remove short ribs and pat dry. Combine ¼ cup braising liquid, molasses, vinegar, hot pepper sauce, and remaining 1 teaspoon salt in small bowl for mop.

PREPARE barbecue (medium heat). Place ribs on grill. Close grill lid or cover ribs with heavy-duty aluminum foil. Grill until ribs are crisp and heated through, turning and basting frequently with mop, about 10 minutes. Transfer ribs to platter and serve.

Beef Stroganoff

ALTHOUGH THIS RUSSIAN DISH has been around for centuries, it wasn't until the 1950s that it caught on in the United States. This modern rendition pays tribute to the classic, while featuring twenty-first century sophistication with Cognac, Dijon mustard, and an elegant cut of meat.

4 SERVINGS

- **1 2½-pound well-trimmed beef tenderloin roast, cut into 2x1x½-inch strips**
- **2 tablespoons vegetable oil**
- **6 tablespoons (¾ stick) butter, room temperature, divided**
- **¼ cup finely chopped shallots**
- **1 pound mushrooms, thickly sliced**

1 cup beef broth
2 tablespoons Cognac or brandy
3/4 cup crème fraîche or whipping cream (about 6 ounces)
1 tablespoon Dijon mustard
1 tablespoon chopped fresh dill

12 ounces wide egg noodles
1 tablespoon Hungarian sweet paprika

SPRINKLE meat with salt and pepper. Heat oil in heavy large skillet over high heat until very hot. Working in batches, add meat in single layer and cook just until brown, about 1 minute per side. Using tongs, transfer meat to rimmed baking sheet.

MELT 2 tablespoons butter in same skillet over medium-high heat. Add shallots and sauté until tender, scraping up any browned bits, about 2 minutes. Add mushrooms. Sprinkle with pepper and sauté until mushrooms brown and juices evaporate, about 12 minutes. Add broth, then Cognac. Simmer until sauce thickens and just coats mushrooms, stirring occasionally, about 14 minutes. Stir in crème fraîche and mustard. Add meat and any accumulated juices from baking sheet. Simmer over medium-low heat until meat is heated through but still medium-rare, about 2 minutes. Stir in chopped dill. Season to taste with salt and pepper.

MEANWHILE, cook noodles in large pot of boiling salted water until tender, but still firm to bite, stirring occasionally. Drain. Transfer hot noodles to bowl. Add remaining 4 tablespoons butter and toss to coat. Season to taste with salt and pepper. Divide noodles among plates. Top with beef and sauce. Sprinkle generously with paprika.

Pork

Marmalade-glazed ham with sweet orange-tea sauce

USE A FULLY COOKED bone-in ham that has the natural shape of the leg, with some fat and rind still attached. Do not substitute a "re-formed" oval canned ham or a deli ham. The marmalade glaze and orange tea sauce provide a memorable variation on familiar honey glaze.

12 SERVINGS

Ham
1 16- to 19-pound smoked fully cooked bone-in ham
36 (about) whole cloves

1 cup orange marmalade
1/4 cup Dijon mustard
2 tablespoons plus 1 1/2 cups water

Sauce
2 cups water
4 orange-spice herb tea bags or orange-spice black tea bags
2 cups low-salt chicken broth
1 cup orange juice
3 tablespoons orange marmalade
1 tablespoon Dijon mustard
1 tablespoon cornstarch dissolved in 1 tablespoon water

Pineapple-Mint Relish (see recipe)

FOR HAM: Position rack in center of oven and preheat to 325°F. Trim any rind and excess fat from upper side of ham, leaving ¼-inch-thick layer. Using long sharp knife, score fat in 1-inch-wide diamond pattern. Insert 1 clove into center of each scored diamond. Place ham in heavy large roasting pan. Bake until thermometer inserted into center of ham registers 120°F, about 3 hours 45 minutes.

MELT 1 cup marmalade in heavy small saucepan over medium heat. Whisk in ¼ cup mustard and 2 tablespoons water. Boil until mixture thickens enough to coat spoon without dripping, about 6 minutes. Set glaze aside.

TRANSFER ham to cutting board. Increase oven temperature to 425°F. Place same roasting pan atop 2 burners on medium heat. Whisk remaining 1½ cups water into pan, scraping up any browned bits. Pour pan juices into 4-cup glass measuring cup. Spoon off fat from top of pan juices. Reserve pan juices.

LINE same pan with aluminum foil. Return ham to pan. Generously spread marmalade glaze over ham. Bake until glaze is set and beginning to caramelize, about 20 minutes. Let ham stand 30 minutes.

MEANWHILE, PREPARE SAUCE: Bring 2 cups water to boil in heavy medium saucepan. Add tea bags. Remove from heat, cover, and steep 10 minutes. Discard tea bags. Add broth, juice, and 3 tablespoons marmalade to tea. Boil mixture until reduced to 3 cups, about 12 minutes. Whisk in 1 tablespoon Dijon mustard and reserved degreased pan juices. Return to boil. Whisk in cornstarch mixture and boil until sauce thickens slightly, about 4 minutes. Season sauce to taste with pepper.

CARVE ham and serve with orange-tea sauce and Pineapple-Mint Relish.

Pineapple-mint relish

THIS REFRESHING COMBINATION of flavors is great with the ham; or try it with grilled fish or chicken.

MAKES 4 CUPS

- **½ large pineapple, peeled, cored, cut into ½-inch cubes (about 3 cups)**
- **½ cup finely chopped green bell pepper**
- **½ cup finely chopped red onion**
- **¼ cup chopped fresh mint**
- **2 teaspoons finely grated lemon peel**

STIR all ingredients in medium bowl to blend. Season relish to taste with salt and pepper. *(Can be made 1 day ahead. Cover and chill.)*

Gratin of endive and ham

GRATINS FEATURE a crust of melted cheese and sometimes breadcrumbs; they're often served as side dishes, but this sophisticated version (which forgoes the breadcrumbs) makes an excellent main course served with good bread and a salad.

4 SERVINGS

- **1 14-ounce can low-salt chicken broth**
- **8 small heads of Belgian endive**
- **8 thin round ham slices (each about 5 inches in diameter)**
- **3 tablespoons butter**
- **3 tablespoons all purpose flour**
- **1½ cups whole milk**
- **¼ cup whipping cream**
- **1½ tablespoons Dijon mustard**
- **Large pinch of ground nutmeg**
- **⅓ cup (packed) coarsely grated Swiss cheese (about 1½ ounces)**

BRING broth to simmer in heavy medium skillet over medium-high heat. Add endive and simmer uncovered until tender, turning occasionally, about 12 minutes. Drain thoroughly. Place endive on paper towels and cool.

PREHEAT oven to 350°F. Butter 11x7-inch glass baking dish. Roll each endive in ham slice to enclose. Arrange rolls in single layer in prepared dish. Melt butter in heavy medium saucepan over medium heat. Whisk in flour; cook 1 minute. Add milk, cream, mustard, and nutmeg; bring to boil, whisking constantly. Boil sauce 1 minute; season to taste with salt and pepper. Spoon sauce over rolls. Sprinkle Swiss cheese evenly over. Bake until sauce is bubbling all over and cheese is beginning to brown, about 30 minutes.

Grilled baby back pork ribs with mustard-bourbon sauce

THESE RIBS get their deep flavor not from hours of slow cooking but from an inventive spice rub and a delicious sauce that is a perfect mixture of sweet and spicy—with a dose of bourbon for good measure. Ancho chiles are sold at Latin markets, specialty foods stores, and some supermarkets. The recipe calls for whole racks of ribs, but if you can find only sections of four to six ribs, they will work fine. Don't buy ribs that have been overtrimmed on top and have bones showing. Begin preparing the ribs a day ahead of time so they can absorb the seasonings overnight after the spice rub has been applied.

4 TO 6 SERVINGS

Sauce

- **1 tablespoon vegetable oil**
- **2 bunches green onions, chopped (about 2¾ cups)**
- **2 cups chopped white onions**
- **8 garlic cloves, chopped**
- **2 cups (packed) golden brown sugar**
- **1 cup ketchup**
- **1 cup tomato paste (about 9 ounces)**
- **1 cup whole grain Dijon mustard**
- **1 cup water**
- **½ cup Worcestershire sauce**
- **½ cup apple cider vinegar**
- **½ cup apple juice**
- **1 large dried ancho chile, stemmed, seeded, cut into small pieces**
- **1 tablespoon ground cumin**
- **1½ cups bourbon**

Spice rub and ribs

- **2 tablespoons ground cumin**
- **1 tablespoon chili powder**
- **1 tablespoon dry mustard**
- **1 tablespoon coarse kosher salt**
- **1½ teaspoons cayenne pepper**
- **1½ teaspoons ground cardamom**
- **1½ teaspoons ground cinnamon**
- **6 pounds baby back pork ribs (3 to 4 whole racks)**

FOR SAUCE: Heat oil in heavy large pot over medium-low heat. Add green onions, white onions, and garlic; sauté until soft, about 15 minutes. Mix in all remaining ingredients, adding bourbon last. Simmer until sauce is thick and reduced to 7 cups, stirring occasionally, about 1 hour. Season sauce to taste with salt and pepper. *(Can be prepared 2 weeks ahead. Cover and refrigerate.)*

FOR SPICE RUB AND RIBS: Mix first 7 ingredients in medium bowl. Rub spice mixture over both sides of all rib racks. Arrange ribs on large baking sheet (they may overlap). Cover and refrigerate overnight.

PREPARE barbecue (medium heat). Cut rib racks into 4- to 6-rib sections. Arrange rib sections on barbecue. Grill until meat is tender, occasionally turning ribs with tongs, about 40 minutes. Using tongs, transfer ribs to work surface.

CUT rib sections between bones into individual ribs. Arrange ribs on clean baking sheet. Transfer 3 cups sauce to small bowl; place remaining sauce in small saucepan and reserve for serving. Brush ribs with sauce from bowl to coat.

RETURN ribs to barbecue. Place pan of reserved sauce at edge of barbecue to rewarm. Grill ribs until edges are brown and crisp, brushing with more sauce from bowl and turning occasionally, about 10 minutes. Mound ribs on platter. Serve ribs with warmed sauce.

Grilled spareribs with cherry cola glaze

BEFORE USING the cherry cola, be sure to pour it into a bowl and allow it to stand until it is no longer bubbling, about four hours. The cola is combined with cherry jam, Dijon mustard, soy sauce, malt vinegar, and hot pepper sauce for an unusual sweet and tangy glaze. Serve the ribs with something cold and thirst-quenching, like lager or iced tea.

6 SERVINGS

- **4 12-ounce cans cherry cola (flat)**
- **2 cups cherry jam or preserves**
- **2/3 cup Dijon mustard with horseradish**
- **3 tablespoons soy sauce**
- **2 tablespoons malt vinegar or apple cider vinegar**
- **1 tablespoon hot pepper sauce**

- **7 1/4 to 7 1/2 pounds well-trimmed pork spareribs**

BOIL cherry cola in heavy large saucepan over medium-high heat until reduced to 1½ cups, about 45 minutes. Stir in next 5 ingredients. Reduce heat to medium and simmer until mixture is reduced to 2½ cups, stirring occasionally, about 35 minutes. Transfer glaze to large bowl. *(Glaze can be made 1 week ahead. Cover and chill. Bring to room temperature before using.)*

POSITION oven racks in top third and bottom third of oven and preheat to 325°F. Sprinkle ribs with salt and pepper. Wrap each rib rack tightly in aluminum foil, enclosing completely. Divide foil packets between 2 large rimmed baking sheets. Bake until ribs are very tender, reversing positions of baking sheets halfway through baking, about 2 hours total. Cool ribs slightly in foil. Pour off any fat from foil packets. *(Ribs can be prepared 1 day ahead. Keep wrapped in foil packets and refrigerate. Let stand at room temperature 1 hour before continuing.)*

PREPARE barbecue (medium-low heat). Cut each rib rack between bones into individual ribs. Spoon 1 cup glaze into small bowl and reserve for serving. Add ribs to bowl with remaining glaze and toss to coat. Grill ribs until brown and glazed, turning to prevent burning, about 5 minutes total. Mound ribs on platter. Serve, passing reserved glaze separately.

Cider-brined pork chops with creamed leeks and apples

OVERNIGHT BRINING is a classic way to prepare pork, and it makes for tender and juicy meat. Since the leeks can be prepared a day ahead while the chops are brining, this is a terrific dinner-party dish.

4 SERVINGS

- **4 1/4 cups apple cider, divided**
- **3 tablespoons coarse kosher salt**
- **6 whole allspice**
- **1 bay leaf**
- **4 10-ounce center-cut pork rib chops**

- **4 tablespoons (1/2 stick) butter, divided**
- **5 large leeks (white and pale green parts only), thinly sliced**
- **1 cup whipping cream**

- **1 1/2 pounds Granny Smith apples, peeled, halved, cored, each half cut into 4 wedges**
- **2 tablespoons sugar**
- **1/2 cup low-salt chicken broth**
- **1/3 cup Calvados or other apple brandy**

- **Olive oil**

BRING 4 cups cider, salt, allspice, and bay leaf to boil in heavy large saucepan, stirring until salt dissolves. Cool brine completely. Place pork in 13x9x2-inch glass baking dish. Pour brine over. Cover and refrigerate overnight.

MELT 2 tablespoons butter in heavy large skillet over medium-low heat. Add leeks and sauté until soft, about 7 minutes. Add cream and simmer until slightly thickened, about 3 minutes. Season to taste with salt and pepper. *(Creamed leeks can be made 1 day ahead. Cover and chill.)*

MELT remaining 2 tablespoons butter in large non-stick skillet over medium heat. Add apples and sauté 10 minutes. Add sugar and sauté until apples are golden, about 6 minutes longer. Add broth, then Calvados and remaining ¼ cup cider. Simmer until sauce thickens slightly and apples are tender, stirring occasionally, about 5 minutes. Set aside.

PREPARE barbecue (medium heat) or preheat broiler. Drain pork. Rinse under cold water; pat dry. Brush pork with oil. Grill or broil to desired doneness, about 5 minutes per side for medium.

MEANWHILE, rewarm leeks, thinning with water by tablespoonfuls if too thick. Bring apples to simmer. Spoon leeks onto plates. Top with pork, then apples.

Pork chops in balsamic cherry sauce

BOTTLED BALSAMIC VINAIGRETTE is a sensational base for this sauce, which is enhanced with dried cherries and chopped shallot. This dish is a snap to prepare and can be a nice weeknight dinner, yet it is special enough for a weekend dinner party.

2 SERVINGS; CAN BE DOUBLED

- **2 5-ounce boneless pork chops (each about 1 inch thick)**
- **⅓ cup bottled balsamic vinaigrette**

- **1 tablespoon butter**
- **1 large shallot, thinly sliced**
- **⅓ cup low-salt chicken broth**
- **¼ cup dried Bing (sweet) or tart cherries (about 1½ ounces)**

PLACE pork and vinaigrette in glass pie dish; turn to coat. Let stand 10 minutes.

MELT butter in heavy medium skillet over medium heat. Using tongs, lift pork from marinade; shake off excess. Transfer pork to skillet, reserving marinade in dish. Sprinkle pork with pepper. Sauté until brown, about 3 minutes per side. Transfer pork to plate. Add shallot to skillet and stir until soft, about 1 minute. Add broth, cherries, and reserved marinade; bring to boil, scraping up any browned bits. Return pork to skillet. Simmer, turning pork once, until pork is cooked through, cherries are tender, and sauce is slightly thickened, about 4 minutes. Season sauce to taste with salt and pepper. Transfer pork to plates; top with sauce and serve.

Grilled Tuscan pork rib roast with rosemary coating and red bell pepper relish

THIS SOPHISTICATED (and amazingly easy) grilled pork roast is prepared in the Tuscan manner, with rosemary, garlic, and a hint of orange. The trick to getting this roast just right is using indirect heat, which cooks the meat more slowly, letting the inside reach the desired temperature without scorching the outside. It's like cooking in the oven, only you get that smoky, grilled flavor. The technique works best with a charcoal grill, but you can also use a gas grill as long as it has a built-in thermometer or a hole in the top for inserting a candy thermometer.

6 SERVINGS

Relish

- **1½ pounds red bell peppers (about 3 large)**
- **2 tablespoons drained capers**
- **1 tablespoon olive oil**
- **4 anchovies, chopped**
- **2 teaspoons grated orange peel**
- **2 teaspoons balsamic vinegar**
- **¼ teaspoon dried crushed red pepper**

Pork

- ½ cup fresh rosemary leaves (from about 2 large bunches)
- ⅓ cup olive oil
- 6 garlic cloves
- Peel from 1 orange (orange part only, removed in strips with vegetable peeler)
- 1 teaspoon salt
- ½ teaspoon ground black pepper
- 1 3½-pound center-cut pork rib roast (6 or 7 rib bones), excess fat trimmed

- 30 charcoal briquettes
- 1 9-inch-diameter disposable foil pan

FOR RELISH: Char peppers directly over gas flame or in broiler until blackened on all sides. Enclose in paper bag 10 minutes. Peel and seed peppers. Transfer peppers to processor; using on/off turns, chop peppers coarsely. Transfer peppers to bowl. Mix in remaining ingredients. Season relish to taste with salt and pepper. Let stand 1 hour. *(Relish can be prepared 1 day ahead. Cover and refrigerate.)*

FOR PORK: Combine rosemary, oil, garlic, orange peel strips, salt, and pepper in processor; blend until thick and almost smooth. Spread rosemary puree evenly all over pork. Let stand while preparing barbecue. *(Pork can be prepared 1 day ahead. Cover and chill. Bring to room temperature before continuing.)*

STAND charcoal chimney on nonflammable surface. Place torn newspaper in bottom of chimney; add charcoal briquettes. Light paper through hole near bottom of chimney. Let charcoal burn until ash is just gray, 30 minutes.

OPEN vents at bottom of barbecue. Remove top grill rack. Carefully turn out hot charcoal from chimney onto bottom grill rack over 1 vent. To make a drip pan, pour water into disposable foil pan to depth of ½ inch. Set pan with water next to charcoal on same rack. Return top rack to barbecue.

PLACE pork roast, bone side down, on top rack over drip pan. Cover barbecue with lid, positioning top vent directly over pork. Place stem of metal candy thermometer through top vent, keeping gauge on outside; thermometer should not touch meat or rack. Leave thermometer in place during cooking. Grill pork 1 hour, maintaining temperature of 325°F by opening top and bottom vents wider to increase heat and closing vents to decrease heat. Leave any other vents closed.

USING tongs, turn pork over. Cover barbecue. Cook pork until instant-read meat thermometer inserted into top center of meat registers 140°F to 145°F, about 15 minutes longer; temperature in barbecue may fall below 325°F during last 30 minutes.

TRANSFER pork to platter, leaving meat thermometer in place. Tent loosely with foil; let stand 15 minutes (temperature of meat will rise to 150°F to 155°F). Cut pork between bones into individual chops. Serve with bell pepper relish.

Hawaiian-style braised pork with stir-fried cabbage

TENDER PIECES of boneless country-style spareribs combine with sophisticated Asian flavors in this version of the classic Hawaiian *kalua* pig. The traditional dish features meat steamed in an underground oven, but here everything cooks slowly in one pot, which means it doesn't need a lot of attention. Chinese five-spice powder is a blend that usually contains ground anise, cinnamon, star anise, cloves, and ginger; it is available in the spice section of most supermarkets.

6 TO 8 SERVINGS

- 3½ pounds boneless country-style pork spareribs, cut into 1½-inch cubes
- 3 tablespoons vegetable oil
- 6 garlic cloves, chopped
- 4 green onions, chopped
- 2 tablespoons chopped peeled fresh ginger

- 1 14-ounce can low-salt chicken broth, divided
- ⅓ cup soy sauce
- 1 tablespoon (packed) dark brown sugar
- ¼ teaspoon dried crushed red pepper
- ¼ teaspoon Chinese five-spice powder
- 1½ tablespoons cornstarch
- Stir-Fried Cabbage (see recipe)

SPRINKLE pork with salt and pepper. Heat oil in heavy large pot over medium-high heat. Add ⅓ of pork to pot and sauté until brown, about 6 minutes; transfer to bowl. Repeat with remaining pork in 2 batches. Add garlic, green onions, and ginger to same pot; sauté 1 minute. Return pork and any accumulated juices to pot. Add 1½ cups broth, soy sauce, sugar, crushed red pepper, and five-spice powder; bring to boil. Reduce heat to medium-low, cover, and simmer until pork is very tender, about 1 hour 15 minutes. Stir remaining broth and cornstarch in small cup until cornstarch dissolves; mix into pork. Simmer until gravy thickens, stirring occasionally, about 3 minutes. Season to taste with pepper. *(Pork can be made 1 day ahead. Refrigerate uncovered until cold, then cover and keep refrigerated. Rewarm over low heat before serving.)* Serve pork with Stir-Fried Cabbage.

Stir-fried cabbage

FRESH GINGER and sesame oil give this easy dish a complex and appealing flavor.

6 TO 8 SERVINGS

- 2 tablespoons vegetable oil
- 1 tablespoon minced peeled fresh ginger
- 1 2-pound green cabbage, quartered, cored, very thinly sliced
- 6 green onions, chopped
- 1 tablespoon Asian sesame oil

HEAT vegetable oil in heavy large pot over medium-high heat. Add ginger and stir 30 seconds. Add half of cabbage and toss until wilted, about 4 minutes. Add remaining cabbage, green onions, and sesame oil. Toss until all cabbage is crisp-tender, about 4 minutes. Season to taste with salt and pepper.

Pork sauté with caramelized pears and pear-brandy cream sauce

THE SAUCE IN THIS DISH is a variation of a classic one from the Normandy region of France, where it is made with apples and Calvados, an apple brandy. Here, pears and pear eau de vie (a clear pear brandy) or pear schnapps provide an intriguing variation.

4 SERVINGS

- 1¼ pounds pork tenderloin, trimmed, cut crosswise into 1 inch-thick slices
- 4 tablespoons (½ stick) butter, divided
- 4 firm but ripe large Anjou pears, peeled, halved, cored, cut into ⅓-inch-thick wedges
- 1 teaspoon sugar
- ½ cup chopped shallots (about 3 large)
- 1¼ teaspoons dried thyme
- ¼ cup pear eau de vie (clear pear brandy) or pear schnapps
- 1 cup whipping cream
- ⅓ cup pear nectar

PLACE pork slices between sheets of plastic wrap. Using meat mallet, pound pork to ¼-inch thickness.

MELT 2 tablespoons butter in large nonstick skillet over high heat. Add pears and sugar; sauté until pears are tender and deep golden, about 8 minutes.

MELT 1 tablespoon butter in another large nonstick skillet over high heat. Sprinkle pork with salt and pepper. Working in batches, add pork to skillet; sauté just until cooked through, about 2 minutes per side. Transfer to plate. Tent loosely with aluminum foil to keep warm. Reduce heat to medium. Melt remaining 1 tablespoon butter in same skillet. Add shallots and thyme; sauté 2 minutes. Add eau de vie; boil until reduced to glaze, scraping up any browned bits, about 2 minutes. Add cream and pear nectar; boil until sauce is thickened enough to coat spoon, about 5 minutes. Season sauce to taste with salt and pepper.

REHEAT pears if necessary; spoon into center of platter. Arrange pork around pears. Pour sauce over pork and serve.

Grilled pork tenderloin with orange-chipotle sauce

PORK TENDERLOINS are very low in fat—almost as low as skinless chicken breasts—and are also very tender. They are quick-cooking and easily absorb flavors, such as the orange juice and chipotle chiles in this recipe. Chipotles (dried, smoked jalapeños), canned in a spicy tomato sauce known as *adobo*, are found at Latin markets, specialty foods stores, and some supermarkets.

10 SERVINGS

3½ pounds pork tenderloins
6 cups orange juice, divided
2 teaspoons salt

2 tablespoons (¼ stick) butter
3 large shallots, finely chopped
1 cup dry white wine
2¾ cups low-salt chicken broth

2 tablespoons chopped fresh cilantro
1 tablespoon chopped fresh chives
1 tablespoon minced canned chipotle chiles

DIVIDE pork between 2 resealable plastic bags. Add 1 cup orange juice and 1 teaspoon salt to each bag; seal. Turn to coat. Chill at least 3 hours or overnight, turning bags occasionally.

MELT butter in heavy large saucepan over medium-high heat. Add shallots and sauté until soft but not brown, about 2 minutes. Add wine and boil until reduced to glaze, about 10 minutes. Add remaining 4 cups orange juice and broth; boil until reduced to 1¾ cups, about 45 minutes. *(Sauce can be made 1 day ahead. Cool, then cover and chill.)*

PREPARE barbecue (medium-high heat). Drain pork; pat dry. Discard marinade. Grill pork until thermometer inserted into thickest part of meat registers 150°F for medium, turning often, about 18 minutes. Transfer to work surface; tent with aluminum foil to keep warm. Let stand 10 minutes.

MEANWHILE, bring sauce to simmer; mix in cilantro, chives, and chipotle chiles. Season sauce to taste with salt and pepper. Slice pork. Serve with sauce.

Brined pork loin with onion, raisin, and garlic compote

BE SURE TO USE a large center-cut loin, which cooks more evenly than two smaller pieces tied together. Begin preparing this recipe a day ahead to accommodate the brining process, which will result in moist, tender meat. This is one dish that would work equally well with a medium-bodied fruity red wine such as Merlot or a fruity white wine such as Australian Sémillon.

8 SERVINGS

8 cups water
½ cup coarse kosher salt
½ cup (packed) golden brown sugar
1 tablespoon fennel seeds
1 tablespoon coriander seeds
1 tablespoon whole black peppercorns
3 bay leaves
1 center-cut boneless pork loin roast (about 4 pounds)

1 **tablespoon olive oil**
2 **teaspoons chopped fresh sage**
2 **teaspoons chopped fresh rosemary**
2 **teaspoons chopped fresh thyme**
2 **teaspoons chopped fresh marjoram**

Onion, Raisin, and Garlic Compote (see recipe)

COMBINE first 7 ingredients in heavy large pot. Bring to simmer over medium heat, stirring until salt and sugar dissolve. Remove brine from heat and cool to room temperature. Transfer brine to very large bowl. Add pork (weight pork with plate to keep submerged in brine). Cover and refrigerate overnight. Drain pork. Return pork to bowl; cover with cold water (weight pork with plate to keep submerged in water). Soak pork at room temperature 2 hours.

POSITION oven rack in top third of oven and preheat to 350°F. Drain pork; pat dry. Transfer pork to rack set in large roasting pan. Rub pork all over with oil. Sprinkle with fresh herbs, pressing to adhere. Sprinkle with pepper. Roast until thermometer inserted into center of meat registers 150°F, about 1 hour 40 minutes. Transfer pork to cutting board; tent loosely with aluminum foil to keep warm. Let stand 15 minutes.

CUT pork crosswise into ¼- to ½-inch-thick slices. Arrange on platter. Serve with compote.

Onion, raisin, and garlic compote

THIS TANGY COMPOTE would also complement broiled lamb chops or sautéed chicken breasts.

MAKES ABOUT 2 CUPS

1 **pound pearl onions**

¼ **cup (½ stick) butter**
24 **garlic cloves, peeled**
1 **bay leaf**
1½ **cups tawny Port**
¼ **cup white wine vinegar**
4 **teaspoons sugar**
½ **teaspoon salt**
½ **cup raisins**
1½ **teaspoons chopped fresh thyme**

BRING large saucepan of water to boil. Add onions and boil 2 minutes. Drain. Rinse onions under cold water to cool. Trim root end slightly, leaving root base intact, and peel onions.

MELT butter in heavy medium saucepan over medium-low heat. Add garlic and bay leaf; sauté until garlic is golden brown, about 6 minutes. Add Port, vinegar, sugar, and salt; simmer 8 minutes, stirring until sugar and salt dissolve. Add onions and raisins. Simmer until onions are tender and liquids thicken enough to coat spoon, stirring occasionally, about 9 minutes. Remove from heat. Stir in thyme. Discard bay leaf. Season compote to taste with salt and pepper. *(Compote can be made 1 day ahead. Cover and refrigerate. Rewarm over medium heat before serving.)* Serve compote warm.

Roast pork tenderloin with cranberry-Port sauce

THE DELICIOUS CRANBERRY SAUCE can be prepared a day before serving, as can the herb rub for the pork. Just before dinner, sear the pork in an ovenproof skillet and then place it in the oven to finish cooking.

8 SERVINGS

3 **tablespoons butter**
2 **cups chopped onions**
4 **garlic cloves, minced**
3 **teaspoons grated orange peel, divided**
1½ **teaspoons dried sage leaves**
5½ **teaspoons dried thyme, divided**
2 **cups low-salt chicken broth**
1½ **cups cranberry juice cocktail**

- **2 cups fresh or frozen (unthawed) cranberries (about 8 ounces)**
- **½ cup sugar**
- **¼ cup tawny Port**
- **1 tablespoon cornstarch**

- **1½ teaspoons salt**
- **1½ teaspoons ground black pepper**
- **3 1-pound pork tenderloins, excess fat trimmed**
- **3 tablespoons vegetable oil, divided**

MELT butter in heavy large skillet over medium-high heat. Add onions and sauté until golden, about 8 minutes. Add garlic, 1½ teaspoons orange peel, sage, and 1 teaspoon thyme; stir 1 minute. Add broth and cranberry juice cocktail; simmer until mixture is reduced to 2½ cups, about 8 minutes. Strain sauce into heavy medium saucepan, pressing on solids in strainer with back of spoon to release as much liquid as possible. Add cranberries and sugar to sauce. Boil just until berries pop, about 5 minutes. Mix Port and cornstarch in small bowl until cornstarch dissolves. Add to sauce and boil until sauce thickens, about 1 minute. Season to taste with salt and pepper. *(Cranberry sauce can be made 1 day ahead. Cover and refrigerate.)*

MIX 1½ teaspoons salt, 1½ teaspoons pepper, and remaining 4½ teaspoons thyme in small bowl. Pat pork dry with paper towels and place in large baking dish. Brush with 2 tablespoons oil. Rub all of thyme mixture over pork. *(Can be prepared 1 day ahead. Cover and refrigerate.)*

PREHEAT oven to 400°F. Heat remaining 1 tablespoon oil in heavy large ovenproof skillet over high heat. Add pork and sauté until brown, turning frequently, about 5 minutes. Transfer skillet to oven and roast pork until instant-read thermometer inserted into thickest part of meat registers 150°F, about 20 minutes. Transfer pork to platter; cover loosely with aluminum foil to keep warm. Add cranberry sauce and remaining 1½ teaspoons orange peel to same skillet and bring to simmer, stirring frequently.

CUT pork on slight diagonal into ½-inch-thick slices. Divide among 8 plates. Spoon sauce over and serve.

Crown roast of pork with stuffing and cider gravy

THIS SPECTACULAR ENTRÉE is ideal for a special-occasion dinner. Ask the butcher to grind any pork trimmings for use in the stuffing.

10 SERVINGS

Pork

- **1 8-pound crown roast of pork (12 ribs tied into circle)**
- **2 tablespoons vegetable oil**
- **1 teaspoon salt**
- **1 teaspoon sugar**
- **1 teaspoon dried thyme**
- **½ teaspoon crumbled dried sage**
- **½ teaspoon ground black pepper**

Apple and Pork Stuffing (see recipe)

Gravy

- **1½ cups beef broth, divided**
- **1 cup apple cider**
- **4 teaspoons cornstarch**
- **2 tablespoons applejack brandy or brandy**

FOR PORK: Position pork atop 9- to 10-inch-diameter tart pan bottom. Transfer pork, still on pan bottom, to large rimmed baking sheet. Brush pork with oil. Combine salt, sugar, thyme, sage, and pepper in small bowl. Rub spice mixture all over pork. Cover with plastic wrap and refrigerate overnight.

POSITION oven rack in bottom third of oven and preheat to 450°F. Fill center of pork roast with enough stuffing to mound. Cover tips of pork bones with aluminum foil. Roast pork 20 minutes. Reduce temperature to 325°F. Continue roasting until thermometer inserted into center of meat registers 150°F, about 1 hour 50 minutes. Remove foil from bones. Continue roasting until thermometer inserted into center of meat registers 155°F, about 15 minutes longer. Carefully transfer roast, still on pan bottom, to platter. Tent loosely with aluminum foil to keep warm. Let stand 15 minutes (temperature of pork and stuffing will rise 5 to 10 degrees).

FOR GRAVY: Add 1 cup broth to baking sheet and scrape up any browned bits. Pour pan juices into 2-cup glass measuring cup. Spoon off fat from top of pan juices and discard. Transfer pan juices to medium saucepan. Add apple cider and remaining ½ cup beef broth; bring to boil. Stir cornstarch and applejack in small bowl until cornstarch dissolves. Whisk into broth mixture. Boil until gravy thickens slightly, stirring, about 3 minutes. Season to taste with salt and pepper. Transfer gravy to sauceboat.

CARVE roast between bones into separate chops. Serve with stuffing and gravy.

Apple and pork stuffing

PART OF THE STUFFING is used to fill the center of the crown roast of pork, and the rest is baked alongside. If you make the stuffing on its own to go with other meats, bake it all in a shallow baking dish until a meat thermometer inserted into the center registers 160°F.

10 SERVINGS

- **2 tablespoons vegetable oil**
- **1¼ cups chopped celery**
- **⅓ cup chopped shallots**
- **3 garlic cloves, minced**
- **2 pounds ground pork**
- **1 cup plain dry breadcrumbs**
- **4 ounces dried apples, chopped (about 1⅓ cups)**
- **3 large eggs, beaten to blend**
- **⅓ cup chopped fresh parsley**
- **2 teaspoons crumbled dried sage**
- **2 teaspoons salt**
- **¾ teaspoon ground black pepper**
- **¼ teaspoon ground allspice**
- **1 cup (about) beef broth**

HEAT oil in heavy medium skillet over medium heat. Add celery and sauté until soft, about 3 minutes. Add shallots and garlic; sauté until shallots are soft, about 2 minutes. Transfer mixture to large bowl. Mix in pork and next 8 ingredients. Mix in enough broth by ¼ cupfuls to moisten stuffing.

SET aside enough stuffing to fill crown roast of pork cavity. Transfer remaining stuffing to buttered 8½x4½x2½-inch loaf pan. Cover with aluminum foil. Bake stuffing in pan alongside roast during last 1 hour of cooking until thermometer inserted into center of stuffing registers 160°F.

INVERT stuffing in pan onto platter. Slice stuffing and serve with roast.

Cumin pork roast with wild mushroom sauce

THE RICH MUSHROOM SAUCE features a surprising Southwestern accent, courtesy of jalapeño chile, cilantro, and oregano. Not only is it sensational with the pork roast, it would also be terrific over mashed potatoes, so serve your favorite version as a side dish.

8 SERVINGS

- **1 3½-pound center-cut boneless pork loin**
- **4 teaspoons ground cumin, divided**

- **3 tablespoons butter, divided**
- **1 pound oyster mushrooms, halved**
- **½ cup plus 1 tablespoon chopped shallots**
- **6 garlic cloves, finely chopped**
- **1 tablespoon plus 1 teaspoon finely chopped jalapeño chile with seeds**
- **2 tablespoons finely chopped fresh cilantro**
- **2 tablespoons finely chopped fresh oregano**

- **1 14-ounce can low-salt chicken broth**
- **¼ cup dry Sherry**
- **2 tablespoons all purpose flour**

Fresh cilantro sprigs

PREHEAT oven to 375°F. Sprinkle pork with salt and pepper. Rub 3 teaspoons cumin all over pork. Place in roasting pan. Roast pork until thermometer inserted into center of meat registers 150°F, about 50 minutes.

MEANWHILE, melt 2 tablespoons butter in large skillet over medium-high heat. Add mushrooms, ½ cup shallots, garlic, and 1 tablespoon jalapeño; sauté until mushrooms are very soft and beginning to brown, about 15 minutes. Remove from heat. Mix in chopped cilantro, oregano, and remaining 1 teaspoon cumin. Season to taste with salt and pepper. Set aside.

TRANSFER pork to platter. Tent loosely with aluminum foil to keep warm. Add broth to roasting pan; scrape up any browned bits. Transfer broth mixture to heavy medium saucepan. Place Sherry in medium bowl; gradually whisk in flour to blend. Whisk Sherry mixture, and remaining 1 tablespoon butter, 1 tablespoon shallots, and 1 teaspoon jalapeño into broth mixture; bring to boil, whisking until smooth. Stir in mushroom mixture and any accumulated juices from pork on platter. Boil until sauce thickens enough to coat spoon, stirring occasionally, about 5 minutes. Season sauce to taste with salt and pepper.

SLICE pork. Garnish platter with cilantro sprigs. Serve pork with sauce.

Pork sauté with apples and Calvados cream sauce

FRANCE'S NORTHWESTERN Normandy region is prime apple-growing country, so when a dish is cooked *à la normande*, it contains butter or cream and one or more of the following: apples, apple cider, or Calvados, an apple brandy. All of those, plus pork–another popular ingredient in Normandy–come together in this stellar dish.

4 SERVINGS

- **1 1-pound pork tenderloin, trimmed, cut into 1-inch-thick rounds**
- **5 tablespoons butter, divided**
- **4 medium Golden Delicious apples (about 1½ pounds), peeled, halved, cored, cut into ⅓-inch-thick slices**
- **1 teaspoon sugar**
- **2 large shallots, chopped**
- **1 tablespoon chopped fresh thyme or 1 teaspoon dried**
- **¼ cup Calvados or other apple brandy**
- **1 cup whipping cream**
- **¼ cup apple cider**

PLACE pork rounds between sheets of plastic wrap. Using mallet, pound pork slices to ¼-inch thickness. *(Can be prepared 4 hours ahead. Cover and refrigerate.)*

MELT 2 tablespoons butter in heavy large skillet over medium-high heat. Add apples and sugar to skillet; sauté until golden brown, about 6 minutes. Set aside.

MELT 2 tablespoons butter in another heavy large skillet over high heat. Sprinkle pork with salt and pepper. Add pork to skillet and sauté until just cooked through, about 2 minutes per side. Transfer to plate; tent loosely with aluminum foil to keep warm.

MELT remaining 1 tablespoon butter in same skillet over medium heat. Add shallots and thyme; sauté 2 minutes. Remove skillet from heat. Add Calvados. Return to heat and boil until reduced to glaze, scraping up any browned bits. Stir in cream and cider; boil until sauce thickens enough to coat spoon, about 3 minutes. Season sauce to taste with salt and pepper.

REHEAT apples. Arrange a few pork slices on each plate. Spoon sauce over. Top with sautéed apples and serve.

Roast pork calypso style

SLICES OF COLD ROAST PORK and avocado fanned around a black bean and corn salad are drizzled with a gingered orange sauce in this colorful Caribbean-style dish. It would be great for a picnic—just carry the components in individual containers, and assemble on-site.

4 SERVINGS

- **3 shallots, chopped**
- **2 bay leaves, crumbled**
- **1½ teaspoons salt**
- **¾ teaspoon ground allspice**
- **¾ teaspoon ground ginger**
- **2 ¾-pound pork tenderloins**

- **1½ cups fresh orange juice**
- **¼ cup minced shallots**
- **3 tablespoons (packed) golden brown sugar**
- **2 tablespoons minced peeled fresh ginger**
- **2 bay leaves**
- **⅜ teaspoon ground allspice**

- **Fresh spinach leaves**
- **Black Bean, Hearts of Palm, and Corn Salsa (see recipe)**
- **2 avocados, halved, pitted, peeled, sliced crosswise**
- **Minced fresh parsley**

PREHEAT oven to 450°F. Mix shallots, bay leaves, salt, allspice, and ginger in small bowl to combine. Add generous amount of ground black pepper. Rub spice mixture over pork. Set pork on rack in roasting pan. Roast pork until thermometer inserted into center of meat registers 150°F, about 25 minutes. Cool slightly. *(Pork can be prepared 1 day ahead. Cover and refrigerate. Bring pork to room temperature before serving.)*

COMBINE orange juice and next 5 ingredients in heavy small saucepan. Simmer until sauce is syrupy and lightly coats spoon, about 10 minutes. Season to taste with salt and pepper. *(Sauce can be prepared 1 day ahead. Cover and refrigerate.)*

LINE platter with spinach. Mound salsa in center. Slice pork. Alternate pork and avocado slices around salad. Discard bay leaves from sauce and drizzle sauce over pork and avocado. Sprinkle with parsley.

Black bean, hearts of palm, and corn salsa

THE THREE MAIN INGREDIENTS in this salsa complete the Caribbean theme of the Roast Pork Calypso-Style. By using canned black beans and hearts of palm, as well as packaged frozen corn, this salsa comes together easily. It would also be nice with grilled chicken or fish.

4 SERVINGS

- **1 15- to 16-ounce can black beans, rinsed, drained**
- **1 10-ounce package frozen corn, thawed, drained**
- **1 7.5-ounce can hearts of palm, drained, cut into ¼-inch-thick rounds**
- **2 large tomatoes, seeded, diced**
- **½ red onion, minced**
- **½ cup chopped fresh cilantro**
- **¼ cup olive oil**
- **3 tablespoons fresh lime juice**
- **1 teaspoon ground coriander**

MIX all ingredients in medium bowl. Season salad to taste with salt and pepper. *(Salad can be prepared 1 day ahead. Cover and refrigerate.)*

Smoked sausage cassoulet

THE COMPLEX AND CLASSIC slow-cooked French stew of beans and meats is streamlined here thanks to the use of canned beans and precooked sausages. The result–not as heavy as the traditional cassoulet–is out of this world; it would make a great party dish. For the best result, begin preparing the dish a day before serving to allow the flavors to meld. To make it easier to eat, take out the ham hocks, trim off the meat, and stir it back into the stew.

8 TO 10 SERVINGS

- **2 tablespoons plus ¼ cup extra-virgin olive oil**
- **4 onions, chopped**
- **10 garlic cloves, chopped**

- **3 pounds assorted fully cooked spicy smoked sausages (such as kielbasa and andouille), sliced into ½-inch-thick rounds**
- **1 cup dry white wine**

- **4 15-ounce cans Great Northern beans, drained**
- **3 14-ounce cans diced tomatoes with roasted garlic in juice**
- **3 cups (or more) low-salt chicken broth**
- **2 smoked ham hocks (about 1 pound)**
- **2 tablespoons herbes de Provence**
- **1 tablespoon chopped fresh rosemary**
- **¼ teaspoon ground cloves**

- **4 cups fresh breadcrumbs made from crustless French bread**
- **2 garlic cloves, minced**
- **½ cup chopped fresh parsley**

PREHEAT oven to 350°F. Heat 2 tablespoons oil in heavy large ovenproof pot over medium heat. Add onions and sauté 10 minutes. Add chopped garlic and continue to sauté until onions are very soft, about 20 minutes longer.

MEANWHILE, sauté sausage in 2 batches in heavy large skillet over medium-high heat until brown, about 10 minutes per batch. Using slotted spoon, transfer sausage to bowl. Add wine to skillet and bring to boil, scraping up any browned bits.

ADD wine mixture from skillet and sausage to pot with onions; then add beans, tomatoes with juice, 3 cups broth, ham hocks, herbes de Provence, rosemary, and cloves. Sprinkle generously with pepper. Bring cassoulet to boil. Cover pot and transfer to preheated oven; bake 1 hour. *(Can be prepared up to 2 days ahead. Uncover and cool 1 hour. If desired, cut meat from ham hocks and return to pot. Refrigerate uncovered until cold, then cover and keep refrigerated. Before continuing, rewarm in covered pot in 350°F oven 40 minutes, adding more broth if dry.)*

HEAT ¼ cup oil in heavy large skillet over medium heat. Add breadcrumbs and minced garlic; sauté until golden brown, about 15 minutes. Mix in parsley. Season topping with salt and pepper.

SPOON cassoulet into bowls. Sprinkle with topping and serve.

La petite choucroute

CHOUCROUTE GARNI, literally translated as "garnished sauerkraut," is also a French dish starring sausage and sauerkraut. This easy version is spiked with aquavit, a Scandinavian caraway-flavored liqueur. Aquavit is available at some liquor stores and specialty foods stores.

4 SERVINGS

- **4 bacon slices, diced**
- **5 cups thinly shredded cabbage (about ½ large head)**
- **1 large onion, thinly sliced**
- **2 large dried pear halves, thinly sliced**
- **2 teaspoons caraway seeds**
- **1 large bay leaf**
- **2 cups sauerkraut, rinsed, drained**
- **8 ounces kielbasa sausage, cut into ½-inch-thick rounds**
- **½ cup aquavit**
- **½ cup low-salt chicken broth**
- **1 teaspoon white wine vinegar**

SAUTÉ bacon in heavy large skillet over medium heat until fat begins to render, about 3 minutes. Add cabbage, onion, pear, caraway seeds, and bay leaf. Cook until cabbage wilts and onion is soft, tossing frequently, about 10 minutes. Add all remaining ingredients. Cover and cook until liquid is almost absorbed, stirring occasionally, about 30 minutes. Season to taste with salt and pepper. Transfer to platter.

Irish "bacon" and cabbage

CALLED IRISH BACON on the Emerald Isle, bone-in pork shoulder—known here as Boston butt—is soaked in a salt-water brine overnight and then cooked for hours until it is falling-apart tender and packed with flavor. The garlic is cooked and served almost like a vegetable. Serve this dish with mashed potatoes and your favorite Irish ale for a satisfying dinner. (Note that the pork can be cooked a day ahead, in case you're planning a St. Patrick's Day party.)

6 SERVINGS

- **4 quarts water**
- **3 cups coarse kosher salt**
- **1 6½-pound bone-in pork shoulder roast (Boston butt), excess fat trimmed**
- **3 large heads of garlic, unpeeled, halved crosswise**
- **1½ teaspoons whole black peppercorns**

- **1 large head of green cabbage, cut into 6 wedges**
- **1 pound large carrots, peeled, cut crosswise in half, then quartered lengthwise**

Fresh thyme sprigs
Spicy mustard

COMBINE 4 quarts of water and salt in heavy large pot. Stir until salt dissolves. Add pork; cover and refrigerate 1 day.

BRING pork in salt water to boil. Boil 10 minutes. Carefully drain salt water. Fill pot with enough fresh cold water to cover pork and bring to boil over high heat. Add garlic and peppercorns. Reduce heat to medium-low, cover, and simmer gently until pork is very tender, about 3 hours. Transfer pork to large pan. Tent with aluminum foil to keep warm.

ADD cabbage and carrots to cooking liquid. Boil until vegetables are almost tender, about 15 minutes. *(Can be made 1 day ahead. Return pork to pot with vegetables. Cool slightly. Chill uncovered until cold, then cover and keep chilled. Before serving, rewarm over medium-low heat.)* Using slotted spoon, transfer vegetables and garlic to serving platter.

TRANSFER pork to cutting board. Cut pork into thick slices; arrange on platter with vegetables. Spoon some hot cooking liquid over pork and vegetables. Garnish with thyme. Serve with mustard.

Carnitas tacos with green onion rajas

CARNITAS TRANSLATES AS "little meats," and this Mexican dish is simply pieces of shredded well-browned pork. *Rajas* is the word for a mixture of sautéed peppers and onion; green onions are a delicious variation on the original. Poblanos are fresh dark green chiles sold at Latin markets and some supermarkets. Accompany the tacos with refried beans and rice and a cold Mexican lager.

6 SERVINGS

- **1 4-pound trimmed boneless pork shoulder (Boston butt), cut into 2-inch pieces**
- **2 14-ounce cans low-salt chicken broth**
- **3 cups (about) water**

- **¼ cup (½ stick) butter**
- **2 garlic cloves, chopped**
- **4 red bell peppers, cut into ¼-inch-thick strips**
- **4 poblano chiles, seeded, cut into ¼-inch-thick strips**
- **12 green onions, cut into matchstick-size strips**
- **1½ cups (packed) coarsely grated Monterey Jack cheese (about 6 ounces)**

3/4 cup whipping cream
1/4 cup coarsely chopped fresh cilantro

18 6-inch-diameter flour or corn tortillas
Lime wedges

PLACE pork in heavy large pot. Add broth, then enough water to cover pork by ½ inch. Bring to boil. Reduce heat to medium, cover partially, and simmer until pork is very tender and liquid is reduced to glaze, about 1 hour 45 minutes. Cool slightly. Shred meat into large bowl. Season to taste with salt. Cover loosely with aluminum foil to keep warm.

MEANWHILE, melt butter in large skillet over medium heat. Add garlic and sauté 1 minute. Add bell peppers and poblanos; sauté until soft, about 12 minutes. Add green onions; sauté until soft, about 4 minutes. Add cheese and cream. Simmer until cheese melts and sauce thickens, stirring occasionally. Stir in cilantro. Season rajas to taste with salt and pepper.

WARM tortillas. Spoon some shredded meat onto half of each warm tortilla. Top with rajas. Fold plain tortilla half over filling. Serve with lime wedges to squeeze over.

Pork chile verde enchiladas

FOR TRADITIONAL ENCHILADAS, the tortillas are fried in oil until soft; this version eliminates the oil by wrapping the tortillas in damp paper towels and heating them in the microwave to soften. Anaheim chiles (sometimes called California chiles), tomatillos (green tomato-like fruits with paper-thin husks), and asadero cheese can be found at Latin markets and many supermarkets. If you cannot find the cheese, Monterey Jack may be substituted.

6 SERVINGS

2 fresh Anaheim chiles

1 14-ounce can low-salt chicken broth
1 1/4 cups chopped onion, divided
4 ounces tomatillos, husked, rinsed, quartered
1 jalapeño chile, stemmed, seeded, coarsely chopped
1 garlic clove, chopped
1/4 cup chopped fresh cilantro
1 tablespoon fresh lime juice
1/4 cup sour cream

12 6-inch-diameter corn tortillas
Pork Chile Verde (see recipe), chilled
2 1/4 cups (packed) coarsely shredded asadero cheese (about 9 ounces)

2 plum tomatoes, seeded, chopped

CHAR Anaheim chiles over gas flame or in broiler until blackened on all sides. Enclose in paper bag 10 minutes. Peel, seed, and coarsely chop chiles.

COMBINE broth, ½ cup onion, tomatillos, jalapeño, and garlic in medium saucepan. Simmer over medium heat until liquid is reduced to 1 cup, about 10 minutes. Transfer to blender and cool to room temperature. Add Anaheim chiles, cilantro, and lime juice to blender; blend until sauce is smooth. Transfer to bowl. Whisk in sour cream. Season to taste with salt and pepper. *(Sauce can be made 1 day ahead. Cover and chill.)*

LIGHTLY oil 15x10x2-inch baking dish. Place 6 tortillas between 2 damp paper towels. Cook in microwave on high until warm, about 1 minute. Dip each warm tortilla into sauce; shake excess sauce back into bowl. Place tortillas on work surface. Spoon scant ¼ cup Pork Chile Verde, 2 tablespoons cheese, and 1 tablespoon remaining onion down center. Roll up tortillas, enclosing filling. Arrange enchiladas, seam side down, in prepared dish. Repeat with remaining 6 tortillas. *(Can be prepared 8 hours ahead. Cover enchiladas and remaining sauce and cheese separately. Chill.)*

PREHEAT oven to 350°F. Top enchiladas with remaining sauce, then remaining cheese. Bake enchiladas uncovered until heated through, about 20 minutes (or 30 minutes if enchiladas have been refrigerated). Sprinkle tomatoes over and serve.

Pork chile verde

THIS CAN ALSO be used to fill burritos or tacos.

MAKES ABOUT 4 CUPS

- **8 fresh Anaheim chiles**
- **1 teaspoon cumin seeds**
- **2 tablespoons vegetable oil**
- **1 cup chopped onion**
- **2 pounds trimmed boneless pork shoulder (Boston butt), cut into ½-inch pieces**
- **3 garlic cloves, finely chopped**
- **4 cups (or more) water**

CHAR chiles over gas flame or in broiler until blackened on all sides. Enclose in paper bag 10 minutes. Peel, seed, and chop chiles.

STIR cumin seeds in heavy small skillet over medium-low heat until fragrant, about 4 minutes. Transfer to spice mill and grind finely.

HEAT oil in heavy large pot over medium-high heat. Add onion and sauté 3 minutes. Add pork; cook until juices evaporate and pork browns, stirring often, about 20 minutes. Add chopped chiles, cumin, and garlic; sauté 5 minutes. Add 4 cups water. Simmer uncovered over medium-low heat until pork is very tender and sauce thickens enough to coat pork, stirring occasionally, about 1 hour. Season chile verde to taste with salt and pepper. *(Can be made 1 day ahead. Chill uncovered until cold, then cover and keep chilled. Before using, rewarm over medium heat, adding ½ cup water to thin if desired.)*

Grilled pork fajitas with chipotle chile sauce

SLICES OF BONELESS PORK LOIN are marinated in lime juice, cumin, and garlic, then grilled and folded into tortillas along with mashed avocado and a spicy chipotle chile sauce flavored with chopped green onions, cilantro, and tomatoes. This is a sensational party entrée. Chipotle chiles are available canned in a spicy tomato sauce called *adobo;* you can find them at Latin markets, specialty foods stores, and many supermarkets.

6 TO 8 SERVINGS

- **1 28-ounce can Italian plum tomatoes in juice**
- **4 canned chipotle chiles plus 1 tablespoon adobo sauce**
- **1 teaspoon salt**
- **5 green onions, sliced**
- **1 cup finely chopped fresh cilantro**

- **1 2½- to 3-pound boneless pork loin, trimmed**
- **¼ cup olive oil**
- **4½ tablespoons fresh lime juice, divided**
- **2 garlic cloves, mashed**
- **2 teaspoons ground cumin**

- **2 large ripe avocados**
- **6 to 8 6- to 7-inch flour tortillas**

COMBINE tomatoes with juice, chiles, adobo sauce, and salt in heavy medium saucepan; bring to boil over medium heat. Reduce heat and simmer until thick, stirring occasionally and breaking up tomatoes and chiles with back of fork, about 40 minutes. Add green onions and simmer 5 minutes. Remove from heat. Stir in cilantro. Season to taste with additional salt if desired. Cool sauce to room temperature. *(Can be prepared 2 days ahead. Cover and refrigerate. Bring to room temperature before using.)*

CUT pork crosswise into ¼-inch-thick slices (about 20). Whisk oil, 3 tablespoons lime juice, garlic, and cumin in medium bowl to blend for marinade. Dip each slice of pork into marinade to coat, then transfer to large bowl. Pour any remaining marinade over pork. Let stand at room temperature 1 hour, stirring twice.

PREPARE barbecue (high heat). Position grill rack 6 inches above coals. Grill pork with some marinade still clinging until lightly browned and just cooked through, about 3 minutes per side. Transfer to plate.

HALVE, peel, pit, and coarsely mash avocados in small bowl. Stir in remaining 1½ tablespoons lime juice. Season avocado mixture to taste with salt and pepper. Heat tortillas on grill, about 30 seconds per side; transfer to basket. To assemble each fajita, spoon about ¼ cup avocado mixture down center of each tortilla. Arrange 3 pork slices atop avocado. Cover with 1 to 2 tablespoons sauce. Fold in sides of tortillas. Serve fajitas immediately.

Spicy stir-fried pork, green onions, and mushrooms

WITH STIR-FRIES, everything cooks very quickly, so it is especially important that you have all your ingredients chopped and ready to go before you put anything in the skillet. Look for hoisin sauce, chili-garlic sauce, and Asian sesame oil in the Asian foods section of the supermarket or at Asian markets.

4 SERVINGS

- **¾ pound pork tenderloin, cut into 2x½x½-inch strips**
- **2 tablespoons soy sauce, divided**
- **1 tablespoon hoisin sauce**
- **1 tablespoon dry Sherry**
- **1 tablespoon cornstarch**
- **1 teaspoon chili-garlic sauce**

- **2 teaspoons Asian sesame oil, divided**
- **3 large eggs, beaten to blend**
- **2 tablespoons vegetable oil, divided**
- **1 tablespoon minced peeled fresh ginger**

- **½ pound fresh shiitake mushrooms, stemmed, caps thinly sliced**
- **6 green onions, cut on diagonal into 1½-inch pieces**
- **¼ cup low-salt chicken broth**

COMBINE pork, 1 tablespoon soy sauce, and next 4 ingredients in medium bowl; stir to combine well. Let stand at least 15 minutes and up to 1 hour.

HEAT 1 teaspoon sesame oil in heavy large skillet over medium-high heat. Add eggs and stir until scrambled, about 1 minute. Transfer eggs to large bowl. Add remaining 1 teaspoon sesame oil and 1 tablespoon vegetable oil to same skillet. Add ginger and stir 30 seconds. Add pork and stir-fry until cooked through, about 5 minutes. Add pork to bowl with eggs.

ADD remaining 1 tablespoon vegetable oil to same skillet. Add mushrooms and green onions; stir-fry until just tender, about 5 minutes. Return pork and eggs to skillet. Add broth and remaining 1 tablespoon soy sauce; toss until heated through, about 2 minutes. Season to taste with salt and pepper.

Lamb

Pan-fried lamb chops with rosemary and garlic

THESE EASY-TO-MAKE lamb chops are perfect for a quick weeknight dinner but are special enough for elegant Saturday-night entertaining. Round out the weekday meal with some roasted or mashed potatoes and boiled green beans, or a party menu with potato gratin and green beans in lemon butter.

6 SERVINGS

- **6 garlic cloves, minced**
- **1½ tablespoons chopped fresh rosemary or 2 teaspoons dried**
- **1 teaspoon dried crushed red pepper**
- **18 small lamb rib chops**

- **3 tablespoons olive oil**
- **Fresh rosemary sprigs (optional)**

MIX first 3 ingredients in small bowl. Sprinkle chops with salt. Rub about ¼ teaspoon garlic mixture over each side of each chop. Place chops on baking sheet; cover and refrigerate at least 30 minutes and up to 4 hours.

HEAT 1½ tablespoons oil in heavy large skillet over medium heat. Add 9 chops to skillet; cook to desired doneness, about 3 minutes per side for medium-rare. Transfer to platter; cover loosely with aluminum foil to keep warm. Repeat with remaining oil and chops. Garnish platter with rosemary sprigs, if desired.

Braised lamb with eggplant tahini

THE RICH BRAISING LIQUID is reduced and acts as one sauce, while the tahini, blended with roasted eggplant, yogurt, lemon juice, and garlic, is an intriguing second sauce. Look for tahini at Middle Eastern and natural foods stores and some supermarkets. Serve the lamb over couscous, accompanied by sautéed spinach.

8 SERVINGS

- **4 pounds lamb shoulder blade chops (each about ¾-inch thick), trimmed**
- **½ cup all purpose flour**
- **1 teaspoon salt**
- **½ teaspoon freshly ground black pepper**
- **2 tablespoons (¼ stick) butter**
- **2 tablespoons olive oil**
- **4 cups (about) low-salt chicken broth**
- **½ cup dry white wine**
- **¼ cup plus ⅓ cup chopped fresh cilantro**
- **3 tablespoons chopped fresh mint**
- **1 teaspoon finely grated lemon peel**

- **2 1-pound eggplants**
- **½ cup tahini (sesame seed paste)**
- **½ cup plain whole milk yogurt**
- **3 tablespoons fresh lemon juice**
- **2 small garlic cloves, minced**

PAT lamb dry. Mix flour, salt, and pepper in shallow dish. Coat lamb with seasoned flour, shaking off excess. Melt 1 tablespoon butter with 1 tablespoon oil in heavy large deep skillet over medium-high heat. Add half of lamb and cook until brown, about 3 minutes per side. Transfer lamb to plate. Repeat with remaining butter, oil, and lamb. Discard drippings from skillet. Add 4 cups broth, wine, ¼ cup cilantro, mint, and lemon peel to skillet. Return lamb and any accumulated juices to skillet. Sprinkle with pepper. Bring just to simmer over medium heat. Cover and cook until lamb is tender, adjusting heat so liquid bubbles gently, about 1 hour 15 minutes.

MEANWHILE, preheat oven to 400°F. Pierce eggplants with fork. Arrange on baking sheet. Bake until very soft, about 45 minutes. Cool slightly. Cut eggplants in half and scoop flesh into processor. Blend eggplant to coarse puree. Add tahini, yogurt, lemon juice, and garlic. Using on/off turns, blend until smooth, scraping down sides of bowl occasionally.

USING tongs, transfer lamb to platter. Cover loosely with aluminum foil to keep warm. Tilt skillet; spoon off fat from cooking liquid. Boil cooking liquid until thickened enough to coat spoon and reduced to 3 cups, about 10 minutes. Season sauce to taste with salt and pepper. Transfer ½ cup sauce to processor and mix into eggplant tahini. Mix in remaining ⅓ cup cilantro. Season eggplant tahini to taste with salt and pepper. Transfer to bowl.

SPOON sauce over lamb. Serve, passing eggplant tahini separately.

Lamb chops with Asian pear and kiwi salsa

THERE ARE more than 100 varieties of Asian pears, but the one most readily available in the United States is called the Twentieth Century. It is large, round, and green to yellow in color, and is slightly sweet, crunchy, and extremely juicy. Look for it at the supermarket, Asian markets, or your local farmers' market.

4 SERVINGS

2 small Asian pears, cored, diced
3 large kiwis, peeled, diced
6 tablespoons dried cranberries (about 2½ ounces)
¼ cup chopped green onions
2 tablespoons fresh lemon juice
3 tablespoons honey, divided
3 tablespoons chopped fresh mint, divided

8 1-inch-thick lamb rib chops

COMBINE pears, kiwis, cranberries, green onions, and lemon juice in medium bowl; mix in 2 tablespoons honey and 2 tablespoons mint. Season salsa to taste with salt and pepper. Let stand 30 minutes, tossing occasionally.

PREHEAT broiler. Brush chops lightly on both sides with remaining 1 tablespoon honey; sprinkle with salt, pepper, and remaining 1 tablespoon mint. Arrange chops on broiler tray. Broil chops until cooked to desired doneness, about 5 minutes per side for medium-rare. Transfer 2 lamb chops to each plate. Spoon salsa alongside and serve.

Braised lamb shanks with caramelized onions and shallots

THE HUMBLE LAMB SHANK, beloved for its rich flavor and buttery texture, is best prepared braised, as in this hearty dish. The caramelized onions and shallots, which provide intense flavor, are enhanced with rosemary and red wine.

6 SERVINGS

4 tablespoons olive oil, divided
1 pound onions, sliced
5 large shallots, sliced (about 1 cup)
2 tablespoons chopped fresh rosemary or 2 teaspoons dried

6 ¾- to 1-pound lamb shanks
All purpose flour
2½ cups dry red wine, divided
2½ cups beef broth
1½ tablespoons tomato paste
2 bay leaves

Potato and Root Vegetable Mash (see recipe)
Additional chopped fresh rosemary

HEAT 2 tablespoons oil in heavy large pot over medium-high heat. Add onions and shallots; sauté until brown, about 20 minutes. Mix in 2 tablespoons chopped rosemary. Remove from heat.

SPRINKLE lamb shanks with salt and pepper; coat lamb with flour, shaking off excess. Heat remaining 2 tablespoons oil in heavy large skillet over medium-high heat. Add 3 lamb shanks and cook until brown on all sides, about 10 minutes. Using tongs, transfer lamb shanks to plate. Repeat with remaining lamb. Add 1 cup dry red wine to same skillet and bring to boil, scraping up any browned bits. Pour into pot with onion mixture. Add remaining 1½ cups red wine, beef broth, tomato paste, and bay leaves to pot. Bring to boil, stirring until tomato paste dissolves. Add lamb shanks and any accumulated juices, arranging in single layer and turning to coat with liquid. Bring mixture to boil. Reduce heat, cover, and simmer until lamb is almost tender, turning lamb occasionally, about 1½ hours. *(Can be prepared 1 day ahead. Refrigerate uncovered until cold, then cover and keep refrigerated.)*

UNCOVER pot, spoon off fat from surface if desired. Boil until sauce thickens enough to coat spoon, turning lamb occasionally, about 30 minutes. Season to taste with salt and pepper.

SPOON Potato and Root Vegetable Mash onto plates. Top with lamb shanks and sauce. Sprinkle with additional chopped rosemary and serve.

Potato and root vegetable mash

ROOT VEGETABLES such as turnips or the rutabagas and parsnips here, make excellent (and healthful) additions to mashed potatoes. This mash is delicious with the braised lamb shanks but would also go well with virtually any meat dish.

6 SERVINGS

- **3 large russet potatoes (about 2½ pounds), peeled, cut into 2-inch pieces**
- **3 rutabagas (about 1¾ pounds), peeled, halved, thinly sliced**
- **6 small parsnips (about 14 ounces), peeled, cut into 1-inch pieces**

- **3 tablespoons olive oil**

BRING large pot of salted water to boil. Add potatoes, rutabagas, and parsnips. Boil until vegetables are tender, about 30 minutes. Drain well.

RETURN vegetables to same pot. Mash until coarse puree forms. Mix in 3 tablespoons olive oil. Season vegetables to taste with salt and pepper. *(Vegetable mash can be prepared 2 hours ahead. Let stand at room temperature. Rewarm over low heat, stirring frequently.)* Transfer vegetables to bowl and serve.

Braised lamb shanks with winter squash and red chard

INSTEAD OF being braised on the stovetop, the lamb shanks are simmered uncovered in the oven. The reason for this unusual cooking method? The dry heat of the oven actually caramelizes the top of the meat, giving it a bit of a crust, which adds appealing texture and color. Be sure to grate the orange peel *before* you remove the peel and pith from the orange. Crushing the fennel seeds in a plastic bag helps contain the seeds and simplifies clean-up.

4 SERVINGS

Lamb and squash

- **4 ¾- to 1-pound lamb shanks**
- **2 tablespoons vegetable oil**
- **4 tablespoons (½ stick) butter, divided**
- **1½ cups chopped onion**
- **1 cup chopped peeled carrots**
- **1 cup chopped peeled parsnips**
- **2 whole heads of garlic, unpeeled, halved horizontally**

4 large fresh thyme sprigs
1 cup dry red wine
5 cups low-salt chicken broth
1 large orange, peel and pith cut away, orange quartered
2 whole cinnamon sticks
2 teaspoons fennel seeds, crushed, divided

1 1¾-pound butternut squash, quartered lengthwise, seeded
½ teaspoon (scant) ground nutmeg

1 medium fennel bulb, trimmed, sliced (about 2 cups)
2 teaspoons finely grated orange peel

Chard

2 bunches red Swiss chard
2 tablespoons (¼ stick) butter

FOR LAMB AND SQUASH: Preheat oven to 375°F. Sprinkle lamb on all sides with salt and pepper. Heat oil in heavy large ovenproof pot over high heat. Add lamb and sauté until brown, turning occasionally, about 10 minutes. Transfer to plate. Add 1 tablespoon butter to drippings in pot. Add onion, carrots, parsnips, garlic, and thyme; sauté until vegetables soften and begin to brown, about 8 minutes. Add wine and boil until reduced almost to glaze, about 4 minutes. Return lamb to pot, arranging in single layer. Add broth, orange, cinnamon, and 1 teaspoon fennel seeds; bring to boil. Place pot in oven. Braise lamb uncovered until tender, turning and basting often, about 2 hours 15 minutes.

MEANWHILE, rub cut sides of squash with 1 tablespoon butter; sprinkle with salt and pepper. Arrange squash, skin side down, on baking sheet. Roast squash on sheet alongside lamb until tender, about 1 hour 15 minutes. Scrape squash from skins into bowl; add nutmeg and remaining 2 tablespoons butter. Mash squash with fork until almost smooth; season to taste with salt and pepper.

TRANSFER lamb to plate. Strain braising liquid into bowl; spoon off fat, if desired. Return liquid to pot. Add sliced fennel, orange peel, and remaining 1 teaspoon fennel seeds. Simmer until fennel is tender and sauce is thick enough to coat spoon, about 15 minutes. Season sauce to taste with salt and pepper. Return lamb to sauce. *(Squash and lamb can be prepared 1 day ahead. Refrigerate separately uncovered until cold, then cover and keep refrigerated.)*

REWARM lamb shanks, covered, over medium-low heat, about 15 minutes. Rewarm squash in saucepan over low heat, stirring often, about 10 minutes.

FOR CHARD: While lamb and squash reheat, cut out center rib from chard leaves; discard ribs. Coarsely tear leaves. Melt butter in heavy large skillet over high heat. Add chard and toss until chard wilts, about 4 minutes. Season to taste with salt and pepper.

DIVIDE squash and chard among 4 plates. Arrange lamb atop vegetables; spoon sauce with fennel over and serve.

Greek-style braised lamb shanks

GARLIC, CINNAMON, NUTMEG, and anchovies give the lamb a Greek accent. The shanks can be prepared completely ahead of time and then reheated before serving, making this dish especially convenient for entertaining. Serve it with orzo, the rice-shaped pasta.

6 SERVINGS

3 tablespoons olive oil
6 12- to 14-ounce lamb shanks
2 celery stalks, chopped
1 large onion, chopped
1 large carrot, peeled, chopped
6 garlic cloves, chopped
3 canned anchovies, drained
2 cinnamon sticks
2 small bay leaves
2 fresh thyme sprigs
5 juniper berries or 2 tablespoons gin

- ¼ teaspoon ground nutmeg
- 1 tablespoon tomato paste
- 1 750-ml bottle Merlot or other dry red wine
- 1 14-ounce can low-salt chicken broth
- 1 14-ounce can low-salt beef broth

PREHEAT oven to 325°F. Heat oil in large ovenproof pot (wide enough to hold lamb in single layer) over medium-high heat. Sprinkle lamb on all sides with salt and pepper. Add lamb to pot and sauté until brown, turning occasionally, about 10 minutes. Transfer lamb to plate. Add celery and next 9 ingredients to pot; sauté until vegetables brown, about 20 minutes. Mix in tomato paste. Add wine and all broth; boil until liquid is reduced by half, stirring occasionally, about 10 minutes. Return lamb to pot, arranging in single layer; add any accumulated juices. Bring to boil.

PLACE lamb in oven and cook uncovered until tender, basting and turning occasionally, about 2 hours. Remove from oven. Transfer lamb to plate. Tilt pot and spoon off any fat from top of roasting liquid. Press all liquid and enough of vegetables through sieve set over large bowl to make sauce with gravy consistency (sieved vegetable puree will thicken juices). Return gravy to pot; add lamb. Season to taste with salt and pepper. *(Can be made 1 day ahead. Cool slightly. Refrigerate uncovered until cold, then cover and keep refrigerated.)* Rewarm lamb over low heat. Transfer lamb and gravy to rimmed platter and serve.

Curried lamb shanks with rice and pine nut pilaf

AN EXOTIC COMBINATION of aromatic spices works wonders in this Indian-style indulgence. The pilaf has special accents like pine nuts, currants, and orange peel and is just the right balance for the lamb. Ask your butcher to crack each lamb shank into three pieces.

6 SERVINGS

Lamb shanks

- 6 12- to 14-ounce lamb shanks, each cracked into 3 pieces
- 6 tablespoons all purpose flour
- 1¼ teaspoons salt, divided
- ¼ teaspoon freshly ground black pepper
- 8 tablespoons olive oil, divided

- 2 large onions, chopped
- ¼ cup minced peeled fresh ginger
- 4 garlic cloves, minced
- 1¼ teaspoons ground coriander
- 1¼ teaspoons ground cumin
- 1¼ teaspoons turmeric
- ¾ teaspoon ground cinnamon
- ½ teaspoon cayenne pepper
- ¼ teaspoon ground cloves
- 2½ cups low-salt chicken broth
- 2 15- to 16-ounce cans whole tomatoes in juice

Pilaf

- 3 tablespoons butter
- 1½ cups long-grain white rice (about 10 ounces)
- ⅓ cup pine nuts
- ¼ cup dried currants (about 1 ounce)
- ½ teaspoon grated orange peel
- ¼ teaspoon salt
- 3 cups low-salt chicken broth

- 1 cup whipping cream

- ¼ cup minced fresh cilantro

FOR LAMB SHANKS: Pat meat dry. Mix flour, ¼ teaspoon salt, and pepper on plate. Coat lamb with seasoned flour, shaking off excess. Heat 6 tablespoons oil in large pot over medium-high heat. Add lamb in batches and brown on all sides, about 10 minutes per batch. Transfer lamb to large bowl.

ADD remaining 2 tablespoons oil to same pot. Reduce heat to medium-low. Add onions and cook until soft and lightly browned, stirring occasionally, about 10 minutes. Add ginger and garlic; stir until golden, 3 to 4 minutes. Mix in remaining 1 teaspoon salt, coriander, cumin, turmeric, cinnamon, cayenne, and cloves. Mix in broth and tomatoes with juice. Bring to boil, breaking up tomatoes with back of fork. Return lamb and any accumulated juices to pot, arranging in single layer. Cover and simmer until lamb is tender, adjusting heat so cooking liquid bubbles gently, about 2 hours.

MEANWHILE, PREPARE PILAF: Melt butter in heavy medium skillet over medium heat. Add rice and pine nuts; stir until rice is translucent and pine nuts are golden brown, about 5 minutes. Stir in currants, orange peel, and salt. Add broth and bring to simmer. Cook uncovered until small holes appear on surface of rice, about 20 minutes. Reduce heat to low, cover, and let steam until broth is absorbed and rice is just tender, about 5 minutes.

TRANSFER lamb to bowl. Tilt pot and spoon off fat from top of cooking liquid. Add cream and boil until sauce thickens and is reduced to 3 cups. Reduce heat to low. Return lamb to sauce and heat through. Season lamb to taste with salt and pepper.

MOUND lamb on platter. Spoon sauce over. Sprinkle with cilantro. Pass pilaf separately.

Grilled butterflied leg of lamb and vegetables with lemon-herb dressing

THIS IMPRESSIVE, COLORFUL DISH is ideal for parties. It begins with lamb that has been marinated in garlic, rosemary, and thyme (the lamb needs to marinate overnight, so start a day ahead), and then grilled, along with assorted vegetables. Grill the vegetables until just tender and use tongs to turn them.

8 TO 10 SERVINGS

Lamb

- **3/4 cup olive oil**
- **12 garlic cloves, chopped**
- **2 tablespoons chopped fresh rosemary**
- **2 tablespoons chopped fresh thyme**
- **1 1/2 teaspoons salt**
- **1 1/2 teaspoons coarsely ground black pepper**
- **1 5- to 5 1/2-pound leg of lamb, boned, butterflied, fat and sinew trimmed**

Dressing and vegetables

- **1 cup fresh lemon juice**
- **5 shallots, minced**
- **3/4 cup olive oil**
- **3/4 cup chopped fresh parsley**
- **1/2 cup chopped fresh mint**

- **6 medium zucchini, trimmed, each quartered lengthwise**
- **6 medium yellow crookneck squash, trimmed, each cut lengthwise into 1/3-inch-thick slices**
- **3 large red bell peppers, stemmed, seeded, each cut lengthwise into 6 strips**
- **4 medium red onions, peeled, halved through root end, each half cut into 3 wedges with some of core attached to each wedge**
- **2 cups red Zinfandel or other dry red wine**

Grilling and serving

- **Nonstick vegetable oil spray**

- **7 ounces feta cheese, crumbled (about 1 3/4 cups)**
- **Fresh rosemary, thyme, and mint sprigs**

FOR LAMB: Whisk first 6 ingredients in medium bowl to blend. Place lamb in 15x10x2-inch glass baking dish. Pour marinade over. Turn lamb, spreading marinade to coat evenly on all sides. Cover dish with plastic wrap and refrigerate overnight, turning lamb occasionally.

FOR DRESSING AND VEGETABLES: Whisk lemon juice, shallots, oil, parsley, and mint in medium bowl to blend. Season dressing to taste with salt and pepper.

PLACE zucchini, yellow squash, and red bell peppers in separate dishes. Sprinkle each lightly with salt and pepper. Spoon ⅓ cup dressing over each and turn to coat; reserve remaining dressing. Arrange red onions in large glass dish; sprinkle with salt and pepper. Pour wine over onions. Let vegetables and onions marinate at least 2 hours and up to 4 hours at room temperature, basting or turning occasionally.

SPRAY grill rack with nonstick spray and prepare barbecue (medium-high heat). Grill vegetables in batches until just tender, turning occasionally, about 15 minutes for onions, 10 minutes for red bell peppers, and 8 minutes for zucchini and yellow squash. Transfer vegetables to baking sheets. Reserve wine from onions to baste lamb.

PLACE butterflied lamb on grill rack with some marinade still clinging. Grill until thermometer inserted into thickest part of meat registers 130°F for medium-rare, turning occasionally and basting with reserved wine from onions, about 35 minutes. Transfer lamb to work surface; let rest 15 minutes.

STARTING at 1 corner and positioning knife at slight angle, slice lamb thinly across grain. Arrange lamb slices on large platter. Arrange grilled vegetables around lamb. Drizzle vegetables with reserved lemon-herb dressing. Sprinkle with feta cheese. Garnish platter with fresh rosemary, thyme, and mint sprigs and serve.

Spice-rubbed butterflied leg of lamb

A MEDLEY OF North African spices—cumin, coriander, turmeric, ginger, and cinnamon—flavors a paste that is rubbed all over the lamb. A butcher can bone, butterfly, and trim the lamb for you. Begin preparing the recipe a day before serving, as the lamb needs to marinate overnight in the refrigerator.

6 TO 8 SERVINGS

- **½ large onion, cut into 2-inch pieces**
- **6 garlic cloves, peeled**
- **2 tablespoons (packed) fresh mint leaves**
- **2 tablespoons paprika**
- **1 tablespoon salt**
- **1 tablespoon (packed) fresh marjoram leaves**
- **2 teaspoons ground black pepper**
- **2 teaspoons ground cumin**
- **2 teaspoons ground coriander**
- **2 teaspoons hot pepper sauce**
- **1 teaspoon turmeric**
- **½ teaspoon ground ginger**
- **¼ teaspoon ground cinnamon**
- **½ cup olive oil**
- **⅓ cup fresh lemon juice**

- **1 4½- to 5-pound boneless leg of lamb, butterflied, fat and sinew trimmed**

COMBINE first 13 ingredients in processor. Using on/off turns, process until coarse paste forms. Add oil and lemon juice; process until well blended.

PLACE lamb in large resealable plastic bag. Pour spice mixture over lamb; seal bag. Turn bag several times and rub spice mixture into lamb. Refrigerate overnight, turning bag occasionally.

PREPARE barbecue (medium heat). Remove lamb from marinade and shake off excess. Discard marinade. Grill lamb to desired doneness or until instant-read thermometer inserted into thickest part of meat registers 125°F to 130°F for medium-rare, about 15 minutes per side. Transfer lamb to cutting board. Cover loosely with aluminum foil and let stand 15 minutes. Cut lamb across grain with knife at slight angle into ⅓-inch-thick slices. Arrange slices on platter and serve.

Roast leg of lamb with potatoes, artichokes, and olives

THIS RECIPE calls for a semi-boneless leg of lamb; ask your butcher to remove most of the aitchbone (rump bone) and leg bone, leaving only the shank bone intact to hold the leg's shape.

8 SERVINGS

- **½ cup (packed) fresh oregano leaves (about 3 large bunches)**
- **8 garlic cloves**
- **1 tablespoon coarse kosher salt**
- **1 tablespoon ground black pepper**
- **1 4-pound semi-boneless leg of lamb, fat trimmed**
- **4 tablespoons olive oil, divided**

- **5 tablespoons fresh lemon juice, divided**
- **4 medium artichokes, stems trimmed, top 1 inch cut off**
- **1 lemon, halved**
- **24 Kalamata olives**

- **6 8-ounce white-skinned potatoes, unpeeled, each cut lengthwise into 6 wedges**

- **Fresh oregano sprigs**

FINELY mince oregano, garlic, salt, and pepper in processor. Place lamb in large roasting pan. Rub lamb with 2 tablespoons oil. Spread 4 tablespoons oregano mixture all over lamb; reserve remaining mixture. Turn lamb fat side up in pan. Let stand at room temperature 1 hour.

MEANWHILE, fill large pot with cold water. Add 4 tablespoons lemon juice to water. Cut 1 artichoke vertically into 8 wedges. Rub cut surfaces of artichoke with lemon half to prevent discoloration. Cut away choke and discard, leaving artichoke wedges intact. Place artichoke wedges in pot with lemon water. Repeat with remaining artichokes. Boil artichokes in lemon water until almost tender, about 15 minutes. Drain. Transfer to large bowl. Add olives, remaining 1 tablespoon lemon juice, and 1 teaspoon reserved oregano mixture to artichokes; toss to coat. Set aside.

PREHEAT oven to 450°F. Roast lamb in pan 10 minutes. Reduce temperature to 350°F.

MEANWHILE, toss potato wedges, remaining 2 tablespoons oil, and remaining reserved oregano mixture in bowl.

ARRANGE coated potatoes around lamb in roasting pan. Roast until thermometer inserted into thickest part of meat registers 135°F to 140°F for medium, about 50 minutes.

TRANSFER lamb to large platter; tent loosely with aluminum foil to keep warm. Add artichoke mixture to roasting pan with potatoes; mix well. Continue roasting until all vegetables are tender, about 20 minutes. Surround lamb with vegetables. Garnish with oregano sprigs and serve.

Grilled lamb with lima bean skordalia

USUALLY MADE WITH mashed potatoes, garlic, and olive oil, the thick Greek sauce called *skordalia* is most often served with meats, fish, fritters, and greens. This more colorful, modern version is excellent with the grilled lamb, which has been simply marinated in the Greek manner—in a mixture of yogurt, garlic, rosemary, and lemon. When mincing the lemon peel, be sure to use only the yellow part, avoiding the bitter white pith.

6 SERVINGS

Lamb

- **¾ cup plain whole milk yogurt**
- **4 garlic cloves, chopped**
- **1 tablespoon chopped fresh rosemary**
- **2 teaspoons minced fresh lemon peel**
- **2 teaspoons ground black pepper**

1 teaspoon ground coriander
1 5-pound leg of lamb, boned, butterflied, fat and sinew trimmed

Skordalia

1 10-ounce package frozen baby lima beans, cooked according to package directions, drained
3 garlic cloves
¾ cup olive oil
Fresh lemon juice
2 tablespoons chopped fresh parsley

Crusty bread

FOR LAMB: Puree first 6 ingredients in blender or processor. Score thickest parts of lamb and press or pound lamb to even thickness. Rub yogurt mixture all over lamb. Transfer lamb to shallow dish. Cover and chill overnight.

FOR SKORDALIA: Place beans in processor. With machine running, add garlic through feed tube and chop. Gradually add oil and puree beans, scraping down sides of bowl occasionally. Season skordalia to taste with lemon juice, salt, and pepper. Stir in parsley. *(Can be made 4 hours ahead. Refrigerate. Bring to room temperature before using.)*

PREPARE barbecue (medium-high heat) or preheat broiler. Sprinkle lamb with salt and pepper. Grill or broil lamb about 10 minutes per side for medium-rare. Let stand 15 minutes. Cut lamb across grain and with knife at slight angle into thin slices. Serve lamb with skordalia and bread.

Olive-stuffed leg of lamb

TO ENSURE that the meat is cooked uniformly, ask the butcher to bone and butterfly the lamb; then score and flatten it where necessary so that it is an even thickness throughout. The Kalamata olive stuffing is enhanced with classic Mediterranean ingredients such as oregano, marjoram, thyme, garlic, and anchovies.

10 SERVINGS

Lamb

1 cup plain dry breadcrumbs
½ cup pitted Kalamata olives
¼ cup olive oil
3 tablespoons chopped fresh oregano
2 tablespoons chopped fresh marjoram
1½ tablespoons fresh thyme leaves
3 garlic cloves
2 anchovy fillets
1 7-pound leg of lamb, boned, butterflied, fat and sinew trimmed

Sauce

1 cup fresh lemon juice
½ cup olive oil
2 teaspoons dried thyme
1 teaspoon cayenne pepper

FOR LAMB: Preheat oven to 400°F. Blend first 8 ingredients in processor until paste forms. Open lamb, boned side up, on baking sheet. Spread paste over lamb. Starting at one long side, roll lamb up tightly and tie at several places with kitchen string to hold log shape. Place lamb in roasting pan.

FOR SAUCE: Whisk all ingredients in medium bowl to blend. Season to taste with salt and pepper. Pour ¾ cup sauce into small bowl and reserve.

BRUSH lamb with 2 tablespoons of remaining sauce in medium bowl. Roast lamb until thermometer inserted into thickest part of meat registers 140°F for medium, basting occasionally with sauce in medium bowl, about 1 hour. Let stand 15 minutes at room temperature.

SLICE lamb and arrange on platter. Drizzle reserved ¾ cup sauce over.

Herb-stuffed leg of lamb with parsnips, potatoes, and pumpkin

FRESH HERB FLAVOR and an innovative trio of vegetables make this centerpiece dish a real stunner. Everything can be prepared ahead of time, so this is an excellent entrée for entertaining.

6 SERVINGS

1 cup (packed) fresh parsley leaves
1/3 cup (packed) fresh rosemary leaves
1/3 cup (packed) fresh oregano leaves
1/3 cup (packed) chopped fresh thyme
6 garlic cloves
1/4 cup (1/2 stick) butter, room temperature
1 5 1/2-pound leg of lamb, boned, butterflied, fat and sinew trimmed

4 medium red-skinned potatoes, quartered
4 large parsnips, peeled, halved lengthwise, cut crosswise into 3-inch pieces
1 small pumpkin or medium butternut squash (about 1 3/4 pounds), peeled, halved, seeded, cut into 2-inch pieces

Assorted fresh herbs (for garnish)

COMBINE first 6 ingredients in processor. Process until herbs and garlic are finely chopped. Open lamb on work surface, boned side up. Sprinkle with salt and pepper. Reserve 2 tablespoons herb butter for vegetables; spread remainder over lamb. Starting at one long side, roll up lamb and tie with string at 3-inch intervals to hold log shape.

BRING large pot of salted water to boil. Add potatoes and parsnips; boil 4 minutes. Add pumpkin and continue to boil until vegetables are tender, about 8 minutes. Drain. Rinse vegetables under cold water; drain again. *(Can be prepared 1 day ahead. Cover lamb, vegetables, and reserved herb butter separately and refrigerate.)*

PREHEAT oven to 375°F. Sprinkle lamb with salt and pepper. Place lamb in roasting pan. Roast until thermometer inserted into thickest part of meat registers 130°F for rare, about 1 hour 10 minutes. Remove from oven; maintain oven temperature.

TRANSFER lamb to platter; cover loosely with aluminum foil to keep warm. Pour off fat from pan. Add vegetables to pan. Sprinkle with salt and pepper. Add reserved 2 tablespoons herb butter to vegetables and toss to coat. Roast until vegetables begin to brown, about 25 minutes. Surround lamb with vegetables. Garnish with fresh herbs.

Greek lamb brochettes with cucumber and tomato tzatziki

CUBED LEG OF LAMB is marinated in traditional Greek ingredients, then skewered and grilled. It is partnered with the classic Greek sauce called *tzatziki;* serve it with rice and sautéed spinach.

6 SERVINGS

3 1/2 pounds boneless leg of lamb, fat and sinew trimmed
6 tablespoons olive oil (preferably extra-virgin)
3 tablespoons fresh lemon juice
1/2 large onion, grated
2 garlic cloves, minced
1 teaspoon dried oregano
1 teaspoon dried thyme

6 10- to 12-inch-long metal skewers
Cucumber and Tomato Tzatziki (see recipe)

CUT trimmed lamb into 1¼- to 1½-inch cubes. Mix lamb and next 6 ingredients in 13x9x2-inch glass baking dish. Cover and refrigerate at least 4 hours and up to 1 day, stirring lamb occasionally.

PREHEAT broiler or prepare barbecue (medium-high heat). Thread lamb cubes on skewers, dividing equally. Sprinkle with salt and pepper. Arrange skewers on broiler pan or grill rack. Drizzle with any remaining marinade from dish. Broil or grill lamb to desired doneness, turning occasionally, about 9 minutes for medium-rare. Transfer skewers to platter. Serve with tzatziki.

Cucumber and tomato tzatziki

THIS COLORFUL VARIATION on the Greek cucumber-yogurt-dill mixture also features sliced tomatoes.

6 SERVINGS

- **3 cups plain whole milk yogurt**
- **1 1-pound English hothouse cucumber, peeled, halved lengthwise, seeded**
- **3 tablespoons finely chopped fresh dill**
- **1 garlic clove, minced**
- **1 large tomato, quartered, seeded, thinly sliced**

PLACE strainer over large bowl. Line strainer with 3 layers of cheesecloth. Spoon yogurt into cheesecloth-lined strainer; let stand at room temperature to drain at least 3 hours, or cover and chill overnight (liquid will drain out and yogurt will thicken). Spoon thickened yogurt into medium bowl; discard drained liquid.

MEANWHILE, grate cucumber coarsely. Place in another strainer; let stand at room temperature until almost all liquid drains out, about 3 hours. Discard drained liquid. Squeeze remaining moisture from cucumber.

MIX cucumber, dill, and garlic into yogurt. *(Can be prepared 1 day ahead. Cover and refrigerate.)*

MIX tomato into tzatziki. Season tzatziki to taste with salt and pepper.

Spiced lamb and vegetable kebabs

THE INDIAN-INSPIRED yogurt marinade will tenderize the lamb slightly and infuse it with wonderful exotic flavor. Yellow summer squash, red bell pepper, and red onion add plenty of color and texture to these easy and appealing kebabs. Basmati rice and a green salad would make fine accompaniments.

4 SERVINGS

- **1 cup plain low-fat yogurt**
- **1 tablespoon fresh lime juice**
- **2 teaspoons minced peeled fresh ginger**
- **1½ teaspoons ground cumin**
- **1 garlic clove, minced**
- **¼ teaspoon cayenne pepper**
- **1¼ to 1½ pounds boneless leg of lamb, cut into 16 large cubes**
- **3 small yellow summer squash, each cut into four ½-inch-thick rounds**
- **1 red bell pepper, cut into 12 squares**
- **½ large red onion, cut into 12 cubes**
- **4 12-inch-long metal skewers**
- **2 tablespoons vegetable oil**

COMBINE yogurt, lime juice, ginger, cumin, garlic, and cayenne in large bowl. Add lamb; stir to coat lamb evenly with yogurt mixture. Marinate at least 20 minutes. *(Can be prepared 1 day ahead. Cover and refrigerate.)*

PREPARE barbecue (high heat). Alternate 4 lamb cubes, 3 squash pieces, 3 red pepper squares, and 3 onion cubes on each skewer. Brush meat and vegetables with oil; sprinkle with salt and pepper. Grill kebabs until vegetables are slightly charred and meat is cooked to desired doneness, turning and brushing with oil occasionally, about 10 minutes for medium-rare.

TRANSFER skewers to platter and serve.

Orange- and lime-marinated lamb kebabs

AN INNOVATIVE Southwestern-style marinade gives the lamb deliciously assertive flavors. In addition to the citrus, the marinade also features oregano, cumin, chipotle chiles, and poblano chiles, which are dark green fresh chiles. Poblanos and chipotles (the latter canned in a spicy tomato sauce called *adobo*) are available at Latin markets, specialty foods stores, and some supermarkets. Be sure to begin preparing this dish a day before serving.

6 SERVINGS

- **1 3½-pound boneless leg of lamb, fat and sinew trimmed, meat cut into 1¼- to 1½-inch cubes**
- **¾ cup orange juice**
- **½ cup olive oil**
- **¼ cup fresh lime juice**
- **¼ cup soy sauce**
- **3 garlic cloves, minced**
- **1 tablespoon chopped fresh oregano**
- **1 tablespoon chopped canned chipotle chiles**
- **2 teaspoons grated lime peel**
- **2 teaspoons ground cumin**
- **2 teaspoons ground black pepper**
- **1 teaspoon salt**

- **1 red onion, cut into 1-inch pieces**
- **3 fresh poblano chiles, seeded, cut into 1-inch pieces**
- **6 12-inch-long metal skewers**

PLACE lamb cubes in large resealable plastic bag. Whisk orange juice and next 10 ingredients in medium bowl to blend. Pour marinade over lamb in bag. Seal bag and refrigerate overnight, turning bag occasionally. Drain lamb; discard marinade.

PREPARE barbecue (medium-high heat). Alternate 4 lamb cubes, 4 onion pieces, and 4 chile pieces on each skewer. Grill until vegetables are slightly charred and lamb is cooked to desired doneness, turning frequently, about 10 minutes for medium-rare. Place skewers on platter and serve.

Lamb Chieti-style

CHIETI IS A CITY in the Abruzzi region of Italy, and this roast features many of the flavors of that area, including rosemary and pancetta, the Italian bacon cured in salt. Pancetta is available at Italian markets and in the refrigerated deli case of many supermarkets.

8 SERVINGS

- **3 ounces pancetta or bacon, coarsely chopped**
- **2 tablespoons plus ½ cup minced fresh Italian parsley**
- **3 garlic cloves, minced**
- **1 tablespoon fresh rosemary leaves or 1 teaspoon dried, crumbled**
- **1 6½-pound bone-in leg of lamb, patted dry**

- **3 tablespoons olive oil**
- **¼ cup red wine vinegar**

- **1½ cups fresh breadcrumbs made from crustless Italian or French bread, toasted**
- **1 tablespoon minced fresh mint**
- **1 cup low-salt chicken broth**
- **½ cup dry white wine**

PREHEAT oven to 400°F. Combine pancetta, 2 tablespoons parsley, garlic, and rosemary in small bowl. Using small sharp knife, cut several 1- to 1½-inch deep slits in lamb. Push handle of wooden spoon into each slit to enlarge. Pack parsley mixture into each hole.

POUR oil into roasting pan. Roll lamb in oil until meat is evenly coated. Sprinkle with salt and pepper. Roast 15 minutes. Reduce oven temperature to 350°F. Continue roasting, sprinkling meat with salt once and basting with vinegar several times, until thermometer inserted into thickest part of meat (but not touching bone) registers 125°F for rare, about 1 hour 10 minutes. Set lamb aside. Maintain oven temperature.

BLEND breadcrumbs, remaining ½ cup parsley, and mint in medium bowl. Using tongs, turn lamb over. Sprinkle with half of crumb mixture. Roast 8 minutes. Turn lamb over to original position; sprinkle with remaining crumb mixture. Roast lamb until golden brown, about 8 minutes longer. Transfer lamb to platter. Let stand 15 minutes. Add broth and wine to roasting pan. Place over 2 burners and bring to boil, scraping up any browned bits. Season pan juices to taste with salt and pepper. Serve lamb with pan juices.

Roasted rack of lamb with parsleyed breadcrumbs

HERE IS EASY ELEGANCE DEFINED: a well-trimmed rack of lamb coated with a tangy mustard–parsley–breadcrumb crust, then roasted less than half an hour. Cut up some very small red-skinned potatoes, coat them with olive oil, and cook alongside the lamb for the perfect side dish.

2 SERVINGS; CAN BE DOUBLED

- **1 well-trimmed 1½-pound rack of lamb, room temperature**
- **3 tablespoons coarse-grained mustard, divided**
- **½ cup fresh breadcrumbs made from crustless French bread**
- **¼ cup minced fresh parsley**
- **2 teaspoons chopped fresh rosemary**
- **1 garlic clove, minced**

POSITION oven rack in center of oven and preheat to 450°F. Sprinkle lamb with salt and pepper. Brush lamb with 1 tablespoon mustard. In small bowl, mix remaining 2 tablespoons mustard with remaining ingredients to combine. Press crumb mixture evenly over rounded side of lamb.

ARRANGE lamb, crumb side up, on rimmed baking sheet. Roast 10 minutes. Reduce oven temperature to 400°F and roast until thermometer inserted into center of meat registers 130°F to 135°F for medium-rare, about 15 minutes longer. Let lamb stand 10 minutes. Cut lamb between bones into individual chops and serve.

Hazelnut-crusted racks of lamb with tomato-olive ragout

THIS DISH manages to be impressive without taking over your life. Ask your butcher to remove the chine bones (backbones) from the racks of lamb to make carving easier. If the lamb has not been trimmed, cut off the outer layer of fat and about two inches of the fat between each bone (the bones will be exposed); this technique is called *frenching.* The pearl onions in the ragout are blanched—or immersed briefly in boiling water—for 30 seconds. Begin preparing this dish a day before serving to allow time for marinating.

4 SERVINGS

Lamb

- **1 cup plus 3 tablespoons olive oil, divided**
- **2 tablespoons chopped fresh rosemary**
- **3 garlic cloves, chopped**
- **2 1⅓- to 1½-pound racks of lamb, trimmed, frenched**

- **5 ounces egg bread (such as challah or brioche), crusts trimmed, bread torn into pieces**
- **½ cup chopped fresh parsley**
- **¼ cup hazelnuts, toasted, skinned**
- **1 large shallot, quartered**

Tomato-olive ragout

- **1 tablespoon olive oil**
- **16 ¾-inch-diameter pearl onions, blanched 30 seconds, peeled**
- **3 garlic cloves, chopped**
- **½ teaspoon dried crushed red pepper**
- **2 cups chopped fennel bulb (about 1 large)**
- **1 28-ounce can Italian-style tomatoes in juice**
- **½ cup Kalamata olives, pitted, halved**

Final preparation

- **3 tablespoons Dijon mustard**

- **¼ cup chopped fresh basil**
- **1 tablespoon butter**

FOR LAMB: Whisk 1 cup oil, rosemary, and garlic in 13x9x2-inch glass baking dish to blend. Sprinkle lamb with salt and pepper. Add to marinade; turn to coat on all sides. Cover and chill overnight, turning occasionally.

FINELY grind bread in processor. Measure 2 cups crumbs (remove any remaining crumbs from processor and reserve for another use). Combine 2 cups crumbs, parsley, nuts, and shallot in processor; process until nuts are finely ground. Gradually add 2 tablespoons oil; process until crumbs begin to stick together. Transfer to bowl. Season with salt and pepper. Add remaining 1 tablespoon oil; toss gently to coat. *(Crumb coating can be made 1 day ahead. Cover and chill.)*

FOR TOMATO-OLIVE RAGOUT: Heat oil in heavy large skillet over medium-low heat. Add onions, garlic, and crushed red pepper; sauté 5 minutes. Add fennel and sauté until translucent, about 3 minutes. Add tomatoes with juice and olives. Increase heat and bring to gentle boil. Cook until onions are tender and juices thicken, breaking up tomatoes with back of fork and stirring occasionally, about 18 minutes. *(Ragout can be prepared 1 day ahead. Cover and chill. Rewarm over medium heat before continuing.)*

PREHEAT oven to 400°F. Heat heavy large skillet over high heat. Remove lamb from marinade. Add lamb to skillet with some marinade still clinging. Sauté until brown, about 4 minutes per side. (If necessary, brown 1 rack at a time.) Using tongs, transfer lamb to rimmed baking sheet; cool 15 minutes. Spread 1½ tablespoons mustard over rounded side of each rack; firmly press half of breadcrumb coating into mustard on each rack.

ROAST lamb until thermometer inserted into center of meat registers 130°F to 135°F for medium-rare, about 25 minutes. Let lamb rest 15 minutes.

MEANWHILE, mix basil and butter into warm ragout; stir until butter melts. Season with salt and pepper.

TRANSFER lamb to cutting board. Cut lamb between bones into individual chops. Divide chops among 4 plates. Spoon ragout alongside and serve.

Pepita-crusted lamb with pomegranate cream

PUMPKIN SEEDS, also known as *pepitas*, provide an interesting crisp crust for the tender lamb. They are available at Latin markets, natural foods stores, and many supermarkets. The unsweetened pomegranate juice lends tang to the creamy sauce; it can be found at Middle Eastern markets, as well as natural foods stores and many supermarkets.

6 SERVINGS

- **½ cup unsalted shelled pumpkin seeds (pepitas) toasted**
- **2 tablespoons all purpose flour**
- **¾ cup fresh white breadcrumbs made from crustless French bread**
- **2 tablespoons chopped fresh cilantro**
- **1½ teaspoons salt**
- **2 tablespoons whole milk**
- **1 large egg**
- **2 2¼- to 2⅓-pound racks of lamb, well trimmed**

- **4 cups unsweetened bottled pomegranate juice**
- **½ cup sour cream**

- **2 tablespoons olive oil**

PREHEAT oven to 400°F. Finely grind pumpkin seeds and flour in processor; transfer to large bowl. Mix in breadcrumbs, cilantro, and salt. Beat milk and egg in medium bowl to blend. Sprinkle lamb with pepper. Brush rounded side of lamb with egg mixture; press breadcrumb mixture over egg mixture on lamb to coat.

BOIL pomegranate juice in heavy medium saucepan until syrupy and reduced to ¾ cup, about 25 minutes. Transfer syrup to small bowl; cool. Whisk in sour cream. Season pomegranate cream to taste with salt.

MEANWHILE, heat oil in heavy large skillet over high heat. Add lamb and cook until brown, about 3 minutes per side. Transfer lamb to rimmed baking sheet. Bake until thermometer inserted into center of meat registers 130°F to 135°F for medium-rare, about 20 minutes. Cut lamb between bones into individual chops. Divide among 6 plates. Spoon pomegranate cream over.

Veal

Family-style veal roast

THE BONELESS VEAL SHOULDER ROAST is first rolled and tied; rubbed with minced garlic, lemon peel, and herbs; and then roasted alongside beef short ribs, ham hocks, and smoked sausage for a hearty home-style meal (that company would love). Serve the meat, vegetables, and sauce alongside mashed potatoes or polenta to complete the rustic supper.

6 SERVINGS

- **9 garlic cloves, minced, divided**
- **3 tablespoons chopped fresh rosemary, divided**
- **2 tablespoons chopped fresh thyme, divided**
- **2 teaspoons finely grated lemon peel**
- **1 3-pound boneless veal shoulder roast, rolled, tied**
- **2 tablespoons olive oil**
- **2 pounds very meaty beef short ribs (each about 3½ inches long)**
- **1 pound smoked ham hocks**
- **1 pound fully cooked smoked sausage (such as kielbasa), cut diagonally into ½-inch-thick slices**
- **2 onions, halved, thinly sliced**
- **6 cups low-salt chicken broth**
- **4 carrots, peeled, cut into 2-inch-long pieces**
- **2 cups dry white wine**
- **3 bay leaves**
- **1 teaspoon caraway seeds**

MIX 6 minced garlic cloves, 2 tablespoons rosemary, 1 tablespoon thyme, and lemon peel in small bowl to combine. Sprinkle veal with salt and pepper. Rub herb mixture over veal. Cover and chill overnight.

PREHEAT oven to 350°F. Heat oil in heavy 8½- to 10-quart ovenproof pot over medium-high heat. Add veal and brown on all sides, about 8 minutes. Using tongs, transfer veal to large bowl. Sprinkle short ribs with salt and pepper. Add ribs and ham hocks to same ovenproof pot. Brown meats on all sides, about 8 minutes. Using tongs, transfer to bowl with veal. Add sausage to pot; sauté until brown, about 3 minutes. Using slotted spoon, transfer sausage to same bowl. Add onions and remaining garlic to pot; reduce heat to low and sauté 5 minutes. Add broth, carrots, wine, bay leaves, caraway, remaining 1 tablespoon rosemary, and remaining 1 tablespoon thyme. Bring to boil. Return all meats to pot, arranging in single layer if possible. Cover; bake until veal is tender, about 2 hours.

USING slotted spoon or metal spatula, transfer meats and vegetables to large platter. Tent loosely with aluminum foil to keep warm. If desired, tilt pot and spoon off fat from top of cooking juices. Boil juices in pot until thickened enough to coat spoon lightly, about 15 minutes. Season sauce to taste with salt and pepper. Cut off string from veal. Slice veal; overlap slices on platter. Spoon sauce over meats and vegetables. Serve, passing remaining sauce separately.

Veal rib roast with orange and rosemary

ASK YOUR BUTCHER to cut and trim this small roast. A simple and elegant main course, this dish is served with an orange juice, white wine, and rosemary reduction—an easy sauce that requires no unusual ingredients. When mincing the orange peel, be sure to get the orange part only, avoiding the bitter white pith underneath.

2 SERVINGS

1 3-bone veal rib roast (about 2 pounds), well trimmed
2 tablespoons minced orange peel
2 garlic cloves, minced
2 teaspoons minced fresh rosemary or 3/4 teaspoon dried

1 tablespoon butter

1 cup beef broth
1 cup low-salt chicken broth
2/3 cup fresh orange juice
1/3 cup dry white wine
1 fresh rosemary sprig

SPRINKLE veal with salt and pepper. Rub veal with orange peel, minced garlic, and minced rosemary. Wrap tightly in plastic wrap; refrigerate overnight.

PREHEAT oven to 425°F. Unwrap veal. Place on rack in roasting pan; dot with butter. Roast 30 minutes. Reduce oven temperature to 375°F; continue roasting until thermometer inserted into center of meat registers 155°F, about 45 minutes longer.

MEANWHILE, combine beef broth, chicken broth, orange juice, wine, and rosemary sprig in heavy medium saucepan. Boil until reduced to 1 cup, about 25 minutes.

TRANSFER roast to platter. Tent loosely with aluminum foil to keep warm. Remove rack from roasting pan. Tilt pan and spoon off fat from pan juices. Stir broth mixture from saucepan into juices in roasting pan; reserve saucepan. Set roasting pan over 2 burners and bring liquids to boil over medium-high heat, scraping up any browned bits. Return roasting juices mixture to reserved saucepan; boil until reduced to ½ cup, about 5 minutes. Season sauce to taste with salt and pepper. Slice roast. Serve with sauce.

Grilled veal chops with onion and red bell pepper chutney

UPSCALE VEAL CHOPS are spiced with an aromatic chutney, made special with red onion, jalapeño, cinnamon, and red wine vinegar.

4 SERVINGS

1/3 cup fresh lemon juice
1/4 cup olive oil
2 tablespoons chopped fresh thyme
2 tablespoons minced shallot
1 garlic clove, minced
4 1-inch-thick veal chops (about 10 ounces each)

Onion and Red Bell Pepper Chutney (see recipe)

WHISK first 5 ingredients in small bowl to blend for marinade. Place veal chops in shallow dish in single layer. Pour marinade over and turn to coat. Let stand 1 hour at room temperature.

PREPARE barbecue (medium-high heat). Remove veal from marinade. Sprinkle veal with salt and pepper. Grill veal, with some marinade still clinging, to desired doneness, about 5 minutes per side for medium-rare. Transfer to plates. Top with chutney and serve.

Onion and red bell pepper chutney

THIS PUNGENT CHUTNEY, which can be prepared up to three days before serving, would also be delicious with pork or chicken.

MAKES ABOUT 1⅓ CUPS

4 red bell peppers

1 tablespoon olive oil
1 red onion, halved, thinly sliced
1 jalapeño chile, halved
2 garlic cloves, chopped
½ cinnamon stick
1 bay leaf
2 tablespoons red wine vinegar
¼ cup low-salt chicken broth
1 teaspoon tomato paste

CHAR bell peppers over gas flame or in broiler until blackened on all sides. Enclose in paper bag and let stand 10 minutes. Peel, seed, and coarsely chop peppers.

HEAT oil in heavy large skillet over medium-high heat. Add onion and sauté until deep golden brown, about 10 minutes. Add roasted bell peppers, jalapeño, garlic, cinnamon stick, and bay leaf; sauté 2 minutes. Add vinegar, then broth and tomato paste. Reduce heat and simmer until chutney is thick and chunky, stirring occasionally, about 20 minutes. Discard jalapeño, cinnamon stick, and bay leaf. Cool. *(Can be prepared 3 days ahead. Cover and chill. Bring to room temperature before serving.)*

Veal chops with tomato-orange-basil sauce

THE SAUCE, which is enriched with just a touch of cream, is also sensational with chicken and shellfish. Prepare it a day ahead of time to make this dish extra-easy. Rice pilaf and sautéed zucchini are good sides.

4 SERVINGS

¾ cup fresh orange juice
½ cup dry white wine
¼ cup minced shallots
2 tablespoons finely grated orange peel, divided
¼ cup whipping cream

5 tablespoons butter, divided
4 6-ounce veal loin chops

1 large tomato, seeded, chopped (about 1 cup)
¼ cup thinly sliced fresh basil
Fresh basil sprigs (optional)

COMBINE first 3 ingredients and 1 tablespoon orange peel in heavy small saucepan. Boil until mixture is reduced to 3 tablespoons, about 10 minutes. Add cream and boil 1 minute. *(Sauce base can be prepared 1 day ahead. Cover and refrigerate.)*

MELT 1 tablespoon butter in heavy large skillet over medium heat. Sprinkle veal with salt and pepper. Add veal to skillet and sauté until cooked to desired doneness, about 4 minutes per side for medium-rare. Transfer to plates; tent loosely with aluminum foil to keep warm.

REWARM sauce base over low heat. Whisk in remaining 4 tablespoons butter. Stir in tomato, sliced basil, and remaining 1 tablespoon orange peel. Season sauce to taste with salt and pepper. Spoon over veal. Garnish with basil sprigs, if desired, and serve.

Veal chops with double mustard sauce

THE "DOUBLE MUSTARD" refers to the Dijon mustard and coarse-grained mustard that team up with shallots, tarragon, and vermouth in a tangy butter sauce that is luscious with the chops. Potato gratin and a frisée salad would be elegant accompaniments to this sophisticated main course.

4 SERVINGS

- **8 tablespoons (1 stick) butter, room temperature, divided**
- **3 tablespoons minced shallots**
- **2 tablespoons plus 2 teaspoons Dijon mustard**
- **1½ tablespoons chopped fresh tarragon**
- **1 tablespoon coarse-grained Dijon mustard**

- **4 8- to 10-ounce veal rib chops (each about ½ to ¾ inch thick)**
- **4 teaspoons whole mustard seeds**
- **⅔ cup dry vermouth or dry white wine**

BLEND 7 tablespoons butter, shallots, 2 tablespoons Dijon mustard, tarragon, and coarse-grained Dijon mustard in small bowl. Season mustard butter to taste with pepper. *(Can be made 4 days ahead. Cover and refrigerate.)*

SPRINKLE veal with salt and pepper; brush with remaining 2 teaspoons Dijon mustard. Press 1 teaspoon mustard seeds onto 1 side of each veal chop. Melt remaining 1 tablespoon butter in heavy large skillet over medium heat. Add veal and sauté until cooked to desired doneness, about 4 minutes per side for medium-rare. Transfer to plate; cover loosely with aluminum foil to keep warm. Add vermouth to drippings in skillet; boil until liquid is reduced to ¼ cup, about 3 minutes. Whisk in mustard butter. Season sauce to taste with salt and pepper. Drizzle sauce over veal and serve.

Grilled veal chops with grape-walnut chutney

THESE SIMPLE GRILLED CHOPS get a delicious accent with the unusual grape-walnut chutney, which is also great with pork. Since veal doesn't have much natural fat, watch the chops closely as they grill, to ensure they don't get overcooked.

8 SERVINGS

- **4 cups halved seedless red grapes (about 1½ pounds)**
- **¼ cup red wine vinegar**
- **3 tablespoons sugar**
- **2 tablespoons balsamic vinegar**
- **½ cup chopped walnuts, toasted**
- **3 tablespoons chopped fresh Italian parsley**

- **8 8- to 10-ounce veal rib chops (each about ¾-inch thick)**
- **Olive oil**

- **Fresh parsley sprigs (optional)**
- **Grape clusters (optional)**

HEAT large skillet over medium-high heat. Add grapes and toss until beginning to warm through, about 2 minutes. Add wine vinegar, sugar, and balsamic vinegar to grapes in skillet. Cook mixture until grape juices reduce slightly, stirring occasionally, about 10 minutes. Mix in walnuts and chopped parsley. *(Chutney can be made to this point 4 hours ahead. Let stand at room temperature.)*

BRING chutney to boil over high heat; boil until juices thicken to syrup, about 1 minute. Season chutney with salt and pepper; transfer to bowl.

PREPARE barbecue (medium-high heat) or preheat broiler. Brush veal chops on both sides with olive oil; sprinkle with salt and pepper. Grill or broil chops until cooked to desired doneness, about 4 minutes per side for medium-rare.

TRANSFER veal chops to platter; garnish with parsley sprigs and grape clusters, if desired. Serve chops with grape-walnut chutney.

Veal shanks with caramelized onions and sage

THE VEAL SHANKS cook a long time and are extremely tender, with a surplus of great-tasting sauce. Soak up that sauce with some polenta and serve sautéed broccoli rabe on the side.

6 SERVINGS

- **6 center-cut veal shank pieces (each about 1½ to 2 inches thick)**
- **½ cup all purpose flour**
- **2 teaspoons dried rubbed sage**
- **4 tablespoons olive oil, divided**
- **3 large onions, sliced**
- **5 garlic cloves, chopped**
- **15 fresh whole sage leaves**
- **1½ cups dry white wine**
- **3 cups beef broth**
- **Chopped fresh sage**

SPRINKLE veal with salt and pepper. Combine flour and dried sage in shallow bowl. Set 3 tablespoons flour mixture aside in small bowl. Coat veal with remaining flour mixture, shaking off excess. Heat 2 tablespoons oil in heavy large very wide pot over medium-high heat. Working in batches, cook veal until brown, about 7 minutes per side. Transfer veal to large bowl.

ADD remaining 2 tablespoons oil to same pot. Add onions and sauté until beginning to brown, about 10 minutes. Reduce heat to medium and sauté onions until very deep brown, about 35 minutes longer. Add garlic and sauté 5 minutes. Add whole sage leaves and reserved 3 tablespoons flour mixture; stir 2 minutes. Add wine and bring to boil, stirring frequently.

ARRANGE veal in single layer in onion mixture in pot. Add broth. Cover and simmer over medium-low heat until meat is very tender but does not fall off bone, about 1 hour 45 minutes. Uncover and simmer until juices thicken enough to coat spoon, about 30 minutes. Season sauce to taste with salt and pepper.

PLACE 1 veal shank on each plate. Spoon onion sauce over. Sprinkle with chopped fresh sage.

Veal sauté with Merlot pan sauce

VEAL CUTLETS are simply enhanced with sage, butter, shallots, and wine. The Merlot can be replaced by Cabernet Sauvignon, if you prefer. This sauté has a deliciously intense flavor that tastes as if the dish took hours to cook—yet it's simple enough for a weeknight dinner.

2 SERVINGS; CAN BE DOUBLED

- **10 ounces veal cutlets**
- **4 teaspoons minced fresh sage, divided**
- **3 tablespoons butter, divided**
- **1 large shallot, chopped**
- **½ cup Merlot or other dry red wine**

USING rolling pin, pound veal between sheets of waxed paper to ¼ inch thickness. Sprinkle veal with 3 teaspoons sage, salt, and pepper. Melt 2 tablespoons butter in heavy large skillet over medium-high heat. Add veal and cook to desired doneness, about 3 minutes per side for medium. Transfer veal to plates. Add chopped shallot to skillet; stir 30 seconds. Add wine and remaining 1 tablespoon butter. Boil sauce until reduced almost to glaze, scraping up any browned bits, about 2 minutes. Season sauce to taste with salt and pepper. Spoon sauce over veal; sprinkle with remaining 1 teaspoon sage and serve.

Veal scallops with wild mushroom, mustard, and tarragon sauce

WHEN PURCHASING VEAL, make sure the color is creamy and pale (avoid any that is dark pink) and the texture is firm and smooth. Serve these veal scallops with orzo tossed with parsley.

6 SERVINGS

- **1½ pounds ⅛-inch-thick veal scallops**
- **4 tablespoons (½ stick) butter, divided**
- **¼ cup chopped shallots**
- **8 ounces assorted wild mushrooms (such as oyster and stemmed shiitake), sliced**
- **2 tablespoons chopped fresh tarragon**
- **½ cup dry white wine**
- **1 cup whipping cream**
- **2 tablespoons coarse-grained Dijon mustard**

SPRINKLE veal on both sides with salt and pepper. Melt 2 tablespoons butter in heavy large nonstick skillet over medium-high heat. Working in batches, sauté veal until golden, about 20 seconds per side. Transfer to plate. Melt remaining 2 tablespoons butter in same skillet. Add shallots and sauté 30 seconds. Add mushrooms and sauté until brown, about 3 minutes. Stir in tarragon, then add wine. Increase heat and cook until almost all liquid evaporates, scraping up any browned bits, about 2 minutes. Add cream and boil until reduced by ¼, about 1 minute. Whisk in mustard. Season sauce to taste with salt and pepper. Using tongs, return veal to pan; simmer until heated through. Divide veal and sauce among 6 plates and serve.

11 Chicken, turkey, and other poultry

Roast a chicken and people think you're a genius. That aroma—*heavenly!* That golden skin—*gorgeous!* That succulent texture, that flavor—*out of this world!* And there you are, saying modestly (and honestly), "It was nothing."

Weeknight, weekend, there's nothing more to delivering a crispy-skinned roast chicken than firing up the oven, seasoning the chicken, and popping it in. Almost as good—better, to some—are the things you can make with leftover chicken: comforting pot pies, spicy enchiladas, and the beginnings of a pot of soup, to name just a few.

But America's love affair with chicken extends well beyond the roast. Chicken breasts are quick-cooking and low in fat (especially when skinless); legs and thighs have a moist, rich flavor that pairs well with bold ingredients. Chicken breast tenders, drumsticks, and wing drummettes (great for appetizers) are also readily available.

If you view cooking as you do investing, it's hard to imagine a better return on your time and money than a roast turkey. Roast turkey does not need a brigade of dishes alongside it; serve this non-holiday meal with a simple pan gravy and a couple of sides. (We've also included a number of great stuffing recipes here, too, for any time of year.) Go on to make turkey sandwiches, then turkey hash, and a salad or two.

There's also a world of turkey parts, from whole breasts, thighs, and legs—which need long, slow roasting or braising—to turkey cutlets from the boneless breasts. And ground turkey has changed forever the way we look at burgers and meat loaf.

Also increasingly easy to find are tastier organically raised birds, and it is worth the effort. Don't overlook duck or goose, either. Both have richer meat and more intense flavor and make a nice change for the centerpiece of a special dinner. The step-by-step instructions here will help you prepare them with excellent results.

One last tip: Even the dullest bird can be transformed by brining—the simple act of soaking a turkey or chicken in salted water and a mix of seasonings. Brined, any bird ends up moist, juicy, and well flavored. Now *that's* genius.

Roast Turkey with Herb Rub and Shiitake Mushroom Gravy (page 359)

Grilled Chicken with Root Beer Barbecue Sauce (page 337)

Arctic Char with Horseradish Cream, Sweet-and-Sour Beets, and Dandelion Greens (page 399)

Grilled Summer Lobster with Chipotle-Lime Oil and Ginger–Green Onion Butter (page 406)

Grilled Corn on the Cob with Chipotle Butter (page 437)

Potato, Leek, Gruyère, and Oyster Mushroom Gratin (page 422)

Green Beans with Walnuts, Lemon, and Parsley (page 439)
Red Cabbage with Apricots and Balsamic Vinegar (page 453)

Rosemary Focaccia with Olives (page 479)
Hazelnut Breadsticks (page 491)

Chicken

Lemon-herb roast chicken

ROAST CHICKEN seems to be more popular than ever, starring on restaurant menus, at take-out shops, and in home kitchens. This recipe not only features simple seasonings and a delicious pan gravy, but also demonstrates an easy trick for ensuring moist, flavorful meat without basting: rubbing an herb butter underneath the skin of the chicken breast as well as all over the outside of the bird.

4 SERVINGS

- **½ cup (1 stick) butter, room temperature**
- **2 tablespoons chopped fresh rosemary or 2 teaspoons dried**
- **2 tablespoons chopped fresh thyme or 2 teaspoons dried**
- **3 garlic cloves, minced**
- **1½ teaspoons grated lemon peel**
- **1 6½- to 7-pound roasting chicken**
- **¼ cup dry white wine**
- **1 cup (about) low-salt chicken broth**
- **2 tablespoons all purpose flour**
- **Lemon wedges**
- **Rosemary sprigs**

COMBINE butter, chopped rosemary, thyme, garlic, and lemon peel in small bowl; stir to combine. Season to taste with salt and pepper. *(Herb butter can be prepared 3 days ahead. Cover and refrigerate. Bring to room temperature before using.)*

PREHEAT oven to 450°F. Rinse chicken; pat dry. Slide hand under skin of chicken breast to loosen skin from meat. Reserve 2 tablespoons herb butter for gravy. Rub half of remaining herb butter over chicken breast under skin. Spread remaining herb butter over outside of chicken. Sprinkle chicken inside and out with salt and pepper. Tie legs together to hold shape.

PLACE chicken in heavy large roasting pan. Roast 20 minutes. Reduce oven temperature to 375°F. Roast chicken until juices run clear when chicken is pierced in thickest part of thigh, about 1 hour 15 minutes. Lift chicken and tilt slightly, emptying any juices from cavity into roasting pan. Transfer chicken to platter. Tent with aluminum foil to keep warm.

POUR pan juices into large glass measuring cup. Spoon off fat from top. Add wine to roasting pan; place over 2 burners and bring to boil, scraping up any browned bits. Pour wine mixture into cup with pan juices; add enough broth to measure 2¼ cups liquid. Melt reserved 2 tablespoons herb butter in heavy medium saucepan over medium-high heat. Add flour; whisk until smooth and beginning to color, about 3 minutes. Gradually whisk in pan juices. Boil until thickened to sauce consistency, whisking occasionally, about 7 minutes. Season gravy to taste with salt and pepper. Arrange lemon wedges and rosemary sprigs around chicken. Serve with gravy.

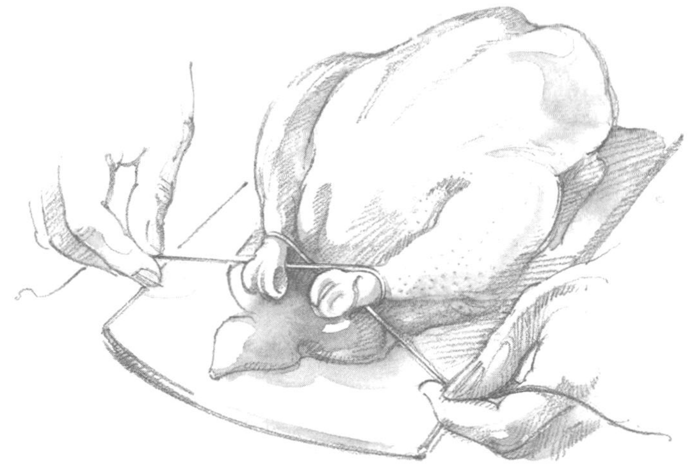

Pesto roast chicken

PESTO—THE SAUCE of pureed basil, pine nuts, and Parmesan cheese—may have originated in Northern Italy, but today cooks everywhere consider it a staple in their culinary repertoire. You can find good-quality pestos ready-made in the refrigerated case of most supermarkets. Here, the pesto dresses up both a roast chicken and its accompanying sauce with lively aroma and flavor.

4 SERVINGS

1 6½- to 7-pound roasting chicken
1 7-ounce container purchased pesto sauce, divided

3 tablespoons dry white wine
¾ cup (about) plus 2 tablespoons low-salt chicken broth
2 tablespoons all purpose flour
3 tablespoons whipping cream
Fresh basil sprigs

RINSE chicken inside and out; pat dry. Slide hand under skin of chicken breast and legs to loosen skin from meat. Reserve 1 tablespoon pesto for gravy; spread remaining pesto under skin and over breast and leg meat of chicken, in cavity of chicken, and over outside of chicken. Tie legs together to hold shape. Tuck wing tips under body. Place chicken in heavy large roasting pan. *(Can be prepared 4 hours ahead. Cover and refrigerate.)*

PREHEAT oven to 450°F. Roast chicken 15 minutes. Reduce oven temperature to 375°F and roast until juices run clear when chicken is pierced in thickest part of thigh, basting occasionally with pan juices, about 1 hour 15 minutes. Transfer chicken to platter. Tent with aluminum foil to keep warm.

POUR pan juices into glass measuring cup; spoon off fat from top. Add wine to roasting pan; set over 2 burners and bring to boil, scraping up any browned bits. Add wine mixture and any drippings from platter to pan juices. Add enough broth to measure 1 cup. Transfer to heavy small saucepan. Combine 2 tablespoons broth and flour in bowl; stir until smooth. Add to saucepan. Bring to boil, whisking constantly. Boil until reduced to sauce consistency, stirring often, about 5 minutes. Mix in cream and reserved 1 tablespoon pesto. Season gravy to taste with salt and pepper. Garnish chicken with basil. Serve with gravy.

Parsley, sage, rosemary, and thyme chicken

A CLASSIC, EVEN LYRICAL combination of herbs, rubbed both inside and outside the chicken as well as sprinkled over the potatoes and shallots that are roasted with it, contributes a pleasingly complex bouquet of flavors. All you need are a simple salad and a light red wine.

4 SERVINGS

1 4½-pound chicken
2 teaspoons dried rosemary
1½ teaspoons ground or dried rubbed sage
1½ teaspoons dried thyme
2 bay leaves, divided
5 tablespoons olive oil, divided
4 small russet potatoes (unpeeled), quartered lengthwise, cut crosswise into ½-inch pieces
8 large shallots, peeled

1¾ cups (about) low-salt chicken broth
¼ cup balsamic vinegar
6 tablespoons (¾ stick) unsalted butter, cut into 6 pieces
Minced fresh parsley

PREHEAT oven to 425°F. Rub chicken inside and out with salt. Combine rosemary, sage, thyme, and generous amount of freshly ground black pepper in small bowl. Rub some of herb mixture inside chicken. Place 1 bay leaf in cavity. Tie legs together to hold shape. Brush chicken with some of olive oil. Sprinkle with half of remaining herb mixture. Place chicken in heavy large roasting pan. Surround with potatoes and shallots. Sprinkle vegetables with remaining olive oil and remaining herb mixture. Add remaining bay leaf and mix well.

ROAST chicken until juices run clear when chicken is pierced in thickest part of thigh, basting chicken with pan juices and turning vegetables occasionally, about 1 hour 15 minutes. Transfer chicken to platter. Using slotted spoon, transfer vegetables to platter with chicken. Discard bay leaf. Tent with aluminum foil to keep warm.

POUR pan juices into large glass measuring cup; spoon off fat from top. Add enough broth to measure 2 cups. Add vinegar to roasting pan; set over 2 burners and bring to boil over medium heat, scraping up any browned bits. Boil until reduced to glaze, about 4 minutes. Add broth mixture and boil until reduced to ½ cup, about 10 minutes. Reduce heat to low and whisk in butter 1 piece at a time. Season sauce to taste with salt and pepper. Stir in parsley. Pour sauce over chicken and vegetables and serve.

Cinnamon-roasted chicken with harissa sauce

MOST AMERICAN COOKS think of cinnamon as a sweet spice used in pastries and desserts. As this traditional North African-style recipe demonstrates, however, the spice adds an intriguing dimension to savory dishes and is especially pleasing in combination with hot cayenne pepper and mild chicken. Overnight marinating in the refrigerator, with the chicken pieces enclosed in a resealable plastic bag that keeps them in contact with the seasonings, allows the flavors to penetrate down to the bone.

8 SERVINGS

- **1 cup olive oil**
- **¼ cup ground cinnamon**
- **1 tablespoon salt**
- **1 teaspoon cayenne pepper**
- **1 teaspoon sugar**
- **8 small chicken breast halves with skin and bones**
- **8 chicken thighs with skin and bones**

- **1 cup (about) all purpose flour**
- **4 tablespoons (about) peanut oil**
- **Harissa Sauce (see recipe)**

MIX first 5 ingredients in small bowl. Place chicken breasts and thighs in 2-gallon resealable plastic bag. Pour oil mixture over; seal bag. Turn bag to coat chicken with marinade. Chill overnight.

PREHEAT oven to 475°F. Transfer chicken to rimmed baking sheet, shaking off excess marinade. Sprinkle chicken with flour, turning to coat. Shake off excess. Heat 1 tablespoon peanut oil in large skillet over medium-high heat. Working in batches, add chicken to skillet. Cook until golden, adding more oil as needed, about 3 minutes per side. Return chicken to baking sheet, skin side up. Roast until cooked through, about 15 minutes. Serve with Harissa Sauce.

Harissa sauce

THE SIGNATURE CONDIMENT of the North African nation of Tunisia, *harissa* (pronounced "hah-REE-suh") is made by pureeing roasted bell peppers with olive oil, garlic, chiles, and other spices. The resulting paste is traditionally served alongside couscous but may be put to a wide range of uses: tossed with hot pasta; spread on sandwiches; or as an accompaniment to seafood, meat, or poultry. While harissa sauce may be purchased in cans and jars at Middle Eastern markets, it will have the best flavor when made at home, a fairly simple process.

MAKES ABOUT 2⅔ CUPS

- **1 tablespoon coriander seeds**
- **1 tablespoon caraway seeds**
- **4 garlic cloves, unpeeled**

4 large red bell peppers
½ cup extra-virgin olive oil
1 tablespoon sugar
2 teaspoons dried crushed red pepper

STIR coriander and caraway in small skillet over medium-high heat until aromatic, about 30 seconds. Transfer to processor. Cook garlic in same skillet, covered, over medium-low heat until tender, turning occasionally, about 10 minutes. Cool. Peel garlic; add to processor.

CHAR bell peppers over gas flame or in broiler until blackened on all sides. Enclose in paper bag 10 minutes. Peel, seed, and coarsely chop peppers. Add peppers, oil, sugar, and crushed red pepper to processor; puree. Season sauce to taste with salt and pepper. *(Can be prepared 1 day ahead. Cover and refrigerate.)*

Spicy roast chicken with tomatoes and marjoram

MARJORAM'S FULL FLAVOR does all the work in this incredibly simple recipe. The sweet little cherry tomatoes that surround the chicken intensify in taste as they roast in the oven, becoming a chunky sauce for the chicken. For a variation, use a mixture of golden and red cherry tomatoes. Serve with crusty bread to soak up all the delicious sauce.

4 SERVINGS

24 ounces whole cherry tomatoes (about 4 cups), stemmed
¼ cup olive oil
5 garlic cloves, pressed
1¼ teaspoons dried crushed red pepper
2 tablespoons chopped fresh marjoram, divided
4 chicken breast halves with ribs

PREHEAT oven to 450°F. Toss tomatoes, olive oil, garlic, crushed red pepper, and 1 tablespoon marjoram in large bowl to combine. Place chicken on rimmed baking sheet. Pour tomato mixture over chicken, arranging tomatoes in single layer on sheet around chicken. Sprinkle generously with salt and pepper. Roast until chicken is cooked through and tomatoes are blistered, about 35 minutes. Transfer chicken to plates. Spoon tomatoes and juices over. Sprinkle with remaining 1 tablespoon marjoram and serve.

Roast chicken with arugula and bread salad

THE JUICES THAT COLLECT in the pan while a whole chicken roasts need not go to waste (nor is gravy the only option): Here the juices are incorporated into a hot dressing for a salad made from oven-toasted bread cubes, green onions, dried currants, and refreshingly peppery-tasting arugula. Most of the fat from the pan juices is skimmed away before the dressing is made by adding chicken broth and vinegar, ensuring clean-tasting yet robust results.

4 SERVINGS

8 cups 1-inch cubes country-style white bread (from about 12 ounces)

1 7-pound whole roasting chicken

½ cup low-salt chicken broth
⅓ cup white wine vinegar
¾ cup thinly sliced green onions
½ cup dried currants
3 bunches fresh arugula leaves, trimmed, halved crosswise (about 2 cups)

PREHEAT oven to 400°F. Place bread on large rimmed baking sheet. Bake until bread is lightly toasted, about 6 minutes. Set aside; maintain oven temperature.

RINSE chicken inside and out; pat dry. Sprinkle inside and out with salt and pepper. Place breast side up on rack in heavy large roasting pan. Tie legs together to hold shape. Roast chicken 1 hour. Reduce oven temperature to 375°F. Roast chicken until juices run clear when chicken is pierced in thickest part of thigh, basting occasionally during last 15 minutes, about 45 minutes longer. Transfer chicken to platter. Tent with aluminum foil to keep warm.

POUR pan juices into 4-cup measuring cup (do not clean pan). Spoon off fat from top of pan juices, returning 2 tablespoons fat to pan. Add pan juices, broth, and vinegar to pan. Set pan over 2 burners and bring to boil, scraping up any browned bits. Add green onions and currants. Simmer 3 minutes to reduce liquid slightly. Remove from heat. Add bread to pan and toss with juices. Mix in arugula. Season to taste with salt and pepper. Serve with chicken.

Chicken marinara

THE JAGGED LITTLE Japanese breadcrumbs called *panko*, available at Asian markets and in the Asian foods section of some supermarkets, give extra crunch to the golden-brown crust of the chicken breasts in this updated version of a traditional Northern Italian recipe. Dredging the chicken breasts in flour and beaten egg before rolling them in the panko-Parmesan mixture ensures that the coating adheres perfectly.

6 SERVINGS

7 tablespoons olive oil, divided
4 garlic cloves, chopped
3 shallots, peeled, chopped
1 28-ounce can crushed tomatoes with added puree
2 teaspoons dried oregano
¼ teaspoon dried crushed red pepper
½ cup chopped fresh basil

¾ cup panko (Japanese breadcrumbs)
¾ cup grated Parmesan cheese
1 cup all purpose flour
2 large eggs, beaten to blend
6 skinless boneless chicken breast halves

¾ cup grated mozzarella cheese (about 3 ounces)

HEAT 4 tablespoons olive oil in heavy large saucepan over medium heat. Add garlic and shallots; sauté until tender, about 4 minutes. Add tomatoes, oregano, and crushed red pepper; simmer until sauce thickens, about 10 minutes. Mix in basil. Season sauce to taste with salt and pepper.

BLEND breadcrumbs and Parmesan cheese in small bowl. Place flour and eggs in separate shallow bowls. Coat chicken with flour, then eggs, then breadcrumb mixture, patting to adhere.

HEAT remaining 3 tablespoons oil in heavy large nonstick skillet over medium-high heat. Add chicken and sauté until golden brown, about 4 minutes per side. Spoon ¼ cup sauce over each chicken breast. Sprinkle with mozzarella cheese. Reduce heat to medium, cover, and cook until chicken is cooked through and cheese is melted, about 5 minutes. Rewarm remaining sauce; serve alongside chicken.

Chicken paprikás

THE TRADITIONAL HUNGARIAN DISH calls for the chicken to be sautéed in bacon drippings and for a sauce made with sour cream. This version is lighter yet still packed with flavor. You can use two of one color bell pepper, or mix and match. Both hot and sweet Hungarian paprikas are used here; look for them at specialty foods stores. Serve this over egg noodles that have been tossed with butter and poppy seeds.

4 SERVINGS

4 large skinless boneless chicken breast halves (about 1⅔ pounds)
All purpose flour

- **3 tablespoons olive oil**
- **2 red, yellow, or green bell peppers, cut into strips**
- **½ medium onion, sliced**
- **4 garlic cloves, chopped**
- **5 teaspoons Hungarian sweet paprika**
- **¼ teaspoon Hungarian hot paprika**
- **1¼ cups low-salt chicken broth**
- **1 cup chopped drained canned Italian plum tomatoes**
- **1 tablespoon tomato paste**

SPRINKLE chicken with salt and pepper. Coat with flour, shaking off excess. Heat oil in heavy large skillet over high heat. Add chicken to skillet and sauté until brown and crisp, about 4 minutes per side. Transfer chicken to plate. Add bell peppers, onion, and garlic to skillet; sauté 5 minutes. Reduce heat to low. Add both paprikas and stir 2 minutes. Mix in broth, tomatoes, and tomato paste. Return chicken to skillet. Bring liquids to simmer. Cover skillet and simmer gently until chicken is just cooked through, about 8 minutes.

TRANSFER chicken to platter; tent with aluminum foil to keep warm. Increase heat to high and boil until sauce coats spoon thickly, about 8 minutes. Season to taste with salt and pepper. Spoon sauce over chicken.

Chicken breasts stuffed with goat cheese and basil

IN THIS EXCEPTIONAL VERSION of stuffed chicken breasts, boneless, skinless chicken breast halves are first flattened to a uniform quarter-inch thickness, then rolled up around a filling of creamy goat cheese, green onions, and fragrant basil. Tying each of the resulting cylinders with kitchen string ensures that the filling stays inside during cooking; the strings are easily snipped off with kitchen scissors or a small sharp knife before serving.

4 SERVINGS

Chicken

- **4 skinless boneless chicken breast halves**

- **½ cup soft fresh goat cheese (about 4 ounces)**
- **2 green onions, thinly sliced**
- **3 tablespoons thinly sliced fresh basil**
- **1 large egg, beaten to blend**
- **½ cup plain dry breadcrumbs**

- **2 tablespoons (¼ stick) unsalted butter, melted**

Mushroom-wine sauce

- **¼ cup (½ stick) unsalted butter**
- **8 ounces mushrooms, sliced**
- **¼ cup dry white wine**
- **⅔ cup low-salt chicken broth**
- **4 tablespoons (½ stick) chilled unsalted butter, cut into 4 pieces**

FOR CHICKEN: Using meat mallet, pound chicken between sheets of waxed paper to thickness of ¼ inch. Pat chicken dry.

MIX cheese, green onions, and basil in small bowl to combine. Season to taste with salt and pepper. Spread cheese mixture lengthwise over half of each chicken piece. Tuck short ends in. Starting at one long side, roll chicken up into tight cylinders. Tie ends with kitchen string to secure. Dip chicken in egg, allowing excess to drip back into bowl. Roll in breadcrumbs, shaking off excess. *(Can be prepared 4 hours ahead. Cover and refrigerate.)*

PREHEAT oven to 350°F. Place chicken in 8-inch square baking dish. Pour 2 tablespoons melted butter over. Bake until cooked through, about 20 minutes.

FOR MUSHROOM-WINE SAUCE: Meanwhile, melt ¼ cup butter in heavy large skillet over medium heat. Add mushrooms and sauté until tender, about 8 minutes. Add wine and boil 3 minutes. Add broth and boil until liquid is reduced by half, about 6 minutes. Remove from heat and swirl in chilled unsalted butter, 1 piece at a time. Season sauce to taste with salt and pepper.

REMOVE string from chicken. Cut rolls crosswise into ½-inch-thick rounds. Fan on plates. Serve immediately, passing sauce separately.

Braised chicken in sun-dried tomato cream

THE FLAVORFUL OLIVE OIL in which sun-dried tomatoes are traditionally packed is a bonus in this Provençal-style entrée: A spoonful of it is used to sauté the chicken breast halves. Though technically a cream sauce, the liquid in which the chicken finishes cooking contains more white wine than cream, providing a perfect balance of fruitiness and richness.

2 SERVINGS; CAN BE DOUBLED

- **2 skinless boneless chicken breast halves**
- **1 tablespoon oil from oil-packed sun-dried tomatoes**
- **3 garlic cloves, thinly sliced**
- **½ cup dry white wine**
- **⅓ cup whipping cream**
- **¼ cup drained oil-packed sun-dried tomatoes, thinly sliced**
- **3 tablespoons thinly sliced fresh basil**

SPRINKLE chicken with salt and pepper. Heat oil in heavy medium skillet over medium-high heat. Add chicken to skillet and sauté until golden, about 4 minutes per side. Add garlic and stir 30 seconds. Add wine, cream, and tomatoes; bring to boil. Reduce heat to medium-low, cover skillet, and simmer until chicken is just cooked through, about 3 minutes. Transfer chicken to plates. Add basil to sauce in skillet. Increase heat and boil until sauce thickens enough to coat spoon, about 2 minutes. Season sauce to taste with salt and pepper; spoon over chicken and serve.

Braised Greek chicken and artichokes

THE MARINADE from jars of purchased artichoke hearts easily enhances the seasoning of this Mediterranean-style stovetop braise. To ensure the most tender results, cook the chicken at a gentle simmer after you brown it. Cooking the chicken breasts with their skins and bones helps keep them moist and flavorful.

4 SERVINGS

- **1 tablespoon olive oil**
- **4 chicken breast halves with skin and bones**
- **2 6-ounce jars marinated artichoke hearts, drained, 2 tablespoons marinade reserved**
- **¾ cup low-salt chicken broth**
- **1 tablespoon fresh lemon juice**
- **1 teaspoon grated lemon peel**
- **¼ teaspoon dried crushed red pepper**
- **3 tablespoons chopped fresh oregano, divided**

HEAT oil in heavy large skillet over medium-high heat. Sprinkle chicken with salt and pepper. Add chicken to skillet and sauté until browned, about 5 minutes per side. Add 2 tablespoons reserved marinade, broth, lemon juice, lemon peel, and crushed red pepper. Reduce heat to low, cover, and simmer until chicken is almost cooked through, about 10 minutes. Uncover; stir in artichokes and 2 tablespoons oregano. Simmer until liquid is slightly reduced and chicken is cooked through, about 5 minutes longer. Stir in remaining 1 tablespoon oregano. Season to taste with salt and pepper.

Spiced Moroccan chicken with onions and prunes

AN EXOTIC MIXTURE of onions, garlic, dried fruit, lemon juice, honey, and spices produces a very flavorful sauce; soak it up by serving the chicken in traditional North African style with couscous, or substitute rice. Sautéing the spices along with the onions for a minute before adding liquid develops the spice flavors more fully.

4 SERVINGS

- **4 skinless boneless chicken breast halves**
- **2 tablespoons olive oil**
- **1¾ cups chopped onions**
- **2 garlic cloves, chopped**
- **1 tablespoon all purpose flour**
- **1 teaspoon ground ginger**
- **1 teaspoon ground cinnamon**
- **1 teaspoon ground cumin**
- **2 cups low-salt chicken broth**
- **1 cup pitted prunes**
- **3 tablespoons fresh lemon juice**
- **2 tablespoons honey**

- **Chopped fresh cilantro**

SPRINKLE chicken with salt and pepper. Heat oil in heavy large skillet over medium-high heat. Add chicken; sauté until brown and just cooked through, about 4 minutes per side. Using tongs, transfer chicken to plate. Add onions and garlic to same skillet. Sauté until onions begin to soften, about 3 minutes. Mix in flour, ginger, cinnamon, and cumin; stir 1 minute. Gradually whisk in broth. Add prunes, lemon juice, and honey. Boil until sauce thickens enough to coat spoon, whisking occasionally, about 8 minutes. Season sauce to taste with salt and pepper. Return chicken to skillet. Simmer until heated through, about 2 minutes.

Transfer chicken and sauce to platter. Sprinkle with cilantro and serve.

Chicken escalopes with watercress–green onion mayonnaise

WITH ITS BRIGHT GREEN COLOR and peppery taste, watercress deserves more respect than being reduced to a garnish. Here, it is blanched in boiling water to preserve its vivid hue, then chopped and combined with mayonnaise, green onions, and lemon juice to make an easy sauce for sautéed chicken breasts. Just place a dollop on top of each hot-from-the-skillet chicken escalope, and the sauce melts and bathes the meat with flavor.

4 SERVINGS

- **3 cups (loosely packed) watercress, thick stems trimmed, coarsely chopped**
- **¾ cup mayonnaise**
- **½ cup thinly sliced green onions (white and pale green parts only)**
- **2 teaspoons plus 2 tablespoons fresh lemon juice**

- **2 large skinless boneless chicken breast halves**
- **3 tablespoons extra-virgin olive oil**

- **4 lemon wedges**

COOK watercress in pot of boiling salted water 30 seconds; drain. Let cool in strainer. Squeeze out excess water. Finely chop watercress. Mix watercress, mayonnaise, green onions, and 2 teaspoons lemon juice in small bowl to blend. Season to taste with salt and pepper. *(Sauce can be made 2 days ahead. Cover and chill.)*

PLACE each chicken breast between sheets of plastic wrap. Using meat mallet or rolling pin, pound chicken to ½-inch thickness. Cut each chicken breast lengthwise in half. Place chicken in glass baking dish. Pour remaining 2 tablespoons lemon juice and olive oil over chicken. Sprinkle with salt and pepper. Turn to coat. Cover and refrigerate at least 1 hour and up to 1 day.

HEAT heavy large skillet over medium-high heat. Remove chicken from marinade. Add chicken to skillet and sauté until cooked through, about 2 minutes per side. Transfer chicken to 4 plates. Garnish each with dollop of sauce and 1 lemon wedge.

Orange-rosemary chicken

IT IS ALMOST AS QUICK to make the citrus-herb glaze that coats this chicken as it is to open a bottle of barbecue sauce—and the glaze tastes far more interesting. The chicken gains extra flavor from the smoke of fragrant wood chips such as hickory or applewood. Sold in cookware, specialty foods, and grilling supply stores (hickory chips may also be available at supermarkets and home-supply stores), they need only be soaked for an hour or so in water (to make sure they smolder rather than burn), then wrapped loosely in aluminum foil and placed directly on the coals before cooking commences.

6 TO 8 SERVINGS

- **1 12-ounce container frozen orange juice concentrate, thawed**
- **1/3 cup dry white wine**
- **1/3 cup honey-Dijon mustard**
- **2 tablespoons finely chopped fresh rosemary or 2 teaspoons dried**
- **4 teaspoons soy sauce**
- **2 teaspoons hot pepper sauce**
- **1 garlic clove, peeled**

- **1 cup hickory wood chips, soaked 1 hour in water to cover, drained**
- **2 7-pound roasting chickens, each cut into 8 pieces (breasts halved if large)**

BLEND first 7 ingredients in processor. Set orange glaze aside.

PREPARE barbecue (medium heat). Place wood chips in 8x6-inch foil packet with open top. Set packet atop coals about 5 minutes before grilling. Sprinkle chicken with salt and pepper. Grill chicken until golden, turning occasionally, about 5 minutes per side. Continue grilling chicken until cooked through, brushing glaze over chicken and turning occasionally, about 25 minutes longer. Transfer to platter and serve.

Grilled chicken with root beer barbecue sauce

EVERY TRICK in the barbecue kit is used to create this incredible dish: a spice rub for deep-down flavor, a mop to keep the chicken moist during cooking, wood chips for old-fashioned smoke taste (you can find hickory chips at supermarkets and home-supply stores), and, of course, a delicious sauce that features a popular soft drink. Ask your butcher to halve the chickens and remove the backbones.

4 TO 6 SERVINGS

- **1 tablespoon salt**
- **1 tablespoon Hungarian sweet paprika**
- **1 tablespoon (packed) dark brown sugar**
- **2 teaspoons ground black pepper**
- **1/4 teaspoon celery seeds**
- **2 3 1/2- to 3 3/4-pound chickens, each cut in half, backbones removed**

- **1 cup water**
- **3/4 cup distilled white vinegar**
- **1/4 cup Worcestershire sauce**

- **45 charcoal briquettes**
- **2 cups hickory wood chips, soaked 1 hour in water to cover, drained**

Root Beer Barbecue Sauce (see recipe)

MIX first 5 ingredients in small bowl. Reserve 4 teaspoons spice mixture for mop. Rub remaining spice mixture all over chicken halves. Refrigerate chicken 1 hour.

MIX 1 cup water, vinegar, Worcestershire sauce, and reserved 4 teaspoons spice mixture in medium bowl to blend for mop.

PLACE 1 handful of torn newspaper in bottom of charcoal chimney. Top newspaper with 30 charcoal briquettes. Remove top rack from barbecue; place chimney on bottom rack. Light newspaper and let charcoal burn until ash on briquettes is gray, about 30 minutes. Open 1 bottom barbecue vent. Turn out hot charcoal onto 1 side of bottom rack. Using metal spatula, spread charcoal to cover approximately ⅓ of rack. Scatter 1 cup drained wood chips over coals (using too many wet chips may douse the fire). Fill foil loaf pan halfway with water and place on bottom rack opposite coals.

RETURN top rack to barbecue. Arrange chicken halves, skin side up, on top rack above loaf pan (not above charcoal). Cover barbecue with lid, positioning top vent directly over chickens. Place stem of candy thermometer through top vent, with gauge on outside of lid and tip near chickens (thermometer should not touch chickens or rack); leave thermometer in place during cooking. Use top and bottom barbecue vents to maintain temperature between 275°F and 325°F, opening vents wider to increase heat and closing to decrease heat. Keep any other vents closed. Check temperature every 10 minutes. Grill chickens until almost cooked through, brushing with mop every 15 minutes, about 1 hour 25 minutes. After 15 minutes, use technique described above to light remaining 15 charcoal briquettes in chimney set atop nonflammable surface.

IF temperature of barbecue falls below 275°F, use oven mitts to lift off top rack with chickens; place rack with chickens on nonflammable surface. Using tongs, add hot gray charcoal briquettes from chimney to bottom rack. Scatter remaining 1 cup drained wood chips over charcoal. Reposition top rack on barbecue, placing chickens above loaf pan. Cover with lid. Brush chickens with some Root Beer Barbecue Sauce and continue grilling until meat thermometer inserted into thickest part of thighs registers 180°F, about 6 minutes longer. Using tongs, move chickens directly over fire. Grill until sauce sizzles and browns, about 2 minutes. Cut chicken into quarters. Serve, passing remaining Root Beer Barbecue Sauce separately.

Root beer barbecue sauce

BARBECUE SAUCES flavored with soft drinks are a long-standing tradition in the South. Although the idea may seem strange at first to non-Southerners, it makes perfect sense, since most barbecue sauces feature not only sugar or other sweeteners, but also the fruit or spices that flavor so many beverages. Root beer is a great choice, being sweet, mellow, and aromatic. Liquid smoke is a smoke-flavored liquid seasoning available at specialty foods stores and many supermarkets.

MAKES 1½ CUPS

- **1 cup root beer**
- **1 cup ketchup**
- **¼ cup fresh lemon juice**
- **¼ cup orange juice**
- **3 tablespoons Worcestershire sauce**
- **1½ tablespoons (packed) dark brown sugar**
- **1 tablespoon mild-flavored (light) molasses**
- **1 teaspoon liquid smoke**
- **½ teaspoon grated lemon peel**
- **½ teaspoon ground ginger**
- **½ teaspoon garlic powder**
- **½ teaspoon onion powder**

COMBINE all ingredients in heavy medium saucepan. Bring to boil over medium heat, stirring occasionally. Reduce heat to medium-low and simmer until reduced to 1½ cups, about 20 minutes. Season sauce to taste with salt and pepper. Cool slightly. Transfer to bowl. Cover and refrigerate. *(Can be made 2 weeks ahead; keep refrigerated.)*

Grilled chicken with tricolor salsa

THIS RECIPE can easily be doubled to serve eight. Offer the chicken with lots of hot tortillas and cold Mexican beer.

4 SERVINGS; CAN BE DOUBLED

Chicken

- **6 large chicken breast halves with skin and bones or one 4-pound chicken, cut into 4 pieces**
- **1/4 cup fresh lemon juice**
- **3 tablespoons olive oil**
- **1/4 red onion, chopped**
- **1 tablespoon grated lemon peel**
- **1 teaspoon ground cumin**

Salsa

- **1 cup fresh corn kernels (from 2 small ears) or frozen, thawed**
- **1 large tomato, seeded, chopped**
- **2/3 cup chopped red onion**
- **1/2 cup chopped fresh cilantro**
- **2 tablespoons olive oil**
- **1 tablespoon fresh lemon juice**
- **1/2 teaspoon ground cumin**
- **1/2 to 1 jalapeño chile, seeded, minced**

- **1 avocado, halved, pitted, peeled, chopped**
- **Fresh cilantro sprigs**

FOR CHICKEN: Place chicken in glass baking dish. Whisk lemon juice and next 4 ingredients in small bowl and pour over chicken; turn to coat. Cover and refrigerate at least 3 hours and up to 1 day, turning occasionally.

FOR SALSA: Combine first 8 ingredients in medium bowl. *(Can be prepared 6 hours ahead. Cover and refrigerate.)*

PREPARE barbecue (medium-high heat) or preheat broiler. Sprinkle chicken with salt and pepper. Grill until cooked through, 12 minutes per side for breasts and 14 minutes per side for leg pieces.

ADD avocado to salsa. Season to taste with salt and pepper. Place chicken on plates. Spoon salsa alongside. Top chicken with cilantro sprigs and serve.

East-West barbecued chicken

HOISIN SAUCE lends this grilled chicken an Eastern flavor; the dried crushed red pepper and chili sauce give it a Western kick. Serve with baked potatoes or garlic bread, and offer cool, refreshing watermelon for dessert. Hoisin sauce is available at Asian markets and in the Asian foods sections of many supermarkets.

2 SERVINGS; CAN BE DOUBLED OR TRIPLED

- **1 2 1/2- to 3-pound chicken, cut into 4 pieces, wings removed**
- **1/4 cup orange juice**
- **1 tablespoon olive oil**
- **2 teaspoons Dijon mustard**
- **1/4 teaspoon dried crushed red pepper**
- **1/4 cup chili sauce**
- **1/4 cup hoisin sauce**

PLACE chicken in glass baking dish. Sprinkle with salt and pepper. Whisk orange juice, oil, mustard, and crushed red pepper in small bowl to blend. Pour over chicken and turn to coat. Let stand 20 minutes. Whisk chili sauce and hoisin sauce in another small bowl to blend.

PREPARE barbecue (medium-high heat) or preheat broiler. Grill chicken until just cooked through, about 12 minutes per side. Brush one side of chicken with chili-hoisin sauce mixture; grill until beginning to brown, about 3 minutes. Brush second side with sauce and grill until chicken is beginning to brown. Serve hot.

Grilled chicken drummettes with ancho-cherry barbecue sauce

THESE OUTSTANDING APPETIZERS—a little fruity, a little spicy—will make you a popular person at the next neighborhood barbecue. Dried ancho chiles are available at many supermarkets, as well as Latin markets and specialty foods stores.

10 SERVINGS

- **1¼ cups apple cider vinegar**
- **¾ cup ketchup**
- **¾ cup chopped onion**
- **¾ cup dried tart cherries**
- **⅓ cup (packed) dark brown sugar**
- **¼ cup water**
- **3 tablespoons mild-flavored (light) molasses**
- **2 large dried ancho chiles (about 1 ounce), stemmed, seeded**
- **2 garlic cloves**
- **1 teaspoon ground coriander**
- **Pinch of ground cloves**

- **3 pounds chicken wing drummettes**

COMBINE all ingredients except chicken in heavy medium saucepan. Bring to boil. Reduce heat to medium-low. Cover; simmer until chiles and cherries are tender, about 20 minutes. Working in batches, puree mixture in blender. Return sauce to pan. If necessary, simmer uncovered until sauce is reduced to 3 cups and thickens. Season with salt and pepper. *(Can be made 3 days ahead. Cover and chill.)*

PREPARE barbecue (medium heat). Sprinkle chicken with salt and pepper. Grill until just cooked through, turning occasionally, about 10 minutes. Brush sauce over; continue grilling until glazed, turning chicken and basting often with more sauce, about 5 minutes longer. Serve with remaining sauce.

Grilled chicken with jerk seasoning

TRADITIONALLY, JERK IS MADE with Scotch bonnet peppers, also known as habanero chiles. This recipe uses the more commonly found jalapeños, but if you do use habaneros (available at Latin markets and some supermarkets), remember that they're 60 times hotter than jalapeños. Reduce the quantity to suit your taste.

8 SERVINGS

- **2 bunches green onions, chopped**
- **⅓ cup red wine vinegar**
- **2 tablespoons vegetable oil**
- **2 tablespoons soy sauce**
- **2 tablespoons whole allspice, ground in spice mill or in mortar with pestle**
- **2 jalapeño chiles, halved**
- **2 teaspoons salt**
- **1 teaspoon ground black pepper**
- **1 teaspoon ground cinnamon**
- **¼ teaspoon ground nutmeg**
- **8 large boneless chicken breast halves with skin**

COARSELY puree first 10 ingredients in processor. Transfer puree to large bowl. Add chicken breasts and turn to coat. Cover and refrigerate at least 3 hours and up to 1 day, turning occasionally.

PREPARE barbecue (medium heat). Remove chicken from marinade. Grill chicken until cooked through, turning occasionally, about 20 minutes. Transfer to plates and serve.

Grilled chicken, red onion, and mint kebabs with Greek salad

THESE COLORFUL KEBABS, featuring the popular Greek flavors of mint and oregano, are extra-easy to prepare thanks to skinless, boneless chicken breast halves: Just cut the meat into one-inch chunks and it's ready to marinate and then skewer. Serve the kebabs over rice or with pita bread that has been lightly brushed with olive oil and briefly toasted on the grill.

4 SERVINGS

1½ pounds skinless boneless chicken breast halves, cut into 1-inch pieces
4 tablespoons extra-virgin olive oil, divided
4 garlic cloves, crushed
1 teaspoon dried mint
1 teaspoon dried oregano
1 teaspoon salt
1 teaspoon ground black pepper
2 tablespoons fresh lemon juice

1 bunch fresh mint
1 red onion, cut into 1-inch pieces
8 12-inch-long metal skewers
Greek Salad (see recipe)

MIX chicken, 2 tablespoons oil, garlic, mint, oregano, salt, and pepper in medium bowl. Let marinate 30 minutes. Whisk remaining 2 tablespoons oil and lemon juice in small bowl to blend.

PREPARE barbecue (medium-high heat). Pull off large fresh mint leaves from stems. Alternate chicken, onion, and mint leaves on skewers; sprinkle with salt and pepper. Grill until chicken is just cooked through, turning and basting occasionally with oil-lemon mixture, about 9 minutes. Transfer skewers to platter. Serve Greek Salad alongside.

Greek salad

KNOWN IN GREECE as *salata horiatiki* ("village-style salad") this traditional and widespread mixture of fresh summer vegetables, black olives, and crumbled feta cheese makes a perfect accompaniment for simple grilled foods. In fact, if the vegetables are chopped into smaller pieces, the same mixture becomes almost like a chunky salsa for Mediterranean-style grilled chicken, meat, or seafood.

MAKES ABOUT 4½ CUPS

12 ounces tomatoes, seeded, diced (about 2 cups)
2 cups diced seeded peeled cucumber (from about 1 large)
1 cup diced red bell pepper (from about 1 large)
¼ cup halved pitted Kalamata olives
¼ cup diced red onion
3 tablespoons chopped fresh Italian parsley
3 tablespoons extra-virgin olive oil
1½ tablespoons red wine vinegar
½ teaspoon dried oregano
¼ cup crumbled feta cheese (about 2 ounces)

TOSS first 9 ingredients in medium bowl to combine. Gently mix in cheese. Season salad to taste with salt and pepper. *(Can be made 2 hours ahead. Let stand at room temperature.)*

Hot and sticky apricot-glazed chicken

TWO KEY STEPS ensure perfect grilled chicken, cooked through and juicy on the inside while perfectly browned (rather than charred) on the outside. First, cook the chicken using *indirect* heat—placing it off to the side of, rather than directly over, the glowing coals or live gas flames, and covering the grill to create an oven-like effect. Second, apply the sweet glaze during the later stages of cooking, to ensure that it is exposed to the heat only long enough to thicken and blacken in spots, but not so long that its sugars burn to a crisp.

4 SERVINGS

2/3 cup apricot preserves
1/4 cup white wine vinegar
2 tablespoons hot mustard
2 garlic cloves, finely chopped

8 chicken thighs with skin and bones, excess fat trimmed

PREPARE barbecue (medium-high heat). Combine first 4 ingredients in small saucepan. Whisk over medium heat until preserves melt. Set glaze aside.

SPRINKLE chicken generously with salt and pepper. Place chicken, skin side down, on outer edges of grill rack. Cover grill and cook chicken until skin is light golden, turning occasionally, about 15 minutes. Continue to grill, brushing with glaze and turning occasionally, until skin is blackened in spots and juices run clear when thighs are pierced with fork, about 10 minutes longer. Divide chicken among 4 plates and serve.

Chicken brochettes with red bell peppers and feta

A LITTLE BIT OF FETA CHEESE goes a long way in the tangy marinade for this dish. Feta tends to be salty, so taste yours first and adjust the amount of salt you sprinkle over the brochettes accordingly. When using wooden or bamboo skewers, always soak them in cold water first so that they will be less likely to scorch over the direct heat of the grill.

6 SERVINGS

1 cup plain nonfat yogurt
5 tablespoons (packed) crumbled feta cheese, divided
2 garlic cloves, minced
1 teaspoon chopped fresh rosemary
1/4 teaspoon ground black pepper
1 1/2 pounds skinless boneless chicken breast halves, cut into 1 1/2-inch pieces

2 large red bell peppers, cut into 1 1/2-inch pieces
6 10- to 12-inch-long wooden skewers, soaked 1 hour in water to cover

MIX yogurt, 3 tablespoons feta cheese, garlic, rosemary, and pepper in large bowl. Add chicken; toss to coat. Let marinate at room temperature 30 minutes.

PREPARE barbecue (medium-high heat) or preheat broiler. Thread chicken and red bell pepper pieces alternately onto skewers. Sprinkle with salt and pepper. Grill or broil until chicken is cooked through, turning occasionally, about 8 minutes.

TRANSFER brochettes to platter. Sprinkle with remaining 2 tablespoons feta cheese and serve.

Tandoori-spiced chicken with tomato-ginger chutney

TANDOORI REFERS TO any food cooked in a *tandoor*, the traditional Indian beehive-shaped clay oven heated by a wood or charcoal fire. By extension, the word also describes any grilled or baked dish marinated or seasoned as it would be for the tandoor. The yogurt in this typical marinade not only is an excellent tenderizer thanks to its natural acidity, but also imparts a nice, mild tang. Begin marinating the chicken one day in advance.

6 SERVINGS

Marinade

- **2 cups plain yogurt**
- **2 tablespoons ground coriander**
- **2 tablespoons mild paprika**
- **1½ tablespoons ground cumin**
- **1½ tablespoons ground ginger**
- **1 tablespoon garlic powder**
- **1 tablespoon ground black pepper**
- **½ teaspoon ground cinnamon**
- **½ teaspoon ground cardamom**
- **¼ teaspoon ground cloves**
- **6 7- to 8-ounce skinless boneless chicken breast halves**

Chutney

- **3 cups chopped seeded tomatoes (about 1¼ pounds)**
- **¾ cup chopped red onion**
- **½ cup chopped fresh mint**
- **3 tablespoons minced peeled fresh ginger**
- **3 tablespoons fresh lime juice**

FOR MARINADE: Whisk yogurt and next 9 ingredients in large bowl to blend. Add chicken and turn to coat. Cover and refrigerate overnight.

FOR CHUTNEY: Combine all ingredients in medium bowl. Season to taste with salt and pepper. *(Chutney can be prepared 1 day ahead. Cover and refrigerate.)*

PREPARE barbecue (medium-high heat). Brush grill rack with oil. Transfer marinade-coated chicken to barbecue grill. Grill chicken until cooked through, about 7 minutes per side. Transfer chicken to cutting board. Cut crosswise on diagonal into ½-inch-thick slices. Transfer to platter. Serve with chutney.

Chianti-braised stuffed chicken thighs on egg noodles

PURE COMFORT FOOD: Skinless, boneless chicken thighs are quickly wrapped around an easy-to-make sausage–breadcrumb–Parmesan stuffing, then browned and simmered in a garlicky mixture of dry red wine, broth, and tomatoes. The results are served over boiled egg noodles, to soak up every last drop of the sauce.

6 TO 8 SERVINGS

- **4 ounces (about 1 link) sweet Italian sausage, casing removed, meat crumbled**
- **½ cup fresh breadcrumbs made from crustless day-old French bread**
- **½ cup freshly grated Parmesan cheese (about 1½ ounces)**
- **1 large shallot, minced**
- **1 large egg**
- **2 tablespoons chopped fresh parsley**
- **2 teaspoons chopped fresh thyme**
- **½ teaspoon salt**
- **¼ teaspoon ground black pepper**
- **8 large skinless boneless chicken thighs (about 2½ pounds total)**

- **2 tablespoons olive oil**
- **¼ cup chopped pancetta or bacon**
- **¾ cup finely chopped onion**
- **6 garlic cloves, minced**
- **1 750-ml bottle Chianti or other dry red wine**

- **3 cups low-salt chicken broth**
- **2 cups canned crushed tomatoes with added puree**
- **1 bay leaf**
- **1 teaspoon dried basil**

- **1 pound egg noodles**

MIX first 9 ingredients in medium bowl. Place 1 chicken thigh on work surface. Fill area where bone was removed with 2 tablespoons stuffing. Wrap chicken thigh around filling and tie with kitchen string to hold together. Repeat with remaining chicken thighs and stuffing. Sprinkle generously with salt and pepper.

HEAT olive oil in heavy large skillet over medium-high heat. Add pancetta; sauté until pancetta is light brown and fat is rendered, about 5 minutes. Transfer pancetta to paper towels to drain. Add chicken to drippings in skillet; cook until golden on all sides, about 10 minutes. Transfer to plate. Add onion and garlic to skillet; sauté until onion is soft, about 10 minutes. Return pancetta to skillet. Add wine and boil until mixture is reduced to 2 cups, about 12 minutes. Add broth, tomatoes, bay leaf, basil, and chicken thighs; bring to boil. Reduce heat and simmer uncovered until chicken is cooked through, about 35 minutes. *(Can be prepared 1 day ahead. Cool slightly. Refrigerate until cold, then cover and keep refrigerated. Rewarm over medium heat before continuing.)*

TRANSFER chicken to bowl; cover to keep warm. Simmer sauce in skillet until slightly thickened and reduced to 4 cups, about 10 minutes. Discard bay leaf. Season to taste with salt and pepper.

MEANWHILE, cook noodles in large pot of boiling salted water until tender but still firm to bite. Drain. Transfer noodles to large platter. Top with chicken and sauce and serve.

Chicken in green pumpkin seed sauce

KNOWN IN SPANISH as *pipián verde,* this classic sauce of the Mexican kitchen combines shelled pumpkin seeds, tomatillos, and green chiles. *Pepitas,* the Spanish term for pumpkin seeds, may be found at Latin markets, natural foods stores, and many supermarkets. Fresh tomatillos, the green tomato-like fruits with paper-thin husks, are available at Latin markets and some supermarkets.

6 SERVINGS

Chicken

- **5 cups water**
- **6 chicken thighs with skin and bones**
- **1/4 large white onion**
- **3 garlic cloves, peeled, halved**
- **3 large fresh cilantro sprigs**
- **1 teaspoon fine sea salt**

Sauce

- **1 2/3 cups shelled pepitas (pumpkin seeds), divided**
- **6 whole black peppercorns**

- **12 ounces tomatillos, husked, rinsed, coarsely chopped**
- **1/4 cup chopped white onion**
- **1/4 cup chopped fresh cilantro**
- **3 medium serrano chiles, stemmed, chopped with seeds**
- **2 garlic cloves, chopped**
- **1 teaspoon fine sea salt**
- **6 tablespoons corn oil, divided**

FOR CHICKEN: Bring all ingredients to boil in large pot. Reduce heat and simmer uncovered until chicken is cooked through, about 30 minutes. Transfer chicken to bowl; cover to keep warm. Reserve chicken broth in pot; spoon off fat from surface of broth.

MEANWHILE, PREPARE SAUCE: Heat heavy large skillet over medium-low heat. Add pepitas; stir frequently until seeds puff and begin to pop, about 15 minutes (do not brown). Transfer to dish and cool. Set aside 2 tablespoons pepitas for garnish. Working in batches, finely grind remaining pepitas with peppercorns in spice mill or coffee grinder.

PUREE tomatillos, next 5 ingredients, and ½ cup reserved chicken broth in blender until almost smooth. Heat 2 tablespoons oil in heavy medium skillet over medium-high heat. Add tomatillo mixture and simmer until sauce is thick and reduced to 1 cup, stirring frequently, about 5 minutes.

HEAT remaining 4 tablespoons oil in heavy large pot over medium heat. Add ground pepita mixture. Stir constantly until mixture resembles very coarse paste and begins to color in spots, about 9 minutes. Add tomatillo mixture and stir 1 minute. Add 2 cups reserved chicken broth and bring to boil. Reduce heat to medium-low and simmer until sauce is thick, stirring constantly, about 3 minutes longer. Season sauce to taste with salt. Spoon some sauce onto platter. Top with chicken. Spoon remaining sauce over chicken. Garnish with reserved 2 tablespoons pepitas.

Sri Lanka chicken curry

THE ISLAND NATION of Sri Lanka, off India's southern tip, typically adds a soothing tropical flourish to curries by using coconut milk as the cooking liquid. Cans of unsweetened coconut milk are available at Indian, Southeast Asian, and Latin markets, and at many supermarkets.

6 SERVINGS

- **⅔ cup chopped onion**
- **5 garlic cloves, peeled**
- **2 tablespoons chopped peeled fresh ginger**
- **1 tablespoon curry powder**
- **1 tablespoon ground cinnamon**
- **¾ teaspoon dried crushed red pepper**
- **½ cup chopped fresh cilantro, divided**
- **12 chicken thighs with skin and bones**

- **2 tablespoons vegetable oil**
- **2 cups canned unsweetened coconut milk**
- **1 cup low-salt chicken broth**
- **½ teaspoon turmeric**
- **Freshly cooked rice**

BLEND first 6 ingredients and ¼ cup cilantro in processor to form paste, stopping frequently to scrape down sides of bowl. Rub paste over chicken.

HEAT oil in heavy large skillet over medium-high heat. Add chicken and brown on all sides, about 6 minutes. Add coconut milk, broth, and turmeric. Reduce heat, cover, and simmer until chicken is cooked through, turning once, about 30 minutes. Transfer chicken to plate. Boil liquid in skillet until reduced to sauce consistency, about 4 minutes. Season to taste with salt. Return chicken to skillet; heat through. Sprinkle with remaining ¼ cup cilantro. Serve over rice.

Chicken with roasted lemons, green olives, and capers

THINK OF THIS RECIPE as a hearty Mediterranean variation on familiar chicken *piccata*. Roasting the lemon slices concentrates their flavor, providing a perfect counterpoint to the pungent green olives and sharp-tasting capers in the sauce that accompanies the quickly sautéed chicken breasts. Be sure that the chicken broth is low in salt, as the liquid is boiled until reduced to a syrupy essence.

4 SERVINGS

Roasted lemons

- **12 thin lemon slices (from 2 lemons)**
- **Olive oil**

Chicken

- **4 large skinless boneless chicken breast halves**
- **All purpose flour**

- **5 tablespoons olive oil**
- **½ cup sliced pitted green Sicilian olives or other brine-cured green olives**
- **2 tablespoons drained capers**
- **1½ cups low-salt chicken broth**
- **4 tablespoons (½ stick) butter, cut into 4 pieces**
- **3 tablespoons chopped fresh parsley, divided**

FOR ROASTED LEMONS: Preheat oven to 325°F. Line baking sheet with parchment paper. Arrange lemon slices in single layer on prepared sheet. Brush lemon slices with olive oil; sprinkle lightly with salt. Roast until slightly dry and beginning to brown around edges, about 25 minutes. *(Lemons can be prepared 1 day ahead. Transfer to container. Cover and refrigerate.)*

FOR CHICKEN: Sprinkle chicken with salt and pepper. Dredge chicken in flour to coat both sides; shake off excess. Heat oil in heavy large skillet over high heat. Add chicken and cook until golden brown, about 3 minutes per side. Stir in olives and capers. Add broth and bring to boil, scraping up any browned bits from bottom of skillet. Boil until liquid is reduced to syrup consistency, turning chicken over after 3 minutes, about 5 minutes. Add butter, roasted lemon slices, and 2 tablespoons parsley; simmer until butter is melted and chicken is cooked through, about 2 minutes. Season to taste with salt and pepper. Transfer to platter. Sprinkle with remaining 1 tablespoon parsley and serve.

Brazilian chicken and rice with olives

A PURCHASED YELLOW RICE MIX becomes the basis for an exotic Brazilian-style chicken pilaf when orange juice and peel, garlic, and olives are added to the skillet, along with strips of skinless, boneless chicken thighs. The garnish of orange wedges may be enjoyed between bites or squeezed over individual portions.

4 SERVINGS

- **1 pound skinless boneless chicken thighs, cut into ½-inch-wide strips**
- **¼ cup olive oil**
- **4 garlic cloves, finely chopped**
- **1 teaspoon grated orange peel**
- **1 cup water**
- **½ cup orange juice**
- **1 cup yellow rice mix with seasoning packet (from 8-ounce box)**
- **½ cup (packed) pimiento-stuffed Spanish olives, halved**
- **1 cup chopped fresh cilantro**
- **Orange wedges**

SPRINKLE chicken lightly with salt and generously with ground black pepper. Heat oil in heavy large skillet over medium-high heat. Add chicken, garlic, and orange peel; sauté until chicken is lightly browned, about 3 minutes. Add 1 cup water and orange juice; bring to boil. Mix in rice, contents of seasoning packet, and olives; return to boil. Reduce heat to medium-low, cover, and cook until liquid is absorbed and rice is tender, about 20 minutes. Remove from heat; let stand covered 10 minutes.

STIR cilantro into rice mixture. Transfer to platter. Garnish with orange wedges and serve.

Pan-seared chicken with goat cheese mashed potatoes

MARINATING THE CHICKEN OVERNIGHT allows the flavors of fresh thyme and rosemary to infuse the meat, with delicious results. The combination of pan-searing and baking ensures that the chicken breasts cook through perfectly, remaining tender and juicy. By all means remove the skin from the chicken breasts if you wish, but only after they are cooked.

6 SERVINGS

10 tablespoons olive oil, divided
½ cup chopped fresh thyme
3 tablespoons chopped fresh rosemary
1 teaspoon crushed black pepper
6 boneless chicken breast halves with skin

2 tablespoons fresh lemon juice
3 bunches arugula, stem ends trimmed
Goat Cheese Mashed Potatoes (see recipe)

WHISK 6 tablespoons oil, thyme, rosemary, and pepper in 13x9x2-inch glass baking dish. Add chicken breast halves and turn to coat. Cover with plastic wrap and refrigerate at least 4 hours and up to 1 day.

PREHEAT oven to 450°F. Scrape herb coating off chicken and sprinkle chicken with salt and pepper. Heat 3 tablespoons oil in heavy large ovenproof skillet over high heat. Place marinated chicken breasts, skin side down, in skillet. Sear chicken until crisp and golden brown, about 5 minutes. Turn chicken over and sear 4 minutes on second side. Transfer skillet to oven and bake until chicken is cooked through, about 6 minutes.

WHISK lemon juice and remaining 1 tablespoon oil in large bowl to blend. Season dressing to taste with salt and pepper. Add arugula to dressing in bowl and toss to coat. Divide mashed potatoes among 6 plates. Top mashed potatoes with arugula salad, then with chicken breasts, and serve.

Goat cheese mashed potatoes

SOFT FRESH GOAT CHEESE not only contributes richness and a hint of tangy taste to these mashed potatoes, but also makes them extra-fluffy. Chopped green onions—their pungency made mild by boiling them in the milk that also enriches the potatoes—add extra flavor. This side dish would also be great with beef or pork.

6 SERVINGS

3 pounds russet potatoes, peeled, cut into 1½-inch pieces

1 cup whole milk
1 bunch green onions, chopped
6 tablespoons (¾ stick) butter

1 cup crumbled soft fresh goat cheese (about 4 ounces)

COOK potatoes in large pot of boiling salted water until tender, about 30 minutes.

MEANWHILE, bring milk, green onions, and butter to boil in small saucepan over medium-high heat. Remove from heat.

DRAIN potatoes and return to pot. Add hot milk mixture and mash. Add goat cheese and mash until blended. Season mashed potatoes to taste with salt and pepper. *(Can be prepared 2 hours ahead. Let stand uncovered at room temperature. Before serving, stir over low heat until heated through.)*

Deviled fried chicken

DEVILED IS A SOUTHERN TERM for a dish that is highly seasoned, especially with mustard and cayenne pepper. If you can't find onion powder with green onion and parsley, regular onion powder will do. To make life easy, have the butcher cut up the chicken; and use a small chicken—about three pounds—so that it will cook through quickly. Plan ahead, because the chicken needs to marinate for at least a day. Transferring the marinated chicken directly to the flour mixture and leaving it there for one hour allows the marinade to keep absorbing more seasoned flour, which then fries up to form an extra-crunchy crust.

4 SERVINGS

2 cups buttermilk
¼ cup Dijon mustard

- **2 tablespoons onion powder with green onion and parsley, divided**
- **5 teaspoons salt, divided**
- **4 teaspoons dry mustard, divided**
- **4 teaspoons cayenne pepper, divided**
- **2½ teaspoons ground black pepper, divided**
- **1 3- to 3¼-pound fryer chicken, backbone removed, chicken cut into 8 pieces, skinned (except wings)**

- **3 cups all purpose flour**
- **1 tablespoon baking powder**
- **1 tablespoon garlic powder**

- **5 cups (or more) peanut oil (for frying)**

IN 1-gallon resealable plastic bag, mix buttermilk, Dijon mustard, 1 tablespoon onion powder, 1 teaspoon salt, 1 teaspoon dry mustard, 1 teaspoon cayenne, and 1 teaspoon black pepper. Add chicken pieces. Seal bag, eliminating air. Turn bag to coat chicken evenly. Refrigerate at least 1 day and up to 2 days, turning plastic bag occasionally.

WHISK flour, baking powder, garlic powder, and remaining 1 tablespoon onion powder, 4 teaspoons salt, 3 teaspoons dry mustard, 3 teaspoons cayenne, and 1½ teaspoons black pepper in 13x9x2-inch glass baking dish. With marinade still clinging to chicken pieces (do not shake off excess), add chicken to flour mixture; turn to coat thickly. Let chicken stand in flour mixture 1 hour, turning chicken occasionally to recoat with flour mixture.

POUR enough oil to reach depth of 1¼ inches into deep 10- to 11-inch-diameter pot. Attach deep-fry thermometer. Heat oil over medium-high heat to 350°F. Add 4 pieces of chicken, skinned side down, to oil. Reduce heat to medium-low and fry 5 minutes, adjusting heat to maintain oil temperature between 280°F and 300°F (oil should bubble constantly around chicken). Using wooden spoons, turn chicken over. Fry 7 minutes. Turn chicken over again. Fry until deep golden brown and cooked through, about 3 minutes longer. Using same spoons, transfer chicken to large rack set over baking sheet.

REHEAT oil to 350°F. Repeat frying with remaining 4 pieces of chicken.

SERVE chicken warm or at room temperature within 2 hours, or chill up to 1 day and serve cold.

Chinese-flavored fried chicken with green onion–ginger dipping sauce

THE CRISPY-CRUSTED CHICKEN is accented with ginger and sesame oil, and served with a simple dipping sauce of soy, cilantro, green onions, and ginger. While the chicken is delicious served hot, it is so packed with flavor that it also makes a perfect cold entrée for a picnic basket. Wrap the chicken in aluminum foil and store the sauce in a plastic container. Hot chili sesame oil, used to season the dipping sauce, is available at Asian markets and in the Asian foods section of some supermarkets.

4 SERVINGS

Dipping sauce

- **½ cup soy sauce**
- **½ cup thinly sliced green onions**
- **2 tablespoons finely chopped fresh cilantro**
- **1½ teaspoons finely chopped peeled fresh ginger**
- **1½ teaspoons hot chili sesame oil**

Chicken

- **3 large eggs**
- **2 tablespoons soy sauce**
- **2 teaspoons Asian sesame oil**
- **1 4- to 4¼-pound whole chicken, cut into 12 pieces**

- **1 quart vegetable oil**
- **1½ cups all purpose flour**
- **3 tablespoons ground ginger**
- **1 teaspoon salt**
- **1 teaspoon ground black pepper**

- **2 1-inch pieces peeled fresh ginger, halved lengthwise**

FOR DIPPING SAUCE: Whisk all ingredients in small bowl to blend. *(Dipping sauce can be prepared 1 day ahead. Cover and refrigerate.)*

FOR CHICKEN: Whisk eggs, soy sauce, and sesame oil in large bowl to blend. Add chicken to egg mixture, turning to coat. Cover and chill at least 2 hours or up to 1 day.

HEAT vegetable oil in heavy large pot over medium-high heat to 375°F. Mix flour, ground ginger, salt, and pepper in another bowl. Add chicken thighs and drumsticks to flour mixture; turn to coat.

ADD fresh ginger to oil. Fry chicken thighs and drumsticks in hot oil until golden and cooked through, about 10 minutes per side. Using tongs, transfer chicken to paper towels to drain. Coat chicken breasts and wings with flour mixture. Fry until golden and cooked through, about 6 minutes per side. Transfer to paper towels. *(Can be prepared 2 hours ahead. Let stand at room temperature.)* Serve with dipping sauce.

Parmesan-Dijon drumsticks

COATING SKINLESS or skin-on chicken drumsticks with mustard-flavored butter and seasoned Parmesan breadcrumbs, then baking them in the oven produces a flavorful finger food that seems fried but isn't. The drumsticks are terrific either hot or at room temperature, which makes them ideal party food. Kids will love them, and so will their parents.

12 SERVINGS

- **3 cups fresh white breadcrumbs made from firm white sandwich bread**
- **1 cup freshly grated Parmesan cheese (about 3 ounces)**
- **6 tablespoons chopped fresh parsley**
- **4 teaspoons onion powder**
- **1 tablespoon Hungarian sweet paprika**
- **1 tablespoon dried oregano**
- **2 teaspoons salt**
- **1½ teaspoons ground black pepper**
- **1½ cups (3 sticks) butter**
- **½ cup plus 1 tablespoon Dijon mustard**
- **24 chicken drumsticks**

PREHEAT oven to 350°F. Butter 2 large rimmed baking sheets. Combine breadcrumbs, Parmesan cheese, parsley, onion powder, paprika, oregano, salt, and pepper in large bowl; stir to combine. Melt butter in small saucepan over medium-low heat. Remove from heat; add all mustard and whisk to blend. Brush drumsticks generously with butter mixture, then roll in breadcrumb mixture, coating drumsticks completely. Arrange drumsticks on prepared baking sheets.

BAKE drumsticks until golden brown and cooked through, about 1 hour. Serve warm or at room temperature within 2 hours.

Chicken and vegetable pot pies with dilled biscuit topping

WITH EACH SERVING prepared in its own individual baking dish and topped with a Pennsylvania Dutch-style buttermilk biscuit, this version of chicken pot pie is exemplary comfort food. Starting the filling the old-fashioned way—by poaching an entire chicken, removing the skin and bones, and tearing the meat into bite-size chunks—ensures incomparably flavorful results.

6 SERVINGS

- **1 4½- to 5-pound chicken, quartered, giblets reserved**
- **6 cups low-salt chicken broth**
- **1 bay leaf**

- **5 tablespoons butter**
- **¾ cup finely chopped red bell pepper**
- **½ cup chopped onion**
- **¾ teaspoon dried thyme**

- **8 ounces mushrooms, coarsely chopped**
- **5 tablespoons unbleached all purpose flour**
- **1¾ cups frozen mixed vegetables (from one 16-ounce bag), thawed**
- **⅓ cup whipping cream**
- **Unbaked dough for Dilled Buttermilk Biscuits (see recipe)**

COMBINE chicken, giblets, broth, and bay leaf in large pot. Cover partially with pot lid; simmer until chicken is just cooked through, rearranging chicken occasionally, about 25 minutes. Transfer chicken to large bowl.

SIMMER broth over medium-high heat until reduced to 2½ cups liquid, about 15 minutes. Strain broth; discard solids. Remove skin and bones from chicken. Tear meat into bite-size pieces; return to bowl.

MELT butter in heavy medium saucepan over medium heat. Add bell pepper, onion, and thyme. Sauté until onion is slightly softened, about 5 minutes. Add mushrooms and sauté until soft, about 7 minutes. Reduce heat to medium-low. Sprinkle mushroom mixture with flour; sauté 2 minutes. Gradually whisk in reduced broth. Add mixed vegetables. Simmer until broth thickens, stirring occasionally, about 5 minutes. Remove from heat. Stir chicken and cream into sauce; season filling to taste with salt and pepper. *(Can be prepared 1 day ahead. Cool slightly. Chill uncovered until cold, then cover and keep refrigerated. Rewarm over medium-low heat before continuing.)*

POSITION rack in top third of oven and preheat to 450°F. Divide filling among six 14-ounce individual casserole dishes or soufflé dishes. Place 1 unbaked 3-inch square of biscuit dough atop each. Bake until filling is bubbling and biscuits are puffed and brown, about 12 minutes. Let stand 5 minutes before serving.

Dilled buttermilk biscuits

ALTHOUGH THE BISCUIT DOUGH makes a perfect topping for chicken pot pies, it is wonderful baked on its own as an accompaniment to roast poultry or meat. Take care not to overmix the dough when combining the moist and dry ingredients; stirring with a light hand will ensure that the biscuits come out absolutely tender.

MAKES 6

- **⅔ cup chilled buttermilk**
- **1 large egg**
- **3 tablespoons minced fresh dill**
- **2½ cups unbleached all purpose flour**
- **4 teaspoons baking powder**
- **2 teaspoons sugar**
- **¼ teaspoon salt**
- **½ cup chilled solid vegetable shortening, cut into ½-inch cubes**
- **7 tablespoons chilled unsalted butter, cut into ½-inch cubes**

WHISK buttermilk, egg, and dill in small bowl to blend. Whisk flour and next 3 ingredients in large bowl to combine. Add shortening and butter to dry ingredients; cut in with fork until mixture resembles coarse meal. Add buttermilk mixture and stir just until moist dough forms.

USING floured hands, gently knead dough on well-floured work surface until dough just holds together. Pat out dough to 9x6-inch rectangle, about ¾ inch thick. Cut dough into six 3-inch squares. Transfer squares to ungreased baking sheet, spacing 2½ inches apart. *(Can be prepared 8 hours ahead. Cover and refrigerate.)*

IF baking separately, preheat oven to 400°F. Bake biscuits until puffed and golden brown, about 12 minutes.

Chicken, ham, and fennel pot pies

WITH THEIR MILD ANISE FLAVOR, fresh fennel bulb and dried fennel seeds make delicious companions to poached white-meat chicken in the light yet creamy filling for these individual pot pies. Let the filling cool completely before topping each serving with pastry; that way the dough won't soften and droop, but will puff up and bake to a golden crispness.

8 SERVINGS

- **5 cups low-salt chicken broth**
- **2 small fennel bulbs, trimmed, halved lengthwise, cored, thinly sliced**
- **1¾ pounds skinless boneless chicken breast halves, cut into 1-inch cubes**
- **½ cup diced peeled carrot**

- **5 tablespoons unsalted butter**
- **5 tablespoons all purpose flour**
- **2½ cups whole milk**
- **3 tablespoons fresh lemon juice**
- **2 teaspoons fennel seeds, crushed**
- **½ teaspoon (or more) salt**
- **4 ounces thinly sliced country ham, cut into matchstick-size strips**

Pot Pie Crust (see recipe)

- **1 large egg white, beaten to blend (for glaze)**

BRING broth to boil in heavy large pot over medium heat. Add fennel and cook 7 minutes. Add chicken and carrot; simmer until fennel, chicken, and carrot are tender, about 10 minutes. Pour chicken mixture into strainer set over bowl; reserve broth for another use.

MELT butter in heavy large saucepan over medium-high heat. Add flour and stir 2 minutes. Gradually add milk and whisk until sauce thickens, about 4 minutes. Add lemon juice, fennel seeds, and ½ teaspoon salt. Add chicken mixture and ham. Season to taste with salt and pepper. Divide filling among eight 10-ounce individual soufflé dishes or custard cups. Cool completely.

ROLL out pie crust on floured surface to ⅛-inch thickness. Cut out 8 rounds, each measuring ½ to 1 inch larger in diameter than soufflé dishes, gathering dough and rerolling as necessary. Cut out leaf decorations from dough scraps, if desired. Lay 1 dough round atop each dish; press dough overhang firmly to adhere to sides and top rim of dish. If using cutouts, brush bottom side with water and place atop dough; cut slits in dough for steam to escape. *(Can be prepared 1 day ahead. Cover each with plastic wrap and refrigerate.)*

PREHEAT oven to 375°F. Place pies on large rimmed baking sheet. Brush crusts with egg white glaze. Bake until pies are heated through and crusts are golden, about 40 minutes.

Pot pie crust

MAKE SURE you don't overprocess the dough—you want small pieces of chilled butter to remain intact (the ice water helps keep the butter and shortening firm), so that it will melt and steam during baking, creating a flaky crust.

MAKES 8 SMALL CRUSTS

- **3 cups sifted all purpose flour**
- **¾ teaspoon salt**
- **¾ cup (1½ sticks) chilled unsalted butter, cut into pieces**
- **4½ tablespoons chilled solid vegetable shortening, cut into pieces**
- **6 tablespoons (about) ice water**

COMBINE flour and salt in processor and blend. Add butter and shortening; using on/off turns, process until mixture resembles coarse meal. Add 4 tablespoons water; blend in. Add enough additional water by tablespoonfuls to form moist clumps.

Gather dough into ball; flatten into disk. Wrap in plastic and refrigerate until cold, at least 1 hour or up to 1 day.

Chicken Normande with mashed apples and potatoes

THE NORTHWESTERN French province of Normandy is famed for its apples, which figure prominently in regional cooking. Here, apples join potatoes in a pale golden puree that forms the crust for a chicken-and-parsnip casserole. Apple cider combines with brandy and cream to form the sauce for the casserole. If you like, further enhance the apple flavor by substituting Calvados, the apple brandy of Normandy, for regular brandy.

4 TO 6 SERVINGS

- **3 cups low-salt chicken broth**
- **1 cup apple cider or apple juice**
- **8 ounces parsnips, peeled, cut into ½-inch cubes**
- **1¾ pounds Yukon Gold potatoes, peeled, cut into ½-inch cubes**
- **12 ounces Golden Delicious apples (about 2 large), peeled, cored, cut into ½-inch cubes**
- **5 tablespoons butter, divided**

- **8 skinless boneless chicken thighs, cut into 1-inch pieces**
- **6 teaspoons minced fresh thyme, divided**
- **2 tablespoons all purpose flour**
- **1 cup frozen peas, thawed**

- **⅓ cup brandy**
- **⅓ cup whipping cream**

COMBINE first 3 ingredients in heavy large pot and bring to boil. Reduce heat to medium, cover, and simmer until parsnips are tender, about 5 minutes. Using slotted spoon, transfer parsnips to small bowl. Add potatoes and apples to same pot. Cover and simmer until very tender, about 20 minutes. Remove from heat. Using slotted spoon, transfer potatoes and apples to large bowl; add 3 tablespoons butter. Mash until almost smooth. Season to taste with salt and pepper. Pour broth mixture from pot into medium bowl; reserve pot.

SPRINKLE chicken with salt, pepper, and 4 teaspoons thyme; dust with flour. Melt remaining 2 tablespoons butter in reserved pot over medium-high heat. Add half of chicken. Sauté until brown and cooked through, turning with tongs, about 5 minutes. Using slotted spoon, transfer sautéed chicken to 11x7x2-inch glass baking dish. Repeat with remaining chicken. Top with parsnips, remaining 2 teaspoons thyme, and peas.

RETURN broth mixture to same pot; add brandy and whipping cream. Boil over medium-high heat until sauce is reduced to 1¼ cups, scraping up any browned bits, about 3 minutes. Season to taste with salt and pepper. Spoon over chicken. Cover with potato-apple mixture. *(Can be prepared 1 day ahead. Refrigerate uncovered until cold, then cover and keep refrigerated.)*

PREHEAT oven to 350°F. Bake casserole uncovered until potato topping is crusty and chicken filling is heated through, about 35 minutes (about 45 minutes if refrigerated).

Chicken and green olive enchiladas

THE SPIRIT OF MEXICO enlivens this home-style, do-ahead main dish, which features a spicy yet subtly sweet sauce enriched with a touch of semisweet chocolate, reminscent of a Mexican *mole.* The enchiladas can be assembled one day in advance and refrigerated. If time is short, use 5 cups of shredded skinless rotisserie chicken from the deli and 4½ cups of low-salt chicken broth. This dish is complemented by the flavorful Three-Chile Rice.

8 SERVINGS

1 4½-pound chicken, quartered
7¼ cups low-salt chicken broth

8 tablespoons (about) olive oil, divided
2 cups finely chopped onions, divided
9 garlic cloves, chopped
1 teaspoon dried oregano
1 teaspoon ground cumin
¼ teaspoon ground cinnamon
5 tablespoons hot Mexican-style chili powder
3 tablespoons all purpose flour
½ ounce semisweet chocolate, chopped

16 5- to 6-inch-diameter corn tortillas

1 pound Monterey Jack cheese, coarsely grated (about 4½ cups)
1 cup sliced drained pimiento-stuffed green olives
Three-Chile Rice (see recipe)

PLACE chicken and broth in heavy large pot. Bring to boil. Reduce heat to medium-low, partially cover pot, and simmer until chicken is cooked through, about 30 minutes. Cool chicken in broth. Strain broth and spoon off fat; reserve broth. Remove chicken skin and bones; discard. Shred chicken coarsely and transfer to large bowl.

HEAT 3 tablespoons oil in heavy large saucepan over medium-low heat. Add 1 cup onion, garlic, oregano, cumin, and cinnamon. Cover and cook until onion is almost softened, stirring occasionally, about 10 minutes. Mix in chili powder and flour; stir 3 minutes. Gradually whisk in 4½ cups broth (reserve remaining broth for Three-Chile Rice). Increase heat to medium-high and boil until mixture is reduced to 3 cups, stirring occasionally, about 35 minutes. Remove from heat. Whisk in chocolate; season sauce to taste with salt and pepper. Cool.

HEAT 1 tablespoon oil in medium skillet over medium heat. Add 1 tortilla and cook until just pliable, about 20 seconds per side. Transfer to paper-towel-lined baking sheet. Repeat with remaining tortillas, adding oil as needed.

SPREAD ⅓ cup sauce in each of two 13x9x2-inch glass baking dishes. Mix 1 cup sauce into chicken. Arrange 8 tortillas on work surface. Spoon 3 tablespoons cheese, 1 tablespoon olives, 1 tablespoon remaining onion, and ¼ cup chicken mixture over center of each. Roll up tortillas. Arrange seam side down in 1 prepared dish. Repeat with remaining tortillas, 1½ cups cheese, and remaining olives, onion, and chicken mixture. *(Enchiladas can be prepared 1 day ahead. Cover sauce and enchiladas separately and refrigerate.)*

PREHEAT oven to 375°F. Top enchiladas with remaining sauce, then sprinkle with remaining cheese. Cover with aluminum foil; bake 20 minutes (30 minutes if refrigerated). Remove foil and bake until sauce is bubbling, about 10 minutes. Let stand 10 minutes and serve with Three-Chile Rice.

Three-chile rice

USE THE CHICKEN BROTH left from making the enchiladas here. Poblanos are fresh dark green chiles available at Latin markets and some supermarkets.

8 SERVINGS

2 large poblano chiles

6 tablespoons olive oil
¾ cup chopped onion
1½ tablespoons minced garlic
1½ tablespoons chopped seeded jalapeño chile
1½ teaspoons dried oregano
1½ teaspoons ground cumin
1 teaspoon chili powder
1½ cups long-grain white rice
2⅔ cups broth reserved from Chicken and Green Olive Enchiladas (see recipe) or low-salt chicken broth
6 tablespoons crushed tomatoes with added puree
1¼ teaspoons salt
1½ cups frozen petite peas, thawed
6 tablespoons chopped green onions

CHAR poblano chiles over gas flame or in broiler until blackened on all sides. Enclose in paper bag 10 minutes. Peel, seed, and chop poblanos.

HEAT oil in heavy large saucepan over low heat. Add poblanos, onion, and next 5 ingredients. Cover and cook until onion is soft, stirring occasionally, about 10 minutes. Add rice and cook 2 minutes, stirring occasionally. Add broth, tomatoes, and salt; bring to boil. Reduce heat to low, cover, and simmer until liquid is absorbed and rice is tender, about 25 minutes. Mix in peas and green onions. Remove from heat. Cover and let stand 10 minutes.

FLUFF rice with fork.

Chicken, black bean, and goat cheese tostadas

WHILE TOSTADAS—the Mexican salads served atop crisply fried tortillas—may never be diet fare, they *can* be streamlined without loss of flavor. Here, the corn tortilla base is fried in vegetable oil rather than in the traditional lard; and the bean and chicken-breast toppings are cooked with just a few spoonfuls of olive oil. A little bit of crumbled goat cheese has a big flavor effect on each serving.

6 SERVINGS

Beans

- **2 tablespoons olive oil**
- **1 red onion, chopped**
- **2 large jalapeño chiles, stemmed, seeded but not deveined, minced**
- **1 teaspoon chili powder**
- **½ teaspoon ground cumin**
- **2 15- to 16-ounce cans black beans, rinsed, drained**
- **2 tablespoons fresh lime juice**

Chicken

- **2 tablespoons olive oil**
- **1½ pounds skinless boneless chicken breast halves, cut into ¾-inch pieces**
- **1½ teaspoons chili powder**
- **¾ teaspoon ground cumin**

Salad

- **4 cups sliced romaine lettuce**
- **1 medium head of radicchio, sliced**
- **½ cup fresh cilantro leaves**

- **Vegetable oil**
- **6 5- to 6-inch-diameter corn tortillas**

- **¼ cup olive oil**
- **1 tablespoon fresh lime juice**
- **2 tablespoons (about) water**
- **8 ounces soft fresh goat cheese, crumbled**
- **Avocado Salsa (see recipe)**
- **6 fresh cilantro sprigs**

FOR BEANS: Heat oil in heavy medium saucepan over medium-low heat. Add onion and chiles; sauté until onion is translucent, about 8 minutes. Add chili powder and cumin; stir 30 seconds. Add beans and lime juice. Cook until heated through, stirring and mashing beans slightly with spoon, about 4 minutes. *(Can be prepared 1 day ahead. Cover and refrigerate.)*

FOR CHICKEN: Heat oil in heavy large skillet over high heat. Add chicken and sprinkle with salt and pepper. Sauté until almost cooked through, about 3 minutes. Add chili powder and cumin; stir until chicken is cooked through, about 30 seconds. Remove from heat.

FOR SALAD: Combine romaine, radicchio, and cilantro in large bowl.

POUR enough vegetable oil into heavy medium skillet to reach depth of ¼ inch. Heat over medium-high heat until just beginning to smoke. Add 1 tortilla and cook until crisp, about 30 seconds per side. Transfer to paper towels to drain. Repeat with remaining tortillas.

ADD olive oil and lime juice to salad; toss. Season with salt and pepper. Rewarm beans over medium-low heat, stirring and thinning slightly with water. Place 1 tortilla on each of 6 plates. Spread beans over tortillas. Sprinkle with cheese. Top with salad, then chicken, Avocado Salsa, and cilantro sprigs.

Avocado salsa

IN PLACE OF the usual generous dollop of guacamole that typically garnishes so many Mexican meals, cooks seeking to lighten their dishes can toss diced avocado with chopped tomatoes, onions, chiles, and cilantro. The salsa showcases avocado's signature richness.

MAKES ABOUT 4 CUPS

2 large tomatoes, seeded, diced
1 large avocado, diced, rinsed with water, drained
½ red onion, chopped
½ cup chopped fresh cilantro
¼ cup olive oil
2 tablespoons fresh lime juice
1 to 2 large jalapeño chiles, stemmed, seeded but not deveined, minced

COMBINE all ingredients in medium bowl. Season to taste with salt. *(Salsa can be prepared 2 hours ahead. Cover and refrigerate.)*

Lemon-sage Cornish game hens with tomato-porcini sauce

THIS DISH CAPTURES all the romance of winter fireside dining, with robust ingredients and an elegant presentation. Serve this with Soft Polenta with Leeks (page 241): Divide the polenta among individual plates, then spoon the tomato sauce over the polenta and place the hens on top. Dried porcini mushrooms are available at Italian markets and specialty foods stores, and in the produce section of many supermarkets.

4 SERVINGS

¾ cup hot water
¾ ounce dried porcini mushrooms

4 tablespoons olive oil, divided
1 tablespoon plus 4 teaspoons chopped fresh sage
2 garlic cloves, minced
1 14.5-ounce can whole peeled tomatoes in juice, pureed in blender with juices
½ cup low-salt chicken broth

4 1¼- to 1½-pound Cornish game hens, giblets removed
4 large fresh sage sprigs
1 lemon, cut into 4 wedges

COMBINE ¾ cup hot water and porcini mushrooms in small bowl. Let stand until mushrooms soften, about 30 minutes. Using slotted spoon, transfer mushrooms to work surface. Coarsely chop mushrooms. Set mushrooms and soaking liquid aside.

HEAT 2 tablespoons oil in heavy medium skillet over medium heat. Add 1 tablespoon chopped sage and garlic; sauté until fragrant, about 1 minute. Add pureed tomatoes, broth, chopped mushrooms, and soaking liquid, leaving any sediment from liquid behind. Simmer over medium-low heat until thickened to sauce consistency, about 25 minutes. *(Sauce can be prepared 1 day ahead. Cover and refrigerate.)*

PREHEAT oven to 450°F. Pat hens dry with paper towels. Sprinkle cavities with salt and pepper. Place 1 sage sprig and 1 lemon wedge in cavity of each hen. Tie legs together to hold shape. Tuck wing tips under hen. Place hens on rack in large roasting pan. Rub remaining 2 tablespoons oil over hens. Sprinkle with salt and pepper. Sprinkle 1 teaspoon chopped sage over breast of each hen. Roast until hens are cooked through and juices run clear when thickest part of thigh is pierced, about 50 minutes. Transfer hens to platter. Tent with foil to keep warm.

POUR pan juices from roasting pan into 1-cup glass measuring cup, scraping up any browned bits from bottom of pan. Spoon off fat from top of juices. Add pan juices to tomato sauce. Simmer 2 minutes to blend flavors. Season sauce to taste with salt and pepper. Serve hens with sauce.

Cornish game hens with pancetta, juniper berries, and beets

JUNIPER BERRIES, which flavor gin, lend piquant flavor to the sauce; look for them in the spice aisle or at specialty foods stores. Place the juniper berries in a resealable plastic bag and coarsely crack them with a rolling pin. The stuffing is flavored with pancetta, an Italian bacon cured in salt, which is available at Italian markets and in the refrigerated deli case of many supermarkets. Sauté any remaining greens from the beets to serve alongside.
4 SERVINGS

- **4 medium beets with greens, beets peeled and cut into ½-inch pieces, greens finely chopped**
- **½ pound ¼-inch-thick slices pancetta, finely chopped**
- **1 tablespoon juniper berries, coarsely cracked**
- **4 1½- to 1¾-pound Cornish game hens, giblets removed**
- **3 tablespoons olive oil, divided**

POSITION 1 rack in top third of oven and 1 rack in bottom third of oven; preheat to 375°F. Mix 1½ cups chopped beet greens, pancetta, and juniper berries in medium bowl. Season to taste with salt and pepper. Fill hen cavities with pancetta mixture, dividing equally. Tie hen legs together. Place hens in heavy large roasting pan. Rub 1 tablespoon olive oil over hens. Sprinkle hens with salt and pepper. *(Can be prepared 8 hours ahead. Cover beets and hens separately and refrigerate.)*

ROAST hens on bottom rack in oven until skin is golden and juices run clear when thickest part of thigh is pierced, about 1 hour 15 minutes.

MEANWHILE, toss chopped beets with remaining 2 tablespoons olive oil on heavy large baking sheet. Season with salt and pepper. Arrange beets in single layer. Roast beets on top rack in oven until tender and beginning to caramelize, stirring occasionally, about 45 minutes.

TRANSFER hens to plates. Remove string. Scrape up any browned bits from bottom of roasting pan. Pour pan juices through sieve into 2-cup glass measuring cup. Spoon off fat from top of pan juices.

SPOON beets around hens. Drizzle pan juices around hens and serve.

Cornish game hens with crab apple–sage glaze

THESE FESTIVE BIRDS are the easiest way to put an elegant dinner on the table in no time at all. Round out the meal with roasted broccoli (it can roast in the oven right alongside the hens) and a wild rice pilaf with sliced green onions. Ask the butcher to cut the hens in half for you.
4 SERVINGS

- **2 1¾-pound Cornish game hens, halved**
- **8 fresh sage leaves**

- **⅔ cup dry white wine, divided**
- **3 tablespoons crab apple jelly**
- **3 tablespoons chopped shallots**
- **2 tablespoons chopped fresh sage**

PREHEAT oven to 450°F. Starting at neck end of hens, slide fingers between skin and breasts to loosen skin. Place 2 sage leaves under skin of each breast half. Sprinkle hens with salt and pepper. Transfer hens, skin side up, to medium roasting pan. Roast hens 15 minutes.

MEANWHILE, simmer ⅓ cup wine, jelly, and shallots in heavy small saucepan until glaze is slightly thickened, about 6 minutes. Stir in chopped sage.

BRUSH half of glaze on roasted hens. Roast hens 5 minutes. Brush with remaining glaze. Roast until hens are cooked through and glaze is bubbling, about 5 minutes longer. Transfer to platter.

SPOON off fat from juices in pan. Place roasting pan directly atop 2 burners over medium heat. Add remaining ⅓ cup wine and boil until liquid is reduced by ⅓, about 5 minutes. Season sauce to taste with salt and pepper. Spoon sauce over hens and serve.

Turkey, duck, and goose

Roast turkey with pomegranate glaze

THE DEEP GARNET GLAZE, made with pomegranate molasses, adds a richly piquant, sweet-tart depth of flavor to the turkey. The molasses—which is in fact a thick pomegranate syrup—is available at Middle Eastern markets and some supermarkets. You can also order it through various Internet purveyors, found by entering "pomegranate molasses" in your computer search engine.

6 SERVINGS

- **6 cups water**
- **1 celery stalk, cut into 2-inch pieces**
- **1 carrot, peeled, cut into 2-inch pieces**
- **1 onion, coarsely chopped**
- **4 fresh parsley sprigs**
- **1 11- to 12-pound turkey; neck, heart, and gizzard reserved**

- **1 cup orange juice**
- **½ cup pomegranate molasses**
- **2 tablespoons extra-virgin olive oil**
- **1 tablespoon coarse kosher salt**
- **1 teaspoon dried crushed red pepper**
- **1 lemon, quartered**
- **1 onion, quartered**
- **10 fresh mint sprigs**

- **3 tablespoons chilled unsalted butter, cut into ½-inch pieces**

COMBINE first 5 ingredients and reserved turkey neck, heart, and gizzard in large saucepan; bring to boil. Reduce heat to medium and simmer until giblet broth is reduced to 3 cups, about 1 hour 10 minutes. Strain; discard solids.

POSITION oven rack in bottom third of oven and preheat to 400°F. Rinse turkey inside and out; pat dry. Whisk orange juice and next 4 ingredients in small bowl to blend for glaze. Place turkey on rack in heavy large roasting pan. Starting at neck end, carefully slide hand between skin and breast, thighs, and legs to loosen skin. Using pastry brush or hand, apply thin coat of pomegranate glaze over meat under skin. Stuff main cavity with lemon, quartered onion, and mint. Tuck wing tips under; tie legs loosely together to hold shape. Brush turkey with some of remaining glaze.

ROAST turkey 20 minutes. Pour 1 cup giblet broth into pan; brush turkey with glaze. Roast 20 minutes; brush with glaze. Roast 20 minutes. Add 1 cup broth to pan, brush with glaze, and cover turkey loosely with aluminum foil. Roast 20 minutes. Brush with glaze and reduce oven temperature to 325°F. Continue to roast until thermometer inserted into thickest part of thigh registers 175°F, brushing with glaze every 20 minutes, about 1 hour 10 minutes longer, about 2½ hours total.

TRANSFER turkey to platter. Tent loosely with aluminum foil. Let stand 30 minutes (internal temperature of turkey will increase by 5 to 10 degrees).

MEANWHILE, tilt roasting pan and spoon off fat from surface of juices. Add remaining 1 cup giblet broth to pan. Place pan over 2 burners. Bring to simmer over medium-high heat, scraping up any browned bits. Add chilled butter and simmer until gravy is smooth, whisking. Season to taste with salt and pepper. Serve turkey with gravy.

Citrus-glazed turkey with chipotle gravy

THE FLAVORS OF honey and orange blend with the popular Latin tastes of cumin and chiles in a glaze that also gives some heat and zip to the gravy. Spreading some of the glaze between the skin and breast helps keep the white meat moist and flavorful, while ensuring richly browned results. Chipotle chiles canned in a spicy tomato sauce called *adobo* are available at Latin markets, specialty foods stores, and some supermarkets.

16 SERVINGS

Glaze

- **3/4 cup (1 1/2 sticks) unsalted butter**
- **1/2 cup honey**
- **3 tablespoons (packed) grated orange peel**
- **3 tablespoons (packed) grated lime peel (from about 12 limes)**
- **2 tablespoons chopped fresh thyme**
- **4 teaspoons chopped canned chipotle chiles**
- **1 tablespoon ground cumin**
- **1 teaspoon salt**

Turkey

- **2 tablespoons (1/4 stick) butter**
- **4 1/2 cups chopped onions**
- **1 22- to 24-pound turkey; neck, heart, and gizzard reserved**
- **2 cups chopped peeled carrots**
- **2 cups chopped celery with leaves**
- **1 1/2 cups chopped plum tomatoes**
- **9 cups (about) low-salt chicken broth, divided**

Gravy

- **1 cup (about) low-salt chicken broth**
- **1/2 cup all purpose flour**

FOR GLAZE: Melt butter in heavy small saucepan over medium heat. Remove from heat. Stir in next 7 ingredients. Freeze until mixture begins to firm up but is still spreadable, about 30 minutes. Set aside ½ cup citrus glaze for gravy.

FOR TURKEY: Melt butter in large nonstick skillet over medium-high heat. Add onions and reserved turkey parts; sauté until onions are very deep brown, about 22 minutes. Add carrots, celery, and tomatoes; toss to combine. *(Glaze and vegetable mixture can be prepared 1 day ahead. Cover separately and refrigerate. Cover turkey and refrigerate.)*

POSITION oven rack in bottom third of oven and preheat to 400°F. Place rack in center of large roasting pan. Sprinkle vegetable mixture with turkey parts around rack. Rinse turkey inside and out; pat dry. Place turkey on rack in roasting pan. Starting at neck end, carefully slide hand between skin and breast meat to loosen skin. Rub ½ cup citrus glaze over breast meat under skin. If stuffing turkey, spoon stuffing loosely into neck and main cavities. Tuck wing tips under turkey; tie legs loosely together to hold shape. Brush ⅓ cup glaze over top and sides of turkey (not bottom); reserve any remaining glaze. Sprinkle turkey generously with salt and pepper. Cover turkey (not pan) loosely with aluminum foil. Roast 30 minutes. Reduce oven temperature to 350°F; add 1 cup broth to pan. Press foil snugly around turkey (not pan). Roast 1 hour 15 minutes. Add 1 cup broth to pan. Roast turkey until thermometer inserted into thickest part of thigh registers 175°F, adding 1 cup broth every 30 minutes, lifting foil to baste with pan juices, and removing foil during last 15 minutes to brown turkey, about 3 hours 30 minutes longer if unstuffed or 4 hours 15 minutes if stuffed. Transfer turkey to platter. Tent with foil; let stand 30 minutes (internal temperature of turkey will increase by 5 to 10 degrees). Reserve pan juices.

FOR GRAVY: Strain pan juices into 8-cup measuring cup, pressing on solids to extract some pulp and as much liquid as possible; discard solids in strainer. Spoon off fat from top of juices; discard fat. Add enough chicken broth to pan juices in cup to measure 6 cups.

STIR reserved ½ cup citrus glaze in heavy large saucepan over medium heat until melted. Gradually add flour; whisk 1 minute. Gradually whisk in pan juices. Bring to boil, whisking until smooth. Reduce heat to medium and boil until gravy thickens slightly, about 5 minutes. Season gravy to taste with salt and pepper. Brush any remaining glaze over turkey. Serve turkey with gravy.

Roast turkey with herb rub and shiitake mushroom gravy

BRUSHING THE TURKEY all over with vegetable oil not only helps the seasoning mixture (herbs, salt, and pepper) adhere to the skin, but it also promotes browning—as does drizzling melted butter over the bird just before it goes into the oven. Because the turkey rests, tented with aluminum foil, for 30 minutes before carving, the bubbling juices settle back into the meat, resulting in more neatly sliced, juicier servings.

14 SERVINGS

Turkey

- **3 tablespoons chopped fresh rosemary or 1 tablespoon dried**
- **3 tablespoons chopped fresh thyme or 1 tablespoon dried**
- **3 tablespoons chopped fresh tarragon or 1 tablespoon dried**
- **1 tablespoon ground black pepper**
- **2 teaspoons salt**
- **1 20- to 21-pound turkey; neck, heart, and gizzard reserved**
- **Fresh herb sprigs (optional)**
- **2 tablespoons vegetable oil**
- **6 tablespoons (¾ stick) butter, melted**
- **4 cups low-salt chicken broth, divided**

Gravy

- **½ cup all purpose flour**
- **½ cup dry Sherry**
- **3 tablespoons butter**
- **12 ounces fresh shiitake mushrooms, stemmed, caps sliced**
- **1 tablespoon plus 1 teaspoon chopped fresh rosemary or 2 teaspoons dried**
- **4 cups (about) low-salt chicken broth**
- **⅓ cup whipping cream**
- **2 teaspoons chopped fresh thyme or 1 teaspoon dried**
- **2 teaspoons chopped fresh tarragon or 1 teaspoon dried**

FOR TURKEY: Mix first 5 ingredients in small bowl; set herb mixture aside. Rinse turkey inside and out; pat dry with paper towels and place on rack set in large roasting pan. If not stuffing turkey, place herb sprigs in main cavity. If stuffing turkey, spoon stuffing into main cavity. Tuck wing tips under; tie legs loosely together to hold shape. Brush turkey with oil. Rub herb mixture all over turkey. Place turkey neck and giblets in roasting pan. *(Can be prepared 1 day ahead if turkey is not stuffed. Cover and refrigerate. Let stand at room temperature 1 hour before roasting.)*

POSITION oven rack in bottom third of oven and preheat to 425°F. Drizzle melted butter all over turkey. Pour 2 cups broth into pan. Roast turkey 45 minutes. Remove turkey from oven and cover breast with aluminum foil. Reduce oven temperature to 350°F. Return turkey to oven; roast unstuffed turkey 1 hour or stuffed turkey 1 hour 30 minutes. Remove foil; pour remaining 2 cups broth into pan. Continue roasting turkey until thermometer inserted into thickest part of thigh registers 175°F, basting occasionally with pan juices, about 1 hour

40 minutes longer. Transfer turkey to platter; tent with foil. Let stand 30 minutes (internal temperature of turkey will increase by 5 to 10 degrees). Reserve pan juices for gravy.

MEANWHILE, PREPARE GRAVY: Mix flour and Sherry in small bowl until smooth paste forms. Melt butter in heavy large saucepan over medium-high heat. Add mushrooms and rosemary; sauté until mushrooms begin to soften, about 3 minutes. *(Can be prepared 3 hours ahead. Cover flour paste tightly. Let paste and mushrooms stand at room temperature.)*

DISCARD turkey neck and giblets from pan juices in roasting pan. Transfer pan juices to 8-cup glass measuring cup. Spoon off fat and discard. Add enough chicken broth to pan juices to measure 5 cups; add to saucepan with mushrooms. Add flour paste and whisk to combine. Bring mixture to boil, stirring frequently. Boil until thickened to light gravy, about 10 minutes. Mix in cream, thyme, and tarragon. Season to taste with salt and pepper. Serve turkey with gravy.

Roast turkey with prosciutto, rosemary, and garlic

THE MIXTURE OF PROSCIUTTO, rosemary, and garlic rubbed under the skin of the turkey gives it a distinctively delicious taste. True garlic lovers can squeeze some of the pan-roasted garlic into their servings of gravy for even more flavor. The saltiness of most prosciutto—a salt-cured, air-dried ham from Northern Italy—makes it unlikely you will need to use additional salt to season the bird or the gravy.

12 SERVINGS

- **1 18- to 20-pound turkey**
- **4 tablespoons, divided, plus ½ teaspoon minced fresh rosemary**
- **4 tablespoons chopped garlic, divided**
- **8 ounces thinly sliced prosciutto, chopped, divided**
- **Olive oil**
- **3 whole heads of garlic, each halved horizontally, divided**
- **2 cups (or more) low-salt chicken broth**
- **½ cup dry white wine**
- **3½ tablespoons all purpose flour**
- **Fresh rosemary sprigs**

RINSE turkey inside and out; pat dry. Starting at neck end, carefully slide hand between skin and breast and thigh meat to loosen skin. Rub 3 tablespoons rosemary and 3 tablespoons chopped garlic under skin over breast and thighs. Carefully arrange half of prosciutto under skin over breast and thighs. Rub 1 tablespoon rosemary and 1 tablespoon chopped garlic inside cavity of turkey. Sprinkle remaining prosciutto into cavity. Place turkey on rack set in heavy large roasting pan. Cover with plastic wrap and refrigerate overnight.

PREHEAT oven 450°F. Rub outside of turkey with oil. Sprinkle generously with pepper. Place 1 head of garlic in cavity of turkey. Place remaining 2 heads of garlic in roasting pan. Tuck wing tips under turkey; tie legs loosely together to hold shape. Roast turkey 30 minutes. Reduce oven temperature to 325°F. Continue roasting turkey until thermometer inserted into thickest part of thigh registers 175°F, basting occasionally with 2 cups broth, about 3 hours. Transfer turkey to platter. Surround with roasted garlic and garlic from turkey cavity. Remove prosciutto from turkey cavity and reserve. Tent turkey with aluminum foil. Let stand 30 minutes (internal temperature of turkey will increase by 5 to 10 degrees).

POUR pan juices into 4-cup glass measuring cup. Skim off fat from surface, reserving 3 tablespoons fat. Set roasting pan over 2 burners over medium-high heat. Add wine and bring to boil, scraping up any browned bits. Add wine mixture to pan juices in cup (liquids should measure 2½ cups; if not, add more broth or boil until reduced to 2½ cups).

HEAT reserved 3 tablespoons fat in heavy medium saucepan over medium heat. Add flour; stir until golden, about 2 minutes. Whisk in pan juice mixture. Mix in remaining ½ teaspoon rosemary. Boil gravy until thickened to sauce consistency, stirring occasionally, about 5 minutes. Mix in reserved prosciutto. Garnish turkey with rosemary sprigs. Serve with gravy.

Herb-roasted turkey with shallot pan gravy

A CLASSIC TRIO of roasting herbs seasons the turkey in two different ways: chopped into an herb butter that is rubbed under and over the skin; and as whole sprigs placed inside the cavity. The natural sugars in shallots cause them to caramelize as they roast alongside the turkey, making them a rich enhancement to the gravy.

10 SERVINGS

¾ cup (1½ sticks) butter, room temperature
3 tablespoons chopped fresh parsley
2 tablespoons chopped fresh sage
2 tablespoons chopped fresh thyme
¾ teaspoon salt
½ teaspoon coarsely ground black pepper

1 15- to 16-pound turkey, rinsed, patted dry
3 sprigs fresh parsley
3 sprigs fresh sage
3 sprigs fresh thyme
1½ pounds shallots, peeled, halved lengthwise through root end

3 cups (or more) low-salt chicken broth, divided

1 cup dry white wine

2 tablespoons all purpose flour

MIX butter, chopped parsley, chopped sage, chopped thyme, salt, and pepper in medium bowl to blend. *(Herb butter can be prepared 3 days ahead. Transfer to small bowl; cover and refrigerate. Bring to room temperature before using.)*

POSITION oven rack in bottom third of oven and preheat to 350°F. Sprinkle main cavity of turkey with salt and pepper. Place whole parsley, sage, and thyme sprigs and 4 shallot halves in cavity. Starting at neck end, carefully slide hand between skin and breast meat to loosen skin. Spread 3 tablespoons herb butter over breast meat under skin. Tuck wing tips under turkey; tie legs loosely together to hold shape. Place turkey on rack set in large roasting pan. Rub 4 tablespoons herb butter over turkey. Cover breast area of turkey only with sheet of heavy-duty aluminum foil. Scatter remaining shallots in pan around turkey.

ROAST turkey 30 minutes; baste with ½ cup broth. Continue roasting turkey for 1½ hours, basting with ½ cup broth every 30 minutes. Remove foil from over turkey breast. Continue to roast until turkey is golden brown and thermometer inserted into thickest part of thigh registers 175°F, basting with pan juices every 20 minutes, about 1 hour longer. Transfer turkey to platter. Brush with 1 tablespoon herb butter. Tent loosely with foil; let stand 20 minutes (internal temperature of turkey will increase by 5 to 10 degrees).

USING slotted spoon, transfer shallots from roasting pan to plate. Pour pan juices into medium bowl; spoon off fat and discard. Add wine and 1 cup chicken broth to roasting pan. Set pan directly over 2 burners and bring broth mixture to boil, scraping up any browned bits. Continue to boil until reduced by half, about 3 minutes; pour into 4-cup glass measuring cup. Add degreased pan juices. Add more broth if necessary to measure 3 cups liquid.

BLEND flour into remaining herb butter. Pour broth mixture into heavy medium saucepan and bring to boil. Gradually whisk in herb butter mixture. Add any accumulated juices from turkey platter. Boil until gravy thickens enough to coat spoon lightly, whisking occasionally, about 6 minutes. Add shallots to gravy; simmer 1 minute. Season gravy to taste with salt and pepper. Serve turkey with gravy.

Molasses-brined turkey with gingersnap gravy

BRINING ENSURES moist, succulent meat. You'll need two 30-gallon plastic bags and one very large (16-quart) bowl that will fit in the fridge. Start a day ahead, as the turkey is brined for 18 to 20 hours. Stuffing this turkey is not recommended: The brine remaining in the meat may soak into the stuffing during roasting.

12 TO 14 SERVINGS

Stock

- **5 cups low-salt chicken broth**
- **2 medium carrots, peeled, chopped**
- **2 large celery stalks, chopped**
- **1 onion, halved**
- **2 small bay leaves**
- **Neck, heart, and gizzard reserved from 18- to 20-pound turkey**

Brine and turkey

- **1 18- to 20-pound turkey**
- **7 quarts water**
- **2 cups coarse kosher salt (about 9 ounces)**
- **1 cup (packed) dark brown sugar**
- **1 cup mild-flavored (light) molasses**
- **2 bunches fresh thyme, divided**
- **1 bunch fresh sage, divided**
- **2 quarts ice cubes**

- **2 large onions, halved**
- **1 head of garlic, halved horizontally**
- **3 tablespoons olive oil**
- **1 tablespoon ground black pepper**
- **1 tablespoon chopped fresh thyme**
- **1 tablespoon chopped fresh sage**

- **4 cups (about) low-salt chicken broth**

Gravy

- **1 cup finely chopped onion**
- **1 tablespoon chopped fresh thyme**
- **20 gingersnap cookies, coarsely crumbled (about 1¾ cups)**
- **3 to 4 tablespoons apple cider vinegar**
- **1 teaspoon Worcestershire sauce**
- **¼ cup whipping cream (optional)**

FOR STOCK: Combine broth, carrots, celery, onion, and bay leaves in large saucepan. Add turkey neck, heart, and gizzard; bring to boil. Reduce heat to medium-low and simmer until stock is reduced to 3¼ cups, about 1 hour. Strain turkey stock into medium bowl. *(Can be prepared 1 day ahead. Cool slightly. Cover stock and refrigerate.)*

FOR BRINE AND TURKEY: Line very large (about 16-quart) bowl with two 30-gallon plastic bags, one inside the other. Rinse turkey inside and out. Place turkey in bag-lined bowl. Combine 7 quarts water, salt, sugar, molasses, 1 bunch thyme, and ½ bunch sage in large bowl or pot. Stir until salt and sugar dissolve. Mix in ice cubes. Pour brine over turkey in bags. Gather tops of bags together, eliminating air space above brine; seal bags. Refrigerate turkey in brine 18 to 20 hours.

POSITION oven rack in bottom third of oven and preheat to 350°F. Remove turkey from brine. Drain very well; discard brine. Pat turkey dry inside and out. Place turkey on rack set in large roasting pan. Fill main cavity with onions, garlic, and remaining 1 bunch thyme and ½ bunch sage. Stir oil, pepper, chopped thyme, and chopped sage in small bowl to form paste; rub all over outside of turkey. Tuck wing tips under; tie legs loosely together to hold shape.

ROAST turkey 1 hour, covering loosely with aluminum foil if browning quickly. Turn pan around; roast turkey 30 minutes. Pour 1 cup broth over turkey; cover loosely with foil. Roast turkey, basting with 1 cup broth every 30 minutes until thermometer inserted into thickest part of thigh registers 175°F, about 2 hours longer. Transfer turkey to platter. Remove vegetables and herbs from main cavity and discard. Spoon any juices from cavity into roasting pan. Tent turkey with foil; let stand 30 minutes (internal temperature of turkey will increase by 5 to 10 degrees).

FOR GRAVY: Strain pan juices into bowl. Spoon off fat; transfer 2 tablespoons fat to heavy large saucepan and heat over medium-high heat (discard remaining fat). Add chopped onion and thyme to saucepan; sauté until onion browns, about 10 minutes. Add turkey stock, gingersnaps, 3 tablespoons cider vinegar, and Worcestershire sauce. Add 2 cups degreased pan juices and bring to boil, whisking to dissolve gingersnaps. Reduce heat to medium-low and simmer until gravy thickens, about 4 minutes. Season gravy to taste with salt and pepper, adding remaining 1 tablespoon vinegar and cream, if desired.

SERVE turkey with gravy.

Turkey tenderloins with pesto and provolone cheese

THIS ULTRA-CONVENIENT RECIPE features ingredients that are both readily available and ready to combine and cook. Turkey tenderloins—skinless boneless strips of white meat from the center of the breast—may be found prepackaged in many supermarkets, and need only be sliced lengthwise almost in half so you can stuff them. Containers of pesto sauce, a Northern Italian blend of basil, garlic, pine nuts, Parmesan cheese, and olive oil, are a common sight in the refrigerated case of supermarkets.

6 SERVINGS

- **4 turkey tenderloins (about 2¼ pounds)**
- **8 tablespoons purchased pesto, divided**
- **3 ounces thinly sliced provolone cheese, cut into ½-inch-wide strips**

Fresh basil sprigs (optional)

PREHEAT oven to 375°F. Starting at 1 long side, cut each tenderloin horizontally almost in half. Open each like book. Sprinkle inside and out with salt and pepper. Spread 1 tablespoon pesto inside each, then insert cheese strips, dividing equally. Using toothpicks, skewer tenderloins closed. Brush each all over with 1 tablespoon remaining pesto. Arrange tenderloins on rimmed baking sheet.

BAKE tenderloins until thermometer inserted near center registers 160°F, about 20 minutes. Slice tenderloins crosswise into ¾-inch-thick slices; arrange on platter. Whisk any juices and browned bits on baking sheet to blend; spoon over turkey. Garnish with basil sprigs, if desired, and serve.

Turkey meat loaf with sun-dried tomatoes

THE CROWD PLEASING STANDARD gets a makeover: This meat loaf is made with ground turkey instead of beef, and sautéed vegetables and sun-dried tomatoes add sophistication as well as flavor. Be sure to use oil-packed sun-dried tomatoes, as their softer texture makes them easier to chop than the dry-packed variety. Tomato ketchup forms a rich glaze during baking—a classic finishing touch for any meat loaf.

6 SERVINGS

- **1½ tablespoons olive oil**
- **1 large onion, chopped**
- **3 celery stalks, chopped**

- **1½ pounds ground turkey**
- **1½ cups fresh breadcrumbs made from soft white bread**
- **⅔ cup chopped drained oil-packed sun-dried tomatoes**
- **½ cup whole milk**
- **2 large eggs**
- **2 teaspoons dried rubbed sage**
- **2 teaspoons dried oregano**
- **2 teaspoons salt**
- **2 teaspoons ground black pepper**
- **Ketchup**

PREHEAT oven to 375°F. Butter 9x5x3-inch glass loaf pan. Heat oil in heavy medium skillet over medium heat. Add onion; sauté 5 minutes. Add celery; sauté until vegetables are very soft, about 15 minutes longer. Transfer to large bowl and cool.

ADD turkey and next 8 ingredients to vegetables in bowl; mix until well combined. Transfer mixture to prepared pan. Bake 1 hour. Brush with ketchup and bake until thermometer inserted into center of meat loaf registers 165°F, about 15 minutes longer. Cool 5 minutes. Invert meat loaf onto platter; slice and serve.

Turkey smothered in wild mushrooms

CONVENIENT, READY-TO-COOK SLICES of turkey breast, usually labeled "turkey breast fillets," may be found packaged at many supermarkets; they make a great starting point for quick-and-easy weeknight recipes like this earthy entrée. For a head start on another quick dinner, sauté some extra turkey to refrigerate and use another day—diced in a tortilla soup made with canned green chiles, hot chicken broth, shredded cheese, and crushed tortilla chips; or diced with apples, celery, toasted walnuts, and ranch dressing for a twist on Waldorf salad.

2 SERVINGS

- **4 3-ounce turkey breast fillets (each about 1/4 inch thick)**
- **3 tablespoons butter, divided**
- **12 ounces assorted fresh wild mushrooms (such as oyster, crimini, and stemmed shiitake), sliced**
- **1/4 cup finely chopped shallots**
- **1/2 cup low-salt chicken broth**
- **2 tablespoons dry Sherry**
- **2 tablespoons chopped fresh tarragon, divided**

SPRINKLE turkey fillets with salt and pepper. Melt 1 tablespoon butter in large nonstick skillet over medium-high heat. Add turkey and cook until golden and cooked through, about 2 minutes per side. Transfer turkey to 2 plates. Tent with aluminum foil to keep warm.

MELT remaining 2 tablespoons butter in same skillet over medium-high heat. Add mushrooms and shallots; stir to coat. Cover and cook until mushrooms soften and release juices, about 5 minutes. Uncover and sauté until soft, about 2 minutes longer. Stir in broth, Sherry, and 1 tablespoon tarragon. Boil until thickened to sauce consistency, scraping up any browned bits, about 2 minutes. Spoon mushroom sauce over turkey. Sprinkle with remaining 1 tablespoon tarragon and serve.

Braised duck with chard and tomatoes

BROWNING THE QUARTERED DUCK in a heavy large pot before braising not only gives it a rich-tasting, attractive surface, but also renders a lot of the deposits of fat beneath the bird's skin, most of which gets poured off before cooking continues. Serve the braised duck with mashed sweet potatoes to soak up all the flavorful juices.

6 SERVINGS

- **2 5- to 5 1/2-pound ducks, quartered**
- **2 tablespoons olive oil**
- **2 onions, chopped**
- **4 garlic cloves, minced**
- **4 teaspoons minced fresh thyme or 1 1/4 teaspoons dried**
- **1 1/3 cups ruby or tawny Port**
- **2/3 cup dry white wine**
- **5 1/2 cups low-salt chicken broth**
- **1 14.5-ounce can diced tomatoes in juice**
- **2 teaspoons grated lemon peel**

- **1 medium bunch Swiss chard, chopped**

PREHEAT oven to 350°F. Sprinkle duck with salt and pepper. Heat oil in heavy large ovenproof pot over high heat. Working in batches, add duck to pot and brown on all sides, turning frequently, about 12 minutes. Transfer duck to plate. Pour off all but 1 tablespoon drippings from pot. Reduce heat to medium. Add onions, garlic, and thyme to pot; sauté until onions are golden brown, about 15 minutes. Increase heat to high. Add Port and wine; boil until reduced to glaze, scraping up any browned bits, about 7 minutes. Add broth, tomatoes with juice, and lemon peel; add duck and any accumulated juices to pot. Bring to simmer. Cover pot and cook in oven until duck is very tender, about 1½ hours.

TRANSFER duck to large bowl. Boil juices in pot until reduced to 4 cups, about 20 minutes. Add Swiss chard and boil until tender, about 3 minutes. Return duck to pot and simmer until heated through, about 5 minutes. Transfer duck to bowl. Pour pan juices over and serve.

Roast duck with potatoes, turnips, and olives

TURNIPS, ESPECIALLY those on the younger and smaller side, have a surprisingly delicate flavor, with an edge of sweetness and just the slightest hint of their cabbage cousins. These qualities make the roots an ideal, and traditional, accompaniment to rich-tasting roast duck. For this rustic main course, look for tiny brine-cured Niçoise olives, available at Italian markets, specialty foods stores, and some supermarkets. Make sure there's plenty of crusty bread for dipping into the sauce made from the pan juices.

6 SERVINGS

2 5-pound ducks
Fresh or dried thyme
2 large onions, sliced, divided

4 russet potatoes, quartered lengthwise, cut crosswise into ½-inch-thick pieces
5 turnips, peeled, quartered lengthwise, cut crosswise into ½-inch-thick pieces
1 cup Niçoise olives
Fresh thyme sprigs (optional)

1½ cups beef broth
½ cup dry white wine

PREHEAT oven to 450°F. Pat ducks dry. Remove fat from body and neck cavities. Sprinkle cavities with thyme, salt, and pepper. Place several onion slices in cavity of each duck. Tie legs loosely together to hold shape. Place each duck in separate large roasting pan. Pierce all over with fork. Rub outside of ducks with generous amounts of thyme, salt, and pepper. Place remaining onion slices around ducks. Roast 15 minutes.

REMOVE roasting pans from oven and add potatoes and turnips. Sprinkle vegetables with thyme, salt, and pepper. Stir vegetables to coat with duck drippings. Return pans to oven and roast 15 minutes longer. Reduce oven temperature to 375°F. Continue roasting until juices run slightly rosy when ducks are pierced in thickest part of thigh or drumstick, turning vegetables occasionally, about 55 minutes longer. Transfer ducks to serving platter. Mix olives into vegetables. Using slotted spoon, transfer vegetable mixture to platter with ducks. Garnish with thyme sprigs, if desired. Tent with aluminum foil to keep warm.

POUR drippings from roasting pans into 4-cup glass measuring cup. Spoon off fat from drippings, reserving 2 tablespoons fat. Add beef broth and wine to 1 roasting pan. Set pan over 2 burners and bring to boil, scraping up any browned bits. Pour broth mixture into second pan. Add reserved 2 tablespoons fat to broth mixture in second roasting pan. Add degreased drippings to same pan. Set over 2 burners and boil until syrupy, scraping up any browned bits, about 5 minutes. Season sauce to taste with thyme, salt, and pepper. Serve sauce with duck and vegetables.

Peppercorn-crusted Muscovy duck with blueberries

THE MUSCOVY BREED OF DUCK is widely prized for its larger size and the succulence of its meat. For this extra-special-occasion entrée, look for ready-to-cook boneless Muscovy duck breasts at specialty foods stores. They may also be ordered for delivery by mail; look for them online or in your favorite specialty foods catalog.

4 SERVINGS

- **1/4 cup sugar**
- **2 tablespoons water**
- **2 1/2 tablespoons balsamic vinegar**
- **1 1/2 cups low-salt chicken broth**
- **1 cup mixed dried fruits, cut into matchstick-size pieces**
- **1 tablespoon minced peeled fresh ginger**
- **2 12- to 16-ounce boneless Muscovy duck breast halves with skin**
- **4 teaspoons crushed mixed peppercorns**
- **2 tablespoons (1/4 stick) chilled butter, cut into 1/2-inch cubes**
- **3/4 cup frozen blueberries, thawed**

STIR sugar and 2 tablespoons water in heavy small saucepan over low heat until sugar dissolves. Increase heat; boil without stirring until mixture is deep amber color, occasionally brushing down sides of pan with wet pastry brush and swirling pan, about 8 minutes. Stir in vinegar (mixture will bubble vigorously). Add broth; simmer until reduced to 1 cup, about 20 minutes. Remove from heat. Stir in dried fruits and ginger. Let sauce stand 30 minutes.

MEANWHILE, pierce duck skin (not meat) all over with fork. Sprinkle with salt. Rub crushed peppercorns over skin side of duck. Heat heavy large skillet over medium heat. Add duck, skin side down, and cook until golden and crisp, about 15 minutes. Turn duck over; cook to desired doneness, about 8 minutes for medium. Transfer to platter and tent with aluminum foil to keep warm. Let rest 10 minutes.

REWARM sauce over low heat. Whisk in butter several pieces at a time. Stir in blueberries. Season to taste with salt and pepper.

SLICE duck breasts; serve with sauce.

Roast duck with prunes and juniper berries

JUNIPER BERRIES—which flavor gin—provide an aromatic, earthy contrast to the sweet prunes, a prized regional product of Bordeaux, the French province where this dish originated. To crush the brittle berries, put them in a heavy-duty plastic sandwich bag and tap them lightly with a kitchen mallet or press down on them with the back of a wooden spoon.

4 SERVINGS

- **3 cups water**
- **30 juniper berries, slightly crushed, divided**
- **1 5-pound duck; neck, heart, liver, and gizzard reserved**
- **5 large fresh thyme sprigs, divided**
- **1 bay leaf**
- **16 large pitted prunes (about 10 ounces)**
- **2 tablespoons red wine vinegar**

BRING 3 cups water, 20 juniper berries, and pinch of salt to boil in large saucepan. Reduce heat to medium; cover and simmer 10 minutes. Set juniper broth aside.

POSITION oven rack in center of oven and preheat to 450°F. Cut wing tips from duck; reserve. Remove excess fat from body and neck cavities. Sprinkle cavity of duck with salt and pepper. Place heart, liver, and gizzard in cavity, then remaining 10 juniper berries, 4 thyme sprigs, and bay leaf. Tie legs loosely together to hold shape. Place duck, breast side up, in roasting pan. Add wing tips and neck to pan.

Pour 1 cup juniper broth over duck. Roast duck until beginning to brown, about 30 minutes.

MEANWHILE, bring remaining juniper broth to boil. Add prunes; reduce heat to medium, cover, and simmer until prunes are soft, about 5 minutes. Using slotted spoon, transfer prunes to small bowl.

TILT roasting pan; spoon off ½ cup fat from top of liquid. Pour ½ cup prune poaching liquid over duck. Turn duck breast side down; pour ½ cup prune poaching liquid over duck. Return to oven; roast 15 minutes. Turn duck breast side up. Arrange prunes around duck; spoon pan juices over prunes. Drizzle vinegar over duck. Return to oven and roast duck until skin is crisp and juices run clear when thigh is pierced, about 20 minutes longer. Transfer duck to cutting board, breast side down; let stand 20 minutes.

DISCARD wing tips and neck. Remove heart, liver, and gizzard from duck cavity; discard. Using slotted spoon, transfer prunes to bowl. Pour pan juices into medium saucepan; spoon off fat. Add remaining thyme sprig. Boil until juices are slightly thickened and reduced to 1¼ cups , stirring occasionally, about 8 minutes. Return prunes to juices to rewarm; season to taste with salt and pepper.

TURN duck breast side up. Cut off legs. Cut off wings with some breast attached. Cut off breasts and thinly slice crosswise. Arrange duck on platter. Spoon juices with prunes over and serve.

Roast goose with Port-thyme gravy

ALTHOUGH THE MEAT of a goose is quite lean, the bird has a generous layer of fat beneath its skin. Frequent basting with hot water (kept at a simmer on the stove while the goose roasts) helps to render the fat. The Port sauce perfectly counterpoints the robust flavor of the meat. Make sure mashed potatoes are among the side dishes.

8 SERVINGS

- **1 12- to 14- pound goose; neck, heart, and gizzard reserved**
- **2 tablespoons vegetable oil**
- **3 cups chopped onions**
- **1 cup chopped peeled carrots**
- **6 sprigs fresh thyme or 1 teaspoon dried**
- **6 sprigs fresh parsley**
- **2 bay leaves**
- **3 cups (or more) low-salt chicken broth**
- **4 cups water, divided**

- **1 cup tawny Port, divided**
- **2½ tablespoons chopped fresh thyme or 2¼ teaspoons dried**
- **3 tablespoons cornstarch**

DISCARD goose liver; remove excess fat from body and neck cavities. Chop reserved heart and gizzard. Cut neck into 2-inch lengths. Heat oil in heavy large pot over medium heat. Add heart, gizzard, and neck; sauté until brown, about 15 minutes. Add onions, carrots, thyme sprigs, parsley, and bay leaves; sauté until onions are golden, scraping up any browned bits, about 20 minutes. Add 3 cups broth and 2 cups water. Bring to boil. Reduce heat, cover partially, and simmer 1 hour 15 minutes, skimming surface occasionally.

STRAIN stock into 4-cup glass measuring cup; discard solids. Skim off fat from surface of stock. Add more chicken broth to stock if necessary to measure 4 cups. Set aside. *(Can be prepared 1 day ahead. Cover and refrigerate.)*

POSITION oven rack in center of oven and preheat to 425°F. Using fork, pierce breast skin (not meat) several times. Pat goose dry with paper towels. Place on rack in large roasting pan. Roast 15 minutes.

BRING remaining 2 cups water to simmer in small saucepan. Reduce oven temperature to 350°F. Using bulb baster, remove fat from roasting pan. Baste goose with simmering water. Return goose to oven. Continue roasting until goose is brown and thermometer inserted into thickest part of thigh registers 175°F and juices run clear when thigh is pierced, removing fat from pan and inside goose and basting with simmering water every 20 minutes, about 2 hours 45 minutes. Drain any liquid from inside goose into roasting pan. Transfer goose to cutting board. Sprinkle with salt and pepper. Tent with aluminum foil to keep warm. Let stand 20 to 30 minutes.

SKIM off fat from surface of pan juices. Set pan over 2 burners on high heat. Add ¾ cup Port and chopped thyme; boil until reduced to glaze, scraping up any browned bits, about 5 minutes. Whisk remaining ¼ cup Port and cornstarch in small bowl until smooth. Add stock and cornstarch mixture to pan; bring to boil, stirring constantly. Reduce heat and simmer until gravy thickens, whisking constantly, about 5 minutes. Strain into serving bowl.

CARVE goose and serve with gravy.

Mustard and garlic roast goose

FOR THIS CLASSIC HOLIDAY FAVORITE, reserved giblets and trimmings from the goose are simmered in chicken broth, which is then reduced to make a flavorful stock that forms the foundation for the gravy. Pass a dish of tart-sweet red currant jelly, a traditional accompaniment, for guests to spoon alongside their servings.

6 SERVINGS

Goose

- **1 13-pound goose (thawed if frozen); neck, heart, gizzard, and wing tips reserved for stock**
- **3 tablespoons Dijon mustard**
- **2 tablespoons fresh lemon juice**
- **2 garlic cloves, minced**
- **1 teaspoon salt**
- **½ teaspoon ground black pepper**
- **½ teaspoon dried savory**

Stock

- **3 14-ounce cans low-salt chicken broth**
- **1 carrot, peeled, cut into 1-inch pieces**
- **1 small onion, sliced**
- **3½ tablespoons balsamic vinegar**
- **3 fresh Italian parsley sprigs**
- **Reserved goose neck (cut into 3-inch pieces), heart, gizzard, and wing tips**

Gravy

- **½ cup plus 2 tablespoons tawny Port**
- **⅓ cup all purpose flour**

FOR GOOSE: Position oven rack in bottom third of oven and preheat to 425°F. Remove excess fat and skin from main body and neck cavities. Pierce goose skin (not meat) with sharp fork, especially where fat is thickest on legs and lower breast. Sprinkle cavities and skin with salt and pepper. Tie legs loosely together to hold shape. Place goose, breast side down, on V-shaped rack set in roasting pan. Add enough water to pan to reach depth of ½ inch. Roast 40 minutes. Spoon off fat from surface of liquid in pan; reserve ¼ cup fat.

REDUCE oven temperature to 350°F. Using tongs as aid, turn goose onto 1 side. Roast 30 minutes. Turn goose onto second side. Roast 30 minutes.

WHISK mustard, lemon juice, garlic, salt, pepper, and savory in small bowl to blend. Turn goose breast side up. Brush goose with mustard-garlic mixture. Roast until thermometer inserted into thickest part of thigh registers 175°F and juices run clear when thigh is pierced, about 50 minutes. Transfer goose to platter; tent with aluminum foil to keep warm. Let stand 20 to 30 minutes. Reserve pan juices.

MEANWHILE, PREPARE STOCK: Bring all ingredients to boil in large saucepan. Reduce heat to medium and simmer uncovered until mixture is reduced to 3 cups, occasionally skimming surface, about 1 hour. Strain stock into bowl; spoon off fat.

FOR GRAVY: Spoon off fat from top of reserved juices in roasting pan. Add ½ cup Port to pan. Place roasting pan atop 2 burners on high heat and boil until mixture is reduced to 1 cup, whisking occasionally, about 5 minutes. Whisk flour and reserved ¼ cup fat in medium saucepan over medium-low heat until roux is light brown, about 5 minutes. Gradually whisk in Port mixture and 2½ cups degreased stock. Simmer until gravy thickens enough to coat spoon, whisking constantly, about 3 minutes. Stir in remaining 2 tablespoons Port. Season to taste with salt and pepper. Carve goose and serve with gravy.

Stuffings

Northwestern wild mushroom stuffing

TWO POPULAR INGREDIENTS from Oregon and Washington—hazelnuts and wild mushrooms—lend terrific flavor and texture to this sophisticated stuffing. Dried porcini mushrooms are available at Italian markets and specialty foods stores, and in the produce section of many supermarkets.

14 TO 16 SERVINGS

- **2 cups hot water**
- **1 ounce dried porcini mushrooms**
- **1 1½- to 1¾-pound loaf unsliced egg bread, crusts trimmed, bread cut into ¾-inch cubes (about 16 cups)**
- **6 tablespoons (¾ stick) unsalted butter**
- **4 cups coarsely chopped leeks (white and pale green parts only; about 4 large)**
- **1 cup chopped shallots (about 6 large)**
- **1¼ pounds crimini or button mushrooms, sliced**
- **8 ounces fresh shiitake mushrooms, stemmed, caps sliced**
- **2 cups chopped celery**
- **1 cup chopped fresh parsley**
- **1 cup coarsely chopped toasted skinned hazelnuts**
- **3 tablespoons chopped fresh thyme or 1 tablespoon dried**
- **2 tablespoons chopped fresh sage or 2 teaspoons dried rubbed sage**
- **2 large eggs, beaten to blend**
- **¾ cup low-salt chicken broth**

COMBINE 2 cups hot water and porcini mushrooms in medium bowl; let stand until mushrooms are soft, about 30 minutes. Drain, reserving soaking liquid but leaving any sediment behind. Squeeze porcini dry; chop coarsely.

PREHEAT oven to 325°F. Divide bread between 2 rimmed baking sheets. Bake until beginning to brown, about 15 minutes. Cool. Transfer to very large bowl.

MELT butter in heavy large pot over medium-high heat. Add leeks, shallots, and crimini and shiitake mushrooms; sauté until golden and tender, about 15 minutes. Mix in celery and porcini; sauté 5 minutes. Transfer mixture to bowl with bread cubes. Mix in parsley, hazelnuts, thyme, and sage. Season to taste with salt and pepper. *(Can be prepared 1 day ahead. Cover and refrigerate porcini soaking liquid and stuffing separately.)* Mix eggs into stuffing.

TO BAKE STUFFING IN TURKEY: Fill main turkey cavity with stuffing. Combine broth and ½ cup reserved porcini soaking liquid in large glass measuring cup. Add enough broth mixture to remaining stuffing to moisten (¾ cup to 1 cup broth mixture, depending on amount of remaining stuffing). Spoon remaining stuffing into buttered glass baking dish. Cover with buttered aluminum foil, buttered side down. Bake stuffing in dish alongside turkey until heated through, about 30 minutes. Uncover stuffing and continue to bake until top is crisp, about 15 minutes longer.

TO BAKE ALL STUFFING IN DISH: Preheat oven to 325°F. Butter 15x10x2-inch baking dish. Mix ¾ cup reserved porcini soaking liquid and ¾ cup broth into stuffing. Transfer stuffing to prepared dish. Cover with buttered aluminum foil, buttered side down, and bake until heated through, about 1 hour. Uncover stuffing and continue to bake until top is crisp, about 15 minutes longer.

Artichoke, sausage, and Parmesan cheese stuffing

SOURDOUGH BREAD complements the vibrant Italian flavors in this stuffing. It's important to use day-old or dry bread in stuffings because it soaks up more liquid, which will result in a more flavorful, less soggy stuffing. Here, fresh bread is used and instructions are included for drying it out; this technique may be applied to other types of fresh bread or stuffings that call for using day-old bread.

12 SERVINGS

- **15 cups 1-inch cubes crustless sourdough bread (from two 1-pound loaves)**
- **3 tablespoons olive oil**
- **1½ pounds sweet Italian sausages, casings removed**
- **2 cups chopped onions**
- **¾ cup chopped celery**
- **2 garlic cloves, minced**
- **1 8-ounce package frozen artichoke hearts, thawed, coarsely chopped**
- **2 teaspoons chopped fresh thyme**
- **1 teaspoon chopped fresh mint**
- **1 cup freshly grated Parmesan cheese (about 3 ounces)**
- **1¼ to 2¼ cups low-salt chicken broth, divided**

PREHEAT oven to 350°F. Divide bread between 2 rimmed baking sheets. Bake until cubes are dry but not hard, stirring occasionally, about 15 minutes.

HEAT oil in heavy large skillet over medium-high heat. Add sausage and sauté until cooked through, breaking up with back of fork, about 5 minutes. Add onions, celery, and garlic; sauté until celery is soft, about 10 minutes. Mix in artichokes, thyme, and mint; sauté 2 minutes longer. Transfer sausage mixture to large bowl. *(Bread and sausage mixture can be prepared 1 day ahead. Cover separately. Store bread at room temperature. Refrigerate sausage mixture and reheat to lukewarm before continuing.)*

ADD bread to sausage mixture; toss to blend well. Mix in cheese, then 1 cup broth. Season to taste with salt and pepper.

TO BAKE STUFFING IN TURKEY: Loosely fill neck and main cavities of turkey with stuffing. Add enough broth to remaining stuffing to moisten slightly (about ¼ cup to ¾ cup, depending on amount of remaining stuffing). Generously butter glass baking dish. Spoon remaining stuffing into prepared dish. Cover with buttered aluminum foil, buttered side down. Bake stuffing in dish alongside turkey and while turkey is resting until heated through, about 25 minutes. Uncover stuffing and continue to bake until top is slightly crisp and golden, about 15 minutes longer.

TO BAKE ALL OF STUFFING IN DISH: Preheat oven to 350°F. Generously butter 13x9x2-inch glass baking dish. Add enough extra broth to stuffing to moisten (between ¾ cup and 1¼ cups). Transfer stuffing to prepared dish. Cover with buttered aluminum foil, buttered side down; bake until heated through, about 40 minutes. Uncover stuffing and continue to bake until top is slightly crisp and golden, about 20 minutes longer.

Apple and sausage stuffing

COOKING STUFFING ALONGSIDE, rather than inside, the turkey is usually a matter of preference, but since this delicious recipe is similar to a bread pudding, it is best baked outside the turkey. When deciding how to cook other stuffings, bear in mind these practical considerations: Unstuffed turkeys cook faster, and there's no danger of overcooking the breast meat while you're waiting for the stuffing to reach a safe temperature.

8 TO 10 SERVINGS

2 tablespoons vegetable oil
1 pound spicy pork bulk sausage
1 cup diced celery
1 cup diced onion
1 cup diced peeled cored apple
2 garlic cloves, minced
1 tablespoon chopped fresh parsley
2 teaspoons minced fresh sage
1 bay leaf

8 cups 1-inch cubes French bread with crusts (from 1-pound loaf)
1 cup whole milk
1 cup low-salt chicken broth
2 tablespoons (¼ stick) butter, melted
3 large eggs, beaten to blend

HEAT oil in heavy large skillet over medium heat. Add sausage; sauté until cooked through and brown, breaking into pieces with back of fork, about 8 minutes. Using slotted spoon, transfer sausage to large bowl. Add celery and next 6 ingredients to drippings in skillet. Sauté over medium heat until vegetables are soft, about 5 minutes. Discard bay leaf. Add mixture to sausage. *(Stuffing can be prepared 1 day ahead. Cover and refrigerate. Reheat to lukewarm before continuing.)*

PREHEAT oven to 350°F. Butter 13x9x2-inch glass baking dish. Add bread to sausage mixture. Whisk milk, broth, and butter in medium bowl to blend. Mix into stuffing; season stuffing with salt and pepper. Mix in eggs; transfer to prepared dish. Bake uncovered until brown and cooked through, about 50 minutes.

Southwestern corn bread stuffing with corn and green chiles

STUFFING THAT IS COOKED inside the turkey is more moist and rich than stuffing that is cooked alongside, because it is basted by the turkey's flavorful juices as it bakes. Don't overstuff the turkey, since the stuffing will expand as it absorbs the juices. When cooking stuffing inside the turkey, follow these two simple safe-handling tips: Stuff the turkey just before roasting it to avoid any bacterial growth, and be sure the center of the stuffing is cooked to a temperature of 165°F. Anaheim (also called California) and poblano chiles are available at Latin markets and many supermarkets. If you can't find petite yellow corn kernels, regular frozen corn will do.

10 TO 12 SERVINGS

10 tablespoons (1¼ sticks) unsalted butter
1¼ cups chopped seeded fresh Anaheim chiles (about 8 ounces)
1¼ cups chopped seeded fresh poblano chiles (about 8 ounces)
3 large jalapeño chiles, seeded, chopped
2 1-pound packages frozen petite yellow corn kernels, thawed, divided
1¼ cups chopped green onions
⅔ cup chopped fresh cilantro

Buttermilk Corn Bread (see recipe), 1 to 2 days old
- 4 large eggs
- ¼ cup sugar
- 2¼ teaspoons salt
- ½ teaspoon ground black pepper
- ¼ to 1¼ cups low-salt chicken broth

MELT butter in heavy large skillet over medium-high heat. Add all chiles; sauté until beginning to soften, about 8 minutes. Stir in 1 package corn and green onions. Transfer to very large bowl. Mix in cilantro. Coarsely crumble corn bread into vegetable mixture and toss to combine.

BLEND remaining package of corn, eggs, sugar, salt, and pepper in processor to coarse puree. Stir mixture into stuffing.

TO BAKE STUFFING IN TURKEY: Loosely fill neck and main cavities of turkey with stuffing. Add enough broth to remaining stuffing to moisten slightly (about ¼ cup to ¾ cup, depending on amount of remaining stuffing). Generously butter glass baking dish. Spoon remaining stuffing into prepared dish. Cover with buttered aluminum foil, buttered side down. Bake stuffing in dish alongside turkey until heated through, about 25 minutes. Uncover stuffing and continue to bake until top is slightly crisp and golden, about 15 minutes longer.

TO BAKE ALL STUFFING IN DISH: Preheat oven to 350°F. Generously butter 13x9x2-inch glass baking dish. Add enough extra broth to stuffing to moisten (¾ cup to 1¼ cups). Transfer stuffing to prepared dish. Cover with buttered aluminum foil, buttered side down. Bake until heated through, about 40 minutes. Uncover stuffing and continue to bake until top is slightly crisp and golden, about 20 minutes longer.

Buttermilk corn bread

BUTTERMILK IS A wonderful moistener and tenderizer for corn bread. Make this sweet, moist corn bread at least one day and up to two days ahead of time if using in the stuffing. It's also delicious on its own, straight out of the oven with a dab of butter.

10 SERVINGS

- ½ cup (1 stick) unsalted butter
- 1½ cups buttermilk
- 2 large eggs
- 2 cups yellow cornmeal
- 1 cup unbleached all purpose flour
- ½ cup sugar
- 4 teaspoons baking powder
- 1 teaspoon salt
- ¼ teaspoon ground black pepper

PREHEAT oven to 400°F. Butter 13x9x2-inch metal baking pan. Melt ½ cup butter in large saucepan over low heat. Remove from heat. Whisk in buttermilk, then eggs. Mix all remaining ingredients in large bowl. Stir in buttermilk mixture. Transfer to prepared pan.

BAKE corn bread until edges are lightly browned and tester inserted into center comes out clean, about 20 minutes. Cool completely in pan. If using in stuffing, cover tightly and store at room temperature at least 1 day and up to 2 days.

Crackling corn bread dressing

WHAT'S THE DIFFERENCE between a dressing and a stuffing? It's a good question and one without a definitive answer. Both terms are used interchangeably; however, some believe a dressing is baked and served alongside the turkey, and therefore "dresses up" the turkey and table, whereas a stuffing is actually stuffed into the turkey and then baked. This particular dressing is best cooked in a dish, which also allows the top to brown and become crisp. Put it into the oven as soon as the turkey comes out to rest before being carved.

8 SERVINGS

8 bacon slices, coarsely chopped
Melted butter (if necessary)

Crackling Corn Bread (see recipe)
2 cups chopped celery
1 cup finely chopped white onion
1 cup pecans, toasted, chopped
3 tablespoons chopped fresh sage
3 large eggs
1¼ cups low-salt chicken broth

PREHEAT oven to 425°F. Sauté bacon in heavy large skillet over medium heat until crisp. Using slotted spoon, transfer bacon to paper towels to drain. Reserve ¼ cup bacon drippings; brush 13x9x2-inch glass baking dish with some remaining bacon drippings (or melted butter, if necessary).

CRUMBLE corn bread into large bowl. Mix in celery, onion, pecans, sage, bacon, and reserved ¼ cup bacon drippings. Season to taste with pepper. Beat eggs and broth in medium bowl to blend; stir into dressing mixture. Transfer dressing to prepared dish. Bake dressing until golden and cooked through, about 35 minutes.

Crackling corn bread

IN THIS RECIPE, the corn bread batter is poured into a hot pan of sizzling bacon drippings, which causes a crackling noise—hence the name. Be sure to use a large heavy skillet that's also ovenproof. A cast-iron pan, which distributes heat evenly and retains high temperatures, is the ideal skillet for making this savory corn bread, which can be prepared one day ahead. Wrap it airtight in aluminum foil and store it at room temperature.

MAKES 8 SERVINGS

12 ounces bacon, coarsely chopped

2 cups white cornmeal
1 teaspoon salt
½ teaspoon baking soda
½ teaspoon baking powder
1½ cups buttermilk
1 large egg

PREHEAT oven to 450°F. Sauté bacon in heavy large skillet over medium-high heat until brown and crisp. Using slotted spoon, transfer bacon to paper towels to drain. Reserve 6 tablespoons drippings from skillet. Brush 10-inch-diameter ovenproof skillet with 2 tablespoons reserved drippings. Place skillet in oven to heat.

WHISK cornmeal, salt, baking soda, and baking powder in medium bowl to blend. Add buttermilk, egg, and remaining 4 tablespoons reserved drippings. Whisk until just blended; mix in sautéed bacon. Pour batter into hot skillet. Bake corn bread until golden and firm to touch, about 25 minutes. Turn corn bread out onto rack and cool completely. *(Can be prepared 1 day ahead. Wrap in aluminum foil; store at room temperature.)*

Wild rice stuffing with pearl onions, dried cherries, and apricots

RICE STUFFING is a delicious alternative to more common bread- and corn-bread-based ones. Here, wild rice and long-grain white rice team up for a marvelous stuffing that goes well with duck, Cornish game hens, or a Thanksgiving turkey. To remove the skins easily from pearl onions, cook them in a saucepan of boiling water for one minute; this loosens the skins and allows them to slip right off.

8 TO 10 SERVINGS

- **6 tablespoons (3/4 stick) butter, divided**
- **18 ounces pearl onions, cooked in boiling water 1 minute, peeled**

- **4 1/2 cups low-salt chicken broth**
- **3 tablespoons chopped fresh thyme, divided**
- **1 1/4 cups wild rice (about 6 1/2 ounces)**
- **1 1/4 cups long-grain white rice**

- **6 ounces dried apricots, coarsely chopped**
- **1 cup dried tart cherries**
- **1 cup raisins**
- **1 cup pecans, toasted, chopped**

MELT 2 tablespoons butter in large skillet over medium heat. Add onions and sauté until brown, about 15 minutes. Set aside.

BRING broth and 1 tablespoon thyme to boil in large saucepan. Add wild rice; return to boil. Reduce heat to medium-low, cover, and simmer 30 minutes. Add white rice; cover and simmer until all rice is tender and liquid is almost absorbed, about 15 minutes longer.

STIR dried apricots, dried cherries, raisins, and remaining 2 tablespoons thyme into rice mixture; cover and simmer 3 minutes. Stir pearl onions and remaining 4 tablespoons butter into rice. Mix in pecans. Season generously with salt and pepper.

TO BAKE STUFFING IN TURKEY: Loosely fill main turkey cavity with cooled stuffing. Butter glass baking dish. Spoon remaining stuffing into prepared dish. Cover with buttered aluminum foil, buttered side down. Bake stuffing in dish alongside turkey until heated through, about 20 minutes.

TO BAKE ALL STUFFING IN DISH: Preheat oven to 350°F. Butter 13x9x2-inch glass baking dish. Transfer stuffing to prepared dish. Cover with buttered aluminum foil, buttered side down, and bake until heated through, about 30 minutes.

12 Fish and shellfish

It wasn't long ago that one could accurately cite a frozen breaded fish stick as America's favorite seafood choice. Now the most popular "fin" fish in the country is, hands down, salmon, thanks to its pronounced but mild flavor and relatively low price. More important: Its fillets or steaks can be accented with ingredients from Rome, Tokyo, Sydney, or New Orleans with equally stellar results.

Farmed Atlantic salmon is the variety most often seen in the market. But there is superior texture and flavor in the wild-caught Alaska and West Coast salmon that appear fresh in warmer months and frozen year-round. The quality of "frozen at sea" Alaskan salmon is kept remarkably high because the fish are flash-frozen very shortly after they are caught and filleted. Keep in mind that when these recipes call for fillets of salmon (or fillets of any other kind of fish), we mean *skinless* fillets—the kind most commonly sold by fishmongers—unless the recipe specifies "with skin."

Slightly firmer and sweeter in taste are fish like red snapper, grouper, and sea bass. Their texture makes them excellent candidates for roasting and grilling, but they also respond beautifully to steaming or braising. While most people prefer the ease of serving "sides" of the fish or even single-portion fillets, a fish cooked whole, then divided into portions, emerges more flavorful and retains moisture.

Tuna and swordfish fall into a category of their own. These large fish are usually cut into thick steaks and are ideal for the barbecue, but other high-heat methods of cooking, like broiling or pan-searing, also work well.

Many shellfish, including clams, mussels, shrimp, and lobster, are often—and best—cooked right in their shells. Mussels and clams even have built-in timers: The shells pop open just as they are done to perfection.

No matter what your seafood of choice, the main concern for home cooks is overcooking. As a *general* rule, the most any seafood should be cooked is just until the center turns opaque. As they say, less is more.

Fish

Salmon with arugula, tomato, and caper sauce

THE PERFECT SUMMER ENTRÉE: The fresh sauce of tomatoes, arugula, and capers requires no cooking at all, and the fish is quickly broiled, keeping temperatures in the kitchen to a minimum. Line the baking sheet with aluminum foil for easy cleanup, and be sure to oil the salmon fillets so that they do not stick to the pan. Position the pan about five inches below the heating element of the broiler to ensure that the salmon cooks through as the top chars slightly. Spread a purchased tapenade over broiled slices of crusty Italian bread and pour a crisp Chardonnay or Sancerre wine to go with the salmon.

4 SERVINGS

1 pound plum tomatoes, seeded, chopped
3/4 cup (lightly packed) chopped fresh arugula, basil, or Italian parsley
1/2 cup olive oil
1 shallot, chopped
1 1/2 tablespoons fresh lemon juice
1 tablespoon drained capers

4 6-ounce salmon fillets
Olive oil
Lemon wedges

COMBINE first 6 ingredients in medium bowl. Season sauce to taste with salt and pepper.

PREHEAT broiler. Brush both sides of salmon with oil; sprinkle with salt and pepper. Arrange salmon on broiler tray. Broil without turning until just opaque in center, about 4 minutes. Transfer salmon to plates. Spoon sauce over. Garnish with lemon wedges and serve.

Salmon and rice wrapped in pastry with dill sauce

THIS IS A SIMPLIFIED but impressive interpretation of a classic Russian salmon dish known as *kulebiaka,* which the French call *coulibiac.* This version can be assembled eight hours ahead and popped into the oven just 30 minutes before serving. Here, six-ounce fillets and a mushroom-rice pilaf are wrapped in puff pastry to make elegant individual servings. Offer caviar and iced vodka for an intimate dinner party, and serve roasted beets as a delicious side dish to the salmon.

4 SERVINGS

1/2 cup long-grain white rice

2 tablespoons (1/4 stick) butter
1/2 cup minced leek (white and pale green parts only)
6 ounces fresh shiitake mushrooms, stemmed, chopped

2 sheets frozen puff pastry (one 17.3-ounce package), thawed
4 6-ounce skinless salmon fillets (each about 4x2 1/2 inches)
1 egg beaten with 1 tablespoon water (for glaze)

Dill Sauce (see recipe)

BRING medium saucepan of salted water to boil. Add rice; boil uncovered until just tender, about 18 minutes. Drain.

MELT butter in heavy medium skillet over medium-low heat. Add leek and sauté until beginning to soften, about 4 minutes. Add mushrooms. Cover skillet and cook until mushrooms release their juices, stirring occasionally, about 5 minutes. Uncover skillet. Increase heat to medium-high and sauté until juices evaporate, about 3 minutes. Transfer leeks and mushrooms to medium bowl. Mix in rice. Season to taste with salt and pepper. Cool completely.

BUTTER large rimmed baking sheet. Roll out 1 pastry sheet on floured surface to 12-inch square. Cut into 4 squares. Divide rice mixture among centers of squares, mounding in oval shape with ends on diagonal toward 2 corners of pastry. Set salmon atop rice mixture. Sprinkle with salt and pepper. Wrap pastry corners up around salmon, forming package. Roll out remaining pastry sheet on floured surface to 13-inch square. Cut into 4 squares. Lay 1 square diagonally atop each package. Turn package over. Fold pastry around salmon to enclose completely. Brush pastry edges with glaze; pinch edges together to seal. Arrange salmon packages, seam side down, on prepared baking sheet. Cover and chill 30 minutes. *(Can be made 8 hours ahead. Keep salmon chilled. Cover and chill glaze.)*

PREHEAT oven to 400°F. Brush top of salmon packets with glaze. Bake until packets are golden and thermometer inserted into salmon registers 145°F, about 30 minutes.

TRANSFER salmon packets to plates. Spoon Dill Sauce around and serve.

Dill sauce

CRÈME FRAÎCHE—a very thick, rich, and slightly tangy French cream—is similar to, and often replaced with, sour cream. But unlike sour cream, crème fraîche can be boiled without curdling, as is done in this recipe. If you can't find crème fraîche at your supermarket, make it at home by heating 1¼ cup of whipping cream until it is lukewarm (about 85°F), then removing it from the heat and mixing in 2½ tablespoons of buttermilk. Cover the cream mixture and allow it to stand at room temperature until it is thick, one to two days, depending on the temperature of the room. Store it in the refrigerator until ready to use, up to one week; it will get more tangy each day. Try substituting fresh basil, chives, or tarragon for the dill.

MAKES ABOUT 1 CUP

- **⅔ cup bottled clam juice**
- **½ cup dry white wine**
- **1¼ cups crème fraîche**
- **3 tablespoons minced fresh dill**

COMBINE clam juice and wine in heavy small nonreactive saucepan. Boil until reduced to ⅓ cup, about 9 minutes. Reduce heat to medium. Whisk in crème fraîche and boil until reduced to 1 cup, about 5 minutes. Remove from heat. Stir in dill. Season to taste with salt and pepper.

Grilled spice-rubbed salmon with corn salsa

THE SPICE MIXTURE of black peppercorns, coriander, cumin, and mustard seeds lends flavor to both the salmon and the corn salsa; it can also be used as a great seasoning for chicken or pork. If time is limited, a purchased Creole spice mixture makes a good shortcut. A large salmon fillet can be difficult to turn over on the grill; to make it easier, place the fish in a metal fish basket before grilling (be sure to oil the basket or coat it with nonstick spray). Or cut the fillet crosswise in half and grill it in two pieces, then reassemble the fish on a platter, and spoon some salsa over the area where the two pieces meet. In this recipe, the salmon is grilled flesh side down first—this makes it easier to turn without tearing the flesh, because the fish will not be flaky yet.

12 SERVINGS

Salmon

- **1½ tablespoons coriander seeds**
- **1½ tablespoons mustard seeds**

- **1½ tablespoons cumin seeds**
- **1 teaspoon whole black peppercorns**
- **3 tablespoons (packed) golden brown sugar**
- **1 4-pound boneless side of salmon with skin**

Salsa

- **6 cups fresh corn kernels (cut from about 9 ears) or frozen, thawed**
- **1 cup finely chopped red onion**
- **½ cup olive oil**
- **½ cup chopped fresh cilantro**
- **¼ cup fresh lime juice**
- **1½ tablespoons minced seeded jalapeño chile**

FOR SALMON: Heat heavy small skillet over medium-high heat. Add coriander, mustard, and cumin seeds; sauté until fragrant and slightly darker in color, about 3 minutes. Add peppercorns. Remove from heat and cool. Finely grind mixture in spice grinder or in mortar with pestle. Transfer to small bowl. Mix in sugar.

PLACE salmon, skin side down, on large baking sheet. Rub ¼ cup spice mixture over salmon, pressing gently to adhere. Cover salmon with plastic wrap and refrigerate at least 1 hour and up to 1 day. Cover remaining spice mixture and let stand at room temperature.

FOR SALSA: Cook corn in saucepan of boiling salted water until just tender, about 2 minutes. Drain. Transfer to large bowl. Mix in remaining ingredients and 2 tablespoons spice mixture (reserve any remaining spice mixture for another use). Season salsa to taste with salt. Cover and chill at least 1 hour and up to 4 hours before serving.

PREPARE barbecue (medium heat). Grill salmon, flesh side down, 6 minutes. Using 2 large spatulas, turn salmon over and grill until just opaque in center, about 6 minutes longer. Transfer salmon to platter. Serve with salsa.

Baked salmon stuffed with mascarpone spinach

WHEN PURCHASING SALMON, select fillets that have a deep salmon-pink color, with meat that is firm and moist and springs back when pressed gently. For this recipe, buy fillets that are thick enough that a ¾-inch-deep pocket can be cut into them for stuffing. If you can't easily find mascarpone, the soft Italian cream cheese, at the supermarket, natural foods store, or Italian market, use all regular cream cheese.

8 SERVINGS

- **1 10-ounce bag fresh spinach leaves**
- **½ cup cream cheese (about 4 ounces), room temperature**
- **½ cup mascarpone cheese, room temperature**
- **Pinch of ground nutmeg**
- **8 6- to 8-ounce salmon fillets with skin (each about 1-inch thick)**
- **Olive oil**
- **2⅔ cups fresh breadcrumbs made from French bread with crust**
- **½ cup (1 stick) butter, melted**
- **½ cup freshly grated Parmesan cheese (about 1½ ounces)**

COOK spinach in large pot of boiling salted water just until wilted, about 30 seconds. Drain; cool briefly. Squeeze spinach dry, then chop finely. Place in small bowl. Mix in cream cheese, mascarpone cheese, and nutmeg. Season to taste with salt and pepper. Cut one ¾-inch-deep, 2½-inch-long slit down center of flesh side of each salmon fillet and press open, forming pocket for spinach mixture. Fill each pocket with spinach mixture, dividing equally. Place fillets on large plate, skin side down. *(Salmon can be prepared 4 hours ahead. Cover and chill.)*

PREHEAT oven to 450°F. Brush rimmed baking sheet with olive oil. Sprinkle salmon with salt and pepper. Mix breadcrumbs, melted butter, and Parmesan cheese in medium bowl. Top each fillet with breadcrumb mixture, pressing to adhere. Transfer fillets, skin side down, to prepared baking sheet. Bake salmon until just opaque in center, about 12 minutes. Transfer to plates and serve.

Roasted salmon with cranberry-mustard sauce

THIS SAUCE IS A TERRIFIC use for cranberry relish left over from Thanksgiving. To enjoy this colorful and delicious entrée any time of the year, use purchased cranberry relish; or replace the relish with a third of a cup of coarsely chopped fresh (or frozen, thawed) cranberries mixed with a couple of tablespoons of sugar.

4 SERVINGS

Nonstick vegetable oil spray
3 tablespoons walnut oil or olive oil
2 tablespoons Dijon mustard
4 6-ounce salmon fillets with skin

⅓ cup cranberry relish, room temperature
2 tablespoons chopped shallot
2 tablespoons red wine vinegar

PREHEAT oven to 450°F. Spray small rimmed baking sheet with nonstick spray. Whisk oil and mustard in medium bowl to blend. Sprinkle salmon with salt and pepper. Place on prepared baking sheet, skin side down. Brush top of salmon with 2 tablespoons mustard mixture. Roast salmon until just opaque in center, about 13 minutes. Set aside.

PREHEAT broiler. Whisk cranberry relish, shallot, and vinegar into remaining mustard mixture. Season sauce to taste with salt and pepper. Broil salmon until top is browning in spots, about 30 seconds. Transfer to plates. Spoon sauce over and serve.

Poached salmon fillets with watercress mayonnaise

WHEN POACHING SALMON or any other fish, use a deep skillet that is wide enough to hold the fillets in a single layer. For this recipe, be sure the cooking liquid comes halfway up the sides of the fish and simmers very gently. If the liquid simmers too vigorously, it can break the delicate fish apart and overcook the outside before the center is done. (Oftentimes, once the fish is cooked, cream is whisked into the poaching liquid–known in French cooking as a *cuisson*–to form a simple sauce. Try it the next time you poach salmon for a quick and easy, but sophisticated, entrée.) Since the salmon here is served cold with a watercress mayonnaise, begin making it at least four hours ahead. You can keep the salmon and mayonnaise covered separately and refrigerated up to one day.

6 SERVINGS

¾ cup mayonnaise
½ cup finely chopped watercress leaves
1 tablespoon coarse-grained Dijon mustard
1 teaspoon fresh lemon juice

⅓ cup water
⅓ cup dry white wine
1 shallot, thinly sliced
4 fresh parsley sprigs
1 fresh thyme sprig
6 6-ounce salmon fillets with skin

MIX first 4 ingredients in small bowl to blend; season to taste with salt and pepper.

COMBINE ⅓ cup water, wine, shallot, parsley, and thyme in large skillet. Place salmon fillets, skin side down, in skillet; sprinkle salmon with salt and pepper. Bring liquid to simmer. Cover skillet tightly and simmer over medium-low heat until salmon is barely opaque in center, about 10 minutes. Remove skillet from heat and let stand, covered, 5 minutes. Transfer salmon to platter; discard liquid. Cover salmon with plastic wrap and chill until cold, at least 4 hours. *(Watercress mayonnaise and salmon can be made 1 day ahead. Cover mayonnaise and chill. Keep salmon chilled.)*

PLACE 1 salmon fillet on each of 6 plates. Serve with watercress mayonnaise.

Grilled salmon fillets with balsamic glaze

GRILLING THE SALMON with the skin on protects the delicate flesh and helps the fish retain its shape. The crispy skin also provides a delicious contrast to the moist and tender fish and syrupy balsamic glaze. If you prefer to discard the skin, do so after the fish is cooked, when the skin will slip off easily.

6 SERVINGS

½ cup balsamic vinegar
½ cup dry white wine
2 tablespoons fresh lemon juice
2 tablespoons (packed) dark brown sugar

6 5- to 6-ounce salmon fillets with skin
Olive oil

COMBINE first 4 ingredients in medium saucepan; stir to dissolve sugar. Boil until reduced to ⅓ cup, about 17 minutes. Season glaze to taste with salt and pepper. *(Can be made 1 week ahead. Cover and refrigerate. Rewarm over low heat before using.)*

PREPARE barbecue (medium-high heat). Brush salmon lightly with oil; sprinkle with salt and pepper. Grill salmon, flesh side down first, until just opaque in center, about 5 minutes per side. Transfer salmon to platter. Drizzle warm balsamic glaze over and serve.

Grilled Asian-style salmon with cabbage and mint slaw

BEFORE LIGHTING THE BARBECUE, brush the grill rack with oil, or spray it with nonstick vegetable oil spray to help keep the fish from sticking. Steamed rice makes a complementary side dish to this Asian-inspired entrée, and small scoops of coconut, pineapple, and passion-fruit sorbets would be a refreshing finish to the meal.

4 SERVINGS

1 cup (packed) fresh mint leaves
2 tablespoons chopped peeled fresh ginger
2 tablespoons soy sauce
2 tablespoons unseasoned rice vinegar
2 tablespoons Asian sesame oil

4 6-ounce salmon fillets with skin

4 cups thinly sliced Napa cabbage

PREPARE barbecue (medium-high heat). Thinly slice enough mint leaves to measure 2 tablespoonfuls. Place in small bowl. Whisk in next 4 ingredients to make dressing.

PLACE salmon in glass baking dish. Add ¼ cup dressing and turn to coat. Sprinkle salmon with salt and pepper. Marinate salmon 15 minutes. Grill salmon, flesh side down first, until just opaque in center, about 5 minutes per side.

MEANWHILE, combine sliced cabbage, remaining mint leaves, and remaining dressing in large bowl; toss to combine. Season slaw to taste with salt and pepper. Divide among 4 plates. Place salmon fillets atop slaw and serve.

Rosemary-roasted salmon

THIS BEAUTIFUL, easy main course can be assembled up to eight hours ahead and kept covered and refrigerated until ready to roast. It goes well with a fennel and orange salad with olives and orange vinaigrette; couscous with garbanzo beans and raisins; and sautéed spinach with pine nuts. Ask your fishmonger for a center-cut salmon fillet, as this cut from the head end of the fish is thicker and more desirable than a flatter piece from the tail end. Use a heavy rimmed baking sheet that will contain any juices and won't buckle under high temperatures.

4 SERVINGS

2 large bunches fresh rosemary
1 large red onion, thinly sliced
1 2-pound center-cut salmon fillet with skin
2 large lemons, thinly sliced
⅓ cup olive oil

ARRANGE half of rosemary sprigs in single layer in center of heavy rimmed baking sheet. Arrange sliced red onion atop rosemary. Place salmon, skin side down, atop onion. Sprinkle salmon with salt and pepper. Cover salmon with remaining rosemary sprigs. Arrange lemon slices over rosemary. Drizzle olive oil over. Sprinkle lemon slices with salt. *(Can be prepared 8 hours ahead. Cover and refrigerate.)*

PREHEAT oven to 500°F. Roast salmon uncovered until just opaque in center, about 20 minutes. Transfer salmon to plates (discarding rosemary). Serve with roasted onion slices and lemon slices.

Broiled salmon with avocado and lime

QUICKLY BROILED salmon fillets are topped with a chunky sauce made from chopped avocado, chives, olive oil, and fresh lime juice, resulting in a delicious and impressive-looking main course for two in just 20 minutes. Serve buttered beets with hazelnuts on the side, and finish up with cookies and ice cream for a satisfying weeknight dinner.

2 SERVINGS; CAN BE DOUBLED

2 6- to 7-ounce salmon fillets with skin (each about 1 inch thick)
5 tablespoons olive oil, divided
½ lime

1 firm but ripe avocado, halved, pitted, peeled, diced
1 bunch fresh chives, finely chopped
1 tablespoon fresh lime juice

RUB salmon with 1 tablespoon oil. Squeeze lime over. Let stand while preparing sauce.

COMBINE avocado, remaining 4 tablespoons oil, chives, and 1 tablespoon lime juice in small bowl. Season sauce to taste with salt and pepper.

PREHEAT broiler. Line broiler tray with aluminum foil. Arrange salmon, skin side down, on foil. Sprinkle with salt and pepper. Broil without turning until just opaque in center, about 9 minutes. Transfer to plates. Spoon avocado sauce over and serve.

Sea bass with tomatoes and onions

OVERSIZE CROUTONS are served alongside the no-fuss sea bass to soak up the delicious sauce of white wine, tomatoes, garlic, onions, parsley, and anchovies. Since this one-skillet entrée is baked in a very hot oven, use an ovenproof skillet with a metal handle. (In a pinch, you can double-wrap a wooden handle with aluminum foil to protect it during this recipe's short baking time.) To avoid burning yourself after the skillet has been removed from the oven, keep the oven mitt over the handle as a reminder that it is extremely hot.

4 SERVINGS

- **7 tablespoons olive oil, divided**
- **4 4½x2x½-inch French bread slices**

- **3 cups thinly sliced onions**
- **½ cup chopped fresh parsley, divided**
- **2 tablespoons chopped canned anchovies (from one 2-ounce can)**
- **5 garlic cloves, minced**
- **¼ teaspoon dried crushed red pepper**
- **1¼ pounds plum tomatoes, seeded, finely chopped**
- **¾ cup dry white wine**
- **4 8-ounce sea bass fillets (each about 1 inch thick)**

PREHEAT oven to 350°F. Brush 2 tablespoons oil over both sides of bread slices. Place on baking sheet; bake until lightly toasted, about 12 minutes. Set croutons aside.

INCREASE oven temperature to 500°F. Heat remaining 5 tablespoons oil in large ovenproof skillet over medium-high heat. Add onions, ¼ cup parsley, anchovies, garlic, and crushed red pepper. Sauté until onions begin to soften, about 5 minutes. Stir in tomatoes and wine. Sprinkle fish with salt and pepper. Arrange fish in same skillet in single layer. Spoon some sauce atop fish. Bring to simmer. Cover skillet and bake until fish is just opaque in center, about 12 minutes. Transfer fish to plates.

STIR remaining ¼ cup parsley into sauce. Boil sauce until slightly reduced, about 2 minutes. Season to taste with salt and pepper. Spoon sauce over fish. Garnish with croutons and serve.

Sea bass with polenta and roasted red bell peppers

THE SILKY, LUXURIOUS TEXTURE of sea bass is paired with a creamy polenta cooked in milk infused with thyme and bay leaf, then served with tender oven-roasted bell peppers. Begin preparing the bell peppers ahead, as they can stand at room temperature for two hours after cooking; just before serving, broil them until they're heated through. A thin layer of tapenade, the robust olive spread, on the sea bass adds a lot of flavor. You can find polenta and tapenade at Italian markets and some supermarkets.

6 SERVINGS

- **3 red bell peppers, quartered**
- **4 tablespoons olive oil, divided**
- **3 garlic cloves, minced**
- **4 teaspoons chopped fresh thyme, divided**

- **3 cups whole milk**
- **2 cups water**
- **1 bay leaf**

- **1 cup polenta (coarse cornmeal)**
- **2 tablespoons whipping cream**

- **6 6-ounce sea bass fillets**
- **6 tablespoons tapenade**

PREHEAT oven to 350°F. Toss peppers, 2 tablespoons oil, garlic, and 3 teaspoons thyme in 13x9x2-inch metal baking pan to coat. Roast until peppers are tender and brown in spots, turning occasionally, about 1 hour. Cut peppers into ½-inch-wide strips and return to pan. Season to taste with salt and pepper. *(Peppers can be prepared 2 hours ahead. Let stand at room temperature.)*

BRING milk, water, bay leaf, and remaining 1 teaspoon thyme to simmer in heavy large saucepan. Cover and remove from heat. Let steep 15 minutes.

GRADUALLY whisk polenta into milk mixture. Bring to simmer over medium-low heat, whisking constantly. Continue cooking until thick and creamy, stirring often, about 20 minutes. Discard bay leaf. Mix in cream. Season polenta to taste with salt and pepper. Cover to keep warm.

MEANWHILE, preheat broiler. Heat remaining 2 tablespoons oil in heavy large skillet over medium-high heat. Sprinkle fish with salt and pepper. Add to skillet; sauté until just opaque in center, about 4 minutes per side. Remove from heat. Spread 1 tablespoon tapenade over each fillet. Broil red peppers in pan until heated through, about 2 minutes.

SPOON polenta onto 6 plates. Top with fish and red peppers and serve.

Sake-marinated sea bass with coconut-curry sauce

STAPLES OF JAPANESE COOKING—mirin, *sake*, tamari soy sauce, miso, rice vinegar, and ginger—team up in this sensational crowd-pleaser. You'll find all of these ingredients at Asian markets, natural foods stores, and some supermarkets. Begin preparations ahead so that the fish can marinate at least two hours. Serve the sea bass with sautéed spinach or bok choy.

6 SERVINGS

½ cup mirin (sweet Japanese rice wine)
¼ cup sake
¼ cup tamari or regular soy sauce
2 tablespoons light yellow miso (fermented soy bean paste)
2 tablespoons unseasoned rice vinegar
1 tablespoon chopped peeled fresh ginger
1 tablespoon (packed) golden brown sugar
6 6-ounce sea bass fillets

1 tablespoon vegetable oil

Steamed white rice
Coconut-Curry Sauce (see recipe)
Chopped fresh cilantro

PUREE first 7 ingredients in blender for marinade. Place fillets in single layer in 13x9x2-inch glass baking dish. Pour marinade over. Cover and refrigerate 2 hours, turning fish occasionally.

PREHEAT oven to 400°F. Remove fillets from marinade; pat dry with paper towels. Sprinkle both sides of fillets with salt and pepper. Heat oil in large ovenproof nonstick skillet over medium-high heat. Add fillets and sear until golden brown on 1 side, about 2 minutes. Turn fillets over in skillet. Transfer skillet to oven. Bake fillets until just opaque in center, about 8 minutes.

PLACE some steamed rice in center of each of 6 plates. Top with fillets. Spoon some sauce around rice on each plate. Garnish with cilantro and serve.

Coconut-curry sauce

PAIR THIS DELICIOUS SAUCE with the sea bass or try it with grilled shrimp or chicken. The mirin, unsweetened coconut milk, and curry paste can be found at Asian markets, natural foods stores, and some supermarkets. You'll find fresh lemongrass in the produce section of these markets. Remove the outside layers of the lemongrass and use the bottom two inches or so of the core. In a pinch, freshly grated lemon peel can be used instead. If desired, strain the sauce through a fine-mesh strainer for a smoother, more refined texture.

MAKES ABOUT 2 CUPS

- **½ cup mirin (sweet Japanese rice wine)**
- **¼ cup chopped fresh lemongrass (about 6 large stalks)**
- **1 tablespoon chopped peeled fresh ginger**
- **¼ cup dry white wine**
- **2 cups whipping cream**
- **¾ cup canned unsweetened coconut milk**
- **2 teaspoons Thai green or red curry paste**

COMBINE mirin, lemongrass, and ginger in heavy medium saucepan. Boil until reduced to ¼ cup, about 6 minutes. Add wine and boil until reduced again to ¼ cup, about 6 minutes. Add cream and coconut milk; bring to boil. Reduce heat to medium. Simmer sauce until slightly thickened, stirring occasionally, about 12 minutes. Whisk in curry paste. Season sauce to taste with salt. *(Can be prepared 1 day ahead. Cover and refrigerate. Rewarm over medium heat before using.)*

Oven-roasted sea bass with ginger and lime sauce

THE EASY-TO-FIND INGREDIENTS in this recipe impart a healthful Asian-inspired flavor to this main course. Store fish properly to keep it fresh for up to two days: Seal the fish in a plastic bag, then set it atop a shallow pan or bowl filled with ice. Place the bowl in the coldest part of the refrigerator.

2 SERVINGS; CAN BE DOUBLED

- **2 tablespoons fresh lime juice**
- **1½ tablespoons soy sauce**
- **1 tablespoon chopped fresh cilantro**
- **1 tablespoon chopped peeled fresh ginger**
- **1 tablespoon minced shallot**
- **5 teaspoons olive oil, divided**
- **2 6-ounce sea bass fillets (each about ¾ inch thick)**

PREHEAT oven to 500°F. Whisk first 5 ingredients and 3 teaspoons oil in small bowl to blend. Season sauce to taste with salt and pepper.

BRUSH 9-inch-diameter glass pie dish with remaining 2 teaspoons oil. Arrange fish in prepared dish; turn to coat. Sprinkle fish with salt and pepper; spoon ½ tablespoon sauce over each fillet. Roast fish until just opaque in center, about 10 minutes. Top fish with remaining sauce and serve.

Sea bass with watercress sauce

THIS DELICIOUS ENTRÉE takes just minutes to prepare, making it a perfect weeknight dinner.

2 SERVINGS

- **1 tablespoon butter**
- **1 tablespoon vegetable oil**
- **2 8-ounce sea bass fillets**
- **3 tablespoons finely chopped shallots**
- **¼ cup dry vermouth or dry white wine**
- **½ cup whipping cream**
- **1 cup (packed) chopped trimmed watercress (from 1 bunch, about 6 ounces), divided**

MELT butter with oil in heavy medium skillet over medium-high heat. Add sea bass to skillet; cook just until opaque in center, about 4 minutes per side. Transfer fish to plate; tent with foil to keep warm. Pour off all but 1 teaspoon drippings from skillet. Add shallots to same skillet; stir 30 seconds. Add vermouth; bring to boil. Continue to boil 1 minute. Add cream; boil until sauce thickens slightly and coats spoon, about 3 minutes. Add ¾ cup watercress to sauce. Season with salt and pepper. Transfer fish to plates. Spoon sauce around fish. Sprinkle with remaining ¼ cup watercress and serve.

Grilled sea bass with anchovy-balsamic dressing

THE ANCHOVY-BALSAMIC DRESSING that flavors the fish would also be delicious served over grilled vegetables such as sliced eggplant, zucchini, yellow crookneck squash, and red onions.

4 SERVINGS

½ cup olive oil
2 garlic cloves, minced
5 canned anchovy fillets, chopped
¼ cup balsamic vinegar
2 tablespoons chopped fresh oregano or 2 teaspoons dried

4 6-ounce sea bass fillets

HEAT oil in heavy small skillet over medium-high heat. Add garlic and sauté 1 minute. Add anchovies and whisk until anchovies dissolve, about 2 minutes. Remove from heat and cool 1 minute. Whisk in vinegar and oregano. Season dressing to taste with salt and pepper.

PREPARE barbecue (medium-high heat) or preheat broiler. Brush sea bass with 2 tablespoons dressing. Sprinkle with salt and pepper. Grill or broil fish until just opaque in center, about 4 minutes per side. Transfer fish to plates. Serve, passing remaining dressing separately.

Steamed whole red snapper with Asian flavors

THIS RECIPE FOR RED SNAPPER steamed with ginger, garlic, and cilantro results in fish with a delicate flavor and a moist texture, and makes a show stopping presentation for a dinner party. The classic Chinese way to steam the fish is in a tiered bamboo steamer set over boiling water in a wok. If you don't have a bamboo steamer or a wok, you can use a vegetable steamer rack –available with other kitchenware at most supermarkets–set in a large pot. Just be sure the pot is large enough to allow steam to circulate around the glass pie dish that holds the fish. Lemongrass is available at Asian markets and in the produce section of some supermarkets.

4 SERVINGS

2 16- to 18-ounce whole red snappers, cleaned, scaled
16 very thin slices peeled fresh ginger
16 very thin slices peeled garlic
16 large fresh cilantro leaves

3 tablespoons chopped fresh cilantro, divided
3 tablespoons chopped shallots, divided
3 tablespoons chopped lemongrass (from about 5 stalks), divided
3 tablespoons chopped green onions, divided
½ cup low-salt chicken broth
3 tablespoons soy sauce, divided

2 tablespoons Asian sesame oil
2 tablespoons vegetable oil
2 tablespoons chopped peeled fresh ginger
6 garlic cloves, chopped

Cooked long-grain white rice

SPRINKLE inside of each fish with salt. Using sharp cleaver or knife, make 4 diagonal slits on 1 side of each fish, spacing equally and cutting to the bone. Insert 1 slice of ginger, 1 slice of garlic, and 1 cilantro leaf into each slit. Turn fish over. Make 4 diagonal slits on second side of each fish and insert remaining sliced ginger, sliced garlic, and cilantro leaves into slits. Arrange fish in 9-inch-diameter glass pie dish. *(Can be prepared 6 hours ahead. Cover and refrigerate.)*

POUR enough water into wok or large pot to reach depth of 1½ inches. Place bottom of 11- to 12-inch-diameter bamboo steamer over water in wok or open a steamer rack and place in pot. Place glass pie dish with fish in bamboo steamer (or on steamer rack). Curl fish tails if necessary to fit. Sprinkle 1 tablespoon each of chopped cilantro, shallots, lemongrass, and green onions into dish around fish. Combine broth and 1 tablespoon soy sauce in cup; pour into pie dish. Bring water to boil. Cover bamboo steamer (or pot). Steam fish until just opaque in center at bone, about 18 minutes.

MEANWHILE, combine sesame oil and vegetable oil in heavy medium skillet. Add chopped ginger and chopped garlic, then remaining 2 tablespoons each of chopped cilantro, shallots, lemongrass, and green onions. Stir over medium heat until oil is hot and seasonings are fragrant, about 3 minutes. Pour seasoned oil into small bowl; whisk in remaining 2 tablespoons soy sauce.

USING oven mitts as aid, transfer dish with fish to work surface. Using large spatula, transfer fish to platter. Spoon juices from dish over fish. Spoon some of seasoned oil over fish. Serve fish with rice, passing remaining seasoned oil separately.

Grilled red snapper with garlic and mint

WHEN GRILLING or broiling fish fillets, brown the more attractive side—known as the "presentation side"—first, not the skin side.

2 SERVINGS

- **¼ cup olive oil**
- **6 garlic cloves, minced**
- **1 tablespoon balsamic vinegar**
- **2 teaspoons minced fresh mint**
- **1 teaspoon salt**
- **1 teaspoon ground black pepper**
- **2 6- to 7-ounce red snapper or orange roughy fillets**

PREPARE barbecue (medium-high heat) or preheat broiler. Whisk first 6 ingredients in small bowl to blend. Place fish on rimmed baking sheet. Brush generously with mint mixture. Turn and brush with more mint mixture. Grill fish or broil on baking sheet until just opaque in center, brushing frequently with mint mixture, about 3 minutes per side. Divide fish between plates and serve.

Red snapper Veracruz-style

A CLASSIC VERACRUZ-STYLE seafood sauce is usually a mixture of tomatoes, garlic, pickled jalapeño chiles, white onion, capers, green olives, oregano, and parsley. The sauce can be made one day ahead and the dish assembled while the oven preheats. Roasted small white potatoes, known in Veracruz as *papas cambray,* and a bowl of white rice are traditionally served alongside this specialty.

6 SERVINGS

- **1 28-ounce can diced tomatoes in juice, well drained, juice reserved**
- **¼ cup extra-virgin olive oil**
- **¼ cup finely chopped white onion**

- **3 garlic cloves, chopped**
- **3 small bay leaves**
- **2 tablespoons chopped fresh parsley**
- **1 teaspoon dried Mexican oregano**
- **¼ cup chopped pitted green olives**
- **2 tablespoons raisins**
- **2 tablespoons drained capers**

- **6 5-ounce red snapper fillets**
- **3 pickled jalapeño chiles, halved lengthwise**

PLACE drained tomatoes in medium bowl. Using potato masher, crush tomatoes to coarse puree. Drain again, reserving juice.

HEAT oil in heavy large skillet over medium-high heat. Add onion and stir 30 seconds. Add garlic and stir 30 seconds. Add coarse tomato puree and cook 1 minute. Add bay leaves, parsley, oregano, and ¼ cup reserved tomato juice. Simmer until sauce thickens, about 3 minutes. Add olives, raisins, capers, and all remaining reserved tomato juice. Simmer until sauce thickens again, stirring occasionally, about 8 minutes. Season sauce with salt and pepper. *(Can be made 1 day ahead. Cover and refrigerate.)*

PREHEAT oven to 425°F. Spread 3 tablespoons sauce in bottom of 15x10x2-inch glass baking dish. Arrange fish atop sauce. Sprinkle fish lightly with salt and pepper. Spoon remaining sauce over. Bake uncovered until fish is just opaque in center, about 18 minutes. Using long spatula, transfer fish with sauce to plates. Discard bay leaves. Garnish with pickled jalapeño halves and serve.

Grilled red snapper and mango with cilantro-lime vinaigrette

THE DELICATE TEXTURE of this fish can make it a bit intimidating to grill. This recipe eliminates the trickiest maneuver—turning the fish over—making it one step easier for the home cook. Keep in mind two key points when preparing this recipe: Use a medium flame so that the fish does not char on the bottom before the top is cooked. Second, close the barbecue lid so that the heat circulates within the barbecue and cooks the fish evenly from all sides. Use a long metal spatula to transfer the fish to serving plates. Serve the fish and mango with warm corn tortillas, Spanish rice, and grilled zucchini.

4 SERVINGS

- **6 tablespoons olive oil**
- **5 tablespoons chopped fresh cilantro, divided**
- **3 tablespoons fresh lime juice**
- **1½ teaspoons grated lime peel**
- **4 5- to 6-ounce red snapper fillets**
- **1 large mango, peeled, pitted, cut into thick wedges**
- **¾ teaspoon cumin seeds**

- **8 large red leaf lettuce leaves**

PREPARE barbecue (medium heat). Whisk oil, 4 tablespoons cilantro, lime juice, and lime peel in small bowl to blend. Season vinaigrette to taste with salt and pepper. Brush fish and mango all over with some of vinaigrette. Reserve remaining vinaigrette. Sprinkle fish and mango with salt, pepper, and cumin seeds. Grill fish and mango with barbecue lid closed, without turning, until fish is just opaque in center and mango is soft and beginning to brown, about 6 minutes. Transfer to plate.

OVERLAP 2 lettuce leaves on each of 4 plates. Top with fish and mango. Drizzle with remaining vinaigrette. Sprinkle with remaining 1 tablespoon cilantro and serve.

Baked cod with tarragon and fennel-seed butter

PLACING THE COD FILLETS on a heavy rimmed baking sheet rather than in a deeper baking dish will provide more direct heat on all sides of the fish and allow the accumulated juices to evaporate, thus baking the fish rather than steaming it. Crushing the fennel seeds in a plastic bag contains the seeds and simplifies clean-up. This entrée is terrific with mashed potatoes and sautéed sugar snap peas.

6 SERVINGS

6 tablespoons (3/4 stick) butter
2 tablespoons chopped fresh tarragon
4 teaspoons fennel seeds, crushed
1 tablespoon grated lemon peel
1 tablespoon fresh lemon juice
6 6- to 7-ounce cod fillets

6 very thin lemon slices
6 fresh tarragon sprigs

STIR butter, chopped tarragon, fennel seeds, lemon peel, and lemon juice in small saucepan over low heat until butter melts. Season to taste with salt and pepper. Arrange cod on rimmed baking sheet; brush all of butter mixture over. *(Cod can be prepared 8 hours ahead. Cover and chill.)*

POSITION rack in center of oven and preheat to 450°F. Bake cod uncovered until just opaque in center, about 12 minutes. Transfer to plates. Garnish with lemon slices and tarragon sprigs and serve.

Miso-marinated cod with cucumber-daikon relish

WHITE MISO—fermented soy bean paste—is milder in flavor than yellow or red miso, thus imparting a more subtle flavor to the fish. You can find the miso, mirin, and nori at Japanese markets and in the Asian foods section or refrigerated deli section of some supermarkets. If you can't find white miso, yellow miso is fine as a substitute. Serve the cod with steamed rice tossed with shelled edamame (fresh soybeans).

6 SERVINGS

1/4 cup white miso (fermented soybean paste)
1/4 cup mirin (sweet Japanese rice wine)
2 tablespoons unseasoned rice vinegar
2 tablespoons minced green onions
1 1/2 tablespoons minced peeled fresh ginger
2 teaspoons Asian sesame oil
6 6-ounce cod fillets

Nonstick vegetable oil spray

Cucumber-Daikon Relish (see recipe)
1 1/2 teaspoons sesame seeds, toasted
1/2 cup radish sprouts
1/2 8x8-inch sheet dried nori, cut with scissors into matchstick-size strips

WHISK miso and next 5 ingredients in 13x9x2-inch glass baking dish to blend for marinade. Add cod and turn to coat. Cover and chill at least 30 minutes and up to 2 hours.

PREHEAT broiler. Line heavy large baking sheet with aluminum foil; spray with nonstick spray. Remove cod fillets from miso marinade; using rubber spatula, scrape off excess marinade. Arrange cod skin side up on prepared baking sheet. Broil 5 to 6 inches from heat source until skin is crisp, about 2 minutes. Using metal spatula, turn cod over. Broil until cod is just cooked through and golden brown on top, about 4 minutes.

TRANSFER cod to plates, skin side down. Spoon Cucumber-Daikon Relish over. Sprinkle with sesame seeds, then sprouts and nori. Serve immediately.

Cucumber-daikon relish

TWO SIMPLE STEPS commonly used in Japanese cookery—salting and soaking—provide optimal results for this Japanese-accented relish. Salting the cucumbers extracts the excess liquid that would otherwise dilute the flavors of the finished relish. Soaking the daikon radish in water mellows its strong flavor so that it doesn't overpower the other ingredients. Make sure the cucumbers and radish are well drained and patted dry before tossing them with the vinegar dressing.

6 SERVINGS

- **2 English hothouse cucumbers, peeled, halved, seeded, cut crosswise into ¼-inch-thick slices**
- **2 teaspoons sea salt**

- **8 ounces daikon (Japanese white radish), peeled, cut into 2x¼-inch sticks**

- **⅔ cup unseasoned rice vinegar**
- **⅔ cup sugar**
- **1 tablespoon minced peeled fresh ginger**
- **⅛ teaspoon cayenne pepper**

TOSS cucumbers with sea salt in colander. Place colander over bowl and let stand 15 minutes. Rinse cucumbers. Drain and pat dry with paper towels.

PLACE radish sticks in medium bowl. Cover with water. Soak 15 minutes. Drain and pat dry with paper towels.

STIR vinegar and next 3 ingredients in large bowl to blend. Add cucumbers and radish; toss to coat. Cover and refrigerate at least 30 minutes and up to 2 hours.

Sautéed cod with creamed corn and summer succotash

SIMPLE FLAVORS come together spectacularly in this special dish. See chapter 1 ("Notes from the Test Kitchen") for tips on cutting corn kernels from the cob and seeding tomatoes.

4 SERVINGS

Succotash

- **1½ pounds fresh fava beans, shelled, or 1½ cups frozen lima beans, thawed**
- **2 large ears of corn, kernels cut from cob (about 2 cups)**
- **1 large tomato, seeded, diced**
- **2 tablespoons chopped fresh Italian parsley**
- **1 tablespoon extra-virgin olive oil**

Creamed corn

- **7 large ears of corn, kernels cut from cob (about 7 cups), divided**
- **3 tablespoons whipping cream**

- **Vegetable oil (for frying)**
- **4 6- to 8-ounce pieces cod fillets, pinbones removed**

FOR SUCCOTASH: Cook beans in large saucepan of boiling salted water until just tender, about 5 minutes. Using slotted spoon or strainer, transfer beans to colander; reserve cooking water. Rinse beans with cold water. If using fava beans, peel off outer skins and discard. Return reserved cooking water to boil; add corn kernels and cook until just tender, about 1 minute. Drain. Return beans and corn to same saucepan. Mix in tomato, parsley, and olive oil. Season to taste with salt and pepper. *(Succotash can be prepared 2 hours ahead. Let stand covered at room temperature. Rewarm over low heat before serving.)*

FOR CREAMED CORN: Place 4 cups corn kernels in processor. Puree until liquid is released from corn, about 3 minutes (mixture will still be coarse). Transfer pureed corn to strainer set over large measuring cup. Press on solids in strainer to extract at least ¾ cup juice; discard solids. Transfer corn juice to medium saucepan. Stir over medium heat just until juice begins to thicken, about 45 seconds (do not boil or juice may curdle). Add remaining 3 cups corn kernels and whipping cream to saucepan and stir just until corn is heated through, about 2 minutes. Season to taste with salt and pepper. Remove creamed corn from heat and cover to keep warm.

POUR enough vegetable oil into heavy large skillet to reach depth of ¼ inch. Heat over high heat. Sprinkle cod fillets with salt and pepper. Add fillets to skillet and cook until golden brown and just opaque in center, about 4 minutes per side.

DIVIDE creamed corn among 4 plates. Top each serving with 1 sautéed cod fillet. Spoon succotash atop each fillet and serve.

Fillet of cod with asparagus and prosciutto

EACH SERVING is baked *en papillote*, or wrapped individually in parchment paper to lock in steam for a more succulent result. Asparagus are best when you pick those with bright green stalks, wash them thoroughly, and use them the same day you buy them.

6 SERVINGS

1½ pounds slender asparagus spears, trimmed to 7-inch lengths

2 garlic cloves, minced
1 teaspoon salt
2 tablespoons (¼ stick) butter
1 tablespoon plus 6 teaspoons olive oil
⅓ cup fresh lemon juice
1½ teaspoons grated lemon peel
½ teaspoon ground black pepper

6 6-ounce cod fillets, pinbones removed
6 ounces paper-thin prosciutto slices, halved lengthwise

COOK asparagus in large pot of boiling salted water until crisp-tender, about 3 minutes. Drain. Transfer to bowl of ice water to cool. Drain well.

MASH garlic and 1 teaspoon salt to paste in small bowl. Melt butter with 1 tablespoon oil in small nonstick skillet over medium heat. Add garlic paste; stir until pale golden, about 1 minute. Stir in lemon juice, lemon peel, and ½ teaspoon black pepper. Remove from heat.

CUT out six 12-inch squares of parchment paper. Place 1 parchment square on work surface. Drizzle 1 teaspoon oil over parchment. Place 1 cod fillet in center of parchment. Spoon ⅙ of garlic-lemon mixture over fish. Cover with ⅙ of asparagus spears. Arrange ⅙ of prosciutto slices over. Fold 2 opposite sides of parchment in over fish and vegetables, then fold in remaining 2 sides, enclosing completely. Fasten parchment edges together with paper clips to seal packet. Place on large rimmed baking sheet. Repeat procedure with remaining parchment, oil, fish, garlic-lemon mixture, asparagus, and prosciutto. *(Can be prepared 6 hours ahead. Refrigerate.)*

PREHEAT oven to 500°F. Bake fish until just opaque in center (parchment will turn golden brown), about 12 minutes. Transfer 1 parchment packet to each of 6 plates. Open parchment packets and serve.

Cod with bok choy and burnt orange–star anise sauce

STAR ANISE are brown star-shaped seedpods available at Asian markets and specialty foods stores. In this recipe, the star anise is used whole, then removed from the sauce before serving. The flavor of star anise is just a bit more bitter than the licorice-like taste of regular aniseed; together with the sautéed orange peel, it gives the subtle cod a wonderfully complex flavor.

6 SERVINGS

- **8 large oranges**
- **7 tablespoons chilled butter, divided**
- **1 tablespoon oil**
- **1 tablespoon unseasoned rice vinegar**
- **6 whole star anise**
- **2 teaspoons minced peeled fresh ginger**

- **6 6-ounce cod or sea bass fillets**

Baby Bok Choy with Garlic (see recipe)

USING swivel-bladed vegetable peeler, remove peel (orange part only) in long pieces from 6 oranges. Cut peel into 2x¼-inch strips. Cut all oranges in half; squeeze enough juice to measure 2¼ cups. Melt 1 tablespoon butter with oil in heavy large skillet over high heat. Add peel and stir until peel turns dark brown on edges, about 4 minutes. Add orange juice, vinegar, star anise, and ginger; boil until reduced to thin sauce consistency, about 12 minutes. Remove sauce from heat.

PREHEAT oven to 450°F. Sprinkle fish with salt and pepper. Melt 1 tablespoon butter in large skillet over high heat. Add 3 fish fillets; cook until golden, about 1 minute per side. Transfer fish to rimmed baking sheet. Repeat with 1 tablespoon butter and remaining fish. Bake fish until cooked through, about 4 minutes.

TRANSFER fish to plates. Remove star anise from sauce. Bring sauce to simmer. Add remaining 4 tablespoons butter and whisk just until melted. Season to taste with salt and pepper. Serve fish with sauce and bok choy.

Baby bok choy with garlic

BABY BOK CHOY is a relative of Chinese cabbage, but looks more like miniature celery stalks with cabbagey leaves. Buy bok choy with firm stalks and colorful leaves, and use it within two or three days (store it in an airtight container in the refrigerator).

6 SERVINGS

- **2 tablespoons (¼ stick) butter**
- **4 teaspoons minced garlic**
- **12 baby bok choy**
- **2 cups low-salt chicken broth**

MELT butter in heavy large skillet over high heat. Add garlic and sauté 1 minute. Add bok choy and broth. Simmer uncovered until bok choy is tender, turning occasionally, about 8 minutes. Season to taste with salt and pepper.

Scrod with herbed breadcrumbs

MOST NEW ENGLANDERS claim that scrod is actually baby cod weighing less than two pounds. However, some contend that baby haddock and pollack, close relatives to cod, may be defined as scrod too. In any case, the fresh breadcrumb topping is delicious on any of these fish. Making the fresh breadcrumbs called for here is simple: Place torn pieces of crustless French bread in a food processor and pulse until they are chopped into crumbs. Six thin slices of the bread will yield about two cups of fresh crumbs.

4 SERVINGS

- **¼ cup (½ stick) butter**
- **2 large shallots, minced**
- **2 cups fresh breadcrumbs made from crustless French bread**
- **¼ cup chopped fresh chives or green onion tops**
- **3 tablespoons minced fresh parsley**
- **2 teaspoons grated lemon peel**

- **4 6- to 8-ounce scrod or true cod fillets (each about 1½ inches thick)**
- **2 tablespoons fresh lemon juice**
- **Lemon wedges**

MELT butter in heavy large skillet over medium heat. Add shallots and cook 1 minute. Add breadcrumbs and stir until butter is absorbed. Remove from heat and mix in chives, parsley, and lemon peel. Season crumb topping to taste with salt and pepper. *(Topping can be prepared 1 day ahead. Cover and refrigerate. Bring to room temperature before using.)*

PREHEAT oven to 450°F. Butter glass baking dish and place fish in pan. Brush fish with lemon juice. Cover fish with breadcrumb topping, dividing equally and pressing to adhere. Bake until fish is just opaque in center, about 20 minutes. Serve with lemon wedges.

Almond-crusted sole with leek-and-lemon cream

BUTTER ADDS a delicious flavor to pan-fried fish, but it burns quickly. Using some oil in addition to the butter helps prevent burning. Lean fish, such as sole, are especially well suited to sautéing because the cooking method provides the fat that the fish lacks. Sautéed fish is often coated first, as in this recipe, to form a crust that browns attractively, helps hold the fish together, and provides a contrast in texture. The cream sauce can be made one day ahead and kept covered and refrigerated. Stir it over medium heat to rewarm just before serving.

4 SERVINGS

- **5 tablespoons butter, divided**
- **2 medium leeks, halved, thinly sliced (white and pale green parts only)**
- **3 tablespoons fresh lemon juice**
- **1 cup whipping cream**

- **1 cup sliced almonds, finely chopped**
- **6 tablespoons chopped fresh parsley**
- **1½ tablespoons grated lemon peel**
- **¾ teaspoon salt**
- **¼ teaspoon ground black pepper**
- **All purpose flour**
- **8 petrale or Dover sole fillets**
- **2 large eggs, beaten to blend**

- **3 tablespoons olive oil**

MELT 2 tablespoons butter in heavy large saucepan over medium-high heat. Add leeks and sauté 2 minutes. Reduce heat to low, cover, and cook until leeks are very tender, stirring occasionally, about 20 minutes. Increase heat to medium; add lemon juice and stir until liquid evaporates, about 1 minute. Mix in cream. Simmer until mixture is slightly thickened, about 2 minutes. Cool 10 minutes. Transfer mixture to blender. Blend until smooth. Strain sauce back into same saucepan, pressing on solids to extract as much liquid as possible. Season sauce to taste with salt and pepper. *(Sauce can be made 1 day ahead. Cover and refrigerate.)*

MIX almonds, parsley, lemon peel, ¾ teaspoon salt, and ¼ teaspoon pepper on large plate to combine. Place flour on another plate and eggs in small bowl. Sprinkle fillets with salt and pepper. Dredge in flour, shaking off excess. Brush 1 side of each with beaten eggs. Press egg side into almond mixture to coat. Arrange fillets, nut side down, on baking sheet.

MELT 1½ tablespoons of remaining butter with 1½ tablespoons oil in each of 2 heavy large skillets over medium-high heat. Add 4 fillets to each skillet, nut side down. Cook until nut crust is brown, about 2 minutes. Turn fillets over and cook until just opaque in center, about 2 minutes longer. Transfer 2 fillets to each of 4 plates.

REHEAT sauce, stirring over medium heat. Spoon around fillets and serve.

Pecan-crusted trout with orange-rosemary butter sauce

WHEN SHOPPING FOR THE TROUT, ask your fishmonger to remove the scales, head, and tail, then cut each trout into two fillets and remove the fine bones, leaving the skin intact. If whole fish are not available, purchase four large fillets with the skin on. Even though this sauce contains some cream to stabilize it, do not allow the sauce to boil after the butter is whisked in, or it may separate.

4 SERVINGS

Trout

- **2 cups pecans**
- **1 cup all purpose flour, divided**
- **2 large (12- to 14-ounce) whole trout, cleaned, heads and tails removed, filleted with skin left intact**
- **3 large egg whites, beaten to blend**

Sauce

- **1½ cups fresh orange juice**
- **1 cup dry white wine**
- **⅔ cup chopped shallots**
- **¼ cup white wine vinegar**
- **8 5-inch-long fresh parsley stems**
- **1½ tablespoons fresh lemon juice**
- **1 large fresh thyme sprig**
- **2 fresh rosemary sprigs**
- **¼ cup whipping cream**
- **¾ cup (1½ sticks) unsalted butter, cut into 12 pieces**

Assembly

- **4 tablespoons olive oil, divided**
- **1 carrot, peeled, cut into matchstick-size strips**
- **1 red bell pepper, thinly sliced**
- **6 cups thinly sliced savoy cabbage**

- **2 tablespoons (¼ stick) butter, divided**

Chopped fresh chives

FOR TROUT: Line baking sheet with waxed paper. Combine pecans and 1 tablespoon flour in processor. Grind pecans finely; transfer to plate. Place remaining flour on another plate. Sprinkle fish with salt and pepper. Dip 1 fillet into flour to coat on both sides; shake off excess. Using pastry brush, brush flesh side with egg whites. Place fillet, egg white side down, on pecan mixture; press to coat with nuts. Transfer to prepared baking sheet, nut side down. Repeat with remaining 3 fillets; cover and chill while preparing sauce.

FOR SAUCE: Combine first 7 ingredients in medium saucepan; boil 10 minutes. Add rosemary and boil until liquid is reduced to ½ cup, about 10 minutes longer. Strain sauce into another medium saucepan, pressing on solids in sieve to extract as much liquid as possible. Add cream to sauce; bring to boil. Reduce heat to low. Whisk in butter 1 piece at a time, allowing each to melt before adding another (do not boil). Season sauce to taste with salt and pepper. *(Sauce can be made 2 hours ahead. Let stand at room temperature.)*

HEAT 2 tablespoons oil in heavy large pot over high heat. Add carrot and bell pepper; toss 2 minutes. Add cabbage; toss until cabbage wilts, about 4 minutes. Season vegetables to taste with salt and pepper. Remove from heat.

MELT 1 tablespoon butter with 1 tablespoon oil in heavy large skillet over medium-high heat. Place 2 fillets, nut side down, in skillet. Cook until crust is golden and crisp, about 2 minutes. Using spatula, turn fillets over. Cook until fish is just opaque in center, about 2 minutes. Transfer to plate. Repeat with remaining butter, oil, and fish.

WHISK sauce over low heat to rewarm (do not boil). Divide vegetables among plates. Top with fish. Spoon sauce around fish and vegetables. Sprinkle with chopped chives and serve.

Cornmeal-crusted trout with warm tomato and tarragon salsa

FRESHWATER RAINBOW TROUT sold in markets are sustainably farm-raised and make a good eco-friendly choice. Select trout with clear and shiny eyes, red or pink gills, moist tail and fins, and a fresh scent. Have your fishmonger scale and bone the trout, leaving the heads and tails intact. Use a combination of yellow, red, and orange vine-ripened tomatoes for a vibrant salsa, and be sure not to overcook them, as they should be just warmed through and holding their shape. Shelled pumpkin seeds, or pepitas, are available at Latin markets, natural foods stores, and many supermarkets. Ancho chili powder is available in the spice section of most supermarkets.

4 SERVINGS

- ½ cup all purpose flour
- ⅓ cup yellow cornmeal
- 1 tablespoon ancho chili powder
- 1 teaspoon salt
- 4 12- to 14-ounce whole trout, cleaned, scaled, left whole (but boned) with heads and tails intact
- 6 tablespoons olive oil, divided

- ½ cup chopped red onion
- 4 garlic cloves, minced
- 2 teaspoons minced seeded serrano chile
- 1½ pounds yellow, red, or orange tomatoes, seeded, cut into ½-inch pieces
- 3 tablespoons bottled clam juice
- 2 tablespoons fresh lemon juice
- 2 teaspoons honey
- 1 tablespoon chopped fresh tarragon

- ¼ cup shelled pumpkin seeds (pepitas), lightly toasted

WHISK flour, cornmeal, chili powder, and 1 teaspoon salt in 13x9x2-inch glass baking dish to combine. Pat trout dry with paper towels. Open trout and sprinkle cavities with salt and pepper; fold trout closed. Coat outside of trout with cornmeal mixture. Heat 2 tablespoons oil in each of 2 heavy large skillets over medium-high heat. Add 2 trout to each skillet and cook until just opaque in center and crisp outside, about 4 minutes per side. Transfer to plates.

WIPE out 1 skillet, then heat remaining 2 tablespoons oil in same skillet over medium-high heat. Add onion, garlic, and serrano chile. Sauté until onion is softened, about 2 minutes. Add tomatoes, clam juice, lemon juice, and honey. Cook just until liquids begin to simmer but tomatoes retain texture, about 2 minutes. Remove skillet from heat. Stir in tarragon. Season salsa to taste with salt and pepper.

SPOON salsa over trout. Sprinkle with pumpkin seeds and serve.

Roasted halibut with tomatoes, saffron, and cilantro

THE HALIBUT cooks directly atop the tomatoes in this flavorful and very easy dish. The saffron adds a lovely aroma and vivid color. Choose Pacific or Alaskan halibut, or substitute another firm white fish, such as Alaskan cod, mahi-mahi, or striped bass. If you can't find red grape tomatoes or teardrop tomatoes, use cherry tomatoes instead. And if you don't have white balsamic vinegar, unseasoned rice vinegar makes a fine substitute.

8 SERVINGS

- 3 pounds plum tomatoes, seeded, cut into 1-inch pieces (about 8 cups)
- 2 cups red grape tomatoes (about 11 ounces), halved
- 1 cup yellow teardrop tomatoes (about 5½ ounces), halved
- 8 8-ounce halibut fillets (each about 1 inch thick)

- ½ cup olive oil
- 3 tablespoons white balsamic vinegar
- 2 green onions, chopped
- 2 tablespoons chopped fresh basil
- 1 tablespoon chopped fresh cilantro
- ¼ teaspoon saffron threads, crumbled

Fresh cilantro sprigs

PREHEAT oven to 450°F. Place all tomatoes in 13x9x2-inch glass baking dish. Sprinkle with salt and pepper; toss to combine. Sprinkle fish with salt and pepper; place atop tomatoes.

WHISK oil, vinegar, green onions, basil, cilantro, and saffron in small bowl to blend. Season dressing to taste with salt and pepper. Pour dressing evenly over fish. Let stand 10 minutes.

BAKE fish until just opaque in center, about 10 minutes. Cool slightly. Place 1 fillet on each of 8 plates. Season tomato mixture to taste with salt and pepper. Top fish with tomato mixture, dividing equally. Garnish with cilantro sprigs and serve warm.

Halibut and red bell pepper skewers with chile-lime sauce

THE MEATY TEXTURE of halibut works well in all sorts of cuisines, from Mediterranean to Indian. It even stands up to skewering in this simple, yet boldly flavored, entrée. You can prepare the skewers and spicy sauce eight hours before serving; keep them covered separately and refrigerated. Be sure to bring the sauce to room temperature before using, to accent the wonderful flavor of fresh lime juice.

6 SERVINGS

½ cup fresh lime juice
4 tablespoons olive oil, divided
3 tablespoons chopped fresh cilantro
2 tablespoons sugar
1½ teaspoons minced serrano chiles with seeds
1½ pounds 1-inch-thick halibut fillets, cut into 1-inch cubes (about 30 pieces)
1 extra-large red bell pepper, cut into 1-inch triangles (about 30 pieces)
6 green onions, cut into 1-inch lengths (about 30 pieces)
6 10- to 12-inch-long metal skewers

WHISK lime juice, 2 tablespoons olive oil, cilantro, sugar, and chiles in small bowl until sugar dissolves. Let sauce stand 1 hour at room temperature to allow flavors to blend. Season sauce to taste with salt and pepper. Alternate halibut pieces, bell pepper pieces, and onion pieces on skewers. *(Sauce and skewers can be made 8 hours ahead. Cover separately and refrigerate. Bring to room temperature before continuing.)*

PREPARE barbecue (medium-high heat). Sprinkle skewers with salt and pepper. Drizzle skewers with remaining 2 tablespoons olive oil. Grill until fish is just opaque in center and vegetables are charred in spots, turning skewers occasionally, about 6 minutes. Transfer skewers to platter. Serve, passing chile-lime sauce separately.

Mustard seed–crusted halibut with mustard cream sauce

THE MUSTARD SEEDS add a crunchy crust around the halibut, and a nonstick skillet helps prevent the crust from sticking to the pan. The sauce can be made one day ahead, covered, and refrigerated, then rewarmed over low heat before serving. Serve steamed broccolini and egg noodles alongside for a satisfying dinner that can be thrown together in less than 45 minutes.

4 SERVINGS

½ cup dry white wine
¼ cup (packed) chopped shallots
3 tablespoons yellow mustard seeds, divided
¾ cup whipping cream
5 tablespoons whole grain Dijon mustard, divided
1 tablespoon chopped fresh tarragon

4 6-ounce halibut fillets
2 tablespoons (¼ stick) butter

BOIL wine, shallots, and 1 tablespoon mustard seeds in heavy small saucepan until mixture is reduced to ½ cup, about 2 minutes. Whisk in cream, 2½ tablespoons Dijon mustard, and tarragon. Boil until sauce is thick enough to coat spoon, about 3 minutes. Season to taste with salt and pepper. Remove from heat; cover to keep warm. *(Sauce can be prepared one day ahead. Cover and refrigerate. Rewarm over low heat, whisking occasionally.)*

BRUSH halibut on both sides with remaining 2½ tablespoons Dijon mustard. Sprinkle remaining 2 tablespoons mustard seeds, salt, and pepper over both sides of halibut. Melt butter in large nonstick skillet over medium heat. Add halibut and sauté until just opaque in center, about 4 minutes per side. Transfer to platter. Spoon warm mustard sauce over and serve.

Teriyaki swordfish with tomato-orange salsa

COLORFUL AND DELICIOUS, yet healthful and low in calories, this entrée will leave no one feeling cheated. Team it with grilled asparagus and a watercress salad. When grilling fish, start with a clean grill and make sure it's hot enough to cook the food quickly.

6 SERVINGS

Salsa

- **3 oranges, all peel and white pith cut away, seeded, diced**
- **1½ cups chopped seeded tomatoes (about 12 ounces)**
- **¼ cup minced red onion**
- **¼ cup chopped fresh parsley**
- **2 tablespoons fresh orange juice**
- **2 garlic cloves, minced**
- **2 teaspoons balsamic vinegar**
- **1 teaspoon minced peeled fresh ginger**
- **⅛ teaspoon cayenne pepper**

Marinade and fish

- **¾ cup bottled teriyaki sauce**
- **⅔ cup dry Sherry**
- **4 garlic cloves, minced**
- **2 teaspoons minced peeled fresh ginger**
- **1 teaspoon Asian sesame oil**

- **6 5- to 6-ounce swordfish steaks (each about 1 inch thick)**

FOR SALSA: Toss all ingredients in large bowl to combine. Season to taste with salt and pepper. Let stand at least 1 hour. *(Salsa can be prepared 4 hours ahead. Cover and refrigerate. Bring to room temperature before using.)*

FOR MARINADE AND FISH: Combine teriyaki sauce and next 4 ingredients in small saucepan. Bring marinade to boil. Set aside to cool.

ARRANGE swordfish in single layer in shallow glass baking dish. Pour marinade over swordfish; turn to coat evenly. Cover and refrigerate fish 1½ hours, turning often.

PREPARE barbecue (medium-high heat). Remove fish from marinade. Grill fish with some marinade still clinging until just opaque in center, about 4 minutes per side. Transfer to platter. Serve with salsa.

Swordfish and red onion spiedini

SPIEDINI IS ITALIAN for skewers of any combination of foods—bread, cheeses, meatballs, fish—that can be grilled or roasted. Look for metal skewers in the supermarket kitchenwares section. Start this meal with bruschetta—chopped fresh tomatoes, basil, and garlic spooned onto toasted baguette slices. Grill slices of potato to have with the swordfish, and follow with biscotti and fresh figs.

2 SERVINGS; CAN BE DOUBLED

- **6 tablespoons garlic-flavored olive oil**
- **2 tablespoons fresh lemon juice**
- **4 teaspoons chopped fresh rosemary**
- **1 12-ounce swordfish steak, cut into 1-inch pieces**
- **12 1x1x¼-inch red onion pieces**
- **8 lemon slices, halved**
- **4 10- to 12-inch-long metal skewers**

- **4 cups mixed baby greens (about 2 ounces)**

PREPARE barbecue (medium-high heat). Whisk oil, lemon juice, and rosemary in small bowl to blend. Season dressing to taste with salt and pepper. Thread fish, onion, and lemon slices onto skewers, dividing equally. Brush skewers with dressing; sprinkle with salt and pepper. Grill until fish is just opaque in center and onion is slightly charred and tender, turning and brushing often with some of remaining dressing, about 8 minutes.

TOSS greens and all remaining dressing in medium bowl to coat. Mound salad on 2 plates; top with swordfish skewers.

Seared tuna with green onion–wasabi sauce

IF YOU'RE A SUSHI LOVER, you'll enjoy this simple recipe at home. Serve the tuna with Jasmine Rice Timbales with Black and White Sesame Seeds (page 232) for a stunning restaurant-style presentation. You'll find wasabi (horseradish) powder at Japanese markets and in the Asian foods section of some supermarkets. It can turn bitter over time, so be sure to use fresh powder. If you can't find it, use prepared wasabi paste (available in the Asian foods section or next to the packaged sushi at supermarkets) to flavor the sauce to your taste.

4 SERVINGS

½ cup water
3 tablespoons wasabi powder (horseradish powder)
⅓ cup reduced-sodium soy sauce
3 tablespoons peanut oil, divided
1 tablespoon dry Sherry
1½ teaspoons Asian sesame oil
1½ teaspoons minced peeled fresh ginger
4 green onions, very thinly sliced

4 6-ounce ahi tuna steaks (each about 1 inch thick)

1 cucumber, peeled, seeded, cut into matchstick-size strips
½ cup radish sprouts

WHISK ½ cup water and wasabi powder in medium bowl to form smooth paste. Whisk in soy sauce, 2 tablespoons peanut oil, Sherry, sesame oil, and ginger. Stir in green onions. Season sauce to taste with salt and pepper.

SPRINKLE tuna with salt and pepper. Heat remaining 1 tablespoon peanut oil in heavy large skillet over high heat. Add tuna and cook to desired doneness, 1 to 2 minutes per side for rare.

SPOON cucumber onto center of plates. Top with tuna. Spoon sauce around. Garnish with radish sprouts and serve.

Pan-seared tuna with ginger-shiitake cream sauce

FRESHLY CRACKED BLACK PEPPER makes a nice crust on the seared tuna. Be sure to trim the stems from the shiitake mushrooms, as they are tough and inedible. If you can't find fresh shiitakes, use dried and rehydrate them in warm water, being sure to trim any stems. Pair the fish with wasabi mashed potatoes or sautéed green beans, and finish the meal with a scoop of green tea ice cream.

6 SERVINGS

6 6-ounce tuna steaks (each about 1 inch thick)
2 tablespoons peanut oil

3 tablespoons butter
⅓ cup thinly sliced green onions
¼ cup chopped fresh cilantro
2 tablespoons finely chopped peeled fresh ginger
4 garlic cloves, chopped
8 ounces fresh shiitake mushrooms, stemmed, caps sliced
6 tablespoons soy sauce
1½ cups whipping cream
3 tablespoons fresh lime juice
Lime wedges (optional)
Fresh cilantro sprigs (optional)

PREHEAT oven to 200°F. Sprinkle 1 side of tuna steaks with freshly cracked black pepper. Heat oil in heavy large skillet over high heat. Place tuna steaks, pepper side down, in hot oil and sear 2 minutes (or less for rare tuna). Turn tuna over and continue cooking to desired doneness, 1 to 2 minutes for rare. Transfer tuna to rimmed baking sheet; keep warm in oven.

ADD butter, green onions, cilantro, ginger, and garlic to same skillet; sauté until fragrant, about 30 seconds. Mix in mushrooms and soy sauce; simmer 30 seconds. Add whipping cream and simmer until sauce thickens enough to coat spoon, about 3 minutes. Stir in lime juice. Season sauce to taste with salt and pepper. Spoon sauce onto plates; arrange tuna atop sauce. Garnish with lime wedges and cilantro sprigs, if desired, and serve.

Beer-battered catfish on vinegar slaw

THE BATTER CAN BE MADE with any flat beer, but choose a good-quality variety, as it will impart a better flavor to the batter. Strips of cod or halibut make excellent substitutes for the catfish. Add frozen steak fries to the skillet after the fish fillets have been fried for a new version of British fish and chips (wrapping in newspaper optional).

2 SERVINGS

2 cups purchased coleslaw mix
2 tablespoons white wine vinegar
1½ tablespoons honey
1 tablespoon vegetable oil plus additional oil (for frying)

⅓ cup plus 2 tablespoons all purpose flour
½ teaspoon salt
¼ teaspoon ground black pepper
⅓ cup flat beer

2 4- to 6-ounce catfish fillets

TOSS coleslaw mix, vinegar, honey, and 1 tablespoon oil in medium bowl to blend. Season slaw to taste with salt and pepper.

WHISK ⅓ cup flour, ½ teaspoon salt, and ¼ teaspoon pepper in medium bowl to blend. Whisk in beer to make batter.

ADD enough additional oil to heavy large skillet to reach depth of ½ inch. Heat oil to 350°F. Place remaining 2 tablespoons flour on plate. Coat fish with flour, then dip in batter, letting excess drip off. Add fish to hot oil and fry until golden brown and crisp, about 4 minutes per side. Transfer fish to paper towels to drain. Divide slaw between plates; top with fish and serve.

Arctic char with horseradish cream, sweet-and-sour beets, and dandelion greens

ARCTIC CHAR is wonderfully delicate fish similar to its salmon cousin, which makes a good substitute in this recipe. If you don't have time to make your own horseradish cream from fresh horseradish, just mix one cup of heavy whipping cream with prepared white horseradish to taste. If dandelion greens are unavailable, any bitter green—such as arugula, watercress, endive, or mustard greens—will work.

4 SERVINGS

Horseradish cream
3 cups ½-inch cubes peeled fresh horseradish root (from 1 pound unpeeled)
1½ cups heavy whipping cream

Beets
8 baby red beets, tops trimmed
8 baby golden beets, tops trimmed

1 cup apple cider vinegar
4 tablespoons sugar

Fish and greens
4 6-ounce arctic char or salmon fillets with skin
3 tablespoons vegetable oil, divided

1 large bunch dandelion greens, stems trimmed

FOR HORSERADISH CREAM: Grate horseradish in processor fitted with coarse-shredder disk. Transfer horseradish to medium saucepan. Add cream. Cover pan and simmer 10 minutes. Remove from heat. Let stand, covered, 30 minutes to infuse. Strain cream into small saucepan, pressing firmly on solids to extract as much cream as possible. *(Cream can be made 2 days ahead. Cover and chill.)*

FOR BEETS: Cook red and golden beets in separate medium pots of boiling salted water until tender, about 18 minutes. Drain and cool. *(Beets can be prepared 2 days ahead. Cover and chill.)*

PEEL red beets; cut each in half and place in medium skillet. Peel golden beets; cut each in half and place in another medium skillet. Mix ½ cup vinegar and 2 tablespoons sugar into each skillet. Cook beets in each skillet over medium-high heat until liquid thickens to syrup and begins to coat beets, stirring often, about 4 minutes. Season beets to taste with salt and pepper. Remove from heat.

FOR FISH AND GREENS: Preheat oven to 350°F. Sprinkle fish with salt and pepper. Heat 1 tablespoon oil in heavy large ovenproof skillet over high heat. Add fish, skin side down. Sear until skin is brown and crisp, about 3 minutes (do not turn fish over). Place skillet with fish in oven. Roast fish until barely opaque in center, about 3 minutes.

MEANWHILE, warm horseradish cream over medium heat. Heat remaining 2 tablespoons oil in another large skillet over medium-high heat. Add greens and sauté until just wilted, about 1 minute. Season greens to taste with salt and pepper.

DIVIDE greens among 4 plates. Top greens with fish, skin side up. Surround fish with beets. Spoon warm horseradish cream over all and drizzle with any remaining beet juices.

Spicy sautéed fish with olives and cherry tomatoes

CHERRY TOMATOES, Kalamata olives, parsley, and garlic dress up quickly cooked tilapia, red snapper, or orange roughy fillets. Diced small plum tomatoes may be used in place of the cherry tomatoes, if desired. Serve herbed orzo pasta alongside the fish, and pour a chilled Pinot Grigio.

4 SERVINGS

- **¼ cup olive oil**
- **2 pounds tilapia, red snapper, or orange roughy fillets**
- **½ cup chopped fresh parsley**
- **½ teaspoon dried crushed red pepper**
- **4 cups cherry tomatoes (about 1 pound), halved**
- **1 cup pitted Kalamata olives, chopped**
- **6 garlic cloves, minced**

HEAT olive oil in heavy large skillet over medium-high heat. Sprinkle fish with salt and pepper. Add half of fish to skillet and sauté until just opaque in center, about 3 minutes per side. Transfer fish to platter. Repeat with remaining fish. Add parsley and crushed red pepper to same skillet; stir 1 minute. Add tomatoes, olives, and garlic; sauté until tomatoes soften and release juices, about 2 minutes. Season sauce to taste with salt and pepper; spoon over fish and serve.

Baja fish tacos

FISH TACOS have been perfected in Baja California, especially from the border town of Tijuana south to Ensenada. Warm, soft corn tortillas are filled with lightly battered and deep-fried fish and topped with crunchy shredded cabbage, a creamy sauce, and a dash of hot pepper sauce for an array of mouthwatering textures and flavors. Green cabbage can be used in place of red cabbage, and other fish such as cod, red snapper, or orange roughy may be substituted for the halibut. A cold *cerveza* is the perfect partner.

6 SERVINGS

Sauce

- **¼ cup mayonnaise**
- **¼ cup ketchup**
- **¼ cup crema mexicana or sour cream**

Batter and fish

- **1 cup all purpose flour**
- **1 teaspoon fine sea salt**
- **½ teaspoon ground black pepper**
- **1 cup dark beer, room temperature**

- **1¾ pounds halibut fillets, cut into 5x¾-inch strips**
- **1 lime, halved crosswise**

12 white corn tortillas

Vegetable oil (for deep-frying)

1½ cups shredded red cabbage
2 large tomatoes, chopped
Lime wedges
Hot pepper sauce

FOR SAUCE: Mix all ingredients in small bowl; season to taste with salt and pepper.

FOR BATTER AND FISH: Whisk flour, salt, and pepper in medium bowl; pour in beer, whisking until batter is smooth. Let stand 15 minutes.

SPRINKLE fish with salt and pepper. Squeeze lime juice from lime halves over each strip of fish. Let stand 15 minutes. Mix fish into batter.

PREHEAT oven to 200°F. Heat skillet over medium heat. Stack 2 tortillas on work surface. Sprinkle top with water. Place stack in skillet, wet side down, and heat 1 minute. Sprinkle top with water. Turn stack over and heat 1 minute. Transfer stack to large sheet of heavy-duty aluminum foil. Repeat with remaining tortillas. Enclose tortillas in foil. Place in oven to keep warm.

POUR enough oil into medium skillet to reach depth of 1 inch. Attach deep-fry thermometer; heat oil to 350°F. Slide 4 batter coated fish strips into oil. Fry until batter is golden and fish is just opaque in center, about 4 minutes. Transfer fish to paper-towel-lined baking sheet; place in oven to keep warm. Repeat with remaining fish strips.

FILL each warm tortilla with 2 fish strips. Top with sauce, cabbage, tomatoes, squeeze of lime from lime wedge, and dash of hot pepper sauce.

New England fish cakes with herbed tartar sauce

THE FOOD PROCESSOR provides the muscle to chop most of the ingredients that go into these delicious fish cakes. Just use the on/off pulse button to help control the amount of chopping. For a quick weekday dinner, serve the fish cakes with home fries, and offer bakery brownies for dessert. Alternatively, the cakes can be formed into hors d'oeuvre sizes for serving with cocktails. The tartar sauce can be made eight hours ahead, and the fish cakes formed two hours ahead; cover them separately and refrigerate.

4 SERVINGS

½ cup purchased tartar sauce
2 tablespoons plus ½ cup finely chopped green onions
2 teaspoons plus 1½ tablespoons chopped fresh thyme
1 teaspoon drained capers

4 slices good-quality firm white bread, torn into pieces (about 1½ cups)
1 celery stalk with leaves, cut into 2-inch lengths
1¼ pounds boneless cod, haddock, or other white fish fillets, cut into 2-inch chunks
1 large egg
¾ teaspoon salt
½ teaspoon ground black pepper

3 tablespoons olive oil
Lemon wedges

STIR tartar sauce, 2 tablespoons green onions, 2 teaspoons thyme, and capers in small bowl to blend.

PLACE bread pieces in processor. Using on/off turns, process until very coarse crumbs form. Transfer breadcrumbs to large bowl. Add celery to processor. Using on/off turns, finely chop celery; add to breadcrumbs. Add fish to processor. Using on/off turns, coarsely puree fish; add to breadcrumbs. Add remaining ½ cup chopped green onions and 1½ tablespoons thyme, then egg, salt, and ground black pepper to breadcrumbs. Mix gently but thoroughly. Shape fish mixture into four ½-inch-thick cakes.

HEAT olive oil in heavy large skillet over medium heat. Add fish cakes and cook until brown on bottom, about 5 minutes. Using large spatula, carefully turn fish cakes over and cook until cakes are brown on bottom and centers are opaque and firm to touch, about 5 minutes longer. Transfer fish cakes to 4 plates; garnish with tartar sauce and lemon wedges and serve.

Shellfish

Garlic shrimp

NEARLY EVERY COUNTRY has its own version of garlic shrimp. This delicious one from Mexico cooks the shrimp in their shells, which protects the prized meat and lends a depth of flavor to the finished dish. White rice flavored with serrano chiles is the traditional accompaniment to soak up the juices. To devein the shrimp while leaving the shells in place, use scissors to cut down the center of each shell from the head end of the shrimp toward the tail. Then open the shell slightly and use the tip of a small knife to remove the vein.

4 SERVINGS

- **3/4 cup olive oil, divided**
- **1/2 cup coarsely chopped white onion**
- **3 garlic cloves, chopped**
- **1 teaspoon fine sea salt**
- **1/2 teaspoon ground black pepper**
- **16 uncooked jumbo shrimp, shells intact, deveined (about 1 pound)**

PUREE ½ cup oil, onion, garlic, salt, and pepper in blender until almost smooth. Place shrimp in large bowl. Stir in oil mixture. Let shrimp marinate 1 hour at room temperature.

HEAT remaining ¼ cup oil in heavy large skillet over high heat. Add shrimp with marinade and sauté until shrimp are just opaque in center, about 4 minutes. Divide shrimp and marinade from skillet among 4 plates and serve.

Hot-and-sour shrimp with watercress and walnuts

BUTTERFLIED SHRIMP provide more surface area for the Sherry and ginger sauce to coat. To butterfly the shrimp, make a deep cut down the back of the shrimp as is done to remove the vein, then gently press the shrimp open as you would a book.

4 SERVINGS

- **1 pound uncooked large shrimp, peeled, deveined, butterflied**
- **4 tablespoons dry Sherry, divided**
- **1 tablespoon grated peeled fresh ginger**
- **1/2 cup low-salt chicken broth**
- **2 tablespoons soy sauce**
- **2 tablespoons ketchup**
- **1 tablespoon cornstarch**
- **1 tablespoon unseasoned rice vinegar or white wine vinegar**
- **1 tablespoon sugar**
- **1 teaspoon Asian sesame oil**
- **1/4 teaspoon cayenne pepper**

- **6 teaspoons peanut oil, divided**
- **2 tablespoons chopped walnuts**
- **3 bunches watercress, thick stems trimmed**
- **2 medium red bell peppers, cut into 1-inch squares**
- **2 garlic cloves, minced**
- **8 green onions, cut diagonally into 1-inch-long pieces**

COMBINE shrimp, 2 tablespoons Sherry, and grated ginger in large bowl; stir to coat. Cover and refrigerate 30 minutes. Stir remaining 2 tablespoons Sherry, broth, soy sauce, ketchup, cornstarch, rice vinegar, sugar, sesame oil, and cayenne in small bowl to blend.

HEAT 2 teaspoons peanut oil in wok or heavy large skillet over high heat. Add walnuts and stir-fry 1 minute. Using slotted spoon, transfer walnuts to plate. Add watercress to wok and stir-fry until just wilted, about 1 minute. Using tongs, divide watercress among 4 plates. Add 2 teaspoons peanut oil, bell peppers, and garlic to wok; stir fry 1 minute. Add remaining 2 teaspoons peanut oil, shrimp mixture, and onions; stir-fry 1 minute. Stir broth mixture to reblend; add to wok and cook until sauce is clear and thick and shrimp are just opaque in center, stirring frequently, about 2 minutes.

SPOON sauce and shrimp over watercress. Sprinkle with walnuts and serve.

Shrimp and mango skewers with guava-lime glaze

NOW IS THE TIME to break out the finest skewers to showcase these shrimp. Weighing in at 1½ to 2 ounces each, colossal shrimp make a stunning presentation; jumbo shrimp, which are about half the size, will also be pretty. Assemble the skewers four hours ahead and keep them covered and refrigerated until ready to grill.

6 SERVINGS

- **3 tablespoons olive oil**
- **1 tablespoon minced peeled fresh ginger**
- **2 garlic cloves, minced**
- **1 teaspoon dried crushed red pepper**
- **18 uncooked colossal shrimp or 36 jumbo shrimp (about 2 pounds), peeled, tails left intact, deveined**
- **2 red bell peppers, each cut into 12 pieces**
- **2 ripe but firm mangoes, peeled, pitted, each cut into 12 wedges**
- **6 12-inch-long metal skewers (for colossal shrimp) or twelve 12-inch-long metal skewers (for jumbo shrimp)**
- **Guava-Lime Glaze (see recipe)**

MIX first 4 ingredients in large bowl. Add shrimp, bell peppers, and mangoes; toss to coat. Alternate bell peppers, mango wedges, and 3 colossal shrimp on each of 6 skewers, or alternate bell peppers, mango wedges, and 3 jumbo shrimp on each of 12 skewers. Arrange skewers on baking sheet. *(Skewers can be prepared 4 hours ahead. Cover and chill.)*

PREPARE barbecue (medium-high heat). Grill shrimp skewers until shrimp are just opaque in center, brushing with Guava Lime Glaze during last 2 minutes, about 4 minutes per side for colossal shrimp and about 3 minutes per side for jumbo shrimp. Arrange skewers on platter.

Guava-lime glaze

THE SUGARY FRUIT NECTAR in this delicious sweet-and-sour glaze caramelizes with heat. Brush it over shrimp, scallops, or fish during the last two minutes of grilling so that it browns nicely but does not burn.

MAKES 1 CUP

- **2 cups canned guava nectar**
- **1 cup orange juice**
- **½ cup red wine vinegar**
- **⅓ cup fresh lime juice**

COMBINE nectar, orange juice, and vinegar in heavy medium saucepan. Boil until reduced to ⅔ cup, about 30 minutes. Cool completely. Mix in lime juice. Season glaze to taste with salt and pepper. *(Glaze can be made 1 day ahead. Cover and chill.)*

Red curry shrimp

THAI RED CURRY PASTE is a blend of intensely flavored ingredients such as dried red chiles, garlic, lemongrass, salt, galangal, shrimp paste, kaffir lime peel or leaves, coriander seed, pepper, cumin, and turmeric. It is available at Asian markets and natural foods stores, and in the Asian foods section of most supermarkets. A green curry paste, which is usually made with green chiles rather than red, may replace the red curry paste for a nice variation on this classic Thai dish. Serve steamed basmati or jasmine rice and a cucumber and red onion salad with the shrimp curry for an easy weeknight meal. Offer sliced tropical fruits such as pineapple, mango, and papaya for dessert.

4 SERVINGS

- **1 tablespoon Thai red curry paste**
- **1 13.5- to 14-ounce can unsweetened coconut milk**
- **1 cup bottled clam juice**
- **1¼ pounds uncooked large shrimp, peeled, deveined**
- **⅓ cup chopped fresh cilantro**
- **1 lime, cut into 8 wedges**

STIR red curry paste in heavy large skillet over medium-high heat until fragrant, about 1 minute. Add coconut milk and clam juice; bring to boil, whisking until paste dissolves and sauce is smooth. Boil until sauce is thick enough to coat spoon, stirring occasionally, about 7 minutes. Add shrimp to sauce. Cook until shrimp turn pink and are just opaque in center, stirring occasionally, about 4 minutes. Stir in cilantro. Season to taste with salt and pepper. Divide shrimp and sauce among 4 shallow bowls. Garnish with lime wedges and serve.

Broiled shrimp with spicy ginger-lime butter

YOU CAN BUY shrimp that are already peeled and deveined to save on preparation time, but expect to pay a bit more. If you peel and devein the shrimp yourself, and especially if you double the recipe, reserve the shells to make a flavorful broth: Place the shells in a saucepan and add enough water to cover them. Cover the pan and simmer gently until the cooking liquid is flavorful, about 30 minutes. Strain the broth and discard the shells. Cover and freeze the broth up to six months for use in other seafood recipes that call for clam juice or fish broth.

2 SERVINGS; CAN BE DOUBLED

- **2½ tablespoons butter**
- **1 tablespoon minced peeled fresh ginger**
- **⅛ teaspoon cayenne pepper**
- **1 tablespoon fresh lime juice**
- **1 teaspoon grated lime peel**

- **½ pound uncooked large shrimp, peeled, deveined**
- **¼ cup chopped green onions**
- **Lemon wedges**

PREHEAT broiler. Melt butter in heavy small skillet over medium heat. Stir in ginger and cayenne. Remove from heat. Stir in lime juice and lime peel. Season ginger-lime butter to taste with salt and pepper.

PLACE shrimp in medium bowl. Add ginger-lime butter; toss to coat. Transfer shrimp to small rimmed baking sheet. Broil shrimp until pink and just opaque in center, about 2 minutes per side. Transfer shrimp to plate; drizzle with ginger-lime butter mixture from sheet. Sprinkle shrimp with onions. Serve with lemon wedges.

Spicy baked shrimp

CAJUN OR CREOLE SEASONING (available in the spice section of most supermarkets) gives these spicy shrimp their kick. The key is to use a spice mix that consists mostly of spices and not a lot of salt. Read the ingredients list on the package and make sure that salt is not one of the first ingredients. Serve the shrimp with French bread to soak up the sauce, or spoon the shrimp over rice or pasta for a simple, sizzling weekday entrée. But don't stop there—this dish has many uses. Try serving the shrimp with toothpicks as a hot hors d'oeuvre, or grill them on skewers during the summer. For an attractive presentation, leave the tails intact. The marinade can be made the night before, kept refrigerated, then tossed with the shrimp one hour before cooking.

4 SERVINGS

- **½ cup olive oil**
- **2 tablespoons Cajun or Creole seasoning**
- **2 tablespoons fresh lemon juice**
- **2 tablespoons chopped fresh parsley**
- **1 tablespoon honey**
- **1 tablespoon soy sauce**
- **Pinch of cayenne pepper**
- **1 pound uncooked large shrimp, peeled, deveined**

- **Lemon wedges**
- **French bread**

COMBINE first 7 ingredients in 13x9x2-inch glass baking dish; whisk to blend. Add shrimp to marinade and toss to coat. Refrigerate 1 hour.

PREHEAT oven to 450°F. Bake shrimp in marinade until just opaque in center, stirring occasionally, about 10 minutes. Garnish shrimp with lemon wedges. Serve with marinade as sauce and with French bread.

Baked shrimp with tomatoes and feta

OUZO, GREECE'S POTENT ANISE-FLAVORED SPIRIT, adds excitement to this recipe. Whenever igniting liqueurs or spirits, keep these guidelines in mind: Never pour the spirit or liqueur directly from the bottle into the pan while on the heat. Instead, remove the pan from the burner, pour the amount of spirit needed into a measuring cup, then add it to the pan. Return the pan to the heat. Use a long fireplace match in order to keep your fingers away from the flames when igniting the sauce. And always use a pan with a high rim to contain the flames.

8 SERVINGS

- **⅓ cup plus 3 tablespoons olive oil**
- **3 medium onions, chopped**
- **2 14.5-ounce cans peeled diced tomatoes in juice**
- **4 tablespoons chopped fresh parsley, divided**
- **1 tablespoon dried oregano**
- **5 garlic cloves, minced**
- **½ teaspoon cayenne pepper**

- **2 pounds uncooked large shrimp, peeled, deveined (tails left intact)**
- **½ cup ouzo (unsweetened anise liqueur)**
- **½ cup Kalamata olives, pitted, halved**
- **8 ounces feta cheese, crumbled**
- **Toasted French-bread slices**

HEAT ⅓ cup oil in large saucepan over medium heat. Add onions and sauté until golden, about 12 minutes. Add tomatoes with juice, 3 tablespoons parsley, oregano, garlic, and cayenne. Bring to boil. Reduce heat to medium-low, cover, and simmer until sauce thickens, about 20 minutes. Season sauce with salt and pepper. Transfer to medium bowl. *(Can be prepared 1 day ahead. Cover and refrigerate. Rewarm before continuing.)*

PREHEAT oven to 400°F. Heat 3 tablespoons oil in heavy large skillet over medium-high heat. Sprinkle shrimp with salt and pepper. Add to skillet and sauté until almost opaque in center, about 3 minutes. Remove skillet from heat. Add ouzo. Carefully ignite ouzo with match. Return skillet to medium heat; cook shrimp until flames subside. Add tomato sauce and olives; stir to combine. Transfer shrimp mixture to 10- to 12-cup baking dish. Sprinkle cheese over. Bake until shrimp are cooked through, about 10 minutes. Sprinkle with remaining 1 tablespoon parsley. Serve immediately with toasts.

Grilled summer lobster with chipotle-lime oil and ginger–green onion butter

PREPARE THE CHIPOTLE-LIME OIL and ginger–green onion butter up to two hours ahead. And for food safety, be sure to grill the lobsters immediately after they have been parboiled and split. If you're uncomfortable cooking live lobsters, use raw lobster tails instead—or pair the delicious sauces with grilled shrimp or scallops. Chipotle chiles, canned in a spicy tomato sauce called *adobo*, are available at Latin markets, specialty foods stores, and some supermarkets.

2 SERVINGS

Chipotle-lime oil

- **½ cup olive oil**
- **6 garlic cloves, chopped**
- **1 tablespoon fresh lime juice**
- **1½ teaspoons minced canned chipotle chiles**
- **1 teaspoon grated lime peel**
- **¾ teaspoon salt**
- **2 tablespoons chopped fresh cilantro**

Ginger–green onion butter

- **2 tablespoons peanut oil**
- **2 teaspoons minced peeled fresh ginger**
- **¼ cup Chinese rice wine or sake**
- **⅓ cup finely chopped green onions**
- **3 tablespoons butter, room temperature**

Lobster

- **2 1½- to 2-pound live lobsters**
- **Olive oil**

FOR OIL: Cook oil and garlic in heavy small saucepan over medium-low heat until garlic begins to brown, about 8 minutes. Carefully mix in next 4 ingredients, stirring until salt dissolves. Remove from heat and cool. *(Can be prepared 2 hours ahead. Let stand at room temperature.)* Mix in cilantro.

FOR BUTTER: Cook oil and ginger in small saucepan over medium-low heat 2 minutes. Carefully add wine; simmer until reduced by half, about 2 minutes. Remove from heat. Add green onions and butter; whisk to blend. Season to taste with salt and pepper. *(Can be made 2 hours ahead. Let stand at room temperature.)*

FOR LOBSTER: Drop 1 lobster headfirst into large pot of boiling salted water. Cover and cook 3 minutes (lobster will not be fully cooked). Using tongs, transfer lobster to large rimmed baking sheet. Return water to boil. Repeat with second lobster.

TRANSFER 1 lobster, shell side down, to work surface. Insert tip of large knife into center of lobster. Cut lobster lengthwise in half from center to end of head (knife may not cut through shell), then cut in half from center to end of tail. If necessary, use poultry shears to cut completely through shell, dividing lobster in half. Repeat with second lobster.

PREPARE barbecue (medium-high heat). Keeping lobster halves meat side up, brush shells with olive oil. Place lobster halves, meat side up, on barbecue. Brush meat with oil; sprinkle with salt and pepper. Place pans with sauces at edge of barbecue to rewarm. Cover barbecue; grill lobsters until just opaque in thickest portion of tail, 7 to 9 minutes. Transfer 2 lobster halves to each plate. Serve, passing warm sauces separately.

Puerto Nuevo–style lobster tacos

PUERTO NUEVO, a Mexican seaside village in Baja California, is famous for its Pacific spiny lobsters, the warm-water relatives of American lobsters from the Northeast, but without the large claws. However, northern lobsters are more widely available outside Baja, and their large claws provide an added bonus to this dish.

6 SERVINGS

6 1½-pound live lobsters

1 cup (2 sticks) butter, melted
Toasted-Garlic Rice with Fresh Herbs and Lime (see recipe)
Crunchy Pear Salsa (see recipe)
Warm flour tortillas
Lime wedges

FILL very large bowl with ice water. Bring large stockpot of water to boil. Plunge 2 lobsters headfirst into boiling water. Cook 3 minutes (lobsters will not be fully cooked). Using tongs, transfer lobsters to ice water to cool. Repeat procedure twice more with remaining lobsters. Using heavy cleaver or large knife, immediately cut each lobster lengthwise in half. Remove intestinal tract and rinse away green tomalley from body cavities. Crack claws; remove claw meat. Arrange claw meat in cleaned body cavities.

PREHEAT broiler. Arrange 6 lobster halves, meat side up, on each of 2 large rimmed baking sheets. Brush lobster meat generously with some of melted butter. Broil 1 sheet of lobster halves until meat is just opaque in center, about 3 minutes. Repeat with second sheet. Arrange lobster halves on platter. Drizzle remaining butter over.

SPOON toasted-garlic rice, then lobster meat and pear salsa onto warm tortillas. Fold up tortillas around filling and serve tacos with lime wedges.

Toasted-garlic rice with fresh herbs and lime

FRESH AND ASSERTIVE FLAVORS make this a great choice to accompany simply grilled or sautéed steaks, lamb chops, or burgers as well as the lobster tacos.

6 SERVINGS

1½ cups uncooked long-grain white rice (about 10½ ounces)
3 cups low-salt chicken broth
2 tablespoons fresh lime juice

2 tablespoons vegetable oil
12 garlic cloves, minced
¾ teaspoon salt
¼ cup chopped fresh cilantro
¼ cup chopped fresh Italian parsley
2 tablespoons chopped fresh mint
1 tablespoon chopped fresh marjoram
1½ teaspoons grated lime peel

PLACE rice in strainer. Rinse under cold water until water runs clear. Drain well. Bring broth and lime juice to simmer in heavy large saucepan.

HEAT oil in large saucepan over medium heat. Add garlic; sauté until golden, about 1 minute. Add rice and stir 2 minutes. Add hot broth mixture and ¾ teaspoon salt; bring to boil. Reduce heat to low, cover, and cook until rice is tender and broth is absorbed, about 25 minutes. Turn off heat; let stand, covered, 10 minutes. Add herbs and lime peel to rice; fluff with fork, mixing gently. Season with additional salt, if desired.

Crunchy pear salsa

MEXICAN LIMES, sold at Latin American markets and some supermarkets, are especially good in this recipe because they are sweeter and more fragrant than Persian limes (the more familiar variety). Mexican limes, which are only about 1½ inches in diameter, are also referred to as Key limes.

MAKES ABOUT 3 CUPS

- **3 8-ounce firm but ripe Bosc pears, peeled, halved, cored, finely chopped**
- **½ cup finely chopped white onion**
- **½ cup chopped fresh cilantro**
- **¼ cup chopped fresh mint**
- **¼ cup fresh lime juice**
- **1 large serrano or jalapeño chile with seeds, minced**
- **1 teaspoon sugar**

COMBINE all ingredients in medium bowl; stir to combine. Season salsa to taste with salt and pepper. *(Salsa can be made 3 hours ahead. Cover and chill.)*

Sautéed scallops with tarragon mashed potatoes and tarragon sauce

SCALLOPS GIVE this terrific main course sophistication with minimal effort, and tarragon lends its distinctive anise-like flavor. Since scallops are always sold shucked (rarely will you find them in their pretty fan-shaped shells), they can be cooked after simply removing any small tough side tendons that may still be attached.

4 SERVINGS

- **2 pounds Yukon Gold potatoes, peeled, cut into 1-inch pieces**
- **1 teaspoon salt**
- **9 tablespoons (1 stick plus 1 tablespoon) butter, room temperature, divided**
- **⅔ cup (or more) whole milk**

- **12 sea scallops**

- **⅓ cup dry white wine**
- **2 tablespoons chopped shallot**
- **2 tablespoons whipping cream**
- **1½ tablespoons plus ¼ cup chopped fresh tarragon**

PLACE potatoes in large pot. Add enough cold water to cover. Add 1 teaspoon salt and bring to boil over high heat. Boil until potatoes are tender, about 8 minutes. Drain and return to pot. Using potato masher, mash potatoes. Mash in 4 tablespoons butter. Stir in ⅔ cup milk. Season to taste with salt and pepper. *(Potatoes can be made 1 hour ahead. Let stand at room temperature. Before serving, stir over medium heat until heated through, adding more milk by tablespoonfuls if potatoes are dry.)*

MELT 1 tablespoon butter in heavy large skillet over medium-high heat. Sprinkle scallops with salt and pepper. Add scallops to skillet and sauté until just opaque in center, about 2 minutes per side. Transfer to plate; tent with aluminum foil to keep warm. Reserve juices in skillet.

PLACE wine and shallot in small saucepan. Simmer over medium heat until reduced to glaze, about 3 minutes. Stir in cream and simmer 1 minute. Gradually whisk in remaining 4 tablespoons butter. Stir in reserved pan juices from skillet. Stir in 1½ tablespoons tarragon. Season tarragon sauce to taste with salt and pepper.

STIR remaining ¼ cup tarragon into warm mashed potatoes. Divide potatoes among 4 shallow bowls. Place scallops atop potatoes. Drizzle with tarragon sauce and serve.

Seared scallops and asparagus with Asian cream sauce

IF SEA SCALLOPS are unavailable, bay scallops—smaller and more delicately flavored than sea scallops—can be used instead. Remove any tough side tendons still attached. Pat the scallops dry before placing them in the skillet so they will caramelize, or brown, on the outside; this helps keep the flesh inside tender and succulent. Szechuan peppercorns are available at Asian markets and some specialty foods stores.

2 SERVINGS

3½ teaspoons Szechuan peppercorns, divided
¾ cup sake
⅓ cup finely chopped shallots
⅓ cup finely chopped peeled fresh ginger
3 tablespoons unseasoned rice vinegar
½ cup whipping cream

12 asparagus spears, trimmed to 4-inch lengths

12 ounces large sea scallops or bay scallops
1 tablespoon butter
1 tablespoon chopped fresh chives

FINELY chop peppercorns in spice grinder or processor. Cook sake, shallots, ginger, vinegar, and ½ teaspoon chopped peppercorns in small saucepan over medium heat until liquid is reduced to 2 tablespoons, about 15 minutes. Add cream and simmer until sauce thickens enough to coat spoon, about 6 minutes. Strain sauce into another small saucepan.

COOK asparagus in large saucepan of boiling salted water 2 minutes. Drain. Rinse under cold water and drain again.

SPRINKLE remaining chopped peppercorns over both sides of scallops, then sprinkle scallops with salt. Melt butter in large nonstick skillet over high heat. Add scallops; cook until golden and almost opaque in center, turning occasionally, about 4 minutes. Add asparagus; sauté until scallops are just opaque in center and asparagus are hot, about 30 seconds. Arrange scallops on plates. Bring sauce to simmer. Spoon sauce around scallops. Garnish with asparagus. Sprinkle with chives and serve.

Scallop brochettes with mango-tarragon salsa

ALMOST EVERY CUISINE has its own name for delicious morsels of skewered meats and vegetables. In Southeast Asia they're called *satay,* in Italy they're referred to as *spiedini;* in Russia they're known as *shashlik,* in Turkey, *shish kebab;* and in France they're called *brochettes.* Americans have come to love each and every one of these national specialties. Serve these brochettes with such globally inspired side dishes as grilled polenta and sautéed squash blossoms.

2 SERVINGS; CAN BE DOUBLED

2 tablespoons olive oil
2 tablespoons chopped fresh tarragon or 2 teaspoons dried
1½ tablespoons fresh lime juice
1 teaspoon grated lime peel
⅔ cup diced peeled, pitted mango
⅓ cup diced red bell pepper
⅓ cup diced sweet onion (such as Vidalia or Maui)

12 sea scallops
2 10- to 12-inch-long metal skewers

PREPARE barbecue (medium-high heat). Whisk first 4 ingredients in medium bowl to blend for dressing. Transfer 1 tablespoon dressing to small bowl and reserve. Mix mango, bell pepper, and onion into remaining dressing in medium bowl. Season salsa to taste with salt and pepper.

THREAD scallops on skewers. Brush reserved 1 tablespoon dressing over scallops; sprinkle with salt and pepper. Grill scallops until just opaque in center, about 3 minutes per side. Transfer scallops on skewers to plates. Spoon salsa alongside and serve.

Teriyaki broiled scallops and green onions

DON'T BE SURPRISED to find scallops that are pale beige, creamy orange, or slightly pink, as they come in an array of these natural colors. Do, however, stay away from stark white scallops; these have been soaked in water, which increases their weight but dilutes their flavor.

2 SERVINGS; CAN BE DOUBLED

- **6 tablespoons bottled teriyaki sauce**
- **1 to 1½ teaspoons wasabi paste (horseradish paste)**
- **12 sea scallops**

- **4 12-inch-long metal skewers**
- **8 whole green onions**

- **Sesame seeds**

PREHEAT broiler. Blend teriyaki sauce and 1 teaspoon wasabi in medium bowl; add more wasabi if desired for spicier sauce. Transfer 3 tablespoons sauce to small bowl and reserve. Mix scallops into remaining sauce in medium bowl; let marinate 10 minutes.

THREAD 6 scallops onto each of 2 skewers. Thread all onions onto remaining 2 skewers by pushing 1 skewer through bulbs of all onions and another skewer (parallel to first) through all onions 2 inches above bulbs.

PLACE scallops and onions on broiler pan; brush with marinade from medium bowl. Broil until scallops are just opaque in center and onions are charred, turning occasionally and brushing with marinade, about 6 minutes total. Place 1 skewer of scallops and 4 green onions on each plate. Sprinkle with sesame seeds. Serve with reserved sauce.

Grilled clams with spaghetti, prosciutto, and mixed greens

THE GRILLED CLAMS lend a smoky nuance and depth of flavor to this dish. Live, fresh clams will close tightly when they're jostled. If the clams do not open when cooked, they are not fresh and should be discarded.

6 SERVINGS

- **½ cup extra-virgin olive oil**
- **4 garlic cloves, chopped**
- **¾ teaspoon dried crushed red pepper**
- **8 large leaves mustard greens, stems cut off and discarded, leaves coarsely torn**
- **4 large leaves Swiss chard, stems cut off and discarded, leaves coarsely torn**
- **4 large leaves collard greens, stems cut off and discarded, leaves coarsely torn**

- **½ pound thinly sliced prosciutto**
- **40 large littleneck clams (about 8¾ pounds), scrubbed**

- **1 pound spaghetti**
- **1 lemon, halved**
- **½ cup chopped fresh parsley**

HEAT oil in heavy large pot over medium-high heat. Add garlic and crushed red pepper; stir until fragrant, about 30 seconds. Add mustard greens, chard, and collard greens; toss until greens are beginning to wilt, about 2 minutes. Remove from heat. *(Greens can be prepared 2 hours ahead. Let stand at room temperature.)*

PREPARE barbecue (medium-high heat). Grill prosciutto slices until beginning to crisp, about 1 minute per side. Transfer prosciutto to plate. Tear each slice lengthwise into 1-inch-wide strips; add to pot with greens. Grill clams in batches, if necessary, and without turning over, until each opens, about 6 minutes (discard any clams that do not open). Transfer clams from grill to pot.

MEANWHILE, cook spaghetti in another large pot of boiling salted water until just tender but still firm to bite. Drain, reserving 2 cups pasta cooking liquid. Add pasta to pot with greens, prosciutto, and clams. Squeeze juice from 1 lemon half over. Add parsley. Toss over medium-high heat until heated through, adding reserved pasta cooking liquid by ½ cupfuls if mixture is dry. Season to taste with salt and pepper and more lemon juice, if desired. Transfer pasta mixture to large shallow bowl and serve.

Steamed mussels with saffron-mustard sauce

BOTH THE STRAINED BROTH and the saffron-mustard sauce can be made one day ahead. Cover them separately and keep them in the refrigerator. Accompany the finished dish with crusty country bread to soak up the delicious cooking juices and sauce. To remove the gritty sand that mussels sometimes carry in their shells, soak them in cold salted water for one hour before using.

2 SERVINGS

- **2 cups fish stock or bottled clam juice**
- **1 cup dry white wine**
- **1 large onion, chopped**
- **1 tablespoon Dijon mustard**
- **1 garlic clove, minced**
- **¼ teaspoon saffron threads, crumbled**
- **¼ cup olive oil**

- **1 pound mussels, scrubbed, debearded**
- **3 tablespoons minced fresh parsley**

SIMMER first 3 ingredients in heavy wide saucepan 15 minutes. Whisk mustard, garlic, and saffron in small bowl to blend. Gradually add oil, whisking until sauce is thick. Thin sauce with 1 tablespoon stock mixture. Strain remaining stock mixture into large skillet. *(Can be prepared 1 day ahead. Cover stock and mustard sauce separately and refrigerate.)*

BRING stock to boil. Stir 1½ tablespoons mustard sauce into stock. Add mussels; cover and cook until mussels open, about 5 minutes. Divide mussels between 2 large shallow bowls (discard any mussels that do not open). Stir parsley into mussel cooking liquid in skillet. Season to taste with salt and pepper. Pour over mussels, then drizzle with mustard sauce and serve.

Seafood paella with alioli

PAELLA IS A Spanish rice specialty that has many variations depending on the region in which it is made. Along the coastal regions of Spain, paella is most often made with fresh fish and seafood, as in this classic version. Inland, where seafood is less abundant, paella often includes chicken, pork, sausage, ham, and even rabbit. It is not unusual, however, to see a paella made with a combination of seafood, chicken, and sausage. If you choose to use lobster in this recipe, ask your fishmonger to split it for you. *Alioli* is the Spanish word for the garlic mayonnaise known in French as *aioli*. Use sweet Spanish paprika in the paella; it has a delicate flavor that won't overwhelm the dish.

6 SERVINGS

Alioli

- **8 garlic cloves, minced**
- **¾ teaspoon salt**
- **2 cups mayonnaise**
- **2 tablespoons extra-virgin olive oil**
- **1 teaspoon fresh lemon juice**

Fish stock

- **1 1½-pound lobster, split lengthwise (optional)**
- **5 cups bottled clam juice**
- **2 cups water**
- **½ pound uncooked medium shrimp, peeled (shells reserved), deveined**
- **2 fresh parsley sprigs**

- **1 bay leaf**
- **½ cup dry white wine**
- **1 teaspoon saffron threads**

Paella

- **3 medium tomatoes**
- **½ cup olive oil**
- **1 pound monkfish or other firm-fleshed white fish fillets, cut into 1-inch pieces**
- **½ pound cleaned squid bodies and tentacles, bodies cut into ½-inch-wide rings**
- **1½ cups finely chopped green bell pepper**
- **12 garlic cloves, minced**
- **2 teaspoons paprika (preferably Spanish)**
- **1 tablespoon minced fresh parsley**
- **1 bay leaf, finely crumbled**
- **3 cups paella rice, arborio rice, or other short-grain rice**
- **½ cup shelled fresh peas or frozen**
- **18 small mussels, scrubbed, debearded**
- **1 4-ounce jar sliced pimientos, drained**
- **Additional minced fresh parsley**

FOR ALIOLI: Mash garlic and salt in medium bowl using back of fork. Whisk in mayonnaise, olive oil, and lemon juice. Season alioli to taste with pepper. Refrigerate until cold. *(Alioli can be prepared 1 day ahead; keep refrigerated.)*

FOR FISH STOCK: Cut lobster tail and claws from body. Cut tail into 4 pieces. Crack claws. Cover and refrigerate tail and claws. Cut lobster body into large pieces. Bring clam juice and water to boil in large pot. Add lobster body pieces, shrimp shells, parsley, and bay leaf; bring to simmer. Reduce heat and simmer 20 minutes. Strain stock into 8-cup measuring cup, pressing on solids with back of spoon. Discard solids. If stock measures more than 5½ cups, return to pot and simmer until reduced to 5½ cups. Mix in wine and saffron. *(Stock can be prepared 1 day ahead. Cover stock and shrimp separately and refrigerate. Keep lobster tail and claws refrigerated.)*

FOR PAELLA: Preheat oven to 375°F. Cut tomatoes in half crosswise. Coarsely grate tomatoes onto large plate, discarding skin. Transfer tomato pulp to sieve and drain. Set aside.

BRING fish stock to simmer. Cover and keep warm over very low heat. Place 14-inch paella pan or heavy 14-inch ovenproof skillet over two stove-top burners or 1 very large burner. Add oil and heat over medium-high heat. Add lobster tail and claws; sauté 2 minutes. Using slotted spoon, transfer tail and claw pieces to large bowl. Add shrimp and monkfish to pan. Sprinkle with salt and sauté 2 minutes, rotating pan occasionally for even heat. Transfer shrimp and monkfish to bowl with lobster. Add squid to pan and sauté 2 minutes. Add bell pepper and sauté 3 minutes. Mix in garlic and cook 1 minute. Add 3 tablespoons alioli and paprika; stir to combine. Stir in tomato pulp, 1 tablespoon parsley, and bay leaf; cook 2 minutes. Add rice and stir to coat with tomato mixture. Add fish stock and peas; cook, uncovered, until rice is partially cooked and liquid is thick, stirring frequently, about 15 minutes. Season with salt. Remove from heat.

ADD shrimp and monkfish with any accumulated juices in bowl to paella. Arrange mussels (on their sides, seam sides up), lobster, and pimientos decoratively atop paella. Transfer paella to oven and bake uncovered until rice is almost tender, about 10 minutes. Remove paella from oven. Cover with aluminum foil and let stand 20 minutes at room temperature. Discard any mussels that did not open. Sprinkle with additional parsley and serve, passing remaining alioli separately.

Chicken, sausage, and shrimp paella

DO-AHEAD TIPS make this rendition of the Spanish classic perfect for entertaining a large group. Usually paella is prepared in a special round two-handled pan—also called a *paella*—that is wide, shallow, and about 14 inches in diameter; it can go from the stove top to the oven to the table. However, this recipe calls for a roasting pan to accommodate the large quantities, so select an attractive pan that can go from the oven to the table for serving.

10 SERVINGS

3 tablespoons olive oil, divided
6 fresh Cajun or hot Italian sausages (about 1¾ pounds)
12 chicken thighs with skin and bones (about 4¼ pounds), excess fat trimmed
2 very large onions, chopped (about 5 cups)
10 garlic cloves, chopped
¾ pound tomatoes, chopped (about 1½ cups)
2 bay leaves
4 medium zucchini, halved crosswise, then quartered lengthwise (about 1¼ pounds)
3 red bell peppers, cut into 1-inch-wide strips

1½ pounds uncooked large shrimp, peeled, deveined
1 garlic clove, minced
Generous pinch plus ¼ teaspoon saffron threads

2½ cups arborio rice or medium-grain white rice (about 17½ ounces)
1½ teaspoons salt

5 cups low-salt chicken broth
2 teaspoons paprika (preferably sweet Spanish paprika)

Chopped fresh parsley

HEAT 1 tablespoon oil in heavy large shallow pot over medium-high heat. Add sausages and sauté until cooked through, turning often, about 10 minutes. Transfer sausages to large bowl. Sprinkle chicken with salt and pepper. Working in batches, add chicken, skin side down, to same pot. Cover and cook until skin is brown, about 6 minutes. Turn chicken over, cover, and cook until brown and cooked through, about 8 minutes longer. Transfer chicken to bowl with sausages. Add onions and 10 chopped garlic cloves to pot; sauté until tender, about 8 minutes. Add tomatoes and bay leaves; stir 2 minutes. Stir in zucchini and bell peppers. Transfer vegetable mixture to another large bowl.

TOSS shrimp with remaining 2 tablespoons oil, 1 minced garlic clove, and generous pinch of saffron in medium bowl. *(Chicken-sausage mixture, vegetable mixture, and shrimp mixture can be prepared 6 hours ahead. Cover separately and refrigerate.)*

PREHEAT oven to 375°F. Brush one 18x12x2¼-inch roasting pan with olive oil. Mix rice and 1½ teaspoons salt into vegetable mixture. Spread rice mixture evenly in prepared pan. Cut sausages diagonally into 1-inch-thick slices. Using wooden spoon, push sausage and chicken pieces into rice mixture; pour any accumulated juices from bowl over. Bring broth, paprika, and remaining ¼ teaspoon saffron to boil in medium saucepan; pour evenly over rice mixture. Cover roasting pan tightly with aluminum foil. Bake until rice is almost tender, about 40 minutes.

SPRINKLE shrimp mixture with salt and pepper. Arrange atop rice mixture. Cover pan with foil; bake until shrimp are just opaque in center, rice is tender, and almost all liquid in pan is absorbed, about 20 minutes longer. Sprinkle with parsley and serve.

Nantucket seafood supper

BEGIN WITH A STARTER of steamed clams, add some crusty bread and a cooling sea breeze, and you've got the makings of an entire New England clambake.

6 SERVINGS

- **18 small red-skinned potatoes**
- **6 small onions, quartered lengthwise**
- **1 fresh fennel bulb (about 1 pound), trimmed, halved lengthwise, thinly sliced crosswise**
- **2 12-ounce bottles pale ale**
- **4 cups water**
- **1 tablespoon Old Bay seasoning**
- **1 tablespoon coarse kosher salt**
- **10 fresh thyme sprigs**
- **1 pound kielbasa or linguiça sausage, cut into 1-inch pieces**
- **6 ears of corn, husked**
- **2½ pounds mussels, scrubbed, debearded**
- **3 1¾-pound live lobsters**
- **1 cup (2 sticks) butter**
- **Lemon wedges**
- **Lemon-Herb Mayonnaise (see recipe)**

FILL very large pot ⅔ full with salted water; bring to boil over high heat. Meanwhile, place potatoes, onions, and fennel in another very large pot. Add beer and 4 cups water; sprinkle with Old Bay seasoning and salt. Add 5 thyme sprigs and sausage. Bring to boil over high heat; reduce heat to medium-high. Cover; cook 15 minutes. Add corn, then mussels and remaining thyme. Cover and cook until mussels open and potatoes are cooked through, about 15 minutes longer.

MEANWHILE, drop lobsters headfirst into salted boiling water; cover. Boil until cooked through and shells turn bright red, about 13 minutes. Using tongs, remove lobsters from pot. Split in half lengthwise.

MELT butter in saucepan and divide among 6 ramekins.

REMOVE corn, fennel, onions, potatoes, and mussels from pot (discard any mussels that do not open). Divide among 6 large bowls. Place ½ lobster atop mixture in each bowl. Season broth with salt and pepper; pour over seafood and vegetables. Serve with melted butter, lemons, and Lemon-Herb Mayonnaise.

Lemon-herb mayonnaise

DELICIOUS WITH the lobster and vegetables, this would also be great just spread on crusty bread.

6 SERVINGS

- **1½ cups mayonnaise**
- **3 tablespoons chopped fresh chives**
- **3 tablespoons chopped fresh tarragon**
- **3 tablespoons chopped fresh parsley**
- **3 tablespoons chopped fresh basil**
- **1 teaspoon fresh lemon juice**
- **½ teaspoon grated lemon peel**

PLACE mayonnaise in food processor. Add next 4 ingredients; process until smooth, about 30 seconds. Transfer to bowl. Stir in lemon juice and peel. Season with salt and pepper. *(Can be made 1 day ahead. Chill.)*

Potatoes 13

The potato is an odd object of affection.

Bumpy and dirt-flecked brown, waxy and dull red, or thin-skinned and yellow, a potato hardly seems to have pulse-quickening potential. But we do adore potatoes. Maybe that's because potatoes try so hard to please. They will be anything we'd like them to be: simply roasted; simmered and whipped or mashed into a fluffy mound; slivered and fried until crisp and golden brown.

And that's just their solo act. Potatoes also have the ability to play well with others. Mashed, they combine with rutabagas or parsley root, or welcome more exotic ingredients such as prosciutto or spicy-smoky chipotle chiles. Roasted, potatoes can be part of a delicious assortment of winter vegetables.

Good mashed potatoes are within the reach of all but the most culinarily challenged. That is probably one reason they hold a special place in the pantheon of American comfort foods—along with their soothing texture and their propensity for canoodling with some of our favorite homey foods, like meat loaf and roast chicken.

Neck and neck with mashed potatoes for all-time comfort foods are gratins. Here sliced potatoes are layered with milk, cream, or broth, cheese of just about any description, and ingredients as diverse as cilantro and wild mushrooms.

When it comes to yams and sweet potatoes, there's a certain amount of confusion about nomenclature—but none about their remarkable versatility and sweetness. Yams and sweet potatoes are actually two separate vegetables from two different families, but supermarkets and years of habit insist that the red-skinned potatoes with the moist orange flesh are "yams" (even if they're really sweet potatoes—got that?). To make life simple, our recipes call for either "tan-skinned sweet potatoes" or "yams (red-skinned sweet potatoes)," so that you'll know exactly what you're looking for.

While potatoes have taken a knocking—think *couch potato* and *low-carb diet*—they show no signs of going anywhere. A never-ending love affair, indeed.

Golden mashed potatoes with parsnips and parsley root

PARSNIPS ADD a hint of sweetness to this dish, and Yukon Gold potatoes not only have an appealing golden color, they also add a subtle buttery flavor. Their slightly starchy, slightly waxy texture makes Yukon Golds ideal for mashing. Exposure to oxygen will turn cut potatoes black, so if you're dicing them more than 30 minutes before cooking, place the potatoes in a bowl of cold water. The parsley root is optional, but if you can find it (it's a tan-colored, carrot-shaped root usually displayed near the parsnips and turnips at the market), this recipe cleverly yields two ingredients from one: the root, plus leafy tops that can stand in for regular parsley leaves. Make these potatoes up to two hours ahead and just reheat before serving.

6 SERVINGS

- **1½ pounds Yukon Gold potatoes, peeled, cut into 2-inch pieces**
- **1 pound parsnips, peeled, cut into 1½-inch pieces**
- **3 ounces trimmed parsley roots (about 3 medium), peeled, cut into 1-inch pieces (optional)**
- **1 garlic clove, halved**
- **3 cups (or more) water**
- **1 14-ounce can low-salt chicken broth**

- **¼ cup whipping cream**
- **2 tablespoons (¼ stick) butter**
- **2 tablespoons minced fresh parsley or parsley root tops**

- **Additional minced fresh parsley**

COMBINE potatoes, parsnips, parsley root if desired, and garlic in heavy large saucepan. Add 3 cups water and broth; if necessary, add additional water to cover vegetables by 1 inch. Boil uncovered until vegetables are tender, about 25 minutes. Drain vegetables, reserving cooking liquid.

RETURN vegetables to pot. Add cream and butter. Over low heat, mash until mixture is smooth and fluffy, adding enough reserved cooking liquid to thin to desired consistency. Mix in 2 tablespoons parsley. Season to taste with salt and pepper. *(Can be prepared 2 hours ahead. Cover; let stand at room temperature. Before serving, stir over low heat until heated through.)*

TRANSFER to bowl. Top with additional minced parsley and serve.

Mashed potatoes with Italian parsley

THESE ARE DEFINITELY NOT your average mashed potatoes—they're an appealing shade of green, thanks to a parsley puree and lots of green onions. It's worth seeking out Italian (flat leaf) parsley for this recipe; the stronger flavor will make a noticeable difference. The potatoes are left unpeeled (the skin adds good texture and flavor), so you'll need to scrub them well and cut out any eyes (those dark, rough indentations). But if you prefer your potatoes peeled, feel free. This dish is wonderful at any time of year—warm and comforting in winter, herby and light in spring—but it would be particularly appropriate with corned beef, cabbage, and a Guinness on St. Patrick's Day.

6 SERVINGS

- **1 large bunch fresh Italian parsley, stemmed**
- **⅓ cup cold water**
- **Large pinch of salt**

- **1½ cups (or more) whole milk**
- **4 large green onions, minced**

- **2½ pounds Yukon Gold potatoes**

- **½ cup (1 stick) butter**

COOK parsley leaves in medium saucepan of boiling salted water 1 minute. Drain. Immediately transfer parsley leaves to blender. Add ⅓ cup cold water and large pinch of salt. Blend until very smooth.

COMBINE 1½ cups milk and onions in medium saucepan. Bring to boil. Reduce heat to medium and simmer until onions are tender, about 5 minutes. Set aside.

PLACE potatoes in large pot of salted water. Bring water to boil over high heat. Reduce heat to medium, cover, and cook until potatoes are tender, about 35 minutes. Drain. Return potatoes to pot.

MEANWHILE, bring milk mixture to simmer. Add butter, parsley puree, and hot milk mixture to potatoes. Mash potatoes with skin. Season to taste with salt and pepper. *(Can be made 2 hours ahead. Cover; let stand at room temperature. Before serving, stir over medium heat until heated through, adding more milk if necessary.)*

Horseradish mashed potatoes with caramelized onions

THE KEY TO making these potatoes as flavorful as possible is really caramelizing the onions. Don't be afraid of browning them too much: Deep, rich color means deep, rich flavor. And horseradish packs these spuds with sophisticated punch. Be sure to use a fresh jar of prepared horseradish (the grated root mixed with vinegar), as an opened jar will get bitter over time even if refrigerated. If you're hosting a dinner party, prepare these potatoes in the morning and warm them up when it's time to eat. Then bring on the prime rib!

6 SERVINGS

- **¼ cup plus 6 tablespoons (1¼ sticks) butter**
- **2¼ pounds white onions, thinly sliced**
- **3 tablespoons balsamic vinegar**
- **2 teaspoons chopped fresh thyme**
- **3½ pounds russet potatoes, peeled, cut into 1-inch pieces**
- **½ cup whole milk**
- **¼ cup prepared white horseradish**

MELT ¼ cup butter in heavy large skillet over medium heat. Add onions and sauté until deep golden, about 30 minutes. Add vinegar and thyme. Reduce heat to low and sauté 4 minutes. Season onion mixture to taste with salt and pepper. *(Can be prepared 1 day ahead. Cover and refrigerate.)*

COOK potatoes in large pot of boiling salted water until very tender, about 20 minutes. Drain. Return to same pot and mash until smooth. Add milk, horseradish, and remaining 6 tablespoons butter; stir to blend. Season to taste with salt and pepper.

MEANWHILE, stir onion mixture in skillet over medium heat until heated through. Transfer potatoes to serving dish. Spoon onion mixture atop potatoes. *(Can be prepared 8 hours ahead. Cover with foil and refrigerate. Rewarm in 350°F oven about 30 minutes.)* Serve hot.

Mashed potatoes with rutabagas and buttermilk

RUTABAGAS ARE ROUND, earth-toned root vegetables that look like giant turnips. They have a very strong flavor, but when used in moderation (as they are here) and cooked, they add a touch of sweetness. (They're cruciferous vegetables like broccoli and cabbage—so they're also good for you.) The tang of buttermilk provides the perfect counterpoint to the sweetness; chives, with their mild oniony flavor, tie the dish together. Serve these with something hearty, like beef stew or meat loaf.

8 SERVINGS

- **1½ pounds rutabagas, peeled, cut into 1-inch pieces**
- **3 pounds russet potatoes, peeled, cut into 2-inch pieces**

6 **tablespoons (¾ stick) butter**
¾ **cup (or more) buttermilk**

Chopped chives or green onion tops

COOK rutabagas in large pot of boiling salted water until very tender, about 20 minutes. Using slotted spoon, transfer rutabagas to strainer. Press gently to release any excess liquid. Add potatoes to same pot of boiling water; cook until tender, about 25 minutes. Drain well. Return potatoes and rutabagas to same pot. Add butter and mash well. Add ¾ cup buttermilk and mash until smooth. Season to taste with salt and pepper. *(Can be prepared 6 hours ahead. Cover and refrigerate. Before serving, stir over low heat until heated through, adding more buttermilk by tablespoonfuls if desired.)*

TRANSFER potatoes to bowl. Sprinkle with chives and serve.

Poblano mashed potatoes

SERVE THESE WITH *carne asada,* or use them as a filling for soft corn tacos sprinkled with Cotija or Monterey Jack cheese. Poblanos are fresh dark green chiles available at Latin markets and some supermarkets. Their heat varies considerably, so taste as you go and add more chiles accordingly. When roasting and peeling the poblanos, it's important that the entire chile get blackened, because only the black bits will peel off easily. After roasting, place the chiles in a paper bag to steam, which encourages the skin to separate from the flesh. Use the sharp side of a paring knife to scrape off the charred bits of peel.

6 SERVINGS

4 **large fresh poblano chiles**

3 **pounds russet potatoes, peeled, quartered**
1 **cup sour cream**
¼ **cup olive oil**

CHAR chiles over gas flame or in broiler until blackened on all sides. Enclose in paper bag and let stand 10 minutes. Peel, seed, and coarsely chop chiles.

COOK potatoes in large pot of boiling salted water until very tender, about 30 minutes. Drain potatoes and return to pot. Mash potatoes until smooth. Mix in sour cream, oil, and chopped chiles. Season potatoes to taste with salt and pepper. Transfer to bowl and serve.

Garlic, white cheddar, and chipotle mashed potatoes

IT'S NO SURPRISE that the cream cheese makes these potatoes exceptionally creamy, and the dish gets a fiery kick courtesy of chipotle chiles—smoked, dried jalapeños canned in a spicy tomato sauce (look for them in the salsa section of the supermarket or at Latin markets). Don't be scared off by the number of garlic cloves; they're roasted until soft, buttery, and mellow. If you don't want to separate all the cloves and peel them individually, you can roast a few heads of garlic and squeeze out the softened cloves. To do so, slice about half an inch off the pointed end of each head of garlic and place the trimmed heads cut side up on a piece of aluminum foil. Sprinkle with salt and pepper and drizzle with olive oil. Wrap the foil loosely around the garlic and seal it. Place the foil packet in a small roasting pan or dish, and roast in a 375°F oven for about an hour or until the garlic cloves are very soft when pierced with a fork. Let the heads cool enough to handle, then turn them upside down and squeeze out the roasted garlic into the mashed potato mixture.

8 TO 10 SERVINGS

36 **garlic cloves (about 3 heads)**
⅓ **cup olive oil**

5 **pounds russet potatoes, peeled, cut into 1-inch pieces**

- **2 cups (packed) grated sharp white cheddar cheese (about 8 ounces)**
- **4 ounces cream cheese, room temperature**
- **¼ cup (½ stick) butter, room temperature**
- **1½ teaspoons minced canned chipotle chiles**

PREHEAT oven to 350°F. Toss garlic with oil in metal pie dish. Cover with aluminum foil and bake 30 minutes. Uncover and bake until garlic is tender, about 15 minutes. Cool; peel and mash garlic.

COOK potatoes in large pot of boiling salted water until tender, about 20 minutes. Drain. Transfer potatoes to large bowl. Add mashed garlic and remaining ingredients. Using electric mixer, beat mixture until smooth. Season to taste with salt and pepper. *(Can be prepared 2 hours ahead. Cover and let stand at room temperature. Before serving, stir over medium heat until heated through.)*

Colcannon

A TRADITIONAL IRISH DISH, colcannon is made by mashing potatoes with onions and cabbage (or sometimes kale). The name comes from the Gaelic word for cabbage, *cál.* Guests will ooh and aah over this when you bring it to the table: It's presented with a big pat of butter melting on top. Serve it with corned beef on St. Patrick's Day or with roasted meats anytime.

6 SERVINGS

- **4 pounds russet potatoes, peeled, cut into 1½-inch pieces**

- **1 1½-pound head of savoy cabbage, thinly sliced**
- **1¼ cups water**

- **1 cup milk**
- **1 bunch green onions, chopped**
- **¾ cup (1½ sticks) butter, room temperature, divided**
- **Chopped fresh chives or green onion tops**

COOK potatoes in large pot of boiling salted water until tender, 20 to 25 minutes. Drain. Return potatoes to pot and mash until smooth. Set aside.

COMBINE cabbage and 1¼ cups water in heavy large skillet. Boil until almost all liquid evaporates, tossing cabbage frequently, about 15 minutes. Mix cabbage into mashed potatoes.

COMBINE milk, green onions, and ½ cup butter in heavy medium saucepan. Bring to boil, stirring to melt butter. Pour over potato mixture and stir to combine. Season to taste with salt and pepper. *(Can be prepared 2 hours ahead. Cover and let stand at room temperature. Before continuing, stir over low heat until heated through.)* Mound mashed potatoes in bowl. Make well in center. Place remaining ¼ cup butter in well. Sprinkle with chopped chives and serve.

Mashed potatoes with prosciutto and Parmesan cheese

PROSCIUTTO AND PARMESAN CHEESE, both born in the Italian region of Emilia-Romagna, are always delicious partners. They're paired here with a New World treat: potatoes, which are native to Peru. Rosemary and garlic complete the Italian flavor profile. Continue the theme by serving these with roast chicken or veal and a bold Sangiovese.

6 TO 8 SERVINGS

- **3¼ pounds russet potatoes, peeled, cut into 1-inch pieces**
- **4 garlic cloves, peeled**

- **½ cup (1 stick) butter**
- **3½ ounces thinly sliced prosciutto, finely chopped**
- **¾ teaspoon minced fresh rosemary**

- **¾ cup (or more) whole milk**
- **1 cup freshly grated Parmesan cheese (about 3 ounces), divided**

COOK potatoes and garlic cloves in large pot of boiling salted water until potatoes are very tender, about 20 minutes. Drain; return potatoes and garlic to same pot.

MEANWHILE, melt butter in heavy small saucepan over medium heat. Add prosciutto and rosemary; sauté until fragrant, about 2 minutes.

ADD prosciutto mixture and ¾ cup milk to potatoes and garlic. Mash well, adding more milk by tablespoonfuls if potatoes are dry. Mix in ¾ cup cheese. Season to taste with salt and pepper. *(Can be prepared 6 hours ahead. Cover and refrigerate. Stir over low heat until heated through, adding more milk by tablespoonfuls if desired.)*

TRANSFER potatoes to bowl. Sprinkle with remaining ¼ cup cheese and serve.

Potato-apple pancakes

APPLE AND CELERY ROOT bring subtle sweetness to these potato pancakes. And since potatoes will discolor soon after they are grated (from exposure to oxygen), onions are added to the mix—their juices prevent the discoloration. The key to great potato-pancake texture is squeezing out as much moisture as possible from the raw grated potatoes. Wrap them in a dish towel and squeeze hard, then do it again. The drier the potatoes, the crisper the potato pancakes. When frying the pancakes, press down a bit; that will help them brown and fry evenly. Serve these as a side dish with brisket, or turn them into an elegant appetizer by topping them with crème fraîche, smoked salmon, and chives.

MAKES ABOUT 16

- **1 pound russet potatoes, peeled, cut into 1½-inch pieces**
- **1 medium onion, peeled, quartered**
- **1 2-inch cube peeled celery root (celeriac)**
- **1 medium unpeeled Granny Smith apple, quartered, cored**
- **1 large egg**
- **1 green onion, finely chopped**
- **1 tablespoon chopped fresh marjoram**
- **¾ teaspoon salt**
- **½ teaspoon ground black pepper**
- **¼ cup all purpose flour**

Vegetable oil (for frying)

PREHEAT oven to 325°F. Place baking sheet in oven. Place colander in large bowl. Line colander with kitchen towel. Using processor fitted with grating disk, coarsely grate potatoes, onion, celery root, and apple together. Transfer potato mixture to towel. Gather towel tightly around potato mixture and squeeze out as much liquid as possible into bowl; discard liquid. Place potato mixture, egg, green onion, marjoram, salt, and pepper in same bowl; toss to combine. Mix in flour.

POUR enough vegetable oil into heavy large skillet to cover bottom, and heat over medium high heat. Working in batches, drop ¼ cup pancake mixture into skillet for each pancake. Using bottom of metal spatula, flatten each mound to 3-inch round. Fry until cooked through and crisp, about 3 minutes per side. Drain on paper towels, then transfer pancakes to baking sheet in oven to keep warm. Repeat with remaining pancake mixture, leaving behind any liquid that collects in bottom of bowl.

Hungarian porcini-potato latkes

TRADITIONAL POTATO LATKES (Yiddish for "pancakes") go spicy and earthy in this recipe. Paprika, the flavorful red powder made from ground dried red peppers, is produced all over the world—Spain, Hungary, California, South America—but the Hungarian variety is considered superior. This recipe calls for the spicier hot paprika, which you'll find right next to the regular (sweet) paprika in the supermarket. Dried porcini mushrooms are available at Italian markets and specialty foods stores, and in the produce section of many supermarkets. After you reconstitute the porcini, save the liquid; it's a broth of sorts that will add delectable flavor to the latkes. Try these potato pancakes with roasted meats, chicken, or fish, or as a light lunch with a salad. Use a food processor fitted with a grating disk to grate the potatoes—it's much easier than doing them by hand.

MAKES ABOUT 10

½ ounce dried porcini mushrooms
¾ cup hot water

7 tablespoons (or more) olive oil, divided
2 garlic cloves, finely chopped
1 teaspoon Hungarian hot paprika

1½ pounds russet potatoes, peeled
1 large egg, beaten to blend
2 tablespoons fresh breadcrumbs made from egg bread
1 teaspoon salt
½ teaspoon ground black pepper

PLACE porcini in small bowl. Add ¾ cup hot water and let stand 45 minutes. Strain through fine sieve, reserving soaking liquid. Coarsely chop porcini.

HEAT 1 tablespoon oil in heavy medium nonstick skillet over medium-high heat. Add chopped porcini and garlic; sauté 2 minutes. Add reserved porcini soaking liquid and paprika; cook until liquid evaporates, stirring frequently, about 3 minutes. Season to taste with salt and pepper. Cool. *(Mushroom mixture can be prepared 1 day ahead. Cover and refrigerate.)*

PREHEAT oven to 325°F. Place baking sheet in oven. Finely grate potatoes by hand or in processor fitted with grating disk. Transfer potatoes to large bowl. Add enough cold water to cover; let stand 5 minutes. Drain potatoes. Wrap in dry kitchen towel; twist ends to squeeze out as much liquid as possible. Place potatoes in large bowl. Mix in egg, breadcrumbs, salt, and pepper. Stir in porcini mushroom mixture.

HEAT 6 tablespoons olive oil in heavy large skillet (preferably cast-iron) over medium-high heat until hot but not smoking. Working in batches, drop potato mixture by ¼ cupfuls into hot oil, spacing apart. Using spatula, flatten each into 4-inch round and cook until crisp and brown, about 4 minutes per side. Using slotted spatula, transfer latkes to paper towels to drain. Keep warm on baking sheet in oven. Add more oil to skillet if necessary and allow oil to get hot before adding more potato mixture. Transfer latkes to plates and serve.

Potato, leek, Gruyère, and oyster mushroom gratin

OYSTER MUSHROOMS, thin and fan-shaped, grow naturally on tree trunks. Look for them in the mushroom section of the supermarket; other wild mushrooms such as shiitake, morel, or portobello can be substituted if you can't find them. When slicing the leeks, use only the white and pale green parts, as the darker green parts are tough. The mushroom-leek mixture can be prepared a day ahead.

8 SERVINGS

4 tablespoons (½ stick) butter, divided
1 pound oyster mushrooms, halved if large
3 garlic cloves, minced
4 cups thinly sliced leeks (white and pale green parts only; about 4 large)
1 tablespoon minced fresh thyme

1¾ cups low-salt chicken broth
1¾ cups whipping cream
¼ cup dry white wine
1 teaspoon salt
½ teaspoon ground black pepper
3¾ pounds russet potatoes, peeled, thinly sliced into rounds (about 8 cups)
2½ cups grated Gruyère cheese (about 10 ounces)

MELT 2 tablespoons butter in heavy large skillet over medium-high heat. Add mushrooms and sauté until almost tender, about 5 minutes. Add garlic and sauté until mushrooms are tender and golden, about 3 minutes longer. Transfer mushroom mixture to bowl. Melt remaining 2 tablespoons butter in same skillet over medium-high heat. Add leeks and thyme; sauté until leeks are tender and beginning to brown, about 8 minutes. Add leek mixture to bowl with mushrooms. *(Can be prepared 1 day ahead. Cover and refrigerate.)*

PREHEAT oven to 400°F. Butter 13x9x2-inch glass baking dish. Whisk broth, cream, wine, 1 teaspoon salt, and ½ teaspoon pepper in large bowl to blend. Arrange ⅓ of potatoes over bottom of prepared dish. Top with half of mushroom-leek mixture, then ¾ cup cheese. Top with half of remaining potatoes. Pour half of cream mixture over. Top with remaining mushroom-leek mixture and ¾ cup cheese. Cover with remaining potatoes. Pour remaining cream mixture over; sprinkle with remaining 1 cup cheese.

BAKE gratin uncovered until potatoes are tender and sauce is bubbling thickly, about 1 hour 20 minutes. Let gratin stand 30 minutes before serving.

Potato gratin with mustard and cheddar cheese

WHITE CHEDDAR is the cheese of choice here, but if you can't find it at the market, yellow cheddar will do (all cheddar starts out pale; yellow-orange coloring is just for aesthetic purposes). Breadcrumbs give the topping a satisfying crunch. To make fresh breadcrumbs, grind white bread in the processor (no need to use day-old bread). This dish calls out for roast chicken, a butter lettuce salad, and a glass of Chardonnay.

10 SERVINGS

1 tablespoon butter
1 cup fresh breadcrumbs made from crustless white bread

1 tablespoon dried thyme
2 teaspoons salt
1 teaspoon ground black pepper
4 cups grated sharp white cheddar cheese (about 1 pound)
¼ cup all purpose flour
5 pounds russet potatoes, peeled, thinly sliced
4 cups low-salt chicken broth
1 cup whipping cream
6 tablespoons Dijon mustard

MELT butter in heavy large skillet over medium heat. Add breadcrumbs and stir until crumbs are golden brown, about 10 minutes. Cool crumbs. *(Can be prepared 2 days ahead. Cover and let stand at room temperature.)*

POSITION oven rack in center of oven and preheat to 400°F. Butter 15x10x2-inch glass baking dish. Mix thyme, salt, and pepper in small bowl. Combine grated cheddar cheese and flour in large bowl; toss to coat cheese. Arrange ⅓ of potatoes over bottom of prepared dish. Sprinkle ⅓ of thyme mixture, then ⅓ of cheese mixture over. Repeat layering of potatoes, thyme mixture, and cheese mixture 2 more times. Whisk broth, cream, and mustard in medium bowl to blend. Pour broth mixture over potatoes.

BAKE potatoes uncovered 30 minutes. Sprinkle buttered crumbs over. Bake until potatoes are tender and topping is golden brown, about 1 hour longer. Let stand 15 minutes before serving.

Scalloped potatoes with goat cheese and herbes de Provence

HERBES DE PROVENCE can be found at specialty foods stores and in the spice section of supermarkets. The dried herb mix is usually some combination of basil, rosemary, thyme, oregano, and lavender; the blends that contain lavender are the most authentic and reminiscent of Provence. A combination of dried thyme, basil, savory, and fennel seeds can be substituted. As with most gratins, this one needs to stand for several minutes after coming out of the oven and before serving. The time allows the dish to cool down a bit–it will be blazing hot straight out of the oven–and the juices have a chance to thicken. If the gratin seems watery even after this resting period, put it back in the oven, uncovered, for about ten minutes.

8 SERVINGS

1½ cups whipping cream
1½ cups low-salt chicken broth
1 cup dry white wine
½ cup minced shallots
3 garlic cloves, minced
4 teaspoons herbes de Provence
¾ teaspoon salt
1 10½- to 11-ounce log soft fresh goat cheese, crumbled
4 pounds russet potatoes, peeled, thinly sliced

PREHEAT oven to 400°F. Butter 13x9x2-inch glass baking dish. Mix first 7 ingredients in large pot. Bring to simmer over medium-high heat. Add half of cheese; whisk until smooth. Cover and refrigerate remaining cheese. Add potatoes to pot; bring to simmer.

SPREAD potato mixture evenly in prepared dish. Cover with aluminum foil and bake 15 minutes. Uncover and bake until potatoes are very tender and liquid is bubbling thickly, about 50 minutes.

DOT potatoes with remaining cheese. Bake until cheese softens, about 5 minutes. Let stand 15 minutes before serving.

Yukon Gold potato and wild mushroom gratin with blue cheese

THE BLUE CHEESE and wild mushrooms in this dish demand a nice, juicy steak and a bottle of big red wine. Use whatever mixture of fresh wild mushrooms you can find. (Make a point of using spongy morels in the spring; they're especially delicious.) If you can't find fresh wild mushrooms, regular button mushrooms will yield excellent results.

8 SERVINGS

1⅓ cups crumbled blue cheese (such as Stilton, Gorgonzola, or Maytag blue; about 5 ounces), room temperature
2½ cups whipping cream, divided
1 teaspoon salt
½ teaspoon ground black pepper

1½ tablespoons butter
1 pound assorted fresh wild mushrooms (such as chanterelle, morel, portobello, stemmed shiitake, oyster, or crimini), thickly sliced

- **1½ teaspoons chopped fresh thyme or ¾ teaspoon dried**
- **1½ teaspoons chopped fresh rosemary or ¾ teaspoon dried**
- **2 pounds Yukon Gold potatoes, peeled, very thinly sliced into rounds**

POSITION oven rack in top third of oven and preheat to 400°F. Butter 13x9x2-inch glass baking dish. Place cheese in medium bowl; add ½ cup cream. Using fork, mash mixture to chunky paste. Mix in salt and pepper. Mix in remaining 2 cups cream.

MELT butter in large pot over medium-high heat. Add mushrooms and herbs; sauté until mushrooms are tender and almost all liquid evaporates, about 8 minutes. *(Cheese sauce and mushrooms can be prepared 8 hours ahead. Cover separately and refrigerate.)*

ARRANGE half of potatoes over bottom of prepared dish. Spoon ¾ cup cheese sauce evenly over. Top with all of mushroom mixture, ¾ cup cheese sauce, and then remaining potatoes. Top with remaining cheese sauce. Cover dish with aluminum foil.

BAKE gratin 30 minutes. Uncover and bake until potatoes are tender, top is golden brown and sauce is thickened, about 30 minutes longer. Let stand 10 minutes before serving.

Southwestern potato gratin

POBLANO CHILES, cilantro, and *queso añejo* put the Southwest in this gratin. Poblanos are fresh dark green chiles; *queso añejo* is a salty, dry, white aged cheese. Both are available at Latin markets and some supermarkets. This gratin would be perfect alongside a Mexican-inspired entrée of pork, chicken, or beef, especially one spiced with chipotle chiles or cumin. And put some Mexican beers on ice.

8 SERVINGS

- **4 large poblano chiles**
- **2 garlic cloves, minced**
- **3½ pounds medium Yukon Gold or russet potatoes, peeled, cut into ⅛-inch-thick slices**
- **¾ cup coarsely chopped fresh cilantro**
- **2 cups low-salt chicken broth**
- **2 cups whipping cream**
- **1½ cups shredded Monterey Jack cheese (about 6 ounces)**
- **½ cup crumbled queso añejo or Romano cheese**
- **Additional chopped fresh cilantro**

PREHEAT oven to 400°F. Char chiles over gas flame or in broiler until blackened on all sides. Enclose in paper bag; let stand 10 minutes. Peel, seed, and chop chiles.

BUTTER 13x9x2-inch glass baking dish. Sprinkle garlic over bottom of dish. Arrange ¼ of potatoes in dish. Sprinkle with salt and pepper, then with ⅓ of chiles and ⅓ of cilantro. Repeat layering of potatoes, chiles, and cilantro 2 more times, seasoning potatoes with salt and pepper. Top with remaining potatoes. Pour broth over, then cream. Sprinkle with salt and pepper.

COVER dish with aluminum foil. Bake until potatoes are tender, about 1 hour 15 minutes. Uncover. Sprinkle cheeses over potatoes and continue baking until liquid thickens, about 15 minutes. Cool slightly. Sprinkle with cilantro.

Carrot and potato gratin

CARROTS MAKE THIS GRATIN count as a vegetable! And they add a lovely smattering of color to the dish. The very versatile Yukon Gold potatoes can be substituted for the russets. It's worth seeking out real Gruyère, a cow's milk cheese from Switzerland. You won't be sorry; the cheese's nutty tang is beyond compare.

8 SERVINGS

2¼ pounds russet potatoes, peeled, thinly sliced
1¼ pounds large carrots, peeled, thinly sliced

1 teaspoon salt
1¼ cups grated Gruyère cheese (about 6 ounces)
1 cup low-salt chicken broth
¼ cup (½ stick) butter

POSITION oven rack in top third of oven and preheat to 375°F. Butter 13x9x2-inch glass baking dish. Bring large pot of salted water to boil. Add potatoes and carrots. Cover and cook 5 minutes. Drain well.

ARRANGE ¼ of cooked vegetables over bottom of prepared dish. Sprinkle with ¼ teaspoon salt and generous amount of pepper. Sprinkle ¼ of grated cheese over. Repeat layering 3 more times with remaining cooked vegetables, salt, pepper, and grated cheese. Pour broth over vegetables. Dot top with ¼ cup butter. Cover with aluminum foil and bake until broth is absorbed and vegetables are tender, about 1 hour. Uncover and bake until top is golden brown, about 10 minutes longer. Let gratin stand 10 minutes before serving.

Potato gratin with Boursin

HERE'S A BRILLIANT USE of Boursin cheese—the French triple-cream that is often flavored with herbs or garlic (try either version here). It adds a wallop of flavor with only one ingredient. Three more ingredients—whipping cream, red-skinned potatoes, and parsley—and voilà, you're done.

8 SERVINGS

2 cups whipping cream
1 5-ounce package Boursin cheese with herbs
3 pounds red-skinned potatoes (unpeeled), scrubbed, thinly sliced
1½ tablespoons chopped fresh parsley

PREHEAT oven to 400°F. Butter 13x9x2-inch glass baking dish. Stir cream and cheese in heavy large saucepan over medium heat until cheese melts and mixture is smooth. Arrange half of sliced potatoes in prepared dish in slightly overlapping rows. Generously season potatoes in dish with salt and pepper. Pour half of cheese mixture over. Arrange remaining potatoes in slightly overlapping rows atop potatoes in dish. Generously season with salt and pepper. Pour remaining cheese mixture over potatoes. Bake until top is golden brown and potatoes are tender when pierced with knife, about 1 hour. Let stand 10 minutes. Sprinkle with parsley and serve.

Garlic-layered potatoes

THIS IS THE one-size-fits-all of potatoes. It's rich, creamy, and satisfying—and it goes with almost anything (roast beef, chicken, pork, fish, to name just a few options). If you don't have fresh thyme on hand, use dried thyme, but remember that drying intensifies the flavor of fresh herbs so use only a third as much (a teaspoon versus a tablespoon in this case).

8 SERVINGS

1 large head of garlic, separated into cloves, unpeeled
2 tablespoons olive oil

4 pounds russet potatoes, peeled, thinly sliced
1 tablespoon chopped fresh thyme or 1 teaspoon dried
1½ teaspoons salt
½ teaspoon ground black pepper
¼ teaspoon ground nutmeg

2 cups whipping cream
1 14-ounce can low-salt chicken broth

PREHEAT oven to 375°F. Place garlic in small baking dish; drizzle oil over. Bake until garlic is tender and brown in spots, about 15 minutes. Cool briefly. Transfer garlic to work surface; reserve oil in dish. Squeeze garlic to release cloves from skin. Coarsely chop garlic. Increase oven temperature to 400°F.

BRUSH 13x9x2-inch glass baking dish generously with reserved garlic oil. Place dish on baking sheet. Arrange ⅓ of potatoes over bottom of prepared dish; sprinkle with half each of garlic, thyme, salt, pepper, and nutmeg. Top with ⅓ of potatoes, then remaining garlic, thyme, salt, pepper, and nutmeg. Cover with remaining potatoes. Bring cream and broth to boil in heavy medium saucepan. Pour cream mixture over potatoes. Bake until potatoes are tender and brown on top and liquid thickens, about 1 hour 20 minutes. Let stand 10 minutes before serving.

Double-baked Roquefort potatoes

STEAKS COULDN'T ASK FOR a better partner—these are like mashed potatoes and a baked potato all in one. The blue cheese and sour cream give the potatoes a rich, smooth texture, and the Parmesan on top forms a nice golden crust. Don't forget to scrub the potatoes before using, and to pierce them a few times with a fork before baking; otherwise, the heat and steam might cause the skins to burst. This is a fantastic dinner-party recipe: The potatoes can be cooked and assembled a day ahead, then popped in the oven and browned for 30 minutes before serving.

8 SERVINGS

6 10- to 12-ounce russet potatoes

⅔ cup crumbled Roquefort cheese
½ cup sour cream
⅓ cup freshly grated Parmesan cheese (about 1 ounce)
2 tablespoons (¼ stick) butter, cut into small pieces

Chopped fresh parsley

PREHEAT oven to 375°F. Pierce potatoes with fork. Place potatoes directly on oven rack and bake until tender, about 1 hour 15 minutes. Transfer potatoes to baking sheet; cool 5 minutes.

HALVE each potato lengthwise. Scoop flesh from potatoes, leaving ¼-inch-thick shell; place flesh in large bowl. Add Roquefort cheese and sour cream to potato flesh; mash until smooth. Season mixture to taste with salt and pepper. Spoon potato mixture into 8 potato shells, mounding slightly and dividing equally (reserve remaining 4 potato shells for another use). Place potatoes on baking sheet. Sprinkle Parmesan cheese over. Dot with butter. *(Can be prepared 1 day ahead. Cover and refrigerate.)*

PREHEAT oven to 400°F. Bake potatoes until heated through and beginning to brown on top, about 25 minutes or up to 30 minutes if chilled. Sprinkle parsley over and serve.

Spicy Parmesan potatoes

THESE REMARKABLY EASY POTATOES fall somewhere between steak fries and baked potato wedges. With the exception of the basil, you probably have all of the ingredients on hand—and if you grow basil in your garden, you're set. Feel free to experiment with this simple combination: For a south-of-the-border alternative, try crushed chipotle pepper flakes instead of the crushed red pepper, Cotija cheese as a stand-in for the Parmesan, and cilantro in place of the basil.

4 SERVINGS

- **4 large russet potatoes, each cut lengthwise into eighths**
- **1/4 cup olive oil**
- **1 teaspoon dried crushed red pepper**
- **1/2 cup freshly grated Parmesan cheese (about 1 1/2 ounces)**
- **Chopped fresh basil**

POSITION oven rack in bottom third of oven and preheat to 375°F. Place potatoes in roasting pan. Add oil and crushed red pepper; toss to coat. Sprinkle with salt and pepper. Bake potatoes until tender inside and crusty outside, turning once, about 1 hour. Sprinkle with Parmesan and basil.

Baked potato wedges with seasoned salt

THIS IS ABOUT AS EASY as it gets: Peel some potatoes; slice 'em into wedges; toss with some melted butter, olive oil, and seasoned salt; then roast and eat. Kids will love them because they're like oversize french fries, so serve them with burgers. Grown-ups might like theirs with steaks and beers.

8 SERVINGS

- **8 large russet potatoes, peeled**
- **1/2 cup (1 stick) butter, melted**
- **1/2 cup olive oil**
- **2 tablespoons seasoned salt**

PREHEAT oven to 450°F. Cut each potato lengthwise into 8 wedges; toss in bowl with butter, oil, and seasoned salt. Arrange in single layer on 2 baking sheets. Bake until tender and golden, turning potatoes and rotating sheets halfway through baking, about 45 minutes. Serve immediately.

Cumin-roasted potatoes

CUMIN, USED SO OFTEN in North African, Asian, Latin American, and Indian cooking (it's integral to curry powder), adds an exotic flavor to these potatoes. They would be a great match for dishes (especially lamb or pork recipes) from those parts of the world. Also try them alongside a Mexican egg dish like huevos rancheros.

4 SERVINGS

- **1 1/2 teaspoons whole cumin seeds**
- **3 tablespoons olive oil**
- **1 1/4 teaspoons salt**
- **3/4 teaspoon paprika**
- **2 pounds russet potatoes, peeled, cut into 1-inch pieces**

PREHEAT oven to 450°F. Stir whole cumin seeds in heavy small skillet over medium heat just until fragrant, about 45 seconds. Transfer cumin seeds to 13x9x2-inch glass baking dish. Add oil, salt, and paprika; whisk to blend. Add potatoes and toss to coat well. Spread out potatoes in single layer. Roast potatoes until brown and crisp around edges, stirring occasionally, about 35 minutes. Transfer to bowl and serve.

Roasted new potatoes with spring herb pesto

THESE ARE JUST RIGHT for a springtime supper, perhaps with spring's favorite fish, salmon. But since most ingredients are available year-round these days, the recipe would be good anytime. Traditional pesto, of course, centers on basil, but this version takes a step outside the box and incorporates parsley, chives, and rosemary. Nice and easy, the pesto can be made a day ahead, so all that's left to do is to halve the potatoes, roast them, and toss them with the pesto.

6 SERVINGS

- **¾ cup chopped fresh parsley**
- **⅓ cup chopped fresh chives**
- **3 tablespoons chopped fresh rosemary**
- **3 tablespoons olive oil, divided**
- **2 garlic cloves, minced**
- **1 tablespoon fresh lemon juice**
- **½ teaspoon grated lemon peel**
- **½ teaspoon salt**

- **2½ pounds red-skinned new potatoes, halved lengthwise**

BLEND parsley, chives, rosemary, 1 tablespoon olive oil, garlic, lemon juice, lemon peel, and ½ teaspoon salt in processor to coarse puree. *(Pesto can be made 1 day ahead. Cover and refrigerate.)*

PREHEAT oven to 400°F. Toss potatoes and remaining 2 tablespoons oil in large bowl. Sprinkle generously with salt and pepper. Arrange potatoes, cut side down, on rimmed baking sheet. Roast until potatoes are golden brown and tender, about 40 minutes. Using spatula, transfer potatoes to large bowl. Add pesto and toss to coat. Serve.

Potato, shallot, and bell pepper packets on the grill

HERE ARE THE PERFECT POTATOES for a camping trip: Just place the aluminum foil packets on the barbecue grate or directly in the fire (use tongs for safe removal). At home, if you don't have an outdoor grill, or if it's the middle of winter, these will work just as well cooked for about half an hour on a baking sheet in a 400°F oven. And feel free to vary the contents of the packets: Try onions instead of shallots, green bell peppers instead of red, rosemary instead of marjoram—almost anything goes.

6 SERVINGS

- **6 medium unpeeled red-skinned potatoes, thinly sliced**
- **2 medium red bell peppers, cut into thin strips**
- **12 garlic cloves, peeled, halved lengthwise**
- **8 shallots, peeled, halved lengthwise**
- **¼ cup olive oil**
- **1 tablespoon minced fresh marjoram**
- **1 teaspoon salt**
- **¼ teaspoon ground black pepper**

PREPARE barbecue (medium-high heat). Oil 6 large sheets of heavy-duty aluminum foil. Combine all ingredients in large bowl and toss to coat. Divide among foil sheets. Gather edges and seal packets tightly. Place packets on edge of grill rack; cover grill and cook until potatoes are tender, turning occasionally, about 20 minutes.

Whole baked yams with spicy molasses-orange butter

THE SWEET AND SPICY MIX of flavors is delightful here, and the roasted sweet potatoes topped with a melting pat of spicy molasses-orange butter are unbelievably succulent. The red-skinned (and orange-fleshed) sweet potatoes called for in this recipe may be labeled either *sweet potatoes* or *yams* at the market. Prepare the butter up to a week ahead to cut the work time on serving day.

6 SERVINGS

- **½ cup (1 stick) butter, room temperature**
- **3 tablespoons mild-flavored (light) molasses**
- **1 teaspoon ground cinnamon**
- **1 teaspoon grated orange peel**
- **1 teaspoon chili powder**
- **¼ teaspoon salt**
- **⅛ teaspoon cayenne pepper**

- **6 9- to 10-ounce yams (red-skinned sweet potatoes)**

USING electric mixer, beat first 7 ingredients in medium bowl until fluffy. *(Spiced butter can be prepared 1 week ahead. Cover and refrigerate. Bring to room temperature before using.)*

PREHEAT oven to 350°F. Line large baking sheet with heavy-duty aluminum foil. Using small sharp knife, make one ½-inch-deep lengthwise slit in each yam, leaving 1 inch of yam uncut at each end. Place yams on baking sheet. Bake yams until tender, about 1 hour 15 minutes.

CUT slits across center of each yam. Press ends toward center to expose flesh. Transfer yams to platter. Spoon 1 tablespoon spiced butter into each. Serve, passing remaining spiced butter separately.

Whole roasted yams with maple-allspice butter

FOR THE RECORD: Allspice is a single spice. It's the dried berry of a particular evergreen tree, but because its flavor has notes of cinnamon, nutmeg, and cloves, people often think allspice is the name of a spice blend. Be sure to pick nicely shaped, uniformly sized yams (red-skinned sweet potatoes) at the market since you'll be serving them whole.

8 SERVINGS

- **½ pound (2 sticks) butter, room temperature**
- **¼ cup pure maple syrup**
- **½ teaspoon salt**
- **½ teaspoon ground allspice**
- **½ teaspoon ground black pepper**

- **8 small yams (red-skinned sweet potatoes)**

MIX first 5 ingredients in medium bowl. *(Spiced butter can be prepared 3 days ahead. Cover and refrigerate. Bring to room temperature before using.)*

PREHEAT oven to 375°F. Lightly pierce yams all over with fork. Set yams directly on oven rack; bake until tender when pierced with skewer, about 1 hour.

CUT cross in top of each yam. Using oven mitts to protect hands, squeeze yams gently in from sides to expose flesh. Spoon 1 tablespoon spiced butter into each yam. Serve, passing remaining spiced butter separately.

Yam puree with ginger and cider

SWEET THROUGH AND THROUGH, this dish is a very sophisticated alternative to the classic marshmallow-topped version. It has the potential to become a new Thanksgiving tradition—but also try it with a pork loin or duck breast. This recipe is great for a party because the whole thing can be made four hours ahead and refrigerated; just reheat before serving.

6 SERVINGS

2½ pounds yams (red-skinned sweet potatoes)

4 cups apple cider
¼ cup minced peeled fresh ginger
2 tablespoons (¼ stick) butter

PLACE yams in large pot; add enough water to cover by 2 inches. Bring to boil over high heat. Reduce heat to medium-low and simmer until yams are very tender, about 40 minutes. Drain; cool. Peel and cut into large chunks. Transfer to processor.

MEANWHILE, bring cider to boil in heavy medium saucepan over high heat. Reduce heat to medium-low and simmer until cider is reduced to 1 cup, about 30 minutes. Transfer cider, ginger, and butter to processor with yams; process until very smooth. Season puree to taste with salt and pepper. *(Can be made 4 hours ahead. Transfer puree to heavy medium saucepan. Cover and refrigerate. Before serving, stir over medium heat until heated through.)*

Yam puree with goat cheese and truffle oil

THIS IS AS EASY AS 1-2-3-4: Four flavor-packed ingredients equal one sweet, rich, earthy side dish. The sweetness of the potatoes is mellowed by the deep earthiness of the goat cheese and truffle oil. Serve these with something rich, such as duck. Truffles are mushroom relatives that grow underground near tree roots (pigs and dogs are trained to sniff them out). The best are black truffles from France's Périgord region and white truffles from the Piedmont in Italy. They're quite a delicacy and quite expensive. The more affordable truffle oil (an infusion of the truffles in olive oil) imparts a similar but less intense flavor. This recipe calls for white truffle oil, which is a touch milder than black. Look for it at well-stocked supermarkets, Italian markets, and specialty foods stores.

6 SERVINGS

2½ pounds yams (red-skinned sweet potatoes), peeled, cut into 1½-inch pieces
4 ounces soft fresh goat cheese, crumbled
2 tablespoons (¼ stick) butter
1 teaspoon white truffle oil

COOK yams in large saucepan of boiling salted water until tender, about 15 minutes. Drain. Transfer to processor. Add cheese and process just until mixture is smooth. Add butter and truffle oil; process just until blended. Season puree to taste with salt and pepper. *(Can be prepared 1 day ahead. Cover and refrigerate.)* Stir puree in large saucepan over medium heat until heated through. Transfer puree to bowl and serve.

Coriander sweet potatoes

SUCH A STRAIGHTFORWARD RECIPE really brings out the best in sweet potatoes: All they need is a little salt and pepper plus a single spice like coriander; then simply roast them to crispy perfection. Coriander and cilantro actually come from the same plant—coriander is the seed and cilantro the leaves (in some cookbooks you'll see cilantro called fresh coriander). These potatoes would be great with Indian-spiced lamb, a pork roast with Mexican flavors, or even an Asian-inspired fish dish. They are delicious left unpeeled, but you can peel them if you prefer.

6 SERVINGS

6 tan-skinned sweet potatoes, cut into ½-inch rounds
5 tablespoons olive oil
2¼ teaspoons ground coriander
½ cup chopped fresh cilantro

PREHEAT oven to 350°F. Mix potatoes and oil in large bowl. Season generously with salt and pepper. Arrange potatoes in single layer on large rimmed baking sheet. Roast until tender and brown, turning after 35 minutes, about 45 minutes total. Transfer to large bowl. Toss with coriander and cilantro and serve.

Sweet potato and celery root gratin with Fontina cheese

A GRATIN IS any dish topped with cheese or breadcrumbs and browned on top, but the term most often refers to a creamy layering of potatoes like this one. And any dish with starch and cheese—like macaroni and cheese or this potato gratin—benefits from a sweet dash of nutmeg. Aside from its nutty flavor, Fontina (an Italian cow's milk cheese) is prized for its "meltability"—which makes it perfect for a gratin.

10 SERVINGS

- **1 teaspoon salt**
- **½ teaspoon ground black pepper**
- **¼ teaspoon ground nutmeg**
- **¾ cup thinly sliced shallots**
- **2 1-pound celery roots (celeriac), peeled, halved, thinly sliced**
- **2 pounds tan-skinned sweet potatoes, peeled, thinly sliced**
- **2 cups whipping cream**
- **1 cup low-salt chicken broth**

- **2 cups grated Fontina cheese (about 8 ounces)**

PREHEAT oven to 400°F. Mix salt, pepper, and nutmeg in small bowl. Sprinkle half of shallots in 16-cup oval gratin dish or 15x10x2-inch glass baking dish. Top with half of celery roots and half of sweet potatoes. Sprinkle half of spice mixture over. Repeat layering with remaining shallots, celery roots, sweet potatoes, and spice mixture. Bring cream and broth to simmer in medium saucepan. Pour over vegetables. Cover tightly with foil.

BAKE until vegetables are almost tender, about 45 minutes. Increase oven temperature to 450°F. Using spatula, press sweet potatoes to even thickness. Bake uncovered until juices thicken, about 10 minutes. Top with cheese and continue baking until cheese melts and browns, about 15 minutes. Let stand 15 minutes before serving.

14 Vegetables

Thanks to the farmers' market revolution of the past decade, it's easy to get excited about cooking with the seasons, tasting the freshest flavors imaginable. Certainly the best vegetables piled high—gleaming bunches of carrots, green beans, pyramids of heirloom tomatoes, and eggplants of every shape and size and hue—are part of the inspiration.

Then the only question is how best to prepare vegetables to enhance their naturally stellar qualities.

The recipes offered here fall into two broad categories:

Some play up or enhance a single vegetable; for instance, releasing the sweetness of onions by roasting them, then balancing that sweetness with a splash of balsamic vinegar. Likewise, a simple sauté of carrots takes on new meaning with the addition of crushed cumin seeds (carrots and cumin have been dating for a very long time—a nice thing to remember the next time you whip up a pot of carrot soup).

Other recipes combine two or more vegetables that are transformed into something greater than the sum of their parts. When paired, sweet green peas and earthy celery root bring out the best in each other—as is the case with any well-matched couple, whether vegetable or human.

Though often we read recipes, pick one that sounds tempting, and *then* shop for the ingredients, when it comes to vegetables we suggest the reverse: Head to the farmers' market, pick whatever looks freshest and most appealing, and then use this chapter to find a great recipe to show it off.

Asparagus with balsamic-shallot butter sauce

BALSAMIC VINEGAR AND SHALLOTS are boiled together until reduced to a rich, syrupy glaze, while asparagus spears are cooked in butter and just enough water to steam them. The best balsamic vinegars are made in Italy from the white juice of the Trebbiano grape. They get their dark color and sharp sweetness from aging in a series of barrels—made from various woods and in various sizes—over a period of years.

8 SERVINGS

- **½ cup balsamic vinegar**
- **2 large shallots, finely chopped**

- **2 pounds asparagus, trimmed**
- **3 tablespoons butter, room temperature**
- **3 tablespoons water**
- **½ teaspoon salt**

COMBINE vinegar and shallots in heavy small saucepan. Boil over medium heat until almost all vinegar is absorbed and about 1 tablespoon liquid remains in pan, stirring frequently, about 6 minutes. Set aside.

COMBINE asparagus, butter, 3 tablespoons water, and ½ teaspoon salt in heavy large skillet. Bring to boil over medium-high heat. Cover and cook until asparagus is almost tender, about 3 minutes. Uncover and cook until all liquid evaporates and asparagus is just tender, stirring occasionally, about 2 minutes longer. Add balsamic-shallot mixture and toss to coat. Season to taste with pepper and additional salt, if desired. Transfer to platter and serve.

Stir-fried sesame asparagus

SESAME SEEDS have a high fat content, which provides a rich, nutty oil. However, the fat content can also make the seeds turn bad quickly, so store them in a cool dark place for no more than three months. The type of oil used in this recipe comes from toasted sesame seeds and is a fragrant accent to virtually any stir-fried dish.

4 TO 6 SERVINGS

- **2 tablespoons soy sauce**
- **2 teaspoons sugar**
- **2 tablespoons Asian sesame oil**
- **2 garlic cloves, chopped**
- **2 pounds asparagus, ends trimmed, cut on diagonal into 2-inch-long pieces**
- **4 teaspoons sesame seeds**

STIR soy sauce and sugar in small bowl until sugar dissolves. Heat oil in heavy large skillet over medium-high heat. Add garlic and stir 15 seconds. Add asparagus and stir-fry until crisp-tender, about 4 minutes. Add soy mixture and toss until asparagus is coated, about 1 minute longer. Season to taste with salt and pepper. Transfer to bowl; sprinkle with sesame seeds and serve.

Roasted asparagus with wild mushroom fricassee

ROASTING THE ASPARAGUS intensifies its flavor and is easy to do. At the market, buy firm, bright green stalks with tight tips. If the asparagus is not cooked the day it is purchased, wrap it tightly in paper towels and then a plastic bag and store it up to four days in the refrigerator. Be sure to wash it well before cooking, as asparagus grows in sandy soil and the sand can get stuck in the tips.

4 SERVINGS

1 pound medium asparagus, tough ends trimmed
2 teaspoons olive oil

3 tablespoons butter
1 large shallot, minced
12 ounces assorted wild mushrooms (such as crimini, oyster, chanterelle, and stemmed shiitake), sliced
½ cup dry white wine
1 tablespoon minced fresh Italian parsley
1 teaspoon minced fresh tarragon

PREHEAT oven to 475°F. Arrange asparagus on rimmed baking sheet. Drizzle oil over and turn to coat. Sprinkle generously with salt and pepper. Roast until just tender, about 10 minutes.

MEANWHILE, melt butter in large skillet over medium-high heat. Add shallot and sauté 1 minute. Add mushrooms and sauté until beginning to brown, about 5 minutes. Cover and cook until mushrooms are tender, about 3 minutes. Add wine and cook uncovered until wine is absorbed, about 2 minutes. Stir in parsley and tarragon. Season to taste with salt and pepper.

DIVIDE asparagus among 4 plates. Top each serving with mushrooms.

Grilled asparagus with saffron aioli

SAFFRON IS one of the most expensive spices in the world—but worth it. Serve this dish for people you really like.

6 SERVINGS

¼ cup red wine vinegar
1 tablespoon honey
Large pinch of saffron threads
1 cup mayonnaise
2 garlic cloves, minced

2 pounds asparagus, tough ends trimmed
3 tablespoons olive oil
1 small red bell pepper, finely chopped

WHISK vinegar, honey, and saffron threads in heavy small saucepan over medium-high heat. Bring to boil. Remove from heat and cool completely. Mix mayonnaise and garlic in medium bowl to blend. Mix in cooled vinegar mixture. Season aioli to taste with salt and pepper. *(Can be prepared 1 day ahead. Cover and refrigerate.)*

PREPARE barbecue (medium-high heat). Toss asparagus with oil on large baking sheet. Sprinkle with salt and pepper. Grill asparagus until crisp-tender, turning occasionally, about 5 minutes. Transfer to platter. Drizzle aioli over asparagus. Sprinkle with chopped bell pepper and serve.

Grilled baby artichokes with olive oil and lemon

HERE'S A SIMPLE and inventive way to serve artichokes, inspired by a Greek preparation. After the vegetables are grilled, they are tossed with an easy lemon dressing that can be made ahead of time. Serve the artichokes with grilled pork or lamb for a sensational summer meal.

4 TO 6 SERVINGS

1 lemon, halved
12 baby artichokes

⅔ cup extra-virgin olive oil
⅓ cup fresh lemon juice

SQUEEZE juice from lemon halves into bowl of cold water. Cut all but 1 inch of stem off 1 artichoke. Snap off bottom 3 rows of leaves. Cut off top ½ inch of artichoke. Halve artichoke lengthwise. Scrape out choke. Place in lemon water to prevent discoloration. Repeat with remaining artichokes.

BRING large pot of salted water to boil. Add artichokes and boil until crisp-tender, about 6 minutes. Drain and pat dry.

PREPARE barbecue (medium heat). Whisk oil and ⅓ cup lemon juice in small bowl to blend. Season dressing to taste with salt and pepper. Brush artichokes with some of dressing. Grill until tender and charred in spots, about 5 minutes per side. Transfer to large bowl. *(Artichokes and dressing can be made 4 hours ahead. Let stand separately at room temperature.)* Mix in enough dressing to coat. Sprinkle with salt and pepper. Transfer artichokes to platter. Serve artichokes warm or at room temperature, passing remaining dressing separately.

Grilled corn on the cob with chipotle butter

THIS RECIPE has a nice balance of sweet and spicy flavors, and a squeeze of lime juice provides tang. Corn is best cooked the day you bring it home from the market, because as soon as it is picked the sugar in the kernels begins to turn to starch, which will lessen the corn's natural sweetness. Chipotle chiles canned in a spicy tomato sauce called *adobo*, are available at Latin markets, specialty foods stores, and some supermarkets.

8 SERVINGS

- **½ cup (1 stick) unsalted butter**
- **1½ tablespoons minced seeded canned chipotle chiles**
- **2 teaspoons fresh lime juice**
- **¼ teaspoon salt**

- **8 large ears of corn, husked**

- **Lime wedges**

MELT butter in small saucepan over medium heat. Add chipotles, lime juice, and ¼ teaspoon salt. Reduce heat to low and cook chipotle butter 1 minute to blend flavors.

PLACE ears of corn on baking sheet. Brush corn all over with chipotle butter. *(Can be prepared 4 hours ahead. Cover corn and refrigerate.)*

PREPARE barbecue (medium-high heat). Grill corn until cooked through and blackened in spots, turning frequently, about 6 minutes. Serve corn with lime wedges.

Fresh corn and cheddar cheese soufflé

SWEET, CRUNCHY CORN and sharp, creamy cheese complement each other in this delicious soufflé. Baked soufflés are very fragile, because the hot air trapped inside the whipped egg mixture begins to escape as soon as the dish is removed from the oven, causing the soufflé to deflate. So handle the dish gently after it is cooked, and serve the soufflé immediately.

4 SERVINGS

- **4 tablespoons (½ stick) butter, divided**
- **1 cup fresh corn kernels (cut from about 2 ears) or frozen, thawed**
- **3 tablespoons all purpose flour**
- **1 cup whole milk**
- **4 large egg yolks**
- **½ teaspoon dry mustard**
- **½ plus ⅛ teaspoon salt**

- **¾ cup (packed) coarsely grated sharp cheddar cheese (about 3 ounces)**
- **1 bunch fresh chives, chopped**

- **5 large egg whites**

MELT 1 tablespoon butter in heavy medium skillet over medium heat. Add corn and sauté until tender, about 3 minutes. Remove from heat. Melt remaining 3 tablespoons butter in heavy medium saucepan over medium heat. Add flour and stir 2 minutes (do not brown). Gradually whisk in milk. Boil until sauce is very thick, whisking constantly, about 1 minute. Remove from heat. Whisk in egg yolks 1 at a time. Whisk in mustard and ½ teaspoon salt.

Season to taste with pepper. *(Corn and soufflé base can be made 2 hours ahead. Let corn stand at room temperature. Press plastic wrap onto surface of soufflé base and let stand at room temperature. Before continuing, rewarm soufflé base over low heat until just lukewarm, stirring constantly.)*

PREHEAT oven to 400°F. Butter 8-cup soufflé dish. Add corn, cheese, and chives to warm soufflé base and stir gently to blend.

USING clean dry beaters, beat whites and remaining ⅛ teaspoon salt in large bowl until stiff but not dry. Fold ¼ of whites into soufflé base to lighten. Gently fold in remaining whites. Spoon into prepared dish. Place soufflé in oven. Reduce temperature to 375°F and bake until soufflé is puffed and golden on top but still moves slightly when top is touched gently, about 30 minutes. Serve immediately.

Calico corn pancakes

GREAT WITH TURKEY OR CHICKEN, these golden pancakes are accented with bacon, pimientos, green onions, oregano, and cumin. Ideal for entertaining, they can be cooked a day ahead and rewarmed just before bringing to the table.

MAKES ABOUT 16

- **4 bacon slices, cut crosswise into ½-inch-wide strips**
- **1 16-ounce bag frozen corn kernels, thawed, drained**
- **¼ cup water**

- **½ cup drained sliced pimientos (about 3½ ounces)**
- **½ cup thinly sliced green onions**
- **¼ cup chopped fresh parsley**
- **1 tablespoon fresh lemon juice**
- **1 teaspoon salt**
- **1 teaspoon sugar**
- **½ teaspoon dried oregano**
- **½ teaspoon ground cumin**
- **Generous pinch of ground black pepper**
- **½ cup whipping cream**
- **3 large eggs, separated**
- **½ cup all purpose flour**
- **¼ teaspoon baking powder**

COOK bacon in heavy large skillet over medium-high heat until crisp. Using slotted spoon, transfer to paper towels to drain. Pour all but 1 tablespoon drippings from skillet into small bowl and reserve. Add corn to skillet and sauté until brown, about 5 minutes. Add ¼ cup water; boil until all liquid evaporates and corn is tender, stirring often, about 3 minutes. Transfer corn to large bowl and cool.

MIX bacon, pimientos, and next 8 ingredients into corn. Mix in whipping cream and egg yolks, then flour and baking powder. Beat egg whites in medium bowl until stiff but not dry. Fold ¼ of egg whites into batter to lighten. Fold in remaining egg whites.

HEAT large skillet over medium heat. Brush with some of reserved bacon drippings. Working in batches, drop batter into skillet by ¼ cupfuls; spread batter with back of spoon to form 3-inch pancakes. Cook until golden and cooked through, brushing skillet with reserved drippings as needed, about 2 minutes per side. *(Pancakes can be made 1 day ahead. Transfer pancakes to large rimmed baking sheet. Cool, then cover and chill. Rewarm on baking sheet in 350°F oven until heated through, about 10 minutes.)*

Green beans with citrus butter sauce

GARLIC LENDS INTRIGUING FLAVOR to the lemon-orange sauce, and chicken broth adds volume but not fat. At the market, buy slender green beans that are crisp and brightly colored. Wrap them tightly in a paper towel and then in a plastic bag, and keep them in the refrigerator for up to five days.

4 TO 6 SERVINGS

- **1 pound slender green beans, ends trimmed**
- **1 tablespoon olive oil**
- **1 tablespoon grated orange peel**
- **2 teaspoons grated lemon peel**
- **2 garlic cloves, minced**
- **¼ cup low-salt chicken broth**
- **2 tablespoons (¼ stick) butter**

COOK green beans in large pot of boiling salted water until crisp-tender, about 4 minutes. Drain well. Heat oil in heavy large skillet over medium-high heat. Add orange peel, lemon peel, and garlic; stir 1 minute. Add broth and simmer 1 minute. Add butter, then beans. Toss until beans are heated through and evenly coated with sauce, about 2 minutes. Season beans to taste with salt and pepper. Transfer to bowl and serve.

Green beans with shiitake mushrooms

THE DARK BROWN CAP of the shiitake mushroom has meaty texture and a full-bodied, steaklike taste. Shiitake stems are very tough and are usually removed before the mushroom is used in a recipe. The best times to buy the mushrooms fresh are spring and autumn; look for plump mushrooms with edges that curl under and set aside any with broken or shriveled caps.

8 SERVINGS

- **6 tablespoons (¾ stick) butter, divided**
- **8 ounces fresh shiitake mushrooms, stemmed, caps sliced**
- **2 shallots, chopped**
- **2 garlic cloves, minced**
- **2 pounds slender green beans, ends trimmed**
- **⅔ cup low-salt chicken broth**

MELT 3 tablespoons butter in large nonstick skillet over medium-high heat. Add mushrooms and sauté until tender, about 5 minutes. Transfer mushrooms to medium bowl. Melt remaining 3 tablespoons butter in same skillet. Add shallots and garlic; sauté until soft, about 2 minutes. Add green beans and toss to coat. Pour broth over green bean mixture. Cover and simmer until liquid evaporates and beans are crisp-tender, about 10 minutes. Stir in shiitake mushrooms. Season to taste with salt and pepper. Transfer to platter and serve.

Green beans with walnuts, lemon, and parsley

RATHER THAN BEING TOASTED, the walnuts in this recipe are sautéed in butter—enhancing the flavor of both the nuts and the butter (which also turns a nice light brown). Lemon peel and parsley provide a fresh, sprightly accent to the green beans. For a variation, try orange peel in place of the lemon.

8 SERVINGS

- **2 pounds slender green beans, trimmed, halved crosswise**
- **5 tablespoons butter**
- **¾ cup chopped walnuts**
- **4 teaspoons grated lemon peel**
- **⅓ cup finely chopped fresh Italian parsley**

COOK green beans in large pot of boiling salted water until crisp-tender, about 4 minutes. Drain. Transfer to bowl of ice water and cool. Drain again and pat dry. *(Beans can be prepared 1 day ahead. Wrap in plastic and refrigerate.)*

MELT butter in large deep skillet over medium heat. Add walnuts; sauté until nuts are crisp and butter is lightly browned, about 3 minutes. Add beans and toss to heat through, about 5 minutes. Mix in lemon peel and toss 1 minute. Mix in parsley. Season beans to taste with salt and pepper. Transfer to bowl and serve.

Green beans with roasted onions

BUTTERY ROASTED ONIONS are stirred into a sweetened vinegar sauce (they can be prepared a day before serving) and then spooned atop buttered green beans. Rich and sophisticated, this side dish is perfect for the holidays or any winter dinner party.

12 SERVINGS

- **Nonstick vegetable oil spray**
- **6 medium onions (about 2½ pounds), peeled, each cut vertically through root end into 12 wedges with some core attached to each wedge**
- **6 tablespoons (¾ stick) butter, divided**

- **2 cups low-salt chicken broth**
- **3 tablespoons sugar**
- **2 tablespoons red wine vinegar**

- **3 pounds slender green beans, ends trimmed**

PREHEAT oven to 450°F. Spray 2 large rimmed baking sheets with nonstick spray. Arrange onions, cut side down, in single layer on prepared sheets. Dot onions with 4 tablespoons butter, dividing equally. Sprinkle with salt and pepper. Bake until onions are dark brown on bottom, about 35 minutes.

MEANWHILE, boil broth in heavy large skillet over high heat until reduced to ½ cup, about 6 minutes. Add sugar and vinegar; whisk until sugar dissolves and sauce comes to boil.

ADD onions to sauce. Reduce heat to medium-low; simmer until liquid is slightly reduced and coats onions, about 5 minutes. Season to taste with salt and pepper. *(Onions can be prepared 1 day ahead. Cover and refrigerate. Rewarm over low heat before continuing.)*

COOK green beans in large pot of boiling salted water until crisp-tender, about 5 minutes. Drain well. Return beans to same pot. Add remaining 2 tablespoons butter and toss to coat. Season beans to taste with salt and pepper. Mound in large shallow bowl. Top with roasted onion mixture and serve.

Chinese-style spicy green beans

LOOK FOR HOISIN SAUCE and chili-garlic sauce in the Asian foods section of the supermarket. Hoisin—a thick, reddish-brown, sweet-spicy sauce—is made from soybeans, garlic, chile peppers, and spices. It teams up with the pungent chili-garlic sauce as well as with soy sauce, sesame seeds, and green onions for an aromatic side dish that would pair well with grilled shrimp, lamb chops, or sauteed chicken breasts. For a variation, use Chinese long beans, cut into 4- or 5-inch lengths.

4 SERVINGS

- **1 pound slender green beans, ends trimmed**

- **1 tablespoon sesame seeds**
- **2 tablespoons hoisin sauce**
- **1 tablespoon soy sauce**
- **1½ teaspoons chili-garlic sauce**
- **3 tablespoons water**
- **2 teaspoons cornstarch**
- **2 green onions, chopped**

COOK green beans in large pot of boiling salted water until crisp-tender, about 4 minutes. Drain beans well.

STIR sesame seeds in large nonstick skillet over high heat until golden, about 1 minute. Transfer seeds to small bowl. Add hoisin sauce, soy sauce, and chili-garlic sauce to same skillet. Stir water and cornstarch in small bowl until cornstarch dissolves; stir into mixture in skillet. Add beans to skillet. Place skillet over medium-high heat. Toss beans until sauce thickens and coats beans, about 2 minutes. Mix in green onions. Transfer to shallow bowl. Sprinkle with toasted sesame seeds and serve.

Grilled vegetables with chipotle chile dressing

CHIPOTLE CHILES are dried, smoked jalapeño chiles that come canned in a delicious *adobo* sauce, a mixture of chiles, herbs, and vinegar. You can find chipotles in adobo sauce at Latin markets, or in the aisle with the salsas at the supermarket. Wear thin disposable gloves when peeling chayote squash—it forms a slime that can be hard to wash off.

6 SERVINGS

- **1/4 cup orange juice**
- **1 tablespoon finely chopped canned chipotle chiles**
- **1 teaspoon ground cumin**
- **1/3 cup olive oil**

- **3 plum tomatoes, quartered lengthwise**
- **1 medium zucchini, trimmed, cut lengthwise into 1/4-inch-thick slices**
- **1 medium yellow crookneck squash, trimmed, cut lengthwise into 1/4-inch-thick slices**
- **1 Japanese eggplant, trimmed, cut lengthwise into 1/4-inch-thick slices**
- **1 red onion, cut crosswise into 1/3-inch-thick slices**
- **1 chayote squash, peeled, pitted, cut into 12 wedges**

WHISK first 3 ingredients in small bowl. Add oil and whisk until well blended. Season dressing to taste with salt and pepper.

PREPARE barbecue (medium-high heat). Place all vegetables on 2 large baking sheets. Brush vegetables with ¼ cup dressing; sprinkle with salt and pepper. Grill vegetables until tender and beginning to brown, turning occasionally, about 5 minutes for tomatoes, zucchini, yellow squash, eggplant, and onion; and 15 minutes for chayote squash.

SEPARATE grilled onion slices into rings. Arrange all grilled vegetables on platter. Drizzle remaining dressing over. Season to taste with salt and pepper. Serve warm or at room temperature.

Grilled summer vegetable medley with fresh herbs

THIS CROWD-PLEASING DISH is outstanding with just about any grilled meat, poultry, or fish. When preparing grilled vegetables, keep in mind a few ground rules: All the vegetables should be marinated or brushed with olive oil before hitting the barbecue; they should be moved around on the grill to compensate for uneven heat; they should be turned often; and the chef should stay close by while they cook.

4 SERVINGS

- **3 tablespoons olive oil**
- **2 garlic cloves, crushed**
- **1 1/2 teaspoons chopped fresh thyme**
- **1 1/2 teaspoons chopped fresh sage**
- **1 1/2 teaspoons chopped fresh rosemary**
- **2 small Japanese eggplants, halved lengthwise**
- **2 small zucchini, halved lengthwise**
- **2 small yellow crookneck squash, halved lengthwise**
- **4 1/2-inch-thick slices red onion**
- **1 red bell pepper, quartered, seeded**

COMBINE first 5 ingredients in small bowl and whisk to blend. Place vegetables on large rimmed baking sheet. Brush with oil-herb mixture; sprinkle with salt and pepper. Let marinate 2 hours.

PREPARE barbecue (medium-high heat). Grill vegetables until just tender, turning occasionally, about 8 minutes. Transfer vegetables to platter. Season to taste with salt and pepper. Serve warm or at room temperature.

Turkish zucchini pancakes

WHEN BUYING ZUCCHINI, look for small vegetables, which will be younger (and therefore more tender) and have thinner skins. The exterior should be bright green and smooth, with no bruises or markings. Zucchini is especially well suited to the pancake treatment. In this dish it is combined with feta cheese, herbs, green onions, and walnuts to make a terrific partner for virtually any Mediterranean-style main course.

MAKES ABOUT 20

- **1 pound zucchini, trimmed, coarsely grated**
- **2 cups chopped green onions (about 9)**
- **4 large eggs, beaten to blend**
- **½ cup all purpose flour**
- **⅓ cup chopped fresh dill or 1½ tablespoons dried dillweed**
- **⅓ cup chopped fresh parsley**
- **2 tablespoons chopped fresh tarragon or 2 teaspoons dried**
- **½ teaspoon salt**
- **½ teaspoon ground black pepper**
- **½ cup crumbled feta cheese (about 3 ounces)**
- **⅔ cup chopped walnuts**
- **Olive oil**

PLACE zucchini in colander. Sprinkle with salt and let stand 30 minutes to drain. Squeeze zucchini between hands to remove excess liquid, then squeeze dry in several layers of paper towels.

COMBINE zucchini, green onions, eggs, flour, dill, parsley, tarragon, salt, and pepper in large bowl. Mix well. Fold in feta cheese. *(Zucchini mixture can be prepared 3 hours ahead. Cover and refrigerate. Stir to combine before continuing.)* Fold walnuts into zucchini mixture.

PREHEAT oven to 300°F. Place rimmed baking sheet in oven. Pour enough oil into large nonstick skillet to coat bottom. Heat oil over medium-high heat. Working in batches, drop zucchini mixture into skillet by heaping tablespoonfuls; flatten slightly. Fry until pancakes are golden brown and cooked through, about 3 minutes per side. Transfer each batch of pancakes to baking sheet in oven to keep warm. Serve pancakes hot.

Zucchini with cilantro and cream

ZUCCHINI GETS AN UNEXPECTED TWIST with whipping cream and fresh cilantro in this simple dish. It is excellent as an accompaniment to poached or baked fish.

4 SERVINGS

- **2 tablespoons (¼ stick) butter**
- **2 garlic cloves, minced**
- **1¾ pounds zucchini, trimmed, cut into ⅓-inch-thick rounds**
- **4 tablespoons chopped fresh cilantro, divided**
- **⅓ cup whipping cream**

MELT butter in heavy large skillet over medium heat. Add garlic and sauté 10 seconds. Add zucchini and 2 tablespoons cilantro; sauté until zucchini is crisp-tender, about 5 minutes. Add cream and simmer until liquid thickens enough to coat zucchini, about 1 minute. Season to taste with salt and pepper; sprinkle with remaining 2 tablespoons cilantro. Transfer to bowl and serve.

Torta de calabacitas

CALABACITAS—A TRADITIONAL Mexican side dish made with zucchini, onions, and peppers—gets a new spin with this recipe. In this version the vegetables are layered with Monterey Jack cheese and tortillas to create a savory tart.

4 TO 6 SERVINGS

5 **tablespoons butter, divided**
1 **large onion, chopped**
2 **teaspoons ground cumin**
3 **large zucchini (about 1¼ pounds), trimmed, grated**
3 **garlic cloves, minced**
3 **tablespoons minced seeded jalapeno chiles**

3 **11-inch flour tortillas**
12 **ounces Monterey Jack cheese, grated**

MELT 3 tablespoons butter in heavy large skillet over medium heat. Add onion and cumin; sauté until tender, about 9 minutes. Add zucchini and garlic to skillet. Sauté until mixture is dry and zucchini is tender, about 14 minutes. Season to taste with salt. Add jalapeños and cook 2 minutes. Transfer to bowl and cool.

PLACE 1 tortilla on large oiled flat plate. Sprinkle ¼ of cheese evenly over. Spread ½ zucchini mixture over cheese. Sprinkle ¼ of cheese over. Top with second tortilla. Repeat layering of cheese and zucchini mixture. Top with last tortilla and press firmly to compact torta.

MELT 1 tablespoon butter in heavy 12-inch skillet over medium heat. Slide torta into skillet. Cover and cook until bottom is golden brown, about 4 minutes. Using spatula, slide torta onto plate. Melt remaining 1 tablespoon butter in skillet. Invert torta into skillet. Cook uncovered until bottom is golden brown, about 4 minutes. Transfer to platter. Let stand 5 minutes. Cut into wedges and serve.

Sautéed baby zucchini with squash blossoms and lemon basil

SQUASH BLOSSOMS—available at farmers' markets and some specialty foods stores—are extremely perishable; it's best to use them the day you buy them. Buy a small pot of lemon basil at a nursery if it's not available at the farmers' market. Fleur de sel is available at specialty foods stores and some supermarkets.

6 SERVINGS

3 **tablespoons butter, divided**
1 **pound baby zucchini, halved lengthwise, each half cut lengthwise into 3 wedges**
1½ **teaspoons chopped fresh lemon basil or regular basil**
Fleur de sel (fine French sea salt)
18 **zucchini squash blossoms**

MELT 1 tablespoon butter in heavy large nonstick skillet over medium heat. Add zucchini; sauté until crisp-tender, about 2 minutes. Stir in basil. Season with fleur de sel. Transfer to plate. Melt remaining 2 tablespoons butter in same skillet. Add squash blossoms and cook until barely wilted and still bright orange, about 2 seconds per side. Arrange atop zucchini and serve.

Red bell pepper and eggplant tian with anchovies

A *TIAN* IS A PROVENÇAL vegetable casserole, as well as the French word for the earthenware dish in which the casserole is baked. The recipe can include a variety of vegetables, herbs, and cheeses; this one is a delicious layering of eggplant, bell peppers, tomatoes, olives, and anchovies. It can be served hot or at room temperature, making it a good choice to go with roasted meats and fish or with sandwiches. If you are not an anchovy fan, leave them out—the tian will still be great.

8 SERVINGS

4 **large red bell peppers (about 2 pounds)**

9 **tablespoons olive oil, divided**
2 **1-pound eggplants, peeled, cut crosswise into ¼- to ½-inch-thick rounds**

3 **cups fresh breadcrumbs made from crustless French bread**

- **3 garlic cloves, minced**
- **3 tablespoons chopped fresh thyme, divided**
- **7 tablespoons coarsely chopped pitted Niçoise or Kalamata olives, divided**
- **6 large plum tomatoes, thinly sliced into rounds**
- **1 2-ounce can anchovy fillets, drained**

ROAST bell peppers directly over gas flame or in broiler until blackened on all sides. Enclose in paper bag and let stand 10 minutes. Peel and seed peppers; cut into scant ½-inch-wide strips. Place in bowl. *(Roasted peppers can be prepared 2 days ahead. Cover and refrigerate.)*

PREHEAT oven to 450°F. Brush each of 2 large rimmed baking sheets with 1 tablespoon oil. Arrange eggplant rounds in single layer on prepared sheets; sprinkle eggplant rounds on each sheet with 1 tablespoon oil. Bake until eggplant begins to soften but not brown, about 15 minutes. Remove from oven; maintain oven temperature.

HEAT 1 tablespoon oil in heavy large skillet over medium heat. Add breadcrumbs and sauté until golden, about 6 minutes. Remove skillet from heat.

ARRANGE half of eggplant rounds in single layer in 12x9x2-inch (9- to 10-cup capacity) oval baking dish. Sprinkle eggplant with half of minced garlic, 1 tablespoon thyme, and 3 tablespoons olives. Top with half each of sliced tomatoes, anchovy fillets, and roasted peppers, spacing evenly. Sprinkle lightly with salt and generously with ground black pepper. Drizzle with 2 tablespoons oil. Repeat layering with remaining eggplant, garlic, 1 tablespoon thyme, and 3 tablespoons olives. Top with remaining sliced tomatoes, spacing evenly and leaving 1½-inch-wide space around edge of baking dish. Arrange remaining roasted peppers and anchovies between tomato slices. Drizzle with remaining 2 tablespoons oil. Sprinkle with remaining 1 tablespoon olives.

BAKE assembled tian 30 minutes. Sprinkle toasted breadcrumbs and remaining 1 tablespoon thyme around edge of baking dish. Continue to bake until vegetables are very tender, about 15 minutes longer. Let tian stand 15 minutes. Serve hot or at room temperature.

Spicy roasted eggplant with tomatoes and cilantro

THIS TRADITIONAL INDIAN DISH, called *baingan bharta,* is scented with many of the spices—ginger, paprika, cumin, coriander, and cayenne pepper—that are the hallmarks of Indian cuisine. Serve it with rice to accompany grilled or roasted meats.

6 SERVINGS

- **2 medium eggplants (2¼ to 2½ pounds total), halved lengthwise**
- **⅓ cup vegetable oil**
- **2 large onions, coarsely chopped**
- **3 tablespoons finely chopped peeled fresh ginger**
- **1 pound tomatoes, coarsely chopped**
- **2 teaspoons ground cumin**
- **1½ teaspoons Hungarian sweet paprika**
- **1 teaspoon ground coriander**
- **½ teaspoon cayenne pepper**
- **⅓ cup chopped fresh cilantro**

PREHEAT oven to 350°F. Oil large rimmed baking sheet. Place eggplant halves, cut side down, on prepared sheet. Roast eggplant until very soft, about 1 hour. Cool slightly. Using spoon, scoop pulp from eggplant halves into medium bowl and mash. Discard skins.

HEAT oil in heavy large skillet over medium-high heat. Add onions and sauté until golden brown, about 8 minutes. Add ginger and stir 1 minute. Add tomatoes and next 4 ingredients; sauté 5 minutes to blend flavors. Add eggplant and cook until slightly thickened, stirring occasionally, about 5 minutes. Remove from heat. Stir in cilantro. Season eggplant mixture to taste with salt and pepper. *(Can be made 2 days ahead. Cool, then cover and refrigerate. Spoon off any accumulated liquids and rewarm before serving.)*

Grilled eggplant with curried yogurt-mint sauce

THE SAUCE is a zesty twist on *raita,* the cooling yogurt condiment that often is served with spicy foods in Indian cooking. The sauce can be made a day ahead of time and the eggplant can be served warm or at room temperature, so this makes a convenient dish for entertaining. Crush the coriander seeds in a plastic bag—this helps contain the seeds and simplifies clean-up.

6 SERVINGS

- **1 cup plain whole milk yogurt**
- **3 tablespoons chopped fresh mint**
- **2 tablespoons fresh lemon juice**
- **1 teaspoon curry powder**
- **1 teaspoon dried crushed red pepper**

- **2 eggplants (each about 1 pound), cut crosswise into 1-inch-thick rounds**
- **¼ cup Asian sesame oil**
- **2 tablespoons coriander seeds, coarsely crushed**

MIX first 5 ingredients in medium bowl; season sauce to taste with salt and pepper. *(Sauce can be made 1 day ahead. Cover and refrigerate.)*

PREPARE barbecue (medium-high heat). Brush eggplant rounds on both sides with sesame oil. Sprinkle with coriander, salt, and pepper. Grill eggplant until tender and slightly charred, about 6 minutes per side.

ARRANGE eggplant rounds on platter. Serve with yogurt-mint sauce.

Lemon-glazed brussels sprouts

BRUSSELS SPROUTS are a classic fall and winter vegetable. They resemble miniature heads of cabbage, and are indeed a member of the cabbage family. They'll keep for up to three days, but don't wash them until just before you plan to use them.

6 SERVINGS

- **2 pounds medium brussels sprouts, trimmed**
- **¾ cup water**
- **¼ cup (½ stick) butter**
- **2 tablespoons olive oil**
- **2 tablespoons fresh lemon juice**
- **2 teaspoons grated lemon peel**

COMBINE first 4 ingredients in large pot. Bring to boil over high heat. Reduce heat to medium, cover, and cook until brussels sprouts are crisp-tender, stirring occasionally, about 10 minutes. Stir in lemon juice. Cook uncovered until sauce is reduced to glaze, stirring occasionally, about 1 minute. Season to taste with salt and pepper. Transfer brussels sprouts to bowl. Sprinkle with grated lemon peel and serve.

Brussels sprouts with garlic, pecans, and basil

THE BRUSSELS SPROUTS are cooked in whipping cream and garlic until the cream is almost absorbed, taking the edge off the vegetable's strong taste and creating a rich texture. Basil and lemon peel provide fresh flavor and toasted pecans add crunch.

6 TO 8 SERVINGS

- **1½ pounds small brussels sprouts, trimmed**
- **¾ cup whipping cream**
- **5 garlic cloves, chopped**

3/4 cup pecans, toasted
3/4 cup (packed) fresh basil leaves
1 1/2 teaspoons grated lemon peel

Fresh basil sprigs (optional)
Lemon wedges (optional)

COMBINE brussels sprouts, cream, and garlic in heavy large skillet. Bring to boil over medium-low heat. Cover skillet tightly and cook until brussels sprouts are crisp-tender but still bright green and almost all cream is absorbed, stirring occasionally, about 10 minutes.

MEANWHILE, finely grind pecans with basil leaves and lemon peel in processor.

ADD pecan mixture to skillet. Toss until brussels sprouts are coated. Season to taste with salt and pepper. Transfer brussels sprouts to serving bowl. Garnish with basil sprigs and lemon wedges, if desired, and serve.

Brussels sprouts and chestnuts with blue cheese

THIS RICH SIDE DISH would be perfect for an elegant fall or holiday dinner party. Smaller brussels sprouts are especially pretty here. Steamed chestnuts can be found at specialty foods stores and some supermarkets.

6 SERVINGS

2 tablespoons olive oil
2 large shallots, halved, sliced
1 pound brussels sprouts, trimmed, halved through stem end
1 7.25- to 7.4-ounce jar steamed chestnuts
1 cup low-salt chicken broth
1/3 cup whipping cream
3 tablespoons chopped fresh chives
1/2 cup crumbled blue cheese

HEAT oil in large nonstick skillet over medium-high heat. Add shallots and sauté 1 minute. Add brussels sprouts and chestnuts. Sprinkle with salt and pepper and sauté 1 minute. Add broth and bring to boil. Reduce heat, cover, and simmer until brussels sprouts are almost tender, about 5 minutes. Uncover and boil until almost all liquid evaporates, about 4 minutes. Add cream and boil until brussels sprouts and chestnuts are coated with cream, stirring frequently, about 3 minutes. Mix in chives. Season to taste with salt and generous amount of pepper. Transfer to bowl. Sprinkle with cheese and serve.

Roasted brussels sprouts and cauliflower with orange

FOR ADDED EASE, you can use frozen brussels sprouts in this festive dish. You'll just need to thaw them and pat them dry before roasting them.

8 SERVINGS

1 large head of cauliflower (about 2 pounds), cut into 1-inch florets
1 pound fresh brussels sprouts, or frozen thawed and patted dry, halved if large
1/4 cup olive oil
1/4 cup minced shallot (about 1 large)
2 garlic cloves, minced
1 tablespoon grated orange peel

1/2 cup fresh orange juice
1/3 cup chopped fresh Italian parsley
Orange slices (for garnish)
Additional chopped fresh Italian parsley (for garnish)

COMBINE first 6 ingredients in large bowl; toss to coat. *(Can be prepared 2 hours ahead. Let stand at room temperature.)*

PREHEAT oven to 450°F. Spread vegetables on large rimmed baking sheet. Sprinkle with salt and pepper. Roast until lightly browned and almost tender, stirring once, about 12 minutes. Pour orange juice over. Roast until vegetables are tender and juices evaporate, about 8 minutes longer. Stir in ⅓ cup parsley. Transfer to serving dish. Garnish with orange slices and additional parsley and serve.

Turnips, brussels sprouts, and beets with hazelnuts

FOR CONVENIENCE, the vegetables can be cooked a day ahead and reheated. You can use regular beets instead of the golden beets called for here, but they should be sautéed separately and combined with the other vegetables just before serving, or they will turn everything red.

8 TO 10 SERVINGS

- **4 medium-size golden beets, tops trimmed**
- **1½ pounds brussels sprouts, trimmed, halved through stem end**
- **1¼ pounds turnips, peeled, each cut into 8 wedges**
- **6 tablespoons (¾ stick) unsalted butter**
- **⅓ cup minced shallots**
- **⅓ cup finely chopped hazelnuts**
- **3 tablespoons chopped fresh thyme**
- **3 large garlic cloves, minced**

PREHEAT oven to 375°F. Wrap beets in aluminum foil and bake until center is tender when pierced with knife, about 1 hour 45 minutes. Cool. Peel; cut each beet into 8 wedges.

COOK brussels sprouts in pot of boiling salted water until crisp-tender, about 6 minutes. Using large slotted spoon, transfer brussels sprouts to bowl of ice water to cool. Drain. Add turnips to pot; boil until crisp-tender, about 7 minutes. Drain. Transfer to bowl of ice water to cool. Drain. *(Beets, brussels sprouts, and turnips can be prepared 1 day ahead. Cover separately and refrigerate.)*

MELT butter in heavy large deep skillet over medium-high heat. Add shallots and hazelnuts; sauté until nuts begin to brown, about 3 minutes. Add thyme and garlic; sauté until nuts are golden, about 2 minutes. Add all vegetables; cover and cook until heated through, stirring occasionally, about 5 minutes. Season to taste with salt and pepper. Transfer to bowl and serve.

Herbed turnips dauphinois

THE TERM *DAUPHINOIS* is often used for a potato gratin made with cream and sometimes cheese. Here it is turnips that are baked with cream, chives, and spices—a pleasantly old-fashioned, comforting dish.

4 SERVINGS

- **1 large garlic clove**
- **1 pound young turnips, peeled, thinly sliced**
- **2 tablespoons all purpose flour**
- **¼ cup chopped fresh chives**
- **1¼ cups whipping cream**
- **½ teaspoon (or more) salt**
- **½ teaspoon ground black pepper**
- **¼ teaspoon grated nutmeg**

PREHEAT oven to 350°F. Rub 11x7-inch glass or ceramic baking dish with garlic. Butter dish generously. Add ⅓ of turnips. Sprinkle with 1 tablespoon flour, then ⅓ of chives. Add ⅓ of turnips, and sprinkle with 1 tablespoon flour and ⅓ of chives. Top with remaining turnips and sprinkle with remaining chives. Bring cream, ½ teaspoon salt, pepper, and nutmeg to simmer in small saucepan. Taste cream mixture, adding more salt if desired. Pour mixture over turnips. Cover with aluminum foil and bake 30 minutes. Remove foil and continue baking until turnips are tender, top browns, and cream thickens, about 20 minutes. Serve immediately.

Sautéed Jerusalem artichokes with sage

ALSO CALLED A SUNCHOKE, the Jerusalem artichoke is not really an artichoke at all—it's a small lumpy, brown-skinned tuber that resembles gingerroot and grows from a sunflower. The name is not a reference to the city of Jerusalem, but comes from the Italian word for sunflower, *girasole*. Butter, lemon juice, and sage flavor the vegetable simply and elegantly.

6 SERVINGS

3 pounds Jerusalem artichokes, peeled

¼ cup (½ stick) butter
4½ tablespoons chopped fresh sage or 2 teaspoons dried rubbed sage
1 lemon, halved

STEAM Jerusalem artichokes until tender, about 20 minutes. Cool slightly. Cut into ¼-inch-thick slices. *(Artichokes can be prepared 4 hours ahead. Cover and refrigerate.)*

MELT butter in heavy large skillet over medium-high heat. Add sage and sauté 1 minute. Add artichoke slices and sauté until heated through, about 5 minutes. Squeeze juice from lemon halves over and toss to coat. Season artichokes to taste with salt and pepper. Transfer to bowl and serve.

Peas with celery root

CELERY ROOT, also known as celeriac, is a brown, knobby root vegetable that tastes like a cross between celery and parsley. Here it lends distinction and crunch to sweet peas, which make a nice accompaniment to roast beef or grilled steak.

6 TO 8 SERVINGS

1 1¼-pound celery root (celeriac), peeled, cut into ½-inch cubes

¼ cup (½ stick) butter
1 shallot, chopped
1 16-ounce package frozen petite peas, thawed
1 teaspoon celery salt

BOIL celery root in large pot of boiling salted water until just tender, about 5 minutes. Drain.

MELT butter in heavy large pot over medium heat. Add shallot and sauté until just tender, about 3 minutes. Add celery root, peas, and celery salt; sauté until vegetables are heated through, about 8 minutes. Season to taste with salt and pepper. Transfer to bowl and serve.

Peas with caraway seeds, pepper, and Parmesan butter

THIS INVENTIVE SIDE DISH is a fine addition to any special-occasion meal. The assertive combination of Parmesan cheese, black pepper, lemon peel, and caraway seeds makes a sensational contrast to the sweet and delicate peas.

8 TO 10 SERVINGS

7 tablespoons freshly grated Parmesan cheese (about 1½ ounces)
6 tablespoons (¾ stick) butter, room temperature, divided
1 teaspoon caraway seeds
¾ teaspoon grated lemon peel
½ teaspoon freshly cracked black pepper

¾ cup chopped shallots (about 3 large)
3 10-ounce packages frozen petite peas, thawed
⅓ cup low-salt beef broth or water
⅓ cup chopped fresh Italian parsley

MIX Parmesan cheese, 4 tablespoons butter, caraway seeds, lemon peel, and pepper in small bowl to blend. *(Parmesan butter can be prepared 3 days ahead. Cover and refrigerate.)*

MELT remaining 2 tablespoons butter in heavy large skillet over medium-high heat. Add shallots and sauté until tender, about 3 minutes. Add peas, broth, and parsley. Simmer until peas are heated through, stirring frequently, about 8 minutes. Add Parmesan butter. Stir until butter melts. Season peas to taste with salt. Transfer to bowl and serve.

Spring peas with lettuce and mint

KITCHEN GARDENERS and apartment dwellers will find good use for that homegrown mint on the windowsill in this light side dish.

4 SERVINGS

- **½ cup low-salt chicken broth**
- **1 10-ounce package frozen peas, thawed**
- **1 cup thinly sliced romaine lettuce**
- **3 tablespoons chopped fresh mint**

BRING broth to boil in medium saucepan. Add peas and simmer until heated through, about 4 minutes. Stir in lettuce and mint. Season to taste with salt and pepper.

Sautéed radishes and sugar snap peas with dill

THIS SIDE DISH would pair beautifully with roast lamb or salmon. To remove strings from fresh peas, just snap off the stem end and pull the string lengthwise down each pod. To make this dish even faster, buy sugar snap peas with the strings already removed; they're sold in 8-ounce packages at some supermarkets.

6 SERVINGS

- **1 tablespoon butter**
- **1 tablespoon olive oil**
- **½ cup thinly sliced shallots**
- **12 ounces sugar snap peas, trimmed, strings removed**
- **2 cups thinly sliced radishes (about 1 large bunch)**
- **¼ cup orange juice**
- **1 teaspoon dill seeds**
- **1 tablespoon chopped fresh dill**

MELT butter with oil in large nonstick skillet over medium heat. Add shallots and sauté until golden, about 5 minutes. Add sugar snap peas and radishes; sauté until crisp-tender, about 5 minutes. Add orange juice and dill seeds; stir 1 minute. Season to taste with salt and pepper. Stir in chopped dill. Transfer to bowl and serve.

Carrot and parsnip puree

THIS CREAMY ROOT-VEGETABLE PUREE has a pleasant nutty taste that makes it an excellent side dish for any number of roasted meats. It is particularly nice at holiday time with turkey, pork, or beef.

8 SERVINGS

- **1½ pounds carrots, peeled, cut into ½-inch cubes**
- **2 pounds parsnips, peeled, cut into ½-inch cubes**
- **8 tablespoons (1 stick) butter, cut into pieces, room temperature**
- **Ground nutmeg**

BRING large pot of salted water to boil. Add carrots, partially cover pot, and simmer carrots 5 minutes. Add parsnips, partially cover, and simmer until vegetables are very tender, about 15 minutes. Drain well. Return vegetables to same pot. Toss over medium heat until any excess moisture evaporates. Transfer vegetables to processor. Add butter and process to smooth puree. Season to taste with nutmeg, salt, and pepper. *(Puree can be made 4 hours ahead. Rewarm in medium saucepan over low heat, stirring often.)* Transfer puree to bowl and serve.

Maple- and tangerine-glazed carrots

TANGERINE JUICE, maple syrup, and lemon juice are boiled with butter until the mixture is reduced to a rich sauce. The carrots are steamed until crisp-tender, then are added to the sauce with a pinch of cayenne pepper—which gives the dish a little bite and curbs the sweetness of the glaze. This is delicious yet simple to prepare.

8 SERVINGS

- **1¼ cups fresh tangerine juice**
- **3 tablespoons pure maple syrup**
- **2 tablespoons (¼ stick) butter**
- **1 teaspoon fresh lemon juice**
- **½ teaspoon grated tangerine peel**
- **2½ pounds large carrots (about 12), peeled, cut on diagonal into ½-inch-thick ovals (about 6 cups)**
- **Pinch of cayenne pepper**
- **½ large tangerine, seeded**
- **Chopped fresh parsley**

COMBINE first 5 ingredients in heavy large skillet over medium-high heat. Boil until sauce coats spoon thickly and is reduced to ⅔ cup, whisking occasionally, about 8 minutes. Set aside.

STEAM carrots until just crisp-tender, about 7 minutes. Mix carrots and cayenne pepper into sauce. *(Can be prepared 1 day ahead. Cover and chill.)*

SIMMER carrots uncovered in sauce over medium heat until heated through and coated thickly with glaze, stirring occasionally, about 5 minutes. Season to taste with salt and pepper. Transfer to bowl. Squeeze juice from tangerine half over. Sprinkle with chopped parsley and serve.

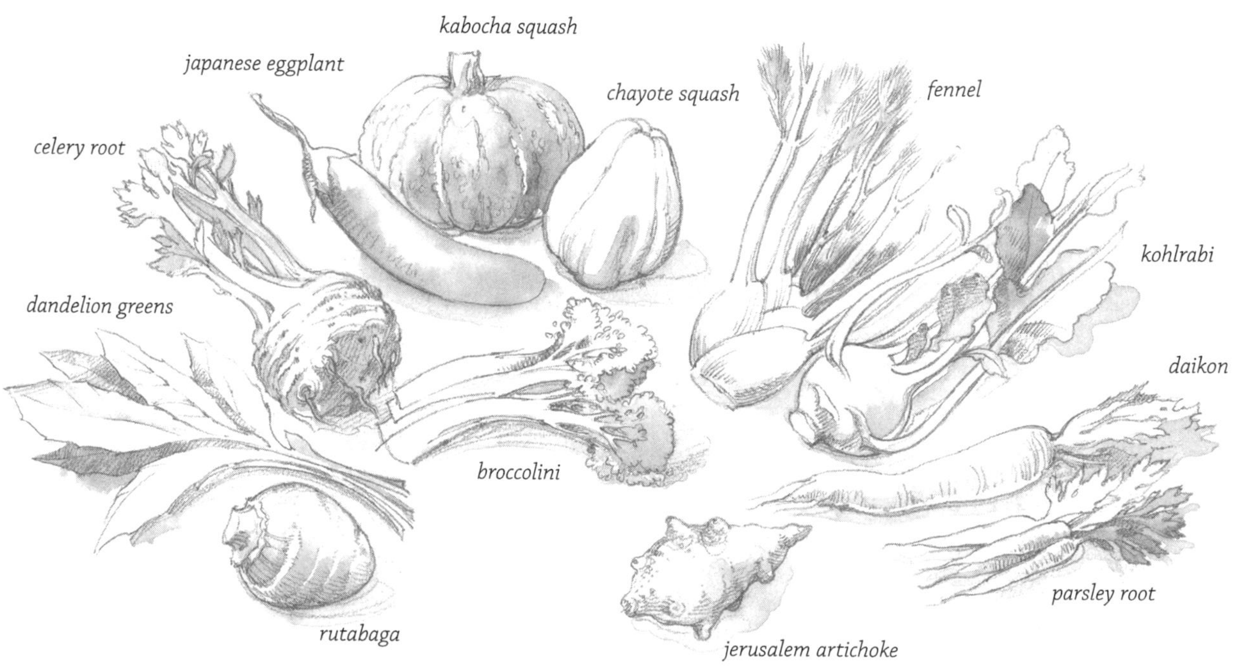

Carrots with cumin and orange

ORANGE IS A CLASSIC PARTNER with carrots, but the addition of cumin and fennel seeds, cloves, garlic, and coriander makes this a truly standout side dish. If you are storing carrots in the refrigerator's vegetable bin, be sure to keep them away from apples, which emit a gas that gives carrots a bitter taste.

4 SERVINGS

2 teaspoons cumin seeds
1 teaspoon fennel seeds
3 whole cloves

3 tablespoons olive oil
1½ pounds medium carrots, peeled, cut diagonally into ⅓-inch-thick ovals
1 cup fresh orange juice
3 garlic cloves, minced
1 tablespoon grated orange peel
1 teaspoon ground coriander

COMBINE cumin seeds, fennel seeds, and cloves in small resealable plastic bag. Using mallet, crush spices finely.

HEAT oil in heavy large skillet over medium-high heat. Add crushed spices, carrots, orange juice, garlic, orange peel, and coriander. Bring to simmer. Reduce heat to medium, cover, and simmer until carrots are crisp-tender, about 5 minutes. Uncover. Increase heat to medium-high and cook until sauce thickens enough to coat carrots, about 5 minutes. Season carrots to taste with salt and pepper. Transfer carrots to bowl and serve.

Carrots and rutabagas with lemon and honey

SWEET CARROTS and earthy rutabagas are refreshed with lemon juice and grated lemon peel. The rutabaga is thought to be a cross between a cabbage and turnip, and in fact looks like a very large turnip; it's slightly sweet when cooked. Buy vegetables that are firm and smooth and refrigerate them in a plastic bag up to two weeks.

6 TO 8 SERVINGS

1¼ pounds rutabagas, peeled, cut into matchstick-size strips
1 pound carrots, peeled, cut into matchstick-size strips

¼ cup (½ stick) butter
¼ cup fresh lemon juice
3 tablespoons honey
1 teaspoon grated lemon peel
½ cup chopped fresh chives

COOK rutabagas in large pot of boiling salted water 2 minutes. Add carrots and continue cooking until vegetables are tender, about 6 minutes. Drain.

MELT butter in large pot over medium-high heat. Add lemon juice, honey, and lemon peel. Bring to boil. Add vegetables and cook until glazed, stirring occasionally, about 6 minutes. Season to taste with salt and pepper. Remove from heat. Mix in chives.

Curried carrots with cilantro

THESE COLORFUL and delicious carrots are both sweet and spicy, thanks to curry and apricot preserves.

4 SERVINGS

- **3 tablespoons butter**
- **1 teaspoon minced peeled fresh ginger**
- **1 garlic clove, minced**
- **3/4 teaspoon curry powder**
- **1/4 cup low-salt chicken broth**
- **2 tablespoons apricot preserves**
- **1 pound carrots, peeled, cut on diagonal into 1/4-inch-thick slices (about 3 cups)**
- **3 tablespoons chopped fresh cilantro**

MELT butter in heavy large skillet over medium heat. Add ginger, garlic, and curry powder; sauté 30 seconds. Stir in broth and preserves, then carrots. Cover and simmer until carrots are crisp-tender and sauce is thick enough to coat, about 6 minutes. Season to taste with salt and pepper. Mix in cilantro. Transfer to bowl and serve.

Carrots glazed with balsamic vinegar and butter

FOR EASE, use the peeled baby carrots sold in plastic bags in the produce section of most supermarkets.

10 SERVINGS

- **1/2 cup (1 stick) butter**
- **3 1/2 pounds peeled baby carrots; or regular carrots, peeled, cut into 2-inch pieces, halved lengthwise**
- **6 tablespoons sugar**
- **1/3 cup balsamic vinegar**
- **1/4 cup chopped fresh chives**

MELT butter in heavy large pot over medium heat. Add carrots and sauté 5 minutes. Cover and cook until carrots are crisp-tender, stirring occasionally, about 7 minutes. Stir in sugar and vinegar. Cook uncovered until carrots are tender and sauce is reduced to glaze, stirring frequently, about 12 minutes longer. Season to taste with salt and pepper. Add chives and toss to combine. Transfer to bowl and serve.

Julienne of sesame carrots and celery root

USE A V-SLICER or mandoline (inexpensive versions are widely available at cookware shops) to julienne the carrots and celery root quickly and easily.

8 SERVINGS

- **2 tablespoons (1/4 stick) butter**
- **1 pound celery root (celeriac), peeled, cut into matchstick-size strips**
- **1 pound carrots, peeled, cut into matchstick-size strips**
- **1 tablespoon black sesame seeds**
- **1 tablespoon white sesame seeds, toasted**
- **1 tablespoon Asian sesame oil**
- **1 tablespoon fresh lemon juice**
- **1/2 teaspoon salt**

COOK butter in heavy large deep skillet over medium heat until golden brown, about 2 minutes. Add celery root and carrots; toss to coat with butter. Reduce heat to medium-low and sauté until carrots and celery root are crisp-tender, stirring occasionally, about 10 minutes. Add all sesame seeds, sesame oil, lemon juice, and ½ teaspoon salt; toss to coat. Sauté 2 minutes longer to blend flavors. Transfer to bowl and serve.

Carrots with spiced pomegranate glaze

BUY CARROTS with the leafy tops still attached. Look for maroon, white, yellow, and red carrots at farmers' markets and include as many colors as you like; or use regular carrots and thin parsnips in whatever proportions you like. Pomegranate molasses, a thick syrup, is available at some supermarkets and Middle Eastern markets, and at online specialty foods shops.

16 SERVINGS

- **1 cup pomegranate molasses**
- **¼ cup (or more) water**
- **¼ cup olive oil**
- **¼ cup (½ stick) butter, melted**
- **¼ cup finely grated peeled fresh ginger**
- **1 teaspoon ground cumin**
- **½ teaspoon ground cardamom**
- **¼ teaspoon ground nutmeg**
- **¼ teaspoon cayenne pepper**
- **4½ pounds medium carrots, peeled, tops trimmed to ½ inch**

- **¾ cup pomegranate seeds**
- **¾ cup pine nuts, toasted**
- **¼ cup thinly sliced fresh basil leaves**
- **¼ cup thinly sliced fresh mint leaves**

PREHEAT oven to 375°F. Whisk pomegranate molasses, ¼ cup water, and next 7 ingredients in large bowl to blend. Add carrots and toss to coat. Divide carrots between 2 large rimmed baking sheets. Roast until carrots are tender and liquids are reduced to glaze, stirring twice and mixing in additional water by tablespoonfuls if needed to prevent burning, about 55 minutes. Season to taste with salt and pepper. *(Can be prepared 4 hours ahead. Let stand at room temperature. Rewarm in 375°F oven 10 minutes before serving.)*

TRANSFER carrots to platter. Sprinkle pomegranate seeds, pine nuts, basil, and mint over and serve.

Braised red cabbage and apples

TART GREEN APPLES, red cabbage, and onion are accented with apple cider, vinegar, and brown sugar. Serve this easy side dish with corned beef, ham, sausages, or Swedish meatballs.

2 SERVINGS; CAN BE DOUBLED

- **1 tablespoon vegetable oil**
- **⅓ cup chopped onion**
- **3 cups (packed) thinly shredded red cabbage**
- **¾ cup chopped peeled tart green apple (such as Granny Smith; from 1 large)**
- **6 tablespoons apple cider or apple juice**
- **2 tablespoons red wine vinegar**
- **1½ tablespoons (packed) dark brown sugar**

HEAT oil in heavy medium skillet over medium heat. Add onion and sauté until beginning to soften, about 3 minutes. Add cabbage and apple; stir 2 minutes. Add apple cider, vinegar, and sugar. Reduce heat to medium-low, cover, and cook until cabbage is tender, stirring occasionally, about 20 minutes. Season cabbage to taste with salt and pepper. *(Can be prepared 1 day ahead. Cover and refrigerate. Rewarm before serving.)*

Red cabbage with apricots and balsamic vinegar

THIS DISH MARRIES THE FLAVORS of dried apricots and apricot preserves with red cabbage—then rounds them out with balsamic vinegar, allspice, and nutmeg. This is a spectacular sweet-tart accompaniment for roast pork or the holiday turkey.

6 SERVINGS

- **6 tablespoons (¾ stick) butter**
- **1 8-ounce red onion, thinly sliced**
- **½ teaspoon ground allspice**
- **¼ teaspoon ground nutmeg**

- **1 1½-pound red cabbage, quartered, cored, very thinly sliced**
- **¾ cup thinly sliced dried apricots**
- **¼ cup apricot preserves**
- **¼ cup balsamic vinegar**

MELT butter in heavy large pot over medium-high heat. Add onion, allspice, and nutmeg; toss 1 minute. Add cabbage and apricots; sauté until well coated, about 2 minutes. Add apricot preserves and vinegar; toss until juices are reduced to glaze and cabbage is crisp-tender, about 6 minutes. Season to taste with salt and pepper. *(Can be prepared 1 day ahead. Cover and refrigerate. Rewarm over medium heat before serving.)*

Baked fennel with goat cheese and sausage

RICH, CREAMY, AND DELICIOUS, this stellar side dish is excellent with roast veal or pork. When buying fennel, select clean and crisp bulbs; at home, wrap the fennel in plastic and refrigerate it up to a week. Licorice lovers will appreciate the flavor of raw fennel; cooked fennel is more delicate. Crushing the fennel seeds in a plastic bag will help contain the seeds and simplify clean-up.

6 SERVINGS

- **½ pound sweet Italian sausages, cut into 1-inch pieces**
- **1½ pounds fresh fennel bulbs (about 2 medium), trimmed, cut vertically into ¼-inch-thick slices**
- **1 teaspoon fresh lemon juice**
- **2 tablespoons (¼ stick) butter, divided**
- **1 tablespoon olive oil**
- **¼ teaspoon fennel seeds, crushed**
- **½ cup water**
- **2 tablespoons all purpose flour**
- **1½ cups whole milk**
- **Freshly grated nutmeg**
- **¼ teaspoon minced fresh tarragon or ⅛ teaspoon dried**
- **4 ounces soft fresh goat cheese**
- **3 tablespoons freshly grated Parmesan cheese (scant 1 ounce)**

SAUTÉ sausage in heavy large skillet over medium heat until just cooked through and golden brown, turning often. Using tongs, transfer sausage to paper towels to drain. Reserve skillet.

TOSS fennel with lemon juice in large bowl. Melt 1 tablespoon butter with oil in same skillet over medium heat. Add fennel and fennel seeds; sauté until fennel is translucent, about 3 minutes. Add ½ cup water. Cover and simmer until fennel is just tender, about 15 minutes. Using slotted spoon, transfer fennel to large bowl; reserve cooking liquid in skillet.

MELT remaining 1 tablespoon butter in heavy medium saucepan over medium heat. Add flour and stir 2 minutes (do not brown). Remove pan from heat. Gradually whisk in milk and reserved fennel cooking liquid. Return to medium heat and whisk until sauce thickens and boils, about 5 minutes. Season sauce to taste with nutmeg, salt, and pepper. Mix in tarragon. Stir sauce into fennel. Transfer mixture to shallow 6-cup glass or ceramic baking dish. Top with sausage and dollops of goat cheese. Sprinkle Parmesan over. *(Can be prepared 8 hours ahead. Cover and refrigerate. Bring to room temperature before continuing.)*

PREHEAT oven to 375°F. Bake until fennel is very tender and heated through, and top is brown, about 20 minutes.

Corn and winter squash with spinach and bacon

THIS HEARTY COMBINATION is a snap to prepare. Basil is stirred in at the last minute for a spark of summer.

10 TO 12 SERVINGS

- **9 bacon slices, chopped**
- **1 2½-pound butternut squash, peeled, seeded, cut into ⅓-inch cubes**
- **2 cups chopped onions**
- **1 16-ounce package frozen corn kernels, thawed**
- **1⅓ 6-ounce packages fresh baby spinach leaves**
- **6 tablespoons chopped fresh basil**

SAUTÉ bacon in large pot over medium heat until crisp, about 10 minutes. Add squash and onions. Sauté until squash is just tender, about 12 minutes. Add corn and spinach. Toss until spinach wilts and corn is heated through, about 5 minutes. Stir in basil. Season vegetables to taste with salt and pepper. Transfer to bowl and serve.

Acorn squash rings with honey-soy glaze

THE BAKED SQUASH is made aromatic with a luscious glaze accented with ginger and garlic. The hard skin of acorn squash protects the sweet orange flesh and allows it to be stored longer than summer squash. Refrigeration is not necessary, and the squash can be kept in a cool dark place for a month.

4 SERVINGS

- **Nonstick vegetable oil spray**
- **2 1¼- to 1½-pound acorn squash**

- **3 tablespoons honey**
- **1 tablespoon reduced-sodium soy sauce**
- **2 teaspoons unseasoned rice vinegar**
- **1½ teaspoons minced peeled fresh ginger**
- **1 garlic clove, minced**

PREHEAT oven to 450°F. Line large rimmed baking sheet with aluminum foil. Spray foil with nonstick spray. Cut off both ends of each squash. Cut each squash crosswise into 4 rings. Scoop out and discard seeds. Place squash rings in single layer on prepared baking sheet. Cover baking sheet tightly with foil. Bake until squash begins to soften, about 15 minutes.

MEANWHILE, whisk honey and next 4 ingredients in small bowl to blend. Remove foil from squash. Brush half of honey mixture over squash. Sprinkle with salt and pepper. Bake uncovered 10 minutes. Brush remaining honey mixture over squash; continue to bake until squash is brown, tender, and thickly glazed, about 10 minutes longer.

Orange- and hoisin-glazed squash with sesame seeds

THE ASIAN FLAVORS of hoisin sauce, fresh ginger, and Chinese five-spice powder find an excellent base in the moist acorn squash. Hoisin sauce is available at Asian markets and in the Asian foods section of some supermarkets. Five-spice powder can be found in the spice section of most supermarkets.

12 SERVINGS

- **2 cups orange juice**
- **¾ cup hoisin sauce**
- **2 garlic cloves, minced**
- **½ teaspoon Chinese five-spice powder**
- **2 teaspoons minced peeled fresh ginger**

- **3 1½-pound acorn squash, each cut vertically into 8 wedges, seeded**
- **3 tablespoons Asian sesame oil**

- **1 cup chopped green onions (about 5)**
- **2½ teaspoons sesame seeds, toasted**

COMBINE first 4 ingredients in heavy medium saucepan. Boil over medium heat until reduced to

1⅓ cups, stirring occasionally, about 30 minutes. Pour glaze into bowl. Mix in ginger. Cool. *(Glaze can be made 1 day ahead. Cover and chill.)*

PREHEAT oven to 400°F. Place squash on baking sheet, skin side down. Brush squash on all sides with sesame oil. Turn squash 1 cut side down and bake 15 minutes. Turn squash skin side down. Brush squash with some of glaze. Bake until tender and well glazed, brushing occasionally with more glaze, about 50 minutes.

PREHEAT broiler. Generously brush squash with more glaze. Sprinkle with salt. Broil until glaze is bubbling, about 2 minutes. Brush with any remaining glaze. Transfer squash to platter. Sprinkle with green onions and sesame seeds and serve.

Butternut squash and orzo with fresh sage

PEELING BUTTERNUT SQUASH and other winter squash can be a little tricky, but if you follow these guidelines, it gets easier: Start by cutting off the stem and base with a chef's knife, then remove the peel with a sharp, good-quality vegetable peeler. Starting at the top, angle the vegetable peeler so that it cuts deeply enough to remove all of the tough exterior, and push the peeler down along the squash to remove the peel in long strips.

4 SERVINGS

- **3 tablespoons butter**
- **1 cup chopped onion**
- **1 garlic clove, minced**
- **1 2-pound butternut squash, peeled, halved, seeded, cut into ½-inch cubes (about 4 cups)**
- **4 cups low-salt chicken broth, divided**
- **½ cup dry white wine**
- **1 cup orzo (rice-shaped pasta; about 6½ ounces)**
- **½ cup freshly grated Parmesan cheese (about 1½ ounces)**

- **2 tablespoons chopped fresh sage**

MELT butter in heavy large skillet over medium heat. Add onion and sauté until softened, about 6 minutes. Add garlic and sauté until fragrant, about 1 minute. Add squash cubes and stir to coat. Add ½ cup chicken broth and wine. Cover and simmer until squash is just tender and liquid is absorbed, about 10 minutes (if necessary, uncover and simmer until excess liquid evaporates).

MEANWHILE, bring remaining 3½ cups broth to boil in heavy large saucepan. Add orzo. Boil uncovered until orzo is tender but still firm to bite, stirring occasionally, about 8 minutes. Drain orzo if necessary.

TRANSFER to large bowl. Stir in squash mixture, then Parmesan and sage. Season to taste with salt and pepper and serve.

Roasted butternut squash with brown butter and nutmeg

NUTMEG IS THE SIGNATURE FLAVOR in this dish, so if possible use freshly grated. Whole nutmeg is a hard, egg-shaped seed about an inch in diameter. When grated, it produces a warm spicy-sweet flavor that is much more delicate than the ground variety.

4 SERVINGS

- **Nonstick vegetable oil spray**
- **1 2-pound butternut squash, peeled, halved, seeded, cut into 1-inch cubes**
- **2 tablespoons olive oil**

- **3 tablespoons butter**
- **¼ teaspoon freshly grated whole nutmeg or ground nutmeg**
- **Additional nutmeg (for garnish)**

PREHEAT oven to 375°F. Spray large rimmed baking sheet with nonstick spray. Place squash on sheet. Drizzle with oil, sprinkle with salt and pepper, and toss to coat. Spread squash in single layer. Bake squash until brown and very tender, stirring occasionally, about 45 minutes. Transfer to bowl.

MELT butter in small saucepan over medium-low heat. Simmer until foam subsides and butter turns nut-brown, swirling pan occasionally, about 4 minutes. Pour brown butter over squash; add ¼ teaspoon nutmeg and stir lightly to coat. Season with salt. Sprinkle with additional nutmeg and serve.

Roasted vegetables with balsamic-lemon vinaigrette

WINTER VEGETABLES—beets, sweet potatoes, acorn squash, and brussels sprouts—are tossed with a tangy dressing to create a satisfying side dish that is a sensational complement to roast chicken or turkey.

10 SERVINGS

- **12 baby beets, trimmed, peeled**
- **2 pounds yams (red-skinned sweet potatoes; about 3 medium), peeled, cut into 1-inch cubes**
- **2 1¼- to 1½-pound acorn squash, unpeeled, quartered lengthwise, seeded, cut crosswise into ½-inch-thick slices**
- **1½ pounds brussels sprouts, trimmed, halved through stem end**
- **2 teaspoons chopped fresh rosemary or 1 teaspoon dried**
- **5 tablespoons, divided, plus 1 teaspoon extra-virgin olive oil**
- **1 whole head of garlic, top ½ inch cut off**

- **¼ cup balsamic vinegar**
- **2 teaspoons grated lemon peel**

PREHEAT oven to 450°F. Cook beets in medium saucepan of boiling salted water until almost tender, about 15 minutes. Drain. Transfer beets to large roasting pan. Add yams, squash, brussels sprouts, and rosemary to roasting pan. Drizzle vegetables with 2 tablespoons oil; sprinkle generously with salt and pepper. Toss to coat. Place garlic, cut side up, on piece of aluminum foil and drizzle with 1 teaspoon oil; enclose in foil. Place wrapped garlic in pan with vegetables. Roast vegetables until tender and brown in spots, turning occasionally, about 45 minutes.

UNWRAP garlic. Peel and chop garlic cloves. Transfer vegetables and garlic to large bowl. Whisk vinegar, lemon peel, and remaining 3 tablespoons oil in small bowl to blend. Season vinaigrette to taste with salt and pepper. *(Vegetables and vinaigrette can be made 8 hours ahead. Chill vegetables; let dressing stand at room temperature. Before continuing, rewarm vegetables in microwave.)* Pour vinaigrette over vegetables and toss to coat. Serve warm.

Pumpkin-cheese pancakes

IF FRESH PUMPKIN is unavailable, any winter squash will work nicely in this recipe, an innovative savory pancake accented with Jarlsberg cheese and green onions. Serve it alongside ham or chicken.

2 SERVINGS; CAN BE DOUBLED

- **3 tablespoons butter**
- **2 large green onions, thinly sliced**
- **2 cups coarsely grated peeled fresh pumpkin or other bright orange winter squash (such as kabocha)**
- **Freshly grated nutmeg or ground nutmeg**

- **2 large eggs**
- **6 tablespoons whole milk**
- **6 tablespoons all purpose flour**
- **¼ cup (packed) coarsely grated Jarlsberg or Parmesan cheese (about 1 ounce)**

- **Additional butter, room temperature**

MELT 3 tablespoons butter in heavy medium skillet over medium-low heat. Add green onions and stir 1 minute. Add pumpkin; sprinkle with salt, pepper, and nutmeg. Sauté until pumpkin is tender, about 6 minutes. Cool pumpkin mixture slightly.

BLEND eggs, milk, flour, and cheese in processor. Add pumpkin mixture. Using on/off turns, blend well.

HEAT heavy large skillet or griddle over medium-high heat. Brush with additional butter. Drop 2 tablespoonfuls batter for each pancake into skillet. Cook until pancakes are brown and set, about 1 minute per side. Transfer pancakes to plates. Spread with additional butter and sprinkle with additional nutmeg. Serve immediately.

Vegetable kebabs with saffron butter

A COLORFUL QUARTET OF VEGETABLES—zucchini, red bell pepper, red onion, and corn—is skewered and then brushed with the delicately scented butter. The kebabs are perfect with roasted chicken or fish.

6 SERVINGS

6 tablespoons (¾ stick) butter
¼ teaspoon saffron threads

3 medium zucchini, trimmed, each cut crosswise into 6 rounds
2 large red bell peppers, cut into ½-inch squares
½ red onion, cut into 1-inch pieces
2 ears of fresh corn, husked, each cut into 6 rounds
6 10-inch bamboo skewers, soaked in water 30 minutes, drained

MELT butter in heavy small skillet over medium heat. Stir in saffron. Cool 1 hour.

ALTERNATE 3 zucchini rounds, 3 red bell pepper squares, 3 red onion pieces, and 2 corn rounds on each skewer.

PREPARE barbecue (medium heat). Brush kebabs with all but 2 tablespoons saffron butter. Sprinkle with salt and pepper. Grill until vegetables are tender and brown, turning frequently, about 20 minutes. Brush with remaining saffron butter and serve.

Roasted root vegetables with green onions

A TOUCH OF MAPLE SYRUP sweetens this outstanding medley of vegetables, which is very simple to prepare. It is nice with roast veal, beef, or pork.

6 SERVINGS

¼ cup olive oil
2 tablespoons pure maple syrup
1 garlic clove, minced
4 large beets, peeled, quartered
2 Yukon Gold potatoes, quartered
2 carrots, peeled, cut diagonally into 2-inch-long pieces
2 parsnips, peeled, cut diagonally into 2-inch-long pieces
1 large tan-skinned sweet potato, peeled, cut into 1½-inch pieces
1 rutabaga, peeled, cut into 1½-inch pieces
1 large onion, peeled, quartered through root end
2 tablespoons (¼ stick) butter, melted
⅓ cup chopped green onions

PREHEAT oven to 350°F. Whisk oil, syrup, and garlic in small bowl to blend. Place all vegetables on heavy large rimmed baking sheet. Pour oil mixture over; toss to coat. Spread out vegetables in single layer. Sprinkle generously with salt and pepper. Roast until vegetables are tender and golden brown, stirring occasionally, about 1½ hours. Transfer vegetables to platter. Drizzle vegetables with melted butter. Sprinkle with chopped green onions and serve.

Parsnips with crispy prosciutto, peas, and mint

PARSNIPS ARE NOT GLAMOROUS vegetables, but they are delicious and versatile—you can whip them into a puree, add them to slow-cooking stews and braises, or quickly boil and then sauté them, as in this dish, which would be very nice with a chicken entrée.

6 TO 8 SERVINGS

- **2 tablespoons (¼ stick) butter, divided**
- **1 tablespoon olive oil**
- **2 large shallots, minced**
- **4 ounces thinly sliced prosciutto, finely chopped (about ½ cup)**
- **12 ounces parsnips, cut into ¼-inch pieces (about 2¼ cups)**
- **2 cups frozen petite peas, thawed**
- **¼ cup chopped fresh mint**

MELT 1 tablespoon butter with oil in small skillet over low heat. Add shallots and prosciutto; sauté until prosciutto is crisp, about 10 minutes. Remove from heat.

COOK parsnips in large saucepan of boiling salted water until crisp-tender, about 2 minutes. Add peas and bring to boil. Drain. Return peas and parsnips to saucepan. Stir in remaining 1 tablespoon butter, mint, and prosciutto mixture. Season to taste with salt and pepper. Transfer to bowl and serve.

Maple-glazed parsnips with popped mustard seeds

THE NATURAL SWEETNESS of parsnips is complemented by the maple glaze and accented by tangy mustard flavors in this recipe. It would be great with roast pork.

6 SERVINGS

- **2 pounds parsnips, peeled, quartered lengthwise, cut into 2-inch lengths**
- **4 tablespoons (½ stick) butter, divided**
- **¼ cup yellow mustard seeds**
- **3 tablespoons pure maple syrup**
- **2 tablespoons Dijon mustard**

STEAM parsnips over medium heat until tender, about 10 minutes. Transfer to paper towels to drain.

MELT 1 tablespoon butter in small skillet over low heat. Add mustard seeds; cover and cook until seeds begin to pop, about 2 minutes. Remove from heat. Let stand until popping stops, about 8 minutes.

MELT remaining 3 tablespoons butter in large nonstick skillet over medium heat. Stir in maple syrup and Dijon mustard. Add parsnips and toss to coat. Sauté until parsnips are glazed, about 8 minutes. Add mustard seeds and toss to coat. Season to taste with salt and pepper. Transfer to platter and serve.

Parsnips and celery root with nutmeg

THIS SIMPLE BUT SATISFYING DISH can be made ahead and just reheated before serving. Keep peeled uncooked parsnips and celery root in cool water to prevent the flesh from darkening.

8 SERVINGS

- **4 tablespoons (½ stick) butter**
- **1 cup chopped onion**
- **2 pounds parsnips, peeled, cut into ½-inch cubes**
- **1¼ pounds celery root (celeriac), trimmed, peeled, cut into ½-inch cubes (about 2 cups)**
- **1¼ cups low-salt chicken broth**
- **½ cup whipping cream**
- **½ teaspoon ground nutmeg**
- **½ cup minced fresh celery leaves**

MELT butter in heavy large skillet over medium-high heat. Add onion and sauté until almost tender, about 4 minutes (do not brown). Add parsnips and celery root; stir to combine. Add broth, whipping cream, and nutmeg; bring to boil. Reduce heat to medium, cover tightly, and simmer until parsnips and celery root are tender and liquid is almost absorbed, stirring occasionally and adding water by tablespoonfuls if mixture is dry, about 10 minutes. Season to taste with salt and pepper. *(Can be prepared 1 day ahead. Cool slightly. Cover and chill. Rewarm vegetables over low heat, stirring often, until heated through before continuing.)* Stir in celery leaves. Transfer to bowl and serve.

Grilled parsnips

THIS QUICK DISH can go with a wide variety of main courses—even a Thanksgiving turkey.

12 SERVINGS

- **3 pounds medium parsnips, peeled, halved lengthwise**

- **⅓ cup olive oil**
- **2 teaspoons chopped fresh thyme**
- **1 teaspoon paprika**

COOK parsnips in large pot of boiling salted water until almost tender, about 5 minutes. Drain and cool. *(Can be prepared 1 day ahead. Cover and refrigerate.)*

WHISK oil, thyme, and paprika to blend in large bowl. Add parsnips and toss to coat.

PREPARE barbecue (medium-high heat). Place parsnips on grill rack; sprinkle with salt and pepper. Grill until cooked through and beginning to brown, turning occasionally, about 5 minutes.

Roasted beets with dill

THIS SIDE DISH with a Russian accent is terrific with roast beef or pork—and it's especially easy to prepare if you roast the beets the day before you plan to serve them. Beets can be stored in a plastic bag in the refrigerator up to three weeks. Wash them just before using.

6 SERVINGS

- **2 pounds beets, trimmed (about 6 medium)**
- **¼ cup water**

- **6 tablespoons (¾ stick) unsalted butter**
- **¼ cup chopped fresh dill**
- **1 tablespoon fresh lemon juice**

PREHEAT oven to 400°F. Place beets in small roasting pan with ¼ cup water. Cover pan tightly with aluminum foil. Bake until beets are tender when pierced with knife, about 1 hour. Cool slightly. *(Can be prepared 1 day ahead. Cover and refrigerate.)* Peel beets. Cut into 1-inch pieces.

MELT butter in heavy large skillet over medium heat. Stir in dill and lemon juice. Add beets and toss until heated through, about 5 minutes. Season to taste with salt and pepper. Transfer to bowl and serve.

Twice-cooked beets in Chianti glaze

ROASTED FIRST AND THEN SAUTÉED, the tender beets are partnered with buttery leeks. The wine glaze balances the natural sweetness of the beets and intensifies their flavor. This Tuscan-style dish is excellent with game or fowl.

6 SERVINGS

- **8 2½-inch-diameter beets, unpeeled, trimmed, scrubbed**
- **4 tablespoons extra-virgin olive oil, divided**

2 **medium leeks (white and pale green parts only), trimmed, halved lengthwise, thinly sliced crosswise (about 3 cups)**
2 **cups Chianti or other dry red wine**
2 **tablespoons (1/4 stick) butter**

PREHEAT oven to 450°F. Toss beets with 2 tablespoons oil in 13x9x2-inch glass baking dish to coat. Roast beets uncovered until tender, about 1 hour. Cool beets slightly, then peel. Cut beets into quarters.

HEAT remaining 2 tablespoons oil in heavy large skillet over medium heat. Add leeks and sauté until translucent and soft, about 12 minutes. Add beets to skillet; sprinkle with salt and pepper. Sauté 5 minutes. Add Chianti and bring to boil. Reduce heat to medium and simmer until wine is reduced to glaze and coats beets, stirring occasionally, about 15 minutes. Add butter and stir until melted. Season beets to taste with salt and pepper. Transfer to bowl and serve.

Sophisticated succotash

WHEN A MENU calls for color and crunch, this side dish fills the bill. The year-round availability of these ingredients—broccoli, carrots, red bell pepper, yellow crookneck squash, and frozen lima beans—makes this dish easy to prepare anytime.

10 SERVINGS

12 **ounces broccoli, trimmed, cut into florets**

10 **tablespoons (1 1/4 sticks) unsalted butter**
1 **pound carrots, peeled, cut diagonally into 1/4-inch-thick ovals**
2 **medium red bell peppers, seeded, cut into 1/4-inch-thick strips**
2 **medium yellow crookneck squash, cut into 1/4-inch-thick slices**
1 **10-ounce package frozen baby lima beans, thawed, drained**

COOK broccoli florets in large pot of boiling salted water until just crisp-tender, about 3 minutes. Drain. Immediately place in bowl of ice water to cool. Drain and pat dry.

MELT butter in heavy large skillet over medium-low heat. Add carrots. Cover and cook until crisp-tender, stirring occasionally, about 15 minutes. Increase heat to medium-high; add bell peppers and sauté 5 minutes. Add squash and stir 1 minute. Add lima beans, then broccoli; sprinkle with salt. Cover and cook until heated through, stirring occasionally, about 4 minutes. Season succotash to taste with pepper and additional salt, if desired, and serve.

Lima beans with ham

NOT FOR NOTHING do Southerners call buttery-rich lima beans "butter beans," which in this recipe are enhanced with hickory-smoked ham. If hickory ham is too hard to find, substitute the more readily available Black Forest ham.

12 SERVINGS

12 **whole black peppercorns**
6 **whole allspice**
3 **large fresh summer savory sprigs or 1 teaspoon dried savory**
2 **whole cloves**

2 **tablespoons (1/4 stick) butter**
1 **large onion, chopped**
1 1/2 **cups coarsely chopped green tomatoes or unripe red tomatoes**
5 **cups frozen baby lima beans (about 1 1/2 pounds)**
1 **pound 1/2-inch-thick slices hickory-smoked ham or Black Forest ham, fat trimmed, meat cut into 1/2-inch cubes**
2 **tablespoons Dijon mustard**
2 **tablespoons (packed) golden brown sugar**
2 **cups low-salt chicken broth**
1 **teaspoon hot pepper sauce**
2 **tablespoons chopped fresh Italian parsley**

WRAP and tie peppercorns, allspice, savory, and cloves in small square of cheesecloth.

MELT butter in heavy large pot over medium-high heat. Add onion and sauté until beginning to soften, about 5 minutes. Add tomatoes and sauté 3 minutes. Stir in lima beans, ham, mustard, brown sugar, and spice packet. Add broth. Reduce heat to medium and boil gently, uncovered, until lima beans are tender and about ½ cup liquid remains, about 25 minutes. Discard spice packet. Stir in hot pepper sauce. Season lima bean mixture to taste with salt and pepper. *(Can be prepared 8 hours ahead. Cool slightly, then cover and chill. Rewarm in microwave before serving.)* Transfer to large bowl; sprinkle with parsley and serve.

Broccoli with mustard butter

THE WORD BROCCOLI comes from the Italian word for "cabbage sprout," because broccoli is related to cabbage, brussels sprouts, and cauliflower. At the market, look for crisp leaves on the stalks and tightly closed buds. The mustard butter is an easy and elegant accompaniment for this popular vegetable.

12 SERVINGS

- **8 tablespoons (1 stick) butter, room temperature**
- **¼ cup Dijon mustard**

- **5 pounds broccoli (about 3 large bunches), stems trimmed, tops cut into florets**

BLEND butter and mustard in small bowl. *(Can be prepared 1 day ahead. Cover and refrigerate. Bring mustard butter to room temperature before using.)*

STEAM broccoli until crisp-tender, about 5 minutes. Transfer to large pot. Add mustard butter and toss over low heat until butter melts and coats broccoli evenly. Season to taste with salt and pepper. Transfer to large bowl.

Broccoli with fennel and red bell pepper

WITH ITS RED AND GREEN COLORS, this would make a good holiday vegetable dish. Crush the fennel seeds in a plastic bag in order to contain the seeds and simplify clean-up. *Herbes de Provence* is a dried herb mixture available at specialty foods stores and in the spice section of some supermarkets. A combination of dried thyme, basil, savory, and fennel seeds can be substituted.

6 TO 8 SERVINGS

- **4 tablespoons extra-virgin olive oil, divided**
- **1 teaspoon fennel seeds, crushed**
- **2 shallots, chopped**
- **1 large fresh fennel bulb, trimmed, halved lengthwise, thinly sliced crosswise**
- **1 large red bell pepper, cut lengthwise into strips**
- **7 cups broccoli florets (from 3 large stalks)**
- **1 teaspoon herbes de Provence**
- **⅔ cup low-salt chicken broth**

HEAT 2 tablespoons oil in heavy large skillet over medium heat. Add fennel seeds and stir until toasted, about 3 minutes. Add shallots and sauté until golden, about 3 minutes. Add sliced fennel bulb and bell pepper; sauté until just tender, about 3 minutes. Add broccoli. Drizzle remaining 2 tablespoons oil over vegetables. Stir in herbes de Provence. Pour broth over. Cover and simmer until broccoli is crisp-tender and liquid evaporates, about 6 minutes. Season to taste with salt and pepper. Transfer to bowl and serve.

Broccoli with sesame seeds and dried red pepper

THIS SIMPLE RECIPE gives everyday broccoli a sophisticated and spicy accent.

4 SERVINGS

3 tablespoons sesame seeds
3/4 teaspoon coarse kosher salt
3/4 teaspoon dried crushed red pepper, divided

1 1/4 pounds broccoli, stems trimmed, tops cut into florets
1 tablespoon Asian sesame oil

STIR sesame seeds in heavy small skillet over medium heat until golden, about 5 minutes. Transfer 1 tablespoon toasted sesame seeds to small bowl and reserve. Place remaining seeds in spice grinder. Add salt and ½ teaspoon crushed red pepper; grind coarsely. Set sesame-red pepper mixture aside.

STEAM broccoli until crisp-tender, about 7 minutes. Transfer to large bowl. Add oil, reserved 1 tablespoon sesame seeds, remaining ¼ teaspoon crushed red pepper, and 2 teaspoons sesame-red pepper mixture; toss to coat evenly. Serve, passing remaining sesame-red pepper mixture separately.

Broccoli rabe with garlic and Pecorino Romano cheese

BROCCOLI RABE, also known as *rapini*, resembles broccoli but has small clusters of florets along its thin stalks. It is available at many specialty foods stores and some supermarkets. Its flavor is more pungent than broccoli, and works well with the bold flavor of Pecorino cheese in this recipe.

6 SERVINGS

2 pounds broccoli rabe (rapini), tough stems peeled

1/4 cup extra-virgin olive oil
5 garlic cloves, coarsely chopped
6 tablespoons freshly grated Pecorino Romano cheese, divided

COOK broccoli rabe in large pot of boiling salted water until crisp-tender, about 2 minutes. Drain. Transfer to bowl of ice water to cool quickly and drain again. *(Can be prepared 1 day ahead. Wrap in paper towels. Enclose in plastic bag and refrigerate.)*

HEAT olive oil in heavy large skillet over medium heat. Add garlic and sauté until fragrant, about 1 minute. Add broccoli rabe and sauté until heated through, about 4 minutes. Remove from heat. Sprinkle 4 tablespoons cheese over and toss to coat. Season to taste with salt and pepper. Transfer to warm platter. Sprinkle remaining 2 tablespoons cheese over and serve.

Broccolini with hazelnut butter

BROCCOLINI IS A CROSS between broccoli and Chinese kale, and is more stalk than floret. Unlike traditional broccoli, the stalk is thin, tender, and just as flavorful as the floret.

6 SERVINGS

1 cup hazelnuts, toasted, skinned, divided
6 tablespoons (3/4 stick) butter, cut into 1/2-inch cubes, room temperature

2 pounds broccolini

FINELY grind ½ cup hazelnuts in processor. Transfer to large bowl. Add butter and mix with spatula until well blended. Season hazelnut butter to taste with salt and pepper. Coarsely chop remaining ½ cup hazelnuts and set aside.

STEAM broccolini until crisp-tender, about 5 minutes. Transfer hot broccolini to bowl with hazelnut butter; toss until butter melts and coats broccolini. Add reserved ½ cup chopped hazelnuts and toss to combine. Season to taste with salt and pepper. Arrange on platter and serve.

Cauliflower and horseradish gratin

THERE'S PREPARED HORSERADISH in the cream sauce and, for good measure, some more in the buttery breadcrumb crust.

8 TO 10 SERVINGS

- **3½ pounds cauliflower, trimmed, cut into florets (about 8 cups)**
- **6 tablespoons butter, divided**
- **3 tablespoons all purpose flour**
- **2 cups half and half**
- **7 tablespoons prepared white horseradish, divided**
- **1 teaspoon white wine vinegar**
- **Ground nutmeg**
- **1 cup (packed) grated Fontina cheese (about 4 ounces)**

- **½ tablespoon Dijon mustard**
- **2 cups fresh breadcrumbs made from crustless French bread**

PREHEAT oven to 375°F. Steam cauliflower until crisp-tender, about 9 minutes. Transfer to 13x9x2-inch glass baking dish. Melt 3 tablespoons butter in heavy large saucepan over medium heat. Add flour and stir 2 minutes (do not brown). Gradually whisk in half and half. Cook until sauce boils and thickens, whisking constantly, about 4 minutes. Mix in 5 tablespoons horseradish and vinegar. Season to taste with nutmeg, salt, and pepper. Pour sauce over cauliflower and mix to coat. Sprinkle cheese over. *(Can be prepared 1 day ahead. Cover and chill.)*

MELT remaining 3 tablespoons butter in heavy medium skillet over medium heat. Mix in mustard and remaining 2 tablespoons horseradish. Add breadcrumbs; stir until crumbs are golden brown, about 9 minutes. Sprinkle over cauliflower.

BAKE until cauliflower is heated through, about 25 minutes.

Deviled cauliflower

DEVILED IS AN OLD-FASHIONED TERM meaning "highly seasoned," and indeed, this dish features a white sauce enlivened with mustard and Worcestershire sauce. The strongly flavored sauce is ideal for the strongly flavored vegetable, which is transformed into a casserole in this impressive recipe. Turkish bay leaves are small, oval-shaped bay leaves from the Mediterranean region; they're available in the spice aisle at the supermarket.

10 SERVINGS

- **2 medium heads of cauliflower, trimmed, cut into florets**

- **3 tablespoons butter**
- **3 tablespoons all purpose flour**
- **1¾ cups whole milk**
- **1 Turkish bay leaf**
- **Generous pinch of ground nutmeg**
- **2 tablespoons Dijon mustard**
- **1 teaspoon Worcestershire sauce**

- **½ cup fresh breadcrumbs made from crustless French bread**
- **2 tablespoons (¼ stick) butter, melted**

COOK cauliflower in large pot of boiling salted water until crisp-tender, about 5 minutes. Drain well.

MELT 3 tablespoons butter in heavy small saucepan over low heat. Add flour and stir 5 minutes. Gradually whisk in milk. Add bay leaf and nutmeg; bring to simmer, stirring often. Cover partially; cook until mixture is thick, stirring often, about 5 minutes. Whisk in mustard and Worcestershire sauce. Season sauce to taste with salt and pepper. Discard bay leaf. Transfer sauce to large bowl. Add cauliflower to sauce and stir until well coated. Place cauliflower mixture in 13x9x2-inch broilerproof baking pan. *(Cauliflower can be prepared 1 day ahead. Cover and refrigerate.)*

PREHEAT oven to 350°F. Sprinkle breadcrumbs over cauliflower in dish. Drizzle with melted butter. Bake until cauliflower is heated through and sauce is bubbling at edges, about 45 minutes.

PREHEAT broiler. Broil until breadcrumb topping is golden, about 2 minutes. Cool slightly and serve.

Indian potatoes, peas, and cauliflower

FRESH GINGER along with small amounts of turmeric, chili powder, and paprika turn ordinary vegetables into an authentic Indian side dish that is so easy to prepare. Serve the vegetables with roasted chicken or lamb.

4 SERVINGS

- **2 tablespoons vegetable oil**
- **1 pound russet potatoes, peeled, cut into ½-inch cubes**
- **1 tablespoon minced peeled fresh ginger**
- **4 cups bite-size cauliflower florets (from 1 medium head)**
- **½ teaspoon salt**
- **½ teaspoon ground turmeric**
- **¼ teaspoon chili powder**
- **¼ teaspoon paprika**
- **½ cup water**
- **½ cup frozen peas, thawed**

HEAT oil in large nonstick skillet over medium heat. Add potatoes and ginger; sauté until potatoes are lightly browned, about 3 minutes. Mix in cauliflower, then salt, turmeric, chili powder, and paprika; sauté 5 minutes, stirring to coat. Add ½ cup water; cover and simmer until vegetables are tender, about 5 minutes. Add peas and simmer until heated through, about 2 minutes. Season vegetables to taste with salt and pepper. Transfer to bowl and serve.

Curried potatoes, tomatoes, and onions

CUMIN SEEDS, mustard seeds, coriander, and turmeric are cooked in a skillet for a couple of minutes to release their aromatic oils, which means the vegetables will be more highly flavored. Jalapeño chiles lend extra kick.

6 SERVINGS

- **⅓ cup vegetable oil**
- **1 teaspoon cumin seeds**
- **1 teaspoon ground coriander**
- **½ teaspoon mustard seeds**
- **½ teaspoon ground turmeric**
- **2 medium onions, thinly sliced**
- **2 tablespoons chopped jalapeño chiles with seeds**
- **1½ pounds white-skinned potatoes, peeled, cut into generous ½-inch cubes**
- **1¼ cups chopped tomatoes (about 2 medium)**

HEAT oil in heavy large skillet over medium heat 1 minute. Add cumin seeds, coriander, mustard seeds, and turmeric to skillet. Cook until seeds are fragrant and darken slightly, stirring occasionally, about 2 minutes. Add onions and jalapeños; sauté until onions soften, about 5 minutes. Add potatoes and stir until well coated with spice mixture. Cover and cook until potatoes are almost tender, stirring occasionally, about 10 minutes. Add chopped tomatoes; cover and cook until potatoes are tender, about 7 minutes longer. Season to taste with salt and pepper. Transfer to bowl and serve.

Creamed spinach with golden breadcrumb topping

THIS STEAKHOUSE FAVORITE is dressed up with a topping of sautéed breadcrumbs and the addition of extra-sharp cheddar cheese to the spinach mixture. It is excellent with grilled steak and roast beef, as well as chicken and turkey.

8 SERVINGS

- **2 tablespoons (1/4 stick) butter**
- **1 cup fresh breadcrumbs made from crustless French bread**

- **3 10-ounce packages frozen chopped spinach, thawed, squeezed dry**
- **2 cups sour cream**
- **1 cup whole milk**
- **1 cup (packed) coarsely grated extra-sharp cheddar cheese (about 4 ounces)**
- **1/2 cup chopped onion**
- **1/4 teaspoon ground nutmeg**
- **1 large egg, beaten to blend**

MELT butter in large nonstick skillet over medium heat. Add breadcrumbs; sauté until golden, about 2 minutes. Set aside.

BUTTER 8x8x2-inch glass baking dish. Mix spinach, sour cream, milk, cheese, onion, and nutmeg in large bowl to combine. Season to taste with salt and pepper. Mix in egg. Transfer spinach mixture to prepared dish. *(Can be made 6 hours ahead. Cover and refrigerate.)*

PREHEAT oven to 350°F. Sprinkle breadcrumbs over top of spinach mixture. Bake uncovered until spinach is set in center and breadcrumbs are browned, about 30 minutes.

Sicilian spinach sauté

THE SWEET, SALTY, and tangy flavor combination of currants, garlic, and capers is a signature of Sicilian cuisine. Here the combination shines in a delicious spinach dish that is a snap to prepare. Partner it with roasted fish, pork, or game.

4 SERVINGS

- **2 10-ounce packages fresh spinach leaves**
- **1/4 cup water**

- **1 tablespoon olive oil**
- **6 garlic cloves, chopped**
- **1/2 cup dried currants (about 2 1/2 ounces)**
- **3 tablespoons drained capers**
- **1/2 cup coarsely grated Romano cheese (about 1 1/2 ounces)**

COMBINE spinach and 1/4 cup water in heavy large pot over high heat. Toss until spinach wilts but is still bright green, about 3 minutes. Transfer spinach to colander; press to release excess liquid. Wipe pot dry.

HEAT oil in same pot over medium heat. Add garlic and stir until fragrant, about 30 seconds. Add currants and capers; stir 1 minute. Mix in spinach, then cheese, and toss until heated through, about 1 minute. Season spinach to taste with salt and pepper. Transfer to bowl and serve.

Collard and mustard greens with bacon

THESE TWO GREENS, both cousins of kale, are prepared with bacon in classic Southern style. The mustard greens add a nice peppery zip. When buying collard and mustard greens, choose those with crisp leaves and healthy green color; store them in a plastic bag in the refrigerator for up to five days.

8 SERVINGS

- 4 **ounces slab bacon, cut into ¼-inch pieces**
- 1 **small onion, minced**
- 2 **large bunches collard greens, leaves stemmed and halved**
- 1 **bunch mustard greens, leaves stemmed and halved**
- ½ **cup low-salt chicken broth**
- **Hot pepper sauce, optional**

COOK bacon in heavy large pot over medium heat until fat is rendered. Reduce heat to low. Add onion and cook until soft, stirring occasionally, about 10 minutes. Add all greens and broth. Cover and cook until greens are just tender, stirring occasionally, about 25 minutes. Season to taste with salt and pepper. *(Can be prepared 2 hours ahead. Let stand at room temperature. Rewarm before continuing.)* Sprinkle greens with hot pepper sauce, if desired. Transfer to bowl and serve.

Sweet-and-sour Swiss chard with dried currants

IN MANY PARTS of the world, dried fruits are paired with vegetables in intriguing savory dishes. This quick Sicilian side dish, in which sautéed Swiss chard is studded with dried currants, can accompany chicken, fish, or meats. The currants become tender as they cook with the vegetables.

4 SERVINGS

- 3 **pounds green and/or red Swiss chard (about 3 large bunches), tough ends trimmed, cut into 2-inch pieces**
- 1 **tablespoon olive oil (preferably extra-virgin)**
- 2 **large garlic cloves, crushed**
- 3 **tablespoons dried currants**
- 1 **tablespoon red wine vinegar**

COOK Swiss chard in large pot of boiling salted water until tender, about 5 minutes. Drain well.

HEAT oil in large nonstick skillet over medium heat. Add garlic and stir 30 seconds. Add Swiss chard and currants; sauté until heated through, about 3 minutes. Drizzle vinegar over and toss to coat. Season to taste with salt and pepper. Transfer to bowl and serve.

Balsamic roasted onions

ROASTED UNTIL THEY ARE SWEET, the onions are drizzled with a luscious balsamic vinegar glaze. Both the onions and the glaze can be prepared a day before serving. To help prevent tearing up while slicing the onions, place them in the freezer first for 20 minutes.

10 SERVINGS

- 4 **pounds medium red onions, peeled**
- ¼ **cup olive oil**

- 6 **tablespoons (¾ stick) butter**
- 3 **tablespoons sugar**
- 6 **tablespoons balsamic vinegar**

- 1 **tablespoon chopped fresh parsley**

POSITION 1 rack in center and 1 rack in bottom third of oven and preheat to 500°F. Line 2 large rimmed baking sheets with aluminum foil. Cut onions through root end into ¾-inch-thick wedges with some core attached to each wedge. Place in large bowl; add oil and stir to coat. Arrange onions, cut side down, on baking sheets. Sprinkle with salt and pepper. Roast until onions are brown and tender, switching position of pans in oven and turning onions once, about 45 minutes.

MEANWHILE, melt butter in heavy small saucepan over medium-high heat. Add sugar and stir until sugar dissolves. Remove from heat; add vinegar. Return to heat. Simmer until mixture thickens to glaze, about 2 minutes. *(Onions and balsamic glaze can be made 1 day ahead. Cool. Cover separately and chill. Rewarm onions in 375°F oven about 15 minutes. Stir glaze over low heat to rewarm.)*

ARRANGE onions on platter. Drizzle glaze over. Sprinkle with parsley and serve.

Wild mushrooms with chestnuts and thyme

RICH IN TASTE (thanks to shallots, garlic, and Madeira) and rich in texture (thanks to butter and cream), this special-occasion dish can pair with virtually any meat or poultry; it could also stand on its own as a meatless main course, served with mashed potatoes or rice pilaf. The chestnuts provide an unusual sweetness that complements the earthy mushrooms.

4 MAIN-COURSE OR 8 TO 10 SIDE-DISH SERVINGS

- **6 tablespoons (3/4 stick) butter, divided**
- **8 large shallots, sliced (about 2 cups)**
- **6 garlic cloves, minced**
- **2 pounds assorted fresh wild mushrooms (such as crimini, oyster, and stemmed shiitake), sliced**
- **2 tablespoons chopped fresh thyme**
- **3/4 cup Madeira**
- **1 7.25-ounce jar roasted peeled whole chestnuts, halved (about 1 1/2 cups)**
- **3/4 cup whipping cream**
- **Chopped fresh chives**

MELT 3 tablespoons butter in large deep nonstick skillet over medium-high heat. Add shallots and sauté until soft and golden, about 6 minutes. Add garlic and stir 30 seconds. Add remaining 3 tablespoons butter and stir until melted. Add mushrooms; sprinkle with salt and pepper. Sauté until mushrooms are tender and brown, about 10 minutes. Add thyme and stir 1 minute. Add Madeira and simmer until almost all liquid is evaporated, about 1 minute. Add chestnuts and cream; simmer until cream thickens and coats mushroom mixture, tossing occasionally, about 1 minute. Season to taste with salt and pepper. Transfer to bowl; sprinkle with chives and serve.

15 Breads, jams, and condiments

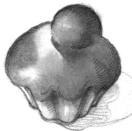

Ubiquitous, ancient, sacred, essential: Bread is more than nutrition. It is a link to our ancestors and, truly, the staff of life.

Over generations, bread has become part of many cultures, moving around the globe with humanity and evolving along with new climates, grains, and technology. Yet bread has also stayed true to regional and local traditions. In an era of global marketing, bread seems to be one of the few foods that has not been homogenized.

France, a country synonymous with bread, gives us loaves that range from *pain ordinaire,* made with white flour, yeast, salt, and water, to brioche, a sunny yellow, chubby round enriched with egg yolks, sugar, and butter. Italy's most famous bread export is focaccia, its dimpled surface readily absorbing a wash of olive oil during baking. It has been baked for centuries in Liguria, the crescent of land that runs along the Mediterranean coast from France to Tuscany. Sometimes focaccia is topped with onions, olives, or sliced tomatoes (it's not hard to make the leap from Liguria's focaccia to the pizza of Naples), sometimes with sweeter toppings like grapes and walnuts.

It is impossible to neatly file the world of bread into compartments. There are, however, two broad categories that work well: breads raised slowly with yeast versus those made without yeast, such as flatbreads and quick breads (the latter prepared in a wink with baking powder or baking soda). For all the appeal that quick breads have in terms of ease, speed, and flavor, don't rule out making yeast breads. Yes, they take time, but they don't require a lot of effort. (Note that, unless otherwise specified, the yeast called for in these recipes is regular active dry yeast.) Probably the most difficult aspect of baking bread is waiting for it to cool before tearing off a piece. Try to resist temptation, and then top it with one of the homemade jams in this chapter. Time tip: Start the jam while waiting for the dough to rise.

Veteran bread bakers know the satisfaction of this most tactile of cooking hobbies—or obsessions. Isn't it time you joined them?

Classic French bread

THIS RECIPE INCLUDES directions to form baguettes, ficelles (smaller, tapered loaves), a country French bread round, or a festive wreath shape, but you can make whatever shapes you like. The versatile dough can be mixed by hand, with a heavy-duty mixer, or even in a food processor. Baking stones are available at cookware stores. Unglazed quarry tiles, available at tile stores and some building supply stores, can also be used. The number of tiles needed will depend on the size of your oven. If tiles are unavailable, heat the baking sheet in the oven for five minutes.

MAKES 2 BAGUETTES, 3 FICELLES, 1 COUNTRY FRENCH LOAF, OR 1 BREAD WREATH

Dough

- **1 cup warm water (105°F to 115°F)**
- **1 envelope dry yeast**
- **1 tablespoon sugar**

- **1 teaspoon salt**
- **½ teaspoon balsamic vinegar or red wine vinegar**
- **2 cups bread flour**
- **¾ cup (about) all purpose flour**

HAND METHOD: Pour 1 cup warm water into large bowl. Sprinkle yeast and sugar over; stir to dissolve. Let stand until foamy, about 5 minutes.

MIX salt and vinegar into yeast. Add 1½ cups bread flour and mix 4 minutes. Stir in remaining ½ cup bread flour. Turn dough out onto work surface sprinkled with all purpose flour and knead until smooth, elastic, and slightly sticky dough forms, using dough scraper as aid and adding more all purpose flour to dough as necessary to prevent sticking, about 10 minutes.

MIXER METHOD: Pour 1 cup warm water into bowl of heavy-duty electric mixer. Sprinkle yeast and sugar over; stir to dissolve. Let stand until foamy, about 5 minutes.

MIX salt and vinegar into yeast. Add bread flour; using paddle attachment, mix 5 minutes. Replace paddle with dough hook. Add ½ cup all purpose flour and knead until soft and slightly sticky dough forms, adding more all purpose flour if dough is very sticky, about 7 minutes.

PROCESSOR METHOD: Measure 1 cup warm water into glass measuring cup. Sprinkle yeast and sugar over to dissolve; stir. Let stand until foamy, about 5 minutes.

ADD vinegar to yeast mixture. Combine salt, bread flour, and ½ cup all purpose flour in processor fitted with steel blade. Add yeast mixture and process until sticky ball forms. If dough does not form ball, add more all purpose flour 1 tablespoon at a time, incorporating each addition before adding next. Add water 1 teaspoon at a time if dough is dry, incorporating each addition before adding next. Process until dough is smooth, elastic, and slightly sticky, about 45 seconds.

OIL hands; transfer dough to floured surface. Knead until elastic, using dough scraper as aid, 2 minutes.

Rising

- **2 tablespoons vegetable oil**

COAT large bowl with 2 tablespoons oil. Add dough, turning to coat entire surface. Cover bowl with plastic wrap. Let dough rise in warm, draft-free area until tripled in volume, about 1½ hours. (To test, press 2 fingers into dough; if fully risen, indentations will remain. If indentations fill in, cover with plastic and let dough rise longer.)

Shaping and baking

- **¼ cup (½ stick) unsalted butter**
- **¼ teaspoon salt**

- **Baking tiles or stones**
- **4 cups boiling water**

MELT butter with salt in saucepan. Keep glaze warm.

BAGUETTES OR FICELLES: Oil or butter double baguette pan or triple ficelle pan. Punch down dough and knead until smooth, about 2 minutes. Divide dough in half for baguettes or in thirds for ficelles. Roll out 1 piece on unfloured work surface to rectangle, about 14x8 inches for baguette or about 12x6 inches for ficelle, oiling rolling pin if dough sticks. Starting at 1 long side, roll up dough jelly-roll style. Roll ends between palms and work surface to taper slightly. Transfer to prepared pan, seam side down. Repeat rolling and shaping with remaining dough.

BRUSH butter glaze over loaves. Let loaves rise in warm, draft-free area 45 minutes. Brush with glaze again. Let loaves rise until tripled in volume, about 35 minutes longer.

POSITION 1 oven rack in bottom third and second rack in center of oven. Place 13x9x2-inch metal baking pan on bottom rack. Place baking tiles on center rack. Preheat oven to 450°F. Brush loaves with glaze again. Using sharp knife, slash each loaf with 3 long diagonal cuts about ⅓ inch deep. Pour boiling water into baking pan in oven (water will steam). Close oven 2 minutes. Place bread in pans on tiles and bake until loaves are golden brown and crisp, dry crust forms, about 20 minutes. Turn out loaves onto rack and cool.

COUNTRY FRENCH LOAF: Oil or butter baking sheet. Punch down dough. Form dough into round ball, smoothing top. Place on baking sheet, flattening slightly. Brush with butter glaze and let rise until tripled in volume as above. Prepare oven as above, preheating to 400°F. Slash dough in tic-tac-toe pattern or with swirled slashes radiating from center. Bake on baking sheet on tiles until loaf is golden brown and sounds hollow when tapped on bottom, about 35 minutes. Cool on rack.

WREATH-SHAPED LOAF: Oil or butter large baking sheet. Punch down dough. Divide dough into 8 pieces. Form each piece into ball. Arrange balls in wreath shape on baking sheet, letting sides just touch. Brush with butter glaze and let rise until tripled in volume as above. Prepare oven as above, preheating to 400°F. Bake bread on baking sheet on tiles until loaf is golden brown and sounds hollow when tapped on bottom, about 25 minutes. Cool on rack. *(Can be made ahead. Cool completely. Double-wrap loaves in aluminum foil and freeze up to 2 weeks. Rewarm thawed loaves wrapped in foil in 350°F oven about 15 minutes, if desired.)*

Golden brioche

MIXING BRIOCHE DOUGH BY HAND requires plenty of muscle power, as the butter must be incorporated into the dough by beating it in bit by bit. The big bowl, tireless motor, and dough-hook attachment of a standing mixer take the heavy work out of preparing these tender loaves.

MAKES 3 LOAVES

⅓ cup warm water (105°F to 115°F)
⅓ cup warm milk (105°F to 115°F)
2 envelopes dry yeast
3¾ cups all purpose flour
2 teaspoons salt
4 large eggs
¼ cup sugar
1½ cups (3 sticks) unsalted butter, each stick cut into 4 pieces, room temperature

1 tablespoon water

COMBINE ⅓ cup warm water, warm milk, and yeast in bowl of standing heavy-duty mixer; stir until yeast dissolves. Fit mixer with dough hook. Add flour and salt to bowl; mix on low speed just until flour is moistened, about 10 seconds. Scrape sides and bottom of bowl. Beat in 3 eggs on low speed, then add sugar. Increase speed to medium and beat until dough comes together, about 3 minutes. Reduce speed to low. Add butter 1 piece at a time, beating until each is almost incorporated before adding next (dough will be soft and batter-like). Increase speed to medium-high and beat until dough pulls away from sides of bowl, about 7 minutes.

COVER bowl with plastic wrap. Let dough rise at room temperature until almost doubled in volume, about 1 hour. Lift up dough around edges and allow dough to fall and deflate in bowl. Cover bowl with plastic and chill until dough stops rising, lifting up dough around edges and allowing dough to fall and deflate in bowl every 30 minutes, about 2 hours total. Cover bowl with plastic; chill dough overnight.

BUTTER and flour three 7½x3½x2-inch loaf pans or three 8½x4½x2½-inch loaf pans. Divide dough into 3 equal pieces. Cut each dough piece into 4 equal pieces. Roll each into 3½-inch-long log, forming 12 logs total. Arrange 4 logs crosswise in bottom of each prepared loaf pan. Place loaf pans on baking sheet. Cover pans with waxed paper. Let loaves rise at room temperature until dough almost fills pans, about 2 hours.

PREHEAT oven to 400°F. Beat remaining 1 egg with 1 tablespoon water for glaze. Gently brush top of loaves with glaze. Bake until loaves are golden brown and sound hollow when tapped, about 30 minutes. Cool in pans on racks 15 minutes. Turn loaves out onto racks; cool at least 1 hour. *(Can be made ahead. Cool completely. Wrap loaves in aluminum foil; enclose in resealable plastic bags and store at room temperature 1 day or freeze up to 1 month. Rewarm room-temperature or thawed loaves wrapped in foil in 350°F oven about 15 minutes, if desired.)*

Braided egg bread

MASHED POTATOES give this bread its moist texture. It would be an excellent addition to a holiday menu or to a brunch table.

MAKES 2 LARGE LOAVES

17 ounces red-skinned potatoes (about 3 medium), peeled
5 cups water
¾ cup sugar
6 tablespoons (¾ stick) butter, room temperature
4 teaspoons coarse kosher salt

½ cup warm water (105°F to 115°F)
3 envelopes dry yeast
Pinch of sugar
4 large eggs
8 cups (about) unbleached all purpose flour

Cornmeal
¾ cup golden raisins (optional)

1 egg, beaten to blend (for glaze)
Sesame seeds or poppy seeds

COMBINE potatoes and 5 cups water in large pot. Cover and boil until potatoes are very tender, about 10 minutes. Ladle 1¼ cups potato cooking liquid into small bowl and reserve; cool reserved liquid to lukewarm. Drain potatoes. Transfer potatoes to medium bowl and mash until smooth. Place mashed potatoes in strainer set over large bowl of heavy duty electric mixer. Using rubber spatula, press mashed potatoes through strainer. Add ¾ cup sugar, butter, coarse salt, and 1¼ cups reserved cooking liquid to mashed potatoes. Using dough hook, beat until well blended.

COMBINE ½ cup warm water, yeast, and pinch of sugar in small bowl. Let stand until foamy, about 10 minutes. Add to potato mixture and beat to blend. Beat in 4 eggs. Mix in enough flour, 1 cup at a time, to form soft dough. Turn dough out onto generously floured surface. Knead until smooth and elastic, adding more flour as necessary to form soft elastic dough, about 10 minutes. Lightly oil large bowl. Place dough in bowl, turning to coat with oil. Cover bowl with plastic wrap, then kitchen towel. Let dough rise in warm, draft-free area until doubled in volume, about 1 hour.

OIL 2 large baking sheets. Sprinkle generously with cornmeal. Turn dough out onto floured surface. Divide dough in half; knead each piece lightly. If desired, knead raisins into 1 piece of dough. Divide each dough piece into 3 equal portions. Roll out each portion between work surface and palms of hands to 15-inch-long rope. Form into braids, using 3 ropes for each braid. Tuck ends under and pinch ends together. Place 1 loaf on each baking sheet. Cover with kitchen towel and let rise in warm, draft-free area until almost doubled in volume, about 30 minutes.

PREHEAT oven to 400°F. Brush loaves with egg glaze. Sprinkle with sesame seeds or poppy seeds. Bake 15 minutes. Reduce oven temperature to 350°F. Continue baking until loaves are deep golden brown and sound hollow when tapped on bottom, about 25 minutes longer. Transfer to racks and cool completely. *(Can be prepared 2 weeks ahead. Wrap tightly in aluminum foil and freeze. Before using, unwrap and let stand at room temperature until thawed.)*

Ciabatta

CIABATTA, A FLAVORFUL PEASANT BREAD from Italy, is also known as "slipper bread" because of its flat, rectangular shape. Begin preparing the bread a day before baking by making a *biga*, the Italian term for starter dough. Unlike standard bread doughs, ciabatta dough is very soft. The resulting dimpled, porous loaves are ideal for sandwiches. Semolina flour (also called pasta flour) is available at specialty foods stores, natural foods stores, Italian markets, and some supermarkets.

MAKES 2 LOAVES

Biga

1 cup plus 1 tablespoon room-temperature water (75°F to 80°F)
1 envelope dry yeast
3⅓ cups bread flour, divided

POUR 1 cup plus 1 tablespoon water into processor. Sprinkle yeast over. Let stand until yeast dissolves, about 8 minutes. Add 1 cup flour; process until blended. Scrape down sides of work bowl. Add 1 cup flour; repeat processing and scraping. Add remaining 1⅓ cups flour; process until small moist clumps form. Gather dough into ball (dough will be firm) and place in large bowl. Cover and chill overnight (biga will soften, resembling thick oatmeal in texture).

Dough

¾ cup plus 2 tablespoons room-temperature water (75°F to 80°F)
Pinch of dry yeast
½ cup plus 3 tablespoons semolina flour (pasta flour)

2½ teaspoons salt

Additional semolina flour

PULL biga into walnut-size pieces; place in clean large bowl. Add ¾ cup plus 2 tablespoons water, yeast, and ½ cup plus 3 tablespoons semolina. Using 1 hand, squeeze ingredients together 2 minutes. Work dough 4 minutes by scooping sections from sides of bowl and pressing into center, blending into very soft, shaggy mass. Using spatula, scrape dough from sides of bowl into center. Let dough rest in bowl, uncovered, 10 minutes.

SPRINKLE salt over dough. Using 1 hand, knead dough by rotating bowl ¼ turn at a time, scooping dough from sides and folding down into center until dough starts to come away from sides of bowl, about 5 minutes. Scrape dough from hand and sides of bowl. Cover bowl with kitchen towel; let dough rest 20 minutes.

ROTATING bowl ¼ turn at a time, fold dough over onto itself 6 times; turn dough over in bowl. Cover with kitchen towel and let dough rest 20 minutes.

PREHEAT oven to 425°F. Sprinkle work surface with additional semolina. Turn dough out onto semolina. Using pastry scraper or large knife, cut dough in half; keep separated. Let stand, uncovered, 20 minutes.

SPRINKLE 2 large baking sheets with additional semolina. Transfer each dough half, semolina side up, to 1 sheet. Stretch out each dough half to 16x4-inch rectangle. Press fingertips into dough in several places to dimple surface. Bake until golden brown, about 25 minutes. Cool completely. *(Can be prepared 2 weeks ahead. Double-wrap in aluminum foil and freeze. Before using, unwrap and let stand at room temperature until thawed.)*

Brown soda bread

IN IRELAND, brown bread is a staple, and according to Irish bakers, a loaf shouldn't take longer than three minutes from measuring to oven. Even if your own doesn't come together quite that quickly, this mixture of whole wheat flour, toasted bran, and wheat germ (a combination that approximates the nutty-textured Irish brown flour) will ensure authentic-tasting results.

MAKES 1 LOAF

- **1¾ cups all purpose flour**
- **1¾ cups whole wheat flour**
- **3 tablespoons toasted wheat bran**
- **3 tablespoons toasted wheat germ**
- **2 tablespoons old-fashioned oats**
- **2 tablespoons (packed) dark brown sugar**
- **1 teaspoon baking soda**
- **½ teaspoon salt**
- **2 tablespoons (¼ stick) chilled unsalted butter, cut into ½-inch cubes**
- **2 cups (about) buttermilk**

PREHEAT oven to 425°F. Butter 9x5x3-inch metal loaf pan. Combine first 8 ingredients in large bowl and mix well. Add butter and rub in with fingertips until mixture resembles fine meal. Stir in buttermilk by ½ cupfuls until soft dough forms. Transfer dough to prepared loaf pan. Bake until bread is dark brown and tester inserted into center comes out clean, about 40 minutes. Turn bread out onto rack. Turn right side up and cool completely on rack. *(Can be made 1 day ahead. Wrap tightly in aluminum foil and store at room temperature.)*

Irish soda bread with raisins and caraway

TRADITIONALLY, THIS SWEET SODA BREAD is baked in a skillet over an open fire. This version simplifies things by putting the skillet into a 350°F oven. The bread goes particularly well with corned beef, braised cabbage, and strong mustard–all the fixings of a St. Patrick's Day feast. On other days, try serving it at breakfast with plenty of butter and orange marmalade.

MAKES 1 LOAF

- **5 cups all purpose flour**
- **1 cup sugar**
- **1 tablespoon baking powder**
- **1½ teaspoons salt**
- **1 teaspoon baking soda**
- **½ cup (1 stick) unsalted butter, cut into ½-inch cubes, room temperature**
- **2½ cups raisins**
- **3 tablespoons caraway seeds**
- **2½ cups buttermilk**
- **1 large egg**

PREHEAT oven to 350°F. Generously butter heavy ovenproof 10- to 12-inch-diameter skillet with 2- to 2½-inch-high sides. Whisk first 5 ingredients in large bowl to blend. Add butter and rub in with fingertips until coarse crumbs form. Stir in raisins and caraway seeds. Whisk buttermilk and egg in medium bowl to blend; add to flour mixture. Using wooden spoon, stir just until well incorporated (dough will be very sticky).

TRANSFER dough to prepared skillet; smooth top, mounding slightly in center. Using small sharp knife dipped into flour, cut 1-inch-deep X in top center of dough. Bake until bread is cooked through and tester inserted into center comes out clean, about 1 hour 15 minutes. Cool bread in skillet 10 minutes. Turn out onto rack and cool completely. *(Can be made 1 day ahead. Wrap tightly in aluminum foil and store at room temperature.)*

Whole wheat porcini soda bread

THE UNUSUAL COMBINATION of mushrooms and dried apricots makes for a deliciously earthy soda bread. It would be good served with a barley and wild mushroom soup for a rustic dinner, or thinly sliced with a selection of cheeses such as fresh goat cheese, Brie, and Manchego. Dried porcini mushrooms are available at Italian markets and specialty foods stores, and in the produce section of many supermarkets. Unsulfured dried apricots can be found at natural foods stores and specialty foods stores.

MAKES 1 LARGE LOAF

- **1 ounce dried porcini mushrooms (about 1½ cups), any grit brushed off, coarsely chopped**
- **½ cup diced unsulfured dried apricots or dried figs (about 4 ounces)**
- **¾ cup warm water**

- **1¾ cups buttermilk**
- **1 cup old-fashioned oats**
- **¼ cup (½ stick) unsalted butter, melted**
- **¼ cup honey**

- **2 cups all purpose flour**
- **1¼ cups whole wheat flour**
- **2 teaspoons baking powder**
- **2 teaspoons coarse kosher salt**
- **1 teaspoon baking soda**
- **1 large egg, beaten to blend (for glaze)**

POSITION oven rack in center of oven and preheat to 375°F. Line baking sheet with parchment paper. Mix porcini mushrooms and apricots in medium bowl; pour ¾ cup warm water over. Let stand until mushrooms and apricots soften and liquid is absorbed, about 15 minutes.

MIX buttermilk, oats, and melted butter in large bowl. Let stand until oats soften, about 15 minutes. Stir mushroom mixture into oat mixture. Stir in honey.

WHISK both flours, baking powder, salt, and baking soda in another large bowl. Make well in center; add oat mixture and stir until dough forms, gradually mixing in dry ingredients. Turn dough out onto work surface and knead gently, about 5 turns. Shape dough into 7-inch round. Transfer to prepared baking sheet. Cut 1-inch-deep X in top center of loaf. Brush loaf with egg glaze.

BAKE until bread is cooked through and tester inserted into center comes out clean, about 1 hour 5 minutes. Transfer to rack and cool. *(Can be made 1 day ahead. Wrap bread tightly in aluminum foil and let stand at room temperature.)*

Whole wheat bread with raisins and walnuts

THIS WONDERFUL WHEAT BREAD is virtually hassle-free: You can make the dough one day before baking using regular yeast, or speed things up with rapid-rising yeast for immediate satisfaction. Spritzing the oven with water creates a more humid environment, which gives the bread a nice crust. Use a standard spray bottle filled with tap water.

MAKES 1 LOAF

- **1¼ cups lukewarm water (85°F to 95°F)**
- **1 tablespoon dry yeast (for do-ahead version) or quick-rising dry yeast (for same-day version)**

- 1 cup warm whole milk (105°F to 115°F)
- 2 tablespoons honey
- 1 tablespoon salt
- 1/4 cup (1/2 stick) unsalted butter, melted, cooled slightly
- 1 1/2 cups whole wheat flour
- 1/2 cup rye flour
- 1/2 cup oat bran
- 1 tablespoon unsweetened cocoa powder
- 2 1/2 cups (about) bread flour
- 1/2 cup raisins
- 1/2 cup chopped walnuts

Nonstick vegetable oil spray

STIR 1 1/4 cups lukewarm water and yeast in large bowl to blend. Stir in warm milk, honey, and salt, then melted butter. Add whole wheat flour and stir vigorously with wooden spoon until well incorporated. Add rye flour, oat bran, and cocoa powder; stir until well blended. Add enough bread flour, 1/2 cup at a time, to form moist and sticky dough, stirring vigorously with wooden spoon until well incorporated. Mix in raisins and walnuts. Cover bowl with plastic wrap. FOR DO-AHEAD VERSION: Refrigerate dough overnight. FOR SAME-DAY VERSION: Let dough rise in warm, draft-free area until doubled in volume, about 1 hour (do not punch down).

SPRAY 9x5x3-inch metal loaf pan with nonstick spray. Transfer dough to prepared pan, being careful not to deflate dough. Cover loaf pan loosely with plastic wrap. Let rise in warm, draft-free area until dough is puffed and almost reaches top of pan, about 45 minutes for refrigerated dough and 20 minutes for room-temperature dough.

MEANWHILE, position rack in center of oven and preheat to 500°F. Generously spray inside of oven with water (about 8 sprays); immediately place bread in oven. Reduce oven temperature to 400°F and bake bread until top is deep brown and crusty and tester inserted into center comes out clean, about 45 minutes. Cool in pan on rack 10 minutes. Turn bread out onto rack and cool completely.

Boston brown bread

ALTHOUGH THIS BREAD has now traveled extensively, it is still associated with Boston. The colonists baked their loaves in various tins; our recipe uses four clean soup or vegetable cans. This modern version is good with Thanksgiving dinner, but it also makes a nice breakfast or tea bread. No matter when you have it, accompany it with lots of the Maple-Molasses Butter. Whole-grain rye flour is available at natural foods stores and some supermarkets.

MAKES 4 SMALL LOAVES

- 1 cup (packed) dried currants (about 5 ounces)
- 1/3 cup brandy

- 1 cup whole wheat flour
- 1 cup unbleached all purpose flour
- 3/4 cup whole-grain rye flour
- 3/4 cup yellow cornmeal
- 2 teaspoons baking soda
- 1 1/2 teaspoons salt
- 1/2 teaspoon ground ginger
- 1 3/4 cups buttermilk
- 2 large eggs
- 1/4 cup pure maple syrup
- 1/4 cup mild-flavored (light) molasses
- 2 tablespoons (1/4 stick) unsalted butter, melted, cooled

Nonstick vegetable oil spray

Maple-Molasses Butter (see recipe)

COMBINE currants and brandy in bowl; let stand until currants plump slightly, about 45 minutes.

GENEROUSLY butter four 14.5- to 16-ounce cans. Place rack in bottom of heavy large pot. Pour enough water into pot to reach depth of 3 inches. Bring water to boil.

MIX whole wheat flour and next 6 ingredients in large bowl. Whisk buttermilk, eggs, syrup, molasses, and melted butter in medium bowl to blend. Mix into dry ingredients. Stir in currant mixture.

DIVIDE batter among prepared cans. Cut out four 12x6-inch pieces of aluminum foil. Fold foil crosswise in half, forming 6-inch squares. Spray foil with nonstick spray. Cover tops of cans with foil, sprayed side down, leaving 2-inch-high space above cans so that bread can rise. Secure foil tightly with heavy heatproof rubber bands or string below rims of cans.

PLACE cans on steamer rack in pot; pour enough additional water into pot for water to come two-thirds up sides of cans. Bring water to boil. Cover pot, reduce heat to medium-low, and simmer until wooden skewer inserted into center of bread comes out clean, occasionally adding more hot water to pot, about 1 hour 45 minutes.

USING tongs, transfer cans to rack. Let cool 10 minutes. Remove rubber bands and foil. Run small knife around sides of bread to loosen. Gently shake to remove breads from cans. *(Can be prepared 1 day ahead. Cool completely. Return breads to cans. Wrap breads tightly with foil. Steam cans, covered with foil and secured with heavy rubber bands, on rack set over simmering water until heated through, about 15 minutes.)* Cut breads into ½-inch-thick slices. Serve warm with Maple-Molasses Butter.

Maple-molasses butter

THIS SWEETENED BUTTER is especially good with the Boston Brown Bread but also tastes great with the Anadama Rolls with Mixed Seeds (page 488).

MAKES ABOUT 1 CUP

- **1 cup (2 sticks) unsalted butter, room temperature**
- **¼ cup pure maple syrup**
- **2 tablespoons mild-flavored (light) molasses**

MIX all ingredients in small bowl until well blended. *(Can be prepared 2 days ahead. Cover and refrigerate. Bring to room temperature before serving.)*

Harvest focaccia

THIS BREAD USES a yeast starter that needs to be made at least one day ahead. Serve the fragrant flatbread for lunch with a salad of arugula and radicchio drizzled with balsamic vinaigrette and topped with large shavings of Parmesan cheese, or with roast chicken for dinner. Raw sugar, also called turbinado or Demerara sugar, is available at natural foods stores and most supermarkets.

MAKES 1 LARGE BREAD

Dough

- **2¼ cups room-temperature water (75°F to 80°F), divided**
- **1¼ teaspoons dry yeast, divided**
- **4¾ cups plus 2 tablespoons unbleached all purpose flour, divided**
- **1½ teaspoons salt**

Topping

- **1 cup seedless red grapes, rinsed, patted dry**
- **1 tablespoon olive oil**
- **2 teaspoons chopped fresh thyme, divided**
- **Yellow cornmeal**
- **Additional olive oil**
- **¼ cup coarsely chopped walnuts**
- **1 teaspoon chopped fresh rosemary**
- **1 teaspoon grated lemon peel**
- **1 tablespoon raw sugar**
- **Coarsely cracked black pepper**

FOR DOUGH: Combine ¾ cup water and ¼ teaspoon yeast in medium bowl. Add 1 cup plus 2 tablespoons flour and whisk until smooth. Cover and let stand at room temperature 3 hours. Refrigerate starter at least 24 hours and up to 3 days.

COMBINE starter and remaining 1½ cups water, and 1 teaspoon yeast in large bowl of heavy-duty electric mixer fitted with dough hook. Beat 1 minute. Add salt and remaining 3¾ cups flour. Beat 5 minutes. Scrape down sides of bowl and dough hook. Continue to beat until very soft, slightly sticky dough forms, about 5 minutes longer. Let stand 5 minutes. Scrape dough into large oiled bowl; cover with plastic wrap. Let dough rise in warm, draft-free area until doubled in volume, about 1 hour 15 minutes.

MEANWHILE, PREPARE TOPPING: Preheat oven to 350°F. Combine grapes, 1 tablespoon oil, and 1 teaspoon thyme in medium bowl; toss to coat. Turn mixture out onto small rimmed baking sheet. Roast until grapes begin to burst, about 10 minutes. Cool completely on sheet.

SPRINKLE large baking sheet lightly with cornmeal. Turn dough out onto prepared sheet. Using floured fingertips, pull and spread dough to approximately 18x10-inch rectangle. Press dough all over with fingertips to dimple. Brush dough with additional oil. Sprinkle with grapes, then remaining 1 teaspoon thyme, walnuts, rosemary, and lemon peel. Sprinkle with raw sugar and lightly with coarsely cracked black pepper. Cover loosely with kitchen towel; let rise until light and puffy, about 45 minutes.

PREHEAT oven to 400°F. Bake focaccia until golden brown, about 25 minutes. Transfer to board; brush edges with additional oil. *(Can be made 4 hours ahead. Let stand at room temperature. If desired, rewarm in 350°F oven about 8 minutes.)* Serve warm or at room temperature.

Rosemary focaccia with olives

THIS VERSION of the popular Italian flatbread is tender and redolent of rosemary and olive oil. Oil-cured olives are available at Italian markets, specialty foods stores, and some supermarkets. You can also try baking the bread sprinkled with 3/4 cup grated Parmigiano-Reggiano cheese. Enjoy it with dinner, as a snack, or even split for a sandwich.

MAKES ONE 13-INCH ROUND BREAD

1 12- to 16-ounce russet potato

2½ cups (or more) bread flour
3 teaspoons fresh rosemary leaves, divided
1 teaspoon salt
1 cup warm water (105°F to 115°F)
¼ teaspoon sugar
1 envelope dry yeast
4 tablespoons extra-virgin olive oil, divided

12 oil-cured black olives, pitted, halved
½ teaspoon coarse sea salt

PIERCE potato in several places with fork. Microwave on high until tender, turning once, about 12 minutes. Cut potato in half. Scoop flesh into small bowl; mash well. Measure ⅔ cup (packed) mashed potato; cool (reserve any remaining potato for another use).

COMBINE 2½ cups flour, 1½ teaspoons rosemary, and 1 teaspoon salt in processor; blend until rosemary is chopped, about 1 minute. Add potato; blend in, using about 25 on/off turns. Combine 1 cup warm water and sugar in 2-cup glass measuring cup; sprinkle yeast over. Let stand until foamy, about 5 minutes. Stir 3 tablespoons oil into yeast mixture. With processor running, pour yeast mixture into flour mixture. Process until smooth, about 1 minute. Scrape dough out onto lightly floured surface. Knead until dough feels silky, sprinkling with more flour as needed, about 1 minute. Place dough in large oiled bowl; turn to coat. Cover with kitchen towel; let rise in warm, draft-free area until doubled in volume, about 1 hour.

POSITION oven rack in center of oven and preheat to 450°F. Brush large baking sheet with oil. Punch down dough; knead 30 seconds on lightly floured surface. Stretch or pat out dough to 12-inch round. Transfer round to prepared baking sheet. Press dough all over with fingertips to dimple. Brush with remaining 1 tablespoon oil. Press olive halves, cut side down, into dough. Sprinkle with sea salt and remaining 1½ teaspoons rosemary. Let rise until just puffy, about 20 minutes.

BAKE focaccia until golden, about 18 minutes. *(Can be made 6 hours ahead. Let stand at room temperature. If desired, rewarm in 350°F oven about 8 minutes.)* Serve warm or at room temperature.

Dilled cheddar cheese batter bread

OLD-FASHIONED BATTER breads require no kneading—just a little beating with an electric mixer and time for rising. Whole wheat flour and dill seeds give this loaf a hearty texture, while the cheddar cheese and fresh dill bump up the flavor. Pair the bread with soup, or enjoy it toasted. It also makes deliciously decadent grilled double-cheddar sandwiches.

MAKES 1 LOAF

- **¾ cup whole milk**
- **1½ tablespoons dill seeds, coarsely chopped**
- **1 tablespoon honey**
- **¼ cup canola oil**
- **3 large eggs, room temperature, beaten to blend**
- **2½ cups whole wheat flour, divided**
- **1 envelope dry yeast**
- **1½ teaspoons salt**
- **3½ cups (packed) grated sharp cheddar cheese (about 14 ounces), divided**
- **3 tablespoons chopped fresh dill**

BRING first 3 ingredients to simmer in small saucepan; cool to 120°F. Whisk in oil and eggs. Combine 1¼ cups flour, yeast, salt, and 2 cups cheese in large bowl of heavy-duty mixer. Add warm liquid mixture and fresh dill; beat 3 minutes. Add remaining 1¼ cups flour and beat 2 minutes. Scrape down sides of bowl. Cover bowl with plastic wrap. Let dough rise in warm, draft-free area until doubled in volume, about 1 hour 15 minutes.

PREHEAT oven to 350°F. Butter 9x5x3-inch metal loaf pan. Do not stir batter. Spoon half of batter into pan; sprinkle remaining 1½ cups cheese over. Cover with remaining batter and smooth top. Cover with plastic and let rise in warm, draft-free area until batter reaches top of pan, about 30 minutes.

BAKE until bread is golden brown and sounds hollow when tapped, about 45 minutes. Turn out onto rack and cool completely. *(Can be made ahead. Wrap in aluminum foil, then enclose in resealable plastic bag and freeze up to 2 weeks. Before using, unwrap and let stand at room temperature until thawed.)*

Corn bread with bacon and green onions

CRACKLING CORN BREAD, made with salt pork or pork rinds, was popular in Colonial days. Here's an updated version that uses bacon; corn kernels are mixed in to enhance the flavor and texture.

12 SERVINGS

- **10 bacon slices**
- **1¾ cups yellow cornmeal**
- **1¼ cups unbleached all purpose flour**
- **¼ cup sugar**
- **1 tablespoon baking powder**
- **¾ teaspoon salt**
- **½ teaspoon baking soda**
- **6 tablespoons (¾ stick) chilled unsalted butter, cut into ½-inch cubes**
- **1½ cups buttermilk**
- **3 large eggs**
- **1⅓ cups chopped green onions**
- **1 8.25- to 8.75-ounce can creamed corn**

PREHEAT oven to 400°F. Working in batches, cook bacon in heavy large skillet over medium heat until brown and crisp, about 6 minutes per batch. Transfer bacon to paper towels to drain. Crumble bacon into small pieces. Reserve 5 tablespoons bacon drippings.

GREASE 9x9x2-inch baking pan with 1 tablespoon reserved bacon drippings. Mix cornmeal, flour, sugar, baking powder, salt, and baking soda in large bowl. Add chilled butter and rub in with fingertips until mixture resembles coarse meal. Whisk buttermilk, eggs, and remaining 4 tablespoons reserved bacon drippings in medium bowl to blend. Add buttermilk mixture to dry ingredients and stir until blended. Mix in green onions, corn, and crumbled bacon. Transfer batter to prepared pan.

BAKE corn bread until top is golden and tester inserted into center comes out clean, about 35 minutes. Cool corn bread in pan on rack. *(Can be prepared 8 hours ahead. Cover tightly with aluminum foil and let stand at room temperature.)* Cut corn bread into squares and serve.

Blue cornmeal sticks with black olive butter

BLUE CORN WAS CULTIVATED by the Hopi centuries ago. Grown primarily in the Southwest and in Mexico, the slightly sweet, nutty-flavored corn is higher in protein, lysine, and zinc than the yellow variety—and it makes products that are purple-blue. Blue cornmeal is available at natural foods stores and some specialty foods stores, but if you find it hard to come by, yellow cornmeal can stand in with good results.

MAKES ABOUT 14

- **1 cup blue cornmeal**
- **1 cup unbleached all purpose flour**
- **1½ tablespoons sugar**
- **2 teaspoons baking powder**
- **¼ teaspoon salt**
- **⅔ cup half and half, room temperature**
- **6 tablespoons (¾ stick) unsalted butter, melted**
- **1 large egg, room temperature**

Vegetable oil
Black Olive Butter (see recipe)

POSITION oven rack in center of oven and preheat to 425°F. Mix first 5 ingredients in medium bowl. Whisk half and half, butter, and egg to blend in large bowl. Add dry ingredients to liquid mixture and stir until just combined.

BRUSH corn stick pans (preferably cast-iron) with vegetable oil. Heat pans in oven until oil smokes slightly, about 10 minutes. Pour off excess oil. Spoon batter into molds, filling each ¾ full. Bake cornmeal sticks until puffed and golden brown, about 15 minutes. Serve hot with Black Olive Butter.

Black olive butter

PLACE KALAMATA OLIVES on a cutting board and whack them firmly with the side of a large chef's knife: The pits will pop out easily. Or you can purchase pitted Kalamata olives for extra convenience. For variety, add a few minced fresh herbs, such as marjoram, thyme, or rosemary, to the butter—and try it on a sandwich of turkey, red onion, and roasted peppers.

MAKES ABOUT 1½ CUPS

- **¾ cup (1½ sticks) unsalted butter, room temperature**
- **12 Kalamata olives, pitted**

Using on/off turns, blend butter and olives in processor until almost smooth. *(Can be prepared 3 days ahead. Cover and refrigerate. Bring to room temperature before using.)*

Maple corn bread

THIS MOIST CORN BREAD gets its sweetness from pure maple syrup. It's wonderful fresh from the oven with maple butter, or it can be featured in a savory spiced apple-sage stuffing for turkey. If you plan to use this bread for stuffing, make it a day ahead.

10 TO 12 SERVINGS

2⅓ cups yellow cornmeal
1 cup all purpose flour
4 teaspoons baking powder
1¼ teaspoons salt
½ cup (1 stick) chilled unsalted butter, cut into ½-inch cubes
1⅓ cups buttermilk
4 large eggs
¾ cup pure maple syrup

PREHEAT oven to 375°F. Butter 9x9x2-inch metal baking pan. Combine cornmeal, flour, baking powder, and salt in processor; blend 5 seconds. Add butter and process until mixture resembles coarse meal. Whisk buttermilk, eggs, and maple syrup in large bowl to blend. Add cornmeal mixture and stir just until evenly moistened (do not overblend). Transfer to prepared pan.

BAKE until bread is golden and cracked on top and tester inserted into center comes out clean, about 45 minutes. Cool bread completely in pan on rack. *(Can be made 8 hours ahead. Cover and store at room temperature.)*

Hush puppies

TRADITIONALLY SERVED WITH FRIED CATFISH, hush puppies are small cornmeal-and-onion dumplings. The name, cooking legend has it, comes from the small fritters that Southern hunters would throw to their dogs to keep them quiet. When frying, make sure the oil reaches 350°F—and don't overcrowd the puppies.

MAKES ABOUT 2½ DOZEN

1 cup yellow cornmeal
1 cup all purpose flour
1 tablespoon baking powder
1 teaspoon salt
Generous pinch of cayenne pepper
Generous pinch of freshly ground black pepper

1 cup cold whole milk
2 large eggs
¾ cup chopped green onions
2 tablespoons minced onion
1 garlic clove, minced
½ teaspoon hot pepper sauce
Dash of Worcestershire sauce

Vegetable oil or corn oil (for deep-frying)

WHISK first 6 ingredients in large bowl to combine. Whisk milk and next 6 ingredients in medium bowl to blend; add to dry ingredients and stir with fork until combined. Let stand 30 minutes.

POUR enough oil into heavy large saucepan to reach depth of 3 inches and heat to 350°F. Working in batches, drop batter by tablespoonfuls into hot oil (do not crowd) and fry until golden brown, about 3 minutes. Using slotted spoon, transfer hush puppies to paper towels to drain. Serve warm.

Chestnut spoon bread with Fontina cheese

ROASTED CHESTNUTS (now conveniently sold peeled and packed in ready-to-use jars) and creamy Fontina cheese enrich the classic southern bread. The semolina flour, also called pasta flour, is available at specialty foods stores, Italian markets, and some supermarkets.

8 SERVINGS

8 tablespoons (1 stick) unsalted butter, divided
1 cup whole peeled roasted chestnuts (from 7.25- to 7.4-ounce jar)
2 tablespoons chopped fresh thyme

3 cups whole milk
¼ teaspoon salt
1 cup semolina flour (pasta flour)
1¼ cups (packed) coarsely grated Fontina cheese (about 5 ounces), divided
5 large eggs, separated

PREHEAT oven to 350°F. Butter 11x7x2-inch glass baking dish. Melt 2 tablespoons butter in heavy medium skillet over medium heat. Add chestnuts and thyme; sauté until heated through, breaking chestnuts into ½-inch pieces with back of spoon, about 4 minutes.

BRING milk just to simmer in heavy large saucepan over medium-high heat. Add salt, then gradually whisk in semolina flour. Reduce heat to medium and stir constantly until mixture is very thick, about 3 minutes. Remove from heat. Add remaining 6 tablespoons butter, then 1 cup cheese, whisking until cheese melts. Whisk in egg yolks 1 at a time; stir in chestnut mixture. Beat egg whites in large bowl until stiff but not dry. Fold whites into warm flour mixture in 2 additions. Transfer to prepared dish; sprinkle with remaining ¼ cup cheese.

BAKE spoon bread until puffed and beginning to brown, about 35 minutes. Let cool 5 minutes, then serve warm.

Popovers with sage butter

POPOVERS ARE basically the American version of Yorkshire pudding. They get their name the obvious way: They swell and "pop over" their baking tins. While popovers are traditionally served with roast beef, this sage-accented version would taste great with roast chicken, pork, or turkey. Don't open the oven while they are baking!

MAKES 12

- **1 cup (2 sticks) unsalted butter, room temperature**
- **1 tablespoon chopped fresh sage**

- **2 cups all purpose flour**
- **1 teaspoon salt**
- **2½ cups cold whole milk**
- **4 large eggs**

MIX butter and sage in small bowl. Season to taste with salt and pepper. Melt 5 tablespoons sage butter in small saucepan. Transfer remaining sage butter to small dish and let stand at room temperature.

PREHEAT oven to 450°F. Using 3 tablespoons melted sage butter, brush inside of 12 standard-size (⅓-cup volume) muffin cups.

WHISK flour and salt in large bowl to blend. Whisk milk, eggs, and 2 tablespoons melted sage butter in medium bowl to blend. Pour egg mixture over dry ingredients. Whisk until batter is smooth. Divide batter among muffin cups.

WITHOUT opening oven door at any time, bake popovers 15 minutes. Reduce oven temperature to 350°F; bake until popovers are puffed and brown, about 20 minutes longer. Transfer popovers to platter; serve immediately with remaining sage butter.

Cheddar-dill scones with honey mustard butter

SCONES ARE USUALLY associated with breakfast or afternoon tea, but these crumbly, mixed grain, dill-flecked versions make an excellent addition to a supper of hearty split pea or potato soup. They can be made ahead and reheated; just be sure to serve them warm—or piping hot.

MAKES 12

- **2 large eggs**
- **⅓ cup plus 1 tablespoon buttermilk**
- **⅓ cup minced fresh dill**
- **1 cup whole wheat flour**
- **1 cup unbleached all purpose flour**
- **1 cup yellow cornmeal**
- **2 tablespoons sugar**
- **2 teaspoons baking powder**
- **1 teaspoon ground black pepper**
- **¾ teaspoon salt**

10 tablespoons (1¼ sticks) chilled unsalted butter, cut into ½-inch cubes
1¾ cups grated sharp cheddar cheese (about 6 ounces)

Honey Mustard Butter (see recipe)

POSITION oven rack in top third of oven and preheat to 375°F. Lightly butter two 9-inch pie dishes. Whisk eggs, buttermilk, and dill in medium bowl to blend. Mix both flours, cornmeal, sugar, baking powder, pepper, and salt in large bowl. Add butter to flour mixture and rub in with fingertips until mixture resembles coarse meal. Add egg mixture and cheese. Stir to mix well (dough will be stiff and crumbly). Knead gently in bowl just until dough holds together.

DIVIDE dough in half. Pat each dough half into 1 prepared pie pan to 1-inch thickness. Using knife or pizza wheel, score each round into 6 wedges. Bake until tester inserted into centers comes out clean, about 30 minutes. Transfer pans to racks and cool scones slightly. Cut through score marks into wedges. *(Can be prepared 6 hours ahead. Cool completely. Wrap in aluminum foil and store at room temperature. Before serving, rewarm scones wrapped in foil in 350°F oven 10 minutes.)* Serve warm scones with Honey Mustard Butter.

Honey mustard butter

DELICIOUS WITH SAVORY SCONES, this butter is also wonderful on ham sandwiches. Using an electric mixer makes it fluffy, but you can also simply stir the ingredients together by hand. Any leftover butter will keep for one week in the refrigerator or up to one month in the freezer.

MAKES ABOUT 1 CUP

¾ cup (1½ sticks) unsalted butter, room temperature
¼ cup honey mustard

USING electric mixer, beat butter in small bowl until fluffy. Add honey mustard and beat until blended. *(Can be prepared ahead. Cover and refrigerate up to 1 week or freeze up to 1 month. Bring to room temperature before using.)*

Stilton and hazelnut drop biscuits

BECAUSE THEY REQUIRE NO kneading, rolling, or cutting, drop biscuits can be prepared whenever the mood strikes you. In a pinch, you could substitute Gorgonzola or another strong blue cheese for the English Stilton, and walnuts make an excellent replacement for the hazelnuts. These tender biscuits also reheat beautifully.

MAKES ABOUT 12

2½ cups unbleached all purpose flour
2 tablespoons sugar
1 tablespoon baking powder
¾ teaspoon cream of tartar
½ teaspoon salt
½ teaspoon ground black pepper
½ cup (1 stick) chilled unsalted butter, cut into ½-inch cubes
¾ cup coarsely crumbled chilled Stilton cheese (about 4½ ounces)
⅔ cup chopped skinned toasted hazelnuts
1 cup chilled buttermilk
1 large egg

POSITION oven rack in center of oven and preheat to 400°F. Butter and flour heavy large baking sheet. Whisk first 6 ingredients in large bowl to blend well. Add butter and rub in with fingertips until mixture resembles coarse meal. Add cheese; rub in with fingertips until cheese is reduced to small pieces. Mix in hazelnuts. Whisk buttermilk and egg in small bowl to blend. Add to flour mixture, stirring just until dough is evenly moistened.

USING ⅓ cup dough for each biscuit, drop 12 mounds onto prepared sheet, spacing 2 inches apart. Bake until biscuits are golden brown and tester inserted into center comes out clean, about 15 minutes. *(Can be made 6 hours ahead. Let stand at room temperature. Rewarm in 350°F oven about 8 minutes.)* Serve warm.

Sour cream and herb muffins

SAY "MUFFIN" and you're likely to visualize the sweet blueberry, bran, or banana-nut varieties. But here is a rich green savory version to get you thinking outside the muffin tin. Serve these with omelets or scrambled eggs at breakfast or brunch, or with soup and salad for a casual lunch or dinner.

MAKES 12

- **2¼ cups unbleached all purpose flour**
- **2 teaspoons baking powder**
- **1¼ teaspoons salt**
- **½ teaspoon baking soda**
- **1 cup buttermilk**
- **2 large eggs**
- **¼ cup sour cream**
- **2 tablespoons olive oil**
- **¼ cup chopped fresh chives or green onions**
- **2 tablespoons chopped fresh basil**
- **1 tablespoon chopped fresh dill**
- **2 teaspoons chopped fresh marjoram**
- **½ teaspoon grated lemon peel**
- **Melted butter**

POSITION oven rack in center of oven and preheat to 350°F. Butter 12 standard-size (⅓-cup volume) muffin cups or line cups with muffin papers. Whisk first 4 ingredients in large bowl to blend. Whisk buttermilk, eggs, sour cream, and oil in medium bowl to blend; whisk in all herbs and lemon peel. Stir buttermilk mixture into flour mixture. Divide batter among prepared cups. Brush tops lightly with melted butter.

BAKE muffins 20 minutes. Brush tops with butter. Continue baking until muffins are golden brown on top and tester inserted into center comes out clean, about 15 minutes longer. Turn muffins out onto rack. *(Can be made 6 hours ahead. Let stand at room temperature. If desired, rewarm in 350°F oven about 5 minutes.)* Serve warm or at room temperature.

Cracked pepper biscuits

BISCUITS ARE THE NATURAL ACCOMPANIMENT to casual family meals. These especially light and buttery biscuits can be made ahead, then reheated when you need one or two for brunch or dinner. You can purchase cracked peppercorns or grind your own using quick on/off turns of an electric spice mill.

MAKES 16

- **2 tablespoons (¼ stick) unsalted butter**
- **2 tablespoons chopped fresh thyme**
- **½ teaspoon coarsely cracked black pepper**
- **½ cup whole milk**
- **1 large egg**

- **2 cups unbleached all purpose flour**
- **1 tablespoon baking powder**
- **1 teaspoon salt**
- **¾ cup (1½ sticks) chilled unsalted butter, cut into ½-inch cubes**

PREHEAT oven to 475°F. Melt 2 tablespoons butter in heavy small skillet over medium heat. Add thyme and cracked black pepper. Sauté until fragrant, about 2 minutes. Transfer thyme mixture to small bowl. Whisk in milk, then egg. Chill until mixture is cold.

BLEND flour, baking powder, and salt in processor 10 seconds. Add ¾ cup chilled butter. Using on/off turns, process until mixture resembles coarse meal. Add milk mixture. Using on/off turns, process just until moist clumps form. Transfer dough to floured work surface. Knead just until dough holds together, about 6 turns. Roll out dough to ½-inch thickness. Using 2-inch-diameter biscuit or cookie cutter, cut out biscuits. Reroll dough scraps and cut out additional biscuits, making 16 biscuits total. Transfer biscuits to large ungreased baking sheet.

BAKE biscuits until golden brown, about 12 minutes. *(Can be prepared 6 hours ahead. Cool completely. Wrap in aluminum foil and store at room temperature. Before serving, rewarm unwrapped biscuits in 350°F oven just until heated through, about 8 minutes.)* Serve warm.

Caraway-dill biscuits

THIS RECIPE IS GREAT for a party or a large crowd at breakfast. Because it calls for self-rising flour, the measuring will be kept to a minimum. (Note that self-rising flour loses its leavening ability over time, so don't let it sit in your cupboard for more than three months or so.) Serve the biscuits with smoked ham as part of a holiday buffet or with Swiss cheese omelets for breakfast.

MAKES ABOUT 48

4 cups self-rising flour
1 tablespoon caraway seeds
1½ cups whole milk
1 cup extra-virgin olive oil, divided
¼ cup chopped fresh dill

PREHEAT oven to 425°F. Mix flour and caraway seeds in large bowl. Make well in center of flour. Add milk, ¾ cup plus 2 tablespoons oil, and dill. Stir just until dry ingredients are evenly moistened. Gather dough into ball. Roll out dough on lightly floured surface to ¾-inch thickness. Using 1¾-inch round cutter, cut out biscuits. Gather scraps and gently reroll dough on lightly floured surface. Cut out more biscuits. Arrange on 2 large ungreased baking sheets. Brush biscuit tops with remaining 2 tablespoons oil.

BAKE until biscuits are puffed and very pale golden on top and tester inserted into center comes out clean, about 15 minutes. *(Can be prepared 6 hours ahead. Cool completely. Wrap in aluminum foil; store at room temperature. If desired, rewarm unwrapped biscuits in 350°F oven just until heated through, about 8 minutes.)* Serve warm or at room temperature.

Butterhorn rolls

THIS BUTTERY CRESCENT-STYLE ROLL is perfect for elegant dinners and holiday gatherings. Any leftovers can be warmed and served for breakfast with fruit preserves. Be careful to cool the milk mixture properly: If added too warm to the yeast mixture, the heat will kill the yeast and the dough will not rise.

MAKES 36

1 cup whole milk
¾ cup (1½ sticks) unsalted butter, cut into pieces
½ cup warm water (105°F to 115°F)
½ teaspoon plus ½ cup sugar, divided
1 envelope plus ½ teaspoon dry yeast

3 large eggs, room temperature
5¼ cups (about) all purpose flour, divided
1 tablespoon salt

½ cup (1 stick) unsalted butter, melted, divided

STIR milk and ¾ cup butter in heavy medium saucepan over low heat until butter melts. Cool to 120°F if necessary. Combine ½ cup warm water and ½ teaspoon sugar in small bowl. Sprinkle yeast over; stir to blend. Let stand until foamy, about 5 minutes.

IN large bowl of heavy-duty electric mixer fitted with whisk attachment, beat eggs and remaining ½ cup sugar at low speed until blended. Beat in milk mixture. Gradually add 2½ cups flour, beating until smooth. Replace whisk with dough hook. Add yeast mixture, salt, and 2 cups flour; beat 8 minutes. Beat in enough flour by tablespoonfuls to form sticky dough that just begins to pull away from sides of mixing bowl.

POUR 1 tablespoon melted butter into large bowl. Scrape in dough; let stand 5 minutes. Using spatula, turn dough over, coating with butter. Cover bowl with plastic wrap, then kitchen towel. Let dough rise in warm, draft-free area until doubled in volume, about 1½ hours.

PUNCH down dough. Cover bowl with plastic wrap, then towel, and let rise again in warm, draft-free area until doubled in volume, about 1 hour. Punch down dough.

DIVIDE dough into 3 equal portions. Roll out 1 portion on floured surface to 12-inch round. Brush with some of melted butter. Cut into 12 triangles. Starting at wide end, roll up triangles toward point. Repeat rolling, cutting, and shaping with remaining 2 dough portions and melted butter. Arrange rolls, point side down, on 2 ungreased heavy large rimmed baking sheets, spacing evenly. Cover rolls with clean kitchen towels; let rolls rise until almost doubled in volume, about 45 minutes.

POSITION 1 rack in bottom third and 1 rack in top third of oven and preheat to 375°F. Brush rolls with melted butter. Bake 15 minutes. Switch top and bottom baking sheets and bake until rolls are golden, about 10 minutes longer. Cool rolls completely on racks. *(Can be made ahead. Wrap in aluminum foil, then enclose in resealable plastic bags and store at room temperature 1 day or freeze up to 2 weeks. Rewarm thawed rolls wrapped in foil in 350°F oven about 15 minutes, if desired.)*

Poppy seed dinner rolls

THESE ALL-AMERICAN ROLLS are so flaky and buttery that everyone will want seconds. Be sure to begin preparing the dough a day before serving because it needs to be refrigerated overnight. You can sprinkle sesame seeds on the rolls instead of poppy seeds, or leave the seeds off altogether.

MAKES 24

1 cup warm water (105°F to 115°F)
2 envelopes dry yeast
¼ teaspoon plus ⅓ cup sugar, divided

⅔ cup whole milk, room temperature
2 large eggs
2½ teaspoons salt
¼ cup (½ stick) unsalted butter, melted, cooled
5⅓ cups (about) all purpose flour, divided
1 cup (2 sticks) chilled unsalted butter, cut into thin slices

1 tablespoon cold water
Poppy seeds

POUR 1 cup warm water into large bowl. Sprinkle yeast and ¼ teaspoon sugar over and stir to blend. Let stand until yeast dissolves and mixture is slightly foamy, about 8 minutes.

WHISK milk, 1 egg, salt, and remaining ⅓ cup sugar into yeast mixture. Add melted butter and whisk until smooth. Add 1 cup flour and mix until smooth. Combine 4 cups flour and 1 cup chilled butter in processor; using on/off turns, process until mixture resembles coarse meal. Add to yeast mixture and stir until dry ingredients are moistened. Knead in bowl until smooth dough forms, adding more flour if dough is sticky, about 5 minutes. Cover bowl with plastic wrap. Refrigerate dough overnight. *(Can be prepared 2 days ahead. Keep refrigerated.)*

BUTTER 24 standard-size (⅓-cup volume) nonstick muffin cups. Turn dough out onto floured work surface; knead briefly until smooth and elastic, about 3 minutes. Divide dough into 4 equal portions. Place 1 dough portion on floured work surface; cover and chill remaining dough. Roll out dough portion to 13x11-inch rectangle (about ⅛ inch thick). Cut rectangle lengthwise into 6 strips, each scant 2 inches wide. Stack strips atop one another, forming 6 layers and pressing slightly to adhere. Cut strips crosswise into 6 equal stacks, each about 2 inches long. Place 1 dough stack, 1 cut side down, in each prepared muffin cup (dough will fan out slightly and fill muffin cups as dough rises). Repeat with remaining chilled dough pieces. Cover rolls with clean kitchen towel. Let rise in warm, draft-free area until rolls are puffed and doubled in volume, about 1 hour 15 minutes.

POSITION 1 rack in center and 1 rack in top third of oven and preheat to 350°F. Beat remaining egg with 1 tablespoon cold water for glaze. Brush rolls gently with glaze. Sprinkle with poppy seeds. Bake until rolls are golden brown, switching top and bottom baking sheets halfway through baking, about 25 minutes total. Transfer pans to racks and cool rolls 5 minutes. Remove rolls from pans and cool on racks. *(Can be prepared ahead. Cool completely. Wrap in aluminum foil, then enclose in resealable plastic bags and freeze up to 2 weeks. If desired, rewarm thawed rolls wrapped in foil in 350°F oven about 10 minutes.)* Serve warm or at room temperature.

Anadama rolls with mixed seeds

ANADAMA BREAD RECIPES, which date back to pre-Revolutionary New England, all call for molasses and cornmeal for substantial results. This contemporary rendition is no exception.

MAKES 16

1½ cups whole milk
⅓ cup mild-flavored (light) molasses
2 tablespoons (¼ stick) unsalted butter
2 teaspoons salt

¼ cup warm water (105°F to 115°F)
2 envelopes dry yeast
¾ cup yellow cornmeal
1½ cups whole wheat flour
2¾ cups (about) bread flour

Additional yellow cornmeal

1 egg, beaten to blend (for glaze)
Assorted seeds (such as fennel, anise, celery, and/or caraway)

COMBINE milk, molasses, butter, and salt in small saucepan. Bring to simmer, whisking until butter melts. Pour milk mixture into bowl of heavy-duty mixer fitted with paddle attachment. Cool to 115°F, about 30 minutes.

MEANWHILE, measure ¼ cup warm water in measuring cup. Sprinkle yeast over and stir to blend. Let stand until yeast dissolves, about 10 minutes. Stir yeast mixture into milk mixture. Mix in ¾ cup cornmeal. Mix in whole wheat flour. Mix in enough bread flour, ½ cup at a time, to form slightly sticky dough. Turn dough out onto floured surface. Knead until smooth and elastic, adding more bread flour if dough is too sticky, about 8 minutes. Form dough into ball.

BUTTER large bowl. Place dough in bowl; turn to coat with butter. Cover bowl with plastic wrap, then kitchen towel. Let dough rise in warm, draft-free area until doubled in volume, about 1½ hours.

SPRINKLE 2 heavy large baking sheets generously with cornmeal. Punch down dough. Turn out onto floured surface and knead until smooth, about 3 minutes. Divide dough into 16 equal portions. Roll each portion between palms and work surface to 8-inch-long rope about ¾-inch thick. Grasping 1 rope at both ends, tie into loose knot. Repeat with remaining ropes. Place on prepared baking sheets, spacing 2 inches apart. Cover with kitchen towels.

Let rise in warm, draft-free area until almost doubled in volume, about 45 minutes.

POSITION 1 rack in center and 1 rack in top third of oven and preheat to 375°F. Brush rolls with egg glaze. Sprinkle with seeds. Bake until rolls are golden and sound hollow when tapped, switching and rotating baking sheets halfway through baking, about 20 minutes. Transfer rolls to racks. *(Can be prepared 2 weeks ahead. Cool. Wrap in aluminum foil and freeze. If desired, rewarm thawed wrapped rolls in 350°F oven 10 minutes.)* Serve warm or at room temperature.

Onion-shallot rye rolls

IF DESIRED, you can prepare these hearty rolls the day before serving, then bake them when you're ready. After shaping the rolls and placing them in the pan, brush them with cooled melted butter. Cover loosely with oiled waxed paper, then wrap tightly with plastic wrap and refrigerate at least two hours and up to one day. Let stand at room temperature 20 minutes before topping and baking. The topping can also be made ahead and refrigerated.

MAKES 12

Dough

- **1 cup warm water (105°F to 115°F)**
- **1 envelope dry yeast**

- **3/4 cup rye flour**
- **1/4 cup (1/2 stick) unsalted butter, melted**
- **2 tablespoons (packed) golden brown sugar**
- **1 large egg**
- **1 1/2 teaspoons salt**
- **3 cups (about) unbleached all purpose flour, divided**

Topping

- **1/4 cup (1/2 stick) unsalted butter**
- **1 large onion, chopped**
- **2 medium shallots, minced**
- **1/4 cup whipping cream**
- **2 teaspoons caraway seeds**

FOR DOUGH: Pour 1 cup warm water into bowl of heavy-duty electric mixer; sprinkle yeast over (dough can also be mixed by hand). Let mixture stand until yeast dissolves, about 10 minutes. Fit mixer with paddle attachment.

ADD rye flour, butter, sugar, egg, and salt to yeast mixture; stir to combine. Add 1 cup all purpose flour. Beat at medium speed until smooth, about 3 minutes. Mix in enough all purpose flour, ½ cup at a time, to form soft dough. Turn dough out onto lightly floured surface and knead until smooth and elastic, about 8 minutes.

BUTTER large bowl. Add dough, turning to coat entire surface. Cover bowl with plastic wrap. Let dough rise in warm, draft-free area until doubled in volume, about 1 hour.

BUTTER 13x9x2-inch metal baking pan. Gently punch down dough. Turn out onto lightly floured surface and knead until smooth. Divide dough into 12 equal pieces. Roll each piece between hands and floured work surface into 6-inch-long oblong roll. Arrange rolls in prepared pan in 2 rows just touching one another. Cover loosely with plastic wrap and let rise in warm, draft-free area until almost doubled in volume, about 40 minutes.

MEANWHILE, PREPARE TOPPING: Melt butter in heavy medium skillet over medium heat. Add onion and shallots; sauté until soft, about 10 minutes. Add cream; increase heat and boil until liquid is reduced by half, about 2 minutes. Scrape onion mixture into small bowl and let cool. Stir in caraway seeds.

PREHEAT oven to 375°F. Gently spoon topping evenly over tops of risen rolls. Bake until golden brown, about 25 minutes. Transfer to rack and cool slightly. *(Can be made ahead. Cool completely. Wrap rolls in aluminum foil, then enclose in resealable plastic bags and freeze up to 2 weeks. Rewarm rolls wrapped in foil in 350°F oven about 10 minutes, if desired.)*

Pesto-potato rolls

THIS RECIPE REQUIRES NO KNEADING and allows you to make the rolls the same day they're to be served; or you can begin the dough a day ahead. The pretty rolls are baked side by side in cake pans. To serve, turn them out of the pans and let your guests pull them apart.

MAKES ABOUT 28 ROLLS

3½ cups water
1 11- to 12-ounce russet potato, peeled, cut into ½-inch pieces
2 teaspoons salt, divided

1 tablespoon dry yeast (for do-ahead version) or quick-rising dry yeast (for same-day version)
6 tablespoons purchased pesto
1 tablespoon sugar
Pinch of ground black pepper
½ cup plus 6 tablespoons (1¾ sticks) unsalted butter, melted, cooled slightly
2 large eggs
4¾ cups (about) bread flour, divided

COMBINE 3½ cups water, potato, and 1 teaspoon salt in large saucepan. Cover and boil until potato is very tender, about 20 minutes. Mash potato with cooking liquid until smooth. Transfer 2 cups potato mixture to bowl (discard any remaining mixture); cool to between 105°F and 115°F.

WHISK yeast, then pesto, sugar, pepper, and remaining 1 teaspoon salt into potato mixture. Whisk in ½ cup melted butter, then eggs. Add enough flour, about ½ cup at a time, to form smooth and sticky dough, stirring vigorously with wooden spoon. Butter large bowl. Transfer dough to bowl; turn to coat. Cover bowl with plastic wrap. **FOR DO-AHEAD VERSION:** Refrigerate dough overnight. **FOR SAME-DAY VERSION:** Let dough rise in warm, draft-free area until doubled in volume, about 45 minutes (do not punch down dough).

BUTTER two 9-inch-diameter cake pans with 1½-inch-high sides. Roll out dough on floured surface to ⅓-inch-thick round. Using floured 2½-inch round cookie cutter, cut out rounds. Reroll dough scraps and cut out additional rounds. Dip top of each dough round briefly into remaining 6 tablespoons melted butter. Fold each dough round into half-circle, buttered surfaces pressed gently together. Arrange half of folded dough rounds side by side, with flared sides turned up, in each prepared pan. Cover loosely with plastic wrap and let rise in warm, draft-free area until folded dough rounds are almost doubled in volume, about 30 minutes for chilled dough and 20 minutes for room-temperature.

MEANWHILE, position rack in center of oven and preheat to 400°F. Bake rolls until golden, about 25 minutes. Cool in pans at least 20 minutes. Turn out onto racks. *(Can be made 8 hours ahead. Cool completely. Wrap in aluminum foil and store at room temperature. If desired, rewarm rolls wrapped in foil in 350°F oven about 8 minutes.)* Serve warm or at room temperature.

Hazelnut breadsticks

START PREPARING THE *BIGA* (the Italian starter) a day before making the breadsticks, as it will need to rise overnight. Right before the last rising, you can give the breadsticks amusing shapes by forming one end of each dough rope into a squiggle, loop, or whatever strikes your fancy.

MAKES 21

- **½ cup plus 1 tablespoon warm water (105°F to 115°F)**
- **2½ cups unbleached all purpose flour, divided**
- **1½ teaspoons dry yeast, divided**
- **¼ cup olive oil**
- **¼ cup fresh sage leaves**
- **½ cup hazelnuts, toasted, skinned, ground**
- **¼ cup warm whole milk (105°F to 115°F)**
- **1 teaspoon salt**

MIX ½ cup warm water, ½ cup flour, and 1 teaspoon yeast in large bowl to blend well. Cover and let starter stand at room temperature overnight.

HEAT oil in heavy small saucepan over medium-low heat. Add sage leaves and sauté until crisp, about 7 minutes. Cool.

COMBINE remaining 1 tablespoon water and ½ teaspoon yeast in small bowl; stir to blend. Let stand until yeast dissolves, about 10 minutes. Transfer to processor.

ADD remaining 2 cups flour, ground hazelnuts, milk, and salt to yeast mixture in processor. Using on/off turns, process until small moist clumps form. Add sage-oil mixture and starter. Process just until large moist clumps form. Transfer dough to clean work surface. Gather dough into ball. Knead until dough is smooth and elastic, about 4 minutes. Form dough into ball.

LIGHTLY oil another large bowl. Add dough; turn to coat. Cover bowl with plastic wrap, then kitchen towel. Let dough rise in warm, draft-free area until doubled in volume, about 1 hour. Punch down dough. Cover and let dough rest 15 minutes.

PREHEAT oven to 400°F. Lightly oil 3 large baking sheets. Turn dough out onto floured work surface and knead briefly until smooth. Divide dough into thirds. Divide first third of dough into 7 equal pieces. Roll 1 dough piece between palms and work surface into 13-inch-long rope. Transfer rope to baking sheet. Repeat with remaining 6 dough pieces, spacing ropes evenly apart. If desired, shape 1 end of each rope decoratively. Let rise 10 minutes. Bake breadsticks until golden and very crisp, about 20 minutes. Transfer to racks and cool.

MEANWHILE, shape second third of dough into 7 breadsticks and let rise 10 minutes. Bake as above. Repeat with final third of dough. *(Can be made ahead. Wrap tightly in aluminum foil and store at room temperature up to 1 day or freeze up to 2 weeks.)*

Crusty breadsticks with rosemary

THESE ITALIAN-STYLE BREADSTICKS are a delicious addition to any meal, Italian or otherwise. You will need a plastic spray bottle filled with water to mist the oven while the breadsticks are baking (the water makes them crusty and chewy on the outside and slightly softer inside).

MAKES 12

- **1¾ cups warm water (105°F to 115°F)**
- **1 envelope dry yeast**
- **Pinch of sugar**
- **1 tablespoon salt**
- **1 tablespoon (generous) chopped fresh rosemary or 1 teaspoon dried**
- **4 cups (or more) bread flour, divided**
- **2 tablespoons cold whole milk**
- **2 tablespoons extra-virgin olive oil**
- **Cornmeal**
- **12 fresh rosemary sprigs**
- **1 egg, beaten to blend (for glaze)**
- **Coarse kosher salt (optional)**

POUR 1¾ cups warm water into large bowl of heavy-duty electric mixer fitted with dough hook. Add yeast and pinch of sugar; stir to blend. Let stand until mixture is foamy and yeast is dissolved, about 10 minutes. Add 1 tablespoon salt and chopped rosemary; beat on medium speed until blended. Add 4 cups flour, 1 cup at a time, beating until well incorporated. Mix milk and oil in small bowl. With mixer running on low speed, gradually add milk mixture. Increase speed to medium; beat 6 minutes. Scrape dough from hook and sides of bowl (dough will be soft and sticky). Let dough rest in bowl 15 minutes.

SPRINKLE 2 heavy baking sheets generously with cornmeal. Turn dough out onto floured surface and knead until soft and slightly sticky, adding more flour if necessary. Divide dough into 12 equal pieces. Let dough rest 10 minutes.

ROLL each dough piece between work surface and palms of hands to form 12-inch-long rope. Arrange 6 ropes on each baking sheet, spacing apart. Break small green clusters off rosemary sprigs. Insert stem end of rosemary clusters along top of breadsticks, spacing rosemary 2 inches apart. Using spray bottle filled with cold water, lightly mist breadsticks. Let breadsticks rise uncovered in warm, draft-free area until puffy and light, about 30 minutes.

POSITION 1 rack in bottom third and 1 rack in center of oven and preheat to 450°F. Brush breadsticks lightly with glaze. Sprinkle very lightly with coarse salt, if desired. Place baking sheets on racks in oven and spray oven with water. Bake 15 minutes, spraying oven with water every 5 minutes. Continue baking without spraying until breadsticks are golden and sound hollow when tapped, about 15 minutes longer. Transfer breadsticks to racks; cool completely. *(Can be made ahead. Wrap tightly in aluminum foil, then enclose in resealable plastic bags and freeze up to 2 weeks. If desired, rewarm thawed breadsticks wrapped in foil in 350°F oven about 15 minutes.)*

Miniature pumpkin breads

YOU'LL NEED six mini loaf pans for this recipe. Look for foil pans at the market; cookware shops also sell paper baking molds. If fresh ginger is difficult to find in your area, substitute ¼ teaspoon ground ginger. Shelled pumpkin seeds (also known as pepitas) are available at Latin markets, natural foods stores, and many supermarkets. These miniature breads make great gifts—just wrap a loaf in cellophane and tie a colorful ribbon around it.

MAKES 6

- **Nonstick vegetable oil spray**
- **3 cups raw (natural) shelled pumpkin seeds (pepitas; about 15 ounces)**
- **3½ cups unbleached all purpose flour**
- **2 teaspoons baking powder**
- **2 teaspoons baking soda**
- **1½ teaspoons salt**
- **1½ teaspoons ground cinnamon**
- **¾ teaspoon ground nutmeg**
- **3 cups canned pure pumpkin (about 24 ounces)**
- **1 cup sugar**
- **1 cup (packed) golden brown sugar**
- **1 cup vegetable oil**
- **4 large eggs**
- **1 teaspoon minced peeled fresh ginger**
- **¾ cup buttermilk**

PREHEAT oven to 350°F. Spray six 5¾x3¼x2-inch baby loaf pans with nonstick spray. Spread pumpkin seeds out on rimmed baking sheet. Roast until beginning to color, stirring twice, about 20 minutes. Cool seeds. Set aside ½ cup whole seeds for topping. Using on/off turns, coarsely grind remaining seeds in processor.

COMBINE flour, baking powder, baking soda, salt, cinnamon, and nutmeg in medium bowl; whisk to blend. Mix in ground pumpkin seeds. Using electric mixer, beat pumpkin and both sugars in large bowl until blended. Gradually beat in oil, then eggs 1 at a time, then ginger. Stir in dry ingredients in 4 additions alternately with buttermilk in 3 additions. Divide batter among prepared pans. Sprinkle with reserved ½ cup whole pumpkin seeds.

BAKE breads until tester inserted into centers comes out clean, about 1 hour. Cool completely in pans. *(Can be made 1 day ahead. Wrap in plastic and store at room temperature.)*

Zucchini spice bread

THIS QUICK BREAD has a sweet, crunchy crust and is moist and tender on the inside. Because it is lighter than traditional zucchini breads, it tastes more like a spice cake flavored with zucchini. This is a good recipe to keep handy in summer, when garden zucchini are abundant.

MAKES 1 LOAF

- **2½ cups all purpose flour**
- **1 teaspoon salt**
- **1 teaspoon ground cinnamon**
- **1 teaspoon baking soda**
- **¼ teaspoon baking powder**
- **3 large eggs**
- **2 cups sugar**
- **1 cup vegetable oil**
- **1 teaspoon vanilla extract**
- **2 cups coarsely grated zucchini (about 10 ounces)**
- **1 cup chopped walnuts, toasted**

PREHEAT oven to 350°F. Butter and flour 9x5x3-inch metal loaf pan. Whisk flour, salt, cinnamon, baking soda, and baking powder in medium bowl to blend. Using electric mixer, beat eggs in large bowl until foamy. Gradually add sugar, beating until mixture is very thick and pale, about 4 minutes. Slowly beat in oil, then vanilla. On low speed, beat in flour mixture in 3 additions. Fold in zucchini, then walnuts. Transfer batter to prepared pan.

BAKE bread until tester inserted into center comes out clean and top is dry and crusty, about 1 hour 30 minutes. Cool 5 minutes in pan on rack. Turn out onto rack and cool completely. *(Can be prepared 2 days ahead. Wrap in aluminum foil and store at room temperature.)*

Banana-walnut bread

TRY STASHING unpeeled ripe bananas (wrapped airtight) in the freezer so that when you're in the mood for moist and comforting banana bread, you can just let the bananas thaw for an hour or two before using. Make this bread at least one day ahead, since the flavor and texture improve overnight.

MAKES 2 LOAVES

- **3½ cups all purpose flour**
- **2 teaspoons baking soda**
- **½ teaspoon salt**
- **3 cups sugar**
- **1 cup solid vegetable shortening, room temperature**
- **1 tablespoon vanilla extract**
- **4 large eggs**
- **½ cup buttermilk**
- **3 cups mashed very ripe bananas (about 6)**
- **1 cup chopped walnuts**

PREHEAT oven to 350°F. Butter and flour two 9x5x3-inch metal loaf pans. Sift flour, baking soda, and salt twice into medium bowl; set aside. Using electric mixer, beat sugar, shortening, and vanilla in large bowl until well blended. Add eggs 1 at a time, beating well after each addition. Mix in flour mixture alternately with buttermilk in 2 additions each. Stir in mashed bananas and nuts. Divide batter between prepared pans.

BAKE bread until tester inserted into center comes out clean, about 1 hour. Cool loaves completely in pans on rack. Remove from pans. Wrap loaves tightly in aluminum foil. Store at room temperature at least 1 day and up to 3 days.

Italian Easter bread

THESE TRADITIONAL HOLIDAY LOAVES are made in several easy steps over about 18 hours. We recommend doing the first four steps on the first day, since step 4 includes an eight- to ten-hour rising that ideally could be done overnight. Then finish the bread the following morning. Dove-shaped paper molds are available at cookware stores, but you can use two buttered and floured nine-inch-diameter springform pans instead. Candied orange peel can be found in some specialty foods stores; during the holidays, you may also be able to find it at some supermarkets and natural foods stores.

MAKES 2 LOAVES

Step 1 (starter)

3 tablespoons plus 1 teaspoon room temperature water (75°F to 80°F)
¼ teaspoon sugar
1½ teaspoons dry yeast
7 tablespoons unbleached all purpose flour

COMBINE 3 tablespoons plus 1 teaspoon water and sugar in bowl of heavy-duty electric mixer. Stir in yeast. Let stand until yeast dissolves and mixture is foamy, about 10 minutes. Using rubber spatula, mix in flour (dough will be firm). Cover bowl with plastic wrap. Let starter rise at room temperature until puffy, about 45 minutes.

Step 2

⅔ cup unbleached all purpose flour
4 large egg yolks
3 tablespoons room temperature water (75°F to 80°F)
2 teaspoons sugar

ATTACH dough hook to mixer. Add ⅔ cup flour and next 3 ingredients to starter. Beat until blended, stopping often to scrape down sides of bowl, about 5 minutes (dough will be soft and thick). Scrape dough off hook; remove hook. Cover bowl with plastic wrap. Let dough rise at room temperature until puffy and bubbly on top, about 1 hour.

Step 3

6 tablespoons (¾ stick) unsalted butter, cut into 6 pieces, room temperature (very soft)
5 tablespoons sugar
2 large egg yolks
2 tablespoons lukewarm whole milk (85°F to 95°F)
1 tablespoon honey
2¼ cups unbleached all purpose flour

REATTACH clean dough hook. Add butter and next 4 ingredients to dough; beat until blended. Add flour. Beat at low speed until smooth, stopping often to scrape down bowl and hook, about 5 minutes (dough will be firm and compact). Scrape dough off hook; remove hook. Cover bowl with plastic wrap; let dough rise at room temperature until lighter in texture and slightly puffed, about 3½ hours.

Step 4

½ cup room temperature water (75°F to 80°F)
1½ teaspoons dry yeast
2 cups unbleached all purpose flour, divided
1 cup (2 sticks) unsalted butter, cut into 12 pieces, room temperature (very soft), divided
6 tablespoons sugar
4 large egg yolks, divided
3 tablespoons lukewarm whole milk (85°F to 95°F)
2 teaspoons vanilla extract
1½ teaspoons fine sea salt
1½ cups chopped candied orange peel (about 10 ounces)

REATTACH clean dough hook. Mix ½ cup water and yeast in small cup. Let stand until yeast dissolves, about 10 minutes; add to dough. Add 1⅓ cups flour, 6 pieces butter, sugar, and 2 egg yolks; beat until dough is smooth, about 3 minutes. Scrape down dough hook and sides of bowl. Add remaining 2 egg yolks, milk, vanilla, and salt. Beat on low speed until blended, about 3 minutes. Scrape down hook. Add remaining ⅔ cup flour, remaining butter, and orange peel. Beat dough until well blended, about 5 minutes. Scrape dough into very large (at least 4-quart) buttered bowl. Cover with plastic wrap. Let dough rise at room temperature until doubled in volume and indentation remains when 2 fingers are pressed about ¼ inch into dough, about 8 to 10 hours.

Step 5

- **½ cup (about) all purpose flour**
- **2 dove-shaped paper baking molds (size C3) or two 9-inch-diameter springform pans**

SPRINKLE ½ cup flour onto work surface. Scrape dough out onto floured work surface (dough will be soft and sticky).

GENTLY toss dough in flour until easy to handle. Brush away excess flour. Divide dough into 3 equal pieces. Divide 1 piece in half; shape each half into 10-inch-long log. Arrange 1 log crosswise in each paper baking mold, curving ends to fit. Roll each remaining dough piece into 11-inch-long log, slightly tapered at ends. Place 1 log across dough in each mold. (If using 2 springform pans, divide dough in half; place half in each prepared pan.) Cover molds (or pans) with plastic wrap. Let stand at room temperature until dough rises to top and indentation remains when 2 fingers are pressed about ¼ inch into dough, about 3¼ hours.

Step 6 (glaze and baking)

- **1 cup sugar**
- **½ cup whole unblanched almonds**
- **3 large egg whites**
- **¼ teaspoon almond extract**
- **1⅓ cups sliced almonds**
- **Powdered sugar**

POSITION rack in bottom third of oven and preheat to 375°F. Finely grind sugar and whole almonds in processor. Add egg whites and almond extract; blend 10 seconds for glaze. Peel plastic off dough. Spoon half of almond glaze over top of each. Sprinkle each with sliced almonds. Sift powdered sugar over. Slide rimless baking sheet under molds; slide molds directly onto oven rack.

BAKE until breads are brown on top and slender wooden skewer inserted into centers comes out clean, about 45 minutes. Cool breads completely on rack. *(Can be made ahead. Wrap in aluminum foil and let stand at room temperature up to 2 days or freeze up to 1 week.)*

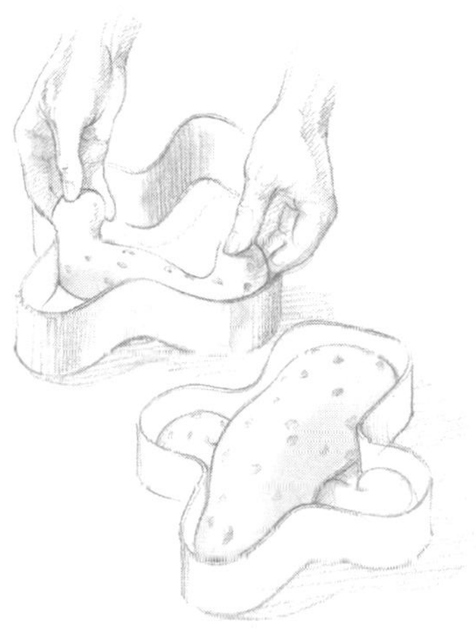

Honey-oat bread

SERVE THICK SLICES of this tender, slightly sweet bread with butter and honey. Or use it to make the ultimate peanut butter and honey sandwich, using natural peanut butter, banana slices, chopped dates, and a drizzle of honey. You can enjoy one loaf fresh and freeze the second loaf for later use.

MAKES 2 SMALL LOAVES

- **1¾ cups warm water (105°F to 110°F), divided**
- **1 tablespoon dry yeast**
- **¾ cup quick-cooking oats**
- **⅓ cup honey**
- **3 tablespoons vegetable oil**
- **2½ teaspoons salt**
- **5 cups (about) all purpose flour, divided**

- **1 large egg, beaten to blend (for glaze)**
- **Additional quick-cooking oats**

STIR ¼ cup warm water and yeast in large bowl. Let stand until yeast dissolves, about 10 minutes. Stir in remaining 1½ cups water, ¾ cup oats, honey, oil, and salt. Stir in enough flour 1 cup at a time to form soft dough. Coat another large bowl with oil. Transfer dough to oiled bowl and turn to coat. Cover with plastic wrap, then kitchen towel, and let rise at room temperature until doubled in volume, about 1 hour.

OIL two 8½x4½x2½-inch loaf pans. Punch down dough; shape into 2 loaves. Place 1 loaf in each pan. Cover and let rise in warm, draft-free area until almost doubled in volume, about 20 minutes.

PREHEAT oven to 350°F. Brush tops of loaves with beaten egg; sprinkle with additional oats. Bake until loaves are brown on top and tester inserted into center comes out clean, about 40 minutes. Cool completely. *(Can be made ahead. Wrap in aluminum foil, then enclose in resealable plastic bag and store at room temperature up to 1 day or freeze up to 2 weeks.)*

Jams and condiments

Fig and grape preserves

PRESERVES IS A SOPHISTICATED term for jam, and this one is definitely sophisticated. The combination of dried Calimyrna figs, red grapes, Zinfandel, and a hint of citrus makes for a luscious grown-up breakfast or afternoon tea snack with whole grain toast or warm, nutty scones.

MAKES ABOUT 1½ CUPS

- **3 cups seedless red grapes, halved**
- **1 cup diced dried Calimyrna figs (about 5 ounces)**
- **1 cup Zinfandel or other dry red wine**
- **¼ cup sugar**
- **2 teaspoons grated orange peel**
- **2 teaspoons fresh lemon juice**

COMBINE first 5 ingredients in medium saucepan. Bring to boil over medium-high heat, stirring occasionally. Reduce heat to medium-low, cover, and simmer 10 minutes. Uncover and increase heat to medium; simmer until liquid is reduced to syrup, stirring frequently, about 10 minutes longer. Transfer to bowl. Stir in lemon juice. Cool. *(Can be made 1 week ahead. Cover and refrigerate.)*

Honey, apricot, and cherry preserves

THESE DELICIOUS PRESERVES can be made with regular honey or with distinctively flavored Greek honey, which is available through specialty foods stores and online specialty foods retailers.

MAKES ABOUT 1¾ CUPS

- **1¼ cups apricot nectar**
- **1 cup chopped dried apricots**
- **1 cup dried tart cherries or cranberries (about 4 ounces)**
- **⅓ cup honey**
- **6 tablespoons sweet white wine (such as Riesling)**
- **2 tablespoons sugar**

MIX all ingredients in heavy medium saucepan. Stir over medium heat until sugar dissolves and mixture comes to simmer. Cover pan and simmer until fruit is tender and preserves thicken, stirring frequently, about 15 minutes. *(Can be prepared 1 week ahead. Cover and refrigerate.)*

Spiced plum jam

CITRUS JUICE and a cinnamon stick add subtle dimensions to this lovely jam. For the best flavor and for a bright violet-red color, use dark-skinned plums with red to purple flesh such as Santa Rosas or Angelinas.

MAKES ABOUT 4 CUPS (ENOUGH FOR FOUR 8-OUNCE JARS)

- **½ cup fresh orange juice**
- **¼ cup fresh lemon juice**
- **2 pounds plums (preferably purple-fleshed), halved, pitted, cut into ½-inch-thick slices**
- **1 cinnamon stick**
- **3½ cups sugar**

COMBINE orange juice and lemon juice in heavy large saucepan; bring to boil. Add plums and cinnamon stick. Cover pan and bring to boil. Reduce heat and simmer covered until plums are very tender, stirring occasionally, about 15 minutes. Add 3½ cups sugar and stir until sugar is dissolved. Simmer uncovered until plum mixture reaches gelling stage, crushing fruit with back of spoon and stirring occasionally, about 1 hour. (To test for doneness, remove pan from heat. Fill chilled spoon with preserves, then slowly pour preserves back into pan; last 2 drops should merge and sheet off spoon. Or spoon 1 tablespoon preserves onto chilled plate and freeze 2 minutes; preserves should wrinkle when pushed gently with fingertips.) Discard cinnamon stick.

RINSE clean jars, lids, and screw bands in hot water. Spoon preserves into hot jar to ¼ inch from top. Immediately wipe rim, using towel dipped into hot water. Place lid on jar; seal tightly with screw band. Repeat with remaining preserves and jars. Arrange jars on rack set in large pot. Cover with boiling water by at least 1 inch. Cover pot and boil 15 minutes.

REMOVE jars from water bath. Cool to room temperature. Press center of each lid. If lid stays down, jar is sealed. Store in cool dry place up to 1 year. Refrigerate after opening. (If lid pops up, store preserves in refrigerator. If preserves have not been processed in water bath as described above, cover and refrigerate.)

Double-berry preserves

A WONDERFUL WAY to capture the flavors of summer. The wide surface of a large skillet reduces the cooking time, which helps keep the fruit flavor at its peak.

MAKES 2 CUPS

- **2 1-pint containers strawberries, hulled, diced**
- **1 ½-pint container fresh raspberries or 1½ cups frozen unsweetened, thawed**
- **¾ cup sugar**

COMBINE all ingredients in heavy large skillet. Stir over low heat until sugar dissolves. Increase heat and boil until preserves are very thick, stirring frequently, about 10 minutes. Spoon into small bowl. Cover and refrigerate. *(Can be prepared 1 week ahead. Keep refrigerated.)*

Lemon-ginger marmalade

THE SEEDS, or "pips" as they call them in Britain (where citrus marmalades date back to the sixteenth century), contain pectin, as does the pith. Gathering the seeds into a cheesecloth bundle and cooking them with the lemons ensures that there will be enough pectin for gelling. Stir carefully after adding the sugar to avoid scorching this distinctive alternative to the traditional orange marmalade.

MAKES ABOUT 3½ CUPS (ENOUGH FOR ABOUT FOUR 8-OUNCE JARS)

- **3 large lemons**
- **3¾ cups cold water, divided**
- **1 4x1-inch piece fresh ginger, peeled, cut into thick slices**
- **4 cups sugar**

CUT off lemon ends. Cut lemons lengthwise into quarters, then cut crosswise into thin slices, removing and reserving seeds. Place lemon seeds in small bowl. Place lemon slices in medium bowl. Add ½ cup cold water to bowl with seeds and 3 cups cold water to bowl with lemon slices. Cover bowls with plastic wrap and let stand 24 hours at room temperature.

TRANSFER lemon slices with their soaking liquid to heavy large saucepan. Strain liquid from bowl with seeds into same saucepan. Wrap seeds in cheesecloth; tie with string and add to saucepan. Bring to simmer over medium-high heat. Cover partially and adjust heat so that mixture barely simmers. Cook 45 minutes, stirring occasionally.

PUREE sliced ginger with remaining ¼ cup water in processor, stopping occasionally to scrape down sides of bowl. Strain mixture through sieve, pressing down on solids with spoon. Reserve ¼ cup ginger juice. Discard solids.

REMOVE cheesecloth bag from saucepan and squeeze it between spoons so that liquid drains back into pan. Add 4 cups sugar to lemon mixture and stir until dissolved. Add reserved ¼ cup ginger juice. Simmer mixture uncovered until gelling stage is reached, about 1 hour. (To test for doneness, remove pan from heat. Fill chilled spoon with marmalade, then slowly pour marmalade back into pan; last 2 drops should merge and sheet off spoon. Or spoon 1 tablespoon marmalade onto chilled plate and freeze 2 minutes; marmalade should wrinkle when gently pushed with fingertip.)

RINSE clean jars, lids, and screw bands in hot water. Spoon marmalade into hot jar to ¼ inch from top. Immediately wipe rim, using towel dipped into hot water. Place lid on jar; seal tightly with screw band. Repeat with remaining marmalade and jars. Arrange jars on rack set in large pot. Cover with boiling water by at least 1 inch. Cover pot and boil 15 minutes.

REMOVE jars from water bath. Cool to room temperature. Press center of each lid. If lid stays down, jar is sealed. Store in cool dry place up to 1 year. Refrigerate after opening. (If lid pops up, store marmalade in refrigerator. If marmalade has not been processed in water bath as described above, cover and refrigerate.)

Five-minute spiced orange marmalade

HONEY, BRANDY, AND WHOLE SPICES give store-bought marmalade an amazing flavor. Make a batch and keep a jar for yourself; then tie gold ribbons around the remaining two for an easy-to-make gift. The brown star-shaped star anise pods are sold at Asian markets and specialty foods stores, and in the spice section of some supermarkets.

MAKES ABOUT 3 CUPS (ENOUGH FOR THREE 8-OUNCE JARS)

- **½ cup honey**
- **½ cup brandy**
- **3 cinnamon sticks**
- **3 whole star anise**
- **1 vanilla bean, cut crosswise into 3 pieces**
- **3 3x1-inch strips orange peel (orange part only)**
- **12 whole cloves**
- **2 14- to 16-ounce jars orange marmalade**

COMBINE first 5 ingredients in large saucepan. Pierce each orange peel strip with 4 cloves, spacing apart; add to pan. Simmer until mixture is reduced to ½ cup, about 5 minutes. Add marmalade; bring to simmer, stirring often. Remove from heat.

USING tongs, transfer 1 star anise, 1 cinnamon stick, 1 vanilla piece, and 1 orange-clove strip to each of three 8-ounce canning jars. Fill each jar with hot marmalade and seal with lids. *(Can be prepared 4 weeks ahead. Refrigerate.)*

Chunky country-style spiced applesauce

THE TART GRANNY SMITH APPLE softens and falls apart as it cooks; the sweet Golden Delicious apple retains its shape when tender and develops a rich buttery flavor as it cooks. Combining the two results in an applesauce with a chunky texture and tart-sweet flavor.

MAKES ABOUT 6 CUPS

2 pounds Granny Smith apples, halved, cored, peeled, sliced
2 pounds Golden Delicious apples, halved, cored, peeled, sliced
2 cups water
2 tablespoons (or more) fresh lemon juice
½ cup sugar
½ teaspoon ground cinnamon
¼ teaspoon (generous) ground cardamom

COMBINE all apples, 2 cups water, and 2 tablespoons lemon juice in heavy large pot; bring to boil over high heat. Reduce heat to medium, cover, and simmer until apples are tender, about 20 minutes. Uncover and cook until mixture is thick, stirring frequently, about 10 minutes longer. Mash apples slightly with potato masher until chunky applesauce forms. Stir in sugar and spices. Cool. Add more lemon juice, if desired. Transfer to bowl; cover and refrigerate overnight. *(Can be prepared 2 days ahead. Keep refrigerated.)*

Cranberry Cumberland sauce

CUMBERLAND SAUCE is an English classic made with red currant jelly, mustard, orange peel, pepper, and Port, and served cold with cold meats. Try this updated version starring the very American cranberry—it's great with hot or cold turkey or ham.

MAKES ABOUT 1½ CUPS

2 cups fresh or frozen cranberries (about 8 ounces)
¾ cup tawny Port
½ cup (or more) sugar
Pinch of salt
2½ tablespoons orange juice
¾ teaspoon cornstarch
½ teaspoon dry mustard
½ teaspoon fresh lemon juice
Pinch of ground cloves
Pinch of ground ginger
¼ cup golden raisins
1 tablespoon grated orange peel
½ teaspoon grated lemon peel

COMBINE cranberries and Port in heavy large saucepan. Bring to boil over medium-high heat. Cook until berries burst, stirring occasionally, about 10 minutes. Add ½ cup sugar and salt; stir 1 minute. Combine orange juice, cornstarch, mustard, lemon juice, and spices in small bowl; whisk until smooth. Stir into berry mixture. Add raisins, orange peel, and lemon peel. Reduce heat to medium and simmer until mixture thickens, stirring occasionally and adding more sugar, if desired, about 5 minutes. Cool. *(Can be made 3 days ahead. Cover and refrigerate. Bring to room temperature before serving.)*

Cranberry sauce with dried cherries and cloves

CRANBERRIES ARE high in benzoic acid, a natural preservative, which means that they can keep for several weeks in the refrigerator without any spoilage. But combining the berries with sweet-tart dried cherries and ground cloves creates a sauce that won't keep long at all—because it will be devoured quickly by guests.

MAKES ABOUT 4½ CUPS

2½ cups cherry cider or black cherry cider or cranberry juice cocktail
8 ounces dried tart cherries (about 2 cups)

- **1 cup sugar**
- **1 12-ounce bag fresh or frozen cranberries**
- **¼ teaspoon (generous) ground cloves**

BRING cider to simmer in heavy large saucepan. Remove from heat. Add cherries and let stand 8 minutes. Mix in sugar, then cranberries and cloves. Cook over medium-high heat until cranberries burst, stirring occasionally, about 9 minutes. Transfer to bowl; cover and refrigerate until cold, about 4 hours (sauce will thicken as it cools). *(Can be prepared 4 days ahead. Keep refrigerated.)*

Gingered cranberry and kumquat relish

MOST THANKSGIVING TABLES would be incomplete without a cooked cranberry sauce and a fresh, raw relish such as this one. Native to China, kumquats are small golden-orange-colored fruits with a pithless, sweet rind and a very sour pulp. They lend a unique citrus-flavored snap, but a small orange, cut into 1-inch pieces, could stand in beautifully.

MAKES ABOUT 3 CUPS

- **1 12-ounce bag fresh or frozen cranberries**
- **16 kumquats, stemmed, rinsed, patted dry, divided**
- **1 cup sugar**
- **½ cup minced crystallized ginger**

USING on/off turns, coarsely chop cranberries in processor. Transfer cranberries to medium bowl. Mince half of kumquats, removing any seeds. Thinly slice remaining kumquats, removing any seeds. Mix all kumquats, sugar, and ginger into chopped cranberries (sugar will dissolve as mixture stands). Cover relish and refrigerate at least 4 hours. *(Can be prepared 1 week ahead. Keep refrigerated.)*

Cranberry sauce with roasted shallots and Port

ROASTED SHALLOTS, balsamic vinegar, ruby Port, and marjoram give this not-too-sweet version of the Thanksgiving classic a unique flavor. The whole sauce can be made ahead, but you could also roast the shallots and refrigerate them a day or two before preparing the rest of the sauce.

MAKES ABOUT 4 CUPS

- **18 large shallots, peeled, quartered lengthwise through root end**
- **1 tablespoon vegetable oil**
- **5 teaspoons minced fresh thyme, divided**
- **5 tablespoons balsamic vinegar, divided**
- **1 tablespoon plus ½ cup sugar**

- **1⅔ cups ruby Port**
- **⅓ cup (packed) golden brown sugar**
- **1 12-ounce bag fresh or frozen cranberries**
- **¼ cup dried currants**
- **1 tablespoon chopped fresh marjoram**

PREHEAT oven to 400°F. Toss shallots with oil and 3 teaspoons thyme on small rimmed baking sheet. Sprinkle with salt and pepper. Bake until shallots are golden, about 25 minutes. Mix 1 tablespoon vinegar and 1 tablespoon sugar in small bowl. Drizzle over shallots; toss to coat. Continue roasting until shallots caramelize, stirring occasionally, about 10 minutes. Remove from oven.

BRING Port, brown sugar, and remaining 4 tablespoons vinegar and ½ cup sugar to boil in heavy large saucepan over medium-high heat, stirring until sugar dissolves. Add cranberries and currants; cook until berries pop, stirring occasionally, about 8 minutes. Mix in marjoram and remaining 2 teaspoons thyme. Mix in shallots. Transfer to bowl. Cover and chill overnight. *(Can be made 1 week ahead. Keep refrigerated.)* Serve cranberry sauce cold or at room temperature.

Cakes 16

Cakes and tortes have their roots in all parts of the world, but they have come to be seen as typically American. And like Americans themselves, American cakes are big, brash, and bold—also understated and elegant, dramatic and subtle, old-fashioned and contemporary. As we said, American cakes are like Americans: all over the map. And that's what we love about them.

Grand celebrations, birthday parties, and holiday feasts call for cakes piled high with frosting, filled with surprises, or gilded with all manner of toppings. More sophisticated events call for dramatic desserts, such as the chocolate lava cake, which has made the leap from restaurant menu to home kitchen because of its elegance and "wow" factor. Essentially a chocolate soufflé baked in individual servings, the cake is cooked just until the outside is set and the center forms a warm, rich, gooey sauce.

Another favorite American indulgence is cheesecake. Having begun as a simple combination of cream cheese, eggs, sugar, and sour cream, the cheesecake can now be found dressed up in flavors from cranberry-orange to coconut candy bar.

Tortes are rich, elegant cakes in which ground nuts or cookie crumbs often replace much of the flour. The word *torte* also encompasses the lattice-topped, world-renowned Linzertorte; our contemporary version is a nut-and spice-enriched cake layered with a white chocolate-cream cheese frosting and raspberry preserves. Some tortes are classical European desserts, others are pure Americana: Where else would there be a white chocolate mousse torte with an Oreo cookie crust?

Finally, at least one version of a spice cake should find its way into every cook's repertoire. With their perfume of ginger, cloves, and nutmeg (which combine especially well with winter's sweet potatoes, pears, and pumpkin), spice cakes satisfy even before they emerge from the oven. And note that a slice of spice cake really needs no big occasion. Just try it with a personal one: relaxing in the living room with a good book and a cup of tea.

Chocolate–toffee crunch layer cake with milk chocolate frosting

MILK CHOCOLATE FROSTING and a generous sprinkling of diced English toffee candy bars separate the moist and tender dark chocolate cake layers, and masses of milk chocolate curls are piled on top of this chocolate-lover's dream. Once assembled, the cake can be chilled for two days before serving.

10 TO 12 SERVINGS

Cake

- **4 ounces unsweetened chocolate**
- **½ cup hot water**

- **1¾ cups cake flour**
- **1 teaspoon baking soda**
- **½ teaspoon salt**
- **½ cup (1 stick) unsalted butter, room temperature**
- **1¾ cups sugar**
- **3 large eggs, room temperature**
- **1 teaspoon vanilla extract**
- **⅔ cup whole milk**

Frosting

- **1¼ cups whipping cream**
- **¼ cup light corn syrup**
- **¼ cup (½ stick) unsalted butter**
- **1 pound imported milk chocolate (such as Lindt), chopped**
- **4 1.4-ounce chocolate-covered English toffee bars (such as Heath or Skor), cut into ¼-inch dice**

- **1 7-ounce bar milk chocolate**

FOR CAKE: Position rack in center of oven and preheat to 350°F. Butter two 9-inch-diameter cake pans with 1¾-inch-high sides. Line bottoms of pans with waxed paper; butter paper. Dust pans with flour; tap out excess. Combine unsweetened chocolate and ½ cup hot water in heavy small saucepan. Stir over low heat until melted and smooth. Cool to lukewarm, stirring often.

WHISK flour, baking soda, and salt in medium bowl to blend. Using electric mixer, beat butter in large bowl until light and fluffy. Gradually beat in sugar. Add eggs 1 at a time, beating well after each, then beat in vanilla. Beat in chocolate mixture. Add flour mixture in 3 additions alternately with milk in 2 additions, beating just to blend after each addition.

DIVIDE batter equally between pans. Bake cakes until tester inserted into center comes out clean and cake just begins to pull away from sides of pan, about 35 minutes. Cool cakes in pans on racks 5 minutes. Cut around pan sides. Turn cakes out onto racks; peel off paper. Cool cakes completely.

FOR FROSTING: Combine cream, corn syrup, and butter in heavy large saucepan. Whisk over medium heat until mixture begins to simmer. Add chopped milk chocolate. Reduce heat to low and whisk until mixture is smooth, about 1 minute. Transfer to large bowl.

FILL another large bowl with ice. Set bottom of bowl with chocolate mixture atop ice; whisk until cool and beginning to thicken, about 8 minutes. Remove bowl from ice. Using electric mixer, beat until color lightens and mixture forms frosting thick enough to make soft peaks when beaters are lifted, about 2 minutes (frosting will continue to thicken as it stands).

PLACE 1 cake layer, flat side up, on 8-inch-diameter tart pan bottom or cardboard round. If desired, place pan bottom with cake atop 8-inch-diameter cake pan to make simple decorating stand. Top layer with 1½ cups frosting, spreading to edge. Sprinkle evenly with diced toffee. Top with second cake layer, flat side down; press slightly to adhere. Spread thin layer of frosting over top and sides of cake to seal and set crumbs. Working quickly, spread remaining frosting over sides then top of cake (if frosting becomes stiff, stir gently with spatula to loosen).

STAND chocolate bar on 1 short end. Using swivel-bladed vegetable peeler and starting at top edge of 1 side, run peeler down length of bar (chocolate will come away from side of chocolate bar in curls). Pile chocolate curls atop cake. Refrigerate at least 2 hours. *(Can be prepared 2 days ahead. Cover with cake dome and keep refrigerated. Let stand at room temperature 1 hour before serving.)*

Fudge layer cake with peppermint mousse

IDEAL FOR A HOLIDAY DESSERT, this triple-layer cake is filled with a mousse made of white chocolate and crushed peppermint candies; a silky chocolate ganache is poured over the top. You'll need an eight-inch cardboard round, available at bakery supply stores, to support the cake for frosting and serving (or use an eight-inch-diameter tart pan bottom).

10 TO 12 SERVINGS

Cake

2 cups all purpose flour
1½ teaspoons baking soda
½ teaspoon salt
1 cup unsweetened cocoa powder
1⅔ cups boiling water

1 cup (2 sticks) unsalted butter, room temperature
2 cups sugar
1½ teaspoons vanilla extract
3 large eggs

Peppermint mousse

10 ounces high-quality white chocolate (such as Lindt or Perugina), chopped
1¾ cups chilled whipping cream, divided
¼ cup sour cream
24 red-and-white-striped peppermint hard candies, crushed (about ⅔ cup)

Ganache

2 cups whipping cream
1 pound bittersweet (not unsweetened) or semisweet chocolate, chopped

FOR CAKE: Preheat oven to 325°F. Butter and flour three 9-inch-diameter cake pans with 1½-inch-high sides. Whisk flour, baking soda, and salt in small bowl to blend. Place cocoa in medium bowl; whisk in 1⅔ cups boiling water. Cool cocoa mixture to room temperature, whisking occasionally.

USING electric mixer, beat butter in large bowl until light and fluffy. Gradually beat in sugar, then vanilla. Add eggs 1 at a time, beating well after each addition. At low speed, beat in flour mixture in 3 additions alternately with cocoa mixture in 2 additions.

DIVIDE batter equally among prepared pans. Bake cakes until tester inserted into center comes out clean, about 25 minutes. Cool cakes in pans 10 minutes. Cut around cakes to loosen; turn out onto racks. Cool completely.

FOR PEPPERMINT MOUSSE: Combine white chocolate, ¾ cup whipping cream, and sour cream in heavy medium saucepan. Stir over low heat just until chocolate is melted and smooth. Transfer white chocolate mixture to large bowl; cool to barely lukewarm, whisking occasionally, about 20 minutes. Mix in candies. Beat remaining 1 cup cream in medium bowl to soft peaks. Fold cream into barely lukewarm white chocolate mixture in 4 additions. Refrigerate mousse until beginning to set, about 2 hours.

PLACE 1 cake layer on 8-inch cardboard round. Spread half of mousse over top of cake. Top with second cake layer, remaining mousse, and third cake layer. Refrigerate assembled cake until mousse is cold and set, about 3 hours.

MEANWHILE, PREPARE GANACHE: Bring cream to simmer in heavy large saucepan. Remove from heat. Add bittersweet chocolate; whisk until melted and smooth. Cool ganache until thick but still pourable, about 45 minutes.

PLACE cake on rack set over baking sheet. Pour ganache over cake, spreading with metal spatula to cover sides evenly. Refrigerate cake until ganache sets, about 1 hour. *(Can be prepared 1 day ahead. Cover with cake dome and keep refrigerated.)*

Chocolate-hazelnut cake

THIS SOPHISTICATED CAKE plays on the idea of gianduja, the luscious paste of hazelnuts and chocolate, by blending those ingredients into a creamy filling. Then the cake is iced with a bittersweet chocolate glaze. Buttermilk adds moisture to the cake layers, while a small amount of espresso powder amplifies the chocolate flavors, making the chocolate taste more chocolaty. This cake can be made one day ahead.

12 SERVINGS

Filling

- **½ cup whipping cream**
- **1 tablespoon light corn syrup**
- **8 ounces imported milk chocolate (such as Lindt), finely chopped**

- **½ cup hazelnuts, toasted, skinned**
- **2 teaspoons powdered sugar**

Cake

- **1 cup sifted all purpose flour (sifted, then measured)**
- **⅓ cup unsweetened cocoa powder**
- **½ teaspoon salt**
- **¼ teaspoon baking powder**
- **¼ teaspoon baking soda**
- **1½ tablespoons hot water**
- **1 tablespoon instant espresso powder or instant coffee powder**
- **½ cup buttermilk**
- **¾ cup (1½ sticks) unsalted butter, room temperature**
- **1⅓ cups sugar**
- **1 teaspoon vanilla extract**
- **3 large eggs**

Glaze

- **6 ounces bittersweet (not unsweetened) or semisweet chocolate, chopped**
- **½ cup (1 stick) unsalted butter, cut into pieces**
- **1 tablespoon light corn syrup**

- **12 whole hazelnuts, toasted, skinned**

FOR FILLING: Bring cream and corn syrup to simmer in heavy small saucepan. Place chocolate in medium bowl. Pour hot cream mixture over and let stand 1 minute. Whisk until chocolate melts and mixture is smooth. Set aside.

BLEND hazelnuts and sugar in processor until paste forms, stopping occasionally to scrape down sides of bowl. Stir paste into chocolate mixture. Refrigerate filling until cool but still spreadable, about 2 hours.

FOR CAKE: Position rack in bottom third of oven and preheat to 350°F. Butter 9-inch-diameter cake pan with 2-inch-high sides. Line bottom with parchment paper. Dust pan with flour; tap out excess. Sift flour and next 4 ingredients into medium bowl. Stir 1½ tablespoons hot water and espresso powder in small bowl until powder dissolves. Mix in buttermilk. Using electric mixer, beat butter in large bowl until light and fluffy. Gradually beat in sugar, then vanilla. Add eggs 1 at a time, beating well after each addition. Beat in flour mixture alternately with buttermilk mixture in 2 additions each.

POUR batter into prepared pan. Bake until tester inserted into center comes out clean, about 45 minutes. Cool cake in pan on rack 5 minutes. Turn cake out onto rack. Peel off parchment. Turn right side up onto another rack and cool.

USING wooden spoon, beat filling until slightly softened and lightened in color, about 30 seconds. Cut cake horizontally in half. Place 1 layer cut side up on platter. Slide waxed paper strips under edges of cake. Spread half of filling over cake. Top with second layer, cut side down. Spread remaining filling over sides and top of cake. Refrigerate 10 minutes.

MEANWHILE, PREPARE GLAZE: Combine chocolate, butter, and corn syrup in top of double boiler set over simmering water. Stir until smooth. Remove from over water. Cool to lukewarm, stirring occasionally.

POUR glaze in pool over center of cake. Using icing spatula, spread over top and sides of cake. Arrange 12 nuts around top edge of cake. Remove waxed paper. *(Can be prepared 1 day ahead. Cover with cake dome and refrigerate. Let stand 1 hour at room temperature before serving.)*

Mississippi mud cake

THIS CLASSIC CHOCOLATE CAKE gets its unlikely moniker from its color: the same as the deep, rich soil that lines Ol' Man River. It's usually made in a single-layer rectangle, but we dressed ours up and fashioned it into a layer cake. Toasted pecans and marshmallows are baked into the top surface of each layer; once it's assembled, only the sides of the cake are frosted, the better to show off the marshmallow-pecan topping. You'll need a candy thermometer (available at cookware stores) to test the temperature of the frosting. The cake can be prepared one day ahead.

12 SERVINGS

Cake

1½ cups (3 sticks) unsalted butter, room temperature
1½ cups (packed) dark brown sugar
1 cup sugar
3 ounces unsweetened chocolate, chopped, melted
¼ cup whipping cream
2 teaspoons vanilla extract
6 large eggs, room temperature
2¼ cups all purpose flour
½ cup unsweetened cocoa powder
½ teaspoon baking soda
¼ teaspoon salt

3 cups mini marshmallows
2 cups coarsely chopped toasted pecans

Frosting

1 cup (packed) dark brown sugar
1 cup whipping cream
½ cup (1 stick) unsalted butter, cut into pieces
5 ounces unsweetened chocolate, chopped
2 ounces bittersweet (not unsweetened) or semisweet chocolate, chopped
2 tablespoons dark corn syrup
1 teaspoon vanilla extract

FOR CAKE: Preheat oven to 350°F. Line two 9x9x2-inch cake pans with aluminum foil, extending foil over sides. Butter and flour foil. Using electric mixer, beat butter and both sugars in large bowl until light and fluffy. Beat in melted chocolate, cream, and vanilla. Add eggs 1 at a time, beating well after each addition. Sift flour, cocoa, baking soda, and salt into medium bowl. Stir flour mixture into batter, which will be very thick.

DIVIDE batter equally between prepared pans; smooth top. Bake cakes until tester inserted into center comes out clean, about 20 minutes. Remove from oven; maintain oven temperature.

SPRINKLE 1½ cups marshmallows and 1 cup pecans over each cake. Bake just until marshmallows begin to melt, about 6 minutes. Transfer to racks. Cool cakes completely in pans.

FOR FROSTING: Combine sugar and cream in heavy medium saucepan. Stir over medium heat until sugar dissolves. Cook without stirring until candy thermometer registers 220°F, about 8 minutes. Remove from heat and whisk in remaining ingredients. Whisk until all chocolate melts and frosting is smooth. Refrigerate frosting until spreadable, about 1 hour 15 minutes.

USING foil as aid, lift cakes from pans. Remove foil. Place 1 cake layer on plate, marshmallow side up. Spread 1½ cups frosting over. Top with second cake layer, marshmallow side up. Spread remaining frosting in waves on sides (not top) of cake. *(Can be prepared 1 day ahead. Cover with cake dome and refrigerate. Bring to room temperature before serving.)*

Chocolate-espresso cake with mocha glaze

HERE'S A SPECIAL-OCCASION CAKE that is surprisingly simple to make. Just be sure to begin one day before you plan to serve it: The lustrous mocha glaze that coats the entire cake needs to set overnight in the refrigerator. Bittersweet and semisweet chocolate are often used interchangeably without any noticeable difference, but in this recipe, use bittersweet chocolate if you want a more intense chocolate flavor.

12 SERVINGS

Cake

3/4 cup plus 2 tablespoons (1 3/4 sticks) unsalted butter
10 ounces bittersweet (not unsweetened) or semisweet chocolate, chopped
4 teaspoons instant espresso powder or instant coffee powder
4 large eggs
1 1/4 cups sugar
1 tablespoon vanilla extract
3/4 cup all purpose flour

Glaze

2/3 cup whipping cream
2 teaspoons instant espresso powder or instant coffee powder
8 ounces bittersweet (not unsweetened) or semisweet chocolate, chopped
1/2 teaspoon vanilla extract

FOR CAKE: Preheat oven to 350°F. Butter and flour 9-inch-diameter springform pan. Stir butter, chocolate, and espresso powder in heavy medium saucepan over low heat until melted and smooth. Transfer to large bowl and cool to room temperature. Add eggs, sugar, and vanilla; whisk until well blended. Add flour and whisk just until blended.

TRANSFER batter to prepared pan. Bake cake until tester inserted into center comes out with moist (not wet) batter attached, about 45 minutes. Cool completely in pan.

FOR GLAZE: Mix cream and espresso powder in medium saucepan. Bring to simmer over medium heat, whisking to blend. Remove from heat. Add chocolate and vanilla; whisk until melted and smooth. Let cool until thickened but still pourable, stirring often, about 20 minutes.

USING small knife, cut around pan sides to loosen cake. Remove pan sides. Place cake on its pan bottom on rack set over baking sheet. Pour glaze evenly over top of cake, allowing glaze to run down sides; smooth glaze over cake with metal spatula. Let cake stand until glaze sets, about 2 hours. Transfer cake to plate. Cover with cake dome and refrigerate overnight. *(Can be prepared 2 days ahead; keep refrigerated.)* Let stand at room temperature 2 hours before serving.

German chocolate cake with coconut-macadamia frosting

THIS CAKE IS GERMAN in name only—literally: The original 1950s recipe called for Baker's German's Sweet Chocolate, named for the Baker employee who developed it, Sam German. Traditionally, it is filled and topped with a pecan-coconut frosting; in this version, macadamia nuts give it a tropical flair. Rounds of parchment or waxed paper ensure that cake layers are easy to remove from the pans. To toast flaked coconut, spread on a rimmed baking sheet and bake in a 350°F oven until just golden, stirring occasionally, about 10 minutes.

12 SERVINGS

Cake

1/2 cup water
1 4-ounce package sweet baking chocolate, chopped

2 cups all purpose flour
1 teaspoon baking soda
1/4 teaspoon salt
2 cups sugar

1 cup (2 sticks) unsalted butter, room temperature
4 large eggs, separated
1 teaspoon vanilla extract
1 cup buttermilk
Pinch of cream of tartar

Frosting

1½ cups (packed) golden brown sugar
1 cup whipping cream
¼ cup whole milk
4 large egg yolks, beaten to blend
1 teaspoon vanilla extract
2 cups sweetened flaked coconut, lightly toasted
1 cup coarsely chopped macadamia nuts, lightly toasted

FOR CAKE: Preheat oven to 350°F. Butter three 9-inch-diameter cake pans with 1½-inch-high sides. Line bottoms with parchment or waxed paper. Butter parchment. Bring ½ cup water to simmer in heavy small saucepan. Remove from heat. Add chocolate and stir until melted and smooth.

COMBINE flour, baking soda, and salt in medium bowl. Using electric mixer, beat sugar and butter in large bowl until light and fluffy. Add egg yolks 1 at a time, beating well after each addition. Add chocolate mixture and vanilla; mix until blended. Add flour mixture alternately with buttermilk, beginning and ending with flour mixture and beating well after each addition. Using clean dry beaters, beat egg whites and cream of tartar in large bowl until stiff but not dry. Fold whites into batter in 2 additions.

DIVIDE batter equally among prepared pans. Bake cakes until tester inserted into center comes out clean, about 35 minutes. Cool cakes in pans on racks 15 minutes. Turn cakes out onto racks. Remove parchment; cool completely. *(Can be prepared 1 day ahead. Cover tightly with aluminum foil and store at room temperature.)*

FOR FROSTING: Combine first 5 ingredients in heavy medium saucepan and whisk until blended. Stir constantly over medium heat until mixture thickens to consistency of caramel sauce and coats spoon, about 10 minutes (do not boil). Remove from heat. Stir in coconut and macadamia nuts. Let frosting stand at room temperature until cool and spreadable, about 1½ hours (frosting will be very sticky but will set up on cake).

PLACE 1 cake layer on platter. Spread ½ cup frosting evenly over top. Top with second cake layer; spread ½ cup frosting over top. Top with remaining cake layer. Spread remaining frosting evenly over top and sides of cake. *(Can be prepared 4 hours ahead. Let stand at room temperature.)*

Old-fashioned chocolate cake with cocoa frosting

WHEN YOU WANT A SLICE (or two) of comforting Americana, this terrific double-chocolate cake offers three moist, dark layers iced with buttery-rich cocoa frosting. Chocolate chips sprinkled atop the batter before baking almost melt into the layers, intensifying the cake's moistness and chocolate flavor. The cake will hold for one day before serving.

8 TO 10 SERVINGS

Cake

3 cups all purpose flour
2 cups sugar
½ cup unsweetened cocoa powder
2 teaspoons baking soda
1 teaspoon salt
2 cups cold water
1 cup corn oil
1 tablespoon vanilla extract
1½ cups semisweet chocolate chips

Frosting

- ½ cup plus 2 tablespoons (1¼ sticks) unsalted butter, room temperature
- 5 cups powdered sugar, divided
- 8 tablespoons (about) whole milk, divided
- 1¼ teaspoons vanilla extract
- ¾ cup plus 3 tablespoons unsweetened cocoa powder

FOR CAKE: Preheat oven to 350°F. Butter and flour three 9-inch-diameter cake pans with 1½-inch-high sides. Sift flour and next 4 ingredients into medium bowl. Mix 2 cups cold water, oil, and vanilla in large bowl. Whisk in flour mixture. Divide batter equally among pans. Sprinkle ½ cup chocolate chips over batter in each pan.

BAKE cakes until tester inserted into center comes out clean, about 25 minutes. Cool cakes in pans on racks 15 minutes. Cut around pan sides to loosen. . Turn cakes out onto racks; cool completely.

FOR FROSTING: Beat butter in large bowl until light and fluffy. Gradually beat in 3 cups sugar. Beat in 6 tablespoons milk and vanilla. Add cocoa and remaining 2 cups sugar; beat until blended, thinning with more milk if necessary.

PLACE 1 cake layer, chocolate-chips side up, on platter. Spread ⅔ cup frosting over. Top with second cake layer, chocolate-chips side up. Spread ⅔ cup frosting over. Top with remaining cake layer, chocolate-chips side down. Spread remaining frosting over sides and top of cake. *(Can be prepared 1 day ahead. Cover with cake dome and let stand at room temperature.)*

Chocolate cake with caramel–milk chocolate frosting

THIS IS A CAKE that begs for a tall pitcher of cold milk. Chocolate chips in the batter add textural contrast and a pure sense of fun, and an inspired combination of milk chocolate and caramel in a thick, rich frosting makes it an instant classic. Once the sugar syrup for the caramel comes to a boil, avoid stirring which can lead to crystallization of the sugar and make the caramel grainy. Use parchment paper to line the pans, and three 9-inch-diameter cardboard rounds (sold at bakery supply stores) to support the delicate cake layers. If you can't find cardboard rounds, use tart pan bottoms instead. The cake will keep up to two days before serving.

12 SERVINGS

Cake

- Nonstick vegetable oil spray
- 2 cups sifted cake flour (sifted, then measured)
- 1 cup unsweetened cocoa powder
- 1¼ teaspoons baking soda
- ¾ teaspoon salt
- ½ teaspoon baking powder
- 1½ cups (packed) golden brown sugar
- 1 cup plus 2 tablespoons (2¼ sticks) unsalted butter, room temperature
- 3 large eggs
- 1 tablespoon vanilla extract
- 1 cup plus 2 tablespoons buttermilk
- ½ cup lukewarm water
- 1 cup semisweet chocolate chips (about 6 ounces)

Frosting

- 24 ounces imported milk chocolate (such as Lindt), finely chopped
- 3 ounces bittersweet (not unsweetened) or semisweet chocolate, finely chopped
- 1½ cups sugar
- ½ cup water
- 2¼ cups whipping cream

FOR CAKE: Preheat oven to 350°F. Spray three 9-inch-diameter cake pans with 1½-inch-high sides with nonstick spray. Line bottom of pans with parchment paper. Whisk flour and next 4 ingredients in medium bowl to blend. Using electric mixer, beat brown sugar and butter in large bowl until fluffy, about 2 minutes. Add eggs 1 at a time, beating well after each addition. Beat in vanilla. Beat in flour mixture in 3 additions alternately with buttermilk in 2 additions. Beat in ½ cup lukewarm water. Stir in chocolate chips.

DIVIDE batter among prepared pans (about 2⅓ cups for each). Smooth tops. Bake cakes until tester inserted into center comes out clean, about 22 minutes. Cool completely in pans on racks. Invert cakes onto 9-inch-diameter cardboard rounds or tart pan bottoms (cakes will be delicate). Peel off parchment.

FOR FROSTING: Combine milk chocolate and bittersweet chocolate in large bowl. Stir sugar and ½ cup water in heavy medium saucepan over medium heat until sugar dissolves. Increase heat and boil without stirring until syrup is deep amber color, occasionally brushing down sides of pan with wet pastry brush and swirling pan, about 10 minutes. Carefully and slowly add whipping cream (mixture will bubble vigorously). Stir over low heat until any hard caramel bits dissolve and mixture is smooth. Pour caramel over chocolate; let stand 1 minute to allow chocolate to soften, then whisk until chocolate is melted and smooth. Refrigerate chocolate-caramel frosting until completely cool, about 2 hours. Let stand 1 hour at room temperature before continuing.

USING electric mixer, beat frosting just until color resembles milk chocolate and frosting is easily spreadable, about 1 minute (do not overbeat or frosting will become stiff and grainy). If necessary to correct graininess, set bowl with frosting over saucepan of simmering water for 10-second intervals, whisking just until frosting is smooth and spreadable.

PLACE 1 cake layer on platter, flat side up. Spread 1 cup frosting evenly over top. Top with second cake layer, flat side up, pressing slightly to adhere. Spread 1 cup frosting over top. Top with third cake layer, rounded side up, pressing slightly. Spread remaining frosting over sides and top of cake, swirling decoratively. *(Can be prepared 2 days ahead. Cover with cake dome and store at room temperature.)*

Triple-layer devil's food cake

SO DECADENT was this dessert when it gained popularity in the early 1900s that it was deemed "devilish" compared to the ethereally light, white, and halo-shaped angel-food cake. A dash of espresso powder in this version amplifies the chocolate flavors and makes the cake even more wicked. The reserved vanilla bean pods can be used to make vanilla sugar, which adds a lovely perfume to pound cakes and other baked goods: Just bury the pods in a jar of sugar, and the vanilla flavor will permeate the sugar. To create the chocolate shavings, run a swivel-bladed vegetable peeler down the narrow edge of a whole chocolate bar.

12 SERVINGS

Cake

1¾ cups water
1 tablespoon instant espresso powder or instant coffee powder
1 cup unsweetened cocoa powder

2¼ cups sifted all purpose flour (sifted, then measured)
1½ teaspoons baking powder
¾ teaspoon baking soda
½ teaspoon salt
1 cup (2 sticks) unsalted butter, room temperature
2 cups (packed) dark brown sugar
2 large eggs
2 large egg yolks

Frosting

- **2 vanilla beans, split lengthwise**
- **1¼ cups whipping cream**
- **½ cup sugar**
- **4 large egg yolks**
- **⅛ teaspoon salt**
- **1 pound bittersweet (not unsweetened) or semisweet chocolate, finely chopped**
- **¾ cup (1½ sticks) unsalted butter, cut into pieces, room temperature**
- **½ cup light corn syrup**
- **¼ cup sour cream**

White chocolate and milk chocolate shavings

FOR CAKE: Preheat oven to 350°F. Lightly butter three 9-inch cake pans with 1¾ inch high sides. Line pan bottoms with waxed paper rounds. Butter waxed paper.

BRING 1¾ cups water and espresso powder to boil in heavy small saucepan. Remove from heat. Add cocoa and whisk until smooth. Cool completely.

SIFT flour, baking powder, baking soda, and salt into medium bowl. Using electric mixer, beat butter in large bowl until light and fluffy. Add sugar ⅓ cup at a time, beating well after each addition and scraping down sides of bowl occasionally. Add eggs and yolks 1 at a time, beating just to blend after each addition. Using rubber spatula, mix flour mixture into butter mixture alternately with cocoa mixture, beginning and ending with flour mixture.

DIVIDE batter equally among prepared pans. Bake cakes until tester inserted into center comes out clean, about 23 minutes. Cool in pans on racks 10 minutes. Turn cakes out onto racks. Peel off paper; cool completely. *(Can be prepared 1 day ahead. Return cakes to pans and cover tightly with aluminum foil. Let stand at room temperature.)*

FOR FROSTING: Carefully scrape seeds from vanilla beans into heavy large saucepan (reserve pods for another use). Add cream, sugar, egg yolks, and salt; whisk to blend well. Stir over medium-low heat until custard thickens and leaves path on back of spoon when finger is drawn across, about 7 minutes (do not let mixture come to boil). Mix in chocolate, butter, and corn syrup. Remove from heat and stir until smooth. Mix in sour cream. Transfer frosting to bowl and refrigerate until spreadable, stirring occasionally, about 1 hour.

PLACE 1 cake layer on platter. Spread 1 cup frosting over top. Repeat with second cake layer and 1 cup frosting. Top with third cake layer. Spread remaining frosting over sides and top of cake, swirling decoratively. *(Can be made 1 day ahead. Cover with cake dome and refrigerate. Let stand at room temperature 1 hour before serving.)*

SPRINKLE white and milk chocolate shavings thickly over top of cake.

Lemon-lattice white chocolate cake

THIS GRACIOUS PARTY CAKE is a springtime scene-stealer: Three layers of fine-crumbed white chocolate cake are filled and topped with white chocolate frosting and a sweet-tart lemon curd, then a lattice pattern in lemon curd is piped decoratively over the top layer. It's impressive and beautiful, but entirely approachable; you can make the frosting and lemon curd a day before assembling the cake.

12 SERVINGS

Lemon curd

- **¾ cup fresh lemon juice**
- **2 tablespoons cornstarch**
- **1 cup plus 2 tablespoons sugar**
- **3 large eggs**
- **6 large egg yolks**
- **½ cup plus 1 tablespoon unsalted butter, cut into small pieces**
- **2 tablespoons grated lemon peel**

Frosting

- **2¼ cups whipping cream, divided**
- **4½ ounces high-quality white chocolate (such as Lindt or Perugina), chopped**
- **¾ teaspoon vanilla extract**

Cake

- **2¾ cups sifted all purpose flour (sifted, then measured)**
- **1 teaspoon baking powder**
- **¾ teaspoon salt**

- **4 ounces high-quality white chocolate (such as Lindt or Perugina), chopped**
- **1 cup whipping cream, divided**
- **½ cup plus 2 tablespoons whole milk**
- **1 teaspoon vanilla extract**

- **½ cup (1 stick) unsalted butter, room temperature**
- **2 cups sugar, divided**
- **4 large eggs, separated**

FOR LEMON CURD: Combine lemon juice and cornstarch in heavy medium saucepan, stirring until cornstarch dissolves. Whisk in remaining ingredients. Cook over medium heat until mixture is thick and smooth and just begins to boil, stirring constantly, about 7 minutes. Transfer to medium bowl. Press plastic wrap directly onto surface of curd to keep skin from forming. Refrigerate until cold, about 6 hours. *(Can be prepared 2 days ahead. Keep refrigerated.)*

FOR FROSTING: Combine ½ cup cream and chocolate in heavy small saucepan. Stir over low heat until chocolate melts and mixture is smooth. Transfer to large bowl. Whisk in remaining 1¾ cups cream and vanilla. Refrigerate until well chilled, about 6 hours. *(Can be prepared 1 day ahead. Keep refrigerated.)*

FOR CAKE: Position rack in center of oven and preheat to 350°F. Butter three 9-inch-diameter cake pans with 1½-inch-high sides. Line bottoms with waxed paper. Butter paper. Dust pans with flour; tap out excess. Sift flour, baking powder, and salt together into medium bowl. Repeat sifting.

STIR chocolate and ½ cup cream in heavy medium saucepan over low heat until chocolate melts and mixture is smooth. Mix in remaining ½ cup cream, milk, and vanilla.

USING electric mixer, beat butter and 1 cup sugar in large bowl until light and fluffy. Beat in egg yolks. Stir flour mixture into butter mixture alternately with white chocolate mixture, beginning and ending with flour mixture. Using electric mixer fitted with clean dry beaters, beat egg whites in medium bowl to soft peaks. Gradually beat in remaining 1 cup sugar. Continue beating until stiff but not dry. Fold whites into cake batter in 2 additions.

DIVIDE batter equally among prepared pans. Bake cakes until tester inserted into center comes out clean and cakes are beginning to pull away from sides of pans, about 24 minutes. Cool cakes in pans on racks 10 minutes. Turn cakes out onto racks; peel off paper and cool completely. *(Can be prepared 4 hours ahead. Cover; let stand at room temperature.)*

USING electric mixer, beat frosting in another large bowl until stiff peaks form. Place 1 cake layer on platter. Spread ⅔ cup lemon curd evenly over top. Spread ¾ cup frosting atop curd. Top with second cake layer. Spread ⅔ cup curd and then ¾ cup frosting evenly over top. Add third cake layer. Frost sides and top of entire cake evenly with 3 cups frosting.

PLACE remaining lemon curd in pastry bag fitted with medium star tip. Pipe circle of curd around top of cake, ½ inch from edge. Pipe evenly spaced diagonal lines inside circle, creating lattice pattern. (Reserve remaining curd for another use.) Spoon remaining frosting into clean pastry bag fitted with medium star tip. Pipe decorative border around top and bottom edges of cake. *(Can be prepared up to 6 hours ahead. Refrigerate.)* Let stand at room temperature 30 minutes before serving.

Lemon-blueberry cake with white chocolate frosting

SWEET SUMMER BLUEBERRIES are the star attraction of this layer cake: Whole fresh berries are folded into the batter and sprinkled atop the frosted cake. Buttermilk makes the cake tender, while cream cheese adds great texture and tang to the frosting. For an attractive garnish, build up a small rim of frosting around the top edge, then fill the center with blueberries; or arrange lemon twists around the edge and sprinkle blueberries in the middle.

10 TO 12 SERVINGS

Cake

3⅓ cups cake flour
½ teaspoon salt
½ teaspoon baking powder
½ teaspoon baking soda
¾ cup (1½ sticks) unsalted butter, room temperature
2 cups sugar
⅓ cup fresh lemon juice
1 teaspoon (packed) grated lemon peel
4 large eggs
1 cup plus 2 tablespoons buttermilk
2½ cups fresh blueberries

Frosting

11 ounces high-quality white chocolate (such as Lindt or Perugina), finely chopped
12 ounces Philadelphia brand cream cheese, room temperature
¾ cup (1½ sticks) unsalted butter, room temperature
2 tablespoons fresh lemon juice

Additional blueberries (optional)

FOR CAKE: Preheat oven to 350°F. Butter and flour two 9-inch-diameter cake pans with 2-inch-high sides; line bottoms with parchment paper rounds.

SIFT flour and next 3 ingredients into medium bowl. Using electric mixer, beat butter in large bowl until light and fluffy. Gradually add sugar, beating until blended and scraping down sides of bowl occasionally. Beat in lemon juice and peel, then eggs 1 at a time, beating until well blended after each addition. Beat in flour mixture in 4 additions alternately with buttermilk in 3 additions. Fold in berries.

TRANSFER batter to pans. Bake cakes until tester inserted into center comes out clean, about 40 minutes. Cool cakes in pans on racks.

FOR FROSTING: Stir white chocolate in top of double boiler set over barely simmering water until almost melted. Remove from over water and stir until smooth. Cool to lukewarm. Beat cream cheese and butter in large bowl until combined. Beat in lemon juice, then cooled white chocolate.

TURN cakes out onto work surface. Peel off parchment. Place 1 cake layer, flat side up, on platter. Spread top with 1 cup frosting. Top with second cake layer, flat side down. Spread remaining frosting over sides and top of cake. Garnish with additional blueberries, if desired. *(Can be prepared 1 day ahead. Cover with cake dome and refrigerate. Let stand at room temperature 1 hour before serving.)*

Whipped cream cake with lemon curd and berries

THIS CLASSIC Swedish summer dessert is all about fresh, bright flavors. And with a cake-to-filling ratio that is about equal, it manages to be both light and luscious. Frozen sweetened sliced strawberries are used deliberately here: Once thawed, they are spooned with their juices over each layer to moisten it. To create the decorative fresh strawberry fans, make thin lengthwise cuts in each berry, from the bottom to just below the stem end, so the stem is still attached; then press the berry to splay the slices. If you make the lemon curd a day (or more) in advance, putting this cake together for a party is surprisingly uncomplicated. Potato starch may also be labeled potato flour; it is available at natural foods stores and in the kosher foods section of most supermarkets.

10 SERVINGS

Lemon curd filling

- ½ teaspoon unflavored gelatin
- 2 teaspoons water
- 1 cup sugar
- 2 tablespoons grated lemon peel
- ½ cup fresh lemon juice
- 6 large egg yolks
- ¾ cup (1½ sticks) chilled unsalted butter, cut into ½-inch cubes

Cake

- ⅓ cup plus 1 tablespoon all purpose flour
- ⅓ cup plus 1 tablespoon potato starch
- 1 teaspoon baking powder
- 4 large eggs, room temperature
- ¾ cup plus 1 tablespoon sugar
- 2 teaspoons grated lemon peel

Whipped cream frosting

- 3½ cups chilled whipping cream
- 6 tablespoons sugar

- 1 10-ounce package frozen sliced sweetened strawberries, thawed
- 3 1-pint containers fresh strawberries, hulled, sliced

- 10 fresh strawberries, fanned
- 1 ½-pint container fresh blueberries

FOR LEMON CURD FILLING: Sprinkle gelatin over 2 teaspoons water in small bowl. Let stand 10 minutes to soften. Blend sugar and lemon peel in processor 2 minutes. Transfer lemon peel mixture to heavy medium saucepan. Whisk in lemon juice and egg yolks. Add butter and cook over medium heat until mixture thickens and leaves path on back of spoon when finger is drawn across, stirring constantly, about 7 minutes (do not boil). Remove from heat. Add gelatin mixture and stir until dissolved. Cover and refrigerate lemon curd until well chilled. *(Can be prepared 3 days ahead; keep refrigerated.)*

FOR CAKE: Position rack in bottom third of oven and preheat to 350°F. Butter and flour 9-inch-diameter springform pan with 2¾-inch-high sides. Sift flour, potato starch, and baking powder into medium bowl. Using electric mixer, beat eggs and sugar in large bowl until mixture is very thick and slowly dissolving ribbon forms when beaters are lifted, about 7 minutes. Mix in lemon peel. Sift flour mixture over egg mixture in 3 additions, folding in after each addition.

POUR batter into prepared pan. Bake until tester inserted into center comes out clean, about 30 minutes. Cool cake in pan on rack 20 minutes. Run small sharp knife around pan sides to loosen cake if necessary. Release pan sides. Cool cake completely. *(Can be prepared 1 day ahead. Wrap tightly and let stand at room temperature.)*

FOR WHIPPED CREAM FROSTING: Beat cream and sugar in large bowl to stiff peaks.

RUN long thin knife between cake and pan bottom to loosen cake. Using serrated knife, cut cake horizontally into 3 equal layers. Place bottom cake layer on plate. Spoon ⅓ cup thawed sweetened berries with juices over cake. Carefully spread generous ⅓ cup lemon curd over. Top with single layer of sliced fresh strawberries. Spread 1 cup frosting over. Top with second cake layer and repeat layering process, using ⅓ cup thawed sweetened berries, generous ⅓ cup lemon curd, single layer of sliced fresh berries, and 1 cup frosting. Top with third cake layer. Spoon 3 tablespoons thawed berry juices over. Spread ⅓ cup curd over top of cake (reserve any remaining curd for another use).

SPREAD 2½ cups frosting over sides and top of cake. Spoon remaining frosting into pastry bag fitted with medium star tip. Pipe cream in vertical columns around sides of cake from top edge to bottom. Pipe rosettes of cream around top edge of cake. Arrange 10 fanned strawberries around edge of cake. Fill center with blueberries. Refrigerate at least 3 hours and up to 6 hours before serving.

Apple spice cake with walnuts and currants

THIS WOULD BE a lovely cake for afternoon tea, a pumpkin-carving party, or any fall occasion. Butter-poached apples are mashed into a homemade applesauce and mixed into the cake batter, adding great texture and pure apple flavor to the cake. A high proportion of butter makes for an extra-smooth and rich icing. The cake can be chilled one day before serving.

8 TO 10 SERVINGS

Cinnamon-sugar walnuts

1 large egg white
1 cup large walnut pieces
2 tablespoons sugar
½ teaspoon ground cinnamon

Cake

1 tablespoon plus ¾ cup (1½ sticks) unsalted butter, room temperature
2 medium Granny Smith apples, peeled, cored, cut into ½-inch pieces
2 medium Jonagold apples, peeled, cored, cut into ½-inch pieces

1¾ cups all purpose flour
1 teaspoon ground cinnamon
1 teaspoon baking soda
½ teaspoon ground allspice
½ teaspoon ground cloves
½ teaspoon salt
1¼ cups sugar
1 large egg
1 cup toasted walnuts, chopped
1 cup dried currants

Icing

1 8-ounce package Philadelphia brand cream cheese, room temperature
½ cup (1 stick) unsalted butter, room temperature
1 cup (packed) powdered sugar
1 teaspoon vanilla extract

1 teaspoon (generous) dried currants

FOR CINNAMON-SUGAR WALNUTS: Preheat oven to 375°F. Line large baking sheet with aluminum foil. Beat egg white in medium bowl until foamy. Mix in remaining ingredients. Spread walnuts in single layer on prepared sheet. Bake until walnuts are golden, about 10 minutes. Cool on baking sheet. Transfer walnuts to work surface and chop coarsely.

FOR CAKE: Melt 1 tablespoon butter in heavy large saucepan over medium-low heat. Add all apples; cover and simmer until apples are juicy and almost tender, stirring occasionally, about 18 minutes. Uncover and simmer until almost all juices evaporate, about 6 minutes. Using potato masher, mash apples in pan. Set applesauce aside and cool.

POSITION rack in center of oven and preheat oven to 350°F. Butter and flour two 8-inch-diameter cake pans with 1½-inch-high sides. Whisk flour and next 5 ingredients in medium bowl. Using electric mixer, beat remaining ¾ cup butter and sugar in large bowl until light and fluffy. Beat in egg. Beat in half of flour mixture on low speed, then all of applesauce, then remaining flour mixture. Mix in 1 cup toasted walnuts and currants.

DIVIDE batter between pans; smooth tops. Bake cakes until tester inserted into center comes out clean, about 40 minutes. Cool cakes in pans on racks 5 minutes. Turn cakes out onto racks and cool completely.

FOR ICING: Using electric mixer, beat cream cheese and butter in large bowl until fluffy. Add powdered sugar and vanilla; beat to blend.

PLACE 1 cake layer on plate; spread ½ cup icing over top. Top with second cake layer. Spread remaining icing over sides and top of cake. Arrange cinnamon-sugar walnuts in ring ½ inch from edge of cake. Sprinkle walnuts with currants. Refrigerate cake until icing sets, about 30 minutes. *(Can be prepared 1 day ahead. Cover with cake dome and keep refrigerated. Bring to room temperature before serving.)*

Triple-layer carrot cake with cream cheese frosting

HERE'S AN EXCEPTIONALLY moist and satisfying version of the classic. Lining the pans with waxed paper keeps the cake from sticking. Grate the carrots finely using the smallest holes on a box grater. An offset-handle metal spatula is also helpful for creating the decorative frosting swirls. The assembled cake can be refrigerated two days before you serve it.

10 SERVINGS

Cake

- **2 cups sugar**
- **1½ cups vegetable oil**
- **4 large eggs**
- **2 cups all purpose flour**
- **2 teaspoons baking powder**
- **2 teaspoons baking soda**
- **1 teaspoon salt**
- **1 teaspoon ground cinnamon**
- **¾ teaspoon ground nutmeg**
- **3 cups finely grated peeled carrots (about 1 pound)**
- **½ cup chopped pecans**
- **½ cup raisins**

Frosting

- **4 cups powdered sugar**
- **2 8-ounce packages Philadelphia brand cream cheese, room temperature**
- **½ cup (1 stick) unsalted butter, room temperature**
- **4 teaspoons vanilla extract**

FOR CAKE: Preheat oven to 325°F. Lightly grease three 9-inch-diameter cake pans with 1½-inch-high sides. Line bottom of pans with waxed paper. Lightly grease waxed paper. Using electric mixer, beat sugar and vegetable oil in bowl until combined. Add eggs 1 at a time, beating well after each addition. Sift flour, baking powder, baking soda, salt, cinnamon, and nutmeg into sugar and oil mixture. Stir in carrots, chopped pecans, and raisins.

POUR batter into prepared pans, dividing equally. Bake until tester inserted into center comes out clean and cakes begin to pull away from sides of pans, about 45 minutes. Cool in pans on racks 15 minutes. Turn cakes out onto racks and cool completely. *(Can be prepared 1 day ahead. Wrap tightly in plastic and store at room temperature.)*

FOR FROSTING: Using electric mixer, beat all ingredients in medium bowl until smooth and creamy.

PLACE 1 cake layer on platter. Spread ¾ cup frosting over top. Top with another cake layer. Spread ¾ cup frosting over top. Top with remaining cake layer. Using icing spatula, spread remaining frosting in decorative swirls over sides and top of cake. *(Can be prepared 2 days ahead. Cover with cake dome and refrigerate.)* Serve cake cold or at room temperature.

Tropical carrot cake with coconut–cream cheese frosting

SPICED UP with crystallized ginger, pineapple, and coconut, this lush carrot cake is beautiful and delicious enough for showers, weddings, and other special occasions. Everyday waxed paper can substitute for the parchment paper rounds when lining the pans. Sweetened cream of coconut is available in the liquor or mixers section of most supermarkets. Crystallized (sometimes called candied) ginger is gingerroot that has been cooked in a sugar syrup and coated with sugar.

8 TO 10 SERVINGS

Cake

- **2⅓ cups sifted all purpose flour (sifted, then measured), divided**
- **1 cup sweetened flaked coconut**
- **1 cup dry-roasted macadamia nuts**
- **¾ cup chopped crystallized ginger**
- **3½ teaspoons ground cinnamon**
- **2½ teaspoons baking powder**

1 teaspoon salt
½ teaspoon baking soda

2 cups sugar
1 cup vegetable oil
4 large eggs
2 teaspoons vanilla extract
2 cups finely grated peeled carrots
2 8-ounce cans crushed pineapple in juice, well drained

Frosting
3 8-ounce packages Philadelphia brand cream cheese, room temperature
¾ cup (1½ sticks) unsalted butter, room temperature
2 cups powdered sugar
¾ cup canned sweetened cream of coconut (such as Coco López)
1 teaspoon vanilla extract
½ teaspoon (scant) imitation coconut extract

14 whole dry-roasted macadamia nuts
¼ cup chopped crystallized ginger

FOR CAKE: Preheat oven to 350°F. Butter three 9-inch-diameter cake pans with 1½-inch-high sides. Line bottom of pans with parchment paper. Combine ⅓ cup flour and next 3 ingredients in processor; blend until nuts are finely chopped. Whisk remaining 2 cups flour, cinnamon, baking powder, salt, and baking soda in medium bowl.

USING electric mixer, beat sugar and oil in large bowl to blend. Add eggs 1 at a time, beating well after each addition. Beat in vanilla. Beat in flour-spice mixture. Stir in coconut-macadamia mixture, then carrots and crushed pineapple.

DIVIDE batter equally among pans. Bake cakes until tester inserted into center comes out clean, about 30 minutes. Cool in pans on racks 1 hour. Run knife around edge of pans to loosen cakes. Turn cakes out onto racks and cool completely.

FOR FROSTING: Beat cream cheese and butter in large bowl until smooth. Beat in powdered sugar, then cream of coconut and vanilla and coconut extracts. Refrigerate frosting until firm enough to spread, about 30 minutes.

PLACE 1 cake layer, flat side up, on platter. Spread ¾ cup frosting over top of cake. Top with second cake layer, flat side up. Spread ¾ cup frosting over. Top with third cake layer, rounded side up, pressing slightly to adhere. Spread thin layer of frosting over top and sides of cake. Refrigerate cake and remaining frosting 30 minutes. Spread remaining frosting over sides and top of cake. Arrange whole nuts and ginger around top edge of cake. Refrigerate 1 hour. *(Can be prepared 1 day ahead. Cover with cake dome and refrigerate. Let stand at room temperature 1 hour before serving.)*

Sweet-potato layer cake with orange–cream cheese frosting

THE LAYERS of this cake are studded with chopped toasted walnuts and dried cranberries. Garnished with still more walnuts and cranberries plus candied orange peel, it's a special-occasion treat that would make a sophisticated alternative to pumpkin pie on the Thanksgiving dessert table. The assembled cake can be chilled one day before serving. Look for parchment paper at cookware stores or in the baking- or paper-goods section of the supermarket. Candied orange peel is sold at specialty candy stores and some specialty foods stores.

10 TO 12 SERVINGS

Cake
2 pounds tan-skinned sweet potatoes (about 3 medium)

- **3 cups cake flour**
- **2 teaspoons baking soda**
- **2 teaspoons baking powder**
- **2 teaspoons ground cinnamon**
- **1 teaspoon ground ginger**
- **½ teaspoon salt**
- **¼ teaspoon ground cloves**
- **1 cup vegetable oil**
- **1 cup sugar**
- **1 cup (packed) golden brown sugar**
- **4 large eggs**
- **⅔ cup chopped walnuts, toasted**
- **⅔ cup dried cranberries**

Frosting

- **1 8-ounce package Philadelphia brand cream cheese, room temperature**
- **½ cup (1 stick) unsalted butter, room temperature**
- **3¼ cups powdered sugar, sifted**
- **2 tablespoons frozen orange juice concentrate, thawed**
- **½ teaspoon vanilla extract**

- **¼ cup chopped candied orange peel**
- **3 tablespoons sugar**
- **¼ cup chopped walnuts, toasted**
- **¼ cup dried cranberries**

FOR CAKE: Preheat oven to 400°F. Pierce potatoes with fork; place on small baking sheet. Roast potatoes until soft, about 1 hour. Cool, peel, and mash potatoes. Measure 2 cups mashed potatoes; cool to lukewarm (reserve any remaining potatoes for another use). Reduce oven temperature to 350°F.

BUTTER and flour two 9-inch-diameter cake pans with 2-inch-high sides; line pans with parchment paper. Sift flour and next 6 ingredients into medium bowl. Combine oil and both sugars in large bowl; whisk until smooth. Whisk in eggs 1 at a time, then sweet potatoes. Whisk in flour mixture in 3 additions. Stir in walnuts and cranberries.

DIVIDE batter equally between prepared pans. Bake cakes until tester inserted into center comes out clean, about 30 minutes. Cool cakes completely in pans on racks.

FOR FROSTING: Using electric mixer, beat cream cheese and butter in large bowl until fluffy. Beat in powdered sugar, scraping down bowl often. Beat in orange juice concentrate and vanilla.

CUT around cake pan sides; turn out cakes. Peel off parchment. Place 1 cake layer, flat side up, on platter. Spread ¾ cup frosting over top of cake. Top with second cake layer, flat side down. Spread remaining frosting over sides and top of cake. Combine orange peel, sugar, walnuts, and cranberries in small bowl. Stir to coat fruit and nuts with sugar. Transfer to sieve; sift off excess sugar. Sprinkle fruit and nut mixture decoratively atop cake. Refrigerate until frosting sets, at least 2 hours. *(Can be made 1 day ahead. Cover with cake dome; keep refrigerated. Let stand at room temperature 1 hour before serving.)*

Gingerbread layer cake with candied pistachios

DARK BEER AND MOLASSES add rich depth of flavor to this moist and delicious cake. If you'd like to use freshly grated nutmeg, which has a sweet and assertive flavor, buy whole nutmeg seeds and swipe them a few times across a spice grater (or the fine-rasp section of a box grater) to yield a quarter teaspoon. To produce finely grated orange peel effortlessly, use a super-sharp Microplane grater (using the smallest holes on a box grater also works). Turn the orange often so that only the orange part of the peel—not the bitter white pith underneath—is grated.

10 SERVINGS

Cake

- **1 cup Guinness extra stout or dark beer**
- **1 cup mild-flavored (light) molasses**
- **1½ teaspoons baking soda**

- 2 cups all purpose flour
- 2 tablespoons ground ginger
- 1½ teaspoons baking powder
- ¾ teaspoon ground cinnamon
- ¼ teaspoon ground cloves
- ¼ teaspoon ground nutmeg
- ⅛ teaspoon ground cardamom
- 3 large eggs
- ½ cup sugar
- ½ cup (packed) dark brown sugar
- ¾ cup vegetable oil
- 1 tablespoon minced peeled fresh ginger

Candied pistachios

- 1 cup finely chopped pistachios
- 1 tablespoon light corn syrup
- 2 tablespoons sugar

Cream cheese frosting

- 2 8-ounce packages Philadelphia brand cream cheese, room temperature
- ½ cup (1 stick) unsalted butter, room temperature
- ¾ teaspoon finely grated orange peel
- 2 cups powdered sugar

FOR CAKE: Preheat oven to 350°F. Butter and flour three 8-inch-diameter cake pans. Bring stout and molasses to boil in heavy medium saucepan over high heat. Remove from heat; stir in baking soda. Let stand 1 hour to cool completely.

WHISK flour and next 6 ingredients in large bowl to blend. Whisk eggs and both sugars in medium bowl to blend. Whisk in oil, then stout mixture. Gradually whisk stout-egg mixture into flour mixture. Stir in fresh ginger.

DIVIDE batter equally among prepared pans. Bake cakes until tester inserted into center comes out clean, about 25 minutes. Cool cakes in pans 15 minutes. Invert cakes onto racks and cool completely. *(Can be prepared 1 day ahead. Wrap each cake layer separately in plastic and keep at room temperature.)*

FOR CANDIED PISTACHIOS: Preheat oven to 325°F. Line large rimmed baking sheet with aluminum foil. Mix pistachios and corn syrup in medium bowl. Add sugar and toss to coat. Working quickly so sugar doesn't melt, spread pistachios on prepared baking sheet. Bake until pistachios are pale golden, about 8 minutes. Cool completely. *(Can be prepared 1 day ahead. Store airtight at room temperature.)*

FOR CREAM CHEESE FROSTING: Using electric mixer, beat cream cheese, butter, and orange peel in large bowl until fluffy. Gradually beat in powdered sugar. Chill frosting 30 minutes.

PLACE 1 cake layer, rounded side up, on platter. Spread ¾ cup frosting over top of cake. Top with second cake layer, rounded side up, and spread ¾ cup frosting over top of cake. Top with third cake layer, flat side up. Spread sides and top of cake with remaining frosting. Sprinkle top of cake with candied pistachios. *(Can be prepared 1 day ahead. Cover and refrigerate. Bring to room temperature before serving.)* Cut cake into wedges and serve.

Flourless chocolate-cassis cake with crème anglaise

EVERY FRENCHWOMAN has a version of this dense and richly chocolaty cake in her repertoire. The addition of crème de cassis, a French liqueur made from black currants, plus a custard sauce and cassis syrup elevates it to a dessert worthy of holiday celebrations or elegant entertaining. For the best flavor, use an imported cassis. The cake can be chilled one day before serving.

12 SERVINGS

Crème anglaise

- 2 cups half and half
- 1 vanilla bean, split lengthwise
- ½ cup sugar
- 4 large egg yolks

Cake

- **½ cup crème de cassis (black currant liqueur)**
- **10 ounces bittersweet (not unsweetened) or semisweet chocolate, chopped**
- **¾ cup (1½ sticks) unsalted butter**
- **½ cup unsweetened cocoa powder**
- **5 large eggs**
- **1 cup sugar**

Icing

- **¼ cup whipping cream**
- **8 ounces bittersweet (not unsweetened) or semisweet chocolate, chopped**
- **6 tablespoons plus ¾ cup crème de cassis liqueur**

Fresh mint sprigs

FOR CRÈME ANGLAISE: Bring half and half to simmer in heavy medium saucepan. Scrape in seeds from vanilla bean; add pod. Whisk sugar and egg yolks in bowl. Gradually whisk in hot half and half mixture. Return mixture to saucepan; stir over medium-low heat until custard thickens and leaves path on back of spoon when finger is drawn across, about 5 minutes (do not boil). Strain sauce. Cover and chill until cold, at least 4 hours.

FOR CAKE: Preheat oven to 350°F. Butter 9-inch-diameter springform pan with 2¾-inch-high sides. Line bottom with parchment paper; butter parchment. Dust pan with flour; tap out excess. Boil crème de cassis in heavy small saucepan until reduced to ¼ cup, about 3 minutes. Cool. Melt chocolate and butter in heavy medium saucepan over low heat, stirring until smooth. Cool slightly. Whisk in cocoa and crème de cassis. Using electric mixer, beat eggs and sugar in large bowl until mixture lightens and triples in volume, about 6 minutes. Add chocolate-butter mixture and fold together.

POUR batter into prepared pan. Bake until top forms crust and tester inserted into center comes out with very moist crumbs still attached, about 40 minutes. Cool cake in pan on rack 5 minutes. Press down on crusty portion of cake to even top. Release pan sides from cake. Turn cake out onto rack; peel off parchment and cool completely.

FOR ICING: Bring cream to simmer in heavy medium saucepan. Add chocolate and 6 tablespoons crème de cassis; whisk until smooth. Let icing stand until cool but still spreadable, about 15 minutes.

PLACE cake on plate. Spread icing over top and sides. Refrigerate 1 hour. *(Can be prepared 1 day ahead. Cover with cake dome and keep refrigerated. Let stand 2 hours at room temperature before serving.)*

SIMMER remaining ¾ cup crème de cassis in heavy small saucepan until reduced to generous ½ cup, about 5 minutes. Cool.

SPOON crème anglaise onto plates, forming pool. Spoon reduced cassis decoratively atop sauce and swirl with knife. Slice cake. Place 1 slice in center of each plate. Garnish with mint sprigs and serve.

Chocolate-espresso lava cakes with espresso whipped cream

FOR A COZY but decadent wintertime treat, these individual soft-centered cakes are baked and served in ovenproof mugs, but you can also use one-cup (eight-ounce) ramekins or soufflé dishes.

6 SERVINGS

- **1 cup all purpose flour**
- **¾ cup unsweetened cocoa powder**
- **6 teaspoons instant espresso powder or instant coffee powder, divided**
- **1½ teaspoons baking powder**
- **1 cup (2 sticks) butter, melted**
- **1 cup sugar**
- **1 cup (packed) golden brown sugar**
- **4 large eggs**
- **1½ teaspoons vanilla extract**
- **¼ teaspoon almond extract**

12 **tablespoons semisweet chocolate chips (about 4½ ounces)**

1 **cup chilled whipping cream**
3 **tablespoons powdered sugar**

SIFT flour, cocoa powder, 5 teaspoons espresso powder, and baking powder into medium bowl. Place butter in large bowl; add both sugars and whisk until well blended. Whisk in eggs 1 at a time, then vanilla and almond extracts. Whisk in flour mixture. Divide batter among six 1-cup ovenproof coffee mugs (using about ⅔ cup in each). Top each with 2 tablespoons chocolate chips. Gently press chips into batter. Cover and refrigerate mugs at least 1 hour and up to 1 day.

COMBINE cream, powdered sugar, and remaining 1 teaspoon espresso powder in medium bowl; whisk until peaks form. Refrigerate up to 1 hour.

POSITION rack in center of oven and preheat to 350°F. Let mugs with batter stand at room temperature 5 minutes. Bake uncovered until cakes are puffed and crusty and tester inserted into center comes out with thick batter still attached, about 30 minutes. Cool cakes 5 minutes. Top hot cakes with espresso whipped cream and serve.

Molten chocolate cakes with mint fudge sauce

WARM, GOOEY, RICH, and luscious, these cakes are slightly underbaked so that the soft chocolate center pools onto the plate when the cakes are cut open. They are also one of the easiest, most impressive entertaining desserts around: Simply mix the batter, fill the soufflé dishes or custard cups, and chill overnight. Then pop them into the oven at serving time (the fudge sauce can also be prepared ahead and quickly reheated).

MAKES 6

Sauce

4½ **ounces bittersweet (not unsweetened) or semisweet chocolate, chopped**
2 **ounces unsweetened chocolate, chopped**
⅓ **cup hot water**
¼ **cup light corn syrup**
¾ **teaspoon peppermint extract**

Cakes

5 **ounces bittersweet (not unsweetened) or semisweet chocolate, chopped**
10 **tablespoons (1¼ sticks) unsalted butter**
3 **large eggs**
3 **large egg yolks**
1½ **cups powdered sugar**
½ **cup all purpose flour**

Vanilla ice cream

FOR SAUCE: Stir both chocolates in top of double boiler over barely simmering water until melted. Add ⅓ cup hot water, corn syrup, and peppermint extract; whisk until smooth. Remove from over water. Cool slightly. *(Can be made 2 days ahead. Cover and refrigerate. Before serving, rewarm in saucepan over low heat, stirring constantly.)*

FOR CAKES: Preheat oven to 450°F. Butter six 6-ounce soufflé dishes or custard cups. Stir chocolate and butter in heavy medium saucepan over low heat until melted. Cool slightly. Whisk eggs and egg yolks in large bowl to blend. Whisk in sugar, then chocolate mixture and flour. Pour batter into dishes, dividing equally. *(Can be prepared 1 day ahead. Cover and refrigerate.)*

BAKE cakes until sides are set but center remains soft and runny, about 11 minutes, or up to 14 minutes for refrigerated batter. Run small knife around cakes to loosen. Immediately turn cakes out onto plates. Spoon sauce around cakes. Serve with vanilla ice cream.

Chocolate-zucchini cake

ZUCCHINI BREAD is really more like a cake than a bread, and this recipe takes that concept to its natural conclusion by adding cocoa powder and chocolate chips. The homey dessert is a snap to bake anytime you want something sweet, or when you need to whip up a quick tea cake or afternoon snack.

12 SERVINGS

- **2¼ cups sifted all purpose flour (sifted, then measured)**
- **½ cup unsweetened cocoa powder**
- **1 teaspoon baking soda**
- **1 teaspoon salt**
- **1¾ cups sugar**
- **½ cup (1 stick) unsalted butter, room temperature**
- **½ cup vegetable oil**
- **2 large eggs**
- **1 teaspoon vanilla extract**
- **½ cup buttermilk**
- **2 cups grated unpeeled zucchini (about 2½ medium)**
- **1 6-ounce package semisweet chocolate chips (about 1 cup)**
- **¾ cup chopped walnuts**

PREHEAT oven to 325°F. Butter and flour 13x9x2-inch baking pan. Sift flour, cocoa powder, baking soda, and salt into medium bowl. Beat sugar, butter, and oil in large bowl until well blended. Add eggs 1 at a time, beating well after each addition. Beat in vanilla. Mix in flour mixture alternately with buttermilk in 3 additions each. Mix in grated zucchini. Pour batter into prepared pan. Sprinkle chocolate chips and nuts over.

BAKE cake until tester inserted into center comes out clean, about 50 minutes. Cool cake completely in pan.

Cappuccino-fudge cheesecake

A THICK DARK-CHOCOLATE GANACHE is poured over the chocolate cookie crust to make a fudgy base layer, then more is piped in a decorative lattice pattern over the sour cream icing to finish the cake. To keep the moist crust mixture from sticking to your fingers, cover your fingers with plastic wrap before pressing the crumbs into the pan. Be sure to make this dessert at least one day (and up to four days) ahead to allow the flavors to blend.

12 SERVINGS

Crust

- **1 9-ounce box chocolate wafer cookies, broken**
- **6 ounces bittersweet (not unsweetened) or semisweet chocolate, coarsely chopped**
- **½ cup (packed) dark brown sugar**
- **⅛ teaspoon ground nutmeg**
- **7 tablespoons unsalted butter, melted, hot**

Ganache

- **1½ cups whipping cream**
- **1¼ pounds bittersweet (not unsweetened) or semisweet chocolate, chopped**
- **¼ cup Kahlúa or other coffee-flavored liqueur**

Filling

- **4 8-ounce packages Philadelphia brand cream cheese, room temperature**
- **1⅓ cups sugar**
- **2 tablespoons all purpose flour**
- **2 tablespoons dark rum**
- **2 tablespoons instant espresso powder or instant coffee powder**
- **2 tablespoons ground espresso coffee beans (medium-coarse grind)**
- **1 tablespoon vanilla extract**
- **2 teaspoons mild-flavored (light) molasses**
- **4 large eggs**

Topping

- **1½ cups sour cream**
- **⅓ cup sugar**
- **2 teaspoons vanilla extract**

Espresso coffee beans (optional)

FOR CRUST: Finely grind cookies, chopped chocolate, brown sugar, and nutmeg in processor. Add butter and process until moist crumbs form, scraping down bowl occasionally, about 1 minute. Transfer crumbs to 10-inch-diameter springform pan with 3-inch-high sides. Using plastic wrap as aid, press crumb mixture firmly up sides to within ½ inch of top edge, then over bottom of pan.

FOR GANACHE: Bring whipping cream to simmer in large saucepan. Remove from heat; add chocolate and Kahlúa. Whisk until chocolate melts and ganache is smooth. Pour 2 cups ganache over bottom of crust. Freeze until ganache layer is firm, about 30 minutes. Reserve remaining ganache; cover and let stand at room temperature.

FOR FILLING: Position rack in center of oven and preheat to 350°F. Using electric mixer, beat cream cheese and sugar in large bowl until combined. Beat in flour. Stir rum, espresso powder, ground coffee, vanilla, and molasses in small bowl until instant coffee dissolves; beat into cream cheese mixture. Beat in eggs 1 at a time, occasionally scraping down sides of bowl.

POUR filling over cold ganache in crust. Place cheesecake on rimmed baking sheet. Bake until top is brown, puffed, and cracked at edges, and center 2 inches moves only slightly when pan is shaken gently, about 1 hour 5 minutes. Transfer cheesecake to rack. Cool 15 minutes while preparing topping (top of cheesecake will fall slightly as it cools). Maintain oven temperature.

FOR TOPPING: Whisk sour cream, sugar, and vanilla in medium bowl to blend. Pour topping over hot cheesecake, spreading to cover filling completely. Bake until topping is set, about 10 minutes. Transfer cheesecake to rack. Refrigerate hot cheesecake on rack until cool, about 3 hours.

RUN small sharp knife between crust and pan sides to loosen cake; release pan sides. Transfer cheesecake to platter. Spoon reserved ganache into pastry bag fitted with small star tip. Pipe 6 diagonal lines atop cheesecake, spacing 1 inch apart. Repeat at right angles to form lattice. Pipe rosettes of ganache around top edge of cake. Garnish with coffee beans, if desired. Refrigerate until lattice is firm, at least 6 hours. *(Can be prepared 4 days ahead. Wrap loosely in aluminum foil, forming dome over lattice; keep refrigerated.)*

Double chocolate–orange cheesecake

THIS SUMPTUOUS CHEESECAKE combines rich white and dark chocolate layers atop a chocolate pecan crust with elegant flourishes added on top: a piped border of whipped cream flavored with Grand Marnier, dark and white chocolate leaves, and slender orange peel threads. Bake the cheesecake one day before serving. The chocolate leaves and orange threads can also be prepared one day ahead.

12 SERVINGS

Crust

- **18 chocolate wafer cookies (about 4 ounces), broken up**
- **1 cup pecans**
- **¼ cup sugar**
- **2 ounces semisweet chocolate, coarsely chopped**
- **¼ cup (½ stick) chilled unsalted butter, cut into pieces**

Filling

- **4½ ounces unsweetened chocolate, chopped**
- **28 ounces Philadelphia brand cream cheese, room temperature (very soft)**
- **½ cup sugar**
- **5 large eggs, room temperature**
- **1 cup plus 2 tablespoons (packed) golden brown sugar**
- **1 tablespoon light corn syrup**

- **¼ cup whipping cream**
- **1 tablespoon plus 1 teaspoon grated orange peel**
- **1 teaspoon grated lemon peel**
- **6 ounces high-quality white chocolate (such as Lindt or Perugina), finely chopped**
- **3 tablespoons Grand Marnier or other orange liqueur**

Dark and white chocolate leaves

- **3 ounces semisweet chocolate, chopped**
- **1 teaspoon solid vegetable shortening, divided**
- **12 medium camellia or lemon leaves, wiped clean, divided**
- **3 ounces high-quality white chocolate (such as Lindt or Perugina), chopped**

Orange threads

- **1 orange**

Whipped cream topping

- **⅔ cup chilled whipping cream**
- **1 tablespoon powdered sugar**
- **2½ teaspoons Grand Marnier or other orange liqueur**

FOR CRUST: Position rack in center of oven and preheat to 350°F. Place cookies, pecans, sugar, and chocolate in processor. Process until finely chopped. Add butter and process until moist crumbs form. Transfer crumb mixture to 10-inch-diameter springform pan with 2¾-inch-high sides. Using plastic wrap as aid, press crumb mixture over bottom and 2 inches up sides of pan. Set on baking sheet and bake 10 minutes. Transfer to rack to cool.

FOR FILLING: Preheat oven to 350°F. Place unsweetened chocolate in top of small double boiler over barely simmering water. Cook until chocolate melts and is smooth, stirring occasionally. Remove from over water. Cool slightly.

USING electric mixer, beat cream cheese with ½ cup sugar in large bowl until light and fluffy. Add eggs 1 at a time, beating until just incorporated and stopping occasionally to scrape down bottom and sides of bowl. Transfer 2½ cups batter to medium bowl and set aside. Add brown sugar to remaining batter in large bowl and beat until combined. Mix corn syrup, then melted chocolate into batter in large bowl. Pour ⅔ cup chocolate batter into small bowl and set aside. Pour remaining chocolate batter into crust. Transfer to baking sheet and bake until filling is barely set, about 15 minutes. Transfer to rack and cool 5 minutes. Maintain oven temperature.

MEANWHILE, bring cream, orange peel, and lemon peel to simmer in heavy small saucepan. Remove from heat. Add chopped white chocolate and stir until melted and smooth. Cool mixture slightly. Add white chocolate mixture to reserved 2½ cups batter in medium bowl and stir to combine. Stir in Grand Marnier.

STARTING at outside edge, carefully spoon white chocolate batter over chocolate layer in pan. Transfer to baking sheet and bake until cake sides are puffed and center moves only slightly when pan is shaken gently, 35 to 40 minutes. Transfer to rack and cool 5 minutes. Maintain oven temperature.

SPOON reserved ⅔ cup chocolate batter by tablespoonfuls over center of white chocolate layer. Using back of spoon, spread chocolate in smooth even circle to within ½ inch of cake edge. Transfer to baking sheet and bake 10 minutes. Transfer to rack. Using small sharp knife, cut around cake pan sides to loosen. Cool cheesecake completely in pan. Cover and refrigerate overnight. *(Can be prepared 2 days ahead. Keep refrigerated.)*

FOR CHOCOLATE LEAVES: Line 2 baking sheets with aluminum foil. Place semisweet chocolate and ½ teaspoon shortening in small bowl. Set bowl over saucepan of barely simmering water. Cook until melted and smooth, stirring occasionally. Remove from over water. Using small metal spatula or spoon, spread thin layer of chocolate over veined underside of 6 leaves, being careful not to drip over edges. Place on 1 prepared baking sheet. Refrigerate until set, about 5 minutes. Spread second thin layer of chocolate over each leaf, remelting chocolate over barely simmering water if necessary. Refrigerate leaves until chocolate sets, about 30 minutes.

PLACE white chocolate and remaining ½ teaspoon shortening in another small bowl. Set bowl over saucepan of barely simmering water. Cook until melted and smooth, stirring occasionally. Remove from over water. Spread thin layer of white chocolate over veined underside of remaining 6 leaves, being careful not to drip over edges. Place on second prepared baking sheet. Refrigerate until set, about 5 minutes. Spread second thin layer of white chocolate over each leaf, remelting chocolate over barely simmering water if necessary. Refrigerate leaves until chocolate is completely set, about 30 minutes.

STARTING at stem end, gently peel leaves off dark and white chocolate. *(Can be prepared 1 day ahead. Refrigerate dark and white chocolate leaves in single layers in airtight containers.)*

FOR ORANGE THREADS: Using vegetable peeler, remove orange peel in large strips. Cut strips into matchstick-size strips. Cook orange strips in saucepan of boiling water 30 seconds. Drain well. Dry thoroughly on paper towels. *(Orange threads can be prepared 1 day ahead. Cover and refrigerate.)*

FOR TOPPING: Beat cream and sugar in medium bowl to soft peaks. Add Grand Marnier and beat topping until stiff peaks form.

RELEASE pan sides from cheesecake. Spoon topping into pastry bag fitted with large star tip. Pipe decorative border around edge of cake. Set alternating white and dark chocolate leaves at a slight angle atop decorative border. Arrange orange threads atop cake. Cut cheesecake into wedges and serve.

Dutch chocolate–mint cheesecake

THE FLAVORS AND SILKY SMOOTHNESS of this cheesecake—named in honor of the Dutch, who are famous for their chocolate—might make you think of an ultra-deluxe after-dinner mint. (If you can't find Dutch process cocoa powder, natural cocoa powder will work as well.) The mousse-like filling contrasts deliciously with the tangy sour cream topping. The pièce de résistance: chocolate ganache piped into a thick lattice pattern over the top. Don't worry if the center sinks slightly as the cake cools; it won't be noticeable when the cake is decorated. To get a neat slice when cutting into the cake, dip a knife or cake server in a glass of hot water, then wipe it dry with a kitchen towel before slicing. Repeat with each serving.

12 SERVINGS

Crust

- **1 9-ounce box chocolate wafer cookies, broken**
- **3 ounces bittersweet (not unsweetened) or semisweet chocolate, coarsely chopped**
- **3 tablespoons sugar**
- **7 tablespoons unsalted butter, melted, hot**

Filling

- **12 ounces bittersweet (not unsweetened) or semisweet chocolate, chopped**
- **4 8-ounce packages Philadelphia brand cream cheese, room temperature**
- **1¾ cups sugar**
- **4 large eggs**
- **¼ cup whipping cream**
- **½ cup unsweetened Dutch process cocoa powder, sifted**
- **1 tablespoon vanilla extract**
- **1 teaspoon peppermint extract**

Toppings

- **2 cups sour cream**
- **⅓ cup sugar**

½ cup whipping cream
1 tablespoon unsalted butter
6 ounces bittersweet (not unsweetened) or semisweet chocolate, chopped
12 fresh mint leaves

FOR CRUST: Finely grind cookies, chocolate, and sugar in processor. Add butter and process until moist crumbs form. Using plastic wrap as aid, press crumb mixture firmly over bottom and up sides of 10-inch-diameter springform pan with 2¾-inch-high sides.

FOR FILLING: Position rack in center of oven and preheat to 350°F. Heat chocolate in top of double boiler set over simmering water, stirring until melted and smooth. Cool to lukewarm. Using electric mixer, beat cream cheese and sugar in large bowl until combined. Add eggs 1 at a time, beating just until incorporated. Add melted chocolate, cream, cocoa powder, and both extracts; beat just until smooth.

POUR filling into crust. Bake until center is just set, about 1 hour. Transfer to rack and cool 20 minutes. Press down gently on puffed edges to flatten. Maintain oven temperature.

MEANWHILE, PREPARE TOPPINGS: Whisk sour cream and sugar in bowl to combine. Spoon sour cream topping over cheesecake. Bake 10 minutes. Run small sharp knife around top edge of pan to loosen. Do not remove pan sides. Place hot cheesecake in refrigerator until cold, at least 6 hours (center may sink as cheesecake cools).

BRING cream and butter to simmer in heavy small saucepan. Reduce heat to low. Add chocolate and whisk until melted. Freeze until firm enough to pipe, whisking occasionally, about 15 minutes. Remove pan sides from cake. Spoon chocolate topping into pastry bag fitted with small star tip. Pipe 6 diagonal lines atop cake, spacing evenly apart. Repeat at right angles, forming lattice. Pipe 12 rosettes of chocolate around top edge of cake. *(Can be prepared 1 day ahead; refrigerate.)* Garnish with mint leaves and serve.

Toffee cheesecake with caramel sauce

A CLASSIC VANILLA CHEESECAKE is topped with caramel sauce, a piped whipped cream border, and English toffee pieces. Since the cheesecake needs to chill at least six hours before serving, it's best to bake it a day ahead of time.

10 SERVINGS

Crust

1½ cups graham cracker crumbs
6 tablespoons (¾ stick) unsalted butter, melted
¼ cup (packed) dark brown sugar

Filling

4 8-ounce packages Philadelphia brand cream cheese, room temperature
1½ cups sugar
5 large eggs, room temperature
2½ teaspoons vanilla extract
2 teaspoons fresh lemon juice

Topping

1¼ cups plus 2 tablespoons sugar
⅓ cup water
1 cup whipping cream
½ cup (1 stick) unsalted butter, cut into small pieces, room temperature
1 teaspoon vanilla extract

¾ cup whipping cream
3 1.4-ounce chocolate-covered English toffee candy bars (such as Heath or Skor), broken into pieces

FOR CRUST: Preheat oven to 350°F. Lightly butter 9-inch-diameter springform pan with 2¾-inch-high sides. Combine crumbs, butter, and brown sugar in small bowl. Using plastic wrap as aid, press crumb mixture over bottom and 1 inch up sides of pan. Refrigerate crust.

FOR FILLING: Using electric mixer, beat cream cheese in large bowl until fluffy. Add sugar and beat until smooth. Beat in eggs 1 at a time. Mix in vanilla and lemon juice.

POUR filling into prepared crust. Bake until cake rises about ½ inch over rim and center moves only slightly when pan is shaken gently, about 1 hour 15 minutes. Cool on rack (cake will fall as it cools, sinking in center). Cover and refrigerate until well chilled, at least 6 hours. *(Can be prepared 1 day ahead. Keep refrigerated.)*

FOR TOPPING: Stir 1¼ cups sugar and ⅓ cup water in heavy medium saucepan over low heat until sugar dissolves. Increase heat and boil without stirring until syrup is deep amber color, occasionally brushing down sides of pan with wet pastry brush and swirling pan, about 8 minutes. Reduce heat to very low. Add cream (mixture will bubble vigorously) and stir until smooth. Mix in butter. Cool caramel sauce slightly. Mix in vanilla.

USING small sharp knife, cut around sides of pan to loosen cake. Release pan sides. Pour ⅔ cup caramel sauce into center of cake. Cover remaining sauce and let stand at room temperature. Refrigerate cake until topping is almost set, about 2 hours. *(Can be prepared 8 hours ahead. Keep refrigerated.)*

WHIP cream with remaining 2 tablespoons sugar in medium bowl until firm peaks form. Spoon cream into pastry bag fitted with medium star tip. Pipe cream decoratively around edge of cake. Arrange toffee pieces in whipped cream border. Cut cake into wedges. Serve, passing remaining caramel sauce.

Coconut candy bar cheesecake

THIS DESSERT RECREATES the flavors of a Mounds bar—turned inside out. A chewy coconut topping and chocolate cookie crust flecked with coconut accent a dense chocolate filling. To toast flaked coconut for garnishing, roast it on a rimmed baking sheet at 350°F, stirring occasionally, until pale golden, about ten minutes. Cream of coconut is available at liquor stores and in the liquor or mixers section of most supermarkets. The cheesecake must chill at least four hours; you can make it one day (and up to two days) ahead.

12 SERVINGS

Crust

26 chocolate wafer cookies (about 6 ounces), broken
1 cup (lightly packed) sweetened flaked coconut
¼ cup sugar
¼ cup (½ stick) chilled unsalted butter, diced

Filling

5 ounces unsweetened chocolate, finely chopped
2 8-ounce packages Philadelphia brand cream cheese, room temperature
1¾ cups sugar
3 tablespoons light corn syrup
1 teaspoon vanilla extract
1 large egg, room temperature
2 large egg yolks, room temperature

Topping

3 cups (lightly packed) sweetened flaked coconut
6 tablespoons sour cream
2 ounces Philadelphia brand cream cheese, room temperature
¼ cup powdered sugar
¼ cup canned sweetened cream of coconut (such as Coco López)
¼ teaspoon (scant) imitation coconut extract

⅓ cup sweetened flaked coconut, toasted

FOR CRUST: Position rack in center of oven and preheat to 350°F. Wrap outside of 9-inch springform pan with 2¾-inch-high sides with heavy-duty aluminum foil. Coarsely grind cookies, coconut, and sugar in processor. Add butter and process until moist crumbs form. Using plastic wrap as aid, press firmly over bottom and 2 inches up sides of pan. Bake crust 10 minutes. Cool crust on rack. Maintain oven temperature.

FOR FILLING: Stir chocolate in top of double boiler over simmering water until melted and smooth. Remove from heat and let cool.

BLEND cream cheese and sugar in processor until thoroughly combined. Add melted chocolate, corn syrup, and vanilla; blend, occasionally scraping down sides of bowl. Add egg and egg yolks; blend 5 seconds. Scrape down sides and blend 5 seconds longer. Spoon batter into crust.

BAKE cheesecake until outer 2 inches are puffed and set and center is only softly set, about 40 minutes. Transfer cheesecake to rack and cool 5 minutes. Maintain oven temperature.

MEANWHILE, PREPARE TOPPING: Blend 3 cups coconut, sour cream, cream cheese, powdered sugar, cream of coconut, and extract in processor until coconut is finely chopped, occasionally scraping down sides of bowl, about 1 minute.

PRESS gently to flatten any raised edges of cheesecake filling. Spoon topping over and spread gently to cover filling. Bake until topping is just set and coconut just begins to brown, about 20 minutes. Transfer cheesecake to rack. Using small sharp knife, cut around cake to loosen crust from pan sides. Cool. Refrigerate cheesecake until very cold, about 4 hours. *(Can be prepared 2 days ahead. Cover and keep refrigerated.)*

SPRINKLE toasted coconut over cheesecake.

Mascarpone cheesecake with roasted cashew crust and passion fruit caramel sauce

ULTRA-RICH MASCARPONE, an Italian cream cheese available at Italian markets and many supermarkets, produces an extraordinarily creamy cheesecake. Baking it in the gentle heat of a water bath (*bain-marie*) ensures a uniform texture; wrapping the springform pan with heavy-duty aluminum foil prevents the water from getting in and making the crust soggy. For convenience, make the cheesecake one day ahead (it needs to chill at least six hours before serving).

12 TO 16 SERVINGS

Crust

- **½ cup salted roasted cashews**
- **¼ cup (packed) golden brown sugar**
- **1 cup all purpose flour**
- **¼ teaspoon salt**
- **⅛ teaspoon ground cinnamon**
- **⅛ teaspoon ground ginger**
- **6 tablespoons (¾ stick) chilled unsalted butter, cut into ½-inch cubes**
- **1 large egg yolk**

Filling

- **2 8-ounce packages Philadelphia brand cream cheese, room temperature**
- **½ cup sugar**
- **Pinch of salt**
- **1 vanilla bean, split lengthwise**
- **2 8-ounce containers mascarpone cheese**
- **½ cup sour cream**
- **4 large eggs**

Passion Fruit Caramel Sauce (see recipe)
Assorted sliced tropical fruits (such as papaya, mango, and pineapple)

FOR CRUST: Preheat oven to 325°F. Wrap outside of 9-inch-diameter springform pan with 2¾-inch-high sides with 2 layers of heavy-duty aluminum foil. Finely grind cashews and brown sugar in processor. Add flour, salt, and spices; blend 5 seconds. Add butter and process until mixture resembles coarse meal. Add egg yolk; using on/off turns, process until moist clumps form. Using plastic wrap as aid, press dough over bottom and ½ inch up sides of prepared pan. Pierce crust all over with fork. Bake until golden brown, about 30 minutes. Cool crust. Maintain oven temperature.

FOR FILLING: Combine first 3 ingredients in large bowl. Scrape in seeds from vanilla bean. Using electric mixer, beat cheese mixture until smooth and fluffy. Add mascarpone cheese and sour cream; beat at low speed just until blended, occasionally scraping down sides of bowl. Add eggs 2 at a time, beating just until blended after each addition. Transfer filling to prepared crust.

PLACE springform pan in large roasting pan. Fill roasting pan with enough hot water to come halfway up sides of springform pan. Place roasting pan with cheesecake in oven; cover roasting pan with foil. Bake cheesecake 30 minutes. Lift edge of foil to allow steam to escape; cover again. Bake cake 30 minutes. Lift foil again; cover again. Bake until cake is loosely set but filling jiggles all over when pan is shaken gently, lifting foil every 10 minutes, about 30 minutes longer. Remove cheesecake from water. Place on rack; cool 1 hour. Refrigerate uncovered until cold, at least 6 hours. *(Can be prepared 1 day ahead. Cover and keep refrigerated.)*

CUT around pan sides to release cheesecake. Cut into wedges. Drizzle each wedge with warm caramel sauce. Spoon some fruit slices alongside and serve.

Passion fruit caramel sauce

OTHER WAYS to enjoy this slightly tropical warm sauce: over ice cream, with grilled pineapple, or as the fondue "dip" for fruit.

MAKES ABOUT 2 CUPS

- **2 cups sugar**
- **½ cup water**
- **2 teaspoons light corn syrup**
- **¼ cup (½ stick) unsalted butter, cut into pieces**
- **1⅓ cups frozen concentrated passion fruit juice cocktail, thawed (from 12-ounce container)**

COMBINE sugar, ½ cup water, and corn syrup in heavy large saucepan. Stir over medium heat until sugar dissolves, occasionally brushing down sides of pan with wet pastry brush. Increase heat and boil without stirring until syrup turns medium amber color, swirling pan occasionally, about 8 minutes. Remove pan from heat. Whisk in butter, then passion fruit concentrate (mixture will bubble up vigorously). Simmer over medium-low heat until color deepens to rich brown and caramel thickens enough to coat spoon thickly, stirring occasionally, about 12 minutes. Transfer sauce to bowl. *(Can be prepared 2 days ahead. Cover and refrigerate. Rewarm slightly before serving.)*

Strawberry-topped cheesecake with graham cracker crust

THIS CLASSIC CREAMY CHEESECAKE features a smooth filling, sour cream topping, and crown of jam-glazed whole strawberries. Begin making this a day before you plan to serve it.

12 SERVINGS

Crust

20 whole graham crackers (10 ounces total), broken
½ cup (1 stick) chilled unsalted butter, diced
½ cup (packed) golden brown sugar

Filling

4 8-ounce packages Philadelphia brand cream cheese, room temperature
1¾ cups sugar
3 tablespoons fresh lemon juice
1 tablespoon vanilla extract
⅛ teaspoon salt
3 tablespoons all purpose flour
5 large eggs

Topping

2 cups sour cream
3 tablespoons sugar
½ teaspoon vanilla extract

2 16-ounce containers strawberries, hulled
½ cup raspberry or strawberry jelly

FOR CRUST: Position rack in center of oven and preheat to 350°F. Finely grind graham crackers in processor. Add butter and sugar; using on/off turns, process until moist crumbs form. Using plastic wrap as aid, press crumbs over bottom and 2¾ inches up sides of 10-inch-diameter springform pan with 3-inch-high sides. Bake crust 8 minutes. Transfer to rack and cool while preparing filling. Maintain oven temperature.

FOR FILLING: Using electric mixer, beat cream cheese, sugar, lemon juice, vanilla, and salt in large bowl until very smooth. Beat in flour. Add eggs and beat just until blended, stopping occasionally to scrape down sides of bowl.

POUR filling into crust. Bake cheesecake until outer 2-inch edge of cake is puffed and slightly cracked, center is just set, and top is brown in spots, about 50 minutes. Transfer cake to rack. Cool 10 minutes. Maintain oven temperature.

FOR TOPPING: Whisk sour cream, sugar, and vanilla in medium bowl to blend.

SPOON topping over cake, spreading to edge of pan. Bake until topping is just set, about 5 minutes. Remove from oven. Run knife between top edge of crust and pan sides to loosen. Cool cake completely in pan on rack. Cover and refrigerate overnight.

RELEASE pan sides from cheesecake. Arrange strawberries, points facing up, atop cheesecake, covering completely. Stir jelly in heavy small saucepan over medium-low heat until melted. Cool to barely lukewarm, about 5 minutes. Brush enough jelly over berries to glaze generously, allowing some to drip between berries. *(Can be prepared 6 hours ahead. Refrigerate cake.)*

Raspberry and blueberry vanilla cheesecake

FRESH RASPBERRIES AND BLUEBERRIES enhance both the filling and the topping of this creamy, summery cheesecake. It also has an especially delicious crust, made of ground shortbread cookies and toasted hazelnuts. Wrapping the springform pan in aluminum foil helps prevent the berry juices and butter from leaking out and burning in the oven. Bake this cheesecake one day before serving.

8 TO 10 SERVINGS

Crust

1½ cups shortbread cookie crumbs
1 cup hazelnuts, toasted, skinned
¼ cup sugar
¼ cup (½ stick) unsalted butter, melted
1 teaspoon vanilla extract

Filling

2 vanilla beans, split lengthwise
⅓ cup whipping cream

- 3 8-ounce packages Philadelphia brand cream cheese, room temperature
- 1 cup sugar
- ½ cup sour cream
- 2 teaspoons vanilla extract
- 4 large eggs

- 1 6-ounce container fresh raspberries
- 1 6-ounce container fresh blueberries
- 1 tablespoon cornstarch

Topping

- 1 cup sour cream
- 3 tablespoons sugar
- 1½ teaspoons vanilla extract

- ⅓ cup seedless raspberry jam
- 1 6-ounce container fresh raspberries
- 1 6-ounce container fresh blueberries

FOR CRUST: Preheat oven to 350°F. Finely grind cookie crumbs, nuts, and sugar in processor. Add butter and vanilla; process until moist crumbs form. Using plastic wrap as aid, press over bottom and up sides of 9-inch-diameter springform pan with 2¾-inch-high sides. Wrap outside of pan with aluminum foil. Bake until crust is light golden, about 15 minutes. Cool. Maintain oven temperature.

FOR FILLING: Scrape seeds from vanilla beans into heavy small saucepan; add pods. Add cream and bring to boil. Cool completely. Discard pods.

USING electric mixer, beat cream cheese and sugar in large bowl until smooth. Add vanilla-cream mixture, sour cream, and vanilla extract; beat until well blended. Beat in eggs 1 at a time.

GENTLY mix raspberries, blueberries, and cornstarch in medium bowl. Pour ⅔ of filling into crust. Sprinkle berry mixture over. Pour remaining filling over berries to cover. Bake until cake is golden and beginning to crack around edges but still moves slightly in center when pan is shaken gently, about 1 hour 10 minutes. Let cool 10 minutes (cake will fall).

MEANWHILE, PREPARE TOPPING: Mix sour cream, sugar, and vanilla in small bowl to blend.

GENTLY press down any raised edges of cake. Spoon topping evenly over cake. Bake 10 minutes. Cool cake on rack. Refrigerate overnight. *(Can be prepared 2 days ahead. Keep refrigerated.)*

MELT jam in small saucepan over low heat. Brush some jam over top of cake. Arrange raspberries and blueberries atop cake. Gently brush berries with remaining jam. *(Can be prepared 8 hours ahead. Refrigerate.)*

RUN small sharp knife around pan sides to loosen. Remove pan sides. Place cake on platter and serve.

Lemon cheesecake with hazelnut crust

AN EASY, NO-HASSLE CHEESECAKE with wonderful flavors; it's so good you won't miss adornments like sauce or topping. Bake this cheesecake one day before you plan to serve it.

8 TO 10 SERVINGS

Crust

- ¾ cup hazelnuts, toasted, skinned
- ¾ cup graham cracker crumbs
- 3 tablespoons powdered sugar
- 5 tablespoons unsalted butter, melted

Filling

- 3 8-ounce packages Philadelphia brand cream cheese, room temperature
- 1 cup sugar
- 3 large eggs
- ¼ cup fresh lemon juice
- 1 tablespoon grated lemon peel

Lemon slices (optional)
Fresh mint sprigs (optional)

FOR CRUST: Position rack in center of oven and preheat to 350°F. Finely grind nuts, graham cracker crumbs, and powdered sugar in processor. Add butter; using on/off turns, blend until moist crumbs form. Using plastic wrap as aid, press crumbs over bottom and ½ inch up sides of 9-inch-diameter springform pan with 2¾-inch-high sides. Refrigerate while making filling.

FOR FILLING: Using electric mixer, beat cream cheese in large bowl until fluffy. Slowly add sugar; beat until smooth. Add eggs 1 at a time, beating 30 seconds after each. Mix in lemon juice and peel.

POUR filling into crust. Bake cake until outer 2-inch portion of top is set and center looks slightly glossy and is barely set, about 45 minutes. Transfer to rack; cool to room temperature. Cover and refrigerate overnight.

RUN knife around pan sides to loosen. Release pan sides. Place cake on plate. Top with lemon and mint, if desired, and serve.

Cranberry-orange cheesecake with chocolate crust

CAPE COD'S CRANBERRY BOGS provided the inspiration for this festive dessert, a vanilla cheesecake scented with orange peel and topped with sweetened fresh cranberries. You can make the cheesecake and the cranberry topping a day or two ahead, then simply assemble the cake an hour before you plan to serve it. To keep the moist crust mixture from sticking to your fingers, cover your fingers with plastic wrap before pressing the crumbs into the pan. Because this cheesecake is cooked in a water bath, you need to wrap the springform pan in aluminum foil; this prevents the water from seeping in and making the crust soggy.

12 SERVINGS

Crust

- **1 9-ounce box chocolate wafer cookies, broken**
- **2 ounces bittersweet (not unsweetened) or semisweet chocolate, coarsely chopped**
- **5 tablespoons unsalted butter, melted**

Filling

- **4 8-ounce packages Philadelphia brand cream cheese, room temperature**
- **1½ cups sugar**
- **3 tablespoons all purpose flour**
- **4 large eggs**
- **2 teaspoons grated orange peel**
- **1 teaspoon vanilla extract**

Topping

- **½ cup sugar**
- **3 tablespoons water**
- **1 teaspoon cornstarch dissolved in 1 tablespoon water**
- **2 cups fresh cranberries**
- **½ teaspoon grated orange peel**

FOR CRUST: Preheat oven to 325°F. Finely grind cookies and chocolate in processor. Add butter and blend until moist clumps form. Using plastic wrap as aid, press crumb mixture over bottom and 1¼ inches up sides of 9-inch-diameter springform pan with 2¾-inch-high sides. Bake until set, about 8 minutes. Cool completely.

FOR FILLING: Increase oven temperature to 350°F. Wrap 2 layers of heavy-duty aluminum foil around bottom and sides of springform pan. Using electric mixer, beat cream cheese and sugar in large bowl until light. Beat in flour. Beat in eggs 1 at a time just until blended. Beat in orange peel and vanilla.

POUR filling into crust. Place springform pan in large roasting pan. Fill roasting pan with enough hot water to come halfway up sides of springform pan. Bake until filling is just set in center but still moves slightly when pan is shaken gently, about 55 minutes. Remove cake from water bath; transfer to rack and cool completely, about 4 hours. Cover and refrigerate overnight.

FOR TOPPING: Stir sugar and 3 tablespoons water in medium saucepan over medium-low heat until sugar dissolves. Increase heat to medium; add cornstarch mixture and bring to simmer. Add cranberries; cook until beginning to pop, stirring often, about 3 minutes. Stir in orange peel. Cool completely. Cover and refrigerate overnight. *(Cheesecake and cranberry mixture can be made 2 days ahead. Keep refrigerated.)*

RUN knife around top edge of cheesecake to loosen. Release pan sides. Top cheesecake with cranberry mixture. Chill until set, about 1 hour.

Triple-cherry cheesecake

ALMONDS AND CHERRIES are a beloved old-world combination; here, an almond-scented cheesecake with an almond and graham cracker crust is topped with a Bing cherry sauce, whose juicy fruit flavors are deepened with dried tart cherries, cherry jam, and a splash of brandy. Begin making this cake one day before serving.

10 SERVINGS

Topping

- **3/4 cup dried tart cherries**
- **1 1-pound bag frozen pitted Bing cherries, thawed, drained, juice reserved**

- **1/2 cup cherry jam**
- **2 tablespoons brandy**
- **1 tablespoon cornstarch**

Crust

- **1/3 cup whole almonds**
- **2/3 cup graham cracker crumbs**
- **1/4 cup sugar**
- **1/4 cup (1/2 stick) unsalted butter, melted**

Filling

- **3 8-ounce packages Philadelphia brand cream cheese, room temperature**
- **1 1/3 cups sugar**
- **4 large eggs**
- **2 tablespoons fresh lemon juice**
- **1/4 teaspoon almond extract**
- **1/4 teaspoon salt**

- **1/2 cup sliced almonds, toasted**

FOR TOPPING: Combine dried cherries and reserved juice from thawed cherries in heavy medium saucepan. Bring to boil. Remove from heat. Cover and let steep 20 minutes.

MIX cherry jam, brandy, and cornstarch in small bowl to blend. Stir into dried cherry mixture. Add thawed cherries. Stir over medium heat until mixture boils and thickens, about 1 minute. Cool slightly, then refrigerate until cold. *(Can be prepared 2 days ahead. Keep refrigerated.)*

FOR CRUST: Finely grind almonds in processor. Add cracker crumbs, sugar, and butter; process until clumps form. Using plastic wrap as aid, press mixture over bottom (not sides) of 9-inch-diameter springform pan with 2¾-inch-high sides. Refrigerate 30 minutes.

FOR FILLING: Position rack in center of oven; preheat to 350°F. Blend cream cheese and next 5 ingredients in processor just until smooth, scraping down sides of bowl several times.

POUR filling over crust. Bake until edges of cheesecake are puffed and center is just set, about 50 minutes. Run knife around pan sides to loosen. Refrigerate cake uncovered overnight.

RELEASE pan sides from cake. Transfer cake to platter. Spoon topping evenly over cake, leaving ½-inch border around edge. Garnish cake with almonds.

Bananas Foster cheesecake

THIS CHEESECAKE FEATURES the flavors of the iconic Big Easy dessert—rum-flambéed bananas spooned over vanilla ice cream—from Brennan's restaurant in New Orleans. Remarkably, this recipe goes (a bit) easy on the decadence by using Neufchâtel, a reduced-fat cream cheese, and low-fat sour cream. It is, however, just as sinfully delicious as the original. Use ripe bananas; when underripe, they can be somewhat astringent. Bananas are ripe when their skins are deep yellow and flecked with tiny dark brown or black spots; to speed up ripening, place them with an apple in a closed paper bag with a few holes. Because this cake is cooked in a water bath, aluminum foil is wrapped around the outside of the pan to prevent water from seeping in. Begin preparing this cheesecake one day before serving.

10 SERVINGS

Crust

3/4 cup all purpose flour
3/4 cup finely chopped pecans
4 tablespoons (1/2 stick) unsalted butter, melted
3 tablespoons sugar
2 tablespoons (packed) golden brown sugar
1 1/2 teaspoons vanilla extract

Filling

2 8-ounce packages Neufchâtel cheese (reduced-fat cream cheese), room temperature
1 1/4 cups sugar
2 tablespoons cornstarch
3 large eggs
2 cups pureed bananas (from about 4 ripe bananas)
1 cup low-fat sour cream
1 1/2 tablespoons fresh lemon juice
1 teaspoon vanilla extract
1 teaspoon ground cinnamon
Pinch of salt

Topping

1 cup low-fat sour cream
1/4 cup sugar
1/4 teaspoon vanilla extract

1 17-ounce jar caramel sauce
2 tablespoons dark rum
2 bananas, peeled, sliced

FOR CRUST: Position rack in center of oven and preheat to 350°F. Wrap outside of 9-inch-diameter springform pan with 3-inch-high sides with 2 layers of heavy-duty aluminum foil. Combine flour, pecans, butter, sugar, brown sugar, and vanilla in large bowl. Mix well. Using plastic wrap as aid, press mixture over bottom (not sides) of prepared pan.

FOR FILLING: Using electric mixer, beat Neufchâtel cheese in large bowl until smooth. Gradually beat in sugar. Beat in cornstarch. Add eggs 1 at a time beating until just blended after each addition. Add pureed bananas, sour cream, lemon juice, vanilla, cinnamon, and salt; beat just until combined.

POUR filling over crust. Place pan in large roasting pan. Add enough hot water to roasting pan to come 1 inch up sides of springform pan. Bake until center of cake is just set, about 1 hour 15 minutes. Remove cheesecake from water bath. Maintain oven temperature.

MEANWHILE, PREPARE TOPPING: Mix together sour cream, sugar, and vanilla in small bowl until well blended.

SPREAD topping over cheesecake. Bake until topping is set, about 10 minutes. Turn off oven. Let cake stand in oven 2 hours. Refrigerate cake until cold, then cover and refrigerate overnight.

CUT around cake to loosen; release pan sides. Transfer cake to platter. Warm caramel sauce in small saucepan over low heat, stirring often. Mix in rum. Drizzle some sauce decoratively over cake. Arrange bananas atop cake. Cut cake into wedges. Serve, passing remaining sauce separately.

Pumpkin cheesecake with Frangelico

A GINGERSNAP CRUST and warm spices give this sophisticated cheesecake a holiday flavor. If you'd like to use fresh nutmeg (which is stronger than jarred), swipe a whole nutmeg seed across a spice grater (or the fine-rasp portion of a box grater). Bake the cheesecake in a nine-inch springform pan at least one day before you plan to serve it; wrapping the outside of the pan (bottom and sides) in aluminum foil catches any melting butter that might otherwise drip into the oven and smoke. For an especially pretty presentation, roast and skin the hazelnuts before arranging them around the edge of the cake; or buy them already skinned at a nut or candy store.

10 SERVINGS

Crust

24 gingersnaps (about 6 ounces)
3 tablespoons sugar
¼ cup (½ stick) unsalted butter, melted

Filling

½ cup Frangelico (hazelnut liqueur)
2 8-ounce packages Philadelphia brand cream cheese, room temperature
1 15-ounce can pure pumpkin
5 large eggs
¾ cup (packed) brown sugar
1 teaspoon ground cinnamon
1 teaspoon vanilla extract
½ teaspoon ground ginger
¼ teaspoon ground nutmeg
¼ teaspoon ground cloves

Topping

16 ounces sour cream
¼ cup sugar
3 tablespoons Frangelico

10 whole skinned hazelnuts

FOR CRUST: Grind gingersnaps and sugar in processor to fine crumbs. With machine running, slowly add butter. Wrap aluminum foil around outside of 9-inch-diameter springform pan with 2¾-inch-high sides. Using plastic wrap as aid, press gingersnap mixture over bottom and 1 inch up sides of pan. Freeze 15 minutes.

FOR FILLING: Position rack in center of oven and preheat to 350°F. Boil Frangelico in heavy small saucepan until reduced to ¼ cup, about 3 minutes. Cool. Blend Frangelico, cream cheese, and next 8 ingredients in processor until smooth, stopping once to scrape down sides of work bowl.

POUR filling over crust. Bake until edges of cake begin to pull away from sides of pan and cake begins to brown, about 1 hour; center will not be firm. Maintain oven temperature.

FOR TOPPING: Whisk together sour cream, sugar, and 3 tablespoons Frangelico.

POUR topping over hot cake, starting at edges. Spread evenly. Continue baking cake until edges begin to bubble, about 10 minutes. Run tip of small sharp knife around cake pan sides to loosen. Place hot cheesecake directly in refrigerator. Chill overnight. *(Can be prepared 2 days ahead. Cover and keep refrigerated.)* Remove foil from pan; release cake pan sides. Press hazelnuts lightly into top edge of cake. Let stand at room temperature for 30 minutes before serving.

Be mine chocolate-truffle heart cake

YOU'LL STEAL SOME HEARTS with this dessert—a heart-shaped layer cake filled with ganache, the mixture of melted chocolate and whipping cream used to frost cakes and make truffles. (To make truffles: Chill the ganache, then shape it into balls. Roll the balls in cocoa and keep refrigerated.) To decorate the cake, arrange whole raspberries or sliced hulled strawberries around the edge, or cluster whole berries in the center of the cake.

8 SERVINGS

Truffle cream

- **8 ounces bittersweet (not unsweetened) or semisweet chocolate, chopped**
- **1/3 cup whipping cream**
- **2 tablespoons (1/4 stick) unsalted butter, room temperature**
- **1/4 cup Chambord or other berry liqueur (such as crème de cassis)**

Cake

- **1 3/4 cups all purpose flour**
- **2 teaspoons baking powder**
- **1/2 teaspoon baking soda**
- **1/2 teaspoon salt**
- **3/4 cup sugar**
- **1/2 cup (1 stick) unsalted butter, room temperature**
- **4 large egg yolks**
- **1 cup buttermilk**

Glaze

- **6 ounces bittersweet (not unsweetened) or semisweet chocolate, chopped**
- **1/4 cup (1/2 stick) unsalted butter, cut into small pieces**
- **1/4 cup light corn syrup**
- **1/4 cup Chambord or other berry liqueur (such as crème de cassis)**

Fresh raspberries or strawberries

FOR TRUFFLE CREAM: Stir chocolate, cream, and butter in heavy medium saucepan over low heat until chocolate and butter melt and mixture is smooth. Mix in Chambord. Let stand at room temperature until very thick and spreadable, stirring occasionally, about 2 hours.

FOR CAKE: Position rack in center of oven and preheat to 350°F. Butter 9-inch heart-shaped pan with 1¼-inch-high sides. Dust with flour; tap out excess. Sift flour and next 3 ingredients into medium bowl. Using electric mixer, beat sugar and butter at high speed in large bowl until light and fluffy. Add egg yolks 1 at a time, beating just to combine after each addition. Using rubber spatula, stir in flour mixture alternately with buttermilk, beginning and ending with flour mixture.

TRANSFER batter to prepared pan. Bake cake until tester inserted into center comes out clean, about 35 minutes. Run small sharp knife around cake pan sides to loosen. Turn cake out onto rack and cool.

USING serrated knife, cut cake horizontally in half. Transfer bottom layer to plate. Spread truffle cream over. Arrange top layer over and press gently to adhere. Run spatula around sides of cake to remove any excess truffle cream. Refrigerate until set, at least 1 hour.

FOR GLAZE: Stir chocolate and butter in heavy medium saucepan over low heat until melted and smooth. Remove from heat. Add corn syrup and Chambord; whisk until smooth. Let glaze stand until slightly thickened, stirring occasionally, about 30 minutes.

PLACE cake on rack set over baking sheet or large piece of aluminum foil. Pour glaze over cake, coating completely. Refrigerate cake on rack until glaze is set, about 30 minutes. Transfer cake to platter. *(Can be prepared 1 day ahead. Cover with cake dome and refrigerate. Bring to room temperature before serving.)* Garnish with berries.

Coconut layer cake

THIS LOVELY WHITE CAKE is the classic choice—deservedly—for ladylike parties, such as bridal showers. If they're available, fresh pansies or violets clustered in the center of the frosted cake add a beautiful touch. Candied violets (from a specialty foods store) or edible flowers (available packaged in the produce section of some supermarkets) are attractive alternatives. Unsweetened coconut milk is available at Indian, Asian, and Latin markets, and many supermarkets.

12 SERVINGS

Cake

- **3 cups cake flour**
- **1 tablespoon baking powder**
- **3/4 teaspoon salt**
- **3/4 cup (1 1/2 sticks) unsalted butter, room temperature**
- **1 3/4 cups sugar**
- **4 large eggs, separated**
- **1 teaspoon vanilla extract**
- **1 teaspoon imitation coconut extract**
- **1 14-ounce can unsweetened coconut milk, divided**
- **1/4 teaspoon cream of tartar**

Frosting

- **6 ounces Philadelphia brand cream cheese, room temperature**
- **1/4 cup (1/2 stick) unsalted butter, room temperature**
- **1 1-pound box powdered sugar, sifted**
- **1 7-ounce package sweetened shredded coconut**
- **Fresh pansies or violets or candied violets (optional)**

FOR CAKE: Preheat oven to 350°F. Line bottom of two 9-inch-diameter cake pans with 2-inch-high sides with waxed paper. Sift flour, baking powder, and salt into large bowl. Using electric mixer, beat butter in large bowl until smooth. Gradually add sugar and beat until light and fluffy. Add egg yolks 1 at a time, beating well after each addition. Mix in vanilla and coconut extracts. Reserve ¼ cup coconut milk for frosting. Add flour mixture to butter mixture alternately with remaining coconut milk, beginning and ending with flour mixture and beating just until combined. Using clean dry beaters, beat egg whites and cream of tartar in another large bowl until medium-firm peaks form. Fold ⅓ of whites into cake batter to lighten, then fold in remaining whites.

DIVIDE batter equally between prepared pans; smooth tops. Bake cakes until tester inserted into center comes out clean, about 30 minutes. Transfer cakes to racks. Cool in pans 15 minutes. Run small sharp knife around pan sides to loosen. Turn cakes out onto racks; peel off waxed paper. Cool completely. *(Can be prepared 1 day ahead. Wrap tightly in plastic and store at room temperature.)*

FOR FROSTING: Using electric mixer, beat cream cheese and butter in large bowl until smooth. Gradually sift powdered sugar over, mixing until well combined. Gradually add enough of reserved ¼ cup coconut milk by tablespoonfuls to make frosting spreadable.

PLACE 1 cake layer on platter. Tuck waxed paper strips under cake to protect platter. Spread ¾ cup frosting over top. Sprinkle ½ cup coconut over. Top with second cake layer. Spread remaining frosting over top and sides of cake. Lightly press remaining coconut over top and sides of cake, covering completely. Remove waxed paper. *(Can be prepared 1 day ahead. Cover with cake dome and refrigerate. Let stand at room temperature 2 hours before continuing.)* Decorate cake with pansies or fresh or candied violets, if desired.

Lemon wedding cake with blackberry sauce

INSTEAD OF STACKED TIERS, this pretty, deconstructed wedding cake is set on three separate stands of varying heights, which makes for an eye-catching arrangement—and much easier assembly. Created with the home cook in mind, this is quite an approachable wedding cake, and it can be made ahead in three stages. A straight icing spatula is helpful for spreading the frosting smoothly and evenly, and an offset spatula is the best tool for making decorative swirls. The cardboard rounds used to support the cakes are available at baking supply stores. For best results, use an imported crème de cassis in the blackberry sauce. Edible flowers are a beautiful garnish.

48 SERVINGS

Lemon curd

- **3 cups strained fresh lemon juice**
- **2 cups (4 sticks) unsalted butter**
- **¼ cup grated lemon peel**
- **12 large egg yolks**
- **8 large eggs**
- **3½ cups sugar**

Cake

- **8 cups cake flour, divided**
- **4 teaspoons baking powder, divided**
- **3 teaspoons baking soda, divided**
- **2 teaspoons salt, divided**

- **2 cups (4 sticks) unsalted butter, room temperature, divided**
- **4 cups sugar, divided**
- **10 large eggs, separated**
- **2 tablespoons grated lemon peel, divided**
- **3 teaspoons vanilla extract, divided**
- **4 cups buttermilk, divided**

- **1 teaspoon cream of tartar, divided**

Frosting

- **3 8-ounce packages Philadelphia brand cream cheese, room temperature**
- **2 cups (4 sticks) unsalted butter, room temperature**
- **4 cups (about 1 pound) powdered sugar**
- **½ cup whipping cream**

Sauce

- **2¼ cups (24 ounces) seedless blackberry jam**
- **½ cup crème de cassis**
- **9 cups fresh blackberries or frozen unsweetened (2¼ pounds), thawed, very well drained**

- **1 7-inch-diameter cardboard round**
- **1 8-inch-diameter cardboard round**
- **1 9-inch-diameter cardboard round**

FOR LEMON CURD: Stir lemon juice, butter, and lemon peel in heavy large nonreactive saucepan over medium heat until butter melts. Whisk egg yolks, eggs, and sugar in large bowl until blended. Gradually whisk in hot lemon mixture. Return mixture to same saucepan; whisk over medium heat until thick and smooth, about 10 minutes (do not boil). Transfer to large bowl. Press plastic wrap directly onto surface to keep skin from forming. Refrigerate overnight. *(Can be prepared 1 week ahead. Keep refrigerated.)*

FOR CAKE: Preheat oven to 350°F. Line bottom of 8-inch-diameter cake pan with 2-inch-high sides and 9-inch-diameter cake pan with 2-inch-high sides with waxed paper. Sift 4 cups cake flour, 2 teaspoons baking powder, 1½ teaspoons baking soda, and 1 teaspoon salt into large bowl.

IN large bowl of electric mixer, beat 1 cup butter until smooth. Gradually add 2 cups sugar, beating until light and fluffy. Add 5 egg yolks 1 at a time, beating well after each addition. Beat in 1 tablespoon lemon peel and 1½ teaspoons vanilla. At low speed, beat in flour mixture alternately with 2 cups buttermilk in 3 batches each, beginning with flour mixture.

BEAT 5 egg whites with ½ teaspoon cream of tartar in large bowl until medium-firm peaks form. Fold ⅓ of beaten egg whites into batter to lighten. Fold in remaining egg whites. Spoon 4 cups cake batter into 8-inch pan. Spoon remaining cake batter (about 5 cups) into 9-inch pan (the batter should be about the same depth in each pan).

BAKE cakes until top is golden and tester inserted into center comes out clean, about 45 minutes for 8-inch cake and 50 minutes for 9-inch cake. Cool cakes 15 minutes. Using small knife, cut around pan sides to loosen. Turn cakes out onto racks and cool completely.

LINE 10-inch-diameter cake pan with 2-inch-high sides and 6-inch-diameter cake pan with 2-inch-high sides with waxed paper. Using remaining ingredients, make second batch of cake batter as described above, using same quantities as for first batch. Spoon 6½ cups batter into prepared 10-inch pan. Spoon remaining batter (about 2½ cups) into prepared 6-inch pan (batter should be the same depth in each pan). Bake cakes until top is golden and tester inserted into center comes out clean, about 45 minutes for 6-inch cake and 1 hour 5 minutes for 10-inch cake. Cool cakes in pans 15 minutes. Cut around pan sides to loosen. Turn cakes out onto racks and cool completely. Peel off paper. *(Cakes can be prepared ahead. Wrap tightly and let stand at room temperature 1 day or freeze up to 2 weeks; defrost in wrapping before continuing.)*

FOR FROSTING: Using electric mixer, beat 1½ packages cream cheese and 1 cup butter in large bowl until fluffy. Gradually beat in 2 cups powdered sugar. Gradually add ¼ cup cream, beating just until blended. Add 1 cup lemon curd and beat just until combined. Transfer to large bowl. Using remaining ingredients, make second batch of frosting as described above, using same quantities as for first batch. Cover frosting; refrigerate until very cold and spreadable, at least 8 hours and up to 1 day.

FOR SAUCE: Whisk jam in large saucepan over medium-low heat until melted and smooth. Whisk in cassis. Transfer to large bowl. Add berries and toss to coat. Chill sauce until cold, stirring occasionally, at least 8 hours and up to 1 day.

USING long serrated knife, cut each cake horizontally into 3 equal layers. Spread dab of frosting on 7-inch cardboard round to anchor cake; transfer bottom 8-inch cake layer to cardboard, cut side up. Spread ¼ cup lemon curd over. Top with second 8-inch layer. Spread ¼ cup lemon curd over. Top with third 8-inch layer, cut side down.

SPREAD 1 tablespoon frosting over top center of assembled 8-inch cake. Center bottom 6-inch layer, cut side up, atop 8-inch cake. Spread 3 tablespoons lemon curd over. Top with second 6-inch cake layer. Spread 3 tablespoons lemon curd over. Top with third 6-inch cake layer, cut side down. Generously frost tiered cake, using about 3 cups frosting.

SPREAD dab of frosting on 8-inch cardboard round to anchor cake; transfer bottom 9-inch cake layer to cardboard, cut side up. Spread 6 tablespoons lemon curd over. Top with second 9-inch cake layer. Spread 6 tablespoons lemon curd over. Top with third 9-inch cake layer, cut side down. Generously frost assembled 9-inch cake, using about 3 cups frosting.

SPREAD dab of frosting on 9-inch cardboard round to anchor cake; transfer bottom 10-inch cake layer to cardboard, cut side up. Spread ½ cup lemon curd over. Top with second 10-inch cake layer. Spread ½ cup lemon curd over. Top with third 10-inch cake layer, cut side down. Generously frost assembled 10-inch cake, using about 3½ cups frosting. Refrigerate cakes at least two hours and up to 1 day. Transfer tiered cake on its cardboard base to tallest cake stand. Transfer 9-inch cake on its cardboard base to shorter cake stand. Transfer 10-inch cake on its cardboard base to platter. Slice cake and serve with sauce.

Chocolate and cherry yule log

IN FRANCE, no Christmas dinner would be complete without a whimsical log-shaped chocolate cake, called *bûche de Noël* ("Yule log"). Its origin can be traced back to winter solstice celebrations, in which a burning log was the symbol of the rebirth of the returning sun. Our version includes dried tart cherries and kirsch, a clear brandy distilled from fresh cherries. You'll need a 15x10x1-inch jelly-roll pan for the cake layer. Traditionally, the *bûche* is garnished with mushroom-shaped meringues and decorated with candies shaped like holly berries, then dusted with powdered sugar to resemble snow. Surround the cake with a selection of holiday greenery (keeping in mind that real holly is poisonous).

8 SERVINGS

Cake

6 large eggs
3/4 cup sugar
3/4 cup cake flour
1/4 teaspoon salt
2 tablespoons (1/4 stick) unsalted butter, melted, cooled

Powdered sugar

Soaking syrup

2 tablespoons sugar
2 tablespoons water
2 tablespoons kirsch (clear cherry brandy)

Filling

2/3 cup dried tart cherries, chopped
1/2 cup water
2 tablespoons kirsch (clear cherry brandy)

3 1/2 ounces high-quality white chocolate (such as Lindt or Perugina), chopped

1 cup chilled whipping cream

Chocolate Icing (see recipe)

Powdered sugar

FOR CAKE: Preheat oven to 350°F. Butter 15x10x1-inch jelly-roll pan. Line pan with parchment paper. Butter and flour parchment. Whisk eggs and ¾ cup sugar in large metal bowl. Set bowl over pot of simmering water (do not allow bowl to touch water). Whisk until just warm, about 2 minutes. Remove bowl from over water. Using electric mixer, beat mixture until tripled in volume, about 3 minutes. Sift flour and salt over; fold just until combined. Gently fold in butter (do not overmix).

POUR into prepared pan. Bake cake until tester inserted into center comes out clean, about 22 minutes.

SIFT powdered sugar over towel. Run knife around cake to loosen. Turn cake out onto towel. Peel off parchment. Starting at 1 long side and using towel as aid, gently roll up cake jelly-roll style. Cool.

FOR SOAKING SYRUP: Stir sugar and 2 tablespoons water in small saucepan over low heat until sugar dissolves. Mix in kirsch. Cool syrup.

FOR FILLING: Simmer cherries, ½ cup water, and kirsch in small saucepan until liquid is absorbed, about 6 minutes. Cool.

STIR white chocolate in top of double boiler over simmering water until melted and smooth. Cool to barely lukewarm.

BEAT cream in medium bowl to soft peaks. Stir ½ cup whipped cream into melted chocolate; fold in remaining cream, then dried cherry mixture.

UNROLL cake. Brush with syrup. Spread filling over, leaving ½-inch plain border on all sides. Reroll cake.

STARTING 1 inch in, cut off 3-inch-long diagonal piece from each end of cake. Place cake on platter, seam side down. Tuck waxed paper under cake. Spread cut side of each 3-inch cake piece with some of icing. Attach 1 cake piece, icing side down, to top of cake near 1 end. Attach other piece, icing side down, to side of cake near opposite end. Spread remaining icing over top and sides of cake. Run fork tines in concentric circles on cake ends. Run fork in lines along length of cake to form bark design. Remove waxed paper. *(Can be prepared 1 day ahead. Refrigerate until icing sets, about 2 hours. Cover cake and keep refrigerated. Let stand 1 hour at room temperature before serving.)* Sift powdered sugar over and serve.

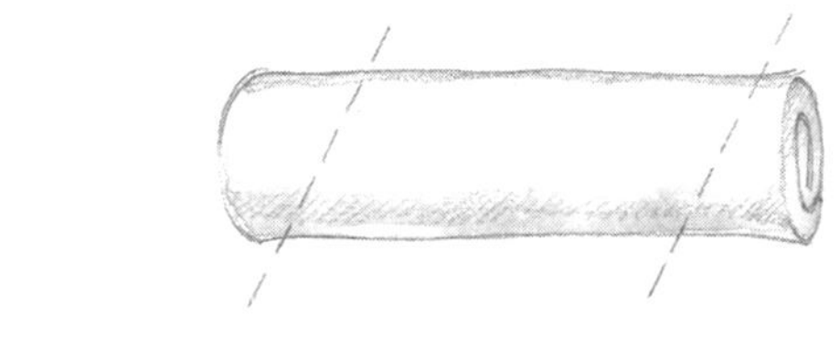

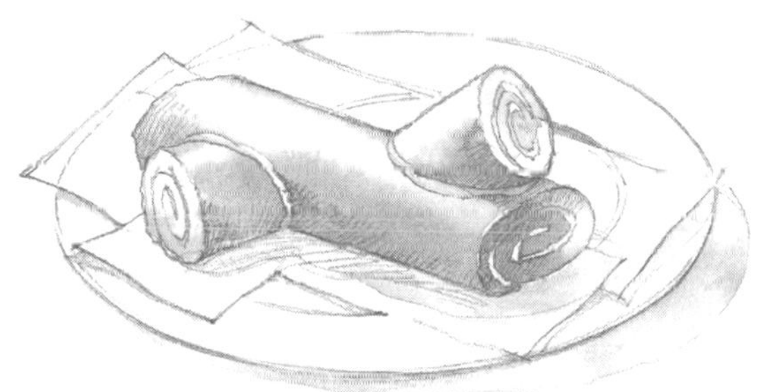

Chocolate icing

THE PERFECT COATING for the Yule log or any cake, this icing would also make a delicious sauce for an ice cream sundae, a great chocolate fondue, or, if chilled, a truffle-like filling for small tart shells.

MAKES ABOUT 2 CUPS

¾ cup chilled whipping cream
3 tablespoons unsalted butter
1½ tablespoons light corn syrup
9 ounces bittersweet (not unsweetened) or semisweet chocolate, chopped
1½ tablespoons kirsch (clear cherry brandy)

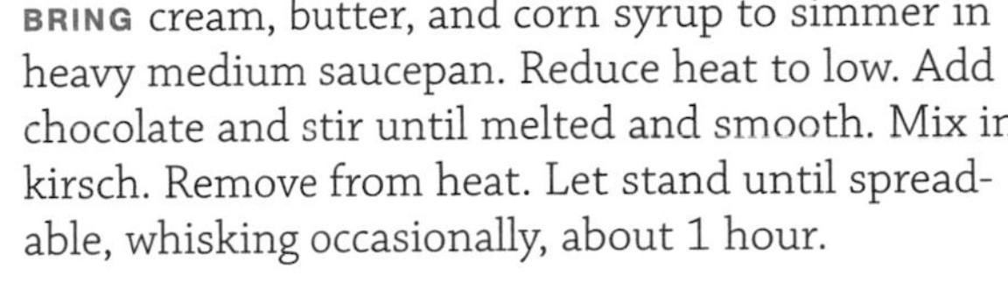

BRING cream, butter, and corn syrup to simmer in heavy medium saucepan. Reduce heat to low. Add chocolate and stir until melted and smooth. Mix in kirsch. Remove from heat. Let stand until spreadable, whisking occasionally, about 1 hour.

Princess cake

LAYERS OF AIRY YELLOW CAKE, vanilla custard, and raspberry jam, all wrapped up like a gift beneath smooth marzipan, make this the national birthday cake of Sweden. These days, most Swedes leave the work to pastry shops, but it's quite manageable for home cooks. The marzipan, a paste of finely ground almonds and sugar, is rolled out like a pie crust and fitted over the cake. If the almond paste (available at specialty foods stores and most supermarkets) seems too crumbly when kneading, return it to the processor and add water by half-teaspoonfuls until it becomes more pliable. Parchment paper works best for rolling out the marzipan, but if it sticks, sprinkle lightly with powdered sugar.

8 TO 10 SERVINGS

Custard filling

1¼ cups half and half
2 large eggs, room temperature
⅓ cup plus 1 tablespoon sugar
¼ cup all purpose flour
2 tablespoons (¼ stick) unsalted butter
2 teaspoons vanilla extract

Marzipan topping

11 ounces almond paste, crumbled
1⅓ cups (or more) powdered sugar, sifted
1 teaspoon almond extract
5 drops green food coloring

Cake

- **4 large eggs, room temperature**
- **3/4 cup plus 1 tablespoon sugar**
- **1/3 cup plus 1 tablespoon all purpose flour**
- **1/3 cup plus 1 tablespoon potato flour**
- **1 teaspoon baking powder**

Assembly

- **2 teaspoons unflavored gelatin**
- **2 tablespoons cold water**
- **2/3 cup chilled whipping cream**
- **1/3 cup raspberry jam**

Powdered sugar
Almond Paste Rose (see recipe)

FOR CUSTARD FILLING: Bring half and half to simmer in heavy medium saucepan. Whisk eggs, sugar, and flour in medium bowl. Gradually whisk in hot half and half. Return mixture to saucepan. Stir over low heat until custard thickens and leaves path on back of spoon when finger is drawn across, about 8 minutes (do not boil). Remove from heat and whisk in butter and vanilla. Transfer custard to medium bowl. Cool filling completely, stirring occasionally. *(Can be prepared 2 days ahead. Cover and refrigerate.)*

FOR MARZIPAN TOPPING: Blend almond paste and 1⅓ cups powdered sugar in processor until crumbly. With machine running, add almond extract and food coloring and process until well blended. Knead on work surface until green color is evenly distributed, adding more powdered sugar if sticky. Shape marzipan into ball; flatten into disk. *(Can be prepared 1 day ahead. Wrap in plastic and store at room temperature.)*

FOR CAKE: Position rack in bottom third of oven and preheat to 350°F. Butter and flour 9-inch-diameter springform pan. Using electric mixer, beat eggs and sugar until pale yellow and slowly dissolving ribbon forms when beaters are lifted, about 5 minutes. Sift both flours and baking powder together. Gently fold into egg mixture 3 tablespoons at a time.

POUR batter into prepared pan. Bake cake until tester inserted into center comes out clean, 25 to 30 minutes. Cool in pan on rack 10 minutes. Remove pan sides and cool cake completely; cake will fall. *(Can be prepared 1 day ahead. Wrap tightly.)*

FOR ASSEMBLY: Sprinkle gelatin over 2 tablespoons cold water in small bowl; let soften 5 minutes. Set bowl in pan of simmering water and stir until gelatin dissolves. Using electric mixer, whip cream in medium bowl until soft peaks form. Gradually add gelatin mixture, beating until stiff peaks form. Fold into filling. Run knife between cake and pan bottom and remove pan. Using serrated knife, cut cake horizontally in half. Place bottom layer on serving platter. Spread jam over, leaving ¼-inch border. Top with a little less than ½ of filling. Add second cake layer; top with remaining filling, mounding slightly in center. Refrigerate 1½ hours.

ROLL marzipan out between sheets of parchment or waxed paper to 13-inch-diameter round. Remove 1 sheet of paper. Using bottom sheet as aid, turn marzipan out onto cake; remove second sheet of paper. Gently wrap marzipan around cake. Trim edges. Refrigerate cake at least 1 hour. *(Can be prepared 6 hours ahead. Keep refrigerated.)* Just before serving, sift powdered sugar over top of cake and place rose in center.

Almond paste rose

ONCE YOU get the hang of making this decorative—and delicious—rose (and it's not difficult), you can use it to accent any other special-occasion cake. Almond paste is available at specialty foods stores and in the baking-products section of most supermarkets.

MAKES 1

1½ ounces almond paste
2 tablespoons powdered sugar
1 drop red food coloring

Knead all ingredients together in small bowl until pale pink. Roll into 1x1½-inch oval log. Cut into eight ⅛-inch-thick slices. Pinch edges to flatten to eight 2¼x1½-inch ovals. Roll 1 oval up lengthwise into cylinder. Wrap second oval around cylinder. Pinch at base to seal. Repeat with remaining ovals, overlapping slightly. Open top of rose by curling petals back slightly. Cut base to flatten. *(Can be prepared 2 days ahead. Store in airtight container.)*

Strawberry cake with whipped crème fraîche

A LIGHT AND BEAUTIFUL CAKE that's perfect for springtime. This recipe calls for a simple garnish of whole strawberries mounded in the center, but if you feel adventurous, save some of the homemade crème fraîche frosting and use a pastry bag to pipe decorations across the top.

10 SERVINGS

2 cups all purpose flour
1 teaspoon baking powder
1 teaspoon baking soda
½ teaspoon salt
¾ cup (1½ sticks) unsalted butter, room temperature
1 cup plus 2 tablespoons sugar
1 cup sour cream
¼ cup orange juice
1½ teaspoons grated orange peel
1 teaspoon vanilla extract
2 large eggs

1½ 1-pint containers strawberries, hulled
⅓ cup strawberry preserves

Whipped Crème Fraîche (see recipe)

PREHEAT oven to 350°F. Butter and flour two 9-inch-diameter cake pans with 2-inch-high sides. Line bottom of pans with parchment paper. Sift flour and next 3 ingredients into medium bowl. Using electric mixer, beat butter and 1 cup sugar in large bowl until light and fluffy. Beat in sour cream, orange juice, orange peel, and vanilla. Add eggs 1 at a time, beating well after each addition. Add flour mixture and beat until well blended.

DIVIDE batter equally between prepared pans; smooth tops. Bake cakes until tops are light golden and tester inserted into center comes out clean, about 28 minutes. Cool cakes in pans on rack 30 minutes. Turn cakes out onto racks and cool completely.

MEANWHILE, slice 1 basket hulled strawberries. Place in medium bowl. Add preserves and remaining 2 tablespoons sugar; toss to combine. Let stand at room temperature until juices form, about 2 hours.

PLACE 1 cake layer, flat side up, on platter. Top with sliced berry mixture in even layer. Spread 1¾ cups Whipped Crème Fraîche over berry mixture. Top with second cake layer, flat side down, pressing slightly. Spread remaining Whipped Crème Fraîche over top and sides of cake. *(Can be made 8 hours ahead. Cover with cake dome and refrigerate.)* Mound remaining whole berries in center of cake.

Whipped crème fraîche

THIS HOMEMADE VERSION of crème fraîche makes a nice alternative to regular sweetened whipped cream; it has a little tang thanks to the sour cream.

MAKES ABOUT 7 CUPS

- **3 cups chilled whipping cream**
- **3/4 cup chilled sour cream**
- **3/4 cup powdered sugar**
- **1 1/2 teaspoons grated orange peel**
- **3/4 teaspoon vanilla extract**

USING electric mixer, beat all ingredients in large bowl until stiff peaks form. *(Can be prepared 3 hours ahead. Cover and refrigerate.)*

Mocha marjolaine

IN THIS VERSION of the classic Parisian gâteau, layers of crisp hazelnut-almond meringue alternate with chocolate ganache and coffee-flavored whipped cream (heavy whipping cream works best). To make the torte, you'll need a 17½x11½x1-inch jelly-roll pan and a pastry bag fitted with a medium star tip. After toasting the hazelnuts, reserve six to eight whole ones for garnishing the cake.

10 SERVINGS

Nut meringue

- **3/4 cup hazelnuts, toasted, skinned**
- **3/4 cup whole almonds, toasted**
- **3/4 cup sugar, divided**
- **1 1/2 tablespoons all purpose flour**
- **6 large egg whites**
- **1/2 teaspoon cream of tartar**

Ganache

- **1 1/4 cups plus 3 tablespoons whipping cream**
- **16 ounces bittersweet (not unsweetened) or semisweet chocolate, finely chopped**

Coffee cream

- **2/3 cup chilled whipping cream**
- **2 teaspoons instant espresso powder or instant coffee powder**
- **2 teaspoons sugar**

Toasted hazelnuts

FOR NUT MERINGUE: Preheat oven to 325°F. Line 17½x11½x1-inch jelly-roll pan with parchment paper. Blend hazelnuts, almonds, ½ cup sugar, and flour in processor until nuts are finely ground. Using electric mixer, beat egg whites and cream of tartar in large bowl until soft peaks form. Gradually add remaining ¼ cup sugar, beating until stiff but not dry. Fold hazelnut-almond mixture into meringue in 2 additions.

SPREAD meringue mixture evenly in prepared pan. Bake meringue until golden brown and dry to touch, about 20 minutes. Cool meringue in pan on rack.

CUT around pan sides. Using parchment as aid, lift meringue onto work surface. Press large sheet of waxed paper onto meringue to cover. Using scissors, cut through waxed paper and parchment to trim meringue to 16-inch-long by 8-inch-wide rectangle. Cut in half crosswise, then lengthwise, forming four 8-inch-long by 4-inch-wide rectangles.

FOR GANACHE: Bring 1¼ cups cream to simmer in heavy medium saucepan. Remove from heat. Add chocolate and whisk until smooth. Transfer ¼ cup ganache to small bowl; add remaining 3 tablespoons cream to make light ganache. Refrigerate light ganache until cold, at least 30 minutes. Refrigerate dark ganache until cold and thick, stirring often, about 1 hour.

FOR COFFEE CREAM: Beat cream, espresso powder, and sugar in medium bowl until peaks form. Refrigerate.

PLACE cake rack on work surface. Peel waxed paper and parchment off 1 meringue rectangle; place on cake rack. Spread with ⅓ cup dark ganache. Peel waxed paper and parchment off second meringue; place atop dark ganache. Whisk light ganache just until thick and stiff. Spread over second meringue. Peel waxed paper and parchment off third meringue; place atop light ganache. Spread with half of coffee cream; cover and refrigerate remaining coffee cream. Peel waxed paper and parchment off fourth meringue; place atop coffee cream. Spread ½ cup dark ganache in thin layer over top and sides of torte to anchor crumbs and smooth surface. Refrigerate on rack 45 minutes.

PLACE torte on rack atop large sheet of aluminum foil. Stir remaining dark ganache over very low heat just until warm enough to pour. Pour dark ganache over torte. Using icing spatula and working quickly, smooth top and sides for even coverage. Refrigerate torte on rack until glaze is firm, at least 2 hours.

(Torte can be made 2 days ahead. Cover loosely and keep refrigerated.)

USING metal spatula, transfer torte to platter. Rewhip remaining coffee cream. Spoon into pastry bag fitted with medium star tip. Pipe cream in decorative pattern atop torte. Garnish with toasted hazelnuts and serve.

Spiced sweet-potato Bundt cake with brown sugar icing

THIS OLD-FASHIONED CAKE makes wonderful use of red-skinned sweet potatoes (otherwise known as yams), an amazingly versatile fall pantry staple. The sweet potatoes' natural sugars tenderize the cake, while their vibrant orange flesh mellows to a warm russet as it bakes. This is nice on a fall afternoon with a cup of coffee.

12 SERVINGS

Cake

- **4 8-ounce yams (red-skinned sweet potatoes)**
- **Nonstick vegetable oil spray**
- **2¾ cups all purpose flour**
- **2 teaspoons ground cinnamon**
- **1¼ teaspoons ground ginger**
- **1 teaspoon baking powder**
- **1 teaspoon baking soda**
- **½ teaspoon salt**
- **2 cups sugar**
- **1 cup vegetable oil**
- **4 large eggs**
- **1 teaspoon vanilla extract**

Icing

- **1 cup powdered sugar**
- **¾ cup (packed) dark brown sugar**
- **½ cup whipping cream**
- **¼ cup (½ stick) unsalted butter**
- **¼ teaspoon vanilla extract**

FOR CAKE: Pierce yams with fork. Microwave on high until very tender, about 8 minutes per side. Cool, peel, and mash yams.

POSITION rack in center of oven; preheat to 325°F. Spray 12-cup Bundt pan with nonstick spray, then generously butter pan. Sift flour, cinnamon, ginger, baking powder, baking soda, and salt into medium bowl. Measure 2 cups mashed yams and transfer to large bowl (reserve any remaining yams for another use). Add sugar and oil to yams; using electric mixer, beat until smooth. Add eggs 2 at a time, beating well after each addition. Add flour mixture and beat just until blended. Beat in vanilla.

TRANSFER batter to prepared pan. Bake cake until tester inserted near center comes out clean, about 1 hour 5 minutes. Cool cake in pan on rack 15 minutes. Run knife around sides of pan and center tube to loosen cake. Turn cake out onto rack and cool completely.

FOR ICING: Sift powdered sugar into medium bowl. Stir brown sugar, whipping cream, and butter in medium saucepan over medium-low heat until butter melts and sugar dissolves. Increase heat to medium-high and bring to boil. Boil 3 minutes, occasionally stirring and swirling pan. Remove from heat and stir in vanilla. Pour brown sugar mixture over powdered sugar. Whisk icing until smooth and lightened in color, about 1 minute. Cool until icing is lukewarm and falls in heavy ribbon from spoon, whisking often, about 15 minutes. Spoon icing thickly over top of cake, allowing icing to drip down sides. Let stand until icing is firm, at least 1 hour. *(Can be prepared 1 day ahead. Cover with cake dome and let stand at room temperature.)*

Sour cream maple cake with lemon glaze

A WONDERFULLY HOMEY Bundt cake that is equally good with afternoon tea, after a meal, or for breakfast with a cup of Italian-roast coffee. Maple sugar is available at some supermarkets and at many natural foods stores.

10 TO 12 SERVINGS

Cake

Nonstick vegetable oil spray
2 cups all purpose flour
2 teaspoons baking powder
½ teaspoon baking soda
¼ teaspoon salt
1⅓ cups sour cream
¼ cup pure maple syrup
½ cup walnuts, toasted, chopped
¼ cup plus 1⅓ cups maple sugar
¼ teaspoon ground cinnamon

13 tablespoons butter (1½ sticks plus 1 tablespoon), cut into pieces, room temperature
2 large eggs
2 teaspoons vanilla extract

Glaze

1⅓ cups powdered sugar
3 tablespoons sour cream
1 tablespoon pure maple syrup
1½ teaspoons fresh lemon juice
1 teaspoon vanilla extract
½ teaspoon grated lemon peel

Whipped cream

FOR CAKE: Preheat oven to 350°F. Butter 12-cup Bundt pan, then spray with nonstick spray. Combine flour, baking powder, baking soda, and salt in medium bowl. Whisk sour cream and maple syrup in another medium bowl. Mix walnuts, ¼ cup maple sugar, and cinnamon in small bowl.

USING electric mixer, beat butter and remaining 1⅓ cups maple sugar in large bowl until fluffy. Gradually beat in eggs and vanilla, occasionally stopping to scrape down sides of bowl. Add flour mixture in 3 additions, alternating with sour cream mixture in 2 additions.

TRANSFER ⅔ of batter to prepared Bundt pan. Sprinkle with walnut mixture. Pour remaining batter into pan. Bake cake until tester inserted near center comes out clean, about 55 minutes. Cool 20 minutes. Run knife around sides of pan and center tube to loosen cake. Turn cake out onto rack and cool completely.

FOR GLAZE: Whisk powdered sugar and next 5 ingredients in medium bowl to blend. Let stand until thickened, about 30 minutes. Pour glaze over cake. *(Can be prepared 1 day ahead. Cover with cake dome and keep at room temperature.)*

SERVE cake with whipped cream.

Almond streusel Bundt cake with coffee glaze

THE ORIGINAL VERSION of this cake was reputed to be a favorite of Abraham Lincoln's. We added more to love: a coffee-cinnamon streusel layer baked into the center of the cake, and a luscious coffee glaze drizzled over the top. Toast the whole almonds (1½ cups total) separately from the sliced almonds, which will brown faster. Almond paste is available at specialty foods stores and in the baking-products section of most supermarkets.

8 SERVINGS

Streusel

½ cup (packed) brown sugar
½ cup whole almonds, toasted, chopped
⅓ cup old-fashioned oats
1½ teaspoons instant espresso powder or instant coffee powder
¾ teaspoon ground cinnamon
¼ cup (½ stick) chilled unsalted butter, cut into pieces

Cake

3 cups sifted cake flour (sifted, then measured)
1 tablespoon baking powder
1 cup whole almonds, toasted
¾ cup (1½ sticks) unsalted butter, room temperature
½ cup almond paste
1⅔ cups sugar, divided
½ teaspoon almond extract
1 cup whole milk
6 large egg whites, room temperature

Glaze

1 cup powdered sugar, sifted
¼ cup whipping cream
1 teaspoon instant espresso powder or instant coffee powder
⅓ cup toasted sliced almonds

FOR STREUSEL: Mix brown sugar and next 4 ingredients in small bowl. Add butter and rub in with fingertips until well combined. Set streusel aside.

FOR CAKE: Preheat oven to 350°F. Butter and flour 12-cup Bundt pan. Mix cake flour and baking powder in small bowl. Finely grind almonds in processor. Using electric mixer, beat butter and almond paste in large bowl until blended. Gradually beat in 1⅓ cups sugar. Continue beating until light and fluffy. Beat in extract. Stir in flour mixture in 3 additions alternately with milk in 2 additions. Mix in ground almonds. Using electric mixer fitted with clean dry beaters, beat egg whites in another large bowl to medium peaks. Gradually add remaining ⅓ cup sugar and beat until stiff but not dry. Fold into batter in 2 additions.

TRANSFER half of batter to prepared Bundt pan. Sprinkle streusel over. Spoon remaining batter over. Bake cake until tester inserted near center comes out clean, about 1 hour. Cool cake in pan on rack 20 minutes. Run knife around sides of pan and center tube to loosen cake. Turn cake out onto rack and cool completely. *(Cake can be prepared 1 day ahead. Cover and let stand at room temperature.)*

FOR GLAZE: Stir powdered sugar, cream, and espresso powder in small bowl until well blended. Drizzle glaze over cake, allowing excess to run down sides. Sprinkle cake with sliced almonds.

Chocolate and peanut butter streusel cake

KIDS OF ALL AGES will find this cake irresistible, and it's super-easy to make. Part of the peanut butter streusel is blended into the cake, adding great flavor and texture.

12 SERVINGS

2¼ cups all purpose flour
2 cups (packed) golden brown sugar
1 cup creamy peanut butter
½ cup (1 stick) unsalted butter, room temperature
3 large eggs
1 cup whole milk
1 teaspoon vanilla extract
1 teaspoon baking powder
½ teaspoon baking soda
1 12-ounce package semisweet chocolate chips (2 cups)

PREHEAT oven to 350°F. Butter 13x9x2-inch metal baking pan. Using electric mixer, beat flour and next 3 ingredients in large bowl at low speed until streusel is blended and crumbly. Transfer 1 cup lightly packed streusel to small bowl and reserve. Add eggs, milk, vanilla, baking powder, and baking soda to remaining streusel in large bowl. Beat at low speed until evenly moist. Increase speed to medium and beat until well blended, occasionally stopping to scrape down bowl, about 3 minutes. Stir in 1 cup chips.

TRANSFER batter to prepared pan. Sprinkle with reserved 1 cup streusel and remaining 1 cup chips. Bake cake until tester inserted into center comes out clean, about 35 minutes. Cool cake in pan on rack.

Vanilla bean pound cake with sour cream ice cream and strawberries

A FAMILIAR DESSERT—buttery-rich and moist pound cake—is made even more satisfying with a few new flourishes: Fresh vanilla bean gives it a deep vanilla flavor, and homemade ice cream and sugared strawberries add style to the comforting favorite. You can make both the cake and the ice cream a couple of days ahead.

12 SERVINGS

2 cups (4 sticks) unsalted butter, room temperature
5 teaspoons grated lemon peel, divided
1 vanilla bean, split lengthwise
2⅓ cups sugar
6 large eggs
4 large egg yolks
1 teaspoon vanilla extract
1 teaspoon salt
3¼ cups all purpose flour

4 1-pint containers strawberries, hulled, halved
1 cup powdered sugar

Sour Cream Ice Cream (see recipe)

PREHEAT oven to 350°F. Butter and flour 10-inch-diameter angel food cake pan. Place butter and 1 teaspoon lemon peel in large bowl. Scrape in seeds from vanilla bean and beat until smooth. Gradually beat in 2⅓ cups sugar. Whisk eggs and egg yolks in medium bowl to blend. Beat egg mixture into butter mixture in 4 additions. Beat in vanilla extract and salt. Sift flour over in 3 additions, mixing just to combine after each.

TRANSFER batter to prepared pan. Bake cake until tester inserted near center comes out clean, about 1 hour 15 minutes. Cool cake in pan on rack 15 minutes. Run knife around sides of pan and center tube to loosen cake. Turn cake out; turn right side up on rack and cool completely. *(Pound cake can be prepared 2 days ahead. Wrap in plastic and let stand at room temperature.)*

TOSS berries, powdered sugar, and remaining 4 teaspoons lemon peel in large bowl to combine. Let stand at least 30 minutes, or cover and refrigerate up to 3 hours.

TOP cake with strawberries and serve with Sour Cream Ice Cream.

Sour cream ice cream

YOU CAN ALSO SERVE this with fruit cobblers and pies, atop dessert waffles, and alongside chocolate cake.

MAKES ABOUT 2 QUARTS

- **1¼ cups sour cream**
- **½ cup powdered sugar**
- **1 tablespoon fresh lemon juice**
- **1½ teaspoons vanilla extract**

- **1¼ cups sugar**
- **6 large egg yolks**
- **2 cups whipping cream**
- **1 cup whole milk**

WHISK sour cream, powdered sugar, lemon juice, and vanilla in small bowl to blend. Cover and refrigerate until ready to use.

WHISK 1¼ cups sugar and egg yolks in medium bowl to blend. Bring cream and milk to simmer in heavy large saucepan. Gradually whisk hot cream mixture into yolk mixture. Return to same saucepan and stir over medium heat until custard thickens and leaves path on back of spoon when finger is drawn across, about 5 minutes (do not boil). Pour into large bowl. Refrigerate until cool, whisking occasionally, about 45 minutes. Mix in sour cream mixture.

PROCESS custard in ice cream maker according to manufacturer's instructions. Transfer to bowl; cover and freeze. *(Can be prepared 3 days ahead. Keep frozen.)*

Buttery pound cake

A CUP OF WHIPPING CREAM adds more delicious indulgence to this wonderful variation on the classic pound cake. Using cake flour gives it an especially fine and tender texture. The cake stays fresh for two days and also freezes well. To make it, you'll need a ten-inch-diameter angel food cake pan.

12 SERVINGS

- **3 cups cake flour**
- **¼ teaspoon salt**
- **1 cup (2 sticks) unsalted butter, room temperature**
- **3 cups sugar**
- **7 large eggs, room temperature**
- **1 cup whipping cream**
- **1 tablespoon vanilla extract**

POSITION rack in center of oven and preheat to 350°F. Generously butter 12-cup angel food cake pan. Dust pan with flour; tap out excess. Sift cake flour and salt into medium bowl. Using electric mixer, beat butter in large bowl until fluffy. Gradually add sugar, beating until mixture is well blended, about 5 minutes. Add eggs 1 at a time, beating just until combined after each addition. Using rubber spatula, fold in flour mixture in 3 additions alternately with cream in 2 additions, beginning and ending with flour mixture. Mix in vanilla.

TRANSFER batter to prepared pan. Bake cake until tester inserted near center comes out clean, covering top loosely with aluminum foil if browning too quickly, about 1 hour 20 minutes. Let cake stand 15 minutes. Run knife around sides of pan and center tube to loosen cake. Turn cake out onto plate. Transfer cake right side up to rack and cool completely. *(Can be prepared 2 days ahead. Cover with cake dome and let stand at room temperature.)*

Old-fashioned gingerbread

SERVED ALONE, this easy-to-prepare cake makes the perfect lunch-box treat or after-school snack. Topped with sweetened whipped cream and sautéed apples, it makes a nice ending to a casual supper. If desired, you can add half a cup of chopped raisins and a quarter-cup of minced crystallized ginger to the batter.

8 SERVINGS

- **2/3 cup solid vegetable shortening, room temperature**
- **1 cup sugar**
- **2/3 cup mild-flavored (light) molasses**
- **2 extra-large eggs**
- **1/3 cup strong brewed coffee**
- **2 teaspoons vanilla extract**
- **1 1/2 teaspoons grated lemon peel**
- **2 cups unbleached all purpose flour**
- **4 teaspoons ground ginger**
- **2 teaspoons ground cinnamon**
- **1 1/2 teaspoons baking soda**
- **1 teaspoon ground cloves**
- **1 teaspoon ground allspice**
- **1/2 teaspoon salt**

PREHEAT oven to 350°F. Butter and flour 9x9x2-inch metal baking pan. Using electric mixer, beat shortening and sugar in large bowl until fluffy. Add molasses, eggs, coffee, vanilla, and lemon peel; beat to combine. Sift flour, ginger, cinnamon, baking soda, cloves, allspice, and salt over shortening mixture. Stir just until combined. Transfer to prepared pan. Bake until tester inserted into center comes out clean, about 45 minutes. *(Can be made 6 hours ahead. Cool in pan. Before serving, cover with aluminum foil and rewarm in 325°F oven 15 minutes.)* Serve warm.

Gingerbread cake with caramelized pear compote

CERTAINLY ONE REASON warm spices like cinnamon and cloves became popular winter seasonings is that they pair so harmoniously with the fruits of the season. This recipe, which incorporates pears into the filling and into a simple compote on the side, beautifully illustrates that combination. We used Bosc pears in the compote, but Anjou or Bartlett varieties would also work well. If the pears are very hard, allow several days to a week at room temperature for them to ripen (you can speed up the process by placing them in a closed paper bag). Pears are ripe when they yield to gentle pressure at the stem end.

8 TO 10 SERVINGS

Cake

- **Nonstick vegetable oil spray**
- **1 15- to 16-ounce can pear halves in syrup, drained well**
- **3/4 cup buttermilk**
- **1 tablespoon vanilla extract**

- **3 cups all purpose flour**
- **1 1/2 teaspoons ground cinnamon**
- **1 teaspoon baking soda**
- **3/4 teaspoon ground ginger**
- **3/4 teaspoon ground allspice**
- **1/2 teaspoon salt**
- **1/4 teaspoon ground cloves**
- **1 cup (2 sticks) unsalted butter, room temperature**
- **1 cup (packed) dark brown sugar**
- **3/4 cup mild-flavored (light) molasses**
- **3 large eggs**

Compote

- **1/4 cup (1/2 stick) unsalted butter**
- **2 1/2 pounds Bosc pears, peeled, halved, cored, cut crosswise into 1/4-inch-thick slices**
- **1/2 cup sugar**

Vanilla ice cream

FOR CAKE: Preheat oven to 350°F. Spray 12-cup Bundt pan with nonstick spray, then butter and flour pan. Puree canned pears in blender until smooth. Place ¾ cup puree in small bowl for cake (reserve any remaining puree for another use); mix in buttermilk and vanilla.

SIFT flour and next 6 ingredients into medium bowl. Using electric mixer, beat butter in large bowl until light and fluffy. Add brown sugar and beat until blended. Gradually beat in molasses. Beat in eggs 1 at a time (batter may appear curdled). Beat in flour mixture in 3 additions alternately with pear mixture in 2 additions.

TRANSFER batter to pan. Bake cake until tester inserted near center comes out clean, about 55 minutes. Cool cake in pan on rack 10 minutes. Turn out onto rack and cool completely. *(Can be prepared 1 day ahead. Cover and let stand at room temperature.)*

FOR COMPOTE: Melt butter in large skillet over high heat. Add pears; sprinkle sugar over. Sauté until pears are tender and juices thicken, stirring often, about 18 minutes. Let stand at room temperature at least 1 hour and up to 4 hours.

REWARM compote over low heat, stirring gently. Cut cake into slices. Place cake slice, compote, and scoop of ice cream on each plate and serve.

Gingerbread with vanilla ice cream and exotic caramel sauce

GINGERBREAD HAS BEEN a European tradition for centuries and came to America with German and other Northern European immigrants. Here, drizzled with a caramel sauce, the homey cake of holidays past is transformed into a contemporary special-occasion dessert.

8 SERVINGS

- **2½ cups plus 2 teaspoons all purpose flour**
- **2½ teaspoons ground ginger**
- **1 teaspoon ground cinnamon**
- **½ teaspoon salt**
- **¾ cup chopped crystallized ginger**

- **½ cup (1 stick) unsalted butter, room temperature**
- **½ cup (packed) golden brown sugar**
- **1 cup mild-flavored (light) molasses**
- **1 cup boiling water**
- **2 teaspoons baking soda**
- **1 large egg, beaten to blend**

Vanilla ice cream
Exotic Caramel Sauce (see recipe)

PREHEAT oven to 375°F. Lightly butter 13x9x2-inch metal baking pan. Sift 2½ cups flour, ground ginger, cinnamon, and salt into medium bowl. Mix crystallized ginger with remaining 2 teaspoons flour in small bowl.

USING electric mixer, beat butter in large bowl until fluffy. Add brown sugar and beat until mixture is light and fluffy. Mix molasses, 1 cup boiling water, and baking soda in another medium bowl to blend. Stir into butter mixture. Stir in flour mixture, then egg and crystallized ginger mixture.

POUR batter into prepared pan. Bake cake 15 minutes. Reduce oven temperature to 350°F and bake cake until tester inserted into center comes out clean, about 12 minutes longer. Transfer pan to rack and cool 30 minutes. Turn cake out onto rack; cool. *(Can be prepared 8 hours ahead. Cover and let stand at room temperature.)*

CUT gingerbread into 8 pieces. Transfer gingerbread to plates. Top each piece with ice cream. Spoon caramel sauce over and serve.

Exotic caramel sauce

PERFUMED WITH an intriguing note of black tea, this luscious sauce also features almonds, pistachios, raisins, and ginger. It would be equally good spooned over a simple baked apple.

MAKES ABOUT 2½ CUPS

- **1 cup plus 5 tablespoons water**
- **1 tea bag (preferably English Breakfast tea)**
- **⅓ cup brown raisins, chopped**
- **⅓ cup golden raisins, chopped**

- **1 cup sugar**
- **1 cup whipping cream**
- **¼ cup (½ stick) unsalted butter**
- **¼ cup slivered almonds**
- **¼ cup shelled roasted pistachios**
- **1 teaspoon minced crystallized ginger**

BRING 1 cup water to simmer in small saucepan. Remove from heat. Add tea bag and steep 5 minutes. Remove tea bag and squeeze to release excess liquid. Add all raisins to liquid. Let stand 30 minutes. Drain and reserve raisins.

COMBINE sugar and remaining 5 tablespoons water in heavy medium saucepan. Stir over low heat until sugar dissolves. Increase heat and boil without stirring until syrup is deep amber color, occasionally brushing down sides of pan with wet pastry brush and swirling pan, about 10 minutes. Remove from heat. Gradually whisk in cream and butter. Stir over low heat until caramel is smooth. Mix in raisins, nuts, and crystallized ginger. *(Can be prepared 1 week ahead. Cover and refrigerate. Rewarm over low heat before serving.)*

Spiced pumpkin cake with caramel icing

DARK RUM moistens the cake layers and adds another festive flavor to this holiday layer cake, which is filled with a caramel icing studded with rum-soaked raisins and cranberries. Use a citrus zester to make the orange peel strips, which are arranged around the edge of the cake as a garnish. The peel can also be removed with a swivel-bladed vegetable peeler and cut into thin strips.

10 TO 12 SERVINGS

Cake

- **3 cups sifted cake flour (sifted, then measured)**
- **2 teaspoons baking powder**
- **1½ teaspoons ground cinnamon**
- **1 teaspoon baking soda**
- **1 teaspoon ground ginger**
- **½ teaspoon salt**
- **¼ teaspoon ground allspice**
- **⅛ teaspoon ground cloves**
- **2 cups sugar**
- **1 cup canola oil or vegetable oil**
- **4 large eggs**
- **1 15-ounce can pure pumpkin**
- **1 teaspoon vanilla extract**

Icing and filling

- **½ cup dark rum**
- **6 tablespoons raisins**
- **6 tablespoons dried sweetened cranberries**

- **¾ cup heavy whipping cream**
- **6 ounces Philadelphia brand cream cheese, cut into small pieces, room temperature**
- **2¼ cups sugar**
- **⅔ cup water**
- **½ cup (1 stick plus 1 tablespoon) unsalted butter, cut into ½-inch cubes**

1½ cups walnuts, toasted, chopped, divided
1 teaspoon grated orange peel

Thin orange peel strips
Vanilla ice cream

FOR CAKE: Position rack in center of oven and preheat to 350°F. Butter and flour two 9-inch-diameter cake pans with 1½-inch-high sides. Sift presifted cake flour and next 7 ingredients into medium bowl. Using electric mixer, beat sugar and oil in large bowl until well blended, about 2 minutes. Add eggs 1 at a time, beating well after each addition. Add pumpkin and vanilla; beat until blended. Gradually add flour mixture; beat just until incorporated.

DIVIDE batter between prepared pans; smooth top with spatula. Bake cakes until tester inserted into center comes out clean, about 30 minutes. Cool completely in pans on racks. Run small knife around cakes to loosen. Turn cakes out onto racks.

FOR ICING AND FILLING: Stir rum, raisins, and dried cranberries in small saucepan over low heat until just warm, about 1 minute. Remove from heat; let stand 30 minutes. Drain, reserving rum and fruit separately.

WHISK whipping cream and cream cheese in small bowl until smooth. Combine sugar and ⅔ cup water in heavy medium saucepan. Stir over medium-low heat until sugar dissolves. Increase heat to high; boil without stirring until syrup is deep amber color, occasionally brushing down sides of pan with wet pastry brush and swirling pan, about 10 minutes. Slowly and carefully whisk in cream cheese mixture (caramel mixture will bubble vigorously). Add butter and whisk until mixture is smooth, about 1 minute. Remove from heat; cool caramel icing 10 minutes, whisking occasionally.

POUR ¾ cup warm caramel icing into bowl. Mix in half of reserved dried fruit mixture, 1 cup walnuts, and grated orange peel. Place 1 cake layer on 8-inch-diameter tart pan bottom or cardboard round. Brush top of cake with half of reserved rum. Spread caramel-nut filling over, leaving ½-inch plain border at edges. Top with second cake layer, flat side down; press to adhere. Brush top of cake with remaining rum; let stand 10 minutes to allow rum to soak in.

POUR generous ½ cup warm caramel icing onto cake and, if necessary, spread over top with offset spatula to cover. Refrigerate cake and remaining caramel icing until icing is firm enough to spread and to adhere to sides of cake, stirring occasionally, about 1 hour.

TRANSFER ¾ cup chilled icing to small bowl and chill for sauce. Using offset spatula, spread remaining 1 cup icing evenly over sides of cake to cover. Mix remaining dried fruit mixture and remaining ½ cup walnuts in another small bowl. Sprinkle mixture in 1½-inch-wide border around top edge of cake. Cover cake with cake dome and refrigerate at least 6 hours. *(Can be prepared 2 days ahead. Keep cake and caramel icing for sauce chilled separately.)*

PLACE cake on platter. Garnish with orange peel strips. Rewarm icing over low heat just until pourable. Serve cake cold with ice cream and warm caramel sauce.

Pear spice cake with pecan praline topping

LOADED WITH holiday flavors and appeal, this single-layer cake is nonetheless easy to make. The secret? Fresh pears, crystallized ginger, and a praline candy topping dress up a boxed spice cake mix. The topping will be soft when warm; it will be firmer, in the style of southern praline, when cool. Serve this warm or at room temperature.

8 TO 10 SERVINGS

- **1 cup (2 sticks) unsalted butter, divided**
- **1 box spice cake mix (1 pound 2.25 ounces)**
- **¾ cup canned pear nectar**
- **3 large eggs**
- **2 tablespoons mild-flavored (light) molasses**
- **½ cup minced crystallized ginger**
- **2 pears, peeled, cored, cut into ½-inch cubes (about 1½ cups)**
- **¾ cup (packed) golden brown sugar**
- **¼ cup whipping cream**
- **1⅓ cups pecan halves, toasted**

POSITION rack in center of oven and preheat to 350°F. Butter 9-inch-diameter springform pan with 2¾-inch-high sides. Stir ½ cup butter in small saucepan over medium heat until melted and brown, about 3 minutes. Pour into large bowl. Add spice cake mix, canned pear nectar, eggs, molasses, and crystallized ginger. Using electric mixer, beat batter 2 minutes. Fold in pears.

POUR batter into prepared pan. Bake until cake is dark brown and tester inserted into center comes out with some moist crumbs attached, about 1 hour 10 minutes.

COOL cake in pan on rack 15 minutes. Run knife between pan sides and cake to loosen. Release pan sides. Place cake on platter.

STIR sugar, cream, and remaining ½ cup butter in heavy medium saucepan over medium-high heat until smooth. Boil 3 minutes, stirring often. Stir in pecan halves. Spoon warm topping over warm cake. Serve warm or at room temperature.

Pear-anise kuchen

THERE'S A WORLD OF VARIETY to *kuchen* (German for "cake" or "pastry"), but it often has a pound-cake-like base—dense and not too sweet—with fresh fruit cooked into the filling or arranged on top of the cake before it is baked. It's the traditional coffee cake in Germany, usually served as a teatime treat. In this version, the rich, anise-flavored crust rises and frames the pears as it bakes. Allow several days to a week for pears to ripen (you can speed up the process by placing them in a closed paper bag with a few holes in it). Pears are ripe when they yield to gentle pressure at the stem end.

8 TO 10 SERVINGS

- **½ cup (1 stick) unsalted butter, room temperature**
- **½ cup plus 2 tablespoons sugar**
- **3 large eggs**
- **1 teaspoon vanilla extract**
- **½ teaspoon aniseed**
- **½ teaspoon anise extract**
- **1 cup all purpose flour**

- **3 large ripe pears**
- **2 tablespoons fresh lemon juice**
- **⅓ cup finely chopped hazelnuts**

Powdered sugar

PREHEAT oven to 375°F. Butter and flour 11-inch tart pan with removable bottom. Using electric mixer, beat butter with ½ cup sugar in large bowl until light. Add eggs 1 at a time, beating until combined after each addition. Continue beating until mixture is fluffy. Blend in vanilla, aniseed, and anise extract. Fold in flour until batter is smooth. Spoon into prepared pan, spreading evenly.

PEEL, halve, and core pears. Cut each half lengthwise into thirds. Arrange pears decoratively in batter, pressing gently. Brush immediately with lemon juice. Sprinkle with hazelnuts and remaining 2 tablespoons sugar.

BAKE until crust is firm to touch, about 40 minutes. Dust with powdered sugar and serve warm.

Lemon crumb cake

THE CRUMB TOPPING and cake are prepared from one simple mixture, so this dessert (or coffee cake) comes together in no time. When grating the lemon, be sure to get the yellow peel only, not the bitter white pith underneath.

8 TO 10 SERVINGS

- **2 cups all purpose flour**
- **1 cup sugar**
- **½ cup (packed) golden brown sugar**
- **4 teaspoons grated lemon peel**
- **¾ teaspoon ground cinnamon**
- **½ cup vegetable oil**
- **2 tablespoons fresh lemon juice**

- **1 cup sour cream**
- **1 large egg**
- **1 teaspoon vanilla extract**
- **1 teaspoon baking powder**
- **1 teaspoon baking soda**

- **Powdered sugar**

POSITION rack in center of oven and preheat to 325°F. Lightly butter and flour 8x8x2-inch glass baking dish. Stir flour, 1 cup sugar, brown sugar, lemon peel, and cinnamon in large bowl to blend. Add oil and lemon juice; mix until flour is evenly moistened and mixture forms clumps. Set aside 1 cup mixture for topping.

WHISK sour cream, egg, vanilla, baking powder, and baking soda in small bowl until well blended. Add sour cream mixture to crumb mixture in large bowl; using electric mixer, beat until batter is smooth.

SPREAD batter in prepared pan. Sprinkle reserved topping over batter. Bake until tester inserted into center of cake comes out clean, about 40 minutes. Transfer pan to rack and cool. *(Can be prepared 1 day ahead. Cover with aluminum foil and let stand at room temperature.)*

SIFT powdered sugar over top of cake. Cut into squares and serve.

Beaumes-de-Venise cake with grapes

THE SWEET, HONEYED FLAVOR of Beaumes-de-Venise, a fortified dessert wine from the southern Rhône village of the same name, infuses this rustic French wine-country cake. You can also use domestic sweet Muscat wines, Vin Santo, sweet Marsala, or a dessert Sherry. Sugar sprinkled over the top of the cake while it bakes gives the crust a delectable crunch. This makes a lovely tea cake on its own, or serve it for dessert with soft whipped cream or whipped crème fraîche.

10 SERVINGS

- **1½ cups all purpose flour**
- **1 teaspoon baking powder**
- **1 teaspoon salt**
- **¼ teaspoon baking soda**
- **¾ cup plus 2 tablespoons sugar**
- **8 tablespoons (1 stick) unsalted butter, room temperature, divided**
- **3 tablespoons extra-virgin olive oil**
- **2 large eggs**
- **1 teaspoon grated lemon peel**
- **1 teaspoon grated orange peel**
- **1 teaspoon vanilla extract**
- **1 cup Beaumes-de-Venise or other Muscat wine**

- **1½ cups red seedless grapes**

PREHEAT oven to 400°F. Brush 10-inch-diameter springform pan with olive oil. Line bottom with parchment paper; brush parchment with olive oil.

SIFT flour and next 3 ingredients into bowl. Whisk ¾ cup sugar, 6 tablespoons butter, and 3 tablespoons oil in large bowl until smooth. Whisk in eggs, lemon peel, orange peel, and vanilla. Add flour mixture alternately with wine in 3 additions each, whisking just until smooth after each addition.

TRANSFER batter to prepared pan; smooth top. Sprinkle grapes over batter. Bake cake until top is set, about 20 minutes. Dot top of cake with remaining 2 tablespoons butter; sprinkle remaining 2 tablespoons sugar over. Bake until cake is golden and tester inserted into center comes out clean, about 20 minutes longer. Cool in pan on rack 20 minutes. Release pan sides. Serve lukewarm or at room temperature.

Plum upside-down cake

UPSIDE-DOWN CAKE probably came into vogue during the 1920s, when the pairing of then-exotic pineapple with an essentially thrifty and simple cake made it a fashionable party dessert. Cooks of that era were onto something: Their novelty turned out to have timeless appeal. Easy to prepare and familiar to everyone, these cakes are delicious and are a great showcase for fresh fruit, such as the summer plums in this recipe.

8 SERVINGS

- **12 tablespoons (1½ sticks) unsalted butter, room temperature, divided**
- **1 cup (packed) golden brown sugar**
- **1 tablespoon honey**
- **6 large plums, halved, pitted, each half cut into 6 wedges**
- **1½ cups all purpose flour**
- **2 teaspoons baking powder**
- **½ teaspoon ground cinnamon**
- **¼ teaspoon salt**
- **1 cup sugar**
- **2 large eggs**
- **½ teaspoon vanilla extract**
- **¼ teaspoon almond extract**
- **½ cup whole milk**

Lightly sweetened whipped cream

PREHEAT oven to 350°F. Stir 6 tablespoons butter, brown sugar, and honey in heavy medium skillet over low heat until butter melts and sugar and honey are incorporated, forming thick, smooth sauce. Pour into 9-inch-diameter cake pan with 2-inch-high sides. Arrange plums in overlapping concentric circles atop sauce.

MIX flour, baking powder, cinnamon, and salt in medium bowl. Using electric mixer, beat remaining 6 tablespoons butter in large bowl until light. Add 1 cup sugar and beat until creamy. Add eggs and beat until light and fluffy. Beat in vanilla and almond extracts. Add flour mixture in 3 additions alternately with milk in 2 additions, mixing just until batter is blended.

SPOON batter evenly over plums. Bake cake until top is golden and tester inserted into center of cake comes out clean, about 1 hour 5 minutes. Transfer to rack and cool in pan 30 minutes.

RUN knife around pan sides to loosen cake. Place platter atop cake pan. Invert cake; place platter on work surface. Let stand 5 minutes. Gently lift off pan. Serve cake warm with whipped cream.

Cherry upside-down cake

WHAT COULD BE a simpler or more satisfying end to a summer dinner? The cake is delicious on its own, but for extra indulgence, serve with whipped cream or vanilla ice cream.

8 SERVINGS

Topping

- **¼ cup (½ stick) unsalted butter**
- **¾ cup (packed) golden brown sugar**
- **14 ounces fresh cherries, halved, pitted**

Cake

- **1½ cups all purpose flour**
- **2 teaspoons baking powder**
- **¼ teaspoon salt**
- **1 cup sugar**
- **½ cup (1 stick) unsalted butter, room temperature**
- **2 large eggs, separated**
- **1½ teaspoons vanilla extract, divided**
- **½ cup whole milk**

- **¼ teaspoon cream of tartar**

- **1 cup chilled whipping cream**
- **1½ tablespoons powdered sugar**

FOR TOPPING: Preheat oven to 350°F. Butter sides of 9-inch-diameter cake pan with 2-inch-high sides. Melt ¼ cup butter in same pan set over low heat. Add brown sugar; whisk until well blended, about 2 minutes. Remove from heat. Spread mixture over bottom of pan. Arrange cherries, cut side down, in single layer in bottom of pan and press lightly to adhere. Set aside.

FOR CAKE: Mix flour, baking powder, and salt in medium bowl. Using electric mixer, beat 1 cup sugar and butter in large bowl until light and fluffy. Mix in egg yolks 1 at a time, beating well after each. Beat in 1 teaspoon vanilla. Mix in flour mixture in 3 additions alternately with milk in 2 additions.

USING electric mixer fitted with clean dry beaters, beat egg whites and cream of tartar in another large bowl until stiff but not dry. Stir ¼ of whites into cake batter to lighten. Using rubber spatula, gently fold remaining whites into batter. Spoon batter atop cherries in pan. Bake cake until top is deep golden and tester inserted into center comes out clean, about 55 minutes. Cool in pan on rack 15 minutes.

WHIP cream, powdered sugar, and remaining ½ teaspoon vanilla in medium bowl to soft peaks.

RUN small knife around edges of pan to loosen cake. Place platter over cake and invert onto platter. Let stand 5 minutes. Remove pan. *(Cake and whipped cream can be prepared 6 hours ahead. Cover cake and let stand at room temperature. Cover and refrigerate whipped cream.)* Serve cake warm or at room temperature with whipped cream.

Layered mocha cream torte

WITH AN EASY press-in crust and alternating layers of mocha meringue mousse, chocolate cookie crumbles, and coffee-flavored whipped cream, this chilled dessert combines the sophistication of a torte with the simple satisfactions of an icebox pie. For convenience, it can be refrigerated overnight before serving.

12 SERVINGS

Crust

- **2½ cups ground chocolate wafer cookies (from two 9-ounce packages)**
- **1½ tablespoons instant coffee powder**
- **6 tablespoons (¾ stick) unsalted butter, melted**

Fillings

- **12 ounces bittersweet (not unsweetened) or semisweet chocolate, chopped**
- **6 tablespoons (¾ stick) unsalted butter, cut into pieces**
- **6 teaspoons instant coffee powder, divided**

- **½ cup sugar**
- **3 tablespoons water**

- **5 large egg whites**

- **2¾ cups chilled whipping cream, divided**
- **¼ cup powdered sugar**
- **¼ teaspoon ground cinnamon**

FOR CRUST: Preheat oven to 350°F. Blend ground cookies and coffee powder in processor. Set aside ¾ cup cookie crumb mixture. Add butter to remaining mixture and process until moist crumbs form. Using plastic wrap as aid, press mixture over bottom and up sides of 9-inch-diameter springform pan with 2¾-inch-high sides. Bake crust until just firm to touch, about 10 minutes. Cool completely.

FOR FILLINGS: Stir chocolate, butter, and 1 teaspoon coffee powder in heavy medium saucepan over medium-low heat until melted and smooth. Transfer to large bowl. Set chocolate mixture aside while preparing meringue.

STIR ½ cup sugar and 3 tablespoons water in heavy small saucepan over low heat until sugar dissolves. Increase heat and boil syrup without stirring until candy thermometer registers 240°F, tilting pan to submerge bulb, about 4 minutes.

MEANWHILE, using electric mixer, beat egg whites in large bowl to soft peaks.

GRADUALLY beat hot syrup into whites. Continue beating until medium-stiff peaks form, about 3 minutes. Fold ⅓ of meringue into lukewarm chocolate mixture to lighten. Fold in remaining meringue. Set chocolate meringue aside.

COMBINE ¼ cup cream and remaining 5 teaspoons coffee powder in large bowl; stir to dissolve. Add remaining 2½ cups cream, powdered sugar, and cinnamon; beat until firm peaks form. Fold 1½ cups coffee whipped cream into chocolate meringue, forming mocha mousse.

SPOON half of mocha mousse over bottom of crust. Sprinkle 3 tablespoons reserved crumb mixture over mousse. Spoon half of coffee whipped cream over crumbs. Sprinkle with 3 tablespoons crumbs. Repeat layering with remaining mocha mousse, crumbs, coffee whipped cream, and crumbs. Cover and refrigerate until set, about 4 hours. *(Can be prepared 2 days ahead. Keep refrigerated.)* Run knife around pan sides to loosen torte. Remove pan sides and serve.

White chocolate mousse torte with Oreo cookie crust

THIS CREAMY NO-BAKE DESSERT is layered like a torte (in this recipe, with chocolate ganache and a white chocolate mousse), but you'll think you're eating a luscious pudding pie. Since the torte needs to chill at least six hours, it's best to make it a day before serving.

10 SERVINGS

Crust

- **24 Oreo cookies**
- **¼ cup (½ stick) unsalted butter, melted**
- **¾ cup whipping cream**
- **8 ounces semisweet chocolate, chopped**

Filling

- **1 pound high-quality white chocolate (such as Lindt or Perugina), chopped**
- **3 cups chilled whipping cream, divided**

- **1 tablespoon unflavored gelatin**
- **¼ cup water**
- **1 teaspoon vanilla extract**

Chopped Oreo cookies

FOR CRUST: Butter 10-inch-diameter springform pan with 2¾-inch-high sides. Finely grind cookies in processor. Add melted butter and blend until combined. Using plastic wrap as aid, press crust mixture over bottom (not sides) of prepared pan. Bring cream to simmer in heavy medium saucepan. Reduce heat to low. Add chocolate and whisk until melted and smooth. Pour chocolate mixture over crust. Chill.

FOR FILLING: Combine white chocolate and 1 cup cream in top of double boiler set over simmering water; stir until melted and smooth. Remove from over water. Cool to barely lukewarm.

SPRINKLE gelatin over ¼ cup water in heavy small saucepan. Let stand 10 minutes to soften. Stir over low heat until gelatin dissolves. Pour into large bowl. Add remaining 2 cups cream and vanilla; stir to combine. Beat cream-gelatin mixture to soft peaks. Fold in white chocolate mixture. Pour filling into crust. Refrigerate until filling is set, at least 6 hours and up to 1 day.

RUN small sharp knife around pan sides to loosen torte. Release pan sides. Sprinkle top with chopped Oreo cookies.

Viennese Linzertorte cake

TORTE USUALLY DESCRIBES a round layer cake, or one that substitutes ground nuts for some or all of the flour, but it also applies to some tart-like desserts—most famously, the Linzertorte, named for the Austrian city of Linz. We've included all the traditional flavors of the hazelnut, spice, and raspberry jam tart in this holiday layer cake, along with modern nuances like Chinese five-spice powder (a blend of ground anise, cinnamon, star anise, cloves, and ginger; it's available in the spice section of most supermarkets). The top is covered with a piped white chocolate frosting that echoes the lattice crust of the classic pastry.

14 TO 16 SERVINGS

Cake

1 cup hazelnuts, toasted, skinned
2 cups unbleached all purpose flour
1 tablespoon baking powder
1½ teaspoons Chinese five-spice powder
½ teaspoon ground nutmeg
½ teaspoon salt
¾ cup (1½ sticks) unsalted butter, room temperature
1½ cups sugar
3 large egg yolks
2 teaspoons vanilla extract
1 teaspoon almond extract
1¼ cups whole milk
5 large egg whites, room temperature

Frosting

6 ounces high-quality white chocolate (such as Lindt or Perugina)
3 8-ounce packages Philadelphia brand cream cheese, room temperature
9 tablespoons (1 stick plus 1 tablespoon) unsalted butter, room temperature
1½ cups powdered sugar
2¼ teaspoons vanilla extract
½ teaspoon almond extract
1 cup raspberry preserves, stirred to loosen

1½ cups finely chopped toasted hazelnuts

FOR CAKE: Preheat oven to 350°F. Butter and flour 15x10x1-inch jelly-roll pan. Finely grind nuts with flour in processor. Transfer to medium bowl. Mix in baking powder, spices, and salt. Using electric mixer, beat butter and sugar in large bowl until light and fluffy. Beat in egg yolks and vanilla and almond extracts. Add nut-flour mixture in 3 additions alternately with milk in 2 additions, beating at low speed after each addition just until combined (batter will be thick). Using clean dry beaters, beat egg whites in another large bowl to stiff peaks. Fold ⅓ of whites into batter to lighten. Fold in remaining whites.

SPREAD batter in prepared pan; smooth top. Bake until tester inserted into center comes out clean, about 25 minutes. Cool cake in pan on rack 20 minutes. Run small knife around pan sides to loosen cake. Turn cake out onto aluminum foil–lined rack and cool.

FOR FROSTING: Stir white chocolate in top of double boiler over barely simmering water until melted. Cool to barely lukewarm. Using electric mixer, beat cream cheese and butter in large bowl until smooth. Beat in white chocolate, then sugar and vanilla and almond extracts (if frosting is too soft, chill until firm enough to spread).

USING serrated knife, cut cake crosswise into three 5x10-inch rectangles. Place 1 cake rectangle on platter. Spread ¾ cup frosting over. Drizzle ¼ cup preserves over; spread over frosting. Top with second cake rectangle. Spread ¾ cup frosting over. Drizzle ¼ cup preserves over; spread over frosting. Top with third cake rectangle. Spoon 1¼ cups frosting into pastry bag fitted with small star tip. Spread remaining frosting over top and sides of cake. Drizzle remaining preserves over top of cake; spread evenly to cover top. Refrigerate cake just until frosting begins to firm, about 20 minutes.

PIPE frosting in 7 diagonal lines atop cake, spacing apart. Repeat at right angles, piping 6 lines to form lattice. Press chopped nuts onto sides of cake. Pipe line of frosting around top edge of cake where nuts and preserves meet. *(Can be prepared 2 days ahead. Cover with dome of aluminum foil and refrigerate. Let stand 2 hours at room temperature before serving.)*

Banana "Turtle" torte

BANANAS AND THE chocolate-caramel-pecan combination of the popular Turtle candy come together in this crowd-pleasing dessert—a chocolate-pecan layer cake filled with caramel, whipped cream, and fresh banana slices. The cake is the texture of a chewy brownie.

10 TO 12 SERVINGS

Caramel

- **1½ cups sugar**
- **½ cup water**
- **¾ cup whipping cream**
- **6 tablespoons (¾ stick) unsalted butter, room temperature**
- **Pinch of salt**

Cake

- **6 ounces unsweetened chocolate, chopped**
- **½ cup (1 stick) unsalted butter**
- **4 large eggs**
- **2 cups sugar**
- **1 cup all purpose flour**
- **1 teaspoon vanilla extract**
- **¼ teaspoon salt**
- **2¼ cups coarsely chopped pecans**

- **1½ cups chilled whipping cream**
- **2 tablespoons banana liqueur (optional)**
- **4 bananas, thinly sliced**
- **Additional coarsely chopped pecans (optional)**

FOR CARAMEL: Combine sugar and ½ cup water in heavy medium saucepan; stir over low heat until sugar dissolves. Increase heat and boil without stirring until syrup is deep amber color, occasionally brushing down sides of pan with wet pastry brush and swirling pan, about 10 minutes. Remove from heat; carefully add cream (mixture will bubble vigorously). Return to low heat and whisk until smooth. Add butter and salt; whisk until smooth. Cool caramel to room temperature. *(Can be prepared 3 days ahead. Cover and refrigerate. Before using, warm over low heat until just pourable.)*

FOR CAKE: Preheat oven to 350°F. Butter three 9-inch-diameter cake pans with 1½-inch-high sides. Line bottom of pans with parchment or waxed paper rounds; butter paper. Combine chocolate and butter in heavy large saucepan. Stir over low heat until melted. Cool. Whisk in eggs and sugar. Stir in flour, vanilla, and salt.

DIVIDE batter equally among prepared pans and smooth top. Sprinkle ¾ cup pecans atop each. Bake until cakes are set and tester inserted into center comes out with a few moist crumbs still attached, about 15 minutes. Cool in pans on rack. Turn out layers onto racks and remove paper. *(Can be prepared 1 day ahead. Store airtight.)*

BEAT whipping cream and liqueur, if desired, in medium bowl to stiff peaks. Place 1 cake layer, pecan side up, on platter. Drizzle ¼ cup caramel over. Cover with layer of bananas. Spread 1 cup whipped cream over bananas. Drizzle 3 tablespoons caramel over cream. Top with second cake layer. Repeat layering with ¼ cup caramel, bananas, 1 cup whipped cream, and 3 tablespoons caramel. Top with remaining cake layer. Drizzle ¼ cup caramel over cake. Transfer remaining whipped cream to pastry bag fitted with large star tip. Pipe rosettes of cream around top edge of torte. Garnish with bananas. Sprinkle with additional pecans, if desired. *(Can be prepared 4 hours ahead. Refrigerate.)* Rewarm remaining caramel. Serve torte, passing caramel alongside.

Banana cupcakes with buttercream frosting

SPREAD AS MUCH or as little frosting as you like over these moist and tender cupcakes. If you wish, garnish each cupcake with one or two slices of fresh banana. Kids will love the buttercream frosting; adults might enjoy a cream cheese frosting such as the one that accompanies the Triple-Layer Carrot Cake on page 516.

MAKES 12

Cupcakes

- **1½ cups all purpose flour**
- **¾ cup sugar**
- **1½ teaspoons baking soda**
- **¼ teaspoon salt**
- **1¼ cups mashed very ripe bananas (about 3)**
- **½ cup (1 stick) unsalted butter, melted**
- **1 large egg, room temperature**
- **¼ cup buttermilk**

Frosting

- **¾ cup (1½ sticks) unsalted butter, room temperature**
- **2½ cups powdered sugar**
- **2 teaspoons whipping cream**
- **½ teaspoon vanilla extract**

FOR CUPCAKES: Position rack in middle of oven and preheat to 350°F. Line 12-cup muffin tin with paper liners. Sift flour, sugar, baking soda, and salt into medium bowl. Whisk mashed banana, melted butter, egg, and buttermilk in large bowl to blend. Add flour mixture and whisk just until combined.

SPOON batter into prepared muffin cups, dividing equally. Bake until toothpick inserted into center of cupcakes comes out clean, about 25 minutes. Remove from oven and immediately invert cupcakes onto rack. Turn cupcakes right side up. Let cool completely.

FOR FROSTING: Using electric mixer, beat butter in large bowl until light and fluffy. Gradually beat in powdered sugar, then cream and vanilla. Spread frosting over cupcakes. *(Can be prepared 2 days ahead. Place cupcakes in single layer in airtight container; cover and refrigerate. Bring to room temperature before serving.)*

Black-and-white cupcakes

THESE WERE INSPIRED by the oversize black-and-white cookies that are practically an institution at delis all over the country. Casual yet stylish, the cupcakes would be a nice finish for a backyard barbecue with friends.

MAKES 12

Chocolate icing

- **1/4 cup whipping cream**
- **1 tablespoon light corn syrup**
- **4 ounces bittersweet (not unsweetened) or semisweet chocolate, chopped**
- **1/2 teaspoon vanilla extract**

White icing

- **1 cup powdered sugar**
- **2 tablespoons whipping cream**
- **2 teaspoons fresh lemon juice**

Cupcakes

- **3 large eggs, room temperature**
- **1 teaspoon vanilla extract**
- **1 teaspoon grated lemon peel**
- **1 1/2 cups cake flour**
- **3/4 teaspoon baking powder**
- **1/4 teaspoon salt**
- **1 1/4 cups sugar**
- **3/4 cup (1 1/2 sticks) unsalted butter, room temperature**
- **1/3 cup buttermilk**

FOR CHOCOLATE ICING: Bring cream and corn syrup just to simmer in heavy small saucepan over medium heat. Remove from heat. Add chocolate and vanilla; whisk until melted and smooth.

FOR WHITE ICING: Whisk powdered sugar, cream, and lemon juice in small bowl to blend.

LET both icings stand 1½ hours at room temperature to thicken.

FOR CUPCAKES: Preheat oven to 325°F. Line 12-cup muffin tin with paper liners. Whisk eggs, vanilla, and lemon peel in medium bowl to blend. Mix cake flour, baking powder, and salt in another medium bowl. Using electric mixer, beat sugar and butter in large bowl until well blended, stopping occasionally to scrape down sides of bowl. Gradually beat in egg mixture. Beat in flour mixture alternately with buttermilk in 2 additions each.

DIVIDE batter among prepared muffin cups. Bake until tester inserted into center of cupcakes comes out clean, about 25 minutes. Cool cupcakes in pan on rack 5 minutes. Invert cupcakes onto rack; turn right side up and cool completely.

SPREAD chocolate icing over half of each cupcake. Spread white icing on second half of each cupcake. Let stand until set, about 1 hour. *(Can be prepared 1 day ahead. Place in single layer in airtight container at room temperature.)*

17 Pies and tarts

Never being ones to let well enough alone, Americans have exhibited typical exuberance when expanding on the theme of pie baking. Unlikely candidates have been drafted into service, from New England's pumpkin (one of America's earliest contributions to the world of pies) to the humble marshmallow. Walnuts, pecans, chocolate, and all manner of cream fillings, along with bananas, meringue, streusel, whipped cream, and more, make for limitless combinations. (Of course, one of the greatest pie combos of all is the pairing of a slice of pie with a scoop of ice cream—whoever thought of that ought to be inducted into the Dessert Hall of Fame.)

Baking fruit pies has become one of our favorite ways to dispatch the best of every season's crop—preserving the very essence of a fruit without gilding it.

The choice to bake a fruit-filled pie with or without a top crust, or with a woven lattice crust, affects more than just the look of the finished pie. Double-crusted pies make for juicier, messier fillings (that's "messier" in a good way). Pies baked without a top crust have denser fillings with more concentrated flavors. Those baked with lattice-top crusts or crumb crusts fall somewhere in between. And let's face it: The aroma of cinnamon-scented apples bubbling away inside a golden-brown crust is so irresistible that apple pie has become a symbol of the country itself.

Tarts differ from pies in style—they're slightly more elegant—and in method of preparation. They are usually baked in a fluted shallow tin with a removable bottom, which gives the tart a compact, slim profile and makes it easy to serve. Tarts can be prepared with spiced fruits, artfully arranged or haphazardly scattered, baked right in the crust. Or the crust can be baked "blind" (without a filling), then lined with rich pastry cream and topped with uncooked fruit. Home-style tarts can be made easily and without special pans: Bake them free-form; that is, by simply rolling out the tart dough, covering it with filling, and folding the edges partway over the filling to make a crust.

Rustic or fancy, pies and tarts should be made, and enjoyed, with exuberance.

Pies

Deep-dish apple pie with cheddar crust

IT'S A TIME-HONORED New England tradition to serve hot apple pie with a wedge of sharp cheddar cheese. This delectable recipe incorporates the cheese right into the crust–but you can still serve a wedge on the side if you like. Quite an unusual "pie," this one has a top crust but no bottom crust (that saves a step), and it's made in an oval baking dish rather than a pie dish. Spiced hard cider would be the perfect accompaniment.

8 SERVINGS

Crust

2½ cups unbleached all purpose flour
½ teaspoon salt
½ cup chilled solid vegetable shortening, cut into ½-inch cubes
6 tablespoons (¾ stick) chilled unsalted butter, cut into ½-inch cubes
1½ cups (packed) coarsely grated extra-sharp cheddar cheese (about 6 ounces)
⅔ cup (about) ice water

Fruit

4 pounds Granny Smith apples, peeled, cored, thinly sliced
⅔ cup raisins
½ cup (packed) golden brown sugar
⅓ cup plus 2 teaspoons sugar
3 tablespoons unbleached all purpose flour
2 tablespoons fresh lemon juice
¾ teaspoon ground cinnamon
½ teaspoon ground ginger
¼ teaspoon ground nutmeg

3 tablespoons unsalted butter, cut into ½-inch cubes

1 egg, beaten to blend with 1 tablespoon water (for glaze)

FOR CRUST: Blend flour and salt in processor. Add shortening and butter; cut in, using several on/off turns. Add cheese and cut in until pea-size clumps form. With machine running, gradually blend in enough water to form soft moist clumps. Gather dough into ball; flatten into disk. Wrap in plastic and chill at least 2 hours. *(Can be prepared 2 days ahead. Keep chilled. Let stand at room temperature 15 minutes before rolling out.)*

FOR FRUIT: Mix apples, raisins, brown sugar, ⅓ cup sugar, flour, lemon juice, and spices in large bowl. Let stand 30 minutes at room temperature, tossing occasionally.

PREHEAT oven to 400°F. Spoon fruit and any accumulated juices into 13x9x2-inch glass or ceramic oval baking dish. Dot fruit with butter cubes.

ROLL out dough on floured surface to oval about ½ inch larger than baking dish. Fold in ½ inch of dough edge to form double-thick border; crimp decoratively. Cut out 1-inch-diameter hole from center of crust. Using tart pan bottom as aid, lift dough and place atop fruit. Tuck in dough around edges.

BAKE pie 15 minutes. Brush crust with egg glaze. Sprinkle with remaining 2 teaspoons sugar. Reduce oven temperature to 375°F. Bake until crust is golden, about 35 minutes. Cool on rack 15 minutes. Serve warm.

Apple-cranberry pie with cornmeal crust

PRETTY LEAF CUTOUTS decorate this welcome-to-fall dessert. If you don't have leaf-shaped cookie cutters, just cut out leaf shapes with a small, sharp knife, then press the blade into the dough to mark the veins in the leaves. Shortening and buttermilk render the crust very tender, and the cornmeal gives it a subtle satisfying crunch. Pumpkin pie spice is one-stop shopping when it comes to flavor: Blends differ, but most feature ground cinnamon, nutmeg, cloves, and ginger.

8 SERVINGS

Crust

2 cups all purpose flour
3/4 cup yellow cornmeal
5 tablespoons sugar
1 1/4 teaspoons pumpkin pie spice
1/2 teaspoon salt
3/4 cup plus 2 tablespoons solid vegetable shortening, room temperature
6 tablespoons (about) buttermilk

Filling

1 cup fresh cranberries
1 cup plus 2 tablespoons sugar
2 teaspoons pumpkin pie spice
3 pounds Pippin apples, peeled, quartered, cored, cut into 1/2-inch-thick slices
1/2 cup dried currants
5 tablespoons all purpose flour

Buttermilk

Rum raisin ice cream

FOR CRUST: Mix first 5 ingredients in processor. Add shortening; using on/off turns, cut in until mixture resembles coarse meal. Blend in buttermilk by tablespoonfuls until dough begins to clump together. Gather dough into ball; divide in half. Flatten each half into disk. Wrap each disk in plastic and chill 45 minutes. *(Can be prepared 1 day ahead; keep chilled.)*

FOR FILLING: Position rack in bottom third of oven and preheat to 375°F. Coarsely chop cranberries with sugar and pumpkin pie spice in processor. Transfer mixture to large bowl. Add apples, currants, and flour; toss to combine.

ROLL out 1 dough disk between sheets of parchment paper to 13-inch round. Peel off top sheet of paper; invert dough into 9½-inch-diameter deep-dish glass pie dish. Peel off paper. Fold dough overhang under, forming double-thick edge. Crimp edge decoratively. Roll out remaining dough disk on lightly floured surface to ⅛-inch-thick round. Using 3-inch-long leaf cookie cutter, cut out leaves. Using knife, mark veins in leaves. Add filling to pie dish, mounding slightly. Arrange leaves around edge of pie and all over top, overlapping decoratively. Brush pastry all over with buttermilk.

PLACE pie on baking sheet. Bake 45 minutes. Cover pie loosely with aluminum foil and continue to bake until filling is bubbling thickly and crust is golden brown, about 35 minutes longer. Transfer pie to rack and cool at least 1 hour. Serve warm or at room temperature with ice cream.

Old-fashioned lattice-top apple pie

THIS IS AN EASY lattice-top crust: The strips are simply laid across each other at right angles to form a crisscross pattern. A squeeze of lemon acts almost like salt in apple pie: It accentuates the apple flavor. In the mood for à la mode? Scoop vanilla or caramel ice cream.

8 SERVINGS

Crust

- **2½ cups all purpose flour**
- **1 tablespoon sugar**
- **¾ teaspoon salt**
- **10 tablespoons (1¼ sticks) chilled unsalted butter, cut into ½-inch cubes**
- **⅓ cup chilled solid vegetable shortening, cut into ½-inch cubes**
- **6 tablespoons (or more) ice water**

Filling

- **½ cup sugar**
- **¼ cup (packed) golden brown sugar**
- **2 tablespoons all purpose flour**
- **1 tablespoon fresh lemon juice**
- **2 teaspoons grated lemon peel**
- **⅛ teaspoon ground nutmeg**
- **3 pounds Golden Delicious apples, peeled, quartered, cored, thinly sliced**

Milk
Additional sugar

FOR CRUST: Blend flour, sugar, and salt in processor. Add butter and shortening; using on/off turns, cut in until mixture resembles coarse meal. Add 6 tablespoons ice water and process until moist clumps form, adding more water by teaspoonfuls if dough is dry. Gather into ball; divide in half. Flatten each piece into disk. Wrap each in plastic and chill 2 hours. *(Can be prepared 2 days ahead. Keep chilled. Let dough soften slightly at room temperature before rolling out.)*

FOR FILLING: Position rack in bottom third of oven and preheat to 400°F. Mix first 6 ingredients in large bowl. Add apples and toss to combine.

ROLL out 1 dough disk on floured surface to 12-inch round. Transfer to 9-inch-diameter glass pie dish. Fold edge under, forming high-standing rim. Crimp edge decoratively. Add filling. Roll out second dough disk on floured surface to 13-inch round. Cut into twelve 1-inch-wide strips. Arrange 6 strips across pie, spacing evenly apart. Form lattice by arranging 6 strips at right angles to first strips. Gently press ends into crust edges. Brush lattice with milk. Sprinkle lightly with additional sugar.

BAKE pie 10 minutes. Reduce oven temperature to 375°F. Continue baking pie until filling is bubbling thickly and crust is deep golden, covering edges with aluminum foil collar if browning too quickly, about 1 hour 20 minutes. Cool on rack at least 1 hour. *(Can be made 8 hours ahead. Let stand on rack.)* Serve warm or at room temperature.

Apple pie with hazelnuts and dried sour cherries

THE FLAVORS of the Pacific Northwest really come through in this delectable pie. You'll need to make a few openings in the top crust—whether simple slits or circles, or creative heart, star, or leaf shapes made with cookie cutters—to allow the steam to escape while baking. Hazelnut or vanilla gelato is just what you'll want alongside.

8 SERVINGS

Cherries

- **¾ cup dried tart cherries**
- **½ cup Merlot or other dry red wine**

Crust

- **3¼ cups all purpose flour**
- **⅞ pound (3½ sticks) chilled unsalted butter, cut into ½-inch cubes**

1/4 cup sugar
1/2 teaspoon salt
2/3 cup ice water

Filling
4 pounds Golden Delicious apples, peeled, quartered, cored, cut into 1 1/2-inch chunks (about 12 cups)
1/3 cup sugar
1/4 teaspoon ground cinnamon
1/2 cup hazelnuts, toasted, skinned, coarsely chopped

1 egg, beaten to blend with 1 tablespoon water (for glaze)
2 tablespoons raw sugar or additional granulated sugar

Vanilla ice cream

FOR CHERRIES: Bring cherries and Merlot to boil in small saucepan over medium-high heat. Remove from heat. Let stand at room temperature overnight. Drain well.

FOR CRUST: Combine flour, butter, sugar, and salt in bowl of electric mixer. Place bowl in freezer 15 minutes. Using electric mixer fitted with paddle attachment, beat mixture on low speed until pea-size clumps form. Drizzle ⅔ cup ice water over mixture and beat just until dough comes together. Gather dough into ball; divide in half. Flatten each piece into disk. Wrap each in plastic; chill at least 8 hours and up to 1 day.

LET 1 dough disk stand at room temperature 15 minutes to soften slightly. Roll out disk on lightly floured surface to 13-inch round. Transfer to 9½-inch-diameter deep-dish glass pie dish. Trim overhang to 1 inch. Fold in overhang, forming double-thick sides. Refrigerate at least 30 minutes and up to 6 hours.

FOR FILLING: Preheat oven to 450°F. Toss apples, ⅓ cup sugar, and cinnamon in large bowl to combine. Transfer to large rimmed baking sheet. Roast until apples soften slightly, about 15 minutes. Cool apple mixture. Reduce oven temperature to 425°F. Toss cherries, apple mixture, and hazelnuts in large bowl.

LET second dough disk stand at room temperature 15 minutes to soften slightly. Roll out disk on lightly floured surface to 13-inch round. Transfer filling to dough-lined dish. Brush edge of crust with egg glaze. Drape dough over filling. Trim top dough overhang to 1 inch. Press top and bottom dough edges together to seal. Crimp edges decoratively. Using sharp knife, cut 4 slashes in top of dough to allow steam to escape during baking. Brush dough with egg glaze; sprinkle with raw sugar.

BAKE pie 30 minutes. Reduce oven temperature to 350°F. Cover pie loosely with aluminum foil. Continue baking until apples are tender and juices are bubbling thickly, about 25 minutes longer. Cool slightly. *(Can be made 8 hours ahead. Let stand on rack at room temperature.)* Serve warm or at room temperature with ice cream.

Deep-dish caramel-apple crumb pie

IF YOU LIKE CARAMEL APPLES, you'll love this pie. Should the crust brown too quickly in the oven, cover the edges with aluminum foil: Tear off a sheet of foil about three feet long and fold it into thirds lengthwise, forming a long three- or four-inch-wide strip. Stand the strip upright around the pie dish, securing the foil at the seam with a metal paper clip. Keeping the foil upright should do the trick, but if the crust begins to burn, fold the collar over the crust edge for more protection.

8 SERVINGS

Crust
1 1/2 cups all purpose flour
2 tablespoons sugar
1/4 teaspoon salt
1/2 cup (1 stick) unsalted butter, cut into 1/2-inch cubes, frozen
4 tablespoons (about) ice water

Streusel

- **3/4 cup all purpose flour**
- **6 tablespoons sugar**
- **1 teaspoon pumpkin pie spice**
- **1/4 teaspoon salt**
- **6 tablespoons (3/4 stick) chilled unsalted butter, cut into 1/2-inch cubes**

Filling

- **3 pounds Golden Delicious apples (about 8), peeled, quartered, cored, cut into 3/4-inch-thick wedges**
- **1/4 cup all purpose flour**

- **1 1/4 cups sugar**
- **1/4 cup plus 2 tablespoons water**
- **3 tablespoons unsalted butter**

FOR CRUST: Mix flour, sugar, and salt in processor. Add butter; using on/off turns, cut in until mixture resembles coarse meal. Blend in enough ice water by tablespoonfuls to form large moist clumps. Transfer dough to work surface. Gather dough into ball. Flatten into disk. Wrap in plastic. Chill dough at least 30 minutes.

FOR STREUSEL: Mix flour, sugar, pumpkin pie spice, and salt in medium bowl to blend. Rub in butter with fingertips until pea-size clumps form. *(Dough and streusel can be made 1 day ahead. Cover and refrigerate streusel. Keep dough chilled. Let dough soften slightly at room temperature before rolling out.)*

FOR FILLING: Combine apples and flour in large bowl; toss to coat apples. Let stand while preparing caramel.

STIR sugar and ¼ cup water in heavy large saucepan over medium heat until sugar dissolves. Increase heat and boil without stirring until syrup is deep amber color, occasionally brushing pan sides with wet pastry brush and swirling pan, about 5 minutes. Remove from heat. Add butter and remaining 2 tablespoons water (mixture will bubble vigorously). Return to heat and stir until smooth. Pour caramel over apples; toss to coat. Let stand until apples release juices, tossing occasionally, about 10 minutes.

POSITION rack in bottom third of oven and preheat to 375°F. Roll out dough on floured work surface to 14-inch round. Transfer to 9 ½-inch-diameter deep-dish glass pie dish. Crimp edges decoratively. Spoon apple mixture into prepared crust. Sprinkle streusel over pie.

BAKE pie until apples are tender and streusel is golden, covering crust edge with aluminum foil collar if browning too quickly, about 1 hour 10 minutes. Transfer pie to rack and cool at least 1 hour. Serve pie warm or at room temperature.

Cherry-berry lattice pie

EGG MAKES THE CRUST tender and pliable—the dough won't crack easily when rolled out—and tapioca nicely thickens the filling. This filling is super-saturated with berry color; if you choose to weave the crust, create the lattice very carefully so as not to stain the crust.

8 SERVINGS

Crust

- **2 cups all purpose flour**
- **5 tablespoons sugar**
- **1/2 teaspoon salt**
- **3/4 cup (1 1/2 sticks) chilled unsalted butter, cut into 1/2-inch cubes**
- **1 large egg**
- **2 tablespoons (or more) whole milk**

Filling

- **4 cups fresh cherries (about 1 1/2 pounds), pitted, halved**
- **2 cups fresh blackberries or boysenberries; or frozen, thawed, drained**
- **3/4 cup sugar**
- **2 tablespoons quick-cooking tapioca**
- **2 teaspoons fresh lemon juice**
- **1/4 teaspoon vanilla extract**

- **2 tablespoons (1/4 stick) unsalted butter**
- **Additional sugar**

FOR CRUST: Blend flour, sugar, and salt in processor. Add butter; using on/off turns, cut in until mixture resembles very coarse meal. Beat egg with 2 tablespoons milk in small bowl; add to processor. Process until moist clumps form, adding more milk by tablespoonfuls if dough is dry. Gather dough into ball; divide into 2 pieces, 1 slightly larger than the other. Flatten each piece into disk; wrap each in plastic and refrigerate 1 hour. *(Can be made 1 day ahead. Keep refrigerated. Let dough soften slightly at room temperature before rolling out.)*

FOR FILLING: Combine first 6 ingredients in large bowl; toss to combine. Let stand until tapioca is translucent, tossing occasionally, about 35 minutes.

PREHEAT oven to 400°F. Roll out larger dough disk on floured surface to 13-inch round; transfer to 9½-inch-diameter deep-dish glass pie dish. Spoon filling into crust; dot with butter. Roll out remaining dough disk to 7x11-inch rectangle. Cut lengthwise into 10 generous ½-inch-wide strips (reserve remaining dough for another use). Arrange 5 strips across pie, spacing evenly apart. Form lattice by arranging remaining 5 strips at right angles to first strips. Cut overhang of bottom crust and strips to ¾ inch. Fold under; crimp edge decoratively. Sprinkle lattice with additional sugar.

PLACE pie on baking sheet; bake 30 minutes. Cover edge with aluminum foil collar to prevent overbrowning. Continue to bake until filling is bubbling thickly, about 50 minutes longer. Cool at least 45 minutes. Serve warm or at room temperature.

Citrus-scented mixed berry pie with oatmeal lattice crust

THIS CRUST gets its cookie-like texture from old-fashioned oats. Cut the strips for the lattice with a very sharp straight-edged knife or, if you have one, a pastry wheel (it looks like a small pizza cutter). When grating peel from citrus fruits, avoid the bitter white pith.

8 SERVINGS

Crust

- **4½ tablespoons ice water**
- **1 large egg yolk**
- **2¼ cups all purpose flour**
- **⅓ cup old-fashioned oats**
- **¼ cup (packed) golden brown sugar**
- **1 tablespoon grated lemon peel**
- **½ teaspoon salt**
- **½ cup (1 stick) chilled unsalted butter, cut into ½-inch cubes**
- **¼ cup chilled solid vegetable shortening, cut into ½-inch cubes**

Filling

- **1 cup plus 1 tablespoon sugar**
- **2½ tablespoons cornstarch**
- **2 teaspoons grated orange peel**
- **¼ teaspoon ground nutmeg**
- **1¾ cups fresh raspberries**
- **1½ cups fresh blueberries**
- **¾ cup fresh blackberries**
- **¼ cup blueberry preserves**

- **1 egg, beaten to blend (for glaze)**

FOR CRUST: Whisk 4½ tablespoons ice water and yolk in small bowl to blend. Blend flour, oats, brown sugar, lemon peel, and salt in processor 30 seconds. Add butter and shortening; using on/off turns, cut in until coarse meal forms. Add yolk mixture; using on/off turns, process until moist clumps form. Gather dough together; divide into 2 pieces, 1 slightly larger than the other. Flatten each piece into disk; wrap each in plastic and chill 1 hour. *(Can be prepared 1 day ahead. Keep chilled. Let dough soften slightly at room temperature before rolling out.)*

PREHEAT oven to 375°F. Roll out larger dough disk on floured surface to 12-inch round. Transfer dough to 9-inch-diameter glass pie dish. Fold overhang under, forming double-thick rim. Crimp, forming high-standing rim. Freeze 15 minutes.

LINE crust with aluminum foil. Fill with dried beans or pie weights. Bake 10 minutes. Remove foil and beans. Continue to bake until crust is set and looks dry, about 8 minutes longer. Cool to room temperature. Maintain oven temperature.

ROLL out remaining dough disk on floured surface to 12-inch round. Cut into ½-inch-wide strips.

FOR FILLING: Mix 1 cup sugar, cornstarch, orange peel, and nutmeg in large bowl. Add all berries and preserves; toss to combine.

MOUND filling in crust. Place dough strips at right angles atop pie, forming lattice; trim excess. Gently press strip ends to crust. Brush lattice with glaze. Sprinkle with remaining 1 tablespoon sugar.

PLACE pie on baking sheet. Bake pie until crust is golden brown and filling is bubbling thickly in center, covering crust edge with aluminum foil collar if browning too quickly, about 1 hour 15 minutes. Transfer pie to rack and cool. Serve pie lukewarm or at room temperature.

Deep-dish strawberry-rhubarb pie with crumb topping

STRAWBERRY AND RHUBARB are made for each other, especially in springtime stunners like this one. To make a nice garnish: After placing the dough into the pie dish and trimming the overhang, gather the dough scraps and roll out on a lightly floured surface to ⅛-inch thickness. Cut out 14 three-inch-long leaves with a knife or pastry cutter. Refrigerate the leaves until ready to use.

8 SERVINGS

Crust

1½ cups plus 1 tablespoon all purpose flour
2½ tablespoons sugar
½ teaspoon (generous) ground cinnamon
Pinch of salt
7½ tablespoons chilled unsalted butter, cut into ½-inch cubes
3½ tablespoons chilled solid vegetable shortening, cut into ½-inch cubes
¾ teaspoon vanilla extract
2 tablespoons (about) ice water

1 egg, beaten to blend (for glaze)
2 tablespoons old-fashioned oats

Topping

⅔ cup plus 2 tablespoons old-fashioned oats
½ cup all purpose flour
½ cup (packed) golden brown sugar
¼ teaspoon ground cinnamon
6 tablespoons (¾ stick) chilled unsalted butter, cut into ½-inch cubes

Filling

¾ pound fresh rhubarb, cut on sharp diagonal into ½-inch-thick slices (3½ to 4 cups)
2 1-pint containers strawberries, hulled, halved
1 cup sugar
¼ cup cornstarch
½ teaspoon ground cinnamon
⅛ teaspoon ground nutmeg

FOR CRUST: Whisk first 4 ingredients in medium bowl to blend. Add butter and shortening; rub in with fingertips until mixture resembles coarse meal. Add vanilla. Mix in enough water by tablespoonfuls to form moist clumps. Gather dough into ball; flatten into disk. Wrap in plastic and refrigerate at least 30 minutes. *(Can be prepared 1 day ahead. Soften dough slightly at room temperature before rolling out.)*

POSITION rack in bottom third of oven and preheat to 350°F. Roll out dough between sheets of lightly floured parchment paper to ½-inch-thick round. Peel off top sheet of paper. Invert dough into 9½-inch-diameter deep-dish glass pie dish; peel off paper. Trim dough overhang to ½ inch. Crimp edges decoratively. Refrigerate 20 minutes.

LINE crust with aluminum foil. Fill with dried beans or pie weights. Bake until crust is set, about 15 minutes. Remove foil and beans. Brush crust bottom and sides (not edge) with some of glaze. Sprinkle with 2 tablespoons oats. Bake until crust is golden, about 20 minutes. Cool crust completely on rack.

FOR TOPPING: Increase oven temperature to 375°F. Blend ⅔ cup oats, flour, sugar, and cinnamon in processor. Add butter; using on/off turns, cut in until mixture is crumbly. Transfer mixture to medium bowl. Stir in remaining 2 tablespoons oats.

FOR FILLING: Mix rhubarb, strawberries, sugar, cornstarch, cinnamon, and nutmeg in heavy large saucepan. Let stand 30 minutes. Bring to boil over medium heat, stirring constantly. Reduce heat and simmer until juices thicken, about 3 minutes.

POUR filling into cooled crust. Cover with crumb topping. Bake 20 minutes. (If using pastry leaves, remove pie from oven and quickly arrange leaves around edge, overlapping slightly. Brush leaves with glaze.) Bake until topping (and leaves) are golden and filling is bubbling thickly, about 15 minutes. Cool pie on rack at least 2 hours. Serve slightly warm or at room temperature.

Berry streusel pie

ALMONDS COMPLEMENT BERRIES beautifully; here they're used in a scrumptious streusel topping, which also includes oats and brown sugar.

8 SERVINGS

Crust

- **2¼ cups all purpose flour**
- **1 tablespoon sugar**
- **½ teaspoon salt**
- **7 tablespoons chilled unsalted butter, cut into ½-inch cubes**
- **⅓ cup chilled solid vegetable shortening, cut into ½-inch cubes**
- **6 tablespoons (about) ice water**

Topping

- **6 tablespoons (packed) golden brown sugar**
- **6 tablespoons whole almonds**
- **6 tablespoons (¾ stick) chilled unsalted butter, cut into ½-inch cubes**
- **4½ tablespoons old-fashioned oats**
- **4½ tablespoons all purpose flour**

Filling

- **1 cup sugar**
- **¼ cup quick-cooking tapioca**
- **2 tablespoons fresh lemon juice**
- **5 cups assorted fresh berries (such as raspberries, blackberries, and blueberries; about 8 ounces each)**

FOR CRUST: Blend flour, sugar, and salt in processor. Add butter and shortening; using on/off turns, cut in until mixture resembles coarse meal. Add 5 tablespoons ice water and process until moist clumps form, adding more water by teaspoonfuls if dough is dry. Gather dough into ball; flatten into disk. Wrap in plastic and chill at least 1 hour.

FOR TOPPING: Combine all ingredients in processor. Process until moist clumps form. *(Dough and topping can be made 1 day ahead. Cover topping and chill; keep dough chilled. Soften dough slightly at room temperature before rolling out.)*

FOR FILLING: Mix sugar, tapioca, and lemon juice in large bowl. Add berries and toss gently to combine. Let stand until tapioca softens slightly, stirring occasionally, about 45 minutes.

PREHEAT oven to 400°F. Roll out dough on lightly floured surface to 13-inch round. Transfer to 9-inch-diameter glass pie dish. Trim dough overhang to 1 inch. Fold overhang under and crimp decoratively, forming high-standing rim. Freeze crust 20 minutes.

SPOON filling into crust. Crumble topping evenly over filling. Bake pie until crust and topping are golden brown and filling is bubbling, covering loosely with sheet of aluminum foil if topping browns too quickly, about 55 minutes. Transfer pie to rack and cool at least 3 and up to 8hours.

Crimson pie

THE CRIMSON COLOR comes from blueberries and cranberries—and because you can use fresh or frozen berries (or a combination of both), this pie is a year-round favorite. Half an orange, including the peel, is ground in a processor and mixed into the filling, imparting a wonderfully refreshing citrus flavor and aroma. Putting the pie on a rimmed baking sheet helps collect any drips and avoids a sticky, smoky mess in the oven.

8 SERVINGS

- **½ small orange (unpeeled), cut into pieces, seeded**
- **4 cups frozen blueberries (about 1½ pounds), thawed**
- **1 12-ounce bag fresh or frozen cranberries**
- **1½ cups sugar**
- **3 tablespoons cornstarch**

- **Sour Cream Pie Crust Dough (see recipe)**
- **2 tablespoons (¼ stick) unsalted butter, cut into ½-inch cubes**

- **Whole milk**

- **Additional sugar**

COARSELY grind orange in processor. Transfer orange to heavy large saucepan. Add blueberries, cranberries, 1½ cups sugar, and cornstarch. Boil mixture over medium-high heat until thick, stirring constantly, about 3 minutes. Cool completely.

POSITION rack in center of oven and preheat to 400°F. Roll out 1 dough disk on lightly floured surface to ⅛-inch-thick round. Roll up dough on rolling pin and transfer to 9-inch-diameter glass pie dish. Trim edges, leaving ½-inch overhang; reserve trimmings. Spoon berry filling into crust, mounding slightly in center. Dot filling with butter.

ROLL out second dough disk on lightly floured surface to 12-inch-diameter round. Roll up dough on rolling pin and unroll over filling. Trim edges. Press edges of bottom and top crust together to seal. Crimp edges decoratively. Make several slashes in top crust to allow steam to escape while baking. Brush crust with milk.

GATHER reserved trimmings and roll out on floured surface to ⅛-inch thickness. Using cookie cutter or small sharp knife, cut out 6 or 7 small leaf shapes. Place leaves decoratively atop pie in center. Press gently. Brush leaves with milk. Sprinkle top of pie with additional sugar.

Place pie on rimmed baking sheet and bake until crust is golden brown, about 50 minutes. Cool on rack at least 1 hour. Serve warm or at room temperature.

Sour cream pie crust dough

THIS CRUST owes its tender texture to sour cream; butter and shortening lend unbeatable flavor and flakiness. The crust is a do-ahead dream: It can be prepared a month ahead and stored in the freezer, so it's worth making a double or triple batch of the dough.

MAKES 2 PIE CRUST DISKS

- **¼ cup plus 2 tablespoons sour cream**
- **2 tablespoons ice water**
- **1 teaspoon sugar**
- **¾ teaspoon salt**
- **2¼ cups all purpose flour**
- **¼ cup cake flour**
- **½ cup (1 stick) chilled unsalted butter, cut into ½-inch cubes**
- **½ cup chilled solid vegetable shortening, cut into ½-inch cubes**

WHISK sour cream, 2 tablespoons water, sugar, and salt in small bowl to blend. Mix both flours in large bowl. Add butter and shortening; rub in with fingertips until mixture resembles coarse meal. Add sour cream mixture and stir just until moist clumps form. Gather dough together; divide in half. Flatten each piece into disk; wrap each in plastic and refrigerate 1 hour. *(Can be prepared ahead and kept refrigerated up to 3 days or frozen up to 1 month. If frozen, thaw overnight in refrigerator. Soften slightly at room temperature before rolling out.)*

Blueberry pie with lattice crust

A PIE THAT'S SURE to become a summer favorite. Pick through the blueberries and remove any stems still attached before adding the berries to the pie. Brushing the edges of the crust with whipping cream results in a beautifully golden crust; and when the filling is bubbling thickly, you'll know the pie is done. Word to the wise: Grate the peel off the lemon *before* you juice it. Vanilla ice cream is a traditional accompaniment–but consider lemon sorbet for a nice variation.

8 SERVINGS

4 ½-pint containers blueberries
¾ cup sugar
¼ cup all purpose flour
2 tablespoons fresh lemon juice
1 teaspoon grated lemon peel
1 teaspoon vanilla extract

Flaky Pie Crust (see recipe)
Whipping cream (for glaze)

Vanilla ice cream

POSITION rack in bottom third of oven and preheat to 400°F. Combine first 6 ingredients in large bowl. Crush a few berries in bowl with back of rubber spatula; toss to combine. Let stand until dry ingredients are moistened, about 15 minutes.

ROLL out 1 dough disk on lightly floured surface to 12½-inch round. Transfer to 9-inch-diameter glass pie dish. Trim dough overhang to ¾ inch. Spoon filling into crust. Roll out second dough disk on lightly floured surface to 12-inch round. Using scalloped pastry cutter, cut dough into generous ½-inch-wide strips. Arrange half of dough strips across top of filling, spacing evenly apart. Form lattice by arranging remaining dough strips at right angle to first strips, weaving strips if desired. Trim dough strips even with overhang on bottom crust. Tuck ends of dough strips and overhang under; press to seal. Crimp edges decoratively. Brush edges and lattice lightly with whipping cream.

PLACE pie on rimmed baking sheet. Bake 40 minutes. Cover crust edge with aluminum foil collar to prevent overbrowning. Continue to bake pie until filling is bubbling thickly in center, about 50 minutes longer. Cool pie on rack at least 2 hours and up to 8 hours. Serve with vanilla ice cream.

Flaky pie crust

FROZEN SHORTENING makes for a flakier crust, and ice water helps keep the fats cool and firm when mixing the dough. Just remember: "Firm fat equals flaky crust."

MAKES 2 PIE CRUST DISKS

2½ cups all purpose flour
1½ tablespoons sugar
1¼ teaspoons salt
⅔ cup solid vegetable shortening, frozen, then cut into ½-inch cubes
½ cup (1 stick) chilled unsalted butter, cut into ½-inch cubes
6 tablespoons (or more) ice water
2 teaspoons apple cider vinegar

BLEND flour, sugar, and salt in processor. Add shortening and butter; using on/off turns, cut in until mixture resembles coarse meal. Transfer mixture to bowl. Mix 6 tablespoons ice water and vinegar in small bowl; pour over flour mixture. Stir with fork until moist clumps form, adding more ice water by teaspoonfuls if dough is dry. Gather dough into 2 balls; flatten each into disk. Wrap each in plastic and chill 30 minutes. *(Can be prepared ahead and refrigerated up to 2 days or frozen up to 1 month. If frozen, thaw overnight in refrigerator. Soften slightly at room temperature before rolling out.)*

Vanilla peach pie

CARDAMOM, WHICH IS native to India, adds an exotic twist to this pie. You can use a tart-pan bottom (very thin and flat) to help transfer the crust to the top of the filling. Alternatively, roll the dough up very loosely on the rolling pin, then unroll it over the pie. Or roll the dough out on a sheet of parchment paper and use the paper to invert the dough onto the pie; then peel off the paper.

8 SERVINGS

- **4 pounds ripe peaches, peeled, halved, pitted, each half cut into 6 wedges (about 8 cups)**
- **½ cup plus 1 tablespoon sugar**
- **¼ cup (packed) golden brown sugar**
- **¼ cup all purpose flour**
- **¼ teaspoon ground cardamom**
- **1 vanilla bean, split lengthwise**

Flaky Pie Crust (see recipe, page 574)
Whipping cream (for glaze)

POSITION rack in bottom third of oven and preheat to 400°F. Combine peaches, ½ cup sugar, brown sugar, flour, and cardamom in large bowl. Scrape in seeds from vanilla bean; discard pod. Toss peach filling to combine well. Let stand until dry ingredients are moistened, about 15 minutes.

ROLL out 1 dough disk on lightly floured surface to 12½-inch round. Transfer to 9-inch-diameter glass pie dish. Trim overhang to ½ inch. Spoon peach filling into crust, mounding slightly in center. Roll out second dough disk to 12-inch round. Drape crust over filling. Trim overhang to ¾ inch. Fold edge of top and bottom crusts under, pressing to seal. Crimp edges decoratively. Cut 4 slits in top crust to allow steam to escape during baking. Brush crust lightly with whipping cream. Sprinkle with remaining 1 tablespoon sugar.

PLACE pie on rimmed baking sheet. Bake 45 minutes. Cover crust edges with aluminum foil collar to prevent overbrowning. Continue to bake pie until crust is golden and filling is bubbling thickly, about 1 hour longer. Cool completely on rack. Serve at room temperature.

Piled-high peach pie

THE NAME SAYS IT ALL: Five sweet, juicy pounds of peaches are dusted with cinnamon, cardamom, and nutmeg, then encased in a buttery, flaky crust (made tender with a bit of acidic vinegar). Look for pretty, unblemished peaches with a strong peach fragrance and that give a little when squeezed gently. On the side, scoop vanilla or cinnamon ice cream; if you can find it, crème fraîche ice cream would add a sophisticated accent.

8 SERVINGS

Crust

- **2⅓ cups all purpose flour**
- **1 tablespoon sugar**
- **1 teaspoon salt**
- **¾ cup (1½ sticks) chilled unsalted butter, cut into ½-inch cubes**
- **¼ cup chilled solid vegetable shortening, cut into ½-inch cubes**
- **1 teaspoon distilled white vinegar**
- **6 tablespoons (about) ice water**

Filling

- **5 pounds medium peaches, peeled, halved, pitted, sliced**
- **¾ cup sugar**
- **¼ cup all purpose flour**
- **¼ teaspoon ground cinnamon**
- **⅛ teaspoon ground cardamom**
- **⅛ teaspoon ground nutmeg**

Vanilla ice cream

FOR CRUST: Whisk flour, sugar, and salt in large bowl to blend. Add butter and shortening; rub in with fingertips until mixture resembles coarse meal.

Add vinegar. Using fork, mix in enough water by tablespoonfuls to form moist clumps. Gather dough into ball; divide dough in half. Flatten each piece into disk. Wrap each in plastic and chill 45 minutes. *(Can be prepared 2 days ahead. Keep refrigerated. Soften slightly at room temperature before rolling out.)*

FOR FILLING: Preheat oven to 400°F. Combine peaches, sugar, flour, and spices in large bowl; toss to mix well.

ROLL out 1 dough disk on floured surface to 13-inch round. Transfer to 9-inch-diameter glass pie dish. Transfer peach mixture to crust, mounding in center. Roll out second dough disk on floured surface to 13-inch round. Roll up dough on rolling pin and unroll atop peach mixture. Trim edges of both crusts to ¾-inch overhang. Fold edges under; press to seal. Crimp edges decoratively. Cut 6 slits in top crust to allow steam to escape during baking.

BAKE pie until crust is golden and juices are bubbling thickly through slits, covering crust edge with aluminum foil collar if browning too quickly, about 1 hour 10 minutes. Cool pie at least 3 hours before serving. *(Can be made 8 hours ahead. Let stand at room temperature.)* Serve with ice cream.

Lattice pie with pears and vanilla brown butter

BROWN BUTTER adds nutty richness to this pie. In France, it's known as *beurre noisette* ("hazelnut butter"), which indicates the golden-brown color to look for when simmering it. Vanilla beans, the fruit pods of a Central American orchid, are hand-pollinated and then cured in a very long and complex process before heading to market—hence their expense. But they're well worth it: The beans are packed with countless tiny seeds that, when scraped out and added to dishes such as the brown butter here, impart unbelievably deep, sweet flavor.

8 SERVINGS

2 tablespoons (¼ stick) unsalted butter
1 vanilla bean, split lengthwise
4 pounds ripe pears (such as Bartlett or Anjou; about 8), peeled, halved, cored, cut into ½-inch-thick slices
⅔ cup golden raisins
½ cup (packed) golden brown sugar
2 tablespoons all purpose flour
1 teaspoon fresh lemon juice

Butter Pie Crust Dough (see recipe)
1 teaspoon whole milk
1 tablespoon sugar

Vanilla ice cream

PREHEAT oven to 375°F. Melt butter in small skillet over medium heat. Scrape seeds from vanilla bean into butter; add pod. Cook until butter is golden brown, stirring often, about 3 minutes. Cool slightly. Remove pod. Gently toss pears, raisins, brown sugar, flour, and lemon juice in large bowl to combine. Stir in vanilla butter.

ROLL out 1 dough disk on lightly floured surface to 12-inch round. Transfer to 9-inch-diameter glass pie dish. Trim overhang to 1 inch. Transfer pear filling to crust. Roll out second dough disk on lightly floured surface to 13-inch round. Using pastry wheel, cut dough into ten 1-inch-wide strips. Arrange 5 strips over filling, spacing evenly apart. Arrange remaining strips at right angles to first strips, weaving if desired. Fold lower crust overhang over strips and seal. Crimp edges decoratively. Brush lattice with 1 teaspoon milk and sprinkle with 1 tablespoon sugar.

BAKE pie until crust is golden brown, pears are tender, and filling is bubbling, covering crust edge with aluminum foil collar if browning too quickly, about 1 hour 20 minutes. Cool at least 1 hour before serving. *(Can be made 6 hours ahead. Let stand at room temperature.)* Serve pie warm or at room temperature with ice cream.

Butter pie crust dough

EVER WONDER WHY pie crust recipes (and lots of dessert recipes) specifically call for unsalted butter, then instruct you to add salt? Salted butters vary widely in their salt content, so by first using unsalted butter and then adding salt separately, the total measure of salt can be controlled precisely—and if there's any cooking method that requires precision, it's baking.

MAKES TWO PIE CRUST DISKS

- **2½ cups all purpose flour**
- **1 tablespoon sugar**
- **1 teaspoon salt**
- **1 cup (2 sticks) chilled unsalted butter, cut into ½-inch cubes**
- **6 tablespoons (or more) ice water**

BLEND flour, sugar, and salt in processor. Add butter; using on/off turns, cut in until mixture resembles coarse meal. Add 6 tablespoons water. Using on/off turns, blend just until moist clumps form, adding more water by teaspoonfuls if dough is dry. Gather dough into ball; divide dough in half. Flatten each piece into disk. Wrap in plastic and refrigerate 1 hour. *(Can be prepared 2 days ahead. Keep chilled. Soften slightly at room temperature before rolling out.)*

Streusel-topped pear and blueberry pie

CALL IT SEASONAL FUSION—or just call it plain delicious. Rarely seen together, pears—the darlings of fall—meet blueberries, some of summer's finest fruits (the use of frozen blueberries makes this possible). Freezing the crust after rolling it out and placing it in the pie dish relaxes the gluten in the dough, resulting in a more tender crust.

8 SERVINGS

Crust

- **1½ cups all purpose flour**
- **1 tablespoon sugar**
- **¼ teaspoon salt**
- **½ cup (1 stick) chilled unsalted butter, cut into ½-inch cubes**
- **3 tablespoons (or more) ice water**

Filling

- **2 pounds firm but ripe pears (about 5 medium), peeled, halved, cored, cut into ¾-inch cubes**
- **9 tablespoons sugar, divided**
- **2 tablespoons orange juice**
- **Pinch of salt**
- **2¼ cups frozen blueberries**
- **6 tablespoons all purpose flour**

Walnut Streusel Topping (see recipe)

FOR CRUST: Blend flour, sugar, and salt in processor. Add butter; using on/off turns, cut in until mixture resembles coarse meal. Add 3 tablespoons ice water and process until moist clumps form, adding more ice water by teaspoonfuls if dough is dry. Gather dough into ball; flatten into disk. Wrap in plastic and refrigerate 30 minutes. *(Can be prepared 2 days ahead. Keep refrigerated. Let soften slightly at room temperature before rolling out.)*

ROLL out dough on lightly floured surface to 12-inch round. Transfer to 9-inch-diameter glass pie dish. Fold edges under, forming high-standing rim ¾ inch above dish sides; crimp edges decoratively. Freeze crust 25 minutes.

PREHEAT oven to 350°F. Bake crust until light golden brown, about 30 minutes. Cool while preparing filling. Maintain oven temperature.

FOR FILLING: Combine pears, 3 tablespoons sugar, orange juice, and salt in large nonstick skillet. Cook over medium heat until pears are tender but still hold their shape, stirring often, about 6 minutes. Transfer pear mixture to large bowl; cool to room temperature. Add blueberries, flour, and remaining 6 tablespoons sugar to pears; toss gently to combine.

TRANSFER filling to pie crust, mounding slightly in center. Sprinkle with Walnut Streusel Topping. Bake pie until filling is bubbling thickly, fruit is tender, and streusel topping is golden brown, about 1 hour 5 minutes. Cool pie on rack until lukewarm. Cut pie into wedges and serve.

Walnut streusel topping

AFTER TOASTING THE WALNUTS, let them cool, then throw everything in the processor and out comes a delectable crunchy topping, or streusel (which means "sprinkle" in German). This topping would be good for coffee cakes and Bundt cakes, too.

MAKES ABOUT 2½ CUPS

1 cup all purpose flour
½ cup (packed) dark brown sugar
½ cup walnuts, toasted
½ cup (1 stick) chilled unsalted butter, cut into ½-inch cubes
¼ teaspoon salt

USING on/off turns, blend all ingredients in processor until coarse crumbs form. *(Can be prepared 1 day ahead. Cover and refrigerate.)*

Pumpkin–apple butter pie with gingersnap crust

APPLE BUTTER—which isn't butter at all but an apple preserve of sorts—imparts a luscious sweetness to this pumpkin pie; you'll find it near the preserves at the market. The rim of this showstopper is covered with overlapping pastry leaves, which aren't nearly as difficult to make as they look. Using a sharp paring knife, cut the leaf shapes from rolled-out dough; then use the same knife to mark lines gently in the leaves to resemble veins. Any leftover pastry leaves would make a nice snack with tea or coffee. If you opt not to make the leaves, place the dough in the pie dish, trim the dough overhang to one inch, and then fold the overhang under (as you would to form a thick-edged crust) and crimp or flute decoratively.

8 SERVINGS

Crust

2 cups all purpose flour
3 tablespoons sugar
2 teaspoons ground ginger
½ teaspoon salt
½ teaspoon ground cinnamon
¼ teaspoon ground cloves
¼ teaspoon ground nutmeg
Large pinch of ground black pepper
2 teaspoons robust-flavored (dark) molasses
7 tablespoons chilled solid vegetable shortening, cut into ½-inch cubes
6 tablespoons (¾ stick) chilled unsalted butter, cut into ½-inch cubes
4 tablespoons (about) ice water

Filling

1¼ cups canned pure pumpkin
¾ cup whipping cream
6 tablespoons apple butter

- 6 tablespoons (packed) golden brown sugar
- 2 large eggs
- 1 large egg yolk
- 1 tablespoon sugar
- ½ teaspoon vanilla extract
- ½ teaspoon ground nutmeg
- ½ teaspoon ground cinnamon
- ½ teaspoon ground ginger
- ¼ teaspoon ground cloves
- ¼ teaspoon salt

Assembly

- 1 egg, beaten with 1 teaspoon water (for glaze)

FOR CRUST: Combine first 8 ingredients in processor and blend 10 seconds. Add molasses and process just to blend. Add shortening and butter; using on/off turns, cut in until mixture resembles coarse meal with some small pea-size pieces remaining. Transfer mixture to large bowl. Add enough water 1 tablespoon at a time to form moist clumps, tossing with fork. Gather dough into ball. Divide dough into 2 pieces, 1 piece about twice as large as second piece. Flatten each piece into disk. Wrap each in plastic and refrigerate until chilled through, about 3 hours. *(Can be made 2 days ahead. Keep refrigerated. Soften slightly at room temperature before rolling out.)*

FOR FILLING: Combine all ingredients in large bowl and whisk to blend. *(Filling can be made 1 day ahead. Cover and refrigerate.)*

TO ASSEMBLE: Roll out larger dough disk on floured surface to 13-inch round. Transfer to 9-inch-diameter glass pie dish. Press dough into dish. Cut off excess dough flush with outer edge of dish; reserve dough scraps. Freeze crust 30 minutes.

ROLL out smaller dough disk on floured surface to ⅛-inch thickness. Using small sharp knife, cut out 30 leaves (each about 2 inches long by 1 inch at widest point) to use as crust border. Transfer leaves to large ungreased baking sheet. Gather all dough scraps; roll out to ⅛-inch thickness. Cut out additional leaves of assorted sizes. Transfer leaves to another large ungreased baking sheet. Using tip of knife, mark veins on each leaf, cutting about ⅓ of way into dough (do not cut through dough). Chill all leaves until cold, at least 30 minutes.

LINE crust with aluminum foil; fill with dried beans or pie weights. Bake crust until sides are set, about 20 minutes. Remove foil and beans. Bake until crust is golden brown and bottom looks dry, piercing with toothpick if bubbles form, about 10 minutes (edge of crust may shrink slightly). Transfer to rack; cool.

PLACE pie dish with crust on work surface. Place baking sheet with 2x1-inch leaves nearby. Brush bottom of 1 leaf with water. Press leaf, wet side down, gently on rim of crust. Brush bottom of another leaf with water. Press onto crust, overlapping first leaf slightly and with tip pointing in a different direction from first. Repeat with enough leaves to cover rim. *(Can be prepared 1 day ahead. Cover and chill.)*

CUT 36x12 inch piece of foil. Fold lengthwise in half twice, forming 36x3-inch strip.

POSITION rack in center of oven and preheat to 350°F. Brush leaves around rim with egg glaze. Pour filling into crust. Transfer pie dish to baking sheet. Stand prepared foil strip around pie like a collar, just touching leaves. Secure overlapping portion of foil with metal paper clip.

BAKE pie until filling is barely set and still slightly shiny in center, about 45 minutes. Remove foil collar. Transfer pie to rack and cool completely (filling may crack as pie cools). Maintain oven temperature.

BRUSH remaining leaves with glaze. Bake until golden brown, about 15 minutes. Using spatula, transfer leaves to racks; cool. Arrange some leaves decoratively atop filling.

Spirited pumpkin pie

DARK RUM gives this pie its spirit, and the filling is spiced with (among other things) mace, the lacy outer covering of nutmeg seeds. Mace tastes like nutmeg but is more intense; if you can't find mace in the spice aisle at your supermarket, you can substitute nutmeg. This is one of the times when using a canned product is better than using fresh: Pure canned pumpkin is actually good-quality pumpkin—very similar to fresh pumpkin, but without the seeds and the mess. Whisk some rum into sweetened whipped cream and add a dollop to each piece of pie.

10 SERVINGS

Crust

- **1½ cups all purpose flour**
- **½ teaspoon salt**
- **5 tablespoons chilled unsalted butter, cut into ½-inch cubes**
- **3 tablespoons chilled solid vegetable shortening, cut into ½-inch cubes**
- **3 to 4 tablespoons ice water**

Filling

- **1 15-ounce can pure pumpkin**
- **½ cup (packed) dark brown sugar**
- **¼ cup sugar**
- **1 tablespoon all purpose flour**
- **1 teaspoon ground cinnamon**
- **½ teaspoon salt**
- **½ teaspoon ground mace**
- **½ teaspoon ground ginger**
- **¼ teaspoon ground allspice**
- **¼ teaspoon ground cloves**
- **3 large eggs**
- **1 cup whipping cream**
- **¼ cup whole milk**
- **3 tablespoons dark rum**
- **1½ teaspoons vanilla extract**

FOR CRUST: Blend flour and salt in processor. Add butter and shortening; process until mixture resembles coarse meal. With machine running, add ice water 1 tablespoonful at a time and process until moist clumps form. Gather dough into ball; flatten into disk. Wrap in plastic and chill 30 minutes. *(Can be prepared 2 days ahead. Keep chilled.)*

ROLL out dough on lightly floured surface to 13-inch round. Transfer to 10-inch-diameter glass pie dish. Fold edge under and crimp decoratively. Pierce crust all over with fork. Freeze 30 minutes.

PREHEAT oven to 450°F. Bake crust until pale golden, pressing with back of fork if bubbles form, about 15 minutes. Transfer to rack and cool. Reduce oven temperature to 375°F.

MEANWHILE, PREPARE FILLING: Whisk first 10 ingredients in large bowl until smooth. Whisk in all remaining ingredients until well blended. Pour filling into crust.

BAKE pie 20 minutes. Reduce oven temperature to 325°F. Bake until filling no longer moves in center when dish is shaken, about 30 minutes longer. Transfer pie to rack and cool completely. *(Can be made 1 day ahead. Cover and refrigerate. Bring to room temperature before serving.)*

Mocha pecan pie with coffee whipped cream

TAKE THE CLASSIC decadent pecan pie, then add chocolate (in the form of cocoa powder) and coffee (in the form of espresso powder). Look for espresso powder in the coffee aisle near the instant coffee powder (which you can substitute if need be). Savor this dessert with a good cup of coffee or a mocha made with some grated Mexican chocolate, which carries hints of almonds and cinnamon.

10 SERVINGS

Crust

- **1¼ cups all purpose flour**
- **1 tablespoon grated orange peel**
- **1 teaspoon sugar**
- **¼ teaspoon salt**
- **¼ cup (½ stick) chilled unsalted butter, cut into ½-inch cubes**
- **¼ cup chilled solid vegetable shortening, cut into ½-inch cubes**
- **1 tablespoon orange juice**
- **2 tablespoons (about) ice water**

Filling

- **3 tablespoons unsalted butter**
- **3 tablespoons unsweetened cocoa powder**
- **1 tablespoon whipping cream**
- **2 teaspoons instant espresso powder or instant coffee powder**
- **1 cup light corn syrup**
- **1 cup sugar**
- **3 large eggs**
- **2 teaspoons vanilla extract**
- **¼ teaspoon salt**
- **1½ cups coarsely chopped pecans**

Coffee Whipped Cream (see recipe)

FOR CRUST: Combine first 4 ingredients in processor. Using on/off turns, cut in butter and shortening until mixture resembles coarse meal. Blend in orange juice; add enough water by tablespoonfuls to form moist clumps. Gather dough into ball; flatten into disk. Wrap in plastic and chill 1 hour. *(Can be prepared 1 day ahead. Keep refrigerated. Soften dough slightly at room temperature before rolling out.)*

PREHEAT oven to 350°F. Roll out dough on lightly floured surface to 12-inch-diameter round. Transfer to 9-inch-diameter glass pie dish. Trim edges and crimp decoratively. Freeze crust 15 minutes. Line crust with aluminum foil; fill with dried beans or pie weights. Bake 15 minutes. Remove foil and beans. Bake crust until pale golden, about 10 minutes. Cool on rack.

FOR FILLING: Melt butter in heavy small saucepan over medium heat. Stir in cocoa, then cream and espresso powder. Transfer to large bowl. Add corn syrup, sugar, eggs, vanilla, and salt; whisk until well blended. Stir in pecans.

POUR filling into pie crust. Bake until puffed and set, about 1 hour. Transfer to rack and cool completely. *(Can be prepared 1 day ahead. Cover and let stand at room temperature.)* Serve with Coffee Whipped Cream.

Coffee whipped cream

WHO KNEW coffee liqueur could make whipped cream taste so good? Using an electric mixer (either handheld or a standing mixer) will make quick work of this topping.

MAKES ABOUT 2 CUPS

- **1 cup chilled whipping cream**
- **3 tablespoons coffee liqueur**
- **1 tablespoon powdered sugar**

POUR chilled cream into medium bowl. Beat until soft peaks form. Add coffee liqueur and powdered sugar and beat until stiff peaks form.

Pecan, caramel, and fudge pie

THIS PIE is as easy as (1) a no-bake, press-in crust, (2) a filling that bakes for only ten minutes, (3) a scoop of chocolate, vanilla, or butter pecan ice cream alongside. And it is versatile enough to end a fancy steak dinner or a kids' burgers-and-fries birthday party.

8 SERVINGS

Crust

- **1½ cups chocolate wafer cookie crumbs (about 7 ounces)**
- **5 tablespoons unsalted butter, melted**
- **½ teaspoon vanilla extract**

Filling

- **¾ cup (1½ sticks) unsalted butter**
- **¾ cup (packed) golden brown sugar**
- **6 tablespoons light corn syrup**
- **3 cups pecan halves**
- **3 tablespoons whipping cream**
- **2 ounces unsweetened chocolate, chopped**

FOR CRUST: Blend all ingredients in processor. Using plastic wrap as aid, press crumb mixture over bottom and up sides of 9-inch-diameter glass pie dish. Freeze while preparing filling. *(Crust can be prepared 1 week ahead. Cover and keep frozen.)*

FOR FILLING: Preheat oven to 350°F. Combine butter, brown sugar, and corn syrup in heavy medium saucepan. Bring to boil, stirring often. Boil 1 minute. Stir in nuts and cream. Boil until mixture thickens slightly, about 3 minutes longer. Remove from heat. Add chocolate and stir until chocolate melts and mixture is well blended.

POUR hot filling into crust. Using spoon, distribute nuts evenly. Bake until filling is bubbling all over, about 10 minutes. Transfer pie to rack and cool.

Marshmallow black-bottom pie

BLACK-BOTTOM PIE is usually dark chocolate custard topped with rum custard. Here the latter is replaced by a billowy pile of homemade marshmallow topping. The name *marshmallow* comes from the root of a plant of the same name, the extract of which used to be made into a sweet, sticky confection. Today marshmallows are made with corn syrup, sugar, water, and gelatin. You'll need a candy thermometer to monitor the marshmallow topping while it cooks. Always ready for a party, this pie can be made a day ahead and chilled; just let it stand one hour at room temperature before serving (it needs to soften a bit).

8 SERVINGS

Crust

- **1½ cups all purpose flour**
- **5 tablespoons chilled unsalted butter, cut into ½-inch cubes**
- **¼ cup chilled solid vegetable shortening, cut into ½-inch cubes**
- **1 tablespoon sugar**
- **¼ teaspoon salt**
- **3 tablespoons (or more) ice water**

Filling

- **½ cup sugar**
- **¼ cup cornstarch**
- **1 tablespoon unsweetened cocoa powder**
- **⅛ teaspoon salt**
- **4 large egg yolks**
- **2 cups whole milk**
- **½ cup whipping cream**
- **5 ounces bittersweet (not unsweetened) or semisweet chocolate, chopped**
- **1 tablespoon unsalted butter**
- **1 teaspoon vanilla extract**

Marshmallow topping

- **1 tablespoon plus ⅓ cup water**
- **½ teaspoon unflavored gelatin**

- 1 cup sugar
- ⅓ cup light corn syrup
- 4 large egg whites (about ½ cup)
- 1 teaspoon vanilla extract
- Chocolate shavings (optional)

FOR CRUST: Combine flour, butter, vegetable shortening, sugar, and salt in processor. Using on/off turns, blend until mixture resembles coarse meal. Add 3 tablespoons ice water and blend until moist clumps form, adding more water by teaspoonfuls if dough is dry. Gather dough into ball. Flatten into disk. Wrap dough disk in plastic and refrigerate at least 1 hour. *(Can be prepared 1 day ahead. Keep refrigerated.)*

PREHEAT oven to 375°F. Roll out dough on lightly floured surface to 13- to 14-inch round. Transfer dough to 9½-inch-diameter deep-dish glass pie dish Fold dough edge under and crimp decoratively, securing dough edge to rim of dish. Pierce crust all over with fork. Freeze crust 15 minutes. Bake until golden brown, pressing with back of fork if bubbles form or crust slips, about 30 minutes. Transfer crust to rack and cool

FOR FILLING: Whisk sugar, cornstarch, cocoa, and salt in heavy medium saucepan to blend. Add egg yolks, milk, and cream; whisk until smooth. Whisk over medium heat until mixture thickens and boils, about 6 minutes. Remove from heat. Add chocolate, butter, and vanilla; whisk until melted and smooth. Pour filling into crust. Cool on rack.

FOR MARSHMALLOW TOPPING: Pour 1 tablespoon water into small heatproof cup; sprinkle gelatin over. Place cup in small skillet; add enough water to skillet to reach depth of ½ inch.

WHISK sugar, corn syrup, and remaining ⅓ cup water in heavy medium saucepan to blend. Bring to boil over medium heat, stirring until sugar dissolves. Attach candy thermometer to side of pan. Boil without stirring until candy thermometer registers 240°F. While continuing to boil syrup, beat egg whites in large bowl with electric mixer until stiff peaks form. When thermometer in syrup registers 248°F, slowly beat hot syrup into egg whites. Continue to beat until whites are stiff and glossy, about 4 minutes. Beat in vanilla.

BRING water in skillet to simmer. Stir gelatin mixture in cup until gelatin dissolves. Gradually pour gelatin over egg whites and beat until topping is cool, about 8 minutes. Using rubber spatula, gently spread marshmallow topping over filling, making decorative peaks.

PREHEAT broiler. Broil pie just until topping is light brown, about 1 minute. Chill pie 1 hour. Garnish with chocolate shavings, if desired. *(Can be made 1 day ahead. Keep refrigerated. Let stand at room temperature 1 hour before serving.)*

Black-bottom banana cream pie

THE THEME HERE is "no baking": Melted chocolate and cookie crumbs are mixed and chilled for a crisp, press-in crust; the crust is then topped with a thin layer of silky chocolate ganache, followed by sliced bananas and vanilla pastry cream. And all of this is done on the stove, not in the oven—just the right recipe for a hot summer day. To create an eye-catching marbled effect, drizzle a little extra chocolate ganache in a fairly tight horizontal zigzag pattern atop the pastry cream, then use a toothpick to draw lines gently in the opposite direction. Your guests won't believe this treat didn't come from the bakery.

8 SERVINGS

Crust

- ½ cup (1 stick) unsalted butter
- 3 ounces semisweet chocolate, chopped
- 1½ cups chocolate wafer cookie crumbs (about 7 ounces)

Chocolate ganache
½ **cup whipping cream**
1 **tablespoon unsalted butter**
4 **ounces semisweet chocolate, chopped**
½ **teaspoon vanilla extract**

4 **ripe bananas (about 1½ pounds), divided**
Vanilla Pastry Cream (see recipe)
Vanilla Whipped Cream (see recipe)

FOR CRUST: Butter 9-inch-diameter glass or ceramic pie dish. Stir butter and chocolate in heavy small saucepan over low heat until melted and smooth. Mix in cookie crumbs. Using plastic wrap as aid, press crumb mixture over bottom and up sides of prepared dish. Chill until crust is firm, about 30 minutes.

FOR CHOCOLATE GANACHE: Heat cream and butter in medium saucepan over medium heat until mixture is hot (do not boil). Remove from heat. Add chocolate and vanilla. Whisk until chocolate is melted and smooth. Reserve 2 tablespoons chocolate ganache in small bowl at room temperature; pour remainder over crust. Chill crust until chocolate ganache is firm, about 30 minutes.

THINLY slice 3 bananas. Arrange banana slices over chocolate. Whisk Vanilla Pastry Cream until smooth. Spread pastry cream evenly over bananas. Drizzle reserved chocolate ganache over pastry cream. Draw toothpick through pastry cream and chocolate to create marbled effect. Refrigerate until pastry cream is set, about 3 hours. *(Can be prepared 1 day ahead. Cover and keep refrigerated.)*

SPOON Vanilla Whipped Cream around edges of pie, or spoon whipped cream into pastry bag fitted with large star tip and pipe cream around edges of pie. Slice remaining banana; garnish pie with slices.

Vanilla pastry cream

PASTRY CREAM is a dreamy sweetened custard of egg yolk and cream (or milk) that's also used as the filling for éclairs and napoleons.

MAKES ABOUT 2 CUPS

1½ **cups half and half**
½ **cup sugar**
2 **large eggs**
1 **large egg yolk**
2 **tablespoons all purpose flour**
2 **teaspoons vanilla extract**

BRING half and half to simmer in heavy medium saucepan. Whisk sugar, eggs, egg yolk, and flour in medium bowl to blend. Gradually whisk in hot half and half. Transfer to same saucepan. Whisk over medium heat until mixture thickens and comes to boil, about 5 minutes. Boil 1 minute. Pour into medium bowl. Stir in vanilla. Press plastic wrap directly onto surface of pastry cream. Cover and chill until cold, about 4 hours. *(Can be prepared 1 day ahead. Keep chilled.)*

Vanilla whipped cream

A DASH OF VANILLA EXTRACT adds a heady note to this whipped cream.

MAKES ABOUT 1¾ CUPS

1 **cup chilled whipping cream**
1 **tablespoon powdered sugar**
½ **teaspoon vanilla extract**

BEAT cream, powdered sugar, and vanilla in large bowl until stiff peaks form. *(Can be prepared 4 hours ahead. Cover and chill.)*

Chocolate Cake with Caramel–Milk Chocolate Frosting (page 509)

Cranberry-Orange Cheesecake with Chocolate Crust (page 532)

Cherry-Berry Lattice Pie (page 569)

Raspberry-Topped Chocolate Tartlets with Pecan Crusts (page 596)

Lemon Curd Mousse with Toasted Coconut and Blueberries (page 627)

Caramelized-Nectarine and Ginger Shortcakes with Sour Cream (page 637)

S'mores Sundaes (page 669)

Chocolate-Dipped Orange and Ginger Florentines (page 696)
Rolled Vanilla Tuiles (page 706)
Classic Bittersweet Chocolate Fudge (page 731)

Lemon meringue pie with hazelnut shortbread crust

THIS SOUPED-UP lemon meringue pie features a buttery shortbread hazelnut crust. (*Short* simply refers to the high proportion of butter to flour in a dough, and the ratio here, combined with the ground hazelnuts, results in an incredibly buttery, dense, cookie-like crust.) Meringue looks fancy, but it's a cinch to make: Egg whites, sugar, and cream of tartar are beaten until stiff peaks form. Stop while the egg whites are still glossy; they shouldn't look dry. Cream of tartar—the white, acidic deposit that forms on the inside of wine barrels—promotes a stable, uniform meringue consistency. Use an offset spatula to spread the meringue on top of the lemon filling, sealing it completely to the edge of the crust so that it doesn't shrink while baking.

8 TO 10 SERVINGS

Crust

- **1/3 cup hazelnuts, toasted, skinned**
- **1 1/4 cups all purpose flour**
- **1/2 cup (1 stick) unsalted butter, cut into 6 pieces, room temperature**
- **1/3 cup powdered sugar**
- **1 large egg yolk**
- **1 tablespoon grated lemon peel**
- **1/2 teaspoon salt**

Filling

- **1 1/2 cups water**
- **1 cup sugar**
- **1/2 cup fresh lemon juice**
- **6 large egg yolks**
- **5 tablespoons cornstarch**
- **2 tablespoons grated lemon peel**
- **1/4 teaspoon salt**
- **2 tablespoons (1/4 stick) unsalted butter**

Meringue

- **7 large egg whites**
- **1/2 teaspoon cream of tartar**
- **1 2/3 cups powdered sugar**

FOR CRUST: Grind nuts fine in processor. Add flour and blend well. Add remaining ingredients; using on/off turns, process just until moist clumps form. Turn dough out onto lightly floured surface. Gather dough into ball; flatten into disk. Wrap in plastic and chill until firm enough to roll out, about 45 minutes.

POSITION rack in center of oven and preheat to 325°F. Roll out dough between sheets of parchment paper to 12-inch round, turning over occasionally to lift and smooth paper. Peel off top sheet of paper. Using bottom paper as aid, invert dough into 9-inch-diameter glass pie dish. Peel off paper. Press dough gently into dish. Fold overhang under; crimp to form decorative edge. Pierce crust all over with fork. Chill 15 minutes.

LINE crust with aluminum foil. Fill with dried beans or pie weights. Bake crust until sides are set, about 15 minutes. Remove foil and beans. Bake until crust is pale golden, about 20 minutes longer. Transfer crust to rack and cool completely. Reduce oven temperature to 300°F.

FOR FILLING: Whisk first 7 ingredients in heavy medium saucepan to blend. Using whisk, stir over medium heat until filling thickens and just begins to boil, about 8 to 10 minutes. Remove from heat. Whisk in butter. Spoon hot filling into prepared crust.

FOR MERINGUE: Using electric mixer, beat egg whites in large stainless steel bowl at low speed until foamy. Beat in cream of tartar and 1 tablespoon powdered sugar. Gradually beat in remaining powdered sugar, 1 tablespoon at a time. Beat at medium speed until stiff glossy peaks form, about 8 minutes. Spread meringue over warm filling, covering completely, sealing meringue to crust edges, and mounding in center.

BAKE pie 30 minutes. Reduce oven temperature to 275°F and continue to bake until meringue is golden brown and set when pie is shaken slightly, about 50 minutes longer. Transfer pie to rack and cool completely, about 4 hours. *(Can be made 1 day ahead. Refrigerate uncovered.)*

Tarts

Chocolate-mint tart

THIS DESSERT is like a giant, sophisticated after-dinner mint. Peppermint extract contributes intense peppermint flavor, which could be complemented by a fresh mint garnish. Baking the crust "blind" (baking it until it browns and sets before any filling goes in) helps keep the creamy chocolate ganache from penetrating the crust and making it soggy. Today's two-for-one special: The same delectable ganache supplies the filling and the shiny glaze.

12 SERVINGS

Crust

- **1 cup unbleached all purpose flour**
- **½ cup powdered sugar**
- **¼ cup cake flour**
- **½ teaspoon baking powder**
- **⅛ teaspoon salt**
- **½ cup (1 stick) chilled unsalted butter, cut into ½-inch cubes**
- **1 large egg, beaten to blend**

Filling

- **1¼ cups whipping cream**
- **3 tablespoons unsalted butter**
- **2 tablespoons sugar**
- **1¼ pounds semisweet chocolate, chopped**
- **1¾ teaspoons peppermint extract**
- **1½ teaspoons vanilla extract**

FOR CRUST: Butter 11-inch-diameter tart pan with removable bottom. Sift unbleached flour, powdered sugar, cake flour, baking powder, and salt into large bowl. Add butter and rub in with fingertips until mixture resembles coarse meal. Add egg. Stir until moist clumps form. Gather dough into ball; flatten into disk. Wrap in plastic and freeze 10 minutes.

PREHEAT oven to 400°F. Roll out dough on floured surface to 14-inch round. Transfer dough to prepared pan. Press dough gently into pan. Trim overhang to ½ inch. Fold overhang in and press, forming double-thick sides. Freeze crust until firm, about 20 minutes.

LINE crust with aluminum foil. Fill with dried beans or pie weights. Bake until sides are set, about 15 minutes. Remove foil and beans. Reduce oven temperature to 350°F. Bake crust until golden brown, about 20 minutes. Cool crust completely.

FOR FILLING: Combine cream, butter, and sugar in heavy large saucepan. Stir over medium heat until butter melts, sugar dissolves, and mixture comes to simmer. Remove from heat. Add chocolate and both extracts. Stir until chocolate melts and mixture is smooth. Pour 1 cup filling into heavy small saucepan and reserve for glaze. Pour remaining filling into medium bowl. Chill until thickened but still spreadable, stirring occasionally, about 1 hour.

WHISK cold filling just until color lightens, about 2 minutes. Spoon into crust. Chill until filling is firm, about 30 minutes.

Stir reserved 1 cup filling over low heat until just lukewarm. Spread over filling in crust to glaze tart. Chill until glaze sets, about 1 hour. *(Tart can be made 2 days ahead. Cover and keep chilled.)* Push up pan bottom to release tart. Serve tart cold.

Dark chocolate and orange tart with toasted almonds

REMINISCENT OF Mexican chocolate, with its cinnamon and almonds, this tart would be great with cinnamon ice cream. Jewel-toned candied orange peel goes into the filling and also does a beautiful job as garnish. The tart can be made a day ahead of time.

12 SERVINGS

Candied orange peel

- **1 orange**
- **¼ cup sugar**
- **2 tablespoons water**

Crust

- **½ cup (1 stick) unsalted butter, room temperature**
- **½ cup sugar**
- **¼ teaspoon ground cinnamon**
- **¼ teaspoon salt**
- **6 tablespoons unsweetened cocoa powder**
- **¾ cup all purpose flour**

Filling

- **1 cup slivered almonds, toasted, coarsely chopped**
- **2 teaspoons sugar**
- **1 teaspoon ground cinnamon**
- **1 cup heavy whipping cream**
- **8 ounces bittersweet (not unsweetened) or semisweet chocolate, chopped**
- **1 tablespoon Grand Marnier or other orange liqueur**

FOR CANDIED ORANGE PEEL: Using swivel-bladed vegetable peeler, remove peel (orange part only) from orange in strips. Cut strips into matchstick-size pieces and place in small saucepan. Add enough cold water to cover; bring to boil. Cook 30 seconds; drain. Rinse saucepan; add sugar, 2 tablespoons water, and peel. Stir over medium-low heat until sugar dissolves. Simmer until peel is translucent and syrup is thick, about 20 minutes. Using tines of fork, transfer peel to plate and cool. *(Can be made 1 day ahead. Cover and store at room temperature.)*

FOR CRUST: Using electric mixer, beat butter, sugar, cinnamon, and salt in large bowl until smooth. Beat in cocoa powder. Add flour and beat until dough comes together in moist clumps. Gather dough into ball; flatten into disk. Wrap in plastic and chill until firm, at least 1 hour. *(Can be prepared 1 day ahead. Keep chilled.)*

ROLL out dough between sheets of parchment paper to 11-inch round. Peel off top sheet of parchment. Invert dough into 9-inch-diameter tart pan with removable bottom; peel off remaining sheet. Gently press dough into pan. Press dough overhang in to form double-thick sides. Pierce dough all over with fork. Refrigerate 30 minutes.

PREHEAT oven to 375°F. Bake crust until sides look dry and bubbles form on bottom, about 14 minutes. Transfer crust to rack. Using back of spoon, press up sides of dough if slipping. Cool completely.

FOR FILLING: Toss almonds, sugar, and cinnamon in small bowl. Chop all but 2 strips of orange peel. Sprinkle chopped orange peel, then almond mixture over bottom of prepared crust. Bring cream to simmer in heavy medium saucepan. Remove from heat; add chocolate and whisk until chocolate melts and mixture is smooth. Mix in Grand Marnier. Pour filling into crust. Refrigerate until filling is firm, at least 3 hours. Garnish with remaining 2 orange peel strips. *(Tart can be made 1 day ahead. Cover loosely with aluminum foil and keep refrigerated.)*

USING small sharp knife, gently loosen crust from pan sides. Push up pan bottom to release tart. Cut tart into wedges and serve cold.

Chocolate-caramel tart

THE FILLING IS GANACHE in its simplest form: velvety chocolate and cream. Make sure to caramelize the sugar mixture until it reaches a true amber color, not just gold; it will have more flavor that way. And as the recipe says, adding the cream and butter to the hot syrup will cause the mixture to bubble vigorously—don't be alarmed. A bit of the ganache is reserved to be piped or drizzled decoratively over the top, so now's the time to get creative.

12 SERVINGS

Crust

- **1 cup all purpose flour**
- **3 tablespoons sugar**
- **1 teaspoon grated lemon peel**
- **⅛ teaspoon salt**
- **½ cup (1 stick) chilled unsalted butter, cut into ½-inch cubes**
- **1 large egg yolk**
- **½ teaspoon vanilla extract**

Chocolate filling

- **¾ cup whipping cream**
- **6 ounces bittersweet (not unsweetened) or semisweet chocolate, finely chopped**

Caramel filling

- **¾ cup sugar**
- **⅓ cup water**
- **⅓ cup whipping cream**
- **5 tablespoons unsalted butter**
- **½ teaspoon vanilla extract**
- **Pinch of salt**

FOR CRUST: Blend flour, sugar, lemon peel, and salt in processor 5 seconds. Add butter, egg yolk, and vanilla; process until large moist clumps form. Gather dough into ball; knead briefly to combine well. Flatten into disk. Wrap in plastic and chill until firm enough to roll out, about 30 minutes.

PREHEAT oven to 400°F. Roll out dough between sheets of parchment paper to 11- to 12-inch round. Peel off top sheet of parchment. Turn dough over; press into 9-inch-diameter tart pan with removable bottom. Peel off parchment. Fold in any excess dough, forming double-thick sides. Pierce crust all over with fork. Freeze 15 minutes.

BAKE crust 10 minutes. Using back of fork, press crust flat if bubbles form on bottom. Continue to bake until crust is golden, about 10 minutes (crust sides may shrink slightly). Transfer to rack and cool.

FOR CHOCOLATE FILLING: Bring cream to boil in heavy small saucepan. Remove pan from heat. Add chocolate and whisk until melted and smooth. Spread 1 cup chocolate filling in prepared crust. Refrigerate until firm, about 45 minutes. Reserve remaining filling in saucepan.

FOR CARAMEL FILLING: Stir sugar and ⅓ cup water in heavy medium saucepan over low heat until sugar dissolves. Increase heat and boil without stirring until syrup is deep amber color, occasionally brushing down sides with wet pastry brush and swirling pan, about 8 minutes. Remove from heat. Add cream, butter, vanilla, and salt (mixture will bubble vigorously). Return pan to very low heat; stir until any caramel bits dissolve, mixture is smooth, and color deepens, about 5 minutes. Refrigerate uncovered until cold but not firm, about 20 minutes.

SPOON caramel filling over chocolate filling. Pipe or drizzle reserved chocolate filling decoratively over caramel (if chocolate is too firm to pour, warm slightly over low heat). Refrigerate tart until caramel is firm, at least 1 hour. *(Can be made 2 days ahead. Cover and keep chilled.)* Push up pan bottom to release tart.

Caramel-banana tart

A SCOOP OF ICE CREAM would make this even more like a banana split. The cookie-like crust is achieved by combining room-temperature butter with sugar.

8 SERVINGS

Crust

- **½ cup (1 stick) unsalted butter, room temperature**
- **¼ cup sugar**
- **1 large egg yolk**
- **1 teaspoon vanilla extract**
- **¼ teaspoon salt**
- **1 cup all purpose flour**

Bananas

- **½ cup plus 1 tablespoon sugar**
- **1 tablespoon light corn syrup**
- **2 tablespoons (¼ stick) unsalted butter, melted, divided**
- **4 large ripe bananas, thinly sliced on diagonal**
- **1 cup chopped lightly toasted macadamia nuts**

FOR CRUST: Using electric mixer, beat butter and sugar in large bowl to blend. Add egg yolk, vanilla, and salt; beat until well blended. Add flour and beat until moist clumps form. Using plastic wrap as aid, press dough evenly over bottom (not sides) of 9-inch-diameter tart pan with removable bottom. Pierce with fork in several places; refrigerate 1 hour.

PREHEAT oven to 450°F. Bake crust until golden, about 15 minutes. Cool on rack.

FOR BANANAS: Fill metal baking pan halfway with ice water. Stir ½ cup sugar, corn syrup, and 1 tablespoon melted butter in heavy small saucepan over medium-low heat until sugar dissolves and mixture boils. Boil without stirring until mixture is medium amber color, occasionally brushing down sides of pan with wet pastry brush and swirling pan, about 7 minutes. Place saucepan in baking pan of ice water to prevent further cooking and to cool caramel to lukewarm.

PREHEAT oven to 375°F. Overlap banana slices on crust, covering completely. Brush remaining 1 tablespoon melted butter over bananas. Sprinkle with remaining 1 tablespoon sugar. Bake until just warmed through, about 3 minutes.

REWARM caramel over low heat, stirring occasionally. Drizzle caramel over bananas; sprinkle with toasted macadamia nuts. Let tart stand until caramel hardens, about 2 minutes. Push up pan bottom to release tart. Transfer tart to platter and serve.

Rustic apple tart with honey, dates, and nuts

THE "RUSTIC" IN THE TITLE comes from the form of the crust: It's just loosely folded and gathered around the filling to hold it in. The nuts are chopped, then sprinkled over the rolled-out dough and pressed in with a rolling pin, to beautiful effect. Medjool dates are at their peak in fall and winter; you'll find them in the produce section of supermarkets and at Middle Eastern and natural foods stores. Any variety of dates will work, though. Here's a tip: To keep the dates from sticking to your knife when you cut them, lightly dust the knife with flour beforehand. Raw sugar, also called turbinado or demerara sugar, is available at natural foods stores and most supermarkets.

8 SERVINGS

Crust

- **1⅓ cups all purpose flour**
- **½ teaspoon salt**
- **½ teaspoon sugar**
- **¼ cup (½ stick) chilled unsalted butter, cut into ½-inch cubes**
- **¼ cup solid vegetable shortening, frozen, then cut into ½-inch cubes**
- **3 tablespoons (or more) ice water**
- **½ teaspoon apple cider vinegar**

Filling

3 tablespoons butter
8 small Granny Smith apples (about 3 pounds), peeled, quartered, cored, each cut into 12 slices
2 teaspoons ground cardamom
⅓ cup plus 2 tablespoons honey

⅔ cup chopped assorted nuts (such as walnuts, almonds, and pistachios)
7 large Medjool dates, pitted, quartered lengthwise
1 large egg
2 tablespoons whole milk
3 tablespoons raw sugar

1 cup chilled whipping cream

FOR CRUST: Whisk flour, salt, and sugar in large bowl to blend. Add butter and shortening; rub in with fingertips until mixture resembles coarse meal. Mix 3 tablespoons ice water and vinegar in small bowl. Pour over flour mixture. Stir with fork until moist clumps form, adding more water by teaspoonfuls if dough is dry. Gather dough into ball; flatten into disk. Wrap in plastic and refrigerate at least 30 minutes. *(Can be prepared 1 day ahead. Keep chilled.)*

FOR FILLING: Melt butter in heavy large skillet over medium-high heat. Add apples and sauté until brown and almost tender, about 15 minutes. Reduce heat to medium; mix in cardamom. Pour ⅓ cup honey over and cook 1 minute.

POSITION rack in top third of oven and preheat to 400°F. Roll out dough between 2 sheets of parchment paper to 12-inch round. Remove top sheet of parchment. Sprinkle crust evenly with nuts. Replace parchment atop crust and roll out to 13-inch round, embedding nuts in dough (crust will be thin). Invert crust onto rimless baking sheet. Remove top sheet of parchment. Spoon half of apple mixture over crust, leaving 2-inch plain border. Sprinkle dates over apples. Top with remaining apple mixture. Using parchment as aid, fold outer edge of crust over apples (dough will be delicate; press together any tears). Whisk egg and milk in bowl to blend. Brush crust edges generously with egg glaze. Sprinkle crust and apples with raw sugar.

BAKE tart until crust begins to brown, about 15 minutes. Reduce heat to 375°F; bake until crust is golden brown, about 10 minutes longer. Loosen tart from parchment paper with spatula. Cool on baking sheet until warm, about 45 minutes.

BEAT cream and remaining 2 tablespoons honey in medium bowl until peaks form.

SLIDE 9-inch-diameter removable tart pan bottom under tart and transfer to platter. Serve with honeyed whipped cream.

Country apple tart with spiced brown butter

THIS RECIPE gets its sultry flavors from steeping whole spices—cloves, star anise, and cinnamon—in simmering butter. In general terms, spices tend to be dried, and are usually the seed, pod, bark, or bud of a plant or tree, whereas herbs are most often leaves. Cloves are dried flower buds, star anise is a dried seedpod, and cinnamon sticks are pieces of tree bark. Look for whole star anise at Asian and Indian markets, at specialty foods stores, or in the spice aisle of well-stocked supermarkets. You can prepare the crust and the roasted apples a day ahead.

12 SERVINGS

Crust

1¾ cups all purpose flour
¼ cup sugar
¼ teaspoon salt
¾ cup (1½ sticks) chilled unsalted butter, cut into ½-inch cubes
2 large egg yolks, beaten to blend

Nonstick vegetable oil spray

Apples

- **Nonstick vegetable oil spray**
- **5½ pounds medium Braeburn or Golden Delicious apples (about 15), peeled, quartered, cored**
- **5 tablespoons unsalted butter, melted**
- **2 tablespoons fresh lemon juice**
- **6 tablespoons sugar**

Spiced brown butter

- **½ cup (1 stick) unsalted butter**
- **1 large vanilla bean, split lengthwise**
- **6 whole cloves**
- **3 whole star anise**
- **1 cinnamon stick**

- **2 large eggs**
- **½ cup sugar**
- **3 tablespoons all purpose flour**
- **⅛ teaspoon salt**

Vanilla ice cream

FOR CRUST: Blend flour, sugar, and salt in processor 10 seconds. Add butter; using on/off turns, cut in until mixture resembles coarse meal. Add egg yolks; using on/off turns, process until dough comes together in large moist clumps. Gather dough into ball; flatten into disk. Wrap in plastic and chill 20 minutes.

SPRAY 10-inch-diameter springform pan with nonstick spray. Divide dough in half. Roll out 1 dough piece on generously floured surface to 10½-inch round. Roll up dough on rolling pin and transfer to pan. Press dough into bottom of pan, patching any cracks in dough. Divide second dough piece into 4 equal pieces. Roll out each piece between palms and generously floured surface to 7-inch rope. Place dough ropes end-to-end to form 1 continuous ring around bottom edge of pan. Press dough ring firmly up sides of pan, forming 1¾-inch-high sides. Press dough seams together to seal. Cover and refrigerate overnight.

PREHEAT oven to 400°F. Bake crust until just set and very light golden around edge, about 10 minutes. Let stand to cool.

FOR APPLES: Position 1 rack in bottom third of oven and 1 rack in center; preheat to 400°F. Spray 2 heavy large rimmed baking sheets with nonstick spray. Toss apples with melted butter and lemon juice in very large bowl. Arrange in single layer on prepared sheets, leaving spaces between apples. Sprinkle 3 tablespoons sugar over apples on each sheet. Bake until apples are tender and golden brown, turning apples occasionally and reversing position of pans halfway through, about 40 minutes. Cool. *(Crust and apples can be prepared 1 day ahead. Cover crust and store at room temperature. Transfer apples to bowl. Cover and refrigerate.)*

PLACE pan with crust on clean baking sheet. Arrange apple wedges close together, standing on short ends, in concentric circles in crust.

FOR SPICED BROWN BUTTER: Melt butter in heavy small saucepan over low heat. Scrape in seeds from vanilla bean; add pod. Add cloves, star anise, and cinnamon stick. Cook over low heat until butter turns golden brown and spices flavor butter, adjusting heat if necessary to prevent burning and stirring frequently, about 25 minutes.

PREHEAT oven to 350°F. Whisk eggs, sugar, flour, and salt to blend in medium bowl. Strain spiced brown butter mixture into egg mixture; whisk to blend. Reserve vanilla bean, star anise, and cinnamon stick; discard cloves. Slowly pour egg mixture over apples in crust. Bake until egg mixture is set, puffed, and light golden and apples are deep golden brown, about 1 hour 5 minutes. Cool on rack at least 30 minutes. *(Tart can be made 8 hours ahead. Let stand at room temperature.)*

RELEASE pan sides. Transfer tart to platter. Garnish tart with reserved vanilla bean, star anise, and cinnamon stick, if desired. Serve tart slightly warm or at room temperature with ice cream.

Tarte Tatin

THIS BRILLIANT DESSERT was created by the Tatin sisters, who lived in France's Loire Valley and made a living selling the treat. *Tarte Tatin* is such an iconic, spectacular dessert that some people spend a lifetime perfecting their recipe and technique. Luckily, this recipe will save you the time. An ovenproof nonstick skillet (one with a metal handle) is essential, as the apples are browned and caramelized on the stove, then the crust is added to the skillet, and the whole thing is placed in the oven to bake. A dollop of crème fraîche or sour cream adds a savory counterpoint. You can always go with vanilla ice cream, though.

10 TO 12 SERVINGS

Sour cream pastry

- **1½ cups all purpose flour**
- **2 tablespoons sugar**
- **½ teaspoon salt**
- **¾ cup (1½ sticks) chilled unsalted butter, cut into ¾-inch cubes**
- **6 tablespoons chilled sour cream**

Apple filling

- **½ cup (1 stick) plus 1 tablespoon unsalted butter, room temperature**
- **1½ cups sugar, divided**
- **11 medium Pippin or Granny Smith apples (about 4¾ pounds), peeled, quartered, cored**
- **1 egg, beaten to blend (for glaze)**
- **Crème fraîche or sour cream**

FOR SOUR CREAM PASTRY: Blend flour, sugar, and salt in large bowl of heavy-duty mixer fitted with whisk attachment. Add butter and beat at medium-low speed until butter is size of small lima beans, about 3 minutes. Add sour cream and beat until moist clumps form, about 1 minute. Gather dough into smooth ball; flatten into 6-inch-diameter disk. Wrap dough in plastic and refrigerate until cold, at least 2 hours. *(Can be prepared 1 day ahead. Keep refrigerated. Let soften slightly before rolling out.)*

FOR APPLE FILLING: Spread butter over bottom of 12-inch-diameter ovenproof nonstick skillet with sloping sides (skillet should be at least 1¾ inches deep). Reserve 2 tablespoons sugar; sprinkle remaining sugar over butter. Place skillet over medium-low heat and cook until butter melts, sugar begins to dissolve, and mixture starts to bubble, about 3 minutes.

REMOVE from heat. Arrange apples on their sides around edge of skillet, placing tightly together. Arrange as many of remaining apples as will fit, pointed ends up, in 2 circles in center of skillet. Sprinkle with reserved 2 tablespoons sugar.

SET skillet over medium-high heat; boil until thick peanut butter–color syrup forms, repositioning skillet often for even cooking and adding remaining apples as space permits, about 45 minutes (syrup will continue to darken during baking). Remove from heat.

MEANWHILE, position rack in center of oven and preheat to 425°F.

ROLL out pastry on floured surface to 12-inch round; place over apples. Cut four 2-inch slits in top of pastry. Press pastry down around apples at edge of skillet; brush pastry with egg glaze.

BAKE tart until pastry is deep golden brown, about 30 minutes. Transfer skillet to work surface; cool 1 minute. Cut around edge of skillet to loosen pastry. Place large platter over skillet. Using oven mitts, hold skillet and platter together tightly and invert, allowing tart to slide out onto platter. Carefully lift off skillet. Rearrange any apples that may have become dislodged. Cool tart 30 minutes.

CUT warm tart into wedges. Serve with crème fraîche or sour cream.

Pear tarte Tatin with vanilla and ginger

THIS IS AN OUTSTANDING VARIATION on the classic apple *tarte Tatin.* Vanilla and ginger give it an exotic twist; purchased puff pastry and the helpful do-aheads make this a piece of cake (or tart). When making the caramel, you'll need to brush down the sides of the pan periodically, using a wet pastry brush, after swirling the pan. That's because the liquid sugar will begin to dry out and re-crystallize; if some of those solid crystals come in contact with the liquid below, they can throw off the chemistry and result in a grainy caramel.

6 TO 8 SERVINGS

1 sheet frozen puff pastry (half of 17.3-ounce package), thawed

½ cup sugar
¼ cup water
1 teaspoon light corn syrup
2 tablespoons (¼ stick) unsalted butter
½ vanilla bean, split lengthwise, seeds scraped into small bowl
1 tablespoon grated peeled fresh ginger
5 medium-size firm Anjou pears (about 2¼ pounds), peeled, halved, cored, each half cut into 4 wedges

Whipped cream

ROLL out puff pastry on lightly floured surface to 10-inch square. Trim edges, making 10-inch-diameter round; pierce round all over with fork. Slide onto rimless baking sheet. Cover and chill pastry while preparing pears. *(Can be prepared 1 day ahead. Keep chilled.)*

FILL large skillet with ice and water; set aside. Stir sugar, ¼ cup water, and corn syrup in heavy 10-inch-diameter ovenproof nonstick skillet over low heat until sugar dissolves. Increase heat and boil until syrup is dark amber color, occasionally swirling pan and brushing down sides of skillet with wet pastry brush, about 5 minutes. Remove from heat; whisk in butter, then vanilla-bean seeds and ginger (caramel will bubble vigorously). Arrange pears, cut side down and overlapping, in circle in skillet, placing a few around edge if necessary. Place skillet over medium heat. Cook until pears are tender and syrup thickens enough to coat spoon, about 23 minutes. Place hot skillet atop ice in large skillet to cool pear mixture quickly. *(Can be prepared 4 hours ahead. Let stand at room temperature.)*

PREHEAT oven to 375°F. Place puff pastry round atop pear mixture in skillet; tuck in edges around pears. Bake tart until pastry is puffed and golden, about 35 minutes. Cool tart completely in pan at least 1 hour and up to 6 hours.

PREHEAT oven to 375°F. Rewarm tart in oven 8 minutes. Place platter atop skillet. Using oven mitts, hold skillet and platter together tightly and invert, allowing tart to slide out onto platter. Carefully lift off skillet. Rearrange any pears that may have become dislodged. Serve tart with whipped cream.

Pear crostata with late-harvest Riesling

RIESLING IS AMONG the world's finest white wine grapes, and German Rieslings are considered the best. Late-harvest Rieslings are sweeter versions of the wine, most often served with or after dessert. The grapes are left on the vine longer than usual and aren't harvested until the very end of growing season, when many of them have shriveled a bit and the sugars have concentrated. Here, the wine is boiled and reduced, intensifying the flavors; some is baked into the tart and some is served in a syrup drizzled over before serving. (And a glass of Riesling on the side couldn't hurt, either.)

6 TO 8 SERVINGS

Crust

- **1½ cups all purpose flour**
- **3 tablespoons sugar**
- **½ teaspoon salt**
- **10 tablespoons (1¼ sticks) chilled unsalted butter, cut into ½-inch cubes**
- **1 large egg yolk**
- **1 tablespoon late-harvest Riesling or other sweet white dessert wine**

Filling

- **3 large ripe Anjou pears, peeled, halved, cored, thinly sliced**
- **1 tablespoon plus ½ cup sugar**
- **1 tablespoon all purpose flour**
- **1 cup plus 2 tablespoons late-harvest Riesling or other sweet white dessert wine**
- **½ cup water**

Vanilla ice cream

FOR CRUST: Blend flour, sugar, and salt in processor until combined. Add butter; using on/off turns, cut in until mixture resembles coarse meal. Add yolk and wine; using on/off turns, mix just until moist clumps form. Gather dough into ball; flatten into disk. Wrap in plastic and chill at least 40 minutes. *(Can be prepared 2 days ahead. Keep chilled. Let dough soften slightly at room temperature before rolling out.)*

POSITION rack in center of oven and preheat to 375°F. Roll out dough between 2 sheets of parchment paper to 12-inch round. Remove top sheet of parchment and transfer dough, with bottom parchment, to rimmed baking sheet.

FOR FILLING: Place pear slices, 1 tablespoon sugar, and flour in large bowl; toss gently to combine. Spoon pear mixture into center of dough, leaving 1½-inch plain border. Using parchment as aid, fold up outer edge of dough over edge of filling. Bake crostata until pears are tender, about 20 minutes.

MEANWHILE, boil 1 cup wine, ½ cup water, and remaining ½ cup sugar in medium saucepan until syrup is reduced to ½ cup, about 10 minutes.

REDUCE oven temperature to 325°F. Drizzle half of syrup over filling. Continue baking crostata until filling is bubbling thickly, about 20 minutes. Run long thin knife under crostata to loosen. Cool crostata on sheet.

WHISK remaining 2 tablespoons wine into remaining syrup. Cut crostata into wedges. Drizzle with syrup. Serve with ice cream.

Strawberry tart with Sherry sabayon

WHETHER IT'S French *sabayon* or Italian *zabaglione,* it's divine. Sabayon is normally a whipped mixture of egg yolks, sugar, and wine—most often Marsala—but Sherry is used here for a change. And there's no getting around it: Sabayon requires a lot of beating (with an electric mixer, thank goodness), but it's well worth it. Any leftovers would be delicious over fruit or pound cake.

6 SERVINGS

Crust

- **1 sheet frozen puff pastry (half of 17.3-ounce package), thawed**
- **1 large egg**
- **1 tablespoon whipping cream**
- **8 teaspoons sugar, divided**

Filling

- **3 1-pint containers strawberries, hulled, divided**
- **2 tablespoons strawberry jam**
- **1 tablespoon sugar**
- **2 teaspoons cornstarch dissolved in ⅓ cup water**
- **1 teaspoon fresh lemon juice**

Sabayon sauce

- **4 large egg yolks**
- **⅓ cup sugar**
- **½ cup dry Sherry or dry white wine**
- **½ cup chilled whipping cream**

FOR CRUST: Position rack in center of oven and preheat to 400°F. Lightly oil heavy large rimmed baking sheet. Roll out puff pastry sheet on lightly floured surface to 15-inch-long rectangle. Cut out 15x6-inch rectangle. Cut two 15x¾-inch strips and two 6x¾-inch strips from remaining pastry.

WHISK egg and cream in small bowl to blend. Brush large pastry rectangle with egg mixture. Sprinkle with 2 teaspoons sugar. Brush rectangle again with egg mixture; sprinkle with 2 teaspoons sugar. Place pastry strips atop edges of pastry rectangle to form border, overlapping corners and trimming to fit. Press strips firmly onto pastry to adhere. Brush pastry strips with egg mixture. Sprinkle strips with 2 teaspoons sugar. Brush strips again with egg mixture and sprinkle with sugar.

TRANSFER pastry to prepared baking sheet. Pierce center (not edges) of pastry all over with fork. Bake 5 minutes. Pierce again with fork to prevent puffing. Bake pastry until golden brown, about 9 minutes longer. Transfer to rack and cool.

FOR FILLING: Coarsely chop enough strawberries to measure 1 cup. Set remaining strawberries aside. Combine chopped strawberries, strawberry jam, sugar, cornstarch mixture, and lemon juice in small saucepan. Bring to boil, stirring constantly. Boil until thick and reduced to ½ cup, stirring frequently, about 3 minutes. Strain glaze into medium bowl. Chill until cold.

CUT remaining strawberries in half. Toss berries with glaze. Arrange berries decoratively in tart. Spoon any remaining glaze in bowl over strawberries. Chill at least 1 hour and up to 6 hours.

FOR SABAYON SAUCE: Fill large saucepan halfway with water and bring to simmer. Using electric mixer, beat egg yolks and sugar in medium metal bowl 2 minutes. Mix in Sherry. Place bowl over simmering water (do not allow bottom of bowl to touch water). Using handheld electric mixer, beat constantly until mixture triples in volume and temperature registers 160°F on candy thermometer, about 10 minutes. Pour into clean bowl; refrigerate until cold, about 1 hour.

BEAT whipping cream in another medium bowl until soft peaks form. Fold whipping cream into sabayon sauce. Slice tart and serve with sabayon sauce.

Raspberry-topped chocolate tartlets with pecan crusts

GOOD THING this recipe makes individual, single-serving tartlets—no fighting over who gets the bigger piece. Pecan-cinnamon crusts provide the backdrop for a simple ganache filling (chocolate and cream) topped with lots of red raspberries.

4 SERVINGS

- **2 cups pecans, toasted**
- **6 tablespoons (packed) golden brown sugar**
- **1/4 teaspoon ground cinnamon**
- **1/4 cup (1/2 stick) unsalted butter, melted**

- **3/4 cup whipping cream**
- **6 ounces bittersweet (not unsweetened) or semisweet chocolate, chopped**

- **2 1/2-pint containers raspberries**
- **1/4 cup seedless raspberry jam**

PREHEAT oven to 325°F. Combine pecans, sugar, and cinnamon in processor. Blend until nuts are finely ground. Add butter and process until moist clumps form. Using plastic wrap as aid, press dough over bottom and up sides of four 4-inch-diameter tartlet pans with removable bottoms.

BAKE crusts until golden brown and firm to touch, about 30 minutes. Transfer to rack and cool completely in pans.

BRING cream to simmer in heavy medium saucepan. Remove from heat. Add chocolate; stir until melted and smooth. Pour mixture into crusts, dividing equally. Chill until chocolate is set, about 1 hour. *(Tartlets can be prepared 1 day ahead. Cover and chill.)*

ARRANGE raspberries over tops of tartlets. Stir jam in heavy small saucepan over low heat until melted. Brush melted jam over raspberries. *(Can be prepared 3 hours ahead. Refrigerate.)* Push up pan bottoms to release tartlets.

Fresh raspberry cream tart

CREAMY AND COOL, this tart's pretty filling requires no baking. A thin layer of raspberry preserves between crust and filling really enhances the raspberry flavor (and makes for a very striking tart when sliced). Mascarpone is a mild-flavored Italian cream cheese available at Italian markets and many supermarkets. Since all you'll be using from the orange is the peel, choose one that has a saturated orange color and smooth, unmarked skin—and give the orange a rinse and a good rub to remove any wax. Use the leftover juice in salad dressing or a smoothie.

8 SERVINGS

Crust

- **1 cup all purpose flour**
- **1/4 cup cornstarch**
- **1/2 teaspoon baking powder**
- **1/4 teaspoon salt**
- **10 tablespoons (1 1/4 sticks) unsalted butter, room temperature**
- **1/4 cup sugar**
- **2 teaspoons grated orange peel**
- **1 1/2 teaspoons vanilla extract**

- **1/3 cup raspberry preserves**

Filling

- **1 8-ounce container mascarpone cheese, chilled**
- **1/2 cup chilled whipping cream**
- **1/3 cup powdered sugar**
- **1 teaspoon grated orange peel**
- **1 teaspoon vanilla extract**
- **1/4 teaspoon almond extract**

- **3 cups fresh raspberries**

FOR CRUST: Preheat oven to 350°F. Butter 9-inch-diameter tart pan with removable bottom. Whisk flour, cornstarch, baking powder, and salt in bowl. Using electric mixer, beat butter, sugar, orange peel, and vanilla in large bowl to blend. Add flour mixture and beat until large clumps form. Gather dough into ball; flatten into disk. Press dough over bottom and up sides of prepared pan. Freeze 15 minutes.

BAKE crust 10 minutes. Remove from oven. Using back of spoon, press crust sides to raise until even with top edge of pan. Bake crust until golden brown, about 15 minutes longer. Spread preserves over bottom of crust. Bake 5 minutes. Cool on rack.

MEANWHILE, PREPARE FILLING: Using electric mixer, beat mascarpone, cream, powdered sugar, orange peel, and both extracts in large bowl until peaks form, about 2 minutes. Spread filling evenly in cooled crust. Chill until firm, at least 2 hours and up to 1 day.

PUSH up pan bottom to release tart. Arrange raspberries in concentric circles atop filling and serve.

Blueberry-almond tart

ALMOND EXTRACT intensifies the subtle flavor of the ground almonds in the crust. The crust is baked "blind," meaning that it gets a turn in the oven all alone, to crisp and brown it, creating a barrier so that it doesn't get soggy when the filling is added. Without its filling, though, the crust may puff up in the oven, so you'll need to fill it with dried beans or pie weights (small metal or ceramic nuggets you can buy in cookware stores). Use a potato masher or the back of a fork to mash the berries. Start making this a day ahead (the filling chills overnight).

8 SERVINGS

Filling

4 ½-pint containers fresh blueberries, divided
½ cup sugar
1 tablespoon fresh lemon juice
2 large egg yolks
2 teaspoons cornstarch
3 tablespoons unsalted butter
1 teaspoon grated lemon peel

Crust

1 cup all purpose flour
¼ cup plus 2 tablespoons sliced almonds, lightly toasted
2 tablespoons sugar
¼ teaspoon salt
½ cup (1 stick) chilled unsalted butter, cut into ½-inch cubes
1 large egg yolk
¼ teaspoon almond extract

½ cup red currant jelly

FOR FILLING: Combine 2 containers berries, sugar, and lemon juice in heavy medium saucepan. Coarsely mash berries. Stir over medium-high heat until sugar dissolves and mixture boils and thickens, about 7 minutes. Whisk egg yolks and cornstarch in medium bowl. Gradually whisk in half of hot berry mixture; return to saucepan. Stir over medium-high heat until mixture boils and thickens, about 3 minutes. Whisk in butter and lemon peel. Transfer filling to bowl. Cover and chill overnight.

FOR CRUST: Lightly butter 9-inch-diameter tart pan with removable bottom. Combine flour, ¼ cup almonds, sugar, and salt in processor; process until almonds are finely ground. Add butter; using on/off turns, cut in until mixture resembles coarse meal. Whisk egg yolk and extract in small bowl; add to processor and blend until moist clumps form. Gather dough into ball; flatten into disk. Press dough over bottom and up sides of prepared pan. Pierce crust all over with fork; freeze 30 minutes.

PREHEAT oven to 375°F. Line crust with aluminum foil; fill with dried beans or pie weights. Bake until crust is set, about 12 minutes. Remove foil and beans. Bake until crust is golden, about 18 minutes longer. Cool crust completely on rack.

SPREAD filling in crust; sprinkle remaining 2 containers berries over. Stir jelly in small saucepan over medium heat until melted; brush over berries. Sprinkle remaining 2 tablespoons almonds around edge of tart. Cover loosely with foil and chill at least 2 hours. *(Can be prepared 1 day ahead. Keep refrigerated.)*

PUSH up pan bottom to release tart. Place tart on platter. Serve cold or at room temperature.

Cranberry-apricot Linzertorte

NAMED FOR its place of birth—Linz, Austria—the classic Linzertorte features a buttery lattice crust filled with jam, most often raspberry. A hazelnut crust and a cranberry-apricot filling give this version fresh perspective.

12 SERVINGS

Filling

- **1 12-ounce bag fresh or frozen cranberries**
- **2 15- to 16-ounce cans apricot halves in light syrup, drained, chopped**
- **1 cup sugar**
- **¼ cup orange juice**

Crust

- **2 cups all purpose flour, divided**
- **1 cup hazelnuts, toasted, skinned**
- **¾ cup sugar**
- **1 teaspoon baking powder**
- **1 teaspoon ground cinnamon**
- **¾ cup (1½ sticks) chilled unsalted butter, cut into ½-inch cubes**
- **2 large egg yolks**
- **2 teaspoons grated orange peel**
- **1 teaspoon vanilla extract**

- **2 tablespoons apricot jam**
- **1 teaspoon water**

FOR FILLING: Combine cranberries, apricots, sugar, and orange juice in heavy large saucepan. Bring to boil over high heat, stirring until sugar dissolves. Reduce heat to medium and simmer, stirring often, until filling is thick, beginning to stick to pan bottom, and reduced to scant 3 cups, about 15 minutes. Cool filling completely. *(Can be prepared 3 days ahead. Cover and chill.)*

FOR CRUST: Preheat oven to 350°F. Combine 1 cup flour and nuts in processor; blend until nuts are finely ground. Add remaining 1 cup flour, sugar, baking powder, and cinnamon; blend 15 seconds. Add butter; using on/off turns, cut in until coarse meal forms. Add egg yolks, orange peel, and vanilla; process until moist clumps form. Gather dough into ball; divide in half. Flatten 1 dough piece into disk; wrap and freeze 10 minutes. Press remaining piece over bottom and up sides of 10-inch-diameter tart pan with removable bottom. Spread cranberry-apricot filling evenly in crust.

ROLL out chilled dough between sheets of parchment paper to 11-inch round. Peel off paper. Cut dough into 1-inch-wide strips. Place 5 strips across top of tart, spacing 1 inch apart. Form lattice by arranging 5 strips at right angles to first strips. Trim ends of strips; press to crust edge to seal.

BAKE tart until golden brown, about 40 minutes. Transfer tart to rack. Stir jam and 1 teaspoon water in small saucepan over medium heat until mixture boils. Brush hot glaze over lattice strips. Cool tart completely. *(Can be prepared 1 day ahead. Cover loosely with aluminum foil and let stand at room temperature.)* Push up pan bottom to release tart. Place tart on platter and serve.

Apricot jalousie with amaretto cream

SO EASY YET SO IMPRESSIVE. *Jalousie* (which means "jealousy" in French) is a French term for Venetian blinds. This dessert gets the name because the topping is made of puff pastry with Venetian blind–like slits cut into it that puff open when baked, giving you a peek at the filling. When you transfer the amaretto cream (made with almond-flavored liqueur) to a bowl to chill, be sure to press plastic wrap directly onto the surface of the cream; otherwise, a skin will form on the surface.

6 SERVINGS

Amaretto cream

- **6 large egg yolks**
- **3 tablespoons sugar**
- **1 cup whipping cream**
- **1 1-inch piece vanilla bean, split lengthwise**
- **2 tablespoons amaretto**

Tart

- **3 tablespoons unsalted butter**
- **12 whole canned apricots, drained well, or very ripe fresh apricots, peeled, halved, pitted**
- **1/4 cup (or more) sugar**
- **1 3-inch piece vanilla bean, split lengthwise**
- **1 sheet frozen puff pastry (half of 17.3-ounce package), thawed**
- **1 egg, beaten to blend (for glaze)**
- **Additional sugar**

FOR AMARETTO CREAM: Whisk egg yolks and sugar in bowl to blend. Pour cream into heavy medium saucepan. Scrape seeds from vanilla bean into cream; add pod. Bring to boil. Gradually whisk hot cream into yolk mixture. Return to saucepan; stir over low heat until mixture thickens and leaves path on back of spoon when finger is drawn across, about 4 minutes (do not boil). Remove from heat and stir in amaretto. Transfer to bowl. Press plastic wrap directly onto surface of cream to keep skin from forming. Chill until cold. *(Can be prepared 4 days ahead. Keep chilled.)* Discard vanilla bean pod.

FOR TART: Melt butter in large skillet over medium heat. Add apricots and ¼ cup sugar. Scrape in seeds from vanilla bean; add pod. Cook until apricots are tender, fall apart, and form thick puree, stirring occasionally, about 15 minutes for canned apricots and 30 minutes for fresh. Cool. Discard vanilla bean pod. Sweeten mixture with more sugar, if desired.

PREHEAT oven to 425°F. Roll out pastry on floured surface to 12x16-inch rectangle. Cut in half lengthwise, forming two 6x16-inch rectangles. Place 1 rectangle in center of rimmed baking sheet. Spread apricot puree evenly over pastry, leaving ¾-inch plain border on all sides. Brush border with egg glaze. Place second rectangle atop filling. Press edges firmly to seal. Brush with glaze. To form rim, fold up ½ inch of edge all around; press to seal. Brush top with glaze; sprinkle with additional sugar. Using small sharp knife, cut diagonal slits 2 inches apart across top of tart, cutting just to filling. Bake until golden, about 25 minutes. Run long thin knife under tart to loosen from baking sheet. Cool on sheet. Cut tart crosswise into 6 slices. Serve with amaretto cream.

Plum tart with marzipan crumble

HOMEMADE MARZIPAN—sweetened almond paste—is a staple in Italian desserts. Sweet and nutty, it's an excellent accompaniment to the sweet tart plums. Look for almond paste in tubes (sold in long rectangular boxes) or in cans in the baking aisle at the supermarket or at specialty foods stores.

10 TO 12 SERVINGS

Crust

- **1 cup all purpose flour**
- **3/4 cup sliced almonds**
- **1/4 cup sugar**

1/8 teaspoon salt
1/2 cup (1 stick) chilled unsalted butter, cut into 1/2-inch cubes
2 tablespoons chilled whipping cream
1 large egg yolk

Crumble
3/4 cup all purpose flour
1/2 cup (packed) almond paste (about 5 ounces)
1/2 cup (packed) golden brown sugar
6 tablespoons (3/4 stick) chilled unsalted butter, cut into 1/2-inch cubes
1/4 cup sliced almonds

Filling
2 1/4 pounds plums (about 12), halved, pitted, thinly sliced
1/2 cup sugar
2 tablespoons plus 2 teaspoons cornstarch

FOR CRUST: Combine first 4 ingredients in processor; blend until nuts are finely ground. Add butter and process until mixture resembles coarse meal. Add cream and egg yolk. Using on/off turns, blend until moist clumps form. Press dough over bottom and up sides of 11-inch-diameter tart pan with removable bottom. Pierce all over with fork. Chill 2 hours. *(Crust can be prepared 1 day ahead. Cover and keep chilled.)*

PREHEAT oven to 400°F. Bake crust until golden, pressing with back of fork every 5 minutes if bubbles form, about 25 minutes. Transfer crust to rack and cool. Reduce oven temperature to 375°F.

FOR CRUMBLE: Blend flour, almond paste, and sugar in processor until almond paste is finely ground. Add butter; using on/off turns, blend until coarse crumbs form. Transfer to bowl; mix in almonds.

FOR FILLING: Place all ingredients in medium bowl; toss to combine well.

SPRINKLE 3/4 cup crumble over cooled crust. Top with plums. Sprinkle with remaining crumble.

BAKE tart until filling is bubbling thickly and top is golden, about 40 minutes. Cool 10 minutes. Push up pan bottom to release tart. Cool. *(Can be prepared 8 hours ahead. Let stand at room temperature.)*

Country-style plum tart

THIS TYPE OF TART, called a *crostata* in Italian cooking, is a breeze to make. The dough is rolled out on parchment paper, which doesn't stick or burn in the oven; the fruit is piled on; and the edges of the crust are simply gathered around the fruit, crimping and folding where necessary, to form a rustic, beautiful treat. A little frozen yogurt or ice cream on the side—vanilla or perhaps cinnamon—is all it needs.

6 TO 8 SERVINGS

Crust
2 cups all purpose flour
1/4 cup sugar
1/2 teaspoon salt
1 cup (2 sticks) chilled unsalted butter, cut into 1/2-inch cubes
5 tablespoons (about) ice water

Filling
1 1/2 pounds red-skinned plums, halved, pitted, sliced
1/3 cup plum jam or preserves
1 teaspoon vanilla extract
1/4 teaspoon ground allspice
3 tablespoons sugar, divided
1 egg, beaten to blend (for glaze)

Vanilla frozen yogurt or ice cream

FOR CRUST: Mix flour, sugar, and salt in processor. Add butter; using on/off turns, cut in until mixture resembles coarse meal. Add water by tablespoonfuls and process just until moist clumps form. Gather dough into ball; flatten into disk. Wrap in plastic and chill 1 hour. *(Can be prepared 1 day ahead. Keep chilled. Let soften slightly at room temperature before rolling out.)*

PREHEAT oven to 375°F. Roll out dough on large sheet of floured parchment paper to ¼-inch-thick round. Trim dough round to 14-inch diameter. Transfer dough on parchment paper to large baking sheet (edges of dough may hang over edges of baking sheet).

FOR FILLING: Mix plums, jam, vanilla, and allspice in large bowl. Mound plum mixture in center of dough, leaving 3-inch plain border. Sprinkle fruit with 2 tablespoons sugar. Fold dough border over fruit, pleating loosely and pinching to seal any cracks. Brush dough with beaten egg. Sprinkle dough with remaining 1 tablespoon sugar.

BAKE tart until crust is brown and filling is bubbling, about 45 minutes. Transfer baking sheet to rack and cool tart slightly, about 20 minutes. Slide metal spatula under all sides of crust to loosen from parchment. Using large tart pan bottom as aid, transfer tart to platter. Serve warm or at room temperature with frozen yogurt or ice cream.

Nectarine and mascarpone tart in gingersnap crust

THIS TART'S appealing zing comes from gingersnap cookies in the crust and crystallized ginger in the filling. Mascarpone is a mild Italian cream cheese; look for it at Italian markets and well-stocked supermarkets. Be sure to finish this at least two hours before guests arrive so that it has enough time to set up properly in the fridge.

8 SERVINGS

Crust

- **25 gingersnap cookies, coarsely broken (about 6 ounces; about 2¼ cups pieces)**
- **¼ cup (½ stick) unsalted butter, melted**

Filling

- **1 8-ounce container mascarpone cheese**
- **6 ounces Philadelphia brand cream cheese, room temperature**
- **¼ cup sour cream**
- **¼ cup sugar**
- **1 tablespoon grated lemon peel**
- **¼ teaspoon vanilla extract**
- **1 tablespoon finely chopped crystallized ginger**

Topping

- **4 to 5 small nectarines, halved, pitted, cut into thin slices**
- **¼ cup peach jam, warmed**
- **2 tablespoons finely chopped crystallized ginger**

FOR CRUST: Preheat oven to 350°F. Finely grind gingersnaps in processor. Add butter and blend until crumbs are evenly moistened. Using plastic wrap as aid, press mixture over bottom and up sides of 9-inch-diameter tart pan with removable bottom. Bake crust until color darkens, pressing sides with back of spoon if beginning to slip, about 8 minutes. Cool completely.

FOR FILLING: Beat first 6 ingredients in medium bowl until smooth. Beat in crystallized ginger. Spread filling in prepared crust. Cover loosely and refrigerate at least 2 hours and up to 1 day.

FOR TOPPING: Overlap nectarine slices atop filling in concentric circles. Brush with jam. Sprinkle with chopped crystallized ginger. *(Can be prepared up to 6 hours ahead. Keep refrigerated.)* Push up pan bottom to release tart.

Nectarine-raspberry crostata with vanilla crème fraîche

THIS CRUST has all the basic elements: flour for body, sugar for sweetness and texture, salt for flavor, chilled butter for flakiness, and enough ice water to keep the butter chilled so that it can do its job. And not only do nectarines and raspberries look beautiful together with their striking, contrasting colors, they taste great together, too.

8 SERVINGS

Crust

- **2 cups all purpose flour**
- **1/4 cup sugar**
- **1/2 teaspoon salt**
- **1 cup (2 sticks) chilled unsalted butter, each stick cut into 4 pieces**
- **2 tablespoons (about) ice water**

Filling

- **1 1/2-pint container raspberries, divided**
- **4 nectarines (about 1 1/4 pounds), halved, pitted, thinly sliced**
- **1/3 cup plus 2 tablespoons sugar**
- **1 tablespoon fresh lemon juice**

- **1 egg, beaten to blend (for glaze)**

Vanilla Crème Fraîche (see recipe)

FOR CRUST: Mix flour, sugar, and salt in processor. Add butter; using on/off turns, cut in until mixture resembles coarse meal. Add ice water by tablespoonfuls and process just until moist clumps form. Gather dough into ball. Flatten into disk. Wrap in plastic and chill at least 1 hour. *(Can be prepared 1 day ahead. Keep chilled. Let soften slightly before rolling out.)*

ROLL out dough on lightly floured parchment paper to ¼-inch-thick round. Trim dough to 14-inch round. Transfer parchment with dough to large baking sheet.

FOR FILLING: Mash ½ cup raspberries in large bowl. Add remaining raspberries, nectarines, ⅓ cup sugar, and lemon juice; toss to combine.

PREHEAT oven to 375°F. Spoon filling into center of dough, leaving 3-inch plain border. Sprinkle fruit with remaining 2 tablespoons sugar. Fold border over fruit, pinching to seal any cracks. Brush dough with some of egg glaze.

BAKE crostata until pastry is golden brown and filling is bubbling, about 35 minutes. Run long thin knife under crostata to loosen. Transfer baking sheet to rack and cool crostata slightly.

SERVE crostata warm or at room temperature with Vanilla Crème Fraîche.

Vanilla crème fraîche

A SUPER-SOPHISTICATED VERSION of sweetened whipped cream (with no whipping!). It's tangy and rich yet subtly sweet, thanks to the vanilla bean.

MAKES ABOUT 1 CUP

- **1 8-ounce container crème fraîche or sour cream**
- **1/2 vanilla bean, split lengthwise**
- **4 1/2 teaspoons sugar**

PLACE crème fraîche in medium bowl. Scrape seeds from vanilla bean into crème fraîche. Stir in sugar. Cover and refrigerate 1 hour. *(Can be prepared 3 days ahead. Keep refrigerated.)*

Lemon-almond tart

PUCKER UP and get ready to be wowed: Almonds add a nice contrasting element to a tangy lemon curd filling. The use of chilled butter helps make the crust flaky.

8 SERVINGS

Crust

1 cup unbleached all purpose flour

¼ cup sliced almonds

1 tablespoon sugar

¼ teaspoon salt

7 tablespoons chilled unsalted butter, cut into ½-inch cubes

1 tablespoon ice water

½ teaspoon almond extract

Filling

4 large eggs

1¼ cups sugar

6 tablespoons fresh lemon juice

2 tablespoons grated lemon peel

2 tablespoons (¼ stick) unsalted butter

⅓ cup sliced almonds

Powdered sugar

FOR CRUST: Blend flour, almonds, sugar, and salt in processor. Add butter; using on/off turns, cut in until mixture resembles coarse meal. Combine 1 tablespoon ice water and extract in small bowl; pour over flour mixture and process just until moist clumps form. Gather dough into ball; flatten into disk. Press dough evenly over bottom and up sides of 9-inch-diameter tart pan with removable bottom. Freeze crust until firm, about 30 minutes. *(Can be prepared 1 day ahead. Cover; keep frozen.)*

FOR FILLING: Combine eggs and 1¼ cups sugar in heavy medium saucepan; whisk to blend. Mix in lemon juice and peel. Whisk over medium-high heat until mixture thickens, about 5 minutes (do not boil). Remove from heat and whisk in butter. Transfer filling to bowl. Chill until cold, stirring occasionally, about 2 hours. *(Can be made 1 day ahead. Press plastic wrap directly onto surface to keep skin from forming and keep chilled.)*

PREHEAT oven to 400°F. Line crust with aluminum foil; fill with dried beans or pie weights. Bake until sides are set, about 15 minutes. Remove foil and beans. Continue baking until crust is golden, about 15 minutes. Transfer to rack and cool completely. Reduce oven temperature to 350°F.

SPREAD filling in crust. Sprinkle almonds over. Bake until filling puffs slightly, begins to crack at edge, and moves slightly in center when shaken gently, about 40 minutes. Cool tart completely on rack. Push up pan bottom to release tart. Sprinkle tart with powdered sugar and serve.

Fresh lime tart with meringue lattice and glazed berries

THANK HEAVENS for summer desserts: Here, homemade lime curd is topped with a vanilla-infused meringue lattice and a selection of the season's freshest berries, which have been tossed in a syrup of fruit-flavored liqueur and sugar. Buy whatever berries look best at the market, and rinse them just before using.

8 TO 10 SERVINGS

Crust

1¼ cups unbleached all purpose flour

2 tablespoons sugar

½ teaspoon grated lime peel

¼ teaspoon salt

½ cup (1 stick) chilled unsalted butter, cut into ½-inch cubes

1 large egg yolk

1 tablespoon ice water

Filling

1¼ cups plus 2 tablespoons sugar

1 cup whipping cream

½ cup dry white wine

4 large eggs

2 large egg yolks

1 tablespoon grated lime peel

1 tablespoon cornstarch

¾ cup fresh lime juice

Meringue

- **½ cup sugar, divided**
- **¼ cup water**
- **1 3-inch piece vanilla bean, split lengthwise**
- **3 large egg whites**

Berry topping

- **2 tablespoons fruit-flavored liqueur, such as crème de cassis (black-currant liqueur), framboise (raspberry liqueur), or Grand Marnier**
- **2 tablespoons sugar**
- **½ teaspoon grated lime peel**
- **2 cups assorted fresh berries (such as blackberries, blueberries, raspberries, boysenberries, and sliced, hulled strawberries)**
- **Mint leaves (optional)**

FOR CRUST: Combine flour, sugar, lime peel, and salt in large bowl. Add butter and rub in with fingertips until mixture resembles coarse meal. Beat egg yolk with 1 tablespoon ice water in small bowl to blend. Pour over flour mixture. Stir with fork until moist clumps form. Gather dough into ball; flatten into disk. Wrap dough in plastic and refrigerate until firm, about 30 minutes.

ROLL out dough on lightly floured surface to 13-inch round. Roll up dough on rolling pin and transfer to 11-inch-diameter tart pan with removable bottom. Press dough into pan; trim edges. Freeze until very firm, about 1 hour. *(Can be prepared 3 days ahead. Cover with plastic wrap and keep frozen.)*

PREHEAT oven to 400°F. Line frozen crust with aluminum foil. Fill crust with dried beans or pie weights. Bake until sides are set, about 12 minutes. Remove foil and beans. Continue baking until crust is golden in center, about 14 minutes. Transfer crust to rack and cool completely. *(Can be prepared 1 day ahead. Cover with plastic wrap and let stand at room temperature.)*

FOR FILLING: Combine sugar, whipping cream, and wine in heavy medium saucepan. Whisk in 3 eggs, 2 egg yolks, and lime peel. Place cornstarch in small bowl. Gradually whisk in lime juice. Add to mixture in saucepan. Stir over medium-high heat until mixture comes to boil. Continue to boil 1 minute, stirring constantly. Transfer mixture to medium bowl. Cool mixture completely. *(Can be prepared 1 day ahead. Cover and refrigerate.)*

PREHEAT oven to 350°F. Beat remaining egg into filling. Pour filling into crust. Bake until filling is set and beginning to bubble around edge, about 40 minutes. Cool completely. Refrigerate tart until well chilled, about 6 hours. *(Can be prepared 1 day ahead. Cover with plastic wrap and keep refrigerated.)*

FOR MERINGUE: Preheat oven to 400°F. Combine ¼ cup sugar and ¼ cup water in heavy small saucepan. Scrape in seeds from vanilla bean; add pod. Stir over medium heat until sugar dissolves. Increase heat and boil until mixture is thick and syrupy, about 3 minutes. Remove vanilla bean pod from saucepan and discard.

MEANWHILE, using electric mixer, beat egg whites in large bowl until soft peaks form. Gradually add remaining ¼ cup sugar and beat until medium peaks form.

GRADUALLY beat boiling syrup into egg whites. Continue beating until stiff peaks form. Using rubber spatula, transfer meringue to pastry bag fitted with large plain tip or star tip. Pipe meringue atop tart in diagonal lattice design, spacing lines of meringue about 2 inches apart. Bake until meringue is golden brown, about 7 minutes. Let tart cool completely. *(Can be prepared up to 4 hours ahead; refrigerate uncovered.)*

FOR BERRY TOPPING: Combine liqueur, sugar, and lime peel in small saucepan. Boil mixture until sugar dissolves and mixture is syrupy, stirring constantly, about 1 minute. Cool slightly. Place berries in bowl. Pour liqueur mixture over. Toss to coat berries. Spoon coated berries decoratively among lattice openings on tart. Push up pan bottom to release tart. Garnish tart with mint leaves, if desired.

Orange custard tart

YOU'VE GROWN UP, so why shouldn't the Creamsicle? Now it's transformed with a crunchy crust, a creamy filling, and a luscious orange and raspberry topping. To prepare the orange peel, use a swivel-bladed vegetable peeler to remove peel in long strips and then mince it; or use a fine grater such as a Microplane to grate the peel. Either way, make sure you use the orange part of the peel only. The white pith beneath is very bitter and will throw the flavors off balance.

8 SERVINGS

Crust

3/4 cup all purpose flour
2/3 cup yellow cornmeal
2/3 cup powdered sugar
2 teaspoons minced orange peel (orange part only)
1/4 teaspoon salt
7 tablespoons butter, room temperature
1 large egg yolk
2 teaspoons vanilla extract

Filling

1 cup whipping cream
1/2 cup fresh orange juice
5 large egg yolks
1/4 cup plus 1 tablespoon sugar
2 tablespoons Grand Marnier or other orange liqueur
1 tablespoon minced orange peel (orange part only)

3 oranges, peeled, white pith removed
2 1/2-pint containers fresh raspberries

FOR CRUST: Combine first 5 ingredients in large bowl. Add butter, egg yolk, and vanilla. Using electric mixer, blend until coarse crumbs form. Knead into ball (dough will be very soft). Pat dough over bottom and up sides of 13½x4¼-inch rectangular tart pan or four 4-inch-diameter tartlet pans with removable bottoms. Press dough into place; trim excess. Freeze 20 minutes.

PREHEAT oven to 350°F. Line crust with aluminum foil and fill with dried beans or pie weights. Bake 15 minutes. Remove foil and beans. Using back of spoon, press crust up sides of pan if slipping. Bake 10 minutes longer. Cool.

FOR FILLING: Whisk first 6 ingredients in medium bowl to blend. Pour filling into crust. Bake until filling is barely set, about 30 minutes. Cool 20 minutes. Refrigerate until custard is firm, about 3 hours. *(Can be prepared 8 hours ahead. Keep refrigerated.)*

USING small sharp knife, cut between membranes of oranges to release segments. Drain well on paper towels. Arrange alternating rows of orange segments and raspberries atop tart. Push up pan bottom(s) to release tart or tartlets.

Mango tartlets with lime curd and tropical nut crust

COCONUT IN THE CRUST gives this tropical treat a chewy, cookie-like quality. Mangoes are often green when they arrive at the market, but ripe ones have turned shades of yellow, orange, and red, with little or no green. Ripe mangoes should give when squeezed and should have a wonderful fragrance. If they're not quite ripe, place them in a paper bag at room temperature to accelerate the process. When making the lime curd, whisk it in a nonreactive metal bowl set over a saucepan of simmering water to cook the eggs properly. The water should be shallow enough that the bottom of the bowl does not come in contact with the water (indirect heat is what's required here; direct heat will curdle the mixture). Using a candy thermometer ensures that the eggs are heated enough for food safety.

8 SERVINGS

Crusts

Nonstick vegetable oil spray

2 cups roasted macadamia nuts (about 10 ounces)

1½ cups sweetened flaked coconut

1¼ cups shelled unsalted pistachios

½ cup (packed) golden brown sugar

3 large egg whites

Lime curd

1 cup sugar

¾ cup fresh lime juice

10 large egg yolks

½ cup (1 stick) chilled unsalted butter, cut into 1-inch cubes

2 mangoes, peeled, halved, pitted, sliced

¼ cup guava jelly or red currant jelly

FOR CRUSTS: Preheat oven to 350°F. Spray eight 4-inch-diameter tartlet pans with removable bottoms with nonstick spray. Combine macadamia nuts, coconut, pistachios, and brown sugar in processor. Process until nuts are finely chopped. Transfer to large bowl. Beat egg whites in another large bowl until soft peaks form. Fold whites into nut mixture in 3 additions (mixture will be thick and sticky). Let mixture stand 10 minutes.

USING plastic wrap as aid, press about ⅓ cup nut mixture over bottom and up sides of each prepared pan. Place pans on rimmed baking sheet. Bake until crusts are puffed and begin to brown, about 20 minutes. Cool crusts in pans 5 minutes. Using oven mitt or pot holders, gently push up pan bottoms to release crusts; cool crusts completely on rack.

FOR LIME CURD: Whisk sugar, lime juice, and egg yolks in large metal bowl to blend. Set bowl over saucepan of simmering water (do not allow bottom of bowl to touch water); whisk constantly until mixture thickens and candy thermometer inserted into mixture registers 180°F, about 9 minutes. Remove bowl from over water. Gradually add chilled butter, whisking until melted and well blended. Press plastic wrap directly over surface of curd. Refrigerate until cold, about 3 hours. *(Crusts and lime curd can be prepared 1 day ahead. Store crusts in airtight container at room temperature. Keep lime curd refrigerated.)*

FILL each crust with 5 tablespoons lime curd. Arrange mango slices decoratively atop tartlets. Whisk guava jelly in heavy small saucepan over low heat until melted. Brush over mango slices. Chill at least 3 hours and up to 1 day. Push up pan bottoms to release tartlets.

Pastry-wrapped raspberry crisps

ALMOST LIKE raspberry crisps inside tart shells, these pretty single-serving desserts are much more elegant than the average crisp–fortunately, they are still a snap to prepare. Serve them with sweetened whipped cream for a luscious treat.

4 SERVINGS

Crust

1¾ cups all purpose flour

1 teaspoon plus 1 tablespoon sugar

¾ teaspoon salt

½ cup (1 stick) chilled unsalted butter, cut into ½-inch cubes

¼ cup frozen vegetable shortening, cut into ½-inch cubes

2 tablespoons ice water

1 tablespoon fresh lemon juice

Filling

6 tablespoons raspberry preserves (with seeds)

1 ½-pint container raspberries

Sweetened whipped cream

FOR CRUST: Combine flour, 1 teaspoon sugar, and salt in processor. Add butter and shortening; using on/off turns, process until mixture resembles coarse meal. Transfer ½ cup of mixture to small bowl; add 1 tablespoon sugar. Cover; chill. Reserve for topping.

ADD 2 tablespoons ice water and lemon juice to mixture in processor. Using on/off turns, blend until moist clumps form. Gather dough into ball; flatten into disk. Wrap in plastic and chill until firm enough to roll, about 30 minutes. *(Can be prepared 1 day ahead. Keep refrigerated. Let dough soften slightly before rolling out.)*

FOR FILLING: Place preserves in medium bowl; stir to loosen texture. Fold in raspberries.

SET rack in bottom position in oven and preheat to 400°F. Roll out dough on lightly floured surface to ⅛-inch thickness. Using 6-inch-diameter saucer as template, cut out four 6-inch-diameter rounds. Spoon ¼ of raspberry filling (about ⅓ cup) in center of each round, leaving 1-inch plain border at edges. Working with 1 pastry at a time, fold border over edge of filling, pinching border at 1-inch intervals. Using spatula, transfer pastries to large rimmed baking sheet, spacing apart. Sprinkle reserved topping mixture over exposed filling of each pastry.

BAKE crisps until crusts are golden, about 35 minutes. Let stand on baking sheet 15 minutes. Transfer to plates; serve warm with sweetened whipped cream.

Fig and raspberry galette

FRESH FIGS are in markets from summer through October, and nothing makes a more alluring tart than these luscious, sensual fruits. This galette offers a particularly pleasing presentation for entertaining (the figs are arranged in concentric circles on top). Serve with small wedges of blue cheese and glasses of Sauternes.

6 SERVINGS

Crust

- **1⅓ cups all purpose flour**
- **½ teaspoon salt**
- **⅓ cup chilled solid vegetable shortening, cut into ½-inch cubes**
- **5 tablespoons chilled unsalted butter, cut into ½-inch cubes**
- **2 tablespoons (about) ice water**

Filling

- **1 pound fresh ripe figs (about 10), quartered**
- **4 tablespoons sugar, divided**
- **½ cup fresh raspberries (from one ½-pint container)**
- **1 large egg yolk, beaten to blend with 1 teaspoon water (for glaze)**

FOR CRUST: Mix flour and salt in processor. Add shortening and butter; using on/off turns, cut in until mixture resembles coarse meal. Mix in ice water 1 tablespoon at a time just until moist clumps form. Gather dough into ball; flatten into disk. Wrap in plastic and refrigerate 30 minutes.

PREHEAT oven to 425°F. Roll out dough between 2 sheets of parchment paper to 12-inch round. Remove top sheet of parchment. Invert dough onto unrimmed baking sheet. Remove parchment.

FOR FILLING: Combine figs and 3 tablespoons sugar in large bowl; toss to coat figs. Toss raspberries with ½ tablespoon sugar in medium bowl. Arrange figs in concentric circles over dough on baking sheet, leaving 2-inch plain border around edges. Sprinkle raspberries over figs. Fold dough border over fruit, pleating loosely and pinching to seal any cracks. Brush dough border with egg glaze. Sprinkle border with remaining ½ tablespoon sugar.

BAKE galette until crust is brown and filling is bubbling, about 35 minutes. Transfer baking sheet to rack and cool galette slightly, about 20 minutes. Slide spatula under all sides of crust to free galette from baking sheet. Using large tart pan bottom as aid, transfer galette to platter. Serve warm or at room temperature.

Fresh fruit tart

THE FLAKY CRUST contains fluffy sweetened cream cheese and a gorgeous topping of fresh fruit. Whatever you're planning—afternoon tea, midnight snack, fancy dinner party—this fills the bill. Use whatever combination of fruit is in season—spring, summer, even winter citrus fruits.

8 TO 10 SERVINGS

Crust

- **1 cup unbleached all purpose flour**
- **1 tablespoon sugar**
- **⅛ teaspoon salt**
- **5 tablespoons chilled solid vegetable shortening, cut into ½-inch cubes**
- **3 tablespoons chilled unsalted butter, cut into ½-inch cubes**
- **3 tablespoons (about) ice water**

Filling

- **1 8-ounce package Philadelphia brand cream cheese, room temperature**
- **¼ cup sugar**
- **2½ teaspoons fresh lemon juice**
- **½ cup chilled whipping cream**

- **3 kiwis, peeled, sliced**
- **Fresh strawberries, hulled, halved**
- **Fresh blueberries**
- **Orange segments, well drained**
- **¼ cup apricot preserves**
- **1 tablespoon water**

FOR CRUST: Combine flour, sugar, and salt in medium bowl. Add shortening and butter; rub in with fingertips until mixture resembles coarse meal. Mix in enough water by tablespoonfuls to form moist clumps. Gather dough into ball; flatten into disk. Wrap in plastic and refrigerate 30 minutes.

ROLL out dough on lightly floured surface to ⅛-inch-thick round. Transfer dough to 9-inch-diameter tart pan with removable bottom. Trim edges and crimp decoratively. Refrigerate 30 minutes.

PREHEAT oven to 375°F. Line crust with aluminum foil; fill with dried beans or pie weights. Bake 15 minutes. Remove foil and beans. Bake until golden brown and cooked through, about 15 minutes longer. Transfer to rack and cool completely.

FOR FILLING: Using electric mixer, beat cream cheese, sugar, and lemon juice in large bowl until well blended. Add whipping cream and beat until light and fluffy. Spread filling in crust. Cover and refrigerate overnight.

ARRANGE fruit in concentric circles atop filling. *(Can be prepared 3 hours ahead. Cover loosely and refrigerate.)* Bring preserves and 1 tablespoon water to boil in heavy small saucepan. Strain into bowl. Brush glaze over fruit. Push up pan bottom to release tart.

18 Custards and puddings

The simplest science can have the greatest results. When eggs are heated slowly–*slowly* being the operative word–with milk or cream, they thicken and enrich the liquid rather than scrambling. Add a little sugar to the milk before you start, chill the whole affair after cooking, and you've got a custard. That simple start is the inspiration for a million and one variations. Whisk the eggs, milk, and sugar together, then pour them into a pan and bake them in the oven at low temperature in a dish set inside a pan of warm water, and the same magic will happen. These slow-baked custards are wonderful on their own, or gilded with caramel or sauces in sophisticated desserts. Crème brûlée–that wonderfully contradictory dessert of silky custard topped with a brittle, paper-thin layer of caramel–is remarkably simple to pull together. And the variations range from the traditional custard flavored with vanilla to more modern versions with praline and chocolate.

A close cousin of the crème brûlée, crème caramel (*flan* in Spain) is even easier to prepare. The fact that crème caramel must be made ahead–so the custard has time to set–makes it an excellent candidate for entertaining. And the layer of caramel that coats the pan ensures that the dessert will slip easily from baking dish to plate, coated with a rich amber liquid that doubles as a sauce.

Pots de crème–which translates, as one might think, to "pots of cream"–are rich custards baked in tiny ceramic pots. Served with a demitasse spoon and a crisp cookie, they are heaven. That's all you need to close out a dinner party–unless, of course, you opt for one of the trifles, mousses, or soufflés also found here.

Puddings share certain qualities with custards–eggs, sugar, and a creamy comfort quotient–but generally add bread, rice, or flour to the mix for a more down-to-earth appeal.

From a baking dish filled with homey bread pudding to the four-star elegance of a chocolate soufflé, a little science makes a lot of people very happy.

Praline-chocolate crème brûlée

A CREAMY CUSTARD and a crackly burnt-sugar topping have made crème brûlée—literally "burnt cream"—one of America's most popular restaurant desserts. In this luxurious version, the hidden cache of extra praline under the creamy chocolate custard is a welcome surprise. Before baking the custards, pour hot water into the baking pan until it reaches halfway up the sides of the baking dishes. Using this method, called a *bain-marie* or water bath, keeps the custards from curdling by cooking them gently until they set. Begin making this a day ahead because it needs to set up in the refrigerator overnight.

4 SERVINGS

Nonstick vegetable oil spray
⅓ cup plus 2 tablespoons hazelnuts, toasted, finely chopped
1½ cups plus 3 tablespoons sugar
⅓ cup water

1¼ cups whipping cream
⅓ cup half and half
3 ounces bittersweet (not unsweetened) or semisweet chocolate, chopped
4 large egg yolks

PREHEAT oven to 350°F. Spray rimmed baking sheet with nonstick spray; sprinkle ⅓ cup nuts in center. Stir 1½ cups sugar and ⅓ cup water in heavy small saucepan over medium-low heat until sugar dissolves. Increase heat and boil without stirring until syrup is medium amber color, occasionally swirling pan and brushing down sides of pan with wet pastry brush, about 9 minutes. Working quickly, pour enough caramel into each of four flameproof 6-ounce soufflé dishes or custard cups to reach depth of ¼ inch. Sprinkle 1 teaspoon nuts over caramel in each dish. Pour remaining caramel over nuts on baking sheet. Let stand until caramel cools completely.

HEAT cream and half and half in medium saucepan over medium heat until beginning to simmer. Remove from heat. Add chocolate and whisk until melted and smooth. Beat egg yolks and remaining 3 tablespoons sugar in medium bowl to blend. Gradually whisk in warm chocolate mixture. Divide custard among prepared dishes. Place dishes in 13x9x2-inch metal baking pan. Pour enough hot water into pan to reach halfway up sides of dishes.

BAKE custards until barely set in center, about 25 minutes. Remove pan with custards from oven; let custards stand in water bath 10 minutes. Transfer custards to rack and cool completely. Cover and refrigerate overnight.

MEANWHILE, break cooled praline into small pieces. Transfer to processor and chop finely. *(Can be prepared 1 day ahead. Store praline in airtight container at room temperature.)*

PREHEAT broiler. Sprinkle 2 teaspoons chopped praline over each custard (reserve remaining praline for another use). Place custards on small baking sheet. Broil until praline begins to melt and bubble, about 1 minute. Refrigerate custards until praline hardens, at least 1 hour and up to 8 hours.

Ginger and vanilla bean crème brûlée

THE ADDITION OF CHOPPED fresh ginger gives this custard a tropical touch and a nice spicy kick. A small handheld blowtorch, made especially for kitchen use and available at some cookware stores, is a useful gadget for caramelizing the sugar topping. If you don't have a blowtorch, broil the custards until the sugar turns dark brown. Watch carefully while they broil, as the topping browns quickly. You can find 4-inch-diameter fluted ovenproof clear glass flan dishes at cookware stores. They are about ⅔ inch deep and hold ½ cup liquid.

6 SERVINGS

- 2 cups whipping cream
- ½ cup plus 12 teaspoons sugar
- 2 tablespoons chopped peeled fresh ginger
- 1 vanilla bean, split lengthwise

- 5 large egg yolks

Assorted sliced tropical fruits (such as mango, papaya, and/or kiwi)

PREHEAT oven to 325°F. Place three 4-inch-diameter fluted ovenproof flan dishes in each of two 13x9x2-inch metal baking pans or place six 6-ounce custard cups in 1 pan.

MIX cream, ½ cup sugar, and ginger in heavy medium saucepan. Using small sharp knife, scrape seeds from vanilla bean. Add seeds and pod to saucepan. Stir over medium heat until sugar dissolves and mixture comes to simmer. Reduce heat to very low, cover pan, and simmer gently 10 minutes to infuse flavors. Strain into 4-cup measuring cup.

WHISK egg yolks in medium bowl until well blended. Gradually whisk in hot cream mixture just until combined. Return custard to measuring cup; divide equally among dishes. Pour enough hot water into baking pans to reach halfway up sides of dishes. Carefully transfer pans to oven.

BAKE custards until centers move only slightly when pans are shaken gently, about 30 minutes for fluted flan dishes and 35 minutes for custard cups. Using metal spatula, transfer custards in dishes to work surface; cool completely. Cover and refrigerate at least 3 hours. *(Can be prepared up to 2 days ahead. Cover and keep refrigerated.)*

SPRINKLE 2 teaspoons sugar evenly over each custard. Working with 1 custard at a time, hold blowtorch so that flame is 2 inches above surface. Direct flame so that sugar melts and browns, about 2 minutes. Refrigerate until custards are firm again but topping is still brittle, at least 2 hours but no longer than 4 hours. Garnish crèmes brûlées with fruit and serve.

Maple crème caramel

THE MAPLE CUSTARD pairs beautifully with the caramel syrup in this superb crème caramel. A key step in making caramel is to cook the sugar syrup to a dark amber color—it will actually look like maple syrup when it's done. If the caramel is too pale, it will be too sweet and lack depth of flavor. If the caramel cooks too long and becomes too dark, it will be bitter and inedible. Using a saucepan with a light-colored interior makes it easy to tell exactly what color the caramel is.

4 SERVINGS

Caramel

- 1 cup sugar
- ½ cup water

Custard

- ½ cup pure maple syrup
- 3 large egg yolks
- 1 large egg
- 1½ cups whipping cream
- ½ cup whole milk

FOR CARAMEL: Preheat oven to 300°F. Lightly butter four 6-ounce soufflé dishes or custard cups. Combine sugar and ½ cup water in heavy small saucepan. Stir over low heat until sugar dissolves. Increase heat and boil without stirring until syrup is deep amber color, occasionally brushing down sides of pan with wet pastry brush and swirling pan, about 10 minutes. Immediately pour caramel into prepared dishes. Using oven mitts, quickly rotate dishes to coat sides with caramel. Set aside.

FOR CUSTARD: Whisk maple syrup, egg yolks, and whole egg in medium bowl to blend. Combine cream and milk in heavy medium saucepan and bring just to boil. Gradually whisk hot cream mixture into yolk mixture. Divide custard among prepared dishes. Place dishes in 13x9x2-inch metal baking pan. Pour enough hot water into pan to reach halfway up sides of dishes. Cover baking pan with aluminum foil.

BAKE custards until set in center, about 55 minutes. Refrigerate custards uncovered until cold, at least 5 hours. *(Can be prepared 1 day ahead. Cover and keep refrigerated.)*

TO SERVE, run small sharp knife around sides of dish to loosen custards; invert onto plates.

Vanilla cream custards with caramel sauce

UNLIKE CRÈMES BRÛLÉES, where the crisp caramel is on top, or crèmes caramels, where the silky caramel sauce is baked underneath, here the caramel sauce is made separately and poured over the custards once they have been chilled. If you're pressed for time, a good-quality purchased caramel sauce, raspberry sauce, or even chocolate sauce makes a convenient stand-in for the homemade caramel sauce. As with most custards, these are cooked when the edges are set but the centers still move slightly when the dishes are shaken gently. This contrasts with the rule for baking cakes, whose centers should be firm and completely cooked through. But unlike cakes, as custards cool the centers set up to a luxurious pudding consistency. If the custards are baked until the centers are completely set, they will be too firm once they are cold and lose the desired creaminess.

12 SERVINGS

Custards

- **12 large egg yolks**
- **¾ cup plus 1 tablespoon sugar**
- **4 teaspoons vanilla extract**
- **5½ cups whipping cream**
- **⅓ cup whole milk**

Sauce

- **2 cups sugar**
- **¾ cup water**
- **1 cup whipping cream**

FOR CUSTARDS: Preheat oven to 350°F. Whisk egg yolks, sugar, and vanilla in large bowl to blend. Gradually whisk in cream, then milk. Divide mixture among twelve 6-ounce soufflé dishes or custard cups.

PLACE 6 dishes in each of 2 roasting pans. Add enough hot water to pans to reach halfway up sides of dishes. Cover pans with aluminum foil and bake until center of custards move only slightly when pans are shaken gently, about 45 minutes. Remove custards from water and cool completely. Cover and refrigerate at least 4 hours. *(Can be prepared 1 day ahead. Cover and keep refrigerated.)*

FOR SAUCE: Stir sugar and ¾ cup water in heavy large saucepan over medium heat until sugar dissolves. Increase heat and boil without stirring until mixture turns deep amber color, occasionally brushing down sides of pan with wet pastry brush and swirling pan, about 14 minutes. Remove from heat. Add cream (mixture will bubble vigorously). Stir over medium heat until any bits of hard caramel melt. Cool sauce. *(Can be prepared 1 day ahead. Cover and refrigerate. Before using, rewarm over low heat, stirring until liquid but not hot.)*

SPOON sauce over custards in dishes and serve.

Maple crème flan with maple-glazed pears

FLAN IS ONE OF the most celebrated Spanish desserts. This one takes on the decadent richness of crème brûlée by using cream instead of milk and egg yolks rather than whole eggs. Begin preparing it a day ahead, as it bakes at a very low temperature for quite a long time and needs to chill overnight. The maple-glazed pears provide a lovely contrast to the smooth texture of the custard, but if you're pressed for time, the flan is delicious on its own.

12 SERVINGS

Flan

- **1 cup pure maple syrup**
- **3½ cups whipping cream**

- **7 large egg yolks**
- **⅛ teaspoon salt**

- **⅔ cup sugar**
- **¼ cup water**
- **½ teaspoon light corn syrup**

Pears

- **1 tablespoon unsalted butter**
- **3 ripe unpeeled Bartlett pears, quartered, cored**
- **¼ cup pure maple syrup**
- **¼ cup crème fraîche or sour cream**
- **⅛ teaspoon salt**

FOR FLAN: Simmer maple syrup in heavy medium saucepan over medium-low heat until reduced to ¾ cup, about 7 minutes. Stir in cream and return to simmer.

WHISK egg yolks in large bowl to blend. Gradually whisk in hot cream mixture. Whisk in salt. Strain custard into another large bowl. Cover and refrigerate until cold, at least 2 hours and up to 1 day.

PREHEAT oven to 300°F. Stir sugar, ¼ cup water, and corn syrup in heavy medium saucepan over low heat until sugar dissolves. Increase heat and boil without stirring until syrup is deep amber color, occasionally brushing down sides of pan with wet pastry brush and swirling pan, about 6 minutes. Pour syrup into 9¼x5¼x3-inch nonstick metal loaf pan, tilting pan carefully to coat sides. Let stand 10 minutes.

POUR custard into pan with syrup. Place loaf pan in large roasting pan. Add enough hot water to roasting pan to reach halfway up sides of loaf pan. Cover roasting pan with aluminum foil; pierce foil all over with fork. Bake flan 1 hour 45 minutes.

INCREASE oven temperature to 325°F. Uncover and bake until flan is set around edges but center moves slightly when pan is shaken gently, about 1 hour longer. Remove flan from water. Transfer to rack; cool completely. Cover and refrigerate overnight.

FOR PEARS: Preheat oven to 375°F. Melt butter in heavy large ovenproof skillet over medium-high heat. Arrange pears, 1 cut side down, in skillet; cook until brown, about 4 minutes. Turn onto second cut side and cook until brown, about 4 minutes longer. Stir in maple syrup and bring to boil. Place in oven and bake until pears are tender, about 25 minutes. Using slotted spoon, transfer pears to plate. Whisk crème fraîche and salt into sauce in skillet. Return pears to skillet and toss to coat.

RUN small sharp knife around edge of flan to loosen. Invert flan onto platter. Surround with pears and sauce and serve.

Caramel-coated cream cheese flan

HERE'S THE PERFECT DESSERT to serve at your next big or small fiesta: The recipe makes two large flans that will serve about 16 people, and also offers flexible instructions that can be adapted for making just one flan. If you have only one roasting pan large enough to fit the cake pan, you can prepare and bake the flans one at a time. The inclusion of cream cheese and sweetened condensed milk makes for an ultra-rich version of flan. Fresh berries or tropical fruits would be perfect partners.

16 SERVINGS

- **Nonstick vegetable oil spray**
- **4 cups sugar**
- **1½ cups water**
- **3½ cups whole milk**
- **2 14-ounce cans sweetened condensed milk**
- **2 teaspoons vanilla extract**
- **1 8-ounce package cream cheese, diced, room temperature**
- **10 large eggs**

POSITION 1 rack in bottom third of oven and 1 rack in center; preheat to 375°F. Spray two 9-inch-diameter cake pans with 2-inch-high sides with nonstick spray. Combine 2 cups sugar and ¾ cup water in heavy large saucepan. Stir over medium heat until sugar dissolves. Increase heat and boil without stirring until syrup is deep amber color, occasionally brushing down sides of pan with wet pastry brush and swirling pan, about 13 minutes. Pour caramel into 1 prepared pan. Using oven mitts, tilt and swirl pan to coat sides and bottom with syrup. Set pan aside. Repeat with remaining 2 cups sugar and ¾ cup water and second pan.

COMBINE 1¾ cups whole milk, 1 can condensed milk, and 1 teaspoon vanilla extract in 5- to 6-cup-capacity blender; blend 15 seconds. With machine running, add half of cream cheese, 1 cube at a time, and blend until smooth. Add 5 eggs, 1 at a time, blending 5 seconds after each. Pour custard into 1 prepared pan. Repeat with remaining whole milk, condensed milk, vanilla, cream cheese, and eggs. Place each pan in separate roasting pan. Pour enough water into each roasting pan to reach halfway up sides of custard-filled pan.

BAKE flans until just set in center, about 50 minutes. Lift each pan from water bath. Place hot flans, uncovered, in refrigerator and refrigerate overnight.

CUT around 1 flan to loosen. Invert platter over flan. Hold platter and pan together and turn over. Carefully lift off pan, allowing flan to settle onto platter and caramel syrup to pour out. Using small sharp knife, loosen any hard caramel from pan bottom. Crack caramel into pieces. Garnish flan with caramel pieces. Repeat with second flan. Serve immediately or refrigerate up to 6 hours.

Coffee-cardamom flans with orange crème fraîche

ONE SUGAR CRYSTAL can turn a satiny-smooth caramel syrup into an undesirable grainy mess. Some caramel recipes, such as this one, include corn syrup, which helps prevent this disaster. Adding a few drops of fresh lemon juice to the sugar mixture before it begins simmering also helps to keep the sugar from crystallizing. If you don't have corn syrup or lemon juice, don't fret. One foolproof way to ensure that the mixture doesn't crystallize is to brush down the sides of the saucepan occasionally with a wet pastry brush, washing away undissolved crystals.

8 SERVINGS

2 cups sugar, divided
⅓ cup water
1 teaspoon light corn syrup

4 cups whole milk
¼ cup finely ground espresso beans
1 tablespoon whole green cardamom pods, each cracked slightly

6 large egg yolks
2 large eggs

Orange Crème Fraîche (see recipe)

STIR 1 cup sugar, ⅓ cup water, and corn syrup in heavy medium saucepan over low heat until sugar dissolves. Increase heat and boil without stirring until caramel is deep amber color, occasionally brushing down sides of pan with wet pastry brush and swirling pan, about 7 minutes. Working quickly, pour caramel into eight 6-ounce custard cups. Tilt and rotate each cup to coat sides and bottom.

STIR milk, ground coffee, cardamom, and ½ cup sugar in heavy medium saucepan over medium heat until sugar dissolves and mixture simmers. Remove pan from heat; let mixture steep 1 hour.

PREHEAT oven to 350°F. Whisk egg yolks, whole eggs, and remaining ½ cup sugar in large bowl to combine. Return milk mixture to simmer; gradually whisk into egg mixture. Line sieve with several layers of moistened cheesecloth; strain custard into bowl, then divide among caramel-lined cups. Arrange cups in 13x9x2-inch metal baking pan. Pour enough hot water into baking pan to reach halfway up sides of cups. Cover pan loosely with aluminum foil.

BAKE flans 20 minutes. Lift foil to allow steam to escape. Replace foil. Bake flans until just set in center, lifting foil every 10 minutes, about 35 minutes longer. Remove flans from water. Refrigerate flans 4 hours, then cover and refrigerate overnight.

RUN small sharp knife around flans; invert onto plates. Serve with Orange Crème Fraîche.

Orange crème fraîche

THE PAIRING of the Coffee-Cardamom Flans with this orange-flavored accompaniment creates an exotic mélange of flavors. Try it with poppy seed cake and fresh berries, with wedges of warm apple tart, with grilled peaches, or as a dip for fresh strawberries. You can find crème fraîche at specialty foods stores and at some supermarkets and health foods stores. If it's unavailable, heat ½ cup of whipping cream to lukewarm (85°F), then remove it from the heat and mix in 1 tablespoon of buttermilk. Cover the mixture and let it stand in a warm draft-free area until it thickens slightly, about 24 to 48 hours, depending on room temperature. Cover and refrigerate it up to two days.

MAKES ABOUT 2 CUPS

- **½ cup whipping cream**
- **1 tablespoon grated orange peel**
- **½ cup crème fraîche**
- **1 tablespoon sugar**

BRING whipping cream and orange peel to simmer in heavy small saucepan over medium heat. Pour into medium bowl. Place bowl inside large bowl of ice water to chill quickly. Whisk in crème fraîche. Refrigerate until mixture is very cold, at least 1 hour. Add sugar and whisk until firm peaks form. Cover and chill up to 3 hours. Rewhip, if necessary, before using.

Champagne zabaglione with fresh fruit compote

THIS PRETTY AND SOPHISTICATED custard sauce is an Italian classic. It gets a dash of elegance from Champagne, while whipped cream enhances its light, airy texture. Be sure to use a large metal bowl when making this sauce, because it triples in volume as it cooks. Allow it to cool completely before folding in the whipped cream to help retain as much volume as possible. Zabaglione can be prepared a day ahead. Serve it over fresh fruit presented in pretty stemware for an impressive dessert.

6 SERVINGS

Zabaglione

- **1 cup dry Champagne or other sparkling wine**
- **¾ cup powdered sugar**
- **5 large egg yolks**
- **2 tablespoons light corn syrup**

- **6 tablespoons chilled whipping cream**

Fruit compote

- **2 large oranges**

- **½ small pineapple, peeled, cored**
- **1 1-pint container strawberries, hulled, quartered**
- **2 kiwis, peeled, sliced into rounds**
- **1 pear, peeled, cored, diced**

- **6 tablespoons chilled dry Champagne or other sparkling wine**
- **6 whole strawberries**

FOR ZABAGLIONE: Whisk Champagne, sugar, egg yolks, and corn syrup in large metal bowl to blend. Set bowl over saucepan of simmering water (do not allow bottom of bowl to touch water). Whisk constantly until mixture has tripled in volume and candy thermometer registers 160°F, about 10 minutes. Remove bowl from over water. Using electric mixer, beat zabaglione until completely cool, about 5 minutes.

BEAT cream to soft peaks in small bowl. Fold cream into cooled zabaglione. Cover and refrigerate until ready to use. *(Can be prepared 1 day ahead; keep refrigerated. Stir lightly to loosen before serving.)*

FOR FRUIT COMPOTE: Using small sharp knife, cut off peel and white pith from oranges. Working over bowl, cut between membranes to release orange segments. *(Oranges can be prepared 6 hours ahead. Cover and refrigerate.)*

USING tip of vegetable peeler, cut out eyes from pineapple; discard eyes. Dice pineapple. Combine pineapple, quartered strawberries, kiwis, and pear in large bowl. Mix in oranges.

SPOON fruit into 6 stemmed glasses. Pour 1 tablespoon Champagne over fruit in each goblet. Top fruit with zabaglione. Garnish each serving with whole strawberry and serve immediately.

Panna cotta with cardamom-poached apricots

LIMONCELLO, THE SWEET LEMON LIQUEUR of Capri (available at some liquor stores and specialty foods stores), adds a new twist to this creamy Italian dessert. If you can't find limoncello, you can make your own (see recipe, page 747). Whipped cream also gives it a fluffy, almost mousse-like consistency. Panna cotta—literally "cooked cream"—is different from other custards in that it's eggless and never baked. Instead, gelatin makes it thicken it as it chills. If unmolding the custards sounds a little tricky, use wide shallow soup bowls or pretty dessert bowls instead of custard cups, and spoon the apricots over the custard just before serving.

4 SERVINGS

2½ tablespoons whole milk
2 teaspoons unflavored gelatin

2¼ cups chilled whipping cream, divided
Peel from 1 orange (orange part only), removed with swivel-bladed vegetable peeler
1 vanilla bean, split lengthwise

Nonstick vegetable oil spray
6 tablespoons powdered sugar
¼ cup limoncello (lemon liqueur) or orange liqueur

Cardamom-Poached Apricots (see recipe)

POUR milk into small bowl. Sprinkle gelatin over. Let stand 10 minutes.

COMBINE 1½ cups cream and peel in saucepan. Scrape in seeds from vanilla bean; add pod. Simmer until cream is reduced to 1¼ cups, about 4 minutes. Strain into bowl. Add gelatin mixture to hot cream mixture; whisk until gelatin dissolves. Chill in freezer until beginning to thicken, whisking occasionally, about 15 minutes.

SPRAY four 6-ounce custard cups with nonstick spray. Beat remaining ¾ cup cream and powdered sugar in bowl until stiff peaks form. Fold into cream-gelatin mixture in 3 additions. Gradually fold in liqueur. Divide among prepared custard cups. Cover and refrigerate until set, at least 4 hours. *(Can be prepared 1 day ahead; keep refrigerated.)*

USING small sharp knife, cut around panna cotta in each custard cup. Place plate atop each custard cup. Invert each cup, allowing panna cotta to settle onto plate. Serve with Cardamom-Poached Apricots.

Cardamom-poached apricots

CARDAMOM, a spice native to India, lends a warm, spicy-sweet flavor to this compote. Look for the pale green cardamom pods in the spice section of the supermarket. The tiny dark cardamom seeds are encapsulated in the pods and can be released easily by crushing the pods gently with a rolling pin to crack them open. Other dried fruits, such as dried cherries, figs, or raisins, make delicious substitutes for the apricots.

4 SERVINGS

- **5 cups water**
- **8 ounces dried apricots**
- **1 cup sugar**
- **2 tablespoons fresh lemon juice**
- **½ teaspoon cardamom seeds (from about 12 whole pods)**

COMBINE all ingredients in heavy large saucepan; let stand 15 minutes. Bring to boil. Reduce heat and simmer gently until apricots are very tender, about 15 minutes.

USING slotted spoon, transfer apricots to medium bowl. Simmer syrup in saucepan until reduced to 1½ cups, about 8 minutes. Pour over apricots in bowl. Refrigerate until cold, about 4 hours. *(Can be prepared 2 days ahead; keep refrigerated.)*

Buttermilk panna cotta with sweetened strawberries

THIS IRRESISTIBLE DESSERT, which gives the basic panna cotta a crème caramel accent, gets tangy flavor from the addition of buttermilk. Be sure to refrigerate the panna cotta at least one day and up to two days, as this will allow enough time for the hardened caramel under the custard to soften into a syrupy sauce.

6 SERVINGS

- **⅓ cup plus 6 tablespoons sugar**
- **2 tablespoons water**

- **2 cups whipping cream, divided**
- **1½ teaspoons unflavored gelatin**
- **½ vanilla bean, split lengthwise**
- **1 cup buttermilk**

- **1 16-ounce container strawberries, hulled, sliced (about 3 cups)**
- **¼ cup (packed) golden brown sugar**

PLACE six 6-ounce custard cups on small baking sheet. Combine ⅓ cup sugar and 2 tablespoons water in heavy small saucepan. Stir over medium-low heat until sugar dissolves. Increase heat and boil without stirring until syrup is deep amber color, occasionally brushing down sides of pan with wet pastry brush and swirling pan, about 8 minutes. Immediately pour caramel into custard cups, dividing equally; tilt cups to cover bottoms evenly (caramel layer will be thin). Cool until caramel is set.

POUR ¼ cup whipping cream into small bowl; sprinkle gelatin over. Let stand until gelatin softens, about 10 minutes. Combine remaining 6 tablespoons sugar and remaining 1¾ cups cream in heavy medium saucepan. Scrape in seeds from vanilla bean; add pod. Bring just to simmer. Remove from heat. Add gelatin mixture and whisk until gelatin dissolves. Strain mixture into 4-cup glass measuring cup. Whisk in buttermilk. Divide mixture among caramel-lined custard cups. Refrigerate panna cotta uncovered overnight. *(Can be prepared 2 days ahead. Cover and keep refrigerated.)*

TOSS strawberries and brown sugar in large bowl. Let stand until juices form, at least 30 minutes and up to 2 hours.

RUN small sharp knife between panna cotta and custard cups to loosen. Invert onto plates. Using rubber spatula, scrape any caramel remaining on bottom of cups over panna cotta. Spoon sweetened strawberries alongside and serve.

Marsala tiramisù

TIRAMISÙ, Italian for "pick-me-up," is often regarded as an Italian trifle—it features layers of espresso-soaked ladyfingers, mascarpone cheese, and the Italian custard known as zabaglione. Tiramisù is best when made one day ahead to allow the flavors to marry. Mascarpone, an Italian cream cheese, is available at Italian markets and many supermarkets.

16 SERVINGS

- **3/4 cup sugar**
- **2/3 cup dry Marsala**
- **8 large egg yolks**

- **3 8-ounce containers mascarpone cheese, room temperature**
- **1 cup chilled whipping cream**

- **3/4 cup freshly brewed very strong espresso coffee**
- **1/3 cup Kahlúa or other coffee liqueur**
- **2 1/2 3.5-ounce packages Champagne biscuits (crisp ladyfinger cookies)**

- **1 1/2 tablespoons unsweetened cocoa powder**

WHISK sugar, Marsala, and egg yolks in medium metal bowl. Set bowl over saucepan of simmering water (do not allow bottom of bowl to touch water). Whisk constantly until candy thermometer registers 165°F and mixture thickens, about 4 minutes. Remove bowl from over water. Cool completely, whisking occasionally.

USING electric mixer, beat mascarpone in another medium bowl just until smooth. Fold mascarpone into marsala mixture. Using electric mixer with clean beaters, beat whipping cream in large bowl to soft peaks. Add mascarpone mixture to whipped cream and fold together.

MIX coffee and Kahlúa in medium bowl. Completely submerge 1 biscuit in coffee mixture for 1 second; shake off excess liquid. Place biscuit in bottom of 8-cup (12x9-inch) oval gratin dish. Repeat with just enough biscuits to cover bottom of pan, trimming biscuits to fit if necessary. Spoon half of mascarpone mixture over biscuits, spreading to cover. Submerge remaining biscuits 1 at a time in coffee mixture and arrange atop mascarpone mixture (discard any remaining coffee mixture). Spoon remaining mascarpone mixture over biscuits, spreading to cover. Sift cocoa powder over, covering mascarpone mixture completely. Cover and refrigerate overnight. *(Tiramisù can be prepared 3 days ahead. Cover and keep refrigerated.)*

Summer fruit trifle

TRADITIONALLY, this British dessert was made with sponge cake, Sherry, custard, jam or fruit, and whipped cream. In this version, cream cheese and whipped cream replace the custard, creating a no-fuss filling and a show-stopping dessert for which no baking or fancy pastry skills are required. Trifle dishes—tall, straight-sided, footed, clear glass bowls—display the layers of fruit, cake, and cream beautifully; but if you don't have a trifle dish, you can use a clear glass bowl or layer the ingredients in wine goblets for individual trifles.

12 TO 18 SERVINGS

- **12 ounces cream cheese, room temperature**
- **1/2 cup plus 2 tablespoons sugar**
- **2 cups chilled whipping cream**
- **2 teaspoons vanilla extract**

- **4 nectarines, halved, pitted, thinly sliced**
- **2 1/2-pint containers raspberries**
- **1 1-pint container blueberries**
- **1 teaspoon ground cinnamon**
- **6 tablespoons apricot jam**
- **3 tablespoons dark rum**

- **1 1/2 (about) 12-ounce purchased pound cakes, cut into 1/2-inch-thick slices**

BEAT cream cheese and ½ cup sugar in large bowl until fluffy. Gradually beat in cream. Add vanilla and beat until medium-stiff peaks form. Spoon ⅔ cup cream cheese mixture into pastry bag fitted with medium star tip and refrigerate. Set remaining cream cheese mixture aside.

COMBINE all fruits, remaining 2 tablespoons sugar, and cinnamon in another large bowl. Mix jam and rum in small bowl to blend.

ARRANGE enough cake slices in bottom of 3-quart trifle dish to cover. Brush with 3 tablespoons jam mixture. Top with 2 cups fruit mixture. Top with half of cream cheese mixture from bowl. Top with another layer of cake slices. Brush with 3 tablespoons jam mixture. Top with 2 cups fruit mixture, then remaining cream cheese mixture. Cover with another layer of cake. Brush with remaining jam mixture. Top with remaining fruit mixture. Cover and refrigerate at least 3 hours and up to 8 hours.

PIPE cream cheese mixture in pastry bag around edge of trifle and serve.

Lemon curd and blueberry trifle

LEMON CURD, a thick and tangy stirred custard, has many uses. Here it's layered between a delicious blueberry compote and a purchased pound cake, making for an ideal summer dessert and make-ahead treat (it can be assembled up to two days before serving and kept refrigerated). Use this lemony custard to fill tartlet shells, as a filling for layered cakes, or to spread on scones. When cooking the curd, stir it constantly and keep it from boiling, or the eggs in the mixture will scramble.

10 TO 12 SERVINGS

Lemon curd

- **1⅓ cups sugar**
- **12 tablespoons (1½ sticks) unsalted butter, cut into ½-inch cubes**
- **⅔ cup fresh lemon juice**
- **1 tablespoon grated lemon peel**
- **⅛ teaspoon salt**
- **5 large eggs, beaten to blend**

Lemon syrup

- **1 cup water**
- **1 cup sugar**
- **⅓ cup fresh lemon juice**
- **1 tablespoon (packed) grated lemon peel**

Filling

- **1 8-ounce package cream cheese, room temperature**
- **¾ cup sugar, divided**
- **2¼ cups chilled heavy whipping cream, divided**
- **¼ teaspoon vanilla extract**

- **3 ½-pint containers fresh blueberries**

- **1 12-ounce purchased pound cake, cut into 1-inch cubes**

FOR LEMON CURD: Combine first 5 ingredients in heavy medium saucepan. Stir over medium heat until butter melts and sugar dissolves. Remove from heat. Gradually whisk in eggs. Whisk constantly over medium-low heat until curd thickens, about 2 minutes (do not boil). Strain curd through sieve into bowl. Press plastic wrap directly onto surface of curd; refrigerate overnight.

FOR LEMON SYRUP: Combine all ingredients in small saucepan. Bring to boil, stirring until sugar dissolves. Reduce heat and simmer 5 minutes. Cool.

FOR FILLING: Using electric mixer, beat cream cheese, ½ cup sugar, ¼ cup whipping cream, and vanilla in large bowl until smooth. Beat remaining 2 cups whipping cream and ¼ cup sugar in another large bowl until peaks form. Fold whipped cream into cream cheese mixture in 2 additions.

PUREE 1 container blueberries and ¼ cup lemon syrup in processor. Transfer to medium bowl. Add 1½ containers blueberries and mash with potato masher until chunky puree forms. Reserve remaining blueberries for garnish.

ARRANGE ⅓ of pound cake cubes (about 2 generous cups) in bottom of 14-cup glass trifle dish. Drizzle with 7 tablespoons lemon syrup. Spoon ⅓ of cream cheese filling (about 2 cups) over cake in dollops; spread to sides of dish. Spoon half of blueberry puree over; spread to sides of dish. Spoon half of lemon curd (about 1¼ cups) over blueberry puree in dollops, then spread to sides of dish. Repeat layering with ⅓ of cake cubes, 7 tablespoons lemon syrup, ⅓ of cream cheese filling, and remaining blueberry puree, then remaining cake cubes, 7 tablespoons lemon syrup, and remaining lemon curd. Spread remaining cream cheese filling over. Sprinkle with reserved blueberries. Cover and refrigerate overnight. *(Can be prepared 2 days ahead. Keep refrigerated.)* Spoon trifle into dessert dishes and serve.

Chocolate, cranberry, and ginger trifle

CREAMY CHOCOLATE PUDDING spiked with Grand Marnier is layered with a ginger-cranberry compote in this festive holiday trifle. Unlike custards, puddings are thickened with flour or another starch, most commonly cornstarch. The addition of starch keeps the pudding from curdling even when it comes to a boil. In fact, for puddings it's important to bring the mixture to a boil in order to achieve the desired consistency. As with most trifles, assemble and refrigerate the trifle at least four hours in advance to allow the flavors to mingle. You'll have a little chocolate pudding left over after assembling the trifle. Spoon it into wineglasses and top it with a dollop of whipped cream.

15 SERVINGS

Cranberry filling

2 12-ounce bags fresh cranberries
1¾ cups sugar
1 cup orange juice
1 tablespoon grated orange peel
1 teaspoon ground ginger
½ cup chopped crystallized ginger

Chocolate pudding

1¾ cups whole milk
6 large egg yolks
¾ cup sugar
¼ cup cornstarch
4 ounces bittersweet (not unsweetened) or semisweet chocolate, chopped
¼ cup Grand Marnier or other orange liqueur

½ cup chopped crystallized ginger
1¾ cups chilled whipping cream

Assembly

1 16-ounce frozen pound cake, thawed, cut crosswise into 16 slices, each slice quartered
9 tablespoons Grand Marnier or other orange liqueur

FOR CRANBERRY FILLING. Combine first 5 ingredients in heavy medium saucepan. Bring to boil, stirring until sugar dissolves. Boil until cranberries pop, stirring occasionally, about 5 minutes. Mix in crystallized ginger. Cover filling and refrigerate until cold.

FOR CHOCOLATE PUDDING: Bring milk to simmer in heavy medium saucepan. Remove from heat. Using electric mixer, beat egg yolks and sugar in medium bowl until very thick, about 3 minutes. Add cornstarch; beat to blend. Gradually beat in hot milk. Return mixture to saucepan; whisk over medium heat until pudding thickens and comes to boil, about 3 minutes (pudding will be very thick). Remove from heat. Add chocolate; whisk until chocolate melts and mixture is smooth. Mix in Grand Marnier. Transfer to medium bowl. Press plastic wrap directly onto surface of pudding. Refrigerate until cold, about 3 hours. *(Filling and pudding can be prepared 1 day ahead. Keep refrigerated.)*

MIX crystallized ginger into pudding. Beat cream in large bowl until firm peaks form. Set aside 1½ cups whipped cream. Fold remaining whipped cream into pudding in 2 additions.

FOR ASSEMBLY: Cover bottom of 8-inch-diameter, 3-quart trifle dish with single layer of cake pieces, turning crusts away from sides of dish. Sprinkle with 3 tablespoons Grand Marnier. Spread 1 cup cranberry filling over cake to sides of dish. Spread 1¼ cups chocolate pudding over cranberry filling to sides of dish. Repeat layering 2 more times (reserve remaining chocolate pudding for another use).

SPREAD reserved 1½ cups whipped cream over trifle, building up whipped cream edges slightly. Spoon remaining cranberry filling atop whipped cream (but not atop whipped cream edges). Cover and refrigerate at least 4 hours. *(Can be prepared 1 day ahead. Keep refrigerated.)*

Sticky toffee pudding

THIS IS A PUDDING not in the American sense of the word, but in the British sense, meaning simply "dessert." It gets its name from the sticky, delicious caramel sauce that is poured over a moist cake—an irresistible combination.

8 SERVINGS

- **1 cup all purpose flour**
- **½ teaspoon baking powder**
- **¼ teaspoon plus ⅛ teaspoon salt**
- **6 tablespoons (¾ stick) unsalted butter, room temperature, divided**
- **½ cup sugar**
- **1 large egg**
- **½ cup boiling water**
- **½ cup pitted dates, finely chopped**
- **1 teaspoon instant coffee powder**
- **1 teaspoon vanilla extract**
- **½ teaspoon baking soda**

- **1 cup whipping cream**
- **½ cup (packed) dark brown sugar**
- **Whipped cream or vanilla ice cream**

PREHEAT oven to 375°F. Butter 11x7-inch flameproof glass baking dish. Whisk flour, baking powder, and ¼ teaspoon salt in medium bowl to combine. Using electric mixer, beat 2 tablespoons butter with ½ cup sugar in large bowl. Beat in egg, then ⅓ of flour mixture. Beat remaining flour mixture into batter. Pour boiling water over dates and coffee powder in small bowl; stir in vanilla and baking soda. Mix into batter. Transfer batter to prepared pan, spreading evenly. Bake until tester inserted into center comes out clean, 20 minutes. *(Can be prepared 1 day ahead. Cool cake completely in pan. Cover and let stand at room temperature.)*

COMBINE 1 cup whipping cream, brown sugar, and remaining 4 tablespoons butter and ⅛ teaspoon salt in heavy medium saucepan over medium-high heat. Bring to boil, stirring constantly. Boil until reduced to 1⅓ cups, stirring occasionally, about 10 minutes.

PREHEAT broiler. Pour hot sauce over hot or room temperature cake. Broil until topping is bubbling, about 1 minute. Spoon cake onto plates. Serve with whipped cream or ice cream.

English pudding with cranberries, figs, and brown sugar hard sauce

THIS IS A LIGHTER VERSION of the traditional English-style steamed pudding: Unlike the original, there are no candied fruits in this rendition, which is nonetheless every bit as delicious—and, depending on your opinion of candied fruit, perhaps even more so. A charlotte mold is a bucket-shaped metal container used for puddings, aspics, ice cream, and more. Look for it at cookware stores.

12 SERVINGS

- **1 cup all purpose flour**
- **1 teaspoon ground cinnamon**
- **1 teaspoon ground ginger**

- **3/4 teaspoon baking powder**
- **1/2 teaspoon salt**
- **1/2 teaspoon ground cloves**
- **1/2 teaspoon ground nutmeg**
- **2 cups dried cranberries**
- **1 1/2 cups coarsely chopped dried Calimyrna figs (about 8 ounces)**
- **1 cup dried currants**
- **4 cups fresh breadcrumbs made from crustless French bread**
- **1 cup (packed) golden brown sugar**
- **3 large eggs**
- **1/2 cup (1 stick) unsalted butter, melted**
- **1/3 cup pure maple syrup**
- **1/4 cup Grand Marnier or other orange liqueur**
- **1/4 cup dark rum**
- **1 tablespoon grated tangerine or orange peel**
- **2 teaspoons vanilla extract**

Tangerine or orange peel twists (optional)
Fresh cranberries, rolled in sugar (optional)
Brown Sugar Hard Sauce (see recipe)

GENEROUSLY butter 2½-quart charlotte mold, pudding mold, or thick ovenproof glass bowl. Sift flour, cinnamon, ginger, baking powder, salt, cloves, and nutmeg into large mixing bowl. Add all dried fruit and toss to coat. Mix in crumbs. Whisk brown sugar, eggs, butter, maple syrup, liqueur, rum, grated tangerine peel, and vanilla in medium bowl to blend. Pour over dry ingredients and stir until well combined (batter will be thick).

SPOON batter into prepared mold. Smooth top. Cover mold tightly with double thickness of aluminum foil. Place rack in large pot and set pudding on rack. Pour enough hot water into pot to reach halfway up sides of mold. Cover pot. Bring water to simmer over medium-low heat. Steam pudding until wooden skewer inserted into center comes out clean, adding more boiling water to pot as necessary, about 5 hours.

TRANSFER mold to cooling rack; uncover and cool 30 minutes. *(Can be prepared up to 2 months ahead. Remove pudding from mold; cool completely. Wrap tightly in plastic and refrigerate. To reheat pudding, unwrap and return to buttered mold; cover. Place mold on rack in large pot. Pour enough hot water into pot to reach halfway up sides of mold. Cover pot; steam pudding over medium-low heat until heated through, about 1 hour. Transfer to cooling rack. Let stand 30 minutes.)*

TURN warm pudding out onto platter. Garnish with tangerine peel twists and fresh cranberries, if desired. Serve with hard sauce.

Brown sugar hard sauce

THIS RICH SAUCE would also be excellent spread over fruitcake or gingerbread. When grating the tangerine or orange peel, turn the fruit often—you want only the orange part of the peel, not the bitter white pith underneath.

MAKES ABOUT 1 3/4 CUPS

- **1/3 cup (packed) golden brown sugar**
- **4 tablespoons dark rum, divided**
- **1 tablespoon grated tangerine or orange peel**

- **1 cup (2 sticks) unsalted butter, room temperature**
- **1/2 cup powdered sugar**

STIR brown sugar and 3 tablespoons rum in heavy small saucepan over medium-low heat until sugar dissolves. Mix in tangerine or orange peel. Cool to room temperature.

USING electric mixer, beat butter in medium bowl until fluffy. Add remaining 1 tablespoon rum, brown sugar mixture, and powdered sugar; beat until well blended and smooth. *(Can be prepared 1 week ahead. Cover and refrigerate. Bring to room temperature before serving.)*

Persimmon pudding

LOOK FOR Hachiya persimmons that have ruby-orange-colored skin and flesh and are soft to the touch, as these signs indicate ripeness. Because they're available from October to February, you'll often find persimmons as part of holiday menus and flavored with holiday spices, as in this old-fashioned baked pudding that's reminiscent of pumpkin pie. To make this year-round, peel and puree the persimmons and freeze them for later use.

8 SERVINGS

- **3 very ripe large Hachiya persimmons**
- **3 large eggs**
- **1 cup (packed) golden brown sugar**
- **1 cup all purpose flour**
- **¾ cup half and half**
- **½ cup (1 stick) unsalted butter, melted, cooled slightly**
- **½ cup raisins**
- **2 teaspoons ground cinnamon**
- **1 teaspoon baking soda**
- **1 teaspoon baking powder**
- **1 teaspoon ground ginger**
- **½ teaspoon ground nutmeg**
- **½ teaspoon salt**

Whipped cream
Chopped toasted walnuts

PREHEAT oven to 325°F. Butter 9x9x2-inch metal baking pan. Cut persimmons in half. Using spoon, scoop out pulp from persimmons and transfer to processor. Puree until smooth. Measure 1½ cups persimmon puree; reserve remainder for another use. Whisk persimmon puree and next 12 ingredients in large bowl to combine. Transfer mixture to prepared pan. Bake until pudding is puffed and tester inserted into center comes out clean, about 45 minutes.

COOL pudding in pan on rack 15 minutes (pudding will fall). Cut pudding into 8 portions. Transfer to plates. Serve warm with whipped cream and nuts.

Individual chocolate croissant bread puddings

INCREDIBLY DECADENT, this bread pudding made with croissants is fancy enough to serve for a special occasion. And since it can be assembled ahead of time, it's perfect for entertaining. To get it ready the day before, simply divide the chocolate and croissants among the custard cups, then prepare and refrigerate the custard mixture. About one hour before serving, pour the custard over the croissants and chocolate and proceed.

6 SERVINGS

- **2 large croissants (about 6 ounces total), cut into ½-inch cubes**
- **5 ounces bittersweet (not unsweetened) or semisweet chocolate, chopped**
- **2 cups whipping cream**
- **½ vanilla bean, split lengthwise**
- **4 large egg yolks**
- **½ cup sugar**

PREHEAT oven to 350°F. Arrange croissant cubes on large baking sheet. Bake until golden, about 10 minutes. Cool. Reduce oven temperature to 325°F.

DIVIDE chocolate among six 6-ounce custard cups. Top with croissant cubes, dividing equally. Pour cream into heavy medium saucepan. Scrape in seeds from vanilla bean; add pod. Bring to simmer over medium heat. Remove from heat. Whisk egg yolks and sugar in medium bowl. Gradually whisk in hot milk mixture. Discard vanilla bean pod. Pour custard over chocolate and croissants, dividing equally.

PLACE cups in large baking pan. Pour enough water into baking pan to reach halfway up sides of cups.

BAKE puddings until set, about 40 minutes. Remove from water; cool slightly. Serve warm or at room temperature.

Buttermilk bread pudding with creamy chocolate sauce

THOUGH CALLED A PUDDING, a bread pudding is actually more closely related to a custard because the mixture does not include flour or cornstarch as a thickener. Here the custard is made of buttermilk and half and half, resulting in a lighter, tangy flavor that makes an excellent foil for the chocolate sauce.

8 SERVINGS

- **3 large eggs**
- **2 large egg yolks**
- **2/3 cup sugar**
- **2 cups buttermilk**
- **2 1/2 cups half and half**
- **2 teaspoons vanilla extract**
- **9 buttermilk bread slices, crusts removed, bread cut into 1-inch pieces (about 6 generous cups)**
- **Ground nutmeg**
- **Creamy Chocolate Sauce (see recipe)**

PREHEAT oven to 325°F. Butter 13x9x2-inch glass baking dish. Whisk eggs, yolks, and sugar to blend in large bowl. Mix in buttermilk, half and half, and vanilla. Add bread; let stand 5 minutes. Transfer to prepared dish. Sprinkle lightly with nutmeg. Place baking dish in large roasting pan. Pour enough hot water into roasting pan to reach 1 inch up sides of baking dish. Bake until pudding is firm in center but still pale in color, about 1 hour 15 minutes. Cool slightly.

SERVE warm or cold, passing warm Creamy Chocolate Sauce separately.

Creamy chocolate sauce

THIS SIMPLE CHOCOLATE SAUCE pairs perfectly with the Buttermilk Bread Pudding, but its uses are nearly endless. Glaze cupcakes or brownies with it, drizzle it over ice cream, or chill it until cold and firm but still spreadable, then sandwich it between two cookies. Add peppermint extract, grated orange peel, or a touch of espresso powder for even more variations.

MAKES ABOUT 1 1/3 CUPS

- **3/4 cup whipping cream**
- **3 tablespoons sugar**
- **1 teaspoon vanilla extract**
- **5 ounces bittersweet (not unsweetened) or semisweet chocolate, chopped**

COMBINE cream, sugar, and vanilla in heavy medium saucepan. Stir over medium-high heat until sugar dissolves. Reduce heat to low; add chocolate and stir until melted. Serve warm.

Bread pudding with dried apricots, dried cherries, and caramel sauce

DON'T WORRY ABOUT using a fancy, rustic French bread for this recipe. The soft, yeasty sliced white bread found in every supermarket's bread aisle gives this pudding an old-fashioned appeal. Reserve the sugar syrup used to soak the dried apricots and cherries, as it lends an intriguing flavor to the caramel sauce.

8 SERVINGS

- **4 cups sugar, divided**
- **2 1/4 cups water, divided**
- **4 ounces dried apricots, thinly sliced**
- **4 ounces dried tart cherries or dried cranberries**
- **3 cups whipping cream, divided**

2 cups whole milk
8 large egg yolks

1½ 24-ounce loaves sliced white bread, crusts trimmed, each slice halved

COMBINE 1 cup sugar, 2 cups water, apricots, and cherries in medium saucepan. Bring to boil, stirring until sugar dissolves. Remove from heat. Cover and let stand 20 minutes. Strain fruit; reserve fruit and soaking liquid separately.

COMBINE 1 cup sugar and remaining ¼ cup water in heavy medium saucepan. Stir over low heat until sugar dissolves. Increase heat and boil without stirring until syrup is deep amber color, occasionally brushing down sides of pan with wet pastry brush and swirling pan, about 12 minutes. Remove from heat. Gradually whisk in 1 cup reserved soaking liquid (mixture will bubble vigorously). Stir over low heat until caramel thickens slightly, about 6 minutes. Add 1 cup cream. Bring to boil and simmer until caramel thickens slightly, about 3 minutes. Remove from heat. Cool caramel sauce 30 minutes, whisking occasionally. *(Can be prepared 1 day ahead. Cover sauce and fruit separately and refrigerate.)*

PREHEAT oven to 350°F. Bring 2 cups cream and milk to simmer in another medium saucepan. Remove from heat. Whisk remaining 2 cups sugar and egg yolks in large bowl to blend. Gradually whisk in warm milk mixture. Cool custard slightly.

LIGHTLY butter 13x9x2-inch glass baking dish. Arrange enough bread in single layer over bottom and up sides of prepared dish to cover completely, trimming bread to fit. Sprinkle reserved fruit over bread. Arrange remaining bread slices over fruit, trimming to fit and overlapping slightly.

POUR custard over bread. Press bread gently to submerge. Let stand until custard is absorbed, about 10 minutes. Bake until custard is set and bread is golden brown on top, about 55 minutes.

REWARM caramel sauce over low heat. Serve pudding warm with sauce.

Rice pudding with raisins and cinnamon

THIS MEXICAN RENDITION of *arroz con leche* includes three types of milk and is rich in fragrance from the cinnamon sticks and vanilla bean. Although any type of cinnamon will work, try using Ceylon or Sri Lanka cinnamon, the one that Mexican cooks prefer—it's less pungent than the cassia cinnamon sold in U.S. markets. Ceylon cinnamon is available at Latin markets, labeled *canela* (Spanish for cinnamon). This rice pudding is best served warm. If you'd like to serve a cold rice pudding, a medium-grain rice provides optimal results.

8 TO 10 SERVINGS

6 cups water, divided
2 cups long-grain white rice

6 2x½-inch strips lemon peel (yellow part only)
½ teaspoon salt

5 cups (or more) whole milk
1 cup sweetened condensed milk
1 cup evaporated milk
2 canela or cinnamon sticks
2 vanilla beans, split lengthwise in half
¾ cup brown raisins or golden raisins
2 tablespoons sugar

Ground cinnamon
Finely grated peel from 1 lemon
Additional canela sticks or cinnamon sticks (optional)

BRING 2 cups water to boil in medium saucepan. Remove from heat. Add rice; let stand 15 minutes. Pour rice into strainer and drain, then rinse rice under cold running water until water runs clear.

BRING remaining 4 cups water to boil in heavy large saucepan. Add rice, lemon peel strips, and salt; return to boil. Reduce heat to low, cover, and simmer until rice is almost tender, about 10 minutes. Drain. Discard lemon peel.

COMBINE 5 cups milk, sweetened condensed milk, evaporated milk, and 2 canela sticks in heavy large saucepan. Scrape in seeds from vanilla beans; add pods. Bring to boil. Reduce heat to medium and boil gently until mixture thickens and is reduced to 2¾ cups, about 30 minutes. Stir in rice, raisins, and sugar. Stir until raisins are plump and flavors blend, about 5 minutes. Discard canela sticks and vanilla bean pods.

SPOON pudding into bowls. Sprinkle with ground cinnamon and grated lemon peel. Garnish with canela sticks, if desired, and serve.

Lemon custards with lemon verbena

THE FRAGRANT HERB lemon verbena is often used in Provence to make herb teas and liqueurs. Although it's optional in this recipe, it lends an exotic flavor to the rich, silky lemon custards. Look for fresh lemon verbena at farmers' markets and nurseries. Dried lemon verbena can be found at specialty foods stores and some health foods stores. If you're unable to locate it, use ¼ cup minced fresh lemongrass instead.

6 SERVINGS

- **1 cup water**
- **14 2- to 2½-inch-long fresh or dried lemon verbena leaves (optional)**
- **10 2x½-inch strips lemon peel (yellow part only)**
- **6 tablespoons sugar**
- **1½ cups whipping cream**
- **6 large egg yolks**
- **1 teaspoon fresh lemon juice**

PREHEAT oven to 325°F. Combine first 3 ingredients in medium saucepan. Boil until mixture is reduced to ½ cup, about 4 minutes. Add sugar and simmer until mixture is reduced to ⅓ cup, about 3 minutes. Stir in cream. Whisk egg yolks to blend in medium bowl. Gradually whisk in hot cream mixture. Whisk in lemon juice.

STRAIN custard through sieve into 4-cup measuring cup. Divide among six ½-cup ovenproof ramekins or soufflé dishes. Cover ramekins with aluminum foil. Place ramekins in 13x9x2-inch metal baking pan. Pour enough hot water into pan to reach halfway up sides of ramekins. Bake custards until just set, about 45 minutes. Remove pan from oven; let custards cool in water in pan. Transfer ramekins to refrigerator. Cover and refrigerate at least 4 hours and up to 1 day.

Lemon curd mousse with toasted coconut and blueberries

WHIPPED CREAM turns luscious lemon curd into a light mousse. You want to add the gelatin to the curd as soon as it's removed from the heat, since the heat will help dissolve the gelatin fully. Be sure the curd is cold before folding in the whipped cream, or else the cream will melt and not impart an airy texture.

8 SERVINGS

- **2 teaspoons water**
- **½ teaspoon unflavored gelatin**
- **1 cup sugar**
- **½ cup fresh lemon juice**
- **6 large egg yolks**
- **2 tablespoons grated lemon peel**
- **¾ cup (1½ sticks) unsalted butter, cut into small pieces**

- **1 cup sweetened flaked coconut**
- **¼ cup (packed) golden brown sugar**

- **1½ cups chilled whipping cream**

- **2 6-ounce containers fresh blueberries**

PLACE 2 teaspoons water in small bowl; sprinkle gelatin over. Let stand 10 minutes. Whisk sugar, lemon juice, egg yolks, and lemon peel in heavy medium saucepan to blend. Add butter; stir constantly over medium heat until mixture thickens and just begins to bubble at edges, about 9 minutes. Remove from heat. Quickly add gelatin mixture; stir to dissolve. Transfer lemon curd to medium bowl. Press plastic wrap directly onto surface. Refrigerate until cold. *(Can be prepared 3 days ahead. Keep refrigerated.)*

PREHEAT oven to 350°F. Spread coconut on baking sheet. Sprinkle brown sugar over. Bake until coconut is golden, stirring occasionally, about 10 minutes. Cool.

BEAT cream in medium bowl until stiff peaks form. Fold 1 cup cream into curd to form mousse.

LAYER 3 tablespoons berries, 3 tablespoons mousse, 1 tablespoon coconut mixture, and 3 tablespoons whipped cream in each of 8 stemmed 10- to 12-ounce glasses. Repeat layering. Top each with 2 tablespoons berries, dollop of cream, some coconut mixture, and more berries. *(Can be prepared 6 hours ahead. Cover and refrigerate.)*

Bittersweet chocolate mousse

THIS VERSATILE MOUSSE lends itself to a variety of presentations and accompaniments. Add half a teaspoon of peppermint extract to the base to create a chocolate-mint mousse. Or accompany the mousse with sweetened whipped cream flavored with grated nutmeg, orange zest, or crystallized ginger and brandy. Or serve it layered in goblets with fresh berries. The myriad possibilities keep the recipe fresh.

6 SERVINGS

- **½ cup whole milk**
- **2 large egg yolks**
- **4 tablespoons sugar, divided**
- **6 ounces bittersweet (not unsweetened) or semisweet chocolate, finely chopped**
- **1 teaspoon vanilla extract**
- **4 large egg whites**
- **Pinch of salt**

- **Whipped cream**
- **Chocolate shavings (optional)**

WHISK milk, egg yolks, and 2 tablespoons sugar in heavy small saucepan to blend. Stir over medium-low heat until mixture thickens enough to coat spoon, about 7 minutes (do not boil). Remove from heat. Immediately add chopped chocolate and whisk until smooth. Whisk in vanilla. Transfer mixture to medium bowl; cool to lukewarm, stirring occasionally, about 10 minutes. Beat egg whites and salt in large bowl until soft peaks form. Gradually add remaining 2 tablespoons sugar, beating until stiff but not dry. Fold whites into cooled chocolate mixture in 3 additions. Divide mousse among 6 goblets or transfer to serving bowl. Cover and refrigerate until cold and set, at least 6 hours. *(Can be prepared 1 day ahead; keep refrigerated.)*

TOP mousse with whipped cream and chocolate shavings, if desired.

Chocolate mascarpone mousse with bananas

MASCARPONE CHEESE, an Italian cream cheese, adds body and richness to this irresistible chocolate mousse. You'll find mascarpone at specialty foods stores, Italian markets, and many supermarkets. Look for evenly colored yellow bananas with a speckling of brown spots, as these are indicators of ripeness. In this recipe, the chocolate mousse atop the bananas seals off the air, which keeps the bananas from discoloring, allowing these desserts to be made up to one day ahead. Keep the desserts covered tightly with plastic wrap and refrigerated. Then slice the remaining banana and use it to garnish the desserts just before serving.

8 SERVINGS

- **12 ounces bittersweet (not unsweetened) or semisweet chocolate, finely chopped**
- **2⅓ cups chilled whipping cream, divided**
- **⅓ cup water**
- **¼ cup dark corn syrup**
- **5 tablespoons dark rum**
- **1 8-ounce container mascarpone cheese**
- **3 bananas, divided**

STIR chocolate, ⅓ cup cream, ⅓ cup water, and corn syrup in heavy medium saucepan over medium-low heat until chocolate melts and mixture is smooth. Let cool until just lukewarm, stirring occasionally, about 20 minutes. Whisk in rum, then mascarpone. Beat 1 cup cream in medium bowl until stiff peaks form. Fold whipped cream into chocolate mixture in 2 additions.

PEEL and thinly slice 2 bananas on diagonal. Arrange 3 slices in each of eight 8- to 10-ounce goblets or coupes. Spoon mousse atop bananas, dividing equally. Cover with plastic wrap and refrigerate at least 4 hours. *(Can be prepared 1 day ahead; keep refrigerated.)*

BEAT remaining 1 cup cream in medium bowl until firm peaks form. Spoon or pipe cream decoratively atop each mousse. Peel and slice remaining banana. Garnish each mousse with banana slices.

Caramel mousse napoleon with caramel sauce and berries

DELICATE LAYERS of puff pastry are filled with caramel mousse and a caramel sauce, making a traditional napoleon even better. Piercing the puff pastry sheets all over with a fork before they're baked keeps them from rising too much and allows thin, flaky layers to form. In this recipe, a portion of the caramel sauce is folded into whipped cream and transformed into a creamy mousse. Adding a bit of dissolved gelatin to the mousse keeps it just firm enough to layer between the pastry.

6 SERVINGS

Pastry layers

- **1 17.3-ounce package frozen puff pastry (2 sheets), thawed**
- **2 tablespoons (¼ stick) unsalted butter, melted**
- **6 teaspoons sugar**

Caramel sauce and mousse

- **3 tablespoons plus ¾ cup water**
- **1 envelope unflavored gelatin**
- **2¾ cups sugar**
- **2 tablespoons light corn syrup**
- **1¾ cups whipping cream, room temperature**
- **½ cup (1 stick) unsalted butter**
- **1½ cups chilled whipping cream**

Assembly and final decoration

- **Powdered sugar**
- **Assorted fresh berries**

FOR PASTRY: Position 1 rack in top third of oven and 1 rack in bottom third and preheat to 400°F. Roll out 1 pastry sheet on lightly floured surface to

15x12-inch rectangle. Using small sharp knife and long ruler, trim sheet to 13x10-inch rectangle. Cut in half lengthwise, forming two 13x5-inch rectangles. Pierce rectangles all over with fork; transfer to 1 ungreased baking sheet. Repeat with remaining pastry sheet, transferring to another ungreased baking sheet. Brush rectangles with melted butter; sprinkle each with 1½ teaspoons sugar.

BAKE pastries 8 minutes. Reverse position of baking sheets and bake until pastries are golden, about 8 minutes longer. Cool pastries on sheets.

FOR SAUCE AND MOUSSE: Pour 3 tablespoons water into ovenproof ramekin or custard cup. Sprinkle with gelatin; let soften while preparing caramel sauce.

COMBINE sugar, corn syrup, and ¾ cup water in heavy large saucepan. Stir over medium-low heat until sugar dissolves, frequently brushing down sides of pan with wet pastry brush. Increase heat and boil without stirring until syrup turns amber, occasionally brushing down sides of pan with wet pastry brush and swirling pan, about 10 minutes. Remove from heat. Add 1¾ cups room temperature cream and butter (caramel will bubble vigorously). Return to low heat; stir until any caramel bits have dissolved.

POUR 1½ cups caramel sauce into glass measuring cup; set aside pan of caramel sauce. Place ramekin with gelatin mixture in small skillet of simmering water. Stir until gelatin dissolves and mixture is clear, about 1 minute. Mix gelatin into measured 1½ cups hot caramel; cool just to room temperature, stirring occasionally.

BEAT 1½ cups chilled whipping cream in large bowl to medium-firm peaks (do not overbeat). Gradually pour cooled caramel-gelatin mixture over cream, folding constantly but gently. Refrigerate mousse 15 minutes.

ARRANGE 3 pastry rectangles on large clean baking sheet; drizzle each with 2 tablespoons caramel from pan. Spread 1 cup mousse evenly over each rectangle. Refrigerate until mousse begins to set, about 1 hour. Reserve plain pastry rectangle.

PLACE 1 pastry layer with mousse on small baking sheet or board. Top with second layer, third layer, then plain pastry, aligning layers. Press assembled pastry slightly so that layers adhere. Cover and refrigerate at least 8 hours and up to 1 day. Cover and chill remaining caramel sauce in pan.

USING serrated knife, cut pastry crosswise into 6 pieces. Dust napoleons with powdered sugar. Transfer to plates. Rewarm sauce over low heat just until pourable; drizzle sauce onto each plate. Garnish with berries and serve.

Lime mousse with lime-vanilla syrup

THE FLECKS OF VANILLA in the clear lime syrup really enhance the simple yet elegant presentation of this refreshing summertime dessert. Beat the eggs with an electric mixer until they form a thick and creamy mixture that falls in slowly dissolving ribbons when the beaters are lifted (it really does take six minutes), as this helps create a delicate, airy mousse. Beating this mixture with the warm lime syrup over simmering water until it reaches 140°F destroys any bacteria in the uncooked eggs.

6 SERVINGS

1½ cups sugar
¾ cup water
1 4-inch piece vanilla bean, split lengthwise
8 tablespoons fresh lime juice, divided

1 teaspoon unflavored gelatin

2 large eggs

1 cup chilled whipping cream
2 teaspoons grated lime peel

COMBINE sugar and ¾ cup water in heavy small saucepan. Scrape in seeds from vanilla bean; add pod. Bring mixture to simmer over medium heat, stirring until sugar dissolves. Simmer until syrup thickens and is reduced to 1¼ cups, about 8 minutes. Cool to room temperature. Discard vanilla bean pod. Transfer ½ cup syrup to small bowl. Whisk in 1 tablespoon lime juice. Cover lime-vanilla syrup and refrigerate.

MIX gelatin and remaining 7 tablespoons lime juice in small bowl. Let stand until gelatin softens, about 10 minutes. Add to syrup in saucepan. Stir over low heat just until gelatin dissolves, about 5 minutes (do not boil).

USING electric mixer, beat eggs in large stainless steel bowl at high speed until mixture falls in heavy ribbon when beaters are lifted, about 6 minutes. Gradually beat in warm lime-gelatin syrup. Place bowl over saucepan of simmering water (do not allow bottom of bowl to touch water); beat until thermometer registers 140°F for 3 minutes, about 5 minutes total. Place bowl over larger bowl of ice water; beat syrup mixture until cold, about 3 minutes longer.

BEAT whipping cream in medium bowl until peaks form. Fold into lime-egg mixture in 2 additions. Fold in lime peel. Cover mousse and refrigerate until set, at least 6 hours and up to 1 day.

USING 2 large soup spoons, form mousse into 12 egg-shaped "dumplings," placing 2 on each of 6 plates. Spoon lime-vanilla syrup over mousse dumplings and serve.

Chocolate-peppermint soufflés

CHOCOLATE AND PEPPERMINT have a natural affinity. Perfect for entertaining the whole family, these individual soufflés can be made up to three days ahead. Wrap the soufflés in aluminum foil and freeze them, then remove the foil just before you're ready to bake them (no need to thaw). When making soufflés, it's important to coat the sides of the baking dishes with butter and sugar so that the soufflé batter won't stick to the sides, and so that it is able to rise high above the rims as it bakes. Make sure not to overbake the soufflés, as they should have moist pudding-like centers.

8 SERVINGS

- **3 tablespoons unsalted butter**
- **3 tablespoons all purpose flour**
- **1 cup reduced-fat (2%) milk**
- **¼ teaspoon salt**
- **6 ounces semisweet chocolate, chopped**
- **½ cup water**
- **⅔ cup sugar, divided**
- **1 teaspoon vanilla**

- **5 large egg yolks**
- **6 large egg whites**
- **¼ teaspoon cream of tartar**
- **⅓ cup crushed peppermint candy canes or other red-and-white-striped peppermint hard candies (about 2 ounces)**

Chocolate-Peppermint Sauce (see recipe)

BUTTER eight 10-ounce soufflé dishes or custard cups. Sprinkle with sugar. Arrange dishes on large baking sheet.

MELT butter in heavy medium saucepan over medium heat. Add flour; whisk until mixture is bubbling and smooth, about 2 minutes. Increase heat to medium-high; gradually whisk in milk. Whisk until mixture boils, thickens, and is smooth, about 1 minute. Mix in salt. Remove from heat. Add chocolate and whisk until melted. Add ½ cup water, ⅓ cup sugar, and vanilla; whisk until blended. Cool to room temperature, about 25 minutes.

WHISK egg yolks into chocolate mixture. Beat egg whites and cream of tartar in large bowl until soft peaks form. Gradually add ⅓ cup sugar, beating until stiff and glossy. Fold ¼ of whites into chocolate mixture. Gently fold chocolate mixture into remaining whites in 3 additions. Divide soufflé mixture among prepared dishes (filling will reach almost to top). Sprinkle crushed candy over soufflés. *(Can be prepared 3 days ahead. Wrap in aluminum foil and freeze; uncover but do not thaw before baking.)*

PREHEAT oven to 400°F. Bake soufflés until puffed and almost firm to touch but still soft in center, about 30 minutes for unfrozen, or 40 minutes for frozen. Serve immediately with Chocolate-Peppermint Sauce.

Chocolate-peppermint sauce

YOU CAN ALSO spoon this chocolate sauce over brownies and vanilla ice cream for a simple but indulgent treat.

MAKES ABOUT 1¾ CUPS

1 cup whipping cream
1 cup crushed peppermint candy canes or other red-and-white-striped peppermint hard candies (about 6 ounces)
¼ cup water
6 ounces semisweet chocolate, chopped

COMBINE cream, crushed candy canes, and ¼ cup water in heavy medium saucepan. Stir over medium heat until candy melts. Remove from heat. Add chocolate and stir until melted and smooth. Serve warm or at room temperature. *(Can be prepared 1 day ahead. Cover and refrigerate. Rewarm over low heat before using.)*

Swiss Toblerone soufflés

THE OLD SAYING IS TRUE: "Kings wait for soufflés; soufflés don't wait for kings." Once soufflés come out of the oven they should be served immediately, as their impressive stature deflates quickly. But we'll bet nobody will mind waiting for these soufflés made with Switzerland's Toblerone chocolate, containing honey-almond nougat. Since they can be assembled three days ahead, then wrapped in aluminum foil and frozen (just unwrap and pop them in the oven 22 minutes before serving), they're ideal for entertaining.

6 SERVINGS

2 tablespoons (¼ stick) unsalted butter
2 tablespoons all purpose flour
1 cup whole milk
8 ounces Toblerone dark chocolate or semisweet chocolate, chopped, divided
1 ounce unsweetened chocolate, chopped
3 tablespoons honey

4 large eggs, separated
¼ teaspoon salt
1 tablespoon sugar
Sliced almonds

Powdered sugar

BUTTER six 10-ounce soufflé dishes or custard cups. Sprinkle with sugar. Arrange soufflé dishes on large baking sheet.

MELT butter in heavy medium saucepan over medium heat. Add flour; whisk until mixture is bubbling, about 2 minutes. Increase heat to medium-high; gradually whisk in milk. Whisk until mixture boils, thickens, and is smooth, about 1 minute. Remove from heat. Add 6 ounces Toblerone chocolate (scant 1¼ cups), unsweetened chocolate, and honey; whisk until melted and smooth. Pour into large bowl. Cool to room temperature, stirring occasionally.

WHISK egg yolks into chocolate mixture. Beat egg whites and salt in medium bowl until soft peaks form. Add 1 tablespoon sugar; beat until stiff and glossy. Fold ¼ of whites into chocolate mixture. Gently fold in remaining whites. Divide half of mixture among prepared dishes. Sprinkle with remaining 2 ounces Toblerone chocolate, dividing equally. Spoon remaining batter over. Sprinkle almonds over soufflés. *(Can be prepared 3 days ahead. Wrap in aluminum foil and freeze; uncover but do not thaw before baking.)*

PREHEAT oven to 400°F. Bake until soufflés are puffed and almost firm to touch but centers still move slightly when dishes are shaken gently, about 17 minutes for unfrozen or 22 minutes for frozen. Sift powdered sugar over and serve immediately.

Bittersweet chocolate soufflé with Earl Grey custard sauce

THE CITRUS FLAVOR and scent of bergamot oranges found in Earl Grey tea create an aromatic custard sauce that pairs well with the bittersweet chocolate soufflé—be sure each serving of soufflé receives a generous dose of this exquisite sauce. Prepare the sauce at least four hours before the soufflé is made.

6 SERVINGS

Sauce

- **6 large egg yolks**
- **2 tablespoons plus ½ cup sugar**
- **1½ cups whole milk**
- **½ cup whipping cream**
- **1 tablespoon Earl Grey tea leaves (from 3 tea bags)**

Soufflé

- **⅓ cup whole milk**
- **8 tablespoons sugar, divided**
- **2½ ounces unsweetened chocolate, chopped**
- **2½ ounces bittersweet (not unsweetened) or semisweet chocolate, chopped**
- **2 large egg yolks**
- **5 large egg whites**

FOR SAUCE: Whisk egg yolks and 2 tablespoons sugar in medium bowl to blend well. Combine milk, cream, tea leaves, and remaining ½ cup sugar in heavy medium saucepan. Bring to simmer over medium heat, stirring until sugar dissolves. Gradually whisk hot milk mixture into egg yolk mixture; return to same saucepan. Stir over medium-low heat until custard thickens enough to leave path on spoon when finger is drawn across, about 8 minutes (do not boil). Immediately strain sauce into small bowl. Refrigerate uncovered until cold, at least 4 hours. *(Can be prepared 1 day ahead. Press plastic wrap directly onto surface of sauce and keep refrigerated.)*

FOR SOUFFLÉ: Preheat oven to 375°F. Generously butter 6-cup soufflé dish; coat dish with sugar. Combine milk and 5 tablespoons sugar in heavy medium saucepan. Stir over medium-low heat until sugar dissolves and milk comes to simmer. Remove from heat; add all chocolate and stir until melted and smooth. Whisk in egg yolks.

USING electric mixer, beat egg whites in medium bowl until soft peaks form. Gradually add remaining 3 tablespoons sugar, beating until stiff but not dry. Fold whites into warm chocolate mixture in 3 additions. Transfer mixture to prepared dish.

BAKE until soufflé is just set in center and top is puffed and cracked all over, about 32 minutes. Serve soufflé immediately with custard sauce.

Chocolate pots de crème with white chocolate whipped cream

POTS DE CRÈME are rich custards typically flavored with vanilla or chocolate. This chocolate version includes a touch of espresso that provides an added depth of flavor. Traditionally, pots de crème are served in small pot-shaped porcelain cups (also referred to as pots de crème), which are available at some specialty cookware stores. Although the little "pots" make a charming presentation, standard six-ounce custard cups or ramekins are easy to find and work just as well.

6 SERVINGS

- **2 cups whipping cream**
- **4 ounces semisweet chocolate, chopped**
- **1 teaspoon instant espresso powder or coffee powder**
- **6 large egg yolks**
- **3 tablespoons sugar**

White Chocolate Whipped Cream (see recipe)

POSITION rack in center of oven and preheat to 325°F. Arrange six 6-ounce custard cups or soufflé dishes in roasting pan. Combine cream, chopped chocolate, and espresso powder in heavy medium saucepan. Bring almost to simmer over medium heat, whisking until chocolate melts and mixture is smooth. Whisk egg yolks and sugar in large bowl to blend. Gradually whisk in hot cream mixture.

DIVIDE custard equally among cups. Pour enough hot water into roasting pan to reach halfway up sides of cups. Bake custards until just set around edges but still soft in center, about 25 minutes. Remove cups from water. Refrigerate pots de crème uncovered until cold, at least 2 hours. *(Can be prepared 1 day ahead. Cover and keep refrigerated.)*

SPOON White Chocolate Whipped Cream atop pots de crème and serve.

White chocolate whipped cream

WITH ONLY TWO INGREDIENTS—cream and white chocolate—in this recipe it's important to use a good-quality white chocolate, as the flavor and melting quality will truly make a difference. Serve it with the Chocolate Pots de Crème or spoon it over steaming cups of hot cocoa.

MAKES ABOUT 1 CUP

- **2 ounces high-quality white chocolate (such as Lindt or Perugina), chopped**
- **2 tablespoons plus ½ cup chilled whipping cream**

COMBINE chopped white chocolate and 2 tablespoons whipping cream in small metal bowl. Set over small saucepan of simmering water and stir until white chocolate melts and mixture is smooth. Remove bowl from over water. Cool white chocolate mixture 10 minutes.

BEAT remaining ½ cup chilled whipping cream in medium bowl until soft peaks form. Whisk in white chocolate mixture. *(Can be prepared 1 day ahead. Cover and refrigerate.)*

19 Fruit desserts

From a slice of watermelon eaten right down to the rind to a sophisticated roasted pear clafouti, desserts featuring fresh fruit have an appeal all their own. Fresh fruit–spiced, marinated in syrup or liqueur, or flavored in other simple ways–can dress up familiar favorites, as when apple wedges spiced with cloves, star anise, and cinnamon are served in a warm caramel sauce over vanilla ice cream, or when old-fashioned dishes like Swedish pancakes or shortcake are transformed with toppings of sweetened berries or brown sugar–glazed nectarines.

In other desserts–cobblers, crisps, and crumbles, for instance–the fruits are lightly sweetened and seasoned, then enclosed or covered to seal in the juices, and cooked until they are bubbling and the flavor is intensified. Cobblers have a biscuit-dough crust (or pie pastry dough) over and sometimes under the spiced fruit. Crisps are topped with a hand-rubbed mix of butter, sugar, flour, and maybe chopped nuts. Crumbles, which resemble crisps, contain oatmeal instead of or in addition to the flour. Any of the three can be made with just about any kind of fruit, from a late-fall apple to a summer peach.

Some of the most delicious desserts are those in which the fruit by itself is the star. Juicy strawberries need no coaxing at all, but a dusting of cardamom-spiked sugar enhances and deepens their flavor. Ditto ripe autumn pears that emerge from a hot bath of Bardolino, the red wine fragrant with the addition of vanilla.

The key to great fruit desserts is so obvious that it's easy to overlook: Follow the seasons in your kitchen. One way to get into the rhythm of nature is through the country's many excellent farmers' markets–or, for that matter, the ever-increasing number of supermarket chains that feature local, seasonal, organic, and *real* produce. Every fruit has its season, and every season its luscious fruit dessert.

Peaches-and-cream shortcakes with cornmeal-orange biscuits

THIS STANDOUT DESSERT is a sensational spin on the summer classic. Cornmeal adds a distinctive crunch to the biscuits; fresh, sweet peaches are simply accented with sugar and vanilla for the filling. If you can't find parchment paper for lining the baking sheet, just butter and flour it instead.

8 SERVINGS

Biscuits

- **¼ cup sugar**
- **1½ teaspoons grated orange peel**

- **1½ cups all purpose flour**
- **½ cup yellow cornmeal**
- **3 tablespoons (packed) golden brown sugar**
- **1 tablespoon baking powder**
- **½ teaspoon salt**
- **½ cup (1 stick) chilled unsalted butter, cut into ½-inch cubes**
- **⅔ cup (or more) chilled whole milk**

Filling

- **2 pounds peaches, peeled, halved, pitted, cut into ½-inch-thick slices**
- **⅓ cup sugar**
- **½ teaspoon vanilla extract**

- **1 cup chilled whipping cream**
- **3 tablespoons powdered sugar**

FOR BISCUITS: Preheat oven to 400°F. Line rimmed baking sheet with parchment paper. Mix ¼ cup sugar and orange peel in small bowl, mashing peel with back of spoon until mixture is pale orange.

WHISK flour, cornmeal, brown sugar, baking powder, and salt in large bowl to blend. Add butter; rub in with fingertips until mixture resembles coarse meal. Add ⅔ cup milk, tossing with fork until moist clumps form and adding more milk by tablespoonfuls if dough is dry. Drop dough by ⅓ cupfuls onto prepared baking sheet, forming 8 mounds and spacing 1½ inches apart. Using floured fingertips, flatten each biscuit to 2-inch round. Sprinkle each with orange sugar.

BAKE until biscuits are golden brown and tester inserted into center comes out clean, about 18 minutes; transfer to rack and cool. *(Can be made 8 hours ahead. Cover loosely and store at room temperature.)*

FOR FILLING: Toss peaches, ⅓ cup sugar, and vanilla extract in large bowl. Let stand 15 minutes, tossing occasionally.

USING electric mixer, beat cream and powdered sugar in medium bowl until peaks form.

USING serrated knife, cut each biscuit horizontally in half. Place bottom halves on plates. Spoon peaches and some juices over each. Top with whipped cream, then biscuit tops, and serve.

Caramelized-nectarine and ginger shortcakes with sour cream

A DOUBLE DOSE OF GINGER—ground and crystallized—pumps up the flavor of the tender biscuits. Instead of the traditional whipped cream, sweetened sour cream is the final touch.

8 SERVINGS

Biscuits

- **2 cups all purpose flour**
- **¼ cup sugar**
- **1 tablespoon baking powder**
- **1 teaspoon ground ginger**
- **½ teaspoon salt**
- **½ cup (1 stick) chilled unsalted butter, cut into ½-inch cubes**
- **½ cup chilled whole milk**
- **1 large egg**
- **¼ cup chopped crystallized ginger (generous 1 ounce)**

Filling

- 2 pounds nectarines (about 8 medium), peeled, halved, pitted, cut into ½-inch-thick slices
- ⅔ cup (packed) golden brown sugar
- 1 tablespoon fresh lemon juice

- 3 cups sour cream (about 24 ounces)
- ⅔ cup sugar

FOR BISCUITS: Preheat oven to 400°F. Line rimmed baking sheet with parchment paper. Combine first 5 ingredients in processor; blend 10 seconds. Add butter; using on/off turns, blend until mixture resembles coarse meal. Whisk milk and egg in small bowl to blend. Add milk mixture to processor and blend, using 5 on/off turns. Add crystallized ginger. Using on/off turns, blend just until dough comes together in moist clumps. Turn dough out onto work surfacc; knead gently 5 turns to combine. Shape dough into log; cut crosswise into 8 rounds. Pat each round to 1-inch thickness; place on prepared baking sheet.

BAKE biscuits until tester inserted into center comes out clean, about 15 minutes. Transfer to rack; cool at least 15 minutes and up to 2 hours.

FOR FILLING: Combine half of nectarines, ⅓ cup brown sugar, and ½ tablespoon lemon juice in heavy large skillet. Cook over high heat until fruit is just tender and juices are bubbling thickly, stirring often, about 5 minutes. Transfer to bowl. Repeat with remaining nectarines, sugar, and lemon juice. Set nectarine mixture aside at least 30 minutes and up to 2 hours.

WHISK sour cream and ⅔ cup sugar in bowl.

CUT biscuits horizontally in half. Place 1 bottom in each of 8 bowls. Spoon fruit mixture and sour cream mixture over each. Cover each with biscuit top and serve.

Lemon-blueberry shortcakes

HOMEMADE LEMON CURD, lemon-cornmeal biscuits, blueberry sauce, fresh blueberries, and whipped cream stack up to a stellar dessert. At the market, look for blueberries that are firm, plump, and dark blue, and rinse and dry the berries just before using them.

6 SERVINGS

Curd

- 7 tablespoons fresh lemon juice
- 6 tablespoons sugar
- 4 large egg yolks

Biscuits

- 1 lemon
- 5 tablespoons sugar, divided
- 1¼ cups all purpose flour
- ¼ cup yellow cornmeal
- 1½ teaspoons baking powder
- ½ teaspoon salt
- ¼ teaspoon baking soda
- 6 tablespoons (¾ stick) chilled unsalted butter, cut into ½-inch cubes
- 8 tablespoons chilled whipping cream, divided

Sauce

- 3¼ cups blueberries (from about four ½-pint containers), divided
- 6 tablespoons water
- 3 tablespoons all-fruit blueberry spread
- 1 tablespoon sugar

- ⅔ cup chilled whipping cream

Fresh mint sprigs (optional)
Lemon slices (optional)

FOR CURD: Combine lemon juice, sugar, and egg yolks in heavy medium saucepan. Whisk over medium heat until mixture thickens and just comes to boil, about 6 minutes. Transfer curd to medium bowl. Press plastic wrap directly onto surface and chill. *(Can be prepared 3 days ahead. Keep chilled.)*

FOR BISCUITS: Preheat oven to 400°F. Using swivel-bladed vegetable peeler, remove peel from lemon in strips. Squeeze 2 tablespoons juice from lemon; reserve juice. Place peel and 3 tablespoons sugar in processor. Blend until peel is finely ground. Add flour, cornmeal, baking powder, salt, and baking soda; process to blend. Add butter; using on/off turns, process until mixture resembles coarse meal. Add 6 tablespoons cream and reserved 2 tablespoons lemon juice. Using on/off turns, process just until moist clumps form. Gather dough into ball; flatten into disk.

PAT out dough on lightly floured surface to ¾-inch-thick round. Using floured 2½-inch-diameter cutter, cut out rounds. Gather dough scraps; pat out to ¾-inch-thick round. Cut out enough additional rounds for total of 6. Place rounds on heavy large baking sheet; brush with remaining 2 tablespoons cream. Sprinkle with remaining 2 tablespoons sugar.

BAKE until biscuits are golden and tester inserted into center comes out clean, about 15 minutes. Transfer to rack and cool. *(Can be prepared 3 hours ahead. Let stand at room temperature.)*

FOR SAUCE: Combine 1½ cups blueberries, 6 tablespoons water, blueberry spread, and sugar in heavy medium saucepan. Stir gently over medium-high heat until mixture comes to boil and berries begin to release juices, about 2 minutes. Remove from heat. Mix in 1½ cups blueberries. Cool sauce.

BEAT cream in medium bowl until cream holds peaks. Fold cream into curd in 2 additions.

CUT biscuits horizontally in half. Place bottoms on 6 plates. Spoon some blueberry sauce, then lemon curd mixture over each. Cover with biscuit tops. Garnish with remaining ¼ cup blueberries, and with mint sprigs and lemon slices if desired, and serve.

Cherry-chocolate shortcakes with kirsch whipped cream

THE DELICATE BISCUITS are flecked with grated semisweet chocolate to enrich the shortcakes, and the chocolate flavor is complemented by the filling: fresh Bing cherries steeped in kirsch and coated with cherry jam. The whipped cream topping is also accented with kirsch to reinforce the cherry flavor.

8 SERVINGS

Filling

- **1½ pounds fresh Bing cherries, stemmed, pitted, halved**
- **¼ cup sugar**
- **1 tablespoon kirsch (clear cherry brandy), divided**
- **⅓ cup cherry jam**

Biscuits

- **2 cups all purpose flour**
- **¼ cup sugar**
- **1 tablespoon baking powder**
- **½ teaspoon salt**
- **½ cup (1 stick) chilled unsalted butter, cut into ½-inch cubes**
- **3 ounces semisweet chocolate, coarsely grated**
- **½ cup chilled whole milk**
- **1 large egg**

Assembly

- **1½ cups chilled whipping cream**
- **2 tablespoons sugar**
- **1 tablespoon kirsch (clear cherry brandy)**

FOR FILLING: Combine cherries, sugar, and kirsch in medium bowl. Let stand until sugar dissolves and juices form, tossing occasionally, about 3 hours. Strain cherry juices into heavy medium saucepan. Mix in jam. Cook over medium heat until jam melts and juices reduce to thick syrup, stirring often, about 8 minutes. Mix syrup into cherries. *(Can be made 2 hours ahead. Let stand at room temperature.)*

FOR BISCUITS: Preheat oven to 400°F. Line rimmed baking sheet with parchment paper. Combine flour, sugar, baking powder, and salt in large bowl; whisk to blend. Add butter and rub in with fingertips until mixture resembles coarse meal. Mix in chocolate. Beat milk and egg in small bowl to blend. Gradually add milk mixture to dry ingredients, tossing with fork until dough comes together in moist clumps. Gather dough together. Turn out onto lightly floured surface and gently knead 5 turns to combine. Shape gently into 8-inch-long log. Cut log crosswise into 8 rounds; shape each into 2½x¾-inch round. Arrange rounds on prepared baking sheet.

BAKE biscuits until bottoms are golden and tester inserted into center comes out clean, about 15 minutes. Transfer to rack and cool 15 minutes. *(Can be made 6 hours ahead. Cool completely. Wrap in foil and rewarm in 350°F oven 10 minutes before continuing.)*

FOR ASSEMBLY: Beat cream, sugar, and kirsch in large bowl until cream holds peaks.

CUT warm biscuits horizontally in half. Place bottom halves in shallow bowls. Spoon cherry filling and kirsch whipped cream over. Cover with biscuit tops and serve.

Chocolate star shortcakes with strawberries

THIS SENSATIONAL TREAT is a cross between a hot fudge sundae and a shortcake dessert. Star-shaped chocolate biscuits studded with chocolate chips are placed alongside a scoop of vanilla ice cream, fudge sauce, strawberries, and whipped cream. The recipe calls for purchased fudge sauce, but you could also use the Fudge Sauce in the Frozen Desserts chapter (page 673). This recipe makes more of the chocolate stars than you'll need; freeze the extras for later use.

8 SERVINGS

2 cups all purpose flour
½ cup sugar
⅓ cup unsweetened cocoa powder
1 teaspoon baking powder
½ teaspoon baking soda
½ teaspoon salt
1 cup semisweet chocolate chips (6 ounces)
1⅔ to 1¾ cups chilled whipping cream

Melted unsalted butter
Additional sugar

2 pints vanilla ice cream or frozen yogurt
Purchased chocolate fudge sauce
2 1-pint containers strawberries, hulled, halved, lightly sweetened
1 cup chilled whipping cream, whipped
Fresh mint sprigs (optional)

PREHEAT oven to 325°F. Sift flour, ½ cup sugar, cocoa, baking powder, baking soda, and salt into large bowl. Mix in chocolate chips. Using fork, gradually mix in just enough chilled cream to form dough that is firm enough to roll out. Turn dough out onto well-floured work surface. Using well-floured hands, pat out dough to ¾-inch-thick rectangle, frequently sliding long knife under dough to prevent sticking. With floured 2-inch star-shaped cookie cutter, cut out stars. Gather dough scraps; pat out to ¾-inch-thick rectangle and cut out additional stars for total of about 24.

BRUSH stars with melted butter; sprinkle with additional sugar. Arrange stars, sugared side down, on 2 large rimmed baking sheets. Brush tops with butter and sprinkle with sugar. Bake until biscuits feel firm and tester inserted into center comes out with a few moist crumbs attached, about 22 minutes. Transfer biscuits to racks and cool. *(Can be made 1 day ahead. Cover; let stand at room temperature.)*

PLACE scoop of ice cream in each of 8 bowls. Garnish with fudge sauce, berries, whipped cream, 1 or 2 stars, and mint if desired, and serve.

Raspberry galettes

HERE'S A FINALE elegant enough for the most special occasion. Galettes—created in France, of course—are delicate round pastries or cakes topped with fruit, jam, or even savory ingredients. Here they are crisp butter-anise cookies stacked with raspberries and honey-flavored cream to create a restaurant-style treat. This recipe makes enough of the tender cookies for four desserts, with extras for nibbling later. Crushing the aniseed in a plastic bag will help contain the seeds. Crème fraîche is available at specialty foods stores and some supermarkets.

4 SERVINGS

Cookies

- **1⅓ cups unbleached all purpose flour**
- **3/4 cup plus 1 tablespoon powdered sugar**
- **3/4 teaspoon aniseed, crushed**
- **1/4 teaspoon (scant) salt**
- **1/2 cup (1 stick) unsalted butter, room temperature**
- **1 large egg yolk**
- **1 tablespoon vanilla extract**
- **1 egg, beaten to blend (for glaze)**

Sauce

- **2 cups frozen whole unsweetened raspberries (about 8 ounces), thawed**
- **3 tablespoons orange blossom or clover honey**

Filling

- **1 cup chilled crème fraîche or heavy whipping cream**
- **3 tablespoons orange blossom or clover honey**
- **2 1/2-pint containers fresh raspberries**
- **Powdered sugar**
- **Fresh mint leaves**

FOR COOKIES: Combine flour, sugar, aniseed, and salt in bowl of heavy-duty mixer fitted with paddle attachment. Add butter, egg yolk, and vanilla; mix on low speed until coarse meal forms. Knead dough into smooth ball. Flatten to disk, wrap in plastic, and refrigerate until firm enough to roll out, about 45 minutes.

PREHEAT oven to 350°F. Roll out dough on lightly floured surface to scant ⅛-inch thickness. Using 3½-inch-diameter fluted cutter, cut out rounds. Transfer rounds to large rimmed baking sheets, spacing evenly apart. Gather dough scraps. Repeat rolling and cutting until all dough is used, chilling dough briefly if soft. Brush cookies with glaze. Bake until light golden, about 12 minutes. Transfer cookies to racks and cool. *(Can be prepared 3 days ahead. Store cookies airtight at room temperature.)*

FOR SAUCE: Puree raspberries and honey in blender. Strain into medium bowl. *(Can be prepared 2 days ahead. Cover and refrigerate.)*

FOR FILLING: Beat crème fraîche and honey in chilled medium bowl until cream holds peaks. Transfer filling to pastry bag fitted with small star tip.

PLACE 1 cookie on work surface. Pipe filling in small stars over cookie. Top with layer of fresh raspberries. Place second cookie atop raspberries. Pipe filling in small stars over second cookie. Top with layer of fresh raspberries. Place third cookie atop raspberries. Sift powdered sugar over. Place 1 raspberry in center. Repeat layering of cookies, filling, and berries to make 3 more galettes. Spoon sauce onto plates. Transfer 1 galette to center of each plate. Garnish with mint leaves and serve.

Swedish pancakes with berry-cardamom topping

THESE DELICATELY SPICED PANCAKES are a typical dessert in Sweden. The classic accompaniment is lingonberries, but this version features a mixture of more readily available raspberries and blackberries. These pancakes would also be great at brunch.

4 SERVINGS

Pancakes

- 2 large eggs
- 1 cup whole milk, divided
- 2/3 cup all purpose flour
- 3/4 teaspoon ground cardamom
- 1/4 teaspoon salt
- 1/3 cup half and half
- 3 tablespoons unsalted butter, melted

Topping

- 1 1/2-pint container raspberries
- 1 1/2-pint container blackberries
- 1/4 cup sugar
- 1/2 teaspoon ground cardamom

Melted unsalted butter

FOR PANCAKES: Blend eggs and ⅓ cup milk in processor until smooth. Add flour, cardamom, and salt; process until mixture is thick and smooth. With machine running, add remaining ⅔ cup milk, half and half, and melted butter; blend until batter is smooth. *(Pancake batter can be prepared 8 hours ahead. Cover and refrigerate.)*

FOR TOPPING: Combine berries, sugar, and cardamom in medium bowl and toss gently. Let mixture stand until berries release juices, stirring occasionally, at least 30 minutes and up to 2 hours.

PREHEAT oven to 200°F. Place baking sheet in oven. Heat heavy large griddle or skillet over medium-high heat. Brush griddle with melted butter. Working in batches, add batter to griddle, using 1 tablespoonful for each pancake and brushing griddle with more melted butter as needed. Cook until pancakes are brown, about 1 minute per side. Transfer to baking sheet in oven to keep warm.

TRANSFER pancakes to plates. Spoon berry topping over and serve.

Roasted pear and cinnamon clafouti

THE FRENCH DESSERT known as *clafouti* is a pancake crossed with a fruit-filled custard. It is best served warm, right from the skillet, just after baking and puffing up in the oven. If you don't have a cast-iron skillet, any ovenproof variety is fine. It would be perfect with vanilla ice cream.

6 SERVINGS

- 4 large Bosc pears, peeled, quartered, cored
- 1/4 cup pure maple syrup

- 3 large eggs
- 1 1/3 cups half and half
- 3/4 teaspoon vanilla extract
- 1/4 cup all purpose flour
- 1/4 cup plus 1 tablespoon (packed) golden brown sugar
- 1 1/2 teaspoons ground cinnamon, divided
- Pinch of salt

PREHEAT oven to 450°F. Butter 9-inch-diameter cast-iron skillet. Heat over medium-high heat. Add pears, rounded side down, to skillet and cook until golden brown, about 3 minutes per side. Spoon maple syrup over pears. Transfer skillet to oven and roast pears until tender, turning and basting once, about 10 minutes. Remove skillet from oven and bring pear mixture to boil over high heat; boil until almost all juices have evaporated, about 2 minutes. Cool to room temperature. Reduce oven temperature to 350°F.

COMBINE eggs, half and half, and vanilla in blender; process until smooth. Add flour, ¼ cup sugar, ¾ teaspoon cinnamon, and pinch of salt; process to blend.

POUR batter over pears in skillet. Bake until center is set and clafouti is puffed and golden brown at edges, about 40 minutes. Mix remaining 1 tablespoon sugar and ¾ teaspoon cinnamon in small bowl. Sprinkle over clafouti; serve warm.

Pear cobbler with almond biscuit topping

NO ONE REALLY KNOWS where the term *cobbler* came from, but the received wisdom is that the term refers to a cook "cobbling"–or patching–together the ingredients for this home-style dessert. The sweet biscuit topping showcases almonds, golden raisins, and cardamom.

12 SERVINGS

Filling

- **2/3 cup sugar**
- **1/4 cup all purpose flour**
- **1 teaspoon ground cinnamon**
- **10 ripe Anjou pears (about 5 1/2 pounds), peeled, halved, cored, thinly sliced**
- **1/2 cup pear nectar**
- **1 tablespoon fresh lemon juice**
- **2 tablespoons (1/4 stick) unsalted butter, cut into small cubes**

Topping

- **1 2/3 cups all purpose flour**
- **1/2 cup slivered almonds**
- **1/4 cup plus 1 tablespoon sugar**
- **1 tablespoon baking powder**
- **1/2 teaspoon ground cardamom**
- **6 tablespoons (3/4 stick) chilled unsalted butter, cut into 1/2-inch cubes**
- **1/2 cup golden raisins**
- **1 cup chilled whipping cream**

Vanilla ice cream

FOR FILLING: Preheat oven to 400°F. Butter 13x9x2-inch glass baking dish. Mix sugar, flour, and cinnamon in large bowl. Mix in pears. Transfer to prepared dish. Pour pear nectar and lemon juice over; dot with butter. Bake filling until pears are tender and juices are bubbling thickly, about 45 minutes.

MEANWHILE, PREPARE TOPPING: Finely grind flour and almonds in processor. Mix in ¼ cup sugar, baking powder, and cardamom. Add butter; using on/off turns, process until mixture resembles coarse meal. Transfer to bowl. Add raisins. Gradually add cream, stirring with fork until soft moist dough forms.

DROP biscuit topping onto hot filling in 12 equal mounds, spacing evenly. Sprinkle with remaining 1 tablespoon sugar.

BAKE cobbler until biscuits are golden brown and tester inserted into center of biscuits comes out clean, about 25 minutes. Cool slightly. Serve with vanilla ice cream.

Blackberry and nectarine cobbler with ginger biscuit topping

TO ENSURE that the biscuit topping stays nice and tender, be sure not to overwork the dough. Knead it gently just a few times to combine. The lemon and crystallized ginger in the topping are accented by a dusting of cinnamon, sugar, and ginger just before the cobbler goes back into the oven. Serve it with whipped cream sweetened with brown sugar.

8 TO 10 SERVINGS

Filling

- **1 cup sugar**
- **3 1/2 tablespoons cornstarch**
- **2 teaspoons grated lemon peel**
- **3/4 teaspoon ground cinnamon**
- **3 pounds firm but ripe nectarines, halved, pitted, cut into 1/2-inch-thick wedges**
- **6 cups fresh blackberries (about five 1/2-pint containers)**
- **1 tablespoon fresh lemon juice**
- **2 tablespoons (1/4 stick) chilled unsalted butter, cut into small cubes**

Topping

2 cups all purpose flour
½ cup plus 1 tablespoon finely chopped crystallized ginger (about 2½ ounces)
⅓ cup plus 1 tablespoon sugar
1 tablespoon baking powder
1 teaspoon grated lemon peel
¾ teaspoon salt
6 tablespoons (¾ stick) chilled unsalted butter, cut into ½-inch cubes
¾ cup plus 2 tablespoons chilled whipping cream

¼ teaspoon ground cinnamon

FOR FILLING: Preheat oven to 375°F. Butter 13x9x2-inch glass baking dish. Mix first 4 ingredients in large bowl. Add nectarines, berries, and lemon juice; toss to combine. Transfer to prepared dish. Dot with butter. Bake until filling begins to bubble, about 30 minutes.

MEANWHILE, PREPARE TOPPING: Mix flour, ½ cup ginger, ⅓ cup sugar, baking powder, lemon peel, and salt in medium bowl. Add butter; rub in with fingertips until mixture resembles coarse meal. Add cream, tossing with fork until dough forms. Turn dough out onto floured surface and knead gently until combined and smooth, about 6 turns. Roll out dough to ¾-inch thickness. Using 2¼-inch star-shaped cookie cutter or round biscuit cutter, cut out biscuits. Gather dough scraps. Roll out to ¾-inch thickness and cut out additional biscuits.

ARRANGE biscuits closely together atop hot fruit. Mix remaining 1 tablespoon crystallized ginger, 1 tablespoon sugar, and ¼ teaspoon cinnamon in small bowl; sprinkle over biscuits. Bake cobbler until fruit is tender, biscuits are golden, and tester inserted into center of biscuits comes out clean, about 25 minutes. Serve cobbler warm or at room temperature.

Peach-strawberry cobbler with buttery lemon crust

THE TOPPING ON THIS COBBLER is unlike the traditional soft biscuit: This one spreads as it bakes, forming a crisp cookie-like layer over the sweet fruit. You can easily peel the peaches by blanching them in boiling water for about 30 seconds and then placing them immediately in ice water until cool enough to handle—the skins will slip right off.

6 SERVINGS

Filling

1¼ pounds firm but ripe peaches (about 5), peeled, halved, pitted, cut into 1-inch-thick wedges
12 ounces strawberries (about 3 cups), hulled
⅓ cup sugar
1 tablespoon cornstarch

Topping

½ cup all purpose flour
¼ teaspoon baking powder
Pinch of salt
½ cup (1 stick) unsalted butter, room temperature
½ cup sugar
1 large egg yolk
1 teaspoon grated lemon peel
½ teaspoon vanilla extract
Vanilla ice cream

FOR FILLING: Preheat oven to 375°F. Butter 8x8x2-inch glass baking dish. Mix all filling ingredients in large bowl. Let stand until sugar dissolves, stirring occasionally, about 5 minutes. Transfer filling to prepared dish.

FOR TOPPING: Mix flour, baking powder, and salt in small bowl. Using electric mixer, beat butter and sugar in large bowl until smooth. Beat in egg yolk, lemon peel, and vanilla. Add flour mixture; mix just until moist dough forms.

USING large spoon, drop dough atop fruit, spacing evenly. Bake until peaches are tender, juices are bubbling thickly, and topping is golden and crisp, about 55 minutes. Cool slightly. Serve cobbler with ice cream.

Peach grunt with caramel sauce

TYPICALLY, GRUNTS ARE composed of stewed fruit with biscuits or dumplings on top. In this baked version, wine-poached peaches are topped with a crunchy layer of chopped almonds and pecans mixed with gingersnap cookie crumbs.

6 TO 8 SERVINGS

Topping

- **½ cup all purpose flour**
- **¼ cup (½ stick) unsalted butter, room temperature**
- **2½ tablespoons (packed) golden brown sugar**
- **1½ teaspoons sugar**
- **½ cup coarsely chopped almonds**
- **½ cup coarsely chopped pecans**
- **½ teaspoon ground ginger**
- **½ cup coarsely crushed gingersnap cookies**

Filling

- **½ cup sugar**
- **¼ cup water**
- **½ cup Muscat or other sweet dessert wine**
- **2¼ pounds firm peaches, peeled, halved, pitted, sliced (about 5 cups)**
- **¼ vanilla bean, split lengthwise**
- **Pinch of salt**

Vanilla ice cream
Caramel Sauce (see recipe)

FOR TOPPING: Preheat oven to 350°F. Stir flour, butter, both sugars, all nuts, and ginger in medium bowl until moist clumps form. Mix in cookie crumbs. Crumble topping onto rimmed baking sheet. Bake topping until golden brown, about 18 minutes. Cool. *(Can be made 1 day ahead. Store airtight at room temperature.)*

FOR FILLING: Stir sugar and ¼ cup water in heavy large saucepan over low heat until sugar dissolves. Increase heat to medium-high and boil without stirring until syrup turns deep amber color, occasionally brushing down sides of pan with wet pastry brush and swirling pan, about 8 minutes. Remove from heat. Gradually add wine (mixture will bubble vigorously). Return to medium-high heat and boil until reduced to ½ cup, swirling pan occasionally, about 2 minutes. Add peaches. Scrape in seeds from vanilla bean. Discard vanilla bean pod. Cook until peaches soften slightly, about 5 minutes. Mix in salt. Set filling aside and cool.

PREHEAT oven to 350°F. Transfer filling to 8x8x2-inch glass baking dish. Sprinkle topping over. Bake until peaches are tender and filling is bubbling thickly, about 40 minutes. Serve with vanilla ice cream and Caramel Sauce.

Caramel sauce

SPOON THIS VERSATILE SAUCE over scoops of ice cream, dessert crepes, or baked apples.

MAKES ABOUT ¾ CUP

- **½ cup sugar**
- **2 tablespoons water**
- **¼ cup whipping cream**
- **¼ cup sour cream**

STIR sugar and 2 tablespoons water in heavy small saucepan over medium-low heat until sugar dissolves. Increase heat to medium-high and boil without stirring until syrup is deep amber color, occasionally brushing down sides of pan with wet pastry brush and swirling pan, about 8 minutes. Remove from heat. Add cream (mixture will bubble vigorously). Stir over low heat until any hard caramel bits dissolve. Cool sauce. Stir in sour cream. *(Can be made 1 day ahead. Cover and chill. Bring to room temperature before using.)*

Pear and dried cherry crisp with coconut-almond topping

CRISPS ARE QUICK AND EASY desserts that are made of sweetened fruit–usually thickened to produce syrupy juices–baked with a crumbly topping sprinkled over. The topping in this crisp is enhanced with extra goodies like coconut and almonds for more crunch and flavor.

8 SERVINGS

Topping

- **3/4 cup all purpose flour**
- **1/4 cup (packed) dark brown sugar**
- **1/4 teaspoon ground cinnamon**
- **1/8 teaspoon ground nutmeg**
- **7 tablespoons chilled butter, cut into 1/2-inch cubes**
- **3/4 cup sweetened shredded coconut**
- **2/3 cup sliced almonds**

Filling

- **3 1/2 pounds pears, peeled, halved, cored, cut into 1/2-inch-thick wedges**
- **1 1/3 cups dried tart cherries or raisins (about 8 ounces)**
- **2/3 cup (packed) dark brown sugar**
- **2 tablespoons all purpose flour**
- **1/4 teaspoon ground cinnamon**
- **1/8 teaspoon ground nutmeg**
- **2 tablespoons (1/4 stick) chilled unsalted butter**
- **Vanilla ice cream**

FOR TOPPING: Mix flour, sugar, cinnamon, and nutmeg in medium bowl. Add chilled butter and rub in with fingertips until mixture resembles coarse meal. Add coconut and almonds. Rub mixture with fingertips until small clumps form. *(Topping can be prepared 1 day ahead. Cover and refrigerate.)*

FOR FILLING: Preheat oven to 375°F. Butter 13x9x2-inch glass baking dish. Toss pears, cherries, sugar, flour, and spices in large bowl to combine. Transfer to prepared dish. Dot with butter. Sprinkle topping over. Bake until topping browns, pears are tender, and juices are bubbling thickly, about 45 minutes. Cool slightly. Serve with ice cream.

Plum and walnut crisp with ginger ice cream

WHEN SHOPPING, look for plums that are firm yet give just a bit to the touch. Select only those without skin blemishes or soft spots, and be sure to store very firm plums at room temperature to ripen slightly and very soft ones in the refrigerator to hold. The crisp goes with a terrific "homemade" ice cream–purchased vanilla ice cream with chopped crystallized ginger mixed in.

6 SERVINGS

Topping

- **1/2 cup all purpose flour**
- **1/2 cup (packed) golden brown sugar**
- **1/2 teaspoon ground cinnamon**
- **1/4 teaspoon ground ginger**
- **1/4 teaspoon salt**
- **Pinch of ground nutmeg**
- **6 tablespoons (3/4 stick) chilled unsalted butter, cut into 1/2-inch cubes**
- **1 cup coarsely chopped walnuts**

- **1 pint vanilla ice cream**
- **1/4 cup finely chopped crystallized ginger (generous 1 ounce)**

Filling

- **2 1/2 pounds plums, quartered, pitted**
- **1/2 cup sugar**
- **1 tablespoon cornstarch**
- **1 teaspoon vanilla extract**

FOR TOPPING: Mix first 6 ingredients in large bowl. Add butter and rub in with fingertips until small moist clumps form. Mix in walnuts. Cover and refrigerate 20 minutes. *(Can be made 3 days ahead. Keep refrigerated.)*

MICROWAVE ice cream on low for 5-second intervals just until slightly softened. Place in medium bowl; mix in ginger. Cover and freeze until firm. *(Can be prepared 1 day ahead. Keep frozen.)*

FOR FILLING: Preheat oven to 400°F. Toss plums, sugar, cornstarch, and vanilla in large bowl to combine. Let stand until sugar dissolves, tossing occasionally, about 5 minutes.

TRANSFER plum mixture to 11x7-inch glass baking dish. Sprinkle topping over. Bake until topping is dark golden brown and crisp and filling is bubbling thickly, about 40 minutes. Transfer crisp to rack and cool 30 minutes.

SPOON warm crisp into shallow bowls. Top with ginger ice cream.

Apple and raisin crisp

THIS IS AS SIMPLE to make as it is good to eat: crisp apples mixed with raisins, sugar, and cinnamon, and then baked with a crumbly topping of oats, walnuts, butter, and brown sugar. Served warm with vanilla ice cream, it is pure, unadulterated, all-American deliciousness.

8 SERVINGS

Topping

- **1¼ cups old-fashioned oats**
- **1 cup plus 2 tablespoons (packed) brown sugar**
- **¾ cup all purpose flour**
- **½ teaspoon ground cinnamon**
- **¼ teaspoon salt**
- **¾ cup (1½ sticks) unsalted butter, room temperature**
- **¾ cup walnuts, chopped**

Filling

- **4 pounds Pippin or Granny Smith apples, halved, peeled, cored, sliced**
- **1½ cups golden or brown raisins**
- **½ cup sugar**
- **1 tablespoon fresh lemon juice**
- **1 tablespoon all purpose flour**
- **¾ teaspoon ground cinnamon**

Vanilla ice cream

FOR TOPPING: Preheat oven to 375°F. Butter 13x9x2-inch glass baking dish. Mix oats, brown sugar, flour, cinnamon, and salt in large bowl. Add butter and rub in with fingertips until coarse crumbs form. Mix in walnuts.

FOR FILLING: Combine apples, raisins, sugar, lemon juice, flour, and cinnamon in large bowl. Mix well.

TRANSFER apple-raisin filling to prepared dish. Spread topping over. Bake until topping is golden brown and apples are tender, about 55 minutes. Serve crisp warm with vanilla ice cream.

Apple-prune crisp with hazelnut topping

HERE'S THE IDEAL cold-weather fruit dessert—one you can make any time, since apples and prunes are available year-round. The aroma, taste, and crunchy texture of the toasted hazelnuts complement the apple filling.

4 SERVINGS

Filling

- **⅓ cup sugar**
- **3 tablespoons (packed) golden brown sugar**
- **1 tablespoon all purpose flour**
- **2 teaspoons ground cinnamon**
- **2 large Granny Smith apples (about 1¼ pounds), peeled, halved, cored, diced**
- **½ cup pitted prunes, chopped**

Topping

- **⅓ cup (packed) golden brown sugar**
- **¼ cup all purpose flour**
- **¼ cup old-fashioned oats**
- **¼ teaspoon salt**
- **¼ cup (½ stick) unsalted butter, diced, room temperature**
- **1 cup hazelnuts, toasted, chopped**

Vanilla ice cream

FOR FILLING: Preheat oven to 375°F. Butter 8x8x2-inch glass baking dish. Mix both sugars, flour, and cinnamon in large bowl. Mix in apples, then prunes. Let filling stand 5 minutes. Transfer to prepared dish. Bake until beginning to bubble at edges, about 20 minutes.

MEANWHILE, PREPARE TOPPING: Mix sugar, flour, oats, and salt in medium bowl. Add butter and rub in with fingertips until moist clumps form. Mix in hazelnuts.

SCATTER topping over filling. Continue baking crisp until topping is golden, apples are tender, and juices are bubbling thickly, about 20 minutes longer. Cool slightly. Serve warm with ice cream.

Apple-pecan crunch

SIMILAR TO A CRISP, this finale has a topping that features graham cracker crumbs along with the traditional ingredients of sugar, butter, nuts, and flour. It all adds up to luscious dessert with homey appeal.

8 SERVINGS

Topping

1½ cups all purpose flour
1 cup coarsely chopped pecans
¾ cup graham cracker crumbs
½ cup plus 2 tablespoons (1¼ sticks) unsalted butter, melted
½ cup (packed) golden brown sugar
2 tablespoons water

Filling

½ cup (1 stick) unsalted butter
1 cup (packed) golden brown sugar
8 small Golden Delicious apples (about 5 ounces each), peeled, halved, cored

Vanilla ice cream

FOR TOPPING: Preheat oven to 350°F. Using back of fork, mix all ingredients in medium bowl until moist clumps form. Set aside.

FOR FILLING: Melt butter in large ovenproof skillet over medium heat. Mix in sugar. Arrange apples, cut side down, over sugar mixture in skillet. Cook apples 2 minutes. Turn cut side up and cook until apples are almost crisp-tender, about 2 minutes. Spoon sugar syrup in skillet over apples; sprinkle topping over apples.

TRANSFER skillet to oven and bake until apples are tender and topping is brown and crisp, about 30 minutes. Serve warm with vanilla ice cream.

Strawberry-rhubarb humble crumble

HERE'S A RUSTIC DESSERT that stars two of the best tastes of spring, their flavors enhanced only by sugar and tapioca added to thicken their juices. The fruit is showcased beneath a tender lattice crust and a cinnamon-scented crumb topping. Choose fresh rhubarb with firm stalks and bright color. Store it in the refrigerator and use it within a day or two.

12 SERVINGS

Crust

¾ cup all purpose flour
1 tablespoon sugar
¼ teaspoon salt
¼ cup (½ stick) chilled unsalted butter, cut into ½-inch cubes
1 tablespoon chilled solid vegetable shortening
½ tablespoon (or more) cold water

Filling

6 cups ½-inch-thick slices fresh rhubarb (from about 3 pounds)
2 1-pint containers strawberries, hulled, thickly sliced
1¼ cups sugar
3½ tablespoons quick-cooking tapioca

Topping
7 tablespoons all purpose flour
5 tablespoons sugar
1/8 teaspoon ground cinnamon
1/8 teaspoon salt
3 tablespoons chilled unsalted butter, cut into small cubes

Vanilla ice cream

FOR CRUST: Combine flour, sugar, and salt in medium bowl. Add butter and shortening; rub in with fingertips until mixture resembles coarse meal. Mix in ½ tablespoon cold water and blend, adding more water by teaspoonfuls if dough is dry, until moist clumps form. Gather dough into ball; flatten into rectangle. Wrap in plastic and chill 30 minutes. *(Can be prepared 2 days ahead. Keep chilled. Let dough soften slightly at room temperature before continuing.)*

FOR FILLING: Generously butter 13x9x2-inch glass baking dish. Place rhubarb, strawberries, sugar, and tapioca in large bowl; toss to combine. Let filling stand until tapioca softens, tossing occasionally, about 40 minutes. Transfer filling to prepared dish.

PREHEAT oven to 400°F. Roll out dough on lightly floured surface to 14x7 inch rectangle. Cut dough lengthwise into ¾-inch-wide strips. Arrange strips in lattice pattern atop filling, spacing 2 inches apart. Trim ends to fit dish. Reroll dough scraps to make additional strips if necessary. Bake 30 minutes.

MEANWHILE, PREPARE TOPPING: Combine flour, sugar, cinnamon, and salt in medium bowl. Add butter and rub in with fingertips until mixture resembles fine meal.

SPRINKLE topping between lattice strips. Continue baking until lattice is golden brown and filling is bubbling in center, about 30 minutes longer. Cool slightly. Serve warm with ice cream.

Vanilla-scented pear strudel with hazelnuts and chocolate sauce

OLD-FASHIONED STRUDEL gets updated with a vanilla-pear filling, crunchy hazelnut phyllo pastry, and a rich chocolate-brandy sauce. Working with phyllo can sometimes be intimidating, but the straightforward instructions here make it easy. Baking the strudel atop two stacked baking sheets keeps the bottom from burning.

6 TO 8 SERVINGS

Vanilla sugar
1 cup sugar
2 vanilla beans, cut into 1/2-inch pieces

Sauce
1/4 cup whipping cream
1/4 cup water
6 ounces bittersweet (not unsweetened) or semisweet chocolate, chopped
2 tablespoons brandy

Filling
2 tablespoons cornstarch
2 tablespoons (1/4 stick) unsalted butter
2 pounds Anjou pears (about 4 large), peeled, halved, cored, cut into 3/4-inch cubes (about 5 cups)
1 teaspoon fresh lemon juice

Strudel and phyllo triangles
3/4 cup hazelnuts, toasted, skinned
12 vanilla wafer cookies

12 sheets fresh phyllo pastry or frozen, thawed (each sheet about 12x17 inches)
1 cup (2 sticks) unsalted butter, melted, cooled

Vanilla ice cream
Fresh mint sprigs (optional)

FOR VANILLA SUGAR: Combine sugar and vanilla in processor. Blend until beans are very finely chopped, about 1 minute. Sift vanilla sugar into bowl; discard contents of sieve. Transfer vanilla sugar to jar and cover. *(Can be made 1 week ahead. Store at room temperature.)*

FOR SAUCE: Combine cream, ¼ cup water and 3 tablespoons vanilla sugar in heavy medium saucepan. Stir over medium heat until sugar dissolves and mixture comes to boil. Remove from heat. Add chocolate and whisk until smooth. Whisk in brandy. *(Sauce can be made 1 week ahead. Cover and chill. Rewarm before serving.)*

FOR FILLING: Mix ½ cup vanilla sugar and cornstarch in bowl. Melt butter in large nonstick skillet over medium heat. Add pears; sauté until tender and golden, about 20 minutes. Sprinkle cornstarch mixture over pears; stir to combine. Simmer until juices are very thick, stirring often, about 6 minutes (longer if pears are very juicy). Remove from heat. Mix lemon juice into filling. Cool.

FOR STRUDEL: Finely grind nuts, cookies, and 2 tablespoons vanilla sugar in processor. Transfer nut mixture to small bowl.

BUTTER 1 large rimmed baking sheet. Place kitchen towel on work surface. Place 1 phyllo sheet on towel (keep remaining phyllo sheets covered with plastic wrap and damp towel to prevent drying). Brush phyllo with melted butter. Top with second phyllo sheet; brush with butter and sprinkle with 3 tablespoons nut mixture. Repeat layering with 6 more phyllo sheets, buttering each and sprinkling with 3 tablespoons nut mixture. Top with another phyllo sheet; brush with butter. Top with another phyllo sheet (for total of 10 sheets); brush with butter. Starting 2 inches in from 1 long side and 2½ inches in from 1 short side, spoon filling in 3-inch-wide by 12-inch-long log parallel to long side. Fold short sides over ends of filling; butter folded edges. Using towel as aid and starting at same long side, roll up strudel, enclosing filling. Using 2 large spatulas, transfer strudel to prepared baking sheet. Brush strudel all over with butter. *(Can be prepared 4 hours ahead. Cover and chill.)*

PREHEAT oven to 375°F. Butter 1 large rimmed baking sheet. Cut remaining 2 phyllo sheets in half crosswise, making 4 pieces, each about 12x8 inches. Place 1 phyllo piece on work surface. Brush phyllo with butter; sprinkle with 1 tablespoon nut mixture and 1 teaspoon vanilla sugar. Repeat layering with 2 more phyllo pieces, buttering and sprinkling each with 1 tablespoon nut mixture and 1 teaspoon vanilla sugar. Top with remaining phyllo piece; brush with butter. Using large knife, trim stack to 12x8 inches. Cut stack into six 4-inch squares. Cut squares diagonally in half. Transfer triangles to prepared baking sheet. Brush sheet of parchment paper with butter; place buttered side down atop triangles. Press 1 large baking sheet atop parchment, anchoring triangles.

BAKE triangles until golden, about 10 minutes. Lift off top baking sheet. Carefully peel off parchment. Transfer triangles to rack and cool. *(Can be made 4 hours ahead. Store airtight at room temperature.)*

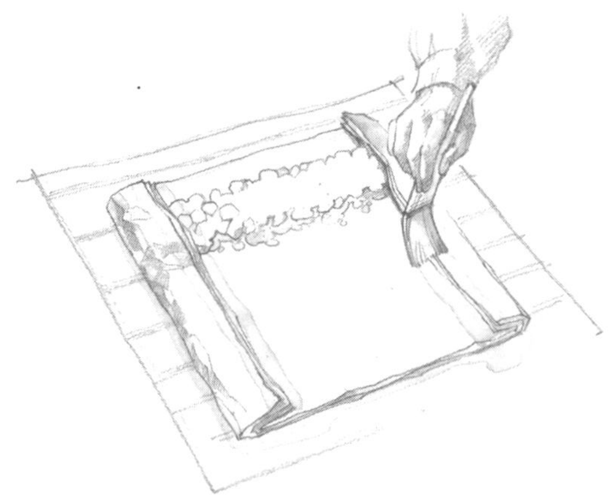

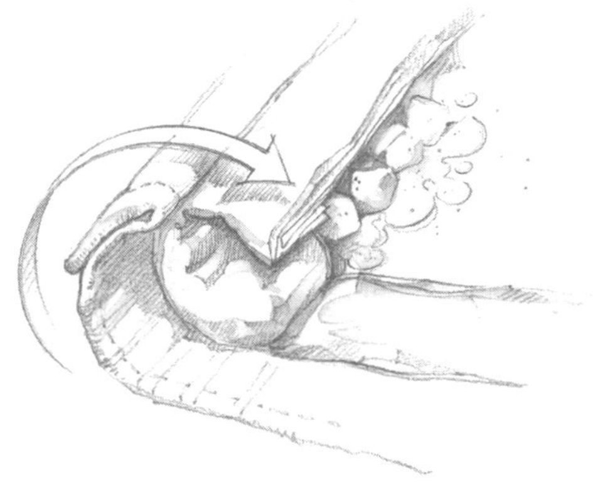

PREHEAT oven to 375°F. Stack baking sheet with strudel in another baking sheet of same size. Bake strudel until golden brown, about 45 minutes. Let stand on sheets at least 15 minutes and up to 4 hours.

SPOON warm chocolate sauce onto each plate. Cut strudel crosswise into 6 to 8 pieces. Place strudel piece atop sauce on each plate. Place scoop of ice cream alongside. Stand 1 or 2 triangles between strudel and ice cream. Garnish with mint, if desired, and serve.

Blackberry-plum turnovers with cardamom

THE FRUIT FILLING is paired with aromatic cardamom and the pastry is spread with rich almond paste, dressing up this down-home treat. The turnovers can be formed ahead, frozen, and then baked just before serving. They are the perfect finale for a picnic lunch or a cozy kitchen supper.

8 SERVINGS

- **12 ounces plums, halved, pitted, sliced**
- **2 cups fresh blackberries (from two ½-pint containers)**
- **½ cup plus 1 tablespoon sugar**
- **⅛ teaspoon ground cardamom**
- **1½ tablespoons cornstarch dissolved in 1½ tablespoons water**

- **1 7-ounce package almond paste, broken into pieces**
- **¼ cup whipping cream**

- **1 17.3-ounce package frozen puff pastry (2 sheets), thawed**
- **1 egg, beaten to blend (for glaze)**

COMBINE plums, berries, ½ cup sugar, and cardamom in heavy medium saucepan. Bring to boil, stirring constantly. Reduce heat to medium and simmer until plums are soft, about 4 minutes. Add cornstarch mixture and stir until fruit mixture thickens and boils, about 1 minute. Cool. Cover and chill until cold, at least 4 hours and up to 1 day.

FINELY grind almond paste in processor. Add cream and puree until smooth.

LINE 2 rimmed baking sheets with parchment paper. Roll out 1 pastry sheet on floured surface to 12-inch square; cut into four 6-inch squares. Spread scant 2 tablespoons almond paste mixture over center 4 inches of each square. Place ¼ cup fruit mixture in center of almond paste on each. Brush 2 sides of pastry edges with glaze. Fold pastry over filling, forming triangle and pressing edges to adhere. Press edges with fork to seal. Transfer turnovers to 1 prepared baking sheet. Repeat with remaining pastry, almond paste mixture, and fruit mixture and transfer to second prepared sheet.

CUT small hole and some slits in top of each turnover to allow steam to escape. Brush turnovers with glaze. Sprinkle with remaining 1 tablespoon sugar. Freeze 20 minutes. *(Turnovers can be prepared 1 week ahead. Cover and keep frozen. Thaw 6 hours in refrigerator.)*

POSITION 1 rack in bottom third and 1 rack in top third of oven; preheat to 375°F. Bake turnovers until golden, reversing positions of baking sheets after 15 minutes, about 30 minutes total. Cool turnovers on sheets. Serve at room temperature.

Pound cake and grilled peaches with burnt-sugar sauce

THIS IS THE IDEAL DESSERT for a summer barbecue. Just be sure the grill is scrubbed clean before the peaches go on, and do not cook them over wood chips because the smoky flavor will overwhelm the fruit. Simply serve the peaches with your favorite purchased pound cake and the easy sauce, which can be made a day before serving. For a delicious homemade pound cake, use the Buttery Pound Cake recipe on page 549.

8 SERVINGS

1 cup sugar
¼ cup water
1¾ cups whipping cream
Pinch of ground nutmeg

4 peaches, peeled, halved, pitted
3 tablespoons vegetable oil

8 pound cake slices

STIR sugar and ¼ cup water in heavy large saucepan over medium-low heat until sugar dissolves. Increase heat and boil without stirring until syrup turns deep amber color, about 7 minutes, occasionally swirling pan and brushing down sides of pan with wet pastry brush to prevent formation of sugar crystals. Gradually add cream (mixture will bubble vigorously). Stir over low heat until any caramel bits dissolve and sauce is smooth. Mix in nutmeg. Cool to room temperature. *(Can be prepared 1 day ahead. Cover and refrigerate. Rewarm over medium-low heat just until pourable before serving.)*

PREPARE barbecue (medium heat). Brush peaches with oil. Place cut side down on grill. Cover and cook until heated through, about 4 minutes.

PLACE cake slices on plates. Top each cake slice with 1 peach half, cut side up. Spoon warm sauce over and serve immediately.

Summer pudding

PUDDING IS A TERM that is applied to many desserts in the United Kingdom, so not all British puddings are the milk-based treats Americans think of when they hear the word. Here is a fine example: a pretty dessert of French bread and assorted sweetened berries. Its name comes from the time of year when these berries are in season—but the pudding can be made just as nicely with frozen berries at any time of year. Begin preparing it a day before serving so that it can set up overnight, and garnish with assorted fresh berries, if desired.

6 SERVINGS

6 ½-inch-thick slices French bread (each about 6x4 inches)

1½ cups hulled halved fresh strawberries (about 6 ounces)
1½ cups frozen unsweetened raspberries, unthawed
1½ cups frozen unsweetened blueberries, unthawed
1½ cups frozen unsweetened blackberries, unthawed
½ cup sugar
¼ cup cranberry juice cocktail

Lightly sweetened whipped cream

PREHEAT oven to 400°F. Place bread slices on baking sheet. Bake bread until slightly dry and firm, about 8 minutes. Trim crusts and discard. Arrange enough bread slices over bottom and up sides of 6- to 6½-cup bowl or pudding mold to line completely; trim overhang and reserve.

COMBINE strawberries, raspberries, blueberries, blackberries, sugar, and cranberry juice cocktail in heavy large saucepan. Stir over low heat just until frozen berries thaw and sugar dissolves, about 10 minutes. Remove from heat. Ladle warm fruit and juices into bread-lined bowl. Cover fruit with reserved bread trimmings. Place small plate atop pudding; weigh down plate with cans or weights. Refrigerate pudding overnight.

REMOVE weights and plate. Invert bowl onto platter and shake gently, allowing pudding to settle onto platter. Cut into wedges and serve with sweetened whipped cream.

Bardolino- and vanilla-poached pears

BARDOLINO IS A LIGHT, dry red wine from Italy's Veneto region. In this simple recipe, sugar, citrus, and spices are added to the Bardolino to make a syrup for poaching Bosc pears. Offer some purchased almond or hazelnut biscotti alongside to dip into the poaching liquid. This recipe can be doubled or tripled easily, and leftover pears will make a terrific breakfast with vanilla yogurt.

2 SERVINGS; CAN BE DOUBLED OR TRIPLED

- **2 cups Bardolino or other dry red wine**
- **3/4 cup sugar**
- **2 1/4-inch-thick orange slices**
- **1 1/4-inch-thick lemon slice**
- **2 whole green cardamom pods (optional)**
- **1 4-inch piece vanilla bean, split lengthwise**
- **1 2-inch cinnamon stick**
- **4 firm but ripe Bosc pears, peeled, halved, cored**

COMBINE first 7 ingredients in heavy medium saucepan over low heat; stir until sugar dissolves. Increase heat and boil 5 minutes. Add pears to syrup and return to boil. Adjust heat so liquid barely simmers, cover pan, and cook until pears are just tender, turning occasionally, 5 to 20 minutes, depending on ripeness of pears. Using slotted spoon, transfer pears to medium bowl. Boil pear syrup until reduced to ¾ cup, about 7 minutes. Pour over pears. Cool completely, turning pears occasionally. *(Can be prepared 1 day ahead. Cover and refrigerate.)* Discard orange and lemon slices and spices. Serve pears with syrup, chilled or at room temperature.

Moroccan orange salad

THIS LIGHT AND REFRESHING DESSERT could also be a nice treat for brunch. Using the orange-flower water, a flavoring extract available at Middle Eastern markets and in the liquor or specialty foods section of supermarkets, will add a lovely grace note.

6 SERVINGS

- **6 large navel oranges, all peel and white pith cut away**
- **1 tablespoon orange-flower water (optional)**
- **1 tablespoon powdered sugar**
- **3/4 teaspoon ground cinnamon**
- **Sliced almonds, toasted**
- **Fresh mint leaves**

CUT oranges crosswise into thin rounds. Arrange orange rounds in concentric circles on serving platter. Sprinkle with 1 tablespoon orange-flower water, if desired. *(Can be prepared 1 hour ahead. Cover and refrigerate.)* Blend sugar and cinnamon in small bowl; sprinkle over oranges. Sprinkle with toasted almonds. Garnish salad with fresh mint leaves and serve.

Mixed fruit compote in ginger syrup

THE GINGERY SYRUP in this compote works well with virtually any fruit—make it all year round with various combinations of seasonal fruits. This dish is rich in flavor, yet contains no fat. Have seconds!

4 SERVINGS

- **2 cups water**
- **1/2 cup sugar**
- **12 quarter-size slices peeled fresh ginger**

- **8 thin slices peeled seeded cantaloupe**
- **4 strawberries, hulled, halved**
- **2 apricots or plums, halved, pitted**

1 **star fruit (carambola), sliced, or 1 cup diced peeled cored pineapple**
1 **kiwi, peeled, sliced**
1 **tablespoon fresh lime juice**

COMBINE 2 cups water, sugar, and ginger in heavy medium saucepan. Bring to boil, stirring until sugar dissolves. Boil until syrup is reduced to 1 cup, about 15 minutes. Cool to room temperature.

Arrange all fruit in shallow bowl. Sprinkle with lime juice. Strain syrup over fruit. Remove 3 ginger slices from strainer; cut into matchstick-size strips. Sprinkle ginger strips over fruit. Cover compote and chill at least 3 hours and up to 8 hours.

DIVIDE fruit among 4 plates. Spoon some syrup over and serve cold.

Honeydew and cantaloupe with cinnamon-clove syrup

THE TYPICAL DESSERT flavors of ginger, cloves, and cinnamon are given a dash of assertiveness with whole black peppercorns—the quartet of spices combines beautifully to complement the melon. This is a cool dessert for a summer evening.

6 SERVINGS

2 **cups water**
1 **cup sugar**
1 **1½-inch-long piece of fresh ginger (about 1 ounce) peeled, sliced into rounds**
3 **whole cloves**
1 **3-inch-long cinnamon stick**
1 **teaspoon whole black peppercorns**
1 **tablespoon dark rum**

1 **honeydew melon, halved, seeded**
1 **cantaloupe melon, halved, seeded**

BRING first 6 ingredients to boil in small saucepan over medium heat, stirring until sugar dissolves. Reduce heat to low and simmer until syrup is reduced to ¾ cup, about 25 minutes. Cool. Strain into small bowl. Add rum and stir to blend. Refrigerate until cold, at least 1 hour. *(Syrup can be prepared 2 days ahead. Keep refrigerated.)*

SCOOP out enough melon balls from honeydew and cantaloupe to measure 4 cups total. Divide melon balls among 6 bowls. Spoon syrup over and serve.

Spiced apple wedges with caramel sauce and vanilla ice cream

WHOLE STAR ANISE are brown star-shaped seedpods sold at Asian markets and specialty foods stores, and in the spice section of some supermarkets. If you don't have a spice mill, place the whole spices in a heavy-duty plastic bag, use a hammer or mallet to crush them, and then grind them finely in the blender.

4 SERVINGS

10 **whole cloves**
2 **whole star anise**
1 **cinnamon stick**
¼ **teaspoon whole black peppercorns**
4 **large Golden Delicious apples (about 2 pounds), peeled, halved, cored, each half cut into 4 wedges**
½ **cup (packed) golden brown sugar, divided**
½ **cup apple cider, divided**
¼ **cup (½ stick) unsalted butter, melted**

¼ **cup whipping cream**
Vanilla ice cream

PREHEAT oven to 400°F. Finely grind first 4 ingredients in spice mill or small coffee grinder. Place apples in 13x9x2-inch glass baking dish. Sprinkle ground spices over apples. Add ¼ cup sugar, ¼ cup cider, and butter. Stir gently to coat apples.

BAKE apples until tender, stirring occasionally, about 40 minutes. Cool 10 minutes. Reduce oven temperature to 300°F. Using slotted spoon, transfer apples to ovenproof bowl and place in oven to keep warm.

SCRAPE all juices from baking dish into medium saucepan. Mix in cream and remaining ¼ cup sugar and ¼ cup cider. Boil until caramel sauce deepens in color and is reduced to ½ cup, whisking occasionally, about 5 minutes. Spoon ice cream into bowls. Top with warm apples and caramel sauce.

Baked apples with toffee, bourbon, and molasses

SIMPLE BAKED APPLES are made sophisticated with bourbon, molasses, ground ginger, and toffee bits spooned over and around the apples. The baked apples and their basting juices are great with vanilla ice cream—the perfect conclusion to a cozy fireside supper.

6 SERVINGS

- **6 tablespoons bourbon**
- **6 7- to 8-ounce Golden Delicious apples**
- **6 tablespoons toffee bits (such as from Skor candy bar), divided**
- **3 tablespoons unsalted butter**
- **1½ cups apple cider**
- **3 tablespoons mild-flavored (light) molasses**
- **1 tablespoon sugar**
- **¼ teaspoon ground ginger**
- **Vanilla ice cream**

PREHEAT oven to 350°F. Boil bourbon in heavy small saucepan until reduced to 3 tablespoons, about 3 minutes. Set aside. Using swivel-bladed vegetable peeler, peel skin off top third of each apple. Using small melon baller, scoop out stem and core, leaving bottom intact. Stand apples in 11x7x2-inch glass baking dish. Place 2 tablespoons toffee bits around apples in dish. Divide remaining bits among cavities of apples. Add ½ tablespoon bourbon and ½ tablespoon butter to cavity of each apple. Whisk cider, molasses, sugar, and ginger in medium bowl to blend. Spoon mixture over and around apples.

BAKE apples until tender, basting often with pan juices, about 1 hour 20 minutes. Transfer apples to bowls. Pour juices from dish into small saucepan. Boil juices until thick enough to coat spoon, about 6 minutes. Spoon sauce over apples. Serve apples warm with vanilla ice cream.

Grilled pineapple with tequila–brown sugar glaze

SKEWERED PINEAPPLE CHUNKS are grilled and basted with a sweet and simple-to-make sauce for a different spin on cookout kebabs. The skewers are an innovative ending to a Mexican or Southwestern-style summer dinner. Look for metal skewers in the supermarket's kitchenware section or at cookware stores.

6 SERVINGS

- **¾ cup tequila**
- **¾ cup (packed) golden brown sugar**
- **1½ teaspoons vanilla extract**
- **¼ teaspoon ground cinnamon**
- **1 large pineapple, peeled, cored, cut into 2x1-inch pieces**
- **6 10- to 12-inch-long metal skewers**

STIR first 4 ingredients in small bowl until sugar dissolves. Thread pineapple pieces onto 6 skewers, dividing equally. *(Tequila mixture and skewers can be prepared 8 hours ahead. Cover separately and chill.)*

PREPARE barbecue (medium heat). Grill pineapple skewers until golden brown, basting with tequila mixture and turning occasionally, about 10 minutes. Push pineapple from skewers onto 6 plates. Serve hot or warm.

Strawberries dusted with cardamom sugar

ELEGANT SIMPLICITY AT ITS BEST. Juicy strawberries are tossed in Grand Marnier, rolled in spiced sugar, and presented in a stemmed glass for a beautiful springtime dessert. It's the perfect finale for a stylish luncheon or brunch. Offer sugar cookies or chocolate truffles alongside as the finishing touch.

6 SERVINGS

- **1/4 cup Grand Marnier or other orange liqueur, or orange juice**
- **2 16-ounce containers strawberries, hulled, left whole**
- **1/2 cup sugar**
- **1/2 teaspoon ground cardamom**
- **Fresh mint sprigs (optional)**

POUR Grand Marnier into large bowl. Add strawberries to bowl and toss to coat. Whisk sugar and cardamom in small bowl to blend. Spread cardamom sugar on small rimmed baking sheet. Using slotted spoon and working in batches, transfer strawberries to baking sheet with cardamom sugar. Roll in sugar to coat well.

DIVIDE strawberries among 6 wineglasses. Pour any remaining Grand Marnier from bowl over berries. *(Can be prepared 2 hours ahead. Cover and chill.)*

PLACE 1 wineglass with strawberries on each of 6 plates. Garnish with mint sprigs, if desired.

Dark chocolate, honey, and almond fondue

CHEESE FONDUE originated in Switzerland, but chocolate fondue was created by a Swiss-born chef, Konrad Egli, working at New York's Chalet Swiss restaurant. Toblerone chocolate from Zurich works well in this dish because its honey-nougat blend echoes the honey and almond flavorings that are also part of the recipe.

4 TO 6 SERVINGS

- **6 tablespoons whipping cream**
- **3 tablespoons honey**
- **2 3.52-ounce bars Toblerone bittersweet chocolate or 7 ounces semisweet chocolate, chopped**
- **1 tablespoon kirsch (clear cherry brandy)**
- **1/4 teaspoon almond extract**
- **Assorted fresh fruits (such as whole strawberries, 1-inch-thick slices peeled banana, peeled pear wedges, and orange segments)**

BRING cream and honey to simmer in heavy medium saucepan. Add chocolate and whisk until melted. Remove from heat. Whisk in kirsch and almond extract. Pour fondue into bowl; place on platter. Surround with fruit. Serve with skewers.

20 Frozen desserts

The next time you're in the frozen foods aisle, trying to decide between triple fudge-peanut butter swirl ice cream and boysenberry sorbet, take a moment to think about the ancient Romans. We owe them, indirectly, a debt of gratitude when it comes to ice creams, sorbets, and all kinds of frozen desserts.

The Romans went to extraordinary lengths to lay in a supply of snow and ice that they kept cold in specially built subterranean containers throughout the year, and which they used to cool beverages, including wine, and to chill certain desserts, including ice flavored with fruit juices. It took a few more centuries before some clever individual (in either China or Europe–legend has it both ways) figured out how to use ice and cream simultaneously to make the world's first ice cream, but today you can see descendants of the enterprising Romans enjoying ice creams and granitas in just about every piazza in the Eternal City. (Granita, a different kind of icy treat, is made without special equipment simply by stirring flavored syrups as they freeze. If you've never tried this easy dessert, the recipes here should prove inspiring.)

But when it comes to enjoying frozen desserts, ice creams and sorbets are just the beginning. Layering them into pies and cakes, to take advantage of contrasting flavors and textures, results in wonderfully festive dinner party finales. Baked Alaska is more than a retro throwback–it's a truly inspired combination of ice creams, sweetened sponge cake, and liqueurs, sheathed in a puffy meringue. A brief trip to a hot oven browns the meringue but keeps the frozen inside intact.

If time is short, there are plenty of other ideas, among them: Scoop lemon sorbet right from its container and top with fresh plums marinated in vodka and sugar; or pile lime ice pops into a bowl, douse them with tequila, and dip them in a little coarse salt for a Margarita-inspired dessert. We don't know what the Romans would have thought of them, but we think they're simple and sublime.

Brown sugar ice cream

TWO KEY STEPS help give this ice cream its ultra-mellow flavor and smooth, creamy texture. First, stirring the sugar over medium heat until it has melted and turned a deep brown color intensifies the caramel-like flavor. And pureeing the egg-yolk-thickened custard in a blender ensures that the mixture has an especially fine consistency.

8 SERVINGS

- **2 cups whole milk**
- **2 cups whipping cream**
- **1¼ cups (packed) golden brown sugar**
- **6 large egg yolks**
- **1 teaspoon vanilla extract**

COMBINE milk and cream in heavy medium saucepan; bring just to simmer. Remove from heat. Place sugar in heavy large saucepan. Stir over medium heat until sugar melts (some soft lumps will remain) and is deep brown, about 5 minutes. Whisk in hot milk mixture. Stir over low heat until caramel bits melt, about 5 minutes (mixture may look curdled). Whisk egg yolks in large bowl to blend. Gradually whisk in brown sugar mixture. Return mixture to same saucepan. Stir over low heat until custard thickens and leaves path on back of spoon when finger is drawn across, about 5 minutes (do not boil). Cool. Mix in vanilla.

WORKING in batches, puree custard in blender until very smooth. Refrigerate custard until cold, at least 1 hour and up to 1 day.

PROCESS custard in ice cream maker according to manufacturer's instructions. Transfer to container; cover and freeze until firm. *(Ice cream can be prepared 3 days ahead. Keep frozen.)*

Brown bread ice cream

YOU CAN USE the Brown Soda Bread on page 475 for the breadcrumbs called for in this recipe (crumbs from crustless whole wheat bread may be substituted). Brown bread ice cream was considered a luxury in nineteenth-century Ireland; this contemporary version, in which the breadcrumbs create a praline, is a modern classic—and it doesn't even require an ice cream maker.

6 TO 8 SERVINGS

- **1 cup crumbs from brown soda bread or crustless whole wheat bread**
- **14 tablespoons sugar, divided**
- **3 tablespoons (packed) dark brown sugar**
- **⅔ cup whole milk**
- **1 3-inch piece vanilla bean, split lengthwise**
- **2 large egg yolks**
- **1⅓ cups chilled whipping cream**
- **2 1-pint containers strawberries, hulled, sliced**

PREHEAT oven to 375°F. Line baking sheet with aluminum foil; butter foil. Mix breadcrumbs, 3 tablespoons sugar, and brown sugar in medium bowl. Scatter over prepared baking sheet. Bake until sugar begins to melt and crumbs are slightly darker, stirring crumbs occasionally with metal spatula to prevent sticking, about 10 minutes. Transfer breadcrumbs to small bowl and cool. Break breadcrumbs into small pieces.

POUR milk into medium saucepan. Scrape in seeds from vanilla bean; add pod. Bring to simmer. Remove from heat; cover and let steep 30 minutes.

WHISK egg yolks and 5 tablespoons sugar in large bowl to blend. Gradually whisk in milk mixture. Return mixture to same saucepan. Stir over low heat until custard thickens and leaves path on back of spoon when finger is drawn across, about 5 minutes (do not boil). Strain into small bowl. Chill custard until cold, stirring occasionally, about 1 hour.

BEAT cream in large bowl until peaks form. Fold custard into cream. Gently fold in breadcrumbs. Transfer to containers; cover and freeze until firm. *(Can be prepared 3 days ahead. Keep frozen.)*

COMBINE strawberries and remaining 6 tablespoons sugar in medium bowl. Let stand until juices form, stirring occasionally, about 20 minutes. Scoop ice cream into bowls. Spoon strawberries and juices over and serve.

Chocolate malted ice cream

THE TOASTED TASTE of malt and chocolate combine in this ice cream to evoke sweet childhood nostalgia. You can make the ice cream up to three days ahead—and for extra indulgence, serve it in chocolate-dipped ice cream cones or in waffle cones.

MAKES ABOUT 3 PINTS

- **8 ounces semisweet chocolate, chopped**
- **2 cups whipping cream**
- **2 cups half and half**
- **4 large egg yolks**
- **¾ cup sugar**
- **¾ cup plain malted milk powder**
- **1 tablespoon vanilla extract**

STIR chocolate in top of double boiler set over simmering water until melted and smooth. Pour chocolate into large bowl. Bring cream and half and half to simmer in heavy medium saucepan. Whisk egg yolks and sugar in medium bowl to blend. Gradually whisk cream mixture into yolks. Return mixture to saucepan and stir over medium-low heat until custard thickens and leaves path on back of spoon when finger is drawn across, about 5 minutes (do not boil). Gradually whisk custard into melted chocolate. Whisk in malted milk and vanilla (custard may appear grainy). Press plastic wrap directly onto surface of custard. Refrigerate custard until well chilled, at least 6 hours and up to 1 day.

PROCESS custard in ice cream maker according to manufacturer's instructions. Transfer to container; cover and freeze until firm. *(Can be prepared 3 days ahead. Keep frozen.)*

Coffee and vanilla ice cream with hot fudge sauce

PURISTS INSIST that a classic hot fudge sundae should feature vanilla ice cream, while many creative types argue for the irresistibly complementary flavor of coffee. This recipe avoids argument by featuring a scoop of each. Of course, the hot fudge sauce will also be delicious over virtually any other flavor of your choosing, from pistachio to peppermint stick, cherry to chocolate chip.

10 SERVINGS

- **1½ cups dark corn syrup**
- **½ cup whole milk**
- **3 tablespoons unsweetened cocoa powder**
- **Pinch of salt**
- **1½ cups semisweet chocolate chips**
- **½ teaspoon vanilla extract**

- **2 pints vanilla ice cream**
- **2 pints coffee ice cream**

BRING corn syrup and next 3 ingredients to simmer in heavy medium saucepan over medium-high heat, whisking occasionally. Boil 2 minutes, whisking frequently. Remove from heat. Add chocolate and vanilla extract; whisk until smooth. Cool slightly. *(Can be prepared 1 week ahead; chill. Rewarm over medium-low heat just until pourable before using.)*

PLACE 1 scoop of each ice cream in each of 10 bowls. Drizzle warm sauce over.

Candied lemon peel ice cream with strawberry compote

THE ICE CREAM'S BRIGHT, intense lemon flavor comes from two sources: thin wisps of candied lemon peel and a syrup made with fresh lemon juice. When cutting the strips of lemon peel, take care to remove only the outermost yellow layer, leaving behind the bitter-tasting white pith. In season, the compote may also be made with juicy fresh raspberries or blackberries, which should be left whole.

12 SERVINGS

10 large lemons
2⅓ cups sugar, divided

8 large egg yolks
4 cups whipping cream
3 cups half and half
¼ teaspoon salt

1 1-pint container strawberries, hulled, quartered

USING 5-hole citrus zester, remove lemon peel in long thin strips. Halve lemons. Squeeze juice into medium bowl; strain. Combine 1⅔ cups lemon juice, lemon peel strips, and 2 cups sugar in medium saucepan. Bring to simmer over medium heat, stirring until sugar dissolves. Simmer gently until liquid is slightly syrupy, about 10 minutes. Strain through sieve into bowl, reserving lemon peel and syrup separately. Transfer peel to small baking sheet; add remaining ⅓ cup sugar and toss to coat. Separate pieces with fork. Let dry 2 hours. Reserve ¼ cup candied lemon peel strips. Coarsely chop remaining candied peel.

WHISK 1 cup syrup and egg yolks in large bowl to blend (cover and chill remaining syrup). Bring cream, half and half, and salt to simmer in large saucepan over medium heat. Gradually whisk hot cream mixture into egg mixture. Return to saucepan. Whisk over medium heat until instant-read thermometer inserted into mixture registers 180°F, about 6 minutes (do not boil). Strain custard into large bowl. Chill until cold, at least 4 hours and up to 1 day.

PROCESS custard in ice cream maker according to manufacturer's instructions; add chopped candied peel during last 5 minutes. Transfer ice cream to container. Cover and freeze at least 4 hours. *(Syrup, candied peel, and ice cream can be prepared 2 days ahead. Keep syrup refrigerated. Store peel in airtight container at room temperature. Keep ice cream frozen.)*

STIR ½ cup syrup in saucepan over medium heat until heated through. Add strawberries. Transfer compote to bowl; refrigerate at least 4 hours and up to 8 hours.

SCOOP ice cream into bowls. Top with compote and reserved candied lemon peel strips.

Lemon curd–blackberry swirl ice cream with blackberry sauce

MAKING THE SWIRLS in this ice cream is actually quite easy. The thick blackberry syrup is simply layered in a loaf pan with the frozen lemon custard, causing them to intermingle slightly. The swirl effect comes mostly from the act of scooping the ice cream out of the pan.

8 SERVINGS

Ice cream
1¼ cups (about 6 ounces) frozen blackberries
1½ cups sugar, divided
1 tablespoon plus ⅔ cup fresh lemon juice
1 tablespoon light corn syrup

1¾ cups whipping cream
1¼ cups whole milk
1 vanilla bean, split lengthwise
8 large egg yolks
2½ teaspoons grated lemon peel

Blackberry sauce
- **2 cups (10 ounces) fresh blackberries, or frozen, thawed**
- **⅓ cup sugar**
- **2 tablespoons fresh lemon juice**

FOR ICE CREAM: Boil berries, ¼ cup sugar, 1 tablespoon lemon juice, and corn syrup in small saucepan over medium-high heat until thick, stirring often, about 8 minutes. Strain berry mixture into small bowl, pressing on solids.

MEANWHILE, combine cream, milk, and ½ cup sugar in heavy large saucepan. Scrape in seeds from vanilla bean; add pod. Bring mixture to simmer. Remove from heat. Whisk egg yolks and remaining ¾ cup sugar in large bowl to blend. Whisk in remaining ⅔ cup lemon juice and lemon peel. Gradually whisk hot cream mixture into yolk mixture. Return mixture to saucepan. Stir over medium heat until custard thickens enough to coat back of spoon (do not boil), about 12 minutes. Strain custard into large clean bowl. Set bowl of custard over large bowl of ice water. Stir custard until cold. Cover blackberry syrup and custard separately and refrigerate overnight.

PROCESS custard in ice cream maker according to manufacturer's instructions. Immediately spoon half of ice cream into 9x5x3-inch loaf pan. Spoon half of blackberry syrup atop ice cream in pan. Spoon remaining ice cream atop blackberry syrup. Top ice cream with remaining blackberry syrup. Cover and freeze until firm, at least 8 hours. *(Can be prepared 2 days ahead. Keep frozen.)*

FOR BLACKBERRY SAUCE: Combine blackberries, sugar, and lemon juice in medium bowl. Let stand until sugar dissolves and juices form, stirring occasionally, about 1 hour. *(Can be prepared 2 days ahead. Cover and refrigerate.)*

SCOOP ice cream into dessert bowls. Serve ice cream with blackberry sauce.

Lemon sorbet with vodka-marinated plums

PROOF POSITIVE that you don't even have to prepare ice cream or sorbet from scratch to enjoy an elegant homemade frozen dessert: This recipe begins with good-quality lemon sorbet purchased at the supermarket. What gives it a special personal touch is the topping, made simply by marinating fresh in-season plums with a little vodka and a sprinkling of sugar. The result is a sophisticated finale that takes almost no time at all to put together.

2 SERVINGS; CAN BE DOUBLED OR TRIPLED

- **4 ripe sweet plums, halved, pitted, sliced**
- **¼ cup vodka**
- **2 tablespoons (or more) sugar**

Lemon sorbet

COMBINE plums, vodka, and 2 tablespoons sugar in medium bowl. Taste and add more sugar if desired. Marinate at room temperature 1 hour.

SCOOP sorbet into glasses. Top with plums and marinade and serve.

Pink grapefruit–Champagne sorbet with pink grapefruit sauce

A SPARKLING SPLASH of Champagne enhances the pretty, pale pink sorbet, which could also be served in small scoops as a palate cleanser between savory dishes at a gala multiple-course meal. Be sure to use a fine strainer to remove the solids from the juice, which will help produce a finer-textured sorbet.

6 SERVINGS

- **5 cups fresh pink grapefruit juice (from about 6 large grapefruits)**
- **1¼ cups sugar**

1/4 cup light corn syrup
1 tablespoon grated pink grapefruit peel
3/4 cup Champagne or other sparkling wine

2 pink grapefruits (optional)

Fresh mint sprigs

STIR pink grapefruit juice and next 3 ingredients in large saucepan over medium heat just until sugar dissolves. Strain into bowl, pressing on solids; mix in Champagne. Pour 2 cups juice mixture into medium saucepan. Refrigerate remaining juice mixture in bowl. Simmer mixture in saucepan until reduced to ¾ cup, stirring occasionally, about 25 minutes. Refrigerate reduced mixture to use as sauce. Process juice mixture from bowl in ice cream maker according to manufacturer's instructions. Transfer sorbet to container; cover and freeze until firm. *(Sauce and sorbet can be prepared 3 days ahead. Keep sauce refrigerated and sorbet frozen.)*

IF using grapefruits, cut peel and white pith from fruit. Working over bowl, cut between membranes to release segments into bowl. *(Can be prepared 6 hours ahead. Cover and refrigerate.)*

CHILL 6 plates in freezer. Scoop 3 ovals of sorbet onto each plate. Spoon sauce around sorbet. Decorate with grapefruit segments, if desired. Garnish with mint and serve.

Apple and blackberry sorbet

WHAT'S THE DIFFERENCE between sorbet and sherbet? Technically, they're the same thing—*sorbet* is French for "sherbet"—but sorbets tend to be a bit softer in texture, and while some sherbets may contain milk, egg whites, or gelatin, sorbets never do. This one is especially delicious and does not require an ice cream maker.

6 TO 8 SERVINGS

2 pounds cooking apples (such as McIntosh), stemmed, unpeeled, cut into 1/2-inch pieces (including cores and seeds)
1 16-ounce bag frozen unsweetened blackberries, unthawed
1 1/2 cups water

3/4 cup sugar
1/4 cup light corn syrup

COMBINE apples, blackberries, and 1½ cups water in heavy large pot. Bring to boil over medium-high heat. Reduce heat to medium, cover, and simmer until fruit is tender, stirring occasionally, about 20 minutes. Transfer to strainer set over large bowl. Press to force through as much fruit and liquid as possible. Discard solids in strainer.

RETURN puree to same pot. Add sugar and corn syrup. Stir over low heat just until sugar dissolves. Spoon puree into 13x9x2-inch glass baking dish. Freeze until almost solid, about 1 hour.

USING spoon, break up frozen puree into chunks. Transfer to processor and puree. Return to same dish; cover and freeze until firm enough to hold shape in spoon, at least 1 hour. Spoon sorbet into bowls and serve.

Rainbow daiquiri sorbet

THE CONTRASTING COLORS of mango and boysenberry are lovely together. If you like, serve the sorbets in frozen "mango boats," made by scooping out the centers of halved mangoes and freezing the shells.

8 SERVINGS

Boysenberry sorbet

1 1/4 cups water
1/2 cup plus 1 tablespoon sugar
2 cups fresh boysenberries or frozen unsweetened boysenberries, thawed

7 tablespoons light rum

Mango sorbet

1¼ cups water
¾ cup sugar
2 cups sliced peeled pitted mangoes

7 tablespoons light rum

8 hollowed-out mango halves (for serving; optional)
Fresh boysenberries
Fresh mango slices

FOR BOYSENBERRY SORBET: Stir 1¼ cups water and sugar in heavy medium saucepan over medium heat until sugar dissolves. Increase heat and bring to boil. Add berries and return to boil. Transfer mixture to processor and puree. Strain through sieve set over bowl, pressing on solids to extract as much liquid as possible. Discard solids in sieve. Refrigerate puree until cold, about 2 hours.

MIX rum into puree. Process sorbet mixture in ice cream maker according to manufacturer's instructions. Spread sorbet evenly in 8x8x2-inch glass baking dish; cover and freeze until firm. *(Can be prepared 2 days ahead; keep frozen.)*

FOR MANGO SORBET: Stir 1¼ cups water and sugar in heavy medium saucepan over medium heat until sugar dissolves. Increase heat and bring to boil. Add 2 cups sliced mangoes and return to boil. Transfer mixture to processor and puree. Pour into bowl. Refrigerate puree until cold, about 2 hours.

MIX rum into puree. Process sorbet mixture in ice cream maker according to manufacturer's instructions. Spread mango sorbet evenly over boysenberry sorbet in dish; cover and freeze until firm, about 2 hours. *(Can be prepared 2 days ahead. Keep frozen.)*

FREEZE 8 hollowed-out mango halves or parfait glasses 1 hour. Using ice cream scooper, scoop both sorbets together for swirled effect and place in mango halves or frozen glasses. Garnish with fresh berries and mango slices and serve.

Quick coconut sorbet

TRY THIS EASY, creamy sorbet in place of vanilla ice cream the next time you serve warm pie, cobbler, or crumble, especially one featuring tropical fruit. Or serve it on its own to cool down the fire after a spicy meal. Canned sweetened cream of coconut is available in the liquor or mixers section of most supermarkets.

MAKES ABOUT 2 CUPS

1 15-ounce can sweetened cream of coconut (such as Coco López)
1 cup ice-cold water
¼ teaspoon rum extract

WHISK all ingredients in medium bowl. Transfer to 11x7x2-inch glass baking dish. Freeze until frozen, stirring every 30 minutes, about 3 hours. *(Can be prepared 2 days ahead. Cover and keep frozen.)*

Pineapple sorbet with minted oranges and fresh pineapple

FRUIT JUICES BLEND with sugar and spices to create a lovely syrup for this icy tropical dessert. If you like, replace the pineapple sorbet with another complementary flavor, such as lemon or strawberry. Orange-flower water is a delicately scented flavoring extract available at Middle Eastern markets and in the liquor or specialty foods section of some supermarkets.

6 SERVINGS

5 oranges, peel and white pith cut away, fruit cubed (about 2 cups)
½ pineapple, peeled, cored, cut into 1-inch cubes (about 2 cups)
⅓ cup chopped fresh mint leaves
3 tablespoons sugar
2 teaspoons orange-flower water

- **1 cinnamon stick, broken in half**
- **4 whole cloves**

- **2 pints pineapple sorbet**
- **Fresh mint sprigs**

COMBINE oranges and next 6 ingredients in large bowl; toss to combine. Cover and chill at least 1 hour and up to 6 hours.

SPOON fruit and syrup into bowls. Top each with scoop of sorbet and mint sprigs and serve.

Plum granita with summer fruit

CINNAMON, ALLSPICE, and the tiny seeds from a vanilla bean add intriguing flavor to a syrup that is combined with pureed and strained plums to make this refreshing granular fruit ice. Red-fleshed plums give the granita dramatic color, but golden or green-fleshed varieties will also produce very good results. Slices of peach (peeled or unpeeled, as you prefer), nectarine, and plum garnish the granita; berries would work well, too.

4 SERVINGS

- **¾ cup water**
- **½ cup sugar**
- **2 whole allspice**
- **1 cinnamon stick**
- **½ vanilla bean, split lengthwise**

- **1½ pounds plums, preferably red-fleshed (about 7 large), halved, pitted, cut into ¾-inch pieces**

- **1 peach, halved, pitted, thinly sliced**
- **1 nectarine, halved, pitted, thinly sliced**
- **1 plum, halved, pitted, thinly sliced**

COMBINE ¾ cup water, sugar, allspice, and cinnamon in heavy small saucepan. Scrape in seeds from vanilla bean; add pod. Bring to boil, stirring until sugar dissolves. Reduce heat and simmer until liquid is reduced to ¾ cup, about 2 minutes. Cool syrup completely.

PUREE 1½ pounds plums in processor. Press enough puree through sieve to measure 1½ cups. Strain syrup into puree and blend well. Transfer mixture to 9x5x3-inch glass loaf pan. Freeze plum mixture until flaky crystals form, stirring mixture with fork and breaking up frozen edge pieces every 30 minutes, about 4 hours. *(Can be prepared 1 week ahead. Cover and keep frozen.)*

SPOON granita into 4 glass goblets. Top with peach, nectarine, and plum slices and serve immediately.

Coffee and orange granita suprema

THE FLAVORS OF orange and cinnamon deliciously highlight the rich taste of espresso in this classic Italian-style frozen treat, for which no ice cream maker is needed. To make the decorative garnishes of chocolate curls and orange peel strips, simply use a swivel-bladed vegetable peeler. Draw the peeler across the narrow side of a bar of room-temperature milk chocolate to make the curls. For the orange, first rinse it thoroughly and dry with a clean towel; then move the peeler's blade across the surface to remove thin strips of just the flavorful, outermost orange-colored layer.

6 SERVINGS

- **4 cups freshly brewed strong coffee (made with ground espresso coffee beans)**
- **½ cup plus 3 tablespoons sugar**
- **1 teaspoon grated orange peel**
- **⅛ teaspoon ground cinnamon**

- **¾ cup chilled whipping cream**
- **2 tablespoons Grand Marnier or other orange liqueur**
- **Milk chocolate curls**
- **Thin orange peel strips**

COMBINE coffee, ½ cup sugar, orange peel, and cinnamon in medium bowl; stir until sugar dissolves. Cool to room temperature. Transfer mixture to 9x5x3-inch loaf pan. Freeze until granita is consistency of shaved ice, stirring mixture with fork and breaking up frozen edge pieces every 30 minutes, about 4 hours. *(Granita can be made 1 day ahead. Cover and keep frozen. Before serving, blend mixture in processor to break up ice.)*

BEAT cream and remaining 3 tablespoons sugar in medium bowl until soft peaks form. Add Grand Marnier and beat until soft peaks form again. Spoon granita into bowls. Top each dessert with dollop of whipped cream. Garnish with chocolate curls and orange peel strips and serve immediately.

Watermelon-berry granita with melon and berry compote

A CLASSIC GRANITA is just flavored, sweetened liquid that has been frozen and then scraped with a fork to make a flaky, icy treat—like a snow cone for grown-ups. In this version, the liquid comes from fresh summertime watermelon to which one plump, ripe strawberry is added, not only to deepen the granita's color but also to add a hint of tantalizingly perfumed flavor. Feel free to substitute other fresh summer berries in the compote that accompanies the granita.

8 SERVINGS

Watermelon-berry granita

- **7 cups ¾-inch cubes seeded watermelon (from 4¼ pounds)**
- **½ cup sugar**
- **2 tablespoons fresh lemon juice**
- **1 large ripe strawberry, hulled**
- **Pinch of salt**

Melon and berry compote

- **3 cups ½-inch cubes seeded watermelon**
- **1 cup diced hulled fresh strawberries**
- **1 cup fresh raspberries**
- **1 cup fresh blueberries**
- **3 tablespoons sugar**
- **1 tablespoon thinly sliced fresh mint**

FOR GRANITA: Working in batches, puree watermelon in blender until smooth. Return 4 cups puree to blender. Add next 4 ingredients. Blend until smooth. Pour mixture into 13x9x2-inch metal baking pan. Freeze until mixture is icy at edge of pan, about 45 minutes. Whisk to distribute frozen portions evenly. Freeze again until icy at edge of pan and overall texture is slushy, about 45 minutes. Whisk to distribute frozen portions evenly. Then freeze until solid, about 3 hours. Using fork, scrape granita down length of pan, forming icy flakes. Freeze at least 1 hour. *(Can be prepared 1 day ahead. Cover and keep frozen.)*

FOR COMPOTE: Mix all ingredients gently in large bowl. Let stand at room temperature at least 30 minutes and up to 1 hour. *(Can be prepared 2 hours ahead. Cover and chill.)*

WORKING quickly, scoop icy flakes into dessert dishes. Spoon compote alongside.

Cantaloupe granita

ASTI SPUMANTE, the fruity sparkling wine of Italy, adds effervescence and flavor to this simple frozen dessert featuring fresh melon. If you like, however, water may be substituted. For a more elaborate but still easy presentation, top off the granita just before serving with a diced melon salad composed of cubes of cantaloupe, honeydew, and watermelon that have been tossed with a light sprinkling of sugar and some thinly sliced fresh mint leaves.

6 SERVINGS

- **4 cups chopped cantaloupe**
- **1⅓ cups Asti Spumante (Italian sparkling wine) or water**
- **¾ cup sugar**
- **2 tablespoons fresh lemon juice**

PUREE cantaloupe in processor; transfer to large bowl. Add next 3 ingredients and stir until sugar dissolves. Pour mixture into 9x9x2-inch metal baking pan. Freeze mixture until partially set, whisking twice, about 2 hours. Freeze uncovered without whisking until completely set, at least 3 hours and up to 1 day. Using fork, scrape granita across surface, forming icy flakes. Cover with aluminum foil and freeze until ready to serve. *(Can be prepared 2 days ahead. Keep frozen.)*

MOUND granita in 6 ice-cold Martini glasses and serve immediately.

Raspberry, strawberry, and orange granita

HONEY ADDS a subtle hint of rich flavor and aroma to an easy frozen dessert starring fresh summer fruit. If you would like an even more lush consistency to the finished granita, pass the pureed fruit through a fine-mesh sieve to remove all of the tiny raspberry and strawberry seeds before freezing.

8 SERVINGS

- **1 cup orange juice**
- **¾ cup water**
- **½ cup honey**
- **¼ cup sugar**
- **1 teaspoon grated orange peel**
- **1 1-pint container fresh strawberries, hulled, quartered (about 3½ cups), divided**
- **2 ½-pint containers fresh raspberries, divided**

COMBINE orange juice, ¾ cup water, honey, sugar, and orange peel in blender. Add half of strawberries and half of raspberries; puree until almost smooth. Add remaining berries; puree until smooth. Transfer mixture to 13x9x2-inch metal baking pan. Freeze until edges are icy and center is slushy, about 1 hour 30 minutes. Stir icy edges into slushy center. Freeze granita until solid, stirring every 45 minutes, about 3½ hours longer.

USING fork, scrape granita across surface, forming icy flakes. Cover and freeze at least 1 hour. *(Can be prepared 2 days ahead. Keep frozen.)*

SPOON granita into glasses and serve immediately.

Blackberry and hazelnut sundaes

JUST ABOUT ALL IT TAKES to transform store-bought ice cream into a spectacular dessert is a selection of ripe seasonal berries. Blackberries star here, but any others may be substituted. Chop the hazelnuts the easy way: in a food processor fitted with the stainless-steel blade, using on/off turns.

4 SERVINGS

- **⅓ cup sugar**
- **⅓ cup (packed) golden brown sugar**
- **⅓ cup water**
- **2 tablespoons (¼ stick) unsalted butter**
- **3 tablespoons Frangelico (hazelnut liqueur) or amaretto**
- **⅓ cup hazelnuts, toasted, skinned, chopped**

Vanilla frozen yogurt or ice cream

- **1 ½-pint container fresh blackberries**

COMBINE sugar, brown sugar, and ⅓ cup water in heavy small saucepan. Stir over medium-low heat until all sugar dissolves. Add butter and stir until melted. Increase heat and boil until sauce is reduced to ½ cup, about 4 minutes. Remove from heat. Mix in Frangelico and nuts. *(Sauce can be prepared 1 day ahead. Cover and refrigerate. Before using, stir over low heat until heated through and smooth.)*

SCOOP frozen yogurt into bowls. Spoon warm sauce over. Top with berries.

Tropical sundaes

THE TWIST TO THESE SUNDAES is a simple ginger-infused sauce sparked with lime. It can be made ahead and rewarmed just before you assemble the desserts. Small jars of crystallized ginger may be found in the spice or Asian foods section of supermarkets; but look also for boxes containing larger slices of crystallized ginger, available at specialty foods stores.

6 SERVINGS

Ginger-lime sauce

½ cup sugar
½ cup (packed) golden brown sugar
6 tablespoons water
¼ cup strained fresh lime juice
3 tablespoons unsalted butter
2 quarter-size pieces crystallized ginger
3 tablespoons minced crystallized ginger

Sundaes

Vanilla ice cream
3 cups assorted diced peeled tropical fruits such as pineapple, papaya, and mango
Toasted sweetened flaked coconut

FOR GINGER-LIME SAUCE: Combine ½ cup sugar and next 5 ingredients in heavy medium saucepan. Stir over medium heat until all sugar dissolves. Simmer until sauce is reduced to 1 cup, stirring frequently, about 15 minutes. Cool to lukewarm. Discard ginger pieces and add minced ginger. *(Can be prepared 1 day ahead. Cover and refrigerate. Before serving, rewarm just until lukewarm, whisking occasionally.)*

FOR SUNDAES: Scoop ice cream into balloon glasses or sundae dishes. Spoon lukewarm sauce over. Top with fruit. Sprinkle with coconut and serve.

Strawberry sundaes with crème fraîche ice cream

CRÈME FRAÎCHE, available in the dairy section of some supermarkets, gives this exceptional ice cream irresistible tang and a silky texture. If unavailable, heat 1 cup whipping cream to lukewarm (85°F). Remove from heat and mix in 2 tablespoons buttermilk. Cover and let stand in a warm draft-free area until slightly thickened, 24 to 48 hours, depending on the temperature of the room. Refrigerate until ready to use.

6 SERVINGS

1 cup half and half
1 cup whipping cream
½ vanilla bean, split lengthwise

¾ cup sugar
6 large egg yolks
1 cup crème fraîche

1 1-pint container fresh strawberries, hulled, sliced
Strawberry Sauce (see recipe)

COMBINE half and half and whipping cream in heavy large saucepan. Scrape in seeds from vanilla bean; add pod. Bring to boil. Remove from heat. Cover and let stand 15 minutes.

USING electric mixer, beat sugar and egg yolks in large bowl until thick and pale yellow, about 4 minutes. Gradually beat in warm cream mixture. Return mixture to saucepan. Stir over medium-low heat until custard thickens and leaves path on back of spoon when finger is drawn across, about 6 minutes (do not boil). Remove from heat. Cool 15 minutes. Discard vanilla bean pod. Whisk in crème fraîche. Cover and chill custard until cold, about 3 hours.

PROCESS custard in ice cream maker according to manufacturer's instructions. Transfer ice cream to container. Cover and freeze until firm. *(Can be prepared 3 days ahead. Keep frozen.)*

PLACE 2 scoops crème fraîche ice cream in each of 6 bowls. Top with sliced strawberries and sauce. Serve immediately.

Strawberry sauce

BESIDES TAKING just a few minutes to prepare, this fresh strawberry sauce is extra-easy because there is no need to spend time searching for the most beautiful-looking berries—the fruit will be chopped up and cooked. Just select strawberries that are ripe, sweet, and juicy, even if a few of them are bruised or less than shapely. In a pinch, you can even make the sauce with frozen fruit.

MAKES ABOUT 2 CUPS

- **1 1-pint container strawberries, hulled, coarsely chopped**
- **1/2 cup sugar**
- **1 teaspoon fresh lemon juice**

STIR strawberries, sugar, and lemon juice in heavy medium saucepan over medium heat until sugar dissolves. Bring to boil. Reduce heat and simmer 3 minutes. Transfer strawberry sauce to bowl. Chill until cold, about 2 hours. *(Can be prepared 1 day ahead. Cover and keep refrigerated.)*

Warm blackberry pie sundaes

ALL THE WONDERFUL TASTES and textures of summer berry pie à la mode come together in these ice cream sundaes, which are incredibly easy thanks to store-bought ice cream and shortbread cookies and a quickly simmered fresh fruit sauce. For a casual party, offer the individual components buffet-style and let guests assemble their own sundaes.

8 SERVINGS

- **4 1/2-pint containers fresh blackberries (about 5 1/2 cups), divided**
- **1 cup orange juice**
- **3/4 cup sugar**
- **2 teaspoons grated orange peel**
- **1/4 teaspoon ground cinnamon**

- **1 7.25-ounce package shortbread cookies (such as Pepperidge Farm Chessmen), coarsely crumbled (about 2 cups)**
- **3 pints vanilla ice cream**

COMBINE 4 cups blackberries, orange juice, sugar, orange peel, and cinnamon in medium saucepan. Bring to boil. Reduce heat to low; simmer until berries are soft and begin to release juices, about 8 minutes. Transfer 2 cups berry mixture to processor and puree until almost smooth. Return mixture to same saucepan. Stir in remaining blackberries. *(Sauce can be prepared 2 hours ahead. Let stand at room temperature. Rewarm over medium heat until just warm before continuing.)*

DIVIDE crumbled cookies among 8 bowls or wineglasses. Add 1 scoop ice cream to each. Spoon warm sauce over each and serve.

S'mores sundaes

IN THIS DELICIOUS INTERPRETATION of the campfire classic, home-baked blondies made with whole wheat flour and chopped walnuts replace the graham crackers, and a luscious hot fudge sauce stands in for the melting chocolate. There is no need, however, to prepare your own marshmallows. And store-bought coffee ice cream adds a cooling touch that would be impossible to duplicate over an open fire.

8 SERVINGS

- **1 cup whole wheat flour**
- **1 cup (packed) golden brown sugar**
- **1 teaspoon baking powder**
- **¼ teaspoon salt**
- **½ cup (1 stick) unsalted butter, melted**
- **1 large egg**
- **1 teaspoon vanilla extract**
- **¾ cup chopped walnuts**

- **¾ cup whipping cream**
- **5 ounces bittersweet (not unsweetened) or semisweet chocolate, chopped**

- **16 large marshmallows**
- **4 metal skewers**
- **1½ pints coffee ice cream**

PREHEAT oven to 350°F. Lightly butter 8x8x2-inch metal baking pan. Mix flour, brown sugar, baking powder, and salt in medium bowl. Whisk butter, egg, and vanilla in large bowl to blend. Add flour mixture. Stir to combine. Mix in nuts.

PRESS dough over bottom of prepared pan. Bake blondie until top is golden and tester inserted into center comes out clean, about 25 minutes. Transfer pan to rack and cool.

BRING cream to simmer in heavy small saucepan. Remove from heat. Add chocolate. Stir until chocolate melts and is smooth. *(Can be prepared 1 day ahead. Store blondie in airtight container at room temperature. Cover and refrigerate chocolate sauce. Rewarm sauce over medium-low heat before using.)*

CUT blondie into 16 squares. Place 2 squares in each of 8 large sundae dishes. Thread 4 marshmallows onto each skewer; hold over gas flame or under broiler until soft and golden. Place 2 scoops ice cream atop blondies in each dish. Spoon sauce over. Top each with 2 marshmallows.

Cherry sundaes with chocolate-cherry sauce

LAYERING FRESH PITTED CHERRY HALVES with ice cream and a warm chocolate-cherry sauce amplifies the pleasures offered by these easy summertime sundaes. Using dried cherries, especially the lightly sugared ones made from the tart Montmorency variety, makes it possible to enjoy the sauce year-round.

4 SERVINGS

- **½ cup whipping cream**
- **5 tablespoons sugar, divided**
- **3 tablespoons kirsch or other clear cherry brandy, divided**
- **4 ounces bittersweet (not unsweetened) or semisweet chocolate, chopped**
- **1 tablespoon unsalted butter**
- **¼ cup dried tart cherries, chopped**

- **2 cups fresh tart or sweet cherries, halved, pitted**

- **Vanilla ice cream**
- **Whipped cream (optional)**
- **4 whole fresh cherries (optional)**

BRING cream, 3 tablespoons sugar, and 2 tablespoons kirsch to simmer in heavy small saucepan, stirring to dissolve sugar. Remove from heat; whisk in chocolate and butter. Stir until chocolate melts and is smooth. Whisk in dried cherries. *(Sauce can be prepared 1 week ahead. Cover and refrigerate. Rewarm over medium-low heat before using.)*

PLACE halved fresh cherries in bowl. Add remaining 2 tablespoons sugar and 1 tablespoon kirsch. Let stand 20 minutes.

LAYER ice cream, halved cherries, and sauce in 4 sundae dishes. Top with second layer of ice cream, sauce, and cherries. Garnish with whipped cream and whole cherry, if desired.

Peanut brittle ice cream sundae with chocolate sauce

AN ICE CREAM-PARLOR SPECIAL comes home in this outstanding treat. The crunchy candy—made by cooking sugar with corn syrup and then stirring in baking soda and salted nuts—has to be cooked to a very high temperature, so be sure to have a bowl of ice water nearby to cool down your fingers in case of any spills.

8 SERVINGS

Peanut brittle

- **3/4 cup sugar**
- **2/3 cup light corn syrup**
- **2 tablespoons water**
- **1/2 teaspoon baking soda**
- **1 1/2 cups salted cocktail peanuts**

Ice cream

- **1 cup whole milk**
- **1 cup sugar**
- **1 vanilla bean, split lengthwise**
- **4 large egg yolks**
- **3 cups chilled whipping cream**

Chocolate Sauce (see recipe)
Whipped cream

FOR PEANUT BRITTLE: Lightly butter large baking sheet. Combine sugar, corn syrup, and 2 tablespoons water in heavy medium saucepan. Stir over medium-low heat until sugar dissolves. Attach clip-on candy thermometer to inside of pan. Increase heat to medium. Using wooden spoon, stir constantly but slowly until temperature reaches 300°F, occasionally brushing down sides of pan with wet pastry brush, about 20 minutes. Remove from heat; immediately add baking soda and stir until very foamy. Quickly stir in peanuts. Working quickly, pour out onto prepared baking sheet. Cool completely. Coarsely chop peanut brittle.

FOR ICE CREAM: Combine milk and sugar in heavy medium saucepan. Scrape in seeds from vanilla bean; add pod. Stir over medium heat until sugar dissolves. Bring to boil. Remove from heat. Whisk egg yolks in medium bowl to blend. Gradually whisk in hot milk mixture. Return mixture to saucepan. Stir over medium-low heat until custard thickens and leaves path on back of spoon when finger is drawn across, about 2 minutes (do not boil). Strain into bowl. Whisk in cream. Chill until cold.

PROCESS custard in ice cream maker according to manufacturer's instructions. Transfer to large container. Mix in 2 cups chopped peanut brittle. Cover and freeze. Reserve remaining brittle for garnish. *(Ice cream and peanut brittle can be prepared 3 days ahead. Keep ice cream frozen. Store remaining peanut brittle in airtight container.)*

SCOOP ice cream into bowls. Top with sauce, whipped cream, and reserved peanut brittle.

Chocolate sauce

THE COMBINATION of semisweet and bittersweet chocolates adds an extra hint of complexity to the flavor of this simple sundae sauce. Be sure to use light corn syrup, which contributes to the sauce's smooth consistency and glossy sheen without imposing any flavor other than its sweetness; dark corn syrup has a distinctive flavor of its own, which can distract from those of the chocolates here. This quick sauce comes in handy for all manner of desserts.

MAKES ABOUT 1 1/2 CUPS

- **2/3 cup water**
- **2 tablespoons light corn syrup**
- **8 ounces semisweet chocolate, chopped**
- **2 ounces bittersweet (not unsweetened) chocolate, chopped**

BRING ⅔ cup water and corn syrup to simmer in heavy medium saucepan. Reduce heat to low. Add both chocolates and stir until melted and smooth. *(Can be prepared 1 day ahead. Cover and refrigerate. Rewarm over low heat before using.)* Serve warm.

Pear-caramel ice cream sundaes

IF YOU LIKE the way the flavor of a juicy, sweet, subtly spicy pear marries with that of rich, mellow caramel, you'll find this recipe doubly pleasing: Those complementary tastes are included in not only the homemade ice cream but also the warm topping spooned over each serving.

6 SERVINGS

Ice cream

- **1½ tablespoons unsalted butter**
- **⅔ cup sugar**
- **3½ cups diced cored halved peeled ripe Bosc pears (about 1½ pounds)**
- **4 large egg yolks**
- **2 cups whipping cream**
- **2 tablespoons poire Williams (clear pear brandy; optional)**

Pears

- **3 tablespoons unsalted butter**
- **6 tablespoons sugar**
- **3 ripe Bosc pears, peeled, halved, cored, each half cut into 6 lengthwise slices**

FOR ICE CREAM: Melt butter in heavy 10-inch-diameter skillet over medium-low heat. Add sugar and cook until sugar melts (mixture will be grainy for first 10 to 12 minutes) and turns deep amber color, stirring occasionally and pressing on sugar lumps to break up, about 20 minutes total. Add diced pears (caramel will bubble and harden). Increase heat to medium-high and boil until liquid thickens and pears are very tender, breaking up large caramel pieces and stirring occasionally, about 14 minutes. Transfer mixture to blender.

BEAT egg yolks to blend in medium bowl. Bring cream to boil in heavy medium saucepan. Gradually whisk hot cream into yolks. Return cream mixture to same saucepan. Stir over low heat until custard thickens slightly and leaves path on back of spoon when finger is drawn across, about 2 minutes (do not boil). Immediately add custard to pear mixture in blender. Add pear brandy, if desired. Blend until smooth. Cover custard and refrigerate until well chilled.

PROCESS custard in ice cream maker according to manufacturer's instructions. Transfer ice cream to container. Cover and freeze until firm, at least 4 hours. *(Can be prepared 1 week ahead. Keep frozen.)*

FOR PEARS: Melt butter in heavy large skillet over medium-low heat. Add sugar and cook until sugar turns deep amber color, stirring occasionally and breaking up sugar lumps, about 20 minutes. Add pears; sauté until pears are tender but not mushy and caramel thickens slightly, about 9 minutes.

ARRANGE 6 pear slices decoratively on each of 6 plates or in shallow bowls. Scoop ice cream atop pears. Drizzle with caramel syrup from skillet.

S'mores coffee and fudge ice cream cake

THIS DECADENT DESSERT appeals to everyone's inner Boy Scout or Girl Scout, recombining the ingredients of the cookout treat in an impressive new way. The graham crackers, finely ground along with toasted almonds, form a crumb crust that holds luscious layers of coffee ice cream and homemade fudge sauce, topped just before serving with a golden brown layer of broiled marshmallows. Begin preparing this cake a day ahead.

10 TO 12 SERVINGS

16 whole graham crackers (about 8 ounces)
1 cup whole almonds, toasted
3 tablespoons sugar
½ cup (1 stick) unsalted butter, melted

3 pints coffee ice cream, softened until spreadable, divided
Fudge Sauce (see recipe)

1 7- to 7.5-ounce jar marshmallow creme
2 cups miniature marshmallows

PREHEAT oven to 350°F. Finely grind graham crackers, almonds, and sugar in processor. Add butter and process mixture until moist crumbs form. Using plastic wrap as aid, press crumb mixture over bottom and up sides of 9-inch-diameter springform pan with 2¾-inch-high sides. Bake crust until edges are golden, about 12 minutes. Cool completely.

SPREAD 1 pint softened ice cream evenly in crust. Spoon ¾ cup cooled Fudge Sauce over. Freeze until sauce is just set, about 10 minutes. Refrigerate or freeze remaining ice cream as necessary to prevent melting. Repeat layering with 1 pint ice cream, then ¾ cup sauce. Freeze until sauce is just set. Spread remaining 1 pint ice cream over. Cover and freeze cake overnight. Refrigerate remaining sauce.

PREHEAT broiler. Warm remaining sauce in small saucepan over low heat. Remove from heat. Place cake in pan on baking sheet. Spread marshmallow creme over top of cake. Sprinkle miniature marshmallows over in single layer. Broil just until marshmallows are golden brown, watching closely to avoid burning, about 1 minute. Run knife between pan sides and cake to loosen. Remove pan sides. Cut cake into wedges. Serve cake immediately with remaining sauce.

Fudge sauce

ALTHOUGH CHOCOLATE can sometimes be difficult to melt, seizing up into hard lumps when subjected to too-high heat, this simple recipe makes the process easy by whisking chopped chocolate into a hot mixture of cream and corn syrup. The sauce can be prepared ahead of time and refrigerated, then gently rewarmed over low heat just until pourable before using.

MAKES ABOUT 2½ CUPS

1 cup whipping cream
½ cup light corn syrup
10 ounces bittersweet (not unsweetened) or semisweet chocolate, chopped

BRING cream and corn syrup to boil in heavy medium saucepan. Remove from heat. Add chocolate and whisk until melted and smooth. Refrigerate until cool but still pourable, stirring occasionally, about 45 minutes.

Chocolate-peppermint ice cream cake

MADE ALMOST ENTIRELY from ingredients that need little preparation, this recipe produces a colorful and festive holiday-season dessert with next to no effort. Nevertheless, begin assembling the cake one day in advance, as it has to freeze overnight. For best results, use a rich, premium ice cream, which will freeze firmly.

12 SERVINGS

Crust
½ cup (1 stick) unsalted butter
8 ounces bittersweet (not unsweetened) or semisweet chocolate, chopped
1½ 9-ounce packages chocolate wafer cookies (about 60 cookies)

Glaze

- **½ cup whipping cream**
- **¼ cup light corn syrup**
- **6 ounces bittersweet (not unsweetened) or semisweet chocolate, chopped**

Filling

- **3½ pints premium vanilla ice cream, slightly softened**
- **1¼ cups coarsely crushed red-and-white-striped peppermint hard candies (about 10 ounces)**
- **2 teaspoons peppermint extract**

Red-and-white-striped peppermint hard candies, whole or broken into pieces

FOR CRUST: Melt butter with chocolate in heavy small saucepan over low heat. Finely grind cookies in processor. Add warm chocolate mixture; blend just until moist crumbs form. Reserve 1 cup crumb mixture in small bowl. Using plastic wrap as aid, press remaining crumb mixture up sides, then over bottom of 9-inch-diameter springform pan with 2¾-inch-high sides. Freeze crust.

FOR GLAZE: Bring cream and corn syrup to boil in heavy medium saucepan. Remove from heat. Add chocolate; whisk until melted and smooth. Let glaze stand until cool but still pourable, about 1 hour.

FOR FILLING: Working quickly, mix ice cream, 1¼ cups crushed candies, and peppermint extract in large bowl just until combined. Spoon half of ice cream into crust; spread evenly (place remaining ice cream mixture in bowl in freezer). Sprinkle reserved 1 cup cookie crumbs over ice cream in pan; press gently to adhere. Pour 1 cup chocolate glaze over ice cream in pan. Freeze 1 hour. Top with remaining ice cream; spread evenly. Freeze until firm, about 4 hours. Stir remaining glaze over low heat just until pourable but not warm. Pour glaze over ice cream; spread evenly. Freeze overnight.

RUN sharp knife between crust and pan sides to loosen cake. Release pan sides. Transfer cake to platter. Garnish cake with candies and serve.

Dulce de leche ice cream cake with strawberries

THE RICH LATIN AMERICAN milk caramel called *dulce de leche* is taking its place as a mainstream flavor favorite in the United States; it may now be found in a wide variety of treats, including familiar brands of quality ice cream. Strawberry sorbet, also purchased, looks and tastes wonderful alongside the dulce de leche in this terrific, uncomplicated dessert.

14 TO 16 SERVINGS

- **5 whole graham crackers, broken into pieces**
- **⅓ cup hazelnuts, toasted, skinned**
- **1 tablespoon plus ⅓ cup sugar**
- **⅛ teaspoon salt**
- **5 tablespoons unsalted butter, melted**

- **4 pints dulce de leche ice cream, divided**
- **2 pints strawberry sorbet, divided**

- **2½ pounds fresh strawberries, hulled, sliced**

Purchased caramel sauce (optional)

PREHEAT oven to 350°F. Combine crackers, nuts, 1 tablespoon sugar, and salt in processor. Blend until nuts are finely chopped. Add butter and blend until mixture is evenly moistened. Using plastic wrap as aid, press mixture over bottom (not sides) of 10-inch-diameter springform pan. Bake crust until golden, about 8 minutes. Cool completely.

SLIGHTLY soften 1¼ pints ice cream; spread over crust. Freeze until firm, about 1 hour. Slightly soften 1 pint sorbet; spread over ice cream. Freeze until firm, about 30 minutes. Slightly soften 1¼ pints ice cream; spread over sorbet. Freeze until firm, about 1 hour. Slightly soften remaining 1 pint sorbet; spread over ice cream. Freeze until firm, about 30 minutes. Slightly soften remaining 1½ pints ice cream; spread over sorbet for top layer.

Cover and freeze ice cream cake until firm, at least 3 hours. *(Can be prepared 1 week ahead. Keep frozen.)*

STIR berries and remaining ⅓ cup sugar in large bowl. Let stand until berries release their juices, about 30 minutes.

CUT around cake to loosen. Release pan sides. Cut cake into wedges; arrange on plates. Spoon berries atop wedges; drizzle with caramel sauce, if desired, and serve.

Caramel ice cream pie with mocha fudge sauce

EACH STEP OF THE PREPARATION goes quickly and easily for this satisfying pie. Start it early enough to allow time for freezing. For the crust, break up purchased vanilla wafers and place in a food processor fitted with the stainless-steel blade, and process using on/off turns until fine crumbs form.

8 SERVINGS

Crust

- **⅓ cup chopped pecans**
- **2 tablespoons sugar**
- **⅔ cup vanilla wafer cookie crumbs (from about 32 cookies)**
- **½ teaspoon ground cinnamon**
- **2 tablespoons (¼ stick) unsalted butter, melted**

Sauce

- **2 tablespoons boiling water**
- **1 tablespoon instant coffee powder or instant espresso powder**
- **1 cup sugar**
- **2 tablespoons unsweetened cocoa powder**
- **1 cup whipping cream**
- **¼ cup light corn syrup**
- **2 ounces unsweetened chocolate, finely chopped**
- **2 tablespoons (¼ stick) unsalted butter**
- **1½ teaspoons vanilla extract, divided**

- **2 pints caramel ice cream (such as dulce de leche), divided**

- **½ cup chilled whipping cream**
- **1 tablespoon powdered sugar**
- **2 tablespoons chopped pecans**

FOR CRUST: Preheat oven to 350°F. Blend pecans and sugar in processor until nuts are finely ground. Add cookie crumbs and cinnamon; process to combine. Add butter and blend until moist clumps form. Using plastic wrap as aid, press crust over bottom and up sides of 9-inch-diameter glass pie dish. Bake crust until lightly toasted, about 10 minutes. Cool completely.

FOR SAUCE: Stir 2 tablespoons boiling water and coffee powder in small bowl until powder is dissolved. Whisk sugar and cocoa in heavy medium saucepan. Whisk in 1 cup cream, corn syrup, and coffee mixture. Add chocolate and butter. Bring to boil over high heat, stirring constantly. Reduce heat to medium and simmer until slightly thickened, stirring occasionally, about 4 minutes. Cool sauce 30 minutes. Stir in 1 teaspoon vanilla.

SOFTEN 1 pint ice cream. Spread evenly over bottom of crust. Drizzle 3 tablespoons sauce over ice cream. Freeze until sauce sets, about 15 minutes.

MEANWHILE, soften remaining 1 pint ice cream. Spread evenly atop sauce. Drizzle with 3 tablespoons sauce. Freeze pie until firm, at least 4 hours. *(Sauce and pie can be prepared 1 day ahead. Cover and refrigerate sauce. Keep pie frozen.)*

REWARM remaining sauce over low heat, stirring often. Beat ½ cup chilled cream, powdered sugar, and remaining ½ teaspoon vanilla in medium bowl until peaks form. Transfer to pastry bag fitted with medium star tip. Pipe rosettes of cream around top edge of pie. Sprinkle with chopped pecans. Cut pie into wedges and serve with sauce.

Coffee-toffee crunch torte

LAYERS OF TOFFEE-STUDDED, coffee-flavored mousse and chocolate ganache fill an almond and sugar-cookie crust. The dark corn syrup adds extra richness to the bittersweet chocolate–cream mixture, helping to make it the perfect complement to the robust tastes of espresso and English toffee.

12 SERVINGS

Crust

- **1 cup whole almonds, toasted**
- **1½ cups ground sugar cookies (such as Pepperidge Farm Bordeaux; about 6¾ ounces)**
- **½ cup coarsely chopped chocolate-covered English toffee (such as Skor or Heath bar; about 3 ounces)**
- **5 to 6 tablespoons butter, melted, hot**

Ganache

- **½ cup whipping cream**
- **2 tablespoons dark corn syrup**
- **6 ounces bittersweet (not unsweetened) or semisweet chocolate, chopped**

Mousse

- **¾ cup plus 2 tablespoons sugar**
- **6 large egg yolks**
- **⅓ cup water**
- **3 tablespoons instant espresso powder**
- **½ teaspoon ground nutmeg**

- **2½ cups chilled whipping cream**
- **2 tablespoons coffee liqueur**
- **1 teaspoon vanilla extract**
- **1½ cups coarsely chopped chocolate-covered English toffee (such as Skor or Heath bar; about 9 ounces)**

- **20 (about) whole almonds, toasted**

FOR CRUST: Preheat oven to 350°F. Grind nuts with ground cookies and toffee in processor. Add 5 tablespoons butter; blend until nuts are finely chopped. To moisten crumbs, if necessary, blend in another 1 tablespoon melted butter. Using plastic wrap as aid, press mixture over bottom and up sides of 9-inch-diameter springform pan with 2¾-inch-high sides. Freeze 15 minutes.

BAKE crust until golden, about 12 minutes. Freeze.

FOR GANACHE: Bring cream and corn syrup to simmer in heavy medium saucepan. Remove from heat. Add chocolate; whisk until melted and smooth. Cool to room temperature.

FOR MOUSSE: Whisk sugar, egg yolks, ⅓ cup water, and espresso powder in large metal bowl. Set bowl over saucepan of simmering water (do not allow bottom of bowl to touch water); whisk constantly until candy thermometer inserted into mixture registers 160°F, about 3 minutes. Remove bowl from over water. Add nutmeg. Using electric mixer, beat mixture until cool and thick, about 5 minutes.

BEAT 2½ cups cream, liqueur, and vanilla in another large bowl until peaks form. Fold cream mixture and toffee into egg mixture. Spoon half of mousse into crust. Drizzle ¼ cup ganache over. Using tip of knife, swirl mixtures together. Carefully spoon remaining mousse over; smooth top. Cover and freeze torte overnight. Cover and refrigerate remaining ganache.

REWARM remaining ganache over low heat, whisking just until slightly softened but not melted. If necessary, let stand until firm enough to pipe. Spoon ganache into pastry bag fitted with medium star tip. Run sharp knife between torte and pan sides to loosen. Release pan sides. Pipe ganache in lattice design atop torte. Pipe ganache in star shapes around border. Garnish torte with almonds. *(Can be prepared 1 week ahead. Freeze until lattice sets, then cover and keep frozen.)*

Halvah and vanilla ice cream torte

HALVAH, a traditional Middle Eastern candy, is made from ground sesame seeds combined with honey or sugar syrup and sometimes other ingredients, including nuts or sweet spices. The source of this easy frozen dessert's rich flavor and pleasing consistency, it is available at many delicatessens and Middle Eastern markets, and in the refrigerated deli case at the supermarket.

8 TO 10 SERVINGS

30 chocolate wafer cookies (about ⅔ of 9-ounce package), broken into pieces
3 tablespoons chilled unsalted butter, cut into ½-inch cubes
3 tablespoons (packed) golden brown sugar
3 cups coarsely crumbled vanilla-flavor halvah (about 12 ounces), divided

3 pints vanilla ice cream, softened slightly

PREHEAT oven to 375°F. Blend cookies, butter, and sugar in processor until cookies are finely ground. Add 1½ cups halvah and blend, using on/off turns. Sprinkle 1¼ cups crumb mixture over bottom of 9-inch-diameter glass pie dish. Using plastic wrap as aid, press remaining crumb mixture firmly over bottom and halfway up sides of 9 inch-diameter springform pan. Bake until crumb mixture in pie dish and crust in pan begin to puff, about 10 minutes. Cool crumb mixture and crust completely.

SPREAD 1½ pints ice cream evenly in cooled crust in springform pan. Sprinkle with 1 cup crumbled halvah. Spread remaining ice cream over. Break up crumb mixture from pie dish. Sprinkle evenly over ice cream; press to adhere for top crust. Sprinkle with remaining ½ cup crumbled halvah. Cover and freeze torte until firm, at least 3 hours. *(Can be prepared 5 days ahead. Keep frozen.)*

Frozen eggnog mousse torte

A CREAMY FROZEN MOUSSE made with whipped cream, white chocolate, egg yolks, brandy, and nutmeg fills a nutty crust lined with bittersweet chocolate. Begin preparing this a day ahead, as it needs to freeze overnight.

8 TO 10 SERVINGS

Crust
2 cups pecans, toasted
1 cup blanched slivered almonds, toasted
½ cup (packed) golden brown sugar
¼ teaspoon ground nutmeg
5 teaspoons unsalted butter, melted
½ teaspoon vanilla extract

3 ounces bittersweet (not unsweetened) or semisweet chocolate, chopped

Filling
4 ounces high-quality white chocolate (such as Lindt or Perugina), finely chopped
1 cup sugar
¾ cup water

8 large egg yolks

2¼ cups chilled whipping cream
¼ cup high-quality brandy
1 tablespoon vanilla extract
¾ teaspoon ground nutmeg

Unsweetened whipped cream

FOR CRUST: Preheat oven to 350°F. Combine pecans, almonds, sugar, and nutmeg in processor. Using on/off turns, process until nuts are finely chopped, stopping once to stir mixture. Transfer mixture to large bowl. Combine butter and vanilla in small bowl. Pour over nut mixture; stir to blend well. Transfer nut mixture to 9-inch-diameter springform pan with 2¾-inch-high sides. Using plastic wrap as aid, press firmly up sides and then over bottom of pan, covering pan completely. Freeze crust 15 minutes.

PLACE pan with crust on rimmed baking sheet and bake 20 minutes. Transfer to rack and cool.

MELT chocolate in top of double boiler set over simmering water, stirring until melted and smooth. Spread over bottom of crust. Cover crust with plastic wrap and freeze until ready to use.

FOR FILLING: Stir white chocolate in top of double boiler set over simmering water until melted and smooth. Remove double boiler with chocolate from heat. Combine sugar and ¾ cup water in heavy small saucepan; stir over medium heat until sugar dissolves. Increase heat and boil without stirring until candy thermometer inserted into syrup registers 238°F (tilting pan slightly to submerge thermometer), about 15 minutes.

MEANWHILE, using electric mixer, beat egg yolks in medium bowl until pale yellow and thick. Gradually beat hot syrup into yolks. Scrape down sides of bowl with rubber spatula. Continue beating until mixture is thick and cool, about 5 minutes. Set aside.

BEAT 2¼ cups cream, brandy, vanilla, and nutmeg in large bowl until peaks form. Fold barely lukewarm white chocolate into yolk mixture. Gently fold in whipped cream. Pour filling into crust; smooth top. Freeze overnight. *(Can be prepared 3 days ahead. Cover pan tightly with plastic wrap and keep frozen.)*

SPOON unsweetened whipped cream into pastry bag fitted with medium star tip. Pipe cream decoratively around edge of cake. Serve immediately.

Brazilian banana and white chocolate ice cream torte

THIS RECIPE TRANSFORMS an irresistible summertime treat—the chocolate-covered frozen banana—into a sophisticated torte, combining the bananas with rich ice cream, a nut crust, and a thick fudge sauce. For the best flavor and consistency, use only very ripe bananas that give to gentle fingertip pressure and have peels well covered in brown spots.

12 SERVINGS

Crust

- 3 cups walnuts
- 1 cup whole almonds
- ⅓ cup (packed) dark brown sugar
- ¼ cup (½ stick) unsalted butter, melted, cooled

Ice cream

- 3 cups whipping cream, divided
- 1 cup half and half
- ¾ cup sugar
- 4 large egg yolks
- 8 ounces high-quality white chocolate (such as Lindt or Perugina), finely chopped

- 1½ pounds very ripe bananas
- 3 tablespoons fresh lemon juice

Sauce

- ¾ cup whipping cream
- ¼ cup light corn syrup
- 8 ounces bittersweet (not unsweetened) or semisweet chocolate, chopped

- 3 large ripe bananas, peeled, cut on diagonal into ¼-inch-wide slices
- 15 small fresh strawberries with stems

FOR CRUST: Preheat oven to 350°F. Finely chop all nuts with sugar in processor. Add butter and process until well blended. Using plastic wrap as aid, press mixture firmly up sides, then over bottom of 9-inch-diameter springform pan with 2¾-inch-high sides. Freeze crust 10 minutes. Bake crust until light brown, about 20 minutes. Cool on rack.

FOR ICE CREAM: Bring 1 cup cream, half and half, and sugar to simmer in heavy medium saucepan, stirring until sugar dissolves. Whisk egg yolks in medium bowl to blend. Gradually whisk in hot cream mixture. Return mixture to saucepan and stir over medium-low heat until custard thickens and leaves path on back of spoon when finger is drawn across, about 5 minutes (do not boil). Strain custard into bowl. Add white chocolate; whisk until melted and smooth. Mix in remaining 2 cups cream. Chill custard until cold.

PEEL and slice bananas. Puree bananas with lemon juice in processor until smooth. Mix puree into custard. Transfer custard to ice cream maker and process according to manufacturer's instructions. Spoon ice cream into cooled crust; smooth top. Cover and freeze torte overnight. *(Can be prepared 1 week ahead; keep frozen.)*

FOR SAUCE: Bring cream and corn syrup to simmer in medium saucepan. Remove from heat. Add chocolate; whisk until melted and smooth. Cool sauce to lukewarm. *(Can be prepared 1 day ahead. Cover and refrigerate. Rewarm over low heat just until pourable before serving.)*

RUN small sharp knife between crust and pan sides to loosen torte. Remove pan sides. Arrange banana slices and strawberries in rows atop ice cream. Serve with chocolate sauce.

Brownie and ice cream sandwiches with chocolate sauce

THICK, NUTTY, FUDGY BROWNIES replace the usual thin chocolate wafers in this brilliant homemade version of the old ice-cream-truck favorite. The sandwiches can be eaten with your fingers, with each bite dipped into the accompanying chocolate sauce laced with hazelnut liqueur and espresso; or present each serving on a plate and drizzle the sauce around it.

MAKES 10

Brownies

- **1 cup plus 2 tablespoons sugar**
- **½ cup (1 stick) unsalted butter**
- **¼ cup water**
- **10 ounces bittersweet (not unsweetened) or semisweet chocolate, chopped**
- **3 large eggs**
- **1 teaspoon vanilla extract**
- **1 cup plus 2 tablespoons unbleached all purpose flour**
- **1½ teaspoons baking soda**
- **1 teaspoon salt**
- **¾ cup chopped macadamia nuts**

- **3 to 4 pints vanilla ice cream, softened slightly**

Sauce

- **8 ounces bittersweet (not unsweetened) or semisweet chocolate, chopped**
- **½ cup freshly brewed strong coffee or 1½ teaspoons instant espresso powder dissolved in ½ cup hot water**
- **6 tablespoons Frangelico (hazelnut liqueur)**

FOR BROWNIES: Preheat oven to 325°F. Line 17x11x1-inch rimmed baking sheet with parchment paper. Bring sugar, butter, and ¼ cup water to boil in heavy large saucepan over medium heat, stirring until sugar dissolves. Reduce heat to low. Add chocolate; stir until melted and smooth. Whisk eggs and vanilla in large bowl to blend. Gradually whisk in hot chocolate mixture. Mix in flour, baking soda, and salt, then nuts.

SPREAD batter over parchment-lined sheet. Bake brownie until toothpick inserted into center comes out clean, about 20 minutes. Cool completely. Freeze on baking sheet until firm.

CUT around brownie to loosen. Turn out onto work surface. Peel off parchment. Trim brownie to 16x10-inch rectangle; cut in half crosswise, forming two 8x10-inch rectangles. Place 1 rectangle on baking sheet. Cover brownie rectangle on baking sheet with ice cream. Freeze until slightly firm.

LIGHTLY score top of remaining brownie in half lengthwise, then score across in 2-inch sections, marking ten 2x4-inch rectangles.

PRESS scored brownie atop ice cream, scored side up. Freeze until ice cream is firm, at least 4 hours. Cut brownie along marked lines into 10 sandwiches.

FOR SAUCE: Stir chocolate and coffee in saucepan over low heat until smooth. Add liqueur. *(Sandwiches and sauce can be prepared 1 week ahead. Wrap sandwiches tightly and keep frozen. Cover and chill sauce. Rewarm over low heat before serving.)*

SERVE sandwiches with sauce.

Individual baked Alaskas

CHEFS HAVE BEEN ingeniously enclosing ice cream inside a hot meringue shell for almost two centuries. The most popular—and lasting—name for such desserts probably came about as a tribute to the purchase of Alaska from Russia in 1867. This elegant version poises meringue-covered coffee ice cream atop individual disks of mocha-flavored cake.

6 SERVINGS

Custard sauce

- **5 large egg yolks**
- **2½ tablespoons sugar**
- **1⅔ cups whole milk**
- **½ teaspoon vanilla extract**

Baked Alaskas

- **1½ cups (packed) dark brown sugar**
- **1¼ cups all purpose flour**
- **½ cup unsweetened cocoa powder**
- **1½ teaspoons baking soda**
- **¾ teaspoon baking powder**
- **¾ cup water**
- **4 teaspoons instant espresso powder or instant coffee powder**
- **¾ cup buttermilk**
- **6 tablespoons vegetable oil**
- **2 large eggs**

- **1½ pints (about) coffee ice cream**

- **6 large egg whites**
- **1½ cups sugar**

FOR CUSTARD SAUCE: Whisk egg yolks and sugar in large bowl to blend. Bring milk just to simmer in heavy medium saucepan. Gradually whisk hot milk into egg mixture. Return mixture to same saucepan and stir over medium-low heat until sauce thickens and coats back of spoon when finger is drawn across, about 7 minutes (do not boil). Pour into bowl. Stir in vanilla. Cool custard sauce, stirring occasionally. Cover and refrigerate until cold.

FOR BAKED ALASKAS: Preheat oven to 350°F. Butter and flour 15x10x1-inch jelly-roll pan. Sift brown sugar and next 4 ingredients into large bowl. Repeat sifting. Combine ¾ cup water and espresso powder in another large bowl; stir to dissolve. Add buttermilk, oil, and eggs; whisk to combine. Add to brown sugar mixture and whisk until blended.

POUR batter into prepared pan. Bake cake until tester inserted into center comes out clean, about 30 minutes. Transfer to rack and cool completely.

(Custard sauce and cake can be prepared 1 day ahead. Keep sauce chilled. Cover cake and refrigerate.)

USING 4-inch-diameter tart pan bottom as guide, cut out 1 cake round. Using metal spatula, transfer cake round to baking sheet. Repeat, forming 5 more cake rounds. Reserve remaining cake for another use. Place large rounded scoop of ice cream atop each cake round. Freeze uncovered until firm, at least 4 hours and up to 8 hours.

USING electric mixer, beat egg whites in large bowl until soft peaks form. Gradually add 1½ cups sugar and beat mixture until thick and glossy. Spoon meringue into pastry bag fitted with medium star tip. Pipe meringue in star shapes atop ice cream, covering ice cream completely but leaving cake visible. Freeze until ready to bake. *(Can be prepared 1 day ahead. Keep frozen.)*

PREHEAT oven to 500°F. Bake desserts until meringue is light brown, about 2 minutes. Using spatula, transfer each baked Alaska to plate. Spoon custard sauce around plates and serve immediately.

Double strawberry baked Alaska

THIS LOVELY SPRING or early summer dessert can be made one day ahead and stored in the freezer; then simply bake it for five minutes before serving. The decorative meringue swirls and peaks may be created with a rubber spatula, table knife, or spoon, but an offset spatula—one with a bend near the handle—works best. A very hot preheated oven and well-frozen ice cream ensure the ideal contrast of hot and cold.

12 SERVINGS

Cake

Nonstick vegetable oil spray
4 large eggs
½ cup sugar
1½ teaspoons vanilla extract
¾ cup sifted cake flour (sifted, then measured)
1 tablespoon poppy seeds
6 tablespoons (¾ stick) unsalted butter, melted, cooled

Filling

2 pints strawberry sorbet, slightly softened
2 pints strawberry ice cream, slightly softened

Meringue

6 large egg whites
¾ cup sugar
½ teaspoon vanilla extract

FOR CAKE: Preheat oven to 325°F. Spray 9-inch-diameter springform pan with nonstick spray. Whisk eggs, sugar, and vanilla in large metal bowl to blend. Set bowl over saucepan of simmering water (do not allow bottom of bowl to touch water); whisk constantly just until mixture is warm, about 2 minutes. Remove bowl from over water. Using electric mixer, beat until mixture is very thick and slowly dissolving ribbon forms when beaters are lifted, about 7 minutes. Add flour in 3 additions, gently folding just to combine after each. Fold in poppy seeds, then quickly fold in butter in 2 additions (do not overmix).

POUR batter into prepared pan. Bake cake until top is golden and tester inserted into center comes out clean, about 28 minutes. Cool completely in pan on rack. Remove pan sides.

FOR FILLING: Line 4-quart 10-inch-diameter bowl with plastic wrap, leaving 8-inch overhang. Spread sorbet in even layer over bottom (not sides) of bowl. Spread ice cream over sorbet. Place cake atop ice cream, pressing slightly to compact. Cover with plastic wrap overhang; freeze at least 4 hours and up to 1 day.

FOR MERINGUE: Using electric mixer, beat egg whites in large bowl until soft peaks form. Gradually beat in sugar, 1 tablespoon at a time; beat until thick and glossy. Beat in vanilla.

UNFOLD plastic wrap from over cake at top of bowl. Invert dessert onto 9-inch-diameter tart pan bottom; remove plastic wrap. Working quickly, spread meringue over dessert, swirling to form peaks and covering completely. Freeze at least 30 minutes. *(Can be prepared 1 day ahead. Keep frozen.)*

PREHEAT oven to 500°F. Place dessert on its tart pan bottom on heavy large baking sheet. Bake just until meringue is light golden, about 5 minutes. Transfer to platter and serve immediately.

Frozen blackberry parfait in hazelnut meringues

THE PARFAIT—a fluffy frozen mixture of berries, egg yolks, crème de cassis, and sugar—is great for special-occasion dinners, as it can be made two days ahead.

8 SERVINGS

- **Vegetable oil**
- **4 large egg whites**
- **1/4 teaspoon cream of tartar**
- **1 3/4 cups, divided, plus 1 tablespoon sugar**
- **1 cup hazelnuts, toasted, skinned, coarsely chopped**
- **24 ounces frozen unsweetened blackberries, thawed, juices reserved**
- **8 large egg yolks**
- **2/3 cup crème de cassis (black-currant liqueur)**
- **Fresh mint sprigs**

PREHEAT oven to 250°F. Line large baking sheet with aluminum foil; brush foil with vegetable oil. Using electric mixer, beat egg whites and cream of tartar in large bowl until soft peaks form. Gradually add 1 cup sugar, beating until thick and glossy, about 7 minutes. Fold in hazelnuts.

USING large spoon, drop meringue onto prepared baking sheet in 8 mounds, spacing 3 inches apart. Using back of spoon, spread each mound to 3-inch round and form indentation in center of each. Bake until meringues are pale but still slightly soft in center, about 1 hour 30 minutes. Cool on sheet. Remove meringues from foil. Wrap individually in foil, then enclose in resealable plastic bag and freeze until firm, at least 2 hours and up to 1 day.

PUREE berries with juice in processor. Strain through sieve set over large measuring cup, pressing on solids in strainer to extract as much puree as possible (about 2¾ cups). Cover puree and chill until cold, at least 1 hour and up to 1 day.

COMBINE egg yolks, crème de cassis, and ¾ cup sugar in medium metal bowl. Set over saucepan of simmering water (do not allow bottom of bowl to touch water). Whisk constantly until thick and billowy and instant-read thermometer inserted into mixture registers 160°F, about 7 minutes. Remove bowl from over water. Add 1¾ cups cold berry puree. Using electric mixer, beat mixture until cool, about 7 minutes. Cover and freeze parfait until firm, at least 6 hours. Whisk remaining 1 tablespoon sugar into remaining berry puree for sauce. *(Meringues, parfait, and sauce can be prepared 2 days ahead. Keep meringues and parfait frozen. Cover and refrigerate sauce.)*

TRANSFER 1 meringue to each of 8 plates. Place 1 large scoop of berry parfait in center of each. Spoon some berry sauce over. Garnish with mint and serve.

White chocolate and Turkish coffee parfaits

SMALL HINTS OF CARDAMOM, cinnamon, and ginger give the coffee flavor an intriguing Middle Eastern personality that is a perfect counterpoint to the smooth, rich white chocolate. Ideal for entertaining, this creamy frozen dessert can be made well in advance. All you have to do before serving is quickly pipe on a decoration of whipped cream.

4 SERVINGS

3/4 cup plus 2/3 cup chilled whipping cream
3 ounces high-quality white chocolate (such as Lindt or Perugina), finely chopped

1 tablespoon instant espresso powder
1/8 teaspoon ground cardamom
1/8 teaspoon ground cinnamon
Pinch of ground ginger

8 large egg yolks
1/2 cup sugar
1/2 cup water
Pinch of cream of tartar
2 teaspoons light corn syrup, divided

2 teaspoons coffee liqueur
4 1/2 teaspoons light rum, divided
1/8 teaspoon vanilla extract

Sweetened whipped cream
Crushed coffee hard candies

BRING ¾ cup cream to simmer in heavy small saucepan over medium heat. Remove from heat. Add white chocolate; stir until melted and smooth. Pour mixture into bowl. Refrigerate until very thick, stirring occasionally, about 3 hours.

MIX espresso powder, cardamom, cinnamon, and ginger in medium bowl. Gradually add remaining ⅔ cup cream, stirring until espresso powder dissolves. Refrigerate coffee cream until well chilled.

USING electric mixer, beat egg yolks in large bowl until pale yellow and slowly dissolving ribbon forms when beaters are lifted. Combine sugar, ½ cup water, and cream of tartar in heavy small saucepan. Stir over medium heat until sugar dissolves. Increase heat and boil without stirring until syrup registers 238°F on candy thermometer (soft-ball stage), tilting pan to submerge thermometer tip, about 5 minutes. Gradually beat hot syrup into yolks in slow steady stream. Beat in 1 teaspoon corn syrup. Continue beating until mixture is completely cool and very light, about 5 minutes. Divide parfait base between 2 bowls.

MIX liqueur, 2 teaspoons rum, and remaining 1 teaspoon corn syrup into coffee cream. Using electric mixer, beat coffee cream until peaks form. Fold into parfait base in 1 bowl. Beat white chocolate cream with remaining 2½ teaspoons rum and vanilla to soft peaks. Fold into parfait base in second bowl. Divide half of coffee parfait among four 8-ounce parfait glasses or slender wineglasses. Divide half of white chocolate parfait among glasses, spooning atop coffee parfait. Repeat layering. Cover and freeze until firm, about 4 hours. *(Can be prepared 2 days ahead. Keep frozen.)*

SPOON sweetened whipped cream into pastry bag fitted with large star tip. Pipe cream decoratively atop each parfait. Sprinkle with candies and serve.

Frozen blackberry and white chocolate terrine

TERRINES, usually savory first courses, take their name from the loaf-shaped French earthenware dishes (*terre* is French for "earth") in which they are traditionally prepared. This terrine is also formed in a loaf pan, with layers of creamy white chocolate and pastel-colored white chocolate–berry frozen mousse. Like any terrine, the mixture is unmolded after it has fully set, then cut into serving slices that reveal its layers. Begin preparing the terrine at least one day ahead.

6 SERVINGS

Terrine
16 ounces frozen blackberries, thawed, juice reserved
1 cup sugar, divided
1 tablespoon crème de cassis (black-currant liqueur) or other berry-flavored liqueur
1/2 teaspoon fresh lemon juice

3 ounces high-quality imported white chocolate (such as Lindt or Perugina), chopped

- **1/4 cup water**
- **6 large egg yolks**
- **2 teaspoons vanilla extract**
- **1 2/3 cups chilled whipping cream**

Sauce

- **16 ounces frozen blackberries, thawed, juice reserved**
- **1/4 cup sugar**
- **2 tablespoons crème de cassis (black-currant liqueur) or other berry-flavored liqueur**

Fresh blackberries or strawberries
Fresh mint sprigs

FOR TERRINE: Line 9x5x3-inch loaf pan with plastic wrap. Puree berries with juice and ¼ cup sugar in blender just until smooth. Strain puree into bowl; discard solids in strainer. Measure 1⅓ cups puree and place in heavy small saucepan (reserve any remaining puree for sauce). Simmer puree in saucepan over medium heat until reduced to scant 1 cup, stirring occasionally, about 8 minutes. Transfer to bowl and chill 30 minutes. Stir in crème de cassis and lemon juice. Refrigerate reduced puree until ready to use.

STIR white chocolate in top of double-boiler set over barely simmering water until melted and smooth. Remove from over water.

COMBINE remaining ¾ cup sugar, ¼ cup water, and egg yolks in medium metal bowl. Set bowl over saucepan of simmering water (do not allow bottom of bowl to touch water). Using handheld electric mixer, beat constantly until instant-read thermometer inserted into mixture registers 140°F for 3 minutes, occasionally scraping down sides of bowl, about 8 minutes total. Remove bowl from over water. Add warm melted chocolate and vanilla to yolk mixture; beat until cool. Beat cream in large bowl until peaks form. Gently mix ¼ of whipped cream into chocolate mixture. Fold in remaining whipped cream.

TRANSFER 1⅓ cups chocolate mixture to another medium bowl. Fold in reduced berry puree. Fill prepared loaf pan with ⅓ of remaining chocolate mixture. Cover with berry-chocolate mixture. Top with remaining chocolate mixture. Smooth top. Cover and freeze terrine overnight. *(Can be prepared 2 days ahead. Keep terrine frozen. Cover and refrigerate any reserved puree.)*

FOR SAUCE: Puree thawed blackberries with juice, sugar, and crème de cassis in blender or processor until smooth. Strain into bowl; discard solids in strainer. Add any puree reserved from terrine.

UNMOLD frozen terrine. Peel off plastic wrap. Slice terrine into ½-inch-thick slices; transfer to plates. Drizzle with sauce. Garnish with berries and fresh mint sprigs and serve.

Toasted almond semifreddo

MEANING "HALF FROZEN" IN ITALIAN, the name for this icy dessert, *semifreddo*, derives from the fluffy frozen mousse on which it is based: It has a soft, creamy consistency that begins to melt tantalizingly almost as soon as it is scooped into individual goblets. If you like, drizzle a little bit of your favorite Italian liqueur over each serving.

12 SERVINGS

- **1 cup sugar**
- **6 large egg yolks**
- **1/4 cup light corn syrup**
- **3 tablespoons amaretto**
- **1/2 cup plus 3 tablespoons finely chopped toasted almonds**

- **2 cups chilled whipping cream**
- **2 teaspoons vanilla extract**

- **2 ounces bittersweet (not unsweetened) or semisweet chocolate, finely chopped**

USING handheld electric mixer, beat sugar, egg yolks, corn syrup, and amaretto in large metal bowl to blend. Place bowl over saucepan of simmering water (do not allow bottom of bowl to touch water). Beat constantly until candy thermometer inserted into mixture registers 160°F and semifreddo base is thick and billowy, about 8 minutes. Remove bowl from over water. Continue to beat semifreddo base until cool, about 7 minutes. Fold in ½ cup almonds.

BEAT cream and vanilla in another large bowl until soft peaks form. Fold cream into cool semifreddo base in 3 additions. Transfer to 13x9x2-inch glass baking dish. Cover and freeze until firm, at least 4 hours. *(Can be prepared 2 days ahead. Keep frozen.)*

SCOOP semifreddo into goblets. Sprinkle with chopped chocolate and remaining 3 tablespoons almonds and serve immediately.

Vacherins with raspberry sorbet and berry-cardamom sauce

MUCH EASIER TO PUT TOGETHER than you might think, these French-style filled meringue cups should nevertheless be started at least a day before you plan to serve them. If you don't have a cookie cutter, use a 3¼- to 3½-inch-diameter can to trace the bases. Do not make the meringues on a humid day, as moisture keeps them from drying properly and staying crisp. If you freeze the sorbet-filled vacherins, the meringues will be tender and chewy.

8 SERVINGS

Meringues

1½ cup sugar
2 tablespoons cornstarch
6 large egg whites, room temperature
¼ teaspoon cream of tartar

Sauce

¾ cup seedless raspberry jam
½ cup sugar
⅓ cup water
16 ounces frozen unsweetened mixed berries (do not thaw)
1 teaspoon ground cardamom

Assembly

3 pints raspberry sorbet
Fresh raspberries
Fresh mint sprigs

FOR MERINGUES: Position 1 rack in bottom third and 1 rack in top third of oven; preheat to 200°F. Line 2 large baking sheets with parchment paper. Using 3¼- to 3½-inch-diameter cookie cutter as template, heavily trace 4 circles on each parchment sheet. Turn parchment over so that marked side faces down (circles will show through).

WHISK sugar and cornstarch in medium bowl to blend. Using heavy-duty or handheld electric mixer at medium-high speed, beat egg whites in large bowl until foamy, about 1 minute. Add cream of tartar; beat until soft peaks form, about 1 minute. Add sugar mixture, 1 tablespoon at a time, beating until whites are very stiff and glossy, at least 4 minutes with heavy duty mixer and 6 to 8 minutes with handheld. Scoop enough meringue into pastry bag fitted with medium star tip to fill ¾ full. Pipe small dot of meringue under parchment in each corner of baking sheets. Press parchment onto dots to anchor.

STARTING in center of 1 marked circle, pipe meringue in continuous spiral to fill circle completely. Pipe 1 meringue circle atop outer edge of base circle, forming standing rim. Repeat, piping 2 more circles atop first, forming meringue cup. Pipe 3 more cups on sheet, filling bag with meringue as needed. Pipe 4 cups on second sheet.

BAKE meringues 3 hours without opening oven door (sides of meringues may settle slightly). Turn off oven; let meringues stand in closed oven overnight to dry completely. *(Can be prepared 1 week ahead. Store in single layer in airtight container.)*

FOR SAUCE: Whisk jam, sugar, and ⅓ cup water in heavy medium saucepan over medium-high heat until sugar dissolves and jam melts. Boil until sauce thickens and is reduced to generous ¾ cup, whisking often, about 7 minutes. Add berries and cardamom; stir gently. Remove from heat; let stand 1 hour to thaw fruit. Cover and refrigerate at least 2 hours and up to 1 day.

SCOOP sorbet into vacherins. *(Can be prepared 2 days ahead. Wrap tightly and freeze.)* Spoon sauce over. Garnish with berries and mint. Serve with remaining sauce.

Frozen blackberry-cream pops with blackberry-mint syrup

HERE'S A SOPHISTICATED grown-up version of the childhood frozen novelties. The sherbet base can be poured directly into pop molds, which are available at many cookware stores. Alternatively, you can churn the mixture in an ice cream maker, transfer it to a resealable freezer container, and simply scoop it into serving bowls. Begin making this dessert one day ahead.

6 SERVINGS

Pops

- **2½ cups frozen unsweetened blackberries (about 10 ounces), thawed, juice reserved**
- **6 tablespoons sugar**
- **1½ cups half and half**
- **½ teaspoon fresh lemon juice**

Syrup

- **¼ cup water**
- **¼ cup sugar**
- **1 tablespoon minced fresh mint**
- **1 cup frozen unsweetened blackberries (about 4 ounces), thawed, juices reserved**
- **2 tablespoons crème de cassis (black-currant liqueur) or berry syrup**

FOR POPS: Puree blackberries with juice in processor until smooth. Pour into strainer set over bowl, pressing on solids to extract as much puree as possible (about 1⅛ to 1¼ cups puree). Discard solids in strainer. Transfer 1 cup berry puree to 4-cup measuring cup (reserve remaining berry puree for syrup). Add sugar to measuring cup and whisk until dissolved. Whisk in half and half and lemon juice.

IF making pops, pour sherbet into six ⅓-cup frozen pop molds, dividing equally. Insert pop-mold handle into each. Freeze overnight. If using ice cream maker, process sherbet according to manufacturer's instructions. Divide mixture equally among six ⅓-cup frozen pop molds. Insert pop-mold handle into each. Freeze pops overnight. *(Can be prepared 1 week ahead. Keep frozen.)*

FOR SYRUP: Stir ¼ cup water, sugar, and mint in medium saucepan over medium heat until sugar dissolves and syrup comes to simmer. Remove from heat. Cover and let steep 5 minutes. Add thawed blackberries with juice, reserved blackberry puree from frozen pops, and crème de cassis. Transfer mixture to blender and puree until smooth. Strain sauce into medium bowl, pressing on solids to extract as much liquid as possible; discard solids in strainer. Refrigerate until cold. *(Can be prepared 2 days ahead. Cover and keep refrigerated.)*

DIVIDE syrup among 6 dessert glasses. Remove cream pops from molds. Place 1 pop in each glass and serve.

Margarita ice pops

FOLLOWING A MEXICAN DINNER, try this clever, made-in-an-instant riff on popular blended Margaritas. For the best results, try to use natural lime pops, sold at natural and specialty foods stores, rather than artificially colored and flavored varieties. Children may still enjoy the contrasts of sweet and salty flavors without the tequila.

6 SERVINGS

- **½ cup tequila**
- **6 tablespoons fresh lime juice**
- **¼ cup coarse kosher salt**
- **6 frozen lime-flavored ice pops or fruit bars, unwrapped**

MIX tequila and lime juice in 1-cup measuring cup. Place coarse salt in small bowl. Place all ice pops, sticks up, in deep bowl, or place 1 pop in each of 6 glasses. Pour tequila mixture over ice pops. Lightly dip 1 edge of each ice pop into coarse salt and serve.

New Orleans banana splits

A HINT OF RUM, a scattering of pecans, sliced store-bought banana bread, and a caramelized coating for the fruit (reminiscent of classic bananas Foster) transform the soda-fountain favorite into an elegant Creole-style dessert. Feel free to vary the ice cream flavors and add your favorite embellishments.

4 SERVINGS

- **4 bananas, peeled, split lengthwise**
- **8 teaspoons plus ¼ cup (packed) dark brown sugar**

- **1 cup chilled whipping cream**
- **2 tablespoons dark rum**

- **4 slices purchased banana bread or pound cake, toasted**
- **4 scoops vanilla ice cream**
- **4 scoops chocolate ice cream**
- **4 scoops chocolate chip cookie dough ice cream**
- **1 cup pecan halves, toasted**
- **Purchased chocolate syrup**
- **Sweetened flaked coconut, toasted**

PREHEAT broiler. Place banana halves, cut side up, on baking sheet. Sprinkle each with 1 teaspoon sugar. Broil bananas until sugar melts and darkens, about 2 minutes. Set bananas aside.

USING electric mixer, beat cream, rum, and remaining ¼ cup sugar in large bowl until peaks form.

PLACE 1 slice banana bread in each of 4 banana split dishes. Place 1 banana half on each side of bread, parallel to long sides of dish. Top bread with 1 scoop of each ice cream. Sprinkle with pecans and drizzle with chocolate syrup. Top bananas with dollop of rum whipped cream and sprinkle of coconut.

Chocolate-dipped ice cream cones

ANY PREMIUM ICE CREAM would be delicious with these white- and dark-chocolate-dipped cones; start with the Brown Sugar Ice Cream or Chocolate Malted Ice Cream in this chapter. You can decorate all the cones the same way or do each one differently.

MAKES 6 CONES

3 pints premium ice cream
6 sugar cones

1½ pounds high-quality white chocolate (such as Lindt or Perugina), chopped
½ cup plus 2 teaspoons vegetable oil

Rainbow mix sprinkles (nonpareil), chocolate sprinkles, and/or dark chocolate shavings

Red, green, and yellow food coloring (optional)

3 ounces bittersweet (not unsweetened) or semisweet chocolate, chopped

SPOON small amount of ice cream into 1 cone, packing gently. Dip large ice cream scoop into hot water. Scoop large ball of ice cream onto cone, pressing gently. Stand cone in small glass; place in freezer. Repeat with remaining cones and ice cream. Freeze 2 hours.

PLACE white chocolate and ½ cup oil in medium metal bowl. Set bowl over saucepan of simmering water; stir until chocolate is melted and smooth. Remove bowl from over water; cool until barely lukewarm, about 5 minutes.

WORKING quickly and tilting bowl, dip ice cream end of cone into chocolate, turning to coat. Shake cone, allowing excess chocolate to drip into bowl.

TO DECORATE WITH SPRINKLES OR CHOCOLATE SHAVINGS: Immediately sprinkle dipped cone with topping of choice. Stand cone in small glass; freeze. Repeat with remaining cones.

TO DECORATE WITH TINTED WHITE CHOCOLATE DOTS: Freeze dipped cones. Rewarm remaining white chocolate in bowl over simmering water, stirring occasionally. Place ¼ cup melted white chocolate in each of 3 small bowls. Mix 3 drops red coloring into first bowl, 3 drops green coloring into second bowl, and 2 drops each of red and yellow coloring into third bowl; stir to blend. Spoon each tinted chocolate into small resealable plastic bags. Cut off tip from corner to form small opening. Pipe tinted dots all over white chocolate-coated cone. Stand cone in small glass; freeze.

TO DECORATE WITH BITTERSWEET CHOCOLATE: Freeze dipped cones. Combine bittersweet chocolate and remaining 2 teaspoons vegetable oil in small metal bowl. Set bowl over saucepan of simmering water; stir until chocolate is melted and smooth. Remove from over water; cool slightly. Spoon some of chocolate mixture into resealable plastic bag and fold wide end to seal. Cut off tip from corner to form small opening. Tilt bowl slightly and dip 1 side of white chocolate-coated cone into melted dark chocolate, allowing excess to drip back into bowl. Pipe chocolate across top of cone in zigzag lines.

STAND cone in glass; freeze until chocolate sets. *(Can be made 1 week ahead. Wrap each cone in plastic and freeze.)*

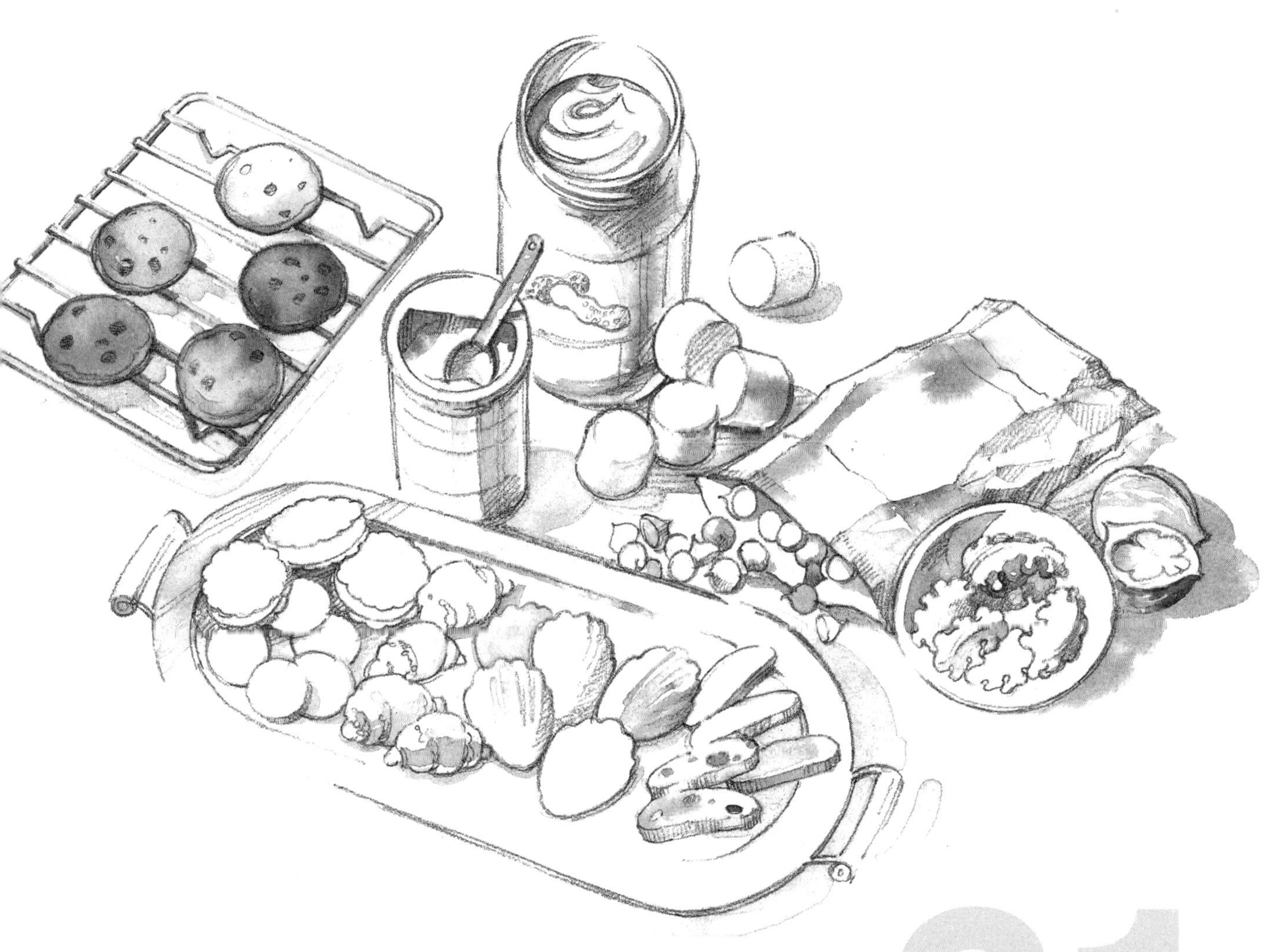

21 Cookies, brownies, and candy

Try walking past a kitchen in which cookies are baking in the oven. You can't. The aroma, the allure, the promise of the cookie draw you closer. You have to have one. That's what makes a cookie a cookie—the power it has over us, and has had over every generation of children and adults.

What else makes a cookie? At their core, all cookies are essentially the same. Butter (or some other fat) is beaten with sugar until fluffy; then eggs, flour, and leavening (usually baking powder) are added to make the basic dough. That's when you start getting creative—and the fun really begins.

Chocolate chip cookies, which add semisweet morsels to the basic formula, are just as popular now as they were when they were invented more than 75 years ago—so we've devoted several pages to combinations of "chocolate" and "cookie."

If the chocolate chip cookie seems uniquely American, some of our other preferences have been influenced by many nations. Italian *biscotti,* for instance: a crunchy, not-too-sweet cookie that is a perfect match for a cup of tea, coffee, or espresso. Spice cookies take their cue from German cookies like *lebkuchen* and from English gingerbreads (a broad term that can signify anything from a rich and moist cake to the cookies shaped like people or "built" into houses).

Of the many varieties of bar cookies, brownies, of course, are the most popular. They are well represented here, indeed. A tip: Bake a double batch of bar cookies next time out. They freeze beautifully and defrost quickly, making them ideal to have on hand in a cookie emergency.

There's another option when you want a fast bite of something sweet and delicious: candy. We tend to think of candy as a kid thing—a big, chewy mouthful of sugar and goo. But these easy recipes will revise your notion of what candy should be.

Cookies, brownies, candy. They've all got the power. Don't try to resist.

Cookies

Classic chocolate chip cookies

THESE CHOCOLATE CHIP COOKIES are perfect as is—but if you like nuts, feel free to add 1½ cups of toasted, chopped pecans or walnuts when you mix in the chocolate chips. Make a double batch of dough and bake half, freezing the rest for later. Just spoon the leftover dough into a gallon-size resealable plastic bag and flatten to a 1½-inch-thick disk, then freeze up to three weeks. Allow the dough to stand 15 to 30 minutes at room temperature before cutting into 1½-inch cubes and baking.

MAKES ABOUT 30

Nonstick vegetable oil spray
3 cups all purpose flour
1 teaspoon baking soda
1 teaspoon salt
1 cup (2 sticks) unsalted butter, room temperature
1 cup sugar
1 cup (packed) golden brown sugar
2 large eggs
2 teaspoons vanilla extract
2 cups semisweet chocolate chips (about 12 ounces)

PREHEAT oven to 325°F. Spray large rimmed baking sheet with nonstick spray. Whisk flour, baking soda, and salt in medium bowl to blend. Using electric mixer, beat butter in large bowl until light and fluffy. Add sugar and brown sugar; beat until well blended. Add eggs and vanilla; beat until mixture is creamy and well blended. Gradually add flour mixture, beating just until incorporated. Stir in chocolate chips.

WORKING in batches, drop dough by heaping tablespoonfuls onto prepared baking sheet, spacing 3 inches apart. Bake cookies until pale brown, about 15 minutes. Cool 5 minutes on sheet. Transfer cookies to racks and cool completely. *(Can be prepared 2 days ahead. Store in airtight container at room temperature.)*

Chocolate chip and peppermint crunch crackles

THESE FUDGY TREATS are sometimes called "crinkles" because of the small wrinkles that form on the cookies as they bake. To crush the peppermint candies, place them in a heavy-duty plastic bag and use a mallet or rolling pin break them into tiny pieces. The cookies are great for the holidays. Try them with scoops of mint-chip ice cream.

MAKES ABOUT 36

8 ounces bittersweet (not unsweetened) or semisweet chocolate, chopped
½ cup (1 stick) unsalted butter, cut into ½-inch cubes
1½ ounces unsweetened chocolate, chopped
½ cup finely crushed red-and-white-striped peppermint hard candies
6½ tablespoons sugar

3 large eggs
2 teaspoons vanilla extract
1 teaspoon peppermint extract
1½ cups all purpose flour
¾ teaspoon baking powder
¼ teaspoon salt
½ cup semisweet chocolate chips (about 3 ounces)

Additional red-and-white-striped peppermint hard candies, coarsely crushed (optional)
Powdered sugar (optional)

COMBINE bittersweet chocolate, butter, and unsweetened chocolate in heavy large saucepan. Stir over low heat until chocolates melt and mixture is smooth. Remove pan from heat. Mix in finely crushed candies and 6½ tablespoons sugar. Cool mixture to lukewarm, stirring occasionally, about 30 minutes.

WHISK eggs into chocolate mixture, 1 at a time, then whisk in vanilla extract and peppermint extract. Whisk flour, baking powder, and salt in small bowl to blend. Whisk flour mixture, then chocolate chips into chocolate mixture. Cover batter; chill until firm enough to shape, at least 3 hours and up to 1 day.

POSITION rack in center of oven and preheat to 325°F. Line 2 large rimmed baking sheets with parchment paper. Using 1 generous tablespoonful for each cookie, roll dough between moistened palms into 1¼-inch-diameter balls, then arrange on prepared baking sheets, spacing 1 inch apart. Bake cookies, 1 sheet at a time, until puffed and cracked on top but still soft to touch in center, about 11 minutes. Let stand on sheets 5 minutes. Press coarsely crushed candies onto tops of warm cookies or sprinkle cookies with powdered sugar, if desired. Transfer to racks and cool completely. *(Can be prepared 1 week ahead. Store in airtight container between sheets of waxed paper in refrigerator.)*

Chocolate-mint melt-aways

ALTHOUGH THERE ARE SEVERAL STEPS involved in making these festive piped cookies, the results are worth the effort. The elegant little swirls are delicious, and they'll keep in the refrigerator for two weeks. Serve them with coffee after dinner, or pack a few in a pretty cookie tin for a special gift.

MAKES ABOUT 42

Cookies

- **1 cup (2 sticks) unsalted butter, room temperature**
- **2 teaspoons vanilla extract**
- **½ teaspoon peppermint extract**
- **½ cup plus 2 tablespoons powdered sugar**
- **2 cups all purpose flour**

Ganache

- **¼ cup plus 2 tablespoons whipping cream**
- **2 tablespoons (¼ stick) unsalted butter**
- **9 ounces high-quality white chocolate (such as Lindt or Perugina), chopped**
- **¼ teaspoon peppermint extract**

Coating

- **9 ounces bittersweet (not unsweetened) or semisweet chocolate, chopped**
- **1 tablespoon solid vegetable shortening**

FOR COOKIES: Preheat oven to 350°F. Butter 2 large rimmed baking sheets. Using electric mixer, beat butter, vanilla extract, and peppermint extract in medium bowl until light and fluffy. Beat in sugar. Beat in 1 cup flour. Stir in remaining 1 cup flour. Spoon half of dough into pastry bag fitted with large star tip. Pipe 2½-inch-long ovals with solid (not hollow) centers on prepared baking sheet, spacing cookies ½ inch apart. Repeat with remaining half of dough. Bake cookies until golden brown at edges, about 12 minutes. Let stand on sheets 5 minutes. Transfer to paper towels and cool.

FOR GANACHE: Bring cream and butter to simmer in heavy small saucepan over low heat. Add white chocolate; stir until melted and smooth. Mix in extract. Refrigerate ganache just until firm enough to spread, stirring occasionally, about 30 minutes.

LINE 2 baking sheets with aluminum foil. Using small metal icing spatula, spread 1 teaspoon ganache over flat side of 1 cookie. Place cookie, ganache side up, on prepared sheet. Repeat with remaining cookies. Refrigerate until ganache is firm, about 30 minutes.

FOR COATING: Stir bittersweet chocolate and shortening in top of double boiler set over simmering water until melted and smooth. Remove chocolate coating from over water.

HOLDING 1 cookie on sides, dip ganache side into chocolate coating and shake cookie to remove excess chocolate. Return cookie to same foil-covered sheet, chocolate-dipped side down. Repeat with remaining cookies. Chill until chocolate coating sets, about 30 minutes. Remove cookies from foil. *(Can be prepared 2 weeks ahead. Store in airtight container between sheets of waxed paper in refrigerator. Let stand 10 minutes at room temperature before serving.)*

Giant chocolate-toffee cookies

A BIG, rich dark chocolate cookie with walnuts and chunks of English toffee—what's not to love? Be sure the batter is properly chilled so that the cookies won't spread too thin while baking; you can even refrigerate the batter overnight. Serve the cookies with your favorite toffee fudge swirl ice cream for a special dessert.

MAKES ABOUT 18

- **½ cup all purpose flour**
- **1 teaspoon baking powder**
- **¼ teaspoon salt**
- **1 pound bittersweet (not unsweetened) or semisweet chocolate, chopped**
- **¼ cup (½ stick) unsalted butter**
- **1¾ cups (packed) golden brown sugar**
- **4 large eggs**
- **1 tablespoon vanilla extract**
- **5 1.4-ounce chocolate-covered English toffee candy bars (such as Heath or Skor), coarsely chopped**
- **1 cup walnuts, toasted, chopped**

COMBINE flour, baking powder, and salt in small bowl; whisk to blend. Stir chocolate and butter in top of double boiler set over simmering water until melted and smooth. Remove from over water and cool to lukewarm. Using electric mixer, beat sugar and eggs in large bowl until thick, about 5 minutes. Beat in chocolate mixture and vanilla. Stir in flour mixture, then toffee and nuts. Chill batter until firm, at least 45 minutes and up to 1 day.

PREHEAT oven to 350°F. Line 2 large rimmed baking sheets with parchment paper. Drop batter by ¼ cupfuls onto prepared sheets, spacing 2½ inches apart. Bake cookies just until dry and cracked on top but still soft to touch in center, about 15 minutes. Cool on sheets. *(Can be prepared 2 days ahead. Store in airtight container at room temperature.)*

Chocolate- and almond-dipped sandwich cookies

THESE BUTTER COOKIES are filled with rich chocolate ganache, dipped in bittersweet chocolate, and garnished with toasted almonds. Because the dough is so delicate, it is best to roll it out between floured sheets of waxed or parchment paper—and be sure to lift off the paper and reflour it occasionally to avoid sticking. The recipe calls for an oval cookie cutter, but any simple shape will work.

MAKES ABOUT 28

Cookies

- **1 cup sugar, divided**
- **¼ cup slivered almonds**
- **1 cup (2 sticks) unsalted butter, room temperature**
- **1 large egg yolk**
- **1½ teaspoons vanilla extract**
- **¼ teaspoon salt**
- **1½ cups all purpose flour**

Filling

- **1 cup whipping cream**
- **12 ounces bittersweet (not unsweetened) or semisweet chocolate, chopped**

Coating

- **6 ounces bittersweet (not unsweetened) or semisweet chocolate, chopped**
- **1¼ cups slivered almonds, toasted, chopped**

FOR COOKIES: Place ¼ cup sugar and slivered almonds in processor; grind almonds fine. Using electric mixer, beat butter and remaining ¾ cup sugar in large bowl until well blended. Beat in egg yolk, vanilla, and salt. Add ground nut mixture and flour; beat until moist clumps form. Gather dough together; divide in half. Shape each half into disk. Wrap in plastic and refrigerate at least 1 hour and up to 2 days.

POSITION 1 rack in top third of oven and second rack in bottom third; preheat to 325°F. Line 2 large rimmed baking sheets with parchment paper. Roll out 1 dough disk between sheets of waxed paper or parchment paper to scant ¼-inch thickness, sprinkling dough lightly with flour as needed to keep from sticking and occasionally peeling off top paper to remove wrinkles. Peel off top paper. Using 2½x1½-inch oval cookie cutter (or cardboard template), cut out cookies. If dough is soft, slide rimless baking sheet under paper and chill dough 10 minutes to firm. Transfer cookies to prepared baking sheets, spacing ½ inch apart. Gather scraps and reroll dough, cutting out more cookies. Chill cookies on sheets 15 minutes.

BAKE cookies 5 minutes. Reverse position of sheets and bake until cookies begin to color, about 6 minutes longer. Cool cookies on sheets 5 minutes. Transfer to racks and cool completely. Repeat with remaining dough.

FOR FILLING: Bring cream to simmer in heavy medium saucepan. Remove from heat. Add chocolate; whisk until melted and smooth. Let filling cool until thick but still spreadable, stirring occasionally, about 2 hours.

PLACE half of cookies, bottom side up, on work surface. Spoon filling into pastry bag fitted with small plain tip. Pipe (or spread) filling over cookies, leaving ¼-inch plain border. Top each with second cookie, bottom side down, and press to adhere.

FOR COATING: Stir chocolate in top of double boiler set over simmering water until melted and smooth. Place toasted almonds in small bowl. Dip end of 1 cookie sandwich in chocolate, then in almonds. Transfer to sheet of aluminum foil. Repeat with remaining cookies. Let stand until coating is set. *(Can be prepared 2 days ahead. Store in airtight container between sheets of waxed paper in refrigerator.)*

Rocky road wedges

THIS RECIPE MAKES TWO LARGE, Frisbee-size cookies that are later cut into wedges. For a deconstructed ice cream sandwich, serve the wedges with rocky road ice cream; or sandwich the whole cookies with one pint of ice cream, freeze for several hours, and then serve as a great alternative to a birthday cake.

MAKES 24

- **1 cup (2 sticks) unsalted butter, room temperature**
- **1 cup (packed) golden brown sugar**
- **2 large eggs**
- **1¾ cups all purpose flour**
- **¼ cup unsweetened cocoa powder**

1 teaspoon baking soda
½ teaspoon salt
3 cups semisweet chocolate chips (about 18 ounces), divided
1 cup whole almonds, coarsely chopped

1 cup mini marshmallows

PREHEAT oven to 350°F. Using electric mixer, beat butter and sugar in large bowl until light and fluffy. Beat in eggs. Whisk flour, cocoa powder, baking soda, and salt in medium bowl to blend. Stir flour mixture into butter mixture. Mix in 2 cups chocolate chips and almonds.

DIVIDE dough in half. Shape each half into 8-inch round on rimless baking sheet. Bake until rounds are set but centers are still soft, about 15 minutes. Sprinkle each round with ½ cup marshmallows and ½ cup of remaining chocolate chips. Bake until marshmallows and chips soften, about 3 minutes longer. Cool 5 minutes. Cut each round into 12 wedges. Let stand 5 minutes. Transfer wedges to racks and cool completely. *(Can be prepared 1 day ahead. Store in airtight container at room temperature.)*

Chocolate chunk, orange, and hazelnut cookies

SOPHISTICATED CHOCOLATE CHIP COOKIES, featuring good-quality bittersweet chocolate given a lift with the aroma of orange zest and the crunch of hazelnuts, would be perfect served with coffee at an outdoor concert.

MAKES ABOUT 24

1¼ cups all purpose flour
½ teaspoon baking soda
⅛ teaspoon salt
¾ cup (packed) golden brown sugar
½ cup (1 stick) unsalted butter, room temperature
4 teaspoons grated orange peel
1 teaspoon vanilla extract
1 large egg
3 3- to 3.5-ounce bars bittersweet chocolate, cut into ⅓-inch chunks
1½ cups hazelnuts, toasted, skinned, chopped

PREHEAT oven to 375°F. Line 2 large rimmed baking sheets with parchment paper. Combine flour, baking soda, and salt in medium bowl; whisk to blend. Using electric mixer, beat sugar, butter, orange peel, and vanilla in large bowl until light and fluffy. Beat in egg. Add flour mixture and beat just until combined. Stir in chocolate chunks and hazelnuts.

DROP batter by heaping tablespoonfuls onto prepared sheets, spacing 2 inches apart. Bake cookies until just firm to touch and beginning to brown, about 13 minutes. Let stand 5 minutes. Transfer to racks and cool completely. *(Can be prepared 2 days ahead. Store in airtight container at room temperature.)*

Chocolate chip cookies with espresso and cinnamon

CRISPY AT THE EDGES and slightly soft in the center, this coffee-flavored cookie features both semisweet and milk chocolate chips. A cookie scoop—which is like a small ice cream scoop with a release mechanism—makes quick work of shaping the dough. You can find one at a good cookware shop.

MAKES ABOUT 48

Nonstick vegetable oil spray
2¼ cups all purpose flour
1 tablespoon ground cinnamon
1 teaspoon baking soda
½ teaspoon salt
1½ cups (packed) golden brown sugar
1 cup (2 sticks) unsalted butter, room temperature
1 large egg
4 teaspoons instant espresso powder
2 teaspoons vanilla extract

1 cup semisweet chocolate chips (about 6 ounces)
1 cup milk chocolate chips (about 6 ounces)
1 cup walnuts, toasted, chopped

PREHEAT oven to 350°F. Spray 2 large rimmed baking sheets with nonstick spray. Whisk flour, cinnamon, baking soda, and salt in medium bowl to blend. Using electric mixer, beat sugar, butter, egg, espresso powder, and vanilla in large bowl until well blended. Beat in flour mixture. Stir in all chocolate chips and walnuts.

DROP dough by rounded tablespoonfuls onto prepared sheets, spacing 2 inches apart (do not flatten dough). Bake cookies until brown on top but still slightly soft to touch in center, about 14 minutes. Cool on baking sheets. *(Can be prepared 3 days ahead. Store in airtight container at room temperature.)*

Chocolate-walnut cookies

BECAUSE THEY CONTAIN so little flour, these cookies have a chewy, brownie-like texture. The espresso powder intensifies the rich chocolate flavor. These cookies are best the day they are baked.

MAKES ABOUT 30

6 tablespoons all purpose flour
1/4 teaspoon baking powder
1/4 teaspoon salt
8 ounces bittersweet (not unsweetened) or semisweet chocolate, chopped
1/2 cup (1 stick) unsalted butter
3/4 cup sugar
2 large eggs
2 1/4 teaspoons instant espresso powder
2 1/4 teaspoons vanilla extract
1 cup semisweet chocolate chips (about 6 ounces)
1 cup coarsely chopped walnuts

PREHEAT oven to 350°F. Mix flour, baking powder, and salt in small bowl. Stir bittersweet chocolate and butter in heavy large saucepan over low heat until melted and smooth. Remove from heat. Using electric mixer, beat sugar, eggs, espresso powder, and vanilla in large bowl until well blended. Stir egg mixture into warm chocolate mixture. Stir in flour mixture. Stir in chocolate chips and walnuts.

IMMEDIATELY drop batter by heaping tablespoonfuls onto 2 large rimmed nonstick baking sheets, spacing 1½ inches apart. Bake cookies until cracked on top but still soft in center, about 12 minutes. Cool cookies on sheets 5 minutes. Transfer cookies to racks and cool completely.

Chocolate-dipped orange and ginger florentines

FLORENTINES—lace cookies—are rich and buttery, a little like candy. This recipe features crystallized ginger and homemade candied orange peel for an exquisite flavor. (The orange syrup that results from making the sugared orange peel would be delicious stirred into hot or iced tea.) If you are short on time, leave out the sugared orange peel and enjoy the cookies undipped. Silicone baking liners work well in place of the aluminum foil on the baking sheets; they need not be buttered.

MAKES 24

Sugared orange peel

3 oranges
1/2 cup plus 4 tablespoons sugar, divided
1/2 cup water

Cookies

1/2 cup plus 2 tablespoons whipping cream
1/2 cup sugar
1/4 cup (packed) golden brown sugar
2 tablespoons (1/4 stick) unsalted butter
2/3 cup sliced almonds, lightly toasted

- **¼ cup all purpose flour**
- **2 tablespoons finely chopped crystallized ginger**
- **6 ounces bittersweet (not unsweetened) or semisweet chocolate, chopped**

FOR SUGARED ORANGE PEEL: Using swivel-bladed vegetable peeler, remove peel (orange part only) from oranges in strips. Mince enough peel to measure 2 teaspoons and reserve for cookie batter. Cook remaining peel in small saucepan of boiling water 2 minutes. Drain. Return orange peel strips to same saucepan. Add ⅓ cup sugar and ⅓ cup water; bring to boil, stirring frequently. Boil 5 minutes. Drain peel (reserve orange syrup for another purpose).

SPRINKLE 2 tablespoons sugar on plate. Arrange orange peel strips atop sugar. Sprinkle with remaining 2 tablespoons sugar. Let stand 15 minutes. Remove peel from sugar. Finely chop enough candied peel to measure 2 tablespoons (reserve any remaining sugared peel for another purpose).

FOR COOKIES: Preheat oven to 350°F. Line 2 large rimmed baking sheets with aluminum foil. Lightly butter foil. Combine cream and next 3 ingredients in heavy small saucepan. Cook over medium heat just until all sugar dissolves, stirring constantly. Add reserved 2 teaspoons minced unsugared peel, 2 tablespoons chopped candied peel, almonds, flour, and crystallized ginger. Bring mixture to boil, stirring frequently.

DROP 1 level tablespoon batter onto 1 prepared sheet (batter will be runny). Repeat 5 more times, spacing cookies about 3 inches apart (cookies will spread). Repeat procedure with second prepared sheet. Bake cookies until edges are pale golden brown, about 8 minutes (cookies will spread). Remove sheets from oven. Using 3-inch round cookie cutter, quickly push cookie sides in to reshape cookies into 3-inch rounds. Slide foil off sheets. Cool cookies on foil. Line same baking sheets with new foil. Repeat with remaining batter. Turn foil over and carefully peel off all cookies.

LINE 2 baking sheets with foil. Melt chocolate in top of double boiler over simmering water, stirring occasionally until smooth. Remove from over water. Dip 1 cookie halfway into chocolate; shake off excess chocolate. Place cookie on 1 prepared sheet. Repeat with remaining cookies. Refrigerate cookies on sheets until chocolate sets, about 30 minutes. *(Can be prepared 2 weeks ahead. Store in airtight container between sheets of waxed paper in refrigerator. Let stand 20 minutes at room temperature before serving.)*

Old-fashioned peanut butter cookies

PEANUT BUTTER was first promoted at the World's Fair in St. Louis in 1904, and it didn't take long for the popular novelty to make its way into a cookie. These cookies, featuring the customary crosshatch fork pattern, are truly—and delightfully—old-fashioned. They make a great afternoon snack served with apple slices and a glass of milk; they're perfect for taking along on a hike; and, of course, they are quintessential lunch-box treats.

MAKES ABOUT 48

- **3 cups all purpose flour**
- **1 teaspoon baking powder**
- **1 teaspoon salt**
- **1 cup (2 sticks) unsalted butter, room temperature**
- **1 cup creamy or chunky peanut butter (do not use old-fashioned-style or freshly ground)**
- **2 teaspoons vanilla extract**
- **1 cup (packed) golden brown sugar**
- **1 cup sugar**
- **2 large eggs**

PREHEAT oven to 350°F. Line 2 large rimmed baking sheets with parchment paper. Whisk flour, baking powder, and salt in medium bowl to blend. Using electric mixer, beat butter, peanut butter, and vanilla in large bowl until well blended. Beat in both sugars. Scrape down sides of bowl. Stir in half of flour mixture. Add eggs 1 at a time, stirring to blend well after each addition. Mix in remaining flour mixture.

FOR each cookie, roll 1 heaping tablespoonful dough into 1¾-inch-diameter ball. Arrange dough balls on prepared baking sheets, spacing 2½ inches apart. Using back of fork, flatten dough balls and form crosshatch design on tops. Bake cookies until dry on top and golden brown on bottom, about 14 minutes. Cool cookies on sheets 5 minutes. Using metal spatula, transfer cookies to racks and cool completely. *(Can be prepared 3 days ahead. Store in airtight container at room temperature.)*

Flourless peanut butter and chocolate chip cookies

THESE ULTRA-RICH COOKIES are slightly dense in texture. Because they contain no flour, they are good for people with allergies to wheat or gluten—and for peanut butter fans in general.

MAKES ABOUT 24

- **1 cup super-chunky peanut butter (do not use old-fashioned-style or freshly ground)**
- **1 cup (packed) golden brown sugar**
- **1 large egg**
- **1 teaspoon baking soda**
- **½ teaspoon vanilla extract**
- **1 cup miniature semisweet chocolate chips (about 6 ounces)**

PREHEAT oven to 350°F. Stir peanut butter and next 4 ingredients in medium bowl to blend. Mix in chocolate chips. Using moistened hands, roll heaping 1 tablespoonful dough into ball for each cookie. Arrange dough balls on 2 ungreased baking sheets, spacing 2 inches apart. Bake cookies until puffed, golden on bottom, and still soft to touch in center, about 12 minutes. Cool on sheets 5 minutes. Transfer to racks and cool completely. *(Can be prepared 2 days ahead. Store in airtight container at room temperature.)*

Peanut butter cookies with milk chocolate chunks

THIS RECIPE CALLS FOR good-quality milk chocolate bars cut into pieces, but you can substitute milk chocolate chips. The Spanish peanuts add crunch and provide a salty contrast to the sweet milk chocolate. Freezing the formed cookies briefly before baking helps them retain their shape.

MAKES ABOUT 24

- **1 cup super-chunky peanut butter (do not use old-fashioned-style or freshly ground)**
- **½ cup plus 2 tablespoons (packed) dark brown sugar**
- **½ cup sugar**
- **6 tablespoons (¾ stick) unsalted butter, room temperature**
- **1 large egg**
- **2 tablespoons dark corn syrup**
- **2 teaspoons vanilla extract**
- **1 cup all purpose flour**
- **¼ cup old-fashioned oats**
- **1 teaspoon baking soda**
- **¾ cup roasted salted red-skinned Spanish peanuts**
- **9 ounces milk chocolate, cut into ½-inch cubes**

PREHEAT oven to 350°F. Butter 2 large rimmed baking sheets. Using electric mixer, beat peanut butter and next 6 ingredients in large bowl until fluffy. Stir flour, oats, and baking soda in small bowl to combine. Add to peanut butter mixture; beat to combine. Stir in nuts and chocolate.

FOR each cookie, drop 1 slightly rounded tablespoonful dough onto 1 prepared sheet; top each with second slightly rounded tablespoonful dough, pressing slightly. Freeze 10 minutes. Bake until cookies are light golden, about 15 minutes. Transfer to racks and cool. *(Can be prepared 2 days ahead. Store in airtight container at room temperature.)*

Butterfinger-chunk cookies

THE BUTTERFINGER CANDY BAR made its debut in 1928, when the Curtis Candy Company held a contest to name the sweet, crunchy, peanutty candy bar. Butterfinger was the popular term for an athlete who couldn't hang on to the ball, and thanks to the bar's peanut butter flavor, the name was a natural winner. Today's version—Butterfinger BB's—make these chewy-crunchy cookies great.

MAKES ABOUT 24

½ cup (1 stick) unsalted butter, room temperature
½ cup sugar
½ cup (packed) dark brown sugar
1 large egg
1 teaspoon vanilla extract
1¼ cups plus 2 tablespoons all purpose flour
½ teaspoon salt
½ teaspoon baking soda
1½ cups Butterfinger BB's candies (about five 1.7-ounce packages)

USING electric mixer, beat butter and both sugars in large bowl until well blended. Add egg and vanilla; beat until light and fluffy. Beat in flour, salt, and baking soda. Stir in candies (dough will be moist). Chill dough at least 30 minutes and up to 1 hour.

PREHEAT oven to 350°F. Line 3 large rimmed baking sheets with parchment paper. Drop dough by heaping tablespoonfuls onto prepared sheets, spacing 3 inches apart (about 8 cookies per sheet; cookies will spread). Bake cookies until golden brown, about 12 minutes. Transfer parchment with cookies to racks and cool completely. *(Can be prepared 4 days ahead. Store in airtight container at room temperature.)*

Oatmeal cookies with raisins, dates, and walnuts

LINING THE BAKING SHEETS with aluminum foil gives this oatmeal cookie the perfect texture. It is chewy, oaty, and packed with dried fruits and nuts. Feel free to experiment with the dried fruit additions: Golden raisins and chopped dried pears—or dried cherries and chopped dried apricots—would make excellent substitutes for the raisins and dates.

MAKES ABOUT 48

2 cups all purpose flour
1 teaspoon baking powder
1 teaspoon ground cinnamon
½ teaspoon baking soda
½ teaspoon salt
¾ cup (1½ sticks) unsalted butter, room temperature
¼ cup solid vegetable shortening, room temperature
1 cup sugar
1 cup (packed) dark brown sugar
2 large eggs
¼ cup honey
1 tablespoon vanilla extract
3 cups old-fashioned oats
1 cup raisins
1 cup chopped pitted dates
1 cup chopped walnuts

PREHEAT oven to 350°F. Line 2 large rimmed baking sheets with aluminum foil; butter foil. Whisk flour and next 4 ingredients in medium bowl to blend. Using electric mixer, beat butter, shortening, and both sugars in large bowl until light and fluffy. Beat in eggs, honey, and vanilla. Gradually beat in flour mixture. Stir in oats, raisins, dates, and walnuts. Drop batter by tablespoonfuls onto prepared sheets, spacing 2 inches apart. Using moistened fingertips, flatten cookies slightly. Bake cookies until golden brown, about 10 minutes. Cool completely on sheets. *(Can be prepared 2 days ahead. Store in airtight container at room temperature.)*

Cosmic apple cookie

THIS ENORMOUS COOKIE, baked in a pizza pan, gets super apple flavor from dried apples reconstituted in apple juice concentrate. Buttering the pizza pan before putting the foil on top makes it easy to slide the cookie and foil off the pan after baking. This is a fun cookie for a party: You can cut it into wedges or let guests pull it apart by hand.

MAKES ONE 12½-INCH-DIAMETER COOKIE

Cookie

- **1¼ cups coarsely chopped unsulfured dried apple slices (about 3½ ounces)**
- **7 tablespoons frozen apple juice concentrate, thawed**
- **1 tablespoon fresh lemon juice**
- **1 tablespoon grated lemon peel**

- **1⅓ cups sifted all purpose flour (sifted, then measured)**
- **¾ cup sugar**
- **1 tablespoon (packed) golden brown sugar**
- **½ teaspoon salt**
- **½ teaspoon ground cinnamon**
- **¼ teaspoon baking soda**
- **Generous pinch of ground cloves**
- **Generous pinch of ground ginger**
- **5 tablespoons chilled unsalted butter, diced**
- **3 tablespoons beaten egg (about 1 large)**
- **1 teaspoon vanilla**
- **1¼ cups coarsely chopped toasted walnuts**
- **2 tablespoons raisins**

Icing

- **5 tablespoons powdered sugar, sifted**
- **1 tablespoon chilled whipping cream**
- **¼ teaspoon (or more) fresh lemon juice**

FOR COOKIE: Combine apples, apple concentrate, and lemon juice in heavy medium skillet over low heat. Cook 5 minutes, stirring occasionally. Increase heat to high. Add lemon peel and boil 15 minutes. Cover tightly and cool mixture completely.

POSITION rack in center of oven and preheat to 350°F. Lightly butter 12½-inch-diameter rimmed pizza pan. Line pan with aluminum foil, leaving overhang. Butter and flour foil. Blend 1⅓ cups flour, both sugars, salt, cinnamon, baking soda, cloves, and ginger in processor 5 seconds. Add butter. Using on/off turns, blend until mixture resembles coarse meal. Transfer mixture to large bowl. Stir egg and vanilla into cool apple mixture. Add apple mixture, walnuts, and raisins to flour mixture. Mix until well combined.

TRANSFER moist batter to prepared pizza pan. Cover with plastic wrap and press dough to within ¼ inch of edge of pan. Peel off plastic. Bake cookie until brown, about 30 minutes. Using overhang as aid, slide cookie with foil onto rack. Cool cookie 30 minutes. Slide large knife between foil and cookie to loosen. Pull foil out from under cookie. Cool cookie completely.

FOR ICING: Whisk powdered sugar, cream, and ¼ teaspoon lemon juice in small bowl to blend. Thin with additional lemon juice if desired. Drizzle icing over cookie. Let cookie stand until glaze sets. *(Apple cookie can be prepared 1 day ahead. Cover tightly with foil; store at room temperature.)* Cut into wedges and serve.

Double lemon bars

CALLED "DOUBLE LEMON BARS" because they feature both lemon juice and lemon peel, these offer the perfect combination of a rich, shortbread-like crust and a tangy lemon curd topping. It is very important to pour the lemon mixture over a hot, just-out-of-the-oven crust so that the filling stays on top of the crust and does not seep underneath while baking.

MAKES 24

- **1½ cups plus 4 teaspoons all purpose flour**
- **½ cup powdered sugar**
- **¾ cup (1½ sticks) unsalted butter, cut into ½-inch cubes, room temperature**

- **4 large eggs**
- **1½ cups sugar**

½ cup fresh lemon juice
1 tablespoon grated lemon peel

Additional powdered sugar

PREHEAT oven to 350°F. Combine 1⅓ cups flour and ½ cup powdered sugar in large bowl. Add butter. Using back of fork, blend until mixture resembles coarse meal. Using plastic wrap as aid, press mixture over bottom of 13x9x2-inch baking pan. Bake crust until golden brown, about 20 minutes. Remove from oven. Maintain oven temperature.

MEANWHILE, beat eggs, 1½ cups sugar, lemon juice, lemon peel, and remaining 4 teaspoons flour in medium bowl to blend.

POUR lemon mixture over hot crust. Bake until lemon layer is set, about 20 minutes. Cool completely in pan. *(Can be prepared 1 day ahead. Cover and refrigerate. Bring lemon bars to room temperature before continuing.)*

CUT pastry into 24 bars. Sift additional powdered sugar over before serving.

Pineapple, mango, and papaya squares

SIMILAR IN TEXTURE to lemon bars, these have a shortbread-cookie base, a delightful tropical-fruit filling, and a pretty lattice crust. If you prefer a smaller-size treat, cut these into sixteen pieces instead of nine. The filling and the dough can be prepared and refrigerated up to two days before baking—just allow the dough to soften a little at room temperature before rolling. Thawed frozen mango chunks would work well in the filling.

MAKES 9 LARGE

Filling

2 cups chopped cored peeled fresh pineapple
1 cup chopped peeled pitted mango
1 cup chopped peeled seeded papaya
¾ cup (packed) dark brown sugar
½ cup orange juice
1 cinnamon stick
½ teaspoon grated orange peel
½ teaspoon grated lemon peel
Pinch of ground cloves

Crust

1¼ cups (2½ sticks) unsalted butter, room temperature
¾ cup sugar
¾ teaspoon vanilla extract
¼ teaspoon salt
2⅔ cups all purpose flour

FOR FILLING: Combine pineapple, mango, papaya, brown sugar, orange juice, cinnamon stick, orange peel, lemon peel, and ground cloves in heavy medium saucepan. Cook over low heat until reduced to 1⅓ cups, stirring frequently, about 1½ hours. Cool filling. Remove cinnamon stick.

FOR CRUST: Using electric mixer, beat butter, sugar, vanilla, and salt in large bowl just until blended. Gradually add flour, beating at low speed just until dough begins to come together. Turn dough out onto floured work surface. Gather dough into ball; divide into 2 pieces, 1 slightly larger than the other. Flatten each piece into square. Wrap each in plastic; chill until firm enough to roll, about 15 minutes.

PREHEAT oven to 375°F. Roll out larger dough piece on lightly floured work surface to 10-inch square. Transfer dough to 9x9x2-inch metal baking pan. Press dough over bottom and ½ inch up sides of pan. Pour filling into crust. Roll out remaining dough piece on floured surface to 9-inch square. Cut into 1-inch-wide strips. Place 4 strips atop filling, spacing evenly apart. Place 5 more strips at right angles atop first 4 strips, forming lattice. Trim lattice edges.

BAKE cookie until crust is golden brown, about 50 minutes. Cool completely in pan. *(Can be prepared 1 day ahead. Cover pan tightly and store at room temperature.)* Cut into 9 squares and serve.

Cherry-almond bars

THESE COOKIES are super-fast to make and wonderfully adaptable. The recipe features an almond cookie crust and a topping made from cherry preserves, but if walnuts and apricots, or hazelnuts and raspberries, suit your fancy (or your pantry), feel free to experiment.

MAKES 30

1½ cups all purpose flour
¼ cup cornstarch
⅛ teaspoon salt
¾ cup (1½ sticks) unsalted butter, room temperature
½ cup sugar
1 teaspoon vanilla extract
¼ teaspoon almond extract
¾ cup toasted slivered almonds, coarsely chopped

1¼ cups cherry preserves

PREHEAT oven to 350°F. Line 11x7x2-inch glass baking dish with aluminum foil. Combine flour, cornstarch, and salt in medium bowl; whisk to blend. Using electric mixer, beat butter in large bowl until light and fluffy. Add sugar and beat until well blended. Beat in vanilla and almond extracts. Add flour mixture and beat just until dough begins to come together. Mix in almonds. Using plastic wrap as aid, press dough over bottom (not sides) of prepared dish. Pierce all over with fork. Bake until just firm to touch, about 45 minutes. Maintain oven temperature.

STIR preserves in small saucepan over medium-low heat until melted and hot; spread over warm crust. Return to oven and bake until preserves are bubbling in center, about 15 minutes. Cool cookie in dish on rack.

USING foil as aid, lift entire cookie from dish; trim edges. Cut into bars. *(Can be prepared 2 days ahead. Store in airtight container in single layer in refrigerator.)*

Blackberry Linzertorte bars

LINZERTORTE IS A CLASSIC Austrian dessert featuring a shortbread-like crust with ground almonds, walnuts or hazelnuts, a lattice top, and, most commonly, a raspberry filling. Here it translates well into an easy-to-make cookie with a walnut topping. The blackberry jam is wonderful, but any jam would do. If you prefer, you can use a pinch of freshly grated nutmeg, which has a stronger flavor and aroma than ground nutmeg.

MAKES ABOUT 32

1½ cups all purpose flour
¾ cup walnut pieces
3 tablespoons cornstarch
1 tablespoon unsweetened cocoa powder
½ teaspoon ground cinnamon
⅛ teaspoon ground nutmeg
⅛ teaspoon ground cloves
⅛ teaspoon salt
¾ cup (1½ sticks) unsalted butter, room temperature
½ cup sugar
1½ teaspoons grated orange peel
1 teaspoon vanilla extract

1 cup blackberry jam
½ cup walnuts, coarsely chopped

PREHEAT oven to 350°F. Line 9x9x2-inch metal baking pan with aluminum foil, leaving overhang. Combine flour and next 7 ingredients in processor. Blend until walnuts are finely ground. Using electric mixer, beat butter in large bowl until light and fluffy. Add sugar and beat until well blended. Beat in orange peel and vanilla. Add flour mixture and beat until dough just begins to come together.

USING plastic wrap as aid, press dough over bottom (not sides) of prepared pan. Pierce all over with fork. Bake crust until just firm to touch, about 45 minutes.

STIR jam in small saucepan over medium-low heat until melted and hot. Spread over crust. Sprinkle with ½ cup coarsely chopped walnuts. Bake until jam is bubbling in center, about 15 minutes. Cool in pan on rack. *(Can be prepared 1 day ahead. Cover tightly and store at room temperature.)* Using foil as aid, lift pastry from pan. Trim edges, if desired. Cut into bars and serve.

Sunflower, oat, and walnut bars

A MOIST, CHEWY BAR COOKIE with walnuts and sunflower seeds for crunch. Rye flour (available at natural foods stores and some supermarkets) adds a unique, nutty flavor, but you could easily substitute whole wheat flour. The not-too-sweet bars will keep well, stored in resealable plastic bags, for several days. They'd be great on a camping trip, and could even make a convenient breakfast on the go with a banana and a glass of milk.

MAKES 16

- **½ cup rye flour**
- **½ cup quick-cooking oats**
- **½ cup chopped walnuts**
- **¼ cup raw sunflower seeds**
- **½ teaspoon baking powder**
- **½ teaspoon salt**
- **1 cup (packed) dark brown sugar**
- **2 large eggs**
- **⅓ cup vegetable oil**
- **1 teaspoon vanilla extract**

PREHEAT oven to 350°F. Oil bottom of 8x8x2-inch glass baking dish. Stir rye flour, oats, walnuts, sunflower seeds, baking powder, and salt in medium bowl to combine. Using electric mixer, beat sugar, eggs, oil, and vanilla in large bowl until smooth, about 3 minutes. Gradually add flour mixture, stirring until combined. Transfer batter to prepared dish, spreading evenly. Bake until cookie is brown and center springs back when lightly touched, about 30 minutes. Cool completely in dish. *(Can be prepared 2 days ahead. Cover tightly and store at room temperature.)* Cut into 16 bars and serve.

Chocolate chip–macadamia nut bars with shortbread crust

EVEN THOUGH macadamia nuts are native to Australia, we tend to associate them with the Hawaiian islands, where they have flourished since their introduction in the early 1890s. For a dessert with a Hawaiian feel, serve these sweet, chewy bars with scoops of coconut ice cream and sliced mangoes. If you prefer, you can make the rich pie-like cookies with toasted chopped pecans or walnuts in place of macadamia nuts.

MAKES 16

Crust

- **1 cup all purpose flour**
- **¼ cup sugar**
- **½ cup (1 stick) chilled unsalted butter, cut into ½-inch cubes**

Filling

- **1 cup sugar**
- **½ cup all purpose flour**
- **2 large eggs**
- **4 tablespoons (½ stick) unsalted butter, melted, cooled**
- **1 teaspoon vanilla extract**
- **1 cup miniature semisweet chocolate chips (about 6 ounces)**
- **1 cup coarsely chopped macadamia nuts**

FOR CRUST: Preheat oven to 350°F. Blend flour and sugar in processor 5 seconds. Add butter. Using on/off turns, blend until moist clumps form. Using plastic wrap as aid, press dough over bottom and ¾ inch up sides of 8x8x2-inch glass baking dish. Bake until crust is golden brown at edges, about 15 minutes. Maintain oven temperature.

MEANWHILE, prepare filling: Whisk sugar, flour, eggs, butter, and vanilla in large bowl to blend. Stir in chocolate chips and nuts.

POUR filling into warm crust, smoothing surface. Bake until filling is golden brown and tester inserted into center comes out with some moist crumbs still attached, about 50 minutes. Transfer dish to rack and cool completely. *(Can be prepared 1 day ahead. Cover and store at room temperature.)* Cut into 16 squares.

Maple-fig pinwheels

THE ADDITION OF CREAM CHEESE makes this tender dough remarkably easy to work with. Both the dough (which must chill overnight) and the filling can be prepared several days in advance and kept in the refrigerator until time to bake. The cookies are crisp when freshly baked, slightly softened after a day or two.

MAKES 48

Filling

- **10 ounces dried moist-pack Calimyrna figs, stemmed, cubed**
- **½ cup pure maple syrup**
- **2 tablespoons water**
- **4½ teaspoons fresh lemon juice, divided**
- **½ teaspoon finely grated lemon peel**

- **1 large egg white**
- **2 drops maple extract**

Dough

- **1¾ cups sifted all purpose flour (sifted, then measured)**
- **½ teaspoon baking powder**
- **½ teaspoon salt**
- **⅔ cup sugar**
- **10 tablespoons (1¼ sticks) chilled unsalted butter, cut into ½-inch cubes**
- **¼ cup (packed) dark brown sugar**
- **2 ounces chilled Philadelphia brand cream cheese, cut into ½-inch cubes**
- **1 large egg**
- **1½ teaspoons finely grated lemon peel**
- **1 teaspoon fresh lemon juice**
- **1 teaspoon vanilla extract**

FOR FILLING: Combine figs, maple syrup, 2 tablespoons water, 3 teaspoons lemon juice, and lemon peel in heavy medium saucepan; bring to simmer. Cover and simmer until figs are soft and liquid is thickened, stirring occasionally, about 15 minutes. Cool filling to lukewarm.

TRANSFER filling to processor and blend until chunky paste forms, about 10 seconds. Add egg white, remaining 1½ teaspoons lemon juice, and maple extract; blend briefly. Transfer filling to small bowl. Cover and refrigerate at least 1 hour. *(Can be prepared 2 days ahead. Keep refrigerated.)*

FOR DOUGH: Whisk flour, baking powder, and salt in large bowl to blend. Using on/off turns, blend sugar and next 7 ingredients in processor, occasionally scraping down sides of bowl. Add mixture from processor to flour mixture and blend well, using back of fork. Gather dough into ball. Wrap in plastic; flatten into square. Chill overnight.

DIVIDE dough in half. Wrap and refrigerate 1 half. Roll half of dough out on floured parchment paper to 8x11-inch rectangle about ⅛ inch thick. Spread half of filling over dough. Starting at 1 long edge and using paper as aid, roll up dough into 1½-inch-diameter log. Wrap log in plastic. Repeat with remaining dough and filling. Freeze logs until firm. *(Can be prepared 2 days ahead. Keep frozen.)*

POSITION rack in center of oven and preheat to 350°F. Line 2 rimmed baking sheets with aluminum foil. Butter foil. Cut each log into 24 slices. Arrange slices on prepared sheets, spacing evenly apart. Bake cookies until light brown at edge and golden on bottom, about 25 minutes. Let stand 3 minutes on sheets. Transfer cookies to rack and cool completely. *(Can be prepared 3 days ahead. Store in airtight container at room temperature.)*

Honey and lemon madeleines

A MADELEINE is a small, seashell-shaped cake from France. Honey gives this version an exceptionally moist texture. You can find the pan at cookware stores, and you'll need to bake the madeleines in two batches to make 24. Consider serving them with a cup of herb tea—the way Proust enjoyed them.

MAKES ABOUT 24

- **Melted unsalted butter**
- **2 large eggs**
- **⅓ cup honey**
- **¼ cup sugar**
- **1½ teaspoons grated lemon peel**
- **⅛ teaspoon ground cloves**
- **½ teaspoon vanilla extract**
- **1 cup sifted all purpose flour (sifted, then measured)**
- **¾ cup (1½ sticks) unsalted butter, melted, cooled to lukewarm**

- **Additional sugar**

PREHEAT oven to 400°F. Generously brush madeleine molds with melted butter; dust with flour. Combine eggs and next 4 ingredients in large bowl. Set bowl over saucepan of simmering water (do not allow bottom of bowl to touch water) and stir until lukewarm. Remove from over water. Using electric mixer, beat until thick and tripled in volume. Beat in vanilla. Reduce speed to low and beat in flour in 3 additions, scraping down bowl occasionally. Transfer ⅓ of batter to medium bowl and fold in ¾ cup cooled melted butter (do not fold in any water at bottom of butter). Gently fold butter mixture into batter in large bowl.

SPOON batter into prepared madeleine molds, filling almost to top. Bake until cookies are golden brown and springy to touch, turning pan after 6 minutes, about 12 minutes total. Invert pan onto rack. Gently pry out cookies with knife tip. Sprinkle with additional sugar. Wipe out molds, grease with melted butter, dust with flour, and repeat with remaining batter. Cool completely. *(Can be prepared 3 days ahead. Store airtight at room temperature.*

Dutch sugar cookies

IN THE NETHERLANDS, Saint Nicholas gives sugar cookies to all the good children on December 5. These cookies can be drizzled with white chocolate as directed, or sprinkled with colored sugar before baking. They're wonderful for any holiday—try hearts sprinkled with red sugar for Valentine's Day. Melting the white chocolate is a little tricky; it's important not to overheat it or else it may "seize," or get too firm. Put the chocolate in a rounded metal bowl over barely simmering water, stirring occasionally and removing it from the heat when the chocolate is almost but not entirely melted. Keep stirring until it has melted completely.

MAKES ABOUT 60

- **1½ cups powdered sugar**
- **1 cup (2 sticks) unsalted butter, room temperature**
- **1 large egg**
- **2 teaspoons vanilla extract**
- **2½ cups all purpose flour**
- **1 teaspoon baking powder**
- **½ teaspoon salt**

- **4 ounces high-quality white chocolate (such as Lindt or Perugina), melted**

USING electric mixer, beat sugar and butter in large bowl until light and fluffy. Beat in egg and vanilla. Add flour, baking powder, and salt; beat just to combine. Divide dough in half. Gather each piece into ball; flatten into disk. Wrap in plastic and chill 1 hour.

PREHEAT oven to 325°F. Roll out 1 dough disk on lightly floured work surface to ⅛-inch thickness. Using assorted cookie cutters, cut out cookies. Transfer cookies to ungreased baking sheets, spacing 1 inch apart. Gather dough scraps; reroll to ⅛-inch thickness. Cut out more cookies. Repeat until all dough is used.

BAKE cookies until pale golden, about 13 minutes. Transfer cookies to racks and cool. Repeat with remaining dough disk.

SPOON melted chocolate into pastry bag fitted with very small plain tip. Pipe chocolate onto cookies. Let cookies stand until chocolate sets. *(Can be prepared ahead. Store in airtight container between sheets of waxed paper at room temperature up to 1 week, or freeze up to 1 month.)*

Pecan and brown sugar crescents

BECAUSE THE DOUGH REQUIRES NO chilling, rolling, or cutting, these tasty little cookies can be put together in minutes. Pair them with ripe pears and a strong blue cheese such as Gorgonzola for an interesting grown-up dessert. To freeze, place the cookies between layers of waxed paper in plastic storage containers or resealable plastic freezer bags and keep for up to one month.

MAKES ABOUT 30

- **1 cup all purpose flour**
- **¾ cup pecans, lightly toasted**
- **½ cup (1 stick) chilled unsalted butter, cut into ½-inch cubes**
- **¼ cup (packed) dark brown sugar**
- **1 teaspoon vanilla extract**
- **½ teaspoon ground cinnamon**
- **Pinch of salt**

- **Powdered sugar**

PREHEAT oven to 325°F. Combine flour and next 6 ingredients in processor. Using on/off turns, process until mixture resembles coarse meal; then process continuously until dough begins to come together in clumps. Gather dough together.

ROLL 2 teaspoonfuls dough between palms of hands to form 2½-inch-long rope, tapering at ends. Place on ungreased baking sheet; curl in ends to form crescent shape. Repeat with remaining dough, spacing cookies 1 inch apart.

BAKE cookies until just firm to touch, about 20 minutes. Cool on sheet 5 minutes. Transfer to rack and cool completely. Sift powdered sugar over. *(Can be prepared 3 days ahead. Store in airtight container at room temperature.)*

Rolled vanilla tuiles

TUILES ARE THIN, crisp wafer cookies. When just out of the oven, the hot, pliable rounds are traditionally draped over a rolling pin, where they cool into a curved cookie that resembles a terra-cotta roof tile—hence the name *tuile* in France, *tegolino* in Italy, and *teja* in Spanish. Here the *tuiles* are smaller, rolled around the handle of a wooden spoon to create elegant cylinder shapes. Use an offset spatula to make spreading the batter easy.

MAKES ABOUT 24

- **1 cup powdered sugar**
- **5 tablespoons unsalted butter, room temperature, divided**
- **2 large egg whites**
- **½ teaspoon vanilla extract**
- **½ cup all purpose flour**

POSITION rack in center of oven and preheat to 350°F. Lightly butter 2 large rimmed nonstick baking sheets. Using electric mixer, beat sugar and 3 tablespoons butter in medium bowl until mixture resembles coarse meal. Beat in egg whites, 1 at a time, then vanilla. Add flour and beat until well blended. Melt remaining 2 tablespoons butter in small saucepan over low heat; mix into batter.

SPOON 1 heaping teaspoonful batter for each cookie onto prepared sheets, spacing 5 inches apart and forming 3 cookies on each sheet. Using small metal offset spatula or back of spoon, spread batter for each cookie to very thin 4-inch round. Bake cookies on 1 sheet until ¾ inch of edge is golden brown, about 5 minutes. Run thin flexible spatula under edge of 1 cookie to loosen and remove from sheet. Working quickly while cookie is still warm and flexible, roll cookie around handle of wooden spoon into cylinder. Slide cookie off handle onto work surface. Shape remaining warm cookies into cylinders, returning sheet to oven briefly to soften cookies if necessary. Cool baking sheet completely.

BAKE cookies on second sheet and roll as above. Repeat with remaining batter, using cool baking sheet each time. Cool all rolled cookies completely. *(Can be prepared 1 day ahead. Store in airtight container at room temperature.)*

Belgian spice cookies

SPECULOOS, A SPECIALTY OF BELGIUM in which flat gingerbread cakes are baked in different shapes, are the inspiration for this recipe. Similar cookies called *speculaas* are made in the Netherlands. These are decorated with melted white chocolate and colored sugar.

MAKES 48

- **2 cups all purpose flour**
- **1 tablespoon ground cinnamon**
- **1½ teaspoons ground ginger**
- **½ teaspoon ground cloves**
- **½ teaspoon baking powder**
- **½ teaspoon salt**
- **1¼ cups (packed) dark brown sugar**
- **½ cup (1 stick) unsalted butter, room temperature**
- **1 large egg**
- **2 ounces high-quality white chocolate (such as Lindt or Perugina), melted**
- **Colored sugar crystals**

WHISK flour and next 5 ingredients in medium bowl to blend. Using electric mixer, beat brown sugar and butter in large bowl until light and fluffy. Add egg and beat until blended. Gradually add flour mixture and beat just until combined. Divide dough in half. Flatten each half into rectangle. Wrap in plastic and refrigerate 1 hour.

PREHEAT oven to 350°F. Lightly butter 2 large baking sheets. Roll out 1 dough piece on lightly floured work surface to 13x9-inch rectangle. Trim edges to form 12x8-inch rectangle. Cut into twenty-four 4x1-inch rectangles.

ARRANGE rectangles on prepared baking sheets, spacing 1 inch apart. Lightly press miniature cookie cutter into each rectangle to make imprint (do not press cutter through dough). Bake until edges begin to darken, about 8 minutes. Transfer cookies to rack and cool. Repeat with remaining dough piece.

WORKING with 1 cookie at a time, brush imprints with melted white chocolate. Sprinkle colored sugar generously over chocolate. Let stand until chocolate sets, about 2 hours. Shake off excess colored sugar. *(Can be prepared ahead. Store in airtight container at room temperature 1 week, or freeze up to 1 month.)*

Gingerbread men

TRY DECORATING THESE with piped icing to outline the shapes of faces or clothes; or spread each one with a thin layer of icing, wait for the icing to dry, then paint on decorations with food coloring. For a simple, adorable, and delicious gingerbread man, use a small dowel or chopstick to mark buttons and eyes on unbaked cookies. Use a spoon to press in a mouth and bake.

MAKES ABOUT 22

Cookies

- **2⅓ cups unbleached all purpose flour**
- **2 teaspoons ground ginger**
- **1½ teaspoons ground cinnamon**
- **½ teaspoon baking soda**
- **¼ teaspoon ground cloves**
- **¼ teaspoon salt**
- **¾ cup (1½ sticks) unsalted butter, room temperature**
- **½ cup (packed) dark brown sugar**
- **½ cup mild-flavored (light) molasses**
- **1 large egg**

Icing

- **¾ cup powdered sugar**
- **4 teaspoons whole milk**

FOR COOKIES: Sift flour and next 5 ingredients into medium bowl. Using electric mixer, beat butter, sugar, and molasses in large bowl until light and fluffy. Beat in egg. Add flour mixture and stir to combine. Gather dough into ball (dough will be soft). Divide into 3 pieces; flatten each into disk. Wrap in plastic and chill until firm, about 1 hour. *(Can be prepared 1 day ahead. Keep refrigerated.)*

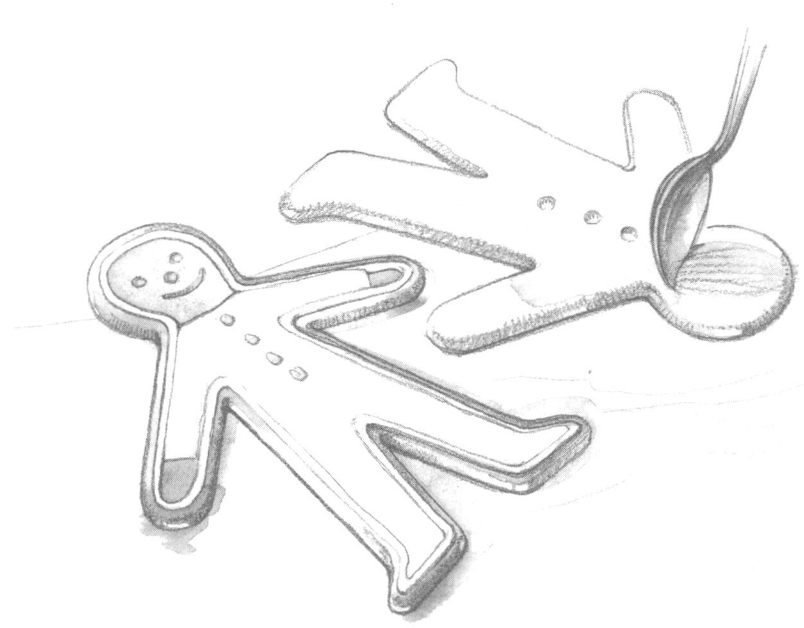

POSITION rack in top third of oven and preheat to 375°F. Grease 2 large rimmed baking sheets. Roll out 1 dough disk on floured surface to ¼-inch thickness. Using 5-inch cookie cutter, cut out gingerbread men. Transfer to baking sheets, spacing 1 inch apart. Gather scraps and chill. Bake cookies until just turning brown at edges, about 10 minutes. Transfer to racks and cool. Repeat rolling, cutting, and baking with all remaining dough, chilling to firm dough as needed while shaping.

FOR ICING: Mix sugar and milk in bowl. Pipe or spread on cookies as desired. Let icing dry 30 minutes. *(Can be prepared 4 days ahead. Store cookies in airtight containers between sheets of waxed paper at room temperature.)*

Gingery spice cookies

THIS IS THE PERFECT ginger cookie, soft and spicy with bits of crystallized ginger. For a variation, you can add a cup of chopped raisins to the batter along with the crystallized ginger. Be sure not to overbake the cookies, as they will become crisp. Pair them with mugs of hot spiced apple cider on a cold day.

MAKES ABOUT 30

- **2 cups all purpose flour**
- **2½ teaspoons ground ginger**
- **2 teaspoons baking soda**
- **1 teaspoon ground cinnamon**
- **1 teaspoon ground cloves**
- **¾ teaspoon salt**
- **¾ cup chopped crystallized ginger (about 4 ounces)**
- **1 cup (packed) dark brown sugar**
- **½ cup solid vegetable shortening, room temperature**
- **¼ cup (½ stick) unsalted butter, room temperature**
- **1 large egg**
- **¼ cup mild-flavored (light) molasses**

Sugar

WHISK flour and next 5 ingredients in medium bowl to blend. Mix in crystallized ginger. Using electric mixer, beat brown sugar, shortening, and butter in large bowl until fluffy. Add egg and molasses; beat until blended. Add flour mixture and beat just until combined. Cover bowl and refrigerate dough 1 hour.

PREHEAT oven to 350°F. Lightly butter 2 large rimmed baking sheets. Spoon sugar in thick layer onto small plate. Using wet hands, form dough into 1¼-inch balls; roll in sugar to coat completely. Place balls on prepared sheets, spacing 2 inches apart.

BAKE cookies until cracked on top but still soft to touch in center, about 12 minutes. Cool on sheets 1 minute. Carefully transfer to racks and cool completely. *(Can be prepared 5 days ahead. Store in airtight container at room temperature.)*

Candied ginger–cardamom bars

THESE LIGHTLY SPICED, chewy bars are reminiscent of old-fashioned blondies. Like most cookies, these can be made ahead and frozen: Wrap the rectangles in aluminum foil, place in freezer bags, and freeze up to 1 week. Thaw unwrapped before cutting into individual bars.

MAKES 24

- **Nonstick vegetable oil spray**
- **2 cups all purpose flour**
- **1 cup sugar**
- **1½ teaspoons ground cardamom**
- **1 teaspoon ground cinnamon**
- **½ teaspoon salt**
- **1 cup (2 sticks) chilled unsalted butter, cut into ½-inch cubes**
- **1 large egg, beaten to blend**
- **¾ cup finely chopped crystallized ginger (about 4 ounces)**

PREHEAT oven to 350°F. Spray 9x9x2-inch metal baking pan with nonstick spray. Blend flour, sugar, cardamom, cinnamon, and salt in processor. Add butter; using on/off turns, process until mixture resembles coarse meal. Add 2 tablespoons beaten egg; blend until moist crumbs form. Add ginger. Using on/off turns, process until moist clumps form. Gather dough together. Using plastic wrap as aid, press dough evenly over bottom of prepared pan. Brush remaining beaten egg over dough. Using small sharp knife, score top of dough with diagonal lines spaced 1 inch apart. Repeat at right angles, forming lattice pattern.

BAKE until pastry is golden and tester inserted into center comes out clean, about 40 minutes. Transfer pan to rack and cool completely. *(Can be prepared 2 days ahead. Store airtight at room temperature.)*

CUT pastry square into 3 long rectangles. Cut each rectangle crosswise into 8 rectangular bars, making 24.

Molasses jumbos with ginger filling

UNSULFURED, OR LIGHT, molasses is made from the first boiling of the sugarcane (and dark molasses from the second boiling). It is rich in iron, adds a pleasing caramel color and flavor to foods, and improves the keeping quality of baked goods. But you might not be able to keep these big, moist sandwich cookies around for long—they're too tasty. If you are unable to find the ginger marmalade, use orange marmalade instead.

MAKES ABOUT 24

Molasses cookies

- **2/3 cup (packed) golden brown sugar**
- **1/2 cup mild-flavored (light) molasses**
- **1/2 cup (1 stick) unsalted butter, room temperature**

- **1 extra-large egg**
- **1 tablespoon apple cider vinegar**
- **2 teaspoons vanilla extract**
- **3 cups sifted all purpose flour (sifted, then measured)**
- **3/4 teaspoon ground ginger**
- **3/4 teaspoon baking soda**
- **3/4 teaspoon ground cinnamon**
- **1/2 teaspoon salt**
- **1/2 teaspoon ground cloves**
- **1/4 teaspoon ground cardamom**

Melted butter

Ginger filling

- **2½ cups powdered sugar**
- **7 tablespoons chopped crystallized ginger (3 ounces)**
- **4 tablespoons ginger marmalade or orange marmalade**
- **4 tablespoons (½ stick) chilled unsalted butter, cut into 4 pieces**

FOR MOLASSES COOKIES: Stir sugar, molasses, and butter in heavy large saucepan over low heat until butter melts. Cool mixture to lukewarm.

STIR egg, vinegar, and vanilla into molasses mixture. Sift flour and next 6 ingredients into molasses mixture; combine well. Cover and chill until dough is firm, about 1½ hours. *(Can be prepared 3 days ahead. Keep refrigerated.)*

LINE 3 baking sheets with aluminum foil. Brush foil with melted butter and dust with flour, shaking off excess. Form dough into 1-inch balls. Arrange on prepared sheets, spacing 3 inches apart. Flatten each to 3-inch round (saucepan bottom wrapped in plastic works well). Chill 1½ hours.

PREHEAT oven to 325°F. Bake cold cookies until honey-colored, about 14 minutes. Gently press each cookie with spatula to flatten. Cool completely on sheets. *(Can be prepared 2 days ahead. Store in airtight container at room temperature.)*

FOR GINGER FILLING: Blend 1¼ cups sugar and 3½ tablespoons chopped ginger in processor until ginger is minced, occasionally scraping down sides of bowl, about 2 minutes. Add 2 tablespoons marmalade and 2 tablespoons butter. Process until thick and well blended, about 1½ minutes. Transfer mixture to small bowl. Repeat with remaining sugar, ginger, marmalade, and butter. *(Can be prepared 1 day ahead. Cover and refrigerate. Bring to room temperature before continuing.)*

SPREAD 1 tablespoon filling on bottom side of 1 cookie, smoothing to edges. Press bottom of another cookie firmly atop filling. Repeat with remaining cookies and filling. *(Can be prepared 6 hours ahead. Let stand uncovered at room temperature to retain crispness.)*

Molasses chewies with brown sugar glaze

THESE MOIST, down-home cookies feature an unbeatable combination of spice and fruit and a chewy texture, as well as a unique glaze: The thin brown sugar topping is honey-colored and translucent when hot, then cools to an opaque, crisp layer. The glaze is the proverbial "icing on the cake," but the bars are also wonderful unadorned.

MAKES 24

Cookie

- **2 cups unbleached all purpose flour**
- **2 teaspoons baking powder**
- **3/4 teaspoon ground cinnamon**
- **1/2 teaspoon baking soda**
- **1/2 teaspoon ground ginger**
- **1/2 teaspoon ground nutmeg**
- **1/4 teaspoon salt**
- **Pinch of ground cloves**
- **Pinch of ground black pepper**
- **1/2 cup (1 stick) unsalted butter, room temperature**
- **1 1/4 cups (packed) golden brown sugar**
- **2 large eggs**
- **1/4 cup mild-flavored (light) molasses**
- **3/4 cup golden raisins**
- **1/2 cup coarsely chopped pecans**

Glaze

- **1 cup (packed) golden brown sugar**
- **3 tablespoons cold water**

FOR COOKIE: Preheat oven to 350°F. Butter and flour 9x9x2-inch metal baking pan. Sift flour and next 8 ingredients into medium bowl. Using electric mixer, beat butter in large bowl until light and fluffy. Add sugar and beat until blended. Beat in eggs 1 at a time. Add molasses and beat until smooth. Add flour mixture and beat just until combined. Stir in raisins and pecans.

TRANSFER dough to prepared pan; smooth top. Bake until top is set but still slightly soft and tester inserted into center comes out with moist crumbs still attached, about 33 minutes.

COOL cookie completely in pan on rack (cookie will sink slightly). Turn cookie out; turn right side up and trim edges.

FOR GLAZE: Fill medium bowl with ice water. Stir brown sugar and 3 tablespoons cold water in heavy small saucepan over low heat until sugar dissolves. Increase heat and boil without stirring until syrup registers 230°F on candy thermometer, about 2 minutes. Set pan in ice water and stir until glaze cools to just warm, about 2 minutes. Pour glaze over top (not down sides) of cookie. Using back of spoon, spread glaze evenly over top. Cool until glaze sets. Cut into 24 bars. *(Can be prepared 1 day ahead. Store in airtight container between sheets of waxed paper at room temperature.)*

Chinese noodle cookies

DEFINITELY A RETRO SWEET. Many will remember noodle cookies from school bake sales–though they are in fact cool, no-bake cookies that can be put together in seconds. This recipe calls for toasted pecans, but chopped peanuts or sliced almonds would work well. Because the recipe is virtually foolproof, this is a great "cooking" project for children.

MAKES ABOUT 24

1 11-ounce package butterscotch chips
1 5-ounce can chow mein noodles
⅔ cup chopped pecans, toasted

HEAT butterscotch chips in large glass bowl in microwave on high until melted, about 2 minutes. Gently stir in noodles, then pecans. Drop mixture by tablespoonfuls onto waxed paper. Let cookies stand until cool and set, about 1 hour.

Honey, anise, and almond biscotti

ANISE AND ALMOND are the traditional flavors of this crisp Italian cookie. Biscotti–*bis* meaning "twice" and *cotti* meaning "cooked"–are baked first in the form of a flat loaf and then sliced and baked again until crisp. Honey gives this version a unique flavor. Enjoy them for dessert with Vin Santo (an Italian dessert wine made from dried Malvasia and Trebbiano grapes), cream Sherry, Port, or Sauternes. Crushing the aniseed is easier if you put the seeds in a plastic bag first.

MAKES ABOUT 48

2 cups all purpose flour
1 teaspoon baking powder
½ teaspoon baking soda
½ teaspoon salt
½ cup vegetable oil
½ cup sugar
½ cup honey
2 large eggs
2 teaspoons grated lemon peel
2 teaspoons aniseed, crushed
1 teaspoon vanilla extract
1½ cups slivered almonds, lightly toasted

WHISK flour and next 3 ingredients in medium bowl to blend. Whisk oil, sugar, honey, eggs, lemon peel, aniseed, and vanilla in large bowl until smooth. Stir in flour mixture, then nuts. Cover and refrigerate dough until well chilled, about 3 hours. *(Can be prepared 1 day ahead. Keep chilled.)*

POSITION 1 rack in top third of oven and another rack in bottom third; preheat to 350°F. Line 2 large rimmed baking sheets with parchment paper. Spoon out dough in 3 equal strips (2 on 1 prepared sheet, spaced well apart, and 1 on second prepared sheet). Using well-floured hands, shape strips into 2-inch-wide by 1-inch-high logs.

BAKE logs until just springy to touch, reversing position of sheets after 10 minutes, about 20 minutes total (logs will spread). Cool 15 minutes on sheets. Maintain oven temperature.

USING large spatula, carefully transfer logs to work surface. Using serrated knife, cut each log on diagonal into ½-inch-thick slices. Remove parchment from baking sheets. Arrange slices, cut side down, on same sheets. Bake until bottom sides brown, about 7 minutes. Turn cookies over. Bake until bottom sides brown, about 7 minutes longer. Transfer to racks and cool (cookies will crisp as they cool). *(Can be prepared 2 weeks ahead. Store in airtight container at room temperature.)*

Chocolate, almond, and dried cranberry biscotti

IDEAL FOR SERVING WITH COFFEE, these biscotti have a delicious white chocolate coating; but the cookies are also wonderful dipped in bittersweet chocolate. It's important to reverse the position of the baking sheets midway through baking to keep the bottom of the logs from overbrowning.

MAKES ABOUT 36

- **1½ cups all purpose flour**
- **¾ cup sugar**
- **½ cup unsweetened cocoa powder**
- **2 teaspoons baking soda**
- **⅛ teaspoon salt**
- **3 large eggs**
- **2 teaspoons vanilla extract**
- **¼ cup (½ stick) unsalted butter, melted**
- **1 cup dried cranberries**
- **1 cup sliced almonds**

- **8 ounces high-quality white chocolate (such as Lindt or Perugina), finely chopped (optional)**

POSITION 1 rack in top third and 1 rack in bottom third of oven; preheat to 350°F. Line 2 rimmed baking sheets with parchment paper. Sift flour and next 4 ingredients into large bowl. Whisk eggs and vanilla in medium bowl to blend. Using electric mixer, beat egg mixture, then melted butter into dry ingredients. Stir in cranberries and almonds.

TURN out dough onto floured surface. Using floured hands, divide dough into 3 equal pieces. Shape each into 8x2x¾-inch log. Place 2 logs on 1 prepared baking sheet, spacing well apart, and 1 log on second prepared sheet.

BAKE logs 12 minutes. Reverse position of baking sheets. Bake logs until firm and dry to touch, about 12 minutes longer. Remove from oven. Cool on sheets 10 minutes. Reduce temperature to 325°F.

TRANSFER logs to work surface. Using serrated knife, cut hot logs on diagonal into ½-inch-thick slices. Remove parchment from baking sheets. Place slices, cut side down, on same sheets. Bake biscotti until dry and slightly darker, about 10 minutes. Transfer to racks and cool completely.

IF DESIRED, stir white chocolate in bowl set over saucepan of barely simmering water until smooth (do not let bottom of bowl touch water). Remove from over water. Dip biscotti 1 at a time into white chocolate, holding cookie at angle and coating 1 inch of end. Return to same baking sheets. Chill until chocolate is set, about 20 minutes. *(Can be prepared 3 days ahead. Store in airtight container between sheets of waxed paper at room temperature.)*

Simple shortbread

SHORTBREAD DATES BACK to sixteenth-century Scotland. It is surprising how the simplest ingredients—sugar, butter, flour—combine to make one of the most satisfying and comforting cookies. Cut the shortbread into wedges while it is still warm, as a cooled "bread" will crack.

MAKES 24

- **½ cup sugar**
- **½ teaspoon salt**
- **1 cup (2 sticks) chilled unsalted butter, cut into ½-inch cubes**
- **¼ teaspoon vanilla extract**
- **2 cups all purpose flour**

BLEND sugar and salt in processor. Add butter; using on/off turns, cut in until blended and smooth. Blend in vanilla. Add flour and process until blended but still slightly crumbly, occasionally scraping down bowl. Gather dough into ball; flatten into disk. Wrap in plastic and refrigerate until dough is cold, about 30 minutes.

POSITION rack in top third of oven and preheat to 250°F. Divide dough in half. Press each half over bottom of 8-inch-diameter cake pan or 9-inch-diameter pie dish. Bake shortbread 30 minutes. Rotate pans and continue baking until shortbreads are cooked through and very pale golden, about 30 minutes longer. Cool in pans on racks 10 minutes. Cut each warm shortbread, still in pan, into 12 wedges. Cool completely in pan. *(Can be prepared 4 days ahead. Cover tightly and store at room temperature.)* Using thin spatula, carefully transfer wedges to platter.

Lemon-nutmeg shortbreads with lemon icing

THIS DELICATE COOKIE is great served with vanilla ice cream. For an interesting variation, try replacing the lemon peel with orange peel and the nutmeg with ground cardamom. The dough can be made ahead, rolled out, and frozen up to one month; just allow it to thaw overnight in the refrigerator before cutting.

MAKES ABOUT 18 SHORTBREADS

Shortbreads

- **1 cup all purpose flour**
- **2½ tablespoons cornstarch**
- **¼ teaspoon ground nutmeg**
- **⅛ teaspoon salt**
- **½ cup (1 stick) unsalted butter, room temperature**
- **⅓ cup sugar**
- **1 tablespoon plus 1 teaspoon grated lemon peel**
- **1 teaspoon vanilla extract**

Icing

- **½ cup powdered sugar**
- **3 teaspoons (about) fresh lemon juice**

FOR SHORTBREADS: Preheat oven to 350°F. Combine flour, cornstarch, nutmeg, and salt in medium bowl; whisk to blend. Using electric mixer, beat butter, sugar, lemon peel, and vanilla in large bowl until light and fluffy. Add flour mixture and mix until dough begins to come together.

TURN out dough onto sheet of parchment paper. Gather dough into ball; flatten into disk. Cover with second sheet of paper. Roll out dough to ¼-inch thickness, turning and freeing paper from dough occasionally. Free bottom sheet of paper; remove top sheet. Cut out cookies using 3-inch cutters. Transfer to 2 ungreased rimmed baking sheets, spacing ½ inch apart. Gather and reroll scraps; cut out additional cookies. Transfer to sheet.

BAKE cookies until firm to touch and just beginning to color, about 15 minutes. Transfer cookies to rack and cool.

FOR ICING: Place sugar in small bowl. Mix in lemon juice by ½ teaspoonfuls to make icing just thin enough to drip off fork. Drizzle icing from fork tines onto cookies. *(Can be prepared 1 week ahead. Store in airtight container in single layer at room temperature.)*

Mexican wedding cakes

CALLED *POLVORONES* IN SPANISH, these are the Mexican version of shortbread cookies. They are often flavored with cinnamon or orange, and they always contain nuts—walnuts, almonds, hazelnuts, or (as in this recipe) pecans. Because the cookies, wrapped individually in tissue paper that is twisted at both ends to resemble a bonbon, are often given as party favors at weddings, they are often referred to as little wedding cakes.

MAKES ABOUT 48

- **1 cup (2 sticks) unsalted butter, room temperature**
- **2 cups powdered sugar, divided**
- **2 teaspoons vanilla extract**
- **2 cups all purpose flour**
- **¼ teaspoon salt**
- **1 cup pecans, toasted, coarsely ground**

- **⅛ teaspoon ground cinnamon**

USING electric mixer, beat butter in large bowl until light and fluffy. Add ½ cup powdered sugar and vanilla; beat until well blended. Beat in flour, salt, then pecans. Divide dough in half; form each piece into ball. Wrap separately in plastic and chill until cold, about 30 minutes.

PREHEAT oven to 350°F. Whisk remaining 1½ cups powdered sugar and cinnamon in pie dish to blend. Set cinnamon sugar aside.

WORKING with half of chilled dough, roll 2 teaspoonfuls dough at a time between palms into balls. Arrange balls on large rimmed baking sheet, spacing ½ inch apart. Bake cookies until golden brown on bottom and just pale golden on top, about 18 minutes. Cool cookies 5 minutes on baking sheet. Gently roll warm cookies in cinnamon sugar to coat completely. Transfer coated cookies to rack and cool completely. Repeat with remaining half of dough. *(Can be prepared 2 days ahead. Store airtight at room temperature; reserve remaining cinnamon sugar.)*

SIFT reserved cinnamon sugar over cookies.

Chocolate chip, cherry, and walnut rugelach

CLASSIC JEWISH COOKIES, rugelach trace their roots to Eastern Europe. Freezing the formed cookies 30 minutes prior to baking helps them maintain their curved shape (*rugelach* means "little horns" in Yiddish). The cookies freeze exceptionally well after baking; they'll keep up to one month and are good to have on hand in the event of an unexpected coffee klatch.

MAKES 32

Dough

- **2 cups all purpose flour**
- **2 tablespoons sugar**
- **¼ teaspoon salt**
- **1 cup (2 sticks) chilled unsalted butter, cut into ½-inch cubes**
- **6 ounces chilled Philadelphia brand cream cheese, cut into ½-inch cubes**

Filling

- **½ cup sugar**
- **1 teaspoon ground cinnamon**
- **12 tablespoons cherry preserves**
- **8 tablespoons dried tart cherries**
- **8 tablespoons miniature semisweet chocolate chips**
- **8 tablespoons finely chopped walnuts**

- **⅓ cup (about) whipping cream**

FOR DOUGH: Blend flour, sugar, and salt in processor. Add butter and cream cheese; using on/off turns, cut in until dough begins to clump together. Gather dough into ball. Divide dough into 4 equal pieces; flatten into disks. Wrap each disk in plastic and refrigerate 2 hours. *(Can be prepared 2 days ahead. Keep refrigerated. Let soften slightly at room temperature before rolling out.)*

FOR FILLING: Line large rimmed baking sheet with parchment paper. Mix sugar and cinnamon in small bowl. Roll out 1 dough disk on floured surface to 9-inch round. Spread 3 tablespoons cherry preserves over dough, leaving 1-inch plain border. Sprinkle with 2 tablespoons dried cherries, then 2 tablespoons chocolate chips, 2 tablespoons cinnamon sugar, and 2 tablespoons walnuts. Press filling firmly to adhere to dough. Cut dough round into 8 equal wedges. Starting at wide end of each wedge, roll up tightly. Arrange cookies, seam side down, on prepared sheet, spacing 1½ inches apart and bending ends slightly to form crescents. Repeat 3 times with remaining dough disks, preserves, dried cherries, chocolate chips, cinnamon sugar, and walnuts. Place baking sheet in freezer 30 minutes.

POSITION rack in center of oven and preheat to 375°F. Brush cookies lightly with whipping cream. Bake frozen cookies until golden brown, about 40 minutes. Transfer cookies to racks and cool completely. *(Can be prepared ahead. Store in airtight container at room temperature up to 1 week or freeze up to 1 month.)*

Double coconut macaroons

MACAROONS WERE POPULAR in Victorian times, and they've never fallen out of favor. This recipe offers a contemporary twist by upping the coconut quotient—the dough contains both flaked coconut and cream of coconut, and the dough balls are rolled and coated in additional flaked coconut—and by dipping the baked and cooled cookies into melted dark chocolate. Be sure to butter and flour the aluminum-foil-lined baking sheet before baking the cookies and to use waxed paper on the baking sheet for the chocolate-dipped cookies—these steps will keep the cookies from sticking to the sheets. Canned sweetened cream of coconut is available in the liquor or mixers section of most supermarkets.

MAKES ABOUT 15

- **2 7-ounce packages sweetened flaked coconut, divided**
- **2/3 cup (packed) powdered sugar**
- **1/4 cup canned sweetened cream of coconut (such as Coco López)**
- **1 ounce Philadelphia brand cream cheese, room temperature**
- **3 tablespoons all purpose flour**
- **1 large egg white**
- **1/2 teaspoon vanilla extract**
- **Pinch of salt**

- **12 ounces bittersweet (not unsweetened) or semisweet chocolate, chopped**

PREHEAT oven to 325°F. Line large rimmed baking sheet with aluminum foil. Butter and flour foil; shake off excess. Blend 1 package coconut and powdered sugar in processor until coconut is finely ground and mixture feels moist. Add cream of coconut, cream cheese, flour, egg white, vanilla, and salt. Process until well blended, scraping down sides of work bowl occasionally (dough will be soft). Transfer dough to medium bowl.

PLACE remaining package of flaked coconut in pie plate. Drop heaping tablespoonful of dough into coconut and roll to coat completely. Using palms of hands, gently roll dough into ball (about 1½ inches in diameter). Place on prepared baking sheet. Repeat with remaining dough and coconut, spacing macaroons evenly apart.

BAKE macaroons until golden brown and just firm to touch, about 35 minutes. Cool cookies completely on sheet on rack.

LINE another large rimmed baking sheet with waxed paper. Melt chocolate in top of double boiler set over simmering water, stirring until thermometer inserted into chocolate registers 115°F. Turn off heat. Dip bottom ½ inch of 1 cookie into melted chocolate. Brush cookie against side of pan to remove excess chocolate. Place cookie, dipped side down, on waxed-paper-lined sheet. Repeat with remaining cookies and melted chocolate. Refrigerate cookies until chocolate sets, about 30 minutes. Remove cookies from sheet. *(Can be prepared ahead. Store in airtight container in single layer in refrigerator up to 3 days or freeze up to 3 weeks. Bring macaroons to room temperature before serving.)*

Almond baklava with rose water syrup

POPULAR THROUGHOUT the Middle East and Mediterranean, the flaky, nut-filled, honey-soaked pastry known as baklava can be made with walnuts or pistachios instead of almonds, or use a combination of all three nuts. Be sure to keep the phyllo dough covered with plastic wrap and a moist towel while assembling the pastry so that the paper-thin layers won't become dry and difficult to work with. And whether you use fresh or frozen phyllo, let it stand at room temperature for a few hours before you work with it—that will make it easier to separate the sheets. Rose water is available at Middle Eastern markets and specialty foods stores.

MAKES 12

1⅔ cups sugar, divided
1½ cups water
⅔ cup honey
2 cinnamon sticks
8 2x½-inch strips orange peel (orange part only)
2 teaspoons rose water

1 cup (2 sticks) unsalted butter, melted
3 cups coarsely chopped almonds
1 teaspoon ground cinnamon
½ teaspoon ground allspice

15 sheets fresh phyllo pastry or frozen, thawed (each about 18x12-inches)

Plain yogurt

STIR 1⅓ cups sugar, 1½ cups water, honey, cinnamon sticks, and orange peel in medium saucepan over medium heat until sugar dissolves. Increase heat and bring to boil. Remove from heat. Mix in rose water. Refrigerate syrup until cold, at least 2 hours. *(Can be prepared 1 day ahead. Keep chilled.)*

PREHEAT oven to 325°F. Brush 13x9x2-inch metal baking pan with some of melted butter. Mix almonds, ground cinnamon, allspice, and remaining ⅓ cup sugar in medium bowl to combine.

FOLD 1 phyllo sheet in half to form 12x9-inch rectangle. Place folded sheet in prepared pan. Brush with melted butter. Repeat with 4 more folded sheets, brushing top of each folded sheet with butter. Sprinkle half of nut mixture over. Top with 1 folded pastry sheet and brush with butter. Repeat with 4 more folded sheets, brushing top of each with butter. Sprinkle remaining nut mixture over. Repeat with 5 more folded sheets, brushing top of each with butter. Using sharp knife, make 5 diagonal cuts across phyllo, cutting through top layers only and spacing cuts evenly. Repeat at right angles to form diamond pattern. Bake baklava until golden brown, about 40 minutes.

STRAIN cold rose syrup into small bowl. Spoon 1 cup cold syrup evenly over hot baklava; cover and chill remaining rose syrup. Recut baklava along lines through layers to bottom of pan. Let stand 4 hours. *(Can be prepared 1 day ahead. Cover and let stand at room temperature.)* Serve baklava with yogurt and remaining rose syrup.

Brownies

Chocolate chip fudge brownies

ALTHOUGH THE ORIGINS of this American classic are unknown, young and old have loved the fudgy treats for more than a century, since the first brownie recipe was published in the 1897 Sears, Roebuck and Co. catalog. Here, chocolate chips add extra richness. Make sure that the batter is not warm when the chips are mixed in.

MAKES 24

- **3/4 cup (1 1/2 sticks) unsalted butter**
- **4 ounces unsweetened chocolate, chopped**
- **4 large eggs**
- **1 3/4 cups sugar**
- **1 1/2 teaspoons vanilla extract**
- **3/4 cup all purpose flour**
- **1 cup semisweet chocolate chips (about 6 ounces)**

Powdered sugar

PREHEAT oven to 350°F. Butter 13x9x2-inch metal baking pan. Stir ¾ cup butter and unsweetened chocolate in heavy medium saucepan over medium-low heat until melted and smooth. Remove from heat. Whisk eggs and 1¾ cups sugar in large bowl until pale yellow and thick, about 3 minutes. Gradually whisk in warm chocolate mixture. Whisk in vanilla, then flour. If necessary, cool batter to room temperature. Mix in chocolate chips.

POUR batter into prepared pan. Bake brownies until tester inserted into center comes out with moist crumbs still attached, about 25 minutes. Cool brownies completely in pan on rack. *(Can be prepared 1 day ahead. Cover tightly and store at room temperature.)* Cut into squares. Sift powdered sugar over brownies and serve.

Rich espresso and cream cheese brownies

AN ESPRESSO–CREAM CHEESE FILLING provides an appealing counterbalance to the deep chocolate brownie. If you don't have a pastry bag, drizzle the reserved batter in thin lines over the filling, spacing evenly, then swirl the mixtures together using the tip of a small, sharp knife.

MAKES 24

- **1/2 cup (1 stick) unsalted butter**
- **3 ounces unsweetened chocolate, finely chopped**
- **2 ounces bittersweet (not unsweetened) or semisweet chocolate, finely chopped**

- **3/4 cup sifted all purpose flour (sifted, then measured)**
- **1/4 teaspoon baking powder**
- **1/4 teaspoon salt**
- **3 large eggs**
- **1 large egg, separated**
- **1 1/4 cups (packed) golden brown sugar**
- **1/3 cup coarsely chopped toasted walnuts**

- **3 1/2 teaspoons instant espresso powder**
- **1 tablespoon coffee liqueur**
- **12 ounces Philadelphia brand cream cheese, room temperature**
- **1 cup powdered sugar**

MELT butter in heavy medium saucepan over low heat. Add unsweetened and bittersweet chocolates; stir until melted. Cool, stirring occasionally.

BUTTER and flour bottom of 13x9x2-inch metal baking pan. Combine sifted flour, baking powder, and salt in small bowl. Using electric mixer, beat 2 eggs, 1 egg yolk, and brown sugar in large bowl until very thick and billowy, about 4 minutes. Fold in chocolate mixture, then flour mixture. Transfer ⅓ cup batter to small bowl and reserve for topping. Fold walnuts into remaining batter. Spread batter with nuts evenly in prepared pan. Refrigerate until firm, about 15 minutes.

POSITION rack in center of oven and preheat to 325°F. Combine espresso powder and liqueur in small bowl and stir until powder is dissolved. Blend cream cheese and powdered sugar in processor until very smooth, stopping occasionally to scrape down bowl. Blend in espresso mixture, remaining egg, and egg white.

SPREAD cream cheese mixture over chilled batter in pan. Transfer reserved ⅓ cup batter to pastry bag fitted with small plain tip. Carefully pipe batter in parallel lines down length of pan, spacing ¾ inch apart. Arrange pan so that 1 short end is facing you. Starting 1 inch from top short end of pan and at top left side, draw toothpick in straight line through piped lines to opposite side of pan, forming V pattern. Repeat process 1 inch down from first line of Vs, starting at opposite side of pan. Repeat down full length of pan, spacing 1 inch apart and alternating directions to make chevron design. Bake until sides of brownie are puffed and center stays firm when pan is shaken gently, about 33 minutes. Cool in pan on rack.

COVER and refrigerate brownie until well chilled. *(Can be prepared 1 day ahead. Keep chilled.)* Using warm knife, cut into 24 pieces. Serve cold.

S'mores brownies

THIS BROWNIE FEATURES all the flavors of the campfire dessert—graham cracker crust, moist milk chocolate brownie filling, and sweet marshmallow topping. Be extra-careful when melting the chocolate and butter, as milk chocolate tends to scorch easily. Lining the pan with aluminum foil ensures moist brownies and easy cleanup.

MAKES ABOUT 24

Crust

- **6 whole graham crackers, broken into small pieces**
- **3 tablespoons sugar**
- **3 tablespoons unsalted butter, cut into pieces, room temperature**

Brownies

- **8 ounces milk chocolate, chopped**
- **6 tablespoons (¾ stick) unsalted butter, cut into pieces**

- **¼ cup sifted all purpose flour (sifted, then measured)**
- **⅛ teaspoon salt**
- **2 extra-large eggs, room temperature**
- **¼ cup plus 1½ teaspoons sugar**
- **4 ounces milk chocolate, cut into ¼-inch pieces**

- **25 large marshmallows, cut crosswise in half**
- **1 ounce milk chocolate, grated**

FOR CRUST: Position rack in center of oven and preheat to 325°F. Fold 18x12-inch piece of aluminum foil in half, making 9x12-inch rectangle. Line 9x9x2-inch nonstick metal baking pan with foil, allowing foil to extend over 2 sides. Butter foil and exposed pan sides. Blend graham crackers, sugar, and butter in processor until moist crumbs form. Using plastic wrap as aid, press crumbs evenly onto foil in bottom of prepared pan. Bake crust until light golden brown, about 7 minutes. Cool crust on rack. Maintain oven temperature.

FOR BROWNIES: Melt 8 ounces chopped milk chocolate and butter in heavy medium saucepan over very low heat, stirring until smooth. Cool chocolate mixture to room temperature.

SIFT flour and salt into small bowl. Whisk eggs and sugar in medium bowl until well blended. Whisk in melted chocolate mixture. Gently fold in flour mixture. Mix in 4 ounces ¼-inch pieces chocolate. Spread batter over crust. Bake until tester inserted in center comes out clean, about 23 minutes (surface may crack).

PLACE marshmallows over hot brownie, spacing evenly. Cover pan tightly with foil and let stand 15 minutes (marshmallows will soften).

REMOVE foil cover from pan. Using wet fingertips, press marshmallows together to fill in any uncovered spaces. Sprinkle 1 ounce grated chocolate over. Cool completely. *(Can be prepared 1 day ahead. Cover tightly and store at room temperature.)* Using foil overhang as aid, lift brownie from pan. Fold down foil sides. Using hot knife (dipped into very hot water) cut brownie into squares, wiping knife clean between slices.

Brownie Newtons

HERE'S A COMBINATION of two old-fashioned favorites: fudge brownies and the classic wholesome fig cookie. The fig filling can be prepared a day or two ahead and refrigerated. Serve the brownies with glasses of milk for a snack, or wrap them individually in aluminum foil to pack along for a picnic.

MAKES ABOUT 24

Filling

1½ cups finely chopped dried stemmed Calimyrna figs (about 8 ounces)
¼ cup water
3 tablespoons sugar
1 tablespoon fresh lemon juice
⅛ teaspoon ground allspice
Pinch of salt

Brownies

3½ ounces unsweetened chocolate
¼ cup (½ stick) unsalted butter

⅔ cup sifted all purpose flour (sifted, then measured)
¼ teaspoon salt
2 extra-large eggs, room temperature
1 cup plus 6 tablespoons sugar
½ teaspoon vanilla extract

FOR FILLING: Combine figs, ¼ cup water, sugar, lemon juice, allspice, and pinch of salt in heavy large saucepan. Bring to boil, stirring until sugar dissolves. Reduce heat to low. Cover and simmer until figs are tender and all liquid is absorbed, stirring occasionally, about 8 minutes. Turn out onto plate and cool fig mixture completely.

FOR BROWNIES: Fold 18x12-inch piece of aluminum foil in half crosswise, making 9x12-inch rectangle. Line 9x9x2-inch metal baking pan with foil, allowing foil to extend over 2 sides. Butter foil and exposed pan sides. Dust pan and foil with flour.

MELT chocolate and butter in heavy small saucepan over very low heat, stirring constantly. Cool chocolate mixture completely.

POSITION rack in center of oven and preheat to 325°F. Sift flour and salt into small bowl. Whisk eggs, sugar, and vanilla in large bowl to blend. Whisk in melted chocolate mixture. Fold in flour mixture. Spread 1¼ cups batter in prepared pan. Scatter fig mixture over. Spoon remaining batter over and spread gently (batter may not cover all figs). Cover pan tightly with foil.

BAKE brownie 15 minutes. Remove foil and bake until tester inserted into center comes out with some moist crumbs still attached, about 30 minutes longer. Transfer to rack and cool 5 hours. *(Can be prepared 1 day ahead. Cover tightly and store at room temperature.)*

USING foil as aid, lift brownie from pan. Fold down foil sides. Cut into squares.

Mexican brownies with brown sugar topping

CHOCOLATE—from the evergreen cacao tree of the genus *Theobroma* (which means "food of the gods")—is native to southern Mexico, where it was valued centuries ago by both the Maya and the Aztecs. Traditionally, Mexican chocolate is flavored with spices such as cinnamon and allspice. These dark chocolate, cinnamon-scented brownies have a topping reminiscent of *piloncillo*, a Mexican brown sugar.

MAKES 16

Brownies

4 ounces unsweetened chocolate, chopped
½ cup (1 stick) unsalted butter
1¼ cups (packed) golden brown sugar
1 tablespoon ground cinnamon
¼ teaspoon salt
3 large eggs
1 teaspoon vanilla extract
¾ cup all purpose flour
1 cup milk chocolate chips (about 6 ounces)

Brown sugar topping

1 cup (packed) golden brown sugar
¼ cup whipping cream
1 tablespoon unsalted butter
¾ teaspoon vanilla extract
½ cup sliced almonds

FOR BROWNIES: Preheat oven to 325°F. Line 8x8x2-inch metal baking pan with aluminum foil, extending foil over sides. Stir unsweetened chocolate and butter in heavy large saucepan over low heat until melted and smooth. Cool 5 minutes. Whisk in sugar, cinnamon, and salt. Whisk in eggs, 1 at a time, then vanilla. Continue to whisk until batter is smooth, about 2 minutes. Add flour and whisk just until combined. Stir in chocolate chips.

POUR batter into prepared pan, smoothing top. Bake until tester inserted into center comes out with a few moist crumbs still attached, about 35 minutes. Cool completely in pan on rack.

FOR BROWN SUGAR TOPPING: Whisk sugar, cream, and butter in heavy small saucepan over low heat until mixture is smooth and comes to boil. Remove from heat; mix in vanilla. Cool 10 minutes. Whisk topping until cooler and thick enough to spread. Spread evenly over brownie. Sprinkle with almonds. Let stand until topping sets, about 1 hour. Refrigerate until cold. *(Can be prepared 1 day ahead. Cover and keep refrigerated.)*

USING foil as aid, lift brownie from pan. Cut brownie into 16 squares. Serve cold or at room temperature.

Grand Marnier brownie bites

THE COMBINATION of Cognac and oranges was considered quite daring when Grand Marnier was created in 1880. Now we consider the orange liqueur a classic—and it makes these rich, do-ahead mini brownies sublime.

MAKES 25

Brownies

4 ounces unsweetened chocolate, chopped
½ cup (1 stick) unsalted butter
1¼ cups sugar
2 teaspoons grated orange peel
1 teaspoon vanilla extract
¼ teaspoon salt
3 large eggs
¾ cup all purpose flour

Topping

½ cup whipping cream
1 teaspoon grated orange peel
5½ ounces bittersweet (not unsweetened) or semisweet chocolate, chopped
3 tablespoons Grand Marnier or other orange liqueur

FOR BROWNIES: Preheat oven to 325°F. Line 8x8x2-inch metal baking pan with aluminum foil, extending foil over sides. Melt unsweetened chocolate and butter in heavy medium saucepan over low heat, stirring until smooth; cool slightly. Whisk sugar, orange peel, vanilla, and salt into chocolate mixture. Whisk in eggs 1 at a time, then continue whisking until mixture is very smooth. Add flour and whisk just to combine.

TRANSFER batter to prepared pan. Bake brownie until top is just springy to touch and tester inserted into center comes out with moist crumbs still attached, about 35 minutes. Cool in pan on rack 10 minutes. If edges are raised, press with metal spatula to level top. Cool completely in pan.

FOR TOPPING: Bring cream and orange peel to simmer in heavy small saucepan. Remove from heat. Add chocolate and whisk until smooth. Whisk in Grand Marnier. Refrigerate topping until thick enough to spread, stirring occasionally, about 45 minutes.

SPREAD topping over brownie. Refrigerate until topping is cold and set, about 1 hour. *(Can be prepared 1 week ahead. Cover tightly and keep refrigerated.)*

USING foil as aid, lift brownie from pan; trim edges. Cut into 25 squares. Let brownies stand at room temperature 30 minutes before serving.

Double chocolate–cherry brownies

DRIED SOUR OR BING CHERRIES and a hint of cinnamon add original twists to the chocolate standard. And you don't even need a mixing bowl: The batter is made in the saucepan used to melt the chocolate.

MAKES 16 OR 32

- **3/4 cup (1 1/2 sticks) unsalted butter**
- **6 ounces unsweetened chocolate, chopped**
- **2 1/2 cups sugar**
- **4 large eggs**
- **1 large egg yolk**
- **1 1/2 teaspoons vanilla extract**
- **1/2 teaspoon almond extract**
- **1 cup plus 2 tablespoons all purpose flour**
- **1 teaspoon ground cinnamon**
- **1 cup halved dried sour or Bing cherries or chopped pitted prunes**
- **1 cup semisweet chocolate chips (about 6 ounces)**

PREHEAT oven to 350°F. Butter and flour 13x9x2-inch glass baking dish. Melt ¾ cup butter and unsweetened chocolate in heavy large saucepan over low heat, stirring until smooth. Remove from heat. Whisk in sugar, then eggs and egg yolk, 1 at a time. Add vanilla and almond extracts, then flour and cinnamon, and whisk until just combined. Mix in cherries and chocolate chips.

SPREAD batter in prepared pan. Bake until brownie is firm around edges and tester inserted into center comes out with moist crumbs still attached, about 35 minutes. Cool in pan on rack. *(Can be prepared 2 days ahead. Cover pan tightly and store at room temperature.)* Cut into 16 or 32 brownies.

Cherry-fudge brownies with chocolate sauce and chocolate-dipped cherries

THIS DECADENT DESSERT teams cherry-sweetened and -studded brownies with cherry-flavored bittersweet chocolate sauce and pretty chocolate-dipped cherries. All of the components, however, are delicious in their own right—the sauce is especially good poured over scoops of cherry vanilla or Burgundy cherry ice cream.

8 SERVINGS

Sauce

- **1/3 cup cherry preserves**
- **3/4 cup whipping cream**
- **8 ounces bittersweet (not unsweetened) or semisweet chocolate, chopped**

Brownies

- 3 ounces bittersweet (not unsweetened) or semisweet chocolate, chopped
- 5 tablespoons unsalted butter
- 3/4 cup sugar
- 2 large eggs
- 1/2 teaspoon vanilla extract
- 2/3 cup all purpose flour
- 1/2 teaspoon baking powder
- 1/4 teaspoon salt
- 3/4 cup dried tart cherries (about 3 1/2 ounces)
- 1/3 cup semisweet chocolate chips (about 2 ounces)
- 1/4 cup cherry preserves

Powdered sugar
Chocolate-Dipped Cherries (see recipe)

FOR SAUCE: Press preserves through fine strainer into heavy medium saucepan. Add cream and bring to simmer. Remove from heat. Add chocolate and whisk until melted and smooth. *(Sauce can be prepared 2 days ahead. Cover and refrigerate. Rewarm before using.)*

FOR BROWNIES: Preheat oven to 350°F. Butter 11x7x2-inch metal baking pan. Stir chopped chocolate and 5 tablespoons butter in heavy small saucepan over low heat until melted and smooth. Remove from heat. Whisk sugar, eggs, and vanilla in medium bowl until blended; whisk in chocolate mixture. Sift in flour, baking powder, and salt; stir to combine. Mix in dried cherries and chocolate chips, then preserves.

SPREAD batter in prepared pan. Bake brownie until tester inserted into center comes out with some moist crumbs still attached, about 35 minutes. Cool completely in pan on rack.

CUT into 8 rectangles. Cut rectangles diagonally in half, forming triangles. Spoon warm sauce onto 8 plates. Place 2 brownie triangles atop sauce on each plate. Sift powdered sugar over. Garnish with Chocolate-Dipped Cherries.

Chocolate-dipped cherries

YOU CAN ENJOY THESE with the Cherry-Fudge Brownies, on their own, or as part of a dessert buffet. When dipping cherries in melted chocolate, be sure the cherries are completely dry, as even a small amount of water can cause the chocolate to "seize," becoming a chalky, semi-solid mass.

MAKES 24

- 6 ounces bittersweet (not unsweetened) or semisweet chocolate, chopped
- 24 large fresh cherries with stems

LINE baking sheet with waxed paper. Place chocolate in top of double boiler set over barely simmering water. Stir until chocolate is melted and smooth. Remove chocolate from over water. Holding 1 cherry by stem, dip cherry halfway into chocolate. Place cherry, chocolate side down, on prepared sheet. Repeat with remaining cherries and chocolate. Chill cherries until chocolate coating is firm, at least 15 minutes. *(Can be prepared 2 days ahead. Cover loosely and keep chilled.)*

Raspberry truffle brownies

THIS BROWNIE is baked in a round cake pan and then cut into wedges for a unique presentation. When baking brownies, be careful to bake them just until the point when a tester inserted into the center comes out with moist chocolaty crumbs still attached; if baked even a minute too long, brownies lose their fudgy texture and become dry.

MAKES 12

Nonstick vegetable oil spray

- 3/4 cup (1 1/2 sticks) unsalted butter
- 4 ounces unsweetened chocolate, chopped

2 cups sugar
3 large eggs
⅓ cup raspberry jam
3 tablespoons black raspberry liqueur (such as Chambord) or other berry liqueur
1 cup all purpose flour
¼ teaspoon salt
1 cup semisweet chocolate chips (about 6 ounces)

Powdered sugar

PREHEAT oven to 350°F. Spray 9-inch-diameter springform pan with nonstick spray. Stir butter and chocolate in large saucepan over low heat until melted and smooth. Remove from heat. Whisk in 2 cups sugar, then eggs, jam, and liqueur. Stir in flour and salt, then chocolate chips.

TRANSFER batter to prepared pan. Bake brownie until tester inserted into center comes out with moist crumbs still attached, about 45 minutes. Cool in pan on rack. Run small knife around edge of pan; remove pan sides. *(Brownie can be prepared 2 days ahead. Wrap tightly in plastic and store at room temperature.)* Dust brownie with powdered sugar. Cut into 12 wedges and serve.

Fudgy chocolate-raspberry bars

THESE "BARS" are actually a dense chocolate cake that is topped with a glaze made from raspberry jam and bittersweet chocolate and garnished with fresh raspberries. Elegant enough to be served at a dinner party, they also make fancy picnic fare for an outdoor concert.

MAKES 12

Chocolate layer

10 ounces bittersweet (not unsweetened) or semisweet chocolate, chopped
¾ cup (1½ sticks) unsalted butter, cut into small pieces
⅓ cup seedless raspberry jam
5 large eggs
1 cup sugar
⅓ cup all purpose flour
1 teaspoon baking powder

Glaze

¼ cup whipping cream
¼ cup seedless raspberry jam
6 ounces bittersweet (not unsweetened) or semisweet chocolate, chopped

2 ½-pint containers fresh raspberries

FOR CHOCOLATE LAYER: Preheat oven to 350°F. Line 9x9x2-inch metal baking pan with aluminum foil. Butter foil; dust with flour. Stir chocolate and butter in heavy medium saucepan over low heat until melted and smooth. Add jam and whisk until melted. Cool slightly.

USING electric mixer, beat eggs and sugar in large bowl until mixture is very thick, about 6 minutes. Sift flour and baking powder over egg mixture and fold in. Gradually fold in chocolate mixture.

POUR batter into pan. Bake until top is slightly crusty and begins to crack, and tester inserted into center comes out with moist crumbs still attached, about 45 minutes. Cool 5 minutes. Gently press down any raised edges to even top. Cool in pan. Invert onto platter. Peel off foil. Trim ½ inch off each edge.

FOR GLAZE: Stir cream and jam in heavy small saucepan over medium heat until jam melts; bring to boil. Remove from heat. Add chocolate and stir until melted. Let stand until cool and thickened but still spreadable, about 15 minutes.

SPREAD glaze over top of chocolate layer. Immediately arrange berries atop glaze, pressing lightly to adhere. Chill until glaze sets, about 10 minutes. *(Can be prepared 1 day ahead. Cover and keep chilled.)*

CUT into 12 bars and serve.

Mint brownies

THESE SMALL, moist peppermint-scented brownies have both a thin, white, peppermint-flavored icing and a dark chocolate coating on top. They can be made ahead and frozen, well wrapped, up to two weeks. Thaw the brownies briefly in the refrigerator and serve cold with mint-chip ice cream for a cool, refreshing treat.

MAKES 25

Brownies

- **½ cup (1 stick) unsalted butter**
- **2 ounces unsweetened chocolate, chopped**
- **2 large eggs**
- **1 cup sugar**
- **½ cup all purpose flour**
- **½ teaspoon peppermint extract**
- **½ teaspoon vanilla extract**
- **Pinch of salt**
- **½ cup chopped pecans**

Toppings

- **1 cup sifted powdered sugar**
- **4 tablespoons (½ stick) unsalted butter, room temperature, divided**
- **1 tablespoon whole milk**
- **¼ teaspoon peppermint extract**

- **4 ounces semisweet chocolate, chopped**

FOR BROWNIES: Preheat oven to 350°F. Lightly butter 8x8x2-inch metal baking pan. Stir ½ cup butter and chocolate in small saucepan over low heat until melted and smooth. Set aside. Using electric mixer, beat eggs and sugar in large bowl until light and fluffy, about 5 minutes. Add chocolate mixture, flour, peppermint and vanilla extracts, and salt; stir until just combined. Mix in nuts.

TRANSFER batter to prepared pan. Bake brownie until tester inserted into center comes out with moist crumbs still attached, about 25 minutes. Cool slightly.

FOR TOPPINGS: Beat powdered sugar, 2 tablespoons butter, milk, and extract in bowl until creamy. Spread over warm brownies. Refrigerate until set, about 1 hour.

STIR chocolate and remaining 2 tablespoons butter in small saucepan over low heat until smooth. Cool slightly. Pour over mint topping, spreading evenly. Cover and refrigerate until set, about 1 hour. *(Can be prepared 8 hours ahead. Cover with aluminum foil and keep refrigerated.)*

CUT into 25 pieces. Serve at room temperature.

Peanut butter and chocolate chunk brownies

THE NAME *BROWNIE* is slightly misleading here: These are golden-brown peanut butter bars with a moist brownie-like texture, studded with chunks of chocolate. Be sure to use the natural, old-fashioned-style or freshly ground peanut butter in this recipe for best results. If desired, you can use ⅔ cup of semisweet chocolate chips in place of the bittersweet chunks.

MAKES 25

- **6 tablespoons (¾ stick) unsalted butter, room temperature**
- **½ cup nutty old-fashioned-style or freshly ground peanut butter, stirred to blend if separated**
- **1¼ cups (packed) golden brown sugar**
- **2 large eggs**
- **2 teaspoons vanilla extract**
- **¾ cup all purpose flour**
- **1 teaspoon baking powder**
- **¼ teaspoon salt**
- **4 ounces bittersweet (not unsweetened) or semisweet chocolate, coarsely chopped**

PREHEAT oven to 350°F. Generously butter and flour 8x8x2-inch metal baking pan. Using electric mixer, beat 6 tablespoons butter in large bowl until smooth. Add peanut butter to bowl; beat until well blended, scraping down sides of bowl occasionally. Beat in sugar. Add eggs 1 at a time, beating well after each addition. Beat in vanilla. Sift flour, baking powder, and salt into medium bowl. Add to peanut butter mixture; beat until blended. Stir in chocolate pieces.

TRANSFER batter to pan and spread evenly. Bake brownies until tester inserted 2 inches from edge of pan comes out with moist crumbs still attached, about 33 minutes. Transfer pan to rack and cool completely. *(Can be prepared 3 days ahead. Cover tightly and store at room temperature.)*

CUT brownie into 25 squares.

Candy

Rich dark chocolate truffles

FOR SUCCESS when making truffles, your kitchen should be no warmer than 70°F. Work quickly, and refrigerate the truffles as soon as possible after dipping. A candy thermometer ensures that the dipping chocolate is just the right temperature–too warm, and the coating will be grainy; too cool, and truffles will develop a white, powdery "bloom." It's easy to dip the truffles with your fingers, but you can also submerge each truffle in the melted chocolate and lift it out with a fork; then tap the fork against the side of the pan to remove any excess chocolate and use a knife to slide the truffle off the fork and onto the baking sheet. Or skip the dipping and simply roll the truffles in cocoa powder or powdered sugar.

MAKES 16

Truffle centers

- **½ cup whipping cream**
- **¼ cup (½ stick) unsalted butter**
- **12 ounces bittersweet (not unsweetened) or semisweet chocolate, finely chopped**
- **½ teaspoon vanilla extract**

Sifted unsweetened cocoa powder

Truffle coating

- **1½ pounds bittersweet (not unsweetened) or semisweet chocolate, finely chopped**

Chocolate curls (optional)
Paper candy cups (optional)

FOR TRUFFLE CENTERS: Bring cream and butter to simmer in heavy small saucepan over medium heat, stirring frequently. Reduce heat to low. Add 12 ounces bittersweet chocolate and whisk until smooth. Pour into small bowl. Stir in vanilla. Freeze chocolate mixture until firm enough to hold shape, about 20 minutes.

LINE 2 rimmed baking sheets with waxed paper. Dust paper on 1 sheet generously with sifted cocoa powder. Spoon 16 mounds chocolate mixture onto prepared sheet, using about 2 tablespoonfuls for each. Freeze until mounds are almost firm, about 8 minutes.

ROLL each mound in cocoa powder on waxed paper, then roll between palms of hands into smooth ball. Set on second waxed paper–lined baking sheet. Cover with plastic wrap. Freeze until ready to dip, up to 1 month.

FOR TRUFFLE COATING: Fill bottom section of small double boiler half-full with water and bring to rolling boil. Turn off heat. Place 1½ pounds chopped bittersweet chocolate in top section of double boiler and place over hot water. Attach candy thermometer. Let stand until chocolate is melted and thermometer registers between 115°F and 120°F, stirring occasionally. Remove top section of double boiler from over water.

LINE clean rimmed baking sheet with waxed paper. Working with 1 truffle center at a time and using thumb and index finger, dip center into melted chocolate. Lift out, shaking gently so excess chocolate drips back into pan. Drop truffle on prepared baking sheet. If necessary, dip index finger into melted chocolate to dab truffle where not completely coated. Attach 1 chocolate curl to truffle, if desired. If temperature of melted chocolate falls below 115°F, rewarm chocolate over hot water in bottom section of double boiler. Refrigerate coated truffles on sheet until coating is set, 30 minutes to 1 hour.

IF DESIRED, transfer truffles to paper candy cups, wrapping fingers in plastic or using rubber gloves to avoid leaving fingerprints on truffles. *(Can be prepared ahead. Store in airtight container in single layer in refrigerator up to 2 weeks, or freeze up to 1 month.)*

Pecan toffee

WHEN MAKING CANDY such as this tasty toffee, use a saucepan of approximately 10- to 12-cup volume, and at least three inches deep; this will allow the ingredients to boil while avoiding a dangerous boil-over. The pan should also have a very heavy bottom so the mixture does not burn. And to avoid burning yourself, use a wooden spoon or spatula with an extra-long handle for the stirring.

MAKES ABOUT 1½ POUNDS

- **1 cup (2 sticks) unsalted butter**
- **1½ cups sugar**
- **¼ teaspoon cream of tartar**
- **6 ounces bittersweet (not unsweetened) or semisweet chocolate, finely chopped**
- **1 cup coarsely chopped pecans**

LINE 9x9x2-inch metal baking pan with aluminum foil, leaving overhang. Butter foil. Melt 1 cup butter in heavy medium saucepan over medium heat. Add sugar and cream of tartar; stir until sugar dissolves. Increase heat to medium-high. Brush down sides of pan with wet pastry brush. Attach clip-on candy thermometer. Cook until mixture registers 310°F, stirring occasionally, about 11 minutes.

IMMEDIATELY pour toffee into prepared pan. Let stand 1 minute. Sprinkle with chocolate. Let stand 2 minutes to soften. Spread chocolate over toffee layer with back of spoon until melted and smooth. Sprinkle with pecans. Refrigerate until firm. Using foil as aid, lift toffee from pan. Break into 3-inch pieces. *(Can be prepared 4 days ahead. Store in airtight container in refrigerator.)*

Buttery hazelnut toffee

BROWN SUGAR AND HONEY add complexity and extra richness to this crunchy favorite. If you love almonds, you can use them in place of the hazelnuts. When cooking the toffee, it is very important to stir the mixture slowly but constantly to keep the butter emulsified.

MAKES ABOUT 1½ POUNDS

- **1¼ cups (2½ sticks) unsalted butter**
- **1 cup sugar**
- **¼ cup (packed) golden brown sugar**
- **¼ cup water**
- **1 tablespoon honey**

1 cup very coarsely chopped skinned toasted hazelnuts
6 ounces bittersweet (not unsweetened) or semisweet chocolate, finely chopped
½ cup finely chopped skinned toasted hazelnuts

BUTTER small rimmed baking sheet. Melt butter in heavy large saucepan over low heat. Add both sugars, ¼ cup water, and honey; stir until sugars dissolve. Attach clip-on candy thermometer. Increase heat to medium and cook until thermometer registers 290°F, stirring slowly but constantly and scraping bottom of pan with wooden spatula, about 15 minutes.

REMOVE pan from heat. Mix in 1 cup coarsely chopped nuts. Immediately pour mixture onto prepared sheet; do not scrape pan. Let stand 1 minute. Sprinkle toffee with chocolate. Let stand 2 minutes to soften. Spread chocolate evenly over toffee with back of spoon until melted. Sprinkle with finely chopped nuts. Refrigerate until firm. Break into 3-inch pieces. *(Can be prepared 4 days ahead. Store in airtight container in refrigerator.)*

Chocolate-hazelnut panforte

PANFORTE (OR "STRONG BREAD")—a specialty of Siena, Italy—is a dense, chewy, candy-like fruitcake. Traditionally associated with Christmas, the confection dates back to the Middle Ages; depending on which legend you prefer, the delicacy was either made by nuns or paid to them as a kind of tithe. The addition of chocolate makes this centuries-old recipe a modern treat. Citron looks like a large lemon but is used almost exclusively for its thick peel, which is candied and sold at specialty foods stores, candy and nut shops, and some supermarkets. This is a rich treat, so slice it into thin wedges. Or wrap entire cakes or wedges in brightly colored cellophane to give as gifts.

MAKES 2 CAKES

¼ cup (½ stick) unsalted butter, melted

1½ cups hazelnuts
1 cup whole unblanched almonds

1½ cups (lightly packed) chopped dried stemmed Calimyrna figs (about 9 ounces)
1½ cups (lightly packed) chopped dried apricots (about 9 ounces)
1 cup diced candied citron (about 5 ounces)
2 tablespoons grated orange peel
1 tablespoon grated lemon peel
¾ cup unbleached all purpose flour
¾ cup unsweetened cocoa powder (preferably Dutch-process)
1½ teaspoons ground cinnamon
1 teaspoon (scant) ground nutmeg
1 teaspoon (scant) ground coriander
¼ teaspoon ground black pepper
¼ teaspoon ground cloves

1 cup plus 2 tablespoons sugar
1 cup plus 2 tablespoons honey

6 ounces bittersweet (not unsweetened) or semisweet chocolate, melted

Additional unsweetened cocoa powder

POSITION rack in center of oven and preheat to 400°F. Brush two 8-inch-diameter cake pans with some of melted butter. Line pan bottoms with parchment paper. Brush parchment generously with melted butter. Reserve remaining melted butter.

PLACE hazelnuts on small rimmed baking sheet; place almonds on another small sheet. Toast nuts in oven until brown and fragrant, stirring occasionally, about 10 minutes for almonds and 14 minutes for hazelnuts. Cool. Gather hazelnuts in kitchen towel. Rub in towel to remove skins. Transfer hazelnuts and almonds to large bowl. Reduce oven temperature to 300°F.

ADD figs, apricots, citron, orange peel, and lemon peel to nuts in large bowl. Whisk flour, ¾ cup cocoa powder, and spices in small bowl to blend. Add to nut mixture.

COMBINE sugar, honey, and reserved melted butter in heavy medium saucepan. Stir over medium heat until mixture is smooth and sugar is almost dissolved, about 5 minutes. Attach clip-on candy thermometer. Bring to boil. Continue to cook, without stirring, until thermometer registers 248°F (firm-ball stage). Immediately pour syrup over nut mixture and stir to combine thoroughly.

DIVIDE batter between prepared pans, using back of buttered spoon to spread evenly. Bake until tops and edges just begin to brown and tops feel dry, about 1 hour 15 minutes. Transfer cakes to racks and cool slightly. Cut around edges of pans to loosen cakes. Turn cakes out onto work surface; peel off parchment. Cool cakes completely.

ARRANGE each cake, right side up, on 8-inch cardboard round. Spread half of melted chocolate over each. Refrigerate until chocolate is set, about 1 hour.

BRUSH tops of cakes with cocoa powder. Wrap tightly with plastic wrap, then aluminum foil. *(Panforte can be prepared up to 1 month ahead. Store at cool room temperature.)*

Cayenne-cashew crunch

CAYENNE—a pungent spice made from ground dried red chiles—and cashews are native to neighboring regions in South America: Guyana and northeastern Brazil, respectively. Perhaps that is why they combine so well in this unique spicy nut brittle. Keep sealed in jars at room temperature up to 10 days.

MAKES ABOUT 1⅓ POUNDS

- **2 cups whole salted cashews**
- **10 tablespoons (1¼ sticks) unsalted butter**
- **½ cup sugar**
- **¼ cup (packed) golden brown sugar**
- **1 tablespoon light corn syrup**
- **1 teaspoon cayenne pepper**
- **¼ teaspoon salt**

BUTTER rimmed nonstick baking sheet. Combine all ingredients in large nonstick skillet. Stir over low heat until butter melts and sugars dissolve. Increase heat to medium and boil, stirring constantly, until mixture turns golden brown, thickens, and begins to come together, about 5 minutes. Immediately pour out onto prepared sheet and spread evenly. Cool completely. Break into pieces. *(Can be prepared 10 days ahead. Store in airtight container at room temperature.)*

Peanut butter–chocolate bark triangles

ORIGINALLY NAMED FOR its resemblance to the bark of a tree, this refined version makes a perfect gift for the peanut-butter-and-chocolate fan. The combination of three chocolates with peanut butter, peanuts, and peanut brittle is inspired. If you have a rimless baking sheet, you can use it instead of an inverted rimmed one.

MAKES 40 PIECES

- **10 ounces bittersweet (not unsweetened) or semisweet chocolate, coarsely chopped**
- **6 ounces high-quality white chocolate (such as Lindt or Perugina), coarsely chopped**
- **½ cup creamy peanut butter (do not use old-fashioned-style or freshly ground)**
- **⅓ cup chopped lightly salted cocktail peanuts**
- **1¾ cups chopped peanut brittle (about 8 ounces), divided**
- **8 ounces high-quality milk chocolate (such as Lindt or Perugina), coarsely chopped**

TURN large baking sheet upside down. Cover tightly with aluminum foil. Mark 12x9-inch rectangle on foil. Stir bittersweet chocolate in medium metal bowl set over saucepan of barely simmering water (do not allow bottom of bowl to touch water) until chocolate melts and thermometer inserted into chocolate registers 115°F. Remove from over water. Spoon 2 tablespoons melted chocolate into small metal bowl and reserve. Pour remaining melted chocolate onto marked rectangle on foil. Using offset spatula, spread chocolate to fill rectangle. Refrigerate to set chocolate while making peanut butter filling.

STIR white chocolate and peanut butter in heavy medium saucepan over medium-low heat until mixture is blended and smooth. Remove from heat. Mix in chopped nuts. Cool mixture to barely lukewarm, about 10 minutes. Pour over bittersweet chocolate rectangle. Working quickly, spread to cover completely. Sprinkle evenly with ¾ cup chopped brittle. Chill until very firm, about 20 minutes.

STIR milk chocolate in medium metal bowl set over saucepan of barely simmering water (do not allow bottom of bowl to touch water) until chocolate melts and thermometer inserted into chocolate registers 115°F. Remove from over water. Pour chocolate over brittle, spreading quickly to cover. Sprinkle evenly with remaining 1 cup brittle. Stir reserved 2 tablespoons bittersweet chocolate over simmering water until just warm. Dip spoon in chocolate and drizzle lines over brittle. Refrigerate bark until firm enough to cut, about 20 minutes.

LIFT foil with bark onto work surface. Cut crosswise into 5 equal strips. Cut each strip crosswise into 4 sections and each section diagonally into 2 triangles. *(Can be prepared 2 weeks ahead. Store in airtight container in refrigerator. Let stand at room temperature at least 30 minutes and up to 1 hour before serving.)*

Double-decker mint patties

WHEN PREPARING these elegant candies, be sure to use peppermint extract, not spearmint extract. If you're looking to make an after-dinner mint in minutes, you can simply cut the white and dark chocolate "bar" into one-inch squares instead of rounds, and forego the chocolate dipping.

MAKES ABOUT 16

¼ cup plus 2 tablespoons whipping cream
2 tablespoons (¼ stick) unsalted butter
22 ounces bittersweet (not unsweetened) or semisweet chocolate, finely chopped, divided
½ teaspoon peppermint extract, divided

6 ounces high-quality white chocolate (such as Lindt or Perugina), finely chopped
2 teaspoons sour cream

16 (about) paper candy cups

LINE 9½x5½-inch loaf pan with aluminum foil, leaving overhang. Bring ¼ cup cream and butter to boil in heavy small saucepan. Reduce heat to low. Add 6 ounces bittersweet chocolate and stir until melted and smooth. Mix in ¼ teaspoon peppermint extract. Pour into prepared pan. Freeze until firm, at least 45 minutes.

BRING remaining 2 tablespoons cream to boil in heavy small saucepan. Reduce heat to low. Add white chocolate and stir until melted and smooth. Remove from heat and stir in sour cream and remaining ¼ teaspoon peppermint extract. Cool to lukewarm. Pour over dark chocolate layer. Smooth with back of spoon. Tap pan on counter to even. Freeze candy until firm, about 1 hour.

LINE rimmed baking sheet with waxed paper. Using foil sides as aid, lift chocolate from pan. Cut into 1¼-inch rounds, using cookie cutter dipped into hot water and wiped clean between cuts. Set rounds on prepared sheet. Freeze until very firm, about 1 hour.

MELT remaining 16 ounces bittersweet chocolate in top of double boiler set over barely simmering water, stirring frequently, until thermometer inserted into chocolate registers 115°F. Remove from over water. Working quickly, submerge 1 patty into chocolate, white chocolate side up. Scoop out using long dinner fork. Tap fork sharply and quickly on sides of pan, allowing excess chocolate to drip back into pan. Using small knife, slide patty off fork and onto prepared sheet. Lightly press back side of fork atop patty and lift off, forming decorative pattern. Repeat with remaining patties, setting double boiler over hot water occasionally if necessary to rewarm chocolate. Refrigerate candies until firm.

SET candies in paper candy cups. *(Can be prepared 1 week ahead. Store in airtight container in single layer in refrigerator.)* Let stand at room temperature 10 minutes before serving.

Classic bittersweet chocolate fudge

FUDGE IS A CLASSIC CANDY made by cooking a mixture of milk and sugar to the soft-ball stage, then adding flavors (such as bittersweet chocolate and vanilla) and beating until the candy develops its characteristic fine, smooth texture. It's an ideal candy for the beginning confectioner—it's simple, can be prepared a week ahead, and makes a lovely gift.

MAKES 24 PIECES

- **6 ounces bittersweet (not unsweetened) or semisweet chocolate, chopped**
- **¼ cup marshmallow creme**
- **1 ounce unsweetened chocolate, chopped**
- **1 teaspoon vanilla extract**
- **1½ cups sugar**
- **¾ cup sweetened condensed milk**
- **⅓ cup water**
- **⅓ cup whipping cream**
- **¼ cup (½ stick) unsalted butter, cut into pieces**
- **¾ cup coarsely broken toasted walnut pieces (optional)**
- **24 paper candy cups**

LINE 9½x5½-inch loaf pan with aluminum foil, leaving overhang. Place bittersweet chocolate and next 3 ingredients in medium metal bowl. Combine sugar, milk, ⅓ cup water, cream, and butter in heavy large saucepan. Stir over medium-low heat until sugar dissolves. Brush down sugar crystals from sides of pan using wet pastry brush. Attach clip-on candy thermometer. Increase heat to high and bring to rolling boil. Reduce heat to medium-high and stir constantly but slowly with wooden spoon until thermometer registers 232°F, about 9 minutes.

POUR mixture over ingredients in bowl; do not scrape pan. Stir vigorously with wooden spoon until chocolates melt and fudge thickens slightly, about 3 minutes (mixture will still be very glossy). Stir in walnuts, if desired. Transfer fudge to prepared pan; smooth top with rubber spatula. Refrigerate uncovered until firm enough to cut, about 2 hours.

USING foil as aid, lift fudge from pan. Fold down foil sides. Trim ends of fudge. Cut into 24 pieces. Place in paper candy cups. *(Can be prepared 1 week ahead. Store in airtight container in refrigerator. Bring to room temperature before serving.)*

Caramel-dipped apples

THESE TREATS are perfect to serve at a Halloween party for kids and grown-ups. Creating clever decorations on the apples adds to the fun. Note that preparing the caramel requires the use of a clip-on candy thermometer.

MAKES 12

- **1 1-pound box dark brown sugar**
- **1 cup (2 sticks) unsalted butter, room temperature**
- **1 14-ounce can sweetened condensed milk**
- **⅔ cup dark corn syrup**
- **⅓ cup pure maple syrup**
- **1½ teaspoons vanilla extract**
- **1 teaspoon robust-flavored (dark) molasses**
- **¼ teaspoon salt**
- **12 chopsticks**
- **12 medium Granny Smith apples, stemmed**
- **Assorted decorations (such as chopped nuts, chopped dried apricots, dried cranberries, toffee bits, mini M&M's, and candy sprinkles)**
- **Melted dark, milk, and/or white chocolates (optional)**
- **Whipping cream (if necessary)**

COMBINE sugar and next 7 ingredients in heavy large saucepan (about 3 inches deep). Stir with wooden spatula or spoon over medium-low heat until sugar dissolves (no crystals are felt when caramel is rubbed between fingers), occasionally brushing down sides of pan with wet pastry brush, about 15 minutes.

ATTACH clip-on candy thermometer. Increase heat to medium-high and cook caramel at rolling boil until thermometer registers 236°F, stirring constantly but slowly with clean wooden spatula and occasionally brushing down sides of pan with wet pastry brush, about 12 minutes. Pour caramel into metal bowl (do not scrape pan). Submerge thermometer bulb in caramel. Cool without stirring to 200°F, about 20 minutes.

WHILE caramel cools, line 2 rimmed baking sheets with aluminum foil; butter foil. Push 1 chopstick into stem end of each apple. Set up decorations and melted chocolates, if desired.

HOLDING chopstick, dip 1 apple into 200°F caramel, submerging all but very top of apple. Lift apple out, allowing excess caramel to drip back into bowl. Turn apple caramel side up and hold for several seconds to help set caramel around apple. Stand coated apple on prepared foil (with chopstick up). Repeat with remaining apples and caramel, spacing apples apart (caramel will pool on foil). If caramel becomes too thick to dip into, add 1 to 2 tablespoons whipping cream, place bowl over low heat, and briefly whisk to thin.

REFRIGERATE apples on sheets until caramel is partially set, about 15 minutes. Lift 1 apple from foil. Using hand, press pooled caramel smoothly around apple; return to foil. Repeat with remaining apples.

WORKING with 1 apple at a time, firmly press decorations into caramel and return apple to foil. Or dip caramel-coated apples into melted chocolate, if desired, allowing excess to drip off, then roll in nuts or candy. Or drizzle melted chocolate over caramel-coated apples and sprinkle with decorations. Refrigerate apples until decorations are set, about 1 hour. *(Can be made 1 week ahead, cover and keep chilled.)*

Pecan Turtles

ANY NUT WILL WORK HERE, so you're welcome to make almond, walnut, or macadamia Turtles if you prefer. For a pretty decoration, drizzle melted white or milk chocolate in a zigzag pattern atop the Turtles. Although these candies are certainly irresistible, do not try to double or triple this recipe, as the results will not be the same.

MAKES ABOUT 26

2 cups (about) pecan halves
1⅓ cups whipping cream
1 cup sugar
½ cup light corn syrup
⅓ cup whole milk
¼ cup (½ stick) unsalted butter
1 teaspoon vanilla extract

12 ounces bittersweet (not unsweetened) or semisweet chocolate, chopped

BUTTER 2 rimmed nonstick baking sheets. On prepared sheets, arrange pecan halves in clusters resembling turtles. Combine cream, sugar, corn syrup, milk, and ¼ cup butter in heavy medium saucepan. Stir over low heat until sugar dissolves. Attach clip-on candy thermometer. Increase heat to high and boil without stirring until mixture turns golden and is bubbling thickly, and thermometer registers 234°F, swirling pan occasionally, about 15 minutes. Remove pan from heat. Stir in vanilla. Immediately drop 1 tablespoon caramel mixture onto center of each pecan cluster. Cool slightly.

STIR chocolate in top of double boiler set over simmering water until melted and warm to touch. Drizzle 1 tablespoon chocolate over each candy. Refrigerate candies until chocolate sets, about 1 hour. *(Can be prepared 1 week ahead. Cover and keep refrigerated. Let stand 30 minutes at room temperature before serving.)*

Drinks 22

No matter what mood you're in, there's a drink to match it.

Leaving aside those dark, brooding moods that lend themselves to straight shots of whiskey—no recipe needed for that—we think there's something inherently positive about mixing up a drink. Measuring, stirring, shaking, blending . . . these are little acts of creativity that transform disparate ingredients into something deliciously new and unexpected. Naturally, you want to share these creations with others.

In this chapter you'll find an entire spectrum of beverage options: cool cocktails for alfresco summer parties; rich, cinnamon-accented hot chocolate for winter evening get-togethers; a flaming Café Brûlot to be presented as a dramatic after-dinner finale; fruity smoothies for weekend brunches.

So when you say, "Stop by for a drink," you're opening the door to all kinds of possibilities—a relaxed evening with friends, a jazzy cocktail party, an impromptu celebration, or just plain kicking back.

And that puts everyone in a *good* mood.

Non-alcoholic

Lime, mint, and honeydew smoothie

PREPARE THE LIME "ICE CUBES" the night before. You can also use them in other drinks and cocktails, like slushy Margaritas and Mojitos, or add them to a bowl of tropical fruit punch.

1 SERVING

- **1/3 cup fresh lime juice**
- **1 1/2 cups cubed peeled seeded honeydew melon, chilled**
- **1/2 cup plain yogurt**
- **1/4 cup sugar**
- **12 large fresh mint leaves**
- **Lime wedge**
- **Mint sprig**

POUR lime juice into 4 individual ice-cube molds or small custard cups, dividing equally. Freeze until firm, at least 8 hours.

COMBINE honeydew and next 3 ingredients with frozen lime cubes in blender. Blend until smooth. Pour into glass. Garnish with lime wedge and mint.

Very berry yogurt smoothie

FROZEN BERRIES work beautifully in this delicious drink and make it a snap to prepare. Stocking the freezer with an assortment of berries means a breakfast on the go can be ready in minutes.

2 SERVINGS

- **1 3/4 cups low-fat blueberry yogurt**
- **1/4 cup grape juice**
- **1 1/2 cups frozen blueberries**
- **1 cup frozen blackberries**

COMBINE yogurt and juice in blender. Add berries. Blend until mixture is thick and smooth. Pour into glasses and serve immediately.

Banana, honey, and soy milk smoothie

IF STORED at room temperature alongside citrus fruit, bananas will go from green to spotted (the sign of ripeness) within a matter of days. In order to use them in this recipe or preserve them for future use, peel the ripe bananas, then wrap them in plastic and freeze. Soy milk contains more protein than cow's milk, yet no cholesterol. This healthful smoothie could make a satisfying breakfast.

2 SERVINGS

- **1 1/2 ripe bananas, peeled, cut into 1/2-inch rounds, frozen**
- **1 cup light (1%) soy milk**
- **1 cup ice cubes**
- **1 tablespoon honey**
- **1/2 teaspoon vanilla extract**

COMBINE all ingredients in blender. Blend until smooth. Pour into 2 glasses and serve immediately.

Watermelon and strawberry smoothie

WITH TWO INGREDIENTS—and no dairy—this drink couldn't be simpler or more refreshing. A ripe watermelon will give a hollow sound when you smack it with your palm. Keep it in the fridge if possible, and use it within a few days.

4 SERVINGS

- **6 cups ½-inch cubes seeded watermelon, divided**
- **1 pint strawberry sorbet, divided**
- **Fresh strawberries**

COMBINE 3 cups watermelon and half of sorbet in blender. Blend until mixture is smooth, about 1 minute. Transfer mixture to pitcher. Repeat with remaining watermelon and sorbet. Divide smoothie among 4 glasses. Garnish with fresh strawberries and serve immediately.

Papaya-pineapple smoothie

WHEN SELECTING PAPAYA, look for those with brightly colored golden skin. The fruit should give just slightly when pressed. Papayas are a good source of vitamins A and C. To boost the calcium and protein content of the smoothie, blend in a few tablespoons of nonfat dry milk or protein powder.

2 SERVINGS

- **1 cup diced peeled fresh or frozen pineapple**
- **1 cup diced peeled seeded papaya**
- **1 cup ice cubes**
- **¾ cup unsweetened pineapple juice**
- **½ teaspoon vanilla extract**
- **2 papaya slices**
- **2 pineapple slices**

COMBINE diced pineapple, diced papaya, ice cubes, pineapple juice, and vanilla in blender. Puree until smooth. Pour smoothie into 2 glasses. Top each smoothie with 1 papaya and 1 pineapple slice.

Double-raspberry malt for two

THIS COULD BE a sweet dessert after a romantic dinner (don't forget two straws and two long spoons) or a summer afternoon treat.

2 SERVINGS

- **1 6-ounce basket fresh raspberries**
- **¼ cup whole milk**
- **¼ cup malted milk powder**
- **1 tablespoon sugar**
- **1 cup vanilla ice cream**
- **1 small scoop raspberry sorbet**

Set aside 4 raspberries for garnish. Combine remaining raspberries, milk, malted milk powder, and sugar in blender; blend until smooth. Add ice cream; blend until smooth, stopping once or twice to scrape down sides of blender, if necessary. Pour malted shake into fluted soda-fountain-style glass. Top with sorbet. Garnish with reserved berries.

Coffee date shake

THE DATES add an intriguing twist—and healthy fiber—to a simple coffee milkshake.

2 SERVINGS

- **½ cup lightly packed pitted dates, minced to paste**
- **½ cup whole milk**
- **2 teaspoons dark corn syrup**
- **4 ice cubes**
- **1 pint coffee ice cream**

COMBINE dates, milk, and corn syrup in blender; blend until smooth. Add ice cubes, then ice cream, and blend until thick and smooth. Pour into 2 chilled glasses and serve immediately.

Cranberry-tangerine cooler

THE CRANBERRY FLAVOR gives this a holiday feel—but since it's prepared with bottled cranberry juice, it's easy to make any time of year. This sunrise-tinted juice can be blended and chilled one day ahead.

6 SERVINGS

- **1 48-ounce bottle cranberry juice cocktail, chilled**
- **3 cups freshly squeezed tangerine juice or purchased tangerine juice, chilled**
- **½ cup fresh lime juice, chilled**

- **2 tangerines, unpeeled**

COMBINE cranberry juice and tangerine juice in large pitcher. Add lime juice and stir to blend. *(Can be made 1 day ahead. Cover and refrigerate.)*

CUT thin slice off tops and bottoms of tangerines. Cut each horizontally into three ¼- to ⅓-inch-thick rounds. Divide cooler among 6 tall glasses. Garnish with tangerine rounds and serve.

Strawberry-kiwi sangria with rose geranium

THE AROMATIC, rose-scented leaves from rose geraniums impart an exotic flavor to this nonalcoholic cooler. If you can't find pesticide-free rose geraniums at your local nursery, use rose water, which is available at Middle Eastern markets and specialty foods stores. A splash of white Muscat or light rum may be added for those who prefer a more spirited sangria.

12 SERVINGS

- **8 cups water, divided**
- **8 wild-berry tea bags**
- **2 cups sugar**

- **4 1-pint baskets strawberries, hulled, divided**
- **2 25.4-ounce (750-ml) bottles chilled sparkling apple cider**
- **6 kiwis, peeled, cut into ½-inch cubes**
- **16 fresh rose geranium leaves, crushed slightly, or ¾ teaspoon rose water**
- **4 cups ice cubes**

BRING 4 cups water to boil in large saucepan. Add tea bags; cover and let steep 10 minutes. Discard tea bags. Add sugar to hot tea; stir until dissolved. Stir in remaining 4 cups water. Chill tea until cold, about 3 hours. *(Can be made 1 day ahead. Cover; keep chilled.)*

PUREE 2 baskets strawberries in processor. Slice remaining 2 baskets strawberries. Place pureed and sliced berries in large pitcher (or divide between 2 pitchers). Add tea and all remaining ingredients. Stir and serve.

Crushed-mint lemonade

THIS THIRST QUENCHER is easily doubled to cool off a crowd. To extract juices from lemons, start with room-temperature fruit, then roll them back and forth on the kitchen counter while pressing down firmly before cutting them in half. Try it with large limes instead of lemons for a refreshing limeade, adding more sugar as needed.

4 TO 6 SERVINGS

- **6 large lemons, scrubbed, thinly sliced**
- **1 small bunch fresh mint, thick stems trimmed (about 2 loosely packed cups)**
- **1¼ cups sugar, divided**
- **½ cup fresh lemon juice**
- **2 cups water**
- **Ice cubes**

USING potato masher, mash sliced lemons, mint, 1 cup sugar, and lemon juice in large bowl until juicy, about 5 minutes. Strain lemon mixture through coarse sieve set over another large bowl, pressing masher on solids in sieve to extract some pulp and as much liquid as possible. Mix 2 cups water and remaining ¼ cup sugar into lemon liquid and pulp in bowl. Fill pitcher with ice; pour lemonade over ice. Let stand 5 minutes. Fill 4 to 6 tall glasses with ice; add lemonade.

Iced espresso–almond latte

ALMOND SYRUP is available at some coffeehouses and in the coffee and tea section of most supermarkets. Other flavored syrups, such as hazelnut, amaretto, and vanilla, make good alternatives to the almond syrup. Serve with biscotti for a light and easy summer dessert.

6 SERVINGS

2 cups plus 1 teaspoon finely ground espresso coffee beans
3 cups water
3 tablespoons golden brown sugar
1½ cups whole milk
5 teaspoons almond syrup (such as Torani)

Ice cubes
Espresso Whipped Cream (see recipe)

FILL coffee filter or basket of coffeemaker with 1 cup ground espresso beans. Add 1½ cups water to coffeemaker and brew. Pour coffee into bowl. Repeat with 1 cup ground espresso beans and remaining 1½ cups water to make total of approximately 2 cups coffee. Mix in sugar, then milk and almond syrup. Refrigerate mixture until cold, at least 2 hours and up to 1 day.

FILL 6 glasses with ice. Divide coffee mixture among glasses. Top each with Espresso Whipped Cream. Sprinkle with remaining 1 teaspoon ground espresso beans.

Espresso whipped cream

THIS VERSION of whipped cream would also add pizzazz to an array of desserts and beverages, including hot fudge sundaes, chocolate puddings or mousses, molten chocolate cakes, and cups of hot cocoa or espresso. If you don't have espresso powder, coffee powder makes a good substitute.

MAKES ABOUT 2 CUPS

1 cup chilled whipping cream
3 tablespoons golden brown sugar
1 teaspoon vanilla extract
1 teaspoon instant espresso powder

BEAT all ingredients in medium bowl to soft peaks. *(Can be made 4 hours ahead; cover and chill.)*

Black currant iced tea with cinnamon and ginger

THIS HERBAL ICED TEA has a nice crimson color. For a frosted look, freeze the glasses about an hour ahead of time, and dip the rims into sugar before pouring the tea.

8 SERVINGS

6 cups water
12 bags of wild black currant herbal tea
2 3-inch-long cinnamon sticks, broken in half
1 tablespoon (packed) minced peeled fresh ginger
6 tablespoons frozen raspberry-cranberry juice concentrate
¼ cup sugar

Ice cubes
8 cinnamon sticks
8 quarter-size pieces crystallized ginger

BRING 6 cups water to boil in large saucepan. Add tea bags, broken cinnamon sticks, and fresh ginger. Remove from heat; cover and steep 10 minutes. Mix in juice concentrate and sugar; stir until sugar dissolves. Refrigerate until cold. Strain tea mixture into pitcher. *(Can be prepared 1 day ahead. Cover and keep refrigerated.)*

FILL 8 wineglasses with ice. Pour tea mixture over. Garnish with cinnamon sticks and ginger pieces.

Homemade chai

A POPULAR COFFEE-BAR ALTERNATIVE to latte, Indian-inspired chai combines black tea, milk, and spices—which in this version include the savory notes of black pepper and cardamom. This would also be delicious served chilled.

6 SERVINGS

- **1 2-inch piece fresh ginger, cut into thin rounds**
- **2 cinnamon sticks**
- **2 teaspoons black peppercorns**
- **10 whole cloves**
- **6 whole cardamom pods**
- **6 cups cold water**
- **6 bags of black tea (preferably Darjeeling)**
- **2 cups whole milk**
- **½ cup (packed) golden brown sugar**

COMBINE first 5 ingredients in resealable plastic bag; close bag. Using mallet, lightly crush or bruise spices. Transfer spices to medium saucepan. Add 6 cups water; bring to boil over high heat. Reduce heat to medium-low, partially cover pan, and simmer gently 10 minutes. Remove from heat. Add tea bags and steep 5 minutes. Discard tea bags. Add milk and sugar to saucepan. Bring tea just to simmer over high heat, whisking until sugar dissolves. Strain chai into teapot and serve.

Mocha-cinnamon hot chocolate

BROWN SUGAR, cinnamon, and espresso are chocolate-friendly ingredients that gussy up a steaming cup of hot milk chocolate. Orange and peppermint are other flavors that partner well with chocolate: To add these flavors to a regular cup of hot cocoa, try steeping orange peels in the milk, or add a dash of peppermint extract to the hot chocolate just before serving.

4 SERVINGS

- **⅓ cup chilled whipping cream**
- **4 teaspoons plus 6 tablespoons (packed) dark brown sugar**
- **1½ teaspoons plus 5 tablespoons instant espresso powder**

- **4 cups whole milk**
- **2 3-inch-long cinnamon sticks, broken in half**
- **¼ cup unsweetened cocoa powder**
- **3 ounces milk chocolate, chopped**

Ground nutmeg
Additional cinnamon sticks (optional)

WHISK cream, 4 teaspoons brown sugar, and 1½ teaspoons espresso powder in medium bowl until stiff peaks form. Cover and refrigerate whipped cream.

BRING milk and 2 cinnamon sticks to simmer in heavy large saucepan over medium-high heat. Add remaining 6 tablespoons brown sugar, 5 tablespoons espresso powder, and cocoa powder. Whisk to blend. Add milk chocolate and whisk until melted and smooth. Discard cinnamon sticks.

LADLE hot chocolate into 4 mugs. Top with whipped cream. Sprinkle with nutmeg. Garnish with additional cinnamon sticks, if desired.

Spiced hot chocolate

"SPICED" IS THE WORD for this exotic hot chocolate that contains seven different spices—including a little crushed red pepper for extra pizzazz. Star anise are brown star-shaped seedpods sold at Asian markets and at some supermarkets.

6 SERVINGS

- **6 cups whole milk**
- **¾ cup (packed) dark brown sugar**
- **15 whole cardamom pods, crushed**
- **12 whole cloves**
- **2 cinnamon sticks, broken in half**
- **2 whole star anise**

3/4 teaspoon whole coriander seeds
3/4 teaspoon ground nutmeg
1/4 teaspoon dried crushed red pepper
1/2 cup unsweetened cocoa powder
3/4 teaspoon vanilla extract

BRING first 9 ingredients to simmer in heavy large saucepan, stirring until sugar dissolves. Remove from heat, cover, and let steep 20 minutes. Add cocoa powder and vanilla. Bring to simmer, whisking until blended. Strain hot chocolate into 8-cup measuring cup; discard spices. Divide hot chocolate among 6 mugs.

Ultra-rich hot chocolate

BITTERSWEET CHOCOLATE adds richness to good old-fashioned hot chocolate topped with miniature marshmallows. Add a splash of brandy or your favorite spirit to give it a more grown-up appeal.

4 SERVINGS

4 cups milk
1/4 cup unsweetened cocoa powder
1/4 cup sugar
4 ounces bittersweet (not unsweetened) or semisweet chocolate, chopped
Pinch of salt

Miniature marshmallows

BRING milk, cocoa powder, and sugar to simmer in heavy large saucepan over medium-high heat, whisking frequently. Add chocolate; whisk until melted and smooth. Add salt; bring to simmer, whisking constantly until frothy.

LADLE into 4 mugs. Sprinkle with marshmallows.

White chocolate and peppermint hot chocolate

PEPPERMINT IS A NATURAL COMPLEMENT to hot chocolate. For a festive holiday-season accompaniment, serve each mug of hot chocolate with a candy cane as a stirrer.

4 SERVINGS

2/3 cup chilled whipping cream
8 round red-and-white-striped peppermint hard candies, coarsely crushed

3 1/2 cups whole milk
8 ounces good-quality white chocolate (such as Lindt or Perugina), chopped
1/2 teaspoon peppermint extract
Additional coarsely crushed peppermint candies

BEAT cream and 8 crushed candies in medium bowl until cream holds peaks. Cover and refrigerate whipped cream.

BRING milk to simmer in heavy large saucepan over medium-high heat. Add white chocolate; whisk until melted and smooth. Bring to simmer, whisking constantly. Mix in peppermint extract. Ladle hot chocolate into 4 mugs. Top with dollops of whipped cream. Sprinkle with additional coarsely crushed candies and serve.

Hot apple cider with ginger and cardamom

CRYSTALLIZED GINGER and cardamom give this cider a sweet, distinctive flavor. If you have trouble finding cardamom pods in your local supermarket, see "Finding Ingredients Online" (page 20) in the "Notes from the Test Kitchen" chapter for sources.

8 SERVINGS

1 lemon
¼ cup sugar
6 quarter-size pieces crystallized ginger, coarsely chopped
20 whole cardamom pods
15 whole cloves
2 cinnamon sticks, each broken in half
8 cups unfiltered apple cider

USING swivel-bladed vegetable peeler, remove peel (yellow part only) in strips from lemon. Heat heavy large pot over medium heat. Add lemon peel, sugar, ginger, cardamom, cloves, and cinnamon and stir until fragrant, about 2 minutes. Add cider and bring to boil. Reduce heat to low and simmer mixture 15 minutes. Strain into mugs and serve.

Alcoholic

Bourbon–ginger ale cooler

A GREAT PARTY DRINK: fast, easy, and refreshing.

10 SERVINGS

Ice cubes
20 tablespoons bourbon (about 1¼ cups)
7½ cups ginger ale

FILL 10 glasses with ice cubes. Add 2 tablespoons bourbon, then ¾ cup ginger ale to each glass; stir and serve.

Crimson royale

CRANBERRY JUICE COCKTAIL and cranberry liqueur add a twist to the traditional Kir royale (an aperitif made with Champagne and crème de cassis) and give this lovely Champagne cocktail a beautiful red color. Use well-chilled brut Champagne or other sparkling wine.

6 SERVINGS

12 tablespoons frozen cranberry juice cocktail concentrate, thawed
6 teaspoons cranberry liqueur
6 teaspoons orange liqueur
1 bottle Champagne or other sparkling wine
12 whole fresh cranberries
6 orange slices, folded in half
6 bamboo skewers

MEASURE 2 tablespoons cranberry concentrate, 1 teaspoon cranberry liqueur, and 1 teaspoon orange liqueur into each of 6 Champagne flutes. Top with Champagne.

THREAD 1 cranberry, 1 orange slice, and then another cranberry onto each skewer. Place skewers atop glasses.

Pomegranate Prosecco cocktail

TO JUICE A POMEGRANATE: Roll the pomegranate on a countertop until the fruit feels slightly mushy, then carefully cut off the flat end. Hold the pomegranate over a bowl in the sink, and squeeze to extract the juice. Strain the juice through a sieve. An 11-ounce pomegranate will yield about ¼ cup of juice. Wear kitchen gloves to avoid staining your hands. Or you can buy pomegranate juice in bottles in the supermarket, year round. If Prosecco (an Italian sparkling wine) is not available, use Champagne or any other sparkling wine. Look for the orange-flower water at Middle Eastern groceries, liquor stores, or in the liquor or mixers section of some supermarkets.

8 SERVINGS

- ½ cup fresh pomegranate juice (from about two 11-ounce pomegranates)
- ¼ cup sugar
- 1 teaspoon orange-flower water

- 2 tablespoons pomegranate seeds

- 2 750-ml bottles chilled Prosecco

BRING juice and sugar to boil in medium saucepan over high heat, stirring until sugar dissolves. Boil 1 minute. Reduce heat to medium and simmer until mixture thickens and reduces to ¼ cup, about 5 minutes longer. Remove from heat and stir in orange-flower water. Refrigerate syrup until cold, about 1 hour. *(Syrup can be made 1 week ahead. Cover and keep refrigerated.)*

PLACE pomegranate seeds in plastic bag and freeze 1 hour.

POUR 1½ teaspoons syrup into each of eight 8-ounce Champagne flutes. Fill flutes with Prosecco; stir gently. Float a few frozen seeds in each glass and serve.

Mango-boysenberry mimosa

THE FAVORITE BRUNCH BEVERAGE—Champagne and orange juice—gets updated. While Valencia oranges produce the best freshly squeezed orange juice, you do not need it in this particular recipe, as its intense taste can overwhelm the other juices.

10 SERVINGS

- 2 cups frozen unsweetened boysenberries, thawed
- 2 tablespoons sugar

- 3 cups chilled orange juice (do not use freshly squeezed)
- 1½ cups frozen orange-peach-mango juice concentrate
- 1 750-ml bottle chilled brut Champagne
- 10 small orange slices

PUREE berries in processor. Strain through sieve over bowl, pressing on solids to extract as much liquid as possible. Mix in sugar. *(Puree can be made 1 day ahead. Cover and refrigerate.)*

WHISK orange juice and concentrate in pitcher to blend. Mix in Champagne. Divide mimosa among 10 Champagne glasses. Drizzle 1½ teaspoons berry puree over each. Garnish with orange slices.

Spiced red wine with brandy and citrus

THIS COUNTRY-FRENCH APERITIF is perfect for the winter holidays. The drink is best at cool room temperature, accompanied by olives, almonds, and crudités. It also makes an excellent gift—just double or triple the recipe, and pour the drink into pretty bottles. Be sure to begin the "winemaking" process at least three weeks before you plan to serve the wine or give it as a present.

MAKES 3 CUPS

- 1 whole orange
- 1 orange, sliced
- ½ lemon, sliced
- 1 vanilla bean
- 6 whole cloves
- 1 750-ml bottle dry red wine (such as Côtes du Rhône or Merlot)

- ½ cup framboise eau-de-vie (clear raspberry brandy) or brandy
- 6 tablespoons sugar

USING swivel-bladed vegetable peeler, remove peel (orange part only) in strips from whole orange. Combine orange peel, sliced orange and lemon, vanilla bean, and cloves in large glass jar. Pour wine over. Cover and place in cool dark place for 2 weeks.

STRAIN wine through several layers of cheesecloth into 4-cup measuring cup. Discard solids in cheesecloth. Add framboise and sugar to wine; stir until sugar dissolves. Pour mixture into wine bottle or decorative bottle. Cork bottle and place in cool dark place for at least 1 week. *(Can be made 6 weeks ahead. Store in cool dark place.)* Serve in small wineglasses.

Frozen limes filled with sangrita and tequila

SANGRITA, MEANING "LITTLE BLOOD" in Spanish, is the traditional chaser for straight tequila and usually includes a splash of tomato juice (hence the name). Serve this spicy, salty mixture with a premium *reposado* tequila, which has a smooth appeal and rich, complex flavor that's best for sipping. The frozen lime cups take some time to prepare, but are well worth it; in a pinch, you can use shot glasses.

12 SERVINGS

12 limes, ends trimmed, cut crosswise in half

2¼ cups fresh orange juice
5 tablespoons grenadine
1 teaspoon (generous) salt
1 teaspoon cayenne pepper

Premium tequila

SQUEEZE lime halves in citrus juicer to extract as much juice as possible. Transfer ¾ cup lime juice to bowl; cover and chill (reserve remaining juice for another use). Using scissors, cut out membranes from hollowed lime halves. Enclose lime cups in resealable plastic bag. Freeze until frozen, about 4 hours.

MIX orange juice, ¾ cup lime juice, grenadine, salt, and cayenne in blender. Transfer mixture to pitcher. Cover sangrita and refrigerate until cold, about 2 hours. *(Can be made 1 day ahead. Keep sangrita chilled. Keep lime cups frozen.)*

ARRANGE frozen lime cups on serving tray. Pour sangrita into 12 lime cups; pour tequila into remaining 12 lime cups and serve immediately.

Bloody Mary with Tabasco-spiked ice cubes

THE PEPPERY ICE CUBES give new meaning to the phrase "fire and ice" and ensure that your Bloody Mary packs a punch to the finish. Tabasco sauce or any other fiery hot red pepper sauce can be used. Another fun way to keep your cocktail cool: Fill an ice cube tray with water and place a slice of red and green jalapeño chile in each.

4 SERVINGS

4 cups tomato juice, divided
6 tablespoons fresh lemon juice, divided
3 tablespoons fresh lime juice, divided
2 teaspoons hot pepper sauce, divided

¾ cup vodka
4 teaspoons Worcestershire sauce
1 teaspoon garlic salt
1 teaspoon dried oregano

4 green onions, trimmed

COMBINE 1 cup tomato juice, 2 tablespoons lemon juice, 1 tablespoon lime juice, and 1 teaspoon hot pepper sauce. Pour into ice cube tray; freeze overnight.

COMBINE vodka, Worcestershire sauce, garlic salt, oregano, and remaining 3 cups tomato juice, 4 tablespoons lemon juice, 2 tablespoons lime juice, and 1 teaspoon Tabasco in pitcher.

DIVIDE Tabasco ice cubes among 4 tall glasses. Pour tomato juice mixture over. Garnish each glass with 1 green onion.

Peach and mango daiquiri

FROZEN FRUIT is often used to replace ice cubes in frozen daiquiris. That's the case in this recipe, where frozen peaches do double duty to add flavor and a slushy texture. For a more prominent mango flavor, use frozen mangoes in place of the peaches.

4 SERVINGS

- **¾ cup frozen mango-peach juice concentrate, thawed**
- **¾ cup light rum**
- **½ cup orange juice**
- **¼ cup sugar**
- **1 16-ounce package frozen unsweetened sliced peaches**
- **Fresh mint sprigs**

COMBINE mango-peach juice concentrate, rum, orange juice, and sugar in blender. Add half of frozen peaches and puree. Add remaining peaches a few at a time, blending until mixture is smooth and thick and stopping to stir as needed.

POUR into chilled daiquiri glasses or wineglasses; garnish with mint and serve.

Mai tai

THIS RECIPE is a classic right down to the fresh juices, the two types of rum, and the use of orgeat syrup. This flavorful syrup, made from a mixture of almonds, sugar, and rose water or orange-flower water, can be found at liquor stores and in the coffee and tea section of some supermarkets. If you can't find it, almond syrup may be used instead.

4 SERVINGS

- **½ cup light rum**
- **½ cup dark rum**
- **½ cup fresh lemon juice**
- **½ cup fresh orange juice**
- **3 tablespoons orange curaçao**
- **3 tablespoons orgeat syrup or almond syrup**
- **Ice cubes**
- **4 fresh pineapple wedges (optional)**
- **4 fresh mint sprigs (optional)**

MIX first 6 ingredients in pitcher. Fill 4 small glasses with ice. Pour rum mixture over; stir to blend. Garnish with pineapple and mint, if desired.

Pink greyhound

PINK GRAPEFRUIT JUICE and a splash of grenadine add a sweet blush to this classic cocktail. Pour it into a glass with a salted rim, and the cocktail becomes a pink Salty Dog. Grenadine, a pomegranate-flavored syrup, can be found in the liquor or mixers section of most supermarkets.

2 SERVINGS

- **⅔ cup pink grapefruit juice**
- **⅔ cup vodka**
- **2 teaspoons grenadine**
- **Ice**
- **2 pink grapefruit twists**

POUR ⅓ cup pink grapefruit juice, ⅓ cup vodka, and 1 teaspoon grenadine into each of 2 glasses. Fill with ice. Garnish each with pink grapefruit twist and serve.

Gin and tonic with Cointreau

CLEAR AND INTENSE from the peels of bitter and sweet oranges, Cointreau pairs well with fresh lime in this sophisticated gin and tonic.

2 SERVINGS

- **2 lime wedges**
- **½ cup gin**
- **½ cup tonic water**
- **4 teaspoons Cointreau**
- **Ice**

PLACE 1 lime wedge and ¼ cup gin in each of 2 small glasses; mash with back of spoon. Add ¼ cup tonic water and 2 teaspoons Cointreau to each; stir to blend. Fill with ice and serve.

Great Martini

PROPORTIONS AND high-quality gin and vermouth are important, but the real secret to a fine Martini is stirring thoroughly but quickly to keep the ice cubes from diluting the drink. It must also be served very cold and straight up. Have some salted nuts on hand to go with your drink.

4 SERVINGS

- **Ice cubes**
- **1 cup gin**
- **1 tablespoon dry vermouth**
- **4 large pimiento-stuffed green olives**

FILL 4-cup glass measuring cup ⅓ full with ice. Add gin and vermouth. Stir gently. Immediately strain mixture into chilled Martini glasses. Add 1 olive to each glass and serve immediately.

Ginger passion Martini

AN EFFERVESCENT COMBINATION of vodka, ginger beer (found at many liquor stores), and passion fruit juice. Swizzle sticks fashioned out of pieces of fresh ginger are a creative touch.

8 SERVINGS

- **1 6- to 7-inch-long piece fresh ginger, peeled**
- **2½ cups vodka**
- **2 cups nonalcoholic ginger beer**
- **2 cups frozen passion fruit juice cocktail concentrate, thawed**
- **Ice cubes**
- **Fresh mint sprigs**

CUT ginger lengthwise into ¼-inch-thick slices. Cut slices lengthwise into ¼-inch-thick sticks, making at least 8. Combine vodka, ginger beer, and juice concentrate in pitcher. *(Ginger sticks and vodka mixture can be prepared 1 day ahead. Cover separately and refrigerate.)*

DIVIDE vodka mixture among 8 Martini glasses. Add ice cubes and 1 ginger stick to each; garnish with mint sprigs.

Pear Martini

THIS PEAR-INFUSED VODKA MARTINI manages to be both classic and contemporary at the same time. The frozen grape clusters used as garnishes add a nice Dionysian note.

2 SERVINGS

- **2 small clusters green grapes**
- **1 cup ice cubes**
- **¾ cup premium vodka**
- **¼ cup premium pear liqueur**

PLACE grape clusters in freezer until frozen, at least 3 hours. Place 2 Martini glasses in freezer and chill at least 2 hours.

COMBINE ice cubes, vodka, and pear liqueur in 2-cup glass measuring cup; stir until well chilled. Strain into chilled Martini glasses. Add 1 frozen grape cluster to each and serve.

Iced vodka with cucumber, lemon, and mint

ALTHOUGH A REGULAR CUCUMBER may be used to make this cocktail, an English hothouse cucumber is preferred since it is virtually seedless. "Muddling" (or mashing) fresh mint leaves and sugar extracts the essential oils from the leaves and releases their aroma and flavor. Allow the muddled sugar mixture and cucumber slices to stand for 30 minutes so that their flavors marry before adding the remaining ingredients. To serve this cocktail as a spritzer, pour it into a tall, slender glass and top it off with a splash of club soda.

8 SERVINGS

1⅓ cups sugar
1 cup (packed) fresh mint leaves
2 lemons, sliced into rounds
½ small cucumber, sliced
2 cups fresh lemon juice
2 cups vodka
½ cup water
3 cups ice cubes

MIX sugar, mint, and lemon rounds in pitcher, mashing slightly with back of spoon. Mix in cucumber. Let stand 30 minutes. Add lemon juice, vodka, and ½ cup water; stir to dissolve sugar. Chill at least 30 minutes and up to 2 hours. Mix in ice and serve.

Homemade sweet-and-sour margarita

CREATING YOUR OWN sweet-and-sour mix is what makes this recipe "homemade." Mix up a batch of the tequila, sweet-and-sour, and triple sec before your guests arrive, so that all you need to do is blend it with ice just before serving. This margarita is great blended or on the rocks.

12 SERVINGS

Lime wedges
Coarse kosher salt

4 cups Homemade Sweet-and-Sour Mix (see recipe)
1½ cups tequila
4 tablespoons triple sec
48 ice cubes
12 lime slices

RUB rims of 12 glasses with lime wedges. Dip rims in coarse salt.

COMBINE 2 cups Homemade Sweet-and-Sour Mix, ¾ cup tequila, 2 tablespoons triple sec, and 24 ice cubes in blender. Process until well blended. Pour into 6 glasses. Repeat with remaining sweet-and-sour mix, tequila, triple sec, and ice cubes. Pour into remaining 6 glasses. Garnish each with lime slice.

Homemade sweet-and-sour mix

FRESH, FROM SCRATCH, and minus the preservatives and chemicals used in store-bought mixes, this easy-to-make sweet-and-sour mix is an indispensable bar staple that can be used in many cocktails. Cool the syrup before adding the lemon and lime juices, as the heat will alter the fresh flavor of the juices. Prepare it at least four hours ahead so that it has plenty of time to chill.

MAKES 4 CUPS

1½ cups water
1½ cups sugar

1 cup fresh lemon juice
1 cup fresh lime juice

COMBINE water and sugar in medium saucepan. Stir over medium heat until sugar dissolves. Bring to boil. Cool syrup.

MIX syrup, lemon juice, and lime juice in pitcher. Cover and refrigerate until cold. *(Can be made 2 days ahead. Keep chilled.)*

Ginger margarita

A MODERN TAKE on the classic margarita, which is given a new twist with lemongrass, ginger, and Cointreau. Lemongrass can be found at Asian markets and in the produce section of some supermarkets.

4 SERVINGS

- **½ cup fresh lime juice**
- **½ cup sugar**
- **¼ cup chopped peeled fresh ginger**
- **1 tablespoon chopped lemongrass**

- **5 lime wedges**
- **Coarse kosher salt**
- **Ice cubes**
- **¾ cup premium white tequila (100% agave)**
- **¾ cup Cointreau or other orange liqueur**

BRING lime juice, sugar, ginger, and lemongrass to boil in small saucepan, stirring until sugar dissolves. Strain ginger syrup; discard solids in strainer. Cover and refrigerate syrup until cold, about 2 hours. *(Can be prepared 2 days ahead. Keep refrigerated.)*

RUN 1 lime wedge around rims of 4 Margarita glasses; dip rims in salt. Fill glasses with ice cubes. Place ginger syrup, tequila, and Cointreau in cocktail shaker. Add ice and shake well. Strain mixture into glasses, garnish with remaining lime wedges, and serve.

Blended citrus gin fizz

THIS VERSION of the classic brunch drink gets its flavor from three types of citrus. For large parties, you can prepare several batches a few hours ahead of time and store in the freezer. Then, before serving, thaw the mixture slightly and whisk to blend.

4 SERVINGS

- **22 ice cubes**
- **½ cup gin or vodka**
- **½ cup whipping cream**
- **½ cup club soda**
- **¼ cup frozen lemonade concentrate**
- **¼ cup frozen limeade concentrate**
- **3 tablespoons frozen orange juice concentrate**
- **3 tablespoons powdered sugar**
- **Ground nutmeg**
- **Lemon- and lime-peel twists**
- **Lemon slices**

PLACE first 8 ingredients in blender and blend until smooth. Pour into 4 glasses. Sprinkle with nutmeg. Garnish with lemon- and lime-peel twists and lemon slices.

Limoncello

THE MEDITERRANEAN ISLAND of Capri is famous for its lemons—many of which find their way into the celebrated local drink known as limoncello. Made by steeping the yellow part of the lemon peel in vodka for an extended period, then adding a sugar syrup, the bright yellow liqueur is most often served as an after-dinner digestif. But you can savor it any time you like.

MAKES 6 CUPS

- **2 pounds lemons**
- **4 cups 100-proof vodka**

- **3 cups sugar**
- **3 cups water**

USING swivel-bladed vegetable peeler, remove peel (yellow part only) in strips from lemons. Combine lemon peel and vodka in large bowl or jar. Let stand, covered, at room temperature 1 week.

STIR sugar and 3 cups water in large saucepan over medium heat until sugar dissolves. Cool syrup. Add vodka mixture to syrup and stir to blend. Strain liquid into bottles; seal and refrigerate limoncello for at least 1 month and up to 2 months. Pour into small glasses to serve.

Tropical fruit and rum punch

MAKE THIS A NONALCOHOLIC party punch by replacing the rum with more pineapple juice, as well as mango and guava nectars. Blend it into slushy cocktails as described below, or serve it in a punch bowl with lots of ice to balance the flavors and keep it cold. You can find sweetened cream of coconut in the liquor or mixers section of most supermarkets.

12 SERVINGS

2 12-ounce cans mango nectar
2 12-ounce cans guava nectar
2 cups canned unsweetened pineapple juice
1½ cups canned sweetened cream of coconut (such as Coco López), well mixed
¼ cup fresh lime juice
2 cups amber (gold) rum

17 cups ice cubes
Fresh pineapple or lime wedges

COMBINE mango nectar, guava nectar, pineapple juice, cream of coconut, lime juice, and rum in large pitcher. *(Punch can be prepared 1 day ahead. Cover and refrigerate. Mix well before using.)*

COMBINE 1 cup punch and 2 cups ice cubes in blender and blend until smooth and thick. Pour into glasses. Repeat with remaining punch and ice cubes in batches. Garnish with fresh pineapple or lime wedges and serve.

Watermelon lemonade with gin

OMIT THE GIN for a kid-friendly drink.

6 SERVINGS

7 cups 2-inch pieces peeled seeded watermelon (from about 4 pounds)
1 cup Simple Syrup (see recipe)
1 cup fresh lemon juice
3 tablespoons grenadine
1 cup gin

3 cups ice cubes
Lemon twists (optional)

PUREE watermelon pieces in processor. Strain watermelon puree into large pitcher, pressing on solids in strainer to extract as much liquid as possible. Discard any solids in strainer. Add syrup, lemon juice, and grenadine to pitcher; stir to blend. Stir in gin. *(Can be prepared 6 hours ahead. Refrigerate.)*

STIR 3 cups ice cubes into watermelon lemonade. Pour into tall glasses. Garnish with lemon twists, if desired.

Simple syrup

IF YOU'RE A COCKTAIL FAN, this syrup is handy to have at the ready in your refrigerator. It's used in many classic cocktails, and is commonly called for in bartending books.

MAKES ABOUT 1½ CUPS

1½ cups water
¾ cup sugar

STIR water and sugar in heavy medium saucepan over medium heat until sugar dissolves. Increase heat and boil 2 minutes. Refrigerate syrup until cold, about 3 hours. *(Can be prepared 1 week ahead. Cover and keep refrigerated.)*

Southern eggnog

THE ADDITION OF BOURBON gives this classic Christmas drink a Southern twist. Be sure the cream–egg yolk mixture does not simmer, or else the yolks will curdle and the mixture will not thicken into a luscious creamy consistency. The eggnog can be served on ice, if desired.

6 SERVINGS

2 cups whipping cream
1 cup whole milk
6 large egg yolks
½ cup sugar
¼ teaspoon ground nutmeg

¼ cup dark rum
2 tablespoons bourbon
2 tablespoons brandy
Additional ground nutmeg

BRING cream and milk to simmer in heavy large saucepan. Whisk egg yolks and sugar in large bowl to blend. Gradually whisk hot cream mixture into yolk mixture. Return mixture to same saucepan. Stir over medium-low heat until mixture thickens and leaves path on back of spoon when finger is drawn across, about 4 minutes (do not boil). Strain into bowl. Stir in ¼ teaspoon nutmeg. Cover and refrigerate until cold, at least 4 hours. *(Can be made 1 day ahead. Keep refrigerated.)*

MIX rum, bourbon, and brandy into cream mixture. Divide mixture among 6 cups or glasses. Sprinkle additional nutmeg over each and serve.

Spirited hot apple cider

THIS WARMING CIDER gets a good kick from the addition of applejack, a strong American apple brandy.

6 TO 8 SERVINGS

1 orange
3 tablespoons unsalted butter
¼ cup (packed) golden brown sugar
3 cinnamon sticks
10 whole allspice
10 whole cloves
6 cups apple cider
¼ cup dark rum
½ cup applejack brandy
Additional cinnamon sticks (optional; for garnish)

USING swivel-bladed vegetable peeler, remove peel (orange part only) in strips from orange. Melt butter in heavy large saucepan over medium heat. Add peel, sugar, 3 cinnamon sticks, allspice, and cloves; stir 1 minute. Add cider; bring to simmer. Reduce heat to low and simmer 15 minutes. Mix in rum and applejack. Strain into mugs. Garnish with additional cinnamon sticks, if desired.

Allspice buttered rum

APPLE CIDER replaces water in this classic cold-weather drink, lending a wonderful aroma and depth of flavor.

2 SERVINGS

2¼ cups apple cider
2 tablespoons fresh lemon juice
36 whole allspice berries
6 whole cloves
1 cinnamon stick, broken into small pieces
1 teaspoon honey
1 tablespoon unsalted butter
6 tablespoons dark rum

BOIL first 6 ingredients in heavy small saucepan 5 minutes. Remove from heat. Add butter and stir to melt. Strain into 2 warm mugs. Add 3 tablespoons rum to each mug and serve.

White chocolate cappuccino

WHITE CHOCOLATE, brandy, and vanilla add a bit of luxury to Italy's famed coffee drink, which is traditionally made with espresso and topped with foamy steamed milk. Use a whisk to create a frothy mixture to float atop the coffee. Serve this cappuccino for weekend brunch or with cookies in place of dessert.

8 SERVINGS

- **4 cups whole milk**
- **1 vanilla bean, split lengthwise**
- **10 ounces high-quality white chocolate (such as Lindt or Perugina), chopped**
- **2½ teaspoons brandy**
- **2½ teaspoons vanilla extract**

- **4 cups freshly brewed strong hot coffee**
- **Unsweetened cocoa powder**

POUR milk into heavy medium saucepan. Scrape in seeds from vanilla bean; add pod. Bring to boil. Remove from heat. Add white chocolate; whisk until melted and smooth. Whisk in brandy and vanilla extract. Using tongs, remove vanilla bean pod. Return white chocolate mixture to low heat; whisk until frothy, about 1 minute.

POUR hot coffee into mugs. Ladle white chocolate mixture over. Sprinkle with cocoa powder and serve.

Café brûlot

A WHIPPED CREAM TOPPING spiked with Grand Marnier adds extra indulgence to this New Orleans specialty, made with dark coffee, brandy, citrus, and spices. The *brûlot*, which means "burnt brandy" in French, should be heated and carefully set aflame in a large saucepan, to help contain the flames.

6 SERVINGS

- **½ cup chilled whipping cream**
- **2 tablespoons plus ½ cup Grand Marnier or other orange liqueur**

- **¼ cup (packed) dark brown sugar**
- **8 2-inch-long, ½-inch-wide lemon peel strips (yellow part only)**
- **8 2-inch-long, ½-inch-wide orange peel strips (orange part only)**
- **2 cinnamon sticks, broken in half**
- **24 whole cloves**
- **⅔ cup brandy**
- **3 cups very strong freshly brewed hot coffee**

BEAT cream with 2 tablespoons Grand Marnier to stiff peaks in medium bowl. Cover and refrigerate up to 3 hours.

COMBINE sugar, citrus peels, cinnamon, cloves, and remaining ½ cup Grand Marnier in heavy large skillet. Stir over medium-low heat until mixture begins to simmer. Simmer 3 minutes. Remove from heat and let stand 30 minutes.

RETURN sugar mixture to simmer over medium heat. Pour mixture into large decorative heatproof bowl. Pour brandy into heavy large saucepan. Set over medium heat; warm to lukewarm. Ignite with long match. Pour flaming brandy over sugar mixture in bowl. Gradually pour coffee down side of bowl (flames will subside).

LADLE coffee into mugs, leaving peel and spices in bowl. Serve with whipped cream.

Hot chocolate with espresso, lemon, and anise

A SPIRITED, Italian-style take on hot chocolate.

4 TO 6 SERVINGS

- **4 cups whole milk (do not use low-fat or nonfat)**
- **¾ cup sugar**
- **4 ounces unsweetened chocolate, finely chopped**
- **2 ounces semisweet chocolate, finely chopped**
- **2 tablespoons instant espresso powder**
- **5 ½-inch-wide strips lemon peel**
- **6 tablespoons anise-flavored liqueur (such as sambuca)**

Combine all ingredients except liqueur in large saucepan. Whisk over medium-high heat until chocolate melts and mixture is smooth and comes to boil. Remove from heat; mix in liqueur. Divide among cups.

Contributors

Recipes

66 in TriBeCa, New York, New York
300 East Boulevard, Charlotte, North Carolina
Bruce Aidells
Elizabeth Allen
Susan Allen
Nicole Aloni
Jean Anderson
Antonio's La Fiamma, Maitland, Florida
Arrows, Ogunquit, Maine
Art Gecko's Southwest Grill, Circus Circus, Reno, Nevada
John Ash
Yvonne Askew
Atalaya, Santa Fe, New Mexico
Automatic Slim's Tonga Club, Memphis, Tennessee
Brad Avooske
AZ, New York, New York
Michelle and David Bach
Nancy Baggett
Lynda Hotch Balslev
Sharmi Banik
Mary Corpening Barber
Karen Barker
Melanie Barnard
Nancy Verde Barr
Barrington Country Bistro, Barrington Hills, Illinois
Joseph Bastianich, Becco, New York, New York
Mario Batali, Babbo, New York, New York
Stephane Beaucamp
Octavio Becerra, Pinot Bistro, Los Angeles, California
Patrice Bedrosian
Marisol Benadayan-Benarroch
Mary Bergin
Deborah Bernstein
Tom Berthiaume
Paul Bertolli
Anne Bianchi
Lena Cederham Birnbaum
Pam Blanton
Carole Bloom
Emily and Dick Boenning
Bombay Club, Cambridge, Massachusetts
Border Grill, Santa Monica, California
Blythe Boyd
Georgeanne Brennan
John Brescio
Marilyn Bright
Meg and Paul Brown
Susan Burnside
Linda Bush
Cafe Spice Namaste, London, England
Cafe Zenon, Eugene, Oregon
Anna Teresa Callen
Misty Callies, Zanzibar, Ann Arbor, Michigan
Georgina Campbell
Susan Campoy
Floyd Cardoz
Fanny Carroll
Penelope Casas
The Castle Inn Riverside, Wichita, Kansas
Mary Cech
Cynthia and Stephen Chaplin
Lauren Chattman
Chez Shea, Seattle, Washington
Bettina Ciacci
Michael Cimarusti
Circa, Philadelphia, Pennsylvania
Eugene I. Cleary
Nicole Coady
Jayne Cohen
Ann Colton
Commander's Palace, New Orleans, Louisiana
Patricia Connell
Stacey Constas
Raphael Conte, Raphael Bar Risto, Providence, Rhode Island
Coquette Cafe, Milwaukee, Wisconsin
Agathe Corby
Shirley Corriher
Cosmos Cafe, Houston, Texas
Cottage Inn, Eureka Springs, Arkansas
Colin Cowie
Coyote Cafe, Santa Fe, New Mexico
Russell Cronkhite
Lane Crowther
Kathi Dameron
Renee and Bruce Davis
Robin Davis
Delfina Studio Café, London, England
Lorenza de' Medici
Jean Louis De Mori
Lori De Mori
Mary Demuth
Marcel Desaulniers, The Trellis, Williamsburg, Virginia
Sara Dickerman
Brooke Dojny
Crescent Dragonwagon
John Dudek
Suzanne Dunaway
Dagny and Tim Du Val
Dorothy and Bill Dworsky
Eat, Somerville, Massachusetts
Elizabeth Clark's, Keokuk, Iowa
Jane and Sandy Elliott
Elizabeth Ellis
Sue Reddin Ellison
Emeril's, New Orleans, Louisiana
Todd English, Olives, Boston, Massachusetts
Elizabeth Falkner
Tarla Fallgatter
Faz Restaurant & Bar, San Francisco, California
Susan Feniger
Barbara Pool Fenzl
Charity Ferreira
Claudia Feurey
Fiddle Heads, Buffalo, New York
Fifty Seven Fifty Seven, Four Seasons Hotel, New York, New York
George Fike
Pamela Fitzpatrick
Bobby Flay
Claudia Fleming
Janet Fletcher
Jamie Elizabeth Flick
Jim Fobel
Margaret and Stephen Gadient
Gale Gand
Joe Gannon, Joe's Bar and Grill, Maui, Hawaii
Ina Garten
Marcella Giamundo
Gerri Gilliland
Debbie Gold
Rozanne Gold
Marcy Goldman
Darra Goldstein
Dorothy Gonzales
Peggy and Bill Grant
The Green Mountain Inn, Stowe, Vermont
Greens, San Francisco, California

Dorie Greenspan
Sophie Grigson
Kathy Gunst
Carlene and Rosendo Gutierrez
Becky Guyton
Dahlia and Andy Haas
Ken Haedrich
Hal's Bar & Grill, Venice, California
Katherine and Laurent Hamon
Charmaine Haravey
Helen and David Hardee
Harmony House Inn, New Bern, North Carolina
Susan Haskell
Julie Hasson
Reed Hearon, Rose Pistola, San Francisco, California
Maida Heatter
Pam and Jim Heavner
Helen's, Richmond, Virginia
Beth Hensperger
Snjezana Hercigonja
Mily Hernandez
Steve Hettleman
Cameron and Gerald Hirigoyen
Inez Holderness
Patricia Hopkins
Hotel Villa Flori, Como, Italy
Thomas Houndalas
Michael Hunter
Inn of the Anasazi, Santa Fe, New Mexico
Miles James
Cheryl Alters Jamison and Bill Jamison
J. Benjamin's, Des Moines, Iowa
Nancy Harmon Jenkins
David Paul Johnson, David Paul's Lahaina Grill, Lahaina, Maui, Hawaii
Blanche Johnson
Mary Jo and Marvin Johnson
Michele Anna Jordan
Julienne, San Marino, California
Cherryl Kachenmeister
Katharine Kagel
Karen Kaplan
Zov Karamardian
Barbara Karoff
Mollie Katzen
Thomas Keller, The French Laundry, Yountville, California
Jeanne Thiel Kelley
Day and Whitney Kerr
Kristine Kidd
Jennifer Kirkgaard
Ron Klein
Elinor Klivans
Kona Village Resort, Kailua-Kona, Hawaii
Aglaia Kremezi
Celeste Kuch
La Brea Bakery, Los Angeles, California
Lakecliff Estate Bed and Breakfast, Hood River, Oregon
Virginia and David Larkin
David Lebovitz
David Leite
Leonard Cohen's Olde Port Inn, Avila Beach, California
Julie Lestrange
Hannah Levitz
Ina Lieb
Eric Lindstrom
Joyce Litz
The Lodge at Koele, Lanai, Hawaii
Susan Herrmann Loomis
Lucca's, Chicago, Illinois
Emily Luchetti
Ronni Lundy
Leslie Mackie
Maison Novelli, London, England
Amy Stafford Malik
Martini Bar, The Raleigh, Miami, Florida
Rosemary Grimes Manell
Marianne Mays
Janet Taylor McCracken
Stephenie McGinnis
Michael McLaughlin
Leigh McLean, Lulu Grille, Memphis, Tennessee
Tory McPhail
Tracey Medeiros
Alice Medrich
Peter Merriman and Beverly Kypfer, Hula Grill, Maui, Hawaii
Mesa Grill, New York, New York
Bonnie Wilkens Metully
Mary Sue Milliken
Ann and Torbjörn Milläng
Mimosa, Los Angeles, California
Crystal and Bob Moll
Mønsoon, Seattle, Washington
Rick Moonen
Jinx and Jefferson Morgan
Selma Brown Morrow
Kitty Morse
Gina and Rich Mortillaro
Kristen and Andrew Murray
John Muse
Cindy Mushet
Myth, Toronto, Canada
Joan Nathan
Micol Negrin
Antonella Nonino
Moshe Nov
Nancy Oakes, Boulevard, San Francisco, California
Beatrice Ojakangas
Mark Okumura
David Page
Gérard Pangaud, Gérard's Place, Washington, DC
Lauren Parrish, East City Grill, Fort Lauderdale, Florida
Patty and Luca Paschina
Leslie Patson
François Payard, Payard Pâtisserie & Bistro, New York, New York
Mark Peel
Caprial Pence
Nellie Petroff-Boyer
Christine Piccin
Alfred Portale, Gotham Bar and Grill, New York, New York
Pam Proto and Rayme Rossello, Proto's Pizzeria Napoletana, Lafayette, Colorado
Provisions, Nantucket, Massachusetts
Wolfgang Puck
Stephan Pyles
Anne Quatrano and Clifford Harrison, Bacchanalia, Atlanta, Georgia
Susan Quick
Patricia Quintana
Steven Raichlen
Lydia Ravello
Victoria Abbott Riccardi
Rick & Ann's, Berkeley, California
Mary Risley
Ristorante Albergo Moretto, Monterosso al Mare, Italy
Tori Ritchie
Deborah and Simon Ritchken
Rick Rodgers
Douglas Rodriguez
Marcela Valladolid Rodriguez
Neil Romanoff
Betty Rosbottom
Anne Rosenzweig, Arcadia, New York, New York
The Royal Hawaiian, Honolulu, Hawaii

Brunella Ruggiero, Terrazza Brunella, Hotel Villa Brunella, Capri, Italy
Gary Rulli
Salish Lodge & Spa, Snoqualmie, Washington
Sally Sampson
Patricia Cohen Samuels
Richard Sax
Sazerac, Seattle, Washington
Abbie Schiller
Chris Schlesinger
Cory Schreiber, Wildwood, Portland, Oregon
Martha Rose Shulman
Carmen Scott
Sarah Patterson Scott
Tracy Scott
Jane Seaman
John Rivera Sedlar
Sharrow Bay Hotel, Ullswater, Cumbria, England
Barbara Shinn
Stacey Siegal
Lana Sills
Marie Simmons
Susan Simon
Prem K. Singh
Skipjack's, Boston, Massachusetts
B. Smith
Michael Smith
Richard Snyder
Debra Sostrin
Marlena Spieler
Candida Sportiello
Stars, San Francisco, California
Galit Stevens
Lorraine Stevenski
Joy and Alex Stewart
Frank Stitt
Sweet Dreams Bakery, Memphis, Tennessee
Sweet Surrender Desserts & Cafe, Louisville, Kentucky
Dan Swinney, Lidia's Kansas City, Kansas City, Missouri
Kate and Carl Swope
Sandy Szwarc
Maureen Tatlow
Marilyn Tausend
Kevin Taylor
Daniela and Gionata Tedeschi
Sarah Tenaglia
Terra, St. Helena, California
Antony Worrall Thompson, Woz, London, England
Mary Jo Thoresen
Susie and Brad Tjossem
Doris Tobias
Rochelle Palermo Torres
Rick Tramonto
Nancy Tringali
Szeto Tze-Bun
Karen and Tom Uhlmann
Union Square Cafe, New York, New York
Mary and Bobby Van Fossan
Mary Vaughan
Juana Vázquez-Gómez
Roger Vergé
William Viets
James Villas
Aidita and Javier Vizoso
Hélène Wagner-Popoff
Charlotte Walker
Patti and Dick Ward
Chris Watson
Maria Watson
Bruce Weinstein
Joanne Weir
Renee Werbin
Jasper White
Sara Corpening Whiteford
Anne Willan
Dede Wilson
Mike Wilson
Colm Wood
Kathryn Dowling Wrye and Donald Wrye
Nancy Zaslavsky
Ricardo Muñoz Zurita

For Bon Appétit

H. Abigail Bok
Alexa Cassanos
Basil Friedman
Gaylen Drucker Grody
Grace Jidoun
Vince LaSpisa
Katy Laundrie
Marcia Hartmann Lewis
Anthony Petrillose
Jordana Ruhland
Giuliana Schwab
Sybil Shimazu Neubauer
Judith Sostrin Strausberg
Angela Phipps Towle
Robin Turk

For John Wiley and Sons

Leslie Anglin
Natalie Chapman
Todd Fries
Gypsy Lovett

Index

A

B

C

D

G

H

I

J

K

L

M

N

O

P

Q

R

S

T

U

V

Y

Z